The Professional Practice of Architectural Working Drawings

The Professional Practice of Architectural Working Drawings

THIRD EDITION

Osamu A. Wakita, Hon. A.I.A.
Professor of Architecture, Los Angeles Harbor College

Richard M. Linde, A.I.A. Architect
Richard M. Linde & Associates, Inc.

JOHN WILEY & SONS

This book is dedicated to the students of architecture and to our families.

Copyright © 2003 by John Wiley & Sons, Inc., New York. All rights reserved.

Published simultaneously in Canada.

Library of Congress Cataloging-in-Publication Data

Wakita, Osamu A.
    The professional practice of architectural working drawings / Osamu A. Wakita, Richard M. Linde.—3rd ed.
        p.   cm.
    ISBN 0-471-39540-4 (alk. paper)
    1. Architecture—Designs and plans—Working drawings.   I. Linde, Richard M.   II. Title.

NA2713   .W34 2002
720'.28'4—dc21   2002003719

Printed in the United States of America.

10 9 8 7 6 5

CONTENTS

PREFACE

This book is designed to teach attitudes, basic drafting skills—both hand and computer-aided (CAD) skills, and fundamental concepts of architectural drafting to persons who will benefit from this information in their professional lives. Beyond this, the authors hope to communicate to readers an understanding of architectural drafting as a means of graphic communication, that is, a language. The professional architect or draftsperson needs a clear and fluent command of the language of architectural drafting.

With the advent of the computer, a new way of approaching working drawings has evolved—that of drawing *full-scale* buildings. Previously, we would draw floor plans, for example, at $\frac{1}{4}'' = 1'0''$. The drafter would have to understand the size of a structure in a fraction of its original size. We presently draw buildings in such a fashion that the computer monitor becomes a type of window through which we are able to view full-size buildings in space. Buildings are drawn in 3-D and rotated into a plan and elevation, or rotated and sliced to produce sections, framing, and floor plans. This rotation and slicing process helps the architectural technician and student better understand what the construction documents entail.

The Professional Practice of Architectural Working Drawings, third edition, is divided into three parts. Part I, "Professional Foundations," consists of Chapters 1 through 7 and is designed to provide basic information about drafting equipment, the process via computer-aided drafting (CAD), foundations in building a better strategy using CAD, office practice and procedures, fundamental skills, and an understanding of the evolution of construction. In this edition, Chapter 3 deals with the standards used in CAD and its impact on architectural drafting. There is a new Chapter 4 on environmental and human considerations, and a chapter dealing with the methods of construction and the various materials used in building—wood, masonry, steel, and the new composite—has been added. The initial preparation of working drawings is also new in Chapter 7, which covers the established game plan for the preparation of working drawings. Part II, "Document Evolution," includes Chapters 8 through 16 and bridges the gap between theory

and practice. These chapters teach the student to prepare site plans, foundation plans, floor plans, exterior elevations, building sections, and other vital drawings. Throughout Part II, the ability to communicate general design ideas and concepts through specific working drawings is emphasized and reinforced through practice.

All of these chapters have been updated with new CAD drawings, including Chapter 16, which discusses elevators, lifts, and stairs as linking forms between floors.

Part III comprises five case studies, including the new Madison Steel Building. In total, there will be access to ten case studies, five of which are new. Palos Verdes condominiums, originally in the *Student Manual*, has four variations in design. These newly developed case studies have been interspersed between Chapters 8 and 16, eliminating the duplication that existed in the previous edition.

Information not included in the book will be available to the reader on a web site for review. Although this book was designed as a stand-alone, the combination of the book and the web site will present ten additional case studies. To understand the total sequencing of the case studies, see the charts in Appendix D at the end of this book or on the web site.

A set of working drawings will be evolved, sheet-by-sheet, layer by layer and at the ends of Chapters 8 through 16. Case studies of real projects, found in Chapters 17 through 20, illustrate the evolution of working drawings from the design concept through the finished construction documents for four different buildings:

1. A hypothetical one-story residence, including the development of a datum layer via a computer-generated 3-D model
2. A two-story beach house
3. A four-plex movie theatre
4. A newly developed all-steel building

These four buildings use a variety of building materials—wood, masonry, and steel systems—and consider environmental and human concerns.

Regional differences affect construction methods, and this is one of the most difficult subjects to address. The authors conducted a national survey to illustrate the diverse problems faced by different regions in the country. The results of this survey are carefully summarized and included in Appendix A at the back of this book. Case studies have also been selected to show extreme conditions such as wind, rain, earthquake, and snow.

Appropriately, the illustrations program in this book is its outstanding feature. An additional 400 computer-generated drawings and photographs have been added to the existing 900-plus illustrations. All the new drawings were generated using the same skills described in this book.

Just as clothes, toys, furniture, and other products are made in foreign countries, construction documents are often contracted out and produced in other countries. Communication is electronically instantaneous and less expensive in other countries, and thus many architectural firms are taking advantage of this cheaper, faster method of producing construction documents. Therefore, it is important for our CAD training not only to provide and equip our drafters with information and skills that will make them more competitive with overseas drafters, but also to train our drafters so that they cannot be replaced by those overseas because they produce a better product. It is for this reason that the information contained in this book becomes the critical foundation on which CAD skills can be built. To this end, we have included, in Appendix D, a chart based on CAD standards that can enable an architectural technician or student to set up layers with the proper standards to produce a set of working drawings.

■ ACKNOWLEDGMENTS

We would like to acknowledge the contribution of the many people who worked on the original manuscript, the second edition, and this third edition of *The Professional Practice of Architectural Working Drawings*.

The two main contributors for the first edition were Marilyn Smith, coordinator and administrative assistant, and Louis Toledo, coordinator of all the hand-drafted illustrations and documents. In addition, Vince Toyama and Gregory Hadden developed additional freehand sketches and case studies; Nancy Nishi was responsible for some of the detailed and tedious checking and typing; and Mark Wakita organized the research questionnaire. Andrea Wakita assisted in the initial proposal and was the resource for research and permissions; William Boggs was responsible for all aerial photography, and Georgia Linde for the preliminary manuscript editing and typing of the original Chapters 3 and 19. Thanks to Art Galvan for coordinating the drafting of all the newly developed images, especially the entire Ryan Residence;

Huey Lim, our project manager and coordinator of the artwork and manuscript; Koya Kameshima for photography and specialty/pictorial drawings; Masaya Okada for translating all design drawings and providing us with images to be used in addressing requirements of the Americans with Disabilities ACT (ADA); John Kanounji, who coordinated work between the student guide and the main text; and Edith Martinez, layout drafter for details and charts.

We would like to acknowledge the contributions of several people to the third edition, two in particular: Steve Fuchs Jr. was the coordinator and drafter for the more than 400 new illustrations developed through CAD, and Joan Chappell was the coordinator and administrative assistant for the entire manuscript both new and revised. We also acknowledge the behind-the-scenes work of Cherrella Chumley, Patricia Castillo, Karla Avila, and Jasmine Molano, who were responsible for the reproduction, manuscript/photo sorting, and countless other tasks necessary in the preparation of a book of this type.

Special thanks to Judy Joseph, our original editor; to Amanda Miller, second edition editor; and to Margaret Cummins, third edition editor, for helping us through the difficult world of electronics via computers.

We are sincerely grateful to the academic reviewers who commented on our manuscript during the course of its development.

Reviewers

J. Sam Arnett, *Pitt Community College*
George T. Balich, *Wentworth Institute of Technology*
Robert J. Berry, *Wentworth Institute of Technology*
James Cates, *Brevard Community College*
Paul J. Chase, Chicago, Illinois
A. W. Claussen Jr., *New River Community College*
Frank Corso Jr., *Illinois Central College*
George E. Coughenoyr, *Erie Community College*
Charles W. Dennis, *Diablo Valley College*
Rushia Fellows, *Arizona State University*
L. J. Franceschina, *City College of San Francisco*
Leonard G. Haeger, Santa Barbara, California
Fred Hassaouna, F.I.A.L., A.I.A., A.I.P., *Saddleback Community College District*
Judith B. Hawk, *Northern Virginia Community College*
Donald A. Hinshaw, *Arizona State University*
Dan Houghtaling, *Delaware Technical and Community College*
William A. Kelly, *Los Angeles Trade-Technical College*

Professional Foundations

chapter

1

THE OFFICE

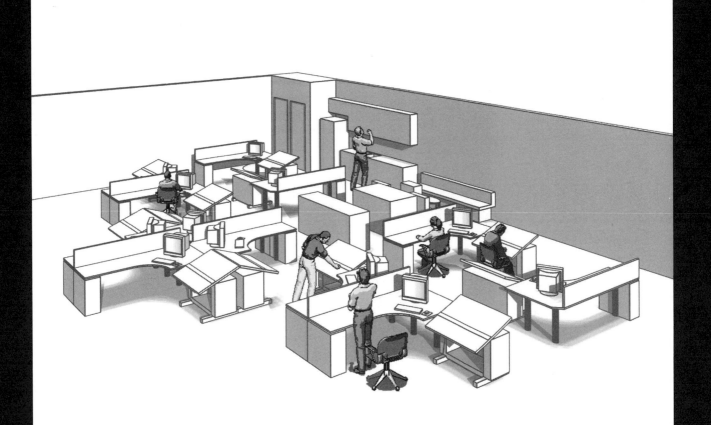

The physical plant of the architectural office has begun to take on a new look. Rows and rows of drafting tables and cubicles are being replaced with mobile stations, giving an entirely new appearance to the work environment. Mobile stations can be reconfigured to the specific needs of a project. The stations can be positioned and repositioned by teams of CAD drafters and designers as the size of a project ebbs and flows. The center for this type of production room may be a conversation area similar to the living room area found in a residence. Here designers and drafters can discuss projects in a relaxed atmosphere. Rather than isolating drafters into small cubicles, as was the case from the 1960s through the 1980s, offices are now beginning to have an open look and feel. The use of low partitions enables the designers and CAD drafters to have eye contact while communicating across the room via computer. Computers are also being networked so that office managers can stay in touch and watch the progress on various projects. For example, if three or more drafters are working on a single project, the information on their individual computers can constantly be upgraded with the latest information as it becomes available. A change in the position of a window on a floor plan will be seen immediately on the different computers where the exterior elevation is being drawn.

Architecture is a small crafts industry in which most offices employ three to eight people. A home office may also be part of the office structure. A single drafter may be hired by two or more firms, and the office then becomes a docking station for the electronic information, such as for construction documents. Because digital images can be rapidly moved electronically, one does not need to live in a city or country to send documents across the world. A suggested office layout is illustrated in Figure 1.1.

■ OFFICE PRACTICE AND HOW IT MAY BE STRUCTURED

How an architectural firm is structured and the office practices it employs depends on the magnitude and type of its projects, the number of personnel, and the philosophies the architects use in their approach to office practice procedures. Normally, the architect or architects are the owners and/or principals of the practice.

In general, an architectural office can be separated into three main departments: the administration department, the design department, and the production department.

The administration department handles all communications between the architectural firm and its clients on items such as contracts, fee schedules billing for services, and the like. This department includes all secretarial duties, such as all written correspondence, payment of operating costs, accounting procedures, paying salaries,

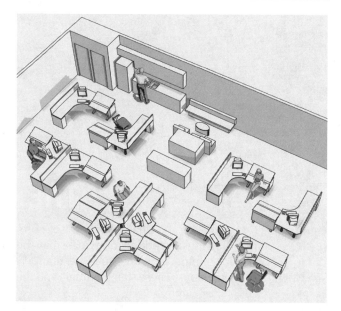

Figure 1.1   Suggested office workstations.

and maintaining records for all the projects relative to their individual costs and procedures. The principal or principals oversee this department in addition to their other duties.

Design Department

The design department is normally headed by either a principal architect and/or an associate architect. This person or persons meets with the client to determine the requirements of a project, the economics of the project, and the anticipated time frame for completing the construction documents. These initial concerns determine the program for the project. The head or heads of this department delegate various work phases of a project to other staff members. The number of staff members depends on the size of the practice and the magnitude of the projects. Staff members may be designated to teams or groups relative to their expertise for specific projects. A team takes a project from the initial design concept stage, through all the revisions and other stages, to the completed working drawings and specifications. These stages may include model building, renderings, coordination between all consulting engineers to meet their individual job requirements, job billing, and reproduction responsibilities. The leader of a project and of the design team staff is designated as the project architect. His or her responsibilities are to develop a game plan for a specific project that will include the following:

1. Design studies and philosophy
2. Initial structural considerations
3. Exterior and interior materials
4. Municipality and building code requirements

5. If applicable, architectural committee reviews
6. Building equipment requirements
7. Manufacturing resources
8. Selection of required engineering consultants such as; soils/geology, structural, mechanical, etc.
9. Planned man-hours, time sheets and billing dates
10. Office standards relative to the representation of items on the working drawings such as; symbols, wall delineations, and other graphic depictions

Production Department

The production department, while supervised by a project architect, prepares all the phases for a set of completed working drawings. Working drawings may be produced by senior draftpersons, intermediate draftpersons, or junior draftpersons. These staff members and the project architect or job captain work as a team to make the transition from the approved preliminary drawings to the implementation and completion of the working drawings. The transition from the approved preliminary drawings to the development of the working drawings is elaborated in Chapter 6 of this book. Other chapters provide step-by-step procedures on how different sections of the working drawings are developed: the site and grading plan, foundation plan, floor plan, building sections, exterior elevations, roof and framing plans, interior elevations, architectural details and schedules. During the process and completion of the various sections, the project architect and/or job captain constantly review the drawings for clarity, accuracy, craftsmanship of detailing, and to see that the drawings reflect all current revisions. These drawings are either created with the use of a computer-aided drafting (CAD) system or are drawn manually using conventional instruments. A suggested organizational chart for the practice of architecture is depicted in Figure 1.2.

■ RESOURCES

To accommodate all the equipment that is required for a structure, such as plumbing, hardware, finishes, and so forth, it is necessary to have access to the various manufacturing resources for specific products. The most widely used product information source is the *Sweet's Catalog File*. This file is provided in a set of volumes that allow architects and engineers to select the equipment necessary for the function of a building. Such equipment may be available from various manufacturers of conveying systems, window and doors, and the like. Information on the various products is now contained on CD-ROMs, which are easier to manipulate than the larger volumes. There are a number of electronic files that can be obtained. The CDs are based on the *Uniform Construc-*

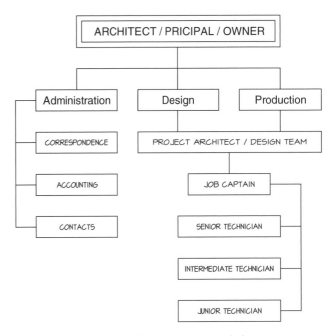

Figure 1.2 Suggested office organizational chart.

tion Index, used widely in the construction industry. These particular systems use the following sixteen major divisions:

1. General data
2. Site work
3. Concrete
4. Masonry
5. Metals
6. Wood and plastics
7. Thermal and moisture protection
8. Doors and windows
9. Finishes
10. Specialties
11. Equipment
12. Furnishing
13. Special construction
14. Conveying systems
15. Mechanical
16. Electrical

Research via the Computer

Almost every large manufacturer has a web site that you can visit via the Internet. One can now research anything from hardware to framing anchors, engineered lumber products to composite building products. Research for building products is done in the same fashion as research for a term paper. The scope of such research can be worldwide. You are limited only by your ability to navigate through the sea of information and your ability to retrieve the necessary information that will satisfy and enhance the completion of the working drawings.

Most manufacturers also provide the architect with a video explaining a product, its specifications, and installation. Digital drawings can also be obtained, making it unnecessary to draw configurations for products such as window sections, stairs, and the like.

Manufacturers' Literature

A wealth of product information is available directly from manufacturers in the form of brochures, pamphlets, catalogs, manuals, and hardbound books. Actual samples of their products may also be obtained. The information available can include the following:

1. Advantages of a particular product over others
2. How the system works or is assembled
3. Necessary engineering
4. Detailed drawings
5. Special design features
6. Colors, textures, and patterns
7. Safety tests
8. Dimensioning
9. Installation procedures

Other Reference Sources

Retail sources such as major book publishers produce architectural reference books. Many art supply and drafting supply stores also carry reference materials. Public libraries contain a variety of professional reference materials—books, journals, and magazines. Colleges and universities offering architecture courses have architectural resource materials. These may include a broad general coverage of such areas as architectural drafting, graphics, engineering, and design principles. An example of a highly technical resource is the *AIA Architectural Graphics Standards* published by John Wiley & Sons. This book includes the maximum, minimum, and average sizes for a variety of items and contains such diverse information as the size of a baseball diamond or a bowling alley, the dimensions of most musical instruments, and the standard sizes for most major kitchen utensils and appliances. This book is found in almost all architectural offices.

Guides and Indexes

Two invaluable general book indexes are the *Subject Guide to Books in Print* (author and title volumes) and the *Reader's Guide to Periodical Literature*. All major bookstores carry these annual reference books. The *Reader's Guide to Periodical Literature* is excellent for locating magazine articles on specific building types, new building techniques, and works of specific architects. Four additional sources of architectural information are the *Art Index, Applied Science and Technology, The Humanities Index,* and the *Social Science Index.* These are available in most college and university libraries and in major public libraries.

■ PROFESSIONAL ORGANIZATIONS

Professional organizations can be an asset to the business performance and office functions of an architectural firm. The American Institute of Architects (AIA) is an example of a professional organization that will provide members with recommended documents, including client and architect contractual agreements, client and contractor agreements, and many others. The institution also provides recommended guidelines relative to fee schedules and disbursements, construction document facets, building specifications, and construction observation procedures and documentation.

Ethical procedures and office practice methods are recommended and defined as part of the many documents that are available from the American Institute of Architects.

It is recommended that associate architects and employees at the various technical levels become involved with a professional organization for a number of reasons, including being made aware of current technical information and activities within the profession of architect. The AIA also offers programs and directions for those in an internship phase of their careers. Student associate member programs are available through the AIA which provide an overall view of the architectural profession.

Other professional organizations for students of architecture can be found in their respective colleges and universities.

■ ARCHITECT/CLIENT RELATIONSHIP

The relationship between the architect and the client, and the procedures for building a project, will vary among architectural offices as different architectural philosophies may be practiced.

In general, the architect/client relationship for a specific building project and the necessary responsibilities and procedures to accomplish the goals of the project will be initiated with the selection of the architect. After the architect is selected, the architect and the client enter into a contract, which defines the services to be performed and the responsibilities of the architect and the client. In many states it is a requirement that the architect use a written contract when providing professional services.

After the contractual agreement is signed and a retainer fee is given, the architect reviews the building site and confers with the client to determine the goals of the building project. Upon establishing the project's goals, there will be meetings with the governing agencies, such as the planning department, the building department, and architectural committees. The primary goal of the architectural team will be to initiate the preliminary planning and design phases.

In most architectural contract agreements, there are provisions for the architect and the consulting engineers to observe construction of the project during the building stage.

Construction Observation

When the construction firm has been selected and construction has commenced, the architect and consulting engineers, according to their agreement in the contract, observe the various phases of construction. These periodic observations generally correspond to the construction phases, such as during construction of the foundation, framing, and so forth. Following their observations, the architect and consulting engineers provide written reports to the client and contractor describing their observations, along with any recommendations or alterations they deem necessary for success of the project.

Preliminary Designs and Reviews

The next step in the architect/client relationship is the architect's presentation of the preliminary planning and design for the project. After the client's initial review of the project's planning and design, there may be some revisions and alterations to the design. In this case, the preliminary drawings are revised and presented again to the client for his or her approval. After the approval of the preliminary design by the client, the architect consults and presents the preliminary drawings to the various governing agencies for their review and comments. Any revisions and alterations that may be required by any one of the agencies are executed and again reviewed by the client for his or her approval. In many offices the preliminary drawings are often used to estimate the initial construction costs that will be submitted for review and approval by the client.

In the preliminary planning and design phase, a conceptual site plan and floor plan of the building areas are reviewed for the building orientation and the preservation of existing landscaping elements such as trees, topography, and other site conditions. An example of a conceptual site and building plan is illustrated in Figure 1.3. The

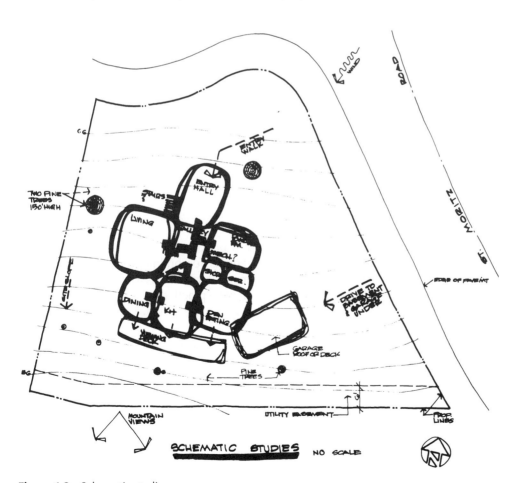

Figure 1.3   Schematic studies.

client for this project desires to build a three-bedroom residence for a young family. The site is located in a mountain area that is subject to heavy snow conditions. Two large pine trees are on the site, which are to be retained.

Besides the large pine trees, the mountain views, wind direction, and the most feasible automobile access to the site are considered, and a schematic study is presented. From this initial schematic study a preliminary floor plan is established, which shows the room orientations and their relationships to one another. This preliminary drawing is depicted in Figure 1.4. A second floor level preliminary plan is studied as it relates to the first floor plan and the room orientation as shown in Figure 1.5. Finally, a basement floor plan is designed to facilitate the use of an artist's studio and a cabinet workshop. This preliminary study is illustrated in Figure 1.6. The studies of the exterior elevations evolved utilizing an insulated aluminum roof material, with a steep pitched roof, and exterior walls of wood siding. The unusual shape of the residence required studies of the roof plan for geometric solutions. As developed from these studies, a roof plan is

shown in Figure 1.7. After the client has approved the preliminary floor plans, the exterior elevations for the North and West are presented in preliminary form to the client for approval, and to the governmental agencies for their required approvals. The North and West elevations are depicted in Figures 1.8 and 1.9. These preliminary drawings and designs are but examples of the architect's studies that may be presented to the client for his or her approval prior to implementation of the working drawings.

■ IMPLEMENTATION OF THE WORKING DRAWINGS

After approval of the preliminary designs and planning for a project by the client and governing agencies, the architect's office initiates the working drawing phase for the construction of the project.

During the working drawing phase a team of architects consult with the engineers required on a specific project.

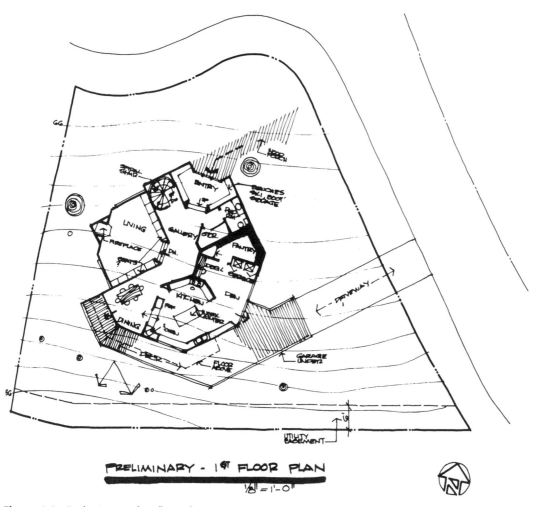

Figure 1.4   Preliminary—first floor plan.

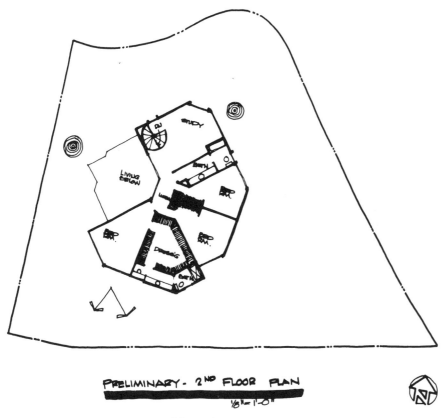

PRELIMINARY - 2ND FLOOR PLAN
1/8"=1'-0"

Figure 1.5 Preliminary—second floor plan.

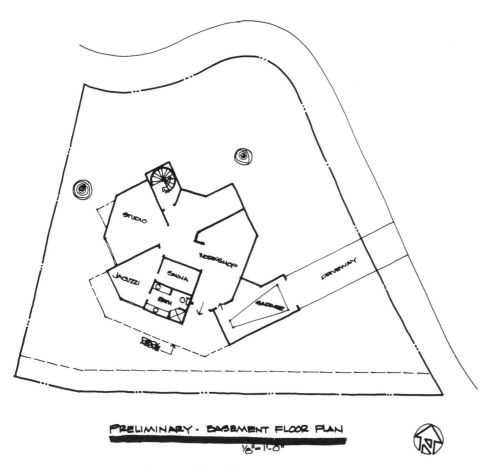

PRELIMINARY - BASEMENT FLOOR PLAN
1/8"=1'-0"

Figure 1.6 Preliminary—basement floor plan.

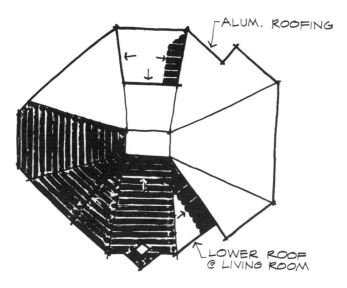

ALUM. ROOFING

LOWER ROOF @ LIVING ROOM

ROOF PLAN

Figure 1.7 Roof plan—conceptual design.

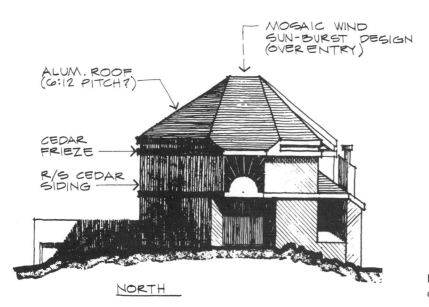

MOSAIC WIND SUN-BURST DESIGN (OVER ENTRY)

ALUM. ROOF (6:12 PITCH?)

CEDAR FRIEZE

R/S CEDAR SIDING

NORTH

Figure 1.8 North exterior conceptual design.

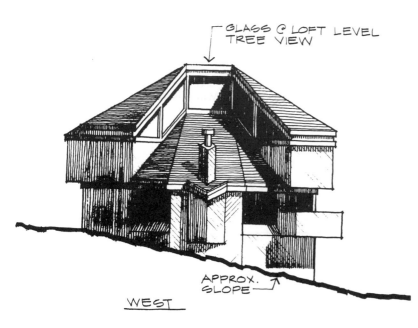

GLASS @ LOFT LEVEL TREE VIEW

APPROX. SLOPE

WEST

Figure 1.9 West exterior conceptual design.

Consulting engineers may be employed directly by the architect, or they may have their own private practice. These consultants may include a soils and geological engineer, a structural engineer, a mechanical engineer, an electrical engineer, and a civil engineer. Other consultants may include a landscape architect and a cost estimator. Periodic conferences with the client are recommended during this phase in order to attain approvals on the various phases of the working drawings. These phases or stages may include lighting and electrical designs, interior cabinetry, wall designs, and many other features that may necessitate review and approval by the client. If these drawings are being developed by use of a CAD system, refer to Chapter 3 for recommended procedures.

Materials and Specifications

There will be numerous conferences between the architect and the client during the working drawing phase to select and determine items such as exterior and interior wall finishes, flooring, plumbing fixtures, hardware design, type of masonry, roofing materials, and so on. During these conferences, the selection of building equipment and systems are also reviewed and determined. The equipment selection may include such items as types of windows and doors and the manufacturer, the elevator type and manufacturer, the mechanical system, electrical fixtures, and so on. Refer to Chapter 6 for related information on the aforementioned items.

Finalization of the Working Drawings and Specifications

Upon completion of the working drawings and specifications, which are now termed construction documents, the architect and/or client may submit the construction documents to financing institutions for building loans, to various construction firms for building cost proposals, and to governing agencies for their final approvals. Finally, the architectural firm will be responsible for submitting the construction documents to the local building department for its approval to obtain the required building permits.

At the completion of the project, the architect and his or her consultants make a final inspection of the construction of the building and prepare what is termed a "punch list." This punch list is in written form and includes graphics indicating to the client and construction firm any revisions, reports, or alterations they deem pertinent and reasonable for a successful building project. After the construction firm makes the revisions, the architect and the consultants again inspect the revisions for approval. If acceptable, a final notice of approval is sent to the client and the construction firm.

■ BUILDING

Building Codes

The purpose of building codes is to safeguard life, health, and the public welfare. Building codes are continually being revised and incorporating additional regulations based on tests or conditions caused by catastrophic events, such as hurricanes, earthquakes, and fires. In most cases, the governing building codes are similar in organization and context. The following building code examples and portions are derived from the current edition of the *Uniform Building Code.*

Building Code Divisions   Primarily, the *Uniform Building Code* is divided into eleven parts with specific chapters and sections incorporated into the various parts. The various parts are as follows:

Part I	Administration
Part II	Definitions and Abbreviations
Part III	Requirements Based on Occupancy
Part IV	Requirements Based on Types of Construction
Part V	Engineering Regulations—Quality and Design of the Materials of Construction
Part VI	Detailed Regulations
Part VII	Fire-Resistive Standards for Fire Protection
Part VIII	Regulations for Use of Public Streets and Projections over Public Property
Part IX	Wall and Ceiling Coverings
Part X	Special Subjects
Part XI	Uniform Building Code Standards

The requirements of various agencies and codes are of paramount influence in the design and detailing of today's structures. There are a great number of codes that govern and regulate the many elements that are integrated into the construction of a building. The major codes that are used in the design and detailing of buildings are the building code, mechanical code, electrical code, fire code, energy code, and accessibility design criteria for persons with disabilities.

Procedures for Use of the Building Codes   There are a number of governing building code requirements that dictate the architectural designs an architect or designer will incorporate in developing a design for a specific structure. For example, to establish the design program for a proposed two-story building having a floor area of 10,000 square feet per floor, it will be necessary to review the governing building code to determine the various requirements that dictate a major portion of the design criteria. The following are the primary steps used in most building codes to determine the classification and requirements for a specific structure.

STEP I. *Building use and occupancy.*   The first step is to classify the building use and to determine the occupancy group that satisfies the use of the building. When the occupancy classification has been determined, the building is assigned a group designation letter. An example of a table found in the *Uniform Building Code,* which determines the description of the occupancy and the group it falls under, is illustrated in Figure 1.10. Note that the proposed office building is designated in the category of group B.

STEP II. *Fire-rated wall assemblies.*   As indicated in Figure 1.11, all the walls of the proposed office building have to be constructed so as to meet the requirements of one-hour fire-rated assemblies acceptable by the governing code. Most codes provide a chapter on acceptable fire-resistive standards for assemblies, so that the architect or designer is able to select an assembly that satisfies his or her specific condition. An example of the assembly of a one-hour fire-rated 2" × 4" wood stud partition is given in Figure 1.14, item 16-1.4. This wall assembly will now be part of the building design program.

STEP III. *Building location on the site.*   The location of the building on the site and the clearances to the property lines and other structures on the site determine the fire-resistant construction of the exterior walls. The openings are based on the distances from the property lines and other structures. Figure 1.11 illustrates the required fire-resistant construction of the exterior walls and openings in the walls based on the distances to the property lines.

STEP IV. *Allowable floor areas.*   The next step is to determine the proposed and allowable floor areas of the building based on the occupancy group and the type of construction. Figure 1.12 indicates the type of construction required based on the allowable floor area for one-story buildings. For multistory buildings, the architect will review another section of the code.

STEP V. *Height and the number of stories or floors in the building.*   The architect computes the maximum height of the building and determines the number of stories and/or floors. The maximum number of stories and the height of the building are determined by the building occupancy and the type of construction.

TABLE NO. 5-A—WALL AND OPENING PROTECTION OF OCCUPANCIES BASED ON LOCATION ON PROPERTY
Types II One-Hour, II-N and V Construction: For exterior wall and opening protection of Types II One-hour, II-N and V buildings, see table below and Sections 504, 709, 1903 and 2203. This table does not apply to Types I, II-F.R., III and IV construction, see Sections 1803, 1903, 2003 and 2103.

GROUP	DESCRIPTION OF OCCUPANCY	FIRE RESISTANCE OF EXTERIOR WALLS	OPENINGS IN EXTERIOR WALLS[1]
A See also Section 602	1— Any assembly building or portion of a building with a legitimate stage and an occupant load of 1,000 or more	Not applicable (See Sections 602 and 603)	
	2— An building or portion of a building having an assembly room with an occupant load of less than 1,000 and a legitimate stage	2 hours less than 10 feet, 1 hour less than 40 feet	Not permitted less than 5 feet Protected less than 10 feet
	2.1— Any building or portion of a building having an assembly room with an occupant load of 300 or more without a legitimate stage, including such buildings used for educational purposes and not classed as Group E or Group B, Division 2 Occupancy		
	3— Any building or portion of a building having an assembly room with an occupant load of less than 300 without a legitimate stage, including such buildings used for educational purposes and not classed as a Group E or Group B, Division 2 Occupancy	2 hours less than 5 feet, 1 hour less than 20 feet	Not permitted less than 5 feet Protected less than 10 feet
	4— Stadiums, reviewing stands and amusement park structures not included with other Group A Occupancies	1 hour less than 10 feet	Protected less than 10 feet
B See also Section 702	1— Repair garages where work is limited to exchange of parts and maintenance requiring no open flame, welding, or use of Class I, II or III-A liquids, motor vehicle fuel-dispensing stations and parking garages not classified as Group B, Division 3 open parking garages or Group M, Division I private garages	1 hour less than 20 feet	Not permitted less than 5 feet Protected less than 10 feet
	2— Drinking and dining establishments having an occupant load of less than 50, wholesale and retail stores, office buildings, printing plants, police and fire stations, factories and workshops using material not highly flammable or combustible, storage and sales rooms for combustible goods, paint stores without bulk handling Buildings or portions of buildings having rooms used for educational purposes, beyond the 12th grade, with less than 50 occupants in any room		

Figure 1.10 Occupancy description.

TABLE NO. 5-A—Continued
TYPES II ONE-HOUR, II-N AND V ONLY

GROUP	DESCRIPTION OF OCCUPANCY	FIRE RESISTANCE OF EXTERIOR WALLS	OPENINGS IN EXTERIOR WALLS[1]
B (Cont.)	3— Aircraft hangars where no repair work is done except exchange of parts and maintenance requiring no open flame, welding, or the use of Class I or II liquids Open parking garages (For requirements, see Section 709) Helistops	1 hour less than 20 feet	Not permitted less than 5 feet Protected less than 20 feet
	4— Ice plants, power plants, pumping plants, cold storage and creameries Factories and workshops using noncombustible and nonexplosive material Storage and sales rooms of noncombustible and nonexplosive materials that are not packaged or crated in or supported by combustible material	1 hour less than 5 feet	Not permitted less than 5 feet
E See also Section 802	1— Any building used for educational purposes through the 12th grade by 50 or more persons for more than 12 hours per week or four hours in any one day	2 hours less than 5 feet, 1 hour less than 10 feet[2]	Not permitted less than 5 feet Protected less than 10 feet[2]
	2— Any building used for educational purposes through the 12th grade by less than 50 persons for more than 12 hours per week or four hours in any one day		
	3— Any building or portion thereof used for day-care purposes for more than six persons		
H	See Table No. 9-C		
I See also Section 1002	1.1— Nurseries for the full-time care of children under the age of six (each accommodating more than five persons) Hospitals, sanitariums, nursing homes with nonambulatory patients similar buildings (each accommodating more than five persons)	2 hours less than 5 feet 1 hour elsewhere	Not permitted less than 5 feet Protected less than 10 feet
	1.2— Health-care centers for ambulatory patients receiving outpatient medical care which may render the patient incapable of unassisted self-preservation (each tenant space accommodating more than five such patients)		
	2— Nursing homes for ambulatory patients, homes for children six years of age of over (each accommodating more than five persons)	1 hour	Not permitted less than 5 feet Protected less than 10 feet
	3— Mental hospitals, mental sanitariums, jails, prisons, reformatories and buildings where personal liberties of inmates are similarly restrained	2 hours less than 5 feet. 1 hour elsewhere	
M[3] See also Section 1102	1— Private garages, carports, sheds and agricultural buildings	1 hour less than 3 feet (or may be protected on the exterior with materials approved for 1-hour fire-resistive construction)	Not permitted less than 3 feet
	2— Fences over 6 feet high, tanks and towers	Not regulated for fire resistance	
R See also Section 1202	1— Hotels and apartment houses Congregate residences (each accommodating more than 10 persons)	1 hour less than 5 feet	Not permitted less than 5 feet
	3— Dwellings and lodging houses, congregate residences (each accommodating 10 persons or less)	1 hour less than 3 feet	Not permitted less than 3 feet

[1]Openings shall be protected by a fire assembly having at least a three-fourths-hour fire-protection rating.
[2]Group E, Divisions 2 and 3 Occupancies having an occupant load of not more than 20 may have exterior wall and opening protection as required for Group R, Division 3 Occupancies.
[3]For agricultural buildings, see Appendix Chapter 11.
NOTES: (1) See Section 504 for types of walls affected and requirements covering percentage of openings permitted in exterior walls.
(2) For additional restrictions, see chapters under Occupancy and Types of Construction
(3) For walls facing yards and public ways, see Part IV.

Figure 1.10 Occupancy description *(continued)*.

TABLE NO. 17-A—TYPES OF CONSTRUCTION—FIRE-RESISTIVE REQUIREMENTS (In Hours)
For details see chapters under Occupancy and Types of Construction and for exceptions see Section 1705.

	TYPE I	TYPE II			TYPE III		TYPE IV	TYPE V	
		NONCOMBUSTIBLE			COMBUSTIBLE				
BUILDING ELEMENT	FIRE-RESISTIVE	FIRE-RESISTIVE	1-HR.	N	1-HR.	N	H.T.	1-HR.	N
1. Exterior Bearing Walls	4 Sec. 1803 (a)	4 1903 (a)	1	N	4 2003 (a)	4 2003 (a)	4 2103 (a)	1	N
2. Interior Bearing Walls	3	2	1	N	1	N	1	1	N
3. Exterior Nonbearing Walls	4 Sec. 1803 (a)	4 1903 (a)	1 1903 (a)	N	4 2003 (a)	4 2003 (a)	4 2103 (a)	1	N
4. Structural Frame[1]	3	2	1	N	1	N	1 or H.T.	1	N
5. Partitions—Permanent	1[2]	1[2]	1[2]	N	1	N	1 or H.T.	1	N
6. Shaft Enclsoures[3]	2	2	1	1	1	1	1	1	1
7. Floors-Ceilings/Floors	2	2	1	N	1	N	H.T.	1	N
8. Roofs-Ceilings/Roofs	2 Sec. 1806	1 1906	1 1906	N	1	N	H.T.	1	N
9. Exterior Doors and Windows	Sec. 1803 (b)	1903 (b)	1903 (b)	1903 (b)	2003 (b)	2003 (b)	2103 (b)	2203	2203
10. Stairway Construction	Sec. 1805	1905	1905	1905	2004	2004	2104	2204	2204

N—No general requirements for fire resistance.　　　H.T.—Heavy Timber.

[1]Structural frame elements in an exterior wall that is located where openings are not permitted or where protection for openings is required shall be protected against external fire exposure as required for exterior bearing walls or the structural frame, whichever is greater.

[2]Fire-retardant-treated wood (see Section 407) may be used in the assembly, provided fire-resistance requirements are maintained. See Sections 1801 and 1901, respectively.

[3]For special provisions, see Sections 1706, 706, 906.

Figure 1.11 Fire-resistive requirements.

TABLE NO. 5-C—BASIC ALLOWABLE FLOOR AREA FOR BUILDINGS ONE STORY IN HEIGHT[1] (in square feet)

	TYPES OF CONSTRUCTION								
	I	II			III		IV	V	
OCCUPANCY	F.R.	F.R.	ONE-HOUR	N	ONE-HOUR	N	H.T.	ONE-HOUR	N
A-1	Unlimited	29,900				Not Permitted			
A-2-2.1[2]	Unlimited	29,900	13,500	Not Permitted	13,500	Not Permitted	13,500	10,500	Not Permitted
A-3-4[2]	Unlimited	29,900	13,500	9,100	13,500	9,100	13,500	10,500	6,000
B-1-2-3[3]	Unlimited	39,900	18,000	12,000	18,000	12,000	18,000	14,000	8,000
B-4	Unlimited	59,900	27,000	18,000	27,000	18,000	27,000	21,000	12,000
E-1-2-3	Unlimited	45,200	20,200	13,500	20,200	13,500	20,200	15,700	9,100
H-1	15,000	12,400	5,600	3,700	Not Permitted				
H-2[4]	15,000	12,400	5,600	3,700	5,600	3,700	5,600	4,400	2,500
H-3-4-5[4]	Unlimited	24,800	11,200	7,500	11,200	7,500	11,200	8,800	5,100
H-6-7	Unlimited	39,900	18,000	12,000	18,000	12,000	18,000	14,000	8,000
I-1.1-1.2-2	Unlimited	15,100	6,800	Not Permitted	6,800	Not Permitted	6,800	5,200	Not Permitted
I-3	Unlimited	15,100	Not Permitted[5]						
M[6]	See Chapter 11								
R-1	Unlimited	29,900	13,500	9,100[7]	13,500	9,100[7]	13,500	10,500	6,000[7]
R-3	Unlimited								

N—No requirements for fire resistance　　**F.R.**—Fire resistive　　H.T.—Heavy timer

[1]For multistory buildings, see Section 505(b).
[2]For limitations and exceptions, see Section 602.
[3]For open parking garages, see Section 709.
[4]See Section 903.

[5]See Section 1002(b).
[6]For agricultural buildings, see also Appendix Chapter 11.
[7]For limitations and exceptions, see Section 1202(b).
[8]In hospitals and nursing homes, see Section 1002(a) for exception.

Figure 1.12 Allowable types of construction.

14

TABLE NO. 5-D—MAXIMUM HEIGHT OF BUILDINGS

OCCUPANCY	TYPES OF CONSTRUCTION								
	I	II			III		IV	V	
	F.R.	F.R.	ONE-HOUR	N	ONE-HOUR	N	H.T.	ONE-HOUR	N
	MAXIMUM HEIGHT IN FEET								
	Unlimited	160	65	55	65	55	65	50	40
	MAXIMUM HEIGHT IN FEET								
A-1	Unlimited	4				Not Permitted			
A-2-2.1	Unlimited	4	2	Not Permitted	2	Not Permitted	2	2	Not Permitted
A-3-4[1]	Unlimited	12	2	1	2	1	2	2	1
B-1-2-3[2]	Unlimited	12	4	2	4	2	4	3	2
B-4	Unlimited	12	4	2	4	2	4	3	2
E[3]	Unlimited	4	2	1	2	1	2	2	1
H-1[4]	1	1	1	1		Not Permitted			
H-2[4]	Unlimited	2	1	1	1	1	1	1	1
H-3-4-5[4]	Unlimited	5	2	1	2	1	2	2	1
H-6-7	3	3	3	2	3	2	3	3	1
I-1.1[5]-1.2	Unlimited	3	1	Not Permitted	1	Not Permitted	1	1	Not Permitted
I-2	Unlimited	3	2	Not Permitted	2	Not Permitted	2	2	Not Permitted
I-3	Unlimited	2				Not Permitted[6]			
M[7]					See Chapter 11				
R-1	Unlimited	12	4	2[8]	4	2[8]	4	3	2[8]
R-3	Unlimited	3	3	3	3	3	3	3	3

Figure 1.13 Maximum building heights.

TABLE NO. 43-B—RATED FIRE-RESISTIVE PERIODS FOR VARIOUS WALLS AND PARTITIONS

MATERIAL	ITEM NUMBER	CONSTRUCTION	MINIMUM FINISHED THICKNESS FACE-TO-FACE[2]			
			4 Hr.	3 Hr.	2 Hr.	1 Hr.
15. Nonumbustible Studs—Interior Partition with Gypsum Wallboard Each Side	15-1.3	No. 16 gauge approved nailable metal studs[10] 24" on center with full-length $\frac{5}{8}$" Type X gypsum wallboard[7] applied vertically and nailed 7" on center with 6d cement-coated common nails. Approved metal fastener grips used with nails at vertical butt joints along studs.				$4\frac{7}{8}$
16. Wood Studs—Interior Partition with Gypsum Wallboard Each Side	16-11[11][16]	2" × 4" wood studs 16" on center wiht two layers of $\frac{3}{8}$" regular gypsum wallboard[7] each side. 4d cooler[12] or wallboard[12] nails at 8" on center first layer, 5d cooler[12] or wallboard[12] nails at 8" on center second layer with laminating compound between layers. Joints staggered. First layer aplied full length vertically, second layer applied horizontally or vertically.				5
	16-1.2[11][16]	2" × 4" wood studs 16" on center with two layers $\frac{1}{2}$" regular gypsum wallboard[7] applied vertically or horizontally each side, joints staggered. Nail base layer with 5d cooler[12] or wallboard[12] nails at 8" on center, face layer with 8d cooler[12] or wallboard[12] nails at 8" on center.				$5\frac{1}{2}$
	16.1.3[11][16]	2" × 4" wood studs 24" on center with $\frac{5}{8}$" Type X gypsum wallboard[7] aplied vertically or horizontally nailed with 6d cooler[12] or wallboard[12] nails at 7" on center with end joints on nailing members. Stagger joints each side.				$4\frac{3}{4}$
	16-1.4[11]	2" × 4" fire-retardant-treated wood studs spaced 24" on center with one layer of $\frac{5}{8}$" thick Type X gypsum wallboard[7] applied with face paper grain (long dimension) paralell to studs. Wallboard attached with 6d cooler[12] or wallboard[12] nails at 7" on center.				

Figure 1.14 Fire-resistive wall assemblies (continued).

TABLE NO. 43-B—RATED FIRE-RESISTIVE PERIODS FOR VARIOUS WALLS AND PARTITIONS

MATERIAL	ITEM NUMBER	CONSTRUCTION	MINIMUM FINISHED THICKNESS FACE-TO-FACE[2]			
			4 Hr.	3 Hr.	2 Hr.	1 Hr.
17. Exterior or Interior Walls	17-1.3[11][16]	2″ × 4″ wood studs 16″ on center with ⅞″ exterior cement plaster (measured from the face of studs) on the exterior surface with interior surface treatment as required for interior wood stud partitions in this table. Plaster mix 1:4 for scratch coat and 1.5 for brown coat, by volume, cement to sand.				Varies
	17-1.4	3⅝″ No. 16 gauge noncombustible studs 16″ on center with ⅞″ exterior cement plaster (measured from the face of the studs) on the exterior surface with interior surface treatment as required for interior, nonbearing, noncombustible stud partitions in this table. Plaster mix 1:4 for scratch coat and 1:5 for brown coat, by volume, cement to sand.				Varies[4]
	17-1.5[16]	2¼″ × 3¾″ clay face brick with cored holes over ½″ gypsum sheathing on exterior surface of 2″ × 4″ wood studs at 16″ on center and two layers ⅝″ Type X gypsum wallboard[7] on interior surface. Sheathing placed horizontally or vertically with vertical joints over studs nailed 6″ on center with 1¾″ by No. 11 gauge by ⁷⁄₁₆″ head galvanized nails. Inner layer of wallboard placed horizontally or vertically and nailed 8″ on center with 6d cooler[12] or wallboard[12] nails. Outer layer of wallboard placed horizontally or vertically and nailed 8″ on center with 8d cooler[12] or wallboard[12] nails. All joints staggered with vertical joints over studs. Outer layer joints taped and finished with compound. Nailheads covered with joint compound. No. 20 gauge corrugated galvanized steel wall ties ¾″ by 6⅝″ attached to each stud with two 8d cooler[12] or wallboard[12] nails every sixth course of bricks.			10	

Figure 1.14 Fire-resistive wall assemblies (continued).

Figure 1.13 illustrates what will be required for the various design criteria. The shaded areas illustrated in Figures 1.10, 1.11, l.12, and 1.13 are applicable to a proposed two-story office building.

Code Influence on Building Design

An example of code-related design requirements is provided by the site plan for the proposed two-story office building. The architect desires that all four sides of the building have windows. To satisfy this design factor, the minimum building setback from the property line will be ten feet, as indicated in Figure 1.10, under openings in exterior walls. Figure 1.15 depicts the proposed site plan for the two-story office building, showing property line setbacks satisfying one design requirement.

As the design program is developed, it is helpful to provide code-required assemblies in graphic form as a visual means for reviewing what is required for the various elements of the office building. An example of such a graphic aid is illustrated in Figure 1.16. As previously illustrated, Figures 1.12 and 1.11 determine the fire-resistive requirements for the various elements of the building, and Figure 1.14 is a partial example of some of the many acceptable construction assemblies that may be

selected for the use of wall assemblies that are found in building codes.

Exit Requirements. Another very important part of a building code is the chapter dealing with egress requirements. This chapter sets forth the number of required exits for a specific occupancy use, based on an occupant load factor. The occupant load will depend on the use of the building. In the case of a two-story building that is designed for office use, the occupant load factor, as illustrated in Figure 1.17, will be 100 square feet. To determine the number of exits required, the 100 square-foot occupant load factor is divided into the office floor area of 10,000 square feet. The resultant occupant factor of 100 exceeds the factor of 30, therefore requiring a minimum of two exits.

The next step in the design program is to plan the location of the required exits, required stairs, and an acceptable egress travel. Egress travel is the path to a required exit. The codes will regulate the maximum distance between required exits, the minimum width of exit corridors, and the entire design of required exit stairways. Figure 1.18 depicts the second level floor plan of the proposed office building, illustrating an acceptable method for the planning of required exits and stair loca-

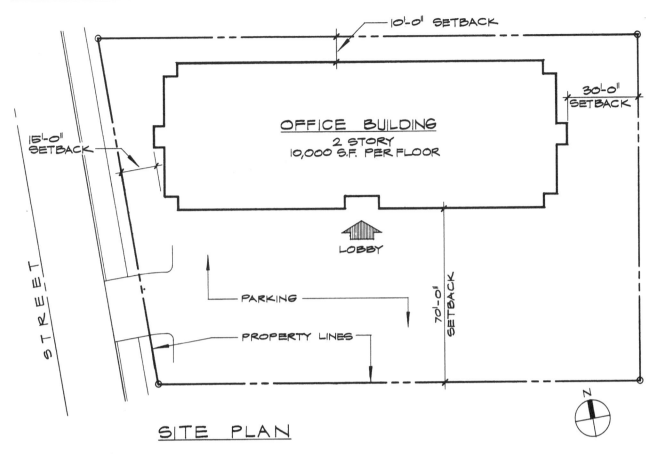

Figure 1.15 Site plan.

tions. An acceptable egress travel will terminate at the first-floor level, exiting outside the structure to a public right-of-way. A public right-of-way may be a sidewalk, street, alley, or other passage. On the first level floor plan, illustrated in Figure 1.19, the egress travel path terminates outside the building through an exit corridor at the east and west walls of the building.

This particular chapter in the *Uniform Building Code*, entitled "Exits," provides a great amount of information to which the architect or designer will continually refer in order to satisfy the many code regulations that will influence the planning and detailing of his or her specific building.

Code Nailing Schedule. In most cases, building code regulations determine minimum standards for the many considerations associated with the construction of a building in order to safeguard public health and welfare. However, this does not mean that the architect or the various engineers cannot increase the quality of these standards to satisfy their design solutions and opinions. An example of a minimum nailing schedule for Type V (wood) construction is illustrated in Figure 1.20. For structures subjected to wind or seismic forces, the engineered design may require more nails and a larger size of nails in order to satisfy the engineered design criteria.

Standards for Wood. The use of wood is prominent in the construction of many types of buildings currently being designed. The building codes have an extensively developed chapter for the various standards required for wood design. This chapter provides an array of tables

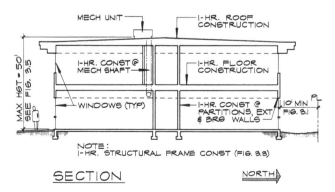

Figure 1.16 Graphic building section.

TABLE NO. 33-A—MINIMUM EGRESS REQUIREMENTS[1]

USE[2]	MINIMUM OF TWO EXITS OTHER THAN ELEVATORS ARE REQUIRED WHERE NUMBER OF OCCUPANTS IS AT LEAST	OCCUPANT LOAD FACTOR[3] (SQ. FT.)
1. Aircraft hangars (no repair)	10	500
2. Auction rooms	30	7
3. Assembly areas, concentrated use (without fixed seats) Auditoriums Churches and chapels Dance floors Lobby accessory to assembly occupancy Lodge rooms Reviewing stands Stadiums Waiting Area	50 50	7 3
4. Assembly areas, less-concentrated use Conference rooms Dining rooms Drinking establishments Exhibit rooms Gymnasiums Lounges Stages	50	15
5. Bowling alley (assume no occupant load for bowling lanes)	50	4
6. Children's homes and homes for the aged	6	80
7. Classrooms	50	20
8. Congregate residences (accommodating 10 or less persons and having an area of 3,000 square feet or less) Congregate residences (accommodating more than 10 persons or having an area of more than 3,000 square feet)	10 10	300 200
9. Courtrooms	50	40

USE[2]	MINIMUM OF TWO EXITS OTHER THAN ELEVATORS ARE REQUIRED WHERE NUMBER OF OCCUPANTS IS AT LEAST	OCCUPANT LOAD FACTOR[3] (SQ. FT.)
10. Dormitories	10	50
11. Dwellings	10	300
12. Exercising rooms	50	50
13. Garage, parking	30	200
14. Hospitals and sanitariums— Nursing homes Sleeping rooms Treatment rooms Health-care center	6 10 10	80 80 80
15. Hotels and apartments	10	200
16. Kitchen—commercial	30	200
17. Library reading room	50	50
18. Locker rooms	30	50
19. Malls (see Chapter 56)	—	—
20. Manufacturing areas	30	200
21. Mechanical equipment room	30	300
22. Nurseries for children (day care)	7	35
23. Offices	30	100
24. School shops and vocational rooms	50	50
25. Skating rinks	50	50 on the skating area; 15 on the deck
26. Storage and stock rooms	30	300
27. Stores—retail sales rooms	50	30
28. Swimming pools	50	50 for the pool area; 15 on the deck
29. Warehouses	30	500
30. All others	50	100

[1]Access to, and egress from, buildings for persons with disabilities shall be provided as specified in Chapter 31.

[2]For additional provisions on number of exits from Groups H and I Occupancies and from rooms containing fuel-fired equipment or cellulose nitrate, see Sections 3319, 3320 and 3321, respectively.

[3]This table shall not be used to determine working space requirements per person.

[4]Occupant load based on five persons for each alley, including 15 feet of runway.

Figure 1.17 Egress requirements.

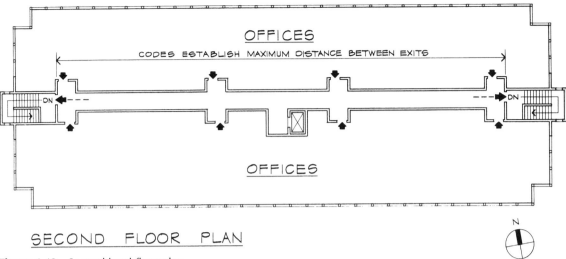

Figure 1.18 Second level floor plan.

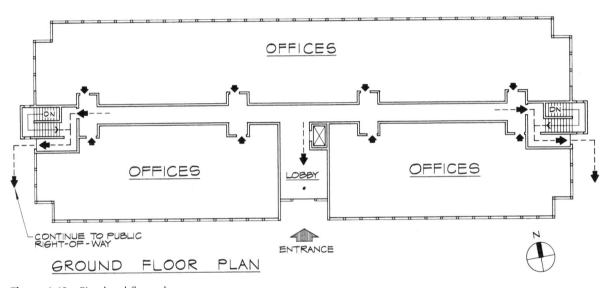

Figure 1.19 First level floor plan.

dealing with examples, such as allowable unit stresses for various types of wood species and their grades, the structural capabilities of plywood relative to its thickness and properties, the numerous species combinations for glued-laminate timber design and allowable spans for roof rafters, ceiling joists, and floor joists. An example of one of the many tables to be found in the chapter on wood is given in Figure 1.21. This table includes the allowable spans for various sizes and spacing of floor joists, based on a specific weight per square foot and on deflection design criteria.

Bolts in Concrete. For the structural design engineer or architect the building codes offer a vast number of working values for wood, concrete, masonry, and structural

steel. These values provide a basis for the selection of the various components that are part of many constructions assemblies found in a specific structure. Figure 1.22 illustrates a value table for various sized anchor bolts embedded in concrete. These design loads would be the maximum allowable pounds per bolt, with a minimum embedded factor.

Minimum Foundation Requirements

As previously mentioned, many code requirements stipulate minimum standards for a specific phase of the construction process. An example is the minimum standards for foundations for wood stud-bearing walls. Figure 1.23 illustrates a table for foundations where there are no

TABLE NO. 25-O—NAILING SCHEDULE

CONNECTION	NAILING[1]
1. Joist to sill or girder, toenail	3-8d
2. Bridging to joist, toenail each end	2-8d
3. 1″ × 6″ subfloor or less to each joist, face nail	2-8d
4. Wider than 1″ × 6″ subfloor to each joist, face nail	3-8d
5. 2″ subfloor to joist or girder, blind and face nail	2-16d
6. Sole plate to joist or blocking, face nail	16d at 16″ o.c.
7. Top plate to stud, end nail	2-16d
8. Stud to sole plate	4-8d, toenail or 2-16d, end nail
9. Double studs, face nail	16d at 24″ o.c.
10. Doubled top plates, face nail	16d at 16″ o.c.
11. Top plates, laps and intersections, face nail	2-16d
12. Continuous header, two pieces	16d at 16″ o.c. along each edge
13. Ceiling joists to plate, toenail	3-8d
14. Continuous header to stud, toenail	4-8d
15. Ceiling joists, laps over partitions, face nail	3-16d
16. Ceiling joists to parallel rafters, face nail	3-16d
17. Rafter to plate, toenail	3-8d
18. 1″ brace to each stud and plate, face nail	2-8d
19. 1″ × 8″ sheathing or less to each bearing, face nail	2-8d
20. Wider than 1″ × 8″ sheathing to each bearing, face nail	3-8d
21. Built-up corner studs	16d at 24″ o.c.
22. Built-up girder and beams	20d at 32″ o.c. at top and bottom and staggered 2-20d at ends and at each splice

Figure 1.20 Nailing schedule.

frost conditions or unfavorable soils and geology reports and no excessive weights acting on the roof and floor systems.

The student or technician should constantly review the many aspects of the governing building code as it relates to the specific region and building techniques.

■ ENERGY CODES

The Council of American Building Officials has published a model energy code that is used by the various building code enforcement agencies throughout the country. The purpose of this code is to regulate the design of various types of new building construction, so that various methods of design can provide high efficiency in the use of energy. The basic energy design criteria for new construction deals with the building envelope, which is defined as all the elements of a building encompassing spaces that are conditioned by various sources of energy. These sources of energy are those that are required to heat, cool, and provide illumination.

Design Methods

The energy code provides methods and techniques and encourages innovative design systems to achieve an effective use of energy. There are three methods of design that are accepted as a means of compliance with the intent of the code:

I. A systems approach for the entire building and its energy-using subsystems that may use nondepletable sources. This method establishes design criteria in terms of total energy use by a building, including all of its systems.
II. A component performance approach for the various building elements and mechanical systems and components. This method provides for buildings that are heated or mechanically cooled. These are constructed so as to provide the required thermal performance of the various components.
III. Specified acceptable practice. The requirements for this method are applicable only to buildings of less than 5000 square feet in gross floor area and three stories or less in height. This method is also limited to residential buildings that are heated or mechanically cooled and to other buildings that are heated only.

Design Influences

If your project falls into the category of Method III, you will be faced with many design decisions as to the construction of the various assemblies within the building envelope, as well as in the selection of mechanical and electrical equipment. Examples of building assemblies include the design and detailing of elements such as the roof, floors, and walls. For these detailed assemblies, it will be necessary to provide the required amount of insulation and to use the method that satisfies the design and energy code criteria.

For the energy design program, it is recommended that the architect or designer develop a typical building section in order to visualize the various building elements that will be affected by the energy design requirements. Figure 1.24 illustrates a building section showing elements of the building envelope that will have to be insulated. In some cases the size of some of the members of the envelope may need to be increased to accommodate the required depth of insulation, such as the depth of wood studs and roof joist. Items such as windows and skylights (in Figure 1.24) will be of major concern in the

TABLE NO. 25-U-J-1—ALLOWABLE SPANS FOR FLOOR JOISTS—40 LBS. PER SQ. FT. LIVE LOAD

DESIGN CRITERIA: Deflection—For 40 lbs. per sq. ft. live load. Limited to span in inches divided by 360. Strength—Live load of 40 lbs. per sq. ft. plus dead load of 10 lbs. per sq. ft. determines the required fiber stress value.

JOIST SIZE (IN)	SPACING (IN)	MODULES OF ELASTICITY, E, IN 1,000,000 PSI													
		0.8	0.9	1.0	1.1	1.2	1.3	1.4	1.5	1.6	1.7	1.8	1.9	2.0	2.2
2×6	12.0	8-6	8-10	9-6	9-9	10-0	10-3	10-6	10-9	10-11	11-2	11-4	11-7	11-11	
		720	780	830	890	940	990	1040	1090	1140	1190	1220	1280	1320	1410
	16.0	7-9	8-0	8-4	8-7	8-10	9-1	9-4	9-6	9-9	9-11	10-2	10-4	10-6	10-10
		790	860	920	980	1040	1090	1150	1200	1250	1310	1360	1410	1460	1550
	24.0	6-9	7-0	7-3	7-6	7-9	7-11	8-3	8-4	8-6	8-8	8-10	9-0	9-2	9-6
		900	980	1050	1120	1190	1250	1310	1380	1440	1500	1550	1610	1670	1780
2×8	12.0	11-3	11-8	12-1	12-6	12-10	13-2	13-6	13-10	14-2	14-5	14-8	15-0	15-3	15-9
		720	780	830	890	940	990	1040	1090	1140	1190	1230	1280	1320	1410
	16.0	10-2	10-7	11-0	11-4	11-8	12-0	12-3	12-7	12-10	13-1	13-4	13-7	13-10	14-3
		790	850	920	980	1040	1090	1150	1200	1250	1310	1360	1410	1460	1550
	24.0	8-11	9-3	9-7	9-11	10-2	10-6	10-9	11-0	11-3	11-5	11-8	11-11	12-1	12-6
		900	980	1050	1120	1190	1250	1310	1380	1440	1500	1550	1610	1670	1780
2×10	12.0	14-4	14-11	15-5	15-11	16-5	16-10	17-3	17-8	18-0	18-5	18-9	19-1	19-5	20-1
		720	780	830	890	940	990	1040	1090	1140	1190	1230	1280	1320	1410
	16.0	13-0	13-6	14-0	14-6	14-11	15-3	15-8	16-0	16-5	16-9	17-0	17-4	17-8	18-3
		790	850	920	980	1040	1090	1150	1200	1250	1310	1360	1410	1460	1550
	24.0	11-4	11-10	12-3	12-8	13-0	13-4	13-8	14-0	14-4	14-7	14-11	15-2	15-5	15-11
		900	980	1050	1120	1190	1250	1310	1380	1440	1500	1550	1610	1670	1780
2×12	12.0	17-5	18-1	18-9	19-4	11-11	20-6	21-0	21-6	21-11	22-5	22-10	23-3	23-7	24-5
		720	780	830	890	940	990	1040	1090	1140	1190	1230	1280	1320	1410
	16.0	15-10	16-5	17-0	17-7	18-1	18-7	19-1	19-6	19-11	20-4	20-9	21-1	21-6	22-2
		790	860	920	980	1040	1090	1150	1200	1250	1310	1360	1410	1460	1550
	24.0	13-10	14-4	14-11	15-4	15-10	16-3	16-8	17-0	17-5	17-9	18-1	18-5	18-9	19-4
		900	980	1050	1120	1190	1250	1310	1380	1440	1500	1550	1610	1670	1780

NOTES:

(1) The required extreme fiber stress in bending (F_b) in pounds per square inch is shown below each span.

(2) Use single or repetitive member bending stress values (F_b) and modulus of elasticity values (E) from Tables Nos. 25-A-1 and 25-A-2.

(3) For more comprehensive tables covering a broader range of bending stress values (F_b) and modulus of elasticity values (E), other spacing of members and other conditions of loading, see U.B.C. Standard No. 25-21.

(4) The spans in these tables are intended for use in covered structures or where moisture content in use does not exceed 19 percent.

Figure 1.21 Floor joist span table.

TABLE NO. 26-H—SHEAR ON ANCHOR BOLTS AND DOWELS—REINFORCED GYPSUM CONCRETE[1]

BOLT OR DOWEL SIZE (INCHES)	EMBEDMENT (INCHES)	SHEAR[2] (POUNDS)
3/8 Bolt	4	325
1/2 Bolt	5	450
5/8 Bolt	5	650
3/8 Deformed Dowel	6	325
1/2 Deformed Dowel	6	450

[1] The bolts or dowels shall be spaced not closer than 6 inches on center.

[2] The tabulated values may be increased one third for bolts or dowels resisting wind or seismic forces.

Figure 1.22 Bolt value table.

TABLE NO. 29-A—FOUNDATIONS FOR STUD BEARING WALLS—MINIMUM REQUIREMENTS[12]

NUMBER OF FLOORS SUPPORTED BY THE FOUNDATION[3]	THICKNESS OF FOUNDATION WALL (Inches)		WIDTH OF FOOTING (Inches)	THICKNESS OF FOOTING (Inches)	DEPTH BELOW UNDISTURBED GROUND SURFACE (Inches)
	UNIT CONCRETE	MASONRY			
1	6	6	12	6	12
2	8	8	15	7	18
3	10	10	18	8	24

[1] Where unusual conditions or frost conditions are found, footings, and foundations shall be as required in Section 2907(a).

[2] The ground under the floor may be excavated to the elevation of the top of the footing.

[3] Foundations may support a roof in addition to the stipulated number of floors. Foundations supporting roofs only shall be as required for supporting one floor.

Figure 1.23 Foundation table.

design of the building envelope. The area of glass and type of glass and the number of skylights will be determined by the energy design computations. These computations may indicate that the windows and skylights will have to be dual-glaze glass rather than single-glazed.

Building Insulation.   Insulation requirements for the roof, wall, and floor assemblies will be determined by the required U factor for that particular element. The **U factor** is defined as the time rate of heat flow per unit area and unit temperature differences between the warm side and cold side air films. The U factor applies to a combination of all the materials that constitute a specific assembly used along the heat-flow path, single materials used for a building assembly, cavity air spaces, and surface air films on both sides of a building assembly. Figure 1.25 depicts an example of an exterior wall assembly with a combination of various materials that establish a U factor.

Mechanical Equipment.   Other influences that will be integrated into the design problem are items such as mechanical and electrical equipment. The heating and cooling systems equipment will be sized according to the required efficiency factor. This factor may be expressed in the maximum allowable Btu (British thermal unit) rating of the equipment, as well as satisfying a prescribed efficiency rating of the equipment. The efficiency rating of the equipment is established by the equipment manufacturer. In Method III, which deals mainly with residential construction, it is required that all heating and cooling equipment be equipped with one thermostat for regulating the space temperature, as well as a readily accessible manual or automatic means to partially restrict or shut off the heating or cooling input to each zone. In general, various control methods may be implemented to reduce the consumption of energy in heating and cooling systems.

Air Leakage in the Building Envelope.   For energy design in the working drawing process, you will be required to provide solutions and details for all exterior joints that are sources for air leakage through the building envelope. These exterior joints are such assemblies as windows, doors, wall cavities, spaces between walls and foundations, spaces between walls and roof-ceiling members, and openings for the penetration of various utility services through the roof, walls, and floors. All these openings and any others must be sealed by means of caulking, gaskets, weatherstripping, or other acceptable methods.

Service Water Heating.   Water heating storage tanks and supply piping will have to be installed in accordance with the energy code. The energy code ordinance will require that specific water heaters be labeled as meeting the established efficiency requirements, as well as being equipped with automatic controls for acceptable temperature settings and a separate switch for shutdown when the use of the system is not required for a specific period of time. It should be noted that an analysis of energy expenditure for electrical power distribution and lighting systems is exempt for detached dwellings and dwelling portions of multifamily complexes and is regulated by Method III.

The foregoing discussion and illustrations have given a few examples of the influencing factors that will have to be resolved in the design and working drawing program. In most cases, because of the complexity of the energy design process, the energy design calculations, the specifications for equipment, insulation, glass, and construction assemblies will be provided by an energy consultant or mechanical engineer. It is recommended that the student or technician obtain a copy of the energy code for reference in conjunction with the building code.

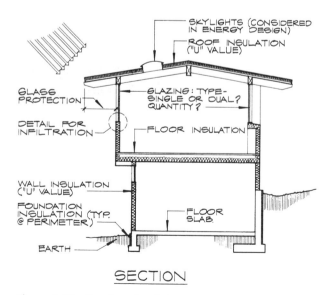

Figure 1.24 Envelope insulation.

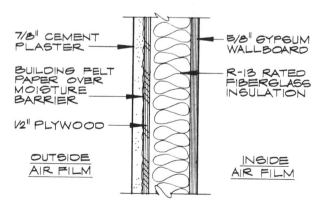

Figure 1.25 Wall assembly combination.

chapter

2

BASIC DRAFTING REQUIREMENTS, STANDARDS, AND TECHNIQUES

Through the 1980s and 1990s the architectural industry produced a legion of CAD drafters, who produced everything from presentation drawings to construction documents. This new breed of architectural drafter, however, could do only what the computer would allow him or her to do. The CAD drafters were controlled by the new tool, rather than using the new tool to their advantage. The reason was that the new tool would not only draw the floor plan, but would also dimension it to tolerances the industry could not hold. It would, for example, dimension a masonry structure to what was drawn rather than to the required block modules for masonry units. And this was just a minor difficulty. Model-making skills (for real models) were being lost. For the drafter constantly working in virtual model space, the concept of real scale in a real world began to diminish.

Frequently, CAD drafters could format a presentation only if it had been done by a computer. As the profession looked to the educational institutions to provide skilled employment for employees, requests of the potential employers were for CAD drafters. Today, the requests are for CAD drafters who can draft manually, sketch, and communicate architectural design concepts in buildable, realistic construction documents.

Manual drafting produces the eye-hand connection needed in designing or producing freehand drafted drawings for subordinates to draft on a computer. Thus, it becomes imperative to learn manual (hand) drafting before attempting to draft on the computer (CAD). To do otherwise produces a disconnect between eye and hand.

■ SKETCHING

Sketching is the process of developing eye-hand coordination that aids in the design process. The designer can accurately maintain the proportions that are so essential in design.

Initially, all elements are sketched, from the design of a structure to a specific architectural detail. This is a way of conveying to the CAD drafter the ideas you are trying to deliver to the men and women in the field. Details, in particular, need to be resolved before the plans, elevations, and building sections are drafted, as they will dictate the shape and configuration of structural components. The decor around a window, the form of a guardrail, and the connection of a column to a roof are but a few conditions exemplifying the control that can be exercised in the freehand detailing process.

Any new idea for assembly needs to be sketched (freehand) and studied before it is hard-lined manually or drafted on the computer. These detail sketches (design sketches) are then sent to the drafter to draw formally. This ability to sketch and communicate puts the employee at a management/supervision level, not at the design level.

When we refer to freehand detail, scale is still used, especially at critical intersections. It is a thing of beauty to see an architect or senior designer freehand a detail (often without a scale), with his or her command of proportion and ability to draw in scale without a scale. Such designers begin to trust their own instincts when sketching, in reference to scale and proportion.

■ DRAFTING

In 2001 the rolling blackouts in California pushed the energy crisis from a threat into a reality and gave new meaning to manual drafting. Hardest hit in northern California were the architectural and aircraft industries and one of the major computer companies. Visualize, if you will, CAD drafters in a sea of computers searching for a pencil. For those firms that hired CAD/manual drafters, little time was lost in production because the work continued. Although most CAD drafting stations are not set up for manual drafting, each station needs a space to lay out drawings, or at least a reference space that can be used for minimal manual drafting. On the other hand, design stations often have CAD drafting as well as a space for manual drafting/sketching/modeling (computer/real) to take place.

The need for this combination CAD/manual drafting can best be realized in the spirit room (a sort of creative think tank), where concept drawings are usually produced. If teams produce the design, the senior designers usually produce sketches and translate the concept sketches into a hard-line drawing via computer or manual drafting.

Drafting manually also develops many positive attributes and skills that are needed to sustain employees in the future. These come in the form of:

A. *Patience.* Drafting manually produces a high degree of understanding of one's own limits and timing.

B. *Appreciation for CAD.* Drafting manually allows the CAD drafter to appreciate the increased productivity CAD affords. For example, those who learned how to drive with a stick shift realize that an automatic transmission is a luxury. Such knowledge is useful if you find yourself in a situation where your vehicle is blocked by a friend's vehicle that is a stick shift and you cannot drive a stick. You are now dependent on another to move the car. Similarly, you become dependent on others who have the capability to draft manually if the computers are inoperable.

C. *Flexibility.* CAD drafters possessing manual drafting skills are more flexible in their ability to create drawings. Suppose, for example, after plotting a plan, one notices a couple of small errors on a drawing. The errors can be quickly corrected manually to meet a deadline or an appointment. On the computer, however, corrections cannot be made as quickly, because first you must locate the file you want to change, make the correction, and then reprint/plot the drawing. Thus, if your manual drafting skills (e.g., lettering) are 80% to 90% as good as the computer's, no one will ever notice the manually performed corrections.

D. *Presentational drawings.* Many CAD drafters are not proficient in the use of standard drafting equipment. Thus, they are not effective in formatting and producing presentation boards and cutting mats.

E. *Model construction.* Construction of actual mock-up design models, massing models, or presentation models are frequently constructed manually for a client's review.

Summary

The following are advantages of the manually drafted drawing process:

1. Eye-hand coordination is developed.
2. Viewers get a look at the drawing as it will appear to the construction workers in the field.
3. Drawing is done at the scale that will be printed.
4. Hard copies allow you to look at all the drawings in a set one at a time, even during development.
5. Line quality can be varied, depending on need and the intent of the drawing.
6. Metes and bounds can be varied, exactly as the civil engineer labels them in the site plan.
7. Hand drawing allows the drafter to think through the drafting process and assess his or her own skills to match the task.
8. Hand drafting enhances other skills needed in the office, such as model making, creating presentation drawings, and even the process of design or translating design.
9. Hand drafting allows assessment of personal human skills, rather than those of machines.
10. Hand drafting promotes a better understanding of how to incorporate the computer into the production drawing.

■ KINDS OF DRAFTING EQUIPMENT

Basic Equipment

The drafting tools needed by a beginning draftsperson and the basic uses of those tools are shown in Figure 2.1 and are as follows:

1. **T-square.** A straightedge used to draft horizontal lines and base for the use of triangles.

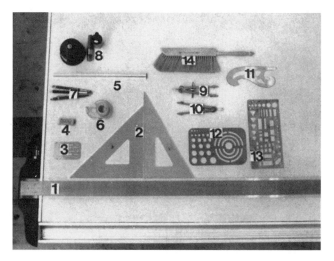

Figure 2.1 Basic drafting equipment.

2. **Triangle.** A there-sided guide used to draft vertical lines and angular lines in conjunction with a T-square. The 30°/60° and 45° triangles are basic equipment.
3. **Erasing shield.** A metal or plastic card with prepunched slots and holes used to protect some portions of a drawing while erasing others.
4. **Eraser.** A rubber or synthetic material used to erase errors and correct drawings.
5. **Scale.** A measuring device calibrated in a variety of scales for ease of translating large objects into a small proportional drawing.
6. **Drafting tape.** Tape used to hold paper while drafting.
7. **Drafting dots.** Circular-shaped tape.
8. **Drafting pencil and lead holders.** Housing for drafting leads.
9. **Lead pointer.** A device used to sharpen the lead in a lead holder.
10. **Divider.** A device resembling a compass, used mainly for transferring measurements from one location to another.
11. **Compass.** A V-shaped device for drafting arcs and circles.
12. **French curve.** A pattern used to draft irregular arcs.
13. **Circle template.** A prepunched sheet of plastic punched in various sizes, for use as a pattern for circles without using a compass.
14. **Plan template.** Prepunched patterns for shapes commonly found in architectural plans.
15. **Dusting brush.** A brush used to keep drafting surfaces clean and free of debris.

Additional Equipment

In addition to the tools listed above, a number of others aid and simplify the drafting process. They are shown in Figure 2.2.

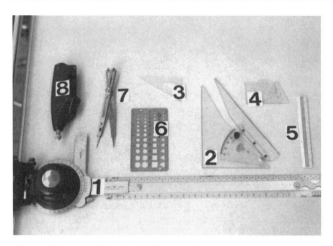

Figure 2.2 Additional drafting equipment.

Figure 2.3 Parallel straightedge. (Courtesy of Kratos/Keuffel & Esser.)

1. **Track drafter.** A device that allows the drafting pencil to rest against the blade of the scale, and be held stationary while the whole track drafter is moved to draw (track) a line. Look at the track on the left side of the drafting table in Figure 2.2.
2. **Adjustable triangle.** A triangle used to draft odd angles such as those found in the pitch (slope) of a roof.
3. **Triangles of various sizes.** Triangles range in size from extremely small ones, used for detailing or lettering, to very large ones, used for dimension lines, perspectives, and so on.
4. **Lettering guide.** A device used for drafting guidelines of varying heights.
5. **Flat scales.** The scales shown in Figure 2.2 are smaller than those shown in Figure 2.1 and are flat. They provide greater ease of handling, but they do not have as many different scales.
6. **Specialty templates.** Specialty templates include furniture, trees, electrical and mechanical equipment, geometric shapes, and standard symbols.
7. **Proportional dividers.** Dividers used to enlarge or reduce a drawing to any proportion.
8. **Electric eraser.** Particularly useful when you are working with erasable sepias or ink.
9. **Parallel straightedge.** Shown in Figure 2.3, this device is often preferred over a T-square, because it always remains horizontal without the user's constantly checking for alignment. This straightedge runs along cords on both sides, which are mounted on the top or the underside of the drafting board. Parallel straightedges are available in lengths up to 72 inches.
10. **Drafting machine.** Shown in Figure 2.4, this machine uses a pair of scales attached on an arm. These scales move in a parallel fashion so parallel, horizontal, and vertical lines can be drawn. A protractor

Figure 2.4 Drafting machine. (Courtesy of Kratos/Keuffel & Esser.)

mechanism allows the drafter to rapidly move the scales to any desired angle. The drafting machine can be mounted onto a drafting board as shown in the illustration or on a drafting desk.

This list is by no means complete. Your selection of tools will be dictated by office standards and the requirements of particular projects.

Using Triangles

Triangles are generally used in conjunction with a straightedge such as a parallel bar, a T-square, or even another triangle (see Figure 2.5). Also note that a combination of triangles can produce 15° and 75° lines in addition to a perpendicular 90° angle, a 45° line, and 30° and 60° lines.

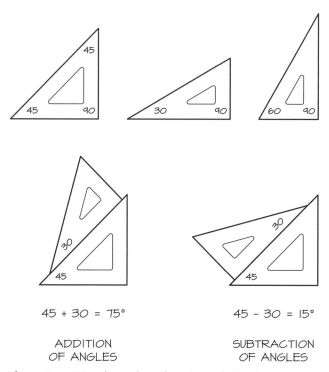

45 + 30 = 75°

ADDITION
OF ANGLES

45 – 30 = 15°

SUBTRACTION
OF ANGLES

Figure 2.5 Triangles and combinations of triangles.

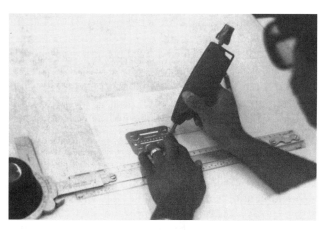

Figure 2.6 Drawing a dotted (hidden) line.

Figure 2.7 The triangle scale.

Figure 2.8 Reading the scale.

Using Erasing Shields and Erasers

Drawing Dotted Lines   Dotted lines, which are usually called **hidden lines** in drafting, can be drawn rapidly by using an erasing shield and an eraser. An electric eraser is more effective than a regular eraser.

First, draw the line as if it were a solid line, using the correct pressure to produce the desired darkness. Second, lay the erasing shield over the line so that the row of uniformly drilled holes on the shield aligns with the solid line. Next, erase through the small holes. The results will be a uniform and rapidly produced hidden (dotted) line.

This technique is particularly effective for foundation plans, which use many hidden lines. See Figure 2.6.

Using the Scale

The Triangle Scale.   The most convenient scale to purchase is a triangular scale because it gives the greatest variety in one single instrument. There are usually 11 scales on a triangle scale, one of which is an ordinary 12-inch ruler. See Figure 2.7.

Reading the Scale.   Because structures cannot be drawn full scale, the 12-inch ruler, which is full scale, is seldom used. Reading a scale is much the same as reading a regular ruler. Translating a full-size object into a reduced scale—1½ scale, for example—is more a matter of your visual attitude than of translating from one scale to another. For example, you can simply imagine a 12-inch ruler reduced to 1½ inches in size and used to measure at this reduced scale. The scale is written on a drawing as 1½″ = 1′-0″. See Figure 2.8.

On an architectural scale, inches are measured to the left of the zero. Numbers are often printed here to indicate the inches to be measured. Note the 1½ standing by itself on the extreme left. The number explains the scale.

All three sides of the triangle scale (except the side with the 12-inch scale) have two scales on each usable surface. Each of these two scales uses the full length of the instrument, but one is read from left to right and the other from right to left. Typically, a scale is either one half or double the scale it is paired with. For example, if one end is a ¼-inch scale, the opposite end is a ⅛-inch scale; if one end is a ⅜-inch scale, the opposite end is a

$^3/_4$-inch scale. The opposite end of the 3-inch scale would be the 1$^1/_2$-inch scale.

Confusion is often caused by the numbers between the two scales. Look carefully at these numbers and notice two sets. One set is closer to the groove that runs the length of the scale and the other is closer to the outside edge. The numbers near the edge will be the feet increments for the smaller scale, and the other numbers will be the feet increments for the larger scale. In Figure 2.8A, notice a lower and a higher 2. The upper, right-hand 2 is 2 feet on the 1$^1/_2$-inch scale, and the lower, left-hand 2 is the number of feet from 0 on the opposite side, which is the 3-inch scale and not seen in the photograph. Because the lower 2 falls halfway between the 0 and the upper 2, in this example, it is read as 1 on the 1$^1/_2$-inch scale. Starting from the opposite direction, the upper 2 is read as 1$^1/_2$ feet because it is found halfway between the 1 and 2 of the 3-inch scale.

Figure 2.8B shows a $^1/_4$-inch scale. Notice, again, the two sets of numbers. Since the opposite end (not shown) contains the $^1/_8$-inch scale, the lower numbers belong to the $^1/_4$-inch side. Notice that they are read 0, 2, 4, 6, 8, etc. In between are numbers that read (from right to left) 92, 88, 84, 80, etc. These numbers belong to the $^1/_8$-inch scale on the opposite side.

An easy error to make is to read the wrong number because the "32" on the $^1/_8$-inch scale is so close to the "32" on the $^1/_4$-inch scale. Similar pitfalls occur in other pairs of scales on the triangle scale.

Most engineering scales use the same principles as architectural scales, except that measurements are divided into tenths, twentieths, and so on, rather than halves, quarters, and eighths. The section on metrics explains these metric scales further.

Using Drafting Tape

A simple but effective method of taping original drawings is to keep the edges of the tape parallel with the edges of the vellum (a translucent high-quality tracing paper), as shown in Figure 2.9. This prevents the T-square or whatever type of straightedge is used from catching the corner of the tape and rolling it off. Vellum taped at an angle creates unnecessary frustrations for the beginning draftsperson. Drafting supply stores sell tape in a round shape (large dot), which is even better.

Rolling Original Drawings

Most beginners begin rolling drawings in the wrong direction. In their attempt to protect the drawings, they often roll the print or the original so that the printed side is on the *inside*, as shown in Figure 2.10A. However, the correct way is to roll the sheet so that the artwork is on the *outside*, as shown in Figure 2.10B.

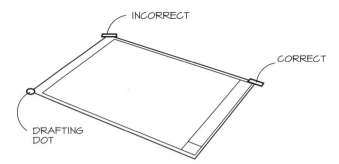

Figure 2.9   Correct placement of drafting tape.

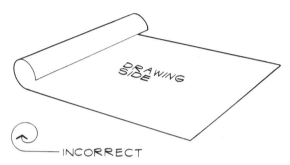

Figure 2.10A   Incorrect way to roll a drawing.

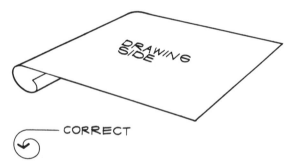

Figure 2.10B   Correct way to roll a drawing.

When a set of prints is unrolled and read, the drawings should roll toward the table and should not interfere with easy reading by curling up. If originals are rolled correctly, the vellum curls toward the drafting table or blueprint machine, preventing it from being torn when drafting equipment slides across it or when it is being reproduced.

■ SELECTING AND USING DRAFTING PENCILS

Types of Leads

Seventeen grades of leads are available, but only a few of these are appropriate for drafting. Harder leads are given an **"H"** designation, while soft leads are given a desig-

Figure 2.11 Lead hardnesses.

nation of **"B"**. Between the "H" and "B" range are **"HB"** and **"F"** leads. The softest "B" lead is 6B (number 6) while the hardest "H" lead is 9H (number 9). See Figure 2.11.

Selection Factors.   Only the central range of leads is used for drafting. 2H, 3H, and 4H are good for light layout, while H is good for a medium-weight line. F leads are excellent for dark object lines.

However, many other factors also determine the choice of pencil. Temperature and humidity may dictate that certain leads be used. Manufacturers vary in what they designate as a particular grade. And the natural pressure that the drafter places on the pencil varies from individual to individual. The reproduction method to be used also determines the grade of lead chosen.

For photography, a crisp line is better than a dark one because a dark, broad line may end up as a blur on the negative. Diazo prints (blue or black lines on a white background) need to block out light, and so a dense line is more important.

Pencils Versus Lead Holders

Wood pencils are fine for the beginner, but serious drafting requires mechanical lead holders. See Figure 2.12. Wood pencils require sharpening of both the wood and the lead, which is time-consuming. More important, a lead holder allows you the full use of the lead, whereas a wood pencil cannot.

Lead Pointers

A lead pointer, a tool used to sharpen drafting leads, is a must. Sandpaper can be used for both wood pencils and lead holders, but it is not nearly as convenient, consistent, or rapid as a lead pointer. A good practice after using a lead pointer is as follows: Take the sharpened lead and hold the pointer perpendicular to a hard surface such as a triangle; crush the tip of the lead slightly; then hone the tip by drawing a series of circular lines on a piece of scratch paper. You can also use this process with a wood pencil. This stops

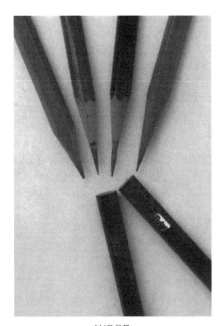

WOOD
PENCILS

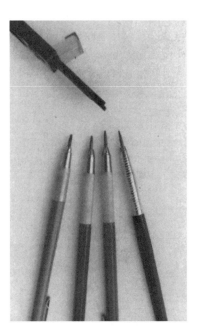

MECHANICAL
LEAD HOLDERS

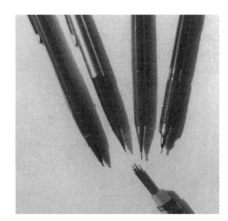

SUPERTHIN (FINE LINE)
LEAD HOLDERS

Figure 2.12 Types of lead holders and pencils.

the lead from breaking on the first stroke. Roll the pencil as you draw to keep a consistent tip on the lead. See Figure 2.13. Draw either clockwise or counterclockwise, depending on whichever produces the best line and is the most comfortable for you. Note the position of the fingers and thumb at the beginning and end of the line.

Superthin Lead Holders

The last type of drafting lead holders, also called fine line lead holders, produces consistent, superthin lines. The diameters of the leads are 0.3 mm, 0.5 mm, 0.7 mm, and 0.9 mm, and the leads come in almost the full range of grades. The most popular of these holders is the 0.5 mm size, because it gives the best thickness of lines. There is no sharpening necessary, so drawing time is maximized. Some drafters still roll this holder as they draw to keep the rounded point, thus avoiding an easily broken chisel point. However, a chisel point is often desirable for lettering. For example, except for the freehand sketches, all of the lettering in this book is done with a chisel end on a superthin holder.

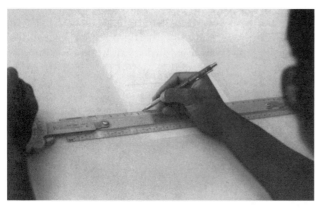

A

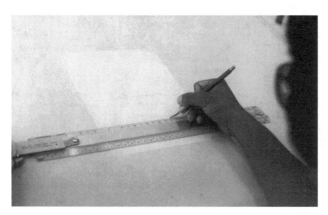

B

Figure 2.13   Rotating the pencil to keep a founded point.

■ DRAWING PRACTICE

The actual practice of drawing must follow standards. Standards are prescribed to the drafter, for both manual and computer drafting, and become the foundation for the translation of drawings from design drawings to construction documents.

With the possible exception of lettering, the following descriptions of line quality, material designation, profiling, dimensioning, and so forth, are for the enhancement of the images (drawings) that we are preparing and as such are not inclusive of manual drafting. Additional office standards can be found in Chapter 6, and CAD standards in Chapter 3.

Lines and Line Quality

Basically, lines can be broken down into three types: light, medium, and dark. Each of these types can be broken down further by variation of pressure and lead.

Light Lines.   The lightest lines used are usually the guidelines drawn to help with lettering height. These lines should be only barely visible and should completely disappear when a diazo print is made. Darker than guidelines but still relatively light are the lines used in dimension and extension lines, leaders, and break lines.

Medium Lines.   Medium-weight lines are used in object and center lines, and in the dashed type of line used for hidden or dotted lines.

Dark Lines.   The darkest lines are used for border lines and cutting plane lines, major sections, and details. See Figure 2.14.

Choosing Line Quality.   Line quality depends on the use of that particular line. An intense line is used to profile and emphasize; an intermediate line is used to show elements such as walls and structural members; and a light line is used for elements such as dimensioning and door swings.

Another way to vary line quality is to increase the width of the line. A thicker line can represent the walls on a floor plan, the outline of a building on a site plan, or the outline of a roof on a roof plan. See Figure 2.14 for line quality examples and uses and Figure 2.15 for an example of the types of lines used to indicate property lines and easements.

Hidden or Dotted Lines.   Hidden or dotted lines are used to indicate objects hidden from view. Solid objects covered by earth, such as foundations, can be indicated with hidden lines. This type of line can also depict future structures, items that are not in the contract, public utilities locations, easements, a wheelchair turning radius, or the direction of sliding doors and windows.

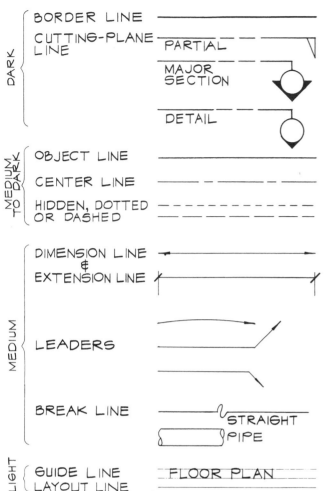

Figure 2.14 Vocabulary of architectural lines.

A floor plan will often show the roof outline, or a balcony above, or a change in ceiling height with a dotted line. On a site plan, dotted lines indicate the existing grades on the site (see Chapter 8).

Arrowheads. Different types of arrowheads are used in dimensioning. These are shown in Figure 2.16. The top one is used architecturally more for leaders than for dimension lines. The second one with the tick mark is the arrowhead most prevalently used in our field. The dot is used in conjunction with the tick mark when you are dimensioning two systems. For example, the dot can be used to locate the center of steel columns, and the tick mark can be used to dimension the secondary structure within a building built of wood. The final wide arrowhead is used as a design arrowhead in many offices.

Material Designation Lines. Material designation lines are used to indicate the building material used. See Figure 2.17 for a sample of tapered or light-dark lines. (This device saves time; complete lines take longer to draw.) Also note the cross-hatched lines between the parallel lines that represent the wall thickness on Figure 2.18. These diagonal lines represent masonry.

Profiling

Architectural profiling is the process of taking the most important features of a drawing and outlining them. Figure 2.19 shows four applications of this concept.

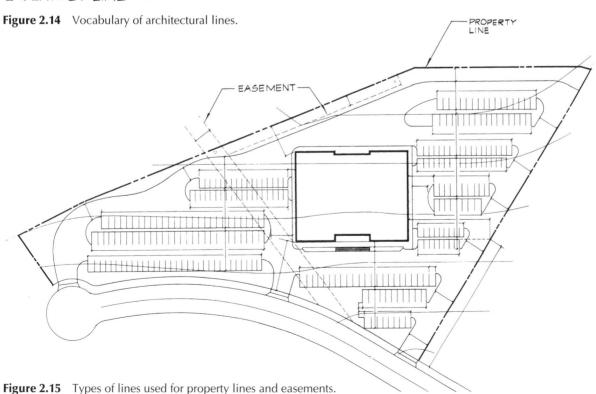

Figure 2.15 Types of lines used for property lines and easements.

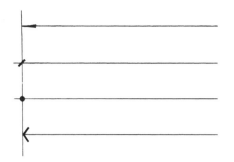

Figure 2.16 Types of arrowheads used in dimensioning.

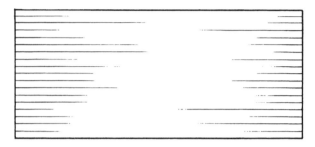

Figure 2.17 Tapered lines.

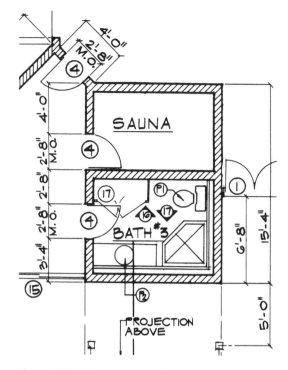

Figure 2.18 Lines representing masonry.

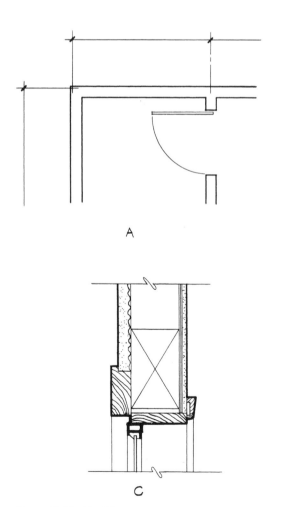

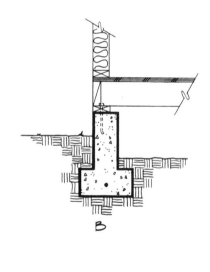

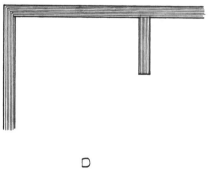

Figure 2.19 Profiling.

Example A illustrates the darkening of the lines that represent the walls of a floor plan. The dimension lines or extension lines are drawn as medium weight lines not only to contrast with the walls but to allow the walls of the particular floor plan to standout. In example B, a footing detail is profiled. Because the concrete work is important here, its outline is drawn darker than any other part of the detail.

Example C shows the top portion (head) of a window. The light lines at the bottom of the detail represent the side of the window. Note how the head section is outlined and the interior parts plus the sides of the walls are drawn lightly.

Example D represents another form of profiling, called "pouché," which enhances the profile technique by using shading. This shading can be done by pencil shading or by lines. Example B also uses this principle: In this instance, the dots and triangles that represent concrete in section are placed along the perimeter (near the profiled line) in greater quantity than toward the center.

In a section drawing, items most often profiled are cut by the cutting plane line. A footing detail, for example, is nothing more than a theoretical knife (a cutting plane) cutting through the wall of the structure. The portion most often cut is the concrete, so it is profiled.

On an elevation, the main outline of the structure should be darkened. See Figure 2.20. This type of profiling is used to simplify the illusion of the elevation to show that the structure is basically an L-shape structure and that one portion does actually project forward.

In the plan view, often the outline of the main structure is heavily outlined (profiled) in order to make the main area stand out more than any other feature of the property. See Figure 2.21 for a finished plan and elevation which have been properly profiled.

■ LETTERING

Importance of Hand Lettering

Being able to hand letter well becomes very important when correcting drawings. This is especially true when correcting computer-generated construction documents. Take, for example, a computer-generated roof framing plan. Let us say the CAD drafter mislabeled a rafter on the plan and posted a 2 × 4 rafter at 12" on center as a note, whereas in reality the rafter should have been a 2 × 6 rafter at 16" on center. For some strange reason, errors of this kind are usually discovered after the document is printed and during the reproduction of multiple field copies. At this point, to locate the drawing in the computer's memory, correct it, and replot the drawing becomes a time-consuming effort, not to mention the cost of supplies. Had the note been printed in an architectural font, it would be a simple matter to erase the error and reletter it by hand. This would be a five-minute task. For this reason, it makes sense not only to use an architectural font on computer-generated drawings for dimensions, notes, and call-outs that may change, but also to master hand lettering and manual drafting as well.

Architectural lettering differs somewhat from the Gothic type letters developed by C. W. Reinhardt about eighty-plus years ago and now called "mechanical lettering." Architectural lettering has evolved from a series of influences, including the demand for speed. We must not, however, interpret speed to mean sloppiness.

Another influence on architectural lettering was style. The architecturally drafted plan was in essence an idea or concept on paper, a creative endeavor. So the lines and the lettering took on a characteristic style of their own. In many firms, stylized lettering serves to identify

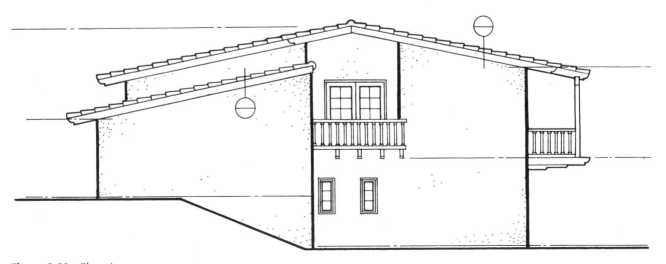

Figure 2.20 Elevation.

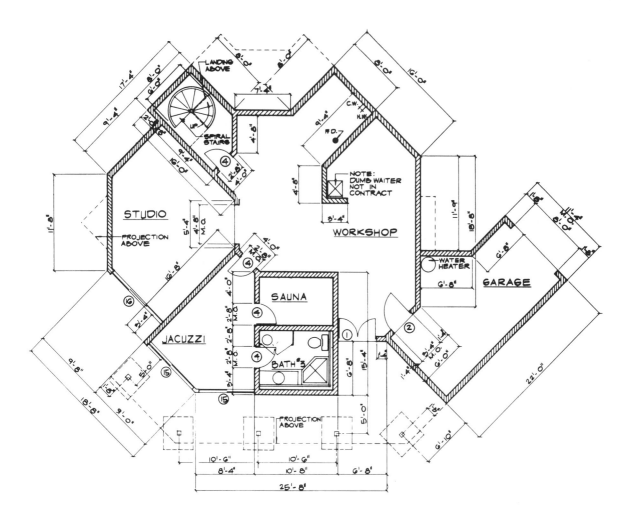

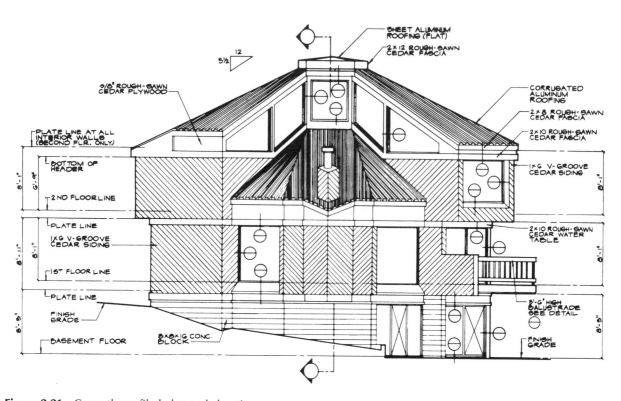

Figure 2.21 Correctly profiled plan and elevation.

the individual draftsperson. However, most firms attempt to create a uniform style of lettering for their entire staff. Stylizing must not be confused with overdecoration. Lettering that looks like a new alphabet should not be justified in the name of stylization.

Basic Rules for Lettering and Numbering

Following are a few simple rules for lettering and numbering:

1. Master mechanical lettering before attempting architectural lettering or any type of stylization. A student who cannot letter well in mechanical drafting has less chance of developing good architectural letters.
2. Learn to letter with vertical strokes first. Sloping letters may be easier to master, but most architectural offices prefer vertical lettering. It is easier to change from vertical to sloping letters than the reverse. See Figure 2.22.
3. Practice words, phrases, and numbers—not just individual letters. Copy a phrase from this book, for example.
4. The shape of a letter should not be changed. The proportion of the letter may be slightly altered but one should never destroy the letter's original image. Although the middle example "W" in Figure 2.23 is in a style used for speed, it can be misconstrued as an "I" and a "V".
5. Changing the proportions of letters changes their visual effect. See Figure 2.24.
6. Certain strokes can be emphasized so that one letter is not mistaken for another. This also forces the draftsperson to be more definitive in the formation of individual strokes. The strokes emphasized should be those most important to that letter; for example, a

"B" differs from an "R" by the rounded lower right stroke, and an "L" from an "I" by the horizontal bottom stroke extending to the right only. The beginning or end of these strokes can be emphasized by bearing down on the pencil to ensure a good reprint of that portion. See Figure 2.25.

7. Many draftspersons have picked up the bad habit of mixing uppercase and lowercase letters. This is not good lettering.
8. Some draftspersons have also developed a style of leaving space within the letter that is not there. This too is to be discouraged. See Figure 2.26.
9. Consistency produces good lettering. If vertical lines are used, they must all be parallel. A slight variation produces poor lettering. Even round letters such as "O" have a center through which imaginary vertical strokes will go. See Figure 2.27.
10. Second only to the letter itself in importance is spacing. Good spacing protects good letter formation. Poor spacing destroys even the best lettering. See Figure 2.28.
11. Always use guidelines and use them to the fullest. See Figure 2.29.

EXAMPLE:

B L I T R K

Figure 2.25 Emphasis on certain strokes.

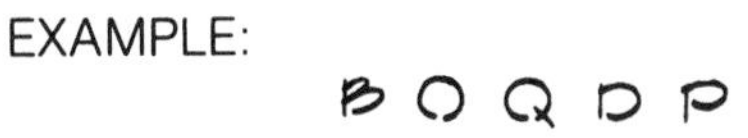

EXAMPLE:

B O Q D P

Figure 2.26 Spaces incorrectly left within letters.

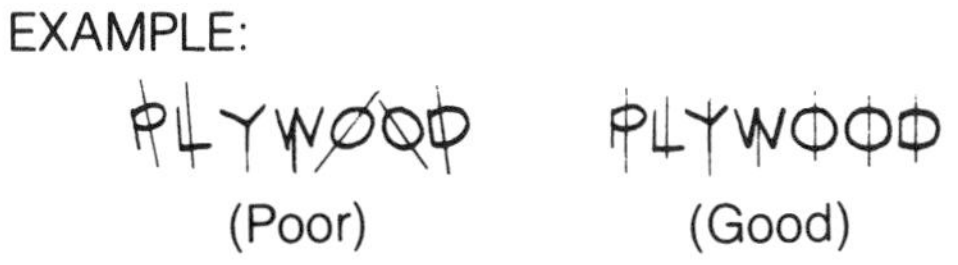

EXAMPLE:

PLYWOOD   PLYWOOD
(Poor)   (Good)

Figure 2.27 Producing consistency.

EXAMPLE:

PLYWOOD   P LY WO OD
(Good)   (Poor)

Figure 2.28 Importance of good spacing.

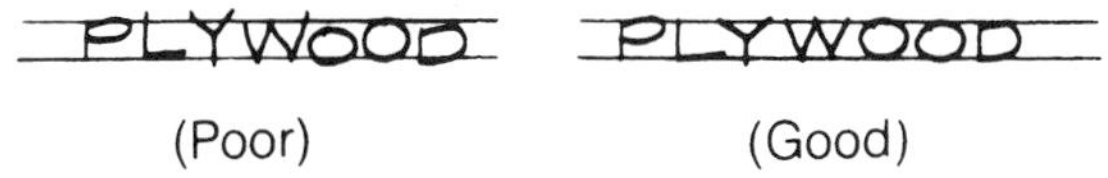

PLYWOOD   PLYWOOD
(Poor)   (Good)

Figure 2.29 Full use of guidelines.

ANCHOR BOLT   ANCHOR BOLT

VERTICAL LETTERS   SLOPING LETTERS

MECHANICAL   ARCHITECTURAL

M W   /\ \/ /\/\ ←(Poor)

Figure 2.23 Overworking architectural letters.

MECHANICAL   ARCHITECTURAL

STUD   STUD STUD

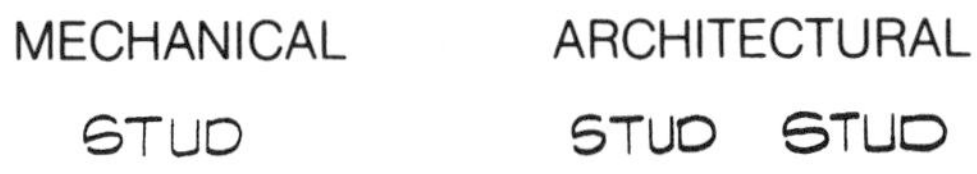

Figure 2.24 Changing proportions to produce architectural effect.

Using Guidelines

Although a purist might frown on the practice, a guideline or straightedge can be used in lettering to speed up the learning process. Horizontal lines are easier for a beginner than vertical lines, and shapes appear better formed when all of the vertical strokes are perfectly perpendicular and parallel to each other. Curved and round strokes are done without the aid of an instrument.

After drawing the guidelines, place a T-square or parallel about 2 or 3 inches below the lines. Locate the triangle to the left of the area to be lettered with the vertical portion of the triangle on the right side. See Figure 2.30. "Eyeball" the spacing of the letter. Position your pencil as if you are ready to make the vertical line without the triangle. Before you make the vertical stroke, slide the triangle over against the pencil and make the stroke. See Figure 2.31 and 2.32. Draw nonvertical lines freehand. See Figure 2.33.

Using a straightedge helps build up skills. Eventually you should discontinue its use as practice improves your lettering skills.

Drafting Conventions and Dimensions

Using Net and Nominal Sizing. Many architectural offices have adopted the practice of separating the **net size** and the **nominal size** of lumber in their notations. The nominal size (call-out size) is used to describe or order a piece of lumber. The net size is the size of the actual piece of wood drawn and used. For example, the nominal size of a "two by four" is 2 × 4, but the net or actual size is $1\frac{1}{2}'' \times 3\frac{1}{2}''$. The distinction between the two sizes is accomplished by the use of inch (") marks. Figure 2.34A would be very confusing because the nominal size is listed but inch marks are used. Compare this notation with that of Figure 2.34B. The 16" o.c. (on center) is to be translated as precisely 16 inches, whereas the 2 × 4 is used to indicate nominal size.

Dimensions. Dimensions in feet are normally expressed by a small mark to the upper right of a number ('), and inches by two small marks (") in the same location. To separate feet from inches, a dash is used. See Figure 2.35. The dash in this type of dimensions becomes very

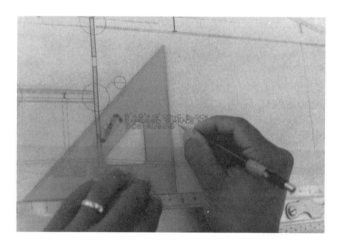

Figure 2.30 Pencil placement for vertical lettering.

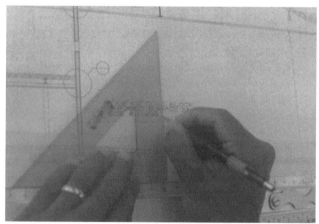

Figure 2.32 Drawing the vertical stroke.

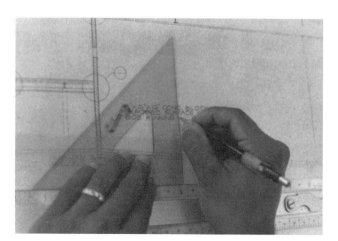

Figure 2.31 Placing the triangle against the pencil.

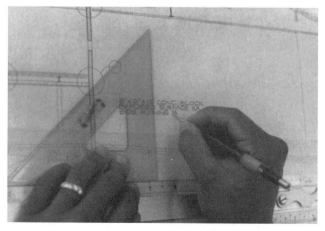

Figure 2.33 Completing the letter.

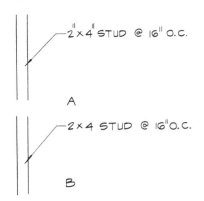

Figure 2.34 Net and nominal notation.

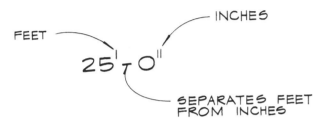

Figure 2.35 Expressing feet and inches.

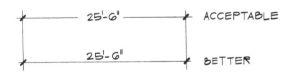

Figure 2.36 Dimensions in a restricted area.

Figure 2.37 Placement of dimensions above or between dimension line.

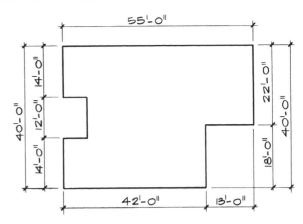

Figure 2.38 Dimensions read from bottom and from the right.

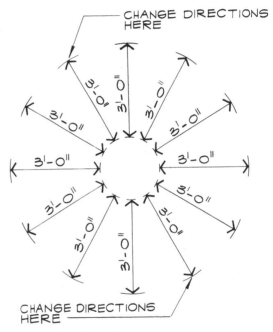

Figure 2.39 Dimension placement.

important because it avoids dimensions being misread and adds to clarity. If space for dimensions is restricted, an acceptable abbreviated form can be used. This is illustrated in Figure 2.36. The inches are raised and underlined to separate them from the feet notation.

Placement of Dimensions. Dimension lines can be broken to show the numerical value, but it is faster simply to put numerical values above the lines. See Figure 2.37. When dimension lines run vertically, place the numbers above the dimension line as viewed from the right. See Figure 2.38.

Not all dimension lines, however, are horizontal or vertical. Often dimension lines are angled, and this can cause problems when you position the numerical value. Figure 2.39 suggests a possible location for such values.

■ USING TERMINOLOGY: MECHANICAL VERSUS ARCHITECTURAL

Mechanical Drafting

Although mechanical drafting resembles architectural drafting, the terms used vary greatly. The basis for mechanical drafting is a method of multiview drawing known as orthographic projection. This method uses a concept in which an object is first housed in a theoretical glass box, as shown in Figure 2.40; second, unfolded as shown in Figure 2.41; and third, viewed in this unfolded form as a flat form. Portions of this six-sided form are given names such as top view, front view, and right side view. The back, left side, and bottom are eliminated, as Figure 2.42 shows.

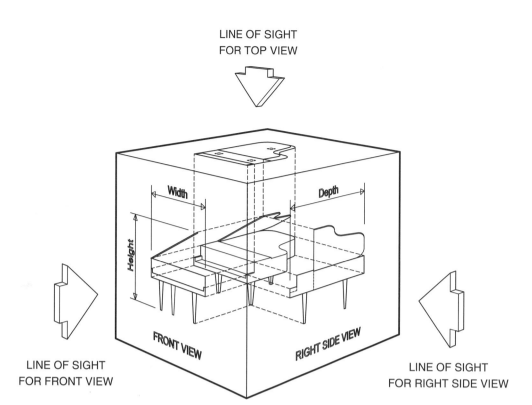

LINE OF SIGHT
FOR TOP VIEW

Width

Depth

Height

FRONT VIEW

RIGHT SIDE VIEW

LINE OF SIGHT
FOR FRONT VIEW

LINE OF SIGHT
FOR RIGHT SIDE VIEW

Figure 2.40 The glass box.

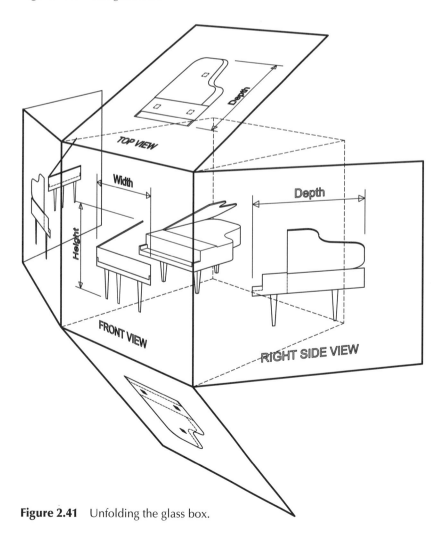

TOP VIEW

Depth

Width

Height

Depth

FRONT VIEW

RIGHT SIDE VIEW

Figure 2.41 Unfolding the glass box.

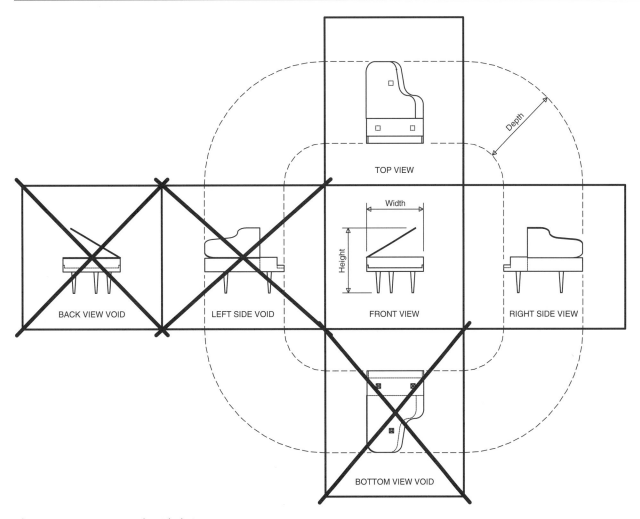

Figure 2.42 Primary and voided views.

Architectural Drafting

The architectural version of orthographic projection is shown in Figure 2.43. The top view (as viewed from a helicopter) is now called the **plan**, and the views all the way around from all four sides are referred to as **elevations**. Each of these elevations has a special name and will be discussed in the chapter on exterior elevations (Chapter 13).

In brief, a top view of the total property is called the site or plot plan. A horizontal section (drawn as if the structure were cut horizontally, the top portion removed, and the exposed interior viewed from above) is simply called a plan. There are many types of plans: floor plans, electrical plans (showing electrical features), framing plans (showing how a floor, ceiling, or roof is assembled), and foundation plans, to mention just a few. A vertical cut through a structure is called a cross-section or a longitudinal section, depending on the direction of the cut. The cross-section is a cut taken through the short end of a structure.

■ REPRODUCTION METHODS

The Blueprint Process

In the first half of the last century, the prevalent method of reproduction was the "blueprint." **Blueprints** have a blue background and white lines. Bond paper was coated with light-sensitive chemicals much like photographic film. The original, drawn on a translucent medium such as vellum, was placed over the paper and exposed to light. The light bleached out the chemicals except where they were screened off by lines. The paper was then dipped in a developing solution which would react to those sections not exposed to the light. The print was then washed and dried. As you can imagine, this process was time-consuming.

The Diazo Process

Today, blueprints are seldom used in architecture. The **diazo** has replaced it, and it also is rapidly disappearing.

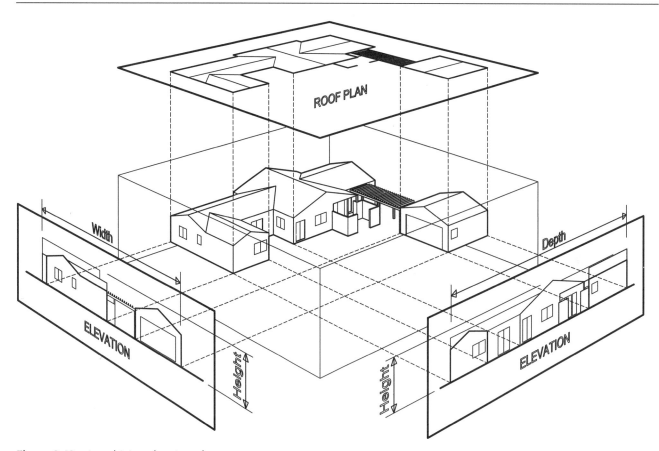

Figure 2.43 A multiview drawing of a structure.

Much as in the blueprint process, an original translucent medium (usually **vellum**) is placed over a bond paper that has a coating of light-sensitive chemicals. As the sheets are exposed to the light, the chemicals are bleached out, leaving only those areas that are screened by lines. The print is then exposed to ammonia or another chemical, which develops the unexposed chemicals. The result is a white background and dark lines. Color lines are also available, including brown and green. This diazo process usually only takes from fifteen seconds to one minute.

The Sepia Process

When diazo chemicals are placed onto vellum instead of bond paper, the resulting print is called a sepia print, or simply a **sepia**. This sepia copy becomes a second master. Sepia displays as reddish-brown lines on a white vellum background. The sepia print can be drawn on or, depending on the type, erased with an electric or chemical eraser called an eradicator. Some sepia papers "ghost" back unwanted lines when the effect of the eradicator wears off.

Transparent and Translucent Films. Diazo chemicals are also used with transparent or translucent film materials; the result is simply called "film." This **transparent** or **translucent** material can also be purchased with an adhesive on one side and is called applique film. After you expose this applique film to the image, you can mount it directly onto a vellum original or sepia. Most types of applique film are erasable.

Plain Paper Copiers

Types and Sizes. A variety of plain paper copiers are now on the open market for sale or lease. Some require special paper; others can copy on almost any paper surface. Some machines can enlarge as well as reduce, but presently only in certain proportions. Some copiers do not copy the original to its exact size; they change the size slightly and often in only one direction. Plain paper copiers usually use the standard paper formats of $8\frac{1}{2}'' \times 11''$ and $8\frac{1}{2}'' \times 14''$. The larger copiers can take copy widths up to 36″ and unlimited length since the machine accepts roll stock. But on most copiers the maximum reproducible size is presently about 24″; a 36″ master must be reduced to a 24″ size for reproduction. A 24″ master can be reproduced full size. Paper copiers can reproduce on bond paper, vellum, or acetate. Therefore, a 24″ × 36″ drawing can be reduced onto vellum and used as a master to produce diazo copies.

Reproducing on polyester is advantageous because prints on polyester can be used with an overhead projector for enlarging sketches or for presentations. Polyester film is also available with an adhesive backing for applique uses.

Appliques. Most adhesive films for plain paper copiers have two sheets: one sheet of adhesive film and a backing sheet or carrier. Since the adhesive film has a sticky substance on one side, the carrier is a nonstick material. This material is either a plastic film or a wax impregnated paper similar to wax paper.

When you use adhesive film on a plain paper copier of the heat developing variety, do not choose a wax carrier type; the heat from the developer portion of the copier melts the wax and jams the copier.

Standard decals can be made with adhesive film for symbols, title block information, and even construction notes.

Computer

The new CAD systems are often combined with a printer or a plotter. The plotters can be used to reproduce a drawing and/or recreate a secondary original that can use the previously mentioned reproduction methods. The advantage is that you can change the size and scale of the reproduction instantly.

Because the industry is moving toward wireless units, both manufacturers and the computer industry are exploring the potential of producing copiers that are programmed directly to the computer. This promises to produce a flexibility heretofore unknown in the office to produce either single or multiple sets instantaneously.

Shortcut Procedures

Freehand Drawing. One of the best shortcuts you can learn is drawing freehand. Most of the preliminary design procedures and conceptual design details in this book were done freehand. You still should use a scale to maintain accuracy, and adhere to the drafting vocabulary of lines and techniques. Freehand skill is useful in field situations, for informal office communications, and for communications with contractors, building department officials, and client. Examples of freehand details can be found in the chapter on architectural details (Chapter 16).

Typewritten Notes. Because of the applique film technique and the ease of reproducing spliced drawings, typing is being used more frequently for working drawings. For example, lengthy construction notes may be typed on applique film. However, hand lettering is *still* encouraged at the beginning.

Computer-Aided Drafting (CAD). Although computers are relatively new to the architectural industry, they have revolutionized the delivery method of construction documents for both the large and personal computers.

Experience has shown, however, that the CAD drafter would be better equipped to handle various tasks if, in addition to his or her skills and knowledge of how to manipulate the computer to the needs of the office, the drafter also mastered the understanding of how architectural information is communicated to the craftsman in the field. Another advantage would be for the CAD drafter to possess the skill to hand draft because there continue to be many office tasks that cannot be done by the computer alone.

Word Processing. The growing popularity of word processing in architectural offices is due mainly to its competitive price and its easy application to architectural uses. Also, the advent of minicomputers has made word processing accessible to even small firms.

Drafting Appliques and Manufacturers' Literature. Architectural offices often use manufacturers' literature and their details. More recently, offices have been using manufacturers' literature and drawings together with applique film. Erasable applique film is used, and the desired drawing supplied by the manufacturer is first printed by a plain paper copier or with the diazo process; second, changed or corrected to meet specific needs; and last, applied to the original vellum sheet. This saves time and the cost of developing the detail from scratch.

Recognizing the practicality of this method, many manufacturers now provide appliques upon request as part of product promotion.

Screen Drafting. This method adds a screen to the printing of the original drawing. The screen is film made up of microscopic dots which produce a partial light barrier. Screens are available in a variety of percentages: some block 20% of the light, others 80%, and so on. When used with an original drawing, the screen produces a gray copy instead of black.

Diazo (Screen) Drafting. For diazo (screen) drafting, a sepia print is made first. The diazo machine is reduced in speed in order to produce a light but readable and reproducible sepia print. This sepia print can now serve as the background for a structural or electrical plan, or a heating and air-conditioning layout, for example. When reprinted on the diazo machine, the reproduction emphasizes the material that has been drafted on and deemphasizes (or "screens") the original drawing, while still showing the relationship between them.

Photography and Drafting. Photography plays a large part in architectural drafting. "Blueprint service" companies have rapidly begun to employ methods of reproduction other than diazo. Many use plain paper copiers and many companies have also added photography. The older photographic method used produced a "photostat." This is rapidly being replaced by the "photo mechanical transfer" (PMT) system. In this process, there is no real negative. Rather, there is an intermediate paper negative that takes about 30 seconds to make; then the image is transferred from this throwaway master to a positive.

Still the best process and the most versatile is regular camera photography. The only limit to the size of print is the equipment itself, and 36" × 42" negatives are now available. Because negatives can be spliced together, the final limit is restricted only by the size of the positive paper available. Uses of photography are described later.

Some stationery suppliers and reproduction centers can take 35 mm slides and produce transparent 8½" × 11" copies by using a 35 mm projector, a plain paper copier, and polyester film.

Reprodrafting

"Reprodrafting" is a term used to describe a number of approaches to improving or revising drafted material in a way that takes advantage of photographic or photocopying processes. These approaches have spawned a number of new terms, including eraser drafting, paste-up drafting, photo-drafting, overlay drafting, pen drafting, and scissors drafting. Reprodrafting, then, actually consists of many processes.

Restoration.   Restoration refers to the process of taking a photograph of an old original or an old print and, by repairing the negative, producing a new master.

Composite Drafting.   Composite drafting is the photographic process of making a single drawing from many, or of taking parts of other drawings to make a new drawing. You will often hear the terms "paste-up," "scissors," "eraser," and "photo-drafting" being used in connection with this process.

Paste-up drafting simply refers to the process of pasting pieces onto a single master sheet, and then photographing and reproducing them. The lines on the negative made by edges of the pieces can be eliminated by the photo retoucher.

Scissors drafting takes an existing drawing and eliminates undesirable or corrected portions by cutting them out before the paste-up process. **Eraser drafting** is similar, but the unwanted portions are simply erased. In both cases, the original is never touched. A good copy on good quality paper is produced first. The copy must be printed in a way that allows easy erasure.

Photo-drafting, as the name indicates, uses drafting and photography. It begins with a photograph of any drawing, such as a plan, elevation, or detail. The drawing is printed on a matte-surfaced film and additional information is drafted onto it.

Photo-drafting is an ideal method for dealing with historical restoration drawings. The building to be restored is photographed and printed (to scale) on a matte-surfaced film. Required information, such as dimensions, and methods of restoration are added to this photographic reprint.

Overlay Drafting.   One of the most significant changes in the production of architectural working drawings is the introduction of overlay drafting or registration drafting. It is a systems approach that works mainly for plans and can be incorporated into CAD. Although this is a difficult procedure to learn, with practice and organization, the time savings can be great. Some governmental agencies require this procedure.

The concept of overlay drafting has been used in the printing industry and in the aircraft industry as well. Overlay drafting combines a base drawing and a series of overlays, ending up with a single drawing.

Computers.   Most computers are equipped with scanners and printers. Older drawings (hard copy), diazo prints, vellum originals, and photographs can be scanned into the computer. These drawings can be altered and changed easily to produce a new master drawing. Layers (overlays) can now be employed to update drawings and produce restoration drawings. Because of the flexibility and speed with which computers operate, they can technically create almost everything that can be done via reprodrafting, composite drafting, paste-up drafting, scissors drafting, photo-drafting, and more.

Other Shortcut Methods

Anytime you combine lines and words in chart form, you can take a number of approaches. Drawing lines in pencil and then lettering directly on the chart is not always the best approach.

Drawing on the Reverse Side.   You can draw lines on the reverse side of the drawing surface and letter on the opposite side. This allows easy correction. You can then erase lettering without disturbing the lines.

This is possible only if you are using the diazo process in reproducing the drawing. With the computer, you keep the office schedule intact and add the lettering on a different layer.

Combining Ink and Pencil.   You can use ink for the lines and pencil for the lettering. The ink lines can be drawn on either side of the vellum, depending on the reproduction method employed.

Saving the Original Drawing. A sepia print can be made from the original, whether it is in pencil or ink. The lettering is then done on the sepia, saving the original. If you are using a plain paper copier, print onto vellum, preferably erasable vellum.

Using Standardized Sheets. If an office uses a standardized sheet for all jobs or specializes in a particular building type that calls for the same information each time, a more permanent procedure can be followed.

A Simple Shortcut

Manual Drafting. Make a copy of all the early stages of the different parts of a building. See Figure 2.44B. The final drawing is shown in Figure 2.44A. If there are no significant changes, tape the drawing to a piece of bond paper, copy it onto the vellum, and then finish the process. If, for example, the pitch (roof slope) is different,

then simply cut out the roof portion, tape it to a sheet of bond paper, and print onto vellum. Manually correct the new roof pitch and proceed to finish the process.

CAD. Simply import a previously constructed drawing, erase the portions that do not apply, and complete the drawing.

A Much Needed Survival Skill

Let us first set up a hypothetical problem and apply a much needed drafting skill:

> Your task as a junior drafter in the office is to produce a workable floor plan and site plan that have been sent to you in a reduced format. The scale is unknown and is similar to that in Figure 2.44.

The solution is to enlarge the drawing back to its original scale of $\frac{1}{8}'' = 1'0''$ for the site plan and $\frac{1}{4}'' = 1'0''$ for the

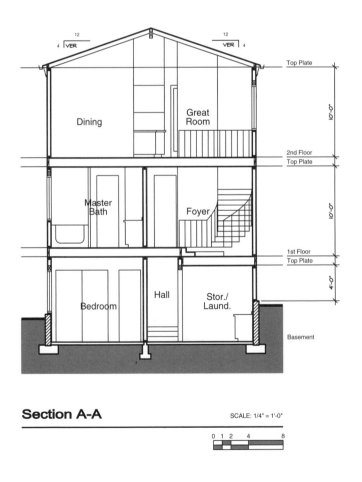

Section A-A

SCALE: 1/4" = 1'-0"

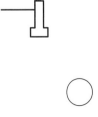

Figure 2.44 Using tracers.

basement floor plan and print it on a 24″ × 36″ sheet of paper.

Manual Drafting Solution.

STEP I. *Establish a measurable datum.* For the site plan, it is a matter of taking one of the known measurements, such as the 70′ property line shown on Figure

2.45. Redraw this measurement on a separate piece of paper at ⅛″ = 1′0″ scale. We will call this our datum line.

STEP II. *Enlarge on the copier.* Enlarge the 70′ property line on the site plan to match the datum line. Do it based on an eyeball estimate.

STEP III. *Compare enlargement to datum line.* Unless you are extremely lucky, the 70′ property line will not

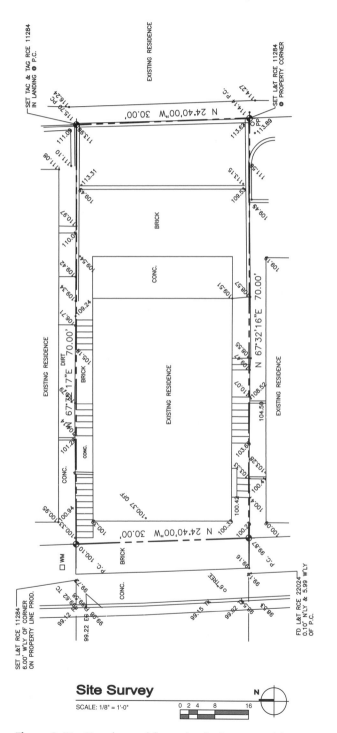

Site Survey

SCALE: 1/8" = 1'-0"

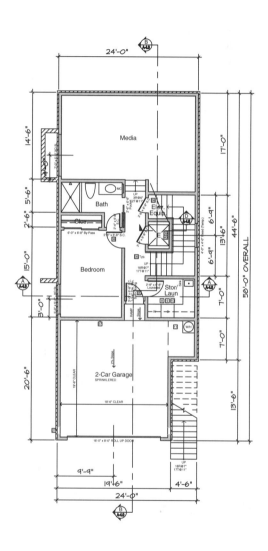

Basement Floor Plan

SCALE: 1/8" = 1'-0"

Figure 2.45 Site plan and floor plan (unknown scale).

exactly match the datum line, so either make another enlargement or a reduction.

STEP IV. *Adjust the enlargement.* You may find, as you get within 1%, that the 1% enlargement is just a bit too large. Try reducing the drawing by a small percentage such as 5%, then enlarge the drawing by 6%.

Basement Floor Plan—Steps are similar to those for the site plan, except you may find that it would be easier to take a small portion, say 20′ 6″ as shown on Figure 2.46.

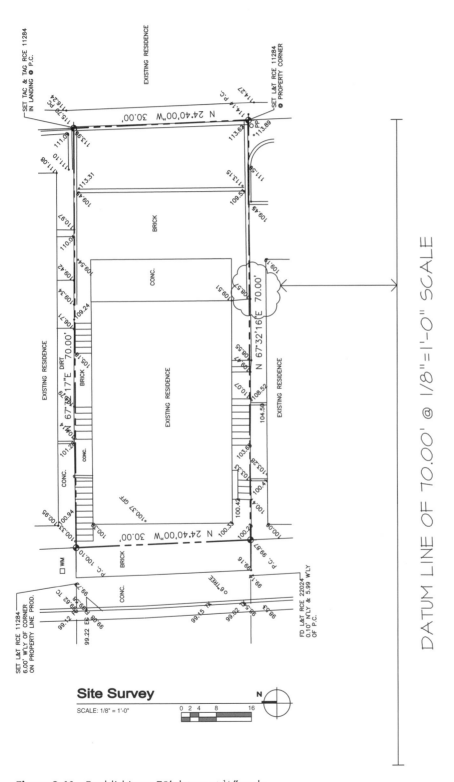

DATUM LINE OF 70.00′ @ 1/8″=1′-0″ SCALE

Site Survey

SCALE: 1/8″ = 1′-0″

0 2 4   8   16

N

Figure 2.46 Establishing a 70′ datum at ¹/₈″ scale.

Using a Computer   The first thing to do is to scan the image into the computer. Isolate one corner of the line to be used as shown on Figures 2.45 and 2.46. Zoom-in on this corner for maximum accuracy. Locate the center of the corner (as shown with a dot). See Figure 2.47.

Next, go to the scale command and scale the datum line with reference. When you type in the reference length, the drawing will automatically resize.

The standardized form can be Xeroxed onto vellum or reproduced photographically in one of two ways. First obtain a negative to make a print plate and print the image on vellum. This can usually be done through a blueprint reproduction service that also provides photographic services. This negative can then be used to expose a sensitized vellum and make a photographic reproduction on vellum.

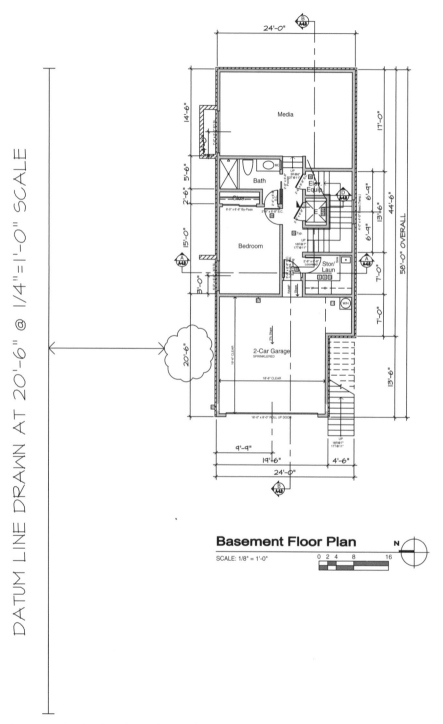

Figure 2.47   Smaller datum line for larger scaled drawing.

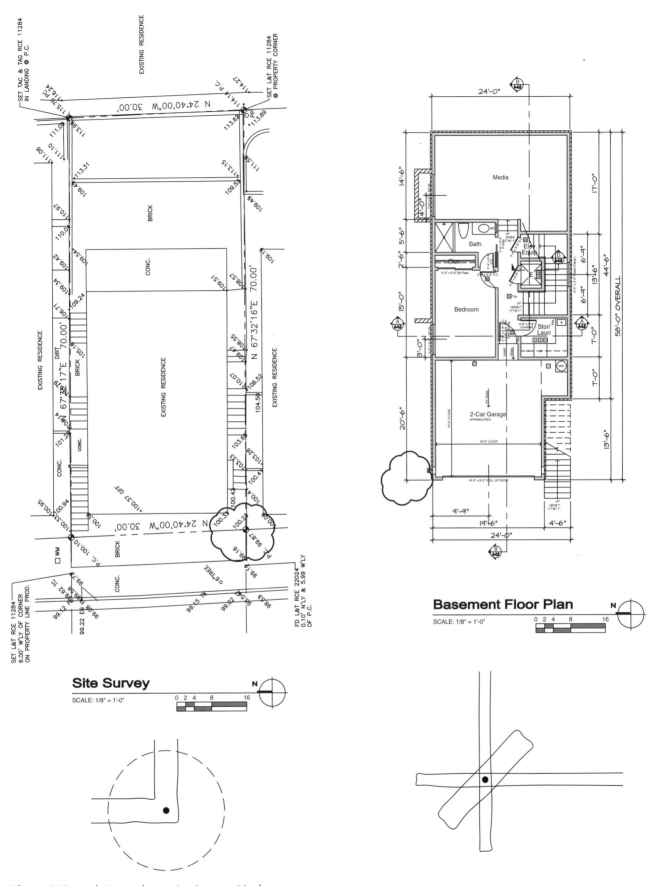

Figure 2.48 Isolating and zooming into a critical area.

Using Standard Titles.   Using any number of the procedures previously described, you can produce standard titles such as those found under a drawing or title block, to keep the lettering of titles uniform. Lettering machines that produce letters on a sticky-backed tape are now available with interchangeable type styles and sizes. The final product resembles rub-on letters on adhesive tape.

For example, you can produce the term "floor plan" with rub-on letters or a lettering machine and then reproduce the term in quantity. You can cut out the multiple copies and position them on a sheet, which you can then use as a master to produce appliques with a plain paper copier and adhesive transparent film. In this way, you can cut titles from the adhesive and apply them to the various sheets as needed.

■ OFFICE STANDARDS

Sheet Size

The drawing sheet size varies from office to office depending on the type of work performed, the method of reproduction used, and the system of drafting used in the office. The most common sheet sizes are 24″ × 36″, 28″ × 42″, and 30″ × 42″.

When sheets are used horizontally, they are usually bound on the left side. Because of this, the border is larger on the left side. A typical border line is $^3/_8$″ to $^1/_2$″ around the three sides and 1″ to 1$^1/_2$″ on the left side.

Title blocks can run the full height of the right side rather than simply filling a square in the bottom right corner, as in mechanical drafting. The long title band contains such information as sheet number, client's name or project title, name of firm, name or title of the drawing, person drafting, scale, date, and revision dates. The title block sheets are usually preprinted or can be applied to sheets in the form of decals or appliques.

This location of the title block allows you to leave a rectangular area for drawing purposes, whereas a title block in the lower right corner produces an L-shaped drawing area. (Even when drawing on a large sheet, take care to draft so that you use the sheet to its fullest.)

Many offices establish a sheet module. Here is an example of this method with a 24″ × 36″ sheet:

Binding side	1$^1/_2$″ border
Other 3 sides	$^1/_2$″ border
Title block	1$^1/_2$″

This leaves a drawing area of 23″ by 32$^1/_2$″. The vertical 23″ distance can be divided into four equal parts, while the horizontal 32$^1/_2$″ can be divided into 8 equal parts. This provides 32 spaces 4$^1/_{16}$″ wide by 5$^3/_4$″ high. This office procedure may be followed so that each sheet has a consistent appearance. Whether the sheet is full of details or a combination of a plan and details and/or notes,

the module gives you parameters within which to work. You should draft from the right side of the sheet so that any blank spaces remaining are toward the inside (on the binding side).

Lettering Height

The height of lettering depends on the type of reproduction used. If you use normal diazo methods, use the following standards as a rule of thumb:

Main titles under drawings	$^1/_4$″ maximum
Subtitles	$^3/_{16}$″
Normal lettering	$^3/_{32}$″–$^1/_8$″
Sheet number in title block	$^1/_2$″

Increase these sizes when you are reducing drawings. For example, increase normal lettering from $^3/_{32}$″ to $^1/_8$″ of $^3/_{16}$″, depending on the reduction ratio.

Lettering

One of the most important office standards to which a drafter must subscribe is lettering. Many offices use a combination of uppercase and lowercase letters for the main titles, such as for room names. Certain fonts, such as Helvetica and Garamond, are very popular. When selecting a font, be sure to find one based on a simple stroking system so as not to impede the printing process. There can be a marked difference in the printing or plotting time for different fonts, especially when the text is very long, as in general notes and framing or energy notes.

The height of the letters is also very important for legibility. Lettering that is $^1/_8$ or $^3/_{32}$″ tall is very readable. Using letters $^1/_4$″ all (maximum) for main titles produces enough contrast between notes and titles to enhance the construction documents.

For general test, we suggest an architectural font. It speeds up the correction process. See "Importance of Hand Lettering" on page 33.

A problem caused by the infusion of electronic equipment into our field is the difficulty in maintaining the lettering size on drawings that are electronically reduced either on a plain paper copier or digitally on a computer.

Scale of Drawings

The scale selected should be the largest practical scale based on the size of the structure and the drawing space available. The following are the most common sizes used by offices, with the most desirable size being underlined where there is a choice.

Site Plan: $^1/_8$″ = 1′-0″ for small sites. Drawings are provided by a civil engineer and scales are expressed in engineering terms such as 1″ = 30′, 1″ = 50′, etc.

Floor Plan: $1/4'' = 1'\text{-}0''$, $1/8''$ or $1/16'' = 1'\text{-}0''$ for larger structures.

Exterior Elevations: Same as the floor plan.

Building Sections: $1/2'' = 1'\text{-}0''$ if possible or the same as exterior elevations.

Interior Elevations: $1/4'' = 1'\text{-}0''$, $3/8'' = 1'\text{-}0''$, $1/2'' = 1'\text{-}0''$.

Architectural Details: $1/2'' = 1'\text{-}0''$ to $3'' = 1'\text{-}0''$, depending on the size of the object being drawn or the amount of information that must be shown. Footing detail: $3/4'' = 1'\text{-}0''$ or $1'' = 1'\text{-}0''$. Eave details: $1\,1/2'' = 1'\text{-}0''$. Wall sections: typically, $3/4'' = 1'\text{-}0''$.

Materials in Section

Figures 2.49, 2.50, 2.51, and 2.52 show the various methods used throughout the United States to represent different materials in section.

In the first column are material designations assembled by the Committee on Office Practice, American Institute of Architects (National) and published in *Architectural Graphic Standards*. The second column designations are prepared by the Task Force on Production Office Procedures of the Northern California Chapter of the American Institute of Architects. The final column lists items from other sources such as pamphlets, manufacturers' literature, textbooks, governmental agencies, and trade and technical organizations or associations.

Clearly, there is standardization and there are variations. For example, all groups agree on the method of representing brick in section, yet there is a great variation in the way concrete block is represented in section.

The last figure shows specialty items from a variety of sources.

Graphic Symbols

The symbols in Figure 2.53 are the most common and acceptable, to judge by the frequency of use by the architectural offices surveyed. This list can be and should be expanded by each office to include those symbols generally used in its practice and not indicated here. Again, each professional is urged to accept the task force recommendation by adopting the use of these symbols.

Abbreviations

Suggested abbreviations compiled by Task Force #1, National Committee on Office Practice, American Institute of Architects, and published in the AIA *Journal* can be found in the Appendix at the end of this book.

Dimensioning

Dimensioning is the act of incorporating numerical values into drawing as a means of sizing various com-

ponents and also locating parts of a building. This is accomplished on dimension lines, in notes, and by referral to other drawings or details.

Grouping Dimensions.　Group dimensions whenever possible to provide continuity. This takes planning. Try running a diazo print of the drawing in question and dimension it on this check print first. This will allow you to identify dimensions and decide how they can be effectively grouped.

Maintaining a Dimension Standard.　The most important dimensions dictate subsequent dimensions. For example, if a wall is dimensioned to the center of the wall first, all subsequent dimensions using this wall as a reference point should be dimensioned at its center.

Size Dimensions and Location Dimensions.　The two basic kinds of **dimensions** are size and location. See Figure 2.54. Size dimensions indicate overall size. Location dimensions deal with the actual placement of an object or structure, such as a wall, a window, a concrete patio slab, a barbecue grill, or a planter.

The Dimensional Reference System.　The dimensional reference system is based on a three-dimensional axis. See Figure 2.55. Critical planes are located by a series of reference bubbles and used as **planes of reference**. Figure 2.56 shows a box; reference bubbles describe the three planes of height, width, and depth. Now examine this box sliced in two directions as shown in Figures 2.57 and 2.58. The first slice produces a **horizontal control plane**, and the second a **vertical control plane**.

The shaded area in Figure 2.59 represents a horizontal plane at a critical point on the structure, such as the floor line. The shaded area on Figure 2.60 represents a vertical plane at a critical point of the structure, such as the location of a series of columns or beams. There is a definite relationship between the vertical control plane and the horizontal control plane. Compare the **plan** and the **section** shown in Figure 2.61. The section is a vertical cut as in Figure 2.60 and the plan is a horizontal cut as in Figure 2.59. The two vertical and one horizontal reference bubbles on Figure 2.59 are an attempt to show this relationship.

Types of Planes.　There are two types of planes. The first is the **axial plane**, which goes through the center of critical structural items as shown in Figure 2.52. Note how the columns are dimensioned to the center. When pilasters (widening of a masonry wall for support) are used, they become a good location for control dimensions, as they support the structural members above.

The second type of plane is called a **boundary control plane**. See Figure 2.63. In this case, columns and walls

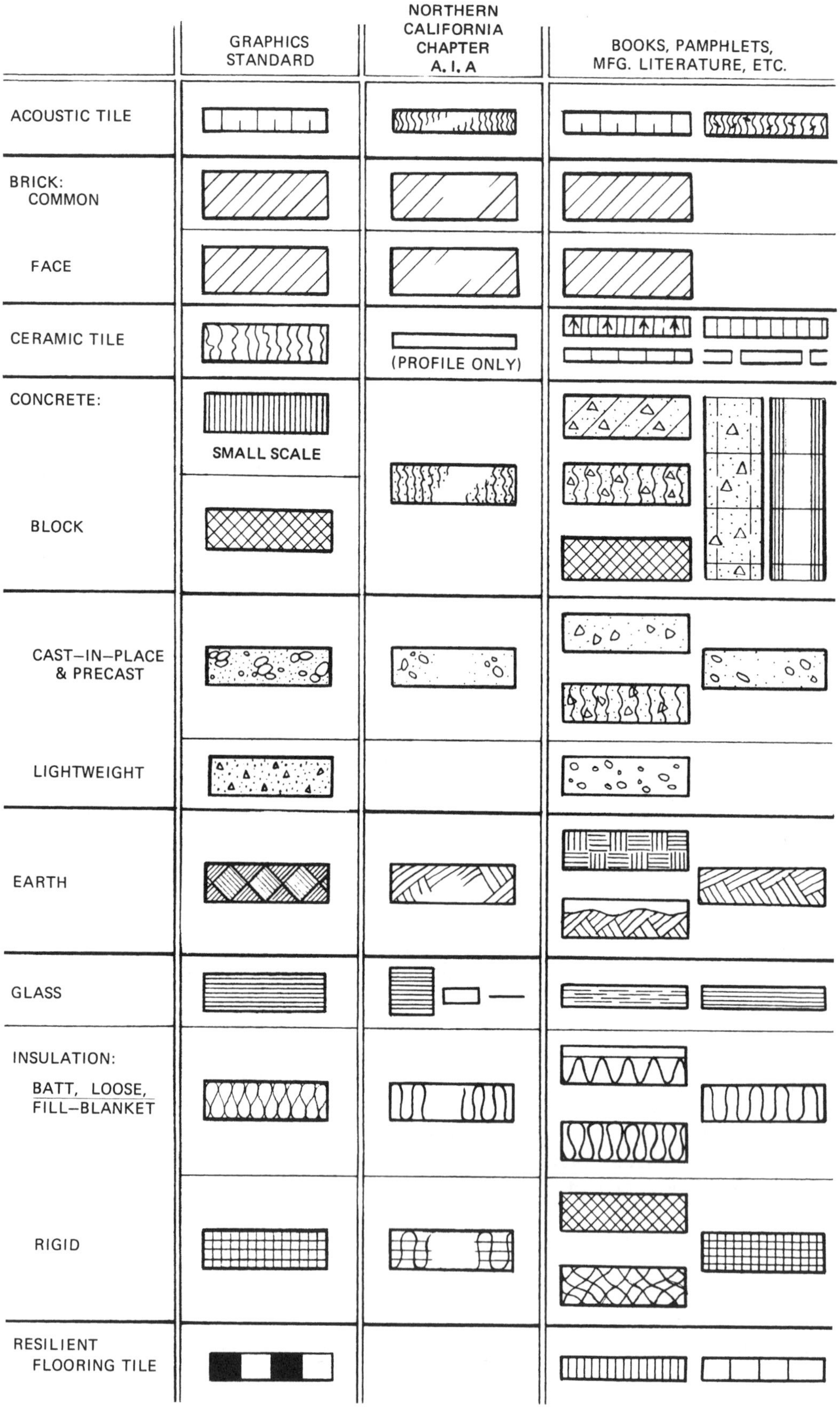

	GRAPHICS STANDARD	NORTHERN CALIFORNIA CHAPTER A.I.A	BOOKS, PAMPHLETS, MFG. LITERATURE, ETC.
ACOUSTIC TILE			
BRICK: COMMON			
FACE			
CERAMIC TILE		(PROFILE ONLY)	
CONCRETE:	SMALL SCALE		
BLOCK			
CAST—IN—PLACE & PRECAST			
LIGHTWEIGHT			
EARTH			
GLASS			
INSULATION: BATT, LOOSE, FILL—BLANKET			
RIGID			
RESILIENT FLOORING TILE			

Figure 2.49 Materials in section.

50

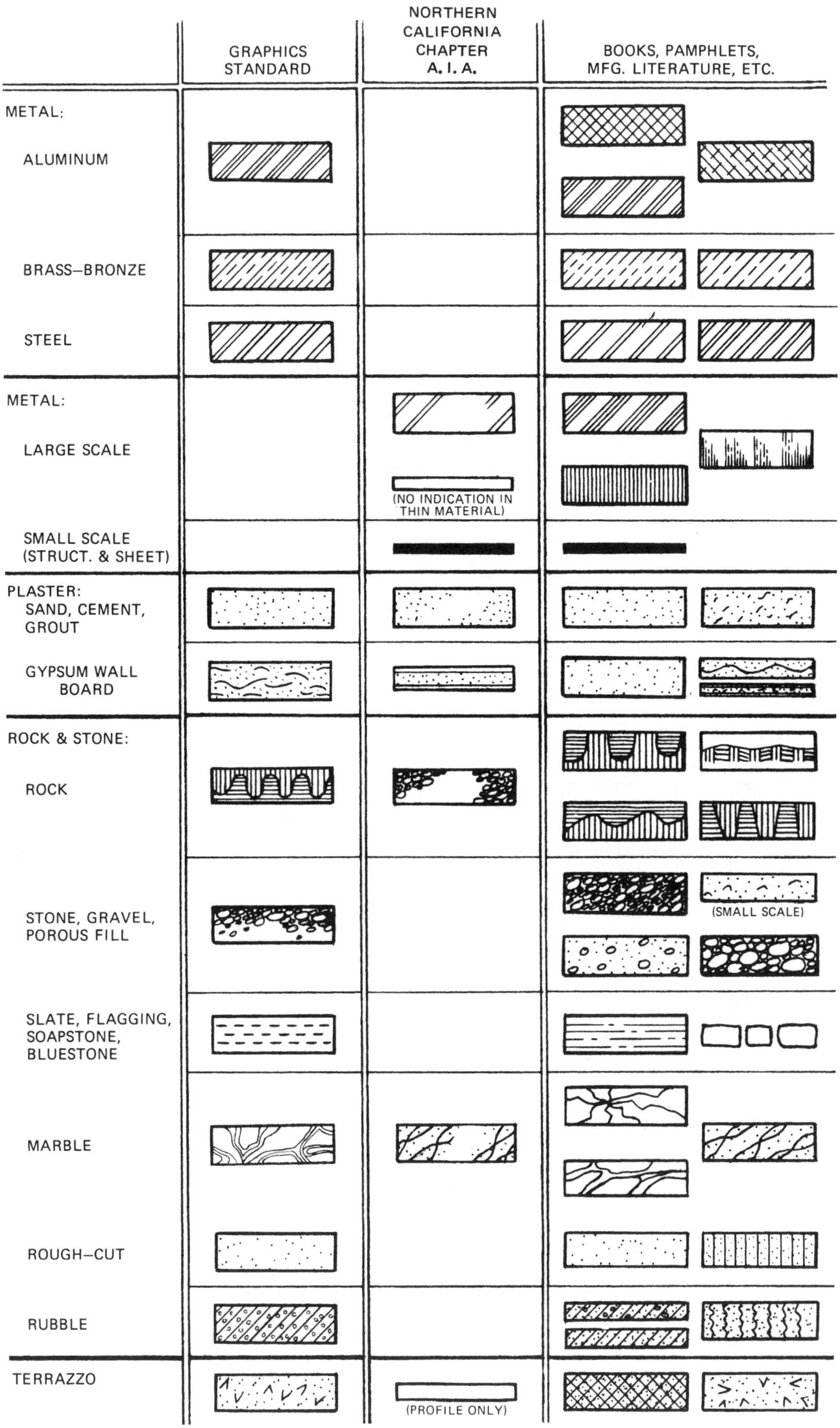

	GRAPHICS STANDARD	NORTHERN CALIFORNIA CHAPTER A. I. A.	BOOKS, PAMPHLETS, MFG. LITERATURE, ETC.	
METAL: ALUMINUM				
BRASS—BRONZE				
STEEL				
METAL: LARGE SCALE		(NO INDICATION IN THIN MATERIAL)		
SMALL SCALE (STRUCT. & SHEET)				
PLASTER: SAND, CEMENT, GROUT				
GYPSUM WALL BOARD				
ROCK & STONE: ROCK				
STONE, GRAVEL, POROUS FILL				(SMALL SCALE)
SLATE, FLAGGING, SOAPSTONE, BLUESTONE				
MARBLE				
ROUGH—CUT				
RUBBLE				
TERRAZZO		(PROFILE ONLY)		

Figure 2.50 Materials in section.

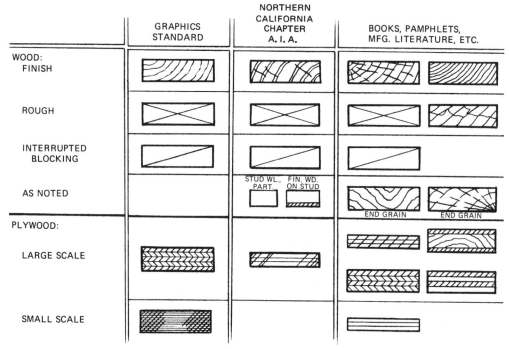

	GRAPHICS STANDARD	NORTHERN CALIFORNIA CHAPTER A.I.A.	BOOKS, PAMPHLETS, MFG. LITERATURE, ETC.
WOOD: FINISH			
ROUGH			
INTERRUPTED BLOCKING			
AS NOTED		STUD WL., PART. / FIN. WD. ON STUD	END GRAIN / END GRAIN
PLYWOOD:			
LARGE SCALE			
SMALL SCALE			

* TO SAVE VALUABLE DRAFTING TIME, THE NORTHERN CALIFORNIA CHAPTER RECOMMENDS THAT THE TOTAL DETAIL IN SECTION NOT BE FILLED IN COMPLETELY BUT JUST ENOUGH TO INDICATE THE MATERIAL IN QUESTION.

Figure 2.51 Materials in section.

ADDITIONAL MATERIALS IN SECTION

BRICK	FIRE BRICK ON COMMON		GLAZED	
CARPET & PAD				
CONCRETE	BRICK	CAST STONE		
GLASS	STRUCTURAL	BLOCK		
GYPSUM BLOCK				
INSULATION: SHEATHING				
METAL LATH				
PLASTIC	CLEAR	FIBERGLASS	GLASS REINF. POLYESTER	
TEMPERED HARDBOARD				
TERRA COTTA	LARGE SCALE	SMALL SCALE		

Figure 2.52 Additional materials in section.

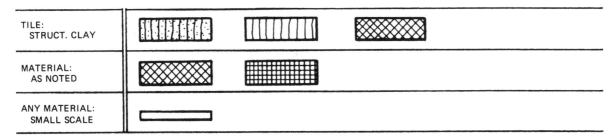

TILE: STRUCT. CLAY	
MATERIAL: AS NOTED	
ANY MATERIAL: SMALL SCALE	

Figure 2.52 Additional materials in section *(continued)*.

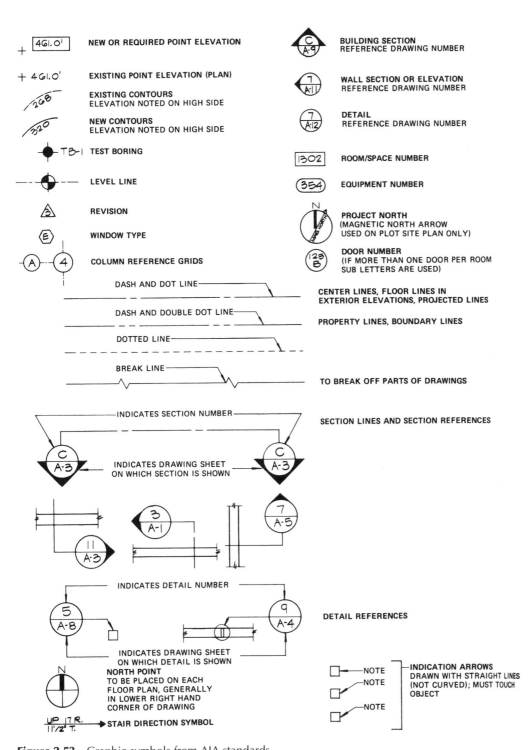

Figure 2.53 Graphic symbols from AIA standards.

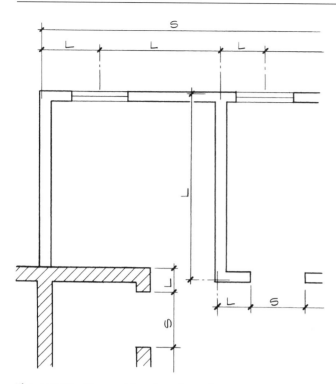

Figure 2.54   Size and location dimensions.

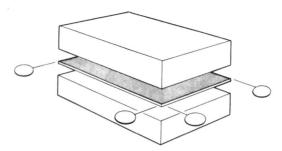

Figure 2.57   Horizontal control plane.

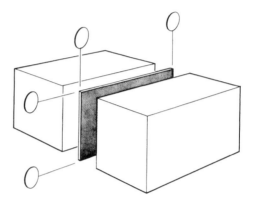

Figure 2.58   Vertical control plane.

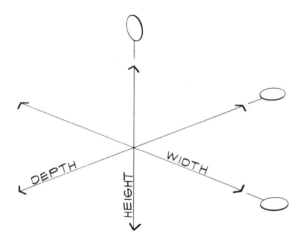

Figure 2.55   Dimensional reference system.

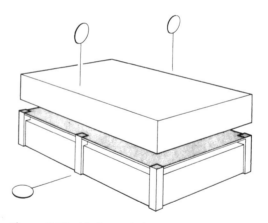

Figure 2.59   Horizontal plane.

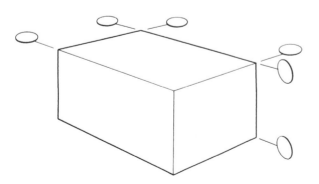

Figure 2.56   Three principal planes using dimensional reference system.

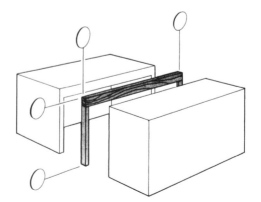

Figure 2.60   Vertical plane.

are not dimensioned to the center; instead, their boundaries are dimensioned. Figure 2.64 shows examples of columns and walls located in the **neutral zone**. These neutral zones are especially valuable in dealing with the vertical dimensions of a section and with elevations. See Figure 2.65. A neutral zone is established between the ceiling and the floor above. The floor-to-ceiling heights can be established to allow the structural mechanical, and electrical consultants to perform their work. Once that dimension is established, the neutral zone and floor-to-floor dimensions follow. See Figure 2.66 for a practical application for the **vertical control dimension** and control zone (another term for neutral zone).

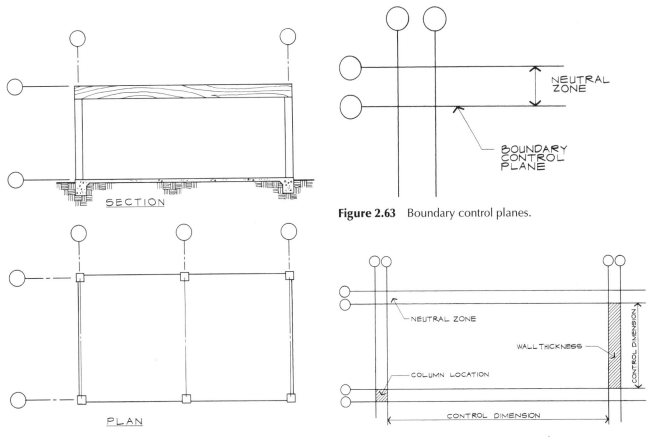

Figure 2.61 Section and plan.

Figure 2.63 Boundary control planes.

Figure 2.64 Column location in a neutral zone.

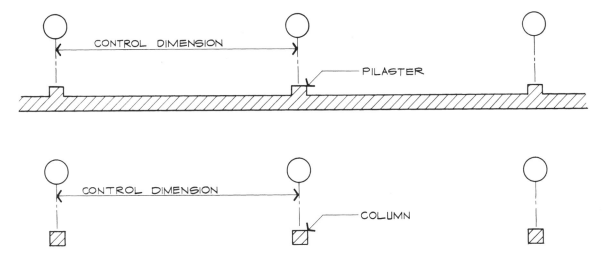

Figure 2.62 Axial control planes.

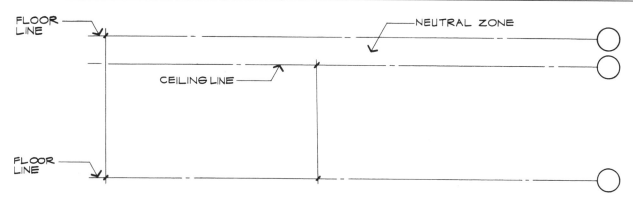

Figure 2.65   Neutral zone in a vertical dimension.

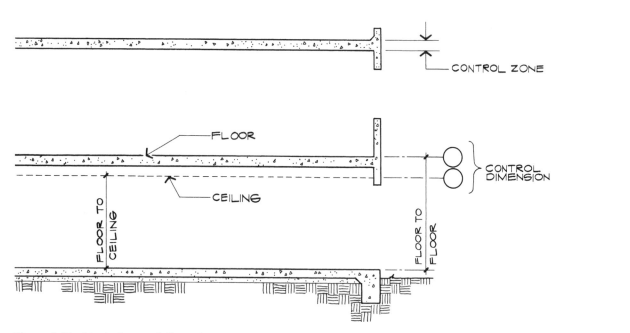

Figure 2.66   Vertical control dimension.

American with Disabilities Act (ADA)

A definite description of the standards established by the Americans with Disabilities Act, which is now a federal law, can be found in Chapter 4, "Environmental and Human Considerations."

■ METRICS

Conversion to metric numbers is a change in total concept and attitude that must be incorporated at the basic design stage. Never design in feet and inches and then convert to metric; it creates undesirable metric measurements. Unfortunately, manufacturers of building materials have not been converting consistently to the metric system. Lumber, steel, and masonry units will soon have standards established, but until they are in effect, there is

an interim period that involves simple conversion of numbers.

The English system uses different basic units. Liquid is measured differently from linear measurements and weight; for example, 4 quarts = 1 gallon, 12 inches = 1 foot, and 16 ounces = 1 pound.

In the metric system, although the names for liquid, weight, and linear measurements are different, their units are based on tenths, which avoids so much memorizing.

Nomenclature

Because the architectural field deals predominantly with linear measurements, this discussion emphasizes the conversion of feet and inches to metric equivalents.

The largest metric unit of measurement for use in the construction industry is the meter. The most recent standard measurement of a meter is the measurement of the swing of a pendulum during a one-second period. This swinging pendulum is made of platinum and is located at 45° latitude in France. Because of the nature of the way the standard meter is measured and the location of this standard, the length of a meter varies slightly throughout the world. It is hoped that attempts at standardization by the International Standards Organization (ISO) will prove successful, because if different lengths are used for the standard meter, building products made in one country might not correspond to the needs of another.

A meter comprises ten decimeters which, in turn, each comprise ten centimeters. The smallest unit of conversion is the millimeter Ten meters make a decameter; ten times that is a hectometer; and ten times that is a kilometer. Here is a chart showing these values:

kilometer	= 1,000 meters	km
*hectometer	= 100 meters	hm
*decameter	= 10 meters	dam
meter		m
*decimeter	= $^1/_{10}$ meter	dm
centimeter	= $^1/_{100}$ meter	cm
millimeter	= $^1/_{1000}$ meter	mm

*Seldom used in modern drawings.

For architectural drafting, the millimeter and the meter are the most desirable units to use.

Notation Method

Locate the decimal point in the center of the line of numerical value rather than close to the bottom of the line. For example, 304.65 is best written 304·65. However, the original notation is acceptable.

Commas are not used. Rather, spaces are left to denote where commas would have been. For example 10·34674 meters would be written 10·346 74 meters, and 506,473·21 meters would be written as 506 473·21 meters.

Abbreviations of metric units do not have special plural forms. For example, fifty centimeters is written 50 cm, *not* 50 cms. Note, also, the space between the number and the letters. It should read 50, space, centimeters: 50 cm.

Once a standard, such as "all measurements shall be in meters," is established for a set of drawings, it need not be noted on each drawing. A 4 by 8 sheet of plywood should be called out not as 121 9·2 m × 243 8·4 m plywood but rather as 121 9·2 × 243 8·4 plywood. However, if a size is in a measure other than meters, this should be noted.

English Equivalents

Here is a quick reference chart for converting linear measurements into metrics:

Length:	inches × 2·54	= centimeters (cm)
	feet × 0·304 8	= meters (m)
	yards × 0·914 4	= meters (m)
	miles × 1·609 34	= kilometers (km)
Mass:	pounds × 0·453 592	= kilograms (kg)
	ounces × 28·35	= grams (g)

General Conversion Rules

Using the equivalent values just given, you can convert by multiplication. For example, 16 inches is:

inches × 2·54 = cm
16 in. × 2·54 = 40·64 cm

To convert 25 feet into metric measurements:

feet × 0·304 8 = m
25 ft. × 0·304 8 = 7.62 m

To convert 5 yards into meters:

yards × 0·914 4 = m
75 yd. × 0·914 4 = 68.58 m

Unit Change

To convert 17 feet 8 inches, follow this procedure:

17 ft. × 0·304 8 = 5·181 6 cm.
8 in. × 2·54 = 20·32 cm

In this example, conversion of feet results in meters, and conversion of inches results in centimeters. You cannot add these quantities unless you convert them to the same unit of measurement. Do this simply by moving the decimal point. In this example, if meters are desired, simply move the decimal point of the centimeter unit two units to the left: 20·32 cm are equal to .203 2 m. Thus,

17 ft.	=	5·181 6 m
8 in.	=	·203 2 m
		5·384 8 m

Actual Versus Nominal

Presently, lumber uses an odd system of notation. When a piece of lumber is drawn, it is drafted to its actual size (net size). In the notes describing this particular piece of wood, it is called out in its nominal size (call-out size). For example, a 2 × 4 piece of wood is drawn at 1½" × 3½", but on the note pointing to this piece, it is still called a 2 × 4.

Therefore, when converting to metric, the 1½" × 3½" size must be converted and drawn to the actual size. There is no set procedure for the call out. Some drawings convert the 2 × 4 size metrically and note this piece of wood with the 1½" × 3½" size converted. A sample note might read as follows:

·0381 × ·0889 (net) STUD

It is hoped that when metric lumber size is established, the net and nominal sizes will be identical.

Using Double Standards

Due to the newness of using metrics in the American architectural profession, we are not yet geared to note things metrically. Lumber, reinforcing, glass, and other materials are still ordered in the English system. Their sizes, weights, and shapes are also still described in the English system.

There are three approaches to this situation. First, we can note only those things we have control over in metrics, such as the size of a room, the width of a footing, and so on, while noting 2 × 4 studs, #4 reinforcing rods, ½″ anchor bolts, and the like, according to the manufacturer until they change to the metric system.

A second method is dual notation. This system requires dimensions, notes, and all call outs to be recorded twice. For example, a 35′-6″ dimension has metric value of 10·820 4 written directly below it. If most workers are operating under the old system, they can ignore the metric value and refer to the English system. If, however, the majority of the workers use the metric figure, you have prepared a value that cannot be measured accurately because the decimal is carried out too far. This problem is dealt with later.

The third and final method is to approach everything metrically. This may not be the best way in an office going through a transition, but it is the best student method because you will eventually be asked to work totally in metrics.

Conversion of Drafting

If we are to convert everything to metrics, there are three procedures to consider. First is that of "holding" certain dimension notes and call outs. If, for example, we are dealing with a #4 rebar (which is a steel reinforcing bar ½″ in size) and the manufacturer has not changed to metrics, we must convert the ½″ by multiplying ½″ × 2·54 and note the rebar as:

1·27 cm rebar
or
0·0.127 rebar

The second procedure requires "rounding off." See Figure 2.67. In this figure, the scale on the top is an enlarged one that you are accustomed to seeing. The scale directly below is in the same enlarged proportion but in metric units. The numbers in this scale are in centimeters. Notice that 2·54 centimeters equal an inch. Notice also that one centimeter is less than ½ inch. Initially, this is a hard proportion to relate to for anyone making the transition. Also note that half a centimeter (0·5 cm) is

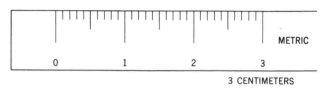

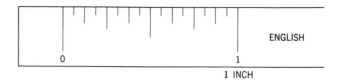

Figure 2.67 Comparison of English and metric scales.

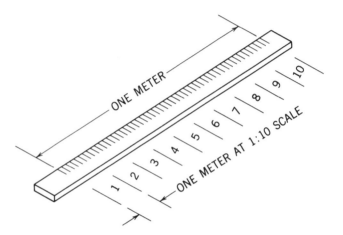

Figure 2.68 Pictorial of reduced metric scale.

smaller than ¼ inch and that one millimeter (one tenth of a centimeter) is less than ¹/₁₆ of an inch.

Now compare this knowledge with an actual number. Assume that you wish to dig a trench 12 inches wide for a footing.

12 inches = (12 × 2·54) = 30·48 cm

Hence, there are 30+ units less than ½ inch in size that we can measure. The .4 is less than ³/₁₆″, which is very difficult to measure and impossible to deal with on the job for a worker. This is the point when we should begin to round off.

The final number (0·08) is even worse. It amounts to just a little more than ¹/₃₂ of an inch—a measurement that a draftsperson would have difficulty even reading on the scale, and that the person digging the trench would have to ignore. The final rounded off value should be 31·0 cm or 0·31. This trench is about ³/₁₆ inches wider than the desired 12 inches but is something the people out in the field can measure with their metric scales.

The third conversion procedure requires judgment about whether to increase or decrease. Certain measurements must be increased in the rounding off process—

the trench discussed previously is a good example. If we round this number off to 30·0 cm or 0·30, the measurement is less than 2 inches. If the 12 inch requirement had been imposed by the local code, you would have thus broken the code. Had it been set at 12 inches for structural reasons, the building could be deemed unsafe. Another example is a planned opening for a piece of equipment. To round off to the smaller number might result in the equipment's not fitting.

You must be aware of situations that are dictated by health and safety. The minimum depth of a step might be $10^1/2"$ or 26·67 cm. If we rounded this off to 26·0 cm, it would not meet the minimum standards for a stair. Another kind of danger lies in *exceeding* a required maximum. For example, the note for an anchor bolt reads:

$1/2" \times 10"$; to anchor bolt embedded 7" into concrete 6'-0" o.c. and 12" from corners.

The spacing of 6'-0" on center is used to maintain a minimum number of anchor bolts per unit of length. If we increase the distance between bolts, we exceed the required spacing, and as stated in the note reduce the number of bolts per unit of length below the minimum required.

The 12-inch measurement has the same effect. The intent is to have an anchor bolt 12 inches or less from each of the corners. We must, therefore, decrease the measurement when we round off after converting to metric, to ensure that there is an anchor bolt closer than 12 inches from every corner. The $1/2" \times 10"$ ⌽ (⌽ is a symbol for round) becomes what is called a "holding" measurement since it comes from the manufacturer that way. The final numerical value that reads "embedded 7 inches into concrete" must be thought out wisely. The bolt must be embedded enough for strength, yet left exposed adequately to penetrate a sill (the first piece of wood to come into contact with concrete) and still leave enough space for a washer and a nut.

The second and third processes are called soft conversion; that is, an English measurement is converted directly into a metric equivalent and then rounded off into a workable metric value. A hard conversion is the name given to changing the total approach. It is not just a numerical conversion but a change of media as well. If bricks are the medium for example, the procedure would be to subscribe to a brick that was sized metrically and dimension accordingly.

Listed below are some of the recommended rounding off sizes:

$1/2"$	= 3·2 mm		$1^3/4"$	= 44·0 mm
$1/4"$	= 6·4 mm		$2"$	= 50·0 mm
$3/8"$	= 9·5 mm		$2^1/2"$	= 63·0 mm
$1/2"$	= 12·7 mm		$3"$	= 75·0 mm
$5/8"$	= 16·0 mm		$4"$	= 100·0 mm

$3/4"$	= 19·0 mm		$6"$	= 150·0 mm
$7/8"$	= 22·0 mm		$8"$	= 200·0 mm
$1"$	= 25·0 mm		$10"$	= 250·0 mm
$1^1/4"$	= 32·0 mm		$12"$	= 300·0 mm
$1^1/2"$	= 38·0 mm			

Zero is used to avoid error in metrics. For example, .8 is written 0.8 or 0·8.

When other conversions are needed, round off fractions to the nearest 5 mm, inches to the nearest 25 mm, and feet to the nearest 0·1 meter.

Metric Scale

The metric scale is used in the same way as the architectural scales. It reduces a drawing to a selected proportion. You can purchase scales with the following metric scales.

1:5	1:50
1:10	1:75
1:20	1:100
1:25	1:125
1:33$1/3$	1:200
1:40	

Although these proportions may not mean anything initially, let us take one example and see what it means. The 1:10 scale indicates that we are taking a known measurement (a meter) and making it ten times smaller. See Figure 2.68. In other words, if you visualize a meter (39·37 inches) and squeeze it until it is only one-tenth of its original size, you have a 1:10 ratio scale. Everything you draw is then one-tenth of its original size.

This also applies to any other scale. A 1:50 scale means that the original meter has been reduced to one-fiftieth of its original length. Figures 2.69 and 2.70 show the visual appearance of a 1:50, 1:10, 1:20, and 1:100 as they might be seen on an actual scale. Notice how the meter is to be located so you can translate decimeters and centimeters. To measure 12 inches or 30·48 cm (0·30·48 m) on a 1:10 scale, see Figure 2.71.

If you find it difficult to transfer a drawing scaled in inches and feet to a metric drawing, the following chart should help.

1:10 is approximately	$1"$ = 1'-0"	(1:12)
1:20 is approximately	$1/2"$ = 1'-0"	(1:24)
1:50 is approximately	$1/4"$ = 1'-0"	(1:48)
1:100 is approximately	$1/8"$ = 1'-0"	(1:96)

Of the four scales in this chart, the 1:50 and 1:100 come closest to being exact conversions.

The conversion charts for feet to meters, and meters to feet, in Appendix B, Tables B.2 and B.3, greatly reduce the need for arithmetical calculations in converting actual dimensions.

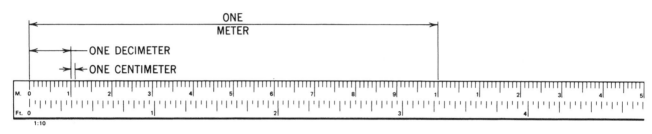

Figure 2.69   How to read an actual scale—1:50 and 1:10.

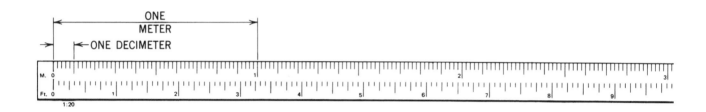

Figure 2.70   How to read an actual scale—1:20 and 1:100.

Figure 2.71   One foot equivalent in metric.

Drawing Sheet Size

When the total conversion to metrics takes place, the change will not only affect the drawing but the sheet size of the drawing paper as well. Listed here are some of the typical sizes used internationally. They are expressed in millimeters (mm).

841 × 1189	105 × 148
594 × 841	74 × 105
420 × 594	52 × 74
297 × 420	37 × 52
210 × 297	26 × 37
148 × 210	

A spot check of the various paper companies that sell reproduction paper as well as drawing paper shows that metrically sized paper is already being used for overseas work.

Possible Sizes

Because the various manufacturers have not converted to a uniform size, it is difficult to predict the final evolution of the various building materials. Suggested sizes and those used by other countries are listed below.

Wood (in mm)

38 × 75	44 × 75	50 × 75	63 × 150
38 × 100	44 × 100	50 × 100	63 × 175
38 × 150	44 × 150	50 × 125	63 × 200
38 × 175	44 × 175	50 × 150	63 × 225
38 × 200	44 × 200	50 × 175	
38 × 225	44 × 225	50 × 200	75 × 200
		50 × 300	75 × 300

Brick (in mm)

300 × 100 × 100	200 × 100 × 100
200 × 100 × 75	200 × 200 × 100

Gypsum Lath (in mm)

9·5   12·7 or 12·00

Miscellaneous

12 mm diameter for rebar	3 mm for sheet glass
25 mm for sheathing	

Modules

As indicated in Figure 2.72, the standard **module** in metrics is 100 mm. Groups of this standard 100 mm module are called a multi-module. When you select the multi-module, you should consider quantities such as 600 mm, 800 mm, 1200 mm, 1800 mm, and 2400 mm. All of these numbers are divisible in a way that allows you flexibility. For example, the 600 mm multi-module is divisible by 2, 3, 4, and 5. The result of this division gives numbers such as 200, 300, 120, and 150. All of these are

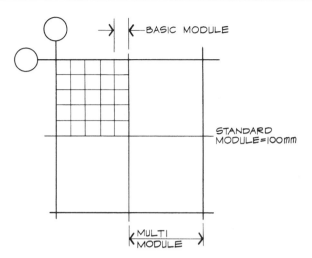

Figure 2.72 Standard module.

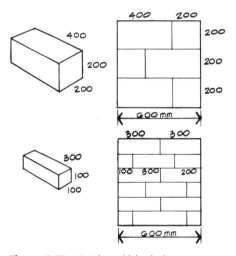

Figure 2.73 Brick and block dimensions.

numbers for which building materials may be available. This is especially true in masonry units. Most of the sizes listed under "Possible Sizes" work into a 600 mm module. See Figure 2.73.

Metrics and Computers

One should understand that the implications for using computers in this metrification process are relatively simple because all of the symbols and conventions remain the same. Line weights, color, and layers also remain the same. In other words, the language remains the same. The only difference is the ruler used to make the changes. Thus, the unit of measurement changes. Structures do not change in size. When we changed from feet and inches to the decimal equivalents, what was being measured did not change, only the instrument used to measure. This means you must first deal with four things on the computer:

A. Settings
B. Grids and Snap
C. Scale
D. Scaling Factors

Setting is simple. Set the computer to metric rather than architectural. Decide to draw in meters, centimeters, or decimeters. Because of the size of structures, the plans, elevations, and sections are usually drawn in meters, whereas details are often drawn in millimeters and centimeters, but seldom in decimeters.

Structures are drawn full size and in model space. Because a scale must be attached when plotting, the CAD drafter must be aware of the typical scales and scale factors for the scale being used.

Desired drawings are often drawn freehand by the office manager, then translated by the CAD drafter. In the case of a foundation plan, the office manager or structural engineer can decide the number of piers, size of girder, and location of access openings, to mention a few of the items that need to be sized and spaced. Figure 2.74 shows a pictorial diagram of a desired foundation plan.

If the drawing has been sketched by the office manager and all of the sizes are listed in metric, the CAD drafter only needs to draw, dimension, and note the plan. As mentioned previously, this is called a hard conversion (see Figure 2.75). The soft conversion becomes a bit more cumbersome. The soft conversion requires a thorough knowledge of the structure and the forces at work.

To become an effective CAD drafter, when asked to perform a soft conversion, you should be able to:

A. Perform simple conversions of wood members.
B. Round off to the nearest desirable measurement based on the work crew's tolerances in the field, while maintaining the strength of the member.

C. Review proportion of lumber and space available in which to work.
D. Select comparable sizes of lumber and rebar based on the available sizes in a particular region. A sampling of sizes available in Europe was listed earlier under the title "Possible Sizes."
E. Check the proportion of the metric wood member.
F. Compute the cross-sectioned area of lumber (or steel by existing charts) and compare this cross-sectioned area in the English system against metrics.
G. Select a scale.

A. *Conversion:* Although it is not the intent to engineer foundation plans, a CAD drafter should be able to convert from the English system (feet and inches) to the metric system. Consider the hypothetical situation shown in Figure 2.76.

The two measurements we will deal with are the 2×6 floor joist at 16" o.c. and the 4' 6" pier spacing.

Pier spacing

$$4'\,6'' \;=\; 4' \times 12'' \text{ per foot} \;=\; 48''$$
$$\qquad\qquad\qquad\qquad\qquad\qquad\qquad\qquad 6''$$
$$\qquad\qquad\qquad\qquad\qquad\qquad\qquad \overline{54''} \text{ total}$$

B. *Rounding Off:*

54" × 2.54 (cm/inch) = 137.16 cm = 137 cm

We will round off small so as not to exceed maximum. To convert to meters:

1 3 7 cm

The decimal point is moved two places to the left, making the measurement 1.37.

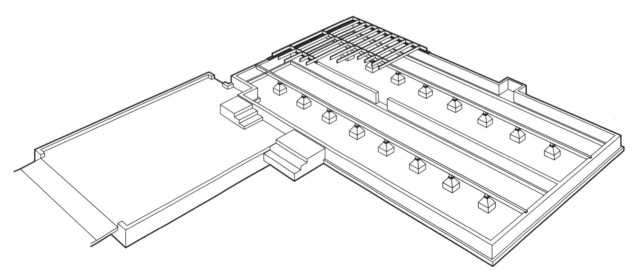

Figure 2.74   Pictorial of pier and girder system.

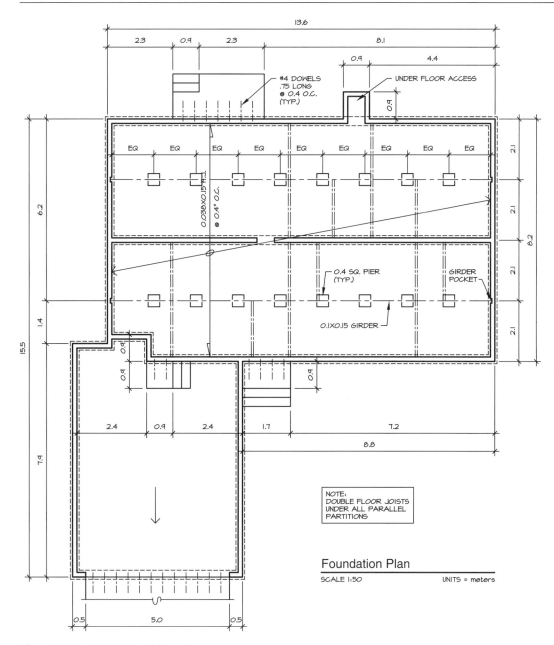

Figure 2.75 Metric foundation plan.

C. *Reviewing Proportion:* Look at Figure 2.77. Notice the minimum dimension between the underside of the girder and the earth (grade) and the distance between the underside of the floor joist and grade. A 6″ space exists, which will accommodate a girder without raising the entire structure. Thus, a 4 × 6 was selected. A 4 × 4 is allowed in many situations, but remember, we are building to increase the strength within the allowable space.

A 2 × 6 was used here because it is often the smallest size allowed by many municipalities and was selected to keep a low building profile.

Converting the 2 × 6 floor joist at 16″ o.c.:

The 2 × 6 is in reality 1.5 × 5.5 inches.
The 2 × 6 member is a 1 to 3 ratio, whereas in reality 1.5 × 5.5 is closer to a 1 to 3.66 ratio.

The larger this ratio (see Figure 2.78), the stronger the member, as you are using the member in the direction of the strength based on the direction of the grain.

Metric Conversion:
1.5 × 2.54 = 3.81 cm
5.5 × 2.54 = 13.97 cm

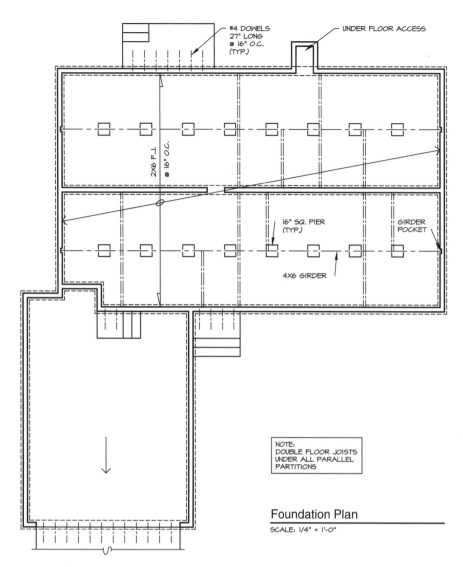

#4 DOWELS
27" LONG
@ 16" O.C.
(TYP.)

UNDER FLOOR ACCESS

2X6 F.J. @ 16" O.C.

16" SQ. PIER
(TYP.)

GIRDER
POCKET

4X6 GIRDER

NOTE:
DOUBLE FLOOR JOISTS
UNDER ALL PARALLEL
PARTITIONS

Foundation Plan
SCALE: 1/4" = 1'-0"

Figure 2.76 Converting English increments to metric.

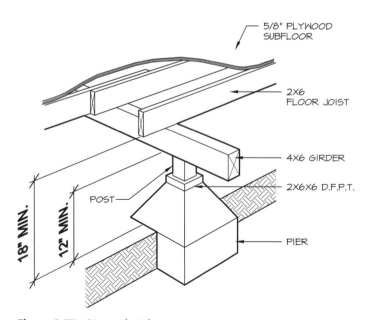

5/8" PLYWOOD
SUBFLOOR

2X6
FLOOR JOIST

4X6 GIRDER

2X6X6 D.F.P.T.

POST

PIER

18" MIN.

12" MIN.

Figure 2.77 Pier and girder.

64

D. *Selecting a Comparable Metric Member:* The 1.5 × 5.5 member converted becomes a 3.81 cm × 13.97 cm unit. When selecting a comparable size from the chart, note that the chart displays sizes in millimeters (mm). The closest is 38 mm × either 100 mm or 150 mm. The 38 mm × 150 mm is used to round off to the strength.

E. *Checking the Metric Proportion:* A 38 mm × 150 mm has a proportion of 1:3.95. Compare this with the 1:3.66 in the English system member. The metric proportion is much better.

F. *Computing Cross-Sectional Area (see Figure 2.78):* The 38 mm × 150 mm member and you have (38 × 150) 5,700 sq mm. The 1.5 (38.1 mm) × 5.5 (139.7 mm) has a cross-sectional area of 38.1 mm × 139.7 mm = 5,322.57 sq mm. Thus, the 38 mm × 150 mm member has a greater cross-sectional area and a better proportion, giving the structure a stronger foundation.

G. *Scale:* If this foundation plan was drawn on a 24″ × 36″ sheet of paper at a scale of ¼″ = 1′ 0″, and now needs to be drawn on a sheet of paper sized in metrics, its nearest size would be 594 mm × 841 mm. A 24″ × 36″ sheet would be 609.6 mm × 914.4 mm in size.

A cartoon of the foundation plan would have to be made and the selected scale implemented. In this situation let us say a 1:50 scale was used; the CAD drafter must be aware that a 1:50 scale is a slight bit larger than that of ¼″ = 1′ 0″. In addition, the paper is a bit smaller, so you cannot use a cartoon of a foundation plan drawn at ¼″ = 1′ 0″ scale and a 24″ × 36″ sheet of paper.

Remember, you are no longer drawing in feet and inches, so you must set your grids and snaps accord-

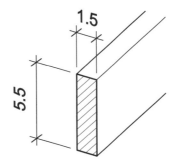

A) CROSS-SECTIONAL AREA:
5.5 X 1.5 = 8.25 SQ. INCHES

Figure 2.78 Ratio and cross-sectional area of a 2 × 6.

ingly. Refer back to Figure 2.75, that shows a typical foundation plan drawn metrically. Notice that the title includes both the scale and unit of measurement used. Also note that all the symbols and conventions look the same as those used in a drawing using feet and inches.

Scaling Factor

The scaling factor in a metric drawing is very easy to compute because the scale is expressed in proportion relative to the meter. In the example 1:50, which means one-fiftieth of a meter, is used to express one meter in the drawing; thus, there are 50 meter increments in one meter. Therefore, the scaling factor is 50.

chapter

3

COMPUTER-AIDED DRAFTING (CAD)

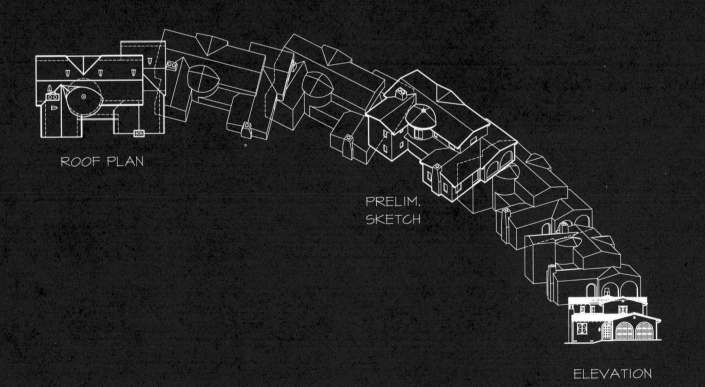

ROOF PLAN

PRELIM.
SKETCH

ELEVATION

In the new millennium, computers are impacting the field of architecture. This chapter is not about how to use specific computer (CAD) systems, but rather how the computer can best be used to become an effective tool in an architectural office. Accepting this premise, a student of architecture will learn:

A. Office set-up and expectation.
B. CAD standards used in the industry, such as line weights, color, and layering.
C. Effective use of 2-D and 3-D spaces. Discussions will allow the beginner to become a more effective user of paper space, or two-dimensional layout space, and model space, or three-dimensional modeling space.
D. Scaling drawings and lettering.
E. Three-dimensional drafting.
F. How to effectively cartoon.
G. The use vectors in the drawing process.
H. The near future of computers in our industry.

The computer is a relatively new tool in the architectural industry, and one that is becoming increasingly important. Just as with other tools, the CAD drafter must learn to use the computer through specific instruction. After the drafter has mastered the techniques the computer can aid in the creative process. The drafter is then controlling the tool, rather than the computer controlling the drafter. There is a corresponding example in the field of music. A trombonist must go beyond thinking about how to position the sliding portion of the instrument to achieve a certain note. Instead, as a musician the trombonist responds to the arrangement of notes on the sheet music and allows his or her hand to move the slide spontaneously to create music. At this point the musician is giving the music emotion, character, or spirit. Similarly, the CAD drafter concentrates on translating the intent of the designer into a workable set of construction documents, with the computer as one of his or her creative tools.

New drawing tools in an architect's office do not drastically change the way in which structures are built. With the introduction of the computer, we may compute the energy requirements for a building differently than we would using a calculator, or we may produce and deliver construction documents differently, but the computer does not change the architectural information necessary to construct a building. To use a car as a metaphor, a car does not change from being a delivery vehicle for passengers or cargo (its function) just because its internal combustion engine has been replaced by an electric engine. A change in energy source to drive the vehicle does not change the car's need for tires, a transmission, or a steering mechanism.

Each computer drafter should be well trained so that he or she can prepare a set of construction documents from scratch. Whether an office hires you as the first CAD operator or the office already has a system incorporated, this training will allow you, the CAD operator, to integrate your understanding of the system and become immediately effective in production.

This chapter is divided into three divisions. The first describes the inner workings of a computer and how a computer actually works. The second section describes the standards used by offices that become the foundation of construction documents. It also discusses such items as standard colors used, line quality, and the subdivisions of a drawing, referred to as layers. The third section shows the evolution of a complete set of construction documents, both two- and three-dimensional.

■ THE COMPUTER

To describe the outer appearance of a computer to anyone in this day and age would be an insult. Students are introduced to the computer as early as the first grade and are thus quite familiar with the cosmetics of the equipment. Add to this the proliferation of video games and other electronic devices, plus the enormous amount of computer advertisement, and we have a population that is very much aware of computers. Here we describe the inner workings of the computer. How often have we seen advertisements that indicate 128MB RAM, 10.0 GB hard drive, 40x CDROM drive, 56k/14.4 V.90 data/fax modem, and wonder whether the computer is sufficient for our purposes. The mystery of the inner workings of a computer is now about to be revealed to you.

We start by comparing and contrasting two parallel worlds: the inner world of a computer and that of an architectural office. The following is a list of elements common in an architectural office, contrasted with their counterparts in a computer (see Figure 3.1).

Office	Computer
1. Architect's office	A. Central processing
2. Production	B. RAM
3. Library	C. Hard drive
4. Hallway	D. Motherboard
5. Clerical	E. Discrete logic
6. Conference	F. Monitor
7. Reception	G. Log-in/out
8. Garage / carport	H. Removable media
9. Kitchen	I. Power
10. Toilet	J. Fan and compressed Air
11. Communication	K. Internet
12. Studio	L. Video card

The three main areas in the computer are central processing (design), RAM (drafting), and the hard drive (storage). All are held together by the motherboard, which can be viewed as the connecting hallway in an architect's office.

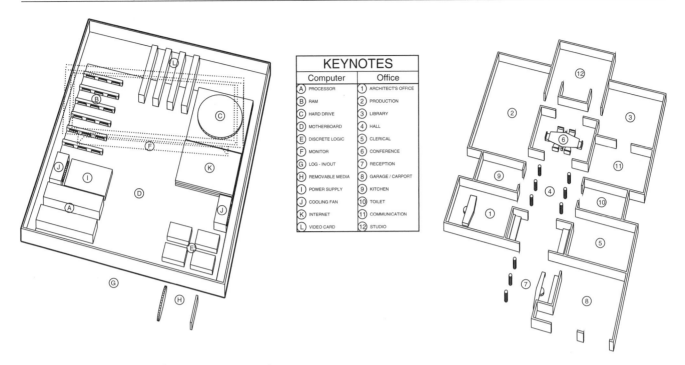

Figure 3.1 Understanding how a computer works.

The user of a computer can be thought of as the client, and the task performed as the job. In the case of the computer, the task may be to word process, draft construction documents, develop schedules, or to chart or render drawings. The job for an architect may be to design a commercial structure, an industrial structure, or a residence.

Processor

The architect's office can be considered the processor or the central processing unit. This is where all of the decisions are made, and it becomes not only the control point of the office, but also the brain of the computer. Because major decisions are made in the architect's office, the architect will make these important decisions at his or her desk. In the computer, this "desk" is called the cache (a high-speed RAM; see the next section on RAM).

RAM (Random-Access Memory). The size of the office is usually dependent on the size and quantity of the jobs entrusted to the architect. To perform these jobs (tasks), drafters (the production area) are hired to meet the need. In the computer this parallel element is the RAM (random-access memory). The greater the number of drafters in an office, the greater the number of jobs that can be handled with greater speed. So it is with RAM. In an office there is no need to hire a large number of drafters if there is not enough work to keep them busy. The overhead is unnecessary for the work performed. Such is the case with the computer. There is very little value in hav-

ing a large amount of RAM if it is never used. However, all offices have the ability to expand production (add drafters) to handle any increased workload. In our parallel computer example, this increased workload creates an increased need for storage space. This is equivalent to the hard drive, which is discussed next.

Hard Drive

Research is done in the library of the architect's office. Samples of materials, names of vendors, product literature, and reference books, among other resources, all are maintained in the library. The library is equivalent to the hard drive in a computer. This is where you get the resource material needed and take it to production (RAM) to produce the construction documents. The greater the amount of resources (hard drive), the more variety of tools you have available to produce a job.

Printed literature and CDs from vendors on available products, along with reference books and other materials, provide the necessary resources to produce a set of construction documents. The work is rarely done in the library. You pick up the materials needed and take them to the production and work areas. In the computer, you visit the computer's hard drive (the library), pick up the needed information, and work in RAM.

If the production area is totally filled with drafters, you can work in the library. As in the computer, the production area is a place of increased productivity. By working in the library, one loses productivity because the space is not designed for rapid drafting.

Discrete Logic

In addition to the three main areas in an architect's office, there are support staff who are not directly involved with the production of construction documents but are critical to the smooth flow of work produced. These are the clerical and support persons, those who were formerly called office boys/girls (now affectionally called "gofers"). They order and move supplies, type reports, file, deliver packages, handle payroll, and carry out other support activities. They are really the connections between spaces, between functions, and do not often get credit for the service they provide the rest of the team. In the computer, this function is called discrete logic, the part of the computer that brings logic to the process. It is the mover of information to its proper location for action.

Monitor

The primary function of the conference room is to provide a place for the visual presentation of the project (job) to the client. The presentation shows the client both progress and the final design of building forms. It is the place where, for the client, reality begins to set in, facilitated by models, drawings, diagrams, and the display of important information. In our parallel computer example, this is the monitor. The monitor allows the user (client) to view various aspects of a project.

Log-in/Out

As you enter an architectural office, the receptionist greets you. This is also the location where you make appointments for future meetings. In the parallel computer example, this is the point at which you spend logging on and off the computer station. One might say that as you log-in/out of the computer, you are dealing with the computer's receptionist.

The user of this office will be the client, and the task to be performed, the job. Thus, to log in to the computer is to make an appointment to discuss the job with the architect.

Removable Media

Most large companies have a company car or van. The van is used to transport models, drawings, and even important clients from an airport to their hotel or office. The larger the vehicle, the greater is the capacity to carry large groups of clients, drawings, and presentation models. Here the computer's equivalents are the CDs, DVDs, and disks. The greater the capacity of the CDs or DVDs, the greater is the ability to transport information. In this manner the garage or carport becomes the place where these vehicles of data transport are inserted, the counterpart of the removable media.

Power

It takes energy to produce work. Without energy or power, there is no work. We chose the kitchen to represent the place where liquids and nourishment are consumed by the employees to produce energy. In the computer, the counterpart is the power supply. The power activates the central processing unit, the hard drive, and RAM.

Cooling Fan (Hot Air Disposal)

A cooling fan that expels hot air from the computer can be used as an example of a toilet that takes user byproducts (waste) to a sewer.

Internet

Communication is vital to the operation of an architectural office. Communication does not occupy a separate space in the office, but flows through the office, allowing for the transfer of information from one entity to another, both inside and outside the office. Architects stay in touch with contractors, vendors, and their associates, such as structural, electrical, and mechanical engineers. The computer counterpart to this means of digital communication—text, voice, video, drawing, and information databases—is the Internet. Through the Internet, the entire world becomes an architect's resource. Designers, drafters, and researchers can surf the world to expand their contacts and resources.

Video Card

More and more frequently, architectural offices are beginning to recognize the need for a specific space set aside for creative thinking, much like a think tank. This creative work space would have all the necessary tools for ideas to flow and flourish. In animation circles, such a space is often called the "spirit room" or "concept space." The video card in a computer allows for creative imaging. It creates a space in the computer where designs and ideas are generated. In the architectural studio, multimedia presentations are assembled, as well as photography and digital photography, along with video presentations. Models are also made in this space. In the computer, slide shows, 3-D modeling, pamphlets and brochures, and a multitude of formatted presentational material are assembled.

■ OFFICE STANDARDS

Every office has a set of standards that all employees must follow. This is essential in the industry not only because many drafters may be working on the same project, but also to ensure uniformity of the language that drafters speak. Adhering to standards helps coordinate drawings and a firm's associates both inside and outside the office.

Standards establish sheet size, scales used, standard line and symbol conventions, placement and positions of drawings, and sheet modules, to mention a few items. These standards are often kept on the drafter's desk and are referred to as the drafting room manual, the office procedure manual, or something similar. Computers are no different. They too have their standards, and although standards may differ slightly from job to job or office to office, they should be rigidly followed. Standards do change, and making or suggesting a revision adds to both their usage and their ability to become viable office solutions.

Although standards are established by individual offices and are often based on existing drafting room manuals, the introduction of computers to the arsenal of production tools has created a need for national and international standards. Associations such as the American Institute of Architects, National Institute of Building Sciences, Construction Specification Institute, and even the military, to mention a few, have in fact produced national CAD standards.

If, for example, you were developing a set of construction documents for a military installation, its standards would prevail and override existing office standards.

When using standards, a drafter should not be so dependent on existing standard templates that he or she is unable to develop new ones that the job calls for. Flexibility and creativity are important. You may find two types of computer drafters in an office. One drafter can develop new office standards as the need requires. This type of drafter is knowledgeable and flexible and knows how to set up line types, lettering size, sheet size, and scales. A second type is the "running scared" CAD employee who will copy office standards from various offices and use a large number of CDs and floppy disks with predrafted, predetermined templates of sheet sizes, lettering, sizing, and so on. This hodgepodge of conflicting standards causes utter chaos and completely disorganizes the existing office communication. Office managers will evaluate individual performance and conformance to standards, and if you do not keep up with the state of the technology or fail to recognize the needs of the office, your job may be jeopardized.

To help drafters avoid this dilemma, the following pages describe the needs of the architectural office and why certain standards are enforced, how to develop them, and how to understand them.

We will describe in this section of the chapter the following topics in regard to standards:

1. A profound change in perception
2. Importance of standards in the electronic world
3. Vector vs. raster
4. Oddly scaled drawings
5. Paper
6. Paper space/virtual space (model space)
7. Scaling factor
8. Layering
9. Pen setting/line weights/color
10. Lettering size
11. Procedure for the preparation of construction documents
12. Advantages
13. Disadvantages
14. Future

A Profound Change

The most profound change caused by the computer is the manner in which we perceive and execute drawings. The first of these changes in perception is the way we view structures. With the use of a computer, structures should be drawn at full scale. This is made possible because we are working in virtual space (model space), which is unlimited. Formerly, we thought of buildings in reduced scale. For example, most floor plans for small structures are drawn at a scale of $1/4" = 1' 0"$. When conceiving the structure, the designer visualizes the building almost as a scaled model of the real thing. Designers will tell you that when sizing rooms, it is important to have a feel of the size of the room at a reduced scale.

When designing and drawing in full scale on the computer, you can now look about the space you are occupying and draw relationships based on the real-world sizes. The monitor becomes a window through which you are viewing this full-size structure. The printer/plotter becomes a photograph of this image displayed on the monitor screen (see Figure 3.2).

Standardization in the Electronic World

Standardization in the electronic world is very important because our whole industry is based on communicating ideas. We can do this only if each of the participants—architects, drafters, associates (mechanical, structural, electrical engineers), and so forth—speak the same language.

With manually drafted documents, a hard copy was usually sent by mail or fax to the client, the contractor, and even between offices. Copies of electronically produced drawings can now be sent as hard copies, or the drawings can be sent electronically. If a set of drawings has been done in layers, as is often the case, the titles of these layers become critical for identification. To aid identification, a CAD drafter must use the office standards (standard titles) to which the office subscribes and plot them out onto a chart similar to that found in Figure 3.3.

Figure 3.2 Drawing and monitor become one and the same relative to perception.

LEGEND		FILE															
A — ARCHITECTURAL																	
M — MECHANICAL																	
P — PRESENTATION		DRAWING															
S — STRUCTURAL																	
E — ELECTRICAL																	
LAYER	NAME																
A.																	
A.																	
A.																	
A.																	
A.																	
A.																	
A.																	
A.																	
A.																	
A.																	
A.																	
A.																	
A.																	
S.																	
S.																	
S.																	
S.																	
S.																	
S.																	
E.																	
E.																	
E.																	
E.																	
E.																	

Figure 3.3 Sample layout for layers.

Generally speaking, drawings are categorized by subject—for example, architectural, mechanical, structural, and the like. In manual drawings, "A" is for architectural, "S" is for structural, and so on. Within each category, there are subdivisions. For example, A-1 may be the number assigned to the site plan, and A-2 may be assigned to the floor plan, A-3 to elevation, A-4 to section, and so on. In electronic drafting, these become file names, with the sheet name preceded by a job number. If this is the first job in the year 2043, that calendar number in conjunction with the category number may be listed as 430101-A1 (year, month, job, sheet). If the same floor plan is used as a furniture plan for the client, a subcategory breakdown is needed and the number may read 430101-A1.3.

This is where the layers and their titles play a significant role. The floor plan becomes a composite of many layers, with each layer producing a different part of the floor plan. Look at Figure 3.4 for such a breakdown. Notice the eleven "A" drawings listed in the left column. The walls of the floor plan are drawn on one layer and given the name A-WALL. All of the appliances (such as plumbing) are drawn on another layer called A-FLOR, windows and doors on A-GLAZ and A-DOOR, dimensions on A-ANNO-DIMS, and so on. To produce a drawing for construction, we must print A-WALL, A-FLOR, A GLAZ/DOOR, and A-ANNO, along with a host of other layers, which contain reference bubbles and titles. To print a furniture plan for the client, you would most certainly need layers A-WALL, A-FURN, and A-ANNO.

Now that we are somewhat familiar with number and layer titles, let us say the structural engineer needs to have a copy of the floor plan. What layers would you send the structural engineer, and how would he or she use this information?

Let us say you sent the engineer the floor plan described earlier: A-WALL, A-FLOR, A-DOOR, A-GLAZ, A-ANNO-DIMS, reference bubbles, notes, titles, and so forth. The engineer will need to enter these particulars into his or her computer system. The engineer has to know how to load the layers needed for an S drawing. If the structural engineer is producing a roof framing plan or a ceiling joist plan, he or she will initially need not only the wall layer, but the dimension layer as well. The dimension layer can be eliminated on the final printing. In this way, the wall (A-WALL) layer is used as a base for a multitude of other drawings. A quick look at Figure 3.4 will reveal the A-WALL layer used for the floor plan, ceiling plan, furniture plan, and finish plan, as well as the floor framing plan, roof framing plan, and, on the simplified chart, the power plan, lighting plan, and the reflected ceiling plan. This is called cross referencing, or X-referencing.

Standardization is also essential in the numbering systems used. Metric versus English system, decimal versus fraction, and engineering versus architectural are but a few of the choices you can make in setting up a computer drawing. All of these factors will affect lumber size, brick size, and the various materials used by the construction industry.

Vector Versus Raster

It is imperative that all CAD drafters know the difference between vector drawings and raster drawings because of the ways in which each file format can be used. Both raster and vector images can be manipulated. Because raster images are made up of pixels, a photo manipulation program must be used with a raster image. You can remove items from the image, elongate, stretch, or compress the image. You can even change the position of the image relative to the paper and format for presentation. However, you cannot easily change the geometry. With advanced computer skills, you can change the drawing. A drafter can do any necessary changes on a drawing by manipulating vectors.

Vector drawings are done both two dimensionally and three dimensionally. Vector drawings are actually lines, planes, and geometric shapes drawn in virtual space. Height, width and depth are described as X, Y, and Z directions. This means you can rotate a three-dimensional form and look at it from any of the six principal directions: front, back, left, right, top, and bottom (or underside) and an unlimited number of views in between.

For importing a digital drawing from a vendor, you should request a vector drawing. Figure 3.5 shows a single-hung window with a transom made of vinyl and imported as a vector file. Such drawings are used to represent the basic change in the manufacturer's configuration on which the header, exterior finish, interior finish, and waterproofing methods are placed so as to produce a construction detail for a specific application.

Figure 3.6 shows a recommended installation detail. The computer drafter can take this detail and adapt it to a specific application while adding pertinent design features. When requesting both basic shapes and installation details, ask for the file format your office typically uses. Usually, that will be DXF or DWG. The majority of CAD programs can easily manipulate these file types.

DXF Versus DWG

In order for a drawing to be sent or received electronically, it must be formatted. Although there are other formatting methods, DXF and DWG are most typically used.

LEGEND
A — ARCHITECTURAL
M — MECHANICAL
P — PRESENTATION
S — STRUCTURAL
E — ELECTRICAL

Note: FILE names carry the prefix "2000_" (e.g., 2000_A-1.0). ● = filled, ○ = open.

LAYER	NAME	A-1.0	A-2.0	A-2.1	A-2.2	A-2.3	A-3.0	A-4.0	A-5.0	A-6.0	S-1.0	S-2.0	S-3.0	S-4.0	E-1.0	E-2.0	E-3.0
		SITE PLAN	FLOOR PLAN	CEILING PLAN	FURNITURE PLAN	FINISH PLAN	ELEVATIONS	SECTIONS	SCHEDULES	INT. ELEVATIONS	FOUNDATION	FLOOR FRAMING	ROOF FRAMING	WALL SECTION	POWER PLAN	LIGHTING PLAN	REFLECTED C.P.
A. SITE	A-SITE	●															
A. WALL	A-WALL		●	○	○						○	○			○	○	○
A. FIXTURES	A-FLOR		●	○	○												
A. DOORS	A-DOOR		●	○	○											○	
A. WINDOWS	A-GLAZ		●	○	○											○	
A. DIMENSIONS	A-ANNO-DIMS		●		○							○	○				
A. CEILING PLAN	A-CEIL			●													●
A. FURNITURE	A-FURN				●												
A. NOTES	A-ANNO					●											
A. BORDER & TITLE	A-TBLK		●	●	●	●	●	●	●		●	●	●	●	●	●	●
A. EXTERIOR ELEVATION	A-ELEV-EXTR						●							○			
A. INTERIOR ELEVATION	A-ELEV-INTR							●									
A. BUILDING SECTION	A-SECT								●								
S. NOTES	S-ANNO										●						
S. DIMENSIONS	S-DIMS										●						
S. FOUNDATION WALLS	S-WALL										●						
S. FOOTING CONVENTIONS	S-FNDN										●						
S. FRAMING MEM. FLOOR	S-FRAM-FLOR											●					
S. FRAMING MEM. ROOF	S-FRAM-ROOF												●				
E. NOTES	E-ANNO														●		
E. EQUIPMENT	E-EQUP														●		
E. WALL FIXTURES	E-FIXT-WALL															●	
E. CEILING FIXTURES	E-FIXT-CEIL																●
E. SUSPENDED CEILING	E-CEIL																●

Figure 3.4   Example of layers and their titles.

The DWG format, which is the most desirable, is the easiest for the AutoCAD drafter to use, change, or correct because it has all the ingredients used to produce the end result.

The DXF (short for drawing exchange format) strips down the total drawing sequence in such a way that it makes it easier to translate. Because it is a stripped-down form, you cannot perform certain tasks because although the final visual image is complete, pertinent information is missing and it thus cannot be easily manipulated. It saves the final geometry, but many of the steps used to produce the final geometry are missing. DXF is easier to exchange with other programs. Not all programs can use DWG formats easily. If you wish to electronically send a drawing or place a drawing on a web site strictly for viewing, then explore a DWF format.

Various AutoCAD programs cannot open DWF-formatted drawings, which provides a level of protection

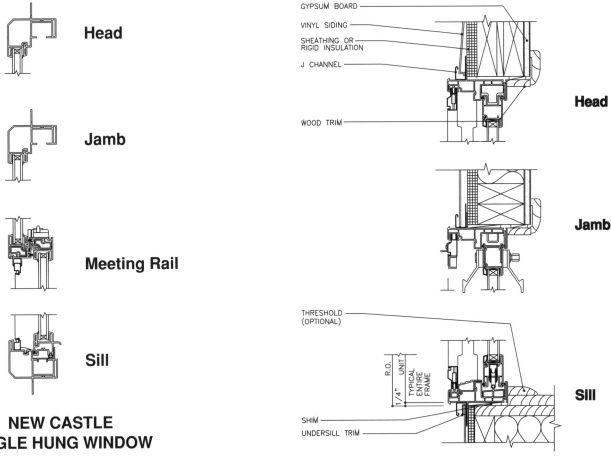

Head

Jamb

Meeting Rail

Sill

**NEW CASTLE
SINGLE HUNG WINDOW**

Figure 3.5 Vinyl window configurations imported from Certainteed.

**NEW CASTLE PATIO DOOR
VINYL SIDING - 2X4 FRAME**

Figure 3.6 Manufacturers' installation details in DWG format.

useful for maintaining a more secure transmission of drawings. Your standards, symbols, layers, sheet set-ups, and so forth, will not be entirely usable by the person to whom you transmit the file.

X-Referencing (XREF)

Cross-referencing in the industry refers to the process of referencing one drawing to another by means of reference bubbles (See figure 3.7A). In the computer industry, the term *X-referencing* (XREF) sounds like *cross-referencing*, but it is not the same. XREF means "externally referenced" drawings. XREF is used to combine drawings and keep the entire set of construction documents updated with the most recent version of a drawing. A secondary datum is now being used to produce drawings. The example shown in Figure 3.7B is an electrical plan. The floor plan (master) becomes the externally referenced drawing and is not directly a part of the electrical plan layers.

Computer-generated drawings, with their intricate network of finely tuned layers, titles, and patterns, are produced almost as if they were a family. Base drawings, such as exterior and interior walls showing some of the basic fixtures and stair locations, are often referred to as masters or parent drawings. Their offshoots, such as framing plans, electrical plans, building sections, and so on, are commonly referred to as children or submasters. The plot sheets serve the parents and children by presenting specific drawings and information (maids or servants). A composite of these drawings may include title blocks, notes, and other features always found on every sheet (e.g., title block) or those features found only on specific sheets. Because CAD drawings can be done using multiple files, the process of delegating certain information to certain drawings is called *XREFing* and allows certain drawings to be used in multiple ways.

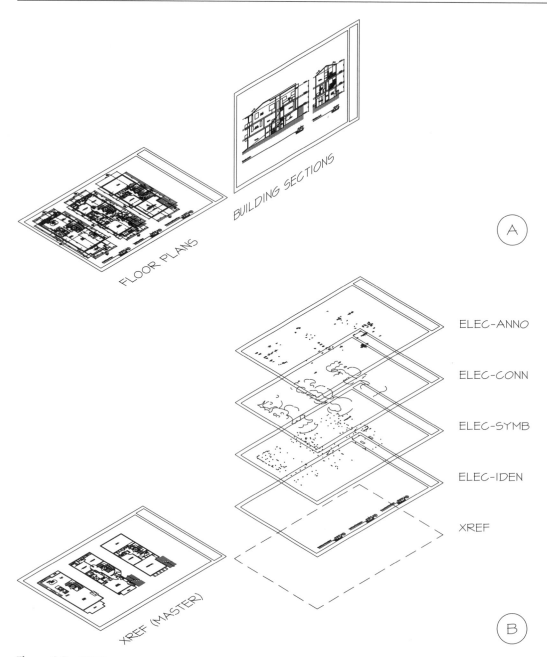

BUILDING SECTIONS

FLOOR PLANS

(A)

ELEC-ANNO

ELEC-CONN

ELEC-SYMB

ELEC-IDEN

XREF

XREF (MASTER)

(B)

Figure 3.7   XREF.

Figure 3.8 shows a sampling of an XREF standard for a hypothetical office. Figure 3.9 provides examples of a master, submaster, and servant. This cross referencing has the same meaning in manual drawings as well as CAD drawings, whereas XREF refers to a special process unique to computer-generated drawings.

Oddly Scaled Drawings

A peculiar group of computer-generated drawings that are beginning to find their way into the construction industry are drawings without a specific or known scale.

These are drawings that may have been drawn to scale initially, but were resized to fit the paper on which they were plotted. Even worse are drawings and notes that have been reduced so that you may need a magnifying glass to read them.

To avoid such a catastrophe, all CAD drafters should be able to cartoon a drawing and adhere to office standards in regard to sizing and heights of lettering.

Cartooning is covered in Chapter 6, but a simple explanation of cartooning can be helpful here. Cartooning or sheet formatting is the process of taking a standard sheet of paper and sizing the drawing on the paper in a standard

Preliminary Documentation of Office XREF Standard

		Schematic Design / Design Development (MASTER)	
		Naming: YearMonthProjectNumber-MAST.dwg (YYMM##-MAST.dwg) 000101-MAST.dwg	
	MAST	Master Design Drawing	Walls, Doors, Windows, Stairs, Fireplaces, Room Labels,
			Plumbing Fixtures, Closets (What you need for the Client)

		Design Development / Construction Documents (Sub-Masters)	
		Naming: YearMonthProjectNumber-FLOR.dwg (YYMM##-FLOR.dwg) 000101-FLOR.dwg	
XREF	**Listed in order of importance**		**Description**
MAST	NBHD	Neighborhood Compatibility	If needed
MAST	FLOR	Floor Plans	Poche, Hatching, Notes, Dimensions
MAST	ROOF	Roof Plan	
MAST	ELEV	Elevations	
MAST	SECT	Building Sections	
MAST	SITE	Site Plan	Modify TOPO to start Could also include a separate Grading Plan
MAST	FRAM	Framing / Foundation	All Structural Drawings
MAST	ELEC	Electrical Plans	
MAST	OTHR	Other Architecture	If in project program
	TBLK	Titleblock	XREF'd to ALL plotsheets
	TOPO	Survey / Topography	Produced by surveyor

		PLOTSHEETS or Layouts w/ modelspaces.	
		It is possible to have all sub-masters drawn on their respective plotsheet modelspaces.	
XREF	**Sheet**	**Sheet Title**	**Description**
	T-1.0	Title Sheet	
	T-1.1	General Notes	
	CF-1R	Title 24 / Energy Calcs	
SITE	A-1.0	Site Plan	
TOPO	A-1.1	Survey / Topography	
NBHD	A-1.2	Neighborhood Compatibility	If required for submittal
SITE	A-1.3	Grading Plan	If not included in Site Plan
FLOR	A-2.0	Floor Plans	
	A-2.1		
ELEV	A-3.0	Exterior Elevations	
	A-3.1		
SECT	A-4.0	Building Sections	
	A-4.1		
MAST	A-5.0	Roof Plan	
INTR	A-6.0	Interior Elevations	
	A-6.1		
OTHR	A-7.0	Other Architecture	
	A-7.1		
	A-8.0	Schedules	
	A-8.1		
	A-D.1	Architectural Details	
	A-D.2		
FRAM	S-1.0	Foundation Plan	
FRAM	S-1.0B	Basement Framing Plan	If needed for space reasons
FRAM	S-1.1	First Floor Framing	
FRAM	S-1.2	Second Floor Framing	
	S-1.3		
FRAM	S-2.0	Roof Framing	
	S-2.1		
	S-D.1	Structural Details	
	S-D.2		
ELEC	E-1.0	Electrical Plans	
	E-1.1		

Figure 3.8 XREF standards.

MASTER
(PARENT)

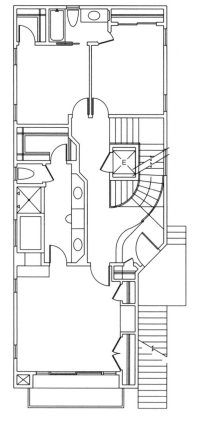

SUB-MASTER
(CHILD)

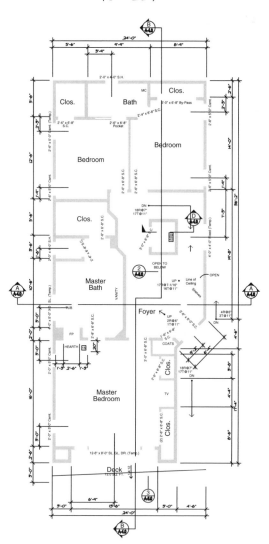

SLAVE
(SERVANT)

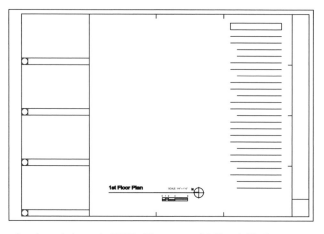

Figure 3.9 A floor plan developed through XREF. (Courtesy of Mike Adli, Owner, Nagy R. Bakhoum, President of Obelisk Architects.)

scale. This can be considered a page layout. The drafter plans the space the drawing will occupy, with the necessary lettering height and other features, so that construction workers can read the print even from a few feet away.

This problem also exists in manual drafting when previously imported details are reduced on a copier to fit the page layout. If the manual drafter understands the percentage reduction of the copier, he or she is able to reduce a $\frac{1}{2}'' = 1'\text{-}0''$ scaled drawing to a $\frac{3}{8}'' = 1'\text{-}0''$ scaled drawing. However, drafters often ignore the height of lettering in the reduction, only to produce drawings that are difficult to read.

The reducing process has found its way into the CAD system with a command that says Print to Fit, printing the drawing on a sheet of paper regardless of scale. If the CAD drafter anticipates how much the drawing will be reduced, lettering height office standards can be maintained.

If a floor plan would fit a 24×36 piece of paper at $\frac{1}{4}'' = 1'\text{-}0''$ and the office standard is to maintain $\frac{1}{8}''$ tall lettering and $\frac{1}{4}''$ tall titles, the drafter must produce lettering at $6''$ in height (at $\frac{1}{4}''$ scale) and titles $12''$ tall.

Paper

Paper comes in various sizes. The standard and nonstandard sizes are listed in Figure 3.10. Nonstandard-sized paper is listed with an asterisk.

Thus, if a final drawing is to be printed/plotted on an $8\text{-}\frac{1}{2}'' \times 11''$ sheet of paper, its template in the computer should be called "A" paper, an $11'' \times 17''$ sheet of paper would be called "B" paper, and so on.

When drafting manually, the drafter has the entire sheet of paper to work with. Such is not the case with computer-generated drawings. The CAD drafter must be aware of the limits of the printer or plotter. For example, an $8\text{-}\frac{1}{2}'' \times 11''$ paper can have a printable area of $8'' \times 10.5''$. This proportion holds true with all paper. Add to the drawing sheet border lines and title blocks, and the actual drawing area of the sheet will be reduced to a given standard used in the office. Figure 3.11 shows a diagram of the printable area and the drawing area of an $8\text{-}\frac{1}{2}'' \times 11''$ sheet of paper (AP for "A"-sized paper).

Knowing that the printable area for an $8\text{-}\frac{1}{2}'' \times 11''$ sheet of paper can be $8'' \times 10.5''$, ideally we would set the margins at $\frac{1}{4}''$ and use a $1''$ or $\frac{3}{4}''$ strip for a title block. Some offices do not even print the borders, but only the title block. If the drawing will be bound, the binding edge is increased to $\frac{3}{4}''$, leaving a drawing area of $7\text{-}\frac{1}{2}'' \times 9\text{-}\frac{3}{4}''$ (see Figure 3.11B and 3.11C, respectively).

Because most computer drawings are done in layers (layering is covered later in this chapter), one layer may contain the limits within which the drafter must stay. These borders may or may not be printed in the final drawing (see Figure 3.11A and 3.11C, respectively).

Typical Paper(s)
"A" Paper (16)
a. 11" x 8.5"
b. 12" x 9"
c. 10.5" x 7.5" **
"B" Paper (8)
a. 17" x 11"
b. 18" x 12"
c. 15" x 10.5" **
"C" Paper (4)
a. 22" x 17"
b. 24" x 18"
c. 21" x 15" **
"D" Paper (2)
a. 34" x 22"
b. 36" x 24"
c. 30" x 21" **
"E" Paper (1)
a. 44" x 34"
b. 48" x 36"
c. 42" x 30" **
(#) = sheets in an "E" size sheet
** = non-standard

Figure 3.10 Typical standard and nonstandard paper sizes.

Paper larger than $8\text{-}\frac{1}{2}'' \times 11''$ is subdivided into drawing modules. In Figure 3.12, a $24'' \times 36''$ sheet of paper is shown with a $1\text{-}\frac{1}{2}''$ left binding border and a $\frac{1}{2}''$ border for the top, bottom, and right side. It will use a $1\text{-}\frac{1}{2}''$ title block. The drawing area left is divided into five horizontal and five vertical spaces, each of which is $4\text{-}\frac{5}{8}'' \times 6\text{-}\frac{1}{2}''$. This now becomes the office standard for all drawings. Notes will be typed so as not to exceed $6\text{-}\frac{1}{2}''$ in width (or $13''$ if two modules are used) and a vertical height of $4\text{-}\frac{5}{8}''$, $9\text{-}\frac{1}{4}''$, $13\text{-}\frac{3}{4}''$, $18''$, or $22\text{-}\frac{5}{8}''$.

Architectural details are drawn to this module of $4\text{-}\frac{5}{8}'' \times 6\text{-}\frac{1}{2}''$. This space may be further divided into drawing areas and keynote areas to further exploit paper usage.

Plans, elevations, building sections, and site plans should be drawn within this established matrix so as to allow for the remaining space to be used by details, notes, charts, and schedules. Figure 3.13 shows a site plan, general notes, details, vicinity map, and an index formatted to a $24'' \times 36''$ sheet of paper with a matrix of five vertical and five horizontal modules.

Figure 3.14 shows this formatting process using a $24'' \times 36''$ divided into a 5×5 module and a 4×5 module, and a $30'' \times 42''$ sheet divided into a 5×5 module and a 6×6 module. Once the formatting process decision is made in the office, the drafter must comply with these limits when drawing, writing notes, and even detailing.

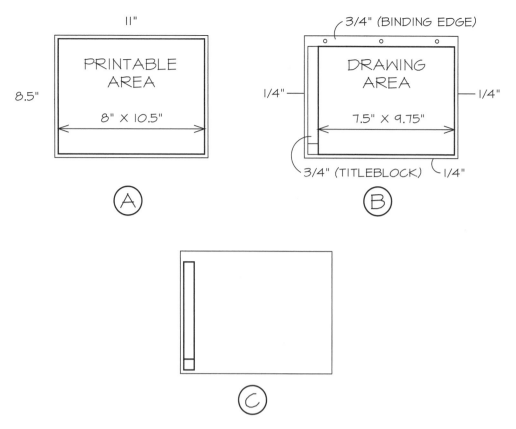

Figure 3.11 Printable and drawing area 8.5 × 11.

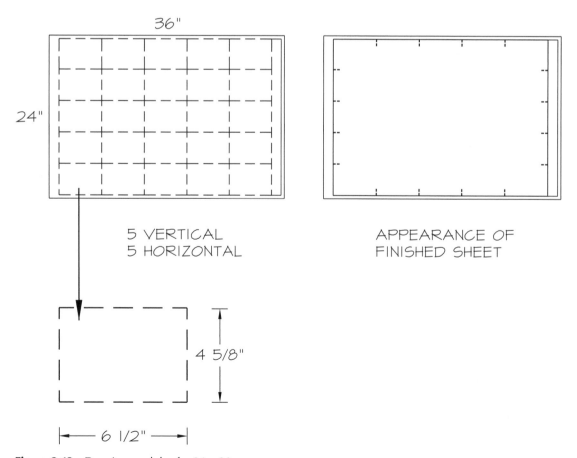

Figure 3.12 Drawing modules for 24 × 36.

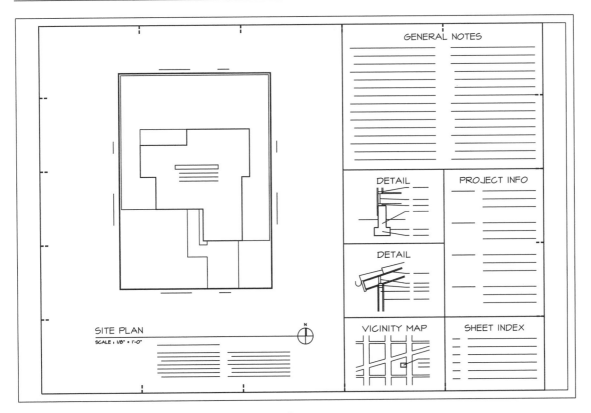

Figure 3.13   Drawing modules for 24 × 36 (registered).

If many drafters are working on one set of working drawings and all subscribe to a single format pattern, not only will the entire set look well organized to the client, but the integral pieces will fit together like a giant puzzle. Clear, precise drawings reduce office liability and increase visual impact of office documents.

As described earlier, a structure is drawn at full scale on the computer and viewed through a window that is actually the monitor. By filling this entire screen area with a standard-size sheet of paper, you have a formatted screen ready to import drawings. The interior of this drawing sheet is now your new window and is called a *viewport*. Each module can also be a view port. Figure 3.15 shows a monitor displaying a 24″ × 36″ sheet of paper. Nine modules (three horizontally and three vertically) have been shaded to show a nine-module viewport into which a drawing can be imported. Thus, a viewport becomes a window on the paper through which you can see a full-size building. The computer allows you to zoom up close or fill the viewport with a graphic image such as a floor plan. In this way, you can fill to the extents of the viewport, but you will not be displaying to any given scale.

The best solution to this nonscaled drawing is to fill the view port with the largest image possible, but to a known scale. This scale may be an architectural scale such as $1/8″ = 1′-0″$, $1/4″=1′-0″$, an engineering scale such as $1″ =$ 20 feet or $1″ = 50$ feet, or a metric scale such as 1:50 or 1:20. This approach is particularly effective because the construction crew in the field is familiar with scale rather than proportion. They need to visualize size and space, so providing them with familiar scaled drawings increases productivity. The ability to manually correct or revise drawings becomes easier because measuring tools are readily available.

2-D (Paper) Versus 3-D (Virtual or Model) Space

The difference between two-dimensional (2-D) and three-dimensional (3-D) space can be compared to the difference between manual drafting and computer-aided drafting (CAD). In paper (2D) space, you fill the monitor with a theoretical piece of paper. This theoretical piece of paper is already unrealistic, because it is a reduction of the actual piece of paper to fit the screen. In manual drafting the paper is actual size. Next, the drawing is done on this unrealistic size to a scale that is also unrealistic until printed. In other words, what you see is not the real size of paper, nor is it at the proper scale (e.g., $1/4″ = 1′)″$ or $1/8″ = 1′-0″$ scale).

In model space or virtual space (3D), you are drawing full size. When you are "modeling" a drawing, you measure exactly the size of the building. You do not work at a reduced scale. It is as if you were inside a room look-

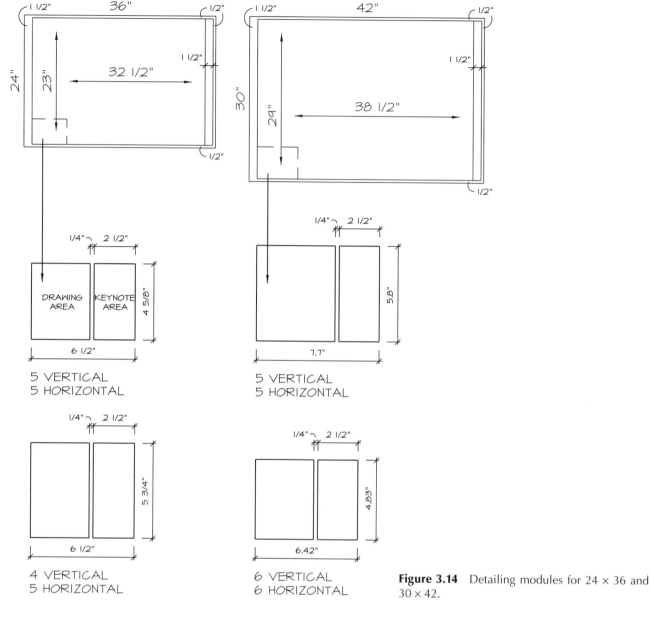

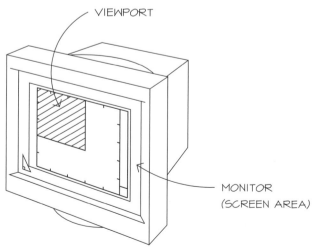

Figure 3.14 Detailing modules for 24 × 36 and 30 × 42.

Figure 3.15 Monitor—paper space and viewport.

ing through a window and seeing the actual structure. The window in this instance is the monitor.

When printing or plotting a drawing, you must reduce this full-size drawing or model to a scale that will fit on the actual paper size. For this reason, we encourage you to draw structures in model space and draw them full scale. Model space, also called virtual space, is the closest thing to the real thing. It does, however, require the drafter to have a working knowledge of paper space because all drawings must eventually be printed and sent to the job site. The drafter must know the size of the paper the project will be printed on, the printable area, the border and title block area used, and the scale in which the project will be printed so as to comfortably fit on the paper.

Figure 3.16 shows various sizes of paper and the drawing area based on scale. Sizes of paper range from a stan-

	AP		BP		CP		DP		EP		FP	
(width) X"	11	8	17	14	24	21	36	33	48	45	42	39
(height) Y"	8.5	7.5	11	10	18	17	24	23	36	35	30	29
Scale	TRUE	ADJ	TRUE	ADJ	TRUE	ADJ	TRUE	ADJ	TRUE	ADJ	TRUE	ADJ
3"=1'	3'8x2'10	2'8x2'6	5'8x3'8	4'8x3'4	8'x6'	7'x5'8	12'x8'	11'x7'8	16'x12'	15'x11'8	14'x10'	13'x9'8
1 1/2"=1'	7'4x5'8	5'4x5'	11'4x7'4	9'4x6'8	16'x12'	14'x11'4	24'x16'	22'x15'4	32'x24'	30'x23'4	28'x20'	26'x19'4
1"=1'	11'x8'6	8'x7'6	17'x11'	14'x10'	24'x18'	21'x17'	36'x24'	33'x23'	48'x36'	45'x35'	42'x30'	39'x29'
3/4"=1'	14'8x11'4	10'8x10'	22'8x14'8	18'8x13'4	32'x24'	28'x22'8	48'x32'	44'x30'8	64'x48'	60'x46'8	56'x40'	52'x38'8
1/2"=1'	22'x17'	16'x15'	34'x22'	28'x20'	48'x36'	42'x34'	72'x48'	66'x46'	96'x72'	90'x70'	84'x60'	78'x58'
1/4"=1'	44'x34'	32'x30'	68'x44'	56'x40'	96'x72'	84'x68'	144'x96'	132'x92'	192'x144'	180'x140'	168'x120'	156'x116'
1/8"=1'	88'x68'	64'x60'	136'x88'	112'x80'	192'x144'	168'x136'	288'x192'	264'x184'	384'x288'	360'x280'	336'x240'	312'x232'
1/16"=1'	176'x136'	128'x120'	272'x176'	224'x160'	384'x288'	336'x272'	576'x384'	528'x368'	768'x576'	720'x560'	672'x480'	624'x464'
1/32"=1'	352'x272'	256'x240'	544'x352'	448'x320'	768'x576'	672'x544'	1152'x768'	1056'x736'	1536'x1152'	1440'x1120'	1344'x960'	1248'x928'

Architectural

	AP		BP		CP		DP		EP		FP	
(width) X"	11	8	17	14	24	21	36	33	48	45	42	39
(height) Y"	8.5	7.5	11	10	18	17	24	23	36	35	30	29
Scale	TRUE	ADJ	TRUE	ADJ	TRUE	ADJ	TRUE	ADJ	TRUE	ADJ	TRUE	ADJ
1/10"=1'	110'x85'	80'x75'	170'x110'	140'x100'	240'x180'	210'x170'	360'x240'	330'x230'	480'x360'	450'x350'	420'x300'	390'x290'
1/20"=1'	220'x170'	160'x150'	340'x220'	280'x200'	480'x360'	420'x340'	720'x480'	660'x460'	960'x720'	900'x700'	840'x600'	780'x580'
1/25"=1'	275'x212'6	200'x187'6	425'x275'	350'x250'	600'x450'	525'x425'	900'x600'	825'x575'	1200'x900'	1125'x875'	1050'x750'	975'x725'
1/30"=1'	330'x255'	240'x225'	510'x330'	420'x300'	720'x540'	630'x510'	1080'x720'	990'x690'	1440'x1080'	1350'x1050'	1260'x900'	1170'x870'
1/40"=1'	440'x340'	320'x300'	680'x440'	560'x400'	960'x720'	840'x680'	1440'x960'	1320'x920'	1920'x1440'	1800'x1400'	1680'x1200'	1560'x1160'
1/50"=1'	550'x425'	400'x375'	850'x550'	700'x500'	1200'x900'	1050'x850'	1800'x1200'	1650'x1150'	2400'x1800'	2250'x1750'	2100'x1500'	1950'x1450'
1/60"=1'	660'x510'	480'x450'	1020'x660'	840'x600'	1440'x1080'	1260'x1020'	2160'x1440'	1980'x1380'	2880'x2160'	2700'x2100'	2520'x1800'	2340'x1740'
1/75"=1'	825'x637'6	600'x562'6	1275'x825'	1050'x750'	1800'x1350'	1575'x1275'	2700'x1800'	2475'x1725'	3600'x2700'	3375'x2625'	3150'x2250'	2925'x2175'
1/100"=1'	1100'x850'	800'x750'	1700'x1100'	1400'x1000'	2400'x1800'	2100'x1700'	3600'x2400'	3300'x2300'	4800'x3600'	4500'x3500'	4200'x3000'	3900'x2900'

Engineering

Adjusted Margins	
Top	0.5"
Bottom	0.5"
Left	1.5"
Right	0.5"
Title Rt.	1"
Title Bot.	0"

Figure 3.16 Paper space maximum.

dard 8-1/2" × 11" to a 36" × 48". These are listed across the top of Figure 3.16, and the various scales (architectural and engineering) are shown to the left. For example, if you were preparing a floor plan for a building 90' deep and 135' at 1/4" = 1'-0" scale (shaded area on chart) and wanted to find a paper sheet size, note that at the intersection of a 24" × 36" column and 1/4" = 1" row, a 96 × 144" figure appears. This means that at a 1/4" scale, and using a 24" × 36" piece of paper, a 96 foot by 144 foot space is available. If a 70 × 90 building were to be drawn, it would occupy approximately 18" × 24" of the 24" × 36" sheet. The rest could be used for details, notes, or schedules.

Scaling Factor

Some computer programs are programmed to deal with scale. The drafter can size or scale a drawing simply by typing in the scale desired or selecting a scale from a menu. For example, if you wish to print or draw a floor plan at 1/4" = 1'0" scale, you simply select this scale and the computer does the rest of the work.

Other programs call for a scaling factor to be used. The CAD drafter must be comfortable with either system. Scaling factor is computed in reference to a foot (12 inches). For example, if a drawing is to be scaled at 1/4" = 1'-0", you divide 12" by 1/4 inch. Forty-eight (48) becomes the scaling factor for 1/4" = 1'-0". Following this logic, and giving a certain size paper a name, most offices use the paper name and scaling factor to describe scale and paper. For example, an 11" × 17" paper with a 1/4" drawing on it will be called BP48. The "B" indicates size, "P" indicates that this is paper, and the 48 is the scale. BP48 is read "Bee paper forty-eight."

Figure 3.17 lists scaling factors for a variety of most typically used architectural and engineering scales. Figure 3.18 shows a 9" × 12" and a 24" × 36" piece of paper. Using a scaling factor (48) for a 1/4" scale, the numbers in the parenthesis indicate how many feet (at 1/4" scale) are available on the 24" × 36" sheet of paper. Now go back to Figure 3.16 and see the figures repeated for a number of different sized sheets of paper and a variety of scales. Next, the drafter must know the same information for the drawing area. See Figure 3.19 and compute.

Scale	Factor
1'=1'	1
3"=1'	4
1 1/2"=1'	8
1"=1'	12
3/4"=1'	16
1/2"=1'	24
1/4"=1'	48
1/8"=1'	96
1/16"=1'	192
1/32"=1'	384
1"=10'	120
1"=20'	240
1"=25'	300
1"=30'	360
1"=40'	480
1"=50'	600
1"=60'	720
1"=75'	900
1"=100'	1200
1"=200'	2400

Figure 3.17   Scaling factor.

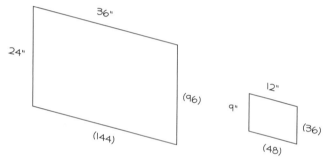

Figure 3.18   Scaling factor (¼") for 24 × 36 and 9 × 12.

Figure 3.20 shows the drawing area for a variety of scales and sheet sizes. The drawing area is now called the viewport.

Layering

Layering is what makes computer drafting so far superior to manual drafting. Layering is the process of creating a series of overlays on which you will display different functions and different types of lines and conventions. Its closest comparable is pin drafting, whereby different features of a single drawing are drafted on different sheets and photographed, and using different combinations of negatives you could obtain a variety of drawings. Cost has been the main drawback of pin drafting. It was also time-consuming and difficult to keep all the sheets registered (aligned) with each other. Drafters used pins that fit into predrilled holes to keep the sheets aligned, in the same manner as a three-hole notebook keeps papers aligned.

The alignment of computer-generated layers is perfect. Selection of the proper layers is done in seconds. Layers

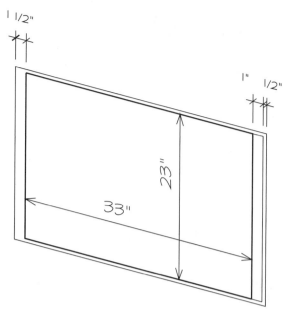

Figure 3.19   Printable area 24 × 36.

may be turned on and off, frozen in place, plotted or not plotted. They can also be grouped and XREFed from other drawings.

Let us now look at a typical set of layers for a construction document. The first layer is often considered the base, unless you are using XREF drawings as a base. It will contain the matrix that will act as a datum for the entire drawing. For example, a steel building such as the Madison Building (Chapter 20) is based on an axial reference system. A matrix will locate and position the steel columns. The matrix will be drawn on the base layer, with the steel columns possibly on the subsequent layer. This base (the datum) can be used for other drawings, so different views subscribe to the same system. Therefore, it becomes even more important that the drafter of tomorrow become familiar with three-dimensional datum drawings (described earlier) so that elevations, building sections, framing plans, and foundation plans can use the same base (datum) layer. In this way, we can cross-reference drawings from the very beginning (XREF drawings).

Subscribing to office standards is not suggested; It is required. If you manage to find a better, faster, more productive way to do things, suggest it to your CAD manager.

Each layer can be done in a different color. The use of various colors helps the drafter stay focused on the specific layer on which a particular task is to be accomplished. Colors also help in identifying drawings. Although most drawings are not printed in color, it does help to identify the layer, because each layer is identified by color. Color also has an impact on the quality of lines, as explained in the next section of this chapter.

If there is an inherent geometry present in the drawing but not used in the finished drawing, the construction

Architectural

			AP		BP		CP		DP		EP		FP	
		(width) X"	11	8	17	14	24	21	36	33	48	45	42	39
		(height) Y"	8.5	7.5	11	10	18	17	24	23	36	35	30	29
Factor	Feet in 1"	Scale	TRUE	ADJ	TRUE	ADJ	TRUE	ADJ	TRUE	ADJ	TRUE	ADJ	TRUE	ADJ
4	1"=0'-4"	3"=1'	3'8x2'10	2'8x2'6	5'8x3'8	4'8x3'4	8'x6'	7'x5'8	12'x8'	11'x7'8	16'x12'	15'x11'8	14'x10'	13'x9'8
8	1"=0'-8"	1 1/2"=1'	7'4x5'8	5'4x5'	11'4x7'4	9'4x6'8	16'x12'	14'x11'4	24'x16'	22'x15'4	32'x24'	30'x23'4	28'x20'	26'x19'4
12	1"=1'-0"	1"=1'	11'x8'6	8'x7'6	17'x11'	14'x10'	24'x18'	21'x17'	36'x24'	33'x23'	48'x36'	45'x35'	42'x30'	39'x29'
16	1"=1'-4"	3/4"=1'	14'8x11'4	10'8x10'	22'8x14'8	18'8x13'4	32'x24'	28'x22'8	48'x32'	44'x30'8	64'x48'	60'x46'8	56'x40'	52'x38'8
24	1"=2'-0"	1/2"=1'	22'x17'	16'x15'	34'x22'	28'x20'	48'x36'	42'x34'	72'x48'	66'x46'	96'x72'	90'x70'	84'x60'	78'x58'
48	1"=4'-0"	1/4"=1'	44'x34'	32'x30'	68'x44'	56'x40'	96'x72'	84'x68'	144'x96'	132'x92'	192'x144'	180'x140'	168'x120'	156'x116'
96	1"=8'-0"	1/8"=1'	88'x68'	64'x60'	136'x88'	112'x80'	192'x144'	168'x136'	288'x192'	264'x184'	384'x288'	360'x280'	336'x240'	312'x232'
192	1"=16'-0"	1/16"=1'	176'x136'	128'x120'	272'x176'	224'x160'	384'x288'	336'x272'	576'x384'	528'x368'	768'x576'	720'x560'	672'x480'	624'x464'
384	1"=32'-0"	1/32"=1'	352'x272'	256'x240'	544'x352'	448'x320'	768'x576'	672'x544'	1152'x768'	1056'x736'	1536'x1152'	1440'x1120'	1344'x960'	1248'x928'

Engineering

			AP		BP		CP		DP		EP		FP	
		(width) X"	11	8	17	14	24	21	36	33	48	45	42	39
		(height) Y"	8.5	7.5	11	10	18	17	24	23	36	35	30	29
Factor	Feet in 1"	Scale	TRUE	ADJ	TRUE	ADJ	TRUE	ADJ	TRUE	ADJ	TRUE	ADJ	TRUE	ADJ
120	1"=10'	1/10"=1'	110'x85'	80'x75'	170'x110'	140'x100'	240'x180'	210'x170'	360'x240'	330'x230'	480'x360'	450'x350'	420'x300'	390'x290'
240	1"=20'	1/20"=1'	220'x170'	160'x150'	340'x220'	280'x200'	480'x360'	420'x340'	720'x480'	660'x460'	960'x720'	900'x700'	840'x600'	780'x580'
300	1"=25'	1/25"=1'	275'x212'6	200'x187'6	425'x275'	350'x250'	600'x450'	525'x425'	900'x600'	825'x575'	1200'x900'	1125'x875'	1050'x750'	975'x725'
360	1"=30'	1/30"=1'	330'x255'	240'x225'	510'x330'	420'x300'	720'x540'	630'x510'	1080'x720'	990'x690'	1440'x1080'	1350'x1050'	1260'x900'	1170'x870'
480	1"=40'	1/40"=1'	440'x340'	320'x300'	680'x440'	560'x400'	960'x720'	840'x680'	1440'x960'	1320'x920'	1920'x1440'	1800'x1400'	1680'x1200'	1560'x1160'
600	1"=50'	1/50"=1'	550'x425'	400'x375'	850'x550'	700'x500'	1200'x900'	1050'x850'	1800'x1200'	1650'x1150'	2400'x1800'	2250'x1750'	2100'x1500'	1950'x1450'
720	1"=60'	1/60"=1'	660'x510'	480'x450'	1020'x660'	840'x600'	1440'x1080'	1260'x1020'	2160'x1440'	1980'x1380'	2880'x2160'	2700'x2100'	2520'x1800'	2340'x1740'
900	1"=75'	1/75"=1'	825'x637'6	600'x562'6	1275'x825'	1050'x750'	1800'x1350'	1575'x1275'	2700'x1800'	2475'x1725'	3600'x2700'	3375'x2625'	3150'x2250'	2925'x2175'
1200	1"=100'	1/100"=1'	1100'x850'	800'x750'	1700'x1100'	1400'x1000'	2400'x1800'	2100'x1700'	3600'x2400'	3300'x2300'	4800'x3600'	4500'x3500'	4200'x3000'	3900'x2900'

Figure 3.20 Paper sizes at specific scales (1/2" top, bottom, and right border, 1-1/2" left border, 1" right titleblock space).

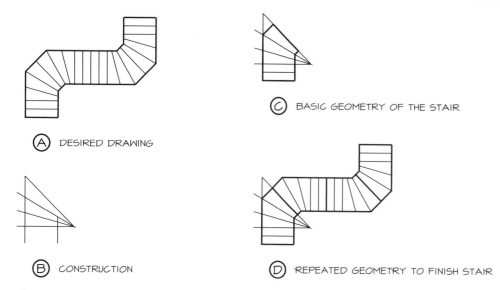

(C) BASIC GEOMETRY OF THE STAIR

(A) DESIRED DRAWING

(B) CONSTRUCTION

(D) REPEATED GEOMETRY TO FINISH STAIR

Figure 3.21 Diagnosing geometry (stair).

lines can be drawn on a layer but never printed, A-NOH plotting layer. Take the case of drawing a winding stair, as shown in Figure 3.21. The construction lines are on one layer, and the drawing of the stair is on another. One need only outline the required portions of the geometry to produce a base drawing, and then repeat the forms to produce the finished drawing.

Setting Up Layers. Look again at the sample of layers and their specific titles in Figure 3.4. Although this is a simplified plan, it does follow many of the examples found in the National CAD Standards pamphlet. You should follow this office standard. Notice the legend and

the letter designations for architectural, mechanical, structural, and so on. Learn to identify the standards so that you can tell the difference between correctly and incorrectly drawn documents.

Correct and uniform titles are important, because as you are laying out the structural members of a building, these members must be cross-referenced with the electrical conduit on the electrical drawing, or the heating or air-conditioning ducts found on the mechanical set, that may occupy the same space.

The strategy employed might be staged similarly to that in Figure 3.22. Note the number of layers produced on the left side, the composite drawing for construction

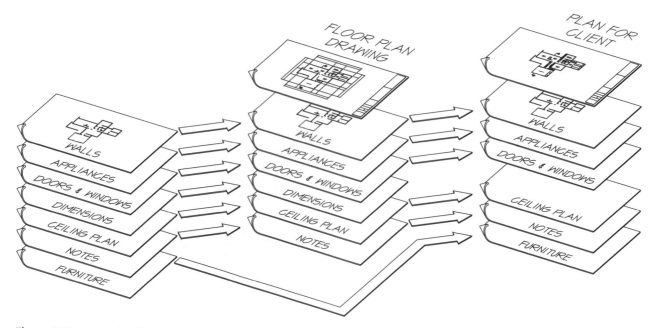

Figure 3.22 Example of the planning for a single file.

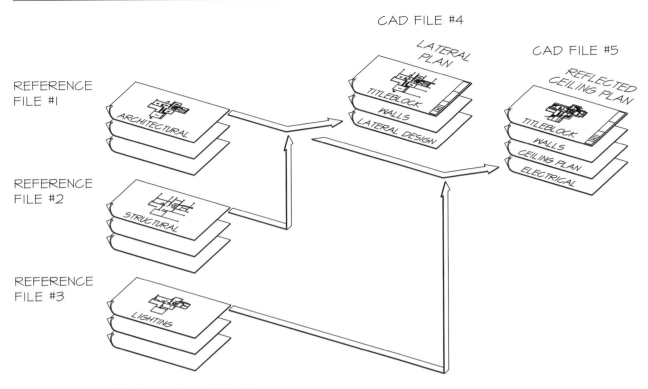

Figure 3.23 Example planning for multiple file.

in the center, and the drawing used for client consumption on the right side. Note the inclusion of the furniture layer for client consumption and voiding the dimensioning layer on the same set.

In the multifile strategy illustrated in Figure 3.23, an example of a three-file system is shown. File No. 1 is the architectural file, which we just looked at in Figure 3.22. File No. 2 is a structural set, and file No. 3 is a lighting plan. Note how various layers are selected to produce still another file. In this example, file No. 4 becomes a lateral plan and file No. 5 becomes the reflected ceiling plan. As indicated earlier, this process is called XREFing.

Pen Setting and Line Weights

Line weights can be produced by establishing and assigning certain colors as desired pen settings. Figure 3.24 shows common AutoCAD pen settings. The number assigned to the pen can be found on the extreme left side of the chart. Directly adjacent to the pen number is the name of the pen. The names are names of colors. As you can see by the width of the pens, magenta is the strongest and should be used for object lines. The thinnest line is red.

The office may have already established these standards, which may be based on a national standard. You need to know the source and why they are established in this fashion. Knowing why allows you to know the office's so-called game plan.

Pen settings and line weights should be saved on the computer or disk immediately when establishing the layers so that you can employ them as needed.

Figure 3.25 is a summary chart of the items discussed in this section of the chapter. Sample standard titles are

Pen Settings

color	name	width
1	red	0.008
2	yellow	0.012
3	green	0.008
4	cyan	0.010
5	blue	0.012
6	magenta	0.030
7	white (high ink)	0.020
8	dark grey	0.015
9	light grey	0.015
15	dark red	0.012
30	orange	0.008
174	dark blue	0.010
250	dark grey	0.015
251	med. dark grey	0.015
252	med. grey	0.015
253	med. light grey	0.015
254	light grey	0.015
255	white (low ink)	0.015

Figure 3.24 Pen settings, line weights, and colors.

Preliminary Documentation of Office LAYERING Standard

NAME	COLOR	LINETYPE	DESCRIPTION
0	WHITE	Continuous	For making Blocks & Unknown
ANNO	CYAN	Continuous	Text (annotation)
ANNO-DIMS	RED	Continuous	Dimensions
ANNO-IDEN	YELLOW	Continuous	Identification (Rooms)
ANNO-KEYN	CYAN	Continuous	Keynotes
ANNO-LEGN	CYAN	Continuous	Legends and Schedules
ANNO-NOTE	CYAN	Continuous	General Notes
ANNO-PATT	RED	Continuous	Hatches (all)
ANNO-PCHE	8 (lt) or 9 (dk)	Continuous	Poche (all)
ANNO-REDL	RED	Continuous	Redlines (Corrections to be made)
ANNO-SYMB	YELLOW	Continuous	Symbols (scale, north, section)
ANNO-TTLB	CYAN	Continuous	Titleblock
ANNO-VIEW	RED	Continuous	Viewports
DOOR	CYAN	Continuous	Doors (plan & elevation)
ELEC	YELLOW	Continuous	Electrical Symbols
ELEC-CONN	CYAN	CENTER2	Electrical Connections
ELEV	CYAN	Continuous	Elevation (colors can vary)
ELEV-BYND	BLUE	Continuous	Objects Beyond
ELEV-OTLN	WHITE	Continuous	Building Outline / Profile
FLOR	CYAN	Continuous	Floor plan (secondary information)
FLOR-DECK	YELLOW	Continuous	Deck
FLOR-HIDD	RED	HIDDEN	Hidden
FLOR-HRAL	RED	Continuous	Handrails & Balcony Railings
FLOR-STRS	CYAN	Continuous	Stairs
FNDN	YELLOW	HIDDEN	Foundation (footings & pads)
FNDN-SHRW	MAGENTA	Continuous	Shearwall
FNDN-SLAB	WHITE	Continuous	Slab
FRAM	YELLOW	Continuous	Framing (posts, headers, rafters)
FRAM-BEAM	WHITE	CENTER	Beams (wood, steel, prefab)
FRAM-JOIS	CYAN	CENTER2	Ceiling Joists
FRAM-SHRW	MAGENTA	Continuous	Shearwall
GLAZ	CYAN	Continuous	Windows (plan & elevation)
ROOF	WHITE	Continuous	Roof Outline (ridges, hips, valleys)
ROOF-BLDG	RED	DASHED	Building Outline
ROOF-OTHR	CYAN	Continuous	Roof (vent, chimney, skylight, etc)
SECT	CYAN	Continuous	Section (colors can vary)
SECT-BYND	BLUE	Continuous	Objects Beyond
SECT-OTLN	WHITE	Continuous	Objects at Section Cut / Profile
SITE	CYAN	Continuous	Site
SITE-BLDG	WHITE	Continuous	Building Outline
SITE-EXST	RED	Continuous	Existing Information
SITE-PLNT	GREEN	Continuous	Plants / Landscape
SITE-PROP	MAGENTA	PHANTOM	Property Line
SITE-RTWL	YELLOW	Continuous	Retaining Wall
TOPO	GREEN	DASHED	Topography (from surveyor)
TOPO-OTHR	BLUE	DASHED2	Topography (faded)
WALL	WHITE	Continuous	Wall (full height)
WALL-HALF	YELLOW	Continuous	Wall (partial height)
XREF	WHITE	Continuous	Cross-Referenced Files (XREFs)
XREF-GHST-OTHER	BLUE	Continuous	Ghost - faded (fixtures, labels, etc)
XREF-GHST-WALL	RED	Continuous	Ghost - light (walls, stairs, etc)

Figure 3.25 Sample preliminary documentation of office layering standard.

listed to the left, then the colors used, followed by the line types and descriptions of their uses.

Lettering Size

One advantage of a computer is its ability to change scale rapidly. With manual drafting, two approaches are used. The first is to redraw, say a floor plan, to a smaller scale by physically changing the scale used. Another is to enlarge or reduce a drawing using an enlarging/reducing copier. Although the latter is easier, it still cannot compete with the computer for speed.

The disadvantage appears, for example, in drawing a floor plan at $1/4'' = 1'-0''$ scale with $1/8''$ tall lettering, then reducing it to a $1/8'' = 1'-0''$ scale without any regard to the final height of the lettering. The lettering in this example

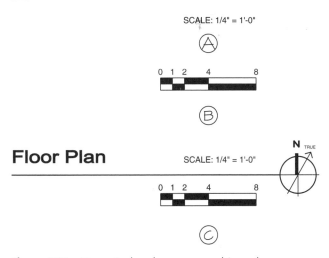

SCALE: 1/4" = 1'-0"

Ⓐ

0 1 2   4   8

Ⓑ

Floor Plan
SCALE: 1/4" = 1'-0"

N TRUE

0 1 2   4   8

Ⓒ

Figure 3.26 Numerical scale versus graphic scale.

will be 1/16" tall and very difficult to read, not to mention that it will not follow the office standard and will look peculiar in a set of drawings.

Graphic scales are often used in lieu of expressing the scale in a proportion (see Figure 3.26A).

Because we are drawing in model space (virtual space), we are able to draw the structure at full scale.

However, every drafter must realize the scale to which the drawing will be reduced and printed. For example, a floor plan can be drawn at full scale but may be reduced to 1/4" = 1' 0" scale when printed on a 24" × 36" sheet of paper. Knowing the final display scale is important, because when notes and dimensions are placed on the final print, they must be readable. If the office standard is to have lettering that is 1/8" tall, with titles 1/4" tall, this lettering height must be translated into a measurement that is full size because we are drawing in full size. At 1/4" = 1' 0", all lettering (1/8" in height) must be scaled at 6" tall and the titles (1/4" tall) 1'-0", because the lettering height is measured in scale. For your convenience, two charts, an engineering scale and an architectural scale, are included to help translate various lettering heights to specific heights (see Figure 3.27).

The scale in which you will print/plot your drawing is read across the top of each chart. The desired height of the final text is read down the left column. The intersection of these columns will tell you the height of the lettering. See the shaded area for the 1/8" tall lettering at 1/4" = 1'-0" scale for the previous example.

A decimal conversion chart in Figure 3.28 includes the height of lettering in decimals. As every schoolchild

Architectural

Scale: Feet in 1": Scale Factor:	3"=1' 1"=0'-4" 4	1 1/2"=1' 1"=0'-8" 8	1"=1' 1"=1'-0" 12	3/4"=1' 1"=1'-4" 16	1/2"=1' 1"=2'-0" 24	1/4"=1' 1"=4'-0" 48	1/8"=1' 1"=8'-0" 96	1/16"=1' 1"=16'-0" 192	1/32"=1' 1"=32'-0" 384
1" Text	4"	8"	12"	16"	24"	48"	96"	192"	384"
3/4" Text	3"	6"	9"	12"	18"	36"	72"	144"	288"
1/2" Text	2"	4"	6"	8"	12"	24"	48"	96"	192"
3/8" Text	1.5"	3"	4.5"	6"	9"	18"	36"	72"	144"
1/4" Text	1"	2"	3"	4"	6"	12"	24"	48"	96"
3/16" Text	0.75"	1.5"	2.25"	3"	4.5"	9"	18"	36"	72"
1/8" Text	0.5"	1"	1.5"	2"	3"	6"	12"	24"	48"
3/32" Text	0.375"	0.75"	1.125"	1.5"	2.25"	4.5"	9"	18"	36"
1/16" Text	0.25"	0.5"	0.75"	1"	1.5"	3"	6"	12"	24"

Engineering

Scale: Feet in 1": Factor:	1/10"=1' 1"=10' 120	1/20"=1' 1"=20' 240	1/25"=1' 1"=25' 300	1/30"=1' 1"=30' 360	1/40"=1' 1"=40' 480	1/50"=1' 1"=50' 600	1/60"=1' 1"=60' 720	1/75"=1' 1"=75' 900	1/100"=1' 1"=100' 1200
1" Text	120"	240"	300"	360"	480"	600"	720"	900"	1200"
3/4" Text	90"	180"	225"	270"	360"	450"	540"	675"	900"
1/2" Text	60"	120"	150"	180"	240"	300"	360"	450"	600"
3/8" Text	45"	90"	112.5"	135"	180"	225"	270"	337.5"	450"
1/4" Text	30"	60"	75"	90"	120"	150"	180"	225"	300"
3/16" Text	22.5"	45"	56.25"	67.5"	90"	112.5"	135"	168.75"	225"
1/8" Text	15"	30"	37.5"	45"	60"	75"	90"	112.5"	150"
3/32" Text	11.25"	22.5"	28.125"	33.75"	45"	56.25"	67.5"	84.375"	112.5"
1/16" Text	7.5"	15"	18.75"	22.5"	30"	37.5"	45"	56.25"	75"

Figure 3.27 Text size for architectural/engineering drawings.

Standard Text Sizes

Standard Text		Optional Text	
1"	1	3/4"	0.75
1/2"	0.5	3/8"	0.375
1/4"	0.25	3/16"	0.1875
1/8"	0.125	3/32"	0.09375
1/16"	0.0625	3/64"	0.046875
1/32"	0.03125		

Figure 3.28 Conversion chart for simple fraction to decimal.

knows, $1/2''$ is equal to $0.5''$, but equivalents for fractions such as $3/16$ and $3/32$ are hard to remember; they are 0.1875 and 0.09375, respectively.

When drawings were archived, manually drafted drawings were often microfilmed or put on microfiche. Lettering size was then computed to a height compatible with the equipment available to preview the drawing. With computer-generated drawings, the consideration is twofold. First is readability on the screen as the drawings are being developed and second, and even more important, is the size of lettering on the printed or plotted sheet. Thus, rigorous standards have been established by various agencies and by individual architectural offices.

The most frequent height for lettering is still $1/8''$ or $3/32''$. However, the computer has one additional dimension that enhances readability: The width of each letter can be changed rapidly to accommodate the space available. For example, the columns in a window or door schedule may be too narrow to house the title, dimensions, or descriptive phrases. With a simple manipulation, the lettering can be compressed to fit the space without having to compromise its height.

Standards are established for general noting, room titles, and the title of the drawing. For example, it is a prevalent practice to use upper- and lowercase lettering for the title of a drawing, such as "Floor Plan." The font may be Helvetica. Room titles may be in all caps, using the same Helvetica font. Notes and general text should be done in all caps, but in an architectural font. An architectural font can simulate a hand-lettered drawing, thus giving the drawing a distinguishing characteristic that separates it from engineering drawings. There are two additional reasons for using an architectural font. Architectural fonts, as compared with other textbook type fonts, are simpler in the geometry used to describe them. Because the shape definition uses less geometry, it prints faster. Although it may take a microsecond less to print each word, the sum total of a complete set of construction notes may save a few minutes, and a complete set of drawings 10 or 15 minutes. Printing productivity is increased, and multiple sets can be completed with hours of time saved.

The other reason to use an architectural font is that because it simulates hand lettering, simple corrections can be done by hand when the computer is down or when speed is of the essence. Of course, the corrections must eventually be done on the computer because manual corrections will not be reflected in the digital image saved on the computer or on the floppy disk.

An office manager, in conjunction with the principal, probably best understands the engineering that goes into font technology. He or she can select the fonts that print faster for the drafter. For example, if the Helvetica font is defined more simply, then by changing the lettering, shape definition without changing the "look," general notes that would take 20 minutes to print can be printed in nearly half the time.

■ A GAME WITHIN A GAME

The idea that there is a game within a game is often found in athletics and can also be seen in the field of architecture. This is evident in the production of construction documents.

Baseball is America's favorite pastime, and everyone knows the basic fundamentals of the game: how it is played, its rules, the number of players, and the number of outs in an inning, along with the basic playing field design. While the baseball game is being played, there is another game going on that may be observed only by those knowledgeable about the subgame. This may be a psychological game between the batter and the pitcher, or a game of strategies between the team managers. There are many such inner games being played within the basic game of baseball.

Similarly, architecture frequently has games within games. There may be a secondary game involved in the financing of a project, or the exploration of new materials and their application to a project, or a game strategy involved in combining materials in a job. Even the production of construction drawings may hold an inner game, such as the study involved to identify the best way to prepare a set of drawings. This may include a game of document standardization and computer productivity and how best to implement both. Another game within the architectural game is that played in model space/virtual space at full scale. We might call this game "Procedure for producing a construction document."

Procedure for Computer Drawings

1. Learn to identify the icons on the screen to determine whether you are in model space or paper space. There will be a "title" (a box) that you can click your cursor on to toggle between model space and paper space. You can verify paper/model space by checking the user coordinate system (UCS) icon

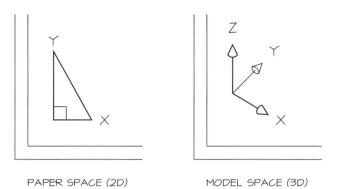

PAPER SPACE (2D) MODEL SPACE (3D)

Figure 3.29 UCS icon.

(usually found on the bottom left corner of the screen) (see Figure 3.29).

2. If your drawing (paper) is set up for ¼″ scale but the building is larger than the paper will allow, go to "Limits" and change the drawing to a different scale. This may have already been done by the office manager on the cartoon (also called *page format* or *page layout*) (see Figure 3.30).

3. Cartooning, as discussed in Chapter 6, should be done for the entire set of working drawings before you start any drawings. In this way, a team of CAD drafters working on a single project will know where each drawing will be positioned before they start a particular drawing.

4. The drawing can be drawn anywhere on the sheet, because it will most likely be repositioned on the paper at a later time.

5. Establish your line weights and pen settings. This information may already be available in the office, but you need to know what and how these standards were established.

6. The next step is to set up the layers for a particular set of drawings. See the discussion in "Layering" earlier in this chapter.

7. Familiarize yourself with the finished drawing (the plot) using the scale you are working with. For example, if the drawing will be plotted at ⅛″ = 1′-0″ scale, and you need to draw a ½″ diagram reference bubble, you will draw it at 4′-0″ in size. Another example using the same ⅛″ = 1′-0″ scale: ⅛″ tall lettering will be drawn at 1′-0″ tall.

8. Consider the following points before you begin drawing:
   a. Confirm the office standard to which you subscribe.
   b. Confirm that all the software you need is operational and registered.
   c. Understand the time constraints and the expectations of your supervisor or administrator.
   d. Review all the preliminary design sketches so you can enhance the design without changing its intent.

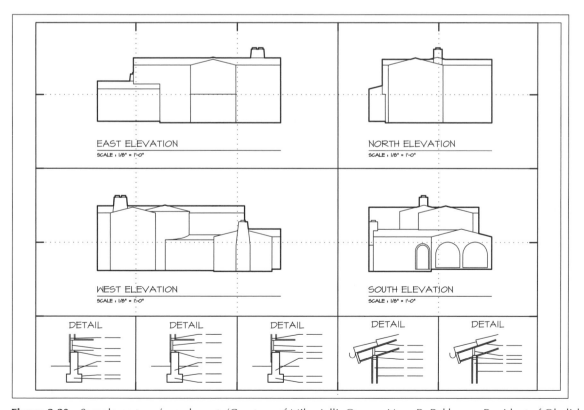

Figure 3.30 Sample cartoon/page layout. (Courtesy of Mike Adli, Owner; Nagy R. Bakhoum, President of Obelisk Architects.)

e. Understand the structure and how the design works into this structural pattern.

f. Study the designer's reaction to the environmental forces to correctly orient windows for the maximum amount of light, orientation to the prevailing view and the part of the view to be showcased, etc.

g. Review the reference resources for construction materials such as the block modules used for masonry, the stud line, dimensioning procedures for lightweight wood structures, etc.

h. Review all of the related drawings such as structural, mechanical, electrical, etc.

Procedure for Preparation of Computer for Computer-Aided Drafting

1. Computer to architectural
2. Setting
   a. Limits
   b. Grids/snap
3. Display
   Zoom all
4. Layer
   Layer standards: line, color, lettering
5. Review paper/model space
6. Saving
7. Printing

■ POWER OF THE CAD DRAFTER

CAD drafters of the past were initially trained in the use of the computer to manipulate lines, textures, and geometric planes and shapes. They failed to understand how architecture communication affected the construction process. These drafters allowed the technology (computers) to dictate what could and could not be done in a set of drawings. They also allowed the computer to establish measurements, rather than allowing the materials and their limits dictate the way we approach a structure. Thus the process of architectural construction must be learned prior to using a computer, so as to translate this process or at least parallel it.

The power of the CAD drafter at all levels is not only understanding the process of how buildings are built, which this book is mainly about, but enabling all CAD drafters to produce the necessary documents to make this process a reality. To that end, all CAD drafters must:

1. Be divided into different levels of proficiency. Table 3.1 defines the four basic levels of CAD drafting and their requirements, found in an architectural office. Level 1 is the equivalent of a junior drafter. Level 2 may be equated to the journeyman drafter, and Level 3 is considered a senior drafter. Level 4 is reserved for management.

2. Be comfortable in working with any version of CAD, not just the latest version. Software programs change so often that it is very difficult to standardize the profession to work in any computer application.

   As you move from office to office, you may be confronted with a large range of programs. We all know that as soon as a 2002 version of any program hits the market, the 2004 or 2006 version is not far behind.

3. Be aware of the program their associates are using, because it does little good to send them drawings that they cannot manipulate or use.

4. Be comfortable in drawing in full scale (model space) and printing in paper space.

5. Be able to send and receive drawings via the computer as easily as making a telephone call; send drawing files that can be opened to receive additional information from their associates or send closed files for viewing only, to protect the office.

   Be able to send drawings on floppy disks, on CDs, via mail, or through any electronic means available, to receive drawings in any format or scale, and to introduce those drawings into an environment that makes them more useful to the office.

6. Be able to draw in 3-D and rotate the 3-D drawing into orthogonals and produce 2-D drawings from them.

7. Be able to work on two different versions of a program without any hindrance to productivity. For example, the office computer may have an older software version than their home computers. They need to know how to save the file at home so that they can open the file at the office and continue to work.

8. Be able to manage their files and know how to compress their files.

This is a list of minimum requirements for an effective CAD drafter. The next level of CAD drafter is a person who can organize and initiate new programs in the office system using existing office standards. The third level of CAD drafter is a person who can troubleshoot the computer and do minimal repair. The final level of computer specialist is the person who can rewrite existing software programs to make them more effective tools for the office.

Setting Up a Computer Drawing
   From scratch:
1. Set Limits to architectural
2. Units
   Grids ⎫
   Snap ⎭ Based on size and scale
3. Set up Layers
   Office Standard
   1. Titles   ⎫
   2. Line type ⎬ Minimum
   3. Color   ⎭

Table 3.1 CAD Drafting in an Architectural Office

Level 1 — Junior Drafter	Level 3 — Senior Drafter

1. Ability to hardline a designer's ideas
2. Mastery of simple commands such as:
  a. LINE, PLINE, DLINE, MLINE
  b. MOVE, COPY, SCALE
  c. TRIM, EXTEND, STRETCH
  d. INSERT BLOCKS
  e. HATCHING
  f. DTEXT, MTEXT
3. Basic 3-D Modeling
4. Use of object snaps
5. Ortho and polar restrictions
6. Keyboard entry (absolute and relative modes)
7. Basic Plan Check revisions (notes, minor geometry changes)
8. File management
9. Layering
10. Dimensions
11. Basic plotting
	1. Attributes (grouping of entities that contain text)
	2. Finding architectural/structural errors based on experience
	3. Manage individuals and projects (ability to "hand off" work)
	4. Advanced 3-D modeling/visualization (thorough understanding of model-centric design)
	5. Thorough understanding of architectural/structural detailing
	6. Complete Plan Check revisions (research and change entire working drawings)
	7. Suggest/modify page setups and templates
	8. Basic program customization
	9. Basic programming
	10. Advanced rendering
	11. Intermediate plotting

Level 2 — Journeyman Drafter	Level 4 — CAD Manager
1. XREF 2. Paper space/model space 3. Can follow a design change throughout a set of working drawings 4. Make appropriate design suggestions 5. Text styles and justifications 6. Intermediate 3-D modeling (including model-based/model centric design) 7. Editing of attributes 8. Filtering 9. Use of object tracking 10. Advanced Plan Check revisions (new geometry/multiple sheets) 11. Program preferences 12. Basic rendering	1. Network/hardware/software installation, upgrades, and troubleshooting 2. Image editing and photo manipulation 3. Template construction 4. Title block construction 5. Custom blocks/symbols 6. Custom hatches and shapes 7. Ability to make purchase suggestions/decisions 8. Ability to make, implement, and suggest changes to office standards 9. Internet and web site development 10. Graphic design skills 11. Advanced program customization 12. Advanced programming 13. Advanced plotting 14. Advanced collaboration and workgroup tools (LAN/WAN/Internet)

4. Work in the paper modules (See Figure 3.12)
  1. Make sure everything fits, including:
    a. Dimension lines
    b. Reference symbols
    c. Titles
5. Work in model space (not in paper space)

As a minimum, a drafter should know:

A. How to set up the computer
  1. Units
  2. Grid
  3. Snap
  4. Limits
  5. Layers
  6. Line types
  7. Styles
B. Establishment of a base layer
C. Check for XREF

Tracking a Drawing via the Computer

A 3-D massing model of the structure is the first step in tracking a drawing via the computer. The office designer will at some stage develop drawings manually or, it is hoped, on the computer. The method that the designer arrives at for a final configuration of the structure varies from office to office, designer to designer. For whatever the process the designer uses, the CAD drafter must translate the 2-D images the designer developed into a 3-D image. If, in fact, the designer has already produced a three-dimensional image on the computer and the structure is rotated into an orthographic view, the CAD drafter must verify that it is a 3-D image. Three-D images are often not 3-D drawings. For example, if the designer sketched or rendered a 3-D image and scanned it into the computer, the model is not 3-D in the truest sense of the word. Look at Figure 3.31A. We will refer to this 3-D

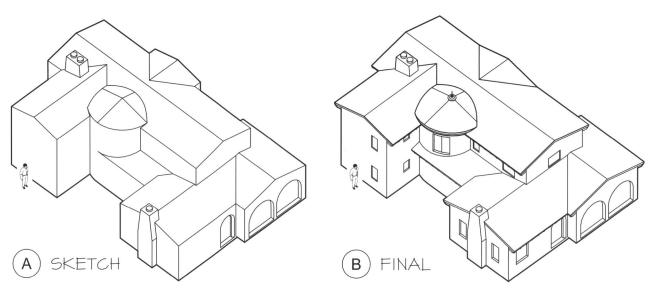

Figure 3.31   Three-dimensional model of Adli Residence. (Courtesy of Mike Adli, Owner, Nagy R. Bakhoum, President of Obelisk Architects.)

model as the preliminary sketch. Because the preliminary model is drawn in 3-D and in full scale, it may be well to incorporate a person standing in front of the structure for scale. This helps the drafter to realize scale. As the model evolves, based on the client's wishes, budgets, and other design-changing factors, a refined 3-D model is created (see Figure 3.31B). Next, we rotate the object

into an orthographic view, a plan view, and a minimum of four elevations. See Figure 3.32.

The structure must now be sliced horizontally to produce a floor plan and/or a reflected ceiling plan, and into a number of vertical slices to produce what are called building sections. See Figures 3.33A and 3.33B, respectively, for these types of slices and their respective solu-

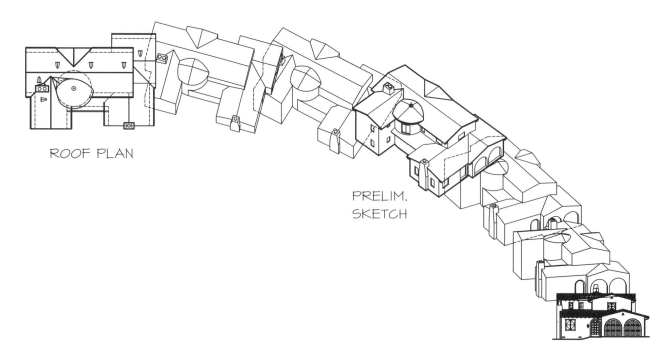

Figure 3.32   Rotation of massing model into ortho view. (Courtesy of Mike Adli, Owner; Nagy R. Bakhoum, President of Obelisk Architects.)

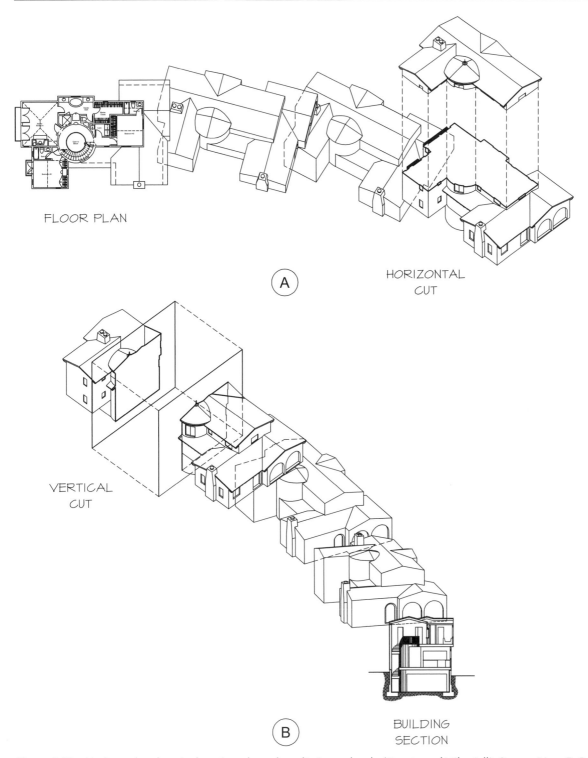

FLOOR PLAN

Ⓐ

HORIZONTAL
CUT

VERTICAL
CUT

Ⓑ

BUILDING
SECTION

Figure 3.33 Horizontal and vertical sections through preliminary sketch. (Courtesy of Mike Adli, Owner; Nagy R. Bakhoum, President of Obelisk Architects.)

tions. Thus, by slicing and rotating, we can produce a roof plan, a floor plan, a number of sections, and at least four elevations, as shown in Figure 3.34.

Other drawings can now be generated from this basic set. The floor plan can become the master drawing (XREF) drawing for the roof-framing plan when used in conjunction with the roof plan; the ceiling joist plan can become the basis for the foundation plan and the base for your associates' drawings, such as an electrical plan, structural plan, and/or mechanical plan. See Figure 3.35.

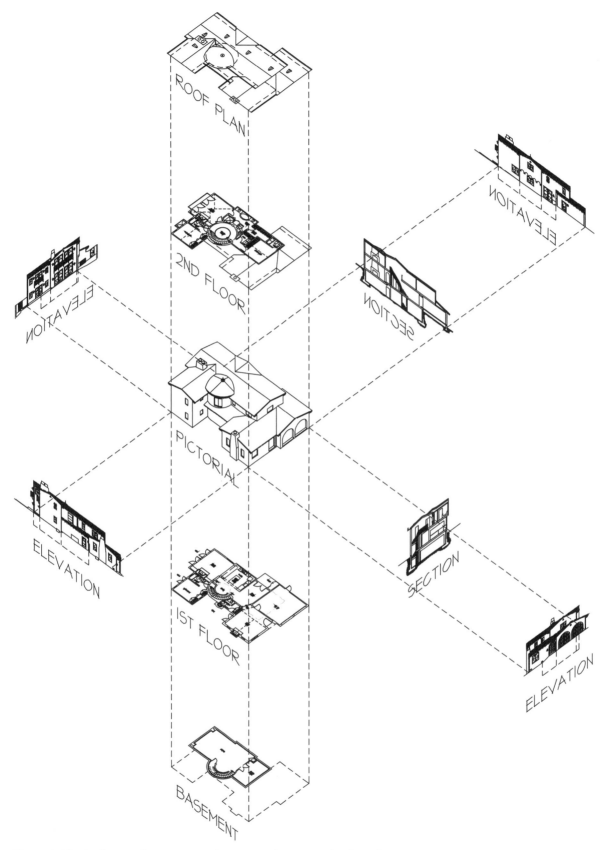

Figure 3.34 Evolution of construction documents. (Courtesy of Mike Adli, Owner, Nagy R. Bakhoum, President of Obelisk Architects.)

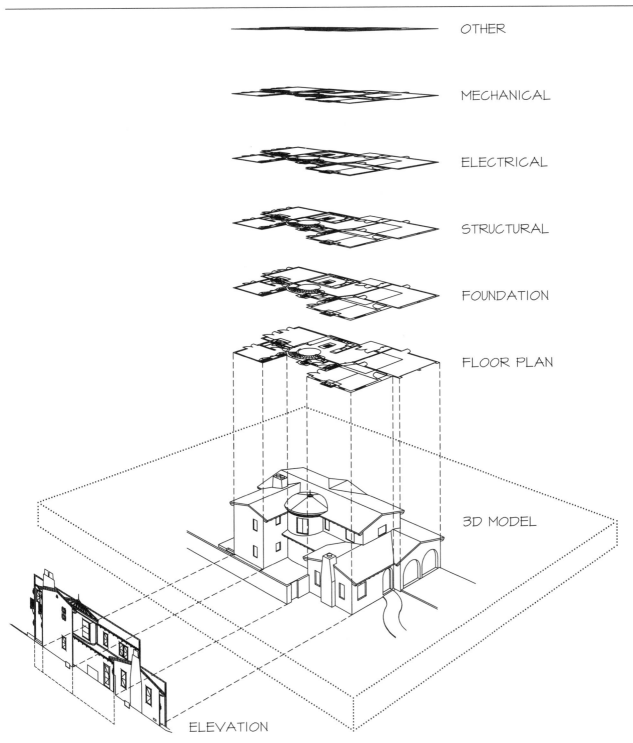

OTHER

MECHANICAL

ELECTRICAL

STRUCTURAL

FOUNDATION

FLOOR PLAN

3D MODEL

ELEVATION

Figure 3.35 Floor plan as a base for other drawings. (Courtesy of Mike Adli, Owner, Nagy R. Bakhoum, President of Obelisk Architects.)

The walls, floors, ceiling, and roof are all initially drawn as solids. Another strategy is to take these planes and further articulate them. Draw the individual rafters, ceiling joist, studs, the concrete slab, and the foundation below it. This can be done on the section before it is rotated into ortho, as shown in Figure 3.36.

The eave can be isolated as shown on Figure 3.37, and then detailed as shown on Figure 3.38.

There is a definite advantage to articulating the structure right on the massing model. The drafter can actually see the construction that is to take place and identify potential problems, which may look as if they are resolved

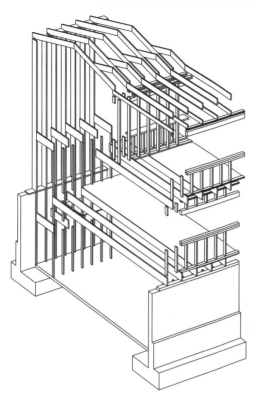

Figure 3.36 Incorporating the individual elements. (Courtesy of Mike Adli, Owner, Nagy R. Bakhoum, President of Obelisk Architects.)

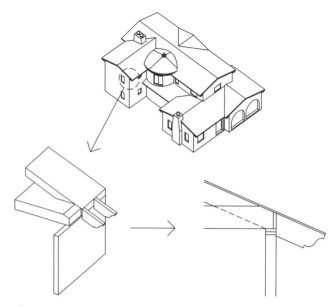

Figure 3.37 Isolating areas for detailing. (Courtesy of Mike Adli, Owner, Nagy R. Bakhoum, President of Obelisk Architects.)

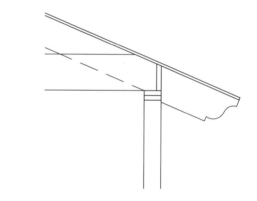

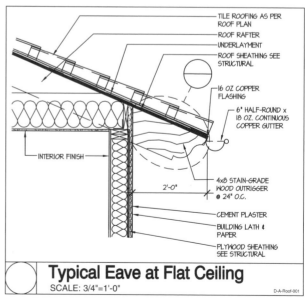

Figure 3.38 Isolating an area and detailing.

on details but reveal themselves only when the whole building is produced. The greater the understanding of the building process, the more effective and valuable the employee is to the office.

If windows, doors, stair, and cabinets are incorporated into the preliminary sketch, the interior elevations and their details will be partly completed. If the preliminary sketch was further evolved to produce presentational drawings, in the form of presentational plans, elevations, renderings, and area sketches, the CAD drafter need only use a stage prior to the rendering to produce the base for elevations, plans, and so on (see Figure 3.39).

Figure 3.39 also shows the reader the stages in producing a 3-D model drawing as shown in Figure 3.31. Whether the designer develops the 3-D model or it is developed by a CAD drafter, the present method is to (see Figure 3.39):

A. Lay out the main masses of the structure as a 2-D drawing.

B. Lay out this drawing in a 3-D image. Obviously, because there are no heights yet, we will be working with the *x* and *y* axes only.

C. From this 3-D form, the heights are extruded.

D. The roof shape is then added to the 3-D rectilinear form.

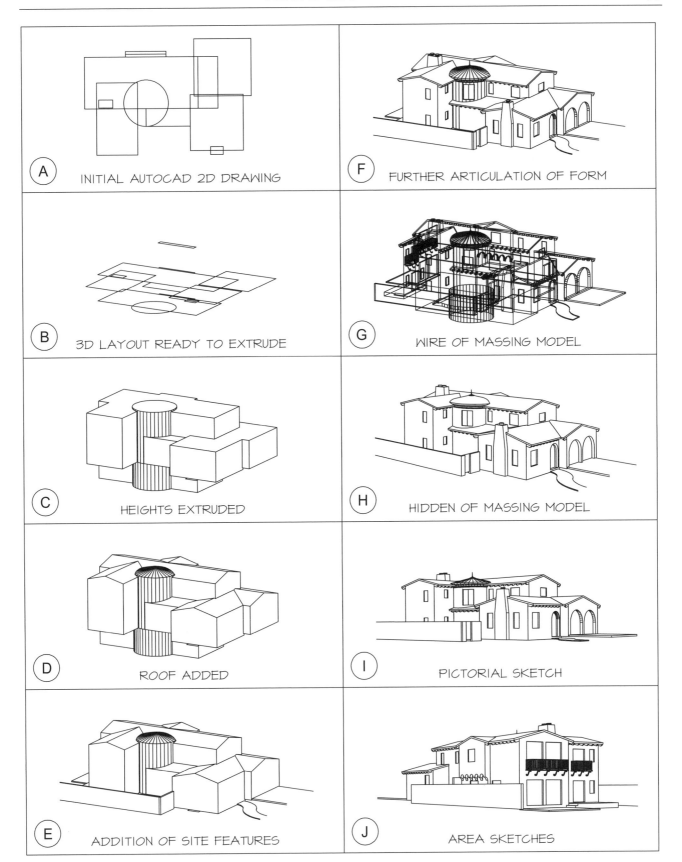

Figure 3.39 Evolution of a 2-D to 3-D sketch. (Courtesy of Mike Adli, Owner, Nagy R. Bakhoum, President of Obelisk Architects.)

E.   Add to this some of the features of the site, such as driveways, walks, and fences.

F.   Further articulation of the form is accomplished by adding windows, doors, fireplaces, skylights, etc.

G.   A wire (short for wire frame) of the massing model is extremely helpful later to locate the interior forms and help the designer understand the intersections of these geometric forms, that will aid not only in the section drawing but in the details as well.

H.   The advantage of the computer is best seen here because we can instantly go from wire frame to (hidden) massing model.

I. & J.   Still another of a 3-D model is that of rotating. To see other views of the building, it is important to rotate in to ortho to produce plans and elevations, which will be explained Chapter 6.

■ DISADVANTAGES OF A COMPUTER

One of the greatest concerns in the industry is the piracy of drawings. If drawings are sent electronically or even on a CD or floppy disk, they can be copied and duplicated. There is always a possibility that people changing jobs may download entire libraries of information and take them with them to their new firms. Drawings can also be changed or altered. For this reason many municipalities require a hard copy (printed on paper) with wet ink signatures. You cannot sign a document, scan it, and send it electronically.

Not all tasks that the computer can perform are organized in an architectural fashion. The drawing of a site plan is an example. Most civil engineers who provide plot plans for architects do so with a notation method that is referenced to North and South. Some civil engineers have moved away from this national standard and orient to North only, which could make some of the listing of angles reach almost 180° and very difficult to understand. The civil engineer should start with a point of beginning (POB) and travel counterclockwise, as illustrated in Figure 8.3A through 8.3H (see Chapter 8). The notation N 18° 50′ 00″ E 180.31′ means a 180.31-foot-long lot line drawn 18° 50′ away from North toward the East. For the computer drafter, the compass bearings are as follows: East is 0°, North is 90°, West is 180°, and South is 270°. Thus, the computer drafter must issue a command of 90 minus 18° 50′, or 71° 10′. This translation is very cumbersome for beginning CAD drafters. All of these settings can be adjusted into AutoCAD's units dialog box. It is a matter of knowing the correct technique.

The computer is forever changing. The life cycle of a computer is said to be three years. Small offices, which are the majority in the architectural industry, cannot financially afford to change computers that frequently.

The percentage of downtime, which is the period when a computer is not operational for one reason or another, is still high and creates a problem for small offices with few computers. The development of better and faster computers is helping to reduce this time, but it is for this reason that all offices need a CAD manager.

Additional Disadvantages to the Drafter, the Office, and Production

Drafters Who Can
1. Not understanding scale (text, viewports, blocks, detail)
2. Not understanding paper size/printable area

Effects on Drafter Health
3. Human health
   - Eye
   - Back
   - Ergonomics
   - Radiation from monitor radiation

Effects on Time Management/Production
4. General loss of time/life (similar to being held captive)
5. Hard to be productive if machine is not in perfect running order

Vulnerability to the Office
6. Ability to erase the work of an entire office in one minute
7. Virus attacks and hackers
8. Difficulty in breaking up a project for multiple drafters

■ ADVANTAGES OF A COMPUTER

The first advantage you may notice with a computer is that you are drawing full size. Fifty-foot-long buildings are drawn 50 feet in length. For the first time in architectural drafting history, we are drawing in full scale. This is possible because we are drawing in model (virtual) space, which is unlimited. Drafters can now think and measure full-size buildings in actual dimensions, rather than in a reduced scale.

Another advantage is the computer's ability to enlarge or reduce a drawing instantly. A drawing can be displayed on the monitor as a single drawing, or the screen can be split and the original drawing can be displayed adjacent to an enlargement (see Figure 3.40). Two monitors can also be used simultaneously: one displaying the original drawing while the second monitor zooms in and shows an enlargement of a given area (see Figure 3.41). A single drawing can be reproduced in a variety of different scales. For example, the intersection of a roof with a wall can be zoomed in for drawing accuracy and then

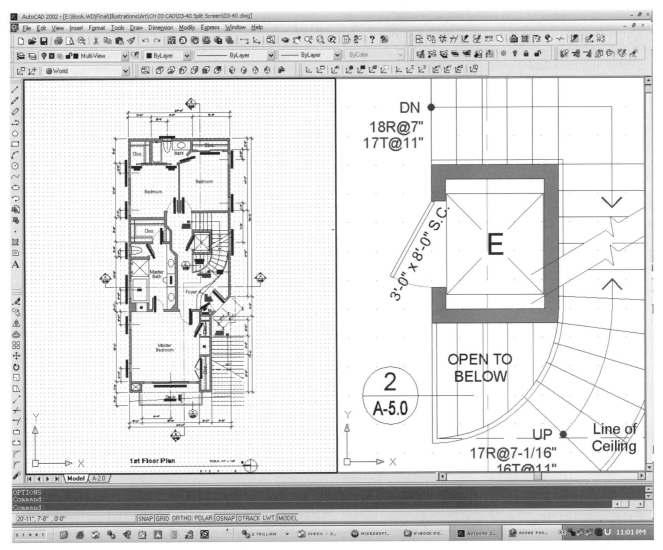

Figure 3.40   Split screen. (Courtesy of Mike Adli, Owner, Nagy R. Bakhoum, President of Obelisk Architects.)

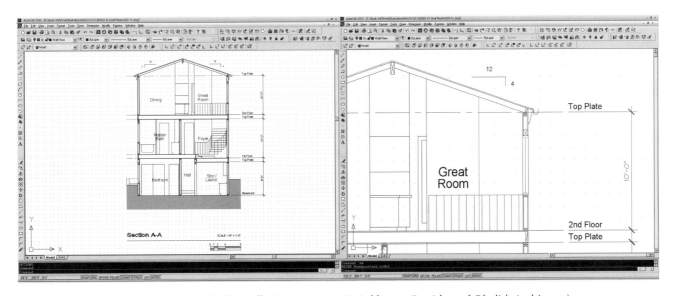

Figure 3.41   Dual screen. (Courtesy of Mike Adli, Owner, Nagy R. Bakhoum, President of Obelisk Architects.)

returned to its original size (zoomed out) with a single command. The computer has the capability to enlarge and reduce much like a paper copier.

The computer was made for repetitive and redundant tasks. If, for example, you were to draft an office layout, the desks can be logically and methodically laid out in just a few seconds. Even with adhesive drafting, this type of drawing would have taken many hours to accomplish in the past.

Computers can be networked so that if many drafters are working on one project, they can communicate with each other. As one drafter changes an element of a drawing, say a window size, the change will be reflected on the drawing of the computers that are networked (review XREF). Although this is the best scenario, it is not easy to implement.

The computer programs of today are doing many tasks simultaneously. As a drafter is outlining a floor plan, the computer is computing the perimeter and the square footage of this polygon. This information not only helps the contractor estimate the board feet of lumber needed or the wall surface area for a stucco estimate, but also helps size windows and doors by computing the maximum glazing area for a structure.

Because the computer can draw in 3-D, any potential problems in construction, installation, and the like, can be identified before they occur. The list of potential problems that can be avoided is endless. An example is positioning air-conditioning ducts in reference to the structural members. Any potential installation problems may be evident before construction begins. We are yet to discover the limits of what the computer can do. There are many advantages yet to be discovered by the architectural industry.

■ FUTURE OF CAD

Advances in the computer industry increased after the turn of the century, making it impossible to accurately forecast the evolution of the computer for the next decade. Soon there will be more computers than there are telephones and televisions, if there are not already. There may be more computers than people, if you count those in appliances, cell phones, and so forth.

This ever morphing industry does, however, provide some clues to the future. One need only look at the cutting edge state-of-the-art computers and plan for offices to incorporate these advances into their operations. There are, for example, seven major movements taking place in the architectural industry:

A. Wireless
B. Skill/toll assessment as a base of compensation
C. The disappearance of the central workspace
D. Model-based or model-centric design as 3-D models, only now being adopted as a base for working drawings
E. Full-size virtual buildings that clients may walk through
F. Software—pay as you use
G. New delivery methods

The impact of wireless components not only is beginning to affect the configuration of the office, but has given more freedom to the CAD drafter. Currently, the only limitation is directional; that is, you need to be sure that the infrared beams are directed toward the equipment you wish to control. Printers and copiers are now beginning to appear on the market that are wireless. A mobile unit is shown in Figure 3.42. A basic diagram

Figure 3.42 Mobile workstation.

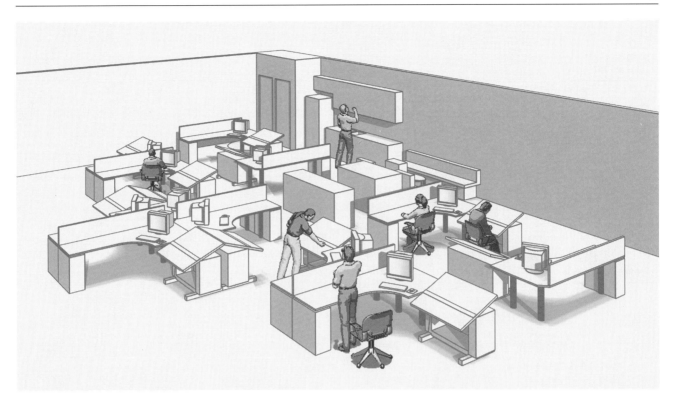

Figure 3.43   A mobile production area without walls.

may look like that shown in Figure 3.43. For example, mobile CAD stations may be grouped to form clusters of two, four, six, eight, or ten units. As jobs arise, the production room will be organized to meet the needs of a specific job by producing the needed grouping of staff required to execute the job. As jobs are completed, the CAD stations will be reconfigured to meet the needs of the next project and future projects. The production room will be forever morphing to meet demands.

As with manual drafting, a hierarchy of skills will be defined and titled with CAD drafting. The CAD drafter will be described or titled based on his or her command of this tool. If you can only CAD draft, you will be on the low end of the spectrum. If you can program and change the nature of some of the existing systems to accommodate the needs of a particular office, you will be on the high end of the spectrum.

Some CAD drafters may choose to work at home and come into the office only for staff meetings. More conventional offices may see this new minimally staffed office as a radical change from the past, with the office acting only as a docking station for the CAD drafter. Technology is making it increasingly easy for the industry to send and receive drawings. The CAD drafter may not even need to come to the office to drop off drawings, but rather may send them electronically.

Some offices may not have CAD drafters at all. CAD drafters may function similarly to a contractor or sub-

contractor and bid on jobs they find on web sites. This can provide greater freedom for drafters, allowing them to spend their daylight hours with their families and perform the contracted work during the evenings or early morning hours.

■ CONCLUSION

Throughout this chapter we have tried to refrain from discussing how to use a computer or the commands used for a specific function. This is because software programs frequently change every three years or so and the new versions have different commands or shortcuts to accomplish a task. Rather, we have deliberately shown the process of how a set of drawings is produced. Certainly, techniques have changed from manual drafting to computer-generated drafting or CAD programs, but the process of building construction has not changed. The changes in the process of building have not resulted from use of the computer or the method of drawing, but rather from changes in building technology.

To help the beginning architectural technician or student set up his or her first set of working drawings, a chart was developed to aid in setting layers, lettering heights, and line quality. This chart can be found in the Appendix (see web site.) It is based on national standards and may even be found in drafting manuals in most offices.

chapter

4

ENVIRONMENTAL AND HUMAN
CONSIDERATIONS

As the title implies, this chapter is about environmental and human concerns. It was written to show students of architecture and prospective employees some of the major concerns of architects as they translate design images into structural reality. One cannot merely place a building on a site without being aware of the impact the structure will have on the immediate environment.

There are many environmental concerns facing the architectural technician, ranging from earthquakes to snow, from the effects of the sun to rainfall, and from the control of termites to frost line depth in certain regions. The results of a national survey conducted by the authors on environmental concerns are printed in the Appendix of this book. An abbreviated list of the most common concerns follows:

1. Wind
2. Snow
3. Seismic activity
4. Fire
5. Energy
6. Foundation design
7. Flooding
8. Distribution of loads
9. Structural design
10. Frost depths
11. Hurricanes
12. Insulation
13. Americans with Disabilities Act (ADA)
14. Water table
15. Roof loads
16. Temperature
17. Rain
18. Frost
19. Exterior finishes
20. Drainage
21. Vertical loading

In addition to the concerns listed, this chapter also addresses sun (light, heat, and ultraviolet), sound, deterioration of materials, termites, and underground gases (see Figure 4.1).

■ SUSTAINABLE ARCHITECTURE

The phrase "sustainable architecture" has different meanings for different individuals. For some, it may be as simple as incorporating a solar unit to heat the water in a structure. To others, it may mean harnessing all the forces nature has to offer to sustain a structure. A third and a more comprehensive approach is to calculate the load a designed structure produces on its immediate surroundings and to provide a successful solution to reduce

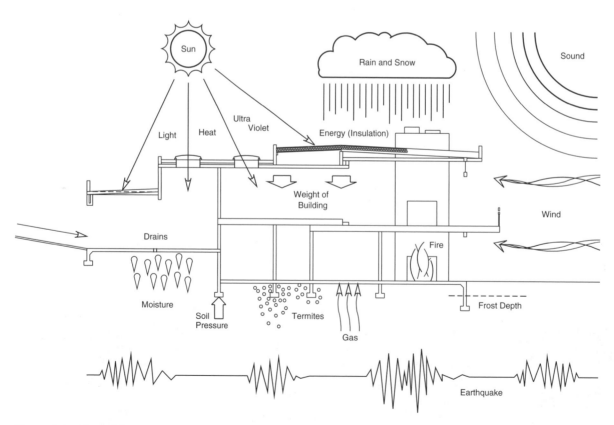

Figure 4.1 Natural forces.

this load via natural forces such as the sun, wind, heat gain and heat loss, or earthquakes, to mention a few.

In any event, this may be a moot point because a responsible architect, through his or her formal training, will in the design process call upon all the applicable and naturally available technology to produce the safest and most efficient structure possible. It is for this reason that this chapter was written—to expose the student/architectural technician to a few of the concerns that may confront an architectural designer and the solutions they may employ to address these concerns.

■ LATERAL INFLUENCES

The considerations for lateral design will deal with structures that are subjected to high wind conditions and earthquakes. Figure 4.2 illustrates a simple rectangular building and the effects of wind pressure on its flat sides. The total wind pressure factor is calculated at the roof and floor diaphragms. This factor is expressed as a force acting on the roof and floor diaphragms, as indicated by F-1, F-2, and F-3. The diaphragms are considered rigid planes and will distribute the forces into vertical bracing units.

The following are three examples of vertical bracing methods that a structural engineer may implement to resist the lateral forces distributed in the building shown in Figure 4.2.

Figure 4.3 depicts a steel frame at the opening at the North side of the first floor level. Because the steel columns are cantilevered from a reinforced concrete grade beam, this method may be considered as a self-stabilizing frame. This frame would be resisting the lateral force F-3.

Another method to resist the lateral force F-3 is the use of steel columns and a steel beam with welded moment connections at the steel columns and beam connection. This method may be termed a *moment frame* and also referred to as a *rigid frame*. Such a resistive system refers to

moment connection joints within the steel-braced frame. This method is illustrated in Figure 4.4.

Figure 4.5 depicts a portion of the West wall in Figure 4.2 where the lateral force F-4 is distributed into the en-

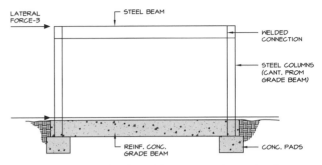

Figure 4.3 Example of steel frame—cantilevered columns.

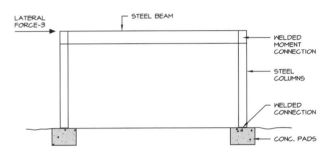

Figure 4.4 Example of steel moment frame.

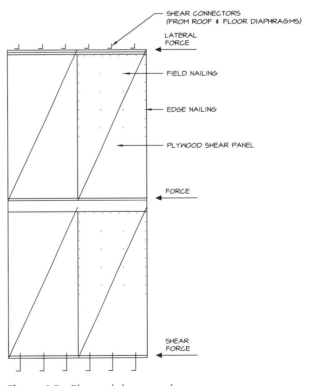

Figure 4.5 Plywood shear panels.

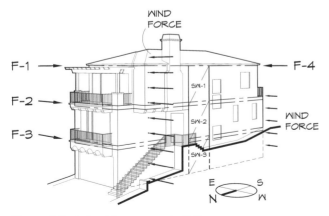

Figure 4.2 Lateral forces on a building.

gineered plywood shear walls. The thickness of the plywood panels, the shear connectors, panel edge nailing, and field nailing are all determined by the force they are to resist. The seismic loads, derived from earthquake forces, are generated by the dead weight of the building construction materials. The force factors distributed throughout the structure are resolved in a manner similar to that done for forces created by wind conditions.

■ ENERGY

The architect, mechanical engineer, and electrical engineer will constantly be designing and providing methods to conserve energy. These methods will primarily deal with the use of insulation allocated to the roof, wall, and floor assemblies for a specific structure. The assemblies will handle both cold and heat, as well as mechanical and electrical systems, and any innovations that will assist in conserving energy.

Figure 4.6 illustrates a three-story residence in which the entire envelope will be calculated, detailed, and constructed with energy-conserving elements designed to address warm and cold weather conditions. The first elements are the roof, ceiling, walls, and floors. These will be insulated with a material that will provide an "R" value that will resist heat loss and heat gain. The R value is the value assigned to a specific insulating material or a combination of materials that have been tested for their resistive capabilities. One method of combating heat and cold is shown in an example of a roof and exterior wall assembly providing insulation at the ceiling and wall locations. This detail is illustrated in Figure 4.7.

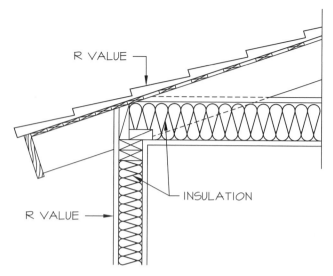

Figure 4.7   Roof/ceiling and wall insulation.

In areas where extreme cold weather conditions prevail in the winter, it is recommended that rigid insulation board be installed at the foundation and around the footing elements. This insulation will prevent excess cold from reaching the floor slab and, ultimately, the inside of the building. Figure 4.8 shows an example of a footing detail where 1" rigid insulation board is incorporated at the footing and concrete slab connection. This detail would lower the need for heating and expenditure of energy.

For exterior wall openings, such as windows and doors, where extreme cold and hot weather conditions prevail, it is recommended and in many governing mu-

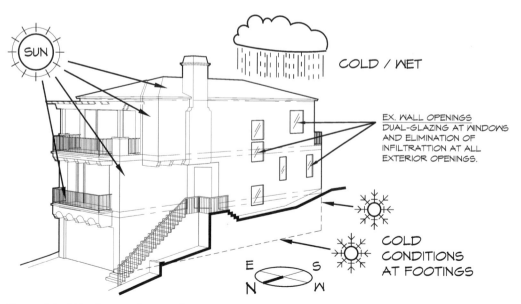

Figure 4.6   Weather conditions affecting energy conservation.

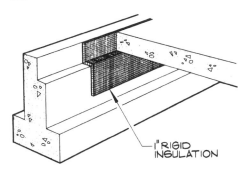

Figure 4.8 Footing insulation. (Reprinted by permission from *Professional Practice of Architectural Detailing*, 3d Ed., copyright © 1999 by John Wiley & Sons, Inc.)

Figure 4.9 Trombe wall.

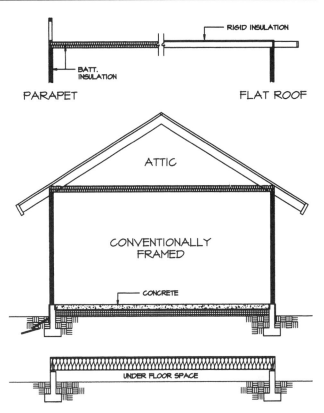

Figure 4.10 Creating an envelope. (Reprinted by permission from *Professional Practice of Architectural Detailing*, 3d Ed., copyright © 1999 by John Wiley & Sons, Inc.)

nicipalities required, that the windows have dual glazing and be installed to prevent air infiltration. Doors will also be installed to prevent air infiltration.

For many building projects there may be methods and innovations for heating and cooling systems whereby energy conservation may be attained. One example of supplemental heating is the use of a trombe wall. A photograph of this supplemental heating innovation is shown in Figure 4.9.

As mentioned previously, the entire envelope in Figure 4.6 will be calculated for energy saving requirements. Envelope is a term referring to the entire enclosure of the interior space of a building. This enclosure may utilize insulation materials to prevent heat loss during the winter and heat gain during the summer. An example of a building section for a one-story residence that creates an insulated envelope is illustrated in Figure 4.10.

For the purpose of augmenting lighting conditions in interior spaces, devices such as manufactured skylights and a unit called a Solatube are recommended. The Solatube, a reflective tube, is attached to the roof, and a lens is directed to an interior space in the structure. The

lens refracts the captured light and disperses it into a specific area. This device can reduce the demand for additional lighting energy. Figure 4.11 depicts a partial building section showing a Solatube installation.

These and other resources are available for conserving energy in building projects.

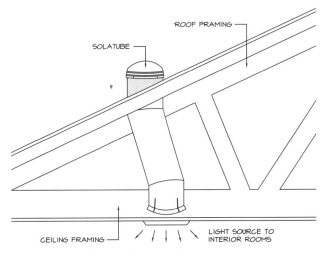

Figure 4.11 Solatube. (Courtesy Solatube.)

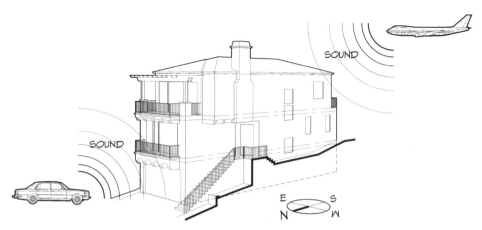

Figure 4.12 Sound-producing forces.

■ SOUND

There are various types of negative sounds that can enter a structure and cause discomfort to the occupants. Aircraft, cars, motorcycles, and trucks are some of the sources of sound that contribute to the need to construct buildings that address the problems of sound infiltration. Figure 4.12 depicts some of the major contributors of negative sound conditions that will be confronted in detailing and construction of a three-story building. The negative sounds coming from above a building, like those created by various aircraft, will necessitate full sound insulation in the roof and ceiling members. A detail for this type of assembly is illustrated in Figure 4.7. Sound infiltration through the exterior walls can be controlled through required sound insulation techniques. Insulation of an exterior wall is achieved either with full insulation placed inside the wall or with sheets applied to the outside of the wall. An example of insulated sheets applied to the outside of exterior walls is shown in Figure 4.13.

In projects where concrete masonry units are used for the exterior walls, the open cells in the masonry units may be filled with a metal baffle or a fibrous filler to deter or eliminate the infiltration of noise. A standard concrete masonry unit with two types of insulation is depicted in Figure 4.14.

An effective method of deterring noise transmission through a floor assembly is with the use of lightweight concrete, carpet, and pad and batt insulation between

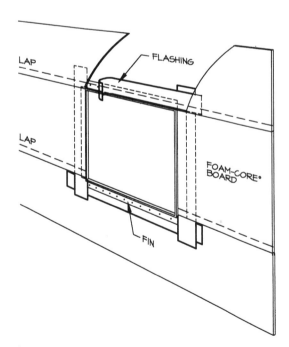

Figure 4.13 Fome-Cor® board as a wrap. Courtesy of International Paper. (Reprinted by permission from *Professional Practice of Architectural Detailing*, 3d Ed., copyright © 1999 by John Wiley & Sons, Inc.)

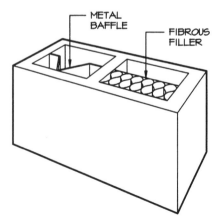

Figure 4.14 Sound insulation in concrete masonry units. (Reprinted by permission from *Professional Practice of Architectural Detailing*, 3d Ed., copyright © 1999 by John Wiley & Sons, Inc.)

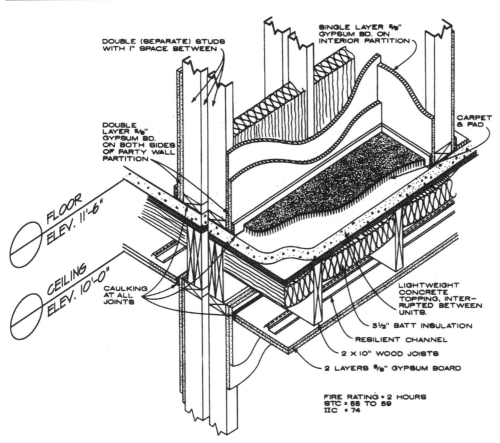

DOUBLE (SEPARATE) STUDS
WITH 1" SPACE BETWEEN

SINGLE LAYER 5/8"
GYPSUM BD. ON
INTERIOR PARTITION

DOUBLE
LAYER 5/8"
GYPSUM BD.
ON BOTH SIDES
OF PARTY WALL
PARTITION

CARPET
& PAD

FLOOR
ELEV. 11'-6"

CEILING
ELEV. 10'-0"

CAULKING
AT ALL
JOINTS

LIGHTWEIGHT
CONCRETE
TOPPING, INTER-
RUPTED BETWEEN
UNITS.

3½" BATT INSULATION

RESILIENT CHANNEL

2 X 10" WOOD JOISTS

2 LAYERS 5/8" GYPSUM BOARD

FIRE RATING = 2 HOURS
STC = 55 TO 59
IIC = 74

Figure 4.15 Soundproofing between floors. (Reprinted by permission from *Professional Practice of Architectural Detailing*, 3d Ed., copyright © 1999 by John Wiley & Sons, Inc.)

the floor joists. The finished ceiling below may contain two layers of 5/8" thick gypsum board attached to the wood joist with resilient channels. The resilient channels will provide a separation between the wood joist, which transmits sound, and the living space below. A pictorial drawing of this assembly is shown in Figure 4.15; a detail of the assembly is shown in Figure 4.16.

There are a few wood construction assemblies recommended to deter sound transmission between the common walls of apartment units or other types of living units. One method is to provide a double-studded wall with a 1" airspace separating the individual stud walls, along with two layers of gypsum board on both sides of the party wall. Batt insulation is installed between the wood studs. This technique is depicted in Figure 4.15.

Another method of interior wall insulation is to construct a wood wall with staggered studs and then continuously weave the sound insulation between the studs. The attachment of gypsum boards to the studs is accomplished with resilient clips. This construction method is shown pictorially in Figure 4.16. This type of assembly is less costly than that shown in Figure 4.15.

An alternative method for deterring sound transmission through a floor assembly is to have a separate ceil-

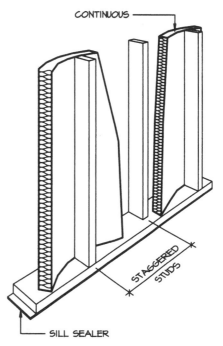

CONTINUOUS

STAGGERED
STUDS

SILL SEALER

Figure 4.16 Interior wall sound insulation. (Reprinted by permission from *Professional Practice of Architectural Detailing*, 3d Ed., copyright © 1999 by John Wiley & Sons, Inc.)

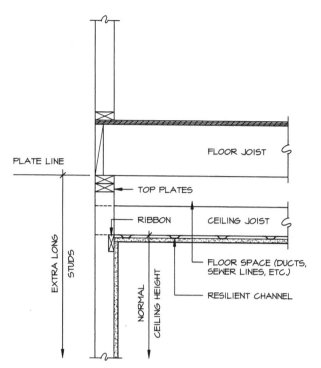

Figure 4.17 Separation of floor joist and ceiling joist. (Reprinted by permission from *Professional Practice of Architectural Detailing*, 3d Ed., copyright © 1999 by John Wiley & Sons, Inc.)

ing independent from the floor joist above. This will necessitate separate ceiling joist members with a higher wall plate line to support the floor joist above. The space between the floor joist and the ceiling joist is an ideal arrangement for preventing sound transmission as well as allowing space for plumbing lines, heating ducts, and other equipment requirements. Resilient channels are recommended for the attachment of the gypsum board to the ceiling joist. This detailed assembly is illustrated in

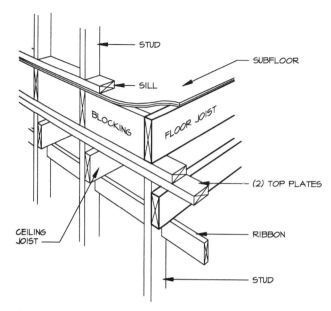

Figure 4.18 Detail of floor-ceiling separation. (Reprinted by permission from *Professional Practice of Architectural Detailing*, 3d Ed., copyright © 1999 by John Wiley & Sons, Inc.)

Figure 4.17. A pictorial drawing depicting this assembly is shown in Figure 4.18.

■ SNOW

In geographic areas where snow and cold climates prevail, it is necessary to address the various sections of a structure that need to be detailed to deal with these climatic conditions.

As shown in Figure 4.19, the roof structure will initially be designed based on the dead load of the snow. This

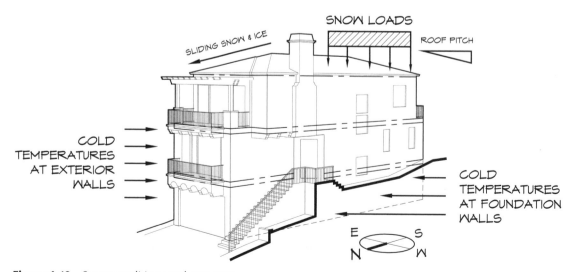

Figure 4.19 Snow conditions and concerns.

dead load figure is usually established by the existing building code in the local municipality. The load may be reduced for each degree of a roof pitch that is more than 20° where snow loads are in excess of 20 pounds a square foot. Special eave requirements are set by the governing building codes. These requirements include a hot or cold underlayment of roofing material on all roofs from the edge of the eave for a distance of up to five feet toward the roof edge.

It should be noted that in areas that are subjected to earthquakes, the building official of the municipality will ask that the snow dead load be calculated into the engineer's lateral design.

It is a good practice, as well as a requirement of the building code, to protect all building exits from sliding ice and snow at the eaves. The use of heat strips and metal flashing at the exit areas in the eave assembly is an

acceptable method to deter ice dams and snow accumulation. Most roof structures with a roof pitch exceeding 70° are considered free of snow loads.

Insulation is required for roof, ceiling, wall, and floor locations. Rigid insulation board is installed at the exterior of the foundation to keep the utility spaces from freezing. The foregoing recommendations are graphically illustrated in Figure 4.20.

■ FIRE

Fire and smoke are major concerns in the design of all types of structures. Building fires may be attributed to both external and internal causes, ranging from brush or forest fires to various internal causes, including electrical or heating fires.

There are various methods and procedures used to prevent the destruction of a building by fire. One method is to protect the various materials used in construction of the building. Under laboratory conditions, various materials or a combination of materials are tested and given fire rating designations. These fire ratings are expressed in the minutes and hours it takes a material to catch fire. For example, a wall may be fire rated as a two-hour firewall, or a specific door may have a rating of 60 minutes. Structural columns can be assembled to provide a 3-hour fire rating, whereas a glass panel may be manufactured with a 20-minute fire rating. Laboratory testing has produced results in a time/temperature chart illustrating temperature in degrees and time in hours.

Figure 4.21 is a chart showing temperatures measured in degrees Fahrenheit (F) and centigrade (C) as they relate

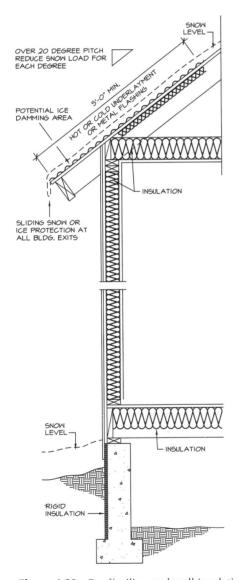

Figure 4.20 Roof/ceiling and wall insulation.

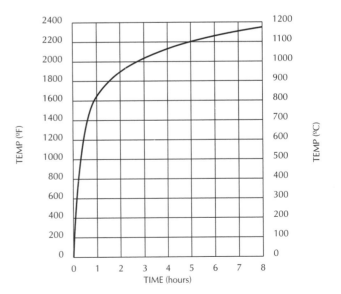

Figure 4.21 Time/temperature curve. (Reprinted by permission from *Professional Practice of Architectural Detailing*, 3d Ed., copyright © 1999 by John Wiley & Sons, Inc.)

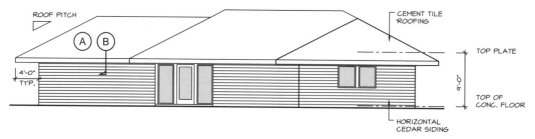

Figure 4.22 Exterior elevation—external fire control.

to a particular length of time measured in hours. An example, using this chart, is a one-hour fire rating for a material or combination of materials that would withstand a fire with a temperature of 1500° F or 860° C.

Although all parts of a structure are vulnerable to fire, the safety of the occupants and the integrity of the structure can be accomplished by providing construction details that incorporate materials that are fire rated to deter a fire or to minimize the spread of a fire. Buildings in high-risk brush fire areas can use exterior materials that will withstand high temperatures. This will give the building's occupants a longer time to evacuate the building in event of a fire. For example, a cement tile roofing material can be used for brush fire protection in a single-family residence. The construction detail of the eave and soffit assembly for this single-family residence is depicted in Figure 4.22 with a reference detail bubble "B" of the construction. Using a nonflammable roof material, the soffit detail is enclosed with a 1″ thick cement plaster finish that will deter a fire from spreading into the attic spaces. This detail is illustrated in detail and pictorial form in Figure 4.23. Note that fireblocking is installed below the soffit area to deter any fire that may occur in the exterior wall. To complete a fire protective envelope of the exterior materials, this residence has a wood-sided exterior wall finish. There is a layer of one-hour-rated fire-resistant hardboard and fire taping at all the joints of the hardboard. This will be installed prior to the installation of the wood siding. A detail and a pictorial drawing are shown in Figure 4.24.

Smoke infiltration is a grave concern because most deaths in a fire are caused by the smoke itself. Detailing the openings in walls, such as those for doors and windows, will reduce the potential of smoke infiltration. One means of reducing the infiltration of smoke through doors is to mill the head and jamb sections and the doorstop from one piece of wood. This feature is required by most building codes and fire protection agencies. A detail of a jamb and head section for a door assembly incorporating a one-piece section is illustrated in detail and pictorial form in Figure 4.25.

Another concern in regard to fire is a building's door and stair exits. The planning of a building requires that the architect and designer provide clearly defined path-

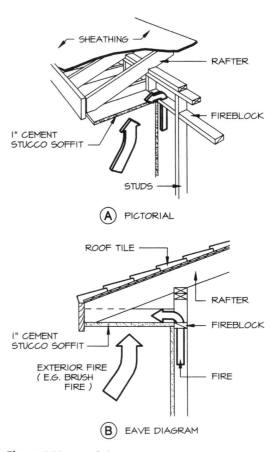

Figure 4.23 Roof tiles, cement stucco soffits, and fireblocking. (Reprinted by permission from *Professional Practice of Architectural Detailing*, 3d Ed., copyright © 1999 by John Wiley & Sons, Inc.)

ways to fire exits. Fire exits and their layouts are determined by the governing fire protection agency and the existing building codes. Distances between stair exits and the number of exits are also established by the governing agencies. In multilevel buildings, a correct stairwell design will allow people to move quickly down the stairs to an outdoor access without any interferences or obstructions in the exiting path. Fire exit arrangements for one-story nonresidential buildings are also governed by the fire protection agency and building codes. Figure 4.26 illustrates an example of a ground floor level of a

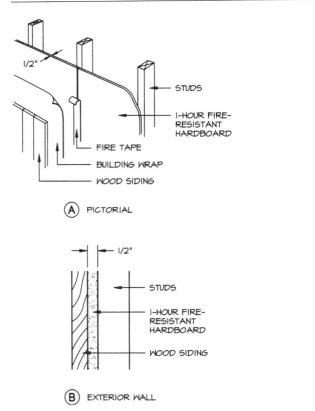

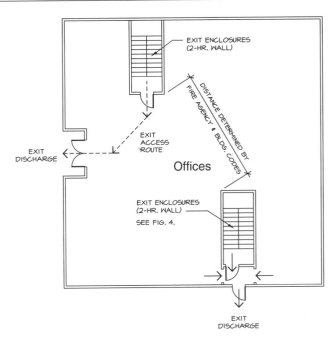

Figure 4.26 Stairway exit access plan.

Figure 4.24 Fire-resistant stud walls. (Reprinted by permission from *Professional Practice of Architectural Detailing*, 3d Ed., copyright © 1999 by John Wiley & Sons, Inc.)

multistory building. Note that the fire protection agency and building code determine the dimensional distances between the exit stairwells. All fire-rated doors must swing in the direction of the exit access. Note, too, in this example the required two-hour wall construction that encloses the stairwell. The local building code establishes requirements for the construction of the stairway walls. An example of a wood constructed two-hour fire wall assembly detail is illustrated in Figure 4.27. A pictorial view of this detail is shown in Figure 4.28.

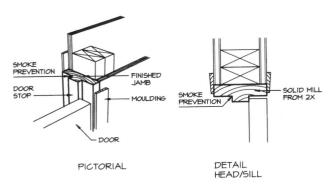

Figure 4.25 Solid-finish jamb and doorstop. (Reprinted by permission from *Professional Practice of Architectural Detailing*, 3d Ed., copyright © 1999 by John Wiley & Sons, Inc.)

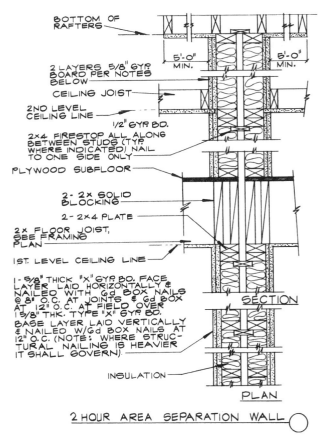

Figure 4.27 Two-hour area separation wall detail. (Reprinted by permission from *Professional Practice of Architectural Detailing*, 3d Ed., copyright © 1999 by John Wiley & Sons, Inc.)

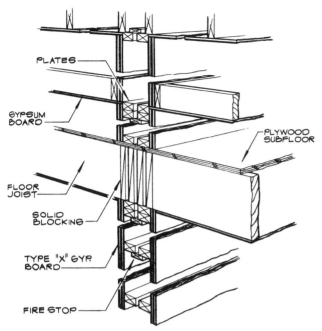

PLATES

GYPSUM BOARD

PLYWOOD SUBFLOOR

FLOOR JOIST

SOLID BLOCKING

TYPE "X" GYP BOARD

FIRE STOP

Figure 4.28 Pictorial view, two-hour area separation wall. (Reprinted by permission from *Professional Practice of Architectural Detailing*, 3d Ed., copyright © 1999 by John Wiley & Sons, Inc.)

■ SMOKE

The exhausting of smoke is a major concern in fires occurring in buildings. It has been determined that smoke kills more people in building fires than heat itself or a structural failure. Therefore, smoke control, whether through deterring smoke infiltration, as previously discussed, or by exhausting smoke from within the structure, is important. A common method for exhausting smoke from a building that is on fire is to use automatic

roof hatch ventilators. These automatic ventilators, which are usually found in smaller buildings, will open individually by means of a device that is activated by either smoke or heat. An example of a roof hatch ventilator that may be installed on a one-story industrial building is illustrated in Figure 4.29. The sizes and locations of these ventilators are determined by the governing fire protection agency and the building code.

Concerning fire and smoke as they relate to the design of a structure, the architect and detailer should be aware of the following:

1. Fire ratings of materials and code requirements
2. Methods of preventing smoke infiltration and the spread of fire
3. Vulnerable areas within a structure
4. Methods of reducing the spread of fire
5. How to protect the integrity of the structural members from fire
6. Methods of exhausting smoke to the outside
7. How occupants can be exited from a building in fire and smoke conditions (the major concern)

■ TEMPERATURE

Outside temperatures affect the design of building structures. In areas with high temperatures, buildings are insulated and provided with various types of mechanical systems to control the temperature within the structure's habitable areas. Temperature also has a large effect on the structural integrity of a building. For example, buildings that are constructed with a concrete frame and a concrete floor system are detailed at various connections to allow for expansion of the various concrete elements affected by temperature increases. Figure 4.30 illustrates a concrete column and a concrete floor beam connec-

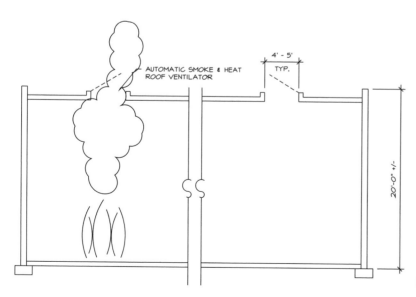

AUTOMATIC SMOKE & HEAT ROOF VENTILATOR

4' - 5' TYP.

20'-0" +/-

Figure 4.29 Smoke and heat roof ventilators.

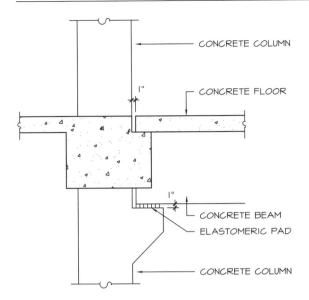

Figure 4.30 Expansion joint detail.

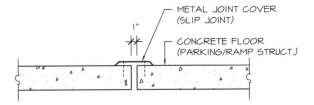

Figure 4.32 Expansion joint cover.

■ DETERIORATION

Many steps are taken in detailing the methods used to reduce or eliminate deterioration of the various building materials used in a structure. As we have seen, the use of metal flashing for foundation details, roof conditions, and other features provides some protection of the wood from deterioration. However, there are other conditions in which wood is subject to deterioration.

For example, wood posts on concrete porches are of concern in regard to future deterioration. Water from rain or hosing down patios is a great catalyst for deterioration at the base of a wood post. One method for detailing this connection to prevent deterioration at the base of the post is to elevate the post base above the concrete patio. An example of this detail is illustrated in Figure 4.33. As shown, a galvanized aluminum prefabricated metal post base is positioned under the post to provide a 1″ clearance above the concrete patio. Openings in the metal base unit will provide for water drainage.

Methods of anchoring exterior wood posts that may be used for fences, balustrades, and wood trellises vary as to how they may be detailed. In regard to preventing deterioration, some methods are recommended and others are not. Figure 4.34 depicts two examples of detailing the an-

tion that provides expansion joint clearances as well as an electrometric pad for ease of movement.

Another example is a floor condition that may require an expansion joint. This may occur when there is a large expanse of floor area, as shown in Figure 4.31. These expansion joints are placed in locations that are visually unobtrusive and will not require expensive covering methods. Concrete parking structures with vast areas of concrete floor require that various locations have expansion joints. The expansion joints are normally covered with an aluminum metal strip to allow for easy automobile traffic. These joints are referred to as slip joints. Figure 4.32 illustrates an expansion joint for a concrete parking structure floor with a metal joint cover.

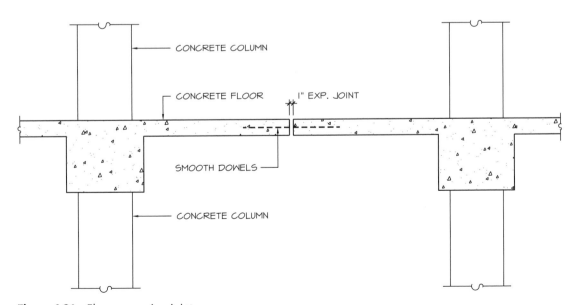

Figure 4.31 Floor expansion joint.

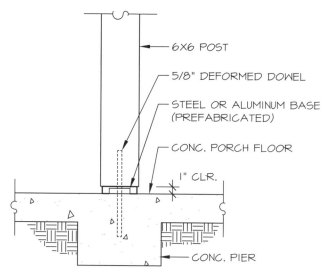

Figure 4.33   Elevated porch post.

chorage of a wooden fence post. Example A is not recommended because, over time the wood post will deteriorate from water damage and/or dry rot. Example B is recommended because the wood post is elevated above the soil and is protected from both soil and water by the concrete pier. Anchorage of the wood post to the concrete pier is achieved by using a manufactured or prefabricated galvanized steel "U" strap and machine bolts. The sloping top perimeter of the concrete pier prevents water from collecting at the base of the post and metal strap.

■ DRAINAGE/RAINFALL

This section deals with the drainage conditions resulting from the accumulation of rainwater that may lead to erosion or flooding problems. Because all regions of the country have particular climatic conditions relative to the amounts of rainfall, the architect and designer will need to anticipate and solve the problems of water drainage that may affect a building's structural areas and site conditions.

Roof Drainage

Roof designs and drainage devices on a roof are designed and detailed to dissipate and control rainwater. For example, a very low pitched roof design will create a slower flow of water runoff, which may reduce the possibility of flooding around a building's foundation. Devices such as acceptable manufactured roof drain units or conventional gutters and downspouts should be placed in key locations on the roof to accommodate and control any amount of rainwater. An example of a roof drain for a low-pitched roof is shown in Figure 4.35. Note that an overflow drain is incorporated as a safety measure in case there is blockage in the roof drain. Blockage may be a result of tree leaves, flying paper, and the like. The solutions for exterior deck drainage are similar to those recommended for a roof drainage system.

Roof drainage that is conducted to the roof eaves or overhangs is detailed in various ways. A recommended

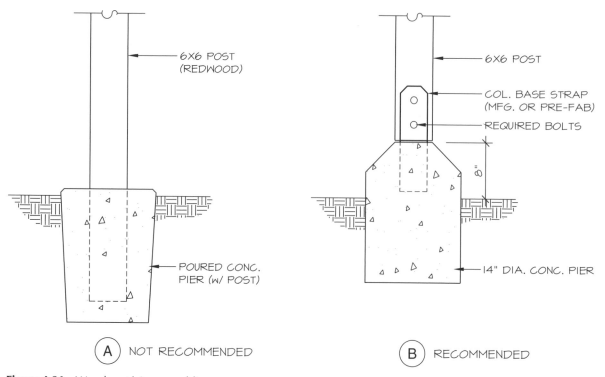

Figure 4.34   Wood post/pier assemblies.

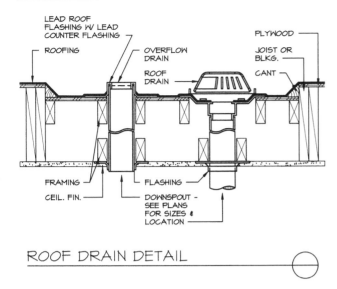

ROOF DRAIN DETAIL

Figure 4.35 Roof drain section. (Reprinted by permission from *Professional Practice of Architectural Detailing*, 3d Ed., copyright © 1999 by John Wiley & Sons, Inc.)

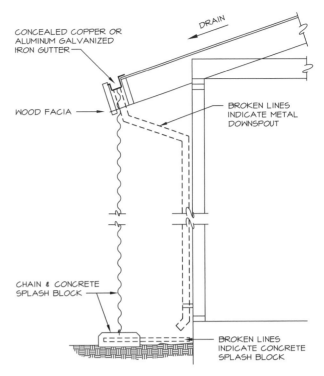

Figure 4.36 Roof draining examples.

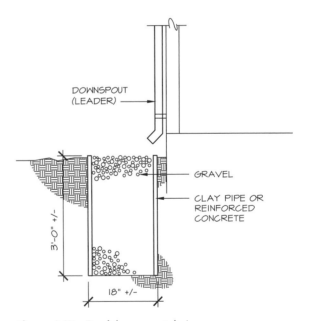

Figure 4.37 Roof downspout drainage.

method of detailing an eave for dispersing water from the roof areas is to provide a concealed gutter and downspouts. This method will control and direct the water to areas that will disperse the water away from the building, thus deterring erosion at the perimeter of the building. The concentration of water caused by the downspouts can be quickly dissipated with use of a splash block. Another method of dispersing the water flow concentrated at the eave, in lieu of metal downspouts, is with the attachment of a steel or aluminum chain from the roof gutter to a concrete splash block. The shape of the chain will act to slow the water flow and further limit the possibility of erosion. These detailed conditions are depicted in Figure 4.36.

Figure 4.37 illustrates another method of dispersing water drainage, which utilizes a gravel-filled pit encased in a concrete or vitreous container. This method may be restricted in areas where the soil conditions are not conducive to dispersing water this way. The enclosed gravel areas are referred to as "drywells."

In areas where soil conditions may dictate how water drainage is dispersed, other methods for roof drainage will be required. Figure 4.38 illustrates a detail in which the downspouts or leaders are connected directly to a vitreous clay pipe that conducts the water to other drainage devices. The sizes of the downspouts or leaders and drainage pipes are determined by the tributary areas of the roof that conduct water to any one of the downspout locations.

When a drainage condition is directing the flow of water to a certain area of a building, such as a garage door, it is recommended that a trough drain, drainage pipes, and an aluminum grate cover be used. This con-

struction assembly will prevent water from entering the garage area. A detail for this condition is shown in Figure 4.39. Note in the detail that cast iron or vitreous clay pipe is located at the ends of the trough to conduct the water away from the building.

A frequent problem of a sloping site is how to control the rainwater and reduce the erosion caused by a concentrated rainwater flow. A recommended method is

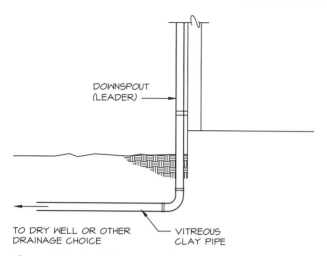

Figure 4.38   Roof downspout drainage.

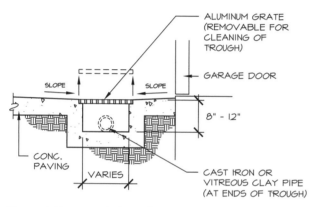

Figure 4.39   Trough drain detail.

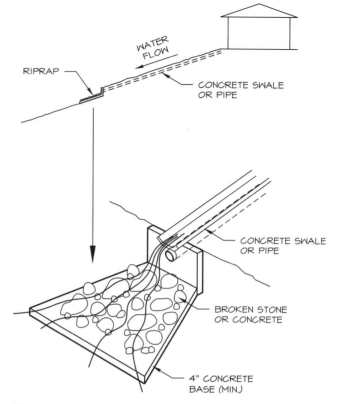

Figure 4.40   Riprap detail.

installation of a concrete swale or drainage pipes on the downslope to collect the rainwater and conduct the flow into recommended drainage or erosion devices. Depending on the slope of the downhill area, numerous swales and drainage pipes may be required.

If the water flow is to be distributed on an existing site, it is recommended that a method of dissipating the flow of water be designed to deter or minimize erosion of the soil. One way to dissipate the concentration of water flow and control soil erosion is to construct a drainage device referred to as a "riprap." This device is constructed in a location that collects the water from swales and/or pipes. It is constructed with a concrete base and inlaid with broken concrete or protruding rocks, which are spaced apart to slow down and dissipate the water flow. A detail of a riprap is illustrated in Figure 4.40.

■ UNDERGROUND GAS CONTROL

Industrial and manufacturing buildings that are constructed on sites where there is evidence of an under-

ground gas, such as methane, will require a method of dissipating the underground gas. A recommended method is to install collector pipes below the concrete floor and vent these pipes to an outside area. To see how this method is achieved, refer to Figure 4.41. This figure illustrates the partial foundation plan for an industrial building. It shows the recommended locations of 4-inch "0" perforated pipes and reference detail symbols for the required pipe and venting installations. Note, in detail A-A, that a 24" × 24" gravel-filled trench encases the 4-inch "0" perforated pipe as a means of collecting the gas. Detail B-B illustrates a method of venting the gas to the outside air through use of a 2-1/2" "0" vent in the exterior wall terminating at a minimum distance of two feet above the roof.

■ WATER TABLE

The term "water table" architecturally has two meanings. The first refers to the elevation (height) at which groundwater is atmospheric. The second designates a projection aboveground that sheds water away from a structure. A sample detail of a water table at a foundation wall is shown in Figure 4.42. It is the former that this section will address.

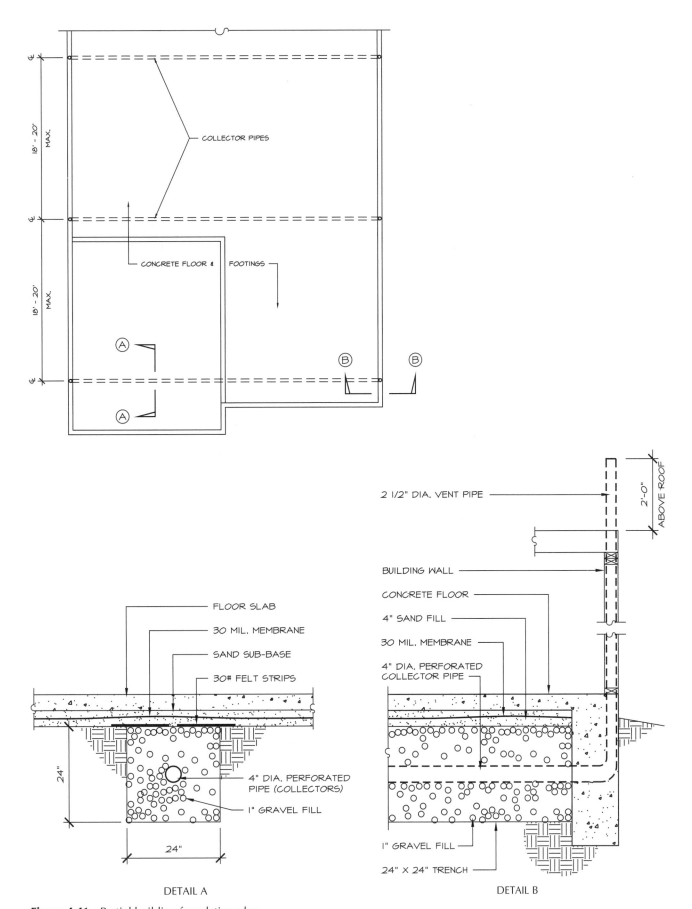

Figure 4.41 Partial building foundation plan.

Labels in the figure:

COLLECTOR PIPES

18' - 20' MAX.

18' - 20' MAX.

CONCRETE FLOOR & FOOTINGS

A

A

B

B

2 1/2" DIA. VENT PIPE

2'-O" ABOVE ROOF

BUILDING WALL

CONCRETE FLOOR

4" SAND FILL

30 MIL. MEMBRANE

4" DIA. PERFORATED COLLECTOR PIPE

1" GRAVEL FILL

24" X 24" TRENCH

DETAIL B

FLOOR SLAB

30 MIL. MEMBRANE

SAND SUB-BASE

30# FELT STRIPS

24"

4" DIA. PERFORATED PIPE (COLLECTORS)

1" GRAVEL FILL

24"

DETAIL A

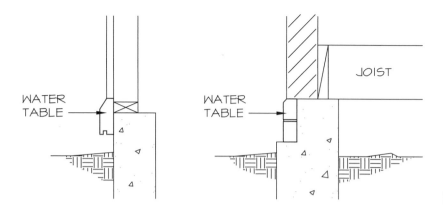

Figure 4.42   Water table at foundation plan.

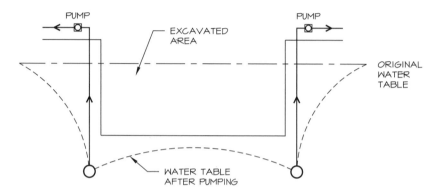

Figure 4.43   Diagram of dewatering.

First, let us establish some basic working facts about water, the movement of water, and water tables:

A. Water will pass easily through clean gravel and sand and seek its own level.

B. Perforated pipe in gravel provides an efficient means for water to travel. A good use for these pipes is under slabs and around basements.

C. Water travels very slowly through silts and very little through clay. Thus, it is important to use gravel to encourage water to flow away from a structure.

D. There are two basic ways of keeping water from penetrating a substructure when the substructure is below the water table. The first is through waterproofing the barrier and draining the water by way of a sump and a pump. Note that waterproofing is not 100% effective.

E. Municipalities require that when work is being done in an excavated area below the water table, the area must remain dry during construction. This can be accomplished with a pump or a series of pumps that change the water table configuration. as shown in Figure 4.43. An example of where this might occur is shown in Figure 4.44. Compacted fill is located in such a manner that the water table is just below the top of the fill. The foundation of a structure with such a fill will be built as shown in Figure 4.45.

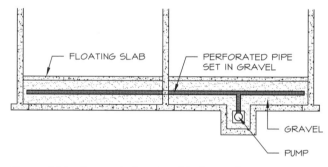

Figure 4.44   Removal of water table from substructure.

■ FROST LINE/FROST DEPTH

In many parts of the world, temperatures fall below freezing. Thus, a new level of measurement is introduced in reference to existing grade. This measurement, called the frost line or frost depth, is a significant datum for building (see Figure 4.46). These lines and numbers on the map represent levels below the grade under which water no longer freezes. This is important, because at these levels the moisture will not become a solid, expand, and cause damage to a foundation system. The figures given on this map are in inches and are for general use only. Frost lines should be checked, because they are estab-

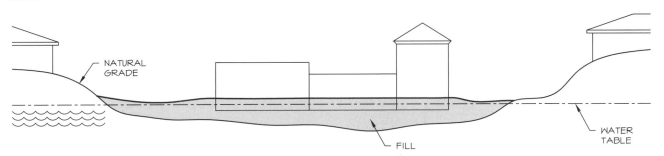

Figure 4.45 Fill at water table.

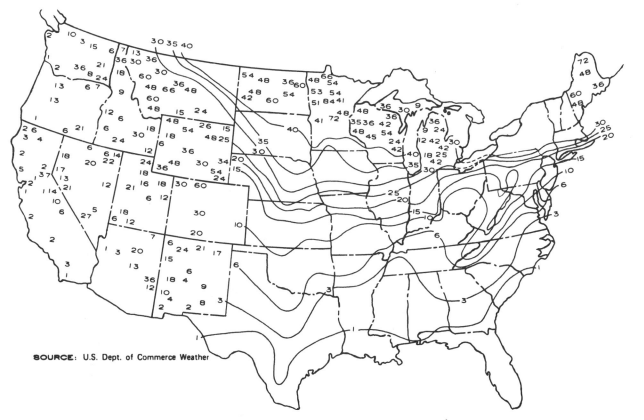

SOURCE: U.S. Dept. of Commerce Weather

Figure 4.46 Frost depths. (Reprinted by permission from *Architectural Graphic Standards*, 6th Ed., copyright © 1970 by John Wiley & Sons, Inc.)

lished by local code. The national code requires that a footing be placed a minimum of 1'-0" below the frost line (see Figure 4.47). The ground will not freeze below the frost line, making this a stable foundation.

■ TERMITES/TREATMENT

The durability and longevity of wood is improved by preservative treatment techniques. The treatment of wood is usually recommended for two reasons: the location of a member that is subject to an unsafe amount of moisture content and the climate or site conditions in regions that are susceptible to decay and termite infestation.

Termites are a major problem in some of our states. California, Hawaii, and the southeastern states have some of the most heavily infested areas. Although not everyone may practice in an infested area, all students and architectural technicians should be somewhat familiar with the methods used to deal with termite infestation. Figure 4.48 shows the termite infestation in the United States. The chart is calibrated in modest, moderate, and heavy infestation areas. The heaviest areas are in our southern states.

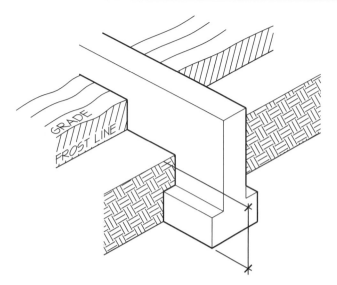

Figure 4.47 Frost line as a datum for footing depth.

When a structure is supported by wood members embedded in the ground, the members should be of an approved pressure-treated wood. Wood is treated by the pressure method when it is impregnated with toxic chemicals at elevated pressures and temperatures. One of the following classes of preservatives is commonly used: (1) creosote and creosote solutions, (2) oil-borne preservatives, (3) water-borne preservatives, and (4) water-repellent preservatives. Standards for preservatives and treatments should be in accordance with the American Wood preservers Association. Water-borne or water-repellent preservatives should be specified when members are to be painted or when finished materials are to be nailed to the members.

Wood members, such as sills, ledgers, and sleeper, that come in contact with concrete or masonry that itself is in direct contact with earth should be of an approved treated wood.

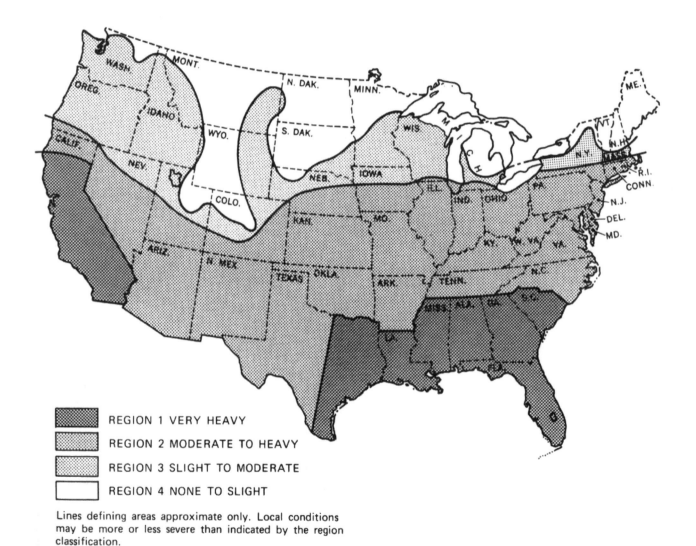

REGION 1 VERY HEAVY

REGION 2 MODERATE TO HEAVY

REGION 3 SLIGHT TO MODERATE

REGION 4 NONE TO SLIGHT

Lines defining areas approximate only. Local conditions may be more or less severe than indicated by the region classification.

Figure 4.48 Regions of termite infestation. (Reprinted by permission from *Architectural Graphic Standards*, 6th Ed., copyright © 1970 by John Wiley & Sons, Inc.)

The effectiveness of treated wood depends on the following factors: (1) type of chemical used, (2) amount of penetration, (3) amount of retention, and (4) uniform distribution of the preservative.

In the course of detailing, the architect should be cognizant of the application of treated wood. Examples of details incorporating a treated wood mudsill, ledger, and sleeper are illustrated in Figure 4.49.

Creosote and creosote solutions for preservation of wood pile foundations are relatively common and therefore should be called out when detailing this assembly. An example of a detail depicting this condition is illustrated in Figure 4.50.

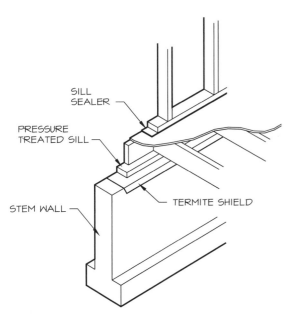

Figure 4.49   Mud sill area.

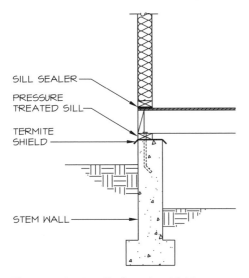

Figure 4.50   Detail of termite shield.

It should be emphasized that damage from decay and termites develops slowly: therefore, inspections should be provided to assure that proper clearances are being maintained and that termite barriers have been implemented correctly.

■ HUMAN CONSIDERATIONS

Architects can deal with forces that affect a structure such as wind, rain, and earthquakes, but they must always stay focused on the main reason the building was designed—for people. It is important to understand the critical anthropometrics data as they affect adult men and women, children, and elderly persons. Architects can provide their clients with the best working environment by producing architecture that makes a daily task a comfortable one. Whether serving food at a counter, working at a computer, or selling tickets for the local philharmonic, it is important to be comfortable. One should also provide an ideal and comfortable setting for dining, relaxing, and, yes, even studying. Providing the best angle for viewing in a museum or a theatre or for watching a favorite television program can contribute significantly to human comfort.

To create comfortable environments, we must first understand the limits of the human body. It is vital to study the measurements for such things as clearances under counters and desks, the maximum height a person can reach when getting a book from an upper shelf, or how far an elderly person can reach down to plug in an electrical appliance. This type of study must be completed for different users, including the people who maintain a facility with considerations for special conditions, such as accommodating those in wheelchairs or children. Dimensions must be considered not only in regard to the limits of individual human bodies, but also in regard to such diverse conditions as clearances for shopping carts at a market, clearances for a person lying down, climbing stairs, squatting, and even kneeling at church.

A sampling of these dimensions can be found in Figures 4.51, 4.52, and 4.53. For a more comprehensive discussion of such dimensions, see the general planning and design data section of *Architectural Graphic Standards*, published by John Wiley & Sons in conjunction with the American Institute of Architects.

However, it should be noted that special studies are performed continually for specific building types such as hospitals, research centers, the service bays of automobile agencies, and so on. It would be helpful to explore the Internet to study people adjusting in their leisure environments as well as in their work environments, and the science of how people adapt to their environments— ergonomics.

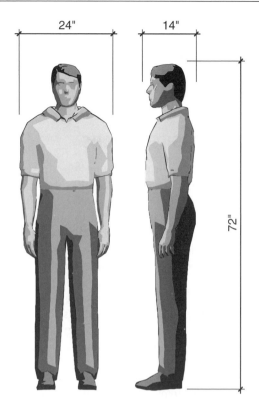

Male : Avg. Width, Depth & Height

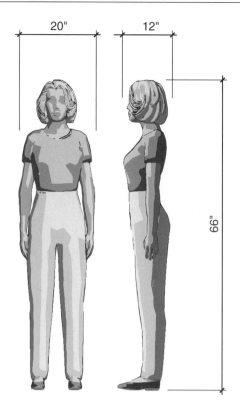

Female : Avg. Width, Depth & Height

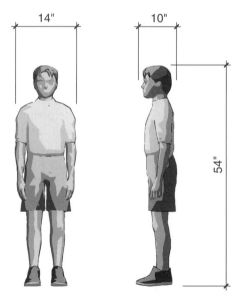

Child : Avg. Width, Depth & Height

Figure 4.51 Understanding the human figure.

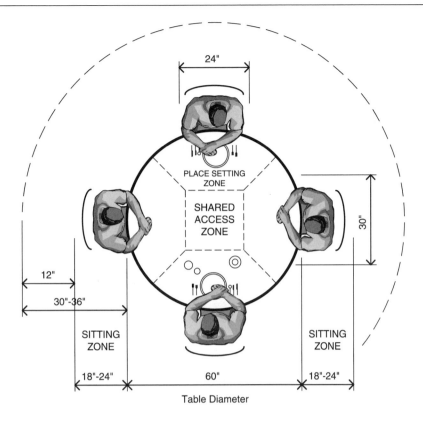

60" Diameter Circular Table for Four / Optimum Seating

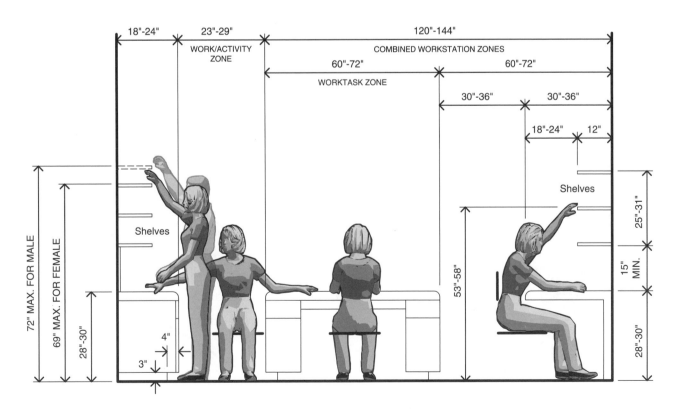

Desk and Workstation Considerations with Shelves

Figure 4.52 Reach.

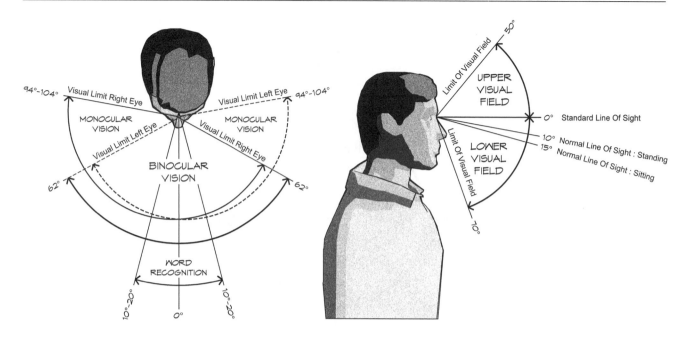

Visual Field in Horizontal Plane   Visual Field in Vertical Plane

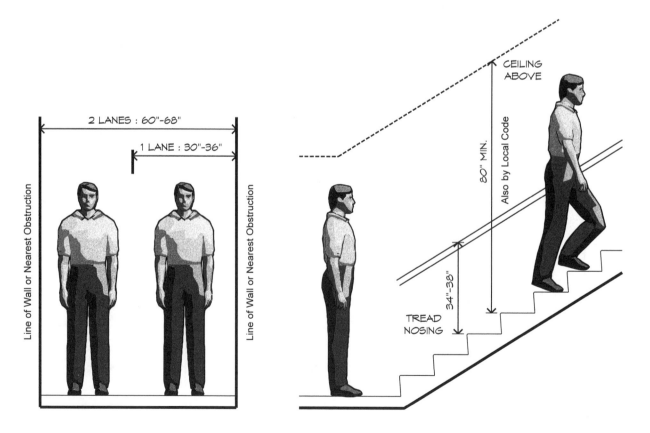

Circulation / Corridors and Passages   General Stair Dimensions

Figure 4.53   Space relative to sight and movement.

■ PUBLIC BUILDING ACCESSIBILITY

The Americans with Disabilities Act (ADA) is a result of legislation for the protection of persons with disabilities. The ADA is a civil rights law—not a building code. This law is divided into four major titles that prohibit discrimination against those who are disabled: Title I, Employment; Title II, Public Services and Transportation; Title III, Public Accommodations; and Title IV, Telecommunications. For the purpose of building design and construction detailing, this chapter discusses Title III, Public Accommodations, and provides graphic illustrations depicting required methods to accommodate the necessary tasks of persons who are disabled in public buildings.

To offer greater accessibility and better accommodations in public buildings for those with disabilities, various representatives of organizations for disabled persons have worked with federal agency officials to establish recommended requirements. These requirements have been compiled in a list of elements that will be of concern to you as you prepare drawings and details to satisfy the various recommended design criteria:

1. Path of travel—exterior accessibility route to the facility
2. Accessible parking
3. Curb ramps
4. Entrances
5. Interior access route
6. Ramps
7. Stairs
8. Elevators
9. Platform lifts
10. Doors
11. Drinking fountains
12. Toilet rooms and bathrooms
13. Water closets
14. Urinals
15. Lavatories and mirrors
16. Sinks
17. Bathtubs
18. Shower stalls
19. Grab bars
20. Tub/shower seats
21. Assembly areas
22. Storage
23. Alarms
24. Signage
25. Public telephones
26. Seating and tables
27. Automatic teller machines
28. Dressing and fitting rooms

There are also recommendations for special applications that apply to the following buildings:

A. Restaurants and cafeterias
B. Medical care facilities
C. Business and mercantile facilities
D. Libraries
E. Transient lodging facilities

Design Elements. The following paragraphs discuss several examples that are applicable to elements derived from the building codes and from representatives and officials of various agencies. The accompanying figures graphically depict the necessary dimensional spaces and other requirements that you will need to plan for in order to accommodate those with disabilities.

Curb Ramps and Parking Stalls. Figure 4.54 illustrates a curb ramp detail, one example of providing an accessible exterior route of travel to a specific facility. For specific buildings, the required number of parking spaces for those with disabilities is determined by the total number of spaces provided for that facility. This determination is based on ratios of the cars required. An example of ratios for handicapped parking may be 2 handicap spaces for 80 required spaces. The planning of a parking space for those with disabilities is illustrated in Figure 4.55. Note that there are provisions for a marked access aisle, a curb ramp, a handicapped parking sign, and a parking surface handicapped symbol. Figure 4.56 depicts separately the freestanding handicapped sign and the parking surface handicapped symbol. In most municipalities a severe fine is imposed on nondisabled persons who use these parking facilities.

Ramps. Another way of providing exterior accessibility to a facility is through the use of ramps. Ramps have

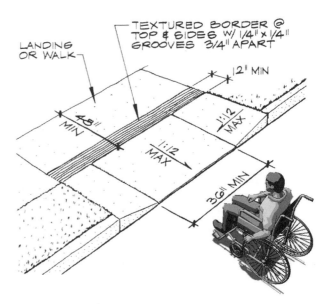

Figure 4.54 Curb ramp.

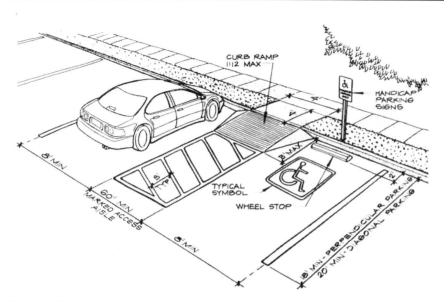

Figure 4.55 Parking spaces.

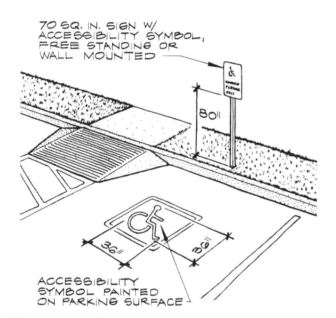

Figure 4.56 Parking sign and symbol.

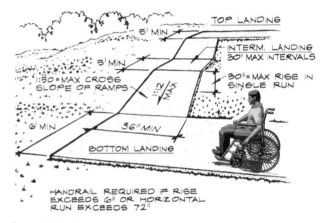

Figure 4.57 Ramp.

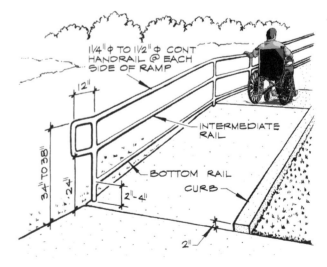

Figure 4.58 Ramp handrail.

proven to be a desirable method to ensure accessibility when there are grade changes in a path of travel to a building. Figure 4.57 illustrates an example of an acceptable ramp with various changes in levels. Handrails are required on both sides of a ramp if the rise exceeds 6 inches or the horizontal projection exceeds 72 inches. If handrails are required, they will have to be drawn and detailed in accordance with the recommended requirements. Figure 4.58 depicts handrail requirements for the ramp shown in Figure 4.57.

Wheelchair Space Requirements

In cases where there are no specific rules for a particular planning situation, it is prudent for the architect or designer to be aware of the space requirements needed for the maneuverability of someone using a wheelchair. Figures 4.59 through 4.63 illustrate some examples of floor space areas and reaching dimensions that are desirable for those who function from a wheelchair.

Locations for Controls and Shelving. As shown in Figures 4.59 and 4.63, there are dimensional limitations in various directions for a person using a wheelchair. Therefore, controls such as thermostats, window controls, electric switches, pullcords, convenience outlets, and so forth, will have to be located within the required reach limitations. Figure 4.64 illustrates such controls. Another con-

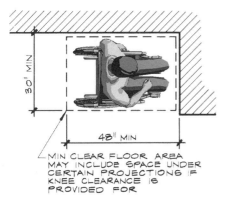

Figure 4.59 Wheelchair space requirements.

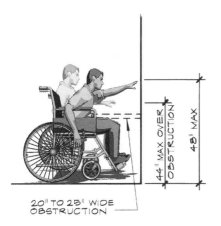

Figure 4.60 Wheelchair space requirements.

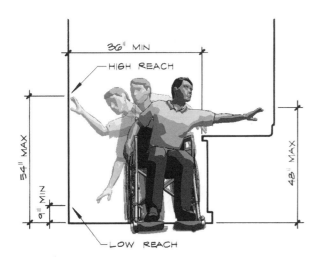

Figure 4.61 Wheelchair space requirements.

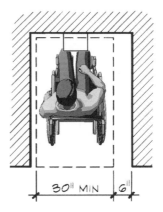

Figure 4.62 Wheelchair space requirements.

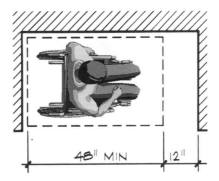

Figure 4.63 Wheelchair space requirements.

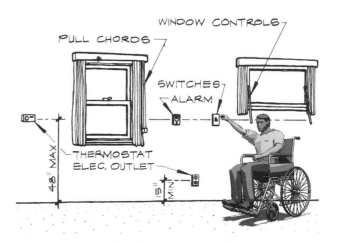

Figure 4.64 Control heights.

cern in regard to reach limitations is accessibility to bookshelves that are found in educational and library facilities. Figure 4.65 illustrates maximum shelf heights and passage dimensions for various types of aisles.

Doors and Doorways. The maneuvering capabilities of a person in a wheelchair when dealing with accessibility in regard to doors and doorways will be determined by minimum required floor plan dimensions. An example of a floor plan configuration involving a door and doorway access is depicted in Figure 4.66. Note that the door clearance does not include the door thickness nor any hardware. Door-swing direction in access corridors will be dictated by required minimum clearances for maneuvering a wheelchair to access doors. If building code requirements specify that certain doors have to swing

into corridors, then corridor dimensions may have to be adjusted to satisfy wheelchair clearances. Figure 4.67 illustrates two examples of door-swing directions that affect the dimensional width of a corridor.

Access doors and the various hardware assemblies required for their functioning must meet certain requirements. For example, the selection of door handle hardware will be regulated to a lever-type U-shaped handle with a minimum and maximum dimensional location above the floor. The slopes and heights of door thresholds will have to satisfy accessibility requirements. An illustration of hardware for door handles and an example of an acceptable threshold is shown in Figure 4.68.

Drinking Fountains. When planning drinking fountain locations, the architect or designer will have to be aware of minimum required dimensions for recessed or projected installation of drinking fountains. Figure 4.69 provides a view of these two types of installation, illustrating dimensional clearances as well as the maximum height to the spout and clearance for knee space.

Plumbing Facility Requirements. An important facet of the building design process is the provision of accessible plumbing facilities in order to accommodate people with disabilities. These facilities, which include such fixtures as water closets, lavatories, and urinals, are planned to ensure accessibility for those who have disabilities. First of all, a floor plan is designed, providing the minimum required space clearances and accessibility to specific plumbing fixtures. Figure 4.70 illustrates an overall pictorial view of a proposed restroom facility in-

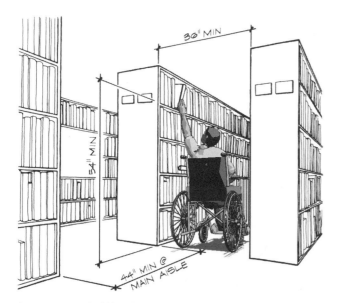

Figure 4.65 Shelf heights.

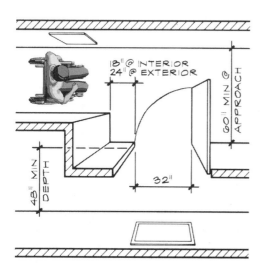

Figure 4.66 Doorway maneuvering clearances.

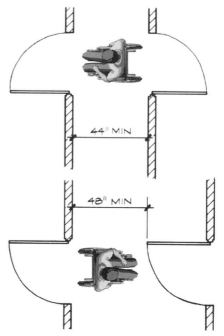

Figure 4.67 Doorway maneuvering clearances.

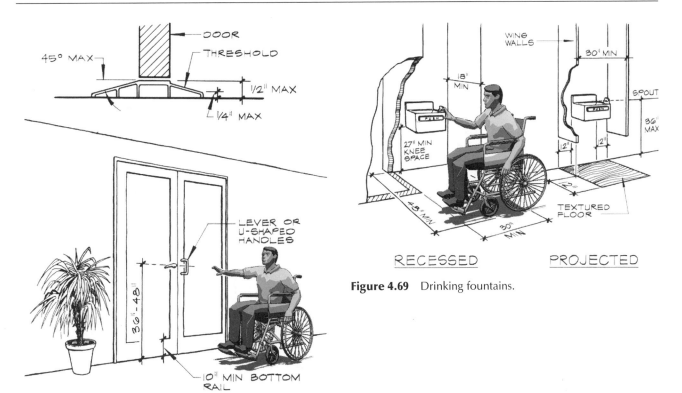

Figure 4.68 Threshold and door hardware.

Figure 4.69 Drinking fountains.

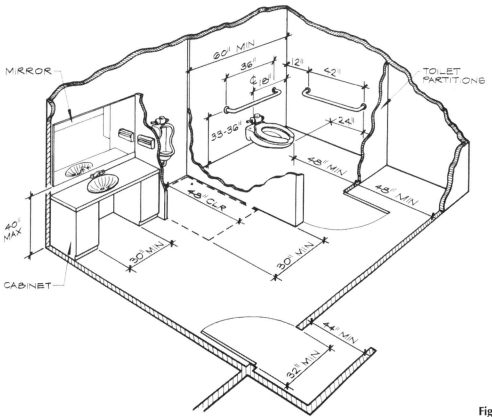

Figure 4.70 Restroom facilities.

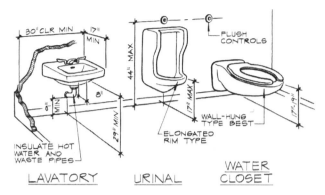

Figure 4.71   Plumbing fixtures.

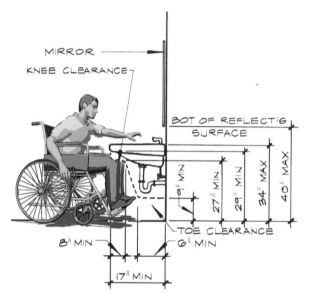

Figure 4.72   Lavatory access.

corporating minimum access clearances for the various plumbing fixtures. Note the required grab bar sizes and locations relative to the water closet. The installation of the various plumbing fixtures is regulated with reference to their dimensional height above the floor, side wall clearances, and knee and toe spaces for the use of lava-

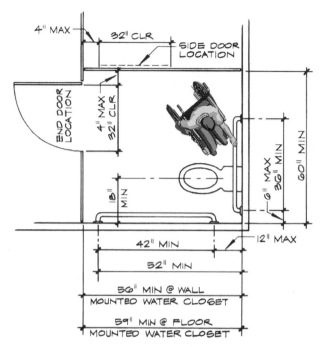

Figure 4.73   Toilet compartment plan.

tories. Figure 4.71 provides pictorial views of a lavatory, water closet, and urinal, illustrating fixture heights and clearances. Note that hot water and drain pipes are required to be insulated in order to protect against contact. Lavatory clearances are most important, because the knee will project under the lavatory fixture and will therefore require additional clearance. To provide a clearer illustration of the required clearances beneath the lavatory, see Figure 4.72. In planning for accessibility to the toilet compartments, the location of the door to the compartment will dictate the required fixture layout. Figure 4.73 shows an example of a toilet compartment plan, illustrating optional door locations.

These illustrations are examples of the elements within a public building that the architect or designer must plan for in order to accommodate people with disabilities.

chapter

5

CONSTRUCTION METHODS AND MATERIALS

Building construction incorporates various building systems, materials, and construction principles. These systems, materials, and principles are generally selected for the following reasons:

1. The type and use of the proposed structure
2. Governing building code requirements
3. Design and planning solutions
4. Structural concepts
5. Economical considerations
6. Environmental influences
7. Energy requirements

The primary materials utilized in construction systems are the following:

1. Wood —sawn lumber and engineered lumber
2. Concrete
3. Structural steel and light steel framing
4. Masonry
5. Composite systems with a combination of materials

The use of one or more of the aforementioned materials for a proposed building may be predicated on reasons such as building code requirements or the building occupancy; architectural design; energy and climatic conditions; and the influence of natural forces, including high winds, earthquakes, infestation, and wetness. The primary components of construction systems include the foundation and floor systems, and the wall and roof systems.

■ WOOD FLOOR SYSTEMS

Sawn Lumber Floor Joist System

The most conventional wood floor systems use sawn lumber floor joists as the supporting structural members. For a single-story residence, these members may be 2″ × 6″ or 2″ × 8″ in dimension. The dimensions will depend on the amount of load and the span of the joists. Plywood of varying thickness is used as a subfloor for supporting the finish floor material. The spacing of the floor joist is usually 16″ on centers. The structural members are supported by the exterior perimeter concrete foundation walls, and the intermediate supports in the interior include the concrete foundation walls and/or wood girders and concrete piers. An example of a foundation plan for a single-story residence using a sawn lumber wood floor joist for its floor system is illustrated in Figure 5.1. Note that a concrete foundation wall and wood girders with concrete piers are used as the interior support for the floor joist members.

Generally, the advantages of utilizing a sawn lumber floor joist system are:

1. Greater span length relative to the size of the joist
2. Requires fewer internal supporting walls and girders

3. Capable of providing floor joist cantilevers.
4. The ability to provide insulation material between the joist members

The major disadvantages of a sawn lumber floor joist system are:

1. Termite infestation and dry rot in regions that are highly susceptible to these conditions
2. For buildings that require a minimum amount of noise transmission
3. In buildings desiring a lower silhouette and the absence of under-floor vents

Construction Principles
1. Ensure that the wood members are not in direct contact with the concrete.
2. Provide recommended under-floor clearances from the soil.
3. Select floor joist sizes that will deter deflection or floor movement.
4. Provide proper metal flashing to protect wood members from possible moisture.
5. Provide recommended under-floor ventilation.

Detail ①, as designated on the foundation plan in Figure 5.1, illustrates an isometric drawing of an exterior concrete foundation wall utilizing a wood floor joist and a plywood subfloor. Note the exterior foundation vent for the under-floor ventilation. This detail is shown in Figure 5.2.

Internal Load-Bearing Foundation. Internal load-bearing foundation assemblies are designed to support heavy loads from the floor system, load-bearing walls, and ceiling and roof loads. Such a foundation assembly may be designed as a concrete wall and footing similar to that in Figure 5.2, or with the use of wood girders and concrete piers. The size of the wood girders and the spacing of the concrete piers are predicated on the amount of structural loading they are required to support. Whenever possible, it is recommended that the wood girders be located directly beneath the load-bearing wall. It is good practice not to extend floor joists to their maximum span, because this approach may cause deflection or movement in the floor system. It is also good practice to add additional rows of girders and piers to provide a stiffer floor system. Figure 5.3 shows an isometric drawing of an internal pier and wood girder assembly. Note the required solid blocking between the floor joist and its placement directly above the girder, and under the wall partition. This is a recommended construction procedure to provide blocking between the joist at all supports, and when possible, under the wall partitions.

Moisture Protection. As mentioned in the list of construction principles for a wood floor system, it is paramount to provide protection for wood members against

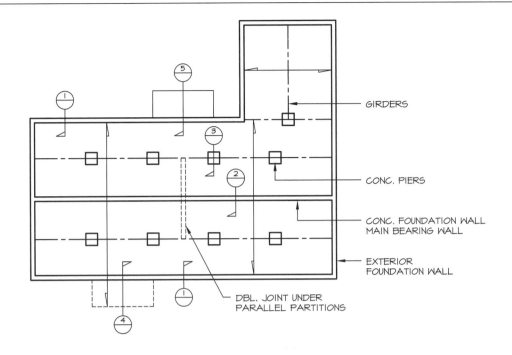

GIRDERS

CONC. PIERS

CONC. FOUNDATION WALL
MAIN BEARING WALL

EXTERIOR
FOUNDATION WALL

DBL. JOINT UNDER
PARALLEL PARTITIONS

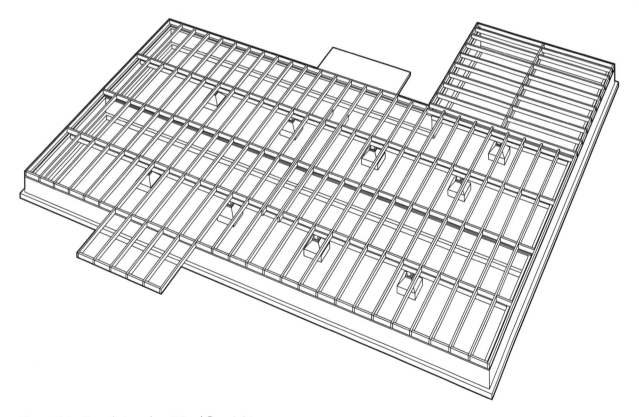

Figure 5.1   Foundation plan: Wood floor joist.

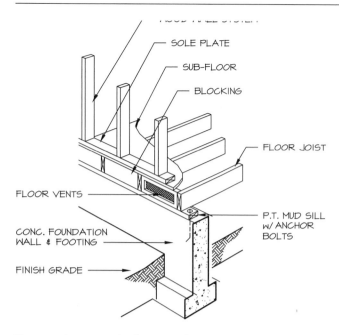

Figure 5.2 Pictorial of exterior foundation wall with wood floor joist.

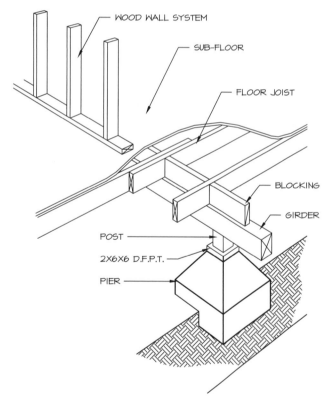

Figure 5.3 Internal pier and girder assembly.

moisture. Moisture infiltration can cause dry rot, swelling, and buckling of wood members. One method of deterring moisture is to provide an adequate sheet metal flashing system in areas subject to water seepage.

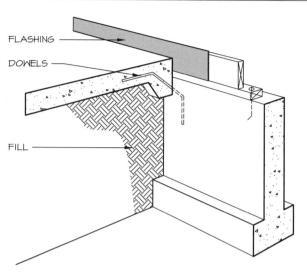

Figure 5.4 Flashing assembly (porch slab and wood floor).

Detail ⑤ in Figure 5.1 illustrates, in an isometric drawing, a recommended sheet metal flashing assembly positioned between a concrete porch and a wood floor system. The drawing is depicted in Figure 5.4.

Wood Plank Floor System

Another wood floor system frequently used is called tongue-and-groove planking. This system utilizes $2'' \times 6''$ or $2'' \times 8''$ wide wood members. These members, with high stress capabilities, are used to span over wood girders and concrete foundation walls. This system requires additional rows of girders and piers because the spans for the 2″ planking is generally limited to spans from 4′ to 5′.

Figure 5.5 illustrates a wood floor system for a one-story residence utilizing 2″ tongue-and-groove planking for structural support. It is recommended that plywood be applied directly over the 2″ planking members for the purpose of providing a subbase for the finish floor materials, as well as developing a tie between the various members. Whenever possible, it is recommended that concrete foundation walls and/or girders be positioned directly under paralleling walls. When bearing walls are parallel with the planking members, it will be necessary to provide a 4″ thick wood girder in the floor system for support. The depth of the girder is governed by the load factor from the wall above and other load-carrying members. Note the bearing cross wall member in Figure 5.5 that will be installed for the support of the load-bearing wall. An isometric drawing depicting the exterior foundation wall for the tongue-and-groove floor system is shown in Figure 5.6.

The advantages of using a tongue-and-groove floor system are as follows:

1. Provides a stiffer floor with the recommended spacing of girders

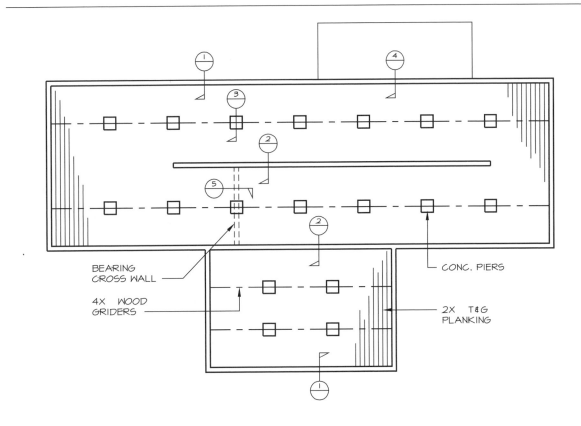

BEARING
CROSS WALL

4X WOOD
GRIDERS

CONC. PIERS

2X T&G
PLANKING

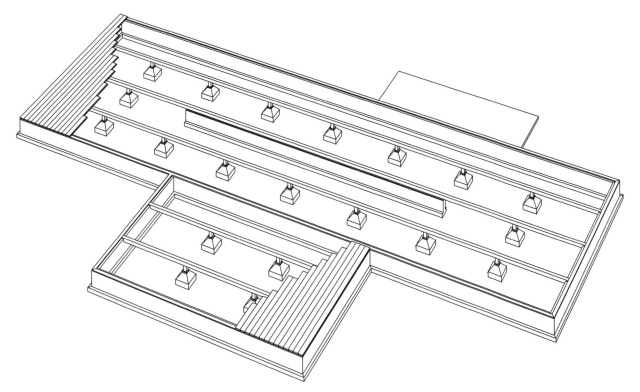

Figure 5.5 Foundation plan: 2″ thick tongue-and-groove planking.

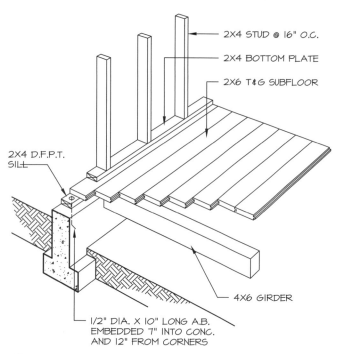

2X4 STUD @ 16" O.C.

2X4 BOTTOM PLATE

2X6 T&G SUBFLOOR

2X4 D.F.P.T. SILL

4X6 GIRDER

1/2" DIA. X 10" LONG A.B. EMBEDDED 7" INTO CONC. AND 12" FROM CORNERS

Figure 5.6 Exterior foundation wall with 2" tongue-and-groove planking.

2. Provides a lower building height silhouette because the added height of the floor joists has been eliminated
3. Has a lower noise factor than a wood floor system
4. Provides a more rigid subfloor for finish floor materials such as ceramic or concrete tiles when they are applied directly on top
5. Availability of tongue-and-groove planking in greater thickness, which can be used when longer spans are required

The disadvantages of using a tongue-and-groove floor system are as follows:

1. Shorter spans will require additional foundation walls, girders, and piers.
2. This system is not conducive to the use of floor cantilevers.
3. The system will be exposed to termite infestation and dry rot in regions subject to these problems.
4. The system does not allow the development of floor beams. A conventional floor joist system may combine a number of floor joists for the purpose of creating a structural beam.
5. The system does not provide space for blanket insulation.

Engineered Lumber Wood Floor System

The use of engineered lumber floor joists has proven to be very successful as a wood floor system. Engineered

floor joists have been approved by all major building codes.

To illustrate the structural capabilities of this floor joist system, the foundation plan illustrated in Figure 5.1 provides a comparison of the span lengths between a sawn lumber floor joist and an engineered lumber floor joist. Two rows of girders and piers have been eliminated from the foundation plan in Figure 5.7 because of the ability of the engineered lumber joist to provide greater strength and load-bearing capacity than sawn lumber. Other engineered lumber wood members that may be used in a wood floor system are girders and floor beams. These members are developed and fabricated with the use of laminated veneer lumber. The laminated members provide a high allowable bearing stress that is accepted by all major building codes and are consistent in size and performance. They also reduce the problems of splitting, warping, and checking. The size of these members may range from 1½" to 7" in thickness and standard depths may range from 7¼" to 24".

An example of the aforementioned engineered lumber joist, illustrating its shape and fabrication components, is shown as an isometric drawing in Figure 5.8. Sizes and structural capabilities will vary with the manufacturers of engineered lumber.

Figure 5.9 depicts a three-dimensional drawing segment of the foundation plan in Figure 5.7, showing the concrete footing, engineered lumber floor joist, engineered plywood subfloor, and wood stud walls.

The advantages of using an engineered lumber wood floor joist system are as follows:

1. Floor joist sizes are uniform.
2. The light weight allows for easier handling on the job.
3. The problems of splitting, checking, warping, and crowns are eliminated.
4. The system has greater structural capabilities.

The disadvantages of using an engineered lumber wood floor joist system are as follows:

1. There are limitations for cutting the members in the framing process.
2. There are restrictions on the location of cutting holes in the web sections.
3. Proper care must be taken to protect these joists prior to installation.
4. The system creates a higher building silhouette because of the depth of the smallest joist.

■ WOOD WALL SYSTEMS

The two most conventional types of wood stud wall framing systems used in construction are the balloon framing system and the Western or platform-framing sys-

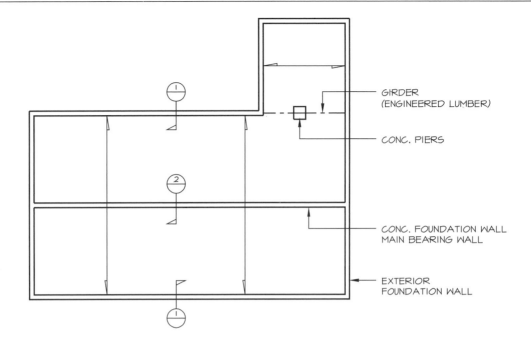

GIRDER
(ENGINEERED LUMBER)

CONC. PIERS

CONC. FOUNDATION WALL
MAIN BEARING WALL

EXTERIOR
FOUNDATION WALL

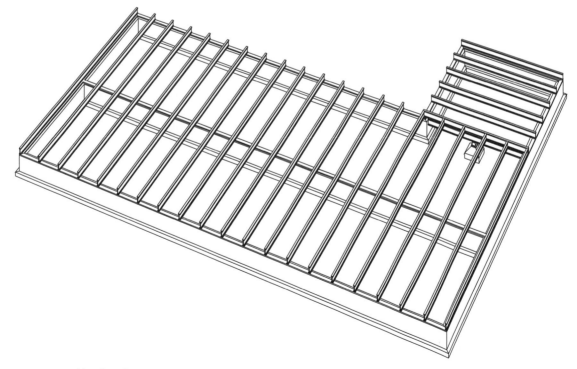

Figure 5.7 Engineered lumber floor joist.

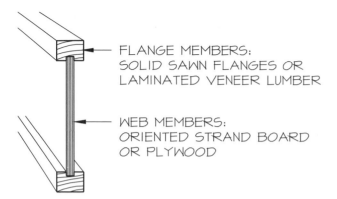

Figure 5.8   Engineered lumber floor joist.

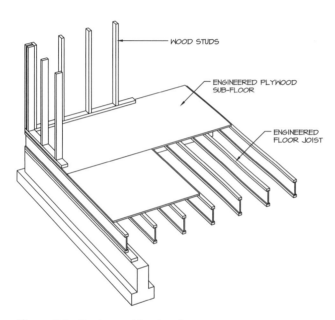

Figure 5.9   Engineered lumber floor system.

tem. The main differences between these two systems are in the construction methods used for the walls and the floor assembly.

Balloon Framing

In the construction of two-story structures, the balloon framing system uses continuous wall studs from the first floor level up to the roof assembly. The second floor supporting members are then framed to the continuous studs. Stud sizes are 2″ × 4″ or 2″ × 6″ at 16″ center to center. Two-inch blocking is fitted to fill all openings to provide fire stops and prevent drafts from one space to another.

Wood or metal members are attached securely at a 45° angle to the top and bottom of the studs and provide hor-

izontal bracing for the walls. In areas subjected to strong lateral forces, plywood shear panels are used for horizontal bracing. The use of plywood panels may be determined by the governing building code or the structural engineering requirements. This system has a minimum amount of vertical shrinkage and vertical movement and may be used with brick veneer or cement plaster exterior finishes. Figure 5.10 illustrates an isometric view of an exterior wall section for this system. It also shows solid sheathing on the exterior walls, in which case its use will be determined according to the region, the building code, and the exterior material that has been selected.

Western or Platform Framing

Western or platform framing uses a different procedure. The lower floor walls are assembled first. Then the supporting floor members and subfloor for the upper floor are framed. The upper subfloor and floor joist provide a platform for assembling the upper floor walls, ceiling joist, and roof framing. The walls are framed with 2 × 4 or 2 × 6 studs at 16″ center to center. Required blocking is 2″ thick and is fitted to prevent drafts between spaces and to provide stiffness to the joist.

Solid sheathing, diagonal braces, or plywood panels may provide lateral bracing. Building code requirements, regional differences, and structural engineering calculations may determine the type of lateral bracing. Figure 5.11 shows an isometric drawing of a wall section using Western framing.

Post and Beam Framing

A third method for framing wood structures is the post and beam system. Less common than platform and balloon framing, this method uses a post and beam spacing that allows the builder to use 2″ roof or floor planking. Figure 5.12 compares this system with more conventional framing systems. For the best use of this system you should establish a specific module of plank-and-beam spacing for planning. Supplementary framing is placed on the exterior walls, with options similar to those used in conventional framing systems.

Planking

The term *planking* is used to refer to members that have a minimum depth of 2″ and a width of 6″ to 8″. The edges of these members are normally tongue and groove. Using such edges enables a continuous joining of members so that a concentrated load is distributed onto the adjacent members. Figure 5.13 illustrates a commonly used planking with tongue-and-groove edges. You must provide a positive connection between the post and beam and secure the post to the floor. Different types of metal framing

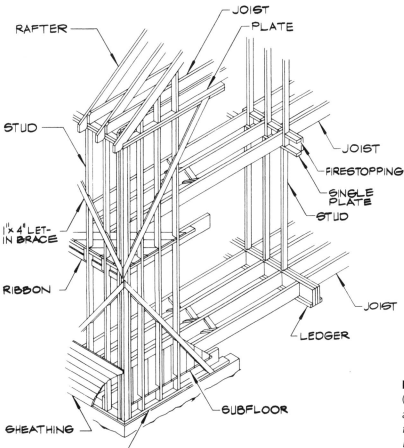

RAFTER

JOIST

PLATE

STUD

JOIST

FIRESTOPPING

SINGLE PLATE

STUD

1"x 4" LET-IN BRACE

RIBBON

JOIST

LEDGER

SUBFLOOR

SHEATHING

SILL

Figure 5.10 Balloon frame construction. (Courtesy of National Forest Products Association. Reprinted by permission from *The Professional Practice of Architectural Working Drawings*, 2d Ed., © 1995 by John Wiley & Sons, Inc.)

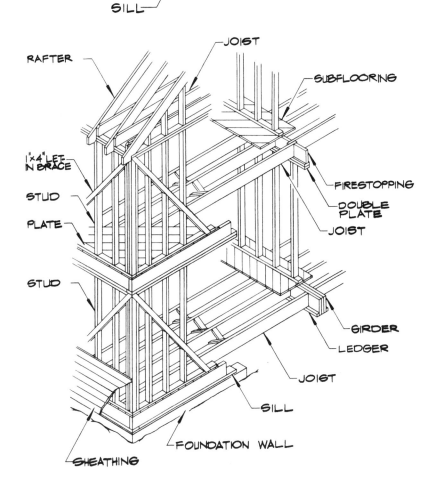

RAFTER

JOIST

SUBFLOORING

1"x 4" LET-IN BRACE

STUD

PLATE

FIRESTOPPING

DOUBLE PLATE

JOIST

STUD

GIRDER

LEDGER

JOIST

SILL

FOUNDATION WALL

SHEATHING

Figure 5.11 Western or platform framing. (Courtesy of National Forest Products Association. Reprinted by permission from *The Professional Practice of Architectural Working Drawings*, 2d Ed., © 1995 by John Wiley & Sons, Inc.)

PLANK-AND-BEAM
FRAMING

CONVENTIONAL
FRAMING

COMPARISON OF PLANK-
AND-BEAM SYSTEM
WITH CONVENTIONAL
FRAMING

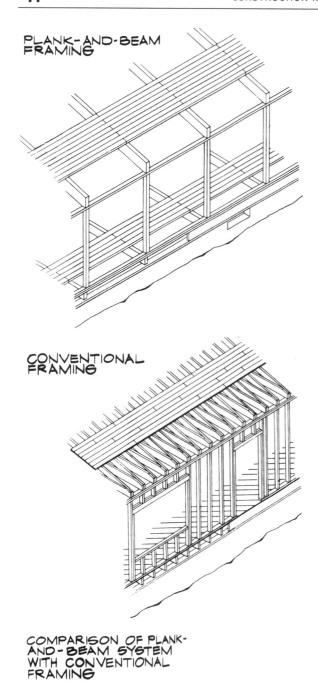

Figure 5.12 Pictorial comparison of plank and beam with conventional framing. (Courtesy of National Forest Products Association. Reprinted by permission from *The Professional Practice of Architectural Working Drawings*, 2d Ed., © 1995 by John Wiley & Sons, Inc.)

connectors may be used to satisfy these connections. If metal framing connectors are undesirable for aesthetic reasons, then steel dowels may be utilized at the post-to-beam connection and the post-to-floor connection. Examples of a doweled post-to-beam connection and a post-to-floor connection are shown in Figures 5.14 and

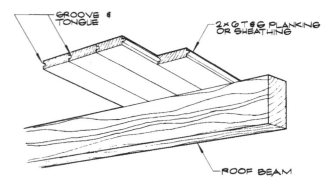

Figure 5.13 Pictorial of roof planking. (Reprinted by permission from *The Professional Practice of Architectural Working Drawings*, 2d Ed., © 1995 by John Wiley & Sons, Inc.)

5.15. Because fewer pieces are used in this system, special attention to post-to-beam connections and connections to other members should be given in detailing these conditions. With proper detailing, such connections will securely fasten components of the building together and act as a unit to resist any external forces.

Engineered Lumber Wall System Panels

Engineered lumber sheathing panels are used in wood stud wall construction to strengthen and stabilize exterior and interior walls. Engineered sheathing panels used for exterior walls should be protected with building paper, wood siding, or other types of exterior cladding to protect the panels from damage caused by water or other moisture conditions. These panels are fabricated in sizes ranging from 4' × 8' to 4' × 9' and 4' × 10'. Panel thickness can range from $3/8$" to $1 1/8$". A three-dimensional example of an engineered sheathing panel is illustrated in Figure 5.16.

■ WOOD ROOF SYSTEMS

The principles underlying wood roof systems, and the construction methods used in developing these systems, may depend on the finish roof material and the requirements of its application. The following are examples of finish roof materials used over roof framing systems:

1. Wood shingles or shakes
2. Asphalt shingles
3. Clay or concrete tiles
4. Built-up composition and gravel surface
5. Aluminum or copper

Wood Roof System Utilizing Sawn Lumber

Traditionally, sawn lumber members of various dimensions have been used for the construction of wood roof

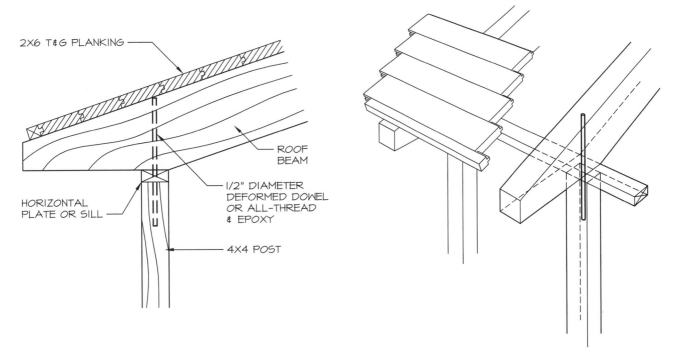

Figure 5.14 Post-to-beam connection.

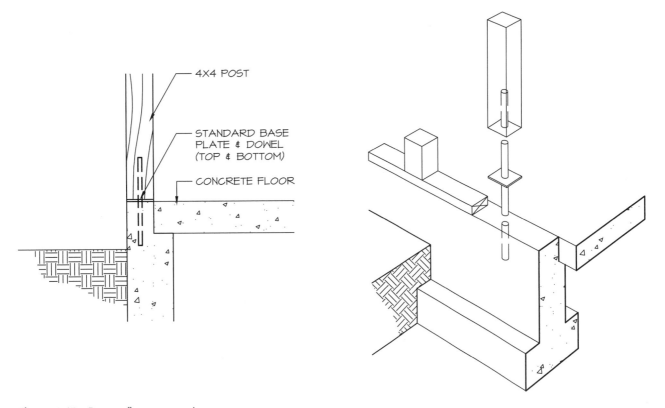

Figure 5.15 Post-to-floor connection.

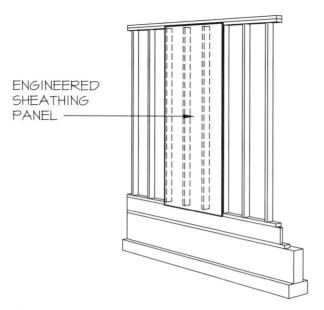

ENGINEERED
SHEATHING
PANEL ——

Figure 5.16   Engineered sheathing panel.

Plank-and-Beam and Heavy Timber Roof Systems

The plank-and-beam roof system is utilized in residential and commercial structures. This system uses heavy wood beam members greater than 2″ in thickness to support roof planking with a minimum of 2″ in thickness and the finish roofing material. The main supporting wood beam members normally have a modular spacing such as 6′ to 8′ on centers. The spacing of these members is determined by the weight of the finish roofing materials. In general, the architect selects this system where he or she wishes to expose the roof structural system for reasons of aesthetics or to meet building code requirements. For roof structural members that need to satisfy heavy timber construction requirements for most building codes, the roof planking must have a thickness of not less than 2″

systems. Utilizing these members can provide more on-the-job flexibility for roof systems because members can be cut and fitted to varying conditions that may occur during the roof framing stage. Members such as required blocking, bracing members, studs, plates, and others are used to fit the job site conditions. An example of sawn lumber roof framing is shown three dimensionally in Figure 5.17. The use of sawn lumber members affords the architect greater latitude in designing the external projections of a roof system, including eave and rake designs. Examples of eave designs are illustrated in Figures 5.18 and 5.19. Further information and illustrations dealing with wood roof framing methods are provided in Chapter 14.

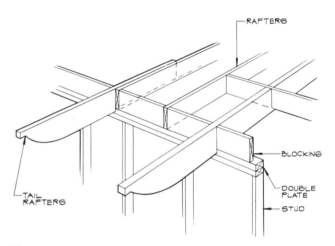

Figure 5.18   Pictorial, eave detail. (Reprinted by permission from *The Professional Practice of Architectural Working Drawings*, 2d Ed., © 1995 by John Wiley & Sons, Inc.)

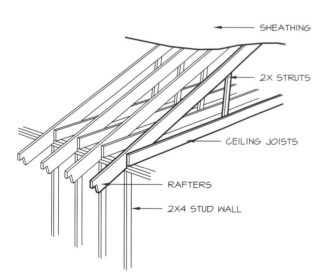

Figure 5.17   Sawn lumber roof system.

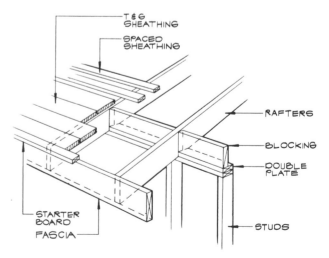

Figure 5.19   Pictorial, eave detail. (Reprinted by permission from *The Professional Practice of Architectural Working Drawings*, 2d Ed., © 1995 by John Wiley & Sons, Inc.)

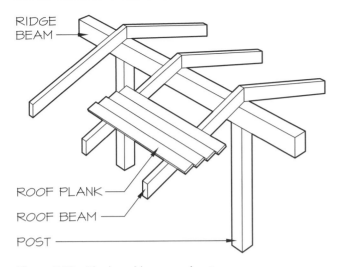

Figure 5.20   Plank-and-beam roof system.

and must provide a tongue-and-groove or splined connection. The size requirements for the main supporting members must not be less than 4″ in width and not less than 6″ in depth. All supporting wood columns must not be less than 8″ in any dimension. A three-dimensional drawing depicting the main supporting members for a heavy timber plank-and-beam roof system is shown in Figure 5.20.

Wood Truss Roof System

Wood roof trusses are available in many sizes, shapes, and lengths. Wood roof trusses are generally fabricated by a manufacturer and delivered to the building site. Trusses are selected according to the manufacturer's stip-

ulated engineered design criteria for the various weights of materials that the trusses need to support. One method of utilizing a wood truss roof system is to place the trusses on a dimensional module spacing that allows the intermediate roof supporting members to span the trusses. An example of a fabricated wood truss supporting intermediate roof members is illustrated three dimensionally in Figure 5.21.

Panelized Wood Roof System

A panelized wood roof system is a construction method whereby plywood roof sheathing panels and intermediate supporting members are prefabricated in a manufacturing plant. Generally, the size of these panels is 4′ × 8′ because this is the standard dimension for plywood sheets. The thickness of the plywood sheathing is governed by the structural engineer's specifications. The supporting intermediate members of the plywood are generally 2″ × 4″ placed at 24″ center to center. Once the panels are fabricated, they are lifted and placed within the 4′ × 8′ module dimensions of the roof's main supporting members. The panels are attached to the main and intermediate supporting members with the metal framing connectors. The main supporting members may be glu-laminated beams, and intermediate members have a minimum thickness of 4″. This roof framing system is generally used in the construction of industrial and manufacturing buildings. Figure 5.22 shows a three-dimensional drawing depicting the installation of a prefabricated panel that fits within the modular spacing of the main and intermediate supporting members.

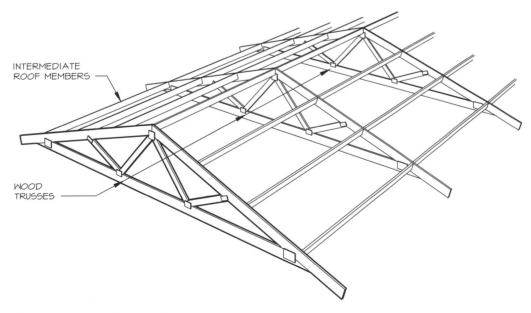

Figure 5.21   Wood truss roof system.

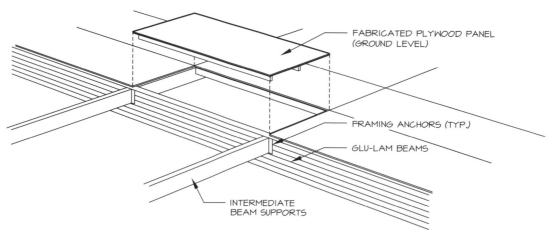

Figure 5.22   Panelized wood roof system.

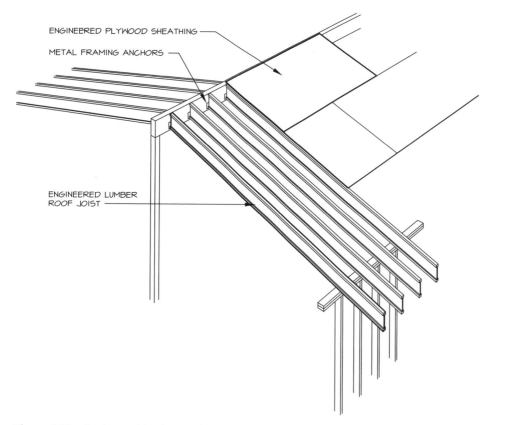

Figure 5.23   Engineered lumber roof system.

Engineered Lumber Roof System

The use of engineered lumber members for roof rafters provides a straighter and stiffer frame for a wood roof system, which is also more consistent in size and shape. The shape and components of an engineered lumber member are shown in Figure 5.8. The structural capabilities of these members allows for the use of different types of roofing materials and can handle snow loading conditions. Roof pitches, when engineered lumber is used, may vary from a low pitch to a steep roof condition. The depth of these members may range from 9½″ to 16″, depending on the particular engineered lumber fabricator or manufacturer. A three-dimensional example of a portion of a roof framing system incorporating engineered lumber roof rafters is shown in Figure 5.23.

■ CONCRETE

Concrete Floor System on Grade

When concrete has been selected for a floor system on grade, factors influencing this selection may be the result of the following factors:

1. Acceptable soil conditions
2. Soundproofing requirements
3. Infestation conditions
4. Desire for a low building silhouette

There are two main types of concrete floors and foundation systems. One type is the monolithic system, also referred to as the one-pour system, in which the concrete floor and foundation are poured in one operation. The other system is referred to as the two-pour system. In this system the foundation walls and footings are poured first, followed by the concrete floor, which is poured separately.

These two systems differ in their construction methods. In the one-pour system, the trenches become the forms for the floor and foundation, as shown in Figure 5.24. For the two-pour system, formwork is required for the foundation wall and footing. A detail of a two-pour foundation wall, footing, and concrete floor is illustrated in Figure 5.25.

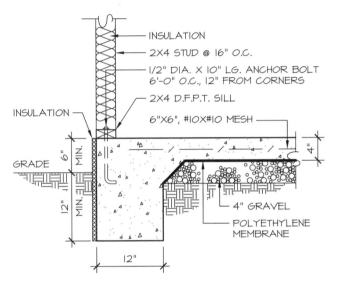

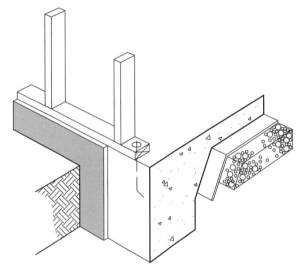

Figure 5.24 Detail of a one-pour footing and floor.

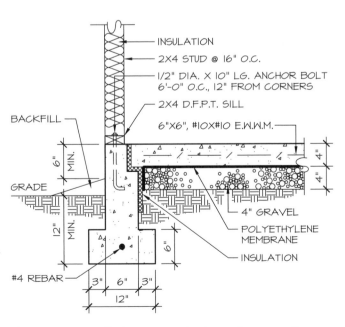

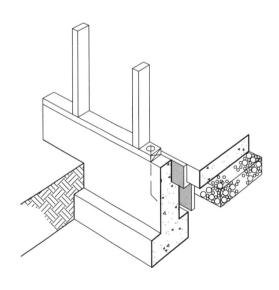

Figure 5.25 Detail of a two-pour footing and concrete floor.

Concrete Floor Steel Reinforcing

Just as a foundation needs to be strengthened with steel reinforcing, a concrete floor needs to be reinforced to prevent cracking. There are primarily two methods of reinforcing concrete floor systems on a grade. One method is to use welded wire mesh, which is usually made of number 10 gauge wires spaced 6″ apart in each direction. Another method of reinforcing a concrete floor is to use deformed steel reinforcing bars with the spacing in each direction recommended by a soils engineer. The designation of the size of reinforcing bars and spacing may be using number 4 bars at 18″ center to center in each direction. The use of deformed steel bars is preferred for most soil conditions. An example of one method of concrete floor reinforcing is depicted in Figure 5.26.

When confronted with having to hold two different pours of concrete together, such as a concrete porch slab and a main concrete floor, it is recommended that deformed steel dowels be used as the holding connection. These dowels may be number 4 bars at 18″ to 24″ cen-ter to center. An example of steel dowels holding a porch slab to the foundation of a structure is illustrated in Figure 5.27.

Concrete Floor Systems Above Grade

There are various types of construction methods for concrete floor systems that are used in above-grade and multilevel concrete floor construction. These concrete floors are erected with the use of various forming and steel reinforcing methods, with assemblies created on the job site in preparation of the concrete placement. One of these methods is referred to as a two-way flat slab. The formwork is completely flat. The concrete slab is reinforced in such a way that the varying stresses are accommodated within the uniform thickness of the slab. The concrete slab thickness may vary from 6″ to 12″ in depth. The depth, as well as the steel reinforcing, is determined by the consulting structural engineer. An example of a two-way flat slab with supporting concrete columns is depicted in Figure 5.28.

Another concrete floor system used in buildings is a two-way solid slab system. In this system, a solid flat slab is supported by a grid of concrete beams running in both directions over supporting concrete columns. In general, a flat slab concrete floor system is very economical because of the simplicity of the formwork. Figure 5.29 illustrates a section of a solid two-way concrete floor system with supporting concrete beams and columns. Steel reinforcing bars, which are not shown, will be incorporated in projects with recommendations from the structural engineer. These systems have limitations on the length of spans for the flat slab.

Precast Prestressed Concrete Systems

The use of precast prestressed concrete structural components for floor systems in buildings has many advan-

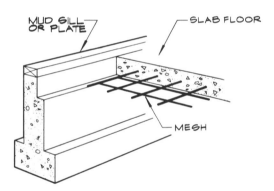

Figure 5.26 Concrete floor reinforcing. (Reprinted by permission from *The Professional Practice of Architectural Working Drawings*, 2d Ed., © 1995 by John Wiley & Sons, Inc.)

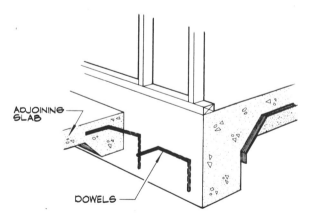

Figure 5.27 Use of steel dowels to tie porch slab to concrete floor. (Reprinted by permission from *The Professional Practice of Architectural Working Drawings*, 2d Ed., © 1995 by John Wiley & Sons, Inc.)

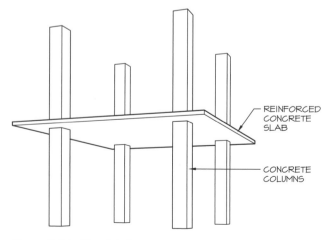

Figure 5.28 Flat slab floor system.

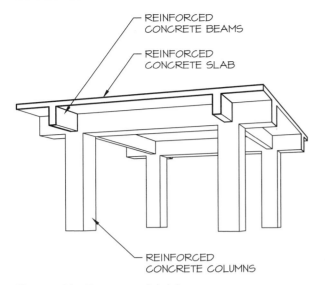

Figure 5.29 Two-way solid slab system.

tages over the use of concrete poured in place at the job site. Precast prestressed concrete components such as slabs, beams, girders, columns, and wall panels are manufactured at a precasting plant and delivered to the building site for erection. Precasting plants offer excellent quality control of materials and workmanship.

An example of a precast prestressed slab floor system utilizing a precast double-tee-shaped floor slab with support beam is illustrated in Figure 5.30. The thickness of the slab and the amount of steel reinforcing are dictated by the length of the span and the weight that will be loaded onto the floor. The solutions are dictated by the structural engineer's findings. Note in Figure 5.30 that the precast double tees are supported on steel-reinforced concrete walls.

Other examples of precast prestressed concrete floor system elements are illustrated in Figures 5.31, 5.32, and 5.33. Figure 5.31 shows a solid flat slab reinforced unit that will be lifted into place and supported by concrete beams and concrete columns. This type of precast slab is used for short span conditions.

Figure 5.32 illustrates a precast prestressed hollow-core slab panel. The hollow cores further reduce the dead weight of the concrete panel. These hollow-core slab panels are best suited for intermediate spans and can be supported by concrete beams and concrete columns. Figure 5.33 depicts a precast prestressed concrete single tee. This type of precast unit and the double tee unit are desirable for longer spans. The single tees are used less frequently than the double tees, because the single tee requires a temporary support to relieve tipping. The examples shown are some of the most commonly used pre-

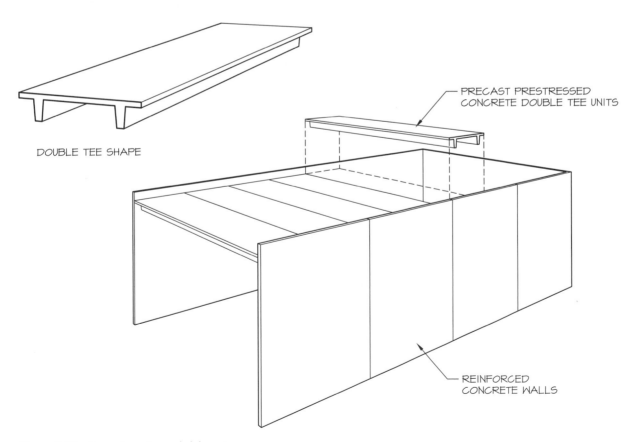

Figure 5.30 Precast prestressed slab system.

Figure 5.31   Precast prestressed solid flat slab.

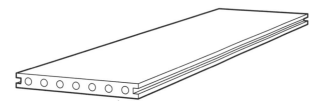

Figure 5.32   Precast prestressed hollow-core slab.

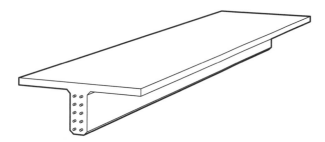

Figure 5.33   Precast prestressed concrete single tee.

cast prestressed concrete elements for floor systems. It should be noted that these concrete elements are also used for concrete roof systems.

Concrete Wall Systems

A commonly used concrete wall system that is poured in place is called a concrete retaining wall. As with most poured-in-place concrete walls, wood forms are constructed on both sides of the wall and tied together to resist the weight and force of the poured concrete. Steel reinforcing bars are required and are attached to the wood forms prior to the concrete being poured. A three-dimensional detail of a poured-in-place concrete retaining wall is illustrated in Figure 5.34. This method is required for poured-in-place concrete walls that are not retaining earth.

Concrete Tilt-Up Wall System

Structurally, tilt-up wall panels are used to support roof and floor loads and serve as shear walls to resist movement due to earthquakes and high wind conditions. Figure 5.35 is a conceptual drawing of the lifting and placement of concrete tilt-up wall panels as they are erected to become the exterior walls of a building.

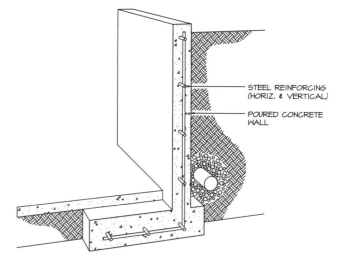

Figure 5.34   Poured-in-place concrete retaining wall.

A

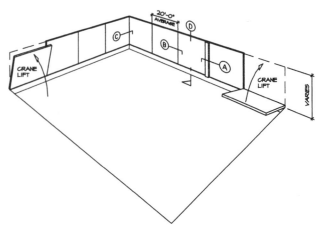

B

Figure 5.35   Tilt-up wall diagram. (Reprinted by permission from *Professional Practice of Architectural Detailing*, 3d Ed., © 1999 by John Wiley & Sons, Inc.)

Tilt-up wall construction is a precast construction method in which the wall panels are cast on the job site. In most cases the concrete floor of the building serves as the casting platform for the wall panels. The panels may be of high-strength concrete and relatively thin. Tilt-up construction is especially suitable for commercial and industrial structures.

Generally, fabrication of a tilt-up wall is accomplished with the use of wood forms, reinforcing steel, and a bond-breaker liquid suitable for the release of the precast panel from the casting platform. After the concrete meets the curing specifications, the panels are lifted into place by a mobile truck crane. This method of construction and the lifting technique are illustrated in Figures 5.36 and 5.37. A photograph of this erection sequence is shown in Figure 5.35A.

A detailed wall section for a two-story concrete tilt-up wall is illustrated in Figure 5.38. Note that a concrete pour strip is used to connect the wall and the casting slab after the tilt-up wall panel is erected.

Precast Concrete Wall System

A highly successful construction method for concrete walls is the use of precast concrete bearing and non-bearing walls. These walls are manufactured at a casting plant and delivered to the building site for erection. The walls may be cast with various openings in them, such as for doors and windows. The wall sizes and shapes vary, based on the designs of the architect and the structural engineer. Figure 5.39 depicts a precast concrete wall arrangement with the use of a precast concrete hollow-core floor system. Note that when wall openings are required, they may be incorporated into the internal and external planning. The connections for precast concrete elements, such as for walls, are dictated by the consult-

ing structural engineer's detail. A wall-to-floor connection (section A) is shown in Figure 5.40. This detail does not show the steel reinforcing and grouting required to connect the walls to the floor system for the structural integrity of the building. There are various methods to achieve the necessary structural requirements.

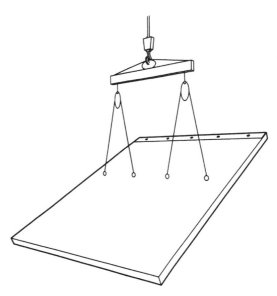

Figure 5.37 Tilt-up wall section. (Reprinted by permission from *Professional Practice of Architectural Detailing*, 3d Ed., © 1999 by John Wiley & Sons, Inc.)

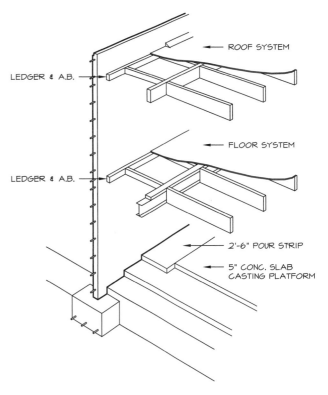

Figure 5.38 Concrete tilt-up wall.

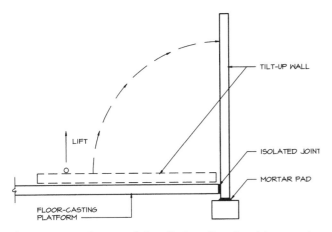

Figure 5.36 Tilt-up wall installation. (Reprinted by permission from *Professional Practice of Architectural Detailing*, 3d Ed., © 1999 by John Wiley & Sons, Inc.)

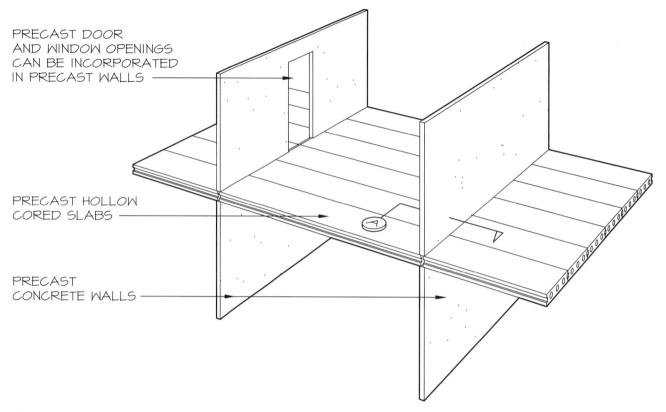

Figure 5.39 Precast concrete bearing walls.

Precast Concrete Roof System

The precast concrete elements used for a structural roof system are similar or identical to those used for precast concrete floor systems. This system is depicted in Figure 5.41, where precast hollow-core planks are supported and incorporated with the use of precast concrete bearing walls. Note that the haunch used to support the hollow-cored planks is part of the precast wall unit. Roofing insulation and the finished roofing application are applied directly over the hollow-core planking.

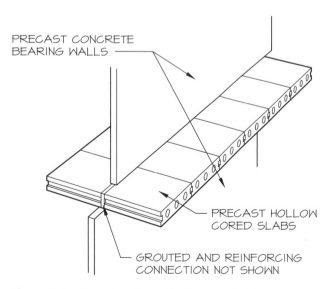

Figure 5.40 Precast walls and hollow-cored slab.

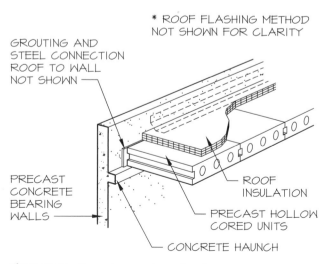

Figure 5.41 Precast concrete roof system.

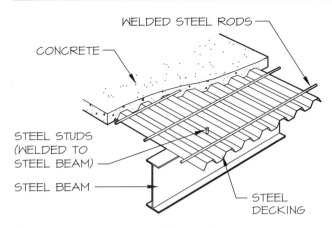

Figure 5.42 Composite steel decking floor system.

STEEL FLOOR SYSTEM

One type of steel floor system is the combination of steel decking and concrete. This type of system is referred to as a composite construction method. The corrugated steel decking sheets provide reinforcing for the concrete, as well as for the form into which the concrete is poured. Corrugated steel decking is available in various shapes, depths, and gauges. One method of attaching the steel decking to the steel supporting beams is with the use of

steel studs welded to the top flange of the steel beams prior to pouring the concrete. Bonding the concrete and steel decking to the steel studs provides the structural capability to withstand horizontal shear forces. The use of this composite steel and concrete floor system provides a lighter and stiffer building as well as an assemblage of incombustible materials. A three-dimensional drawing of this floor system is shown in Figure 5.42.

STEEL STUD WALL FRAMING SYSTEM

The use of lightweight, cold-formed steel stud members provides a solid wall framing system for load-bearing and non-load-bearing walls. These walls provide an incombustible support for fire-related construction and are well suited for preassembling. Moreover, shrinkage is not a concern with steel stud walls. The material of the studs varies from 14-gauge to 20-gauge galvanized steel, with sizes ranging from 3 5/8″ to 10′ in depth. These walls are constructed with a channel track at the bottom and top of each wall and steel studs attached to the channels. Horizontal bridging is achieved with the use of a steel channel positioned through the steel stud punch-outs and secured by welding. An isometric drawing of a steel stud wall assembly is shown in Figure 5.43. The attachment of wood sheathing to steel framing members can be

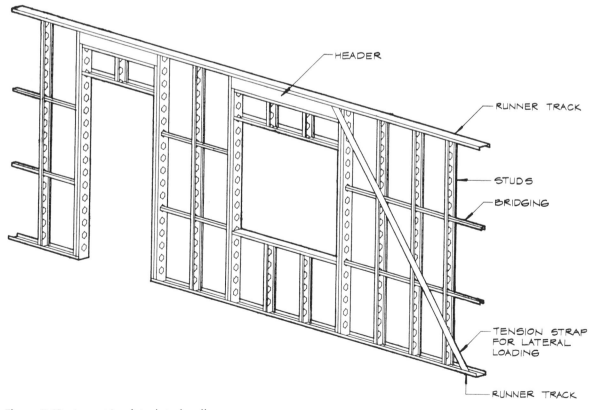

Figure 5.43 Isometric of steel stud wall.

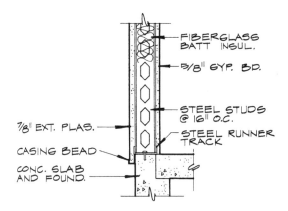

Figure 5.44 Partial steel stud wall section.

achieved with the use of self-tapping screws. A partial section of a steel stud wall using exterior stucco is shown in Figure 5.44.

STEEL DECKING ROOF SYSTEM

Corrugated steel decking that is used in steel roof systems is available in various shapes, with steel gauges ranging from 18 to 24 gauge and depths from $1\frac{1}{2}''$ to 3". Steel decking roof systems are mainly found in the construction of commercial, industrial, and institutional-type buildings. Figure 5.45 illustrates a three-dimensional roof-to-wall assembly incorporating a 20-gauge galvanized steel decking, which in this case has a fire protection coating to satisfy a building code requirement. For insulation purposes, a $2\frac{1}{2}''$ thick rigid insulation board is installed directly above the steel decking, followed by installation of the built-up roof system.

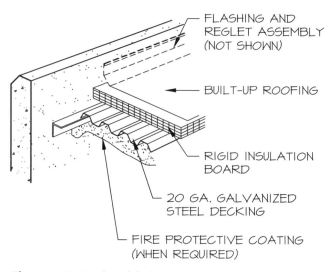

Figure 5.45 Steel roof decking system.

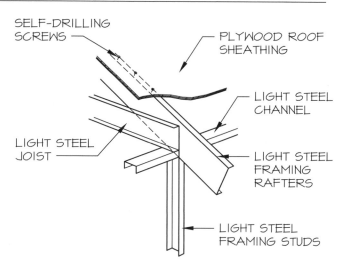

Figure 5.46 Light steel roof framing system.

LIGHT STEEL ROOF FRAMING SYSTEM

Light steel framing members are used in the construction of roof framing systems. These members are available in web depths of $3\frac{5}{8}''$ to $13\frac{1}{2}''$. These light steel members are manufactured from 18-gauge to 24-gauge steel. The attachment of plywood sheathing and other wood members may be accomplished with the use of self-tapping screws. A three-dimensional example of a roof-to-wall detail utilizing light steel framing members is depicted in Figure 5.46.

MASONRY AS A WALL SYSTEM

Masonry is widely used for exterior structural walls in commercial, industrial, and residential construction. The main masonry units used are bricks and concrete blocks. These are available in many sizes, shapes, textures, and colors.

Masonry is fire resistant and provides excellent fire ratings, ranging from two to four hours or more. The hour rating is based on the time it takes a fire-testing flame temperature to penetrate a specific wall assembly. Masonry also acts as an excellent sound barrier. When solid brick units are used for an exterior structural wall, the primary assembly is determined by regional geophysical conditions such as earthquakes and high winds. For example, steel reinforcing bars and solid grout may be needed to resist lateral forces. Figure 5.47 shows a steel-reinforced brick masonry wall. The size and placement of the horizontal and vertical reinforcing steel are determined by the structural engineer and the governing building code. In regions without high wind conditions or earthquakes, reinforcing steel and grout are not needed. The unreinforced masonry wall or brick cavity wall is excellent for insulating exterior walls. Two 3" or

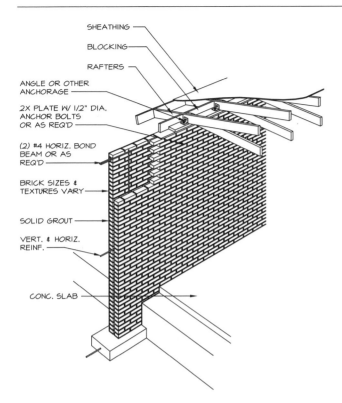

SHEATHING

BLOCKING

RAFTERS

ANGLE OR OTHER
ANCHORAGE

2X PLATE W/ 1/2" DIA.
ANCHOR BOLTS
OR AS REQ'D

(2) #4 HORIZ. BOND
BEAM OR AS
REQ'D

BRICK SIZES &
TEXTURES VARY

SOLID GROUT

VERT. & HORIZ.
REINF.

CONC. SLAB

Figure 5.47   Section of reinforced grouted brick masonry wall.

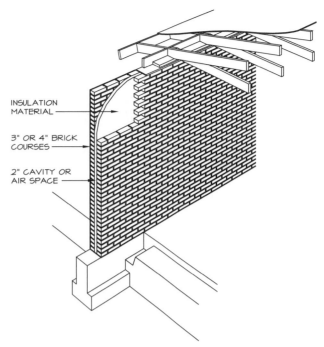

INSULATION
MATERIAL

3" OR 4" BRICK
COURSES

2" CAVITY OR
AIR SPACE

Figure 5.48   Brick cavity wall section.

4" walls of brick are separated by a 2" air space or cavity. This cavity provides a suitable space for insulating materials, and the two masonry walls are bonded together with metal ties set in the mortar joints. A wall section illustrating the cavity wall is depicted in Figure 5.48.

Concrete block units for structural walls are generally 6" to 8" thick, depending on the height of the wall. The hollow sections of these units are called "cells". These vertical cells may be left empty or filled solid with grout and reinforcing steel. As in brick wall construction, the use of unreinforced or reinforced walls will depend on the structural engineer's calculations and the building code requirements. In regions where reinforcing steel and grout are not required, the open cells may be filled with a suitable insulating material. When you detail a concrete block wall, dimension the height of the wall to satisfy the modular heights of the masonry units selected. Figure 5.49 illustrates a reinforced concrete block wall.

Masonry Veneer Wall

Masonry veneer includes the use of brick, concrete block units, or stone. The maximum thickness of masonry veneer is regulated by most building codes and is generally recognized as 5". "Masonry veneer" may be defined strictly as a masonry finish that is nonstructural and generally used for its architectural appearance.

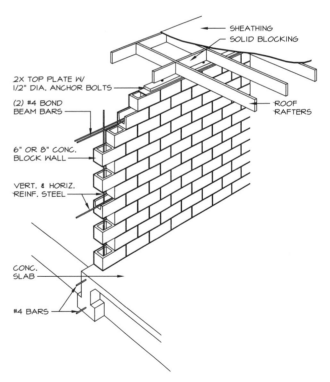

SHEATHING

SOLID BLOCKING

2X TOP PLATE W/
1/2" DIA. ANCHOR BOLTS

(2) #4 BOND
BEAM BARS

ROOF
RAFTERS

6" OR 8" CONC.
BLOCK WALL

VERT. & HORIZ.
REINF. STEEL

CONC.
SLAB

#4 BARS

Figure 5.49   Reinforced concrete block wall section.

Building code requirements for the attachment of masonry or stone veneer may vary, depending on regional differences. In regions with seismic disturbances, a positive bond between the veneer and a stud wall is re-

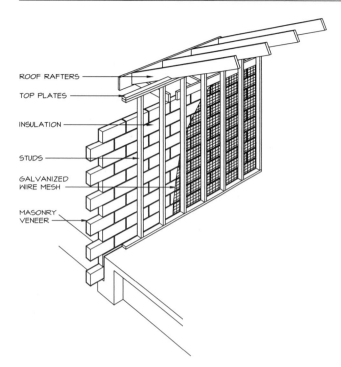

ROOF RAFTERS
TOP PLATES
INSULATION
STUDS
GALVANIZED
WIRE MESH
MASONRY
VENEER

Figure 5.50 Wall section/masonry veneer.

quired. A wall section using masonry veneer as an exterior wall finish is shown in Figure 5.50.

A partial example of the assemblage using concrete block units for exterior and interior walls is illustrated in the three-dimensional drawing in Figure 5.51. Note that the wall height and window and door openings satisfy the dimensions of the modular units. Partial ceiling and roof framing is also shown.

COMPOSITE SYSTEMS AND COMBINATIONS OF MATERIALS

Some construction methods incorporate systems that are assembled with various materials. These are called composite systems and may include a combination of materials such as steel and concrete; aluminum and insulation panels; polystyrene, galvanized steel, and concrete; and plastic and wood. These are just a few of the material combinations utilized in building construction. An example is the combination of steel floor and roof panels and concrete that is depicted in Figure 5.42. Another example of a composite system is the use of polystyrene

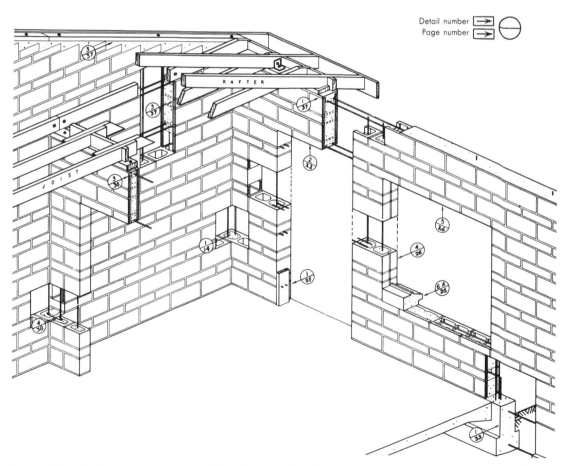

Detail number
Page number

RAFTER

JOIST

Figure 5.51 Typical concrete block residential construction. (Reprinted by permission from *Professional Practice of Architectural Detailing*, 3d Ed., © 1999 by John Wiley & Sons, Inc.)

and galvanized steel forms for construction of poured concrete walls. This system provides a form for the poured concrete and also possesses excellent insulation qualities, as the polystyrene forms are retained in the structural wall. They are designed to serve as an anchor for the finish materials that will be applied to the exterior and interior faces of the wall. The exterior and interior finishes may be anchored to galvanized steel furring strips that are an integral part of the form unit. An example of an exterior wall section depicting the use of "polysteel forms" in a composite system is illustrated three-dimensionally in Figure 5.52. Figure 5.53 depicts a single polysteel form unit in three dimensions.

For structures that are designed to incorporate exterior wall insulation qualities, the architect may select a composite exterior wall system that utilizes a substrate material insulation board and a moistureproof exterior finish. The thickness of an acceptable substrate may be at least 1/2", and an expanded polystyrene insulation board may be from 1" to 2" in thickness. The selected thickness may be determined by the required or desired "R" factor. The R factor designates the assigned insulation capability. It is recommended that the supporting exterior wall members for this system be galvanized steel studs at 16" center to center or 24" center to center. The attachment of this composite system to the steel studs and the approved substrate can be achieved with the use of an approved adhesive or a mechanical attachment. The mechanical attachment incorporates a metal screw and washer. An example of the primary composite materials for this exterior wall panel is depicted in Figure 5.54.

Figure 5.55 illustrates an exterior wall assembly utilizing the aforementioned wall panel. Note that the polystyrene selected is 2" thick. The Madison Building, illustrated in Chapter 20, utilized this particular exterior composite wall system. The parapet detail of that building, depicted in Figure 5.56, incorporates the various requirements in using this system.

Another example of combining materials to develop a composite system is the use of wood and plastic. The use of these two materials is found in a product developed

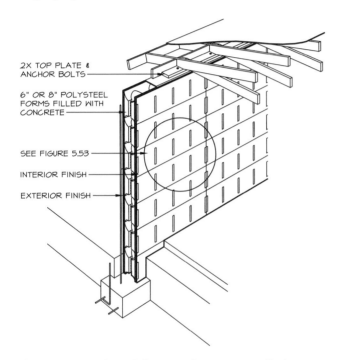

Figure 5.52 Polysteel forms and concrete wall. (Courtesy American Polysteel, Inc.)

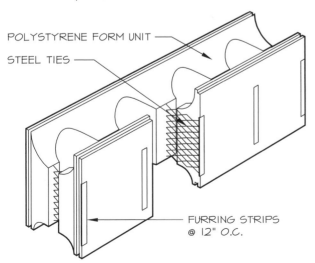

Figure 5.53 Polysteel form unit. (Courtesy American Polysteel, Inc.)

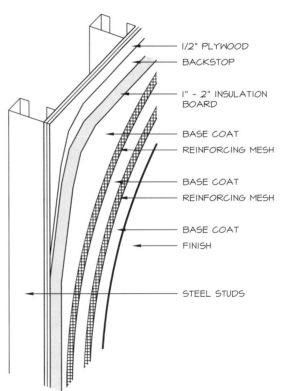

Figure 5.54 Composite wall panel. (Compliments of Dryuit Systems, Inc.)

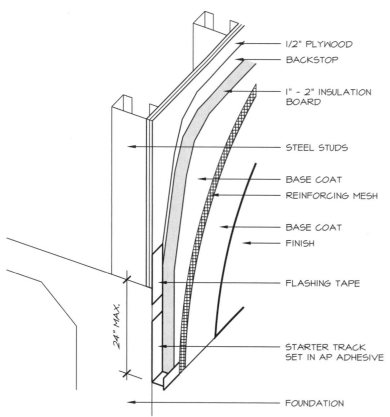

1/2" PLYWOOD

BACKSTOP

1" - 2" INSULATION
BOARD

STEEL STUDS

BASE COAT

REINFORCING MESH

BASE COAT

FINISH

FLASHING TAPE

24" MAX.

STARTER TRACK
SET IN AP ADHESIVE

FOUNDATION

Figure 5.55 Composite wall panel attachment. (Compliments of Dryuit Systems, Inc.)

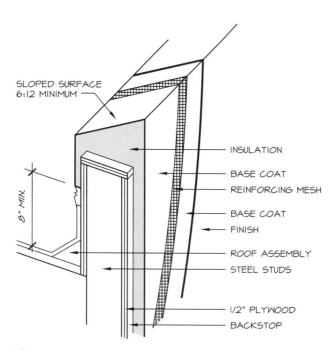

SLOPED SURFACE
6:12 MINIMUM

INSULATION

BASE COAT

REINFORCING MESH

BASE COAT

FINISH

ROOF ASSEMBLY

STEEL STUDS

1/2" PLYWOOD

BACKSTOP

8" MIN.

Figure 5.56 Composite parapet detail. (Compliments of Dryuit Systems, Inc.)

for exterior decking and handrails in residential construction. This composite product requires virtually no maintenance and is manufactured from a sturdy wood composite. The decking material will not splinter, split,

or crack, is resistant to termites, dry rot, and decay, and is available in a wood-tone finish. The individual members are straight and true, having smooth finish with no splinters or knots. The members can be attached using the same method as that used for sawn lumber; however, predrilling and the use of screws are recommended. This decking material is available in two types. One is a solid unit that is 4" × 6" in size and can be supported with structural members spaced at 16" center to center. The other type is a 2" × 6" unit that is hollowed to provide a lighter weight for ease of handling. The hollowed member may span over the joist spaced at a maximum of 24" center to center.

These two products do not require painting, staining, or sealing. Because all members are of exactly the same size and shape, the installation process is made easier. Figure 5.57 illustrates the two types of composite decking materials that are used in the construction of decks.

The composite handrail system incorporates 2" × 6" handrails, 2" × 4' side rails, and 2" × 2" balusters. The use of screws with countersunk-type heads is recommended for the connection of the various members. All screws must be predrilled. The composite handrail system is depicted in Figure 5.58. This handrail assembly shows the various member sizes that are available for construction of an exterior handrail system. Figure 5.59 illustrates a section through the handrail assembly.

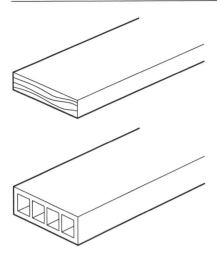

Figure 5.57 Composite decking members. (Courtesy Lousiana Pacific Corp.)

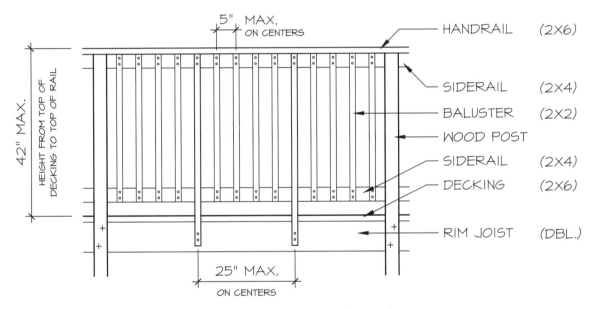

Figure 5.58 Composite handrail system. (Courtesy Lousiana Pacific Corp.)

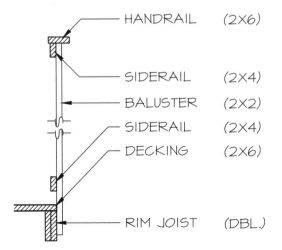

Figure 5.59 Section through handrail.

chapter

6

INITIAL PREPARATION PHASE FOR CONSTRUCTION DOCUMENTS

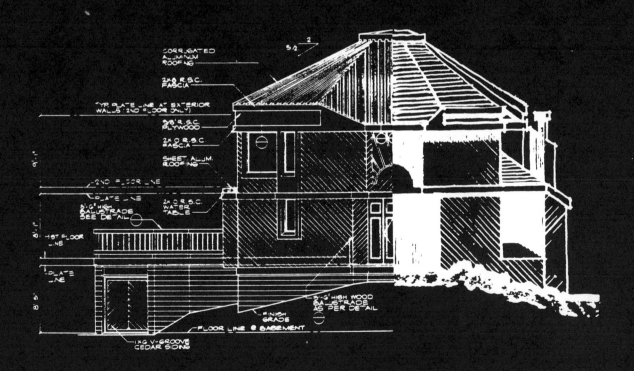

■ WORKING GUIDELINES FOR PREPARING CONSTRUCTION DOCUMENTS

In this time of technological advance and specialization, you might easily assume that working guidelines would be precise and mathematically logical. This is not the case. Guidelines are too important to reduce to a series of steps and formulas to memorize. In fact, working guidelines for drafting are actually attitudes and ideals that are fundamental to good communication. It is this ingredient that makes a success or failure out of a basically skilled draftsperson.

You may well think that much of this material is obvious, common knowledge, or common sense. Yet if these guidelines are assumed but *not acted upon*, mass confusion and anguish result! They have been arrived at through research in supervision, communication, human relationships, and field experiences, particularly with prospective employers. This material is, therefore, not original, but its application often is.

The Rules in Drafting Construction Documents
1. Plan every step of your drawing.
2. Establish some manner in which you can check your work.
3. Understand the decisions you will be asked to make.
4. Find out the standards under which you will function.
5. Draft from the other person's point of view.
6. Cooperate, communicate, and work with others.
7. Find out your primary and secondary responsibilities. Don't assume.
8. Think for yourself.
9. Concentrate on improving one aspect of your skills with each task.
10. Be sure to follow office standards.

The Rules in Drafting Construction Documents
1. *Plan every step of your drawing.* Do not get a piece of vellum and start immediately on the top left corner. Each drawing has a distinct procedure and an order. Use your mind's eye to completely draw the object first. Picture yourself at the drafting desk. Watch yourself perform the task. Make mental and/or written notes about the sequence and anticipated problems. Every sheet of a set of architectural plans subscribes to a basic system. The system may be based on the materials used, methods of erection, limits of the technology at the present time, or even the limits of the person, to mention just a few. Whatever the control factors, be aware of them, understand them, digest them intellectually, and put them into effect.

2. *Establish some manner in which you can check your work.* Every office has some method of checking. The method may be a check sheet developed by the principal draftsperson or a person whose primary function is that of checking others. Whatever the system, establish a method to check yourself before you submit a drawing to a senior in the firm. This does two things. First, it builds trust, trust between you and your employer. If your employer thinks that you not only perform the task asked of you but are conscientious enough to double-check your work, the rapport built between you and your employer will be enhanced. Second, it builds the employer's confidence that you have done your best to perform your duty.

   This checking method differs with each person and each drawing. However, remember that the checking method is also based on the construction system used. If you understand the system, you will usually discover the method needed to check it.

   Accuracy transcends all systems—accuracy of representation as well as of arithmetic, grammar, and spelling. Nothing causes as many problems in the field as an "L" that looks like an "I," and an "E" that looks like an "F," or arithmetical tools that are not equal to their parts, or dimensions that do not reflect an established module.

3. *Understand the decisions you will be asked to make.* Know your job. Know what decisions you will be allowed to make, and know when to ask a superior.

   If, every time you are confronted with a decision, you ask a superior for help, you are taking that person's valuable time and reducing the superior's effectiveness. On the other hand, making decisions that are not part of your job will also create problems. For example, if a production draftsperson (a person drafting working drawings) were to change a design decision, the draftsperson might not be aware of all the factors that led to that decision and might make the wrong decision. It might seem obvious to the draftsperson that a particular change would produce a better effect, but the original may have been based on a code requirement, a client's request, cost of production, or any one of hundreds of reasons of which the draftsperson may not be aware.

   Make sure your duties, responsibilities, and, above all, the decisions you are allowed to make are clearly defined by your superior.

4. *Find out the standards under which you will function.* There are many standards you will encounter. Just as there are office dress and behavior standards, so there are drawing standards.

   Each sheet you draw will have a set-up standard. Certain sheet sizes are used by certain offices. Title blocks, border lines, and sheet space allocation are usually set up in advance. Certain drawing conventions are used by each office. Certain symbols and abbreviations are acceptable. In fact, some offices produce what is called a manual of "office standards." The standard may call for something as simple as all vertical lettering, or as professional as a standard based on building erection procedures followed by a particular contractor. Again, whether it be a building code or state regulated requirement, or a personal whim of an employer, you must immediately incorporate this standard into your assignments.

5. *Draft from the other person's point of view.* Your work involves three people: the person in the field, the person who assigns you your duties, and the client. All of these people influence your attitudes. For example, when you draft for the person in the field, your work becomes a medium of communication between the client's needs and the people who execute those needs, but it must also express an understanding of the limits and capabilities of the workers themselves. Prior to drafting, for example, a detail, plan, or section, you must sufficiently understand the trade involved so that you do not ask a person or machine to perform an unreasonable task.

As for drafting from your employer's point of view, first and foremost understand what your task is. It is better to spend a few minutes with your supervisor at the beginning of a drawing, outlining your duties, and his objectives and needs, than to spend countless hours on a drawing only to find that much of the time you have spent is wasted. We are often so eager to "get on" with a job that we have not spent the proper amount of time understanding what is expected of us. As the ironic saying goes, "There is never enough time to do a job but always enough time to do it over, CORRECTLY."

Finally, look at things from the client's standpoint. The client and the designer have made a number of design and construction decisions. No matter what the reasons are for these decisions, the office and the client have an understanding, which must be respected by you. In other words, you, as a technician, must abide by and subscribe to these decisions and do everything you can to support them. This is not to say you cannot question a decision, but do not make changes without approval. If you know of a better solution or method, verify its appropriateness with a superior before you employ it.

6. *Cooperate, communicate, and work with others.* One of the main criticisms that comes from employers is that employees do not know how to work as members of a team. While education requires you to perform as an individual, each person in an office is a member of a team and has certain responsibilities, duties, and functions on which others rely. There may be many people working on a single project, and you must understand your part and participate with others toward achieving a common goal.

The method of communication is as important as the need for it. Be clear about the way you communicate your ideas. Sketch ideas when possible so others can visualize them. If the office is large, write memos and notes; write formal letters to other companies. Keep in mind that you are a representative of your firm and that proper presentation, grammar, spelling, and punctuation reflect the abilities in the firm.

Communication helps you know what the other people in the firm are doing. The more you understand the overall picture, the more you can participate. Communication also helps you to develop an appreciation of attitudes, goals, and aims of others with whom you will be working. Know what is going on in the office.

7. *Find out your primary and secondary responsibilities. Don't assume.* Nothing gets an office or an employee in as much trouble as making assumptions. Phrases such as "I thought John was going to do it" or "I didn't think, Kay; I assumed you would do it" not only break down the communication process in an office but can create discord and disturb the office harmony. Many bad feelings emerge and ultimately break down office morale.

Know your responsibilities and how and whom to ask for guidance in case of a change in your responsibilities.

A classic example of this was a large office that had two divisions: an architectural division and a structural engineering division. Each prepared a set of drawings: the architectural drawings and the structural drawings. Each division assumed the other would develop a set of details for the project. Thus, on the architectural drawings there were notations that read, "See structural drawings for details." The structural group did the same but made the detail reference to the architectural set. Needless to say, the details were never drawn, and when the total set was assembled and the lack of details discovered, a great delay followed and caused much embarrassment to the firm. The client was obviously unhappy.

The size of the firm is not always to blame. Any time there is more than one person working on a project, you need to understand not only your primary responsibilities, but your not-so-obvious secondary responsibilities as well.

8. *Think for yourself.* There is a natural tendency for a draftsperson to feel that all decisions should be made by a superior. However, your supervisor will tell you that certain decisions have been delegated to you.

The process of thinking for yourself also involves fully understanding your primary and secondary responsibilities.

If, each time a problem arises, you ask Bob for help, Bob will not be able to do his job effectively. There is also a cost factor involved. Your immediate supervisor or head draftsperson is earning two to five times as much as you are because of additional responsibilities. Therefore, each time you ask a question and stop production, the cost is that of your salary plus that of your supervisor.

The solution to this dilemma is a simple one. Research the solution before you approach your seniors, look through reference and manufacturers' literature, construction manuals, *Sweet's Catalog File*, reference books, and so on. Make a list of problems and questions and work around them until your superior is free and available to deal with them. Arrange your time to suit your supervisor's convenience. THINK and be able to propose solutions or suggestions yourself. In this way, you will be prepared to understand the answers you are given, and a potential frustration will have become a learning situation.

Above all, don't stop production and wait around for superiors to be free; don't follow them around. Employers react very negatively to this.

9. *Concentrate on improving one aspect of your skills with each task.* Make a special effort with each new assignment to improve some part of your skills. Constantly improve your lettering, your line quality, your accuracy. As athletes work to perfect some part of their ability, so should you. Work on your weakness first. Because it is your weakness, you may want to shy away from it. For example, if spelling is your problem, carry a dictionary around with you. If sketching is your weakness, practice and use it as a communication method whenever possible. The most valuable athlete is often the most versatile one—the person who can throw and catch and play defense as well as offense. A draftsperson who can draft, sketch, do simple engineering, and do research is a valuable commodity in an office and will always be employed, because an office cannot afford to lose such a versatile person.

An employer wants an employee who is punctual, dependable, and accurate, has a high degree of integrity, and is able to work with a minimum amount of supervision.

We have said many of the principles listed here are obvious. Yet if they are so obvious, why do teachers, employers, and supervisors lament the absence of these principles when desirable employee traits are discussed? To admit to your shortcomings is to confront and deal with them. To ignore them and act as if they don't exist is to run away from them.

10. *Be sure to follow office standards.* Office standards are an integral part in the evolvement process of construction documents. It is not sufficient merely to follow the standards; it is also necessary to understand why they are used. Certain standards are possibly used because associates such as structural engineers use the same documents as those used in the architectural office. Layer titles, basic symbols, and conventions must be the same from office to office.

■ MAKING THE TRANSITION FROM PRELIMINARY DRAWINGS TO CONSTRUCTION DOCUMENTS

Making the transition from approved preliminary drawings to construction documents is important because it completes the process of making decisions about the physical characteristics of the building. Once this transition is made, the production of construction documents can proceed.

Accomplishing this transition—the design development phase—requires that the following basic requirements be satisfied and thoroughly investigated:

1. Building code and other requirements, such as those set by the zoning department, fire department, health department, planning department, and architectural committees
2. Primary materials analysis
3. Selection of the primary structural system
4. Requirements of consultants, such as mechanical and electrical engineers
5. Regional considerations (see Appendix A on web site)
6. Energy conservation considerations and requirements (see Chapter 4)
7. Interrelationship of drawings
8. Project programming

■ BUILDING CODE REQUIREMENTS

Building code requirements are extremely important to research. Figure 6.1, for example, shows a small office building with a code requirement of a minimum dimension between required exit stairs. The correct placement of these stairs is important because the whole structural concept, the office layouts, and many other factors will be affected by their location.

Many people frequently overlook the building code requirements for correct stair dimensions. Often they give a little attention to the width of stairs and landings or to the provisions for the necessary number of risers (stair height) and treads (step width) to satisfy the vertical dimensions between floors. See Figure 6.2.

Two further examples of satisfying the physical requirements dictated by the code are illustrated in Figure 6.3, which shows corridor dimensions, and Figure 6.4, which shows handicapped toilet access.

In multiple housing projects as well as in residential projects, building codes establish minimum physical requirements for various rooms. Figure 6.5 shows the minimum floor areas and dimensions required for the bedroom and kitchen.

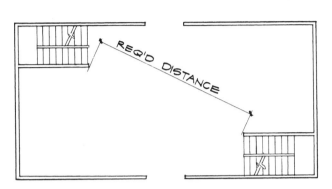

Figure 6.1 Stair separation (commercial).

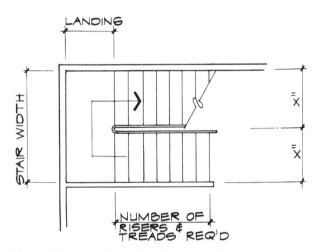

Figure 6.2 Stair dimensions (commercial).

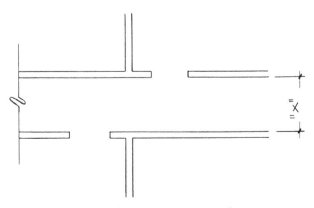

Figure 6.3 Corridor dimension (commercial).

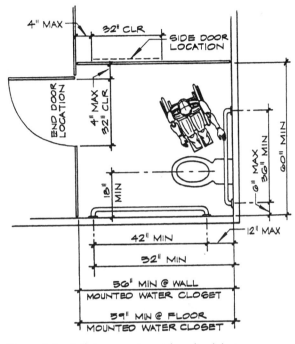

Figure 6.4 Toilet compartment for wheelchair use.

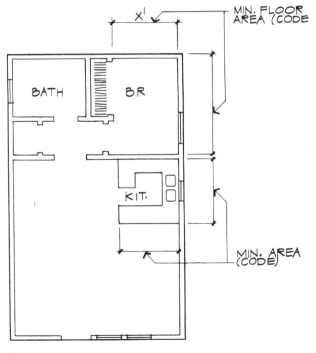

Figure 6.5 Apartment unit.

■ PRIMARY MATERIALS ANALYSIS

The most important building materials to be selected are for foundations and floors, exterior and interior walls, and ceiling and roof structures. There are several factors that influence selection, and many of these require considerable investigation and research:

A. Architectural design
B. Building codes
C. Economics
D. Structural concept
E. Region
F. Ecology
G. Energy conservation

An example of the importance of selection is given in Figure 6.6. Concrete block units have been selected as the material for the exterior walls of a structure. Using this material affects the exterior and interior dimensions because concrete blocks have fixed dimensions. Establishing the exterior and interior dimensions *before* the production of construction documents is most important because other phases, such as the structural engineering, are based on these dimensions.

Modular and Nonmodular Units

The term "module" refers to a predetermined dimension from which structures are designed. "Block module" is usually used in conjunction with masonry units, such as bricks, concrete blocks, or structural clay tiles.

Masonry units can be broadly classified as either modular or nonmodular. The mortar joint between two units is usually either ⅜", ⁷⁄₁₆", or ½" thick. Modular sizes are designed to ensure that final measurements including mortar joints are in whole numbers. Nonmodular units result in fractional measurements.

For example, an 8 × 8 × 16 modular concrete block unit measures 7⅝" × 7⅝" × 15⅝", so that a ⅜-inch mortar joint produces a final 8 × 8 × 16 measurement to work with. There are also half sizes available, so that when the units are stacked on top of each other, lapping each other by one half the length of the block, the end of the structure comes out even. See Figure 6.7.

Certain lengths are commonly available. See Appendix B, Table B.6, left column, on web site. These measurements follow three rules: First, all even numbers of feet are available (2'-0", 8'-0", 2'-0", etc.); second, all odd-numbered feet have four inches added to them (for example, the length closest to 3 feet is 3'-4"; the length closest to 9 feet is 9'-4"; etc.); third, all even-numbered feet are also available in 8" increments, such as 4'-8", 8'-8", and 32'-8".

Using the preceding rules or Appendix B, Table B.6, left column, Table A (on web site), check to see if the following measurements are good for lengths of a concrete block structure using an 8 × 8 × 16 modular construction.

A. 28'-8"
B. 42'-9"
C. 101'-4"
D. 89'-4"
E. 93'-8"

All but B and E are correct, B should be 42'-8" and E should be 93'-4".

The height in the left column of Table B.6 is calculated in the same way and presented in two columns—one for 4"-high blocks and one for 8"-inch blocks. The 4"-inch blocks do not completely follow the rules mentioned earlier. A careful examination of the chart will reveal a single rule: all modular dimensions will be 4", 8", or 0" (for example, 3'-4", 6'-8", or 10'-0").

Tables B and C (on web site) are for a nonmodular system. The same size concrete block is used here but with a different mortar joint. Odd fractions begin to appear.

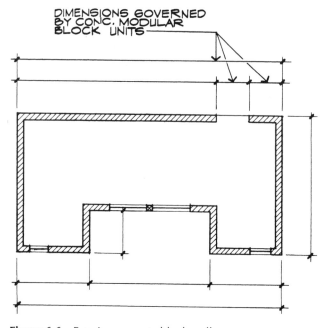

Figure 6.6 Exterior concrete block walls.

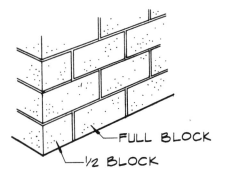

Figure 6.7 Use of half block.

Only heights are shown. The mortar joints—both $^7/_{16}''$ and $^1/_2''$—affect window and door sizes and heights.

Brick also comes in modular and nonmodular sizes. Examples of sizes for a modular unit are $5^5/_8'' \times 2^1/_4'' \times 7^5/_8'' \times$ for a $^3/_8''$ joint and $3^1/_2'' \times 2^3/_{16}'' \times 7^1/_2''$ for a $^1/_2''$ joint. $2^1/_2'' \times 3^7/_8'' \times 8^1/_4''$ is a nonmodular size. See Appendix B, Table B.7 on web site, for an interpretation of nonmodular height and length applications.

Here are some of the things you should consider when deciding whether or not to use the block module system:

1. Heights of the structure
2. Ceiling heights
3. Size of foundation if walls are masonry units
4. Size of floor plan if foundation wall is made of masonry units
5. Window and door openings
6. Window and door heights

If you have a choice of modular or nonmodular materials, use modular. The dimensions are easier to figure out, and, as contractors report, the structure is faster, easier, and cheaper to build.

Why, then, would you choose nonmodular? You may be forced into nonmodular sizes. For example, building function might dictate overall size, as in an assembly plant. The client may require that a building occupy the full width of depth of a piece of property to maximize the site use. An auditorium size is often dictated by seating arrangement or acoustics. A fire department regulation may determine certain size corridors for schools. These are only a few of the reasons for using a nonmodular system. If all these kinds of restraints can be satisfied by using modular units, use modular units.

Because of the state of technology, the cost of cutting masonry units is rapidly decreasing, thus giving greater selection for almost any size structure. Cutting reduces the visual unity of the building and should be used with discretion.

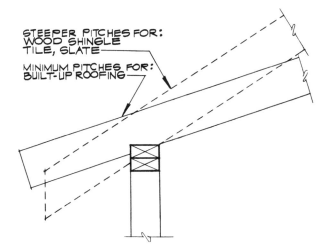

Figure 6.8 Roof material and roof pitches.

The importance of selecting primary building materials is further shown in Figure 6.8. The roofing material selected here actually governs the roof pitch. This in turn establishes the physical height of the building and also dictates the size of the supporting members relative to the weight of the finished roof material.

■ SELECTING THE PRIMARY STRUCTURAL SYSTEM

The selection of a structural system and its members is influenced by the following: meeting building code requirements, satisfying design elements, and using the most logical system based on sound engineering principles, economic considerations, and simplicity.

For most projects, the architect consults with the structural engineer about systems or methods that will meet these various considerations. Figures 6.9 and 6.10 illustrate the importance of establishing a structural concept before producing construction documents. Figure 6.9 shows a residential floor plan in which an exposed wood post and beam structure system has been selected. Here, the walls should fall directly beneath the beam module. To achieve these desired wall locations and to accommodate the modular structural system, you may need to adjust the floor plan.

Another example of structural factors is the need, at times, for shear (earthquake resistant) walls to resist lateral forces. Figure 6.10 shows a retail store floor plan which has an extensive amount of glass. However, preliminary structural engineering calculations also require the use of shear walls at various locations in order to resist earthquake (seismic) or wind forces. To satisfy these requirements, you would need to make a physical adjustment to the floor plan.

■ REQUIREMENTS OF CONSULTANTS

Early involvement of structural, electrical, mechanical, and civil engineering consultants is highly recommended. Their early involvement generally results in physical adjustments to the finalized preliminary drawings in order to meet their design requirements. For example, the mechanical engineer's design may require a given area on the roof to provide space for various sizes of roof-mounted mechanical equipment. See Figure 6.11. For projects that require mechanical ducts to be located in floor and ceiling areas, necessary space and clearances for ducts must be provided. Figure 6.12 shows a floor and ceiling section with provisions for mechanical duct space.

The electrical engineer should also be consulted about any modifications to the building that may be required to provide space for electrical equipment. In most cases,

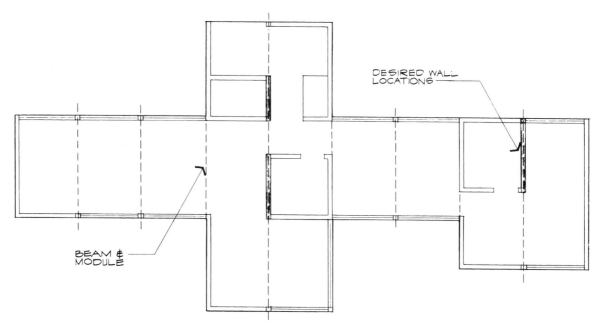

Figure 6.9 Wood post and beam structural system.

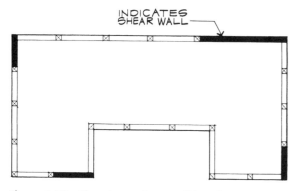

Figure 6.10 Plan view—shear wall locations.

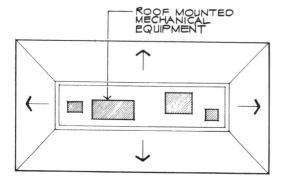

Figure 6.11 Roof plan—mechanical equipment area.

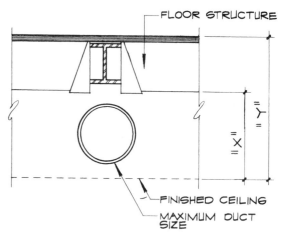

Figure 6.12 Mechanical duct space equipment.

electrical room dimensions may require a floor plan adjustment, which can even result in a major or minor plan modification. Figure 6.13 illustrates a floor plan modification to satisfy space requirements for electrical equipment.

■ REGIONAL CONSIDERATIONS

Regional differences in construction techniques are mainly controlled or influenced by climatic conditions, soil conditions, and natural events such as very high winds and earthquakes. These are considered in greater detail later.

the architect or project manager provides for an electrical equipment room or cabinet in the plans. However, with the increasing sophistication and size of equipment, additional space may be required. This increase in the

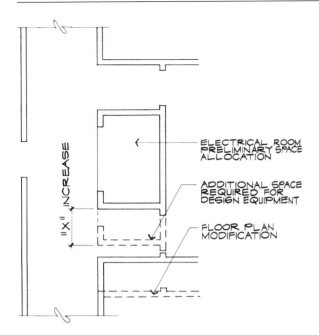

Figure 6.13 Electrical equipment room modification.

In brief, regional differences influence:

1. Foundation design
2. Exterior wall design
3. Framing system
4. Roof design
5. Structural considerations
6. Insulation

Figure 6.14 illustrates a type of foundation used in regions with cold climatic conditions: an exterior founda-

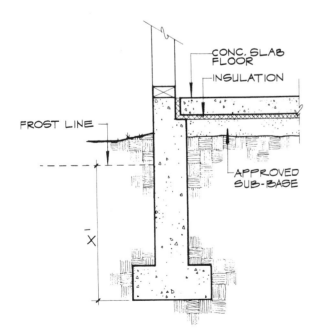

Figure 6.14 Foundation—cold climate conditions.

tion wall and footing with a concrete floor. The depth of the foundation is established from the frost line, and insulation is required under the concrete floor.

Where temperatures are mild and warm, the foundation design and construction techniques are primarily governed by soils investigations and local building codes. Figure 6.15 illustrates an exterior foundation detail where the depth of the footing is established to a recommended depth below the natural grade.

Another example of regional influence is the change in exterior wall design. Figure 6.16 shows a section of an exterior wall with wood frame construction. This open frame construction is suitable for mild climates. A wood frame exterior wall recommended for Eastern regions is shown in Figure 6.17. Here, solid sheathing is used, and this in turn requires the wood studs to be set in from the

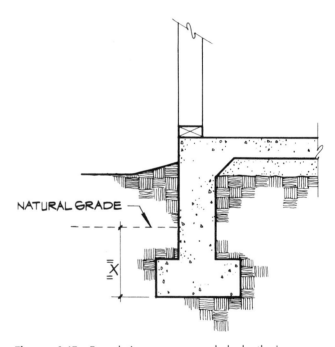

Figure 6.15 Foundation—recommended depth in warm climate.

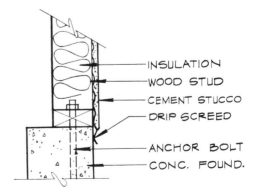

Figure 6.16 Exterior wall—open frame construction.

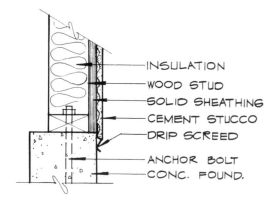

Figure 6.17 Exterior wall—sheathed frame construction.

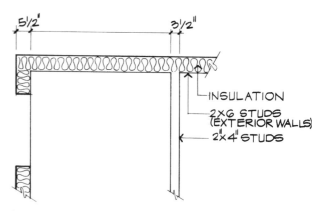

Figure 6.18 Floor plan wall thickness.

face of the foundation wall. This one regional difference can affect many procedures and detailing throughout the construction documents such as wall dimensioning, window details, and door details.

■ ENERGY CONSERVATION

To determine what you must do to satisfy local and federal energy conservation requirements, you must complete preliminary research. These requirements can affect exterior wall material and thickness, amount and type of glazing, areas of infiltration (leakage of air), amount of artificial lighting to be used, thickness and type of insulation, mechanical engineering design, and so forth. For example, a wood building requires exterior walls to be 2 × 6 studs instead of 2 × 4 to allow for the thickness of the building insulation. This particular requirement dictates procedures in the construction document process, such as floor plan wall thickness and dimensioning, window

and exterior door details, and other related exterior wall details. Figure 6.18 shows a segment of a floor plan and indicates the thickness of walls and the locations of required insulation.

An excellent example of an award-winning mechanical system that produces energy savings is an ice bank. The use of storage tanks in the design of a mechanical system can increase operating efficiency and considerably reduce both the electrical costs and amount of energy used. An example of this storage tank approach is the use of ice storage tanks to produce cooling for a large office building. Ice usually forms around the piping that carries the refrigerant located in a tank. The ice is produced during off-peak hours, such as during the night, when energy costs are at their lowest. This then provides the necessary coolant during the following day's peak-use hours. The use of this mechanical cooling design is incorporated in the steel office building discussed in Chapter 20. Figure 6.19 depicts the basic equipment necessary in this system in pictorial form in diagram form.

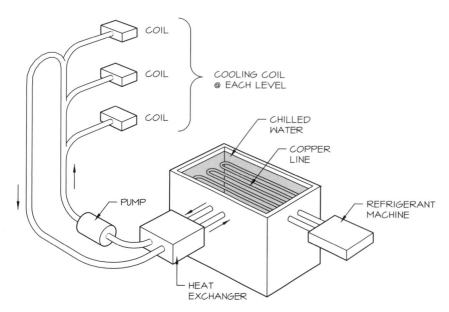

Figure 6.19 Ice bank.

■ INTERRELATIONSHIP OF DRAWINGS

When you develop construction documents, you must have consistent relationships between the drawings for continuity and clarity. These relationships vary in their degree of importance.

For example, the relationship between the foundation plan and the floor plan is most important because continuity of dimensioning and correlation of structural components are both required. See Figure 6.20. The dimensioning of the floor plan and the foundation plan are identical, and this provides continuity for dimensional accuracy.

The relationship between drawings for the electrical plan and the mechanical plan is also important. This relationship is critical because the positioning of electrical fixtures must not conflict with the location of mechanical components, such as air supply grilles or fire sprinkler heads.

Cross-reference drawings with important relationships such as these and constantly review them throughout the preparation of the construction documents. Only in this way will you avoid conflicts.

This cross-referencing and review is not as critical with drawings that are not so closely related, such as the electrical plan and the civil engineering plans, or the interior elevations and the foundation.

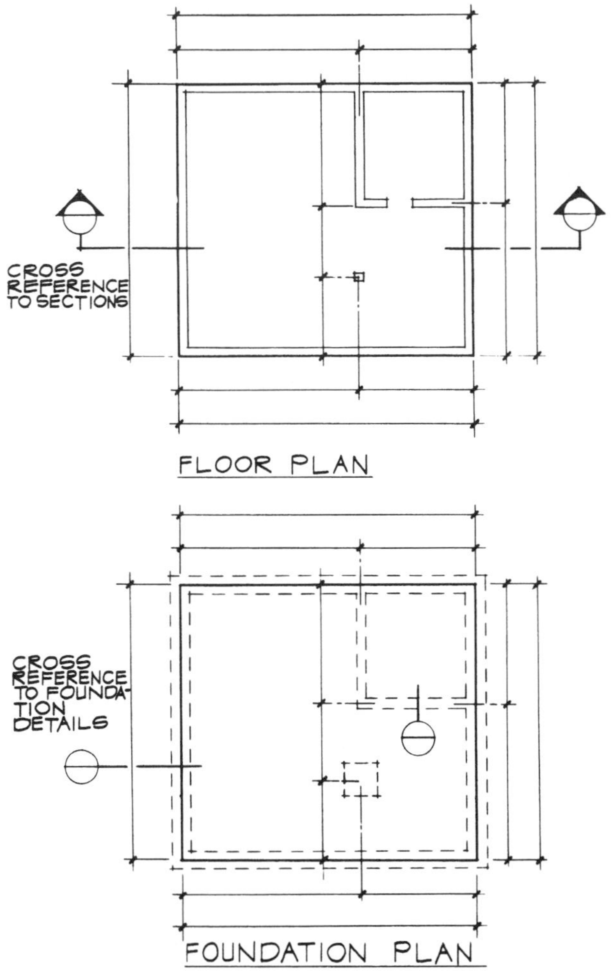

■ PROJECT PROGRAMMING

For many construction projects, a construction firm uses a time schedule process to coordinate all trades and services necessary to finish the project on the scheduled completion date. Architects also use a time schedule for programming phases of a project.

The primary phases of a project are preliminary design, client review, preliminary budget, agency review (when required), construction documents, final construction bids, and building department approvals and permits.

■ OFFICE PROCEDURE AND PLANNING STRATEGY

Most offices have a set procedure for planning the transition from preliminary drawings to the development and execution of working drawings. In a small office it may be a simple matter of the principal giving verbal commands to employees until a specific system is understood. In a large office the system may be an intricate network of planned procedures.

There are two items in any office with which the beginner will be confronted. These are described herein as **standards**, standard graphic and written patterns to which the office subscribes, and **procedures**, the methods that are instituted during this transition.

Standards

Many offices have a booklet called *Office Standards* or *The Drafting Room Manual*. It contains such items as the following:

A. A Uniform List of Abbreviations for working drawings
B. Material designations in plan, section, and elevation
C. Graphic symbols
D. Methods of representing doors and windows in both plan and elevation
E. Electrical and plumbing symbols
F. Graphic representations of appliances and fixtures
G. Sheet standards and drawing modules

These standards might be presented in an informal packet, photocopied and stapled, or housed in a binder

Figure 6.20 Relationship of foundation plan and floor plan.

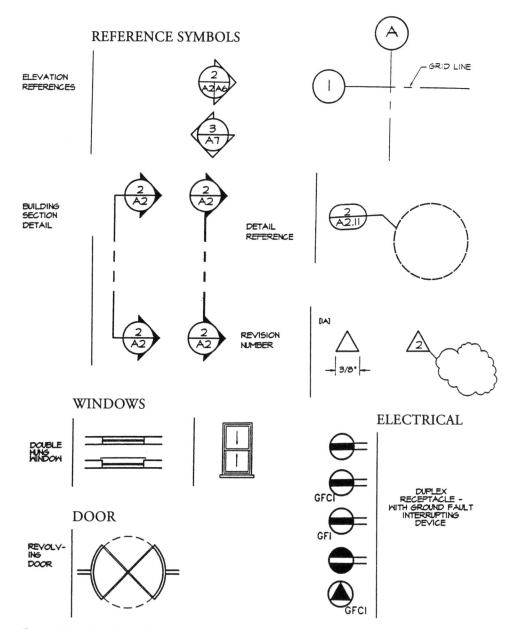

Figure 6.21 Sampling of standard conventions.

with division for specific standards to be followed. A sampling is shown in Figure 6.21.

Procedures

For a beginner, the transition process of changing design proposals to working drawings appears to be a complex one, because there are so many pieces to the puzzle. If you understand the system, then not only will you understand the steps to follow but you will begin to comprehend how you fit into this system.

As in sports, there is a game plan (the procedure) with specific plays (standards) for the individual player

(drafter). One must know how the game is to be played, the specific play being incorporated, and each player's individual responsibility within each specific plan. Standardization is critical, because if an injury occurs (illness), another player must be able to take over without missing a beat.

Think of the process, as described here, as parallel to a basketball, football, or even a baseball game. It is important to understand the role of the owner of the team, the manager, the offense and defense coaches, and the team members, including the team captain. In this comparison the owner might be viewed as the principal, the manager as the person in charge of the specific job, the offense and defense coaches as professional associates such as the electrical engineer and structural engineer, and, finally, the players as the drafters. The more seasoned the player (drafter) the more responsibility he or she takes on. These players often become the spirit, the determination, and the core around whom new players rally.

To take the analogy a step further, the spectators are the clients with certain expectations and the umpires and referees can be compared with the building inspectors who check for violation of the rules of the game.

There are, however, large differences: the duration of the project, the cost/investment, and the life span of the project being executed. Moreover, our profession also addresses the health and safety, as well as the creative needs, of generations of clients.

Datum Base

All construction documents should be datum based. If the documents are to be executed on CAD, the first layer should be a datum layer.

The datum is usually based on the material to be used in the construction and the system best suited for that selected material. For example, if steel is selected as the material for constructing a structure, then a matrix system such as the dimensional reference system is best suited for constructing with steel. This is described in Chapter 2 and revealed in Figures 6.22 and 6.23. Horizontal and vertical control planes are used on these examples, giving us control dimensions to the centers of the steel columns.

For ceilings and floors, neutral zones are used to control the space in between and are referred to as the con-

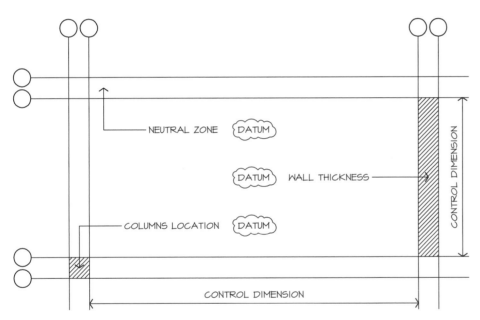

Figure 6.22 Horizontal (X, Y) datum.

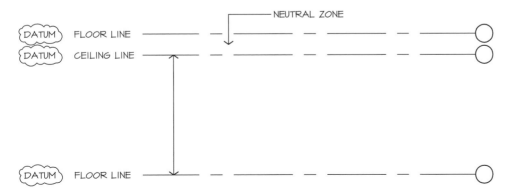

Figure 6.23 Vertical (Z) Datum.

trol zones or control dimensions. Thus, the entire dimensioning process is dictated by this matrix datum, even to the drafting of details, which also should be datum based.

■ TRACKING A SET OF WORKING DRAWINGS

The process of tracking a drawing is similar to that of tracking a package en route to a distant city. One should be able to locate, at a moment's notice, the precise progress of a set of construction documents. This is particularly critical for the office manager or job captain, because this person must be able to track the progress of a set of drawings for budgetary reasons. He or she must be able to know whether an entire set will meet the deadline, as well as the progress of a single drawing. In this way, the manager can check the productivity of employees, give an extra push to those falling behind, compliment those working ahead of schedule, and even recommend some for a quarterly raise.

It is important to understand the total sequence followed by drafters so that individual participants can track their progress in relation to their colleagues to ensure that all drawings produced by the team will progress equally. For an overview of where areas of participation fit into the whole scheme of things in an office, see Figure 6.24. The initial design phase is done either by hand or by computer.

By Hand

During the design phase, models, renderings, presentational floor plans, elevations and sections are developed. These are altered or changed after being viewed by the client. Subsequent to this stage, the drafter must realize that design changes cannot be made without the approval of the designer in conjunction with the client.

Cartoons that are reduced on formatted sheets are produced to show, on each drawing, the allocation of the various other drawings.

The easiest way to transfer the design to working drawings is to establish a series of datum lines on each sheet. If the original design drawings were drawn to a matrix or block module (refer to the earlier section "Datum Base" in this chapter), the design drawings only need to be reproduced via an engineering copier onto a bond copy. The need for bushes, tree shadows, and design features to help the client understand scale, is then eliminated. An erasable vellum copy is again made on an engineering copier.

The drafter then builds up each drawing through the developmental stages, following basic office standards. The specific stages for the plans, elevations, building sections, and details are covered later in this chapter.

By Computer

If the design phase includes a computer 3-D model, the drafter's task is simple. The 3-D model is rotated (as described in Chapter 3), into an ortho position to obtain plan, elevation, and building sections. The floor plan, which is a horizontal section, is then used as a datum base for other drawings such as the framing plan, mechanical plan, electrical plan, or any other associate (i.e., electrical engineer, structural engineer) you might enlist to aid you in the completion of this set of working drawings. This datum base drawing should be imported as a XREF drawing [see "Externally Referenced Drawing (X REF) section in Chapter 3]. Thus, every time a drawing is accessed, the most recent version of, say, the floor plan, is loaded. The various stages now become layers and any combination of layers can be sent to the associates. In fact, these layers in progress can be placed on a web site and downloaded with a specific code given only to the associates.

Designing Working Drawings Both Manually and on a Computer

Design images that have been drawn manually should be changed to digital images. This can be done by scanning in the presentational plans, elevations, and building sections. Although this drawing cannot be manipulated, it can be used as a tracer or corrected by erasing any undesirable information, with the correction done on a different layer.

■ FORMAT/CARTOON

During the planning phase of developing working drawings, someone in the office may be responsible for the layout of the individual document sheets. The planning phase is most affectionately called the *cartooning* of a set of working drawings. *Mock-up, page format,* and *sheet layout* are other terms used interchangeably.

Although the cartooning of a set of drawings can be done on a full-size sheet of paper, on which it is to be drafted, a more expedient method is to draw it at a reduced sheet size, 8-$\frac{1}{2}$" × 11" being the most convenient size. This can be performed manually or by CAD. In either case, determining the scale at which, say, a floor plan, will be drafted is the biggest problem (see Figure 6.25).

Hand Drafting a Cartoon

When hand drafting (manual drafting) a cartoon, everything is based on proportion. For example, the proportion of the full-size sheet (24" × 36") on an 8-$\frac{1}{2}$ × 11" cartoon. The best way to start is by establishing a ratio of

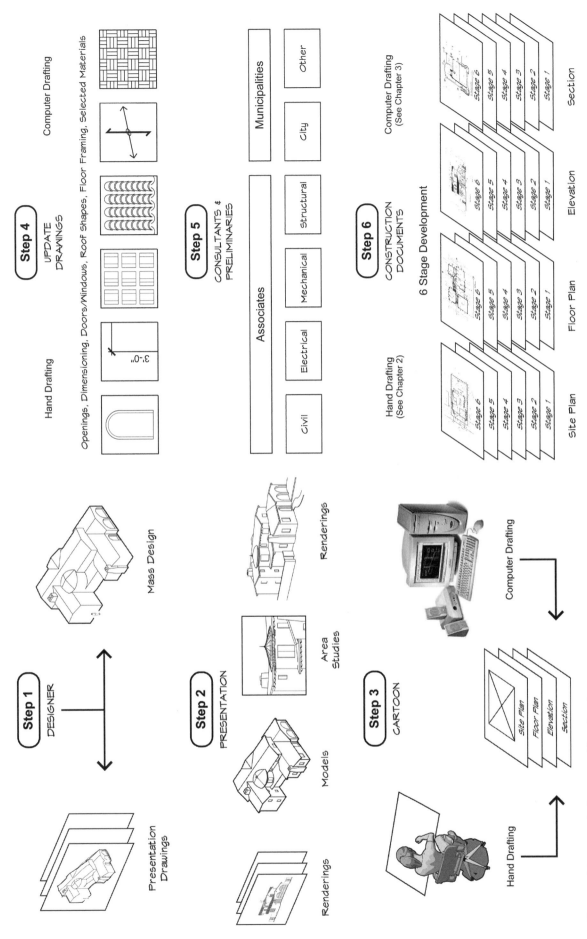

Figure 6.24 From design to working drawings.

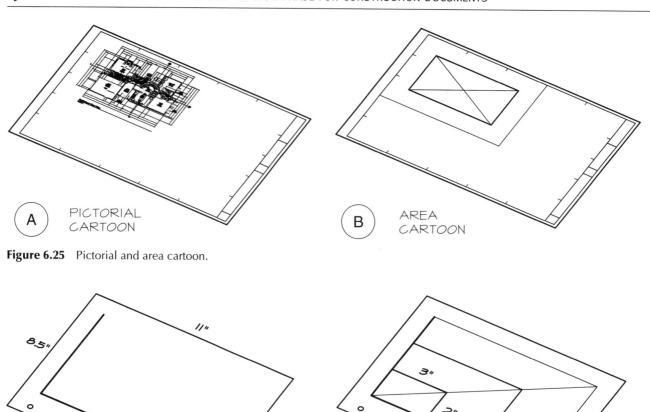

Figure 6.25 Pictorial and area cartoon.

Figure 6.26 Setting up sheet proportion.

the full-size sheet to the cartoon. For example, if the final drawing is to be drafted onto a 24″ × 36″ sheet, the ratio you are dealing with is two feet (24″) by three feet (36″). This is expressed as a ratio of 2 to 3. Start by drawing a datum (see Figure 6.26A). This is a horizontal line along the bottom of the horizontally oriented sheet, and with a vertical line to the left. A 2″ × 3″ rectangle is drafted onto this datum, as shown in Figure 6.26.B. Next, draw a diagonal through the corners of this rectangle to produce an even larger rectangle. Be sure the diagonal line runs through the corners of the new rectangle to maintain the 2 to 3 ratio. This rectangle represents a 24″ × 36″ sheet of paper.

If you divide this space into three equal parts, you will have the equivalent of a 12″ measurement of this rectangle (see Figure 6.27). Subdivide this 12″ unit into twelve equal divisions, and each unit will represent one inch (full-scale) or one foot at a scale of 1″ = 1′ 0″ (see Figure 6.27). In addition, this theoretical 12″ measure-

ment can be divided into 48 divisions for a ¼″ scale, 96 divisions for a ⅛″ scale, or 32 divisions for a ⅜″ scale.

In scaling with a computer, these division numbers are called scale factors, which are discussed later in regard to cartoons produced on a computer.

The typical office sheet, as seen in Figure 6.28, is drawn using the proportion used in Figure 6.27 as drafted. This needs to be done only once for all cartoons. If a cartoon of the floor plan sheet is needed, take the presentational floor plan of the project and, using a known measurement such as the width of the garage—say 24′ 0″, reduce the image on an enlarger/reducer to the desired scale. For a 24′ 0″ measurement at ¼″ = 1′ 0″ scale, you must use the measuring device developed in Figure 6.27. See Figure 6.30 for a composite cartoon of the floor plan shown in Figure 6.29. Note that the space occupied by the floor plan stays within the modules established on this sheet and is found by noting the small tick marks on the sheet.

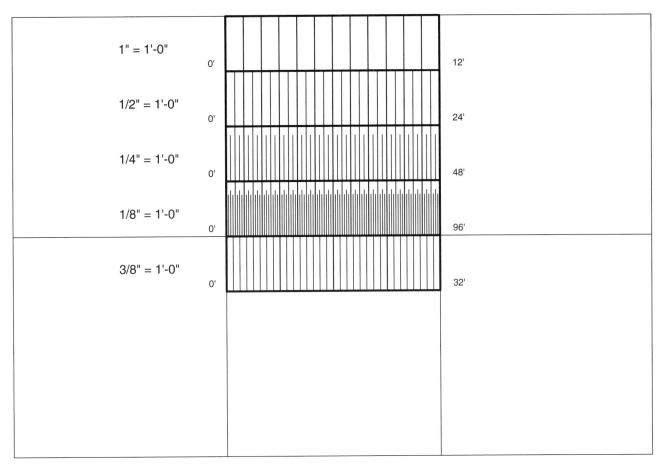

Figure 6.27 Establishing scale relative to sheet size.

Figure 6.28 Typical 24 × 36 construction document sheet.

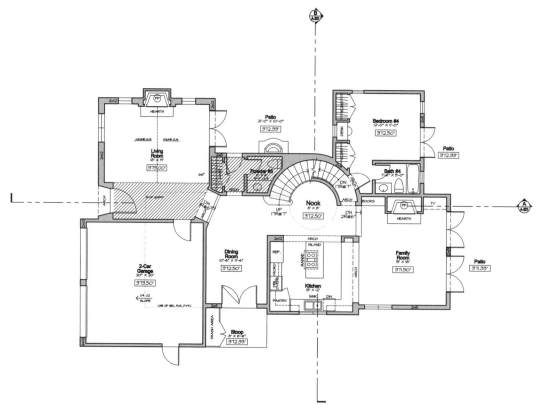

Figure 6.29 Floor plan to be cartooned. (Courtesy of Mike Adli, Owner; Nagy R. Bakhoum, President of Obelisk Architects.)

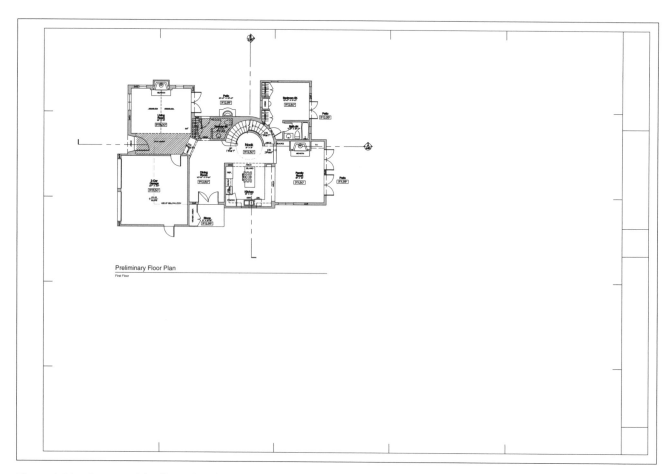

Preliminary Floor Plan
First Floor

Figure 6.30 Cartoon of the floor plan sheet. (Courtesy of Mike Adli, Owner; Nagy R. Bakhoum, President of Obelisk Architects.)

Figure 6.31 shows a cartoon of the exterior elevation sheet with additional measurements for positioning the elevations for the drafter.

Computer Cartoon

Computer cartoons are much easier to produce than hand-drafted cartoons. The paper (24 × 36) is drawn at full scale in model space, and the drawings are im-ported into the theoretically full-size sheet in the desired scale to fit. If the plans, elevations, and sections are drawn full scale, the scaling factor previously discussed is used to create an image in the proper scale (see Figure 6.32).

If drawings are not available, as is usually the case with interior elevations, rectangles can be drawn at the desired scale to occupy the space allocated for a cartoon. See Figure 6.33 for an example of such a cartoon.

Figure 6.31 Cartoon of exterior elevation.

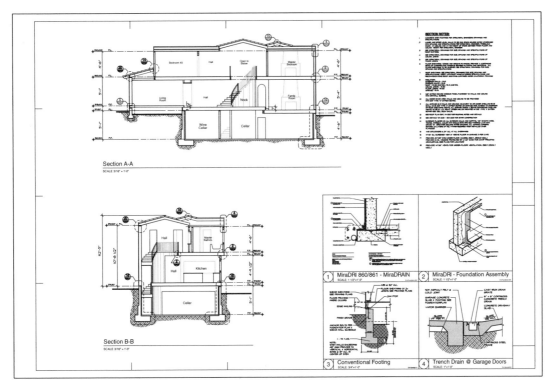

Figure 6.32 Cartoon of building section. (Courtesy of Mike Adli, Owner; Nagy R. Bakhoum, President of Obelisk Architects.)

Hand-Drafted Preliminary to Computer Cartoon

When the preliminary floor plans, elevations, and sections are drawn by hand or freehand, the images can be scanned and positioned onto the sheet at any desired scale. The computer has the capability to enlarge or reduce drawings merely by inputting a scale factor or a proportion ratio.

■ PROJECT BOOK

All information about a specific project, the materials selected, the structural system chosen, the exterior finishes

and interior finishes, plus all correspondence relative to the project, is documented and placed in a project book. Lists of structural considerations, exterior finishes, and interior finishes are shown in Figures 6.34, 6.35, and 6.36, respectively.

Exterior Finishes

In the development of the exterior elevation, the drafter must be able to identify the various materials used on the exterior surface, as well as the type of fenestration via windows and doors. As with structural considerations, a chart is again the instrument used to convey the information to the drafter. See Figure 6.25.

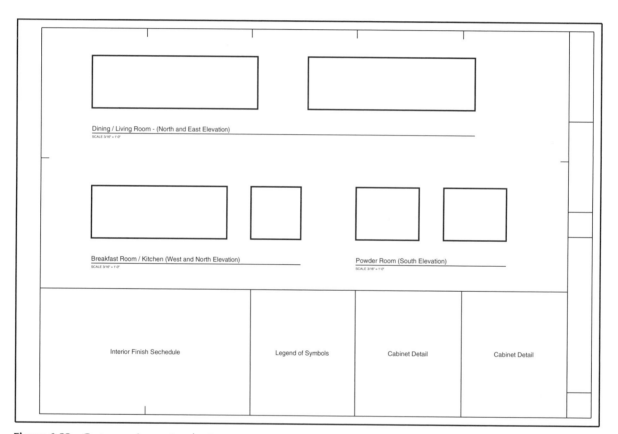

Figure 6.33   Cartoon using rectangles to reserve space.

STRUCTURAL

1. FOUNDATION	2. TYPICAL WALL FRAMING	3. TYPICAL FLOOR FRAMING	4. TYPICAL ROOF FRAMING
a. Conventional slab-on-grade	a. 2 x ___ wood studs	a. 2 x wood floor joists	a. Conventional (wood rafters & beams)
b. Post-tensioned slab	b. Lap with corner boards	b. 2 x wood floor joists per structural consultant	b. TJI
c. Wood floor	c. Other	c. TJI	c. Trusses
d. Other		d. 1-1/2" lightweight concrete over	d. Trusses and conventional framing
		e. Other	
		Note: Specify any minimum sizes	Note: Specify any minimum sizes

Figure 6.34   Listing of structural considerations.

EXTERIOR FINISHES

A. WALLS

1. STUCCO	2. CEDAR SIDING	3. MASONITE SIDING	4. MASONRY VENEER
a. Sand texture	a. Lap with mitered corners	(specify other manufacturers)	a. Thin set brick (mfg.)
b. Other	b. Lap with corner boards		b. Full brick (mfg.)
		a. Lap with metal corners	c. Stone
		b. Lap with corner boards	d. Stucco stone
		c. V-groove with corner boards	e. Other
		d. Other	

B. TRIMS, BARGES, AND FASCIA

1. SIZE	2. TEXTURE
a. X ____ Trim at windows and doors	a. S4S
____ Whole house	b. Resawn
____ Front elevation only	c. Rough sawn
b. X ____ Barge and fascia with ____ X ____ Trim over	d. Other

C. ROOFING

1. MATERIAL	2. GUTTERS	3. DIVERTERS AT DOORS	
a. Wood shakes	a. At whole house	Composition shingle	
b. Wood shingle	b. At doors only	Wood shake and shingle	Only
c. Concrete "s" tile　　　(mfg.)		Flat concrete tile	
d. Clay "s" tile　　　(mfg.)			
e. Clay 2-piece mission tile　　(mfg.)	*Note:*　Gutters will be assumed		
f. Flat concrete tile　　(mfg.)	at all tight eave		
g. Composiiton shingle　　(mfg.)	conditions.		
h. Built-up			
i. Built-up with gravel surface			
j. Other　　　(mfg.)			

D. DECKS AND BALCONIES

1. TYPE
a. 2 X spaced decking
b. Dex-o-Tex waterproof membrane decking
c. Other

E. STAIRS

1. THREADS	2. STRINGERS
a. Open wood treads	a. Steel stringers
b. Precast concrete threads	b. Wood stringers
c. Conc.-filled metal pan treads	
d. Dex-o-Tex waterprf. membrane	

F. DOORS

1. ENTRY	3. PATIO / DECK
a. 3068 1-3/4" S.C.　　(mfg.)	a. Aluminum sliding glass door
b. 3080 1-3/4" S.C.　　(mfg.)	b. Aluminum French doors
c. Other	c. Wood sliding glass door
2. GARAGE	d. Wood French doors
a. Overhead	e. Other
b. Wood roll-up　　(mfg.)	
c. Metal roll-up　　(mfg.)	

G. WINDOWS

1.	Aluminum	Wood	2. MUNTINS
a. Sliding			a. All Windows
b. Single-hung			b. Front elevation and related rooms
c. Double-hung			3. Dual Glazed
d. Awning			4. Single and dual glazing per Title 24
e. Casement			5. Other

H. SKYLIGHTS

1. GLASS (mfg.)	2. ACRYLIC (mfg.)		3. GLAZING
Color	Color	Shape	a. Single
a. Bronze	a. Bronze	a. Flat	b. Double
b. Gray	b. Gray	b. Dome	c. Per Title 24 report
c. Clear	c. Clear	c. Pyramid	d. Other
d. White	d. White	d. Other	
e. Other	e. Other		

Figure 6.35　Listing of exterior finishes.

INTERIOR FINISHES

A. WALLS

1. Drywall - Texture
2. Plaster - Texture
3. Other
4. Bullnose Corners

B. FLOORS

	Carpet	Sheet Vinyl	Ceramic Tile	Other
Entry				
Living				
Dining				
Family				
Den				
Kiitchen				
Nook				
Hall				
Master Bedroom				
Second Bedroom				
Master Dressing Room				
Second Bathroom				
Powder				
Service				

C. CEILING

1. Drywall - Texture
2. Plaster - Texture
3. All dropped beams shall be drywall wrapped
4. All dropped beams shall be exposed
5. Other

D. CABINET TOP AND SPLASH

	Ceramic Tile	Corian	Cult. Marb	Cult. Onyx	Plastic Lam.	Wood	Other	Splash Hght.
Kitchen								
Service								
Wet Bar								
Powder								
Linen								
Master Bathroom								
Second Bathroom								

E. INTERIOR DOORS

1. Passage	2. Wardrobe
Master Bedroom	a. 6'-8" high siding
a. 3068	b. 8'-0" high siding
b. 2868	c. 6'-8" high bifold
c. Other	d. 8'-0" high bifold
Secondary Bedrooms	e. Other
a. 2868	
b. 2668	
c. Other	

3. Mirrored
  a. Master Bedroom
  b. Secondary Bedroom
  c. Other

F. BATHROOM FIXTURES

	Master Bath	Second Bath
1. Tubs and Tub/Showers		
a. 3'-6"x5'-0" cast iron oval tub		
b. 3'-6"x5'-0" porc/stl. oval tub		
c. 3'-6"x5'-0" fiberglass oval tub		
d. 3'-6"x5'-0" 1-piece fiberglass oval tub and surr.		
e. 2'-8"x5'-0" cast iron tub		
f. 2'-8"x5'-0" porc./stl. Tub		
g. 2'-8"x5'-0" 1-piece fiberglass oval tub and surr.		
h. Other		
Note : Specify surrounding material		
2. Showers		
a. Fiberglass pan and surround		
b. Hot mopped ceramic tile pan with ceramic tile surrounding material		
c. Precast pan with surround		
Specify: Type Pan		
Type Surround		
d. Shatterproof enclosure		
e. Curtain rod		
3. Mirrors		
a. 3'-0" high		
b. 3'-6" high		
c. 3'-8" high		
d. 4'-0" high		
e. Full height to ceiling		
4. Medicine Cabinets		

G. KITCHEN APPLIANCES

1. Sink
  a. Double
  b. Double with garbage disposal
  c. Triple
  d. Triple with garbage disposal
2. Built-In Oven
  a. Double - gas
  b. Double - electric
  c. Single with microwave
3. Built-in Cooktop
  a. Gas
  b. Electric
  c. Downdraft - gas
  d. Downdraft - electric
  e. Hood, light and fan above
  f. Microwave above
4. Slide-in Range/Oven (30")
  a. Gas
  b. Electric
  c. Downdraft - gas
  d. Downdraft - electric
  e. Hood, light and fan above
  f. Microwave above

Figure 6.36   Listing of interior finishes.

G. KITCHEN APPLIANCES (continued)

5. Hi/Low Slide-in Range/Oven (30")	
	a. Gas
	b. Electric
	c. Oven below and above
	d. Oven below, microwave above
6. Dishwasher	
	a. Included
7. Trash Compactor	
	a. Included
	Size
8. Refrigerator	
	a. 3'-3" wide space
	b. 3'-0" wide space
	c. Other
	d. Stub-out for ice maker
	e. Recessed stub-out for ice maker

H. LAUNDRY

1. Dryer	
	a. Gas
	b. Electric 220V
	c. Both

I. MECHANICAL

1. F.A.U.	
	a. Gas
	b. Electric
	c. Zoned - Specify number of units _____
1. Air Conditioner	
	a. Included
	b. Optional

J. PLUMBING

1. Water Heater - Gas	
	a. Recirculating
	b. Water softener - included
	c. Water softener - loop only
2. Exterior Hose Bibb	
	a. Total Required _____
	b. Locations: _____

L. FIREPLACES

1. Prefab Metal	
	a. Manufacturer
	b. Size
	c. Gas stub-out
2. Precast Concrete	
	a. Manufacturer
	b. Size
	c. Gas stub-out
3. Masonry Sizes	
	b. Size
	c. Gas stub-out

K. ELECTRICAL

	Surface Mounted	Rec. Can Light	Square Flush Light	Lum. Clg. (Fluor.)	Lum. Soffit (Fluor.)	Lum. Soffit (Incand.)	Wall Mounted	Pendant	Other
1. Location									
Entry									
Living									
Dining									
Family									
Den									
Kitchen									
Nook									
Stair									
Hall									
Master Bedroom									
Second Bedroom									
Master Dress									
Second Dress									
Master Bath									
Second Bath									
Powder									
Service									

2. Outlet for Garage Door Opener	
3. Exterior W.P. Outlets	
	a. Total Required:_____
	b. Location: _____
4. Phone Outlets - Locations	
	a. _____
	b. _____
5. TV Outlets - Locations	
	a. _____
	b. _____
6. Intercom System	
	a. Wired
	b. Option
7. Security System	
	a. Wired
	b. Option

M. Miscellaneous Amenities

1. Safe	
	a. Wall - location _____
	b. Floor - location _____
2. Wet Bar - Plans	
	Under-counter
	Ice maker _____
	Refrigerator,_____
3. Other (specify)	
	a.
	b.

Figure 6.36 *(continued)*.

Interior Finishes

To allow an accurate drawing of the floor plan, interior elevation, and finish schedule, interior finishes are selected by the client in conjunction with the designer. The drafter can find this information in the project book on a chart similar to the one found in Figure 6.36. Although this list is called "Interior Finishes," it often includes appliances and other amenities such as fireplaces, a security system, a safe, and so on.

■ NUMBERS—LEGAL, JOB, TASK

Legal Description

Every project has some type of legal description. A simple description might look like this:

Lot # _____ Block # _____

Tract # ____ , as recorded in book ____ , page ____ ,
_____ county recorder's office.

This is a description that must appear on the set of working drawings. It may be on the first sheet or, more appropriately, on the site plan sheet.

The legal description is used when researching the zoning requirements of your client's site, setback requirements, or any other information you might need for a specific design feature of the project.

Job Number

Every office has its own way of identifying a specific project. Generally, each project is assigned a job number which might reveal the year of the project, the month a job was started, or even the order in which the project was contracted. For example, job #9403 might reflect the third project received in an office in the year 1994. By

using this system, an office can rapidly identify the precise year a job was constructed and never duplicate a number.

Task Number

In all offices, a time card or some such form is used to keep track of the performance of the drafter. In a small office, a drafter might log the time spent on a project by simply writing the date, the job number, a written description of the task performed, and amount of time, such as:

6–14   Job #9403—Ryan Floor Plan   2 hrs.

If you are working on one or two projects at one time, this method might suffice, but in a large office each task is also numbered. Figure 6.37 displays a chart describing

ADDITIONAL SERVICE CHECK LIST
SINGLE-FAMILY SUMMARY OF PLANNED MAN-HOURS

PROJECT NAME: _____

PROJECT NO: _____

PROJECT MANAGER: _____

START DATE: _____

	WORK PACKAGE NAMES	PLANNED MAN-HOURS
110	BUILDING DEPARTMENT PLAN CHECK	
120	BUILDING DEPARTMENT SUBMITTAL	
130	IN-HOUSE PLAN CHECK	
140	SITE VISIT	
150	PRODUCTION ASSISTANT/PRINTING	
160	CONSTRUCTION DOCUMENTS (DIR. & ASSOC. DIR.)	
170	FOUNDATION LAY-OUT (ARCHITECTURAL)	
180	FLOOR PLAN	
190	ARCHITECTURAL BACKGROUND	
200	EXTERIOR ELEVATIONS	
210	BUILDING SECTIONS	
220	DETAILS	
230	INTERIOR ELEVATIONS	
240	ROOF PLAN	
250	STAIR PLANS	
260	NOT USED	
270	NOT USED	
280	FOUNDATION PLAN (STRUCTURAL INFORMATION)	
290	FRAMING PLAN (STRUCTURAL)	
300	TITLE SHEET	
310	SITE PLAN	
320	SCHEDULES	
330	PLAN CHANGE (SINGLE FAMILY)	
340	PROJECT MANAGEMENT (PROJECT MGR./ARCHITECT)	
350	PROJECT MEETINGS (TEAM MEMBERS)	
360	CAD COORDINATION (DIR. OF CAD SERVICES)	
370	CAN BE USED FOR ADDITIONAL WORK	
380	CAN BE USED FOR ADDITIONAL WORK	
390	CAN BE USED FOR ADDITIONAL WORK	
	TOTAL PLANNED MAN-HOURS	

APPROVED BY: _____

Figure 6.37   Task numbers and summary of planned man-hours.

Summary of Planned Man-Hours

Project Name: The Professional Practice or Architectural Drawings
Case Study—Mr. And Mrs. _____ Residence

Task No.	Work Package Names	Planned Man-Hours
310	Site Plan, Root Plan, and Energy Notes	10
170	Foundation Plan and Details	20
180	Floor Plan and Electrical Plan	20
220/320	Door Window Details and Schedules	32
200	Exterior Elevations and Details	20
210	Building Sections	10
290	Roof Framing and Details	20
230	Interior Elevations	16
130	Project Coordination and Plan Check	18
	Total Hours	166
	166 hours $ _____ Hr. =	$ _____

Figure 6.38 Planned man-hours for a project.

the work to be performed as "work packages," the task number at the left assigned to the specific package, and a column at the right indicating the total man-hours planned for the particular work package. The task numbers jump by ten, allowing the flexibility, on a complex project, to have sub-work packages. For example, 140 Site Visit might use 141 as a task number for measuring an existing structure to be altered.

Figure 6.38 is an example of the total man-hours for a particular job, such as the Ryan Residence. Note the task numbers and the computer display of the corresponding work package names.

Each week as the drafters turn in their time cards, the man-hours and tasks performed are loaded into a computer, allowing the project manager to ascertain instantly the progress on a particular job or check to see if the project has been budgeted correctly. Figure 6.39 provides an example of such a spot check.

Summary of Man-Hours Through 12-15-93

310	Site Plan	2 hrs. 40 min.
310	Vicinity Map	20 min.
310	Roof Plan	1 hr. 15 min.
170	Foundation Plan	3 hrs. 15 min.
320	Foundation Details	3 hrs. 55 min.
180	Floor Plan	4 hrs. 5 min.
200	Exterior Elevations	3 hrs. 55 min.
210	Sections (Garage)	15 min.
290	Roof Framing Plan	40 min.
130	Projection Coordination	2 hrs. 5 min.
	Total NqNqNqNqNqNqNqNq22 hrs. 25 min.	

Figure 6.39 Progress for a specific time period.

Document Numbering System

Although this book is mainly concerned with architectural working drawings, it includes other drawings which constitute a complete set of construction documents. To keep all of the drawings in their proper spaces, they are numbered differently. For example, the set of architectural drawings can easily be identified by the letter A: Sheets A-1, A-2, A-3, and so on. In contrast, S can be used for structural drawings (S-1, S-2, S-3), E for electrical, L for landscape, and M for mechanical, to mention but a few categories.

A typical sheet number might look like this:

It is extremely important also to indicate the number of sheets in the set. In this example there are 15. If the total number of sheets is not indicated, the recipient of the set will never know whether there is a sheet missing should Sheet 15 accidentally be excluded.

■ DRAWING SEQUENCE

Now to the actual performance—the development of the drawings themselves. As indicated previously, most offices have a game plan. Although such plans may vary slightly from one office to another, Figure 6.40 displays

Working Drawing Procedures

PROJECT

1. Lay out Unit Floor Plans—$\frac{1}{4}$"
   - ____ Block out walls.
   - ____ Doors and windows.
   - ____ Cabinets, appliances, and fixtures.
   - ____ Dimension overalls.
   - ____ Calculate square footages.

2. Lay Out Roof Plan—$\frac{1}{8}$"
   - ____ Indicate exterior line of building.
   - ____ Indicate roof lines and pitch.

3. Lay Out Building Sections—$\frac{1}{4}$"
   - ____ Indicate type of framing.
   - ____ Dimension floor and plate heights.

4. Lay Out Exterior Elevations—$\frac{1}{4}$"
   - ____ Indicate doors and windows.
   - ____ Indicate exterior materials.
   - ____ Dimension floor and plate heights.

5. Lay Out Addenda Plans—$\frac{1}{4}$"
   - ____ Partial floor plans.
   - ____ Exterior elevations (per step #4).
   - ____ Roof plan (per step #2).

6. Project Manager to Select Keynotes
   - ____ Floor plans.
   - ____ Exterior elevations.
   - ____ Interior elevations.
   - ____ Sections.

7. Project Manager to Select Details
   - ____ Doors and windows.
   - ____ Exterior elevations.
   - ____ Interior elevations.

8. Project Manager to Lay Out Framing and Mechanical Study
   - ____ Overlays.

9. Plot
   - ____ Floor plans.
   - ____ Addenda plans/exterior elevations/roof plans.
   - ____ Sections.
   - ____ Submit package to structural, T-24 engineers, and applicable consultants.
   - ____ In-house back check of package (designer and project architect).

50% Complete

10. Floor Plans—$\frac{1}{4}$"
    - ____ Lay out electrical plan.
    - ____ Finish interior/exterior dimensions.
    - ____ Note plans.
    - ____ Reference details.

11. Lay Out Interior Elevations and Fireplaces—$\frac{1}{4}$"
    - ____ Indicate ceiling heights.
    - ____ Dimension cabinet heights.
    - ____ Dimension appliances.
    - ____ Note interiors.
    - ____ Dimension fireplaces.
    - ____ Note fireplaces.

12. Architectural Detail Sheets
    - ____ Finish all details.
    Consultant design information due for in-house plan check and application to drawings.

13. Addenda
    13.1 Partial Floor Plans
    - ____ Electrical.
    - ____ Dimension.
    - ____ Note—Plans.
    - ____ Reference details.
    13.2 Roof Plans—$\frac{1}{4}$"
    - ____ Reference details.
    - ____ Reference notes.
    13.3 Exterior Elevations
    - ____ Reference details.
    - ____ Reference notes.
    - ____ Exterior materials finish schedule.

14. Sections
    - ____ Reference notes.
    - ____ Coordinate consultant design.

15. Title Sheet
    - ____ Code tabulation.
    - ____ Consultant information.
    - ____ Vicinity map.
    - ____ Sheet index.

16. Final Coordination
    - ____ Building department submittal information.
    - ____ Final plotting for building department.
    - ____ Submit for plan check.

90% Complete

17. Formal In-House Plan Check
    - ____ Plan check.

18. Building Department Plan Check
    - ____ Incorporate correction into plans.
    - ____ Coordinate client/cyp in-house plan checks and incorporate into plans.
    - ____ Final plot for building department submittal.

19. Signatures
    - ____ Upon building department approval (permit), route plan set for consultant approval and signatures.

100% Complete

Ready for plotting and submittal

Figure 6.40 Working drawing procedures—the game plan.

what we feel is a rather typical sequence. The term *lay out* or *block out* in this list means to draw lightly so that changes and corrections can easily be implemented. Key or special notes (*Keynotes*) refers to the fact that noting is vitally important. The drafter should respond to this or any list just as it's written. Proceed *no* further than what is listed and assigned, because at certain intervals a spot check will be made by the project manager. Some of these checks are noted on the "Working Drawing Procedures" list.

Also note that in between numbers 9 and 10 is a "50% Complete" note. This is a point at which the time sheets are checked in the computer to validate that the drawing budget is approximately 50% used.

The Development of Working Drawings

Although the total development of a set of working drawings is not addressed in this chapter, we will take a skeletal look at the general process here. For development of individual working drawing sheets, refer to the sections at the ends of Chapters 8, 9, 10, 12, 13, and 14. For a look at the development of a set of working drawings using different materials and different building types, see Chapter 17 for a simple one-story single-family residence, Chapter 18 for a two-story beach house, Chapter 19 for a six-plex theatre complex constructed of masonry, Chapter 20 for a steel office building, and Chapter 21 for a tenant improvement project in an existing building.

Preliminary Approach with Computer Model

Following the initial design stages of whatever process is chosen, a massing study is used as a bridge between the design and construction documents (see Figure 6.41). If this massing study was sketched, the computer drafter must know how to translate the study into the computer as a three-dimensional drawn object. If the massing study was initially formed as a three-dimensional model on the computer, the journey is much easier. Review the steps described in Chapter 3 to better understand the process we will now embark upon.

Initially the 3-D massing model is refined and adjusted to the client's needs (see Figure 6.42). The next step is to convert the refined 3-D model into a series of ortho views. The top view becomes the roof plan, and the front, rear, and side views become the elevation (see Figure 6.43). The next step is one that can be performed by only the most highly trained CAD drafter. This is the process of taking a building (drawn in 3-D) and slicing it. The horizontal slice produces a floor plan when the inside is detailed. The vertical slice becomes a building section when rotated into an ortho position (see Figure 6.44). A summary of the various views available via ro-

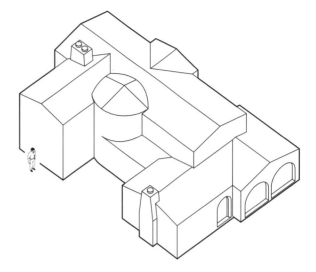

Figure 6.41   3-D model of Adli Residence (sketch). (Courtesy of Mike Adli, Owner; Nagy R. Bakhoum, President of Obelisk Architects.)

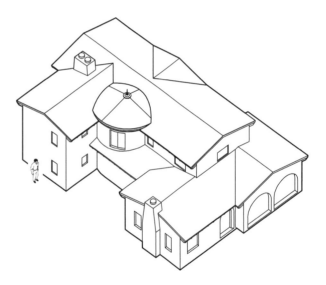

Figure 6.42   3-D model of Adli Residence (final). (Courtesy of Mike Adli, Owner; Nagy R. Bakhoum, President of Obelisk Architects.)

tation can be seen in Figure 6.45. Further rotation of isolated areas produces the details as seen in Figure 6.44.

Stages and Layers of Production Drawings

The pictorial and preliminary floor plan shown in Figure 6.47 can be used as a tracer for the hand drawings or scanned and used as a construction layer for computer drawings. If the 3-D model is digital, we can then rotate the object into the required views as described earlier.

Producing the initial stage of working drawings by rotation sets the stage for the following five to six stages of

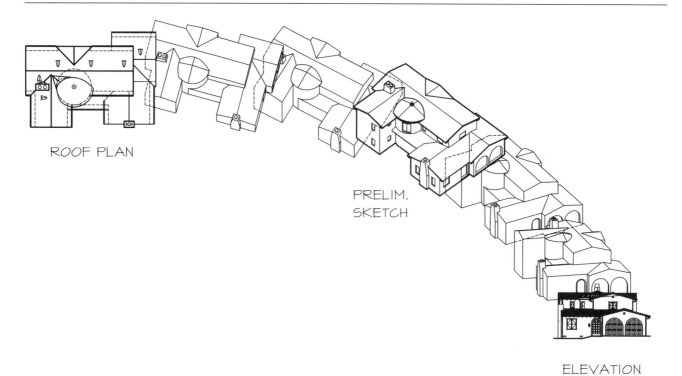

ROOF PLAN

PRELIM.
SKETCH

ELEVATION

Figure 6.43 Rotation of massing model into ortho view. (Courtesy of Mike Adli, Owner; Nagy R. Bakhoum, President of Obelisk Architects.)

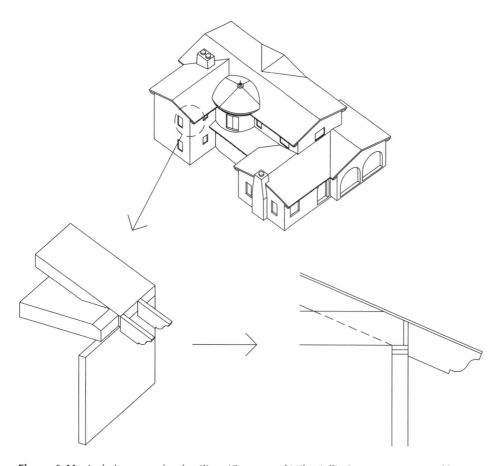

Figure 6.44 Isolating areas for detailing. (Courtesy of Mike Adli, Owner; Nagy R. Bakhoum, President of Obelisk Architects.)

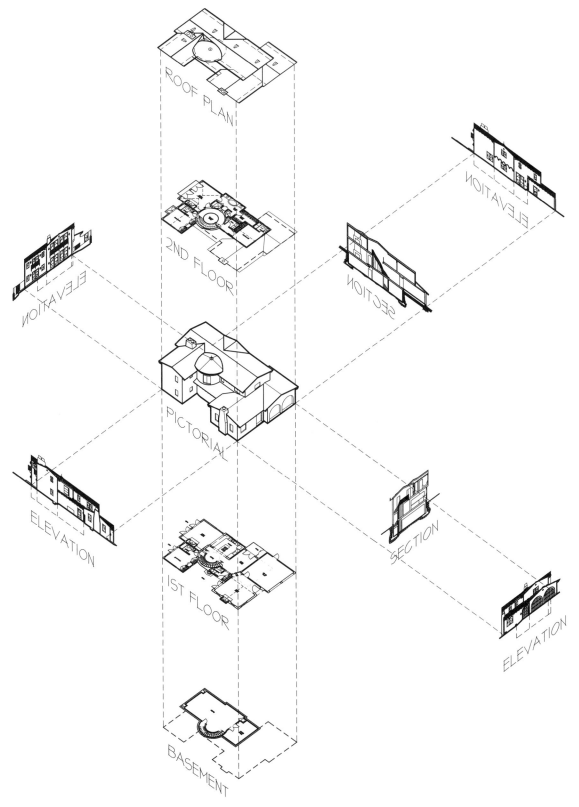

Figure 6.45 Evolution of construction documents. (Courtesy of Mike Adli, Owner; Nagy R. Bakhoum, President of Obelisk Architects.)

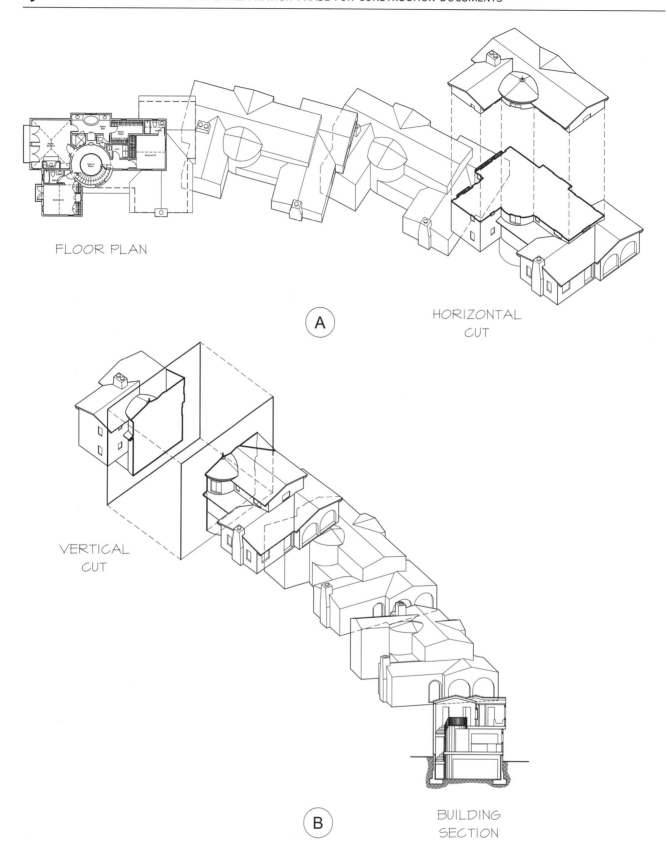

FLOOR PLAN

HORIZONTAL
CUT

A

VERTICAL
CUT

BUILDING
SECTION

B

Figure 6.46 Horizontal and vertical sections through preliminary sketch. (Courtesy of Mike Adli, Owner; Nagy R. Bakhoum, President of Obelisk Architects.)

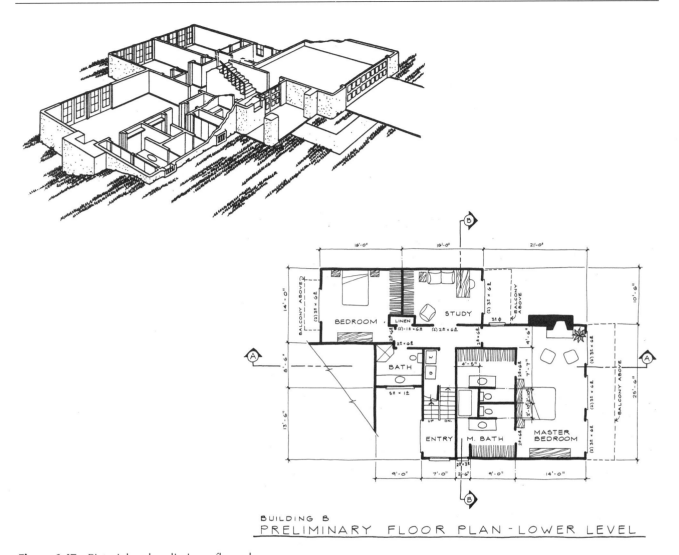

BUILDING B
PRELIMINARY FLOOR PLAN-LOWER LEVEL

Figure 6.47 Pictorial and preliminary floor plan.

layers that are produced by the CAD drafter. More complex projects may call for more stages, but we think that five is the absolute minimum number of stages for any set of working drawings.

Stages

STAGE I (Figure 6.48). The floor plan becomes the basic pattern for all other drawings in the set. If a computer is used, grids and snaps are set to produce the preestablished modules, such as a block module when masonry is used or a matrix for steel.

STAGE II (Figure 6.49). The interior and exterior walls with their limits are drawn in this stage. Columns and openings should also be included at this stage. The designer called for rounded corners. Figure 6.50 shows a pictorial and a detail of how this is accomplished. This stage may become the datum stage for the foundation plan.

STAGE III (Figure 6.51). Stair positioning is critical at this stage. Plumbing appliances also become a critical part of the drawing. For an office, partitions are frequently drawn at this stage, as are nonbearing walls and the positions for openings and doors not previously positioned by rotation of the 3-D model.

STAGE IV (Figure 6.52). This is a crucial stage, because sizing and location (positioning) occurs at this time. Dimensioning, including values, is also accomplished here. You must dimension to face or center of stud for wood, follow a block module for masonry, and position the columns correctly using the axial reference plane method for steel.

STAGE V (Figure 6.53). This is the communication level. The drawing is cross-referenced with other drawings, plans, sections, and details.

STAGE VI (Figure 6.54). All text and titles should be placed on one layer. Refer to the standard for type face, size, and positioning.

Stages and layers may appear to be the same to the beginning CAD drafter, but in reality they are different. An

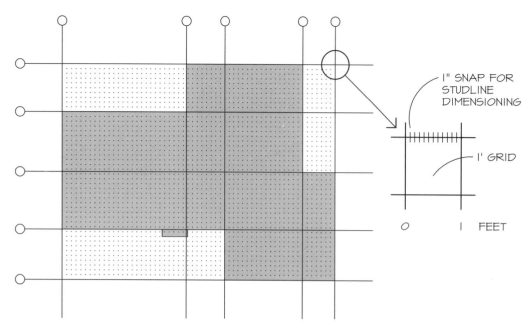

Figure 6.48 Floor plan datum layer.

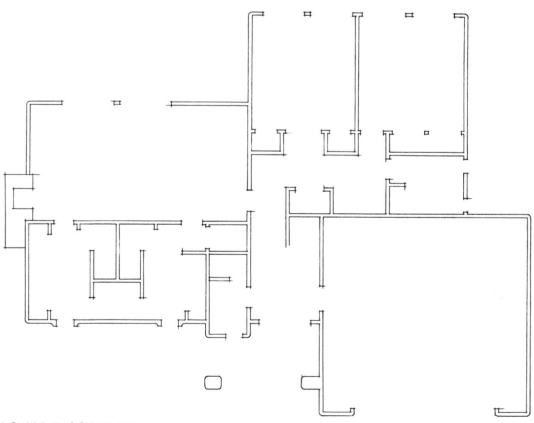

LOWER FLOOR PLAN

Stage II

Step A. Lay out basic shape from preliminary lower floor plan.
Step B. Special attention to columns at entry.
Step C. Note special round corners.

Figure 6.49 Stage II.

194

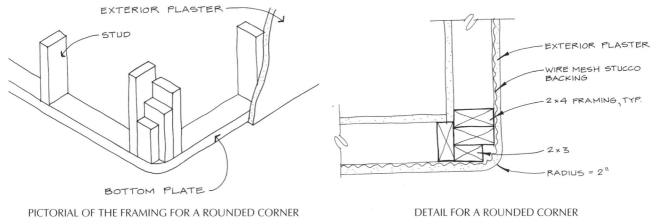

EXTERIOR PLASTER

STUD

BOTTOM PLATE

PICTORIAL OF THE FRAMING FOR A ROUNDED CORNER

EXTERIOR PLASTER

WIRE MESH STUCCO BACKING

2 x 4 FRAMING, TYP.

2 x 3

RADIUS = 2"

DETAIL FOR A ROUNDED CORNER

Figure 6.50 Framing at rounded corners.

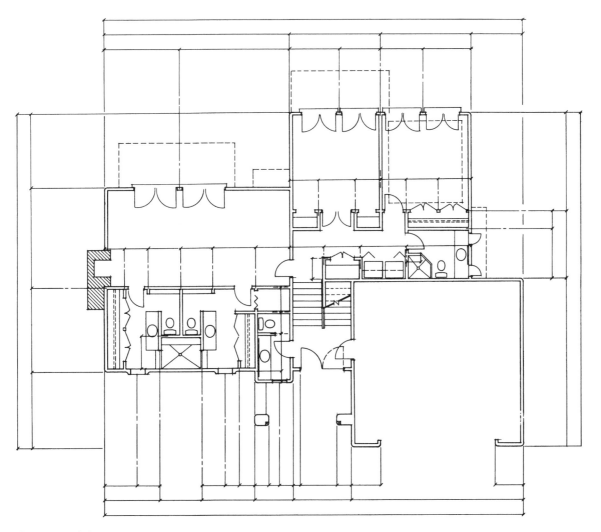

LOWER FLOOR PLAN

Stage III

Step A. Darken walls.
Step B. Show all built-ins and equipment.
Step C. Show decks at rear of structure.
Step D. Show stairs.

Figure 6.51 Stairs and plumbing appliances.

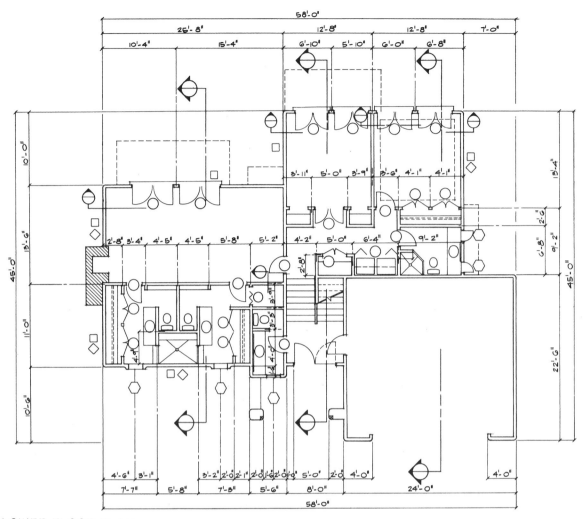

LOWER FLOOR PLAN

Stage IV

Step A. Show door swings and windows.
Step B. Dimension lines added.
Step C. Column at entry added.
Step D. Material designation for fireplace.

Figure 6.52 Dimensioning and material designation.

example is the floor plan shown in Figure 6.47. This is a drawing done in six or seven stages, but there are as many as fifteen layers. The greater the number of layers, the easier it is to change or alter the drawing. As any office employee will tell you, there is nothing more constant than change. The client may find a better piece of equipment that needs to be dimensioned into the drawing, the Department of Building and Safety may require a greater clearance than originally expected, the structural engineer may request a longer wall for a shear wall, or any number of changes may develop. The importance

of being able to alter a drawing easily then becomes very evident.

Some layers may contain similar conventions—for example, text on one layer and dimensions on another. The CAD drafter may work a little on each layer as the drawing process progresses, as described in the stages of evolution. Additional layers may have to be developed as needed. An example of this is the text titled "ANNO." The text layer can be divided into a multiple number of layers. One layer may be used for room titles only, a second layer may be used for general construction notes,

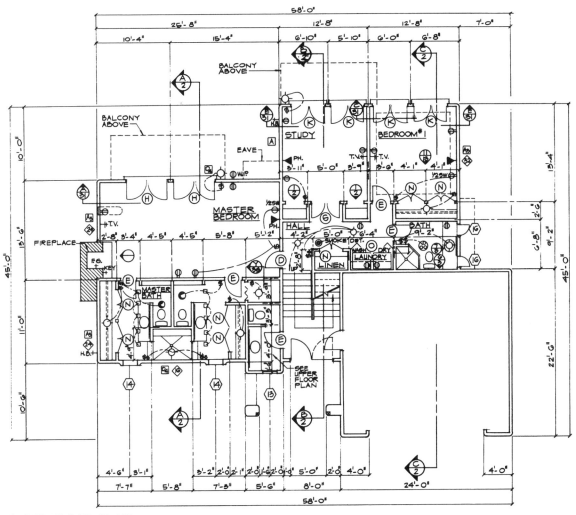

LOWER FLOOR PLAN

Stage V

Step A. Reference bubbles for doors and windows added.
Step B. Numerical values added on dimension lines (verify with foundation plan).
Step C. Special noting around exterior (square and diamond shape indicate finish and other nailing).
Step D. Building section references bubble.

Figure 6.53 Referencing.

and all other incidental notes may be on a third. The same can be said about dimensions. Column dimensions may be on one layer, and bearing wall dimensions may be on a second layer. Nonbearing walls and the dimensions for partitions may be on a third. In this manner, the CAD drafter can finish each layer in his or her sequential order. An architectural office may utilize a standard layering practice as proposed in the national standards, or it may develop its own method.

The final plot sheet of the first floor plan of the Adli Residence is shown in Figure 6.55. This sheet has twenty

layers, but many of the layers have been combined, resulting in a set of drawings with eleven layers:

A. Plot Sheet. Figure 6.55 includes the title block and the notes on separate sheets.
B. The floor plan is divided into the following layers:
  1. Datum Layer—Figure 6.56. This layer shows the perimeter layout for a block module if the building is made of masonry. Space is plotted at the given module if a module is used (e.g., 5'0" module). The module at which the steel

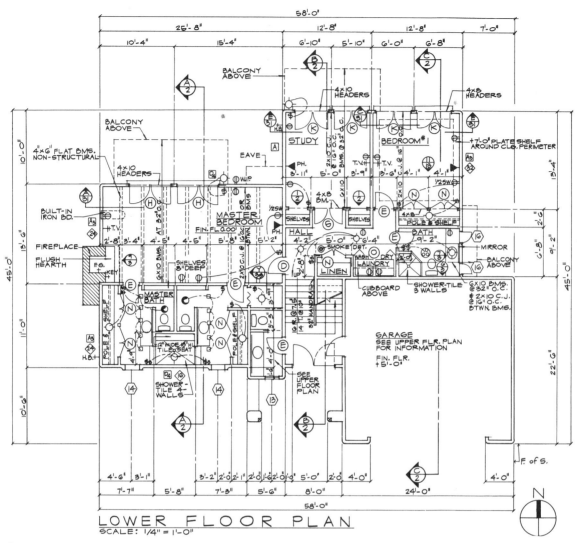

LOWER FLOOR PLAN
SCALE: 1/4" = 1'-0"

LOWER FLOOR PLAN

Stage VI

Step A. Fill in reference bubbles.
Step B. Show all electrical.
Step C. Show roof tile.
Step D. Interior elevation reference symbols.
Step E. Special noting (see legend of symbols on foundation plan).
Step F. Add second floor framing information on lower floor plan and roof framing information on upper floor plan.

Figure 6.54 Final plot sheet of lower floor plan.

columns are set by the structural engineer (e.g., 10'–0" o.c.) if steel is used, or setting the grid at one-foot increments and the snap at one-inch increments for stud line dimensioning when the structure is to be framed in wood. Whatever the game plan for the structure in question, the datum layer becomes the pattern to which all other drawings are established. This perimeter drawing can be used to estimate square footage or to estimate the perimeter of this form.

2. Figure 6.57. All walls are drawn on this layer. It may be split further into two additional layers, one showing bearing walls only, and nonbearing walls on the other. If walls are moved, one can decide immediately whether it is a load-bearing wall that affects the structure, or a non-

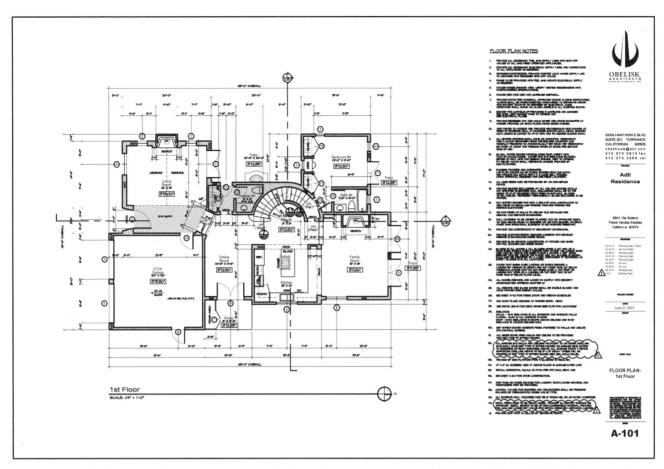

Figure 6.55 Plot sheet: First floor plan. (Courtesy of Mike Adli, Owner; Nagy R. Bakhoum, President of Obelisk Architects.)

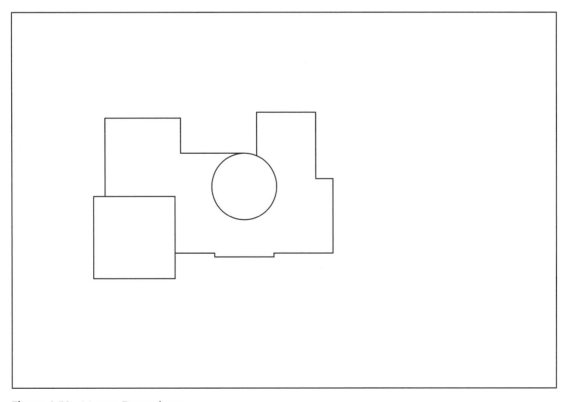

Figure 6.56 Master: Datum layer.

bearing wall that does not affect the calculation or engineering of the structure. If the walls were already drawn in 3-D, validate that indeed they were extruded from the massing model. A rotation of the 3-D model can be used for this layer. All openings can be done in this stage or again on another layer.

3. Figure 6.58. Plumbing appliances, stairs, cabinets, and fireplaces are drawn on this layer. They can also be drawn on separate layers.

4. Figure 6.59. All hidden lines are drawn on this layer. They may be outlines of cabinets, soffits, or ceiling level changes. Whatever the reason for using hidden lines, they are placed on this level, voiding the need to change line types within a layer. They too can be divided into wall and floor layers.

5. Figure 6.60. Because openings were positioned on a previous layer, the conventions used to identify doors, windows, and, in some instances, large cabinets are drawn at this stage. As can be seen on this layer, the doors that lap are identified. It will also help later in the positioning of light switches to ensure that none are placed behind doors.

6. Figure 6.61. This is the most critical of all of the layers in this set because it sets the parameters and limitations for all the other drawings, elevations, sections, framing, and so forth. The numerical values must adhere to the module being used. If the structure is a wood stud construction, the dimensions must be set to face of stud (outside walls) or center of stud (inside walls). They must be positioned so the workers in the field (carpenters in this instance) can immediately find them and use the measurements efficiently and accurately. Dimension everything. Do not leave anything to chance. Do not force the carpenter to compute figures. Be sure the total equals the sum of its parts. See Chapter 10, "Floor Plan," and review the sections on dimensioning practices.

7. Figure 6.62. This is the lettering layer. In most instances it is split into two layers, room titles and other lettering. The name of the drawing, North arrow, scale, and any other office standard titling identification can be placed on a third lettering layer.

8. Figure 6.63. Walls can be pouchéd (darkened) on this layer. For the floor plan, all walls are

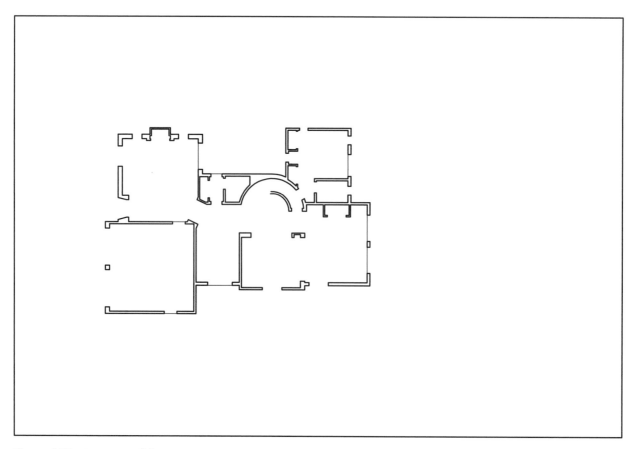

Figure 6.57 Master: Wall layer.

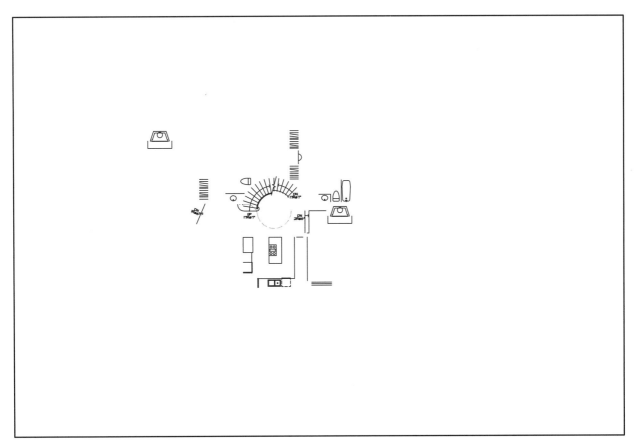

Figure 6.58 Master: Floor layer.

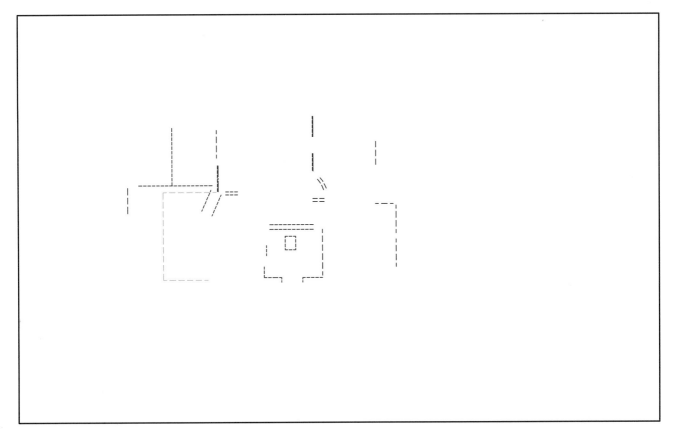

Figure 6.59 Master: Wall and floor hidden layer.

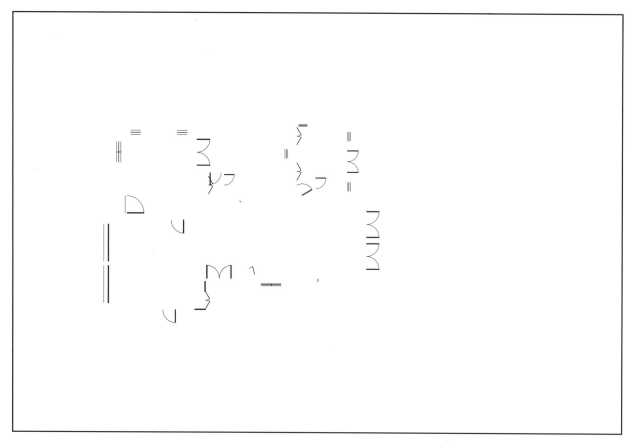

Figure 6.60 Master: Door and glazing layer.

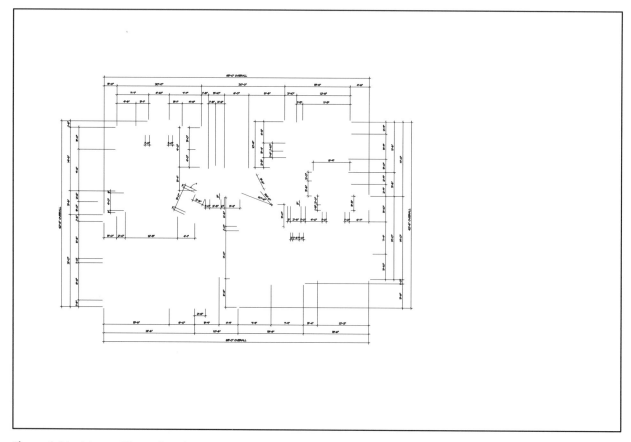

Figure 6.61 Master: Dimensions layer.

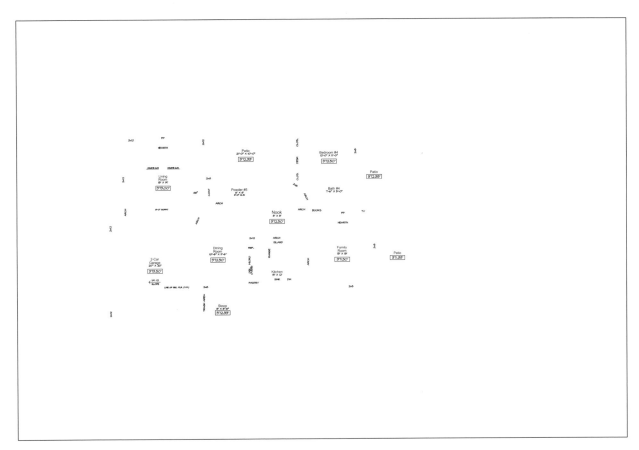

Figure 6.62 Master: Annotation layer.

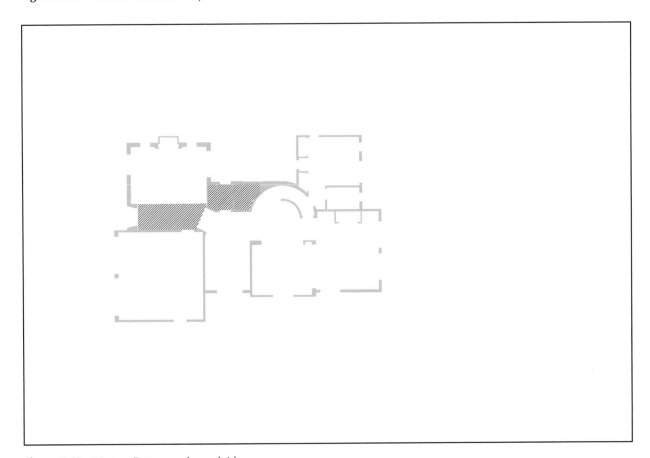

Figure 6.63 Master: Pattern and pouché layer.

shaded in the same intensity. On a framing plan, the bearing walls can be shaded dark and the nonbearing walls are not pouchéd. Patterns for furred ceilings, floor material, fireplace hearths, and any other patterns can be done on this layer or, again, as in previous layers, split into multiple layers if the patterns are complex.

9. Figure 6.64. This is a critical communicative layer. This layer references one area of a drawing to a detail, schedule, or building section. You will notice reference bubbles for a variety of referrals. Each of these can be placed on a separate layer.

10. Patios, barbeques and other outside forms that do not affect the floor plan yet, set the proper context for the floor plan, can be done on another layer. The outside forms on this floor plan were so minimal that an example is not shown.

11. Figure 6.65A. XREF(ed) and positioned on all sheets is the standard office title block and notes (Figure 6.65B).

12. As can be seen in Figure 6.55, there is a set of notes positioned on the extreme right side. As with details, these may be predrawn or preformatted notes and should be placed on a layer by themselves.

13. Please note the revisions on the notes and in the revision portion of the title block on Figure 6.55. All revisions should be placed on a separate layer.

Chapters 8 through 16 have been organized to dovetail with this chapter, in conjunction with Chapter 2 ("Basic Drafting Requirements, Standards, and Techniques") and Chapter 3 ("Computer-Aided Drafting (CAD)"), as well as the five case studies at the end of this book along with drawings on the web site.

■ DELIVERY METHODS

The method of actually printing or plotting a drawing is called the delivery or reproduction method. With manually drafted documents, the originals are drawn on vellum and then copied onto a light-sensitive paper (most often by a diazo method). This requires the drafting technique to keep all parts of the vellum translucent so that

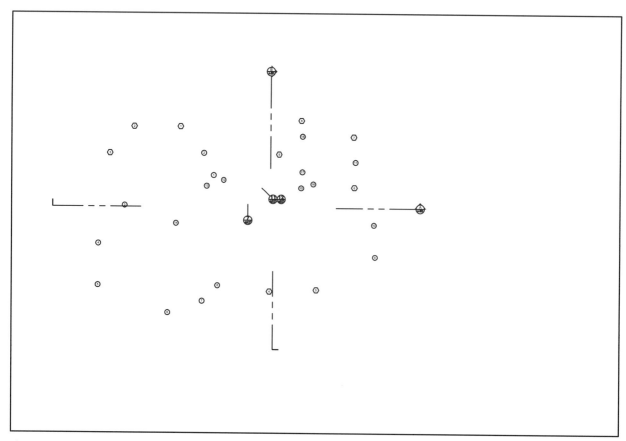

Figure 6.64   Master: Section and symbol layer.

Figure 6.65A   XREF: Title block.

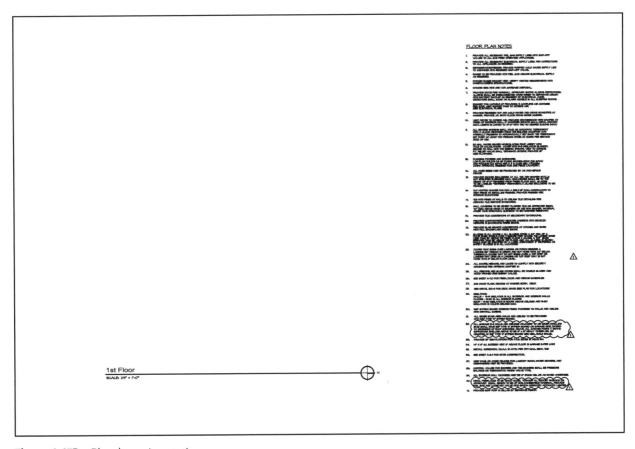

Figure 6.65B   Plot sheet: Annotation.

light can penetrate the originals and print the lines, much like a negative from a camera. Other drawings should not be pasted onto the vellum unless they are spliced into the drawing or translucent adhesive materials are used.

If an engineering copier is used (which reproduces much like a large plain paper copier), a drafter can paste drawings, notes, and charts onto one large sheet and produce a composite drawing. Even photographs and vendors' literature can be pasted or taped on with page-mending tape. Corrections can be done easily with the use of white correction fluid or simply a cutout.

With CAD, the delivery system employed takes on a completely new look. Because the entire drawing is electronic, any electronic device can be used as a delivery method, starting with plotters and printers for a hard copy, or sent via telephone lines with a modem or e-mailed.

At one time there was a cardinal rule in our industry: "Never give the client the originals!" Today we are essentially giving up our originals by sending electronically based drawings. There are both positives and negatives to sending electronic copies of our documents.

On the positive side:

A. Our consultants get the exact base sheet on which they can compute and draw the framing plans and structural details.
B. For an out-of-stage project, multiple copies can be at another location.
C. Corrections can be made instantly in the field and relayed to the home office.
D. There is no downtime for mail delivery as was the case with hard copy.

On the negative side:

A. There is a potential for piracy of the drawings.
B. Building departments require wet copy signatures for permits.
C. Viruses can destroy parts of an image, creating an incorrect set of drawings.

chapter

7

GAME PLAN FOR MATERIALS SELECTED

In the practice of architecture, an architectural firm will be confronted with the issue of selecting a material for a specific project. This selection process is generally dictated by such factors as the governing building codes, fire department requirements, the architect's design philosophy, environmental influences, and economical considerations. For most structures the main materials used are wood, concrete, structural steel, masonry, light steel framing, and composite materials. For many structures a combination of materials may be utilized.

Once a material has been chosen for a specific project, the architect and staff members will then develop a game plan for work with the selected materials.

■ WOOD AS A MATERIAL

When a conventional wood stud framing system has been selected for the floor, walls, and roof systems, it will require that the floor plan drawings are graphically correct. For example, a wood stud wall system is shown with the use of two parallel lines, which may be drawn to scale, incorporating the wood stud size in combination with the exterior and interior finishes. An example of a floor plan for a small dwelling using two parallel lines to represent a conventional 2" × 4' wood stud wall in plan view is illustrated in Figure 7.1. The exterior walls are dimensioned from the face of the wood stud as ab-

breviated with the letters 'f.o.s.' indicating "face of stud." The interior walls are dimensioned to the centerline of the walls, as indicated in Figure 7.1. Note that the 4' × 4' post is dimensioned to the center line in both directions.

Figure 7.2 represents a pictorial view of the corner framing condition for this small dwelling. This is shown to illustrate the actual dimension line as it relates to the stud face dimension. This method of dimensioning will correspond to the face of the concrete foundation footing, thus providing a good dimensional check for both the floor plan and the foundation plan. For layout purposes, the width of the two parallel lines will be the stud width of $3\frac{1}{2}$" plus the thickness of the exterior and interior wall finishes.

In laying out the interior walls of the floor plan, the two parallel lines will be drawn to scale, incorporating the width of the wood stud plus the thickness of the interior wall finishes. The dimensioning of the interior walls will be the centerline of the wood stud wall, as depicted in Figure 7.1. A pictorial view of an exterior wood stud wall and the intersection of an interior wall are shown in Figure 7.3. Note that the exterior dimension lines are to the center of the interior stud wall line. The centerline dimensioning of the interior walls will correspond with the centerline dimensioning for concrete foundation footings that may be found directly under an interior load-bearing wall. In general, the layout of a floor plan using a wood stud framing system is very flexible in comparison to that

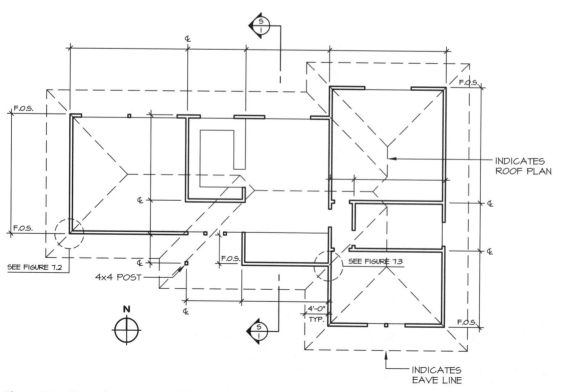

Figure 7.1   Floor plan—2 × 4 stud framing.

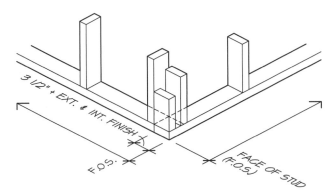

Figure 7.2 Corning framing layout.

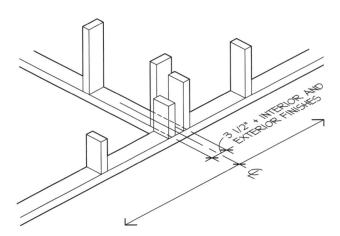

Figure 7.3 Exterior and interior wall intersection.

of a floor plan using other material. This is because openings in the exterior and interior walls are not restricted to a modular unit or other material considerations.

Exterior Elevations

The design and layout for the exterior elevations are developed in conjunction with the floor plan exterior wall openings, exterior wall material, roofing material, and roof pitch. The initial building section concept is also considered in the design development of the exterior elevations. Another aspect to be included in the layout process for the exterior elevations is the design and layout of the roof plan. The architect for this small dwelling has chosen to use a hip roof design utilizing cement tiles as a finish roof material. The roof plan is illustrated in Figure 7.1. Based on the foregoing considerations, the design and layout for the exterior elevations may then proceed. Figure 7.4 illustrates the design and layout of the South elevation. The height of 9' from the top of the concrete floor to the top plate has been dictated by the 4' overhang, the roof pitch, and the horizontal soffit at the eaves, which terminate just above the exterior window and exterior door trims. This was done to satisfy a design principle. From the South and West elevations, a pictorial view is developed on the computer to allow for further study and presentation. The pictorial view is shown in Figure 7.5.

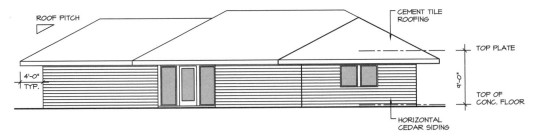

Figure 7.4 South elevation.

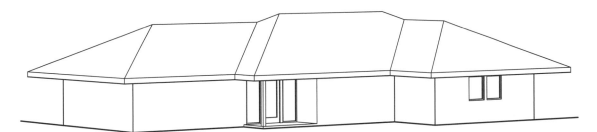

Figure 7.5 Pictorial—South/West view.

Building Section

It is recommended that a preliminary building section be studied prior to the development of the exterior elevations. As discussed in regard to the development of the exterior elevations, the architect developed a roof pitch, an eave overhang, and a soffit so as to terminate the finish soffit material directly above the exterior window and door trims. This design requirement also established a 9' height dimension from the top of the concrete floor to the top plate. Generally, the plate heights for light residential wood structures are from 8' to 8'2". However, as mentioned earlier, a wood stud framing system provides flexibility in the design and construction process. Figure 7.6 illustrates a building section that is cut through the floor plan at the building section symbol location on the floor plan. As indicated by the building section symbol, the section cut is looking in the westerly direction.

Figure 7.6 shows the various components that are utilized to formulate this wood structure. Note that the horizontal soffit at the roof eave terminates just above the normal window and door height of 6'8". The size and grade of the wood supporting members in the roof system will be determined later in the working drawings by the architect and the structural engineer.

Wood Post and Beam

Another project to be built with wood may have a different format with a conventional wood stud construction system. For example, after the preliminary design has been approved, the use of a wood modular system for the structure may be selected. This system will incorporate the use of posts and beams spaced at a preferred

dimensional distance. The modular distance will depend on the type and size of the floor and roof members that will span between the modular beam systems. These members may use, for example, solid tongue-and-groove planking, sawn lumber joists, or engineered lumber joists. Modular post and beam systems may be used in light construction projects, such as a residence, or in the heavy timber construction of a public building.

Floor Plan. The initial approach for development of a floor plan to be used in the working drawings for a project utilizing a wood post and beam system, is to create a matrix system. This may also be referred to as an *axel reference plane* for the supporting post in each direction. Once the matrix system has been established, the architect begins the required interior and exterior planning for the specific project. The matrix for the wood post and beam system now provides the basic structural skeleton for the building's structure.

In most cases, this system is used to expose the wood structural members and the simplicity of the structural design. The dimensioning of this wood system is different from that of the conventional wood stud system. All the structural wood posts are dimensioned to the centers of the posts. This method is accomplished by utilizing a matrix system. A matrix system layout for a post and beam building is shown in the plan view in Figure 7.7.

As shown in Figure 7.7, the post and beam construction method that utilizes a matrix system allows the location of any of the supporting columns and their corresponding concrete pier foundation supports. An example of locating a specific column is illustrated in Figure 7.7, where column B-3 has been defined for referencing. Any one of these specific columns can be uti-

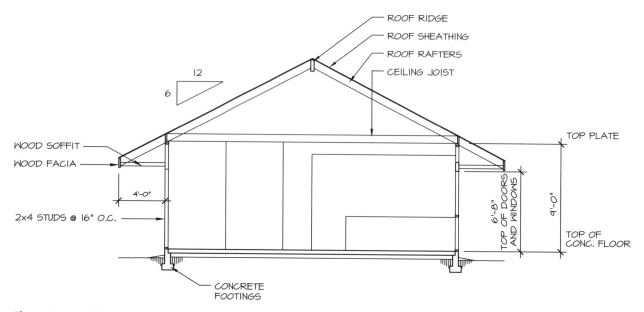

Figure 7.6 Building section.

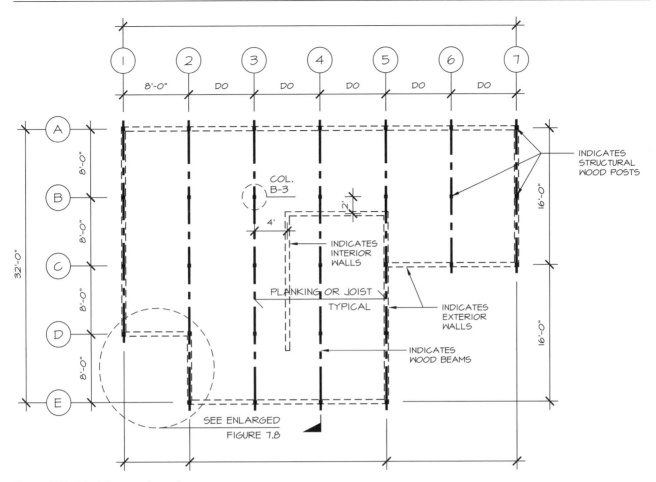

Figure 7.7 Modular wood post layout.

lized for the purpose of referencing dimension lines to the interior wall locations. An example of dimensioning an interior wall from a designated matrix point is shown in Figure 7.7, as referenced from column B-3. To further illustrate the game plan for the initial modular post layout, a partial pictorial drawing is provided in Figure 7.8.

Exterior Elevations. Development of the exterior elevations for a modular wood post and beam system would depict the wood columns according to the matrix layout, while also establishing the desired wall and bottom of beam heights. In addition, the dimensioning of roof overhangs may be referenced from a specific matrix designa-

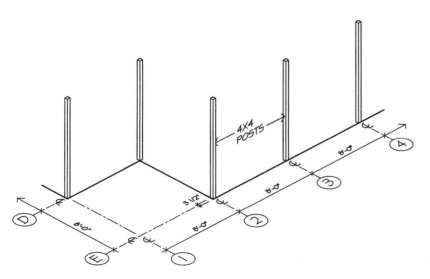

Figure 7.8 Partial modular post layout.

tion. Figure 7.9 illustrates one view of the exterior eleva-tion. A partial pictorial drawing of Figure 7.9 is shown in Figure 7.10.

Building Section.   The next major item to consider and analyze is the building sections for the post and beam wood framing method. This process may be concurrent with the development of the exterior elevations inas-much as the beam and column sizes may be determined at this stage. As previously mentioned, the selection of the roof and floor system may consider the use of tongue-and-groove planking, sawn lumber joist, or engineered lumber members. For this project it was decided to use tongue-and-groove planking spanning over the exposed beams, which are to be spaced 8' center to center. Nailed directly over the tongue-and-groove planking will be one layer of ³⁄₈″ exterior grade plywood. To meet en-ergy conservation standards, one layer of insulation board, such as urethane, will be applied over the ply-wood and will be the substrate for the applications of a built-up roofing system. For a graphic illustration of a building section utilizing the aforementioned wood members, refer to Figure 7.11. This building section is viewed along the matrix axis line ④. Figure 7.12 depicts pictorially a view along the matrix line ④.

■ CONCRETE AS A MATERIAL

Once concrete has been selected as the structural mate-rial for a building project, it is necessary to decide whether the concrete will be poured in place or whether precast concrete members will be used. If precast con-crete units have been selected for construction of the exterior and interior walls and the roof system, it is para-mount to have a consultation with the project's structural engineer. From the approved preliminary building de-sign, the structural engineer will determine the thickness of the interior and exterior walls. This will allow the ar-chitect and his or her design team to lay out the exact wall thickness on the floor plan. The thickness of a wall will depend on whether it is a load-bearing or non-load-bearing wall. The procedural steps for development of a floor plan layout for a light manufacturing building using precast concrete members is shown in Figure 7.13. This initial drawing of the floor plan establishes the wall thick-ness for the load-bearing and non-load-bearing precast concrete walls. The walls shown on matrix lines A, B, and D are non-load-bearing walls and have been deter-mined to be 5″ thick. The wall thickness for the load-bearing walls along matrix lines 1 through 9 are to be 7″ thick. The load-bearing walls have been engineered to

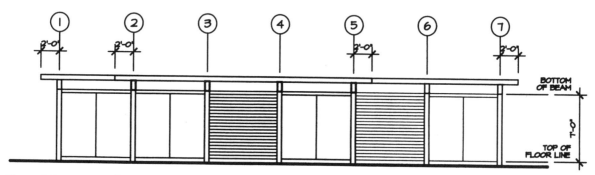

Figure 7.9   Exterior elevation—post and beam system.

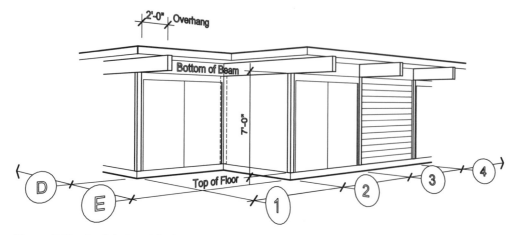

Figure 7.10   Partial pictorial of Figure 7.9.

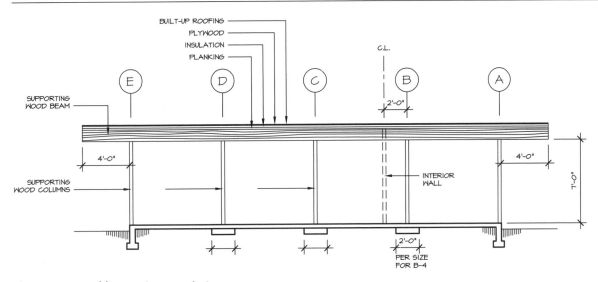

Figure 7.11 Building section on axis 4.

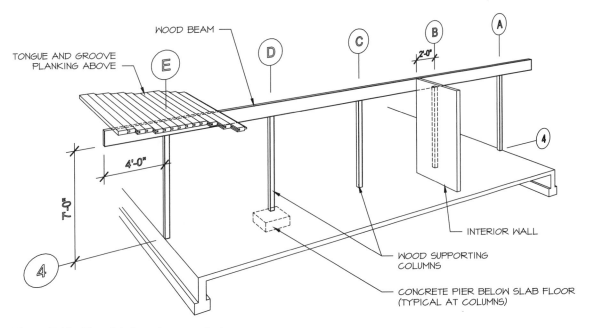

Figure 7.12 Pictorial view along matrix 4.

support 6" precast concrete cored slab panels, which will span 21'. Refer to Chapter 5 for information and drawings illustrating precast concrete cored slab panels. As shown in Figure 7.13, the use of a matrix system provides clarity for identifying the various precast concrete panel locations.

The next step in developing the floor plan layout is to provide the building dimensions and the various wall thickness dimensions. Also noted at this time are the directional arrows for the spans of precast hollow-cored panels that will support the roof. Indicated on the span directional arrows are the thickness of the concrete cored slab panels, which is 6", and the abbreviation HC, that

means hollow core. A directional arrow is drawn between the matrix symbols ① and ⑨ to further illustrate the bays that the hollow-cored precast panels are spanning. On this arrow are noted four bays at 21' with an overall length of 84'. At this stage the basic floor plan layout shows the primary structural members.

Exterior Elevations

For most projects, the exterior elevations and the initial building sections may be designed and formulated concurrently inasmuch as wall heights and other features are decided in the initial stages. Because this is a light

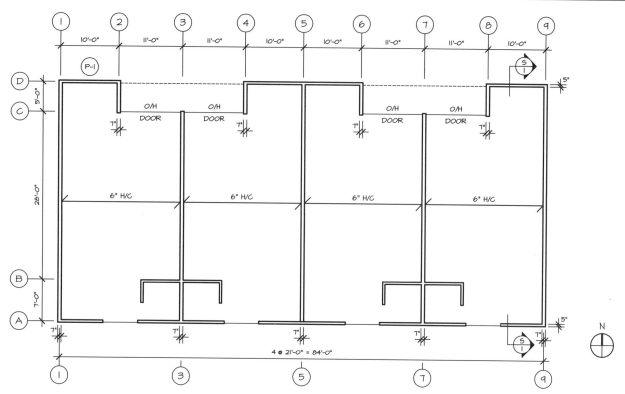

Figure 7.13 Plan layout—precast concrete walls.

manufacturing building, it was decided to provide 14' high ceilings. The ceiling heights will then dictate the wall heights. The initial study of the exterior elevations is illustrated in Figures 7.14 and 7.15. Figure 7.14 depicts the North elevation, and Figure 7.15 illustrates the West elevation. As shown in Figures 7.14 and 7.15, these exterior elevations illustrate the dimensioning of such items as the top of the parapet, the ceiling level height above the concrete floor, and the height of the steel overhead doors. These dimensions provide the necessary information for the sizes of the precast concrete wall panels, which will be manufactured and delivered to the build-

ing site. Also indicated on the North elevation are the precast sections that are to be finished in a textured scored concrete. A pictorial representation of the combined North and West elevations is shown in Figure 7.16. Other exterior elevations will show similar architectural features.

Building Sections

In conjunction with the necessary drawings for the building sections, it will be important to develop the precast panel drawings illustrating the wall dimensions and wall

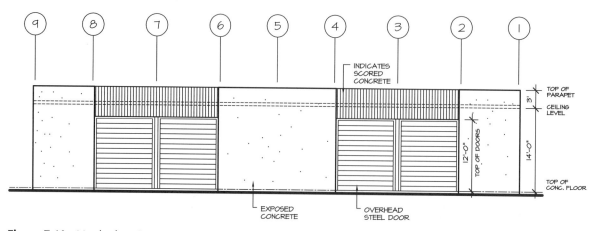

Figure 7.14 North elevation.

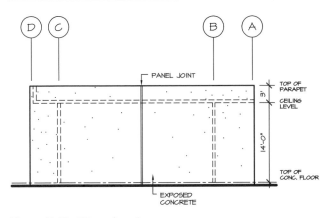

Figure 7.15 West elevation.

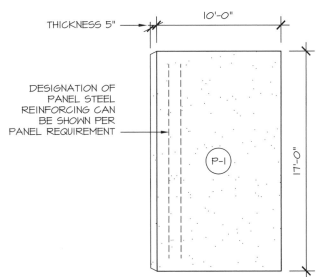

Figure 7.17 Precast concrete panel.

thickness for each specific panel. These panels should be identified with an elevation drawing and a panel identification number. An example of a method for identifying a specific panel is illustrated in Figure 7.17. The precast panel occurring between matrix numbers ① and ② is defined as panel P-1. Panel identification may be shown on the floor plan, or a key plan may be provided.

The number of building sections to be illustrated on a set of working drawings will be the number needed to clearly explain and show the various conditions that exist for a specific building. In our example of a light manufacturing building, Figure 7.18 depicts a building section cut in the north-south direction as referenced on the floor plan. The figure illustrates the dimensional heights for the ceiling and parapet and identifies the di-

rection of the precast concrete cored roof panels. At the east and west outside walls, a corbel or haunch, which is formed in the precast wall panel, will be necessary to support the precast cored panels at the end wall conditions. The shape and dimensions of the corbel and how it may appear are depicted in Figure 7.19. Similar requirements and drawings will be necessary for a project using a poured-in-place concrete construction method. These requirements will pertain to wall height dimensions, wall thickness, steel reinforcing, and any type of architectural feature.

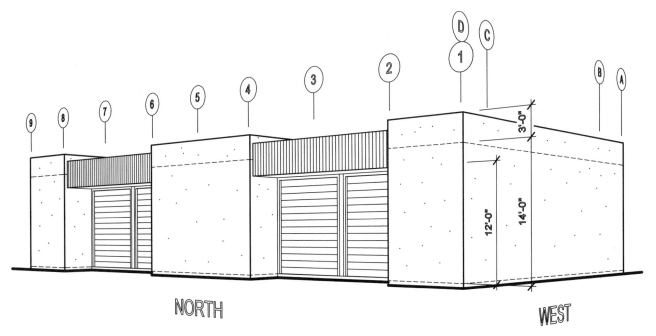

Figure 7.16 Pictorial view of North/West elevations.

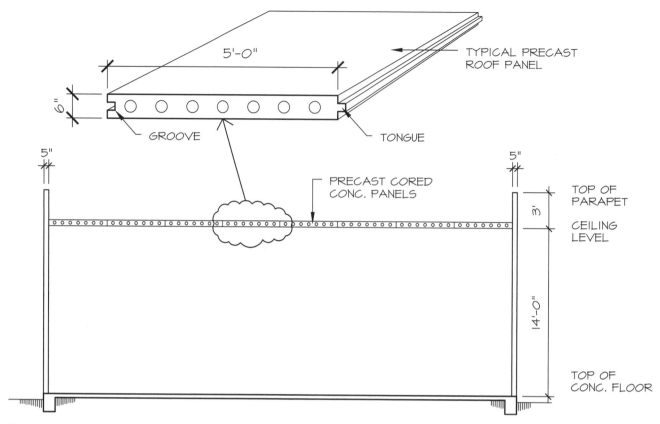

Figure 7.18   Building section on S-1.

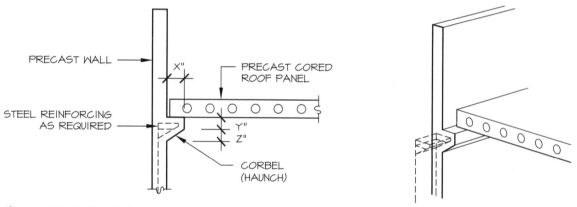

Figure 7.19   Wall corbel.

■ STEEL AS A MATERIAL

When selecting steel as a construction material for a building project, it is necessary to decide whether the steel components are to be structural steel members or light steel framing members. The initial layout approach will differ from the use of light steel framing members. The use of structural steel members, such as "W" shapes, "S" shapes, or channels, will probably dictate the use of a matrix identification system. In a light steel framing system, the approach will be similar to that found in a wood stud framing system.

If an architectural firm has been commissioned to design and prepare working drawings for an office building incorporating structural steel members, then the game plan for the floor plan layout is to establish a matrix identification system. A matrix system will identify the column and beam locations as well as spread concrete footings and concrete piers. Prior to formulating a floor plan layout with the steel column locations, it is neces-

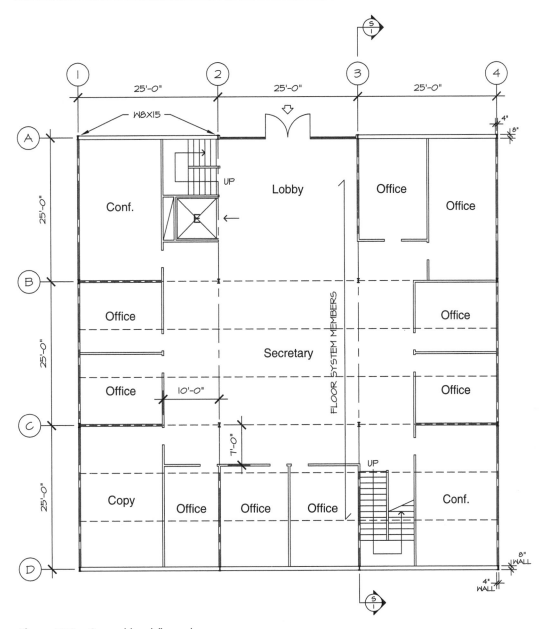

Figure 7.20 Ground level floor plan.

sary to consult with the project's structural engineer for his or her recommended span lengths between the supporting steel columns. With the structural engineer's preliminary recommendations, the architectural design team may proceed with the preliminary studies, incorporating the client's requirements and the other design facets necessary in designing a building.

Floor Plan

When creating a floor plan for a building using structural steel members, it is desirable to incorporate continuity and simplicity in the column and beam spacing. This allows for standardization of column and beam sizing

while developing simplicity in the steel fabrication process. Figure 7.20 illustrates a simple approach in the floor plan layout for a two-story office building using structural steel members. This figure depicts the ground level floor plan, using a matrix system to identify the column and beam locations. To enclose the steel columns in the finished north or south walls, it will be necessary to have a wall 8" thick or more. The columns along the matrix lines A and D are a minimum of 8" in thickness. Their call-out size is W8 × 15. W describes their shape; 8 is the depth measured in inches; 15 represents the weight in pounds per linear foot. The east and west walls will be dictated by the flange width of the steel columns along matrix lines ① and ④ . These flanges are 4" wide.

The interior wall partition layout may be dimensioned from the various matrix line identifications. An example is shown on the ground floor plan where the office partition walls are dimensioned from the column identified at matrix lines ② and C .

Second Level Floor Plan

The second level floor plan columns and beams will align directly over the ground floor steel members. However, the column and beam sizes will be different because they are not supporting as much weight as the ground floor members. The steel columns on the second floor level will be W6 × 12 members. The finished wall thickness, on the North and South walls, will then need to be a minimum of 6" to enclose the columns along matrix lines A and D . The finished wall thickness along the matrix lines ① and ④ will need to be a minimum of 4" because the flange width of the W6 × 12 steel column is 4" wide. When dimensioning the wall thickness for the enclosure of steel columns, it is recommended that the properties of the steel members be verified by referring to the *Manual of Steel Construction*. Figure 7.21 illustrates the second level floor plan.

Exterior Elevations

The process or game plan approach in developing preliminary exterior elevations is to coordinate the basic requirements established by the structural and mechanical

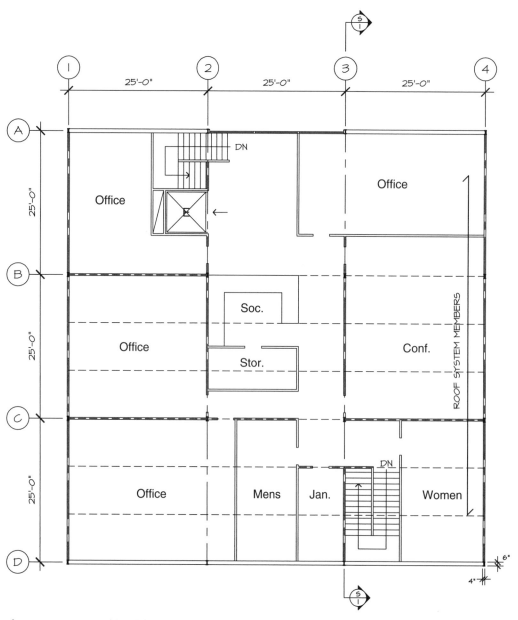

Figure 7.21   Second level floor plan.

engineers. For example, the structural engineer may establish the unsupported heights for selected steel columns, and the mechanical engineer may provide a recommended dimensional clearance in the plenum area. The plenum area is the allocated space between the top of the finished ceiling and the bottom of the floor and roof system members. This space is used for heating and cooling ducts and various plumbing lines. These dimensional requirements are needed for the layout of the preliminary exterior elevations relative to their building heights. The North elevation of this all-steel building is illustrated in Figure 7.22. Note that the various established floor lines and ceiling heights were predetermined by recommendations from the consulting engineers and the architectural design team. This figure also illustrates the matrix identification symbols used for referencing the exterior wall material and architectural features. Figure 7.23 is a pictorial view of the North and West elevations with accompanying designated information.

Building Sections

For most projects the building sections may be developed concurrently with the design of the exterior elevations. As previously mentioned, various preliminary information recommended by engineering consultants is incorporated into the layout of the building sections. For example, the initial layout illustrates dimensionally the recommended floor to finished ceiling height while also showing the recommended dimensional space for the

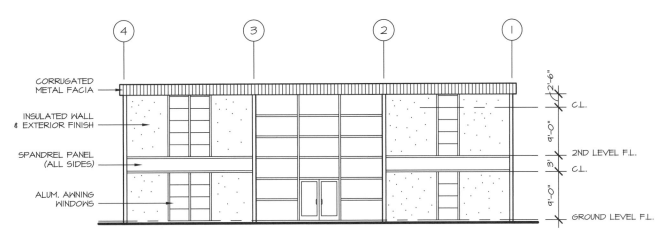

Figure 7.22 North elevation.

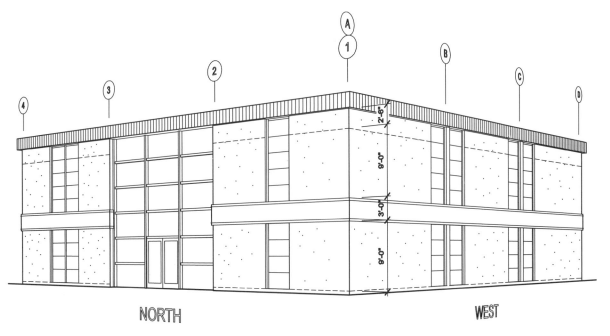

Figure 7.23 Pictorial view—exterior elevation.

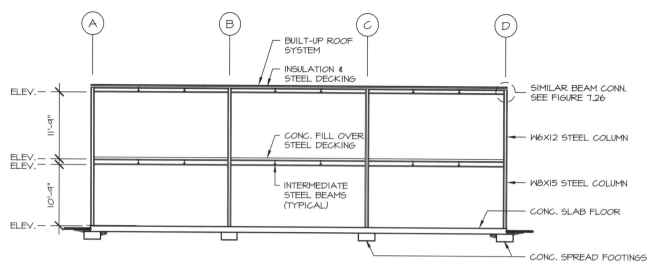

Figure 7.24 Building section.

plenum area. Preliminary engineering calculations provide the approximate steel column and beam sizes necessary for the development of the building sections. In some cases the modification of column and beam sizes may occur later in the project design because of unforeseen requirements and solutions that may enhance the architectural and structural design and detailing.

A building section is provided in Figure 7.24. This section is taken along matrix line ③, which is in the north-south direction looking eastward. Refer to the ground level floor plan in Figure 7.20 for the building section designation symbol.

It was decided to use a composite floor and roof system utilizing corrugated steel decking and concrete fill

as indicated on the building section. As shown in Figure 7.24, dimensions are provided for the heights of the concrete floor to the bottom of the second floor and the top of the second floor to the bottom of the roof beams. This may also be achieved with the use of vertical elevations relative to the ground floor concrete slab elevation. A pictorial view of the building section is given in Figure 7.25. A photograph taken at the job site illustrates a typical corner first floor steel column and beam. A second floor beam connection is shown in Figure 7.26.

Another job site photograph illustrates a beam and columns found along matrix line A at the first floor level is Figure 7.27.

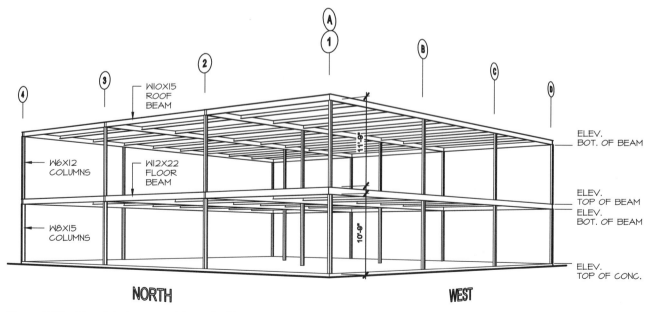

Figure 7.25 Pictorial view—steel frame building section.

Figure 7.26 Photograph similar corner-column and beam connection. (Courtesy of Rich Development.)

Figure 7.27 Photograph ground floor steel columns and beam.

■ MASONRY AS A MATERIAL

Masonry has proven to be a versatile and durable construction material. There are various types of masonry products available for the construction of buildings. In general, reinforced grouted brick masonry units and reinforced concrete masonry units are widely used in the construction of residential, commercial, and industrial structures.

The game plan in the initial approach of a floor plan layout is for the architect to first select the type of masonry material that will be used in the building project. Wall thickness and modular layout will depend on whether reinforced grouted brick masonry or concrete

masonry units are selected. Brick masonry units are manufactured in a great range of sizes, starting with the standard brick size of 2-1/2″ × 3-7/8″ × 8-1/4″ and ranging to a brick block size of 7-5/8″ × 5-1/2″ × 15-1/2″. Concrete masonry units are often referred to as concrete block units. Though sizes vary, a typical modular concrete block unit is rectangular with dimensions of 8″ wide, 8″ high, and 16″ long.

Floor Plan

An architectural firm has selected concrete masonry units for the exterior walls of a small industrial building, utilizing an 8″ × 8″ × 16″ modular concrete block unit. This selection will now dictate the initial floor plan layout. Because the architectural design team is dealing with a precast modular unit, they will delineate the exterior walls to 8″ wide while recognizing the length of the modular unit as it relates to dimensioning and wall openings. When possible, it is more practical and efficient to lay out the walls and vertical wall heights with the standard concrete block modular sizes. This will eliminate the need for saw cutting the concrete units, which will lessen the construction costs of the structure and save construction time.

An example of a light industrial building floor plan layout using 8″ × 8″ × 16″ concrete block units is illustrated in Figure 7.28. This floor plan has used standard size masonry units in order to eliminate the process of saw cutting any of the modular units. The dimensioning of the door and window openings adhere to the length of the modular units, also referred to as "stretchers." An acceptable method of delineating concrete block units in plan view is shown in the enlarged portion of Figure 7.28. A pictorial view showing a part of the floor plan is depicted in Figure 7.29.

Exterior Elevations

Architects may design the exterior elevations of a building project in conjunction with developing the building sections. Because concrete block modular units have been selected for this project, it is paramount to develop and design the exterior wall heights to accommodate the height of the concrete blocks. In this case the modular concrete block units are 8″ in height, and therefore a multiple of these units will dictate the height to the top of the concrete block wall. Figures 7.30 and 7.31 illustrate a wall height of 16′ which translates to 24 courses of 8″ high concrete block units. The window and door heights are at the height of a multiple of concrete block units. In this case, the tops of the doors and windows will be a height of 10′, which is established with the use of fifteen 8″ high concrete masonry units. A pictorial view of the North and West elevations is given in Figure 7.32.

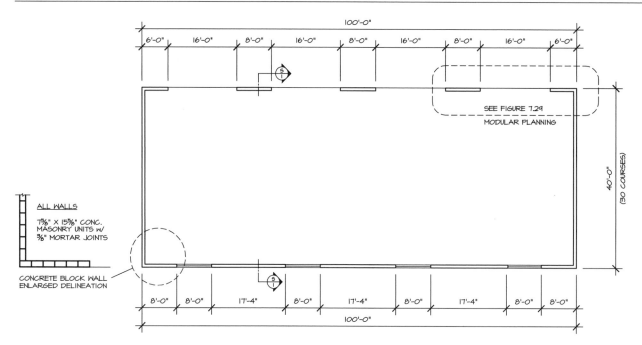

Figure 7.28 Floor plan—concrete masonry modular units.

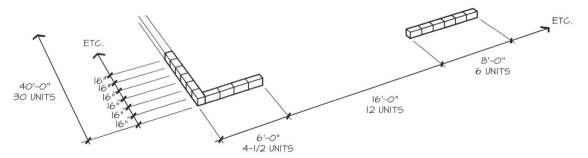

Figure 7.29 Pictorial—modular floor planning.

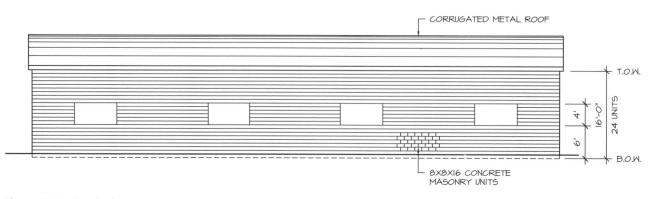

Figure 7.30 South elevation.

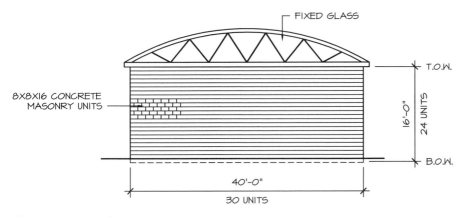

Figure 7.31 East elevation.

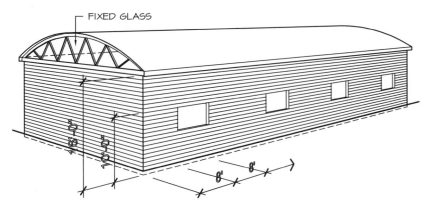

Figure 7.32 Pictorial—North/West elevation.

Building Sections

The study of the preliminary building sections usually coincides with the development of the exterior elevations in order to determine the wall heights and the wall material. The study also includes the type of roof system and its material. In the example of the light industrial build-

ing, a building section S-1 has been taken in the North-South direction, as indicated in Figure 7.28. This building section delineates the top and bottom of the concrete masonry wall, in which case the height of the masonry wall is established by the desired number and height of the modular concrete masonry units. The building section is illustrated in Figure 7.33. As previously indicated,

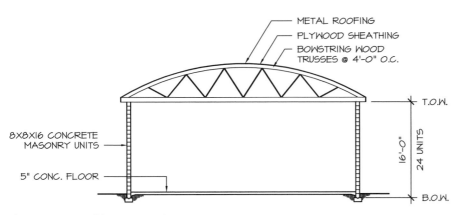

Figure 7.33 Building section S-1.

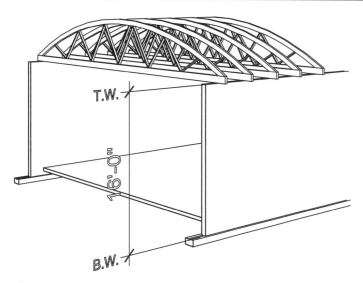

T.W.

16'-0"

B.W.

Figure 7.34 Partial pictorial—building section.

the wall height has been established by the height and number of concrete block units while addressing the requirements for this type of building. In this case, the use of twenty-four modular units translates into a wall height of 16'. A partial pictorial drawing illustrating this building section is given in Figure 7.34.

Document Evolution

chapter

8

SITE AND GRADING PLAN

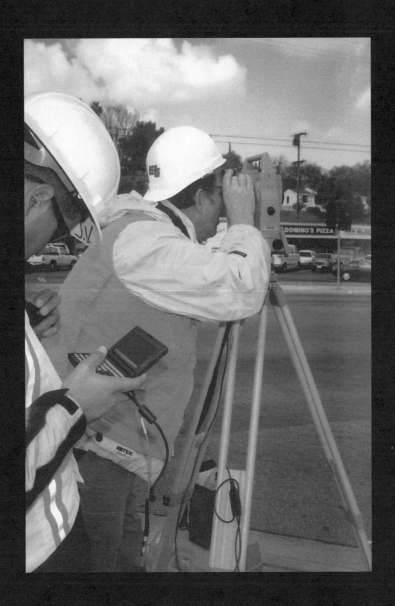

■ THE PLAT MAP

The Function of a Plat Map

The site plan is developed through stages, each dealing with new technical information and design solutions. The first step in site plan development is the **plat map**. This map, normally furnished by a civil engineer, is a land plan which delineates the property lines with their bearings, dimensions, streets, and existing easements. The plat map forms the basis of all future information and site development. An example of a plat map is shown in Figure 8.1. The property line bearings are described by degrees, minutes, and seconds; the property line dimensions are noted in feet and decimals.

Even when the architect or designer is furnished with only a written description of the metes and bounds of the plat map, a plat map can still be delineated from this information. Lot lines are laid out by polar **coordinates**; that is, each line is described by its length plus the angle relative to the true North or South. This is accomplished by the use of compass direction, degree, minutes, and seconds. A lot line may read N 6° 49′ 29″ W. The compass is divided into four quadrants. See Figure 8.2.

Drawing a Plat Map

Figure 8.3A shows a plat map with the given **lot lines**, **bearings**, and dimensions. To lay out this map graphi-

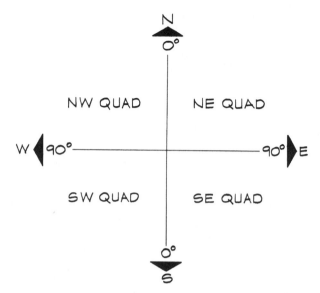

Figure 8.2 Compass quadrants. (Reprinted by permission from *The Professional Practice of Architectural Working Drawings*, 2d Ed., © 1995 by John Wiley & Sons, Inc.)

cally, start at the point labeled **P.O.B. (point of beginning)**. From the P.O.B., you can delineate the lot line in the North-East quadrant with the given dimension. See Figure 8.3B. The next bearing falls in the North-West quadrant, which is illustrated by superimposing a compass at the lot line intersection. See Figure 8.3C. You can delineate the remaining lot lines with their bearings and dimensions in the same way you have delineated the previous lot lines, closing at the P.O.B. See Figures 8.3D, 8.3E, and 8.3F. For a plat map layout, accuracy within ½° is acceptable.

With the completion of the plat map layout, there is now a specific plot of ground that has been established for locating building **setbacks**, existing setbacks, and other factors that will influence the development of the property. For the purpose of the architectural working drawings, this portion of the drawings will be called the **site plan**. In some offices, "plot plan" is the term used for this part of the working drawings. In Figure 8.3G, the front yard, side yard, and rear yard setbacks are illustrated for the purpose of defining the governing building setback locations. The next step in site plan development is to provide a dimensional layout for a proposed building. One method, as shown on Figure 8.3H, is to provide a dimension along the west and east property lines. Starting from the front property line, a line joining these two points will establish a parallel line with front of the building, thus eliminating the problem determining the angle of the front of the house to the front property line. In addition, from this parallel line dimensional **offsets** of the building can be established. Note also in Figure 8.3H that all required yard setbacks will be maintained with no encroachments.

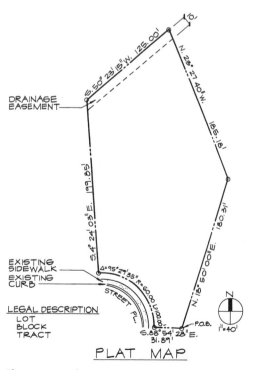

Figure 8.1 Plat map. (Reprinted by permission from *The Professional Practice of Architectural Working Drawings*, 2d Ed., © 1995 by John Wiley & Sons, Inc.)

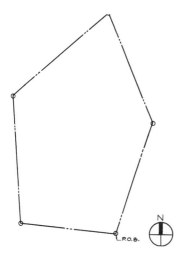

Figure 8.3A Point of beginning. (Figure 8.3 A through H reprinted by permission from *The Professional Practice of Architectural Working Drawings*, 2d Ed., © 1995 by John Wiley & Sons, Inc.)

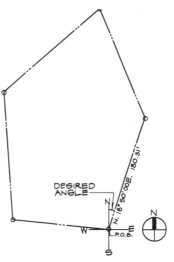

Figure 8.3B Point of beginning and first angle.

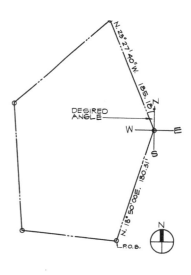

Figure 8.3C P.O.B. and second angle.

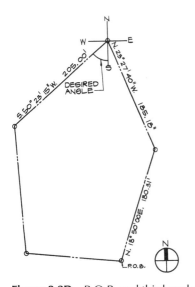

Figure 8.3D P.O.B. and third angle.

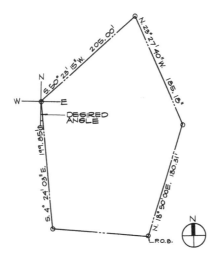

Figure 8.3E P.O.B. and fourth angle.

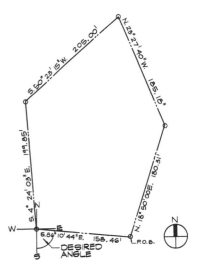

Figure 8.3F P.O.B. and fifth angle.

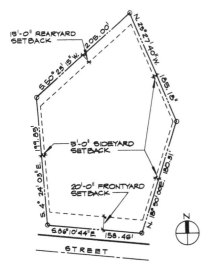

Figure 8.3G Site plan—building setbacks.

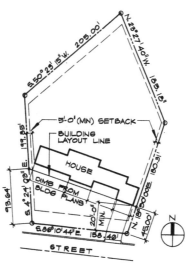

Figure 8.3H Site plan—building layout.

Drawing a Site Plan on the Computer

In this world which we travel, it is hoped that your associates are also on the same journey. In drawing a site plan, the easiest way is to call your civil engineer and ask for a copy of a digital site plan of the project in question. This drawing becomes the datum drawing on which various layers are drawn, such as setbacks, building location, dimensions, noting, and so on.

If a drawing is available as a hard copy but not digitally available, you can scan the drawing into the computer, size and scale it as described in Chapter 3. This drawing then becomes the datum drawing or datum layer on which the other layers are built. However, if you have a need to initiate the drawing from scratch, you must first check and see what type of program you have installed in your computer. If you are fortunate enough to have your system programmed to draw site plans as previously described, then it's just a matter of following the procedure outlined in Figures 8.3A and 8.3H.

In most CAD programs, this is not the case, and the drafter must adjust his or her thinking to accommodate the computer. For example, in the majority of instances, the computer has been programmed to view the East compass bearing as 0°, North as 90°, West as 180°, and South as 270°. For example, if you need to draw a property line N 18° 50' 00" E, you must understand that this line will be drawn in the upper right quadrant of your compass and that the shaded area shown in Figure 8 is the measurement. For the purpose of giving the computer the proper command, you must subtract 18° 15' from 90° and instruct the computer to draw a line 71° 10'. Let us continue drawing this lot (developed on Figure 6.3) and construct the second line of 23° 27' 40". As can be seen on Figure 8, this shaded area describes the desired line in reference to north. Since north is 90°, we must add 23° 27' 40" to 90°, giving us 113° 27" 40' and relay this instruction to the computer.

A final note: you will find no key for degree unless it has been programmed into the computer. For the degree symbol, type in % % d.

The final line of any site is drawn with the Close command. This insures that the polygon is totally closed and you can hatch texture without the fear of the texture bleeding outside of the site boundaries.

■ THE TOPOGRAPHY MAP

The Function of a Topography Map

For most projects, the architect adjusts the existing contours of the site to satisfy the building construction and site improvement requirements. Because **finish grading**—

that is, the adjusting of exiting contours—is a stage in the site improvement process, the architect or designer needs a topography map to study the slope conditions which may influence the design process. Usually, a civil engineer prepares this map and shows in drawing form the existing **contour lines** and their accompanying numerical elevations. Commonly, these contour lines are illustrated by a broken line.

The **topography** map is, therefore, actually a plat map, and its broken lines and numbers indicate the grades, elevations, and contours of the site. Figure 8.4 is a topography map showing existing contour lines.

Site Cross-Sections

A topography map can appear complex. However, a cross-section through any portion of the site can make the site conditions clearer and will also be valuable for the finish grading. Figure 8.5 shows a **cross-section** of a portion of a topography map. The fall of the contours from the front of the site to the rear is almost as high as a two-story building. This site slopes to the North at approximately 1' for every 15'.

To make a cross-section, draw a line on the topography map at the desired location. This is called the section line. Next, on tracing paper, draw a series of horizontal lines using the same scale as the topography map and spacing equal to the grade elevation changes on the topography map. Project each point of grade change to the appropriate section line. Now connect the series of grade points to establish an accurate section and profile through that portion of the site.

■ THE SOILS AND GEOLOGY MAP

Soils and geology investigations evaluate soil conditions such as type of soil, moisture content, expansion coefficient, and soil bearing pressure. Geological investigations evaluate existing geological conditions as well as potential geological hazards.

Field investigations may include test borings at various locations on the site. These drillings are then plotted on a plat map, with an assigned test boring identification and a written or graphic report. This report provides findings from the laboratory analysis of boring samples under various conditions.

When there are geological concerns and soil instability, the particular problem areas may be plotted on the **soils and geology map** for consideration in the design process. Figure 8.6 shows a plat map with each test boring identified. This map becomes a part of the soils and geological report. Sometimes, the architect or structural engineer requests certain locations for borings according

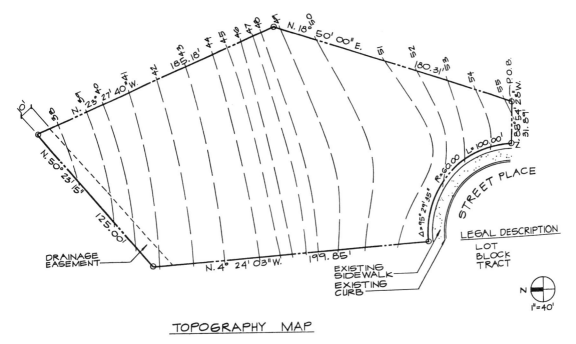

TOPOGRAPHY MAP

Figure 8.4 Topography map. (Reprinted by permission from *The Professional Practice of Architectural Working Drawings*, 2d Ed., © 1995 by John Wiley & Sons, Inc.)

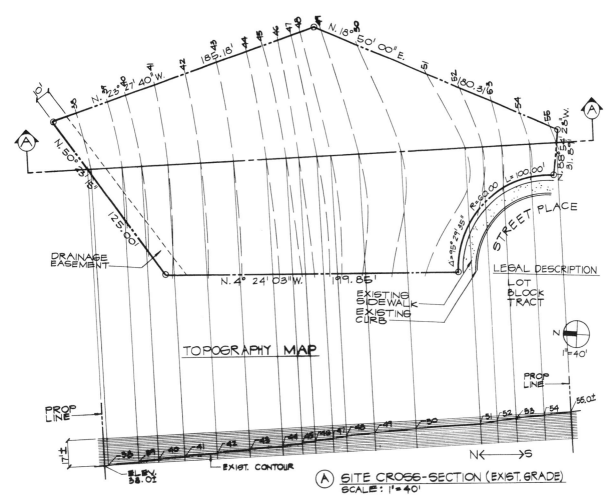

Figure 8.5 Topography map with section lines and cross-section. (Reprinted by permission from *The Professional Practice of Architectural Working Drawings*, 2d Ed., © 1995 by John Wiley & Sons, Inc.)

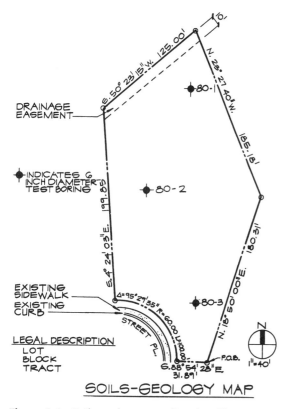

Figure 8.6   Soils-geology map. (Reprinted by permission from *The Professional Practice of Architectural Working Drawings*, 2d Ed., © 1995 by John Wiley & Sons, Inc.)

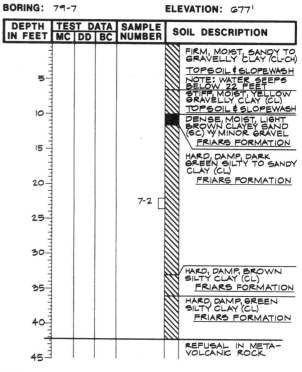

Figure 8.7   Example of a boring log. (Reprinted by permission from *The Professional Practice of Architectural Working Drawings*, 2d Ed., © 1995 by John Wiley & Sons, Inc.)

to building location or area of structural concern. Figure 8.7 shows a **boring log** in graphic form. Notice the different types of information presented in the sample boring log. Figure 8.8 shows a geological cross-section.

Normally, architectural technicians are not involved in *preparing* drawings for geology and soils information; however, it is important to have some understanding of their content and presentation.

■ THE UTILITY PLAN

Plotting existing utilities is necessary to the site improvement process. See Figure 8.9. Such a plan should show the location of all existing utilities, including sewer laterals, water and gas lines, and telephone and electrical services. This drawing then provides a basis for new utility connections. It may also influence the locations of electrical rooms and meter rooms in the structure itself.

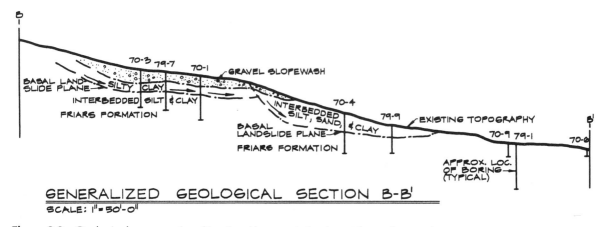

Figure 8.8   Geological cross-section. (Reprinted by permission from *The Professional Practice of Architectural Working Drawings*, 2d Ed., © 1995 by John Wiley & Sons, Inc.)

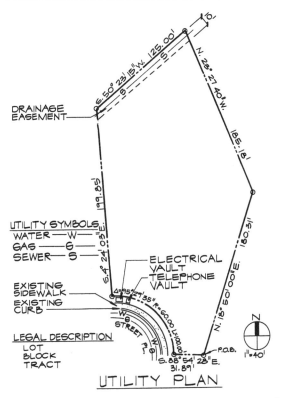

Figure 8.9 Utility plan. (Reprinted by permission from *The Professional Practice of Architectural Working Drawings*, 2d Ed., © 1995 by John Wiley & Sons, Inc.)

■ THE GRADING PLAN

The grading plan shows how the topography of the site will be changed to accommodate the building design. This plan shows the existing grades and new grades or finished grades. It should also indicate the finished grade elevations and the elevations of floors, walks, and walls. Existing grade lines are shown with a broken line, and finished grades with a solid line. Finished grading lines show how the site is to be graded. See Figure 8.10.

Floor Elevations

Once the orientation and location of the building has been established, the process of preparing a grading plan may begin. The first step is to designate tentative floor-level elevations, which will be determined by the structure's location in relation to the existing grades. It should be noted that in the process of designing a grading plan, tentative floor elevations may have to be adjusted to satisfy the location of the finished contours and their elevations. This particular building has two different floor levels, which provides greater compatibility with the existing sloping grades. The upper floor Level-2 elevation has tentatively been set at 44.5, and the lower floor Level-1 has been set at 42.5, providing a two-foot floor transition. With the establishment of the floor-level ele-

vations it will then be necessary to reshape the existing grade lines to satisfy floor clearances and site drainage control. Figure 8.10 illustrates that the existing grades, at the South side of the building, will need to be cut back, in which case finished grades will need to be lower in elevation than the floor Level-1, which is tentatively set at an elevation of 44.5.

For the purpose of providing proper drainage around the building, a high-point elevation of 44.3 has been established at the middle portion of the building, as shown in Figure 8.10A. This grade elevation is below the finished floor elevation of Level-1 and higher than the finished grades at the East and West sides of the building, in which case surface drainage will flow to each side of the building, continue around, and follow the natural slope of the site. Finished contour elevations 42.0, 43.0, and 44.0 at the East and West sides have been contoured to provide a gentle slope at the front and sides of the building.

At the rear of the building a floor-level change has been incorporated to accommodate the natural slope of the site. This floor elevation is set a +42.5 feet, which is two feet below Level-1. The adjacent natural grade at this level will be reshaped to provide a more gradual slope and maintain proper drainage and floor clearances. The remaining finished grading will be reshaped, using a 8:1 slope ratio, providing a slope that is consistent with the existing grades and will not cause grading in the drainage casement. The design of slope ratios, like that of floor elevation, may be only tentative as a starting point for the shaping of the finish contours.

A starting point for the design of slope ratios is laid out with horizontal scaled increments for the tentative slope ratio. As depicted in Figure 8.10B, a 12:1 slope ratio is anticipated for the grade cut at the south side of the building. In this case, 12-foot horizontal increments will start from the established grades adjacent to the building. At the front of the building (South side), from an elevation grade of +44.0, twelve horizontal increments will be plotted at three locations. These increments will start at grade elevation +44.0 and stop at grade elevation +49.0, inasmuch as there would be no finish grade intrusion at the existing grade elevation +50.0. Once the various increments have been plotted, these points can be connected with a french curve or other instruments to delineate the finished contour or other instruments to delineate the finished contour line elevation. A similar procedure will be used for the rear of the building (North side), illustrating finished contours and slope ratios. The cut section of the site will occur at the south portion of the building, whereas the fill portion will be to the north of the building. In most cases, all finished grade elevations will start at an existing or natural grade elevation and terminate at the respective existing grade elevation, as illustrated in Figure 8.10C.

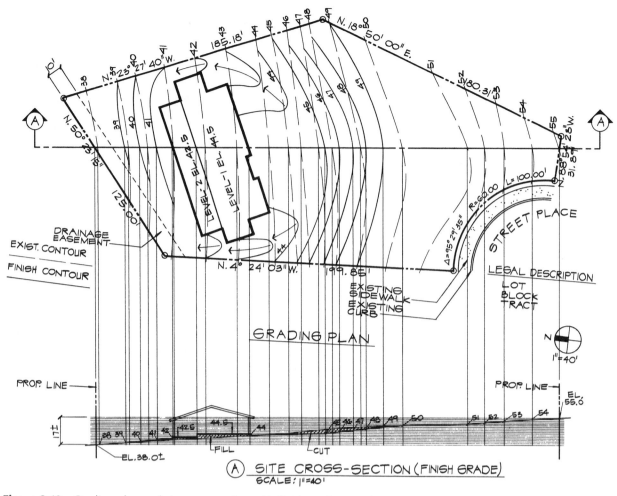

Figure 8.10 Grading plan and site cross-section with finish grades. (Reprinted by permission from *The Professional Practice of Architectural Working Drawings*, 2d Ed., © 1995 by John Wiley & Sons, Inc.)

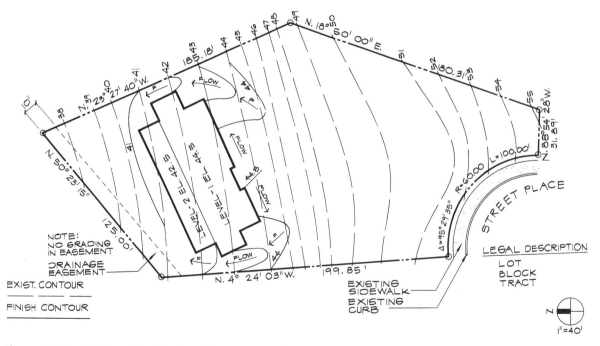

Figure 8.10A Initial grading. (Reprinted by permission from *The Professional Practice of Architectural Working Drawings*, 2d Ed., © 1995 by John Wiley & Sons, Inc.)

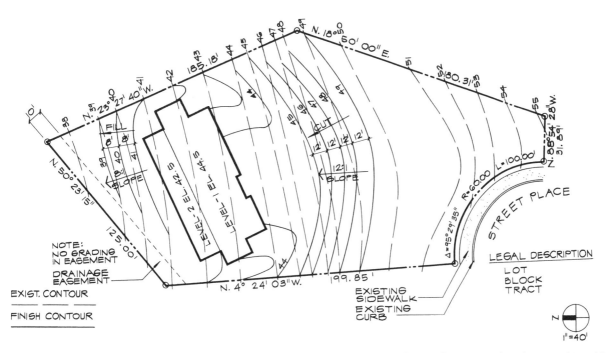

Figure 8.10B Finished slope designs. (Reprinted by permission from *The Professional Practice of Architectural Working Drawings*, 2d Ed., © 1995 by John Wiley & Sons, Inc.)

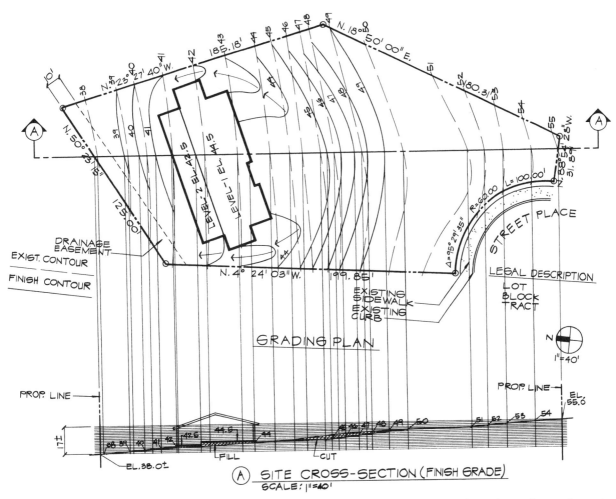

Figure 8.10C Grading plan and cross-section with finish grades. (Reprinted by permission from *The Professional Practice of Architectural Working Drawings*, 2d Ed., © 1995 by John Wiley & Sons, Inc.)

235

Cut and Fill Procedures

The contour changes previously described require a removal of soil—a "cut" into the existing contours. The opposite of this situation, which requires the addition of soil to the site, is called a "fill." In Figure 8.10C, reshaping contours with cut and fill procedures has provided a relatively level area for construction. Depending on the soil's condition and soil preparation, the maximum allowable ratio for cut and fill slopes may vary from 1½:1 to 2:1. A ratio of 2:1 means that for each foot change in elevation, there is a minimum 2-foot separation of the horizontal. To clarify grading conditions, grading sections should be taken through these areas. See Figure 8.10C.

■ DEVELOPING OPTIONS FOR A SITE PLAN

Site Grading and Options

As previously mentioned, the grading plan drawing illustrates and defines the various alterations of the land contours in order to satisfy the site development for a specific structure. It is an important and powerful tool that helps the architect or designer understand grading techniques in order to incorporate grading into architectural planning and site development.

The drawings that follow illustrate various examples of grading options for the site development and architectural planning for a specific residential lot. Initially, the architect or designer is furnished with a topography map depicting the existing grade elevations and contours for this residential site.

Figure 8.11 illustrates the topography map and depicts the contours and assigned grade elevations. The grade elevations are in 1-foot intervals representing changes in heights. As in most cases, the slope ratio, which represents the relationship between the horizontal dimension and the vertical dimension, will vary at different locations on the site. For example, area A as shown on the topography map depicts the grade condition and slope ratio in this area, which is adjacent to the access street. Figure 8.12 illustrates a cross-section in this area and also provides the determination of the slope ratio. Since the grade rises 5 feet in 25 feet, this can be interpreted as a 1:5 slope ratio and further defined as a 20% slope. Figure 8.3 depicts a cross-section of grade condition that is found in the site area designated B on the topography map. Note that this area has a slope ratio of 1:8. Figures 8.12 and 8.13 illustrate an example of varying grade conditions that are discovered on this site. Figure 8.14 depicts a overall cross-section of a major portion of this site, providing a clearer picture of the general grade conditions.

■ GRADING OPTION I

Option I calls for the design and orientation of the residence to be developed on the site with a minimum amount of grading. The existing grades and contour lines will then dictate the building configuration and floor transitions in order to accommodate the changes in grade elevation. The first step is to develop the grading for a driveway that will provide acceptable slopes for access to the garage, which will determine the garage location and floor elevation. As a means of reference for an explanation of the finish grading for the driveway design, see Figure 8.15. Starting at the street grade elevation of 542.0', the initial grade transition from the street to the driveway should not be so steep as to scrape the front bumper of an automobile. The initial slope ratio is approximately 1 foot vertically to 10 feet horizontally, or 10% slope. A slope of 20% or a one 1:5 ratio would be too steep at this transition. To proceed with the driveway slope design, we have selected an average slope of 9% or a ratio of 1:11 for relative ease of access to the garage. The finished driveway grades from 542.0 feet to 549.0 feet are now drawn at approximately 11-foot intervals. Note in Figure 8.15 that there are approximately 20 feet between the finished grade elevation of 548.0 feet and the garage floor elevation of 549.0 feet. This will provide a minimal slope condition in front of the garage for the parking of automobiles.

The finished driveway grades on the south side of the driveway will be joined to their respective existing grade elevations, providing a natural conformity with this area of the site. Along the north side of the driveway, a steep condition exists that will necessitate a 3-to-1 fill condition, as indicated in Figure 8.15. Because of this condition, 1-foot high concrete curb is recommended for directing surface water to the street and to eliminate possible water erosion on the 3:1 slope condition. The finished grading on the east side of the garage has been contoured in order to decrease the height of retaining walls that would be necessary at that portion of the garage. The slope ratio at this location is approximately 4:1.

For further clarity, a cross-section through the garage and the adjacent existing grades is shown in Figure 8.16. It should be emphasized that it may take numerous attempts to solve all facets of the grading design—somewhat like attempts to solve architectural planning designs.

The next step in Option I is to orientate a predetermined size residence on the site with a minimum amount of finished grading. Since the primary location and floor elevation have been established for the garage, the formation and planning for the residence may now proceed, with the intention of providing compatibility with the existing grade elevations and the contour configurations of the existing grades. In view of the fact that a city view exists to the north of the site and that the existing

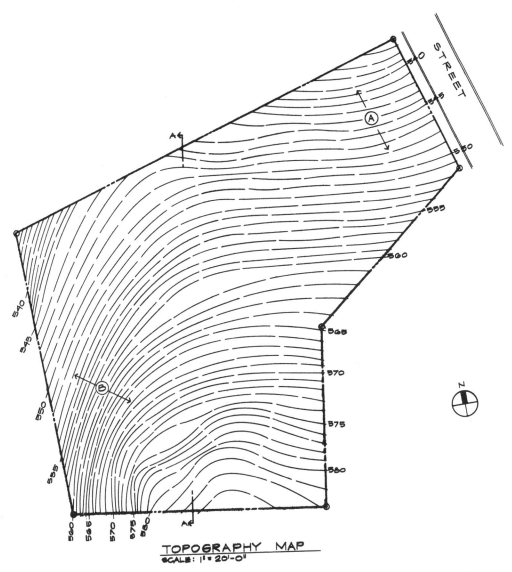

Figure 8.11 Topography map. (Reprinted by permission from *The Professional Practice of Architectural Working Drawings*, 2d Ed., © 1995 by John Wiley & Sons, Inc.)

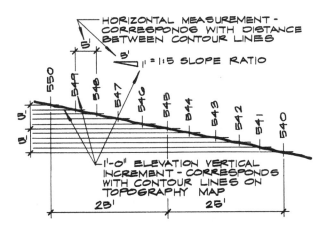

Figure 8.12 Site area A. (Reprinted by permission from *The Professional Practice of Architectural Working Drawings*, 2d Ed., © 1995 by John Wiley & Sons, Inc.)

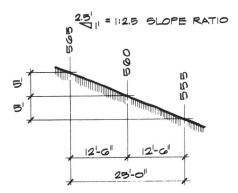

Figure 8.13 Site area B. (Reprinted by permission from *The Professional Practice of Architectural Working Drawings*, 2d Ed., © 1995 by John Wiley & Sons, Inc.)

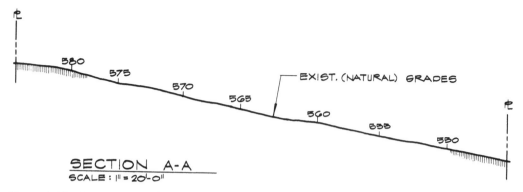

Figure 8.14 Cross-section of existing grades. (Reprinted by permission from *The Professional Practice of Architectural Working Drawings*, 2d Ed., © 1995 by John Wiley & Sons, Inc.)

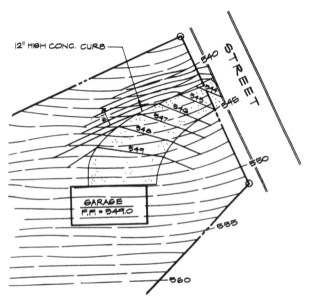

Figure 8.15 Driveway grading and design (1″ = 20). (Reprinted by permission from *The Professional Practice of Architectural Working Drawings*, 2d Ed., © 1995 by John Wiley & Sons, Inc.)

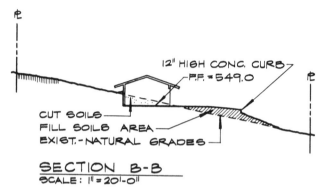

Figure 8.16 (Reprinted by permission from *The Professional Practice of Architectural Working Drawings*, 2d Ed., © 1995 by John Wiley & Sons, Inc.)

grade contours slope to the north, we decided to develop a rectilinear building configuration that would accommodate minimal finished grading conditions and that would provide a more compatible development with the natural terrain. Figure 8.17 illustrates graphically a rectangular shape that falls within a grade transition area of 5 to 8 feet. This condition is depicted in a cross-section in Figure 8.18. Note on Figure 8.18 that floor elevation changes are utilized to further the compatibility between the structure and the existing grades. As shown on Figure 8.17, the westerly portion of the residence has been pivoted to the south in order to follow the contours of the existing grade elevations. This is another method of site planning if one wishes to minimize the finished grading in the development of a site. A cross-section through this area is illustrated in Figure 8.19. Note that some excavation will occur below the floor levels in order to provide

under-floor clearances that are required by building codes for wood floors.

After completing an analysis of the existing grades and their contours in conjunction with the architectural planning of the residence, a grading plan can be prepared for Option I. It should be mentioned that if you are working on a topography plan in which the natural grade lines are erasable on the top sides of the drawing, it is advisable to trace the natural grades on the back of the drawing, since you will find that the finished grade lines may need adjustment and you would not want to erase the natural grade lines during this process.

Figure 8.20 illustrates a grading plan for Option I that incorporates a minimum amount of finished grading. In order to describe the procedure for reshaping the contours and finished grade elevations, four key areas are shown on the grading plan. Area 1, which is on the south side of the residence, illustrates that a minimum cut will be necessary to accommodate minimum grade clearances below the desired floor elevation of 562.0 feet located at that portion of the residence. This cut condition is depicted by reshaping the existing contours of 561.0 feet through 564.0 feet, resulting in a 4:1 slope ratio.

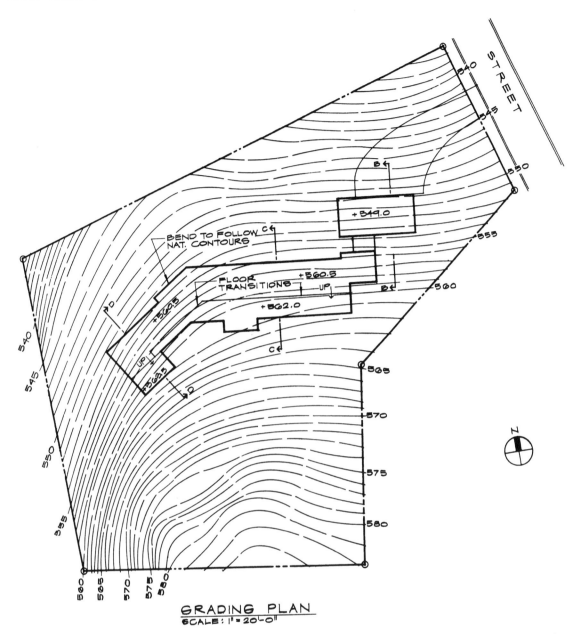

GRADING PLAN
SCALE: 1" = 20'-0"

Figure 8.17 Planning house for existing contours. (Reprinted by permission from *The Professional Practice of Architectural Working Drawings*, 2d Ed., © 1995 by John Wiley & Sons, Inc.)

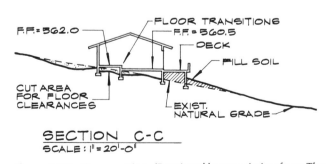

SECTION C-C
SCALE: 1" = 20'-0"

Figure 8.18 Cross-section. (Reprinted by permission from *The Professional Practice of Architectural Working Drawings*, 2d Ed., © 1995 by John Wiley & Sons, Inc.)

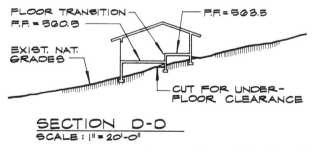

SECTION D-D
SCALE: 1" = 20'-0"

Figure 8.19 Cross-section. (Reprinted by permission from *The Professional Practice of Architectural Working Drawings*, 2d Ed., © 1995 by John Wiley & Sons, Inc.)

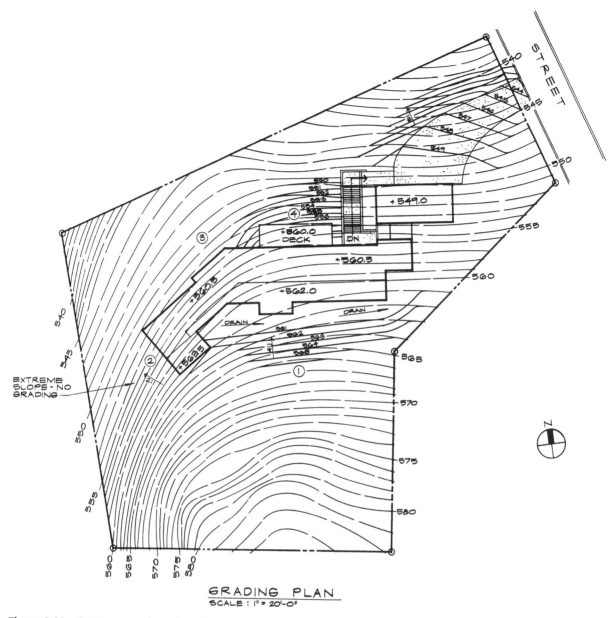

Figure 8.20 Option I—grading plan. (Reprinted by permission from *The Professional Practice of Architectural Working Drawings*, 2d Ed., © 1995 by John Wiley & Sons, Inc.)

Note that the finish grades are again connected to their respective existing grade elevations. Figure 8.18 provides a cross-section that incorporates this area.

Area 2 on the west side of the residence has an existing 2:1 slope ratio. It will remain in its natural state, since this is an extreme slope condition and any changes in these grades may result in the use of retaining walls. Refer to Figure 8.19 for a visual inspection of the grade condition in this area.

Another portion of a site where the finish grading is not mandatory is in area 3. The slope ratio in this area is approximately 4:1. Area 4 will require some grading in

order to ensure that the finished grade elevations will be compatible and will relate to the entry stairs and landing elevations. Since the established garage floor elevation is 549.0 feet and the residence entry is at an elevation of 560.5 feet, this translates into a stair and landing design that will satisfy this 10'-6" height difference between the floor elevations. The method of relating floor elevations to existing and finished grades also pertains to the stair design. The location of the risers, treads, and landing relate to the adjacent grade elevations. In area 4, note that the existing grade elevation s550, 551, 552, 553, and 554 have been contoured to provide finished grades that relate to the stair run and landings. The remaining area to be graded, which is the garage and driveway, is illustrated in Figure 8.15.

■ GRADING OPTION II

The approach in Option II is to develop a level area on this site for the construction of a residence. The level area is defined as a building pad that will have a minimal slope for drainage. The creation of a building pad will provide the architect or the designer with more flexibility in the design, since he or she will not be dictated by grade elevations, floor transitions, building shapes, or other considerations.

One approach in developing a building pad is to try to create a balance cut and fill. In this approach, the earth that is cut from the site slope will be dispersed for the use of fill material to increase the building pad site. The fill material must then be compacted to an acceptable soil-bearing capacity if a structure is to be founded in the fill area. To develop the size, shape, and grading for the building pad, it is recommended that an assumed pad elevation be established. This pad elevation may be determined by what is referred to as a "daylight grade elevation." The term **daylight grade elevation** may be defined as that point or elevation where the cut-and-fill portions of the grading of the site intersect at a given grade elevation. To illustrate this graphically, see Figure 8.21, which is a cross-section of the proposed grading for the building pad.

The grading plan for the building pad development is shown in Figure 8.22. A building pad elevation of 536.5 feet has been established with 1% slope for drainage. Note that pad elevation is at the approximate daylight grade elevation. As mentioned previously, it may take various preliminary design approaches in order to satisfy

a cut-and-fill balance. Another option in the cut-and-fill process would be to instigate the use of a retaining wall. Figure 8.21 illustrates in cross-section that the use of a retaining wall at the south portion of the pad would reduce the amount of earth to be cut from the slope. In this case, the grading plan will reflect a 2:1 ratio cut slope condition.

The finished slope designs and the grade elevations have been shown at a 2:1 slope ratio. To lay out these contour lines, start at the top of the fill slope and scale off 2-foot increments in order to establish the grade elevations for a 2:1 fill condition. The identical process will be done at the toe of the slope for the cut portion of the site. Again, note that the finished contours will be drawn and connected to their respective existing grade elevations. The amount of grading for Option II is substantially greater than that for Option I, as depicted on the grading plans.

■ GRADING OPTION III

The grading approach for Option III is to develop the site that will incorporate two building pads. This approach will necessitate the greatest amount of finished grading in comparison to Options I and II.

The grading design procedure for pad 2 will differ from the initial approach for the grading of pad 1, because the pad elevation will not originate from an approximate daylight elevation. For this situation, the pad 2 elevation will be determined by the top of the slope elevation located at the top of the south slope of pad 1, which is illustrated on the grading plan shown in Figure 8.23. From the top of slope elevation 571.0 feet, a graded pad will be developed to an approximate distance that will be determined by the toe of a 2:1 cut slope on the remaining portion of the site. The approximate North-South dimen-

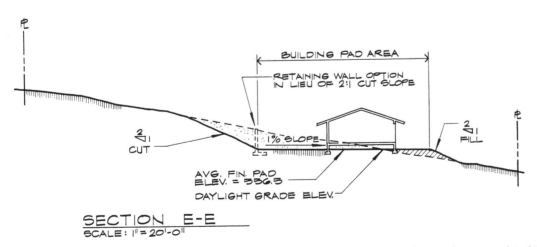

Figure 8.21 Cross-section building pad-I. (Reprinted by permission from *The Professional Practice of Architectural Working Drawings*, 2d Ed., © 1995 by John Wiley & Sons, Inc.)

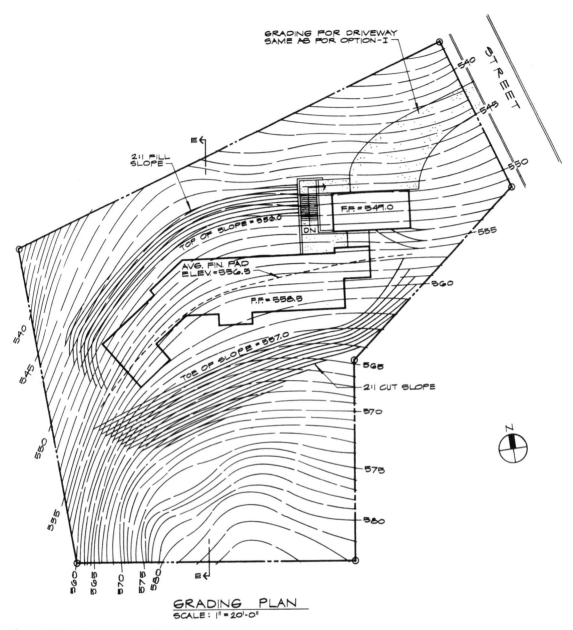

GRADING FOR DRIVEWAY
SAME AS FOR OPTION-I

E
2:1 FILL
SLOPE
TOP OF SLOPE = 556.0
AVG. FIN. PAD
ELEV. = 556.5
F.F. = 558.5
TOE OF SLOPE = 557.0
F.F. = 549.0
DN
2:1 CUT SLOPE

GRADING PLAN
SCALE: 1" = 20'-0"

Figure 8.22 Option II—Grading plan and building pad. (Reprinted by permission from *The Professional Practice of Architectural Working Drawings*, 2d Ed., © 1995 by John Wiley & Sons, Inc.)

sion of pad 2 will be determined by the remaining horizontal dimension of the site that will comfortably provide for a maximum 2:1 slope, as is shown on the grading plan. The approach for determining the North-South pad dimension is to start at the rear property line with a gradual slope and then dimensionally lay out 2-foot horizontal increments for the finished contour lines that will depict a 2:1 slope condition, as shown in Figure 8.23. Again, note that all of the finished contour elevations will be connected to their respective existing grade elevations.

For projects on which there are steep slopes that will necessitate many contours lines, the use of a French curve and other similar graphic tools is recommended for the drawing of contour lines.

To illustrate graphically the cut-and-fill conditions that will occur for the grading of pad 1 and pad 2, a cross-section is shown in Figure 8.24. Note that there is a balanced cut-and-fill condition for the development of pad 1 where the forming of pad 2 is totally reliant on a cut slope condition. This means that the earth from pad 2 will be exported rather than be used for fill conditions on

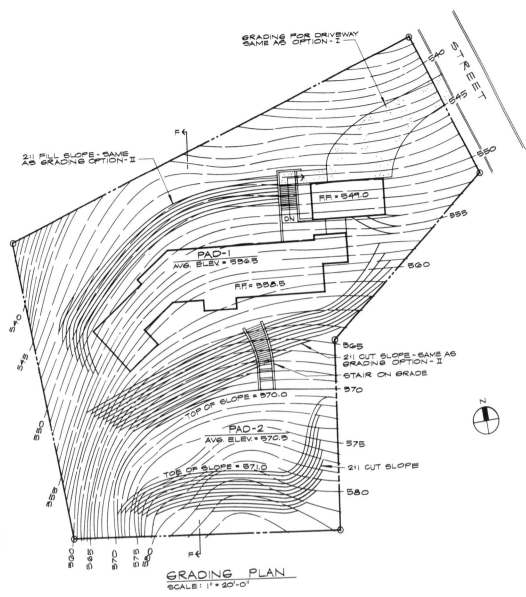

GRADING FOR DRIVEWAY
SAME AS OPTION - I

STREET

2:1 FILL SLOPE - SAME
AS GRADING OPTION - II

F

540

545

550

555

F.F. = 549.0

DN

PAD-1
AVG. ELEV. = 556.5

560

F.F. = 558.5

540

545

565

2:1 CUT SLOPE - SAME AS
GRADING OPTION - II

STAIR ON GRADE

570

TOP OF SLOPE = 570.0

550

PAD-2
AVG. ELEV. = 570.5

575

TOE OF SLOPE = 571.0

2:1 CUT SLOPE

555

580

560 565 570 575 580

F

N

GRADING PLAN
SCALE : 1" = 20'-0"

Figure 8.23 Option III—Grading plan with two building pads. (Reprinted by permission from *The Professional Practice of Architectural Working Drawings*, 2d Ed., © 1995 by John Wiley & Sons, Inc.)

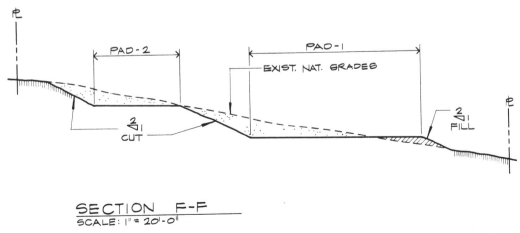

PL

PAD - 2

PAD - 1

EXIST. NAT. GRADES

2
1
CUT

2
1

2
1
FILL

PL

SECTION F-F
SCALE : 1" = 20'-0"

Figure 8.24 Cross-section of building pads I and II. (Reprinted by permission from *The Professional Practice of Architectural Working Drawings*, 2d Ed., © 1995 by John Wiley & Sons, Inc.)

the site. These two conditions illustrate grading options for the development of building pads.

■ THE SITE AND GRADING PLAN

Another example of grading design and the various criteria that dictate design solutions are discussed and illustrated for a two-story residence. The topography map for this project is illustrated in Figure 8.25. Note that the natural or existing grades are indicated with a broken line and a designated number indicating the grade elevation of each contour line.

For this project the initial concern was the driveway access and slope relative to the garage floor elevation. The desired maximum slope of the driveway does not exceed one foot in ten feet (1:10). This translates into a slope of 10%. Starting at the southerly property line, or front property line, the existing contour grade elevation is 375.00'. From this existing grade elevation of 375.00', it is desirable to maintain a maximum driveway slope of 10% within the 15'-0") building setback area. This design

solution will then establish the garage floor elevation to be 372.50'. This condition is illustrated in Figure 8.26. Note that a trench drain is located in front of the garage to divert any water accumulation from the sloping driveway. This trench drain will have a grate cover and drain lines to dissipate the water.

Another concern in dealing with sloping driveways is the transition from the street and the driveway apron elevation to the sloping portion of the driveway. This concern is illustrated graphically in the driveway transition section shown in Figure 8.27. Note the hypothetical driveway transition depicted with a broken line, showing steep slope transitions that may cause under-car damage and/or bumper scraping.

It is not recommended to exceed a 20% driveway slope, which is a one-foot transition for each five feet horizontally. A maximum of 4% slope is recommended for the side-to-side slope of the driveway. As mentioned previously, the garage floor elevation has been established at 372.50. From the garage floor elevation, a 6" floor transition will determine the first floor elevation to be 373.00'. The garage floor and first floor elevations will

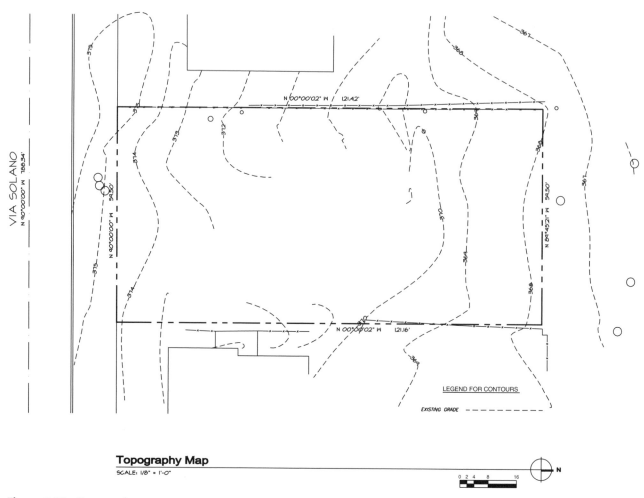

Topography Map

SCALE: 1/8" = 1'-0"

Figure 8.25 Topography map.

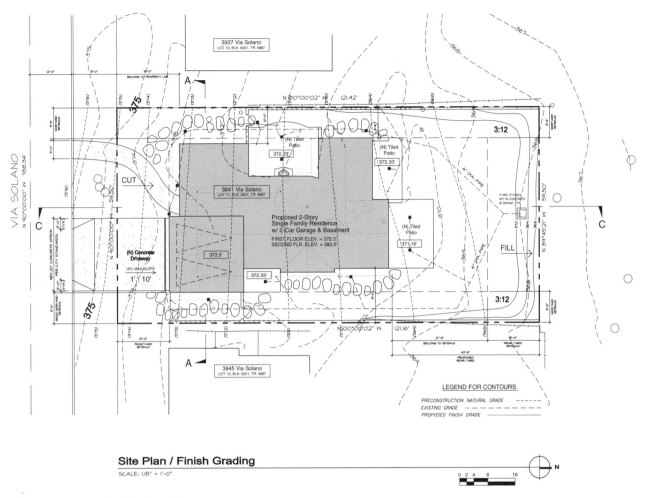

Site Plan / Finish Grading
SCALE: 1/8" = 1'-0"

0 2 4 8 16

N

Figure 8.26 Site plan/finish grading.

now be the basis for the finish grading design. As illustrated in Figure 8.26, the existing grade lines of the site are gently sloping down from the southerly property line to the northerly property line. This condition, based on the established garage and first floor elevations, will require an earth cut at the front or southerly area of the site, with the removed soil being relocated to the rear or northerly portion of the site, which now becomes a fill area. The solid lines illustrate the finish grade contours as

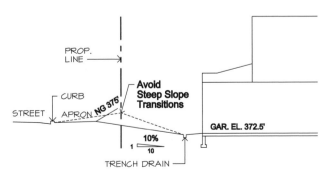

Figure 8.27 Driveway transition section.

depicted in Figure 8.26. Note that the finish grade line elevations connect to the existing grade line elevations. Figure 8.28 shows graphically a cross-section of the building site cut in a South-to-North direction. The broken line depicts the approximate existing grade, and the solid line and shaded areas show the finish grade line and fill areas. Additional cross-sections in relationship to abutting properties are illustrated in Figure 8.29.

The maximum slope or gradient for cut and fill slope conditions may be determined by the type of soil found on the site. Various soil types react differently to potential soil erosion. For most cases, the maximum slope or gradient may range from one and one-half to one ($1\frac{1}{2}$:1) to two to one (2:1). These ratios translate into a 66% and 50% slope conditions. These are illustrated graphically in Figure 8.30.

Commercial Site Grading

For sloping sites that are going to be developed for commercial and office use, the grading design will need to address automobile and pedestrian access to the build-

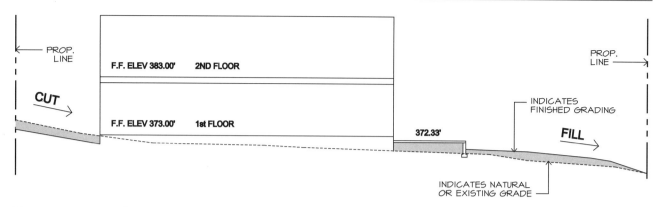

Figure 8.28 Site grading cross-section C-C.

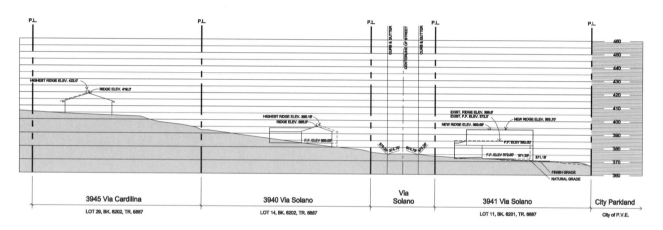

Cross Section "B-B"

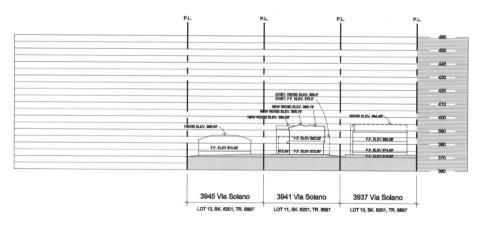

Cross Section "A-A"

Site Sections

SCALE: 1" = 30'-0"

Figure 8.29 Site sections.

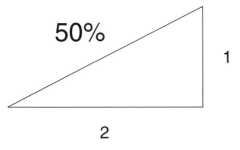

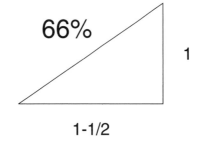

Figure 8.30   Slope ratios.

ing. Access from the street to the parking area should provide an ease of access relative to the driveway slope and the slope of the parking area. Grade transitions that require stairs and landings will also require ramps for people using wheelchairs and others with disabilities. Figure 8.31 illustrates an existing topography plan for a site that is developed for use by a small medical building. The governing planning department requires parking for eight cars and one stall for handicapped use. The car stall sizes and turning radii have also been established by the planning department.

As shown in Figure 8.31A, the existing grades are delineated with a broken line and the finish grades are shown with a solid line. Where does one start to develop and reshape the existing grades to satisfy automobile and pedestrian access to the building? It is recommended to start the driveway access at the higher grade elevation adjacent to the street. First, this will afford a more gradual driveway slope to the parking area. For this site, the highest grade elevation is approximately 80.00'.

Second, it will provide a relatively flat area along the driveway for the ease of site ingress and egress. From this area, the driveway slope has a rise ratio of approximately one foot in eight feet (1:8) or 12.5%. This slope will satisfy a recommended pedestrian walk ratio of one foot in eight feet. Note that the desired contour lines at driveway elevations 80.0', 82.0', and 83.0' are connected to their respective existing grade contour elevation lines. From the top of the driveway grade elevation 83.0', the parking lot has been designed for a slope of one foot in ten feet (1:10), which provides an ease of access for pedestrian travel. From this selected slope of 1:10, the finished grades are contoured to the slope of the parking area. The rise of elevation from 83.0' with a 1:10 slope translates to an elevation of 86.30' at the east end of the parking area.

The next elevation transition will be from the parking area highest grade of 86.30' to the entry walk of the medical office, which has a grade elevation of 90.50'. This transition translates into an approximate rise of 4'-4". That transition will require stairs and ramps for public access. Starting at the top of paving grade (TP) 86.30' in the

parking area, four 6" risers terminate at a landing elevation of 88.30', which falls closely to the existing grade of 88.0'. From this landing grade, four more 6" risers are required to adjoin the landing and walk elevation of 90.00'. From this point a walk slope to elevation 90.50' terminates at the entrance of the medical office. The finish floor elevation of the building has been established at 90.00'. Note that the finish contour lines have been connected to the various landing, stair, and walk locations.

Another public access device is a ramp for people with disabilities and those who rely on the use of a wheelchair. The maximum slope for this ramp is one foot in twelve feet (1:12), which translates to an 8.3% slope. The minimum width of the ramp is 3'. This ramp will be designed with a width of 4' and a slope of one foot in twelve feet (1:12). The ramp slope of 1:12 will require a linear length of 48' to reach the entry walk elevation. There is a 4' rise from the top of paving elevation 86.30' to 90.30'. The first section of the ramp rises to an elevation of 87.50', which is closely related to the existing contour elevation of 87.00'. The ramp then turns and rises to a grade elevation of 89.50'. Note that at this elevation of 89.50', the existing grade contour of 87.00' indicates that there will be a need for approximately two feet of fill at the ramp landing.

The entry walk to the medical office has an established elevation of 90.50'. From this elevation the finish floor elevation for the medical office is designated as 91.00'. With this established floor elevation the finish grading contour lines can now be shaped to illustrate a cut and fill condition that will be necessary to satisfy the established finish floor elevation. The cut portion at the east side of the building will be approximately 3'-0" with a maximum slope of one foot in three feet (1:3). Note the existing grade contour of 93.00' at the northeast corner of the building. When freehanding the finish elevation contour lines for their connections to the existing corresponding grade contour lines, it is recommended that the sculpting of the site should be aesthetically pleasing. Note that the west side of the building will require a maximum fill of approximately 3'-0" and the three-foot cut requirement provides a desired balance of cut and fill.

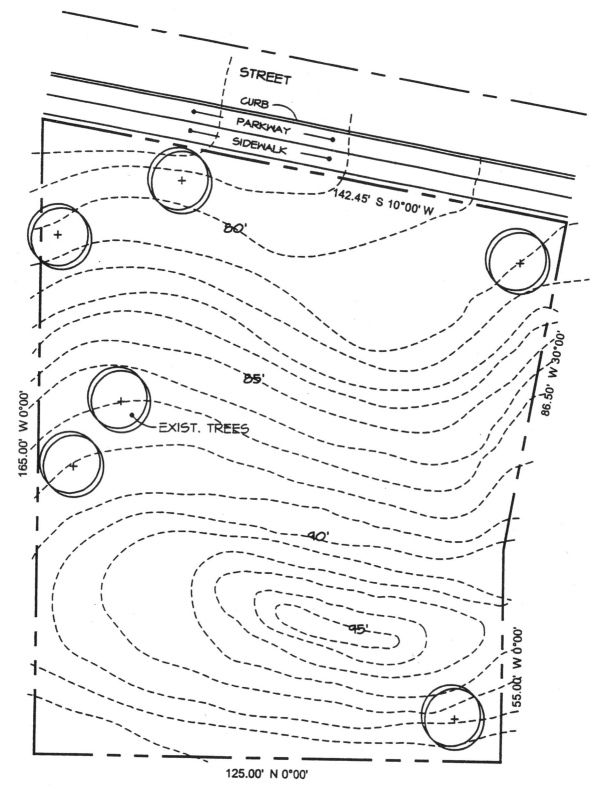

Figure 8.31 Existing grade.

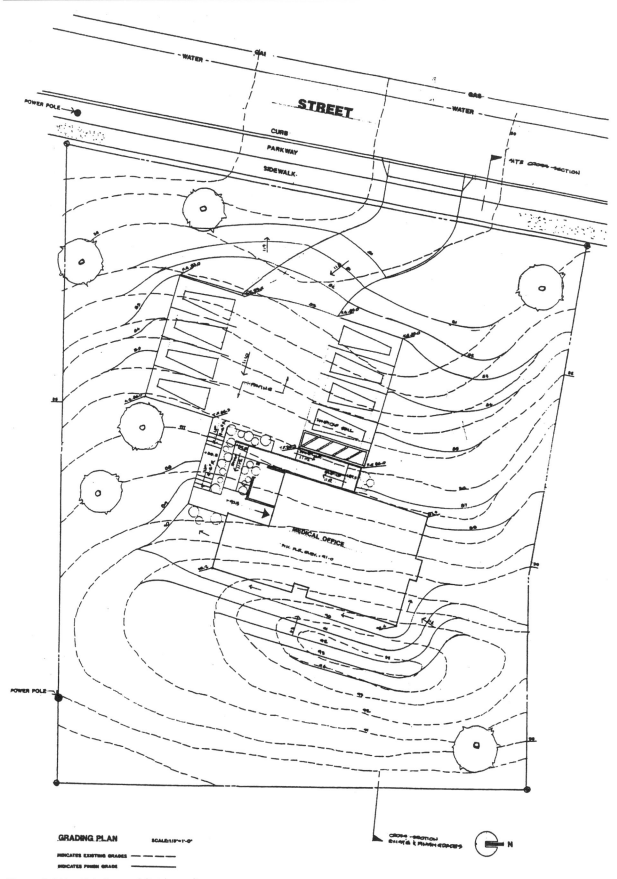

Figure 8.31A   Existing and finish grading.

Site Cross-Section : Existing Grade
Scale : 1/8" = 1'-0"

Figure 8.32   Existing grade.

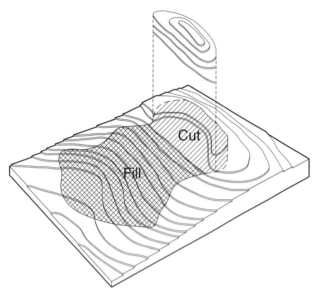

Figure 8.32A   Pictorial of existing and finish grades.

A visual analysis of this site is illustrated with a West-to-East cross-section showing the existing grade contours and elevations. This section is depicted in Figure 8.32. It is recommended that prior to site development, various cross-sections should be delineated in order to allow further visualization of the existing site contours.

Upon completion of the finish grading plan and building layout, it is recommended that a cross-section is provided to illustrate the cut and fill areas. This is shown in Figure 8.33. As discussed earlier in this chapter, site design and grading mechanics can sometimes result from a trial-and-error approach where various studies are analyzed.

Figure 8.32A illustrates a three-dimensional drawing of the existing topography and the finish grading contours at the cut and fill locations as shown in Figure 8.31A.

■ THE LANDSCAPE PLAN AND THE IRRIGATION PLAN

Landscape Plan and Plant List

The final stage of site development for most projects is landscaping. The landscape drawing shows the location of trees, plants, ground covers, benches, fences, and walks. Accompanying this is a **plant list**, identifying plant species with a symbol or number and indicating the size and number of plants. See Figure 8.34.

Irrigation Plan

An irrigation plan often accompanies the landscape plan. This shows all water lines, control valves, and types of watering fixtures needed for irrigation.

■ THE SITE IMPROVEMENT PLAN: AN OVERVIEW

The basic requirement for all construction documents is clarity. The site improvement plan is no exception. It can incorporate any or all of the plans just discussed, depending on the complexity of the information and on office practice.

Site Cross-Section : Finish Grading
Scale : 1/8" = 1'-0"

Figure 8.33   Existing and finish grade (cut and fill) section.

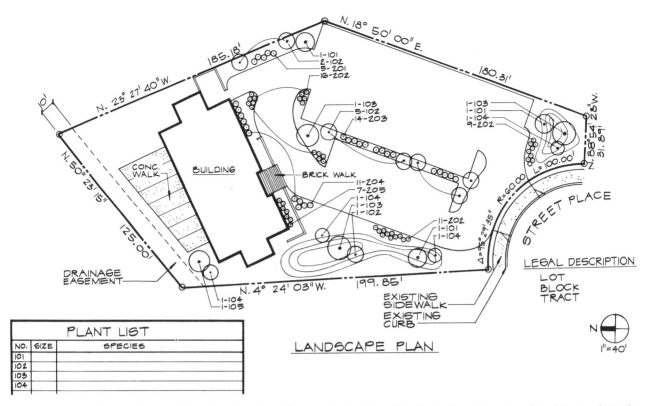

Figure 8.34 Landscape plan and plant list. (Reprinted by permission from *The Professional Practice of Architectural Working Drawings*, 2d Ed., © 1995 by John Wiley & Sons, Inc.)

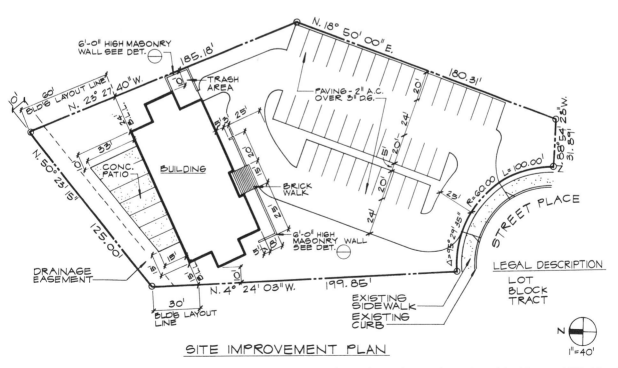

Figure 8.34A Site improvement plan. (Reprinted by permission from *The Professional Practice of Architectural Working Drawings*, 2d Ed., © 1995 by John Wiley & Sons, Inc.)

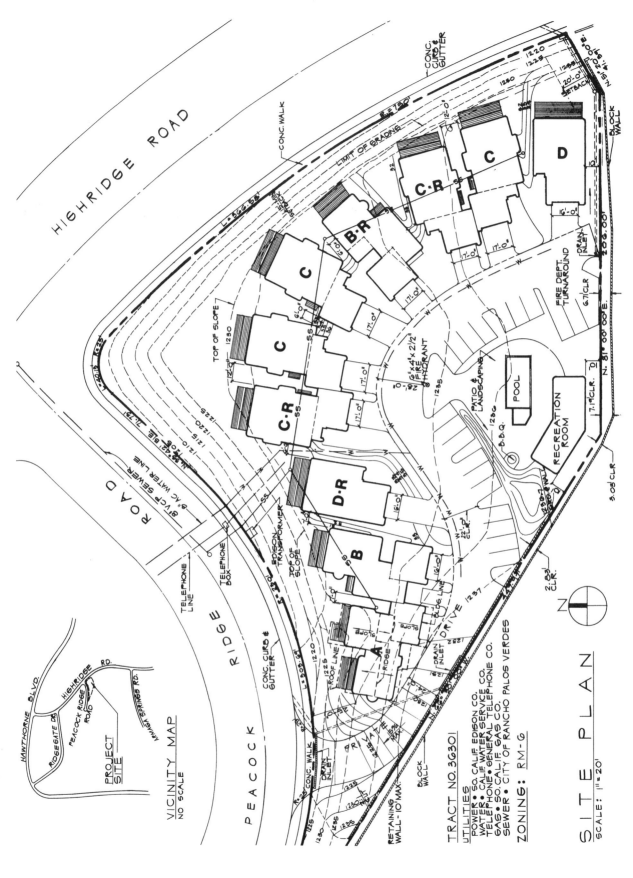

Figure 8.35 Site development plan for multiple housing. (Reprinted by permission from *The Professional Practice of Architectural Working Drawings*, 2d Ed., © 1995 by John Wiley & Sons, Inc.)

The primary information to be found in the site improvement plan is as follows:

1. Site lot lines with accompanying bearings and dimensions
2. Scale of the drawing
3. North arrows
4. Building location with layout dimensions
5. Paving, walks, walls with their accompanying material call-outs, and layout dimensions

Figure 8.34A shows the primary information found on a site improvement plan. The building layout dimension lines at the East and West property lines are parallel to their respective property lines, providing two measuring points at the East and West property lines. This, in turn, provides offset dimensions to each corner of the building. This is helpful when the property lines do not parallel the building. This method may apply to patios, walks, paving, and walls, also dimensional on the site improvement plan.

Site plans for large sites such as multiple-housing projects must show primary information such as utility lo-cations, driveway locations, and building locations. See Figure 8.35. Further examples of site development plans appear in later chapters. See Figure 8.36 for a Site Plan Checklist.

■ SIZE AND LOCATION

As you position the structure on the site and subsequently position architectural features adjacent to the building, two considerations come to mind: size and location.

Size includes width, length, and thickness (sometimes even height), plus location dimension. See Figure 8.37; in this illustration S refers to the size and L refers to the positioning that we call "location dimension."

Consider the example of the freestanding wall. S (size) refers to the length, the note indication, the height, and the two "L" dimensions that position the wall with respect to the building. This is a very generic note, which depends on a written description (specifications) about the size of the block unit, how it is stacked, and the size

---

1. Vicinity Map
2. Property lines
   a. lengths—each side
   b. correct angles if not 90°
   c. direction
3. Adjoining streets, sidewalks, parking, curbs, parkways, parking areas, wheel stops, lanes and lighting
4. Existing structures and buildings and alleys
5. Structures and buildings to be removed
   a. Trees
   b. Old foundations
   c. Walks
   d. Miscellanea
6. Public utilities locations
   a. Storm drain
   b. Sewer lines
   c. Gas lines
   d. Gas meter
   e. Water lines
   f. Water meter
   g. Power line
   h. Power pole
   i. Electric meter
   j. Telephone pole
   k. Lamp post
   l. Fire plugs
7. Public utilities easements if on property
8. Contours of grade
   a. Existing grade—dotted line
   b. Finish cut or fill—solid line
   c. Legend
   d. Slopes to street
9. Grade elevations
   a. Finish slab or finish floor
   b. Corners of building (finish)
   c. Top of all walls
   d. Amount of slope for drainage
10. Roof plan—new building
    a. Building—hidden line
    b. Roof overhang—solid line
    c. Garage
    d. Slopes (arrows)
    e. Projecting canopies
    f. Slabs and porches
    g. Projecting beams
    h. Material for roof
    i. North arrow
    j. Title and scale
    k. Show ridges and valleys
    l. Roof drains and downspouts
    m. Parapets
    n. Roof jacks for TV, telephone, electric service
    o. Note building outline
    p. Dimension overhangs
    q. Note rain diverters
    r. Sky lights
    s. Roof accessways
    t. Flood lite locations
    u. Service pole for electrical
11. New construction
    a. Retaining walls
    b. Driveways and aprons
    c. Sidewalks
    d. Pool locations and size
    e. Splash blocks
    f. Catch basins
    g. Curbs
    h. Patios, walls, expansion joints, dividers etc.
12. North arrow (usually toward the top of sheet.)
13. Dimensions
    a. Property lines
    b. Side yards
    c. Rear yards
    d. Front yards
    e. Easements
    f. Street center line
    g. Length of fences and walls
    h. Height of fences and walls
    i. Width of sidewalks, driveway, and parking
    j. Utilities
    k. Locations of existing structures
    l. Note floor elevation
    m. Dimension building to property line
    n. Set backs
14. Notes
    a. Tract no.
    b. Block no.
    c. Lot no.
    d. House no.
    e. Street
    f. City, county, state
    g. Owner's name
    h. Draftman's name (title block)
    i. materials for porches, terraces, drives, etc.
    j. Finish grades where necessary
    k. Slope of driveway
    l. Scale (1/8", 1"-30', 1"-20' etc.)
15. Landscape lighting, note switches
16. Area drains, drain lines to street
17. Show hose bibs
18. Note drying yard, clothes line equipment
19. Complete title block
    a. Sheet no.
    b. Scale
    c. Date
    d. Name drawn by
    e. Project address
    f. Approved by
    g. Sheet title
    h. Revision box
    i. Company name and address (school)

Figure 8.36 Site Plan Checklist. (Reprinted by permission from *The Professional Practice of Architectural Working Drawings*, 2d Ed., © 1995 by John Wiley & Sons, Inc.)

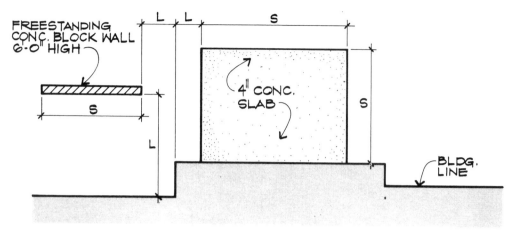

Figure 8.37 Size and location dimension. (Reprinted by permission from *The Professional Practice of Architectural Working Drawings*, 2d Ed., © 1995 by John Wiley & Sons, Inc.)

and appearance of the joint. Another type of note might read:

> 8 × 8 × 16 conc. Block freestanding wall, stretcher, running bond, V-jointed, 6'-0" high

The patio slab at the center of the illustration shows one location dimension and three size dimensions. Two are marked with S, and the third comes in the form of a note at the center which describes thickness. The composition and quality of the concrete will be dealt with in the specifications, and the shape of the footing around the perimeter will be dealt with in the footing detail, as will the size and frequency of the dowels that hold the slab to the building.

Driveway and Curb

Often one side of your site is bound with a sidewalk, parkway, and a small curb. In most cities this portion, adjacent to a street, is maintained by the Department of Public Works or some such agency. To break the curb for a driveway, permits are obtained from such an agency or a subdivision, perhaps the Road Department Bureau. Based on the size of the curb, the agency will configure an angle at which you can cut the curb to form the driveway. Figure 8.38 is a before-and-after type drawing showing the appearance of a driveway.

Procedural Stages for a Site Plan Development

STAGE I   The architect requests a digital drawing of the site plan illustrating the property lines, existing grade contours, and any major physical features such as trees, utility poles, or any other feature that may dictate the site plan process. This digital drawing is provided by a civil engineer (see Figure 8.39).

STAGE II   At this stage any easements that are allocated for utility purposes, such as sewers, are depicted on the drawing with a broken line. This stage of the drawing also shows the adjacent streets, street curbs, sidewalks, and pathways. This stage is illustrated in Figure 8.40.

STAGE III   After the final preliminary building designs and their relationship to the influencing factors of the

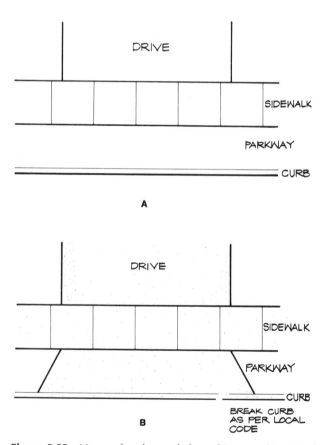

Figure 8.38 How to break a curb for a driveway. (Reprinted by permission from *The Professional Practice of Architectural Working Drawings*, 2d Ed., © 1995 by John Wiley & Sons, Inc.)

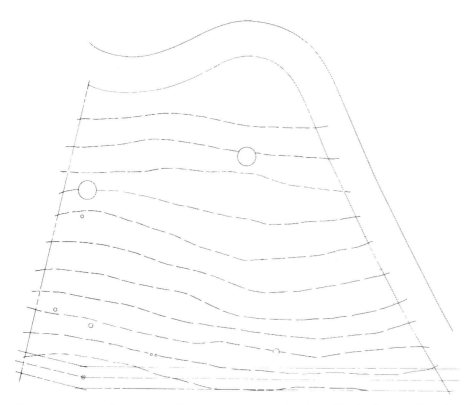

Figure 8.39 Site plan—Stage I. (Reprinted by permission from *The Professional Practice of Architectural Working Drawings*, 2d Ed., © 1995 by John Wiley & Sons, Inc.)

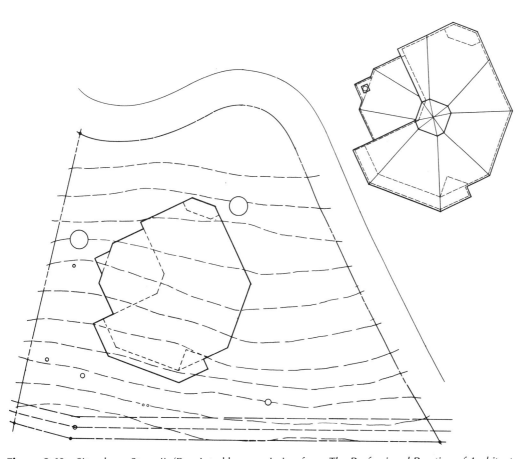

Figure 8.40 Site plan—Stage II. (Reprinted by permission from *The Professional Practice of Architectural Working Drawings*, 2d Ed., © 1995 by John Wiley & Sons, Inc.)

building site are determined, the building is placed on the site plan. The placement of the building is derived from the final preliminary designs relative to the orientation of the sun, prevailing winds, governing setback requirements, and any existing easements. A solid line depicts the perimeter lines of the building, and a broken line indicates walls beneath. A roof plan is drawn separately for clarity so as not to confuse the building wall lines with the perimeter roof eave line. This is done to ensure that the setback dimension lines are to the perimeter wall lines. This stage is depicted in Figure 8.41.

STAGE IV   The procedure at this stage was to show items such as the driveway, patio slab on the east side, and the garage roof deck. The trees and the roof texture have been delineated for more clarity. Also shown is the water meter location at the northwest corner of the site, and a concrete slab is provided for the use of a propane tank. Many of the major lines have been darkened for clarity. Stage IV is illustrated in Figure 8.42.

STAGE V   The next procedure was to provide the finish contour lines, which are drawn with a solid line and connected to their correlating grade elevations. The

numerical elevation grades have been added, representing one-foot intervals. Dimension lines and their values are now shown from the property lines to the perimeter wall lines of the building for layout purposes. Also shown in this stage are the property line dimensions and their bearings. The utility easement is shown and dimensioned at the southerly property line (See Figure 8.43).

STAGE VI   The final stage includes all the required noting, such as the roof material and roof slope directions and the roof flashing locations. These notes are shown on the roof plan. The finish noting on the site plan indicates the driveway finish material, the walkway material, balustrade reference detail, the wood porch deck material, and the size of the sewer pipe.

All the various floor elevations have been labeled on a chart below the site plan. This has been done for clarity. In addition, a chart for symbol designations has been provided to define those symbols on the site plan. Finally, the title of the drawing is shown, along with the North orientation arrow, the street name, and the scale for the site and roof plan drawing.

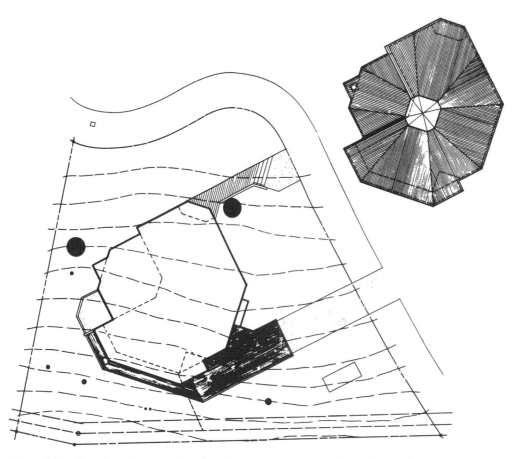

Figure 8.41   Site plan—Stage III. (Reprinted by permission from *The Professional Practice of Architectural Working Drawings*, 2d Ed., © 1995 by John Wiley & Sons, Inc.)

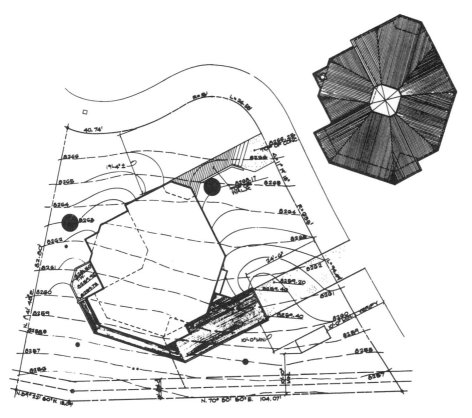

Figure 8.42 Site plan—Stage IV. (Reprinted by permission from *The Professional Practice of Architectural Working Drawings*, 2d Ed., © 1995 by John Wiley & Sons, Inc.)

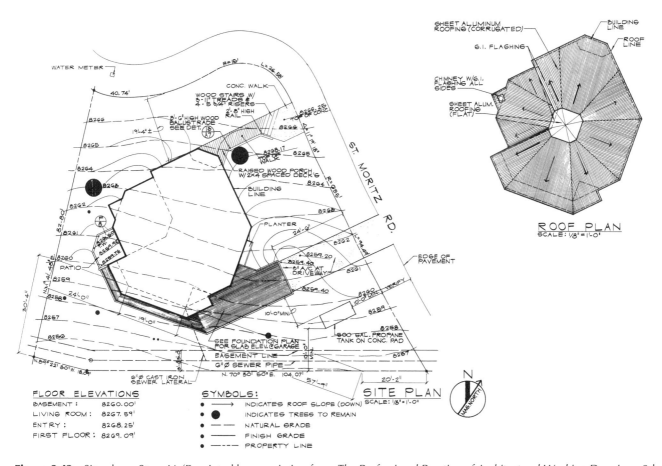

ROOF PLAN
SCALE: 1/8" = 1'-0"

FLOOR ELEVATIONS
BASEMENT : 8260.00'
LIVING ROOM : 8267.59'
ENTRY : 8268.25'
FIRST FLOOR : 8269.09'

SYMBOLS:
• → INDICATES ROOF SLOPE (DOWN)
• ● INDICATES TREES TO REMAIN
• — — NATURAL GRADE
• — FINISH GRADE
• — — — PROPERTY LINE

SITE PLAN
SCALE: 1/8" = 1'-0"

Figure 8.43 Site plan—Stage V. (Reprinted by permission from *The Professional Practice of Architectural Working Drawings*, 2d Ed., © 1995 by John Wiley & Sons, Inc.)

chapter

9

FOUNDATION PLAN

A foundation plan is a drawing that shows the location of all concrete footings, concrete piers, and structural underpinning members required to support a structure. The main purpose of all the foundation footings is to distribute the weight of the structure over the soil.

■ TYPES OF FOUNDATIONS

Two types of floor systems are usually used in foundation plans. These floor systems are constructed of concrete or wood or a combination of both. Each floor system requires foundation footings to support the structure and the floor.

Concrete Slab Floor: Foundation Plans

If you have selected concrete as the floor material for a specific project, first investigate the types of **foundation footing details** required to support the structure before drawing the foundation plan. The **footing design** will be influenced by many factors such as the vertical loads or weight it is to support, regional differences, allowable soil bearing values, established frost line location, and recommendations from a soils and geological report as reinforcing requirements. Figure 9.1 illustrates a concrete footing and concrete floor with various factors influencing design.

You may sketch the foundation details in freehand form. Figure 9.2A shows a freehand drawing with an exterior bearing wall footing and concrete slab floor. The sketch then becomes the guide for drawing an exterior bearing footing on the foundation plan. See Figure 9.2B. The broken line represents the footing and foundation wall, located under the concrete slab or grade. This broken line, as you will remember, is referred to as a hidden line. The solid line shows the edge of the concrete floor slab as projected above the grade level. Broken lines are mainly used to show footing sizes, configurations, and

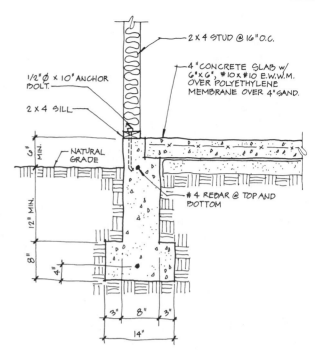

Figure 9.2A Exterior bearing—Beach House.

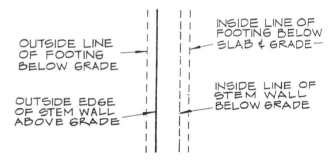

Figure 9.2B Plan view of foundation detail.

their locations below grade level or below a concrete floor; solid lines show those above.

The investigation and freehand sketch for a required interior bearing footing might look like Figure 9.3A. If it does, draw the plan view of this detail only with broken lines, because all the configurations are under the concrete slab floor and grade. See Figure 9.3B.

An interior nonbearing footing (a footing that supports a much lighter load than a bearing footing) is drawn in the plan view as the section configuration dictates. Figure 9.4A shows a section through a nonbearing footing. Figure 9.4B shows this footing in the plan view. Note here that only the width of the footing is shown since the foundation wall and footing are in this case one and the same.

Often, concrete curbs above the concrete floor levels are used, as, for example, in garage areas where wood studs need to be free from floor moisture. As with the

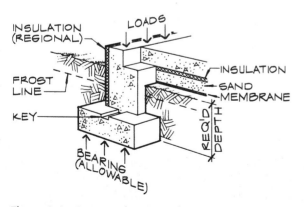

Figure 9.1 Concrete footing and concrete floor with various influencing design factors.

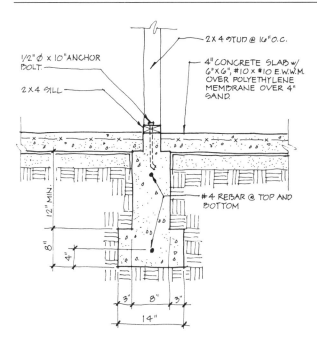

Figure 9.3A Detail of interior bearing footing—Beach House.

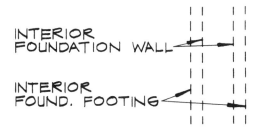

Figure 9.3B Plan view of interior bearing footing.

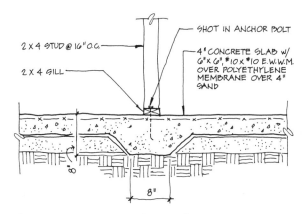

Figure 9.4A Interior nonbearing footing.

Figure 9.4B Plan view of interior nonbearing footing.

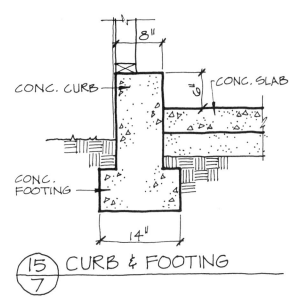

Figure 9.5A Concrete curb and footing.

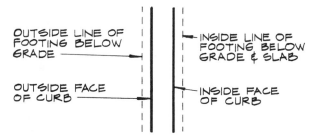

Figure 9.5B Plan view—concrete curb.

other foundation conditions, draw a freehand sketch of this detail. See Figure 9.5A for an example. The plan view of this detail is shown in Figure 9.5B, and Figures 9.6A and 9.6B show this photographically.

When you are faced with drawing concrete steps and a change of floor level, a freehand sketch of the section clarifies this condition. See Figure 9.7A. A plan view may then be drawn reflecting this section. See Figure 9.7B.

In order to visualize the foundation of the structure and its various components, a three-dimensional image was produced. Two major segments were then removed to help the designer visualize the interior shapes and connections. For this model, we selected the Ryan Residence, which is fully developed in Chapter 17. One can actually see the exterior bearing footing, the change in level, and even the depressed slab in the bathroom. See Figure 9.8.

Drawing the Foundation Plan

You are now ready to draw the **foundation plan** for a concrete slab floor. Lay your tracing over a tracing of the floor plan drawing, then lightly draw the configuration of

Figure 9.6A   Forms for concrete curb.

Figure 9.6B   Poured concrete curb.

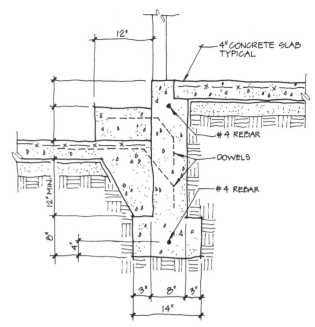

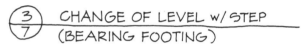

CHANGE OF LEVEL w/ STEP
(BEARING FOOTING)

Figure 9.7A   Change of level with step (bearing footing).

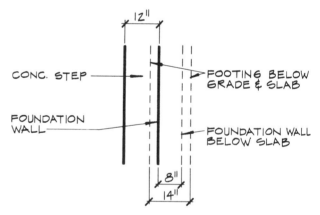

Figure 9.7B   Plan view—steps and level change.

the floor plan, as well as the internal walls, columns, fire-places, and so on, that require foundation sections. (Do not trace the foundation plan from a reproduction of the floor plan, because reproductions alter the scale of the original drawing.) After this light tracing, you are ready to finalize the drafting.

The final drafting is a graphic culmination in plan view of all the foundation walls and footings. Start with all the interior bearing and nonbearing foundation conditions. Represent these with a dotted line according to the particular sections in plan view. Figure 9.9 shows an example of a foundation plan for a residence, incorporating the plan views similar to Figures 9.2B and 9.3A, 9.3B, 9.5A, and 9.5B as previously discussed. Note reference symbols on foundation details and Figure 9.9.

Usually, various notes are required for items to be installed prior to the concrete pouring. An item like a **post hold-down**, (a U-shaped steel strap for bolting to a post

and embedded in concrete for the use of resisting lateral forces) should be shown on the foundation plan because its installation is important in this particular construction phase. Note the **call-out** for this item on Figure 9.9. A photograph of this is shown in Figure 9.10.

Drawing Fireplaces.   A drawing of a masonry fireplace on the foundation plan should have the supporting walls crosshatched. (To **crosshatch** is to shade with crossed lines, either diagonal or rectangular.) Show its footing with a broken line. When numerous vertical reinforcing

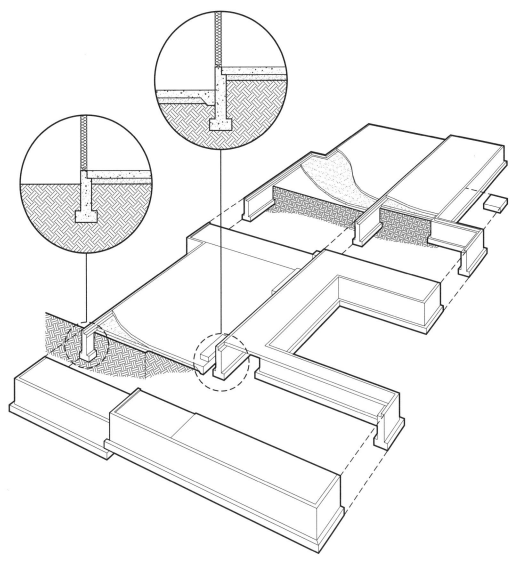

Figure 9.8 Pictorial of Ryan Residence foundation.

bars are required for the fireplace, show their size and location, because they are embedded in the fireplace.

Strengthening Floors. Requirements for strengthening concrete floors with reinforcing vary for specific projects, so it is important to show their size and spacing on the foundation plan. Figure 9.8's foundation plan calls for a 6″ × 6″—#10 × #10 welded wire reinforcing mesh to strengthen the concrete floor. This call-out tells us that the mesh is in 6″ × 6″ squares and made of number 10 gauge wire. Figure 9.11 shows how the reinforcing mesh and a plastic membrane are placed before the concrete is poured. Deformed reinforcing bars are also installed to strengthen concrete slab floors. The size and spacing of these bars are determined by factors such as excessive weights expected to be carried by the floor and unfavorable soils conditions.

Sloping Concrete Areas. When concrete areas have to be sloped for drainage, indicate this, too, on the foundation plan. You can do this with a directional arrow, noting the number of inches the concrete is to be sloped. See Figure 9.9; here a garage slab is sloped to a door.

Your foundation plan dimensioning should reflect the identical dimension line locations of the floor plan. For example, center line dimensions for walls above should match center line dimensions for foundation walls below. This makes the floor and foundation plans consistent. When you lay out dimension lines, such as perimeter lines, leave space between the exterior wall and first dimension line for foundation section symbols. As Figure 9.9 shows, you must provide dimensions for every foundation condition and configuration. Remember people in the field do not have the luxury of protrac-

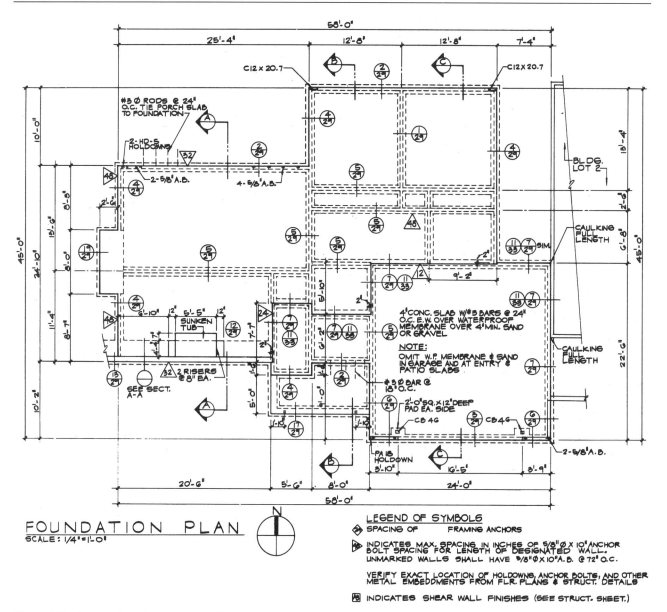

FOUNDATION PLAN
SCALE: 1/4" = 1'-0"

LEGEND OF SYMBOLS

◇ SPACING OF   FRAMING ANCHORS

▷ INDICATES MAX. SPACING IN INCHES OF 5/8"Ø X 10"ANCHOR BOLT SPACING FOR LENGTH OF DESIGNATED WALL. UNMARKED WALLS SHALL HAVE 5/8"ØX10"A.B. @ 72" O.C.

VERIFY EXACT LOCATION OF HOLDOWNS, ANCHOR BOLTS, AND OTHER METAL EMBEDDMENTS FROM FLR. PLANS & STRUCT. DETAILS

▲ INDICATES SHEAR WALL FINISHES (SEE STRUCT. SHEET.)

Figure 9.9 Foundation plan—concrete floor.

tors or other measuring devices and therefore rely on all the dimensions you have provided on the plan.

In some cases, the foundation dimensioning process may require you to make adjustments for stud wall alignments. For example, if studs and interior finish need to be aligned, be sure to dimension for foundation offset correctly to achieve the stud alignment. See Figure 9.12. In this figure, the 3½" stud, the foundation wall, and footing of the exterior wall are not aligned with the interior foundation wall and footing.

Provide reference symbols for foundation details for all conditions. Provide as many symbols as you need, even if there is some repetition. Remove any guesswork for the people in the field. As Figure 9.9 shows, the reference

symbol will have enough space within the circle for letters and/or numbers for detail and sheet referencing.

Foundation Details for Concrete Slab Floor

You can now draft finished drawings of the foundation details, using freehand sketches as a reference. For most cases, foundation details are drawn using an architectural scale of ½" = 1'-0", ¾" = 1'-0" or 1" = 1'-0". Scale selection may be dictated by office procedure or the complexity of a specific project.

Different geographical regions vary in depth, sizes, and reinforcing requirements for foundation design. Check the requirements for your region.

Figure 9.10 Post hold-down.

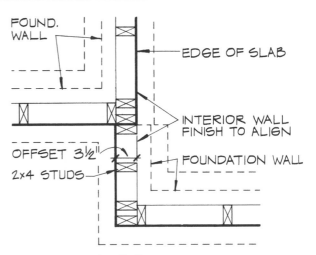

Figure 9.12 Stud wall alignment.

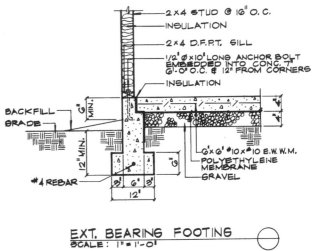

EXT. BEARING FOOTING
SCALE: 1" = 1'-0"

Figure 9.13 Drafted detail of a two-pour footing.

Figure 9.11 Reinforcing mesh and plastic.

Foundation details for the residence shown in Figure 9.13 are drawn to incorporate a **two-pour system**; that is, the foundation wall and footing are poured first and the concrete floor later. Figure 9.13 shows the exterior bearing footing drawn in final form. Notice the joint between the foundation wall and concrete floor is filled with insulation.

The interior bearing footing detail should also be drawn to reflect a two-pour system with call-outs for all the components in the assembly. See Figure 9.14. The nonbearing footing is drafted differently from the exterior and interior bearing footings. This detail, Figure 9.15, is shown as one pour, because it is only deep enough to accommodate the **anchor bolt embedment** and can therefore be poured at the same time as the floor slab. The remaining foundation details are drafted using the freehand sketches for reference.

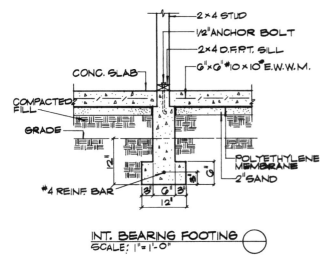

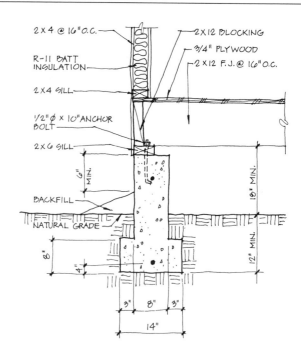

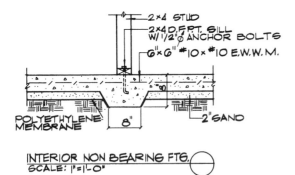

Figure 9.14 Drafted detail of a two-pour interior bearing footing.

Figure 9.16A Exterior bearing footing detail.

Figure 9.15 Drafted detail of an interior nonbearing footing.

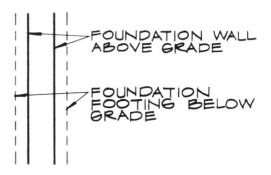

Figure 9.16B Plan view of exterior bearing footing.

Powder actuated bolts, or shot-ins as they are often called, can be used to replace the anchor bolts in some municipalities. Because the bolts, which look more like nails, are only a few inches long, a footing may not be required. However, they should be used only on nonbearing walls in the interior of a structure.

Wood Floor: Foundation Plans

Prepare a foundation plan for a wood floor the same way you do for a concrete floor. Sketch the different footings required to support the structure.

Your first sketch should deal with the exterior bearing footing, incorporating the required footing and wall dimensions and depth below grade. Show earth-to-wood clearances, sizes and treatment of wood members, floor sheathing, and the exterior wall and its assembly of components above the sheathing or subfloor level. See Figure 9.16A. Figure 9.16B describes the exterior bearing footing in plan view. An investigation of the interior bearing footing requirements can be done with a scaled freehand sketch. See Figure 9.17. In the plan view the interior

bearing footing looks similar to the exterior bearing footing in Figure 9.16B.

When laying out the foundation plan for a wood floor system, provide intermediate supporting elements located between exterior and interior bearing footings. You can do this with a pier and girder system, which can be spaced well within the allowable spans of the floor joists selected. This layout will be reviewed later in the discussion of the foundation plan. The girder-on-pier detail can be sketched in the same way as the previous details. See Figure 9.18A. Figure 9.18B describes the concrete pier in plan view. The pier spacing depends on the size of floor girder selected. With a 4 × 6 girder, a 5' or 6' spacing is recommended under normal floor loading conditions.

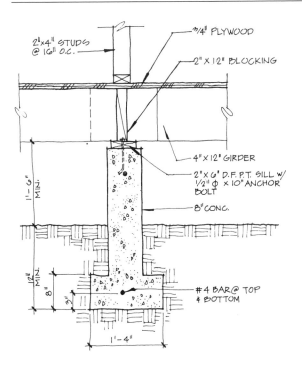

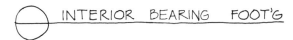

INTERIOR BEARING FOOT'G

Figure 9.17 Interior bearing footing detail.

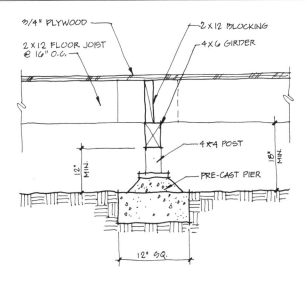

PIER AND GIRDER DETAIL

Figure 9.18A Pier and girder detail.

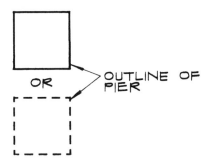

OR

OUTLINE OF PIER

Figure 9.18B Plan view of concrete pier.

Regional building codes help you to select floor joists and girder sizes relative to allowable spans.

Drawing the Foundation Plan

Begin the foundation plan drawing by laying the tracing directly over the floor plan. Lightly trace the outside line of the exterior walls, the center line of the interior load bearing walls (walls supporting ceiling, floor, and roof), and curb and stud edges that define a transition between the wood floor members and the concrete floor. It is not necessary to trace nonbearing wall conditions for wood floors because floor girders can be used to support the weight of the wall.

Refer to your freehand sketches of the foundation details to help finalize the foundation plan. As a review of this procedure, Figure 9.19 shows a pictorial of a foundation plan with wood floor construction, incorporating

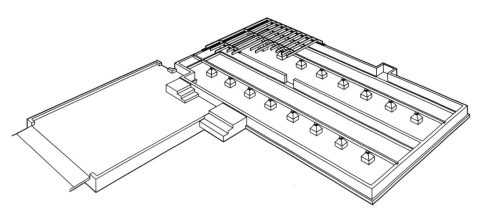

Figure 9.19 Foundation plan—wood floor.

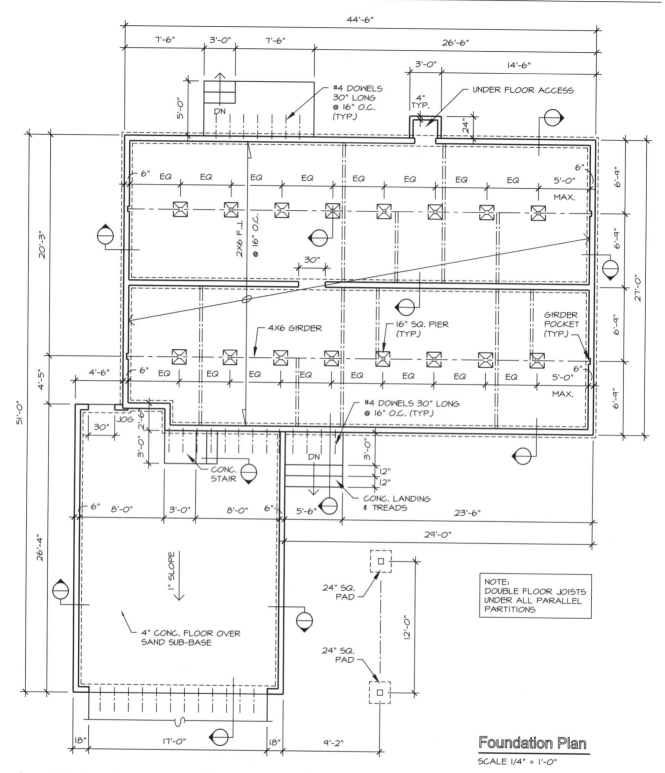

Figure 9.20 Foundation plan—wood floor.

the plan views shown in Figures 9.16B and 9.18B. The floor plan is the same one used for the concrete floor foundation plan. The spacing for floor girders and the concrete piers supporting the girders is based on the selected floor joist size and girder sizes. The floor girders can be drawn with a broken line while the piers, being above grade, can be drawn with a solid line. Dimension the location of all piers and girders. Wherever possible, locate floor girders under walls. Show the direction of the floor joists and their size and spacing directly above the floor girders. The fireplace foundation and reinforcing information can be designated as indicated earlier.

In Figure 9.20 a foundation plan shows a concrete garage floor connected to a house floor system with #3 dowels at 24″ on center. This call-out should also be designated for other concrete elements such as porches and patios. If a basement exists, the supporting walls can be built of concrete block. The concrete block wall will be crosshatched on the foundation plan to indicate masonry construction. A sample of this condition can be seen in Figure 9.21 and in Chapter 19. The detail of a basement footing can be seen in Figure 9.32.

Incorporate dimensioning and foundation detail symbols the same way you did for a concrete foundation. This instance, however, the detail reference symbol shows arrowheads on the circular symbols as recommended by state and national standards. An important note to be located on the foundation plan drawing is the number of foundation vents required, and their sizes, material, and location. This requirement is regulated by governing building codes.

The foundation plan is ideally suited to be drawn on the computer. There are two main reasons for this. As every trained manual drafter knows, the repetitious

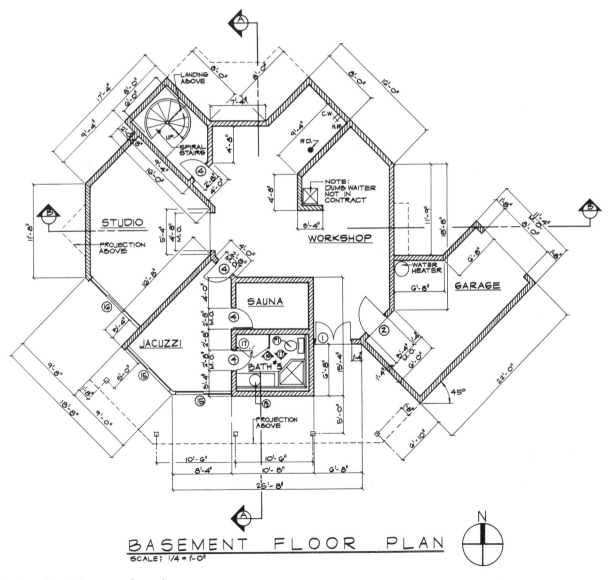

Figure 9.21 Basement floor plan.

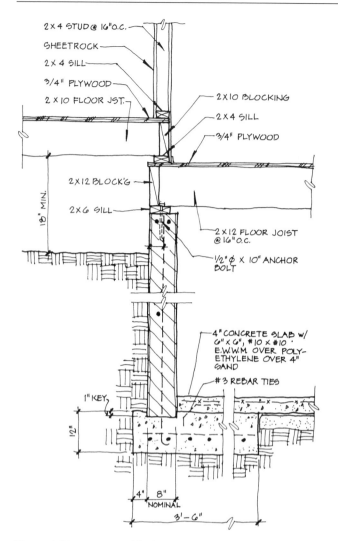

Figure 9.22 Concrete block wall and basement—wood floor.

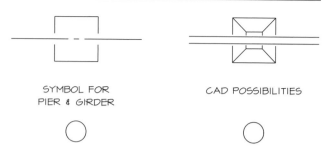

Figure 9.23 Comparison of hand-drafted/CAD-developed.

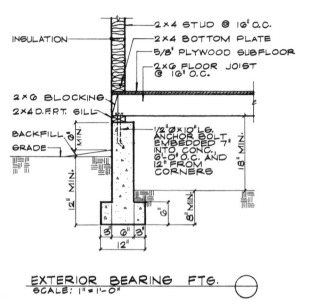

Figure 9.24 Drafted detail of typical exterior.

drawing of piers and girders is a thing of the past, as is the drawing of dotted or hidden lines around the perimeter of the stem wall on the foundation. Just change the layer and line type, and offset lines, and you immediately have the outline of a footing or foundation. Figure 9.23A shows a typical hand-drafted pier. An abstracted pattern is used for speed. Figure 9.23B shows a girder with a fully drawn pier, which is blocked (computer term for *saved*) and displayed in multiple.

Foundation Details for a Wood Floor Foundation

Finished drawings for the foundation details can be drafted with call-outs and dimensions for each specific detail. As with concrete floor foundation sizes, depths and reinforcing requirements vary regionally. Finished details for exterior and interior bearing footings as well as a typical pier and girder are shown in Figures 9.24, 9.25 and 9.26. Figure 9.27 illustrates the use of concrete block

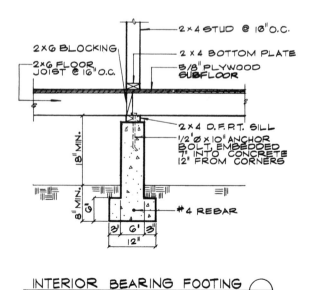

Figure 9.25 Drafted detail of interior bearing footing with wood floor.

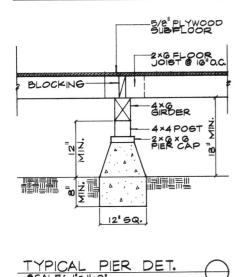

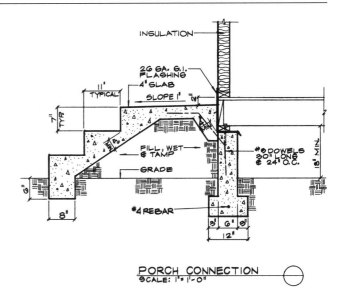

Figure 9.26 Pier detail perpendicular to girder.

Figure 9.28 Drafted detail of a porch connection.

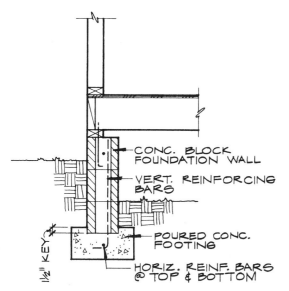

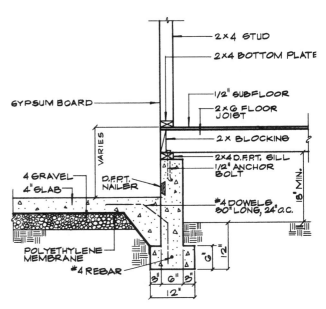

Figure 9.27 Concrete block foundation wall supporting a wood floor.

Figure 9.29 Drafted detail of change of level from a wood floor to a concrete slab.

for a foundation wall supporting a wood floor. Figure 9.28 combines Figure 9.24 with a porch and stair connected to the exterior foundation detail. Here dowels have been added to tie the concrete porch to the building and metal flashing has been used to protect against dryrot from water seepage.

A foundation detail through the garage concrete floor and house floor is shown in Figure 9.29. This important detail shows the placement of dowels and provisions for a nailer in which a finished interior material can be secured at the concrete foundation wall. Remaining foundation sections are drafted in the same way using investigative sketches for reference.

■ EXAMPLES

Example 1: A Building with Masonry Walls

When projects use concrete or masonry for exterior and interior walls, the walls may continue down the concrete footing. Figure 9.30 shows an exterior masonry wall and concrete footing. If interior walls are constructed of masonry, the foundation section is similar to Figure 9.30. Drawing the foundation plan using masonry as the foundation wall requires delineation of the foundation walls by crosshatching those areas representing the masonry.

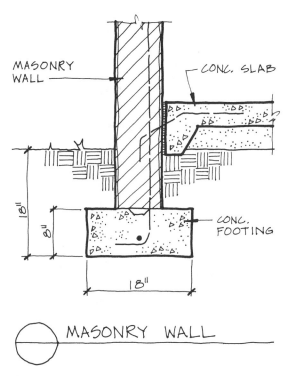

MASONRY WALL — CONC. SLAB — CONC. FOOTING

18"   8"   18"

MASONRY WALL

Figure 9.30 Exterior masonry wall and footing.

The building in this example is a theatre with exterior and interior masonry walls. Its foundation plan, details, and photographs of the construction of the foundation follow.

The foundation plan, shown in Figure 9.31, defines all the masonry wall locations as per Figure 9.30 and 9.32. The footings are drawn with a broken line. For this project **pilasters** are required to support steel roof beams. A pilaster is a masonry or concrete column designed to support heavy axial and/or horizontal loads. See Figure 9.32. The footing width is not called out but refers to the foundation plan for a specific pilaster footing dimension. Many projects do this because the total loads acting on the pilaster vary.

Steel columns are also required to support heavy axial loads and they, in turn, require a foundation. These foundation members are commonly referred to as concrete piers or **concrete pads**. The size of these pads varies with different loading conditions. Because of the various pad sizes, you may need to use a column pad schedule. This schedule should note the column designation, size, depth, and required steel reinforcing.

An example of a pad schedule is shown in Figure 9.31. Locate the pad schedule directly on the foundation plan sheet for ease of reference. It should show dimensions for all footings, walls, and pad locations with reference symbols clearly defined for specific conditions. Similar notes are provided for items such as ramp and floor slopes, pilaster sizes, and required steel reinforcing.

From the information on the foundation plan, the various foundation conditions are laid out on the site using chalk lines. In Figure 9.33, the footing for the masonry walls and pilasters is clearly visible on the right side of the structure.

When **chalking** has been completed for the footing locations, trenching for these details is dug and made ready for the pouring of the concrete. Once the reinforcing rods and footings are installed, the masonry work can begin. Figure 9.34 shows masonry work in progress. Note the pilasters and chalking for the various concrete pads.

Example 2: A Foundation Using Concrete Pads and Steel Columns

Drawing foundation plans varies depending on the foundation requirements of the method of construction for a specific structure. The example that follows uses a structure requiring concrete pads to support steel columns with a continuous footing to support masonry walls.

This foundation plan, as Figure 9.35 shows, is handled differently from the foundation plan in Example 1. As you place the tracing paper directly over the floor plan tracing, first establish the column locations as they relate to the **axial reference locations**. Masonry walls are then drawn and delineated. Concrete pads, located under a concrete floor, are represented with a broken line. See Figure 9.35. Figure 9.36 provides a visual example of this column pad footing detail in section. The column pad sizes may vary due to varying loads, and may be sized using a pad schedule or noted directly on the foundation plan. In this case, sizes are noted on the foundation plan. These pads are drawn to scale, relative to their *required* sizes, rather than their actual sizes. Provide, at the bottom of the foundation plan drawing, a **legend** defining the size and shape of the steel column and the base stem that supports it.

Because of all the critical information required in the field, a schedule for column base plates and their required anchorage may be necessary. Put this at the bottom of the plan. Dimensioning this type of foundation depends on the axial reference locations, which are identical to the floor plan referencing. Other foundation conditions are dimensioned from these axial reference lines. See Figure 9.35.

After you complete all the necessary dimensioning, show section reference symbols and notes. Figure 9.35 has a double broken line representing a continuous footing underneath, which connects to all the concrete pads. The main purpose of this footing is to provide continuity for all the components of the foundation.

The concrete pads are the main supports for this structure. Figure 9.37 shows the trenching and some formwork for a concrete pad. Note particularly the placement

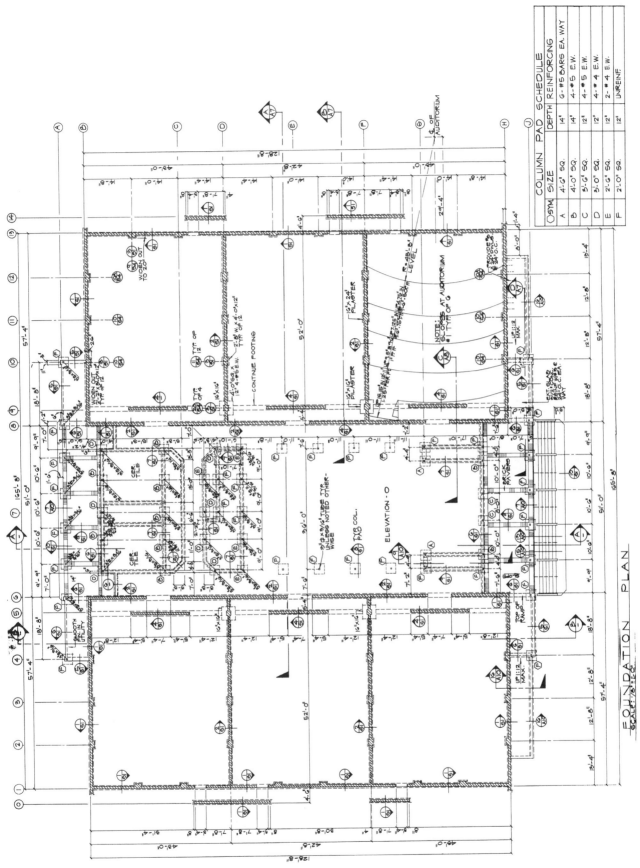

Figure 9.31 Foundation plan—masonry walls. (Courtesy of AVCO Community Developers, Inc., and Mann Theatres Corporation of CA.)

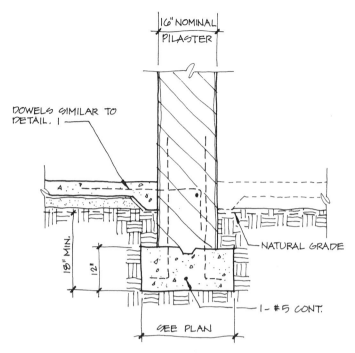

Figure 9.32 Pilaster footing detail.

Figure 9.33 Chalking for foundation layout. (Courtesy of AVCO Community Developers, Inc., and Mann Theatres Corporation of CA.; William Boggs Aerial Photography. Reprinted with permission.)

Figure 9.34 Foundation development. (Courtesy of AVCO Community Developers, Inc., and Mann Theatres Corporation of CA.; William Boggs Aerial Photography. Reprinted with permission.)

of the reinforcing steel and the footing, which is used to tie all the pads together. After the concrete is poured and anchor bolts embedded, the steel column with the attached base plate is bolted to the concrete pad. See Figure 9.38.

When columns are used for structural support, **concrete caissons** may be needed in unfavorable soil conditions. A concrete caisson is a reinforced column designed specifically for the loads it will support and is located at a depth that provides good soil bearing. The concrete caisson shown in Figure 9.39 is used on a sloping site to provide firm support for a wood column which in turn is part of the structural support for a building. Figure 9.40 shows a job site drilling rig providing holes for concrete caissons.

Example 3: A Concrete Floor at Ground-Floor Level

This foundation plan is for a small two-story residence with a concrete floor at the ground-floor level. See Figure 9.44. The plan view drawing of the foundation sections is similar to those in Figures 9.2B, 9.3B, 9.4B, 9.5B, and 9.7B.

Note on the foundation plan everything that is to be installed prior to the pouring of the concrete. If terms are located somewhere else in the drawings, the foundation contractor may miss these items, causing problems after the pouring. Specific locations call for anchor bolt placement, steel column embedment, post hold-down hardware, and other symbols, all explained in the legend below. Dimensions for the location of all foundation

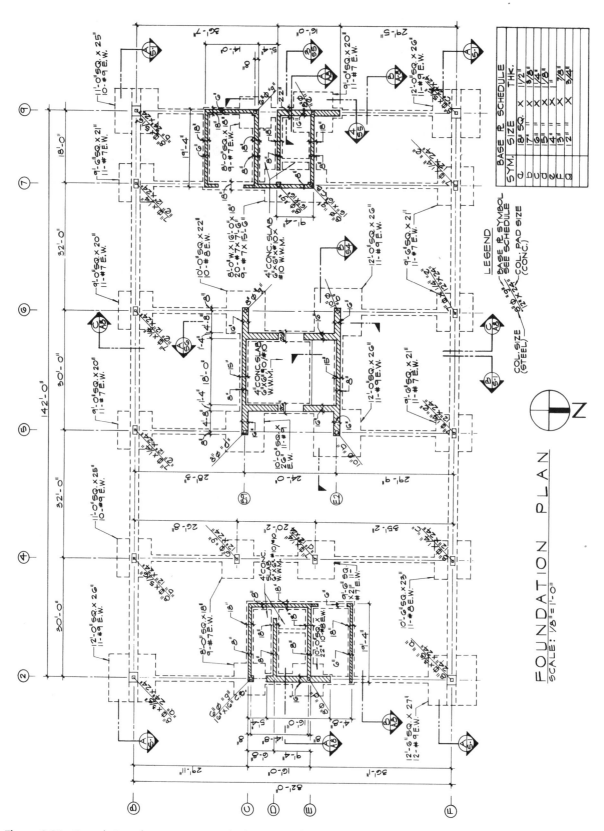

Figure 9.35 Foundation plan—concrete pads. (Courtesy of Westmount, Inc., Real Estate Development, Torrance, CA.)

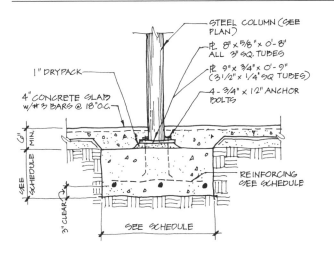

Column footing detail labels:
- STEEL COLUMN (SEE PLAN)
- PL 8" x 5/8" x 0'-8" ALL 3" SQ. TUBES
- PL 9" x 3/4" x 0'-9" (3 1/2" x 1/4" SQ TUBES)
- 4 - 3/4" x 12" ANCHOR BOLTS
- 1" DRYPACK
- 4" CONCRETE SLAB w/ #3 BARS @ 18"O.C.
- REINFORCING SEE SCHEDULE
- 6" MIN.
- SEE SCHEDULE
- 3" CLEAR
- SEE SCHEDULE

COLUMN FOOTING DETAIL

Figure 9.36 Column footing detail.

Figure 9.37 Forming for concrete pad. (William Boggs Aerial Photography. Reprinted with permission.)

Figure 9.38 Steel column on concrete pad.

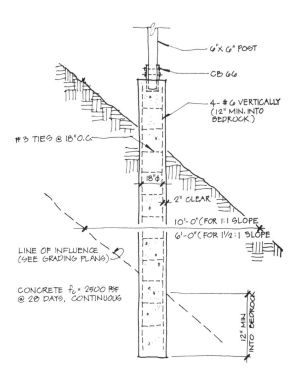

Concrete caisson labels:
- 6" X 6" POST
- CB 66
- 4 - #6 VERTICALLY (12" MIN. INTO BEDROCK.)
- #3 TIES @ 18"O.C.
- 18"∅
- 2" CLEAR
- 10'-0" (FOR 1:1 SLOPE)
- 6'-0" (FOR 1 1/2:1 SLOPE)
- LINE OF INFLUENCE (SEE GRADING PLANS)
- CONCRETE f'c = 2500 PSF @ 28 DAYS, CONTINUOUS
- 12" MIN. INTO BEDROCK

CONCRETE CAISSON

Figure 9.39 Concrete caisson.

Figure 9.40 Drilling holes for concrete caissons. (William Boggs Aerial Photography. Reprinted with permission.)

walls and footings are shown with reference symbols for the various footing conditions.

Figure 9.42 demonstrates the importance of noting all the required hardware or concrete accessories on the foundation plan. You can well imagine the problems that would arise if these items were not installed before the concrete was poured! Trenching and formwork for the foundation (see Figure 9.41) is shown photographically in Figure 9.43. The next step in completing the foundation phase of this residence is the pouring of the concrete and finishing of the concrete floor in preparation for the wood framing. See Figure 9.43. Often, a checklist also is furnished that provides specific information required for a project. See Figure 9.44.

■ SUMMARY OF TYPICAL CONVENTIONS—FOUNDATION PLAN (FIGURE 9.45)

A. Plan view of an exterior bearing footing for a slab-on-ground. For a description, see Figures 9.2A and 9.2B.

B. Plan view of a footing with a concrete curb as seen in Figure 9.5A and 9.5B. Also represents bearing footing for a wood floor system original, as seen in Figures 9.16A and 9.16B.

C. Plan view of an interior bearing footing for a slab-on-the-ground system. Originally shown in Figures 9.3A and 9.3B.

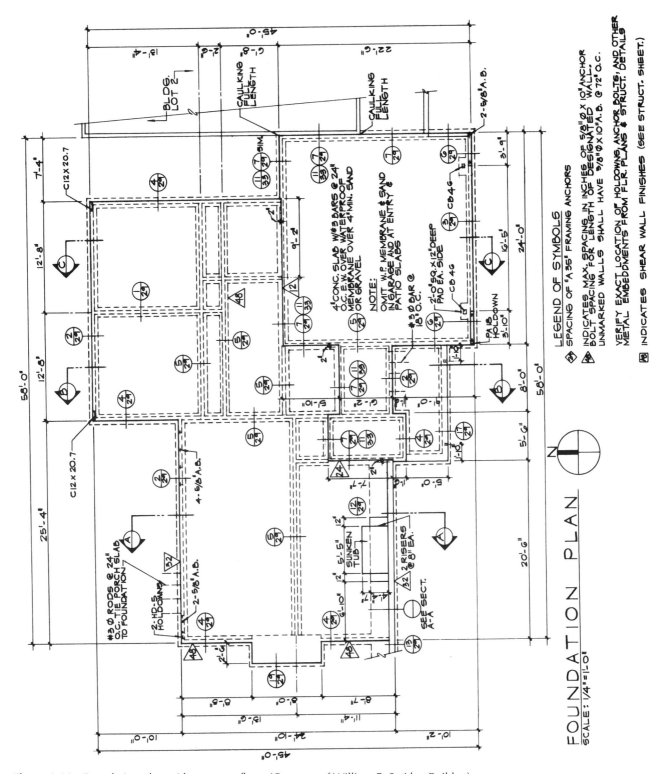

Figure 9.41 Foundation plan with concrete floor. (Courtesy of William F. Smith—Builder.)

Figure 9.42 Embedded hardware (concrete accessories). (Courtesy of William F. Smith—Builder.)

Figure 9.43 Foundation trenching—poured concrete floor and foundation. (Courtesy of William F. Smith—Builder; William Boggs Aerial Photography. Reprinted with permission.)

FOUNDATION PLAN AND DETAIL CHECKLIST

1. North arrow
2. Titles and scale
3. Foundation walls 6" (solid lines)
   a. Overall dimensions
   b. Offset dimensions (corners)
   c. Interior bearing walls
   d. Special wall thickness
   e. Planter wall thickness
   f. Garage
   g. Retaining Wall
4. Footings—12" (hidden lines)
   a. Width of footing
   b. Stepped footing as per code
   c. fireplace footing
   d. Belled footing
   e. Grade beams
   f. Planter footing
   g. Garage
   h. Retaining will
5. Girder (center line)
   a. Size
   b. Direction
   c. Spacing (center to center)
6. Piers
   a. Sizes
   b. Spacing (center to center)
   c. Detail
      (1) 8" above grade (finish)
      (2) 8" below grade (natural)
      (3) 2 × 6 × 6 redw'd block secure to pier
      (4) 4 × 4 post
      (5) 4 × 6 girder
      (6) 2 × ? floor joist (o/c)
      (7) Subfloor 1" diagonal
         (a). T & G
         (b). Plyscord
      (8) Finished floor *usually in finished schedule)
7. Porches
   a. Indicate 2" lip on foundation (min.)
   b. Indicate steel reinforcing ($3/8$"–24" o/c)
   c. Under slab note: Fill, puddle, and tamp
   d. Thickness of slab and steps
8. Sub floor material and size
9. Footing detail references
10. Cross section reference
11. Column footing location and sizes
12. Concrete floors:
    a. Indicate bearing and non-bearing footings
    b. Concrete slab thickness and mesh size
13. Fireplace foundation
14. Patio and terrace location
    a. Material
    b. See porches
15. Depressed slabs or recessed area for ceramic tile, etc.
16. Double floor joist under parallel partitions
17. Joist—direction and spacing
18. Areaways (18" × 24")
19. Columns (center line dimension and size)
20. Reinforcing—location and size
    a. Rods
    b. Wire mesh
    c. Chimney
    d. Slabs
    e. Retaining walls
21. Apron for garage
22. Expansion joints (20' o/c in driveways)
23. Crawl holes (interior foundation walls)
24. Heat registers in slab
25. Heating ducts
26. Heat Plenum if below floor
27. Stairs (basement)
28. Detail references
    a. "Bubbles"
    b. Section direction
29. Trenches
30. Foundation details
    a. Foundation wall thickness (6" min.)
    b. Footing width and thickness (12" min.)
    c. Depth below natural grade (12" min.)
    d. 8" above finish grade (FHA) (6"—UBC)
    e. Redwood sill or as per code (2 × 6)
    f. $1/2$" × 10" anchor bolts, 6'-0" o/c. 1' from corners, imbedded 7"
    g. 18" min. clearance bottom, floor joist to grade
    h. Floor joist size and spacing
    i. Sub-floor (see pier detail)
    j. Bottom plate 2 × 4
    k. Studs—size and spacing
    l. Finish floor (finish schedule)
31. All dimensions—coordinate with floor plan dimensions
32. Veneer detail (check as above)
33. Areaway detail (check as above)
34. Garage footing details
35. Planter details
36. House-garage connection detail
37. Special details
38. Retaining walls over 3'-0" high (special design)
39. Amount of pitch of garage floor (direction)
40. General concrete notes
    a. Water-cement ratio
    b. Steel reinforcing
    c. Special additives
41. Note treated lumber
42. Special materials
    a. Terrazzo
    b. Stone work
    c. Wood edge
43. Elevations of all finish grades
44. Note: solid block all joists at mid-span if span exceeds 8'-0"
45. Specify grade of lumber (construction notes)
46. Pouché all details on back of vellum
47. Indicate North arrow near plan
48. Scale used for plan
49. Scale used for details
50. Complete title block
51. Check dimensions with floor plan
52. Border lines heavy and black

Figure 9.44 Foundation plan checklist.

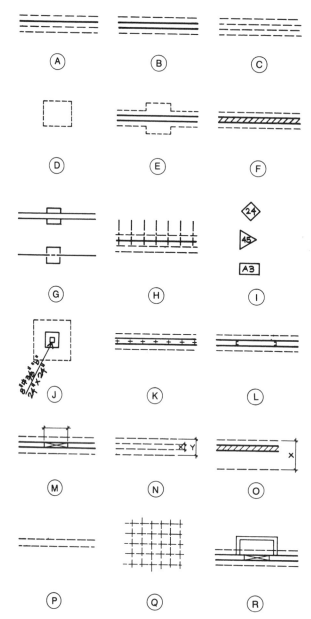

Figure 9.45 Conventions used on foundation plan.

I. The diamond shape, triangle, and rectangle are used to identify such things as anchor bolt spacing, shear wall finishes, and spacing of framing anchors. See Figure 9.41 and note how they are positioned.

J. This is a multiple convention, indicating pad, pedestal, steel column, and base plate sizes. The letter refers you to a schedule in which the plate size, pad size, or even the reinforcing are described.

K. The (+) symbols represent anchor bolt locations for shear walls. This symbol should be accompanied with a note similar to the following:

$\frac{1}{2}''$ dia. A.B. @ 12'' o.c. (shear wall)
Note: All hardware in place prior to pouring of concrete.

L. The (|) shapes represent hold-downs at shear walls. It is critical to include a note to the effect of "all hardware in place prior to pouring of concrete."

M. Shows the location of underfloor vents and/or crawl hole from one chamber of underfloor space to another. As shown, the rectangle should be dimensioned.

N. The four hidden lines shown in this convention represent an interior bearing footing for a slab-on-the-ground system. If the stem wall and width of the footing vary from location to location, dimensions for them are indicated right at the location on the foundation plan. This negates the need to draw a separate detail for each condition, but rather a single generic detail with a dimension that includes a note such as "See foundation plan."

O. This convention represents a retaining wall. As in the previous example, the plan view could be dimensioned if they are of varying sizes throughout a structure.

P. A convention for a nonbearing (footing for a slab-on-the-ground system.

Q. This matrix is used to represent concrete slab reinforcement. The size of the reinforcing is to be determined by the structural engineer, for example, #4 @ 18'' o.c. ea./way. It is not shown throughout the foundation plan, but only on a portion of it.

R. This convention represents an underfloor access, with the rectangle having an X as the actual opening through the foundation wall. This symbol can also be used for a transom window in a basement area.

D. Convention could represent a pier, as shown in Figures 9.18A and 9.18B, or as a concrete pad for a column.

E. A widening of the footing portion of a foundation for a column, actually a combination of B and D.

F. A plan view of a masonry wall, such as shown in Figure 9.30.

G. A system showing a pier and girder convention, such as seen in Figure 9.20.

H. Short perpendicular center lines as shown here represent dowels. This convention can be seen in Figure 9.20.

■ EXTERIOR/INTERIOR WALLS

As we overlay the vellum over the floor plan for alignment, the walls should be directly translated, except for those that start as exterior and continue as interior walls. Figure 9.46 shows a partial floor plan of the living room wall adjacent to the master bedroom that begins as an exterior wall and turns into an interior wall. A model was constructed to show this translation, as seen from above in Figure 9.47. The problem reveals itself when we remove the slab, as seen in Figure 9.48. Note that the stem wall is not aligned, but that the plates are. If we align the foundation as shown in Figure 9.49, the plates (sills) are out of alignment, thus creating a framing problem. On the surface the solution might appear to be easily resolved by moving the plate and the anchor bolt, but the bearing surface for the plate is the same width as the plate, making this impossible.

For a quick look at the details of this condition, see Figures 9.13 and 9.14 and review the text in reference to Figure 9.12. There are a couple of ways of representing this condition. One, as shown in Figure 9.50A, is to actually show the offset by jogging the hidden lines. An-

other method, as shown in Figure 9.50B, is to show the exterior/interior foundation wall as continuous and identify the job with a note. A third option (not shown) is to use means—actually show the job and so noting.

The stem wall (vertical portion of the footing for the Ryan Residence) is 8 inches wide with a 2 × 4 (actually 3½″ wide) plate on top. The exterior bearing wall has the plate along the edge, and the interior bearing footing has the plate located in the center, or, to put it another way, 2¼ inches from the edge. This becomes the amount of the job—2 inches as we round off the 2¼ inches measurement. On this surface, it appears that the need for a

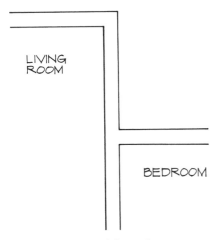

Figure 9.46 Partial floor plan.

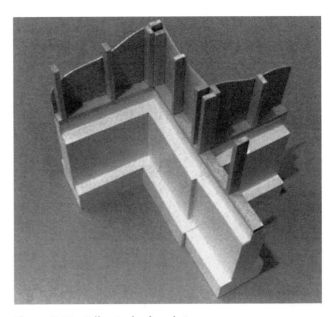

Figure 9.48 Offset in the foundation.

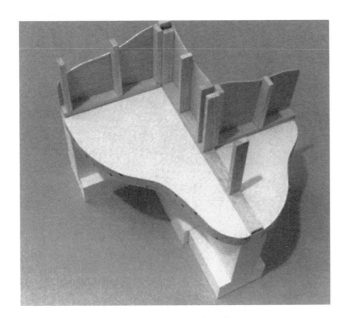

Figure 9.47 Exterior/interior framed wall.

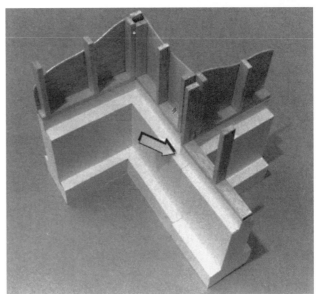

Figure 9.49 Wall plates out of alignment.

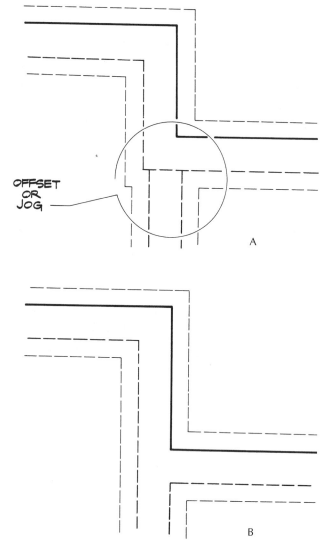

Figure 9.50 Partial foundation plan.

jog can be solved by merely moving the plate. Yet this cannot be done, because the anchor bolt will miss the plate completely.

Remember, this problem does not exist with the interior nonbearing walls, because there will be no footings under them and the plates can be positioned with powder-actuated bolts with case-hardened nails shot through a solid washer and used on interior walls only.

Drafting a Foundation on the Computer

STAGE I (Figure 9.51). The first stage is always the datum or base stage. Although the foundation plan is often the second sheet, the floor plan, which is often the third sheet, is developed first. Therefore, the floor plan must be used for the base or datum stage. XREF the floor plan. Incidentally, the foundation plan can often be found as a part of the structural set.

STAGE II (Figure 9.52). The second stage involves outlining the structure with a single line and positioning the interior bearing walls. Care must be taken in identifying any exterior walls that become interior walls for sill (bottom plate) placement.

STAGE III (Figure 9.53). Additional items such as concrete pads are located and the configuration of the footing is established.

STAGE IV (Figure 9.54). If depressed slabs are needed to accommodate materials such as ceramic tile or brick pavers, concrete steps or stairs, and elevator shafts, they are shown at this or an earlier stage. Solid lines may be changed to dotted lines at this point. It is just a matter of changing layers and changing line type.

STAGE V (Figure 9.55). Dimensioning takes place at this stage. Remember, the dimensions on the floor plan are to face-of-stud (FOS) and should be the same as those on the foundation plan. This may be just a bit confusing, but refer back to Figure 9.2A and note the

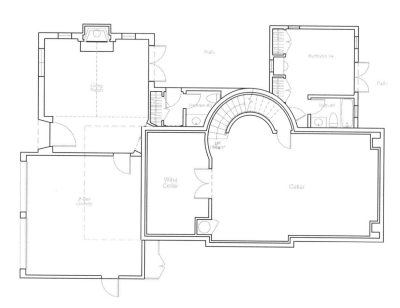

Figure 9.51 Stage I: Establishing datum (using floor plan).

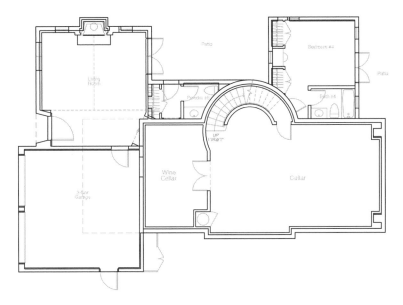

Figure 9.52 Stage II: Outline structure.

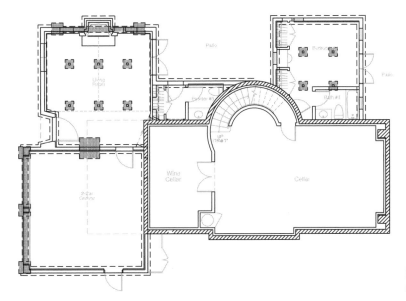

Figure 9.53 Stage III: Positioning bearing walls and post/pads.

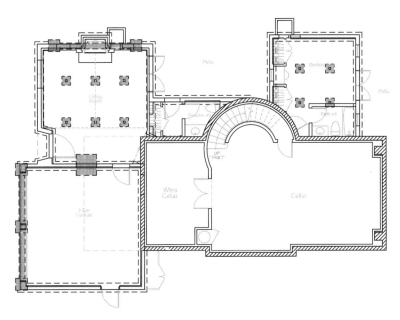

Figure 9.54 Stage IV: Steps, depressed slabs.

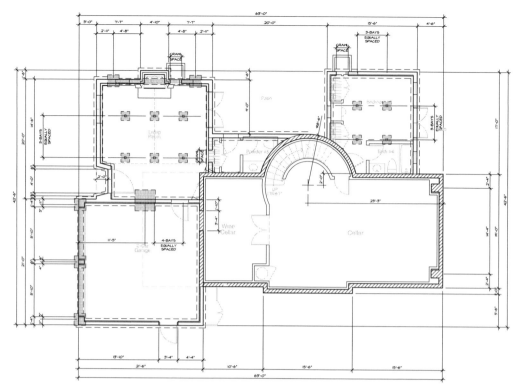

Figure 9.55 Stage V: Dimensioning.

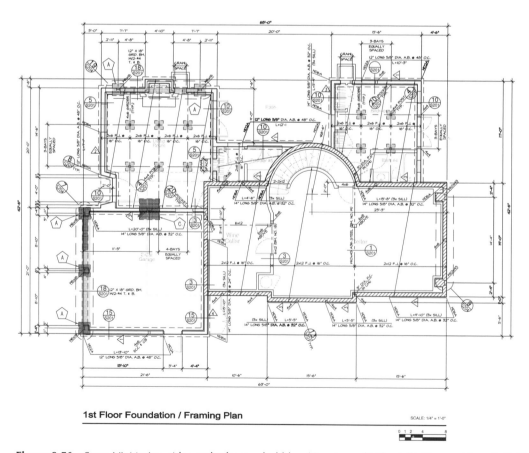

1st Floor Foundation / Framing Plan

SCALE: 1/4" = 1'-0"

Figure 9.56 Stage VI: Noting, titles and reference bubbles. (Courtesy of Mike Adli, Owner; Nagy R. Bakhoum, President of Obelisk Architects.)

alignment of the stud and its respective sill with the stem wall.

STAGE VI (Figure 9.56). All noting takes place at this, the final, stage. It should be remembered that main titles should conform to the standard office font, and all other noting should be done with an architectural lettering font that allows for ease of manual correction.

■ A STEEL STRUCTURE

The foundation plan for the Madison Steel Building, found in Chapter 20, and used for the tenant improvements in Chapter 21, is presented on the following pages as an example of a foundation plan for a commercial building.

Stage I

Stage I (Figure 9.57) . For this all-steel building, all drawings were produced using the dimensional reference system. Thus, the datum or base for the foundation plan will be the matrix shown in Figure 9.57.

Stage II

The foundation plan shown in Figure 9.58 is unusual because we can see on it an approximation of the basic shape and configuration of the upper levels of the buildings. At this stage, the structural engineer has established the size of the various concrete pads and pipe columns and provided us with engineering details. These important pieces of information would be translated into a drawing in the next stage.

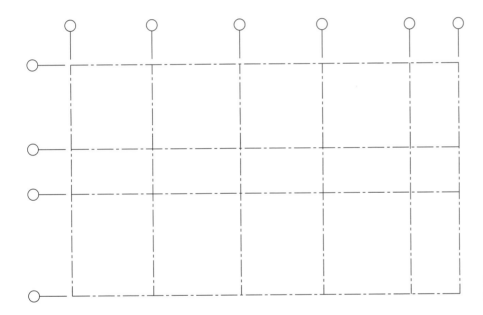

Figure 9.57 Stage I: Establishing datum.

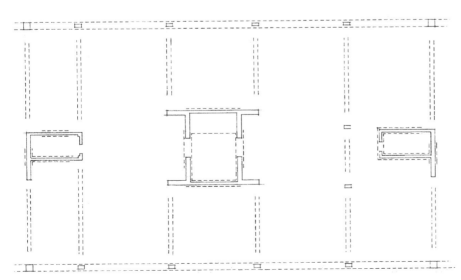

Figure 9.58 Foundation plan— Stage II.

Stage III

As you compare the beginning stages of the ground level plan and the ground floor plan, you will probably be confused because of differences at the stair area. See Figure 9.59. When the complete set of drawings was submitted for Building Department plan check, changes were made. One of these was the addition of a trash area and the requirement for those using the stairs to exit to the outside of the building instead of under the building. We considered the area below the structure as a continuation of the parking area, but the Building Department interpreted it as the ground level parking garage and so made the stair egress requirement.

All other plans and elevations show this change at the last stage. We sent the foundation plan back to the structural engineer because the change was, in effect, a new item requiring structural revisions.

We next drew columns (circles) and their respective support pads (squares). We obtained their sizes and shapes from the structural engineer.

Stage IV

Dimension lines were the first addition to the drawing at this stage. We used the reference plane system. See Figure 9.60. All subsequent dimensions were referenced to

this basic set on the top and to the left. In the lobby area (central portion of the plan), where the walls do not align with the existing reference bubbles, we added new bubbles. We showed partial and full section designations, but only the full sections are included in the set of drawings in this chapter.

Stage V

Dimensions were added for the concrete block foundation walls. We also dimensioned the width of all footings. A single detail is used for all of the foundation walls and footings. This detail does *not* have dimensions for the foundation wall or footing, just a note saying "See plan." In this way, a single typical detail took care of every condition and the foundation plan accounted for the variation. At this stage, the material designation for the concrete block walls and variations in dimensions in the footing and width of the walls were added. See Figure 9.61. Also, the section reference notations were filled in, in the section designation symbols.

Stage VI

At this stage we added all remaining numerical values and filled in the reference bubbles. See Figure 9.62. Of interest is the method of naming locations on the matrix

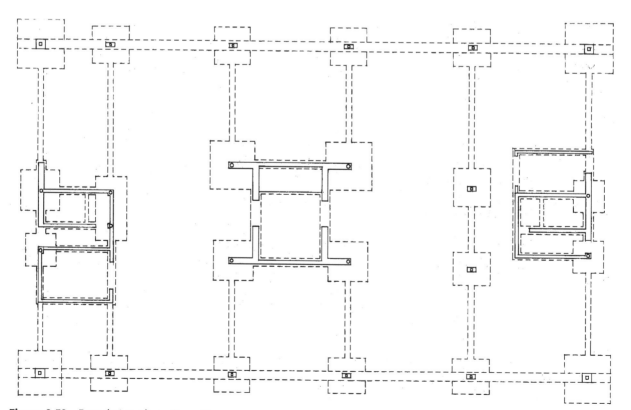

Figure 9.59   Foundation plan—Stage III.

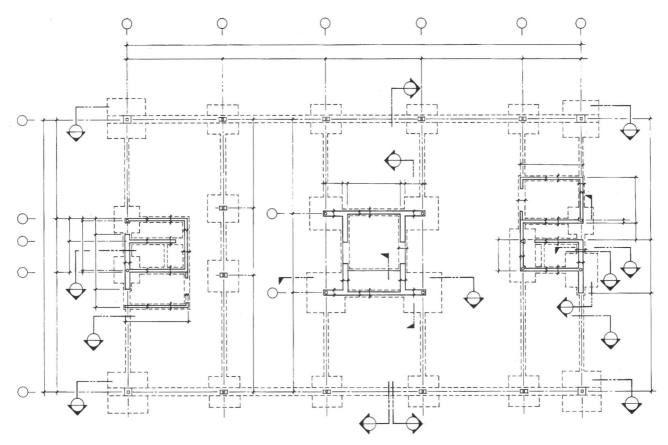

Figure 9.60 Foundation plan—Stage IV.

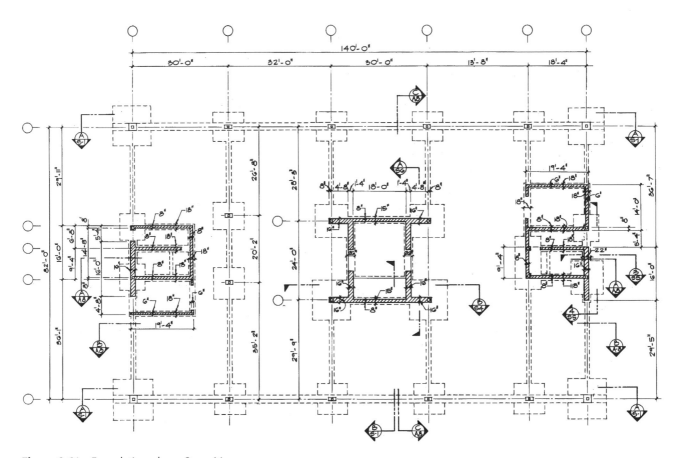

Figure 9.61 Foundation plan—Stage V.

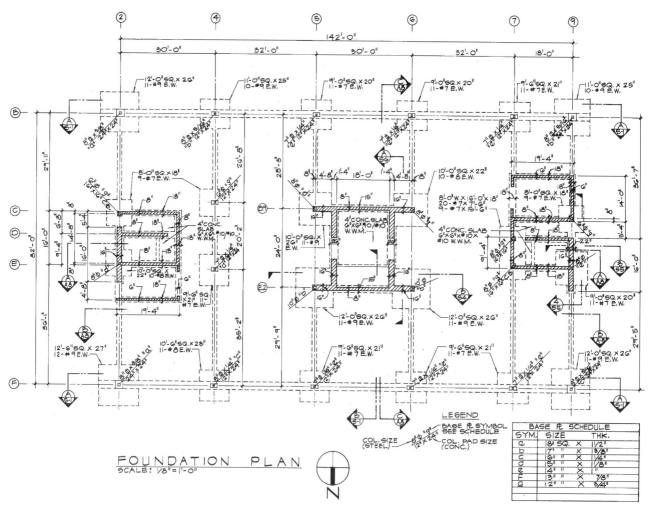

Figure 9.62 Foundation plan—Stage VI.

in the dimensional reference system. The reference B.9, for example, indicates there is a column at an intermediate distance between B and C of the axial reference plane. B.9 is approximately ⁹/₁₀ of the distance between B and C. If there were another column that was ⁸/₁₀ of the way between B and C, it would be designated B.8.

Around the perimeter of the structure are a series of squares drawn with dotted lines. These represent concrete pads that distribute the weight bearing down on the columns. A special type of noting is used here. The leader pointing to the hidden line indicates the size and thickness of the concrete pad and reinforcing. For example, 9'-0" sq. × 20", 11—#7 EW, means the concrete pad is 9' square and 20" thick and that there are 11 Number 7 (⁷/₈") reinforcing bars running each way.

At the center of these hidden lines is another rectangle with a smaller rectangle inside, representing a steel column. The leader pointing to this area explains these. For example, 7" ⊄ × ¼" "e", 12 " × 24 ", means that the column is a 7"-square column, ¼" thick (wall thickness), mounted onto an "e" base plate. This "e" base plate size can be found in the base plate schedule below Figure 9.62. Here, "e" is equal to a 14"-square by 1"-thick plate. This plate rests on another concrete pad often called a pedestal, 12" by 24".

Contained within the masonry walls are some steel columns, with concrete pads that are also noted using the schedule. Next to the schedule is a legend explaining the noting method. The title and North arrow finished this sheet.

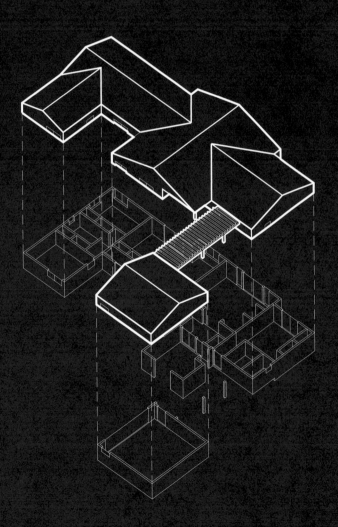

■ TYPES OF FLOOR PLANS

A floor plan is a drawing viewed from above. It is called a plan, but actually it is a horizontal section taken at approximately eye level. See Figure 10.1.

To better understand this, imagine a knife slicing through a structure and removing the upper half (the half with the roof on a single-story structure). The remaining half is then viewed from the air. This becomes the floor plan. See Figure 10.2.

The floor plan for a split-level residence is more complicated. This plan requires a lower, middle, and upper level. In the example, the entry, powder room, and garage are at the mid-level, which is also the level of the street and sidewalk. Use this level as a point of reference.

The stairs at the rear of the entry lead to the upper and lower levels. The lower level contains the master bedroom, master bath, study, bedroom, laundry, and bathroom. See Figure 10.3. The upper level contains the living room with a wet bar, and the dining room, kitchen, breakfast room, and foyer. See Figure 10.4. When these are translated into a floor plan, they appear as in Figures 10.5 and 10.6. The mid-level is duplicated and common to both drawings. A second approach is to use a **break line** (a line with a jog in it to indicate that a portion has

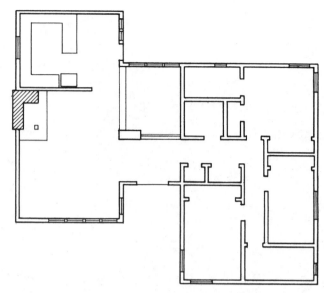

Figure 10.2   Floor plan. (Courtesy of William F. Smith—Builder.)

been deleted), showing only a part of the garage on one of the plans. Another approach is to use a straight break line, through the garage shown on Figure 10.7A and draft it as showing only part of the garage on one of the plans. (See Figure 10.7B.)

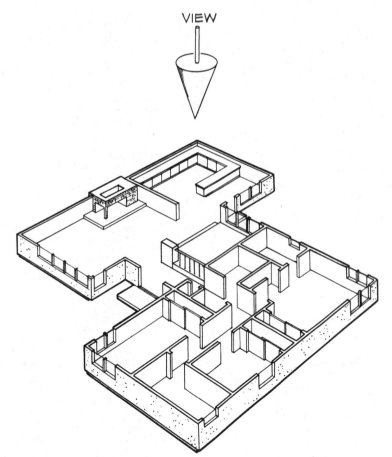

Figure 10.1   Cutaway view of a floor plan. (Courtesy of William F. Smith—Builder.)

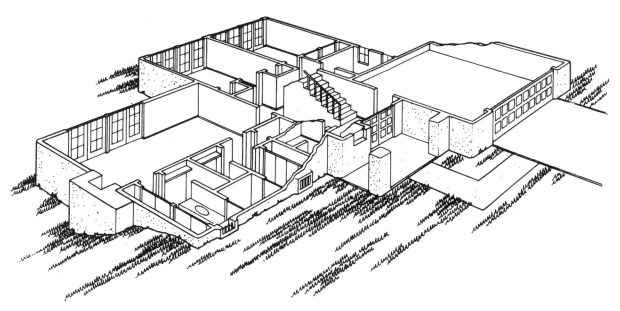

Figure 10.3 Pictorial of lower floor plan. (Courtesy of William F. Smith—Builder.)

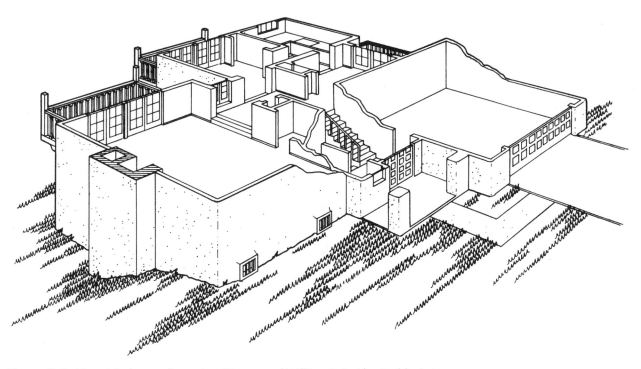

Figure 10.4 Pictorial of upper floor plan. (Courtesy of William F. Smith—Builder.)

In a two-story building, a single room on the first floor is sometimes actually two stories high. If this room were a living room, for example, it would be treated as a normal one-story living room on the first floor plan; however, the area would be repeated on the second floor plan and labeled as upper living room or just labeled "open."

To simplify the image to be drafted, not every structural member is shown. For example, in a wood-framed struc-ture, if every vertical piece of wood were shown, the task would be impossible. Simplifying this image of the wood structure is done with two parallel lines. Sometimes the insulation is shown in symbol form and is not shown through the total wall. See Figure 10.8. The same parallel series of lines can also be used to represent a masonry wall by adding a series of diagonal lines. See Figure 10.9. Steel frame can be represented as shown in Figure 10.10.

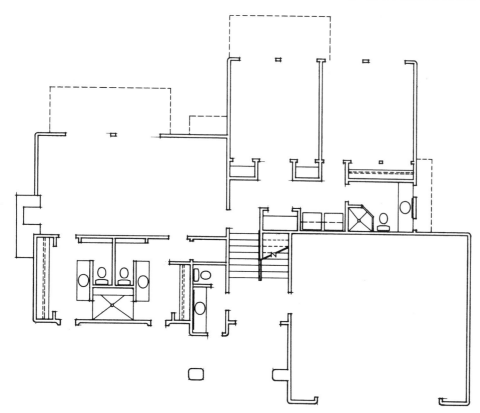

Figure 10.5   Lower floor plan. (Courtesy of William F. Smith—Builder.)

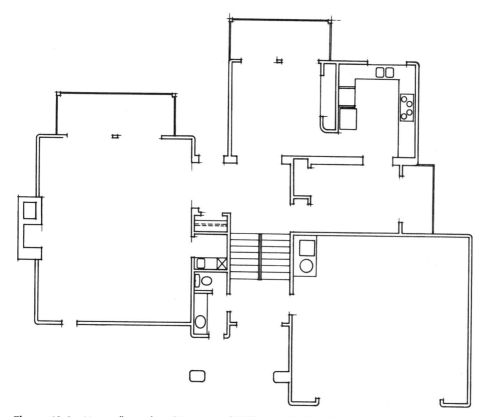

Figure 10.6   Upper floor plan. (Courtesy of William F. Smith—Builder.)

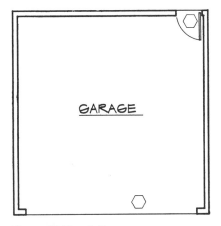

Figure 10.7A Full garage.

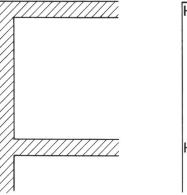

Figure 10.9 Representation of masonry.

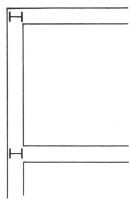

Figure 10.10 Representation of steel frame.

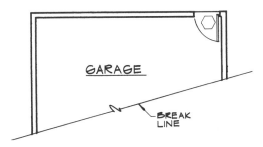

Figure 10.7B Partial garage shown with break line.

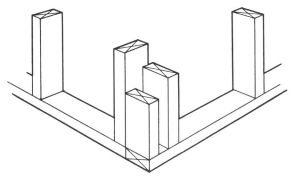

Figure 10.11 Corner at sill.

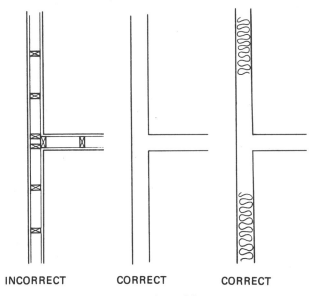

INCORRECT   CORRECT   CORRECT

Figure 10.8 Representation of wood frame.

Figure 10.12 Corner at sill.

Wood Framing

Figures 10.11 and 10.12 show the appearance of a corner of a wood frame structure. Each side of the wall is built separately. An extra stud is usually placed at the end of the wall; it extends to the edge of the building. It therefore acts as a structural support, and gives a greater nail-

ing surface to which wall materials can be anchored. Figure 10.13 shows a plan view of the condition at the corner of the wall.

Figures 10.14 and 10.15 show the intersection of an interior wall and an exterior wall. Figure 10.16 is the plan view of this same intersection.

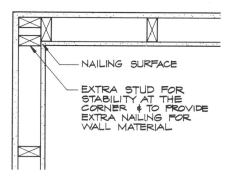

Figure 10.13 Actual appearance of the corner of a wood-framed wall.

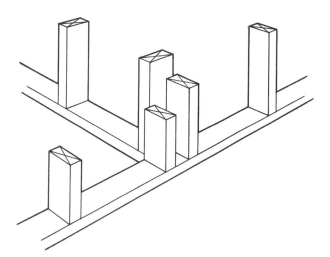

Figure 10.14 Intersection of exterior wall and interior wall.

Figure 10.15 Intersection of exterior wall and interior wall.

Walls are not the only important elements in the framing process, of course. You must also consider the locations of doors and windows and the special framing they require. See Figure 10.17.

Various photographic views of interviews are shown in Figures 10.18, 10.19, and 10.20. Figure 10.21 shows how **sills** and **headers** are precut and aligned with the anchor bolts. (A sill is the bottom portion of a door or window. Headers are the structural members above a door or window.)

Interior Dimensioning. Because a wood-framed wall is a built-up system, that is, a wall frame of wood upon which plaster or another wall covering is added, dimension lines must sometimes be drawn to the edge of studs and sometimes to their center.

Figure 10.22 shows how the corner of a wood-framed wall is dimensioned to the stud line. Figure 10.23 shows how an interior wall intersecting an exterior wall is dimensioned. It is dimensioned to the center so that the two studs which the interior wall will join can be located.

The process of drawing each stud in a wall becomes tiresome. So usually two lines drawn 6″ apart (in scale)

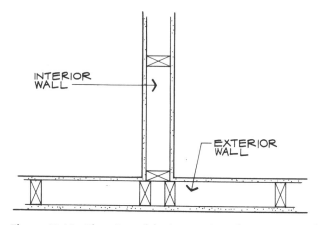

Figure 10.16 Plan view of the intersection of an exterior and an interior wall.

are used to represent wood. To make sure that the person reading this set of plans does know that the stud is being dimensioned and not the exterior surface, the extension is often brought inside the 6″-wide wall lines. Another way to make this clear is to take extension lines

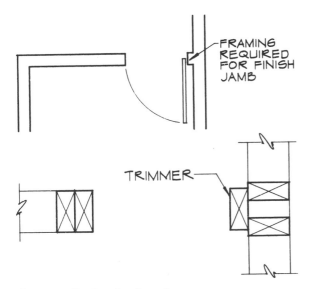

Figure 10.17 Framing for a door.

Figure 10.18 Intersection of interior walls at the sill.

Figure 10.19 Intersection of interior walls at the top plates. (Courtesy of William F. Smith—Builder.)

A

B

Figure 10.20 Top plates showing intersections of exterior and interior walls. (Courtesy of William F. Smith—Builder.)

Figure 10.21 Precutting of sills and headers. (Courtesy of William F. Smith—Builder.)

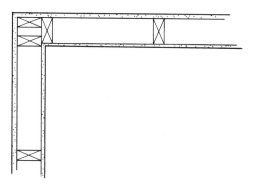

Figure 10.22 Dimensioning a corner of a wood-framed wall.

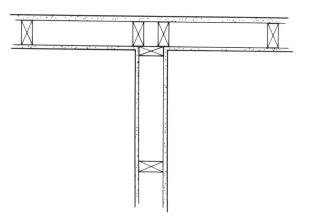

Figure 10.23 Dimensioning an intersection of an interior wall and an exterior wall.

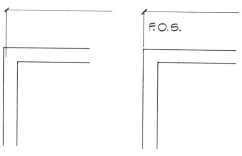

Figure 10.24 Dimensioning corners.

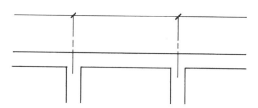

Figure 10.25 Dimensioning interior walls.

to the outside surface and write **"F.O.S." (face of stud)** adjacent to the extension lines. See Figure 10.24.

Dimensioning interior walls requires a center line or an extension line right into the wall intersection, as shown in Figure 10.25. A center line is more desirable than a solid line.

Windows and doors are located to the center of the object, as shown in Figure 10.26. When a structural column is next to a window or door, the doors and windows are dimensioned as in Figure 10.27. The size of a particular window or door can be obtained from a chart called

a schedule. This schedule can be found by locating the sheet number on the bottom half of the **reference bubble** adjacent to the window or door. See Figure 10.28. (A reference bubble is a circle with a line drawn through it horizontally.)

Exterior Dimensioning. There are normally three dimension lines needed on an exterior dimension of a floor plan. The first dimension line away from the object includes the walls, partitions, centers of windows and doors, and so forth. See Figure 10.29. The second dimension line away from the object (floor plan) includes walls and partitions only. See Figure 10.30. If, in establishing the second dimension line, you duplicate a dimension, eliminate the dimension line closest to the object. See Figure 10.31. The third dimension line away from the object is for overall dimensions. See Figure 10.32. The first dimension line away from the structure should be measured ¾" to 1½" from the outside lines of the plan to allow for notes, window and door reference

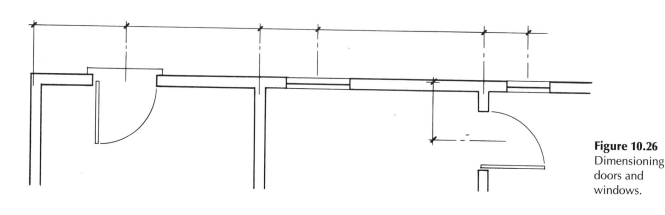

Figure 10.26 Dimensioning doors and windows.

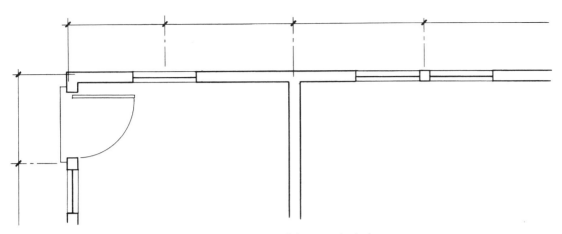

Figure 10.27   Dimensioning structural members around doors and windows.

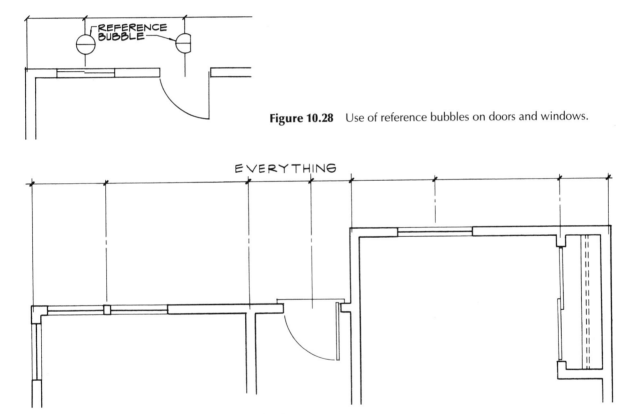

Figure 10.28   Use of reference bubbles on doors and windows.

Figure 10.29   First dimension line away from the object.

bubbles, equipment that may be placed adjacent to the structure, and so on. The second dimension line away from the structure should be approximately ³/₈″ to ½″ away from the first dimension line. The distance between all subsequent dimension lines should be the same as the distance between the first and second dimension lines.

A large jog in a wall is called an **offset**. Because the jog is removed from the plane that is being dimensioned, you must decide whether to use long extension lines or whether to dimension the offset at the location of the jog. See Figure 10.33.

Objects located independently or outside of the structure, such as posts (columns), are treated differently. First, the order in which the items are to be built must be established. Will the columns be built before or after the adjacent walls? If the walls or the foundation for the walls are to be erected first, then major walls near the columns are identified and the columns are located from

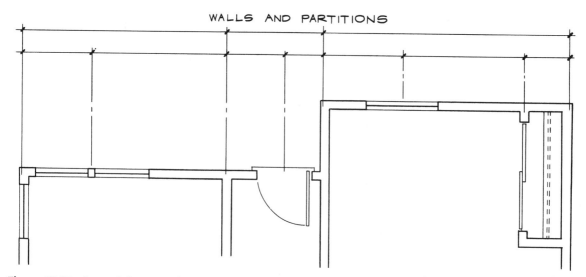

Figure 10.30 Second dimension line away from the object.

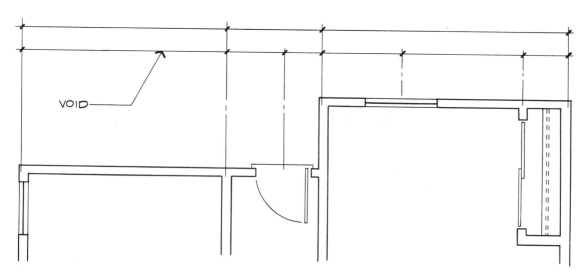

VOID

Figure 10.31 Void duplicating dimension lines.

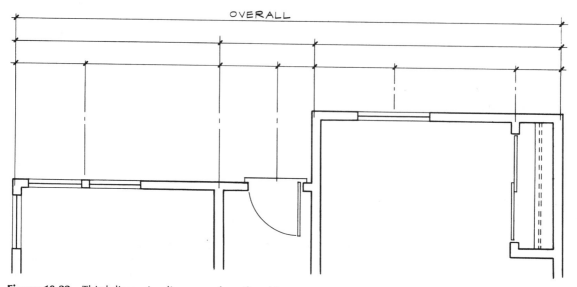

OVERALL

Figure 10.32 Third dimension line away from the object.

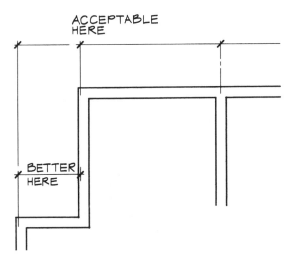

Figure 10.33 Offset dimension locations.

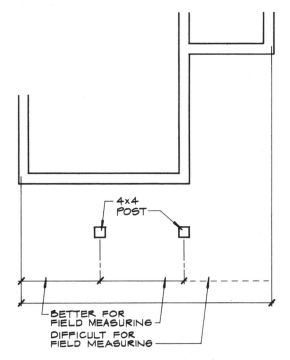

Figure 10.34 Locating columns from the structure.

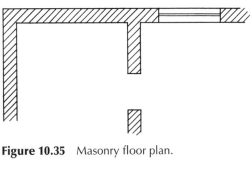

Figure 10.35 Masonry floor plan.

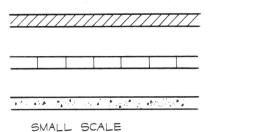

Figure 10.36 Concrete block material designations used on floor plans.

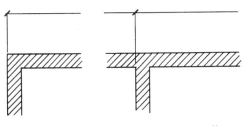

Figure 10.37 Dimensioning masonry walls.

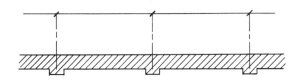

Figure 10.38 Dimensioning plasters.

them. Never dimension from an inaccessible location! See Figure 10.34.

Masonry

When walls are built of bricks or concrete block instead of wood frame, the procedure changes. Everything here is based on the size and proportion of the masonry unit used. Represent masonry as a series of diagonal lines. See Figure 10.35. Show door and window openings the same way you did for wood frame structures. You may represent concrete block in the same way as brick for small scale drawings, but be aware that some offices do

use different material designations. See Figure 10.36. (These methods of representing concrete blocks were obtained from various sources, including association literature, AIA standards, and other reference sources.) Extension lines for dimensioning are taken to the edge (end) of the exterior surface in both exterior and interior walls. See Figure 10.37. Pilasters, that is, columns built into the wall by widening the walls, are dimensioned to the center. The size of the pilaster itself can be lettered adjacent to one of the pilasters in the drawing. Another method of dealing with the size of these pilasters is to refer the reader of the plan to a detail with a note or reference bubble. See Figure 10.38. All columns consisting of masonry or masonry around steel are also dimensioned to the center.

Windows and Doors. Windows and doors create a unique problem in masonry units. In wood structures, windows and doors are located by dimensioning to the center and allowing the framing carpenter to create the proper opening for the required window or door size. In masonry, the opening is established before the installation of the window or door. This is called the **"rough opening"**; the final opening size is called the **"finished opening."**

The rough opening, which is the one usually dimensioned on the plan, should follow the masonry block module. See Figure 10.39. This block module and the specific type of detail used determine the most economical and practical window and door sizes. See Figure 10.40. Therefore, you should provide dimensions for locating windows, doors, and interior walls or anything

of a masonry variety to the rough opening. See Figure 10.41.

Steel

There are two main types of steel systems: **steel stud** and **steel frame**. Steel studs can be treated like wood stud construction. As with wood stud construction, you need to dimension to the stud face rather than to the wall covering (skin).

There are various shapes of steel studs. See Figures 10.42 and 10.43. Drawings A and B in Figure 10.43 show how these shapes appear in the plan view. Drawing each steel stud is time-consuming and so two parallel lines are drawn to indicate the width of the wall. See drawing C in Figure 10.43. Steel studs can be called out by a note.

If only a portion of a structure is steel stud and the remainder is wood or masonry, you can shade (**pouché**)

Figure 10.39   Rough opening in masonry wall.

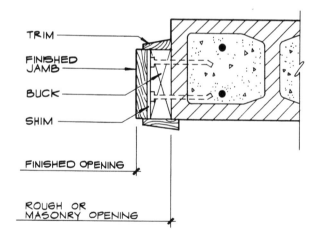

Figure 10.40   Door jamb at masonry opening.

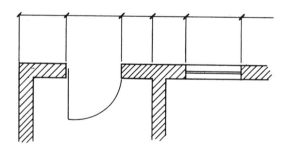

Figure 10.41   Locating doors and windows.

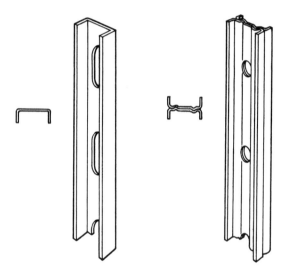

Figure 10.42   Basic steel stud shapes.

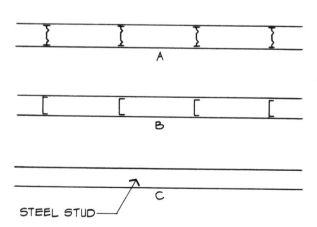

Figure 10.43   Method of representation of steel studs in a floor plan.

the area with steel studs or use a steel symbol. See Figure 10.44.

Dimensioning Columns. Steel columns are commonly used to hold up heavy weights. This weight is distributed to the earth by means of a concrete pad. See Figure 10.45. This concrete pad is dimensioned to its center, as Figure 10.46A shows. When you dimension the steel columns, which will show in the floor plan, dimension them to their center. See Figure 10.46B. This relates them to the concrete pads. Dimensioning a series of columns follows the same procedure. See Figure 10.47. The dimensions are taken to the centers of the columns in each direction.

Sometimes, the column must be dimensioned to the face rather than to the center. As Figure 10.47 shows, the extension line is taken to the outside face of the column. Axial reference planes are often used in conjunction with steel columns as shown in Figure 10.48 and the column may be dimensioned to the face. (The dimensional reference system was discussed in Chapter 2.) A sample of a portion of a floor plan dimensioned with and without a series of axial reference planes is shown in Figures 10.49A and 10.49B. Because of the **grid** pattern often formed by the placement of these columns, a center line or a plus (+) type symbol is often used to help the drawing. See Figure 10.50.

Dimensioning Walls. Walls, especially interior walls that do not fall on the established grid, need to be dimensioned—but only to the nearest dimension grid line. Figure 10.51 is a good example of an interior wall dimensioned to the nearest column falling on a grid.

Combinations of Materials

Due to design or code requirements for fire regulations or structural reasons, materials are often combined: concrete columns with wood walls; steel mainframe with

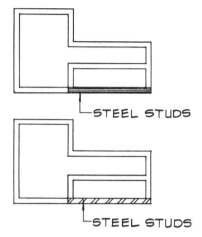

Figure 10.44 Combination of wood and steel.

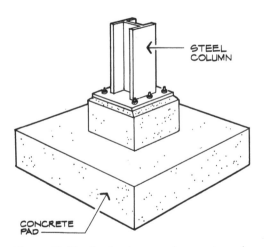

Figure 10.45 Steel column and concrete pad.

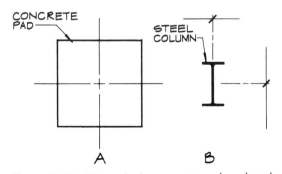

Figure 10.46 Dimensioning concrete pads and steel columns.

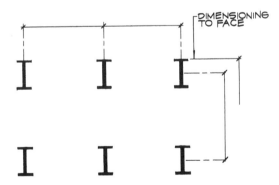

Figure 10.47 Dimensioning a series of columns.

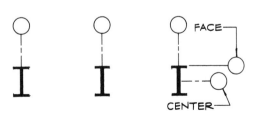

Figure 10.48 Dimensioning a series of columns by way of the axial reference plane.

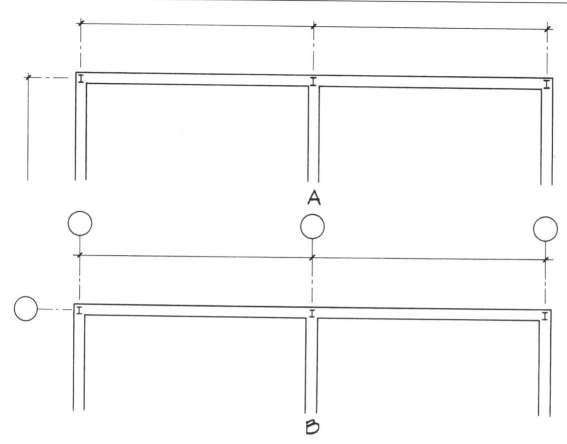

Figure 10.49 Dimensioning a floor plan with steel columns.

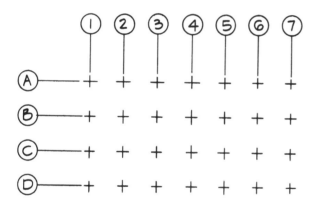

Figure 10.50 Columns forming a grid pattern.

wood walls as secondary members; masonry and wood; steel studs and wood; and steel and masonry, for example. Figure 10.52 shows how using two different systems requires overlapping dimension lines with extension lines. Since dimension lines are more critical than extension lines, extension lines are *always* broken in favor of dimension lines. The wood structure is located to the column on the left side once, then dimensioned independently.

Wood and Masonry. Wood and masonry, as shown in Figure 10.53, are dimensioned as their material dictates: the masonry is dimensioned to the ends of the wall and the rough opening of windows, while the wood portions are dimensioned to the center of interior walls, center of doors, and so forth. The door in the wood portion is dimensioned to the center of the door and to the inside edge of the masonry wall. This assumes the block wall will be built first.

Masonry and Concrete. Masonry walls and concrete columns, in Figure 10.54, are treated in much the same way as wood and concrete columns. In both instances, the building sequence dictates which one becomes the reference point. See Figure 10.55. Here, steel and masonry are used in combination. Using the dimensional reference system, the steel is installed first. The interior masonry wall is then located from the nearest axial reference plane, and dimensioned according to the block module for that kind of masonry. Additional axial reference plane sub-bubbles are provided. Numbers are in decimals. Since one face of the masonry wall is between 1 and 2, 7/10 of the distance away from axial reference plane 1, the number 1.7 is used in the sub-bubble. And, since the same wall is also halfway between A and B, A.5

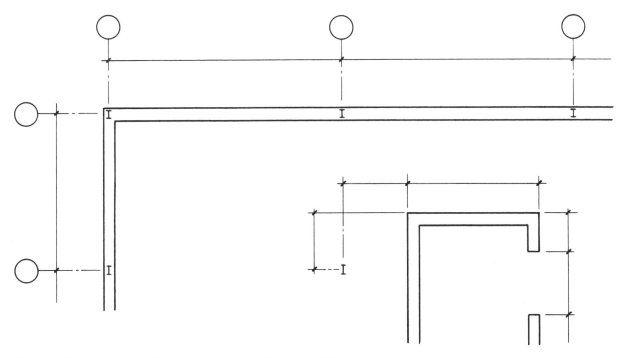

Figure 10.51 Locating interior walls from axial reference bubbles.

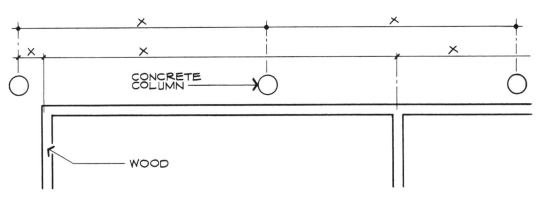

Figure 10.52 Concrete and wood.

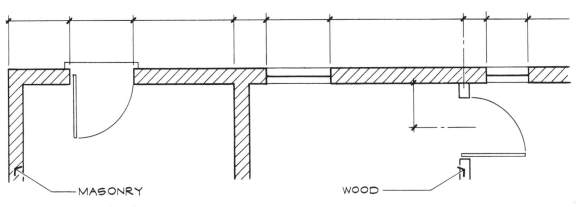

Figure 10.53 Wood and masonry.

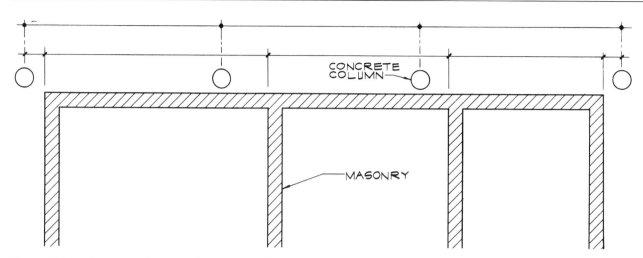

Figure 10.54   Concrete columns and masonry walls.

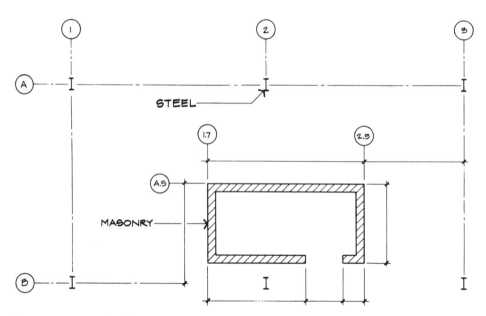

Figure 10.55   Steel and masonry.

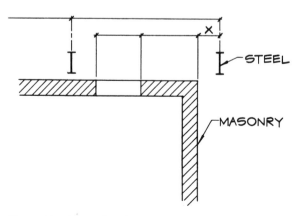

Figure 10.56   Steel and masonry.

is used as a designation. Another example of the process is found in Figure 10.56. The fabricators will locate the steel first, then the masonry wall. Dimension "X" relates one system to another.

Doors in Plan View

The general method of dimensioning a window or a door was discussed earlier. Here, we examine a variety of doors and windows and how to draft them. Figure 10.57 shows a sampling of the most typically drafted doors.

Hinged.   Doors A and B in Figure 10.57 show the main difference in drafting an **exterior and interior hinged**

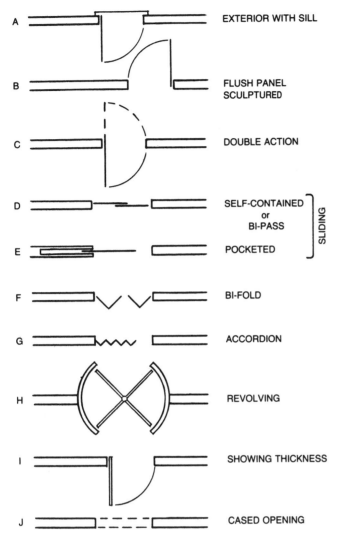

Figure 10.57 Doors in plan view.

Sculptured and Decorative. Sculptured and decorative doors can be carved forms put into the doors in the form of a panel door or added onto a flush door in the form of what is called a "planted" door. Different types of trim can also be planted onto a slab door.

Double Action. Door C in Figure 10.57 represents a double action door, a door that swings in both directions. Double action doors can be solid slab, panel, or sculptured.

Sliding. Two types of sliding doors are shown in Figure 10.57. Door D, when used on the exterior, typically is made of glass framed in wood or metal. Pocketed sliding doors are rarely found on the exterior because the pocket is hard to weatherproof, and rain, termites, and wind are hard to keep out of the pocket.

Folding. Doors F and G are good doors for storage areas and wardrobe closets.

Revolving. Where there is a concern about heat loss or heat gain, a revolving door is a good solution. See door H, which shows a cased opening, that is, an opening with trim around the perimeter with no door on it.

Windows in Plan View

Typical ways of showing windows in the plan view are shown in Figure 10.58. When a plan is drawn at a small scale, each individual window, of whatever type, may simply be drawn as a fixed window (Window A, Figure 10.58), depending for explanation on a pictorial drawing (as shown in Chapter 11). Ideally, casement, hopper, and awning-type windows should be used only on the second floor or above, for the sake of safety. If they are used on the first or ground floor, they should have planters or reflection pools or something else around them to prevent accidents.

Sizes of Door and Windows

The best way to find specific sizes of windows and doors (especially sliding glass doors) is to check *Sweet's Catalog File*. There you will find interior doors ranging from 1'-6" to 3'-0" and exterior doors from 2'-4" to 3'-6". Sizes of doors and windows also depend on local codes. Local codes require a certain percentage of the square footage to be devoted to windows and doors to provide light and ventilation. These percentages often come in the form of minimum and maximum areas as a measure of energy-efficient structures. Still another criterion for door size is consideration of wheelchairs and the size required for building accessibility (ADA compliance).

door. A straight line is used to represent the door and a radial line is used to show the direction of swing. Door "I" shows the same kind of door with its thickness represented by a double line. Doors A, B, and I are used in the floor plans to show flush doors, panel doors, and sculptured doors (decorative and carved).

Flush. Flush doors, as the name indicates, are flush on both sides. They can be solid on the interior (solid slab) or hollow on the inside (hollow core).

Panel. Panel doors have panels set into the frame. These are usually made of thin panels of wood or glass. A variety of patterns are available. See *Sweet's Catalog File* under Doors for pictures of door patterns. Also see the earlier discussion of elevations for a drafted form of these doors.

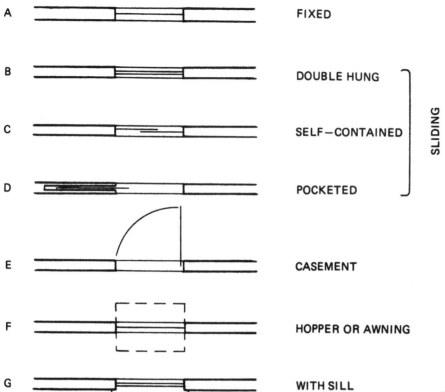

A — FIXED

B — DOUBLE HUNG

C — SELF–CONTAINED

D — POCKETED

SLIDING

E — CASEMENT

F — HOPPER OR AWNING

G — WITH SILL

Figure 10.58 Windows in plan view.

■ SYMBOLS

Just as chemistry uses symbols to represent elements, architectural floor plans use symbols to represent electrical and plumbing equipment. Figure 10.59 shows the most typical ones used. These are symbols only. They do not represent the shape or size of the actual item. For example, the symbol for a ceiling outlet indicates the *location* of an outlet, not the shape or size of the fixture. The description of the specific fixture is given in the specifications document.

Electrical and Utility Symbols

Some symbols are more generally used than others in the architectural industry. A floor plan, therefore, usually contains a legend or chart of the symbols being used on that particular floor plan.

Number Symbols

Symbols 1, 2, and 3 in Figure 10.59 show different types of switches. Symbol 2 shows a weatherproof switch, and symbol 3 shows a situation in which there might be a number of switches used to turn on a single light fixture or a series of light fixtures. See Figure 10.60. A center-line type line is used to show which switch connects with which outlet. This is simply a way of giving this in-

formation to the electrical contractor. (However, Figure 10.60 is not a wiring diagram.) If one switch controls one or a series of outlets, it is called a two-way switch. A three-way switch comprises two switches controlling one outlet or a series of outlets. Three switches are called a four-way, and so on. Thus you will name switches by the number of switches plus one. For example, the number 3 is placed next to the switch when there are two switches, the number 4 for three switches, and so on. See Figure 10.60 for examples of switches, outlets, and their numbering system.

Symbol 4 represents a duplex convenience outlet with two places to plug in electrical appliances.

Numbers are used to indicate the number of outlets available other than the duplex, the most typical. For example, if a triplex (3) outlet is required, the number 3 is placed beside the outlet symbol. A number in inches, such as 48", may be used to indicate the height of the outlet from the floor to the center of the outlet. See Figure 10.59, symbols 6, 7, and 9.

Letter Symbols

A letter used instead of a number represents a special type of switch. For example, "K" is used for key-operated, "D" for dimmer, "WP" for weatherproof, and so forth.

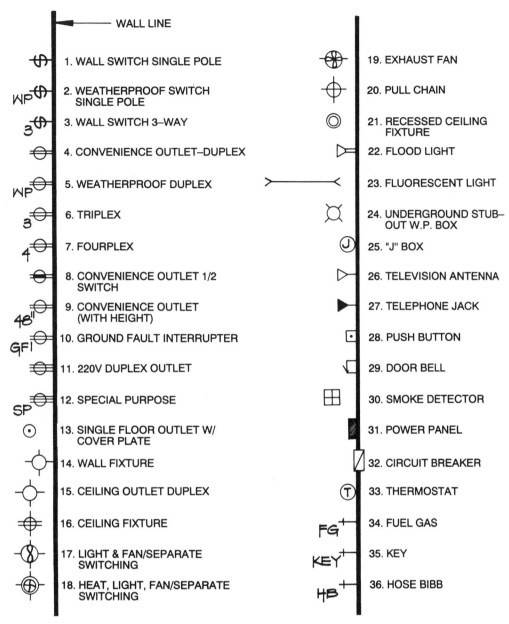

Figure 10.59 Electrical and utility symbols.

As with switches, letter designations are used to describe special duplex convenience outlets: "WP" for waterproof, and so on. A duplex convenience outlet is generally referred to by the public as a wall plug.

The call letters "GFI" mean ground fault interrupt. They designate a special outlet used near water (bathrooms, kitchens, etc.) to prevent electric shock. "SP" designates special purpose—perhaps a computer outlet on its own circuit and unaffected by electrical current flowing to any other outlet.

A combination of a switch and a regular outlet is shown in Figure 10.59, #8. This illustration shows a du-

plex convenience outlet that is half active (hot) at all times. In other words, one outlet is controlled by a switch and the other is a normal outlet. The switch half can be used for a lamp, and the normal outlet for an appliance.

Other Symbols

A round circle with a dot in it represents a floor outlet. See symbol 13, Figure 10.59. The various types of light outlets are shown by symbols 14 through 18.

A flush outlet is one in which the fixture will be installed flush with the ceiling. The electrician and carpenter must address the problem of framing for the fixture in the members above the ceiling surface. See symbol 21.

A selection of miscellaneous equipment is shown in symbols 22 through 36.

Special Explanation

Symbols 24, 25, 26, 28, 31, and 32 in Figure 10.59 require special explanation.

Symbol 24—Used for electrical connections (usually on the outside) for such things as outdoor lighting and sprinkler connections.

Symbol 25—An "I" box is an open electrical box allowing the electrician to install later such things as fluorescent light fixtures.

Symbol 26—This is not the TV antenna itself, but the point at which you connect a television antenna line at the wall.

Symbol 28—Location at which you push a button to ring a doorbell or chime.

Symbol 31—The connection between the utility company and the structure where the power panel is installed.

Symbol 32—As the structure is zoned for electrical distribution, circuit breaker panels are installed. This allows you to reset a circuit at a so-called substation without going outside to the main panel or disturbing the rest of the structure.

Symbol 34 represents a gas outlet, and 35 a control for fuel gas. Symbol 34 would be used to indicate a gas jet in a fireplace, and 35 would be used to indicate the control for the gas, probably somewhere near the fireplace. Symbol 36 is a hose bib, a connection for a water hose.

Electrical and Computers

Although most residences are still being wired in the conventional manner, use of the computer to control circuitry is beginning to find its way into the architectural construction world. Similarly, the approach to lighting a small structure is rapidly changing. Today we are being asked to think in terms of the following:

A. What type of general lighting would be appropriate for a given structure

B. What wall washes, by color and intensity, to use in a specific area

C. What specific tasks are to take place in an area, and what kind of lighting would satisfy this task

D. What type of mood to create, and how to dim or employ color lights to produce that specific mood

E. How to light the floor area to facilitate the safe movement of people through a corridor at night or during the day, as in a school environment

F. How to efficiently light stairs—both to identify the positions of the steps and to show where they begin

G. How to employ specialty lighting, such as fiber optics or neon lighting to identify an entry area or light located to produce a light beacon to the heavens at night

Electrical wiring falls into three basic categories:

A. Conventional—This system presently exists in the majority of today's structures. Lights are hardwired from switch to outlet, and the system is not very flexible (see Figure 10.60).

B. Retrofit

1. Radio Frequency—An old conventional toggle-style switch is replaced by what we will refer to as a "smart switch." The smart switch is capable of transmitting and receiving signals to and from other outlets (modules). This system is ideal in building additions and alterations where the cost of rewiring can become prohibitive. Radio wave signals can be disturbed by steel studs, chicken wire in older walls for stucco or plastic, or by distance (approximately 25 feet distance limits).

2. Power Line Carrier (PLC)—Also uses smart switches, but rather than sending a radio wave signal, it sends an electrical pulse through the existing wiring. A single switch can be replaced

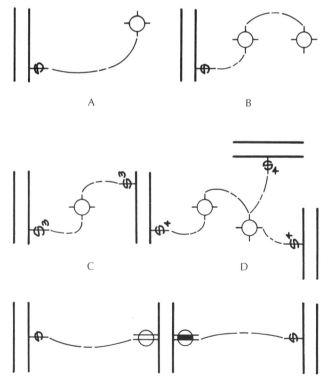

Figure 10.60 Switch to outlet (conventional).

OLD SWITCHES　　　NEW CONTROL SWITCHES

Figure 10.61 Comparison of old switches and new control stations.

(A)　　　(B)

Figure 10.62 Symbol for smart switch.

with a smart switch with multiple controls. This enables one smart switch location to control multiple outlets, fixtures, appliances, and so forth. HomeTouch by Lite-Touch, Inc., is an example of such a system.

C. Centralized Controller (Computer)—Using low-voltage wires, the switches are connected to a central processor. We no longer think in terms of a single light switch controlling a bank of lights but, rather, a single control station with as many as nine buttons that can control any or all lights in a structure. These control stations, which are wall-mounted keypads, replace the old-fashioned switches and dimmers (see Figure 10.61). Note that nine switches and dimmers are replaced with one control station the size of a single-gang toggle switch.

Figure 10.62A is a conventional switch similar to that shown in Figure 10.59-1. With a simple circle added to an existing switch, a drafter can show the installation of a smart switch. Thus, you can easily adjust an existing drawing. Figure 10.62B shows a slight variation of the same smart switch that is drafted from scratch.

The first major change is in the way we think about lighting. Do not think of a room with its lighting controlled by a single switch, but rather plan lighting scenes. Position the lighting to create a visual pathway through a structure. Consider how you would light the exterior of the structure for visual impact or to deter possible intruders with flashing lights. Think in terms of how best to secure your house electrically, by opening or closing windows or draperies. Controls can also be programmed

to provide music throughout a structure, to activate a television, or even to dramatically showcase works of art.

The next step to take with your client is to decide from which locations you would like to control these various lighting scenes. Let us now look at the three basic components in this type of control system. As mentioned before, the first are the control stations that are wall-mounted keypads suitable for use in both the wet and dry areas of a structure. The second is the central control unit (CCU). The CCU is the brain of the system, that is, where programming resides. It receives signals from the control stations and then processes them. Each control station is connected to the CCU with low-voltage wire. This is very different from the old system in which the lights were hooked up to the control station. Once programmed, the CCU will maintain the information even during a power outage or spike. And, yes, the CCU can be programmed for times when you may be away for a vacation. Lighting can be programmed to give the structure an appearance of being occupied and then returned to its original setting upon your return. The client can be trained to program his or her own system, or the system installer can be called and can reprogram the system via the telephone. Thus, a technician does not need to come to your structure to reprogram the CCU.

Control modules make up the third component. These are self-contained modules that actually do the work. Receiving their instructions from the CCU, they dim lights; drive motorized devices to open skylights, windows, and drapery; raise or lower the screen in a home theater; or merely turn on the garden and pool lights (see Figure 10.63). For the visual appearance of the central control unit and modules, see Figure 10.64. The installation of modules can be seen in Figure 10.64C.

Drawing for the Installer

The next task is to convey the information to the installer about the system you have designed, the location of the control stations, and the number of control points you have at one location. The number of control points at a given location can be dealt with using a chart. A chart similar to that shown in Figure 10.65 is called a routing schedule and can be easily developed and become part of the electrical plan. The first column identifies the location of the control station in the structure, and the second column actually tells the manufacturer the actual number of control points needed. Each control station in that location (say #1) is then labeled, such as 1A, 1B, 1C, 1D, and so on.

Each group of outlets—for example, six outlets in the ceiling in the living room—is then given a call letter. In this chart, the letter E-1 is used for the general light in the living room, E-2 is used for mood lighting, and E-3 may be used as a spotlight for paintings.

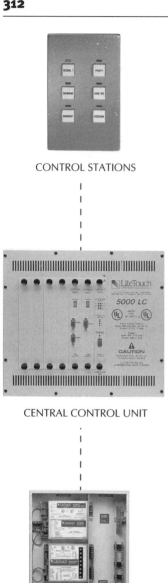

CONTROL STATIONS

CENTRAL CONTROL UNIT

CONTROL MODULES

Figure 10.63 Three components of the Lite-Touch system.

A. CENTRAL CONTROL UNIT

B. CONTROL MODULE

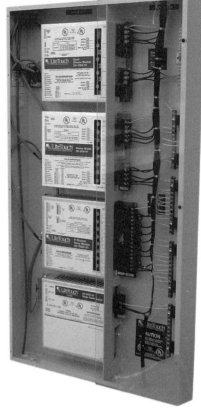

C. INSTALLATION OF CONTROL MODULES

Figure 10.64 Central control unit and control modules.

Routing Schedule							
Number of Housed	Individual	Connected to System	Number of Outlets	Dimmer % (100% is Full)	Location	Type	Remarks
1 6	1A	E-1	4	100	LIVING	GENERAL	-
	1B	E-2	6	60	LIVING	SPOT	-
	1C	E-3	2	40	LIVING	MOOD	-
	1D	C	1	100	OUTSIDE	SECURITY	-
	1E	M	2	40	HALL	PATH	-
	1F	L	2	80	DINING	GENERAL	-

Figure 10.65 Routing schedule.

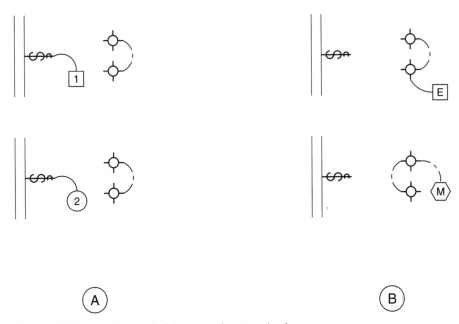

Figure 10.66 Routing symbol for control stations/outlets.

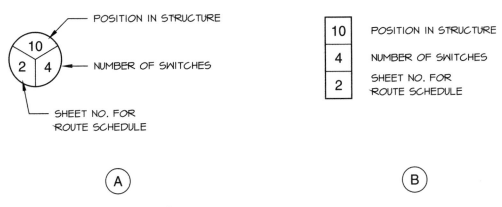

Figure 10.67 Symbol for switch.

Control station groups can be identified with a single number (see Figure 10.66A). The symbol may be a square or a circle. The outlets are connected as in the conventional method, but are not connected to the control stations identified by a C or S with a line through it. Now look at Figure 10.66B. The outlets are connected to a symbol that may be a hexagon, a circle, or even a square, if the symbol does not duplicate those already used for the control stations.

The chart can be incorporated into the symbol (See Figure 10.67A). A circle is divided into three parts. The top one-third indicates the location in the structure. The right one-third displays the number of control points at this location, and the left one-third, the sheet number on which the route schedule is located. Figure 10.67B uses a rectilinear stacking symbol with the same results. Now

you can understand the display of symbols used on Figures 10.68A through 10.68F.

Appliance and Plumbing Fixture Symbols

Many templates are available for drafting plumbing fixture and kitchen appliances. A good architectural template contains such items as:

Circles	Various kitchen appliances
Door swings	Various plumbing fixtures
Electrical symbols	Typical heights marked along edges

Figure 10.69 shows some of these fixtures and appliances.

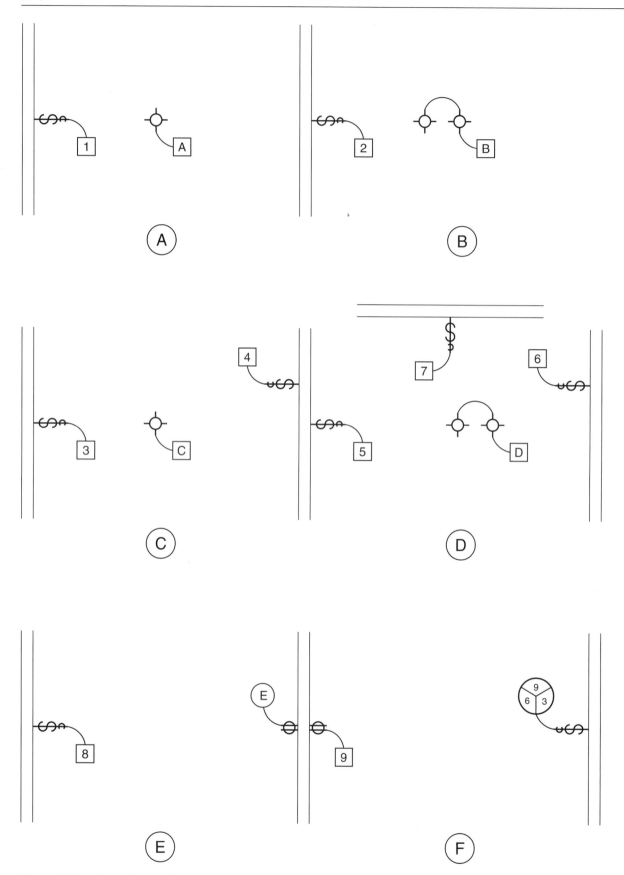

Figure 10.68   Symbol examples.

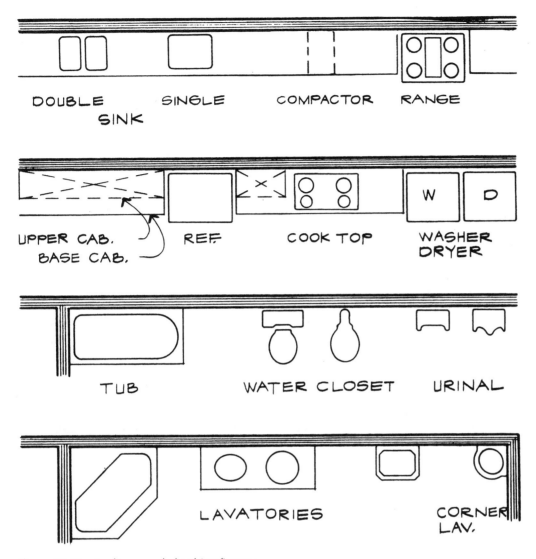

Figure 10.69 Appliance and plumbing fixtures.

■ OTHER FLOOR PLAN CONSIDERATIONS

It is often necessary to show more than one or two building materials on a floor plan. Let us take a college music building as an example of a structure that has a multitude of walls of different materials, including:

1. Masonry
2. Wood studs
3. Two types of soundproof partitions
4. Low walls
5. Low walls with glass above

We need to establish an acceptable symbol for each material and to produce a legend similar to that in Figure 10.70. A sample of a partial floor plan using some of these materials symbols is shown in Figure 10.71.

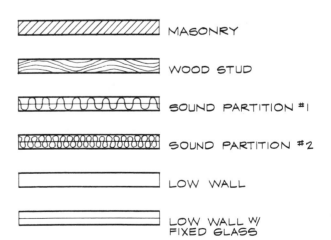

Figure 10.70 Legend for music building floor plan.

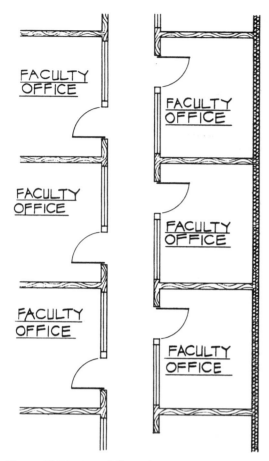

Figure 10.71   Partial floor plan—music building.

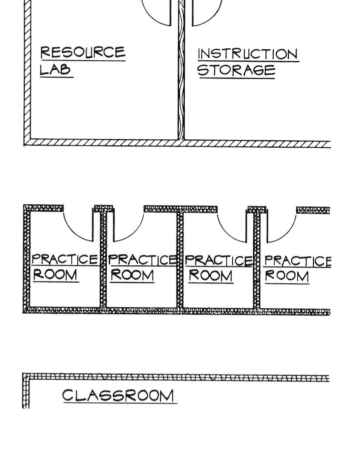

Combining Building Materials

Because of ecological requirements (such as insulation); structural reasons; aesthetic concerns; and fire regulations, materials must often be combined. For example, insulation may be adjacent to a masonry wall, a brick veneer may be on a wood stud wall, and steel studs may be next to a concrete block wall. Figure 10.72 shows examples of what some of the walls will look like on the floor plan.

Repetitive Plans and Symmetrical Items

If a plan or portions of a plan are symmetrical, a center line can be used and half of the object dimensioned. If a plan is repetitive—for example, an office building or an apartment or condominium—each unit is given a letter designation (Unit A, Unit B, etc.). These are then referenced to each other and only one is dimensioned.

For example, suppose you were drafting a floor plan for an eight-unit apartment structure; these eight units are to be divided into four one-bedroom units and four two-bedroom units, all using the same basic plans. Your ap-

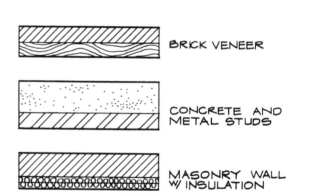

Figure 10.72   Combinations of building materials.

proach could be to draft the overall shape of the structure and then to draft the interior walls only on one typical unit and label it completely. The remaining units (three of each) are referenced to the original unit by a note such as "See Unit A for dimensions and notes."

This type of plan lends itself well to the use of adhesives (see Chapter 2). A typical unit is drawn at the proper scale; then a series of adhesives are made of this plan.

The whole plan is made by putting the adhesive plans in the proper position to produce the overall shape.

Dimensional Reference Numbers and Letters

The dimensional reference system has been discussed earlier. Responsibility for placement of the letters and numbers, and often the drafting of the dimensional reference bubbles, rests with the structural engineer. Because the structural engineer is responsible for sizing and locating the columns for proper distribution of the building weight, only the structural engineer can make the proper decision. This information can then be taken and put in the reference bubbles on the foundation plan, building section, framing plans, and so forth.

Pouché Walls

The word *pouché* was mentioned earlier. This is the process of darkening the space between the lines which represent wall thickness on a floor plan. Special pouché pencils can be purchased at most drafting supply stores. Graphite pencils, like drafting pencils or colored pencils, can be used to pouché. Do not use red, yellow, or orange; they will block light in the reproduction of the plan and leave the walls black. Do not use wax-based pencils.

Stairs

An arrow is used on the plan of the stair to show the direction in which the stair rises. See the partial floor plan, Figure 10.73. Notice how the arrowheads show direction and how the number and size of the treads and risers are indicated.

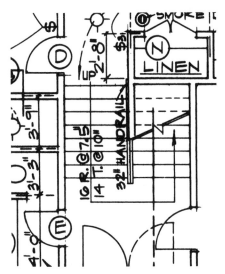

Figure 10.73 Stair direction and number of treads. (Residence of Mr. And Mrs. Ted Bear.)

Noting Logic

The basic approach used here is to show a complete set of working drawings as if a complete set of specifications were included. Specifications are the written documentation of what is drafted; they give information that is not given in the drawings. Brand names, model numbers, installation procedures, and quality of material are just a few of the items discussed in a set of specifications. So the inclusion of the specifications affects the noting of the floor plan.

Because of the precise descriptions contained in the specifications, only general descriptions are necessary on the floor plan. For example, it is sufficient to call out a "cook top" as a generic name and let the specifications take care of the rest of the description. "Tub" and "water closet" are sufficient to describe plumbing fixtures. Further description would only confuse the drawing, and these items should be described in the "specs", short for "specifications."

In other words, specific information should not be duplicated. If it is, changes can present problems. For example, suppose brand "A" is selected for a particular fixture and is called brand "A" on the floor plan rather than by its generic term. Later, it is changed to brand "B." Now both the floor plan and specs need to be changed; if one is missed, confusion results.

Electrical Rating

Many architectural firms that superimpose the electrical plan on top of the floor plan note the **electrical rating** necessary for a particular piece of equipment; for example, range 9KW, oven 5KW, dishwasher 1.5KW, and refrigerator 110V. Electrical ratings can also be included in an electrical appliance schedule if one exists.

Room Sizes

Because sizes of rooms are often found on presentation drawings (scaled drawings), some people think that sizes of rooms (9 × 12, 10 × 14) belong on a floor plan. They do not. These approximate sizes are fine for client consumption but are useless in the construction process.

Providing Satisfactory Dimensions

One of the most common criticisms from the field (workers on the job) is that the floor plans do not contain enough dimensions. Because these people cannot scale the drawings (something we would not want them to do anyway), they are dependent on dimensions, so be sure they are all included. Remember that notes take precedence over the drawing itself. If a member is called a 2 × 10 but is drawn as a 2 × 8, the note takes precedence.

OTHER FLOOR PLAN CONSIDERATIONS

1. Walls
   a. Accuracy of thickness
   b. Correctness of intersections
   c. Accuracy of location
   d. 8-inch wall
   e. Openings
   f. Phony walls designated
   g. Pouché
2. Doors and windows
   a. Correct use
   b. Location
   c. Correct symbol
   d. Schedule reference
   e. Header size
   f. Sills, if any
   g. Show swing
   h. Direction of slide if needed
3. Steps
   a. Riser and treads called out
   b. Concrete steps
   c. Wood steps
4. Dimensioning
   a. Position of line
   b. All items dimensioned
   c. All dimensions shown
   d. All arrowheads shown
   e. Openings
   f. Structural posts
   g. Slabs and steps
   h. Closet depth
   i. Check addition
   j. Odd angles
5. Lettering
   a. Acceptable height and appearance
   b. Acceptable form
   c. Readable
6. Titles, notes, and call-outs
   a. Spelling, phrasing, and abbreviations
   b. Detail references
   c. Specification references
   d. Window and door references
   e. Appliances
   f. Slabs and steps
   g. Plumbing fixtures
   h. Openings
   i. Room titles
   j. Ceiling joist direction
   k. Floor material
   l. Drawing title and scale
   m. Tile work
      (1) Tub
      (2) Shower

   (3) Counter (kitchen and bath)
   n. Attic opening — scuttle
   o. Cabinet
   p. Wardrobe
      (1) Shelves
      (2) Poles
   q. Built-in cabinets, nooks, tables, etc.
7. Symbols
   a. Electric
   b. Gas
   c. Heating, ventilating, and air conditioning
8. Closets, wardrobes, and cabinets
   a. Correct representation
   b. Doors
   c. Depths, widths, and heights
   d. Medicine cabinets
   e. Detail references
   f. Shelves and poles
   g. Plywood partitions and posts
   h. Overhead cabinets
   i. Broom closets
9. Equipment (appliances)
   a. Washer and dryer
   b. Range
   c. Refrigerator
   d. Freezer
   e. Oven
   f. Garbage disposal
   g. Dishwasher
   h. Hot water
   i. Forced draft vent
10. Equipment (special)
    a. Hi-Fi
    b. TV
    c. Sewing machine
    d. Intercom
    e. Game equipment (built-in)
    f. Others
11. Legend
12. Note exposed beams and columns
13. Special Walls
    a. Masonry
    b. Veneers
    c. Partial walls, note height
    d. Furred walls for plumbing vents
14. Note sound and thermal insulation in walls
15. Fireplaces
    a. Dimension depth and width of fire pit
    b. Fuel gas and key
    c. Dimension hearth width

16. Mail slot
17. Stairways
    a. Number of risers
    b. Indicate direction
    c. Note railing
18. Medicine cabinet, mirrors at bath
19. Attic and underfloor access ways
20. Floor slopes and wet areas
21. Hose bibbs
22. Main water shut-off valve
23. Fuel gas outlets
    a. Furnace
    b. Range
    c. Oven
    d. Water heater
    e. Fireplace
24. Water heater: gas fired
    a. 4" vent through roof
    b. 100 sq. in. combustion air vent to closet
25. Furnace location: gas fired
    a. Exhaust vent through roof
    b. Combustion air to closet
26. Electric meter location
27. Floodlights, wall lights, note heights
28. Convenience outlets, note if 220V, note horsepower if necessary
29. Note electric power outlets
    a. Range 9 KW
    b. Oven 5 KW
    c. Dishwasher 1.5 KW
    d. Refrigerator 110 V
    e. Washer 2 KW
    f. Dryer 5 KW
30. Clock, chime outlets
31. Doorbell
32. Roof downspouts
33. Fire extinguishers, fire hose cabinets
34. Interior bathroom, toilet room fans
35. Bathroom heaters
36. Kitchen range hood fan and light
37. Telephone, television outlets
38. Exit signs
39. Bathtub inspection plate
40. Thermostat location
41. Door, window, and finish schedules
42. Line quality
43. Basic design
44. Border line
45. Title block
46. Title
47. Scale

Figure 10.74 Floor plan checklist.

Checklist: Checking Your Own Drawing

There are so many minute things to remember in the development of a particular drawing that most offices have worked out some type of checking system. A **checklist** (or check sheet) is one frequently used device. It lists the most commonly missed items in chart form, making it easy for you to precheck your work before a checker is asked to review a particular drawing. See Figure 10.74 for a floor plan checklist.

■ DRAWING A FLOOR PLAN WITH A COMPUTER

The procedure of drawing a floor plan on a computer is somewhat different from that used a few years ago to draw a floor plan manually. However, the information placed on the floor plan, as well as the dimensioning techniques and the representation formally used, remains valid for construction purposes.

The floor plan should be layered out on the grid the designer used. The structure may be built on a four- or five-foot grid, and this grid should be drawn on the datum layer. If there is no set module, the datum grid can be set to one- or two-foot increments (see Figure 10.75). If the structure is built of masonry, there may be a block module to which this grid can be set.

Multiples of 16 inches has become a favorite spacing inasmuch as most building products come in multiples of 16 inches. Thus, 16, 32, and 48 become easy modules to locate. In working with steel, the columns may be set to a larger grid, such as 12'-6" spacing. If the grid is this large, set your snaps (spacing where the cursor will momentarily stop) to a smaller spacing. If you are rounding off walls to the nearest 3", then 3" will be a good distance to set your snaps. In dimensioning conventional stud

construction, the snap should be set at 1", allowing the drafter to dimension to the face of stud (FOS) (see Figure 10.76).

Let us take a look at the computer drawings done in six stages for the first floor plan of the Adli Residence. Remember, there may be more than ten layers to accomplish these six stages:

STAGE I (Figure 10.77). This is the most critical stage because it sets the field of work and the basic outlines for the structure. If we were working with steel, the columns would be set and positioned in this stage. The properties of the outline can be listed, whereby one can immediately find the square footage of the structure and its perimeter. This outline can be used to position the structure on the site, to verify the required setbacks, or to compare this figure with the allowable buildable area of a particular site.

STAGE II (Figure 10.78). All walls are established at this stage. Exterior walls and interior bearing walls can be

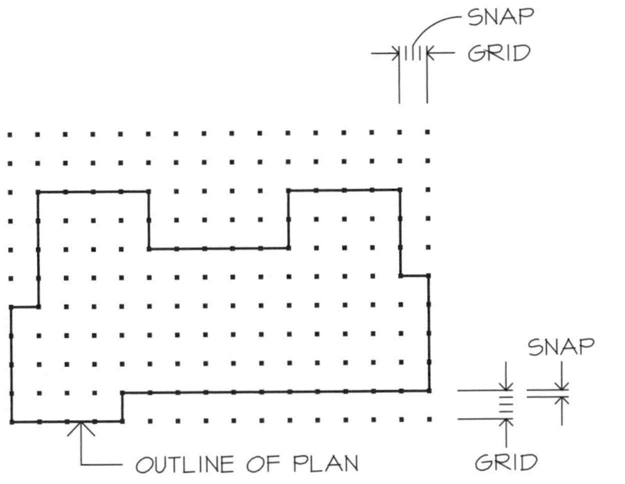

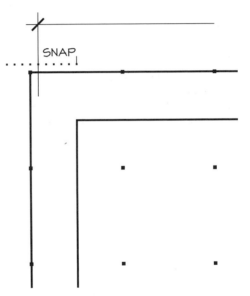

Figure 10.76 Grid versus snap.

Figure 10.75 Setting grids and snaps to a module.

OUTLINE OF PLAN

GRID

SNAP

SNAP
GRID

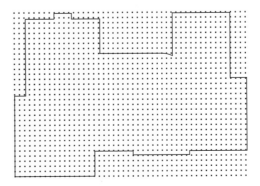

Figure 10.77 Stage I: Setting the datum and building outline.

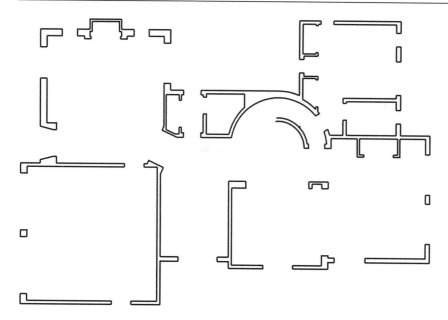

Figure 10.78 Stage II: Exterior/interior wall and openings.

put on one wall layer, and all nonbearing walls can be placed on a secondary wall layer. Column locations and all openings are drawn on still another layer. Openings for doors and windows can also be placed on separate layers. Completion of this stage may produce four to six layers. Preliminary energy calculations can be done easily at this stage.

STAGE III (Figure 10.79). Door and window conventions are drawn, along with any connectors such as for stairs, ramps, escalators, elevators, and lifts, at this stage. Partitions for office layouts are done here, as

well as indications for plumbing appliances such as sinks and toilets, and built-in cabinets such as kitchen cabinets, shelves and poles in wardrobe closets, built-in bookcases, reference tables, and the like.

STAGE IV (Figure 10.80). This is the sizing and location stage. All the necessary dimensioning is done here. You must verify block modules and stud line dimensioning, or adhere to the dimensional reference system if used. Work to numerical values (maximum and minimum) and tolerances to which the workers in the field can build.

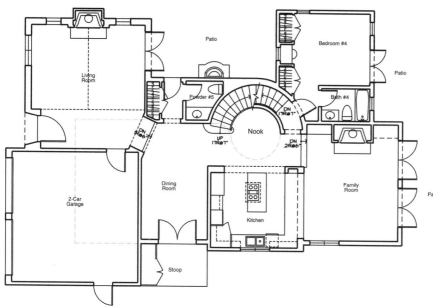

Figure 10.79 Stage III: Plumbing, stairs, windows/doors, and partitions.

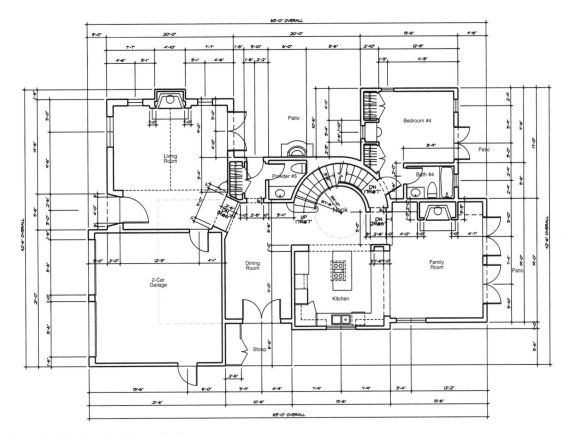

Figure 10.80 Stage IV: Dimensioning.

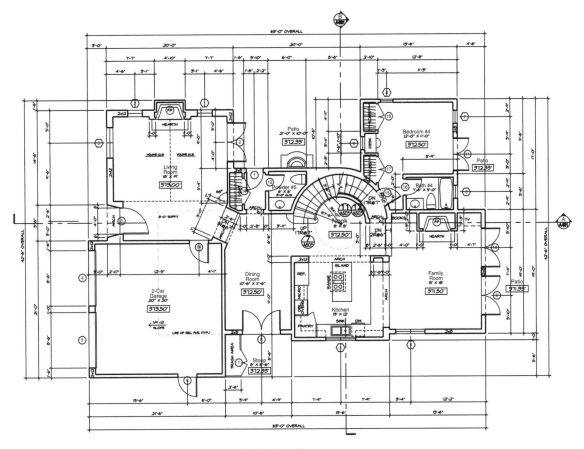

Figure 10.81 Stage V: Noting and references, both detail and section.

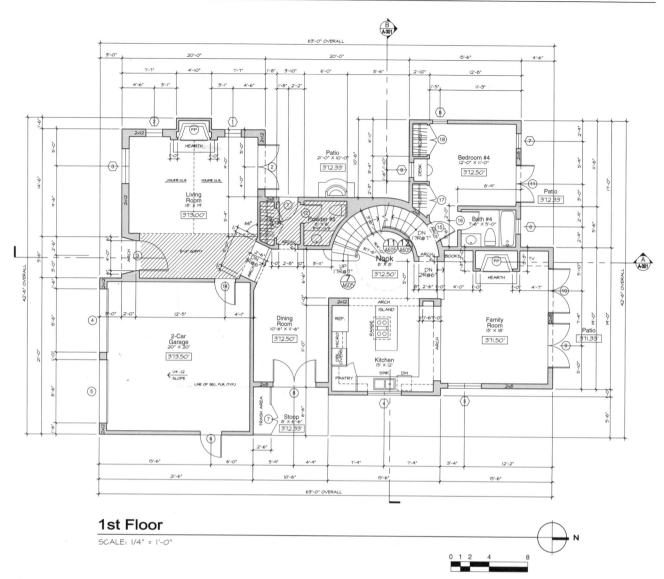

1st Floor

SCALE: 1/4" = 1'-0"

Figure 10.82 Stage VI: Finish work—titles, pouché, scale. (Courtesy of Mike Adli, Owner; Nagy R. Bakhoum, President of Obelisk Architects.)

STAGE V (Figure 10.81). This may easily be called the communication stage, because this stage must communicate with all the other drawings. Reference symbols are used to connect one drawing with another. Detail reference, reference to schedules, and building section reference bubbles are drawn at this stage. This allows the reader to look to other sources for additional information about a portion of the floor plan. Section symbols refer us to the multiple building sections through this plan. Detail reference bubbles explain in greater detail the nature of the cabinets and columns and how they are connected with other structural members. Interior elevation reference bubbles show, for example, how a fireplace may be finished, or the appearance of cabinets in an examination room of a medical facility, or can be used to reference win-

dows and doors to schedules for size or for details on the physical makeup of a particular window or door.

STAGE VI (Figure 10.82). All noting and titles are added in this stage, but in many instances the designer may have inserted the room titles when presenting the floor plan to the client. These titles can then be moved at this stage for clarity. The titles can be relocated so that they do not interfere with the dimensions, appliances, and so forth. Room titles can be placed on one layer, and other notes, such as those identifying columns or materials, can be placed on another layer. Lettering size can be a determinant for the different layers or the font being used. Main titles should be of existing fonts in the computer program, and all construction notation should be done with an architectural lettering font for ease of correction.

SCHEDULES: DOOR, WINDOW, AND FINISH

■ THE PURPOSE OF SCHEDULES

A schedule is a list or catalog of information that defines the doors, windows, or finishes of a room. The main purpose for incorporating schedules into a set of construction documents is to provide clarity, location, sizes, materials, and information for the designation of doors, windows, roof finishes, plumbing and electrical fixtures, and other such items.

■ TABULATED SCHEDULES: DOORS AND WINDOWS

Schedules may be presented in **tabulated** or **pictorial** form. While tabulated schedules in architectural offices vary in form and layout from office to office, the same primary information is provided.

Figures 11.1 and 11.2 are examples of tabulated **door and window schedules**. The door schedule provides a space for the symbol, the width and height, and the thickness of the door. It also indicates whether the door is to be solid core (SC) or hollow core (HC). The "type" column may indicate that the door has raised panels, or that it is a slab door or french door, and so forth.

Information

The material space may indicate what kind of wood is to be used for the door, such as birch or beech. Space for remarks is used to provide information such as the closing device or hardware to be used, or the required fire-rated door. In some cases, where there is insufficient space for remarks, an asterisk (*) or symboled number may be placed to the left of the schedule or in the designated box and referenced to the bottom of the schedule with the required information. This information must under no circumstances be crowded or left out. For any type of schedule including lettering, provide sufficient space in each frame so that your lettering is not cramped or unclear.

Symbols

Symbol designations for doors and windows vary in architectural offices and are influenced by each office's procedures. For example, a circle, hexagon, or square may be used for all or part of the various schedules. Figure 11.3 illustrates symbol shapes and how they may be shown. There are various options, such as using a letter or number or both, and choosing various shapes. Door

DOOR SCHEDULE

SYM	WIDTH	HEIGHT	THK.	TYPE	MATERIAL	HC/SC	GLAZ. AREA	REMARKS
1	PR. 2'-9"	7'-0"	1 3/4"	SLAB	WOOD	SC		
2	PR. 2'-10"	"	"	FRENCH	"	"	11.3 ⌗	1/4" TEMP. GL. / TINTED GL.
3	PR. 3'-1"	"	"	"	"	"	"	" "
4	3'-6"	"	"	"	"	"	13.8 ⌗	" "
5	3'-0"	"	"	SLAB	"	"		
6	2'-8"	"	"	"	"	"		
7	2'-8"	"	"	"	"	"		1 HOUR SELF-CLOSING
8	2'-6"	"	"	"	"	"		
9	2'-4"	6'-8"	1 3/8"	SLAB	WOOD	HC		
10	2'-0"	"	"	"	"	"		
11	2'-6"	"	"	"	"	"		
12	PR. 3'-7"	"	"	BI-FOLD	WOOD	"		
13	PR. 3'-8"	"	"	"	"	"		
14	PR. 3'-2"	"	"	"	"	"		
15	8'-8"	8'-0"	3"	GARAGE	WOOD	—		2x3 W/ 1x6 T&G R/S CEDAR
⬡								
⬡								

Figure 11.1 Door schedule. (Reprinted by permission from *The Professional Practice of Architectural Working Drawings*, 2d Ed., © 1995 by John Wiley & Sons, Inc.)

WINDOW SCHEDULE

SYM.	WIDTH	HEIGHT	TYPE	FRAME	SCR.	GLAZ. AREA	VENT. AREA	REMARKS
A	5'-8"	7'-0"	FIXED/AWNING	WOOD	YES	39.6 ☐	9.9 ☐	PR. 1'-9" HIGH AWNING BELOW
B	4'-6"	"	FIXED	"	NO	31.5 ☐		¼" TEMP. GLASS
C	5'-6"	"	"	"	"	38.5 ☐		"
D	4'-0"	3'-0"	AWNING	"	YES	12.0 ☐	12.0 ☐	
E•	5'-8"	7'-0"	FIXED	"	NO	39.7 ☐		¼" TEMP. GLASS
F	4'-0"	3'-6"	GARDEN	WOOD	YES	14.0 ☐	5.0 ☐	OPERABLE SIDE VENTS
G	1'-8"	3'-3"	CASEMENT	"	"	5.4 ☐	5.4 ☐	
H	PR. 2'-0"	4'-0"	"	"	"	16.0 ☐	16.0 ☐	
I	4@1'-4"	5'-8"	FIXED	"	NO	30.2 ☐		
J	3@1'-8"	4'-0"	FIXED/CASEMENT	WOOD	YES	20.0 ☐	6.7 ☐	MIDDLE IS CASEMENT
K	PR. 1'-3"	"	CASEMENT	"	"	10.0 ☐	10.0 ☐	
L•	5'-6"	7'-0"	FIXED	"	NO	38.5 ☐		¼" TEMP. GLASS

NOTES: ALL WINDOWS DOUBLE GLASS-THERMAL EXCEPT WINDOW Ⓕ
ALL WINDOWS TINTED GLASS, EXCEPT WHERE NOTED BY •

Figure 11.2 Window schedule. (Reprinted by permission from *The Professional Practice of Architectural Working Drawings*, 2d Ed., © 1995 by John Wiley & Sons, Inc.)

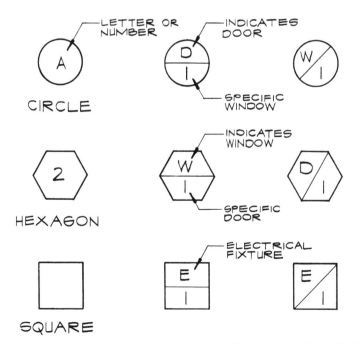

Figure 11.3 Symbol designation. (Reprinted by permission from *The Professional Practice of Architectural Working Drawings*, 2d Ed., © 1995 by John Wiley & Sons, Inc.)

and window symbol shapes should be different from each other. To clarify reading the floor plan, the letter "D" at the top of the door symbol and the letter "W" at the top of the window symbol are used. The letter "P" is used for plumbing fixtures, "E" for electrical fixtures, and "A" for appliances. Place the letter in the top part of the symbol. Whatever symbol shape you select, be sure to make the symbol large enough to accommodate the lettering that will be inside the symbol.

Whenever possible, the door and window schedules should be on the floor plan sheet. This helps locate the various doors and windows on the floor plan. If you cannot place these schedules on the floor plan sheet, use an adjacent sheet.

Draw the lines for the schedules with ink on the front side of the vellum or with lead on the reverse side of the sheet. In this way, when changes are made in the schedule information, you run no risk of erasing the lines. When you provide lines for the anticipated number of symbols to be used, allow extra spaces for door and window types that may be added.

■ PICTORIAL SCHEDULES: DOORS AND WINDOWS

Pictorial Representation

In many cases, tabulated schedules cannot clearly define a specific door or window. In this case, you can add to a schedule a call-out with a pictorial drawing of a door or window adjacent to your schedule, as in Figure 11.4. Door 1 is difficult to explain so a pictorial representation makes it clearer.

Pictorial Schedules

A pictorial schedule, as distinct from a pictorial representation, is totally pictorial. Each item is dimensioned and provided with data such as material, type, and so forth. Figure 11.5 provides a pictorial schedule of a window. A pictorial schedule provides section references for the head, jamb, and sill sections, so you no longer need to reference the exterior elevations. (The head is the top

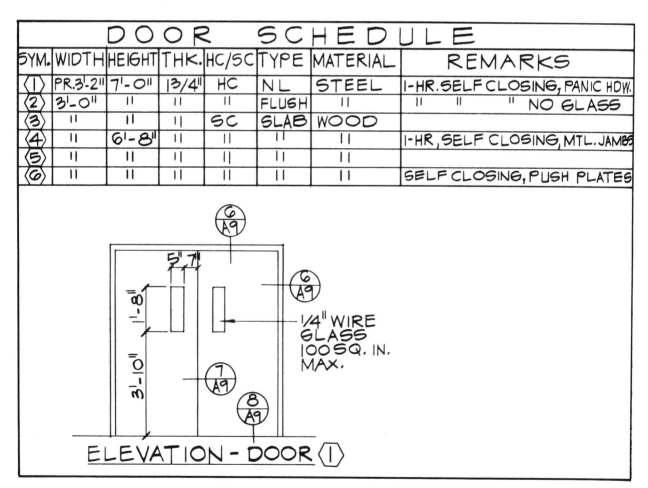

Figure 11.4   Pictorial representation on a tabular schedule. (Reprinted by permission from *The Professional Practice of Architectural Working Drawings*, 2d Ed., © 1995 by John Wiley & Sons, Inc.)

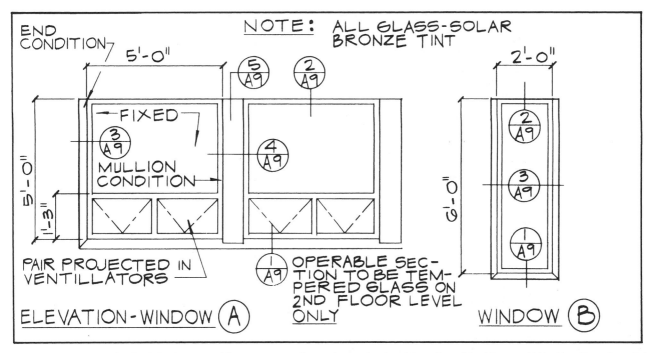

Figure 11.5 Pictorial schedule. (Reprinted by permission from *The Professional Practice of Architectural Working Drawings*, 2d Ed., © 1995 by John Wiley & Sons, Inc.)

of a window or door, the jamb refers to the sides of a window or door, and the sill is the bottom of the window or door.)

■ CHOOSING A TABULATED OR PICTORIAL SCHEDULE

Tabulated

Your choice of a tabulated schedule may involve the following factors:

1. Specific office procedures
2. Standardization or simplicity of doors and windows selected
3. Large number of items with different dimensions
4. Ease of changing sizes

Pictorial

Choice of a pictorial schedule may involve the following factors:

1. Specific office procedures
2. Unusual and intricate door or window design requirements
3. Very few doors and windows in the project or very few types used
4. Desired clarity for window section referencing

■ INTERIOR FINISH SCHEDULES

Interior finish schedules provide information such as floor and wall material, trim material, and ceiling finish. Architectural offices vary in their layout of an interior finish schedule because of their office philosophy and specific information they receive for various types of projects.

Figure 11.6A shows an interior finish schedule. The column allocated for room designation may show the room name or an assigned space number or both. This selection may be dictated by the project itself. See Figure 11.6B. Another method of defining finishes combines the room finish schedule with a room finish key, which uses numbers and letters to indicate the various materials to be used for floors, walls, and so forth. An example of this type of schedule is shown in Figure 11.6C. Using space numbers is more logical for a large office building, for example, than for a very small residence. Once again, when extensive information is required in the remarks section of the schedule, use an asterisk (*) or footnote number for reference at the bottom of the schedule.

■ ADDITIONAL SCHEDULES

Other types of schedules used depend on office procedure and the type of project. For example, if a project has many types of plumbing and appliance fixtures in various

INTERIOR FINISH SCHEDULE

ROOM	RESILIENT FLR	CARPET	EXP.CONC.	LINOLEUM	VINYL ASBES	HARDWOOD	CER. TILE	TERRAZZO	TOPSET	WOOD	CER. TILE	COVED	CER. TILE	TERRAZZO	PAINT	PLASTER	EXP.MASONRY	EXP. WOOD	5/8 DRYWALL	WALL PAPER	PAINT	CEILING HEIGHT	PLASTER	AC PLASTER	EXP. WOOD	5/8 DRYWALL	ILLUM.	EXP.JST.&SUBFLR	REMARKS
	FLOOR								BASE				WAINSCOT			WALLS							CEILING						
ENTRY							●					●							●							●			
GALLERY							●					●							●							●			
LIVING ROOM		●				●					●								●						●				
DINING ROOM						●					●								●						●				
DEN					●						●								●						●				
KITCHEN					●						●								●						●				
PANTRY					●						●								●						●				
POWDER RM.					●						●								●							●			
STORAGE																													
MASTER BEDRM.		●							●										●						●				
WARDROBE		●							●										●						●				
VANITY NO. 1					●						●								●						●				
BATH NO. 1					●						●								●							●			USE WATER PROOF DRYWALL
BEDROOM NO.2		●							●										●							●			
BEDROOM NO.3		●							●										●							●			
VANITY NO. 2					●						●								●							●			
BATH NO. 2					●						●								●							●			USE WATER PROOF DRYWALL
STUDIO NO. 1						●						●					●			●					●				
HALL						●											●			●					●				
STUDIO NO. 2						●						●					●			●					●				
WORKSHOP			●									●					●			●					●				
SAUNA			●															●							●				
JACUZZI							●					●						●							●				
BATH NO.3					●						●								●							●			USE WATER PROOF DRYWALL
SHOP			●														●									●			
STAIR (BASEMENT)		●																	●							●			
STAIR (1ST FLR)						●					●								●							●			
STAIR (2ND FLR)						●					●								●							●			

Figure 11.6A Interior finish schedule. (Reprinted by permission from *The Professional Practice of Architectural Working Drawings*, 2d Ed., © 1995 by John Wiley & Sons, Inc.)

INTERIOR FINISH SCHEDULE

ROOM		CARPET	LINOLEUM	TILE	WOOD	VINYL TOPSET	COVED	5/8" SHEETROCK	CEILING HEIGHT	5/8" SHEETROCK	SQUARE FEET	REMARKS
		FLOOR			BASE			WALLS	CEILING		AREA	
101	ENTRY			●		●		●	17'-6"	●	73	
102	KITCHEN		●			●		●	8'-0"	●	184	
103	LIVING	●				●		●	9'-3"	●	270	CEILING SLOPES
104	DINING	●				●		●	8'-6"	●	284	
105	FAMILY	●				●		●	7'-9"	●	167	
106	BAR		●			●		●	8'-0"	●	26	
107	LAUNDRY		●			●		●	"	●	39	
108	MUD ROOM		●			●		●	"	●	28	
201	MASTER BATH		●			●		●	7'-6"	●	77	
202	DRESSING	●				●		●	"	●	60	
203	MAST. BEDROOM	●				●		●	8'-0"	●	380	
204	BATH		●			●		●	7'-6"	●	55	
205	BEDROOM	●				●		●	8'-0"	●	146	
206	STAIRS	●				●		●	—	●	54	

Figure 11.6B Interior finish schedule. (Reprinted by permission from *The Professional Practice of Architectural Working Drawings*, 2d Ed., © 1995 by John Wiley & Sons, Inc.)

ROOM FINISH SCHEDULE

NO.	ROOM	FLOOR	BASE	WALLS	CEILING	CEIL. HGT.	ROOM AREA	REMARKS
101	RECEPTION	B	1	A	2	9'-0"	110□'	
102	OFFICE	A		B	2	8'-0"	70□'	
103	OFFICE	A		B	2	"	180□'	
104	OFFICE	A		B	2	"	185□'	
105	WOMENS TOIL.	C	1	A	1	7'-6"	30□'	
106	MENS TOILET	C	1	A	1	7'-6"	25□'	

ROOM FINISH KEY

FLOORS		BASES		WALLS		CEILINGS	
A	CARPET	1	WOOD	A	5/8" SHEETROCK	1	5/8" SHEETROCK
B	OAK PARQUET			B	1x6 T&G CEDAR	2	SUSP. AC. TILE
C	CERAMIC TILE						

Figure 11.6C Room finish schedule—key type. (Reprinted by permission from *The Professional Practice of Architectural Working Drawings*, 2d Ed., © 1995 by John Wiley & Sons, Inc.)

areas, provide additional schedules to clarify and to locate items with their designated symbols.

Figures 11.7 and 11.8 show a **plumbing fixture schedule** and an **appliance schedule**. If these types of schedules are not used in a project, the fixture types, manufacturers, catalog numbers, and other information needed must be included in the project specifications.

For most projects, the specifications will augment information found in the schedules. Examples of information usually found in the specifications include the window manufacturer, the type and manufacturer of the

PLUMBING FIXTURE SCHEDULE

SYM.	ITEM	MANUFACTURER	CATALOG NO.	REMARKS
1	WHIRLPOOL BATH	FIXTURES INC.	2640.061	FITTING 1108.019
2	LAVATORY	"	0470.039	FAUCET 2248.565
3	BIDET	"	5005.013	FITTING 1852.012
4	TOILET	"	2109.395	

Figure 11.7 Plumbing fixture schedule. (Reprinted by permission from *The Professional Practice of Architectural Working Drawings*, 2d Ed., © 1995 by John Wiley & Sons, Inc.)

APPLIANCE SCHEDULE			
SYM.	ITEM	MANUFACTURER	CATALOG NO.	REMARKS
1	COOKTOP	APPLIANCES INC.	RU38V	WHITE
2	MICROWAVE	"	JKP65G	
3	DISHWASHER	"	GSD2500	WHITE
4	DISPOSER	"	GFC510	
5				

Figure 11.8 Appliance fixture schedule. (Reprinted by permission from *The Professional Practice of Architectural Working Drawings*, 2d Ed., © 1995 by John Wiley & Sons, Inc.)

door hardware, and the type and manufacturer of paint for the trim.

■ SCHEDULES AS THEY RELATE TO STRUCTURAL ENTITIES

Shear Wall Finish Schedule

For building projects that may require various structural components such as shear walls resisting lateral forces or spread concrete footings of various sizes carrying different loads, it is good practice to provide schedules for the various structural entities for clear drawings.

An example of a shear wall finish schedule is shown in Figure 11.9. This schedule and the various finishes reflect the need for this kind of schedule to provide clarity in reviewing the structural drawings. A partial lateral floor plan is shown in Figure 11.10 to illustrate the symbolizing of the shear walls.

Pier/Spread Footing Schedule

Another example of a schedule that is related to a structural entity is a pier and/or spread footing schedule. This type of schedule is recommended when there are numerous spread footings of various sizes. This occurs on many commercial buildings, as shown in Chapter 20.

Shear Wall Finish Schedule

Sym	Wall Material	Blocked / Unblocked	Nailing Size & Spacing	Stud Size	Anchor Bolts & Number	Remarks
S 1	1/2" GYPSUM WALLBOARD	UNBLOCKED	5d COOLER @ 7" O.C.	2 X 4	(6) 1/2" DIA. X 10"	-
S 2	5/8" GYPSUM WALLBOARD	BLOCKED	6d COOLER @ 7" O.C.	2 X 4	(8) 1/2" DIA. X 10"	-
S 3	3/8" PLYWOOD STRUCT - 1	BLOCKED	8d @ 3"	2 X 4	(5) 5/8" DIA. X 10"	FIELD NAILING : 8d @ 12" O.C.
S 4	1/2" PLYWOOD STRUCT - 1	BLOCKED	10d @ 3"	3 X 4	(8) 5/8" DIA. X 10"	FIELD NAILING : 8d @ 12" O.C.
S 5	- -	-	- -	-	-	-
S 6	- -	-	- -	-	-	-
- -	- -	-	- -	-	-	-
- -	- -	-	- -	-	-	-

Figure 11.9 Shear wall finish schedule example.

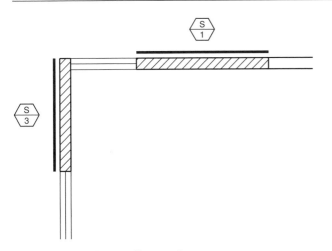

Figure 11.10   Shear wall example.

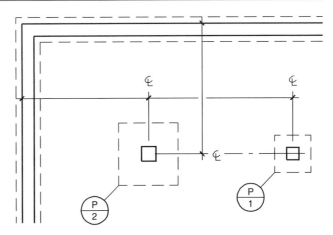

Figure 11.12   Pier/spread footing example.

Figure 11.11 illustrates an example of a pier/spread footing schedule. Note the variances in the steel reinforcing requirements, the sizes of the base plates, the number and sizes of the anchor bolts and other items. Figure 11.12 depicts how the schedule symbols may be shown on a structural foundation plan.

A further refinement is to make a transparency of the schedule on a plain paper copier. This transparency is turned over and placed back onto a plain paper copier, and a reverse image, similar to Figure 11.13, is made and filed. When a schedule is needed, this reverse image is reproduced onto an adhesive sheet and mounted onto the back side of the vellum, as shown in Figure 11.14. You then letter the desired information on the front side. This means that you are lettering on vellum, and not on the slick adhesive material.

The best of all solutions is to type the information (if known in advance) onto a regular copy of a schedule,

transfer onto an adhesive, and place this on your drawing. The main drawback to this method is that the finished product is so final. It is difficult to add or delete information and nearly impossible to remove the adhesive. However, there is solution: If a change, addition, or deletion is necessary, a xerographic copy can be made of the whole sheet onto erasable vellum and this product can be altered.

Preprinted Sheets

Many offices prepare preprinted sheets that contain many of the standards established by them, along with schedules, abbreviations, standard symbols, and so on. A simple way of preparing one of these sheets is to ink a schedule onto a sheet of vellum. Lettering can be done with a mechanical lettering machine that produces words and phrases on a transparent adhesive material. Standard symbols can also be drafted on a separate (pos-

Pier / Spread Footing Schedule

Sym	Size	Depth	Reinforcing	Base Plate Size	Anchor Bolts & Number	Remarks
P 1	1'-6" X 1'-6"	10"	(3) 1/2" DIA. BARS ONE WAY	N.A.	N.A.	KEEP STEEL 3" CLR. OF EARTH
P 2	2'-6" X 2'-6"	12"	(4) 1/2" DIA. BARS EACH WAY	6" X 6" x 1/4"	(2) 5/8" DIA.	KEEP STEEL 3" CLR. OF EARTH
P 3	3'-6" X 3'-6"	12"	(5) 1/2" DIA. BARS EACH WAY	7" X 7" X 3/8"	(4) 5/8" DIA.	KEEP STEEL 3" CLR. OF EARTH
P 4	-	-	- -	-	-	-
- -	-	-	- -	-	-	-
- -	-	-	- -	-	-	-

Figure 11.11   Pier/spread footing schedule example.

WINDOW SCHEDULE

SYM.	WIDTH	HEIGHT	TYPE	FRAME	SCR. AREA	GLAZ. AREA	VENT.	REMARKS
○								
○								
○								
○								
○								
○								
○								
○								
○								
○								
○								
○								
○								
○								

A

WINDOW SCHEDULE

SYM.	WIDTH	HEIGHT	TYPE	FRAME	SCR. AREA	GLAZ. AREA	VENT.	REMARKS
○								
○								
○								
○								
○								
○								
○								
○								
○								
○								
○								
○								
○								
○								
○								
○								

B

Figure 11.13 Predrawn schedules. (Reprinted by permission from *The Professional Practice of Architectural Working Drawings*, 2d Ed., © 1995 by John Wiley & Sons, Inc.)

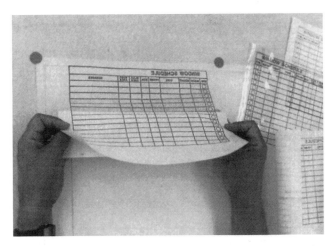

Figure 11.14 Using an adhesive to generate the schedule. (Reprinted by permission from *The Professional Practice of Architectural Working Drawings*, 2d Ed., © 1995 by John Wiley & Sons, Inc.)

sibly $8^1/_2 \times 11$) sheet, the written portion typed, and attached to the original sheet to produce a composite drawing. Much of the work described in Chapter 17 uses this method.

The final assembled sheet is sent to a reproduction company that can produce a vellum copy the same size as the original.

Thus the original can be filed and the new information, such as the schedule, is performed on the xerographic vellum copy and becomes an original for that specific set.

Computer

When done by CAD, the schedules, symbols, abbreviations, and so on can be drawn and merged by the computer and plotted on a sheet of vellum. The information to appear on the schedules can even be placed on the schedules in the computer, and the result is a finished sheet when plotted.

■ CAD-GENERATED SCHEDULES

To illustrate a project utilizing the abilities of a CAD-generated plotting system in developing schedule layouts, three examples are given in the following figures.

Figure 11.15 shows an example of a computer drawing for an interior finish schedule. This schedule can be revised quickly with a computer while still preserving the basic layout for future projects.

A window schedule with drawings of some of the window types that will be incorporated in this project is depicted in Figure 11.16. As discussed previously in this chapter, windows in pictorial form provide for clarity

INTERIOR FINISH SCHEDULE

ROOM	CARPET	HARDWOOD	STONE	CERAMIC TILE	CONCRETE	PAINT GRADE 8" BASE	PAINT GRADE 5" BASE	STAIN GRADE 8" BASE	STONE	CERAMIC TILE	NONE	5/8" GYP. BD. W/SKIM-COAT	CERAMIC TILE WAINSCOT	WAINSCOT	STAIN-GRD WOOD PANELING	FULL-HEIGHT CERAMIC TILE	STUCCO	5/8" TYPE 'X' GYP. BD.	STAIN GRD. WOOD PANELING	STAIN GRD. T&G AND BEAMS	STAIN GRD WOOD BEAMS/PLAST	STUCCO	RED BRICK	STAIN GRADE ALDER	PAINT GRADE	MELAMINE	WALLS PAINT	WALLS ENAMEL	WALLS FAUX FINISH	WALLS WALL PAPER	CEIL PAINT	CEIL ENAMEL	CEIL STAIN	NOT APPLICABLE	TRIM PAINT	TRIM ENAMEL	TRIM STAIN	CAB PAINT #	CAB ENAMEL	CAB STAIN #	REMARKS
LIVING RM.	X					X						X						X									X															
DINING RM.	X					X						X						X									X															2X6 WOOD PLANK DECKING AT FAM. RM. DECK
FAMILY RM.	X					X						X									X						X				X										
KITCHEN				X		X						X												X			X					X						X			
NOOK				X		X						X															X				X										
POWDER				X		X						X											X				X				X					X					
LAUNDRY				X		X						X															X				X										
2-CAR GARAGE					X						X							X									X							X							
STAIRWELL	X					X						X						X									X								X						
HALL	X					X						X						X									X								X						
MAST. BDRM.	X					X						X						X									X								X						
MAST. BATH				X						X		X															X					X			X						
WALK-IN CLOSET	X					X						X						X									X								X			X			
BED RM. #2	X					X						X						X									X								X						
BATH #2				X						X		X															X					X			X				X		
BED RM. #3	X					X						X						X									X								X						
BATH #3				X						X		X															X					X			X			X			
BED RM. #4	X					X						X						X									X								X						
BATH #4				X						X		X															X					X			X				X		
CELLAR					X			X				X						X									X								X						
WINE					X			X				X						X									X								X						

Figure 11.15 Interior finish schedule.

WINDOW SCHEDULE

KEY	WIDTH	HEIGHT	TYPE	MATERIAL	GLAZING	HEAD HGT. FROM F.F.	REMARKS
①	2'-4"	5'-0"	D	PAINT GRD. WOOD		8'-0"	CASEMENT
2	2'-4"	5'-0"	D	"		8'-0"	CASEMENT
3	4'-8"	5'-2"	A	"		8'-0"	FRENCH CASEMENT
4	4'-8"	4'-0"	A	STAIN GRD. WOOD	TEMPERED	6'-8"	FRENCH CASEMENT
5	4'-8"	5'-0"	A	PAINT GRD. WOOD		8'-0"	FRENCH CASEMENT
6	2'-0"	4'-0"	D	"	TEMPERED	6'-8"	CASEMENT
7	2'-0"	4'-0"	D	"		6'-8"	CASEMENT
8	2'-0"	4'-0"	D	"		6'-8"	CASEMENT
9	2'-0"	3'-0"	B	"		8'-0"	CASEMENT
10	6'-0"	4'-0"	C	"		6'-8"	FIXED
11	2'-0"	4'-0"	D	"		6'-8"	CASEMENT
12	4'-0"	4'-0'	A	"		6'-8"	FRENCH CASEMENT, EGRESS (12.25 SQ. FT.)
13	4'-0"	3'-6"	A	"		6'-8"	FRENCH CASEMENT
14	2'-0"	3'-0"	B	"	TEMPERED	6'-8"	CASEMENT
15	2'-0"	4'-0"	E	"		6'-8"	FIXED, SEE ELEV
16	4'-0"	4'-0"	A	"	TEMPERED	6'-8"	FRENCH CASEMENT
17	2'-0"	4'-0"	D	"		6'-8"	CASEMENT
18	2'-0"	4'-0"	E	"	TEMPERED	6'-8"	INSWING CASEMENT, SEE ELEV
19	2'-0"	4'-0"	D	"	TEMPERED	6'-8"	CASEMENT
20	2'-0"	4'-0"	E	"		6'-8"	INSWING CASEMENT, SEE ELEV
21	2'-0"	3'-0"	B	"		6'-8"	CASEMENT

WINDOW TYPES

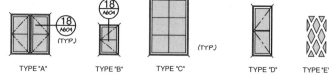

TYPE "A"   TYPE "B"   TYPE "C"   TYPE "D"   TYPE "E"

NOTES:

1. ALIGN TOP OF WINDOWS WITH TOP OF DOORS SO THAT TOP EDGES OF DOORS AND WINDOWS ALIGN IN A LEVEL PLANE ABOVE FINISH FLOOR.

2. ALL ESCAPE OR RESCUE WINDOWS SHALL HAVE A MINIMUM NET CLEAR OPENABLE AREA OF 5.7 SQ. FT.. THE MINIMUM NET CLEAR OPENABLE HEIGHT DIMENSION SHALL BE 24". THE MINIMUM NET CLEAR OPENABLE WIDTH DIMENSION SHALL BE 20" WHEN WINDOWS ARE PROVIDED AS A MEANS OF ESCAPE OR RESCUE. THEY SHALL HAVE A FINISHED SILL HEIGHT NOT MORE THAN 44" ABOVE FIN. FLR..

3. SKYLIGHTS SHALL HAVE A NON-COMBUSTIBLE FRAME GLAZED WITH DUAL GLAZING OF HEAT STRENGTHENED OR FULLY TEMPERED GLASS OR SHALL BE A 3/4-HOUR FIRE-RESISTIVE ASSEMBLY

4. WINDOWS WITH SILLS LESS THAN 5'-0" ABOVE TUB OR SHOWER FLOOR SHALL BE TEMPERED

Figure 11.16 Window schedule and types of windows.

and symbolizing for window sections. Note in the glazing column that the clouded areas refer to tempered glass. This has been done to satisfy a building department requirement and is referenced to as a delta one symbol, which is a building a department requirement. Additional notes have been added by the architect to indicate his or her directions for the alignment of the windows and doors. Notes relating to building code requirements are also shown below the window types.

Figure 11.17 is an example of a door schedule. The types of doors specified for this project are shown in pictorial form. A clouded area for a specific door illustrates a revision and requirement by the governing building department. Types of doors have been depicted pictorially for clarity and referencing. These types of doors are keyed with a letter on the door schedule. The computer offers the flexibility to alter or revise the schedule layouts for projects that may have different requirements.

■ SCHEDULES ON THE COMPUTER

If a set of construction documents was produced on the computer, chances are that a basic office standard template (pattern) was produced. Every CAD drafter should be able to produce a new basic template as office standards change. The new pattern will change as the technology changes for architectural installation of windows, doors, and so forth.

Schedule templates can be produced on the computer by simply drawing lines and arranging them horizontally and vertically. The text for the main title and the column titles is entered by typing the word key in all the positions. If the first phase is positioned and centered carefully, the remaining columns will also be centered. Next, edit the word key with the desired column titles and change the size if necessary. The text will automatically center the new titles. The word key is our placeholder. Look at Figure 11.18. Because we are producing a generic schedule,

DOOR SCHEDULE

KEY	WIDTH	HEIGHT	THICK.	TYPE	MATERIAL	GLAZING	REMARKS
1	2'-8"	6'-8"	2 1/4"	C	PAINT GRD. WOOD	TEMP.	FRENCH DOORS (SEE ELEVATIONS)
2	(2)-3'-0"	8'-0"	2 1/4"	E	"	TEMP.	FRENCH DOORS (SEE ELEVATIONS)
3	4'-0"	8'-0"	2 1/4"	A	STAIN GRD. WOOD		
4	8'-6"	8'-3"		D			GARAGE OVERHEAD SECTIONAL DOOR (SEE ELEVATIONS)
5	8'-6"	8'-3"		D	"		GARAGE OVERHEAD SECTIONAL DOOR (SEE ELEVATIONS)
6	3'-0"	6'-8"	2 1/4"	K	PAINT GRD. WOOD		
7	(2)-2'-0"	5'-0"		F	"		TRASH AREA, GATE
8	(2)-3'-0"	8'-0"	2 1/4"	E	"	TEMP.	FRENCH DOORS (SEE ELEVATIONS)
9	(2)-3'-0"	8'-0"	2 1/4"	E	"	TEMP.	FRENCH DOORS (SEE ELEVATIONS)
10	(2)-3'-0"	8'-0"	2 1/4"	E	"	TEMP.	FRENCH DOORS (SEE ELEVATIONS)
11	(2)-2'-6"	6'-8"	2 1/4"	E	"	TEMP.	FRENCH DOORS (SEE ELEVATIONS)
12	2'-6"	6'-8"	1 3/4"	J	"		
13	(2)-2'-0"	6'-8"	1 3/4"	G	"		
14	3'-0"	6'-8"	1 3/4"	J			20 MIN. RATED, SELF-CLOSING & TIGHT FITTING
15	2'-8"	6'-8"	1 3/4"	J	"		
16	2'-6"	6'-8"	1 3/4"	J	"		
17	(2)-2'-0"	6'-8"	1 3/4"	G	"		
18	(2)-2'-0"	6'-8"	1 3/4"	G	"		
19	2'-6"	6'-8"	1 3/4"	J	"		
20	(2)-2'-6"	6'-8"	1 3/4"	G	"		
21	(2)-3'-0"	8'-0"	1 3/4"	E	"	TEMP.	FRENCH DOORS (SEE ELEVATIONS)
22	(2)-3'-0"	8'-0"	1 3/4"	E	"	TEMP.	FRENCH DOORS (SEE ELEVATIONS)
23	(2)-2'-6"	6'-8"	1 3/4"	E	"	TEMP.	FRENCH DOORS (SEE ELEVATIONS)
24	(2)-2'-0"	6'-8"	1 3/4"	G	"		
25	(2)-2'-0"	6'-8"	1 3/4"	G	"		
26	2'-6"	6'-8"	1 3/4"	J	"		
27	2'-8"	6'-8"	1 3/4"	J	"		
28	2'-8"	8'-0"	1 3/4"	J	"		
29	2'-6"	8'-0"	1 3/4"	J	"		
30	(2)-1'-6"	8'-0"	1 3/4"	G	PAINT GRD. WOOD		
31	2'-6"	8'-0"	1 3/4"	J	PAINT GRD. WOOD		
32	(2)-1'-0"	8'-0"	1 3/4"	G	"		
33	2'-6"	8'-0"	1 3/4"	J	"		
34	2'-8"	6'-8"	1 3/4"	H	"		
35	2'-8"	6'-8"	1 3/4"	J	"		
36	(2)-4'-0"	6'-8"	1 3/4"	B	"		
37	2'-6"	6'-8"	1 3/4"	J	"		

DOOR TYPES

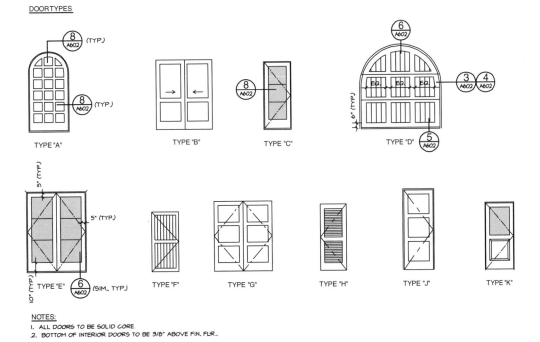

TYPE "A"   TYPE "B"   TYPE "C"   TYPE "D"

TYPE "E"   TYPE "F"   TYPE "G"   TYPE "H"   TYPE "J"   TYPE "K"

NOTES:
1. ALL DOORS TO BE SOLID CORE.
2. BOTTOM OF INTERIOR DOORS TO BE 3/8" ABOVE FIN. FLR.

Figure 11.17 Door schedule and types of doors.

Window Schedule

Key	Width	Height	Type	Material	Glazing	
⬡ -	-	-	-	-	-	
-	-	-	-	-	-	
-	-	-	-	-	-	
-	-	-	-	-	-	
-	-	-	-	-	-	
-	-	-	-	-	-	
-	-	-	-	-	-	
-	-	-	-	-	-	
-	-	-	-	-	-	
-	-	-	-	-	-	

Figure 11.18   Partial template of a schedule with placeholder.

Window Schedule

Key	Width	Height	Type	Material	Glazing	
⬡ 1	2'-4"	5'-0"	D	PAINT GRADE WOOD	-	
2	2'-4"	5'-0"	D	-	-	
3	4'-8"	5'-2"	A	-	-	
4	4'-8"	4'-0"	A	STAIN GRADE WOOD	TEMPERED	
5	4'-8"	5'-0"	A	PAINT GRADE WOOD	-	
6	2'-0"	4'-0"	D	-	TEMPERED	
7	2'-0"	4'-0"	D	-	-	
8	2'-0"	4'-0"	D	-	-	
9	2'-0"	3'-0"	B	-	-	
10	6'-0"	4'-0"	C	-	-	

Figure 11.19   Replacing the placeholder with required text.

put a hyphen (dash) in the unused spaces as a placeholder. The user of this schedule need only edit the hyphens and change them to the desired height, width, material, and so on. All of the information will be automatically centered or placed with the margin to the left, as shown in the Remarks column. See Figure 11.19.

Of course, you can take an example from a previous job that has been produced manually and scan it into the computer. Whichever method you use, it is best to put the information on a separate layer. This allows ease of change, revision, or correction.

If, as a CAD drafter, you are able to develop a spreadsheet, the technique can be applied directly to the development of specialized schedules. Certain projects call for a job-specific schedule (chart). A spreadsheet is ideal for this custom development.

12

BUILDING SECTIONS

■ BUILDING SECTIONS

A building section cuts a vertical slice through a structure or a part of a structure. For the computer, it is a cut along the z-x axis or the z-y axis. It is also an integral part of the dimensional reference system described earlier in this book. Figure 12.1 shows a vertical slice cut through a wood-framed, two-story residence. To further examine the various roof, floor, and wall conditions found at that particular slice location, we can separate the two elements as viewed in Figure 12.2

Drawing a Building Section

Drawing a building section is done by making a cross-section giving relevant architectural and structural information. When given the task of drawing a building section, you first need to gather basic information including:

1. Type of foundation
2. Floor system
3. Exterior and interior wall construction

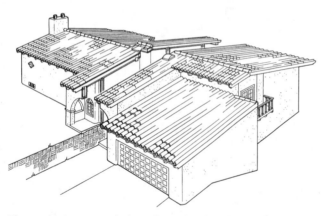

Figure 12.1 Vertical slice through a building. (Courtesy of William F. Smith—Builder.)

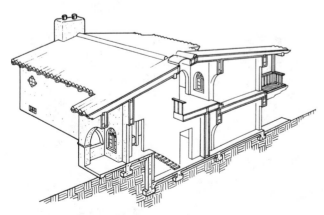

Figure 12.2 Vertical slice separated. (Courtesy of William F. Smith—Builder.)

4. Beam and column sizes and their material
5. Plate and/or wall heights
6. Floor elevations
7. Floor members (size and spacing)
8. Floor sheathing, material and size
9. Ceiling members (size and spacing)
10. Roof pitch
11. Roof sheathing, material and size
12. Insulation requirements
13. Finished roof material

When you have gathered this information, select a suitable architectural scale. Usually, the scale ranges from $3/8'' = 1'-0''$ to $3/4'' = 1'-0''$. The scale depends on the size and complexity of a project and should also be chosen for clarity.

As you draw the building section, visualize the erection sequence for the structure and the construction techniques of the material being used. Figure 12.3 shows a building section derived from Figures 12.1 and 12.2.

The first step is to show the concrete floor and foundation members at that particular location. While foundation details should be drawn accurately, they do not need to be dimensioned or elaborated upon; all the necessary information will be called out in the larger scale drawings of the individual foundation details.

Next, establish a **plate height**. (A plate is a horizontal timber that joins the tops of studs.) Here the plate height is 8'-0", measuring from the top of the concrete floor to the top of the two plates (2—2 × 4 continuous) of the wood stud wall. This height also establishes the height to the bottom of the floor joist for the second floor level. Once the floor joists are drawn in at the proper scale, repeat the same procedure to establish the wall height that will support the ceiling and roof framing members.

As indicated, the roof pitch for this particular project is a ratio of 3 in 12; for each foot of horizontal measurement, the roof rises 3 inches (for every 12 feet, the roof rises 3 feet). You can draw this lope or angle with an architectural scale, or you can convert the ratio to an angle degree and draw it with a protractor or adjustable triangle. Draw the roof at the other side of the building in the same way, with the intersection of the two roof planes establishing the ridge location. Mission clay tile was chosen for the finished roof member for this project and is drawn as shown.

When you have drawn in all the remaining components, such as stairs and floor framing elevation changes, note all the members, roof pitch, material information, and dimensions.

Figure 12.3 shows various reference symbols. These symbols refer to an enlarged drawing of those particular assemblies. To demonstrate the importance of providing enlarged details, Figure 12.4 shows a building section of a wood-framed structure with critical bolted connec-

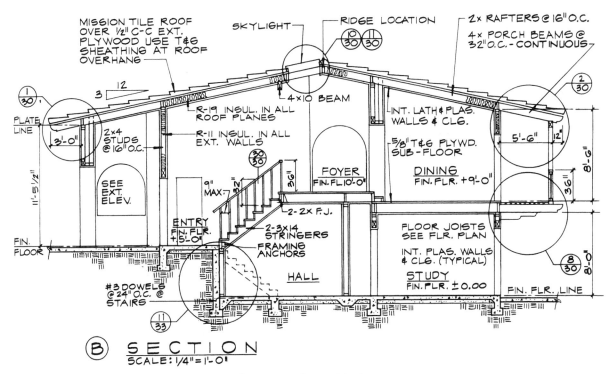

Figure 12.3 Building section. (Courtesy of William F. Smith—Builder.)

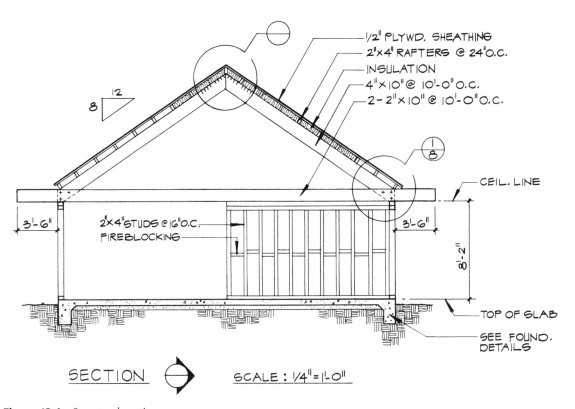

Figure 12.4 Structural section.

tions. A reference symbol (the number 1 over the number 8, in a reference bubble) is located at the roof framing and wall connection. This connection is made clear with an enlarged detail showing the exact location and size of bolts needed to satisfy the engineering requirements for that assembly. See Figure 12.5.

Number and Place of Sections

Draw as many building sections as you need to convey the greatest amount of information and clarity for those building the structure.

Usually, building sections are used to investigate various conditions that prevail in a structure. These sections can point out flaws in the building's structural integrity, and this information can lead to modifications in the initial design.

The number of building sections required varies according to the structural complexity of the particular building. Figures 12.6 and 12.7 illustrate two buildings varying in complexity. Figure 12.6 shows a rectangular building, which probably needs only two building sections to clearly provide all the information required. However, the building in Figure 12.7 requires at least five sections to provide all the structural information.

■ TYPES OF SECTIONS

Because the design and complexity of buildings vary, types of sections also vary.

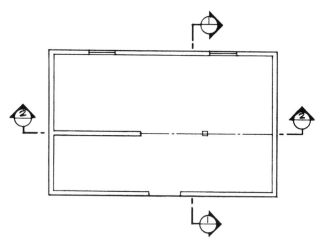

Figure 12.6   Two structural sections.

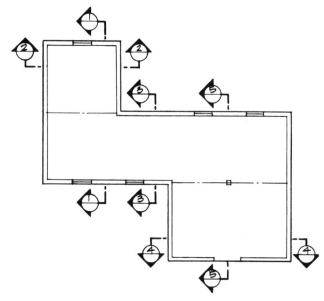

Figure 12.7   Five structural sections.

Wall Sections

Simple structural conditions may only require wall sections to convey the necessary building information. Structural sections for a small industrial building, for example, might use wall sections.

In most cases, wall sections can be drawn at larger scales such as $1/2'' = 1'-0''$. These larger scale drawings allow you to clearly elaborate building connections and call-outs without having to draw separate enlarged details.

Figures 12.8, 12.9, 12.10, 12.11 show an industrial building and also show how wall sections are incorporated into a set of construction documents. Figure 10.8 shows the floor plan with two main exterior and one in-

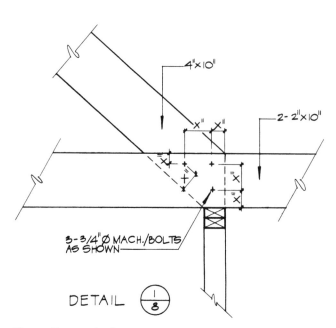

Figure 12.5   Bolted connection.

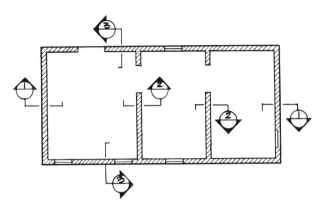

Figure 12.8 Floor plan—industrial building.

terior bearing wall conditions. These wall conditions are referenced to wall sections and are shown in Figures 12.9, 12.10, and 12.11.

To draw a wall section, first select a scale that clearly shows the wall and foundation assembly details as well as

adjacent structural members and components. Then, using wall section 1, Figure 12.9, as an example, draw and dimension the footing for the masonry wall. Because you are drawing at a large scale, you can note all the footing information directly on the wall section, thereby making separate foundation details unnecessary. Next draw the masonry wall using $8 \times 8 \times 16$ concrete block as the wall material. Because a modular unit is being used for the wall construction, a wall height is established that satisfies the 8" concrete block increments. Draw the roof-to-wall assembly at the desired height above the concrete floor, with the various framing connections and members needed to satisfy the structural requirements. After you finish the drawing, add notes for all members, steel reinforcing, bolts, and so forth. Other wall sections, as shown in Figures 12.10 and 12.11, are drawn and noted similarly. Note that while Figure 12.11 is similar to Figure 12.9, different roof framing conditions exist.

In short, large-scale wall sections allow the structural components and call-outs to be clearly drawn and usu-

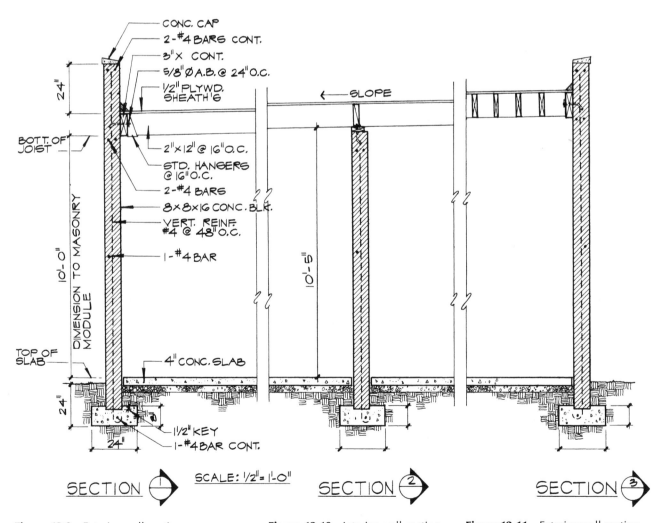

Figure 12.9 Exterior wall section.   **Figure 12.10** Interior wall section.   **Figure 12.11** Exterior wall section.

Full Sections

For projects with complex structural conditions you should draw an entire section. This gives you a better idea of the structural conditions in that portion of the building, which can then be analyzed, engineered, and clearly detailed.

Figure 12.12 shows a building section through a residence that has many framing complexities. Here you can clearly understand the need for a full section to see the existing conditions. To show the full section, you should draw this type of section in a smaller architectural scale, ¼" = 1'-0". Again, when you use a smaller scale for drawing sections, you must provide enlarged details of all relevant connections. The circled and referenced conditions in Figure 12.12, for example, will be detailed at a large scale.

Partial Sections

Many projects have only isolated areas of structural complexities. These areas are drawn in the same way as a cross-section, but they stop when the area of concern has been clearly drawn. This results in a partial section of a structural portion.

Figure 12.13 shows a partial section that illustrates the structural complexities existing in that portion. Additional detailing is required to make other assemblies clear.

One of these assemblies, for example, may require a partial framing elevation to show a specific roof framing condition. This condition may be referenced by the use of two circles—each with direction arrows, reference letters, and numbers—attached to a broken line. Figure 12.14 shows this partial framing elevation as referenced on Figure 12.13.

Steel Sections

For buildings built mainly with steel members, use elevations to establish column and beam heights. This approach coincides with the procedures and methods for the shop drawings provided by the steel fabricator.

Figure 12.15 shows a structural section through a steel-frame building. In contrast to sections for wood-frame buildings, where vertical dimensions are used to establish plate heights, this type of section may establish column and beam heights using the top of the concrete slab as a beginning point. Each steel column in this section has an assigned number because the columns are identified by the use of an axial reference matrix on the framing plan, shown in Figure 12.16.

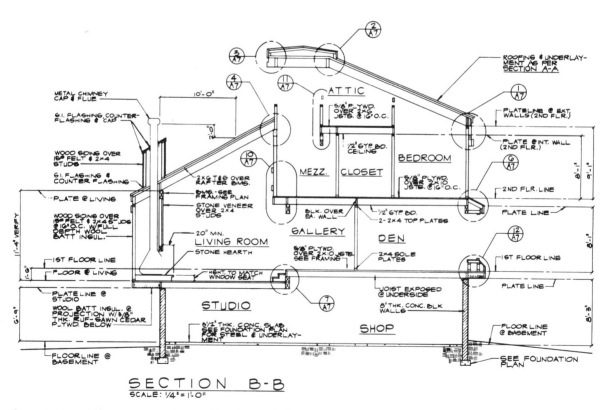

Figure 12.12   Full section. (Courtesy of Steve L. Martin.)

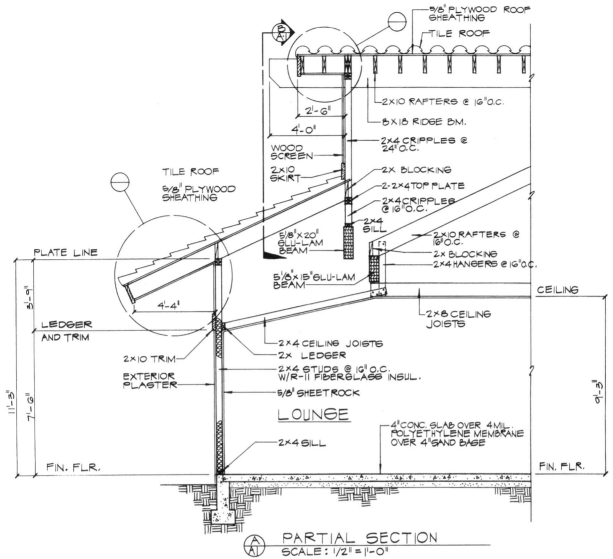

Figure 12.13 Partial section.

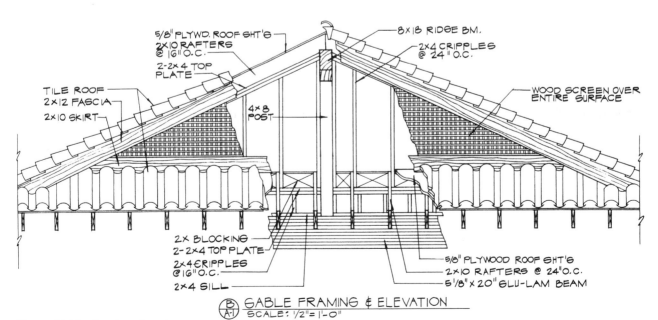

Figure 12.14 Framing elevation.

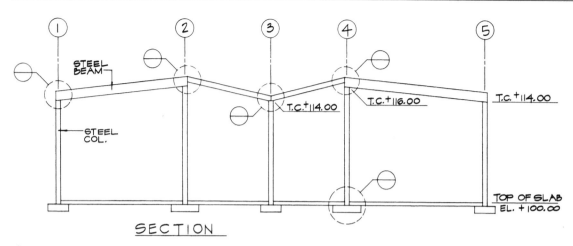

Figure 12.15 Steel frame section.

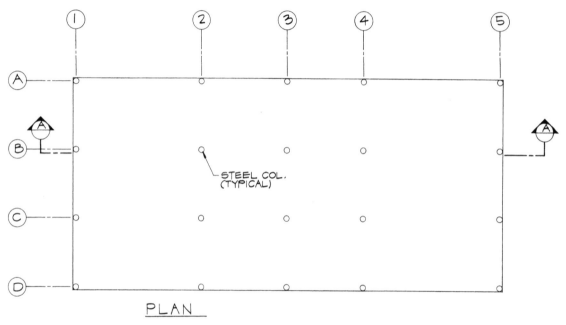

Figure 12.16 Column matrix.

■ EXAMPLES

These two examples of buildings show how their unique structural systems dictate different ways of showing a building section.

Example 1: A Theatre

The first building, constructed of masonry and steel, has a mainly symmetrical floor plan. Therefore, the structural design is similar for both sides, if not identical. As Figure 12.17 shows, the symmetry of this theatre may mean that only two major building sections are required. The first section has been taken through the lobby in the

East-West direction. The other has been taken through one side of the lobby in the North-South direction.

Draw the first building section, Figure 12.18 shows, by first lightly laying out the dimensional reference planes to accurately locate beams, columns, and walls relative to those shown on the floor plan in the East-West direction.

For this type of structure and its overall dimensions, a scale of ¼" = 1'-0" gives enough clarity for the members and required assemblies. Because the overall dimensions of the building are large and the area through the lobby is mainly open space, you may simply provide break lines between supporting members, as indicated between dimensional reference planes Ⓓ and Ⓔ, Ⓔ and Ⓕ,

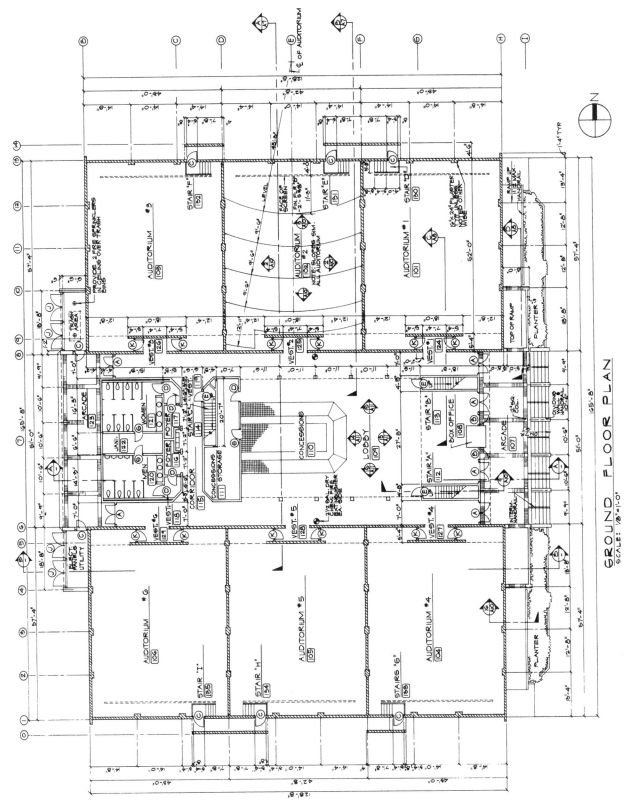

Figure 12.17 Theatre floor plan. (Courtesy of AVCO Community Developers, Inc.)

Ⓕ, and Ⓖ. This helps when the size of the vellum is restricted.

When you have drawn the foundation members and concrete floor, then draft wall locations and their respective heights in place. In this way, the second floor members are shown in their respective locations. The finished ceiling is attached directly to the bottom of the steel joist. Steel decking with a 2½″-thick concrete topping is drawn in as shown. From the second floor level, plate heights are set and then minimum roof pitches are drawn, establishing the roof height at reference planesⒹ and Ⓖ. You can now draw all the remaining structural members at their respective locations and heights.

Because the North and South auditoriums are identical in size and structural design, you may simply provide a section through one auditorium and the lobby. See Figure 12.19. This partial building section is delineated in the same way as Figure 12.18; first, the reference planes are laid out, and the foundation sections and the concrete floor are drawn relative to the foundation plan. The concrete floor slopes in the auditorium area. This slope ratio is determined by recommended seating and viewing standards for cinema theatres. Next, draw in the various walls and their heights.

The exterior masonry wall height at reference ⑬, established by the recommended interior ceiling height of 22′-0″, satisfies the required height for the viewing screen. From the top of this wall, you can draw in the steel decking and roof assembly at a roof pitch of 4 in 12. The ridge location is established by the reference number ⑩. From this point, a roof pitch of 10 in 12 is drawn to where it intersects the lobby roof along the dimensional reference line ⑨. All the structural members for the roof and walls within the lobby area are now drawn in and noted.

For reference, show a portion of the opposite identical side for this type of partial section. In Figure 12.19 this is indicated at reference line ⑤, the back wall of the opposite auditorium. Use the correct material designation for the wall, floor, and roof materials.

Example 2: A Three-Story Office Building

This three-story office building has structural steel beams and columns as the main supporting members. Spanning the steel beams, open web **trusses** are used for the floor joists. Plywood and lightweight concrete are installed directly above the joists. Supporting members, at the ground floor level, are composed of steel columns encased in concrete, and masonry walls located at the lobby and stairway areas.

Figure 12.20 shows the ground floor plan for this structure and the dimensional axial reference planes for column and wall locations. Building section cuts have been referenced in the North-South and East-West directions.

The floor plan for the second and third levels, which are similar, is provided so that the building sections can be drawn. See Figure 12.21.

The first section to draw is SectionⒶ. This is taken between reference planesⒹ and Ⓔ in the East-West direction. Begin the drawing by lightly laying out the reference planes and incorporating section break lines between the reference planes as indicated between beam lines ④ and ⑤ as well as between ⑥ and ⑦. See Figure 12.22A, building sectionⒶ.

Starting from the lobby's finished floor elevation of 100.0, we establish a clearance height of approximately 8′-0″ in the parking area, in which the **soffit** (finished underside of spanning members) framing elevation is designated at 108.00. Now, consult with the structural and mechanical engineers about what space is required for structural members and plumbing lines. In this case, a height of 4′-10″ satisfies their requirements, thus establishing a second floor elevation of 112.8. From the second to the third floor level, a height of 14′-0″ is required to satisfy the space requirements for structural and mechanical members, as well as for the desired suspended ceiling height. The space required for mechanical and electrical components is called the **plenum area**. An example of this is shown on Figure 12.22B.

A top plate height of 12′-0″ or an elevation of 139.33 establishes the exterior wall height, from which point the roof pitch will be drawn. Roof rafters are drawn in with a roof pitch of 4 in 12, extending 2 feet beyond the exterior walls to provide support for the soffit framing. The steel roof beams at the various reference numbers are drawn in at various elevations to provide adequate roof drainage for the various drains located in the roof well area.

These elevations are shown at the various beam locations. From these locations, wood members are framed between the main steel beams which provide the required roof pitches. When all the required members have been drafted in, the various notes and dimensions can be lettered accordingly. When you provide notes, organize lettering as shown on reference lines ⑤, ⑦, and ⑩ in Figure 12.22A.

Building sectionⒸ, cut in the North-South direction, is shown in Figure 12.23. This section is drawn in the same way as building sectionⒶ. However, many of the notes have not been shown because they are identical to those noted in sectionⒶ. This is acceptable practice as long as you make clear they are identical, as is done in his case at the bottom of reference Ⓕ. In this way, changes can be made on one drawing and also corrected elsewhere. The section shown in Figure 12.23 was taken through an area with many elements relevant to the construction process.

The checklist (opposite, top) covers the basic information that should be found on building sections as well as characteristics of a well-thought-out set of sections.

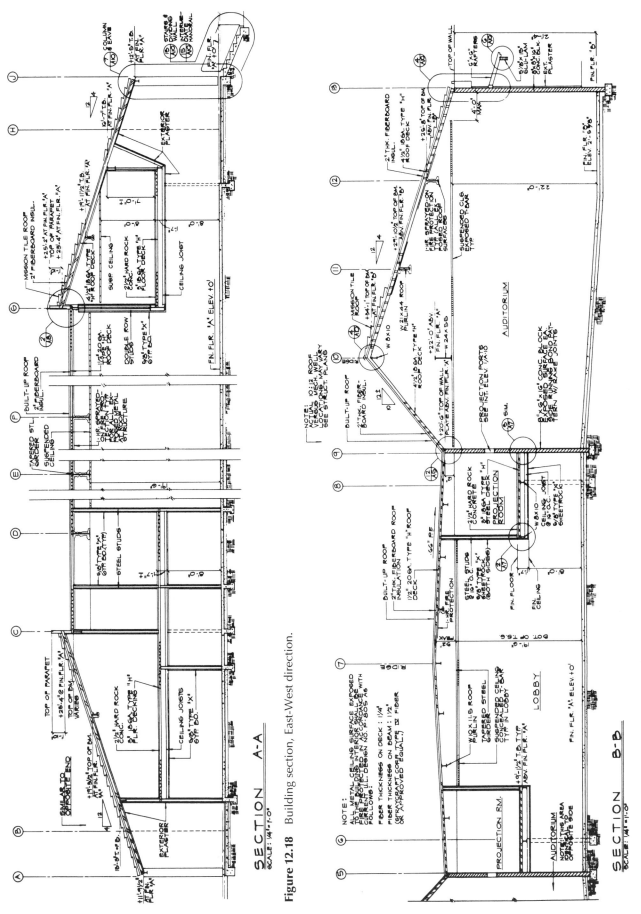

Figure 12.18 Building section, East-West direction.

Figure 12.19 Building section, North-South direction.

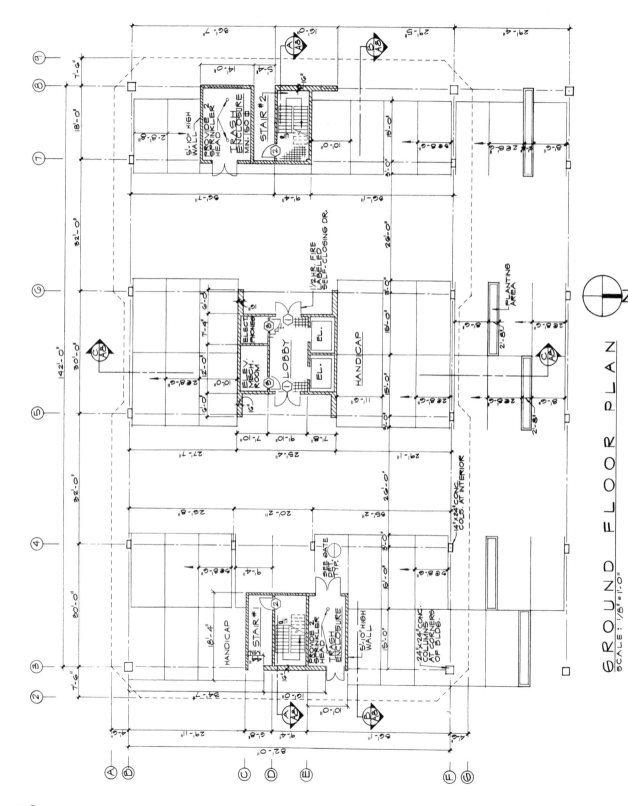

Figure 12.20 Ground floor plan—office building. (Courtesy of Westmount, Inc., Real Estate Development, Torrance, CA.)

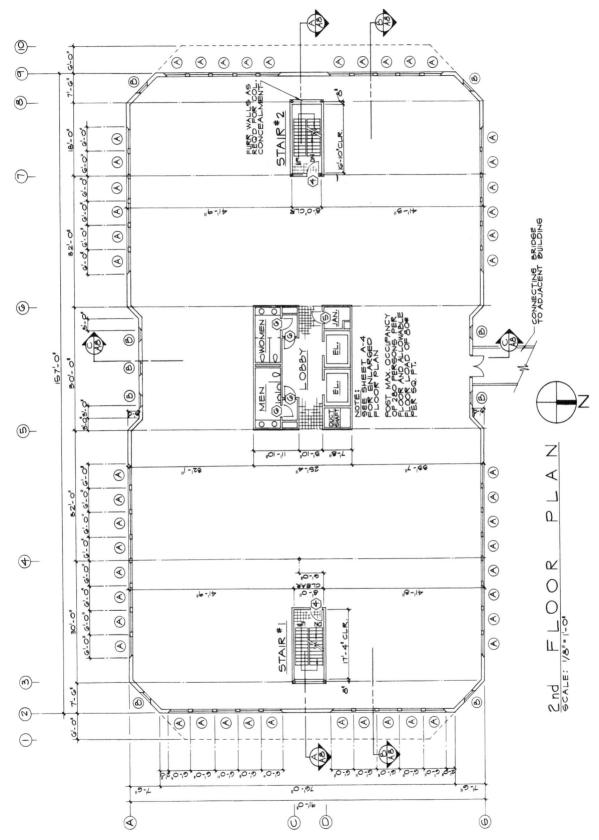

Figure 12.21 Floor plan—second level of office building. (Courtesy of Westmount, Inc., Real Estate Development, Torrance, CA.)

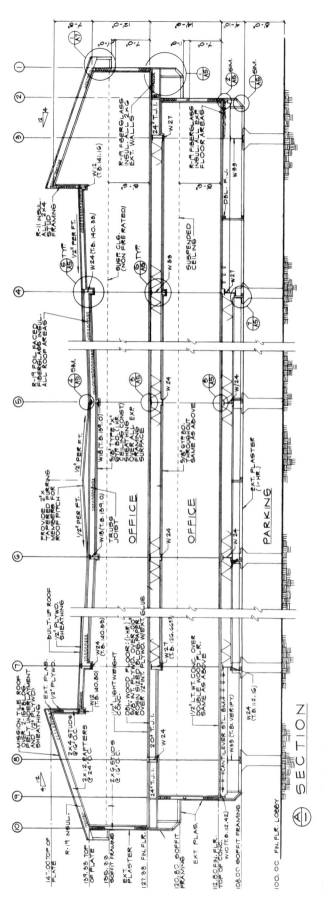

Figure 12.22A Office building section—East-West direction. (Courtesy of Westmount, Inc., Real Estate Development, Torrance, CA.)

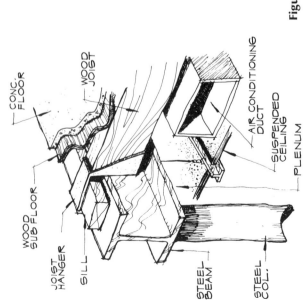

CONC. FLOOR

WOOD JOIST

WOOD SUB FLOOR

JOIST HANGER

SILL

AIR CONDITIONING DUCT

SUSPENDED CEILING

PLENUM

STEEL BEAM

STEEL COL.

Figure 12.22B Plenum area.

Building Sections Checklist

1. Sections that clearly depict the structural conditions existing in the building
2. Sections referenced on plans and elevations
3. Dimensioning for the following (where applicable):
   a. Floor to top plate
   b. Floor to floor
   c. Floor to ceiling
   d. Floor to top of wall
   e. Floor to top of column or beam
   f. Cantilevers, overhangs, offsets, etc.
   g. Foundation details
4. Elevations for top of floor, top of columns and beams
5. Call-out information for all members, such as:
   a. Size. material, and shape of member
   b. Spacing of members
6. Call-out information for all assemblies if enlarged details are not provided
7. Column and beam matrix identification if incorporated in the structural plan
8. Call-out for sub-floor and sheathing assembly
9. Roof pitches and indication of all slopes
10. Reference symbols for all details and assemblies that are enlarged for clarity
11. Designation of material for protection of finish for roof, ceiling, wall, and structural members
12. Structural notes applicable to each particular section, such as:
    a. Nailing schedules
    b. Splice dimensions
13. Structural sections corresponding accurately to foundation, floor, and framing plans
14. Scale of drawing provided

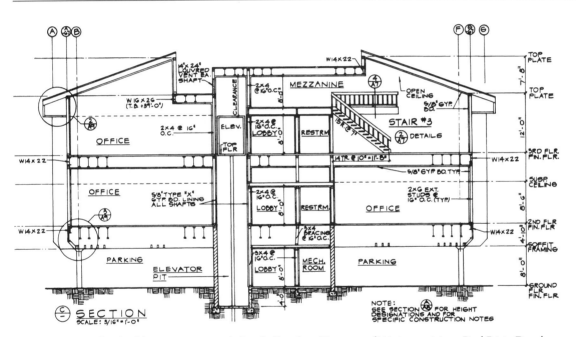

Figure 12.23 Office building section—North-South direction. (Courtesy of Westmount, Inc., Real Estate Development, Torrance, CA.)

■ DRAFTING A BUILDING SECTION

After deciding where a section is to be taken that reveals the greatest amount of the structure, a grid pattern is drafted. The horizontal lines of the grid represent the floor line and the plate line (at the top of the two top plates). All of the vertical lines represent the walls of the structure or column locations. See Figure 12.24.

The section should be drawn at as large a scale a the drawing sheet allows. A scale of ½" = 1'-0" is ideal, but because of the size of the structure or the limits of the sheet, a scale of ³/8" = 1'-0" or even ¼" = 1'-0" might be used.

Before you decide on a smaller scale, explore the possibility of removing portions of the building that are re-dundant by virtue of break lines. See Figures 12.9, 12.18, and 12.22A. If the building is symmetrical, a partial section, as shown in Figure 12.13, may suffice.

Looking at the cartoons, the project manager may have already made this decision.

From Floor Plan to Building Section

If the building section is to be drawn at the same scale as the floor plan, the drafter need only transfer measurements by scaling, or, better yet, by using a pair of dividers. If the building section is drafted at twice the size of the floor plan, one can simply transfer the measurements by reading the ½" scale or, as mentioned earlier,

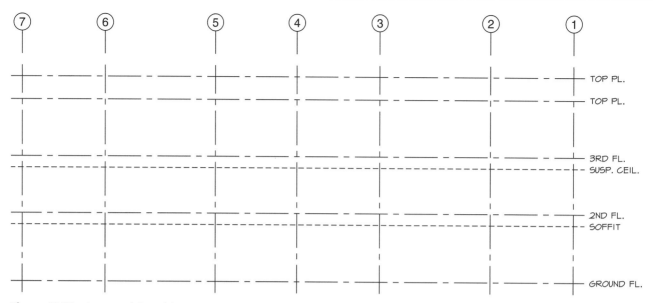

Figure 12.24 Layout of the grid pattern.

by using a divider and pace the distance off twice with the divider.

Let's say that the floor plan was drawn at $^1\!/_4''$ scale and the building section is to be drawn at $^3\!/_8''$ scale. A proportional divider is used. See Figure 12.25. There is a set of numbers on this particular instrument, which are proportions; $^1\!/_4$ is two-thirds of $^3\!/_8$, the proportional divider is set at the $^2\!/_3$ setting. If 6'-0" is measured on the top (the smaller side) at $^1\!/_4''$ scale, the instrument will translate the 6'-0" distance on the bottom side, but at a $^3\!/_8''$ scale. Thus, by using the proportional divider, one can easily transfer measurements from one drawing to another even if the scale is different.

With the computer you do not have a problem with scale, because the floor plan and the building section, along with the entire set of construction documents, are drawn full-scale in model space. Only when you import the drawings into paper space do you need to add a scaling factor (see Chapter 3). To reproduce a drawing at a $^1\!/_4'' = 1'\,0''$ scale and a building section at $^3\!/_8'' = 1'\,0''$ to fit the paper becomes as easy to do as when plotting.

If the floor plan was drawn in paper space at a scale of $^1\!/_4'' = 1'\,0''$ rather than full-scale in model space, the scaling factor can be changed quickly from the $^1\!/_4''$ plan to a $^3\!/_8'$ scale. It can be changed to any scale with ease on a computer.

Pitch

If there is a pitch (an angle) involved and it is constant, an adjustable triangle is handy. If the building section is drafted at the top of the sheet, the adjustable triangle can be positioned with ease. Had the building section been drafted at the bottom of the sheet, using the adjustable

triangle can be cumbersome. See Figure 12.26. This is because of the distance between the base of the triangle and the desired angle. In this instance it would be easier to actually measure the pitch. If you have a template, look for a pitch scale printed on its side. If you are in the market for a plan template, check the various brands carefully, because there are templates that will measure

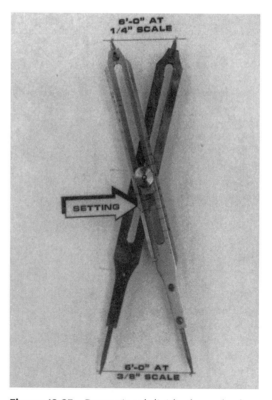

Figure 12.25 Proportional divider for scale change.

pitch, have markings for typical heights of equipment from the floor, and even plot spacing, such as for 4" and 6" tile, 16, spacing for stud and joist position, and door swings, among other items.

Another alternative is to make your own pitch template using an ink marking on your triangle. This ink tick mark can be saved by covering it with clear fingernail polish. See Figure 12.27A. Still better would be to start with an index away from the end or point of the triangle, which might be slightly rounded, and because of the rounded form it might be difficult to find the beginning point of the pitch. See Figure 12.27B.

If you understand the process of drafting a building section, you might develop a shortcut method. For example, if you have access to a plain paper copier that enlarges and reduces, it would be a simple matter of reproducing, to the proper scale, an eave detail with the same pitch on an acetate sheet, place it under the building section, and trace. It is reproduced onto an acetate sheet so that it can be flipped over and used on the opposite side of the building section as the shape and pitch reverse direction. See a sample being used in Figure 12.28.

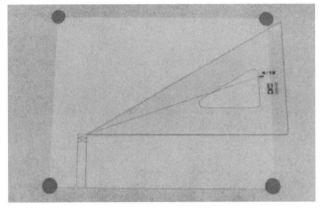

A

Figure 12.26 Use of adjustable triangle at the bottom of the drawing.

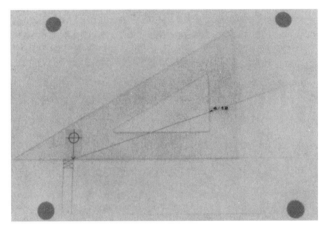

B

Figure 12.27 Triangle formatted for pitch.

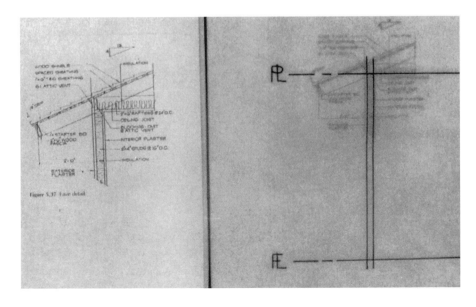

Figure 12.28 Acetate template.

■ DRAFTING A BUILDING SECTION OF ADLI RESIDENCE

The building section is second only to the floor plan in importance because it reveals how the building is assembled and describes the individual parts. The building section becomes the source for the discovery of essential details such as the base for the exterior elevation. In many instances the building section reveals potential problems in the intersection of walls, floors, ceilings, and roof.

From a three-dimensional model, the building section can be sliced or sectioned, flattened and drafted. The various construction members, such as the studs and rafters, can then be rotated in a three-dimensional model to explain the construction features that are not readily obvious in a two-dimensional drawing.

STAGE I (Figure 12.29). If a flattened 3-D section is available, this then becomes the datum for future stages. All wall locations, plate heights, and level changes must be verified and corrected at this stage. If a flattened model is not available, the first stage of a 2-D drawing, as shown in Figure 12.29, will establish the base or datum. The drafter may start by establish-

ing the grade and its relationship with the floor line. Using this floor line as the main baseline, the plate lines and floor lines of subsequent floors can be established and measured. In larger buildings, measurement may be in decimals. This is particularly true in steel structures where the tips of the columns and tops of the floor girders are critical during installation.

STAGE II (Figure 12.30). The outline of the structure is now positioned, including the roof. On 3-D drawings the walls are already positioned, but in a 2-D drawing, the walls need to be positioned by aligning the datum lines with a partial floor plan where the cut occurs (see Figure 12.31).

STAGE III (Figure 12.32). The thicknesses or widths of the foundation, walls, ceiling, and roof are drawn in this stage. Everything is drawn to net size, not nominal

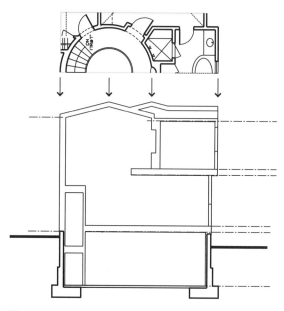

Figure 12.31   Stage III: Aligning datum with floor plan.

Figure 12.29   Stage I: Establishing datum.

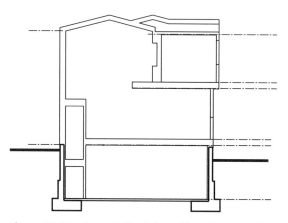

Figure 12.30   Stage II: Outlining of foundation, walls, and roof.

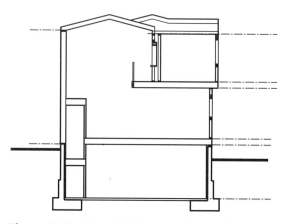

Figure 12.32   Stage III: Sizing members and outlining configuration.

size, to produce an accurate assembly drawing. Previously drafted details showing similar shapes and parts can be imported and used.

STAGE IV (Figure 12.33). This is said to be the most enjoyable stage, because the building begins to take on character with the addition of material designations and the array of the end views of ceiling joists, floor joists, and rafters. Concrete takes on its own character adjacent to grade (soil).

STAGE V (Figure 12.34). If Stage IV is the most enjoyable stage, Stage V is the most critical to the accuracy of the project. All vertical dimensions are established at this stage. The most critical aspects are the dimensions for the floor to plate and defining the neutral zones on the project (see the section on the dimensional reference system in Chapter 2). Horizontal dimensions should not appear in this stage, but rather on the floor plan, with the exception of describing the

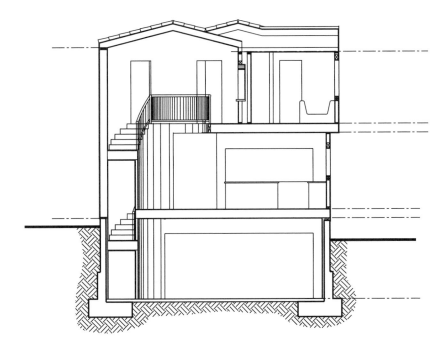

Figure 12.33 Stage IV: Materials designation, array joists.

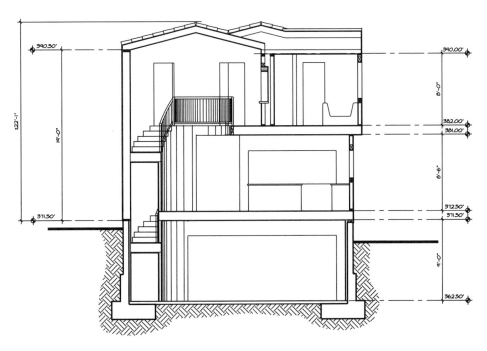

Figure 12.34 Stage V: Dimensioning.

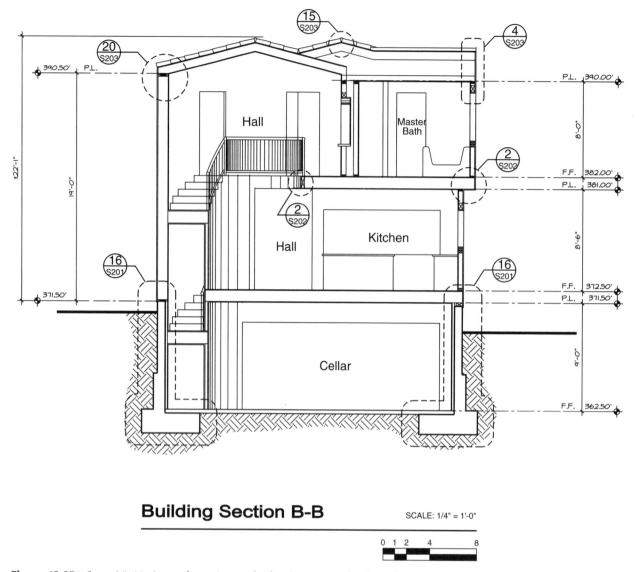

Building Section B-B

SCALE: 1/4" = 1'-0"

0 1 2   4   8

Figure 12.35 Stage VI: Noting, referencing, and titles. (Courtesy of Mike Adli, Owner; Nagy R. Bakhoum, President of Obelisk Architects.)

shape of a soffit or any other feature not seen in the floor plan.

STAGE VI (Figure 12.35). All notes and referencing are included in this stage. Notes should be generic if the specific materials are described in the specifications. Titles must be given to all of the parts, including the names of rooms through which the section cut occurs.

Reference bubbles are positioned and are referred to footing details, eave details, stair details, and so on. Remember, the title is a name given to this building section. If it is a full section, as in our example, two letters are used—for example, X-X, Y-Y, Z-Z. The first letter indicates the beginning of the section, and the second letter, the end of the cut.

EXTERIOR ELEVATIONS

■ INTRODUCTION TO EXTERIOR ELEVATIONS

Purpose

Exterior elevations are an important part of a set of construction documents because they can show information not found anywhere else in the set.

The exterior elevations will:

1. Describe exterior materials found on the structure.
2. Provide a location for horizontal and vertical dimensions not found elsewhere.
3. Show, by using hidden lines, structural members that are found inside the walls. (Diagonal bracing is a good example of such hidden members.)
4. Show the relationship of two elements such as the height of the chimney in relationship to the roof of the structure.
5. Incorporate reference bubbles for building, window, and door sections.
6. Show any exterior design elements that cannot be shown elsewhere.

Basic Approach

In mechanical or engineering drafting, the elevations are described as the front, side, and rear. In architecture, exterior elevations are called North, South, East, and West. See Figure 13.1. Figure 13.2 shows how we arrive at the names for exterior elevations.

Orientation

The North, South, East, and West elevations may not be true North or true East. They may have been taken from

an "orientation North," or as it has been called in other regions, "Plan North," which may not be parallel to true North. For example, if a structure's boundaries are not parallel with true North, an orientation North is established, and used from then on to describe the various elevations. See Figure 13.3.

These terms, then, refer to the direction the structure is facing. In other words, if an elevation is drawn of the face of a structure that is facing south, the elevation is called the South elevation; the face of the structure that is facing west is called the West elevation, and so on. Remember, the title refers to the direction the structure is facing, *not* to the direction in which you are looking at it.

Finally, because of the size of the exterior elevations, they are rarely drawn next to the plan view as in mechanical drafting. See Figure 13.4.

Method 1: Direct Projection

Exterior elevations can be drafted by directly projecting sizes from the plan views or sections. Figure 13.5 shows

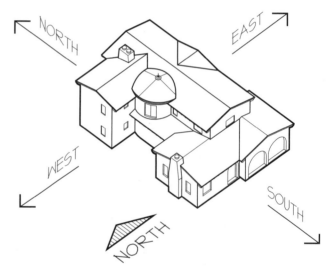

Figure 13.2 Names of elevations. (Courtesy of Mike Adli, Owner; Nagy R. Bakhoum, President of Obelisk Architects.)

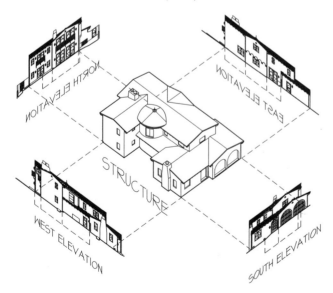

Figure 13.1 Multiview drawing of a structure. (Courtesy of Mike Adli, Owner; Nagy R. Bakhoum, President of Obelisk, Architects.)

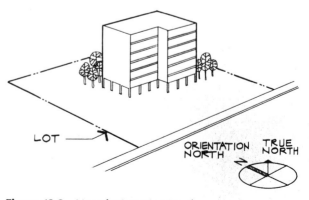

Figure 13.3 Use of orientation North.

East Elevation

North Elevation

West Elevation

South Elevation

Figure 13.4 Elevation arrangement. (Courtesy of Mike Adli, Owner; Nagy R. Bakhoum, President of Obelisk Architects.)

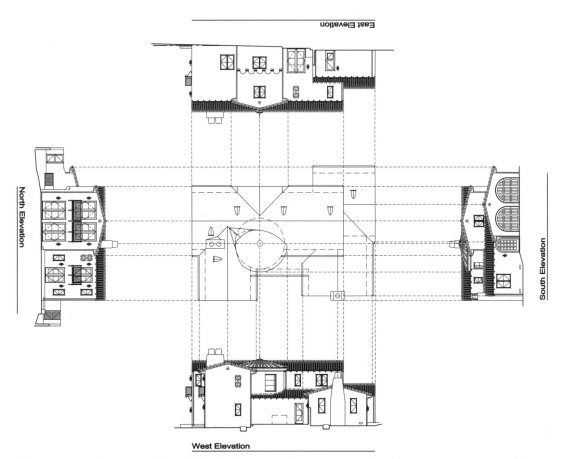

East Elevation

North Elevation

South Elevation

West Elevation

Figure 13.5 Obtaining width and depth dimensions. (Courtesy of Mike Adli, Owner; Nagy R. Bakhoum, President of Obelisk Architects.)

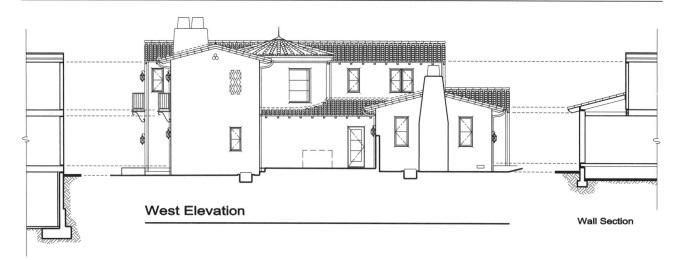

West Elevation

Wall Section

Wall Section

Figure 13.6 Heights from wall sections. (Courtesy of Mike Adli, Owner; Nagy R. Bakhoum, President of Obelisk Architects.)

how elevations can be directly projected from a plan view (a roof plan in this case). Figure 13.6 shows how the heights are obtained. Locations of doors, windows, and other details are taken from the floor plan. Figure 13.7 shows a slightly more complex roof being used to form the roof shape on an elevation.

Method 2: Dimensional Layout

Exterior elevations can also be drafted by taking the dimensions from the plans and sections and drafting the elevation from scratch. First, lightly lay out the critical

vertical measurements. In the example shown in Figure 13.8, these measurements are the subfloor line and the plate line (top of the two top plates above the studs). See Figure 13.9A. This measurement is taken directly from the building section.

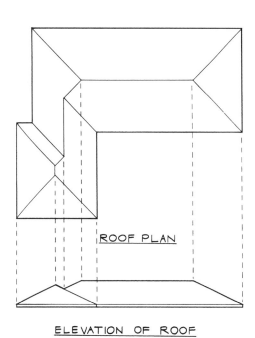

ROOF PLAN

ELEVATION OF ROOF

Figure 13.7 Roof elevation from roof plan.

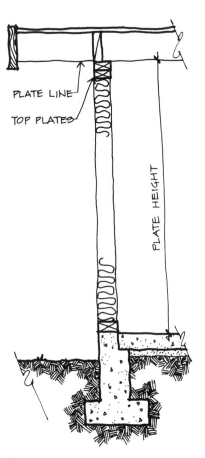

PLATE LINE

TOP PLATES

PLATE HEIGHT

Figure 13.8 Subfloor to plate line.

The second step establishes the location of the walls and offsets in the structure from the floor plan. Draw these lines lightly because changes in line length may be required later. See Figure 13.9B.

Third, establish the grade line (earth) in relationship to the floor line. See Figure 13.9C. This dimension is from the building sections or footing sections.

Next, as Figure 13.9D shows, the roof configuration is added. To better understand the relationship between the roof and structure, draw the **eave** in a simple form as shown in Figure 13.9E. These dimensions are found on the building section. The finished roof shape depends on the roof framing plan or the roof plan for dimensions. See Figure 13.9F.

Finally, windows and doors are located. Sizes are found on the window and door schedule, and locations on the floor plan. Material designations, dimensions, notes, and structural descriptions complete the elevation. See Figure 13.9G.

To help you visualize the transition from a drafted elevation to the actual building, see Figures 13.10 and

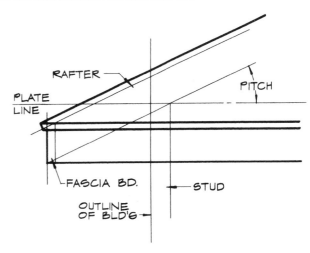

Figure 13.9E   Rough eave detail.

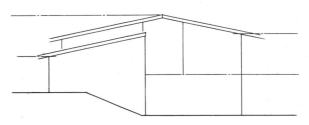

Figure 13.9F   Finishing the roof shape.

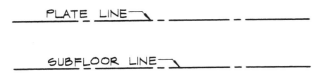

Figure 13.9A   Establishing floor and plate lines.

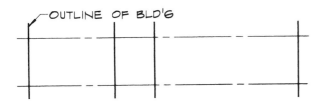

Figure 13.9B   Drafting exterior outline.

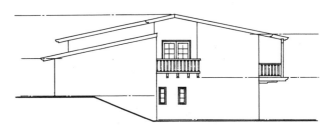

Figure 13.9G   Locating doors and windows.

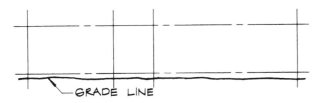

Figure 13.9C   Establishing the grade line.

Figure 13.9D   Incorporating the roof structure into the exterior elevation.

13.11. Compare the drafted elevation with the photograph.

Choice of Scale

Selection of the scale for elevations is based on the size and complexity of the project and the available drawing space. For small structures, $1/4'' = 1'-0''$ is a common scale. For a larger project, a smaller scale can be used. The exterior elevation is usually drawn at the same scale as the floor plan. For medium and large elevations, you may have to decrease the scale in relationship to the floor plans.

Because we are dealing with small structures, two to four stories in height, we are using the largest scale allowed by the available drawing space not exceeding $1/4'' = 1'0''$.

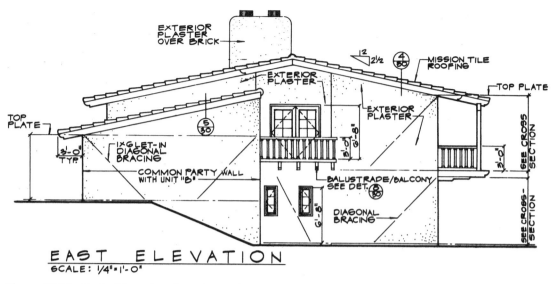

EXTERIOR
PLASTER
OVER BRICK

12
2½

MISSION TILE
ROOFING

4
30

EXTERIOR
PLASTER

TOP PLATE

EXTERIOR
PLASTER

TOP
PLATE

5
30

3'-0"
TYP.

1×6 LET-IN
DIAGONAL
BRACING

COMMON PARTY WALL
WITH UNIT "B"

6'-0"

3'-0"

BALUSTRADE/BALCONY
SEE DET.
8
30

DIAGONAL
BRACING

6'-0"

3'-0"

SEE CROSS SECTION

SEE CROSS SECTION

EAST ELEVATION
SCALE: 1/4" = 1'-0"

Figure 13.10   Drafted East elevation of a condominium. (Courtesy of William F. Smith—Builder.)

Figure 13.11   Pictorial view of South elevation of a condominium. (Courtesy of William F. Smith—Builder; Aerial photography by William Boggs. Reprinted with permission.)

Odd-Shaped Plans

Not all plans are rectangular; some have irregular shapes and angles. Figure 13.12 shows several building shapes and the North designation. For these kinds of conditions, all elevations are drawn.

Shape A.   Figure 13.13 shows the exterior elevations for a relatively simple L-shaped building and how these elevations were obtained using the projection method.

Shape B.   The elevations for Shape B in Figure 13.14 present a unique problem on the East and particularly the South elevation. Because the fence is in the same plane

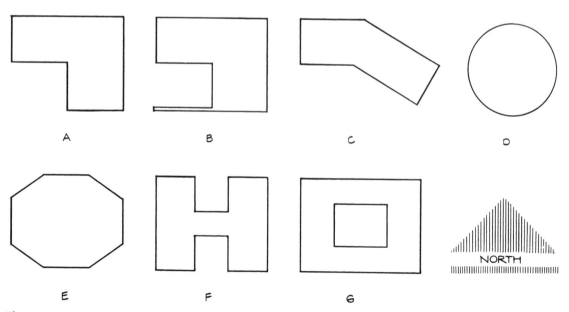

A   B   C   D

E   F   G

NORTH

Figure 13.12   Irregularly shaped plans.

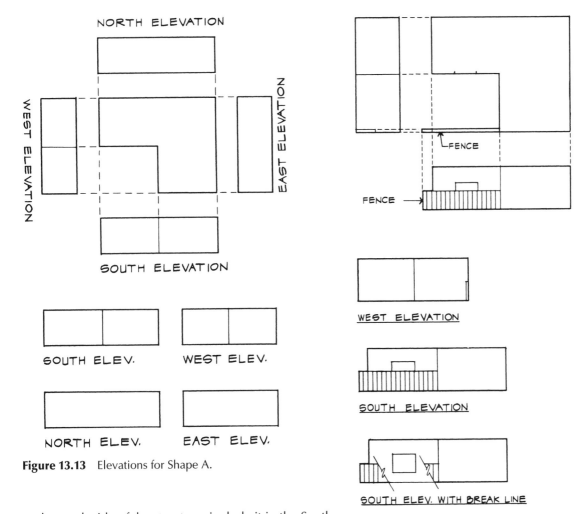

NORTH ELEVATION

WEST ELEVATION

EAST ELEVATION

SOUTH ELEVATION

SOUTH ELEV.   WEST ELEV.

NORTH ELEV.   EAST ELEV.

Figure 13.13 Elevations for Shape A.

FENCE

FENCE →

WEST ELEVATION

SOUTH ELEVATION

SOUTH ELEV. WITH BREAK LINE

Figure 13.14 Elevations for Shape B.

as the south side of the structure, include it in the South elevation. Had the fence been in front of the structure, you could either delete it or include it in order to show its relationship to the structure itself.

The inclusion of the fence may pose additional problems, such as preventing a view of portions of the structure behind. You can overcome this difficulty in one of two ways: Either eliminate the fence altogether (not show it) or use a break line, as shown in Figure 13.14. This allows any item behind it, such as the window, to be exposed, referenced, and dimensioned. Break lines still allow dimensioning and descriptions of the fence.

Shape C.   The two portions on the right of the South elevation and all of the East elevation are *not* true shapes and sizes because they are drawn as direct 90° projections from the *left* portion of the plan view. This is sometimes a problem. See Figure 13.15. The West and North elevations will also have distortions. See Figure 13.12.

To solve this problem, we use an auxiliary view: a view that is 90° to the line of sight. The elevations are projected 90° to the sight lines and a break line is used to stop that portion which is not true. Notice on Figure 13.16 how the break line splits the South elevation into

two parts. Each part is projected independently of the other, and its continuation, which is not a true shape, is voided.

The South elevation in Figure 13.15 appears to have three parts rather than two, as in Figure 13.16. In the latter case, the third part will be left to the East elevation. With a more complex shape, a break line beyond the true surface being projected can be confusing. See Figure 13.17. To avoid confusion, introduce a pivot point (P.P.) and show it as a dotted (hidden) line or a centerline type line (dots and dashes). See Figure 13.18. Use a **pivot point**. (A pivot point is the point at which the end of one elevation becomes the beginning of another elevation.)

Pivot points can cause a problem in selecting a title for a particular elevation. To avoid confusion, introduce a **key plan**. The key plan is usually drawn on the bottom right corner of the drawing sheet. See Figure 13.19. Draw and label a reference bubble for every necessary elevation. These reference bubbles will become the title for

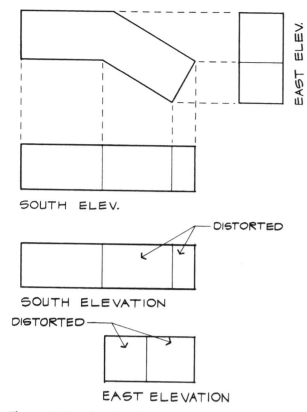

SOUTH ELEV.

DISTORTED

SOUTH ELEVATION

DISTORTED

EAST ELEVATION

Figure 13.15 Elevations for Shape C.

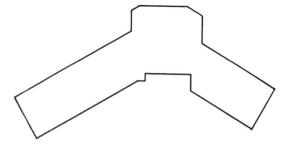

Figure 13.17 Complicated shape.

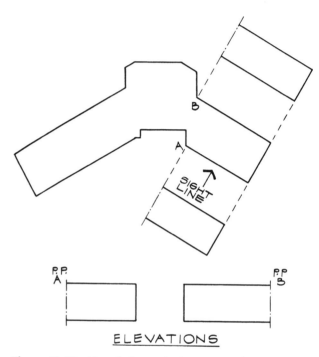

B

A

SIGHT LINE

P.P. A

P.P. B

ELEVATIONS

Figure 13.18 Use of pivot point in exterior elevations.

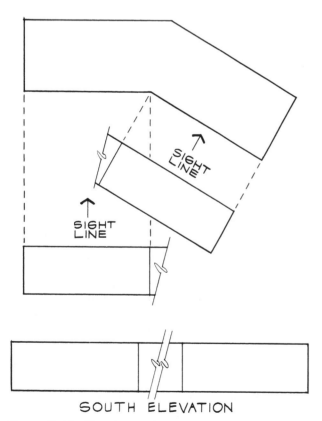

SIGHT LINE

SIGHT LINE

SOUTH ELEVATION

Figure 13.16 Elevations with new sight line. (William Boggs Aerial Photography. Printed with permission.)

the elevation. If the surface contains important information about the structure or surface materials, it deserves a reference bubble. Figure 13.20 shows how these elevations are represented with titles and pivot point notations.

Shape D. With Shape D, in Figure 13.12, nothing is true shape and size, regardless of the direction of the elevation. See Figure 13.21. Figure 13.22 shows a pivot point together with a fold-out (called a "development drawing" in mechanical drawing).

Shape E. Shape E in Figure 13.12 can be drawn in one of three ways: first, drawing it as a direct projection so that one of the three exposed faces will be in true shape and size; second, using a key plan and drawing each surface individually; and third, drawing it as a fold-out similar to Figure 13.22. Choose the method that will explain the elevations best. For example, if all other sides are the

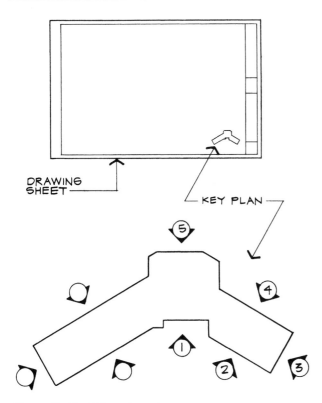

Figure 13.19   Using a key plan.

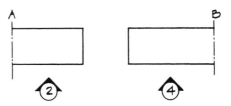

Figure 13.20   Elevations using key plan.

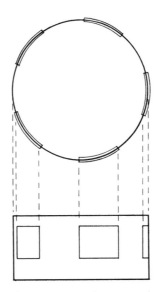

Figure 13.21   Elevations of a cylinder.

same, the direct projection method may be the best. If every wall surface is different, then the key plan or fold-out method is best.

Shape F.   Surfaces that will be hidden in a direct projection, such as some of the surfaces of Shape F in Figure 13.12, can effectively be dealt with in one of two ways.

The first uses a key plan and the second uses a combination of an elevation and a section. Both methods are shown in Figure 13.23. The combination of the section and the elevation shows the structure and its relationship to the elevation more clearly.

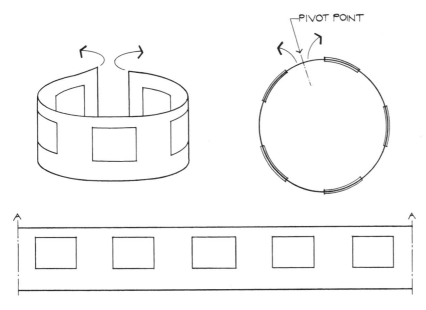

Figure 13.22   Elevation of cylinder using pivot point.

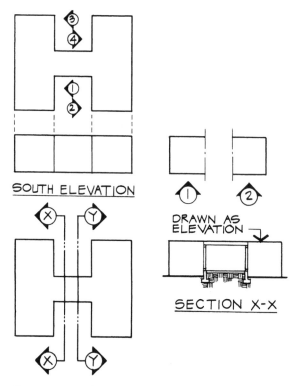

Figure 13.23 Elevations for Shape F.

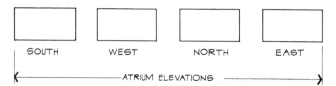

Figure 13.24 Simplified elevation titles.

Shape G. Shape G in Figure 13.12 can be drawn simply as the South elevation, North elevation, East elevation, and West elevation using a direct projection method. The interior space (atrium) can also be drawn as a direct projection with titles "Atrium North Elevation," "Atrium South Elevation," "Atrium East Elevation," and "Atrium West Elevation." A way to simplify this is shown in Figure 13.24.

■ DRAWING DOORS AND WINDOWS

Draw doors and windows on elevations as closely as possible to the actual configuration. Horizontal location dimensions need not be included because they are on the floor plan; and door and window sizes are contained in the door and window schedule. However, vertical location dimensions are shown with indications of how the doors and windows open.

Doors

Doors and their surface materials can be delineated in various ways. Illustrations A and B in Figure 13.25 show the basic appearance of a door with and without surface materials—wood grain in this instance. Illustration C shows the final configuration of a dimensioned door. Note that the 6'-8" dimension is measured from the floor line to the top of the floor. The other line around the door represents the trim. For precise dimensions for the trim, consult the door details. Illustrations D and E of Figure 13.25 show how a door opens or slides. Panel doors are

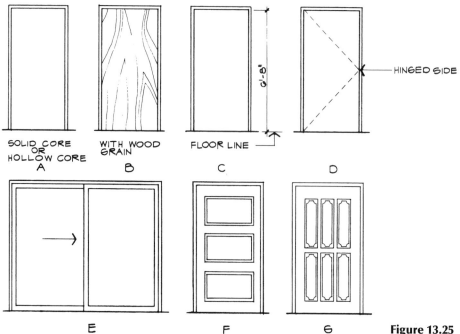

Figure 13.25 Doors in elevation.

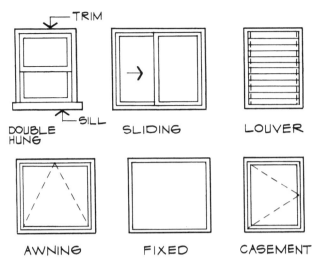

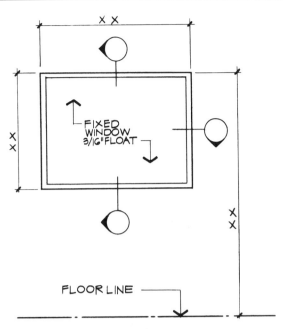

Figure 13.26 Windows in elevation.

Figure 13.27 A fixed window.

shown in illustration F, and plant-on doors (doors with decorative pieces attached) are shown in illustration G.

Windows

Windows are drafted much like doors. Their shape, their operation, and the direction in which they open are represented. Double-hung windows and louver windows are obvious exceptions because of their operation. See Figure 13.26.

On the double-hung and the sliding windows, one portion of the window is shown in its entirety, whereas the moving section shows only three sides of the window. Using the sliding window as an example, the right side of the window shows all four sides because it is on the outside. The left section shows only three sides because the fourth is behind the right section.

Fixed Windows. If the window is fixed (nonopening), as shown in Figure 13.27, you must know whether the window is to be shop made (manufactured ahead of time) or constructed on the job. If the frame can be ordered—in aluminum, for example—treat it like other manufactured windows and include it in the window schedule. If the window is to be job made (made on the site), provide all the necessary information about the window on the window schedule or exterior elevations as shown in Figure 13.28. However, keep all this information in one place for consistency and uniformity.

Referencing Doors and Windows

Reference doors and windows with bubbles. Bubbles can refer to details or to a schedule for size. See Figure 13.28. If, for some reason, there are no schedules or details for a set of drawings, all information pertaining to

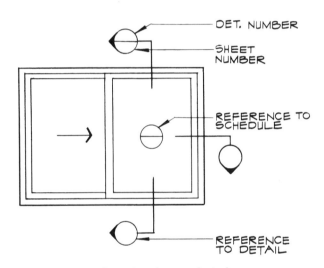

Figure 13.28 Referencing doors and windows.

the windows or doors will be on the exterior elevations near or on the windows and doors. See Figure 13.27.

■ MATERIAL DESIGNATIONS

Describing the Materials

The exterior elevations also describe the exterior wall surface material. For a wood structure, describe both the surface covering and any backing material. **Wood siding**, for example, is described with the backing behind it. See Figure 13.29.

In some cases, one word, such as "stucco," describes the surface adequately unless a special pattern is to be

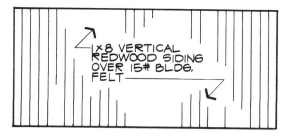

Figure 13.29   Wood siding in elevation.

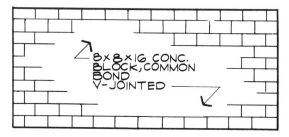

Figure 13.30   Concrete block in elevation.

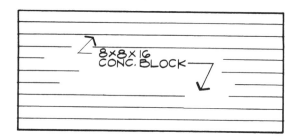

Figure 13.31   Abbreviated concrete block pattern.

applied. Here, the draftsperson assumes that the contractor understands that the word "stucco" implies building paper (black waterproof paper) mesh (hexagonal woven wire), and three coats of exterior plaster. Often a more detailed description of the material is found in the specifications.

Even if the complete wall is made up of one material such as concrete block (as opposed to a built-up system as in wood construction), describe the surface. See Figure 13.30.

Drawing the Materials

In both Figures 13.29 and 13.30 a facsimile of the material is shown. The material represented does not fill the complete area but is shown in detail around the perimeter only, which saves production time. Figure 13.31 shows more of the area covered with the surface material but in a slightly more abstract manner. Another

method is to draft the surface accurately and erase areas for notes.

Figure 13.32 shows other materials as they might appear in an exterior elevation. These are only suggestions. Scale and office practice dictate the final technique. See Figure 13.33.

Eliminating Unnecessary Information

Because exterior elevations are vital in the construction document process, unnecessary information should be eliminated. Shades and shadows, cars, bushes and trees, people and flowers add to the looks of the drawings but serve no purpose here.

■ NOTES

Order of Notes

Notes on elevations follow the same rules as notes on other drawings. The size of the object is first, then the name of the material, and then any additional information about spacing, quantity, or methods of installation. For example,

1″ × 8″ redwood siding over 15# (15 lb) building felt
or
Cement plaster over concrete block
or
Built-up composition gravel roof
or
1″ × 6, let-in bracing

In the second example, there are no specific sizes needed, so the generic name comes first in the note.

Noting Practices

Noting practices vary from job to job. A set of written specifications is often provided with the construction documents. Wall material on a set of elevations may be described in broad, generic terms such as "concrete block" when the specific size, finish, stacking procedure, and type of joint are covered in the specifications.

If there are differences between the construction documents and the specifications, the specifications have priority. In the construction documents, often the same material note can be found more than once. If an error is made or a change is desired, many notes must be revised. In the specifications, where it is mentioned once, only a single change has to be made.

There are exceptions. When there are complicated changes and variations of material and patterns on an elevation, it is difficult to describe them in the specifications. In this case, the information should be located on the exterior elevations. See Figure 13.33.

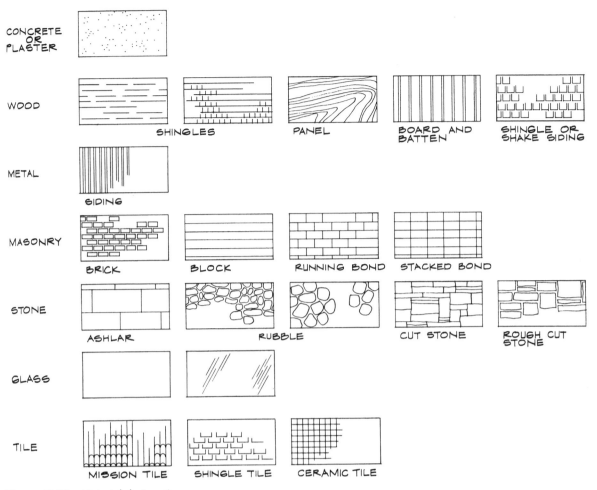

Figure 13.32 Material designations.

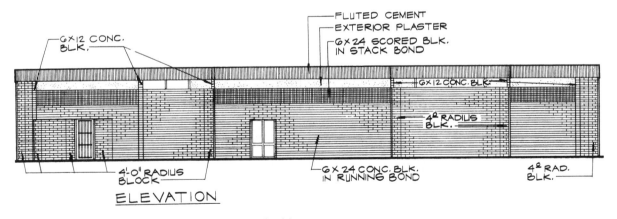

Figure 13.33 Masonry structure with variations in building patterns.

■ DOTTED LINES

Doors and Windows

Dotted lines are used on doors and windows to show how they operate. See illustration D of Figure 13.25 and the awning and casement windows in Figure 13.26. These dotted lines show which part of the door or window is hinged. See Figure 13.34. Not all offices like to show this on an elevation. One reason is that the direction the door swings is shown on the floor plan and therefore does not need to be indicated on the elevations.

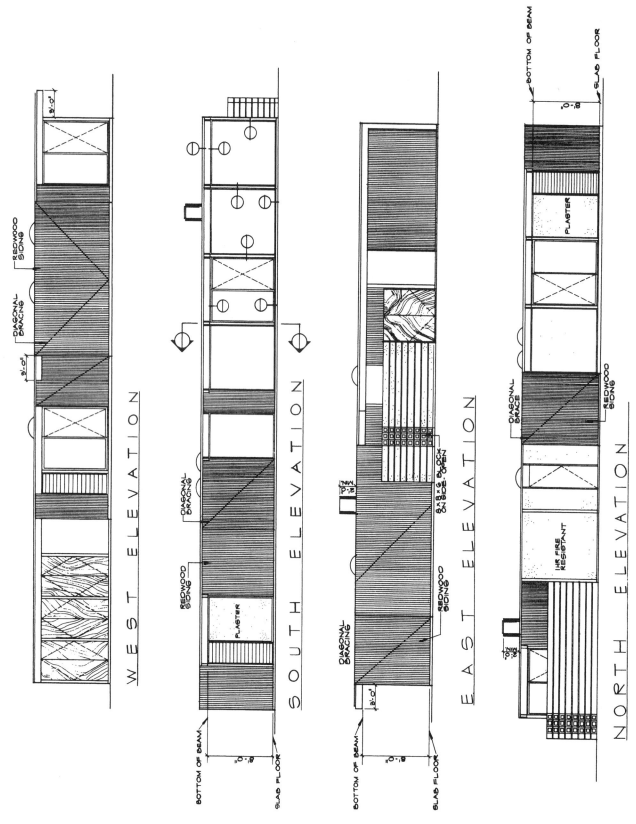

Figure 13.34 Elevation in wood.

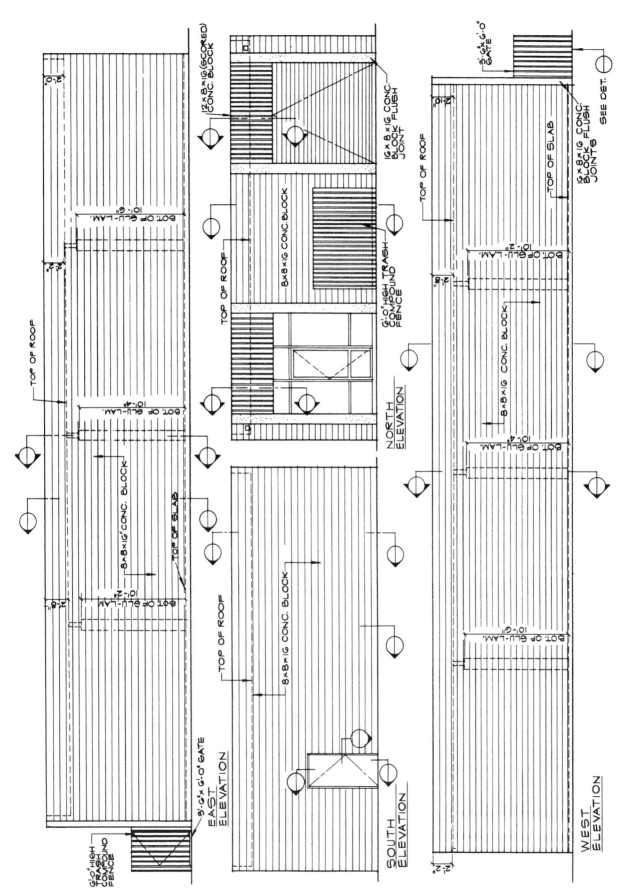

Figure 13.35 Elevation in masonry.

Foundations

At times you may have to delineate the foundation on the elevations in order to explain the foundation better. Dotted lines are used in various ways relating to the foundation. Dotted lines (centerline-type lines are also used) show the top of a slab as in Figure 13.35. They are used to show the elevation of the footings. See Figure 13.36 for elevations of a two-pour footing and a one-pour footing.

Dotted lines are also used to describe a **stepped footing**. When the property slopes, the minimum depth of the footing can be maintained by stepping the footing down the slope. See Figure 13.37.

Structural Features

Structural features below the grade can be shown by dotted lines if this helps to explain the structure. See Figure 13.38. Dotted lines can also be used to help show structural elements of the building. In Figure 13.10, centerline type lines (which can also be used) show **let-in braces** (structural angular braces in a wall). (The plate line is the top of the two horizontal members at the top of the wall, called **top plates**.) In Figure 13.35, dotted lines show the top of the roof, which slopes for drainage, and a pilaster (a widening of the wall for a beam) and beam (here, a laminated beam called a Glu-lam).

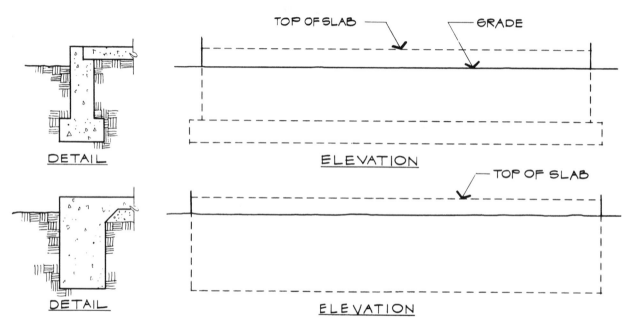

Figure 13.36 Showing the foundation on an elevation.

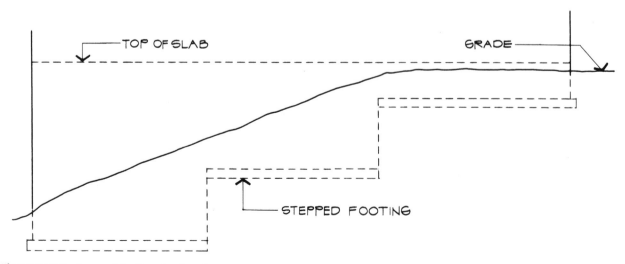

Figure 13.37 Stepped footings in elevation.

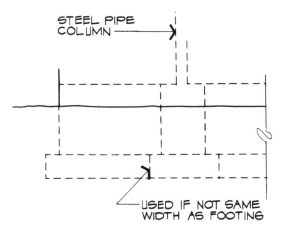

Figure 13.38 Structural features below grade.

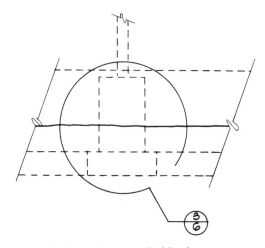

Figure 13.39 Referencing hidden lines.

As with doors and windows, the footing on an elevation can be referenced to the foundation plan, details, and cross sections. The system is the same. Reference bubbles are used. See Figure 13.39.

Whatever the feature, the dotted line is used for clarity and communication. How can you keep the message clear for construction purposes? How can you communicate this best on the drawings?

■ CONTROLLING FACTORS

Each type of construction has unique restrictive features that you need to know about to effectively interpret the transition from design elevations to production of exterior elevations in the construction documents.

Wood Frame Structures

With wood frame structures, elevations are usually dictated by plate line heights. The **plate height** is measured from the floor to the top of the two top plates. See Figure 13.8. Efficient use of material is dictated by this dimension because studs are available in certain lengths and sheathing usually comes in 4′ × 8′ sheets.

Floor, Plate, and Grade Lines. When the floor elevations and plate heights are established, the first thing to draw is the floor line and its relationship to the grade. Next, draw the plate line. If the structure is of post and beam construction, measure from the floor line to the bottom of the beam. Some offices prefer these dimensions on the building sections.

Find the distance between the floor line and the grade line from the grading plan, foundation plan, footing details, and building sections. If the lot is relatively flat, just draw a grade line with the floor line measured above it and the plate line height above the floor as a start. If the site is not flat, carefully plot the grade line from the grading plan, foundation plan, and details or the site plan.

Some site plans, grading plans, and foundation plans indicate the grade height, marked F.G. (finished grade), in relation to the structure at various points around the structure. In Figure 13.40, the grade line is figured by making a grid where the horizontal lines show grade heights and vertical lines are projected down from the structure. Once this grade line is established, the top of the slab—that is, the floor line—is drawn. The plate line is then measured from the floor line. There is no need to measure the distance between the grade and the floor line. See Figure 13.41.

Masonry Structures

Masonry structures such as brick or concrete block must be approached differently. The deciding factor here is the size of the concrete block or brick, the pattern, the thickness of the joint, and the placement of the first row in relationship to the floor. Unlike wood, which can be cut in varying heights, masonry units are difficult to cut, so cutting is minimized. As Figure 13.33 shows, dimensions of the masonry areas are kept to a minimum. Refer to the discussion of noting, earlier in this chapter, for suggested practices and sample illustrations.

Steel Structures

Structures where the main members are steel and the secondary members are, for example, wood, are treated differently from wood structures or masonry. The configuration is arrived at in the same way and representation of material is the same, but dimensioning is completely different.

In a wood frame structure, the lumber can be cut to size on the job. In masonry, the size of the masonry units often dictates such things as the location of windows and

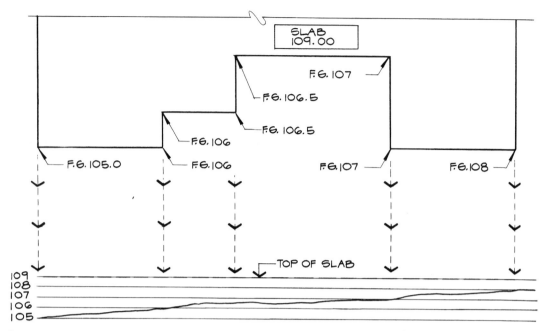

Figure 13.40 Plotting grade lines for an elevation.

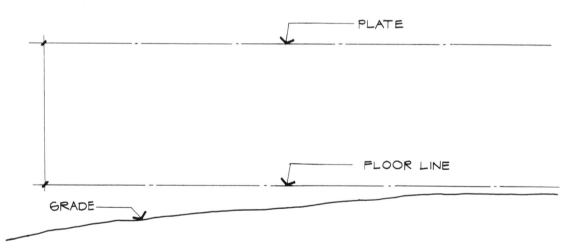

Figure 13.41 Preliminary steps for drafting an elevation with grade variation.

doors, the modular height, and so on. Some of the controlling factors in steel construction are: the size of the structural members; the required ceiling heights; and the **plenum** area (the space necessary to accommodate the mechanical equipment and duct work). See Figure 13.42.

Drawing an exterior elevation for a steel structure is a relatively simple task. Usually, the floor elevations on a multistory structure of steel are established by the designer. The building section usually provides the necessary height requirements. See Figure 13.42. Figure 13.43 is a checklist for exterior elevations.

■ DRAFTING AN EXTERIOR ELEVATION

The drafting of an exterior elevation is a straightforward procedure, because most of the structural and shape descriptions have been completed by the time it is drafted: the shape of the roof, the size of the site component parts, the shape and size of the foundation, and all of its vertical heights were determined when drafting the building section. For a small structure, such as those contained in this book, we believe it is the easiest drawing to accomplish.

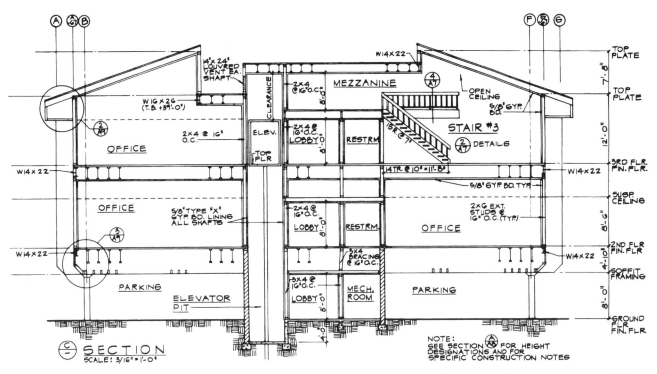

Figure 13.42 Section of a steel and wood structure. (Courtesy of Westmount, Inc., Real Estate Development, Torrance, CA.)

EXTERIOR ELEVATIONS

1. Natural grade
2. Finish grade
3. Floor elevations
4. Foundation (hidden lines)
   a. Bottom of footing
   b. Top of foundation (stepped footing)
   c. Detail reference
5. Walls
   a. Material
      (1) Wood
      (2) Stucco
      (3) Aluminum
      (4) Other
   b. Solid sheathing
      (1) Plywood
      (2) 1 × 6 diagonal
      (3) Other
   c. Diagonal bracing (hidden lines)
6. Openings
   a. Heights
      (1) Door and window min. 6'- 8"
      (2) Post and beam special
   b. Doors
      (1) Type
      (2) Material
      (3) Glass
      (4) Detail reference
      (5) ey to schedule
   c. Windows
      (1) Type
      (2) Material

(3) Glass   obscure for baths
(4) Detail reference
(5) ey to schedule
   d. Moulding, casing and sill
   e. Flashing (gauge used)
7. Roof
   a. Materials
      (1) Built-up composition, gravel
      (2) Asphalt shingles
      (3) Wood shingles or shake
      (4) Metal-terne-aluminum
      (5) Clay and ceramic tile
      (6) Concrete
   b. Other
8. Ground slopage
9. Attic and sub floor vents
10. Vertical dimensions
11. Window, door fascia, etc. detail references
12. Roof slope ratio
13. Railings, note height
14. Stairs
15. Note all wall materials
16. Types of fixed glass and thickness
17. Window and door swing indications
18. Window and door heights from floor
19. Gutters and downspouts
20. Overflow scuppers
21. Mail slot
22. Stepped foundation footings   if occur
23. Dimension chimney above roof

Figure 13.43 Exterior elevations checklist.

Figure 13.44   Using the floor plan as a base for the exterior elevation.

Figure 13.45   Revealing let-in brace.

The hand drafter, as well as the CAD drafter, can use all of the shortcuts previously described in other chapters. Acetate templates, reduced building sections, and a base layer for the building section are but a few of the shortcuts available to produce the base layer for the elevations.

Because exterior elevations are drafted at the same scale as the floor plan, a diazo copy of the floor plan can be positioned under the plate line and floor line to position the walls. See Figure 13.44.

Guide to Dimensioning

Do not dimension anything on the exterior elevation that has been dimensioned elsewhere. For example, the distance between the floor line and the plate line is dimensioned on the building section and should not be repeated on the exterior elevation. In contrast, windows have been described (width and height) on the schedule, yet their positions in relation to the floor line have not. This makes the exterior elevation an ideal place to dimension these positions, as well as architectural features such as signage on a commercial building.

Descriptions

Anything that can be described better by drawing should be drawn, and anything that would be better as a written description should be included in the specifications. Noting should use generic terms. It would be sufficient to label the exterior covering (called skin) "redwood siding" or "stucco" (exterior plaster), rather than describing the quality of the siding or the number of coats and quality of the stucco.

Concerns

Compare the exterior elevation to the human body. In both instances the outside cover is called the skin. Di-

rectly below the skin is the muscle. The muscle might be comparable to the substructure that strengthens a structure, such as metal straps, let-in braces, and shear panels. See Figure 13.45. The purpose of these members is to resist outside forces such as wind, hurricane, and earthquake. Our skeleton might parallel the "bone structure" of a building, which is in the form of a network of wood pieces called studs.

The exterior elevation addresses the "skin and muscle," and the building section emphasizes the skeletal form.

Use of Hidden Lines

Hidden lines are used on an exterior elevation to reveal structural members behind the surface. See Figure 13.35. Notice, in this figure, the used of hidden lines to show the slope of the roof, the pilaster, the hinged side of doors and windows, and, in Figure 13.34, to show diagonal bracing.

Now look at Figure 13.46. The outline of a gable roof (roof plan) is translated into elevations. Notice that in the front view the small bend in the roof at the top-right corner does not show, whereas in the rear view the entire shape is shown and the right side view shows only a single roof but nothing behind it. All hidden roof lines are not shown.

Pictorial vs. Written Description

It often takes a combination of a drawing and a generic description to describe a material used for covering the outer surface of a structure. For example, a series of horizontal lines are used to describe siding, a row of ma-

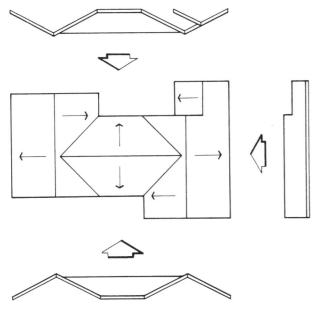

Figure 13.46 Visualizing roof in elevation.

RAISED
WINDOW FRAME

EAST ELEVATION
RYAN RESIDENCE

Figure 13.47 Preliminary exterior elevation.

A

B

Figure 13.48 Hardboard siding.

sonry units, or possibly a texture pattern on exterior plaster.

The preliminary East elevation of the Ryan Residence shown in Chapter 17 has been redrawn in Figure 13.47, showing an example of horizontal siding as a finish. Wood siding as shown here can be applied in two ways: first, with individual pieces of (possibly) redwood over solid sheathing and a waterproof membrane, or second, in sheet form. Sheets of simulated horizontal siding may be purchased in 16'-0" lengths that are preprimed with paint. See Figure 13.48.

Material Designation

The designation of material on the surface of the elevation will be done with a template called Burnish-On, distributed by the Alvin Company. These high-impact templates are available in a variety of scales and textures,

among which are stone, cedar shake, brick, and river rock. The material designations are shown in the plan as well as in the elevational view.

As shown in Figure 13.49A, the template is placed under the vellum and burnished with a sharp pencil, as you would do to tracing paper over a coin to reveal the

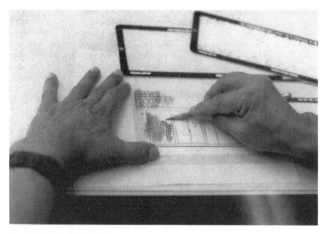

A ADDING TEXTURE

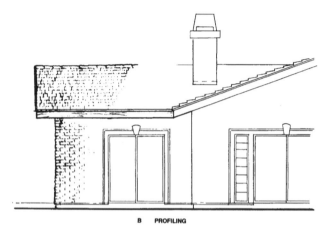

B PROFILING

Figure 13.49 Using template for material designation. (With permission from Alvin Company, distributor of Burnish-On templates.)

pattern beneath. Even if the texture goes beyond the limit of the border, it can easily be removed with an eraser and the border of the material redrawn when profiling, as was done in Figure 13.49B. The patterns are better placed on the back side of the vellum if a diazo print is to be used, and on the top side if photographic or plain paper copies are made.

If CAD drafting is used, you will find that most of these patterns already exist in the library of many of the programs. These can be rapidly employed by setting borders, selecting patterns, and allowing the computer to do the rest.

■ WEATHERPROOFING

Weatherproofing a structure basically means keeping out wind, rain, and ultraviolet rays (UVR) of the sun. UVR reduction is necessary because these rays are harmful to

our skin and will fade the color from drapery, furniture, and carpets. The solution is rather simple in a residence. Large overhangs on roofs can eliminate these harmful rays, as can the newly developed high-performance glass used in windows.

Windows and doors are now made, or can be retrofitted, with weatherstripping. This keeps the structure energy efficient and prevents dust from entering the structure as a result of driving winds. The selection of the type of window or door for wind control is addressed in Chapter 16 in the section on window detailing. The present discussion focuses mainly on wind and rain, with an emphasis on water control.

As you may have learned in a science course, the structure of water is different in its various phases: solid, liquid, and vapor. Therefore, a variety of materials are used to combat the migration of moisture from the outside to the inside of structures.

Generally, a cover is placed over the structure (especially the walls) much like a raincoat on a human. Yet, depending on the material of the raincoat, the wearer's body heat, the temperature of the air, and especially the humidity (moisture in the air), the inside surface of the raincoat will react differently. So it is with buildings. Building do perspire. Consider the following scenario: Driven by wind, moisture migrates from the outside to the inside of a structure in the form of vapor. This moisture changes its state through condensation because of temperature change and is unable to leave the inside of the wall. As night approaches the temperature drops drastically, and the moisture now expands as it becomes a solid (ice). If moisture happens to be inside the wood or insulation within the wall, it can cause terrible deterioration and damage. Had a vapor barrier been used, moisture might come from the inside of the structure and condense along this membrane as it tried to escape.

Solution to Condensation

A solution to condensation in the attic and underfloor space in a wood floor system can easily be achieved by proper ventilation and recirculation of the air. This is done with small openings through which venting can take place, using the wind as an ally, or the air can be recirculated mechanically, as is often done for bathroom ventilation.

Figure 13.50 is a map of the United States. Notice how it is divided into three major zones. Zone A experiences severe damage to structures as a result of condensation. Zone B experiences moderate damage, whereas the damage in Zone C is slight to almost none. This does not mean that there will never be moderate-to-severe damage in mountainous areas in Zone C; rather, this is a more generalized look at large geographic areas. Therefore, the drafter must be aware that a building in South-

Figure 13.50 U.S. condensation hazard zones.

ZONE A—Severe

Zone B—Moderate

Zone C—None to Slight

ern California will *not* be dealt with in the same way as a building in the Dakotas, nor can a building in southern Texas be treated the same as one in Colorado.

Waterproofing

Waterproofing can be achieved in four ways:

1. The use of admixtures that render concrete impermeable.
2. Hydrolithically: this is done by applying a coat of asphalt or plastic to a surface, making it waterproof.
3. Chemically: a specially formulated paint is applied to a basically porous surface such as concrete. Upon contact with water this chemical explodes into crystals, sealing the pores. Such products are used more often for a retro-fix.
4. The use of a membrane. Older houses used bituminous-saturated felts (called building felts), which have recently been replaced with asphalt-saturated kraft paper.

For a structure in Zone A, you may wish to select a material that will keep the colder side of the wall wind resistant and airtight and require that the material be a vapor retarder. On the warm side of the wall, you might wish to stop the migration of moisture into the wall by using a foil-backed lath product. There are a number of products on the market today that can be specified by the project architect, including a vaporproof membrane, a membrane that can breathe, and a self-sealing membrane for ice and water, as shown in Figure 13.51.

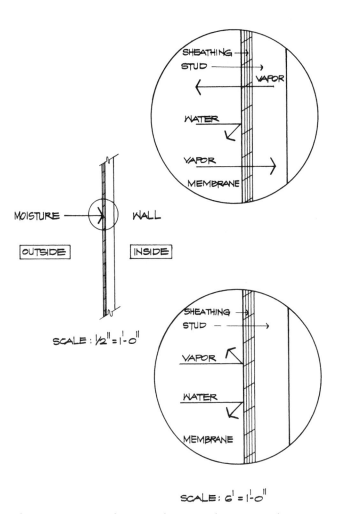

Figure 13.51 Breathing membranes and vapor membranes.

A drafter must know what is being used to properly ensure that he or she uses the correct convention and notation for drawings and details.

Counterflashing

Anytime you break the surface of a waterproof membrane, whether it is plastic or paper, a second sheet (usually of heavier weight) is used. This sheet, called counterflashing, is found around openings and at the ends of the membrane, inasmuch as these are the places most likely to leak. In Zone C, for example, where asphalt-saturated (grade D) kraft paper is often used, a heavier-grade band of kraft paper, called sisal-kraft, is used. In other instances, a strip of self-sealing vapor membrane may be used around the opening. In either case it should be done carefully so as to shed water; lapping and overlapping so as to let gravity take its natural course and help us eliminate moisture. See the section on window detailing in Chapter 16 for a discussion on how the overlapping and installation sequence is performed and shown in detail by the drafter.

Referencing

Referencing is the process of referring a specific area to an enlarged detail. Thus, the top half of the reference bubble indicates the name of the detail, and the bottom number indicates the sheet on which the particular detail can be found. Had this been a complete set with details of all conditions, you would see detail reference bubbles around all windows, doors, beam connections and so on.

Noting

Whenever possible, noting was done outside the elevation within the right margin. You cannot fit all of the notes in one place without having to use long leaders pointing to the subject. Therefore, certain notes were made inside the elevation to reduce the length of the leaders. A good rule of thumb in regard to leaders is not to allow them to cross more than one object line, never cross a dimension line, and keep the leader length to a minimum.

Keynoting is used by many offices. This is a procedure of numbering and placement of all of the notes on one side (usually the right). You then place a leader in the desired location and, rather than placing the note at the end of the leader, you use a reference bubble that refers to the correct note. A detail used to show the keynoting procedure can be seen in Chapter 16.

Keynoting can be done with either hand-drafted or CAD-drafted elevations. If computers are not available in an office, keynoting can still be done by word processing and positioned on the sheet with adhesives.

The advantage of keynoting is the standardization of the notes. Keynoting also allows the drafter to make direct references to the specification numbers right on the notes. Numbering systems recommended by the American Institute of Architects are similar to the numbering system used by libraries and can be incorporated here.

■ DRAWING AN ELEVATION WITH A COMPUTER

With a 3-D Model

If a 3-D model is available, the base or datum drawing can be easily created. You begin by rotating the 3-D model to ortho, as shown in Figure 13.52. Although this drawing shows itself as a 2-D drawing, depth does exist. Thus, the CAD drafter should flatten the image into a single plane. This will not change the appearance of the displayed image, but it will change the geometry from 3-D to 2-D. This step is important to the drafter, as offset lines can be used for other construction. Because all lines fall on the same plane, the geometry of the drawing can be altered or changed within the confines of the two-dimensional plane. This flattening process can best be understood if you can visualize the structure caught in a giant vice and flattened to a paper-thin image. See Figure 13.53.

Without a 3-D Model

If a 3-D mode is unavailable, the CAD drafter should use the base layer of the building section for the geometry layer under the base layer (datum layer) for the elevation.

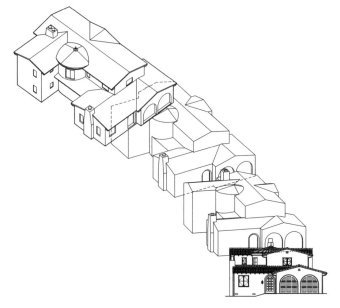

Figure 13.52 Rotation of 3-D model into elevation view. (Courtesy of Mike Adli, Owner; Nagy R. Bakhoum, President of Obelisk Architects.)

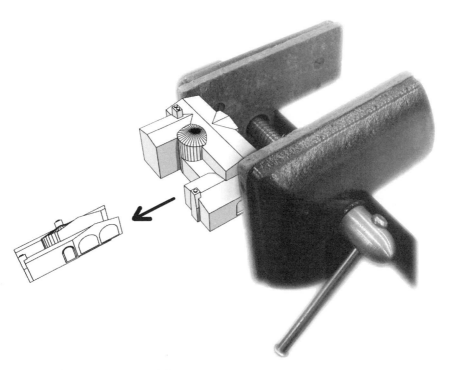

Figure 13.53 Flattening a 3-D model.

Because we are drawing the structure full-scale, the drawings will transfer directly. If the drawings are prepared in paper space and the scale of the building section and elevation are to be drawn differently, the first stage of the building section must be changed in scale to suit the elevation.

The next move is to import the floor plan and position the walls as shown on Figure 13.54. The floor plan is temporarily positioned above the datum elevation draw-

ing and rotated for each of the respective North, South, East and West elevations. This drawing constitutes the base or datum stage of a set of elevations.

STAGE II (Figure 13.55). The total outline of the structure is accomplished in this stage, as well as the incorporation of the geometry of the roof and additional floor lines and plate lines as they change throughout the structure.

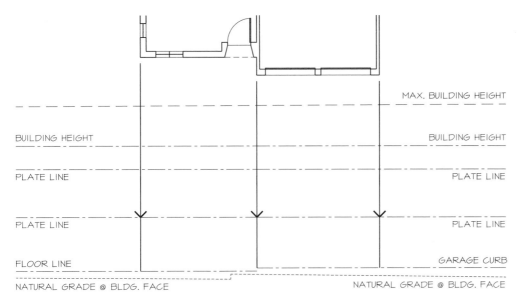

Figure 13.54 Stage I: Establishing a base (datum).

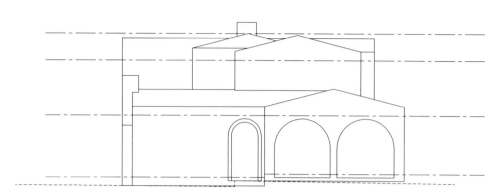

Figure 13.55 Stage II: Outline of structure.

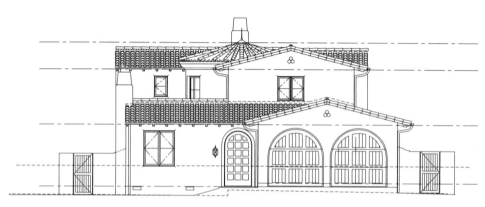

Figure 13.56 Stage III: Positioning doors, windows, etc.

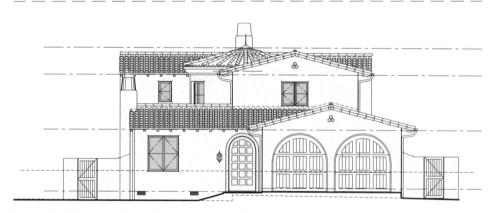

Figure 13.57 Stage IV: Adding texture and adjusting line quality.

STAGE III (Figure 13.56). Doors and windows are positioned. It is best to get digital images from the manufacturer, and then size and position them. If the structure is subject to lateral loads, shear walls may be included at this stage as stepped footing or any other structural components.

Stage IV (Figure 13.57). Line weight should be adjusted at this stage while adding texture. Adding texture may be fun, but it is recommended that restraint be used so as not to disturb any notes or dimensions.

STAGE V (Figure 13.58). Dimension Stage. Remember, the floor line to plate line dimension should be noted

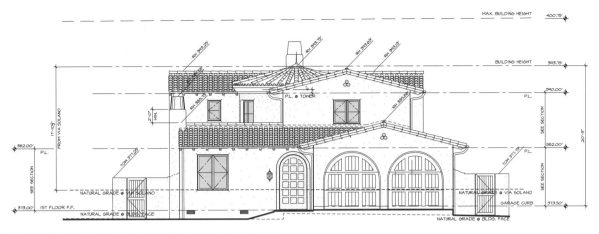

Figure 13.58 Stage V: Dimensioning, stairs, handrails, etc.

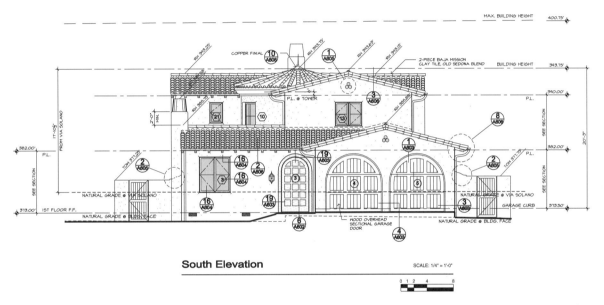

South Elevation

SCALE: 1/4" = 1'-0"

Figure 13.59 Stage VI: Noting and referencing. (Courtesy of Mike Adli, Owner; Nagy R. Bakhoum, President of Obelisk Architects.)

once on the building section and should not be repeated here. Simply refer the floor to plate line dimension to the section. Only those vertical dimensions that do not appear on the building section should appear here. Header height, ridge heights, handrail and guardrail dimensions, heights of fences and walls adjacent to the structure are examples of -

actual dimensions that will occur on the exterior elevation.

STAGE VI (Figure 13.59). This is the noting, titling, and referencing stage, as well as the exterior elevations final stage. Notes should be generic, allowing for the specifications to cite the precise quantity, brand names, model numbers, and so forth.

chapter

14

ROOF PLAN
AND FRAMING SYSTEMS

■ METHODS OF REPRESENTATION

There are two main ways to represent floor, ceiling, and roof framing members as part of construction documents: drawing framing members on the floor plan and drawing them separately.

Drawing Framing Members on the Floor Plan

This first method illustrates and notes ceiling and/or floor framing members directly onto the finished floor plan. It is a good method to use when the framing conditions are simple and do not require many notes and reference symbols that might be confused with the other finished floor plan information.

Figure 14.1 shows the lower floor plan of a two-story residence. This plan contains all the information and symbols needed: No separate drawing of the ceiling framing members is required. Note how the ceiling joist size, spacing, and direction are illustrated in bedroom #1 and the study. Note also the use of broken lines to represent exposed ceiling beams in the master bedroom. As you can see, if a great deal more framing information were required, the drawing would lose its clarity.

The upper floor plan of this residence designates ceiling joist sizes, spacing, and direction, as well as roof

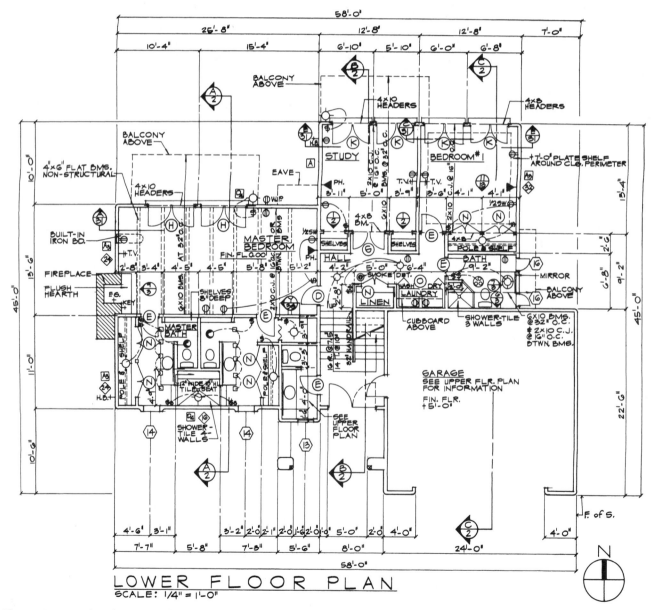

Figure 14.1 Ceiling framing on finished floor plan. (Courtesy of William. F. Smith—Builder.)

framing information such as rafter sizes, spacing, and direction; ridge beam size; and the size and spacing of exposed rafter beams in the living room. See Figure 14.2A. **Headers** and beams for framing support over openings are also shown in this figure. If you are using this method to show framing members, you can delineate beams with two broken lines at the approximate scale of the beam or with a heavy broken line.

The structural design of beams and footings is calculated by finding the total loads that are distributed to any specific member. This total load is found by computing the tributary area affecting that member. Figure 14.2B illustrates a cross-section showing the various tributary areas which accumulate loads to the ridgebeam, floor beam, and foundation pier.

Drawing Framing Members Separately

The second way to show ceiling, floor, and roof framing members is to provide a separate drawing that may be titled "Ceiling Framing," "Floor Framing," or "Roof Framing." You might choose this method because the framing is complex or because construction document procedures require it.

The first step is the same as that of the foundation plan's. Lay a piece of tracing paper directly over the floor plan tracing. Trace all the walls, windows, and door openings. The line quality of your tracing should be only dark enough to make these lines distinguishable after you have reproduced the tracing. In this way, the final drawing, showing all the framing members, can be

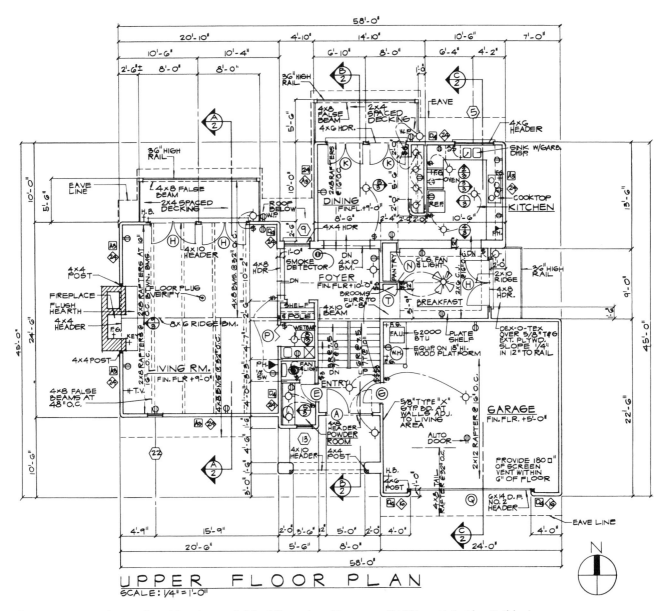

Figure 14.2A Ceiling and roof framing on finished floor plan. (Courtesy of William. F. Smith—Builder.)

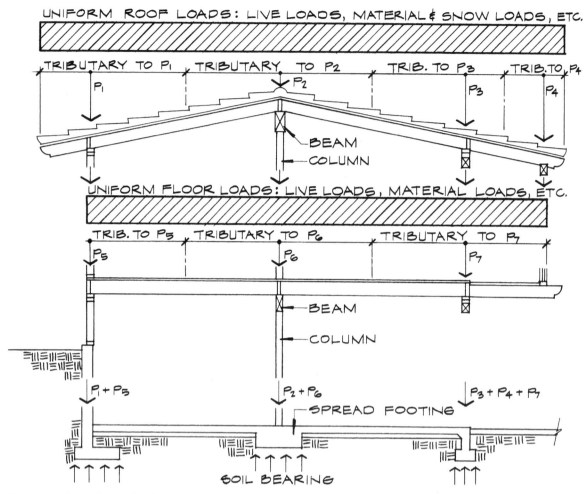

Figure 14.2B Tributary loading section.

drawn with darker lines like a finished drawing. This provides the viewer with clear framing members, while the walls are just lightly drawn for reference.

Another way to provide a basis for a framing plan is to reproduce the floor plan from the initial line drawing with a mylar or sepia print. By doing this, you can print the floor plan drawing when only the walls and openings have been established. Later, when you are prepared for framing plans, you can go back to these prints and incorporate all the required information to complete the framing plan.

Figure 14.3 shows the floor plan of the first floor of a two-story, wood-framed residence with all the framing members required to support the second floor and ceiling directly above this level. Because the second floor framing and ceiling for the first floor are the same, this drawing is titled "Upper Floor Framing Plan."

First draft in all the floor beams, columns, and headers for all the various openings. Then incorporate the location and span direction of all the floor joists into the drawing. In Figure 14.3, the floor joist locations and span

directions are shown with a single line and arrowhead at each end of the line. This is one way to designate these members. Another method is shown later when the roof framing plan is discussed.

Dimensioning for framing plans mainly applies to beam and column locations. Provide dimensioning for all floor beams and columns located directly under load-bearing members. These members, such as walls and columns, are located on the second floor. Dimensioning for these members is similar to that on a floor plan. When you have finished the drawing, provide the required notes for all the members included in the drawing.

Drawing the ceiling plan for the second floor level involves only the immediate ceiling framing members. See Figure 14.4. This drawing deals only with headers over openings and with ceiling joist location, span, direction, size, and spacing for a specific ceiling area. Where applicable, notes and dimensioning are shown as in Figure 14.3.

The final framing plan for this project is the roof framing plan. See Figure 14.5. As mentioned previously, an-

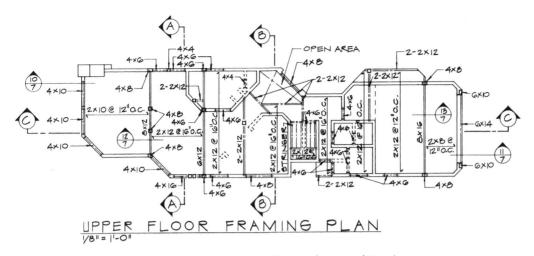

UPPER FLOOR FRAMING PLAN
1/8" = 1'-0"

Figure 14.3 Upper floor framing plan. (Residence of Mr. and Mrs. Ted Bear.)

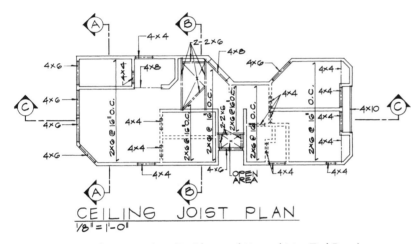

CEILING JOIST PLAN
1/8" = 1'-0"

Figure 14.4 Ceiling joist plan. (Residence of Mr. and Mrs. Ted Bear.)

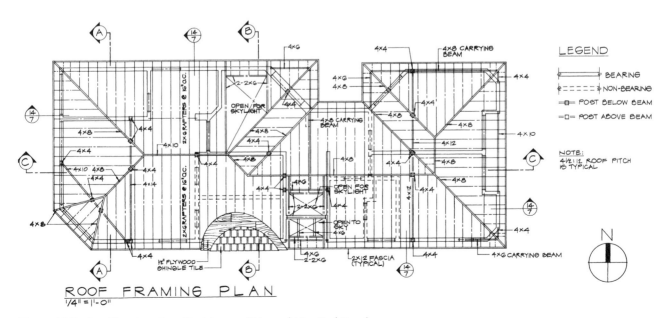

ROOF FRAMING PLAN
1/4" = 1'-0"

Figure 14.5 Roof framing plan. (Residence of Mr. and Mrs. Ted Bear.)

other way to show framing members is to draw in all the members that apply to that particular drawing. This obviously takes more time to draw but is clearer for the viewer.

■ FRAMING WITH DIFFERENT MATERIALS

Framing Plan: Wood Members

When wood structures have members spaced anywhere from 16″ to 48″ on centers, show them with a single line broken at intervals. Figure 14.6 shows the roof framing plan for this residence incorporating all the individual

rafters, ridges, **hip rafters** (the members that bisect the angle of two intersecting walls), and supporting columns and beams under the rafters. Show the rafters, which are closely spaced, with a single line. Lightly draft the walls so that the members directly above are clear. Provide dimensioning for members with critical locations as well as call-outs for the sizes, lumber grade, and spacing of all members.

Framing Plan: Steel Members

When you are using steel members to support ceilings, floors, and roof, show all the members on the framing

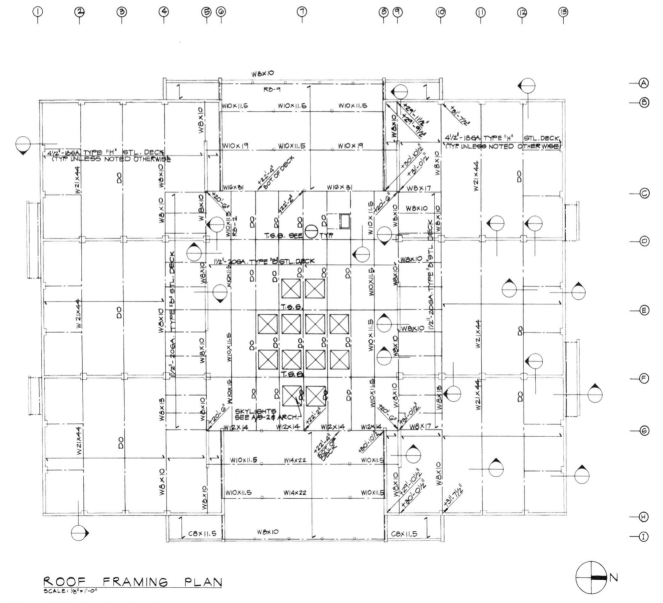

Figure 14.6 Roof framing plan—steel members. (Courtesy of AVCO Community Developers, Inc., and Mann Theatres Corporation of California.)

plans. The method of drawing the framing plan is similar to the method for drawing wood framing plans.

After you have selected a method, show steel members with a heavy single line. See Figure 14.6, which is a roof framing plan for a theatre using various size steel members and steel decking. The interior walls have been drawn with a broken line, which distinguishes the heavy solid beam line and the walls below. As you can see, all the various beam sizes are noted directly on the steel members. Some members have an abbreviated "DO" as their call-out; this tells the viewer that this member is identical to the one noted in the same framing bay.

In some cases, a beam may also be given a roof beam number, noted as "RB-1", "RB-2", and so on. The structural engineer uses this beam reference in the engineering calculations. It can also be incorporated into a roof beam schedule, if one is needed. Any elements that require openings through a roof or floor should be drawn directly on the plan. On Figure 14.6, an open area for skylights and a roof access hatch are shown with a heavy solid line.

A framing plan can also be useful to show detail reference symbols for **connections** of various members that cannot otherwise be shown on the building sections. Figure 14.6 shows several detail symbols for various connecting conditions. Show building section reference symbols at their specific locations.

Axial reference lines form the basis for dimensioning steel framing members. These lines provide a reference point for all other dimensioning. In Figure 14.6, axial reference symbols are shown on all the major beam and wall lines. From these, subsequent dimension lines to other members are provided. These same reference lines are used on the foundation plan.

Beam and column elevation heights are often shown on the framing plan. See the axial reference point H-10 in Figure 14.6. The diagonal line pointing to this particular beam has an elevation height of 31'-7½" noted on the top of the diagonal line. This indicates that this is the height to the top of the beam. If the height at the bottom of that beam were required, you would note it underneath the diagonal line. Columns usually only require the elevations to the top of the column.

An aerial photograph showing a stage of the roof framing is shown in Figure 14.7. You can clearly see the main supporting steel members, as per axial reference lines ②, ③, ④, ⑩, ⑪, and ⑫, and some placement of the steel decking on top of these members.

Framing Plan: Wood and Steel Members

Framing plans using wood and steel members to support ceilings, floors, and roof are drawn in a similar fashion to framing plans using steel alone. Steel members are

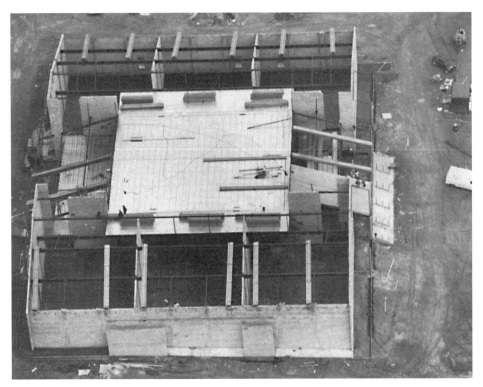

Figure 14.7 Roof framing. (Courtesy of AVCO Community Developers, Inc., and Mann Theatres Corporation of California; William Boggs Aerial Photography. Reprinted with permission.)

drawn with a heavy solid line and the wood members with a lighter line broken at intervals. You can also show wood members with a solid line and directional arrow.

Figure 14.8 shows a floor framing plan using steel and wood members to support the floor. This particular building is supported mainly on round steel columns, with the wall being used only to enclose a lobby and stairwells. For clarity, draw these columns in lines, and be careful to align them with each other. After you have laid out the required columns and walls below, draw in the main steel members with a solid heavy line. The designation of floor trusses spaced at 24″ on centers is shown between these steel members.

Because these members are closely spaced, a solid line is used with directional arrows at the end and the size and spacing of trusses noted directly above the solid line. The bottom of the line shows a notation, "FJ-3." This is the abbreviation for floor joist number 3, which is referenced in the structural engineer's calculations and may be used in a floor joist schedule. When you are asked to

draw a similar framing plan, be sure to show the joist for all bay conditions. As we saw earlier, "DO" is shown between axial reference lines ⑦ and ⑧. When you use this abbreviation, be sure it is clear. Detail reference symbols are shown for the connections of various members. Sizes and shapes for all the steel columns have been designated as well as the elevation height to the top of each column. Building section reference symbols and locations are shown. Whenever possible, take these sections directly through an axial reference plan.

Dimensioning for this type of project relies totally on axial reference planes as they relate to the column locations. Usually, you should locate notes satisfying various requirements on this same drawing. For example, these notes might designate the thickness, type, and nailing schedule for the plywood subfloor or the location of the fire draft stops within the floor framing.

To understand this structure better, look at the series of framing photographs. Figure 14.9 gives a general view of the overall steel and wood skeleton used in the erection

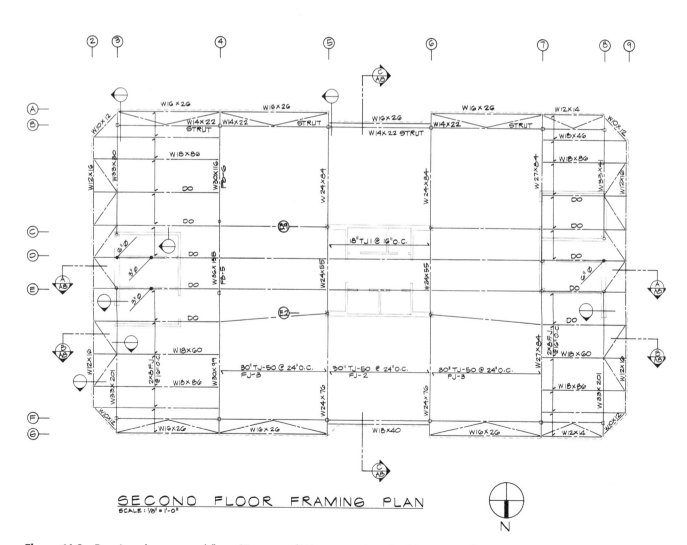

Figure 14.8   Framing plan—second floor. (Courtesy of Westmount, Inc., Real Estate Development, Torrance, CA.)

Figure 14.9 Steel beams for floor framing. (Courtesy of Westmount, Inc., Real Estate Development, Torrance, CA; William Boggs Aerial Photography. Reprinted with permission.)

Figure 14.10 Main steel floor beam and column with joist hangers. (Courtesy of Westmount, Inc., Real Estate Development, Torrance, CA; William Boggs Aerial Photography. Reprinted with permission.)

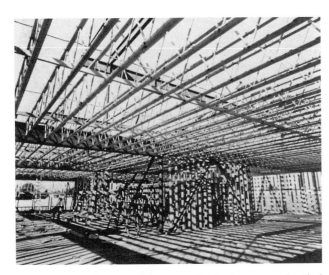

Figure 14.11 Floor joist trusses attached to hangers and nailed in place. (Courtesy of Westmount, Inc., Real Estate Development, Torrance, CA; William Boggs Aerial Photography. Reprinted with permission.)

of this building. The floor joist truss member seen in the foreground will eventually be attached between the main steel beams. Figure 14.10 is a close-up view of a main steel floor beam and column with joist hangers located at the top of the beam in preparation for the attachment of the floor truss members.

In Figure 14.11, floor joist trusses have now been attached to the hangers and nailed in place. Reference symbols for connection details should be located throughout the framing plan drawings. Figure 14.12 and 14.13 give examples of what these details may look like in their construction phase.

Framing Plan Checklist

1. Titles and scales.
2. Indicate bearing and nonbearing walls.
   a. Coordinate with foundation plan.
   b. Show all openings in walls.
3. Show all beams, headers, girders, purlins, etc.
   a. Note sizes.
4. Show all columns, note sizes and materials.
5. Note accessway to attic—if occurs.
6. Note ceiling joist sizes, direction, spacing.
7. Draw all rafters, note sizes and spacing.
8. Draw overhangs.
   a. Indicate framing for holding overhangs up.
   b. Dimension width.
9. Note shear walls.
10. Note roof sheathing type and thickness.
11. Indicate all ridges, valley. Note sizes.
12. Note all differences in roof levels.

Figure 14.12 Beam and column connection. (Courtesy of Westmount, Inc., Real Estate Development, Torrance, CA.)

Figure 14.13 Floor beam to main beam assembly. (Courtesy of Westmount, Inc., Real Estate Development, Torrance, CA.)

■ ROOF PLAN FRAMING SYSTEMS

As you look at the various framing plans, there may be many conventions that require clarification. For this reason we have included a chart of typical conventions in Figure 14.14. You may find it helpful to flag this chart as you look at the various framing plans and use it as you would a dictionary; that is, a reference table that defines the conventions used. The explanations to these conventions are listed below (letters correspond to the chart).

A. A beam, header, or lintel over an opening, door, or window within a wall.

B. Used to show the direction of a framing member or a system of framing members, such as floor joist, rafters, or ceiling joist. Lettering occurs right along the line indicating size, name, and spacing, for example, "2 × 6 ceiling joist at 16" o.c." Note that a half arrowhead is on one side and another half on the opposite side.

C. The line with the half arrowheads is the same as described in definition B. The diagonal line with a full arrowhead on both ends indicates the duration of the system, for example, where a particular system of ceiling joists begins and ends. When sizes of the ceiling joists vary on the structure, for example, this

symbol is used to convey to the contractor where one size ends and another begins.

D. A beam, girder, or joist over a post.

E. A beam, girder, or joist under and supporting a post.

F. The employment of a framing anchor or joist hanger at the intersection of two members.

G. A structural post within a wall.

H. Two framing systems on the drawing. For example, one might represent ceiling joists, and the other roof rafters.

I. "W12 × 44" is a call-out for a steel beam or girder. When these members are sequentially repeated the center lines are still drawn to represent them, but the description (call-out) is abbreviated with the letters DO, which is short for "ditto."

J. In using conventional wood framing, which is subject to lateral forces such as wind and earthquake, a plywood membrane is often placed on a portion or on the complete wall surface. The adjacent hexagon symbol refers you to a nailing schedule to ensure minimums for nails to secure the plywood to the studs. These are called shear walls or shear panels, a drawing of which can be found in a companion to this book, *The Professional Practice of Architectural Detailing.*

K. Still another way to show a shear wall. The space within the wall that is designated as a shear wall is pouchéd in pencil.

L. The rectilinear box that contains the 8'-2" dimension is a convention used to indicate height of an object in plan view. In this example, the two dotted lines may represent the top of a beam or the plate line at a wall, and the numbers indicate height.

M. The use of three lines instead of two to represent a partition designates a double joist at the partition.

N. Shows a post on top of a beam similar to E with a post size notation.

O. This is the method architects use to represent an opening in a floor, ceiling, or roof system. The three lines surrounding the opening represent the doubling of the joists, and the dark L-shape indicates the use of framing anchors. The large X is the area of the opening. This convention is used for skylights and openings in the ceiling or roof for chimneys, a hatch, or attic access.

Roof Plan

A roof plan is a simple look at the top of a structure, as if you were aboard a helicopter. Unless you are looking at a flat roof, the view is usually a distorted one. The reason is that a roof plan cannot reveal the entire surface of the roof in its true shape and size if there are slopes involved.

There are a multitude of roof forms. Among the most commonly known are domes, gable, hip, Dutch gable, and shed roofs.

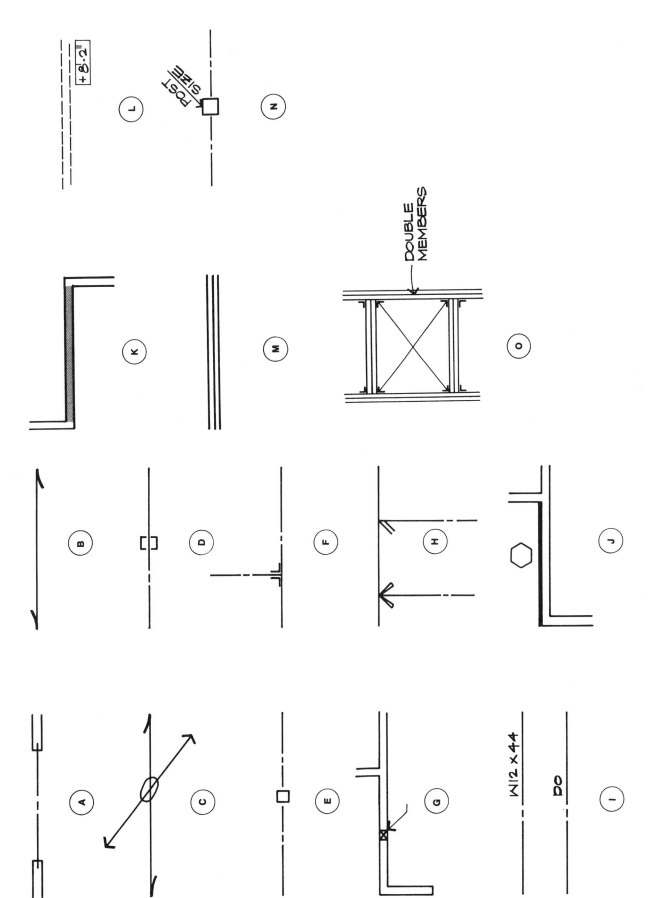

Figure 14.14 Summary of typical framing conventions.

Most small structures, especially residential structures, use a flat, gable, or hip roof. See Figure 14.15. Throughout this section we will devote most of our attention to the hip roof. If you can configure a hip roof, a gable or Dutch gable becomes a simple task.

Our approach will be to create a roof system that is geometrically correct and consistent in pitch, and avoiding flat areas that can entrap rain, thus causing leaks through the roof structure. Note the roof structure in Figure 14.16(A). Between the two roof systems, you will notice a flat (parallel to the ground) line. This space can entrap water, causing deterioration of the roof material and, eventually, leaks. A short-term solution is to place a triangular metal form to induce the water to travel outward. Figure 14.16(B) shows a standard solution to a roof that was configured incorrectly to begin with. See Figure

14.17 for the geometrically correct way to solve the problem in this roof outline.

So that you may configure the most complex of roof systems, we describe here the procedure you should follow in even the simplest of roof outlines. With this knowledge, you will be able to create the most complex outline. Once you know the system, you may even alter the building configuration slightly to avoid tricky problems in your plan.

The approach we use always solves the roof as a hip roof. Even if the desired roof was a gable or Dutch gable, in its initial form it will be a hip roof. Once having configured the roof as a hip roof, the conversion to a gable or Dutch gable is a simple one, as you will discover later.

Solution to Problem 1

STEP I.   Identify the perimeter of the roof as shown in the plan view in Figure 14.18. Be sure to indicate the overhang.

STEP II.   Reduce the shape into rectilinear zones. This is done by finding the largest rectilinear shape that will fit into the space. Figure 14.19A shows an outline of a roof, and Figure 14.19B shows the selection of the major area, as designed by the number 1. The major area is not selected according to square footage, but by greatest width. Look at another shape, similar to the preceding outline, in Figure 14.20A. Had the dimension of the base, designated by the letter B, been larger

Figure 14.15   Hip and gable roof systems.

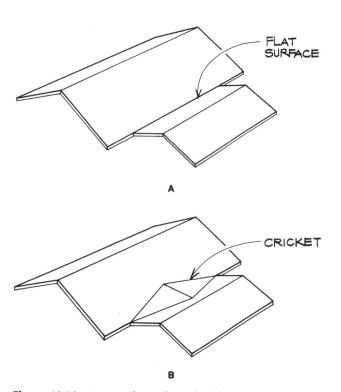

Figure 14.16   Incorrectly configured roof.

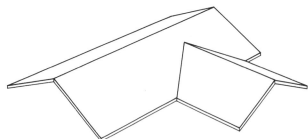

Figure 14.17   Ideal solution to avoid water problem.

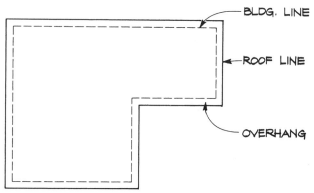

Figure 14.18   Draft the perimeter of the roof to be configured.

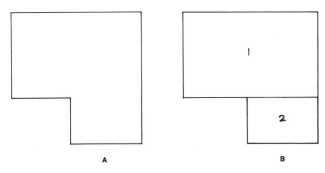

Figure 14.19 Finding the major zone.

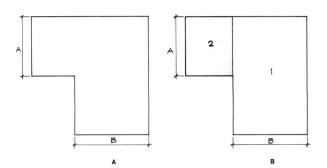

Figure 14.20 Letting the largest width determine the major zone.

than A, the major zone would be zone 1, as shown in Figure 14.20B.

STEP III. At this stage, you will locate both the hip rafter and the ridge. See Figure 14.21A. A 45° triangle is used to ensure the same pitch (angle of roof) on both sides of the roof, as shown in Figure 14.21B. This is possible when the corners are at 90° to each other.

Note, in Figure 14.22, that the outline has been organized into three zones: the main zone (1) in the center, with zones 2 and 3 above and below. These angles have been identified by the letters A, B, and C. For the sake of this solution, any angle such as A, which is 90°, will be called an "inside" corner. The other two corners (nos. 2 and 3) have angles greater than 90° and will be referred to as "outside" corners.

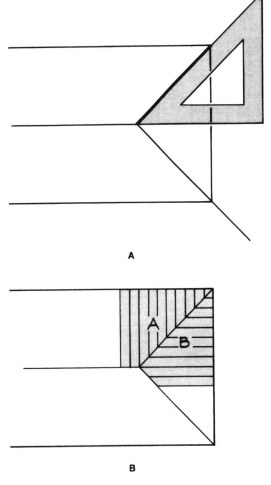

Figure 14.21 Use of 45° to maintain pitch.

STEP IV. Configure the roof. Let us take this configuration and develop it into a hip roof with the information already learned.

- Figure 14.23A: Taking the major zone identified as zone 1, we strike 45° hip lines from each of the floor's inside corners to form the main structure around which the other two zones will appear.

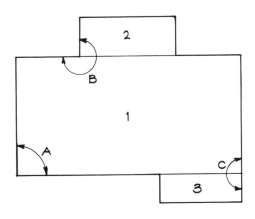

A - INSIDE (ANGLE) CORNER
B - OUTSIDE (ANGLE) CORNER
C - OUTSIDE (ANGLE) CORNER

Figure 14.22 Defining inside and outside corners.

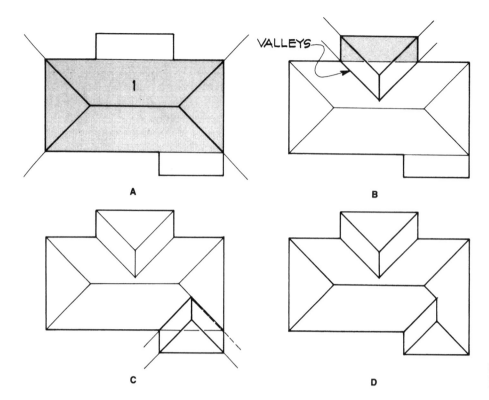

VALLEYS

A

B

C

D

Figure 14.23 Solving hip roof Problem 1.

• Figure 14.23B: We now approach zone 2 with an eye out for inside and outside corners. There are two of each. The inside corners at the top are drawn toward the center of the rectangle. The outside corners have their 45° lines going away from the zone 2 rectangle, thus forming the valleys of the roof.

• Figure 14.23C: The same approach is used for zone 3 as was used for zone 2. In the process of drawing the outside corners, you will notice that the one on the right overlaps an existing line. When this happens, the lines cancel each other, creating a continuous plane. See Figure 14.23D, which displays the final roof shape.

As you look at the final roof form, it may appear foolish to have gone through such an elaborate system, because you may have been able to visualize the finished roof from the beginning. Let's reinforce and validate the procedure by attempting roofs of varying complexities.

Solution to Problem 2

Step I. Figure 14.24A. The figure displays an area in the center that appears to be the major zone. By square footage, it might be, but remember, the major zone is the zone with the greatest width.

Step II. Figure 14.24B. Notice the relocation of the major zone by greatest width. Compare zone 1 with zone 2. The one with the greatest width will produce the highest ridge because it takes longer rafters in the framing of this roof. Knowledge of the highest point is

often helpful in staying within code limits or obstructing someone's view.

Step III. Figure 14.24C. This shows all of the zones with roofs outlined. Remember the outside/inside corner rule.

Step IV. Figure 14.24D. As can be seen in the previous step, many of the lines overlap. We show them side by side for ease of understanding, but in reality they are on top of each other. This means they cancel each other and are erased.

To continue this exploration of problems, we have selected an outline whose major roof configuration will all but disappear as we develop the roof.

Solution to Problem 3

Step I. Figure 14.25A. The main zone is situated vertically through the center of the total form. Check this area, in width, with a horizontal rectangle drawn through the top.

Step II. Figure 14.25B. Draw the hip and ridge lines. Identify inside and outside corners, and proceed with drawing the hip lines as well as the valley lines.

Step III. Figure 14.25C. As the lines overlap each other, which happens in three locations, these locations are identified with dotted lines. Notice that three of the four hip lines of the major zone are eliminated in the process.

There are configurations in which the major zones are well hidden. There are also shapes that have overlapping

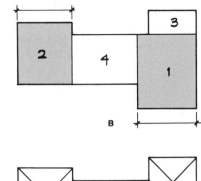

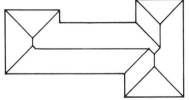

A

B

C

D

Figure 14.24 Problem 2.

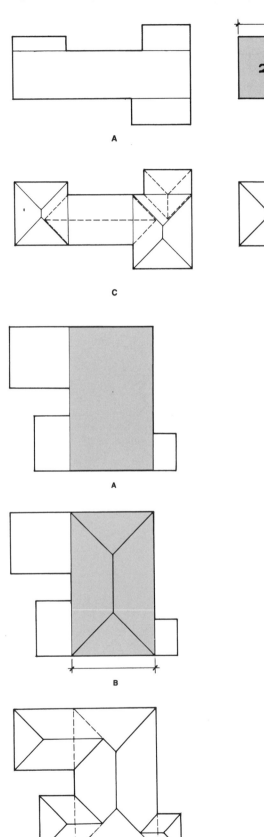

A

B

C

Figure 14.25 Problem 3.

zones. These are by far the most difficult challenges. The following five-step example demonstrates.

Solution to Problem 4

STEP I. Figure 14.26A. Covering all but the top illustration, see if you can identify the major zone on this outline of the structure.

STEP II. Figure 14.26B. Validate your initial selection with this figure. Next, identify the second largest zone which has been "X"ed out. Notice the overlap of zones 1 and 2.

STEP III. Figure 14.26C. Solve zones 3 and 4 next. Two lines will overlap, causing their removal.

STEP IV. Figure 14.26D. Zone 2 has inside corners only. Solve zone 2 as you did zone 1. The points that overlap have been identified with the letters W and X. These are outside corners, which become valleys. Extend point X toward zone 1, and W toward zone 2. These lines will intersect a hip line, identified by the letters Y and Z, respectively.

STEP V. Figure 14.26E. Y and Z are connected to form a ridge. This ridge is slightly lower than the ridge of zones 1 and 2. The hip lines below points Y and Z are also eliminated to form the final roof configuration.

Saving the most challenging for last, we encounter a shape that includes an angle other than 90° around the perimeter. At first glance the task of roofing this outline seems difficult, but if you apply the principles learned in this chapter, the solution is easier than it may first appear.

Solution to Problem 5

STEP I. Figure 14.27A. Extending the center portion toward the left does not produce the rectangle with the largest width, so change your approach and solve the major zoning as explained in the next step.

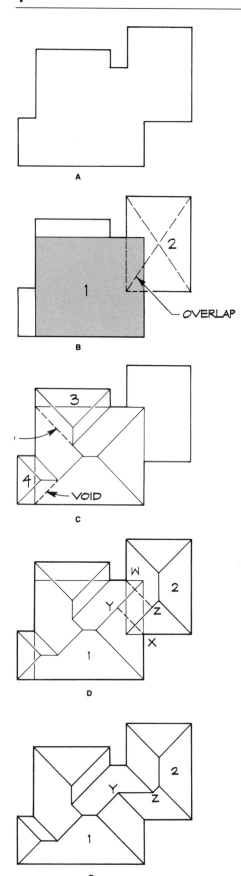

Figure 14.26 Problem 4.

STEP II. Figure 14.27B. After you have checked the various possible zones, we hope you have selected zone 1 and zone 2 as shown in this figure.

STEP III. Figure 14.27C. With all inside corners in zones 1 and 2, the solution is simple. Zone 3 should also be easy, with two inside and two outside corners, and thus will be shown as a finished section in the next step.

STEP IV. Figure 14.27D. Zone 4 has four outside corners, two of which overlap zone 1. To find the ridge, use the upper two outside corners and extend the ridge well into zone 1, as shown in this figure. The valleys will start at points X and Y.

Because points X and Y are not the normal outside angles (180° or 270°), they must be bisected. It is easier to bisect the outside rather than the inside angle around points X and Y because these angles are less than 180°. This can be accomplished by measuring the angle with a protractor and mathematically dividing the angle, or by

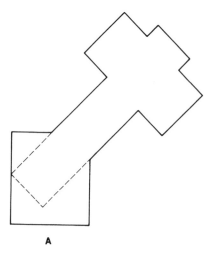

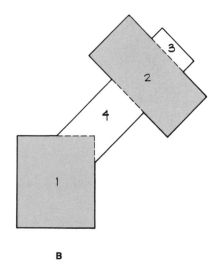

Figure 14.27 Problem 5.

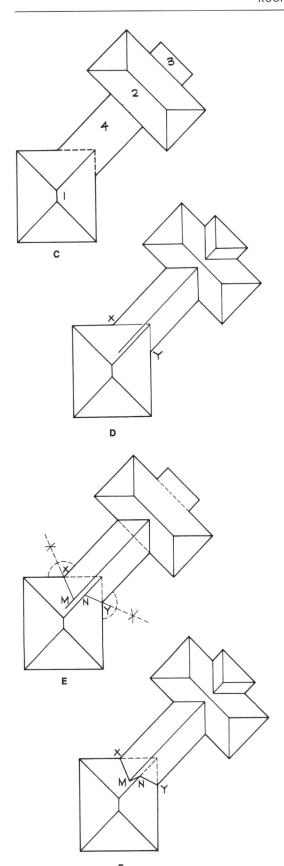

Figure 14.27   Problem 5 *(continued).*

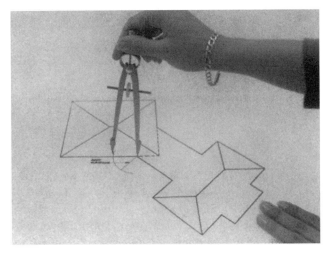

A

B

Figure 14.28   Bisecting an angle.

using a method, which you may have learned in a basic drafting class or in a geometry class, that requires use of a compass.

The compass is set at any radius, and an arc is struck, using X and Y as the center of the arc. See Figure 14.28A. Next, open the compass wider than the original settings and strike two more arcs, starting where the original arc struck the angular lines. See Figure 14.28B. Let's call this new intersection Z. When a line is drawn through Z and X (or Z and Y, depending on which angle you are bisecting), you have bisected the angle.

STEP V.   Figure 14.27E. Extend the bisecting lines from X and Y to the inside until they hit the ridge. We have identified these points as M and N.

STEP VI.   Figure 14.27F. Next, connect M and N. This line represents another valley at a different angle and defines the true geometric shape of zones 1 and 4 as they collide into each other. The dotted line, which is the underside of the hip of zone 1, is eliminated in a roof plan but may be shown on a subsequent roof framing plan.

Changing Configuration

After having configured an outline of a roof to its correct geometric shape, you can readily convert it to other than a hip roof. For example, consider the roof shown in Figure 14.29A.

Gable Roof.   To change this roof to a gable roof is accomplished by simply extending the ridges to the edge of the roof, as shown by the arrows. The final gable roof is displayed in Figure 14.29B. Notice the return of the valley lines (marked X).

In the next example, found in Figure 14.30, a slight bit of interpretation is needed for the top right corner of the structure.

Dutch Gable Roof.   The procedure for converting a hip roof to a Dutch gable is almost the same as for gable conversion, except that the ridge stops short of the perimeters of the building. The extension of the ridge can stop anywhere. The limiting factor may be the designer's de-

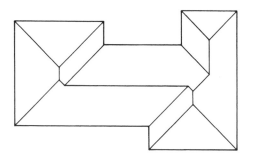

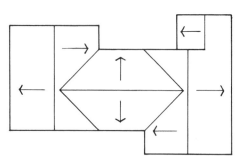

Figure 14.30   Hip to gable conversion.

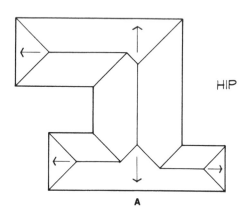

A

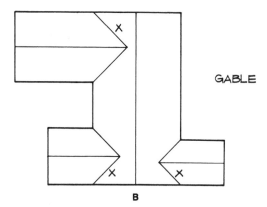

B

Figure 14.29   Changing configuration.

sire to produce a particular proportion for the gable portion of this roof. See dimensions X and Y in Figure 14.31.

Skylight Attic Location—Ventilation

A roof plan in conjunction with an exterior elevation gives the designer a perfect opportunity to position and check the appearance of such things as an attic ventilating system that must comply with energy standards. Standards have been instituted by local, state, and even federal commissions for energy conservation. An effective system may simply be a screened opening or a screened opening enhanced with a mechanical device.

Because heat rises, it is best to place ventilating systems as high as possible, at the ends of a roof, for thorough ventilation—also taking into consideration the prevailing winds and any other environmental factors that may dictate their position.

Traditionally, ventilation systems were placed on the ends of gable roofs, on the gable portion of a Dutch gable roof, or at the eaves of a hip roof. There are presently available roof-surface-mounted units and ridge ventilating systems, as well as numerous mechanical systems for industrial, commercial, and residential structures. As a drafter, you should be aware of the ventilating system used by your particular place of employment.

The position of skylights must always be verified on the roof plan. This will ensure that you are not cutting through a strategic area, such as a hip or valley of the

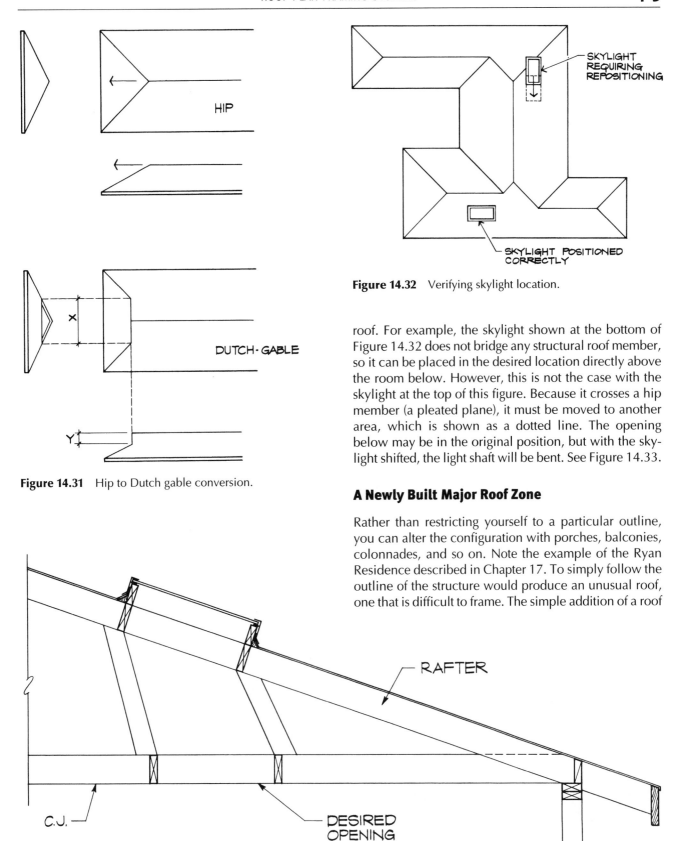

Figure 14.31 Hip to Dutch gable conversion.

Figure 14.32 Verifying skylight location.

roof. For example, the skylight shown at the bottom of Figure 14.32 does not bridge any structural roof member, so it can be placed in the desired location directly above the room below. However, this is not the case with the skylight at the top of this figure. Because it crosses a hip member (a pleated plane), it must be moved to another area, which is shown as a dotted line. The opening below may be in the original position, but with the skylight shifted, the light shaft will be bent. See Figure 14.33.

A Newly Built Major Roof Zone

Rather than restricting yourself to a particular outline, you can alter the configuration with porches, balconies, colonnades, and so on. Note the example of the Ryan Residence described in Chapter 17. To simply follow the outline of the structure would produce an unusual roof, one that is difficult to frame. The simple addition of a roof

Figure 14.33 Skylight with bent light shaft.

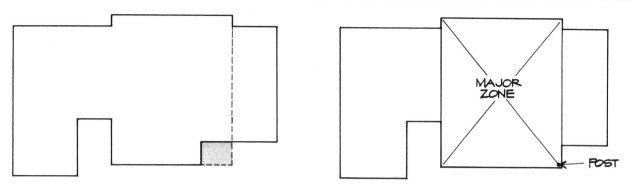

Figure 14.34   Changing the outline.

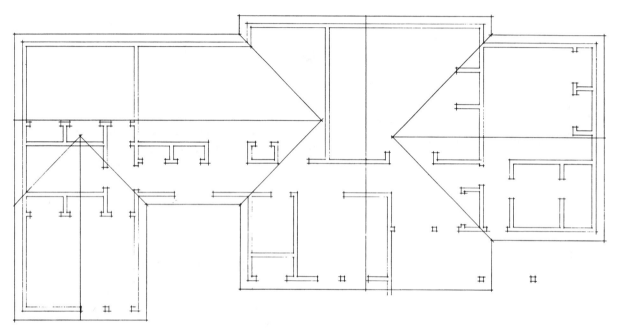

Figure 14.35   Roof to match zoning.

over the entry can protect the entry, create the basis for a better structural form, and even simplify the roof form. A simpler roof allows ease of construction, a system that is structurally stable, and, if it answers a functional need (covered entry), the best of all solutions. See Figure 14.34 for the transition from a simple outline to an extension of the roof over the entry and the beginning of a structural system that improves the strength of the total structure (See Figure 14.35).

■ DRAWING A ROOF PLAN ON THE COMPUTER

STAGE I   (Figure 14.36). This is the roof plan datum stage. It requires an accurate drawing of the perimeter of the structure. One of the initial stages of the floor plan becomes the datum and should be XREFed into the system.

STAGE II   (Figure 14.37). Add to the outline the various zones to be roofed by isolating the geometry used by the designer and later used by the structural engineer to properly structure this geometric form with its component parts.

STAGE III   (Figure 14.38). The chimney to the fireplace and skylights are positioned, and the roof ridges and valleys are added to the roof structure.

STAGE IV   (Figure 14.39). Skylights and chimneys that cut through ridges and valleys are resolved through detailing. Roof slopes and venting of the attic are done at this stage. Heat rises, so it is recommended that the ridge vents be placed as high atop the roof as possible. A portion of the roof may be hatched to show the roof material covering this structure.

STAGE V   (Figure 14.40). This is the plotting and titling stage. Elevations of the top of the roof may be noted if the municipality calls for height restrictions.

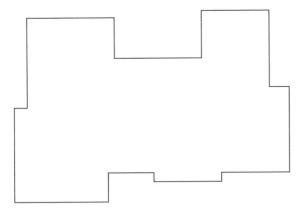

Figure 14.36 Stage I: Datum.

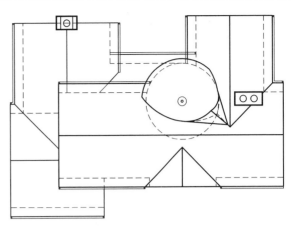

Figure 14.38 Stage III: Defining roof shape.

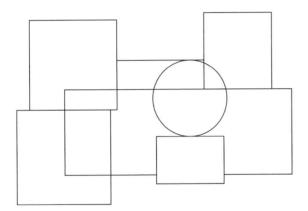

Figure 14.37 Stage II: Isolating geometry.

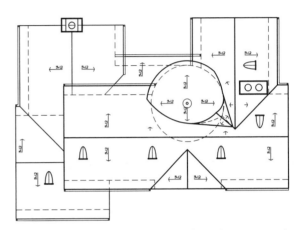

Figure 14.39 Stage IV: Chimney, slope direction, and vents.

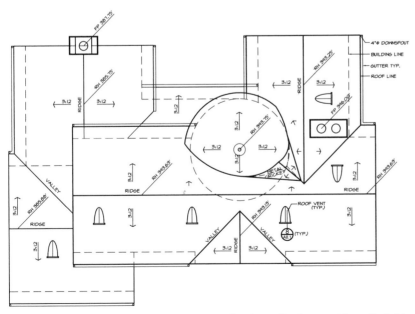

Figure 14.40 Stage V: Noting. (Courtesy of Mike Adli, Owner; Nagy R. Bakhoum, President of Obelisk Architects.)

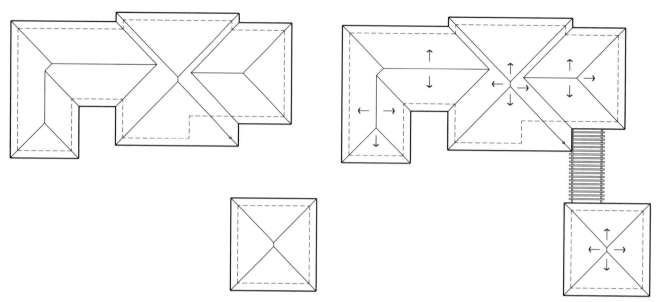

Figure 14.41   Stage I: Developing a hip roof.

Figure 14.42   Stage II: A hip roof with a trellis spline.

As an extension of Figure 14.35 and the roof of the Ryan Residence found in Chapter 17, a roof plan of a hip roof is developed here in three stages. The five stages previously discussed are still valid for a beginning drafter.

STAGE I   (Figure 14.41). The datum stage and the description of the geometry are combined in one stage.

STAGE II   (Figure 14.42). The trellis connecting the garage and the residence are immediately incorporated, and the direction of the flow of rainwater is

drawn with an arrow. This is an excellent time to check for any flat spots that can trap water.

STAGE III   (Figure 14.43). This stage finishes this roof plan with the inclusion of skylights, cricket/saddles, chimneys, and roof drains, plus all of the necessary reference symbols and final written descriptions.

To illustrate another roof plan, a drawing of a mountain cabin with heavy snow loads is included and displayed in Figure 14.44.

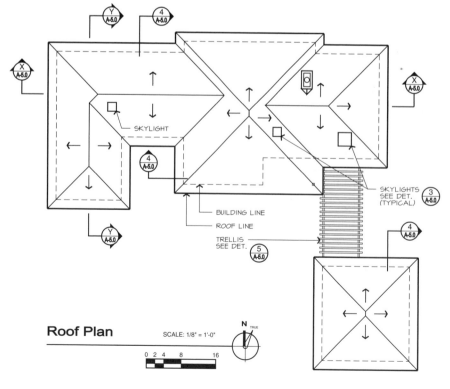

Roof Plan

SCALE: 1/8" = 1'-0"

0 2 4   8   16

Figure 14.43   Stage III: Completing a roof plan for a hip roof.

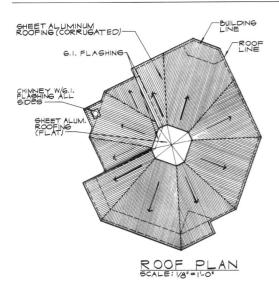

Figure **14.44**   Stage IV: Roof plan using sheet aluminum.

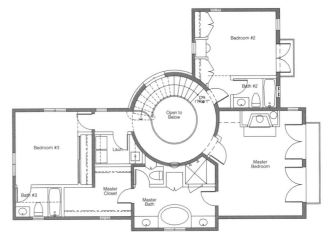

Figure **14.46**   Stage II: Identifying bearing and nonbearing walls.

DRAWING A ROOF FRAMING PLAN ON THE COMPUTER

The roof framing plan may be drafted by a structural engineer, or a less expensive move may be to provide the structural engineer with a set of digital drawings on which the engineer may calculate the sizes needed for all of the structural components (rafters, headers, sheet walls, etc.). These can then be translated in the architectural office as a CAD drawing.

For a better understanding of the system that will be used to build the roof structure, refer to Chapter 17 and the framing analysis prior to the drafting of the Ryan Residence roof framing plan.

STAGE I   (Figure 14.45). An early stage of the second floor plan becomes the datum for the evolution of this drawing.

STAGE II   (Figure 14.46). After looking at the engineer's sketch, the CAD drafter may separate the bearing walls from the nonbearing walls by pouché. The walls that are bearing the weight of the roof are hatched (textured). This can make the drawing easier to understand and help the drafter proceed to the next stage.

STAGE III   (Figure 14.47). Because the bearing and nonbearing walls have been identified, the drafter will not have any trouble in also placing the direction and duration symbols on the drawing. Because the bearing walls are located, the drafter can also isolate the most important headers and beams listed by the engineer and isolate critical beams that may be missing on the engineer's sketch. Shear walls are also located, drawn, and referenced to a schedule (also shown in Figure 14.47).

STAGE IV   (Figure 14.48). All noting and referencing occurs in this stage.

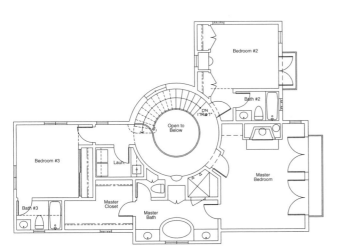

Figure **14.45**   Stage I: Floor plan as datum.

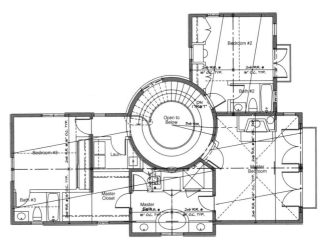

Figure **14.47**   Stage III: Direction, duration, shear, and beams.

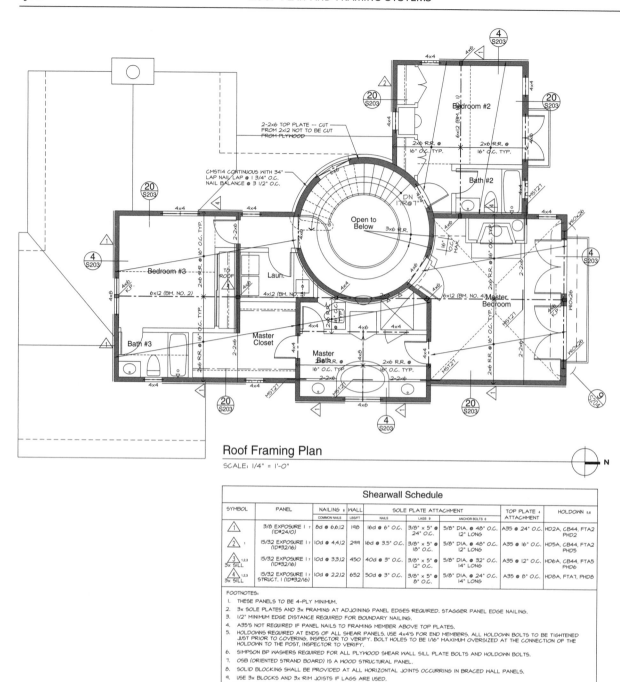

Roof Framing Plan

SCALE: 1/4" = 1'-0"

N

SYMBOL	PANEL	NAILING 8		WALL	SOLE PLATE ATTACHMENT			TOP PLATE 4 ATTACHMENT	HOLDDOWN 5,6
		COMMON NAILS	LBS/FT	NAILS	LAGS 9	ANCHOR BOLTS 8			

Shearwall Schedule

SYMBOL	PANEL	NAILING 8 COMMON NAILS	LBS/FT	WALL NAILS	SOLE PLATE ATTACHMENT LAGS 9	ANCHOR BOLTS 8	TOP PLATE 4 ATTACHMENT	HOLDDOWN 5,6
1	3/8 EXPOSURE 1 7 (ID#24/0)	8d @ 6,6,12	198	16d @ 6" O.C.	3/8" x 5" @ 24" O.C.	5/8" DIA. @ 48" O.C. 12" LONG	A35 @ 24" O.C.	HD2A, CB44, FTA2 PHD2
2 1	15/32 EXPOSURE 1 7 (ID#32/16)	10d @ 4,4,12	299	16d @ 3.5" O.C.	3/8" x 5" @ 18" O.C.	5/8" DIA. @ 48" O.C. 12" LONG	A35 @ 16" O.C.	HD5A, CB44, FTA2 PHD5
3 1,2,3 3x SILL	15/32 EXPOSURE 1 7 (ID#32/16)	10d @ 3,3,12	450	40d @ 3" O.C.	3/8" x 5" @ 12" O.C.	5/8" DIA. @ 32" O.C. 14" LONG	A35 @ 12" O.C.	HD6A, CB44, FTA5 PHD6
4 1,2,3 3x SILL	15/32 EXPOSURE 1 7 STRUCT. 1 (ID#32/16)	10d @ 2,2,12	652	50d @ 3" O.C.	3/8" x 5" @ 8" O.C.	5/8" DIA. @ 24" O.C. 14" LONG	A35 @ 8" O.C.	HD8A, FTA7, PHD8

FOOTNOTES:
1. THESE PANELS TO BE 4-PLY MINIMUM.
2. 3x SOLE PLATES AND 3x FRAMING AT ADJOINING PANEL EDGES REQUIRED. STAGGER PANEL EDGE NAILING.
3. 1/2" MINIMUM EDGE DISTANCE REQUIRED FOR BOUNDARY NAILING.
4. A35'S NOT REQUIRED IF PANEL NAILS TO FRAMING MEMBER ABOVE TOP PLATES.
5. HOLDOWNS REQUIRED AT ENDS OF ALL SHEAR PANELS. USE 4x4'S FOR END MEMBERS. ALL HOLDDOWN BOLTS TO BE TIGHTENED JUST PRIOR TO COVERING, INSPECTOR TO VERIFY. BOLT HOLES TO BE 1/16" MAXIMUM OVERSIZED AT THE CONNECTION OF THE HOLDDOWN TO THE POST, INSPECTOR TO VERIFY.
6. SIMPSON BP WASHERS REQUIRED FOR ALL PLYWOOD SHEAR WALL SILL PLATE BOLTS AND HOLDDOWN BOLTS.
7. OSB (ORIENTED STRAND BOARD) IS A WOOD STRUCTURAL PANEL.
8. SOLID BLOCKING SHALL BE PROVIDED AT ALL HORIZONTAL JOINTS OCCURRING IN BRACED WALL PANELS.
9. USE 3x BLOCKS AND 3x RIM JOISTS IF LAGS ARE USED.

Figure 14.48 Stage IV: Noting. (Courtesy of Mike Adli, Owner; Nagy R. Bakhoum, President of Obelisk Architects.)

■ ROOF FRAMING—HIP ROOF

The roof plan for an alternate hip roof for the Ryan Residence (Chapter 17) is evolved as a roof framing plan. To avoid redundancy in describing the stages, the four previous stages have been reduced to two.

STAGE I (Figure 14.49). The floor plan shown in Figure 17.45, used as a datum, and the layer showing the roof shape (Figure 14.41), were used in conjunction with each other. Bearing walls were pouchéd at this stage.

STAGE II (Figure 14.50). This drawing shows the finished display. In particular, note:

A. The shaded areas showing California Frame (see Figure 17.78).

B. Detail and building section bubbles.

C. Title—both graphic and scale called-out.

D. North arrow.

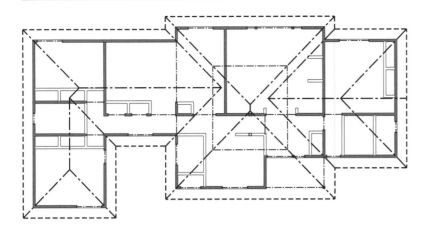
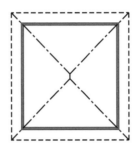

Figure 14.49 Stage I: Roof framing plan—hip roof.

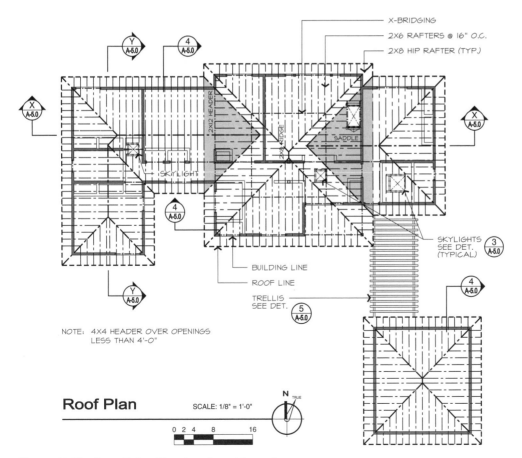

Figure 14.50 Stage II: Roof framing plan—hip roof.

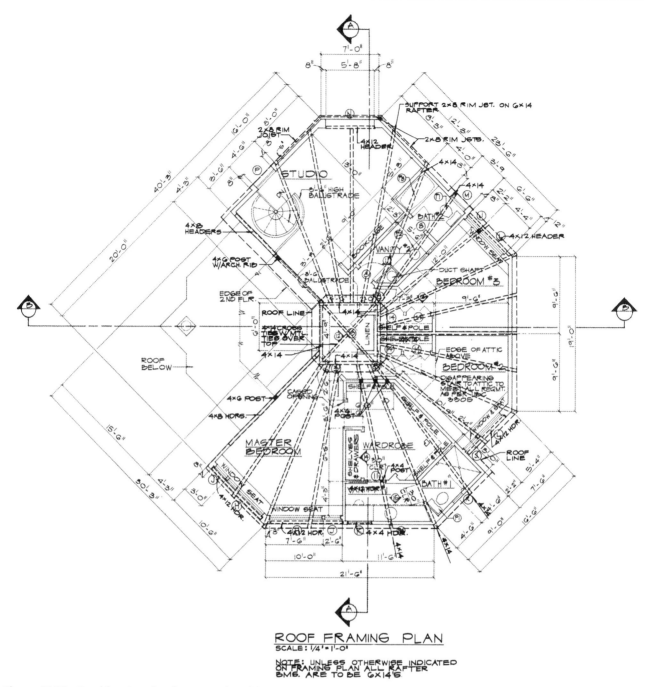

Figure 14.51   Roof framing plan for mountain cabin.

E. Location and framing around the fireplace and the skylights.

Mountain Cabin

The roof framing plan for a mountain cabin is shown using a single finished drawing stage (see Figure 14.51). An earlier stage of the floor plan was adjusted with lighter lines so that the principal framing lines would be clearly displayed.

■ FLOOR FRAMING

The basic conventions for floor framing are generally the same as those used in roof or ceiling framing plans.

When drawing floor framing plans with CAD, the architectural technician should be aware of the datum that is the floor plan. The floor plan should be used, with XREF as discussed in Chapter 3. In this manner, not only do you keep the size of the file small, but any corrections or changes in the floor plan will be reflected in the framing plan.

This section discusses a second floor framing plan that will be drawn onto the first floor plan. Two systems will be shown. The first will be conventional framing. The second will be drawn with engineered lumber, as discussed in Chapter 5. In discussing engineered lumber, we will show how to use the computer framing program developed by Boise Cascade called "BC Framer."

Conventional Floor Framing Plan

STAGE I   (Figure 14.52). Use an early stage of the floor plan that shows all the walls and openings in the structure. Fireplaces, elevators, and stairs should be included and externally referenced in the drawing set so that the framing around them can be included.

STAGE II   (Figure 14.53). The various areas to be framed include openings and are identified as zones. An example of the framing that will be employed for openings is shown in Figure 14.54. If not already done, any bearing walls should be identified with hatching (texturing).

STAGE III   (Figure 14.55). Shear walls are drawn at this stage and referenced to a schedule that is shown directly below the framing drawing. Headers, beams,

and openings are defined, using a centerline. Critical columns and posts should also be identified.

STAGE IV   (Figure 14.56). This stage shows the direction of the floor joist and its duration. A half arrowhead is used to indicate direction, and a full arrowhead indicates the duration. They are connected with an ellipse.

STAGE V   (Figure 14.57) . The direction lines receive information as to size and space. Headers, beams, and columns are identified, along with the hardware and the connectors used. Referencing and titling complete the drawing.

Floor Framing Above Masonry

The graphic display of the floor framing on a masonry wall looks similar to the previously discussed roof framing plan in that it also uses the same symbols and conventions. An example of a first floor framing plan over a basement whose walls are made of concrete block (masonry) is shown in Figure 14.58. Figure 14.59 is a photograph of the framing in progress for this mountain cabin.

The drawing was done by hand. The basement floor plan was printed on an engineering copier, using a thin

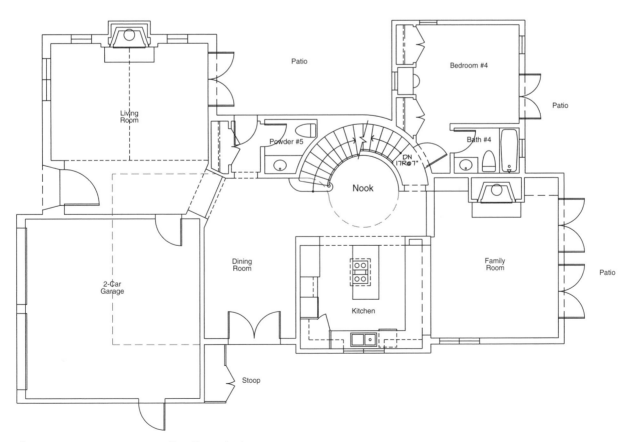

Figure 14.52   Stage I: Datum (first floor plan).

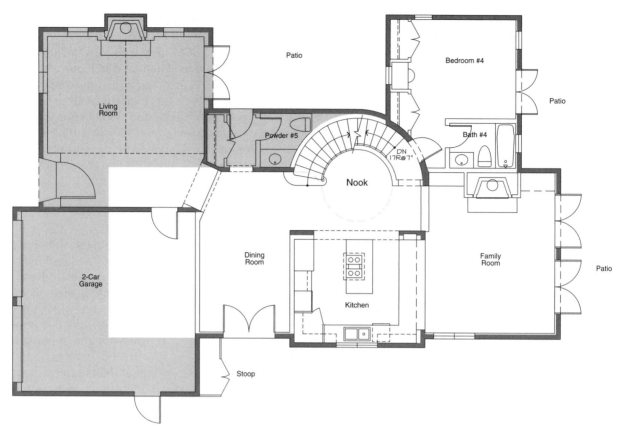

Figure 14.53   Stage II: Selecting zones.

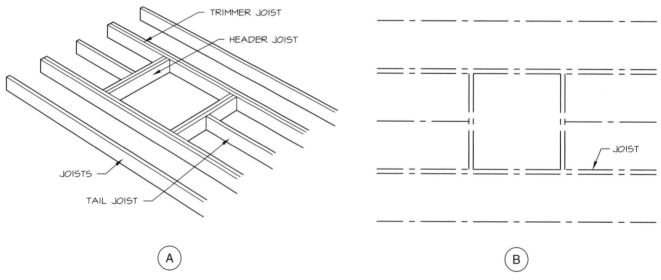

Figure 14.54   Framing an opening.

tissue overlay to reduce the intensity of the lines. It was printed on vellum as a base for this new master. The beam, headers, and framing members were drafted over this plan, and one can easily see the difference of line weights.

If the drawing had been done on a computer, the basement floor plan could have been scanned, sized, and put on a base layer, with the framing portion done on a second layer and the text line done on a third layer.

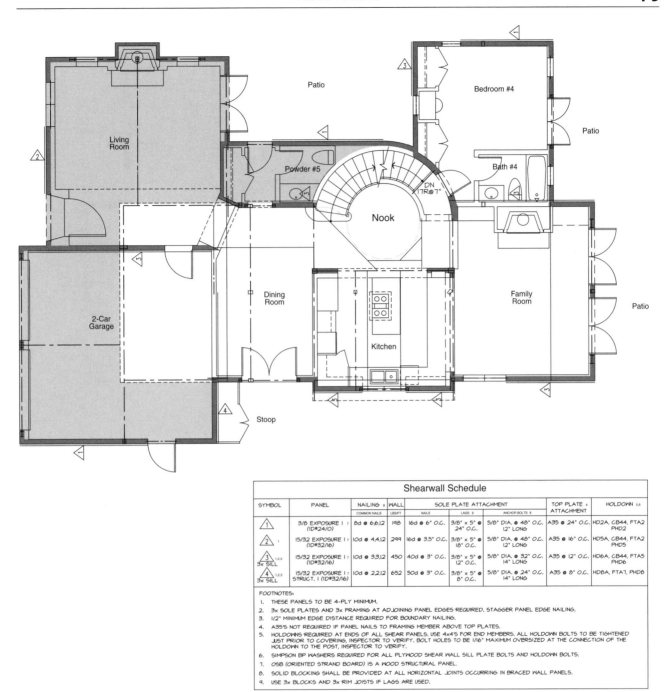

Shearwall Schedule								
SYMBOL	PANEL	NAILING 8	WALL	SOLE PLATE ATTACHMENT			TOP PLATE 4 ATTACHMENT	HOLDOWN 5,6
		COMMON NAILS	LBS/FT	NAILS	LAGS 9	ANCHOR BOLTS 6		
△1	3/8 EXPOSURE I 7 (ID#24/O)	8d @ 6,6,12	198	16d @ 6" O.C.	3/8" x 5" @ 24" O.C.	5/8" DIA. @ 48" O.C. 12" LONG	A35 @ 24" O.C.	HD2A, CB44, FTA2 PHD2
△2 1	15/32 EXPOSURE I 7 (ID#32/16)	10d @ 4,4,12	299	16d @ 3.5" O.C.	3/8" x 5" @ 18" O.C.	5/8" DIA. @ 48" O.C. 12" LONG	A35 @ 16" O.C.	HD5A, CB44, FTA2 PHD5
△3 1,2,3 3x SILL	15/32 EXPOSURE I 7 (ID#32/16)	10d @ 3,3,12	450	40d @ 3" O.C.	3/8" x 5" @ 12" O.C.	5/8" DIA. @ 32" O.C. 14" LONG	A35 @ 12" O.C.	HD6A, CB44, FTA5 PHD6
△4 1,2,3 3x SILL	15/32 EXPOSURE I 7 STRUCT. I (ID#32/16)	10d @ 2,2,12	652	50d @ 3" O.C.	3/8" x 5" @ 8" O.C.	5/8" DIA. @ 24" O.C. 14" LONG	A35 @ 8" O.C.	HD8A, FTA7, PHD8

FOOTNOTES:
1. THESE PANELS TO BE 4-PLY MINIMUM.
2. 3x SOLE PLATES AND 3x FRAMING AT ADJOINING PANEL EDGES REQUIRED. STAGGER PANEL EDGE NAILING.
3. 1/2" MINIMUM EDGE DISTANCE REQUIRED FOR BOUNDARY NAILING.
4. A35'S NOT REQUIRED IF PANEL NAILS TO FRAMING MEMBER ABOVE TOP PLATES.
5. HOLDOWNS REQUIRED AT ENDS OF ALL SHEAR PANELS. USE 4x4'S FOR END MEMBERS. ALL HOLDOWN BOLTS TO BE TIGHTENED JUST PRIOR TO COVERING, INSPECTOR TO VERIFY. BOLT HOLES TO BE 1/16" MAXIMUM OVERSIZED AT THE CONNECTION OF THE HOLDOWN TO THE POST, INSPECTOR TO VERIFY.
6. SIMPSON BP WASHERS REQUIRED FOR ALL PLYWOOD SHEAR WALL SILL PLATE BOLTS AND HOLDOWN BOLTS.
7. OSB (ORIENTED STRAND BOARD) IS A WOOD STRUCTURAL PANEL.
8. SOLID BLOCKING SHALL BE PROVIDED AT ALL HORIZONTAL JOINTS OCCURRING IN BRACED WALL PANELS.
9. USE 3x BLOCKS AND 3x RIM JOISTS IF LAGS ARE USED.

Figure 14.55 Stage III: Structural support.

Floor Framing Plan with Engineered Lumber

Rather than using the conventional method of framing described throughout this chapter, here we introduce the second floor framing system via engineered lumber. These drawings will become part of the structural set under normal circumstances, and not part of the architectural set of construction documents.

Normally, the first floor plan is sent to the manufacturer of the engineered lumber, as described in Chapter 5. For an example, we will use a plan drawn by Boise Cascade that utilizes the 9-1/2" high Boise Cascade 400 series. This will be noted as 9-1/2BCI-400.

The drawing is done by Boise Cascade drafters on a system similar to that of a standard AutoCAD program. The BC Framer, as it is called, reconciles the space allo-

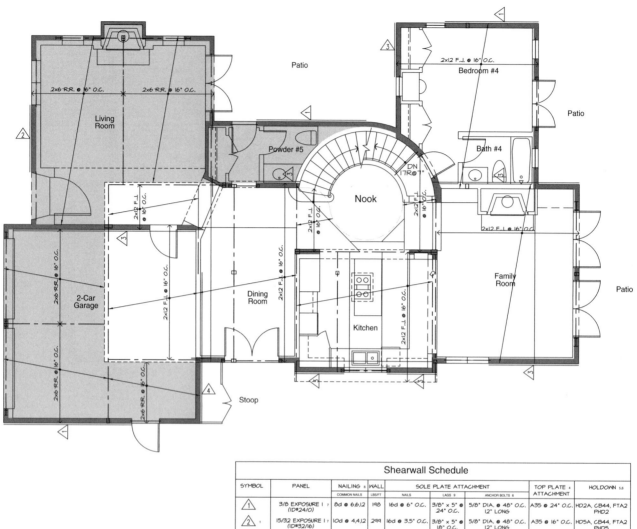

				Shearwall Schedule				
SYMBOL	PANEL	NAILING 8	WALL	SOLE PLATE ATTACHMENT			TOP PLATE 4 ATTACHMENT	HOLDOWN 5,6
		COMMON NAILS	LBS/FT	NAILS	LAGS 9	ANCHOR BOLTS 6		
△1	3/8 EXPOSURE I 7 (ID#24/0)	8d @ 6,6,12	198	16d @ 6" O.C.	3/8" x 5" @ 24" O.C.	5/8" DIA. @ 48" O.C. 12" LONG	A35 @ 24" O.C.	HD2A, CB44, FTA2 PHD2
△2 1	15/32 EXPOSURE I 7 (ID#32/16)	10d @ 4,4,12	299	16d @ 3.5" O.C.	3/8" x 5" @ 18" O.C.	5/8" DIA. @ 48" O.C. 12" LONG	A35 @ 16" O.C.	HD5A, CB44, FTA2 PHD5
△3 1,2,3 3x SILL	15/32 EXPOSURE I 7 (ID#32/16)	10d @ 3,3,12	450	40d @ 3" O.C.	3/8" x 5" @ 12" O.C.	5/8" DIA. @ 32" O.C. 14" LONG	A35 @ 12" O.C.	HD6A, CB44, FTA5 PHD6
△4 1,2,3 3x SILL	15/32 EXPOSURE I 7 STRUCT. I (ID#32/16)	10d @ 2,2,12	652	50d @ 3" O.C.	3/8" x 5" @ 8" O.C.	5/8" DIA. @ 24" O.C. 14" LONG	A35 @ 8" O.C.	HD8A, FTA7, PHD8

FOOTNOTES:
1. THESE PANELS TO BE 4-PLY MINIMUM.
2. 3x SOLE PLATES AND 3x FRAMING AT ADJOINING PANEL EDGES REQUIRED. STAGGER PANEL EDGE NAILING.
3. 1/2" MINIMUM EDGE DISTANCE REQUIRED FOR BOUNDARY NAILING.
4. A35'S NOT REQUIRED IF PANEL NAILS TO FRAMING MEMBER ABOVE TOP PLATES.
5. HOLDOWNS REQUIRED AT ENDS OF ALL SHEAR PANELS. USE 4x4'S FOR END MEMBERS. ALL HOLDOWN BOLTS TO BE TIGHTENED JUST PRIOR TO COVERING. INSPECTOR TO VERIFY. BOLT HOLES TO BE 1/16" MAXIMUM OVERSIZED AT THE CONNECTION OF THE HOLDOWN TO THE POST. INSPECTOR TO VERIFY.
6. SIMPSON BP WASHERS REQUIRED FOR ALL PLYWOOD SHEAR WALL SILL PLATE BOLTS AND HOLDOWN BOLTS.
7. OSB (ORIENTED STRAND BOARD) IS A WOOD STRUCTURAL PANEL.
8. SOLID BLOCKING SHALL BE PROVIDED AT ALL HORIZONTAL JOINTS OCCURRING IN BRACED WALL PANELS.
9. USE 3x BLOCKS AND 3x RIM JOISTS IF LAGS ARE USED.

Figure 14.56 Stage IV: Direction of joist and duration.

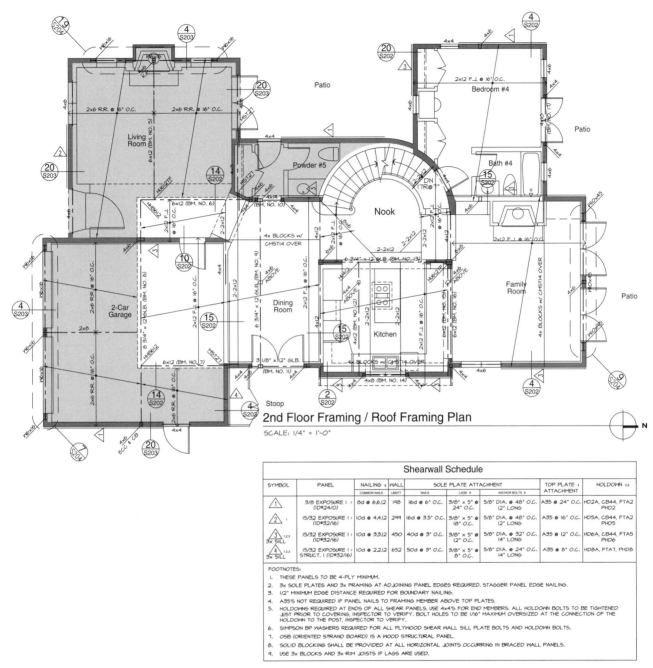

2nd Floor Framing / Roof Framing Plan

SCALE: 1/4" = 1'-0"

Shearwall Schedule

SYMBOL	PANEL	NAILING 8	WALL	SOLE PLATE ATTACHMENT			TOP PLATE 4 ATTACHMENT	HOLDOWN 5,6
		COMMON NAILS 7	LBS/FT	NAILS	LAGS 9	ANCHOR BOLTS 6		
△1	3/8 EXPOSURE 1 7 (ID#24/0)	8d @ 6,6,12	198	16d @ 6" O.C.	3/8" x 5" @ 24" O.C.	5/8" DIA. @ 48" O.C. 12" LONG	A35 @ 24" O.C.	HD2A, CB44, FTA2 PHD2
△2 1	15/32 EXPOSURE 1 7 (ID#32/16)	10d @ 4,4,12	299	16d @ 3.5" O.C.	3/8" x 5" @ 18" O.C.	5/8" DIA. @ 48" O.C. 12" LONG	A35 @ 16" O.C.	HD5A, CB44, FTA2 PHD5
△3 1,2,3 3x SILL	15/32 EXPOSURE 1 7 (ID#32/16)	10d @ 3,3,12	450	40d @ 3" O.C.	3/8" x 5" @ 12" O.C.	5/8" DIA. @ 32" O.C. 14" LONG	A35 @ 12" O.C.	HD6A, CB44, FTA5 PHD6
△4 1,2,3 3x SILL	15/32 EXPOSURE 1 7 STRUCT. 1 (ID#32/16)	10d @ 2,2,12	652	50d @ 3" O.C.	3/8" x 5" @ 8" O.C.	5/8" DIA. @ 24" O.C. 14" LONG	A35 @ 8" O.C.	HD8A, FTA7, PHD8

FOOTNOTES:
1. THESE PANELS TO BE 4-PLY MINIMUM.
2. 3x SOLE PLATES AND 3x FRAMING AT ADJOINING PANEL EDGES REQUIRED. STAGGER PANEL EDGE NAILING.
3. 1/2" MINIMUM EDGE DISTANCE REQUIRED FOR BOUNDARY NAILING.
4. A35'S NOT REQUIRED IF PANEL NAILS TO FRAMING MEMBER ABOVE TOP PLATES.
5. HOLDOWNS REQUIRED AT ENDS OF ALL SHEAR PANELS. USE 4x4'S FOR END MEMBERS. ALL HOLDOWN BOLTS TO BE TIGHTENED JUST PRIOR TO COVERING, INSPECTOR TO VERIFY. BOLT HOLES TO BE 1/16" MAXIMUM OVERSIZED AT THE CONNECTION OF THE HOLDOWN TO THE POST, INSPECTOR TO VERIFY.
6. SIMPSON BP WASHERS REQUIRED FOR ALL PLYWOOD SHEAR WALL SILL PLATE BOLTS AND HOLDOWN BOLTS.
7. OSB (ORIENTED STRAND BOARD) IS A WOOD STRUCTURAL PANEL.
8. SOLID BLOCKING SHALL BE PROVIDED AT ALL HORIZONTAL JOINTS OCCURRING IN BRACED WALL PANELS.
9. USE 3x BLOCKS AND 3x RIM JOISTS IF LAGS ARE USED.

Figure 14.57 Stage V: Complete floor framing plan. (Courtesy of Mike Adli, Owner; Nagy R. Bakhoum, President of Obelisk Architects.)

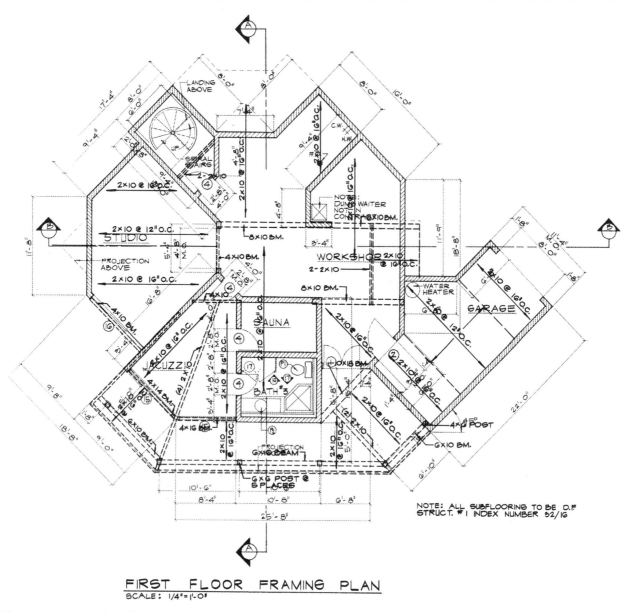

FIRST FLOOR FRAMING PLAN
SCALE: 1/4"=1'-0"

Figure 14.58 First floor framing plan.

cated for the thickness of the floor determined by the designer, which is given to the manufacturer along with the floor plan. The manufacturer then takes the information provided by the office and translates it into the framing plan, as shown in Figure 14.60A. A pictorial of the assembly is shown in Figure 14.60B. Samples of the series of pictorial details are shown in Figure 14.60C, and a list of required materials and hardware is in Figure 14.60D. A separate cost estimate is provided to the office, along with any engineering calculations required by the governing department of building and safety. The service is total and makes the preparation of framing plans a delight for the office. However, the senior drafters must be able to not only read the framing plans but also ensure

their proper integration with the rest of the drawings. The drafters must also consider that space must be provided for any overlooked items such as duct space for heating and air-conditioning units; space for venting appliances such as ranges and hot water heaters; space for electronic appliances and access for electrical lines from the fixtures to the computers and for the drainpipes that run from the roof through the floors and walls. All of these problems should be resolved before you submit the plans for framing drawings. Such thoroughness will also provide the workers in the field with a clear picture of potential problems that can be averted. This is further accomplished with comprehensive details, partial sections, and full sections.

Figure 14.59 First floor framing.

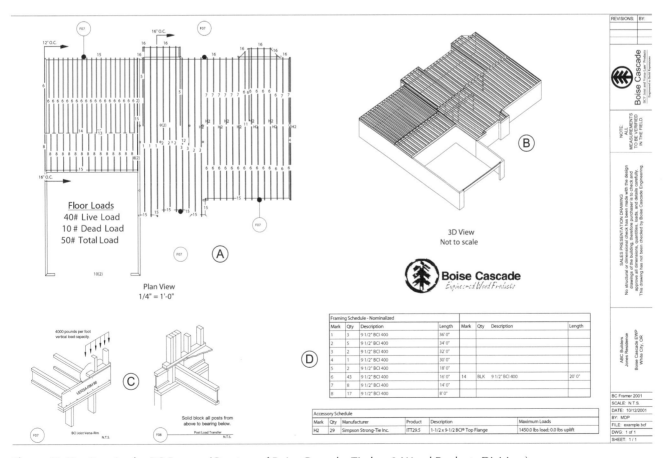

Figure 14.60 Drawing by BC Framer. (Courtesy of Boise Cascade, Timber & Wood Products Division.)

chapter

15

INTERIOR ELEVATIONS

■ PURPOSE AND CONTENT OF INTERIOR ELEVATIONS

The drawing process for **interior elevations** resembles the drafting procedure for exterior elevations. You should be familiar with the chapter on exterior elevations before proceeding with this chapter.

Sources of Measurements

Use the floor plan and building sections for accurate measurements of the width and height of an interior elevation wall. When you use these plans, remember that these dimensions are usually to the stud line or center line of the wall. Interior elevations are drafted to the plaster line.

Interior elevations may not always be drafted at the same scale as the floor plans or sections. Because this requires a scale transition, use caution to avoid errors. In this chapter, if the same scale is used and the drawings are directly projected from the plan and section, it is done only to show the theory of where to obtain shapes and configurations.

Information Shown on Interior Elevations

Some architectural offices draft interior elevations for every wall of every room. Although this can guard against errors, many wall surfaces are so simple that they do not need a formal drafted interior elevation. These simple walls depend primarily on the interior finish schedule for their proper description.

Use interior elevations when you need to convey an idea, dimension, construction method, or unique feature that you can better describe by drafting than by a written description in the specification. For example, in a residence, the kitchen, bathrooms, special closets, and wet bars have walls that are usually drafted. On a commercial structure, you may select typical office units showing bookcases, cabinets, display cases, and so on. In an industrial structure you may draw the locations of equipment, conveyor belts, and special heights for bulletin boards or tool racks.

In other words, interior elevations are the means of controlling the interior walls of a structure in terms of construction, surface finishes, and the providing of information to subcontractors.

Naming Interior Elevations

In exterior elevations, the titles assigned—North, South, East, and West—are based on the direction the structure faces. In interior elevations this is reversed: The title is based on the direction in which the viewer is looking. For example, if you are standing in a theatre lobby facing north, the interior wall you are looking at has the title "North Lobby Elevation." See Figure 15.1. To avoid confusion when you are naming an interior elevation, you should use reference bubbles like those in Figure 15.2.

The reference symbol shown on the left is the same as the one used in the foundation plans and framing plans when you need to refer to details. Remember that the reference bubble is a circle with a darkened point on one side which points to the elevation being viewed and drawn.

The reference symbol shown on the right in Figure 15.3 shows a circle with a triangle inside it. The point of

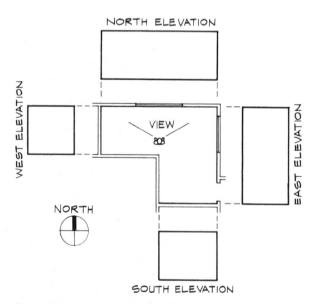

Figure 15.1 Naming interior elevations.

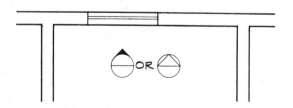

Figure 15.2 Interior elevation reference bubbles.

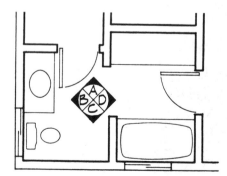

Figure 15.3 Symbol used to show multiple interior elevations.

triangle tells the viewer which elevation is being viewed, and the placement of the triangle automatically divides the circle in half. The top half contains a letter or number, which becomes the name of that interior elevation. The lower half contains the sheet number on which the interior elevation can be found.

Figure 15.3 shows a floor plan and a symbol used to show multiple elevations. Letter "A" is for the North elevation, "C" is for the South elevation, "B" for the West elevation, and "D" for the East elevation. Figure 15.4 shows two types of **title references**.

Choosing a Scale

The most desirable scale to use on an interior elevation is ½" = 1'-0". Most floor plans are drafted at ¼" = 1'-0", so using the scale makes the translation from floor plan to interior elevation easy because you only need to use a pair of dividers and double every measurement. Interior elevations are seldom drawn larger than this.

If the drawing space does not permit you to use a ½" = 1'-0" scale, or if the scale of the drawing calls for a smaller interior elevation, you may use a ⅜" = 1'-0" or ¼" = 1'-0" scale. The scale could also depend on the complexity of the wall to be shown.

Using Dotted Lines

Dotted lines are used extensively on interior elevations. As in the drafting of exterior elevations, the dotted line is used to show door-swing direction—for example, for cabinets or for bi-fold doors on a wardrobe closet. See Figure 15.5. Dotted lines are also used to represent items

Figure 15.4 Interior elevation titles.

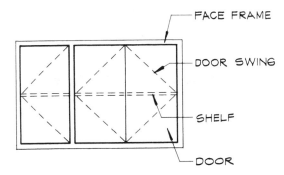

Figure 15.5 Typical elevation of cabinet.

hidden from view, for example, the outline of a kitchen sink, shelves in a cabinet, or the vent above a hood vent, range, or cook top.

Dotted lines are also used to show the outline of objects to be added later or those **not in the contract** (designated as "**N.I.C.**"). For example, the outline of a washer and dryer or refrigerator is shown. Even though the appliances themselves are not in the contract, space must be allowed for them. The wall behind the appliance is shown, including duplex convenience outlets, and moulding or trim at the base of the wall.

Other Drafting Considerations

To draft interior elevations of cabinets, you must know the type, countertop material, heights, general design, and number of cabinet doors.

Types of Cabinet Doors. There are three main types of cabinet doors: **flush**, **flush overlay**, and **lip**. As Figure 15.6 shows, flush overlay doors cover the total face of the cabinet. The front surface, called the **face frame** of the cabinet, does not show. The flush door is shown in Figure 15.7 and the lip door in Figure 15.8. Because the face

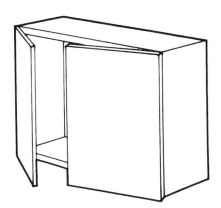

Figure 15.6 Flush overlay doors.

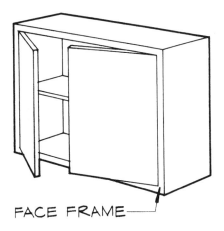

Figure 15.7 Flush doors.

frame of the cabinet shows in both the lip and flush cabinet doors, they appear the same in the interior elevation.

Material Designation and Noting

Materials for interior elevations are represented like the materials for exterior elevations. Refer to Chapter 13, on exterior elevations, for samples.

Noting is kept simple and generic terms are often used. Specific information, brand names, workmanship notes, procedures, applications, and finishes are placed in the specifications. Later in this chapter you will see examples of generic noting for such items as ceramic tile countertops, an exhaust hood (with a note to "See specs."), and metal partitions.

Outline of Interior Elevations

The outline of an interior elevation represents the outermost measurement of a room. Objects that project toward the viewer, such as cabinets, beams, and air-conditioning ducts, are drawn. Some architectural offices deal with these as if they were in section, but most prefer to treat them as shown in Figures 15.9 and 15.10. Note in Figure 15.10 that the tops of the cabinets have been eliminated in drafting the outline of the cabinet.

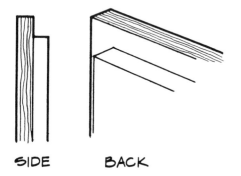

Figure 15.8 Up door.

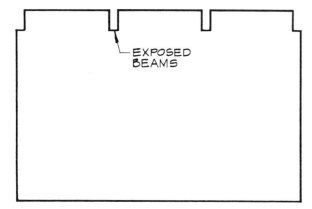

Figure 15.9 Exposed beams.

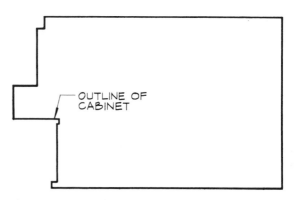

Figure 15.10 Outline of cabinet.

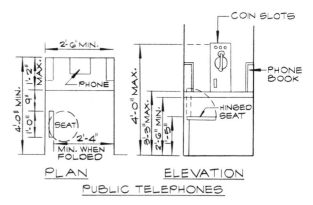

Figure 15.11 Public telephone for disabled persons. (Courtesy of AVCO Community Developers, Inc., and Mann Corporation of California.)

Planning for Children and Persons with Disabilities

Always have information available on standards affecting facilities that should be usable by children and persons with disabilities. Here are some of the standards established by several states for disabled persons:

1. Door opening: minimum size 2'-8" clear
2. Restroom grab bars: 33–36" above the floor
3. Towel bars: 3'-4" maximum above floor
4. Top of lavatory: 34" maximum above floor
5. Drinking fountains: 3'-0" maximum

Many standards can be obtained by writing to the proper authority, such as the State Architect's office. Most standards are presented in the form of a drawing; see Figure 15.11 for an example.

■ DIMENSIONS AND INTERSECTIONS

Dimensions

When you draft a set of interior elevations, do not repeat dimensions that appear elsewhere. For example, you do not need to indicate the width of rooms on the interior elevation. In fact, avoid repeating dimensions at all costs.

In this way, if you need to make changes on one plan—such as the floor plan—you do not risk forgetting to change the interior elevations.

In a similar way, you do not need to dimension the interior elevation of the counter of Figure 15.12, because it will occupy the total width of the room. The boundaries, which are the walls, are already dimensioned on the floor plan.

The interior elevations for Figure 15.12 will show a counter, walls, a window, and an opening. The portion of the counter that returns toward the opening should be dimensioned either on the floor plan or on the interior elevations, but not on both. See Figure 15.13.

Notice how the base cabinet is dimensioned; in fact, the space between the door and the cabinet could have been dimensioned instead. Deciding whether to dimension the space or the cabinet is based on which is more important. If the space is left for an appliance or some other piece of equipment, then the space should be dimensioned.

The interior elevation is also the place to provide such information as the location of medicine cabinets, the heights of built-in drawers, the locations of mirrors, the required clearance for a hood above a range, and the heights of partitions.

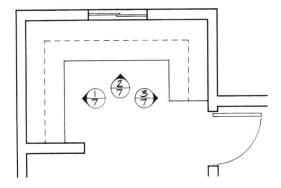

Figure 15.12 Partial plan of food preparation area.

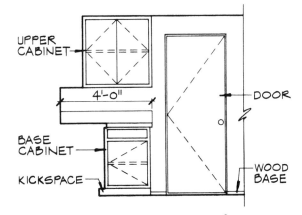

Figure 15.13 Partial interior elevation of $\frac{3}{2}$.

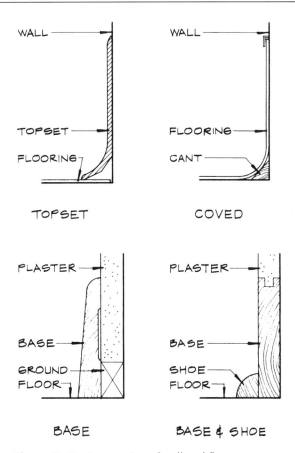

Figure 15.14 Intersection of wall and floor.

Intersection of Wall and Floor

Interior elevations can also show, in a simple way, the wall and floor intersection. This can be achieved by applying a topset, covering the floor, or using a base or a base and a shoe. This creates a transition between the floor and wall planes. **Topset** is made of flexible material such as rubber and placed on the wall where it touches the floor. **Coving** is a method whereby the floor material is curved upward against the wall. A **base** is used to cover or as a guide to control the thickness of the plaster on the wall, and a **shoe** covers the intersection between the wall and floor. See Figure 15.14.

■ DRAFTING AN INTERIOR ELEVATION: EXAMPLES

A Kitchen

Figure 15.15 shows a perspective view of a kitchen. The main portion has lip doors on the cabinets, and the extreme left side (not shown in the perspective) has flush overlay doors. Different types of cabinet doors are not usually mixed on a single project; here the intention is simply to show the different methods used to represent them on an interior elevation. Figure 15.16 shows a floor plan of the perspective drawing in Figure 15.15. Note the flush overlay cabinet on the left and the lip or flush cabinets on the right. The upper and base cabinets, slightly left of center, project forward.

Figure 15.17 shows the drafted interior elevation of one side of the floor plan of the kitchen. You should take careful note of these points:

1. The difference in the method of representing a flush overlay and a lip door on the cabinets
2. The outlining of the cabinet on the extreme right side of the drawing
3. The use of dotted lines to show door swing, shelves, and the outline of the sink
4. The handling of the forward projection of the upper and base cabinets slightly to the left of center
5. Dimensions and, eventually, the location of notes

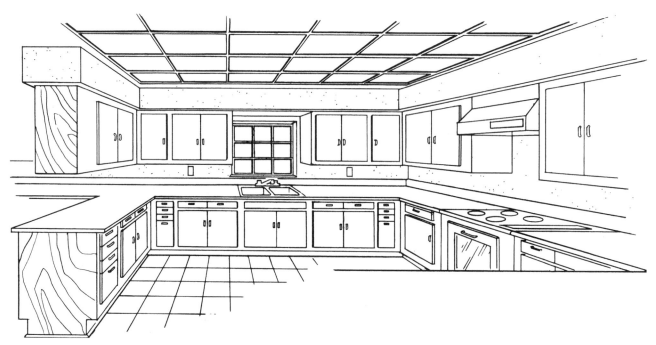

Figure 15.15   Perspective of a kitchen.

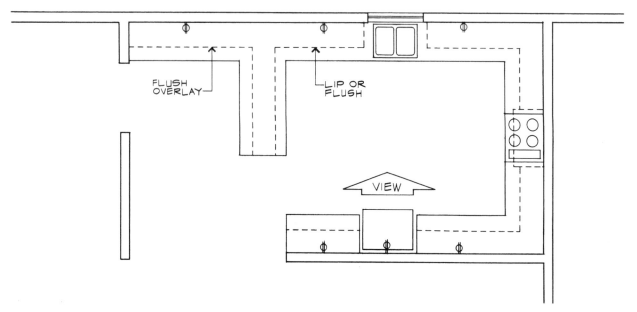

Figure 15.16   Partial floor plan of kitchen.

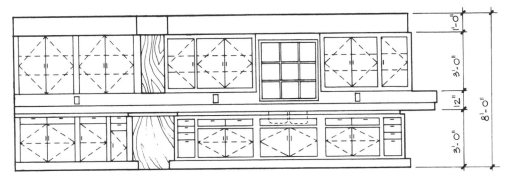

Figure 15.17 Interior elevation of Figure 15.16.

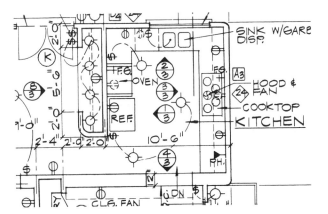

Figure 15.18 Partial floor plan of kitchen. (Courtesy of William F. Smith—Builder.)

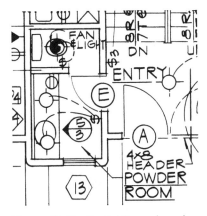

Figure 15.19 Partial floor plan of powder room. (Courtesy of William F. Smith—Builder.)

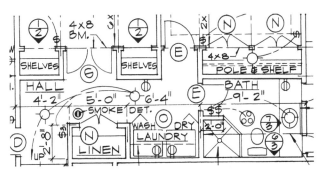

Figure 15.20 Partial lower floor plan. (Courtesy of William F. Smith—Builder.)

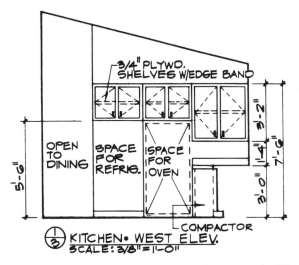

Figure 15.21 Kitchen: West elevation. (Courtesy of William F. Smith—Builder.)

A Condominium

Figures 15.18 and 15.20 are partial floor plans of a two-story condominium project. The corresponding interior elevations can be found in Figures 15.21 through 15.28. Different ways of showing door openings, cabinets, appliances, partial walls, open shelves, and other features are given. Notice the dimensioning procedure and the noting method used.

A Lobby and Restroom

Figure 15.29 shows a partial floor plan for the lobby and restroom area of an office building. Figure 15.30 shows the North elevation of the men's toilet. Because this is a public facility, access for persons with disabilities is shown on both the partial floor plan and the interior elevation.

Additional interior elevations for a beach house and for a threatre are found in later chapters.

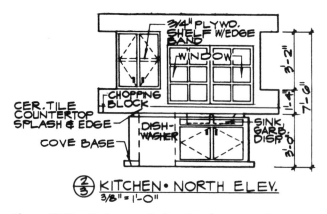

Figure 15.22 Kitchen: north elevation. (Courtesy of William F. Smith—Builder.)

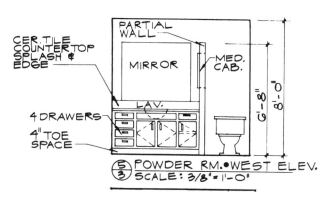

Figure 15.25 Powder room: West elevation. (Courtesy of William F. Smith—Builder.)

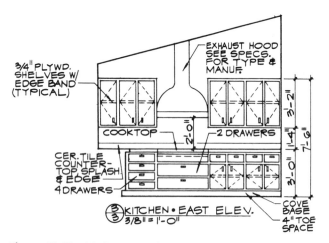

Figure 15.23 Kitchen: East elevation. (Courtesy of William F. Smith—Builder.)

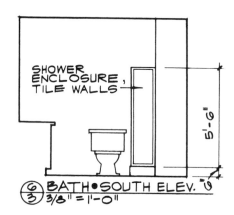

Figure 15.26 Bath: South elevation. (Courtesy of William F. Smith—Builder.)

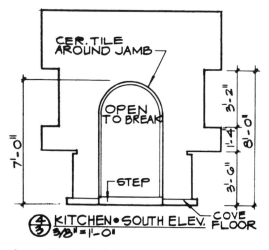

Figure 15.24 Kitchen: South elevation. (Courtesy of William F. Smith—Builder.)

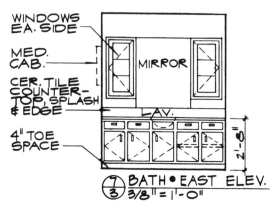

Figure 15.27 Bath: East elevation. (Courtesy of William F. Smith—Builder.)

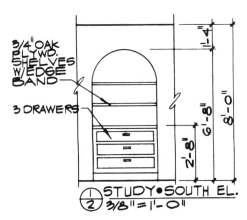

Figure 15.28 Study elevation. (Courtesy of William F. Smith—Builder.)

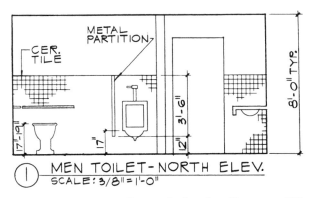

Figure 15.30 Men's toilet: North elevation. (Courtesy of Westmount, Inc., Real Estate Development, Torrance, CA.)

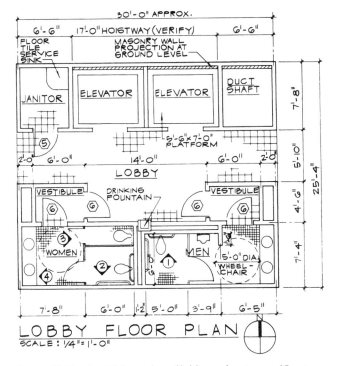

Figure 15.29 Partial floor plan of lobby and restroom. (Courtesy of Westmount, Inc., Real Estate Development, Torrance, CA.)

■ TEMPLATES

One of the best time-saving devices available for the drafting of interior elevations is a template, especially for plumbing fixtures. Plumbing fixtures have very difficult shapes to replicate with normal instruments, thus the use of a template similar to that shown in Figure 15.31 speeds up the drafting process.

If you need to draw ceramic tile, this template can provide you with ceramic tile spacing, as can be seen at the left of the figure. Shower heads and faucets are also

positioned in relationship to a baseline at the bottom, which is the floor line.

■ INTERIOR ELEVATION DRAFTING

The best way to transfer room sizes from a floor plan to an interior elevation manually is with the use of a pair of dividers. Dividers are most effective when the scale of the interior elevation is the same or as double the floor plan. See Figure 15.32. As seen in the building section, a proportional divider can be used if the scale is other than ¼" or ½". A scale of ⅜", a typical in-between scale used in drafting an interior elevation, can be accomplished by setting the proportional divider at ⅔.

Computers and Interior Elevations

The drafting of a set of interior elevations for any structure, be it commercial, industrial, or residential, becomes a relatively painless task when you enlist the aid of a computer. Textures are easily applied to a drawing by using the Hatch command. If you are drawing full-scale in model space, you can transfer heights from the datum layer of the sections and the width and depth of a room from the floor plan.

Cabinet outlines, plumbing appliances, and many other outlines can be imported from a set of previously developed drawings or frequently can be found in a collection of shapes. A collection may include such configurations and conventions titled as electrical, cabinetry, plumbing, and other categories stored in a library file of symbols and conventions.

The unique shapes of fireplaces, elevators, lifts, handrails, stairs, and so on, can be purchased in a generic format, or exact sizes can be obtained from the manufacturers.

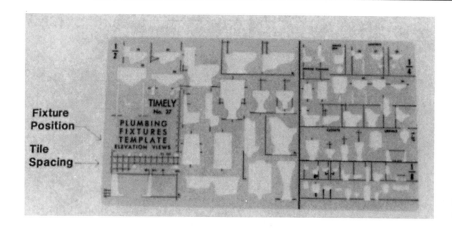

Fixture
Position

Tile
Spacing

Figure 15.31 Plumbing fixture template. (Courtesy of Timely Products Co.)

Figure 15.32 Drafting an interior elevation at ¹/₂″ scale from a ¹/₄″-scale drawing.

■ EVOLUTION OF A SET OF INTERIOR ELEVATIONS

This section is devoted to the various development stages of interior elevations. To illustrate this, the Kavanaugh Residence was selected. It has an exposed ridge and vaulted ceilings in some of its rooms, including the master suite, dining room, family room, library, kitchen, living room, and guest room. See Figure 15.9 and its accompanying text for a description of how to pictorially draw exposed beams in drawing an interior elevation. The early stages of the floor plan are shown in Figure 15.33.

STAGE I   (Figure 15.34). Stage I, called the ease or datum stage, sets the parameters. These include the width from wall to wall and the height, and the changes that may exist in the floor or ceiling level. Prior to this stage, the drafter should consult the project book and become familiar with the sizes and shapes of the various kitchen appliances, plumbing fixtures, cabinets, washer and dryer, and so forth.

STAGE II   (Figure 15.35). Once the maximum size of the room is determined, the real outline of the interior elevation is established by drawing in the soffits, cabinets, fireplaces, and so on. Doors and windows may

also be included in this stage. The total outline is now converted to a dark outline. See Figures 15.22 and 15.26 for examples.

STAGE III   (Figure 15.36). This is the stage at which various products are added to what is basically an empty room: bathtubs, toilets, built-in bookshelves, fireplaces, and so on.

STAGE IV   (Figure 15.37). Material designations and patterns such as ceramic tile wainscots, fire extinguishers, bulletin boards, and decorative added forms are included along with texturing. Some of the shapes for such items as plumbing appliances can often be obtained from the manufacturer. Swings on cabinet doors and outlines (dotted) of fixtures behind the exposed face, such as a sink, flues from fireplaces, and shelves, are also added at this stage.

STAGE V   (Figure 15.38). This is the dimensioning stage. Remember, we must locate and size all items. A good example is a mirror. It must first be sized, and its placement or position on a wall must be given to the installer. If the installation is at all complex, a detail should be drawn. If a description is needed, the detailer must know whether it is described in the specifications. If it is, a generic title is all that is needed at this stage.

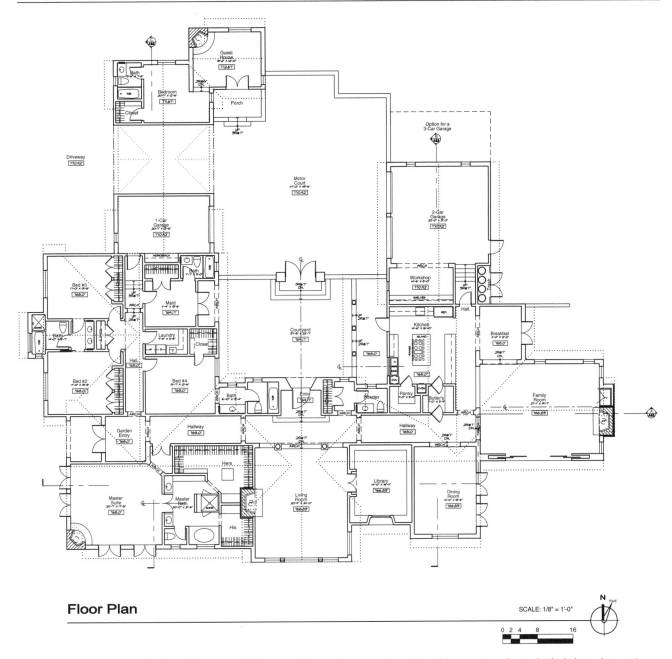

Floor Plan

SCALE: 1/8" = 1'-0"

0 2 4   8   16

Figure 15.33 Kavanaugh plans. (Courtesy of Kavanaugh Development; Nagy R. Bakhoum, President of Obelisk Architects.)

Dimensioning also calls for setting limits, such as the clearance of a water closet (toilet) between a wall and a cabinet. Some building codes require a minimum 15-inch distance between the center of the water closet and the adjacent wall.

STAGE VI (Figure 15.39). Notes, references, and titles are included at this stage. Use the following checklist as a guide or develop your own.

    A. Call-outs for all surface materials, other than those included on the finish schedule.

    B. A description of all appliances, even those that are not on the surface facing the observer—for example, sinks, garbage disposals, recessed medicine cabinets.

    C. A description of items that are not standard. The open shelves in a master bedroom is a classic example.

    D. The use of standard conventions to denote shelves, cabinet door swings, drawers, and so forth.

    E. Any clearances that must be maintained. Those needed for refrigerators and microwave ovens are good examples in this instance.

Figure 15.34   Stage I: Datum.

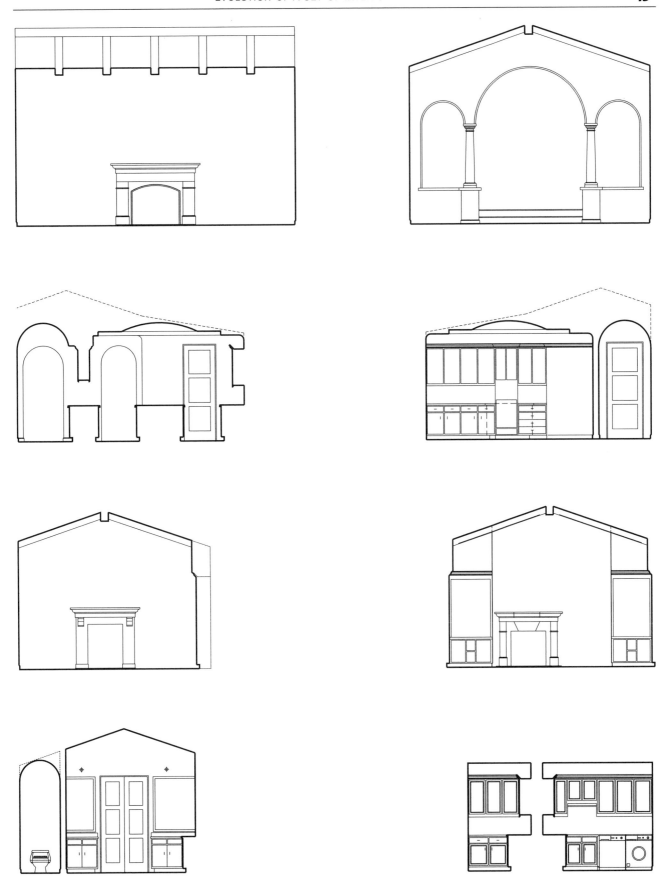

Figure 15.35 Stage II: real outline and doors and windows.

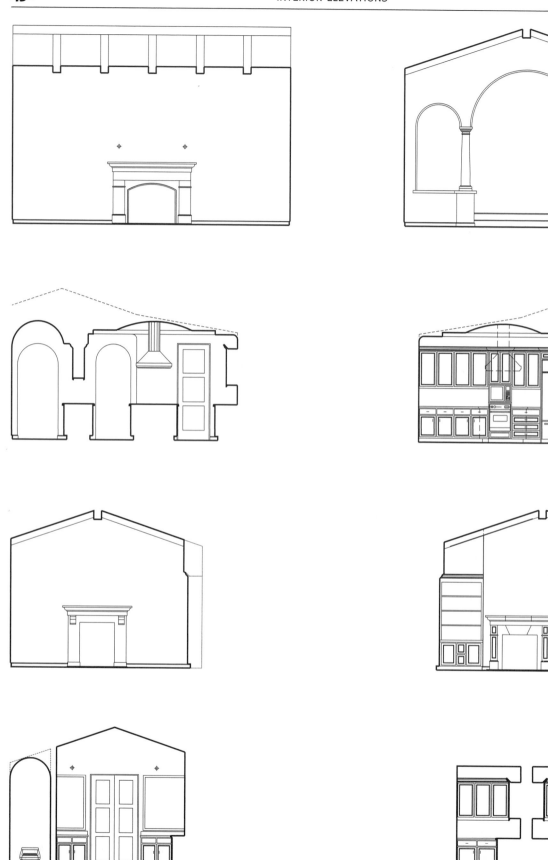

Figure 15.36 Stage III: Products and appliances.

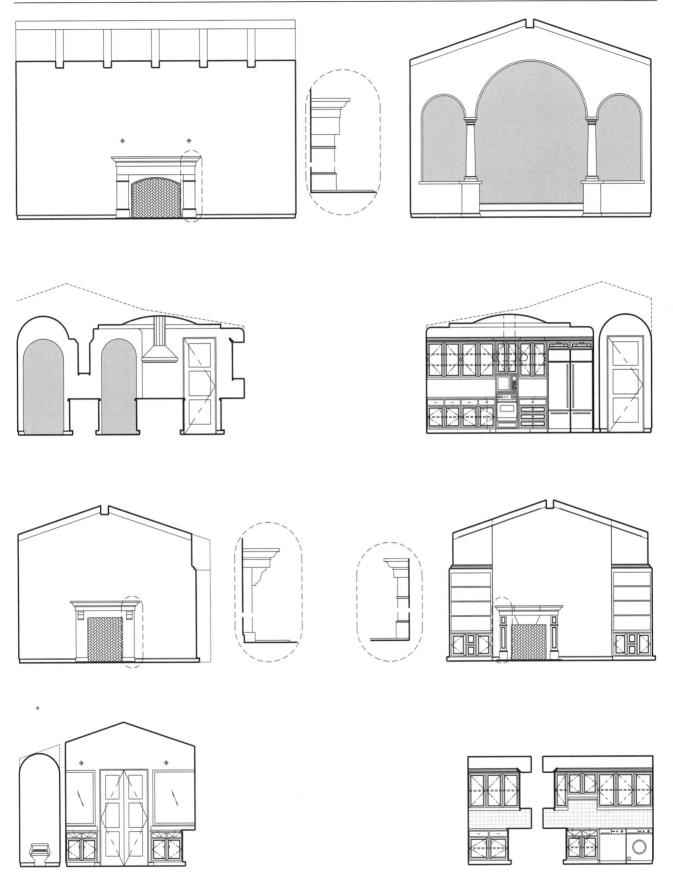

Figure 15.37 Stage IV: Material designation and patterns.

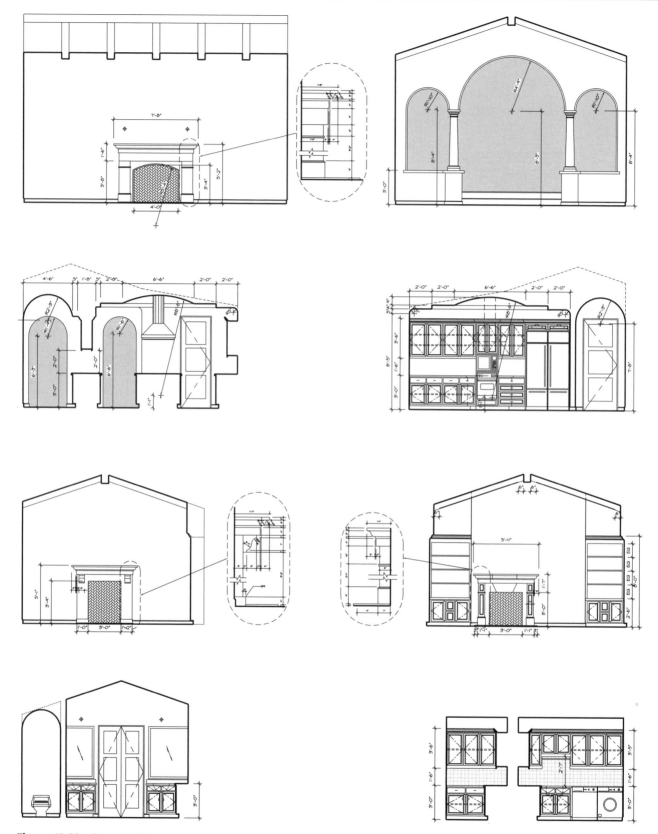

Figure 15.38 Stage V: Dimensioning.

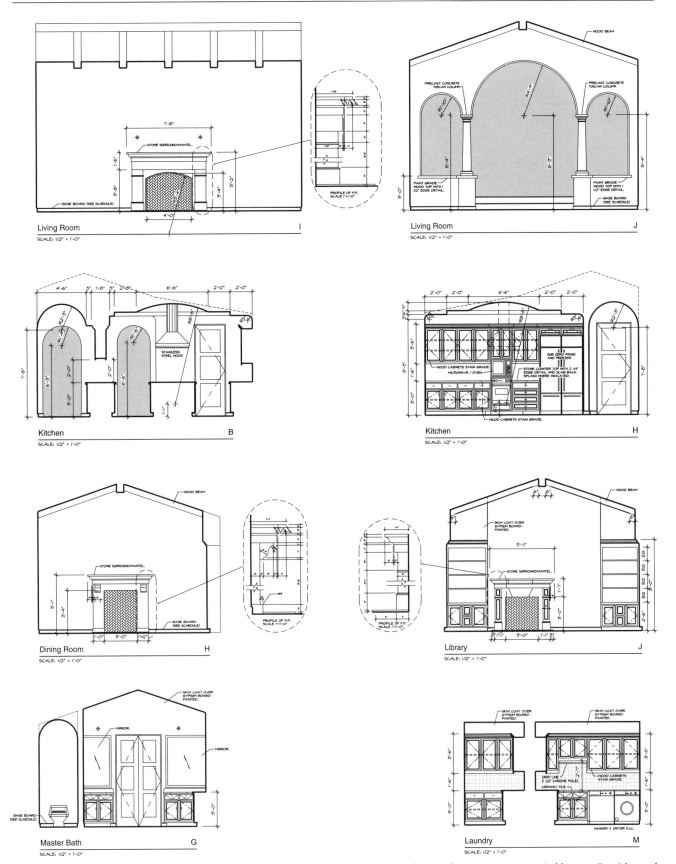

Figure 15.39 Stage VI: Noting, referencing, and titles. (Courtesy of Kavanaugh Development; Nagy R. Bakhoum, President of Obelisk Architects.)

chapter

16

ARCHITECTURAL DETAILS
AND VERTICAL LINKS
(STAIRS/ELEVATORS)

■ THE PURPOSE OF ARCHITECTURAL DETAILS

Architectural **details** are enlarged drawings of specific architectural assemblies. These details are usually provided by the architect, and structural details are furnished by the structural engineer.

Architectural details are done for many different construction assemblies, including door and window details, fireplace details, stair details, and wall and roof assemblies. The number and kind of details needed for a given project depends entirely on the architect's or designer's estimate of what is needed to clarify the construction process. The contractor may request additional architectural details in the construction stage.

Architectural details often start with **freehand sketches** and an architectural scale in order to solve different construction assemblies in a structure. Once the details have been formulated in a scaled freehand sketch, they are then ready to be drafted in final form. Many details, such as standard foundation and wall assemblies, are relatively straightforward and do not require freehand sketches. The following sections provide examples of residences to give you an understanding of what is required.

The drawing of details from scratch requires a drafter who understands detailing relative to the detail area available. One should not draft a detail and plot it to fit the space, but should rather begin with the office format sheet and then decide whether keynotes will be used and what type of noting will be used. The steps required to create a detail and to determine what formatting to use are covered later in this chapter.

■ USING DETAILS IN CONSTRUCTION DOCUMENTS

Freehand Detail Sketches: Mountain Residence

Architectural details encompass many construction assemblies, such as this mountain residence with unique foundation details. This residence was selected because of its unusual geometric shape, similar to that of a pentagon. Figure 16.1 shows a freehand sketch detail of an exterior bearing footing for this residence. Parts of the residence are seen throughout this book. Refer to the chart in the Appendix, on the web site for the figure numbers and their location in this book and, when available, on the web site. There are some nonstandard conditions in this detail, such as steel anchor clips for the connection of the floor joists to the mudsill (for lateral support), steel reinforcing placement in the wall for earth retention, and location of (and installation requirements for) a footing drain. Figures 16.2 and 16.3 show two other exterior footing conditions: Figure 16.2 shows a concrete

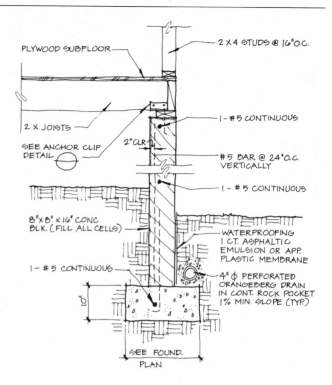

EXTERIOR BEARING FOOTING

Figure 16.1 Detail of exterior bearing footing.

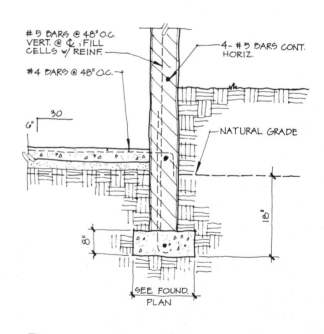

EXTERIOR FOOTING

Figure 16.2 Detail of exterior footing.

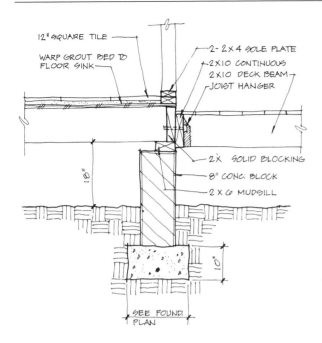

Figure 16.3   Detail of deck at exterior footing.

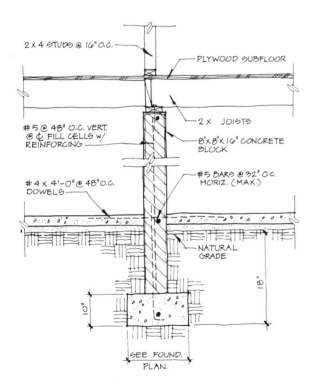

Figure 16.4   Detail of interior concrete block wall.

floor condition below grade, and Figure 16.3 shows the wood deck connection to the exterior footing.

An interior foundation and masonry wall are also sketched in detail, showing steel reinforcing placement and floor joist assembly in Figure 16.5. Figures 16.5 and 16.6 show other interior footing conditions: Figure 16.5 shows a bearing footing with a concrete floor; Figure 16.6 shows a square concrete pier and reinforcing bars required to support a heavy concentrated load distributed by a 6 × 6 post. Study each of these carefully before proceeding further.

If you are asked to detail a wood beam and masonry wall connection, with the required assembly information, first draw a freehand sketch including the necessary information. Figure 16.7 shows such a sketch. The size

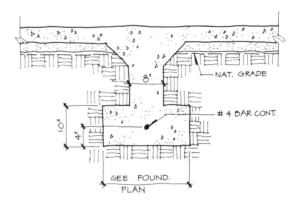

Figure 16.5   Detail of interior bearing footing.

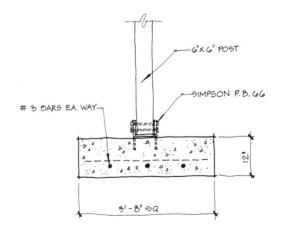

Figure 16.6   Detail of footing at wood post.

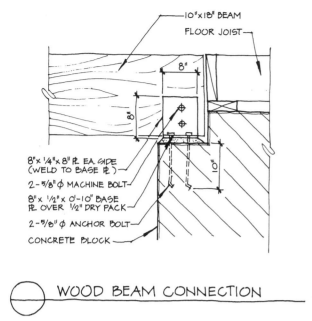

WOOD BEAM CONNECTION

Figure 16.7   Detail of wood beam connection.

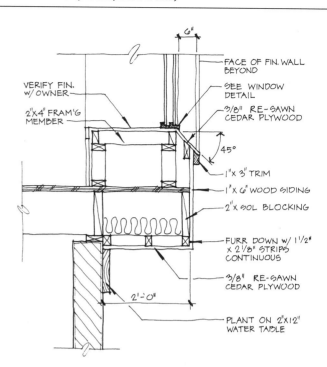

FLOOR FRAMING CANTILEVER

Figure 16.8   Detail of floor framing cantilever.

of the steel plate dictates the masonry wall offset, and the embedment of the anchor bolts is 10″.

An important factor in architectural detailing is providing details that are an integral part of the architectural design of the building. For example, if floor cantilevers and wood soffits are an integral part of the design, first design and solve these assemblies in sketch form, as shown in Figure 16.8, before completing the final detail. As this figure shows, creativity and craftsmanship in architectural detailing are as important as any other factors in designing a structure.

In this particular residence, we thought that the top of the head section of the windows and doors should have a direct relationship with the eave assembly. So we detailed the eave assembly with the various wood members forming a wood soffit directly above the head section of the window. See Figure 16.9. We sketched in detail the windowsill and exterior wall assembly projecting down from the head section. From both these figures 16.8 and 16.9, it was possible to design and detail the **jamb** section for this particular opening, using the established head and sill section as a guide for the detailed assembly. Figure 16.10 shows a freehand sketch of the jamb details. We used two wood stud walls at the window area to provide a deep architectural relief at the openings. See Figure 16.9.

Details: Beach Residence (For additional details, see Chapter 9.)

Foundation Details.   The architectural details for this project were fairly conventional but were still worth in-

vestigating with freehand drawings. To better understand these details, refer to Chapter 18 for a description of the evolution of the construction documents to which these details pertain. For example, we detailed the foundation details for this two-story residence to satisfy the sandy soil requirements. Figure 16.11 shows a detail for the exterior bearing wall. Because this soil did not provide good bearing qualities, we used horizontal reinforcing rods at the top and bottom of the foundation wall. Non-bearing walls still required a minimal footing to support the weight of the wall and a depth of concrete to receive the anchor bolts. See Figure 16.12. Because this residence has a change of floor levels, we provided a detail through the floor transitions. Figure 16.13 shows a detail at a location that has incorporated the **risers** and **tread**. (A riser is the vertical dimension of a stair step and the tread is the horizontal dimension.) The risers and tread are dimensioned, as are rebar ties for the connection of the upper concrete floor. (Rebar ties act as dowels to join two concrete elements.)

A large storage area and a mechanical room were located in the basement. A detail was needed to show the assembly for the basement and floor level changes. See Figure 16.14. The wood stud wall has been offset in front of the upper level concrete floor to provide a nailing surface for the wall finishes at both levels.

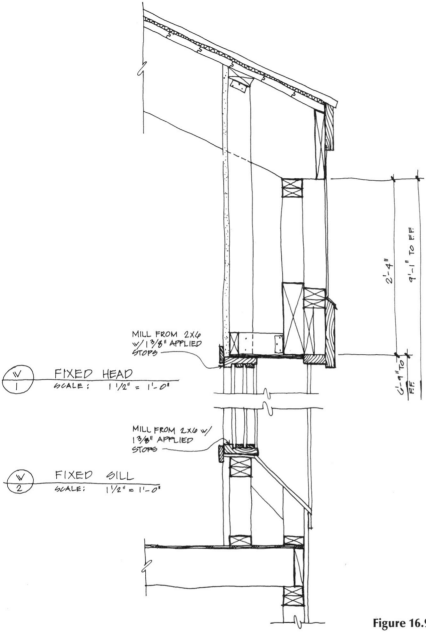

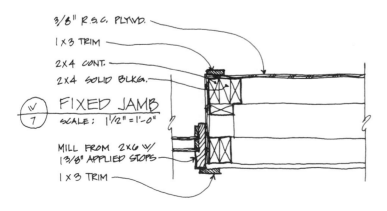

W
1 FIXED HEAD
   SCALE: 1 1/2" = 1'-0"

MILL FROM 2X6
W/ 1 3/8" APPLIED
STOPS

2'-4"

9'-1" TO F.F.

6'-9" TO
F.F.

MILL FROM 2X6 W/
1 3/8" APPLIED
STOPS

W
2 FIXED SILL
   SCALE: 1 1/2" = 1'-0"

Figure 16.9 Detail of eave and window head sill.

3/8" R.S.C. PLYWD.

1 X 3 TRIM

2X4 CONT.

2X4 SOLID BLKG.

W
7 FIXED JAMB
   SCALE: 1 1/2" = 1'-0"

MILL FROM 2X6 W/
1 3/8" APPLIED STOPS

1 X 3 TRIM

Figure 16.10 Detail of window jamb.

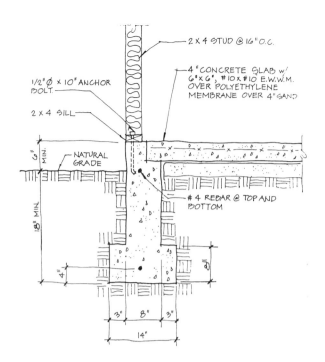

2 X 4 STUD @ 16"O.C.

1/2"Ø x 10" ANCHOR BOLT.

4" CONCRETE SLAB w/ 6"x 6", #10x#10 E.W.W.M. OVER POLYETHYLENE MEMBRANE OVER 4"SAND

2 x 4 SILL

NATURAL GRADE

6" MIN.

18" MIN.

#4 REBAR @ TOP AND BOTTOM

4"

8"

3" 8" 3"

14"

EXTERIOR BEARING

Figure 16.11   Detail of exterior bearing footing.

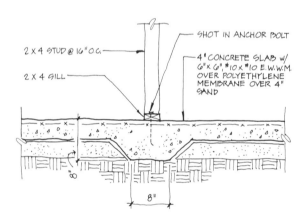

2 X 4 STUD @ 16"O.C.

SHOT IN ANCHOR BOLT

4" CONCRETE SLAB w/ 6"x 6", #10x#10 E.W.W.M. OVER POLYETHYLENE MEMBRANE OVER 4" SAND

2 x 4 SILL

8"

8"

5/7   INTERIOR NON-BEARING

Figure 16.12   Detail of interior nonbearing footing.

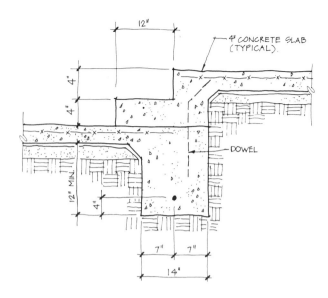

12"

4"

4"

4" CONCRETE SLAB (TYPICAL)

12" MIN.

DOWEL

7" 7"

14"

4/7   CHANGE OF LEVEL w/STEP

Figure 16.13   Detail of change of level with step.

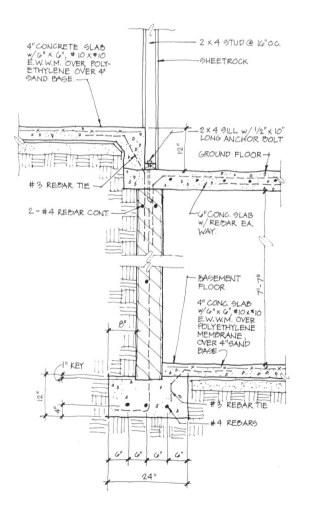

4"CONCRETE SLAB w/6"x 6", #10x#10 E.W.W.M. OVER POLY-ETHYLENE OVER 4" SAND BASE.

2 X 4 STUD @ 16"O.C.

SHEETROCK

2 x 4 SILL w/ 1/2"x 10" LONG ANCHOR BOLT

12"

#3 REBAR TIE

GROUND FLOOR

2 - #4 REBAR CONT.

6"CONC. SLAB w/ REBAR EA. WAY.

BASEMENT FLOOR

8"

4" CONC. SLAB w/6"x 6", #10x#10 E.W.W.M. OVER POLYETHYLENE MEMBRANE OVER 4"SAND BASE

7'-1"

1" KEY

12"

4"

#3 REBAR TIE

#4 REBARS

6" 6" 6" 6"

24"

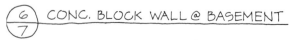

6/7   CONC. BLOCK WALL @ BASEMENT

Figure 16.14   Detail of concrete block wall at basement—slab.

Details for Framing Assemblies. Architectural details for framing assemblies were also provided in these construction documents. One example is the eave detail. First, the project designer did a freehand drawing. Then this freehand drawing was given to a draftsperson for final drawing. Figure 16.15 shows the freehand sketch.

Figure 16.16 shows a study of a deck and handrail detail located directly above a recessed garage door. The deck assembly at the building wall is also detailed, because proper flashing and drainage are needed to prevent water leaks. Figures 16.17 and 16.18 resemble each other but show different floor framing conditions. Other deck and handrail conditions are also detailed. Figure 16.19 shows the flashing and handrail assemblies and a continuous wood soffit to be used at the wall cantilever.

Details: Theatre (See Chapter 19.)

In some projects, structural complexities may dictate various construction assemblies. For example, a masonry and steel structure has many architectural details that are governed by structural engineering requirements. The detailer must coordinate these details with the structural engineer. Figure 16.20 shows a detail for a steel beam connection where the beam, steel decking, and concrete floor thickness have been designed by the structural engineer. From these required members, the architectural

detail is developed, showing wall materials, ceiling attachment, and underfloor space for mechanical and electrical runs. Figure 16.20 has a note to "SEE STRUCTURAL." This refers the reader to the structural engi-

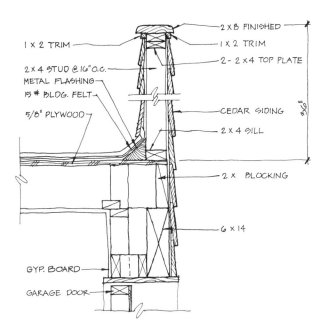

Figure 16.16 Detail of deck railing and header at garage.

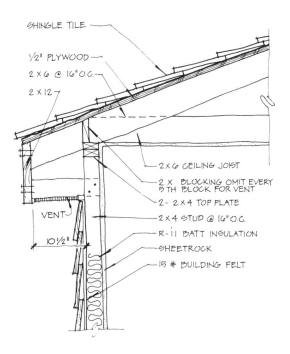

Figure 16.15 Eave detail.

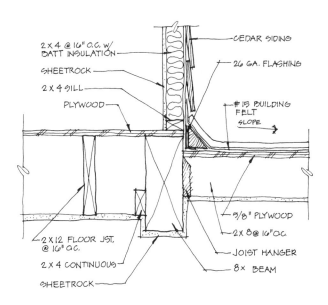

Figure 16.17 Detail of beam and deck at garage.

neer's drawings, which provide such information as type and length of welds for steel connections, and size and weight of steel members. Note the call-out on the steel beam of "W 8 × 10." The "W" refers to the shape of the

beam (here a wide **flange**), the "8" refers to the depth of the beam (here 8 inches), and the "10" refers to the weight of the beam per lineal foot (here 10 lb per linear foot).

A second example is shown in Figure 16.21. The steel stud framing is terminated at the bottom of the steel beam, and extensive galvanized iron flashing has been used to cover and protect the intersection of the various members at the ridge.

Figure 16.18 Detail of beam and deck at living room.

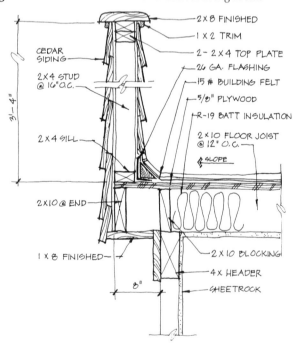

Figure 16.20 Detail of typical connection at a steel beam. (Reprinted by permission from *The Professional Practice of Architectural Working Drawings*, 2d Ed., © 1995 by John Wiley & Sons, Inc.)

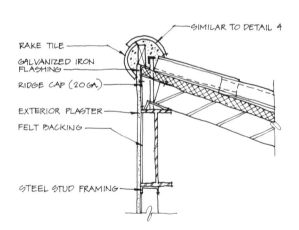

Figure 16.19 Detail of deck railing above living room. (Reprinted by permission from *The Professional Practice of Architectural Working Drawings*, 2d Ed., © 1995 by John Wiley & Sons, Inc.)

Figure 16.21 Detail of ridge at mechanical well. (Reprinted by permission from *The Professional Practice of Architectural Working Drawings*, 2d Ed., © 1995 by John Wiley & Sons, Inc.)

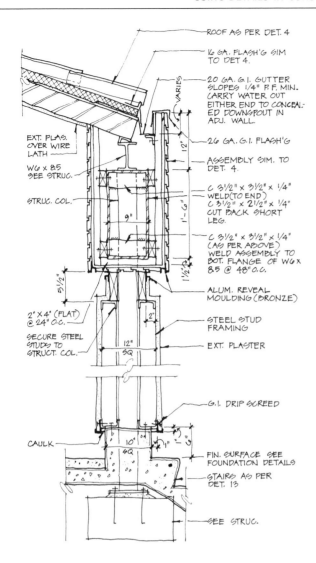

EAVE AND COLUMN DETAIL

Figure 16.22 Eave and column detail. (Reprinted by permission from *The Professional Practice of Architectural Working Drawings*, 2d Ed., © 1995 by John Wiley & Sons, Inc.)

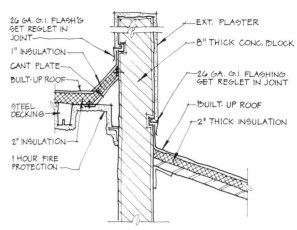

PARAPET DETAIL

Figure 16.23 Parapet detail. (Reprinted by permission from *The Professional Practice of Architectural Working Drawings*, 2d Ed., © 1995 by John Wiley & Sons, Inc.)

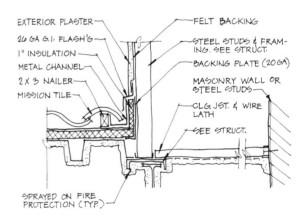

BASE FLASHING DETAIL

Figure 16.24 Base flashing detail. (Reprinted by permission from *The Professional Practice of Architectural Working Drawings*, 2d Ed., © 1995 by John Wiley & Sons, Inc.)

Some architectural details become complex and require much study before the finished detail is drafted. See Figure 16.22. This eave and column detail is intricate and shows the entire column assembly from the foundation to the roof, including the eave detail. Notes refer the viewer to other details for more information. Usually, it is unnecessary and unadvisable to repeat all the information from one detail to another; changes made on one detail must be made on any other affected.

Many projects require a specific architectural detail to show conditions that will satisfy a governing building code requirement. Figure 16.23, for example, shows ex-

actly where a fire protection coating is required under a steel roof decking that covers the structural steel angle on a masonry wall. This information is combined with a roof parapet detail. Figure 16.24 shows another detail for areas requiring fire protection.

Figure 16.25 shows a third example of this kind of detail. This detail of a handicapped ramp shows the required number of handrails, the height of the handrails above the ramp, and the clear space required between the handrail and the wall. This information has also been combined with the structural requirements for the support of a low wall on the outside of the ramp.

Footing details may also be sketched for various conditions as an aid to the finished drawings. Figure 16.26 shows a footing detail supporting a steel stud wall, and

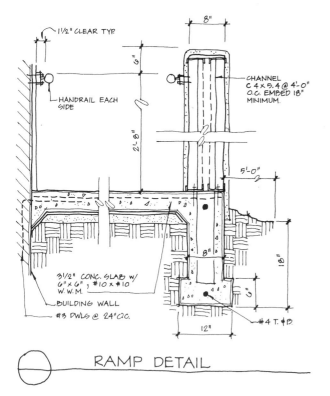

RAMP DETAIL

Figure 16.25   Ramp detail. (Reprinted by permission from *The Professional Practice of Architectural Working Drawings*, 2d Ed., © 1995 by John Wiley & Sons, Inc.)

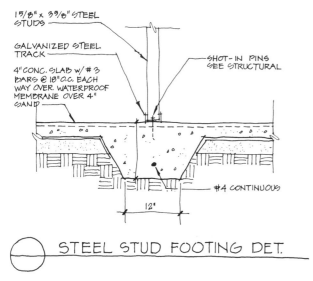

STEEL STUD FOOTING DET.

Figure 16.26   Steel stud footing detail. (Reprinted by permission from *The Professional Practice of Architectural Working Drawings*, 2d Ed., © 1995 by John Wiley & Sons, Inc.)

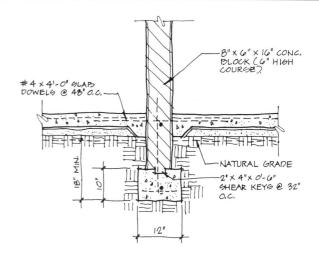

BLOCK WALL FOOTING

Figure 16.27   Block wall footing detail. (Reprinted by permission from *The Professional Practice of Architectural Working Drawings*, 2d Ed., © 1995 by John Wiley & Sons, Inc.)

Figure 16.27, a footing detail supporting the masonry wall that separates the auditoriums.

■ HARD-LINE (HAND-DRAFTED AND CAD)

Actually, this chapter should begin here, with hard-lining of details, because that is what the final appearance of details should be. We hope we have not led you to believe that most detailing is done freehand—quite the contrary. Detailing is done freehand only at the conceptual level and confirmation stage to check whether, in fact, what was seen in the mind's eye really works. Freehand details are also used as a means of communication from the mind of the designer to the real world of the drafter. We hope you will view the first few pages of this chapter as just that, a visual communication with the reader, analyzing assembly ideas and confirming them practically with sketches.

Henceforth, we will explore three details, from sketch to final hard-line, to convey the proper method of translating freehand details into usable hard-line details.

Finally, we will display a set of hard-lined details from the Ryan Residence for a window, footing, and a fireplace.

Approach to Detailing

Before you hard-line draft a detail, you must understand its primary and secondary functions. Although functions vary, they may be categorized within a few divisions.

A. Structural—The intent of a detail may be to reveal the method of connection between two structural members or to show the transition between wood and steel members and the connective device between them.

B. Architectural—The purpose of a detail may be to ensure that a particular architectural feature is explained, to maintain a certain aesthetic quality to a part of the building.

C. Environmental—A detail may reveal how to deal with environmental and natural forces such as sun, rain, wind, snow, and light, as well as human-made problems of noise, pollution, and so on.

D. Human Needs—A detail may ensure that a particular human need is meet. Stairs are a good example of this type of need, configured so as to allow a person to safely ascend or descend with the least amount of energy expended so as to avoid fatigue. This is done by formatting the proper angle of tread and riser. Special needs are explained in Chapter 4 (ADA), such as those of elderly or physically impaired persons.

E. Connection—It is critical to detail a transition of one plane into another; for example, the connection between the wall and the floor, or between the wall and the roof or ceiling.

F. Material Limits—A detail may reveal the limits of the material with which you are dealing. You can drill a hole into a 2 × 6 floor joist, but how large a hole before you weaken the member too much? The limits can be dimensioned or noted right in the detail.

G. Facilitation—In a tenant improvement drawing, a floor may be elevated to allow housing of computer cables. A detail can be drafted through this floor, showing the floor system support and the minimum clearances needed to accommodate the cables for maintenance.

Detailing Based on a Proper Sequence

STEP 1. The drafter can accomplish the crucial *block-out* stage by blindly copying the freehand sketch provided. Although this approach may be the most expedient, it misses two very important points: The drafter will never catch errors in the sketch, and the drafter becomes a tracer rather than a significant and valuable employee of the firm. Quickly outline the functional constraints of the detail, and check to see that the sketch complies.

STEP 2. Once you have laid out the most significant form, its adjacent parts can now be drawn. For example, in drafting an exterior bearing footing for a wood floor system, do not draft the floor first and then add the footing; rather, draft the footing first as it is built.

STEP 3. Critical dimensioning is added.

STEP 4. Now notes should be strategically placed so they easily convey the message.

STEP 5. Designation of materials for the various pieces (wood, steel, earth, etc.) can be added at this point or at any of the previous stages.

STEP 6. Profiling and outlining are almost synonymous. Darken the perimeter of the most important shape or shapes in the detail.

STEP 7. Using the proper method described earlier in this book, add reference symbols, a title, and a scale so that each detail has a "name" and scale.

Shortcut

When details were drafted by hand, copies were often kept on file. A specific detail could then be copied, corrected by scissor drafting, recopied on vellum, and then put onto an adhesive that could be applied to the construction documents. Some offices may still follow this practice of working with details.

In offices that use computers, each detail produced in the architect's office can be archived and later retrieved when it is needed. These digital images can be changed to meet any new application needs.

Offices using computers and hand drafting prepared tracers with a minimal amount of information so that a drafter could later add new information to this so-called bare bones detail. This practice is still used in some offices, but it is best done electronically. These bare bone details are developed, filed, and later retrieved as a datum stage to be updated with new and pertinent information.

Sizing Details

If you are working with a 24″ × 36″ sheet of vellum similar to that formatted in Chapter 3 and you extend the tick marks to form a matrix for detail placement, you will discover that the space measures $4^5/_8$″ high × $6^1/_2$″ wide. These spaces can be doubled in both width and height, or in both directions, depending on the scale of the detail.

With the availability of word processing and CAD, the drawing zone has been further subdivided into the drawing area and the note or keynote area. See Figure 16.28. The detail placed on one side allows the noting (done by CAD, word processor, etc.) to be done with ease. The drafter finishes the detail by drawing the leaders, thus connecting the notes with the drawing. See Figure 16.29. A further refinement is the use of keynoting. This refers to the practice of giving each note a number or a letter. When the detail is drafted, the leaders will have the corresponding number or letter pertaining to the note. See Figure 16.30. This method can be used by a manual drafter or by CAD, expediting the drawing procedure.

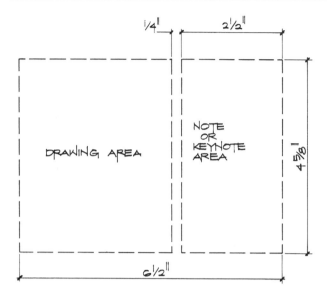

Figure 16.28 Detail format with noting area. (Reprinted by permission from *The Professional Practice of Architectural Working Drawings*, 2d Ed., © 1995 by John Wiley & Sons, Inc.)

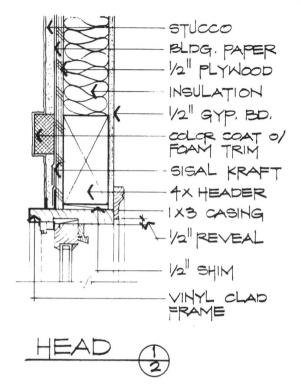

Figure 16.29 Window detail with noting format. (Reprinted by permission from *The Professional Practice of Architectural Working Drawings*, 2d Ed., © 1995 by John Wiley & Sons, Inc.)

■ FOOTING DETAIL

The exterior bearing footing for the Ryan Residence is not unlike the freehand sketch found in Figure 16.11 and evolved in Figures 16.35 through 16.38. The difference between one footing and another can be so subtle that it takes a trained eye to distinguish them. As you compare the freehand detail with the hard-line detail mentioned in these two figures, note the size difference at the bottom, the thickness of the foundation wall, the number of rebars, backfill, and sand versus gravel under the slab. These are two details that look alike but are really totally different in how they react to the various forces acting on them.

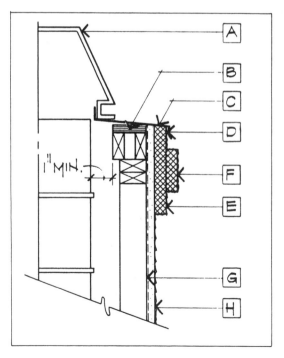

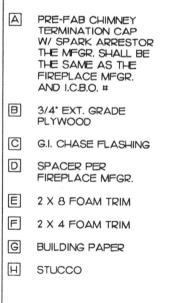

A	PRE-FAB CHIMNEY TERMINATION CAP W/ SPARK ARRESTOR THE MFGR. SHALL BE THE SAME AS THE FIREPLACE MFGR. AND I.C.B.O. #
B	3/4" EXT. GRADE PLYWOOD
C	G.I. CHASE FLASHING
D	SPACER PER FIREPLACE MFGR.
E	2 X 8 FOAM TRIM
F	2 X 4 FOAM TRIM
G	BUILDING PAPER
H	STUCCO

Figure 16.30 Chimney detail with keynoting format. (Reprinted by permission from *The Professional Practice of Architectural Working Drawings*, 2d Ed., © 1995 by John Wiley & Sons, Inc.)

Before we hard-line the exterior bearing footing for the Ryan Residence, let's look at four considerations for this type of footing:

A. *Configuration.* Most typically used is a two-pour inverted "T" shape. Through the years the industry has found this to be the best distributor of weight while using the least amount of material. Much like snowshoes distributing concentrated loads through the legs onto a wide platform, the inverted T distributes weight over a vast area as long as it does not break. Notice how the weight from above is distributed on the soil in Figure 16.31A. Surrounding the example are dimensions: "X" is based on the weight of the structure and the ability of the soil to hold up this weight by virtue of its quality.

As a rule of thumb, the thickness should be, as the example shows, $\frac{1}{2}$X. The depth of the footing, marked "A," is again a matter of the stability of the soil or the frost line, or even a requirement of building officials, as a minimum. The prevailing attitude is, however, that rather than use established maximums, soundness of construction should prevail. The amount of the stem of the inverted "T" that extends above the soil might be a matter of how high it should be to keep moisture from the first piece of wood to come in contact with the concrete or to prevent termite infestation.

B. *Soil.* The cost of a piece of property might be a matter of the view it provides, its convenience to various major streets, its slope, and so on, but many clients overlook the condition and quality of the soil. If a property has loosely filled soil (not permitted in many areas), the depth of the footing may have to extend far beyond the fill to firm soil, making the foundation very expensive. Moreover, in a marshy area where the bearing pressure of the earth (weight that can be put onto the soil measured in pounds per square foot) is minimal, the type and shape of the foundation may dictate a prohibitively expensive system, making the property impractical if not unbuildable. See Figure 16.31.

C. *Strength.* Concrete, an excellent material in compression, is very brittle in tension. The load imposed from above puts the concrete in compression, which is its strength. However, the footing travels the length of a wall, and with expansive soil or irregular loading, forms a beam that is in tension. This beam will break or shatter along the top or bottom, depending on the forces at work—thus the introduction of reinforcing bars, which are strong in tension, like a rope or chain, but rather weak in compression. By combining the two materials, we have strength in both tension and compression. See Figure 16.31C.

D. *Energy.* In this era of energy-efficient buildings, architects are paying extra attention to areas through which heat is lost. The movement of heat, as any physics major will tell you, is from hot to cold. In colder weather, we must heat structures such as the Ryan Residence using whatever natural resources are available: natural gas, petroleum products, or in some cases, electricity. To keep it from leaving the structure, heat is contained by means of insulating floors, walls, and ceilings. Notice the various locations for insulation on the footing in Figure 16.31D.

There are numerous other factors to consider in designing a footing. Where should the plastic membrane be put (if one is to be used)? Between the slab and the sand? Below the sand? How is the thickness of the slab determined? Does it require reinforcing? Backfill is still another factor—how much?—and so on. The answers to these questions relate to strength, energy conservation as a reaction to soil, and/or to the selected shape as mentioned before.

Ryan Residence—Exterior Bearing Footing

STAGE I (Figure 16.32). The grade line should be drawn first. This becomes the datum from which you can establish all of the necessary vertical dimensions, such as the distance to be placed between the floor and the grade. The width of the footing (bearing surface) is the next item to be measured. Half this width is centered for the stem wall. Footing thickness and slab thickness are positioned, and finally the beginning of the stud above the stem wall is drawn to create the slot for the slab.

STAGE II (Figure 16.33). After checking the accuracy of the first stage, proceed to the inclusion of the adjacent parts: insulation, sand or gravel, sill, the stud with its sheathing, and the termination points of the detail, which will be turned into break lines at a later stage.

STAGE III (Figure 16.34). This stage is actually a combination of Steps 3 and 5, dimensioning and material designation. Be sure to use the correct designation of material for each of the seven or so differing materials used here: plywood, batt insulation, rigid insulation, concrete, rebars, and so on.

STAGE IV (Figure 16.35). This is the final stage, which includes additional profiling and noting. To keep the noting consistent from detail to detail, many offices have a standard set of notes. The project manager may select the proper notes from this standard list and make them available to the drafter. In other offices, especially small offices, this practice may not be used at all; rather, the drafter is presumed to have the necessary training and ability to note a detail properly. Detailing

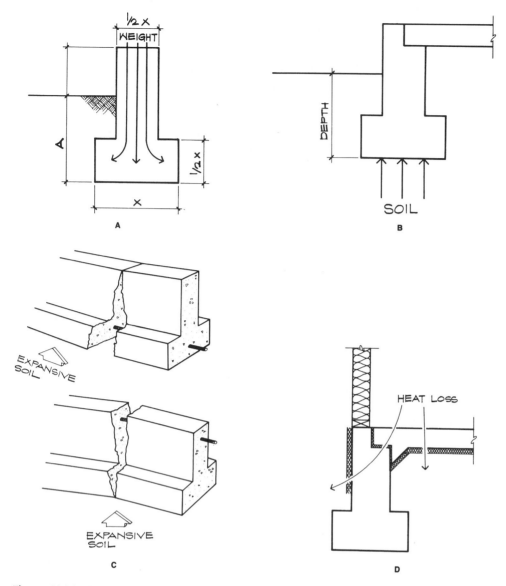

Figure 16.31 Footing concerns. (Reprinted by permission from *The Professional Practice of Architectural Working Drawings*, 2d Ed., © 1995 by John Wiley & Sons, Inc.)

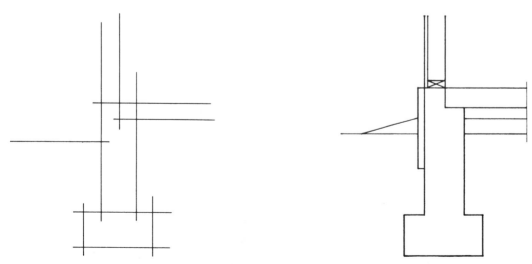

Figure 16.32 Exterior bearing footing—Stage I. (Reprinted by permission from *The Professional Practice of Architectural Working Drawings*, 2d Ed., © 1995 by John Wiley & Sons, Inc.)

Figure 16.33 Exterior bearing footing—Stage II. (Reprinted by permission from *The Professional Practice of Architectural Working Drawings*, 2d Ed., © 1995 by John Wiley & Sons, Inc.)

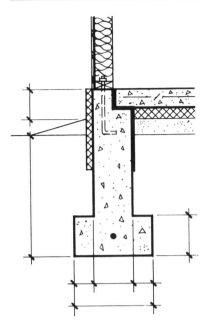

Figure 16.34 Exterior bearing footing—Stage III. (Reprinted by permission from *The Professional Practice of Architectural Working Drawings*, 2d Ed., © 1995 by John Wiley & Sons, Inc.)

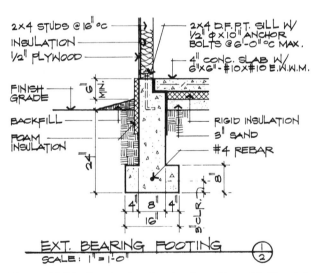

Figure 16.35 Exterior bearing footing—Stage IV. (Reprinted by permission from *The Professional Practice of Architectural Working Drawings*, 2d Ed., © 1995 by John Wiley & Sons, Inc.)

on a CAD system is merely a matter of recalling the proper notes, which have been stored in the computer, and positioning them.

If the notes are word processed, the drafter merely prints the necessary notes onto an adhesive and applies them to the drawing in the form of a chart called "keynotes." See Figure 16.30. This procedure can easily be adapted to the computer as well.

■ WINDOW DETAIL

Before drafting a window detail, the drafter should understand the action of the window's moving parts, its attributes, the installation procedure, and how to prepare the surrounding area before and after installation.

The window selected for the Ryan Residence is an Atrium double-tilt window. See Figure 16.36. It was selected because it is not the typical double-hung, casement, or sliding window, and because of its special features.

Action and Features

As seen in the diagram in Figure 16.36, the window tilts inward, creating a wind scoop as diagrammed in Figure 16.37A. This makes the window ideal for placement adjacent to a bed or a desk, positioned on the windward side of the site, or, for that matter, anywhere you do not want direct wind. The windows pivot at the base, and the mechanism allows for ease of cleaning and removal. The insulated high-performance glass includes two sheets of glass with air space between them, making this a $^3/_4''$ thick glazing. See Figure 16.36B. The glass blocks ultraviolet rays to prevent damage to drapery, carpets, furniture, and humans. See Figure 16.37B.

The exterior is vinyl clad with full bulb weatherstripping around its perimeter, and the interior is pine, which

Figure 16.36 Atrium double-tilt window. (Courtesy of the Atrium Door & Window Company, a Division of Fojtasek Companies, Inc. Reprinted by permission from *The Professional Practice of Architectural Working Drawings*, 2d Ed., © 1995 by John Wiley & Sons, Inc.)

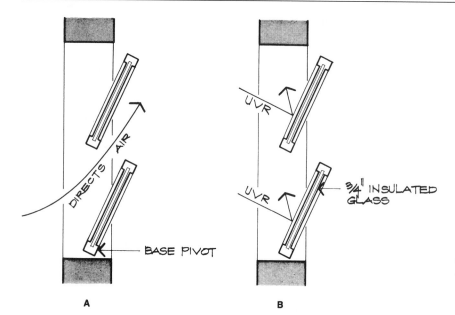

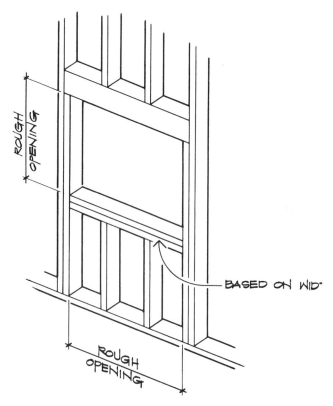

Figure 16.37 Diagram of atrium double-tilt window. (Reprinted by permission from *The Professional Practice of Architectural Working Drawings*, 2d Ed., © 1995 by John Wiley & Sons, Inc.)

can be stained or painted to match the interior decor. Finally, removable wood grilles can be ordered to create a matrix pattern for a divided look. These divisions in a window are called lites. As with the main frame, these grilles are finished on the exterior and unfinished on the inside face. The grilles are clipped into place and are easily removed for window cleaning.

Insulation

By studying the installation method, the detailer can better emphasize certain features of the detail. As seen in the original photograph, there are fins around the perimeter that will be used to nail the window in place. Therefore, the rough opening (the rough framed opening) must have enough clearance to accommodate the preconstructed window. In this case the clearance will be 1/2" both vertically and horizontally, compensating for any irregularity in the framing members and allowing the window to be placed into the rough opening perfectly level. See Figure 16.38. The wood shim under the windowsill in this sketch functions as a leveling device while sealing the space between the rough sill and the finished sill of the window. See Figure 16.39.

Before and after the fin of the window is nailed to the wall, a moisture/vapor barrier is placed around the frame. The "Weatherproofing" section in Chapter 13 can acquaint you with the various materials used to waterproof windows and the reasons for the positioning of particular pieces of waterproofing material.

For the installation of this window, we use an asphalt-saturated kraft paper to cover the building and a secondary strip (a band of about 6"–8") of heavily saturated heavy weight kraft-type paper called sisal-kraft.

In Figure 16.40, note the positioning of the building paper and its secondary member, the sisal-kraft. Both sheets are placed under the fin on the jamb and both

Figure 16.38 Rough opening for window installation. (Reprinted by permission from *The Professional Practice of Architectural Working Drawings*, 2d Ed., © 1995 by John Wiley & Sons, Inc.)

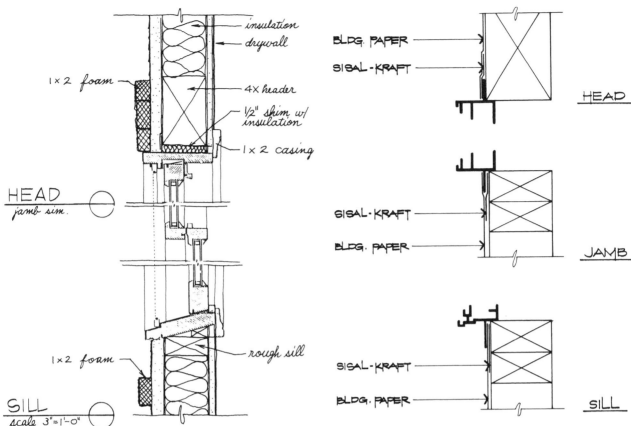

Figure 16.39 Finished sketch of window context. (Reprinted by permission from *The Professional Practice of Architectural Working Drawings*, 2d Ed., © 1995 by John Wiley & Sons, Inc.)

Figure 16.40 Placement of building paper around window. (Reprinted by permission from *The Professional Practice of Architectural Working Drawings*, 2d Ed., © 1995 by John Wiley & Sons, Inc.)

sheets over the fin on the head. This strategic placement acts to shed water and prevent its penetration. This method is unique to zone C (see the map in Figure 13.50).

Raised Frame

There will be raised plaster frame around the windows. Such frames, affectionately called "stucco bumps," can be produced in a number of ways. Two possible solutions are described as follows. The first is to use one or more pieces of wood to raise the surface, as seen in Figure 16.41. Notice how the building paper is carried completely around the wood (including the metal mesh, which is not shown). The exterior plaster (stucco) follows the contour of the complete unit.

A second possible solution is the use of Styrofoam. See Figure 16.42. In this example two pieces of foam have been placed over the first two coats of stucco, which are called the scratch coat and the brown coat. The final coat (called the color coat) is placed over the entire unit, completing the image as a whole. Notice the position of the building paper.

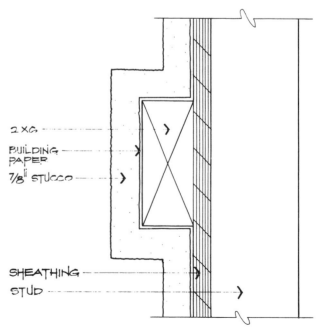

Figure 16.41 Raised surface using wood as a backing. (Reprinted by permission from *The Professional Practice of Architectural Working Drawings*, 2d Ed., © 1995 by John Wiley & Sons, Inc.)

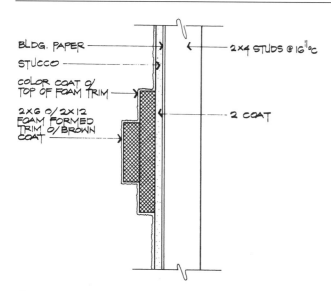

BLDG. PAPER

STUCCO

COLOR COAT O/ TOP OF FOAM TRIM

2x6 O/ 2x12 FOAM FORMED TRIM O/ BROWN COAT

2x4 STUDS @ 16"O.C

2 COAT

Figure 16.42 Raising a surface with foam. (Reprinted by permission from *The Professional Practice of Architectural Working Drawings*, 2d Ed., © 1995 by John Wiley & Sons, Inc.)

For the Ryan Residence, the second method is used and a keystone is placed at the top of this raised frame, as can be seen in elevation in Figure 16.43. Figure 16.44 shows the placement of the building paper and the sisal-kraft (called counterflashing).

Rough Opening Size

Most brochures provided by manufacturers contain written descriptions of a window itself and its various features, the available stock sizes, suggested details depending on the context, and a drawing of the window at 3" = 1'-0" scale, which can be used as tracer or scissor-drafted into the detail. Figure 16.45 shows a drafter checking typical installation details and identifying the different features. This sheet is replicated on Figure 16.46. Figure 16.47 shows the drafter checking on the rough opening sizes. Many manufacturers list the available sizes in terms of rough opening so that the actual size of a window is 1/2" smaller than the call-out size. For

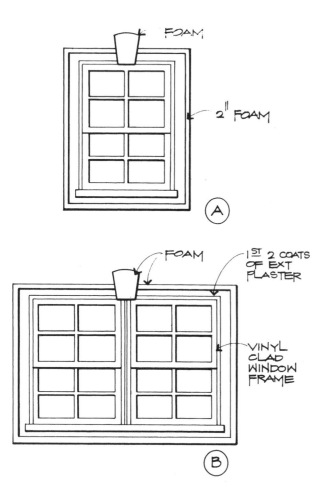

FOAM

2" FOAM

Ⓐ

FOAM

1ST 2 COATS OF EXT PLASTER

VINYL CLAD WINDOW FRAME

Ⓑ

Figure 16.43 Raised frame of foam. (Reprinted by permission from *The Professional Practice of Architectural Working Drawings*, 2d Ed., © 1995 by John Wiley & Sons, Inc.)

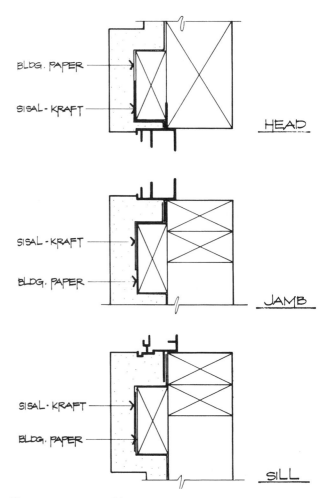

BLDG. PAPER

SISAL-KRAFT

HEAD

SISAL-KRAFT

BLDG. PAPER

JAMB

SISAL-KRAFT

BLDG. PAPER

SILL

Figure 16.44 Raised frame of wood. (Reprinted by permission from *The Professional Practice of Architectural Working Drawings*, 2d Ed., © 1995 by John Wiley & Sons, Inc.)

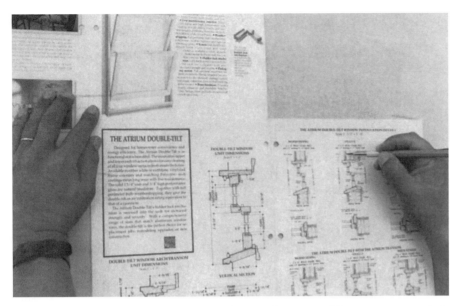

Figure 16.45 Suggested detailing by manufacturer. (Courtesy of the Atrium Door & Window Company, a Division of Fojtasek Companies, Inc. Reprinted by permission from *The Professional Practice of Architectural Working Drawings*, 2d Ed., © 1995 by John Wiley & Sons, Inc.)

example, a DW2030 is really $19\frac{1}{2}'' \times 29\frac{1}{2}''$. Notice the drawing above the left hand on this photograph. It is drawn at $3'' = 1'\text{-}0''$ scale and can be used as a tracer or scissor-drafted, as is the case in the Ryan Residence project.

Ryan Residence—Window Detail

STAGE I (Figure 16.48). Actually, this is not a drawing stage but, rather, a preparation stage. The $3'' = 1'\text{-}0''$ vertical section provided by the manufacturer's literature is reproduced on a plain paper copier. See Figure 16.48A. Unwanted information is removed with white-out correction fluid or white acrylic artist paint or is cut out with scissors. The remaining detail might look like Figure 16.48B. This drawing is positioned on a piece of white bond paper and reproduced xerographically onto vellum. The first time you do this, it will take you longer than outright tracing, but if this Atrium Double-Tilt window is used again, you have a head start in the drawing process. Also note that we are using a double module.

STAGE II (Figure 16.49). The rough framing is drawn on the drawing of the window. If you were tracing the outline of the window, this process would be reversed: rough framing would be drawn first, then the window would be traced within this context. Care must be taken in redrawing any important line that was inadvertently eliminated or has faded away. The fin is especially important. Finally, the rough opening is established.

STAGE III (Figure 16.50). As we look at this detail, we should be able to see the lines of the jamb. To save time and for the sake of clarity, some offices do not put these lines into the detail. A true detail should include such lines, thus our choice to include them here. The interior and exterior wall coverings (skin) were drafted at this stage. Note the lining of the building felt over the fin for moisture control and the inclusion of insulation below the header. Finally, the raised window frame is drafted.

STAGE IV (Figure 16.51). Noting and referencing complete the detail. The positioning of notes is critical for ease of reading. Don't crowd the detail, but also avoid long leaders. Be sure to create a margin for uniformity of appearance.

■ FIREPLACE

Fireplaces have gone through quite an evolution over the past century: from masonry fireplaces, which are still built, to metal; from fully vented fireplaces using chimneys to those that do not. Some varieties burn wood as fuel, and others burn natural gas or, more recently, gelled alcohol.

Fireplaces can be built with remote control starters much like those used for television and VCRs. They can also be constructed to recirculate warm air. Fireplaces can be made to look like fireplaces or designed to look like furniture. And, much to the surprise of many clients, portable fireplaces are now manufactured, which burn

THE ATRIUM DOUBLE-TILT WINDOW INSTALLATION DETAILS
Scale 1 - 1/2" = 1' - 0"

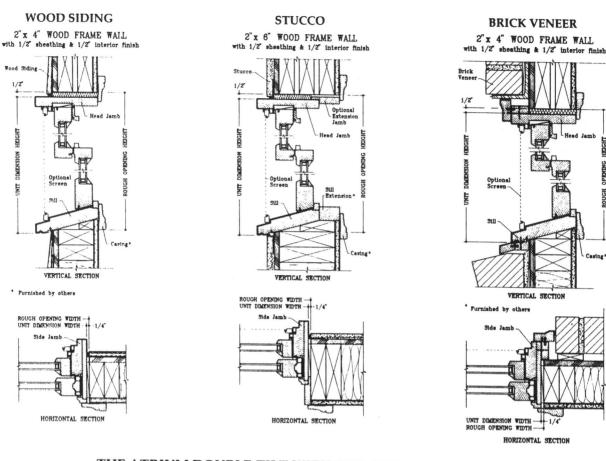

THE ATRIUM DOUBLE-TILT WITH THE ATRIUM TRANSOM

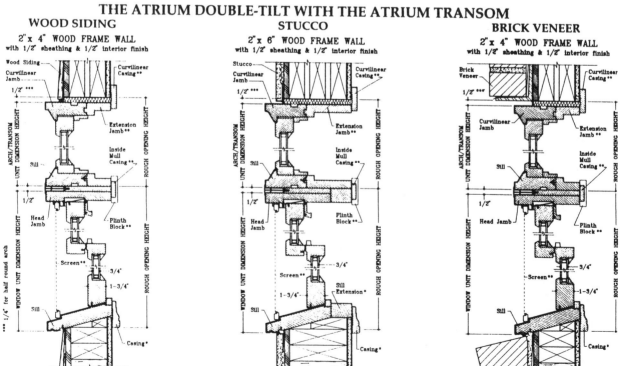

Figure 16.46 Installation examples. (Courtesy of the Atrium Door & Window Company, a Division of Fojtasek Companies, Inc. Reprinted by permission from *The Professional Practice of Architectural Working Drawings*, 2d Ed., © 1995 by John Wiley & Sons, Inc.)

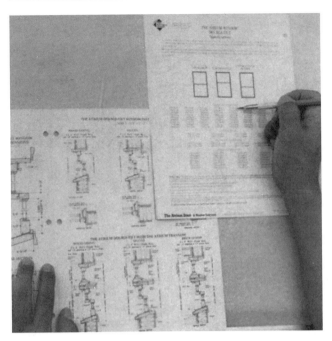

Figure 16.47 Rough opening sizes. (Reprinted by permission from *The Professional Practice of Architectural Working Drawings*, 2d Ed., © 1995 by John Wiley & Sons, Inc.)

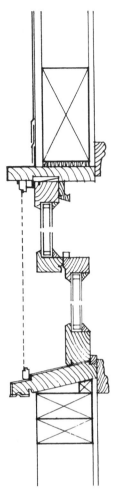

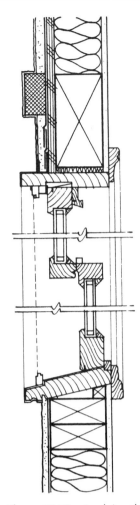

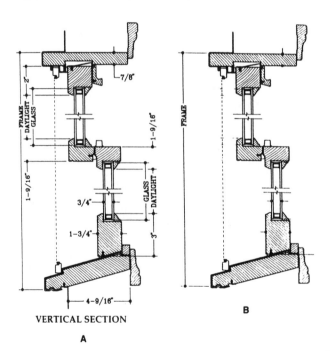

VERTICAL SECTION

A

B

Figure 16.48 3″ = 1′-0″ drawing by manufacturer. (Reprinted by permission from *The Professional Practice of Architectural Working Drawings*, 2d Ed., © 1995 by John Wiley & Sons, Inc.)

Figure 16.49 Laying out the rough frame. (Reprinted by permission from *The Professional Practice of Architectural Working Drawings*, 2d Ed., © 1995 by John Wiley & Sons, Inc.)

Figure 16.50 Applying the interior and exterior skin onto the wall surface. (Reprinted by permission from *The Professional Practice of Architectural Working Drawings*, 2d Ed., © 1995 by John Wiley & Sons, Inc.)

gelled alcohol and can be moved from room to room, much the way furniture is rearranged. When you move, you take the fireplace with you.

Many of the metal fireplaces are fitted with recirculating air pockets. The air around the fire chamber is heated and redirected back into the room. You can even have a thermostat-controlled blower installed, which increases the movement of the warm air, thus achieving greater efficiency in heat circulation. This means that 20,000 to 75,000 Btu/hr of heat can be recaptured. See Figure 16.52.

For the sake of this discussion, fireplaces are categorized as follows:

Standard fireplace. The normal masonry units that are usually job-built and require the detailer to draft the fireplace from the throat. Often built of concrete block, brick, or stone.

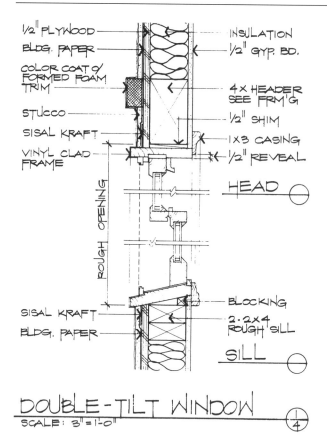

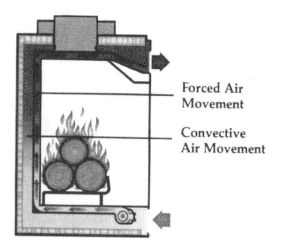

Figure 16.52 Heat circulation. (Courtesy of Majco Building Specialties, L.P. Reprinted by permission from *The Professional Practice of Architectural Working Drawings*, 2d Ed., © 1995 by John Wiley & Sons, Inc.)

Figure 16.51 Noting and finishing the window detail. (Reprinted by permission from *The Professional Practice of Architectural Working Drawings*, 2d Ed., © 1995 by John Wiley & Sons, Inc.)

Prefabricated fireplaces. Built of steel, with the chimney built of double or triple wall units that snap together. A typical unit can be seen in Figure 16.53.

Direct vented fireplaces. Built of steel and similar to the prefabricated fireplaces previously described, except that they are vented directly out an adjacent wall. See Figure 16.54 and 16.55. Note the uninterrupted windows surrounding the fireplace in the photograph.

Portable fireplaces. Made of metal and built much like an oven, so that the outer surface gets warm but not hot to the touch. Can be housed in a cabinet like a television set and uses a clean-burning gelled alcohol.

Ryan Residence Fireplace

For the Ryan Residence, the Majestic 42 unit was selected for its heat-circulating features. See Figure 16.53.

Much like the Atrium window discussed earlier, this fireplace has a metal fin (tab) around the perimeter of the front face that can be nailed to the surrounding framing. The metal fireplace must not come into contact with the

Figure 16.53 Majestic heat-circulating fireplace. (Courtesy of Majco Building Specialties, L.P. Reprinted by permission from *The Professional Practice of Architectural Working Drawings*, 2d Ed., © 1995 by John Wiley & Sons, Inc.)

framing around it. The manufacturer suggests a minimum clearance of about 1/2", but the local codes should be checked.

The chimney is a triple wall unit and does not necessarily go straight up through the ceiling and/or roof.

Figure 16.54 Majestic wall-vented fireplace. (Courtesy of Majco Building Specialties, L.P. Reprinted by permission from *The Professional Practice of Architectural Working Drawings*, 2d Ed., © 1995 by John Wiley & Sons, Inc.)

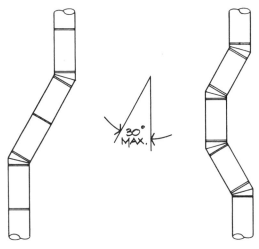

Figure 16.56 Bends in chimney section. (Reprinted by permission from *The Professional Practice of Architectural Working Drawings*, 2d Ed., © 1995 by John Wiley & Sons, Inc.)

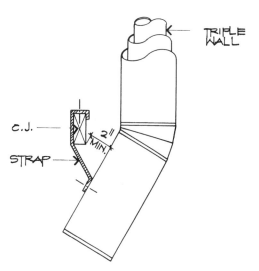

Figure 16.57 Attached to adjacent members. (Reprinted by permission from *The Professional Practice of Architectural Working Drawings*, 2d Ed., © 1995 by John Wiley & Sons, Inc.)

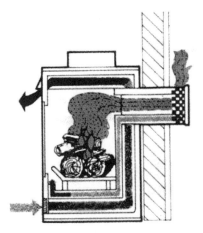

Figure 16.55 Wall-vented schematic. (Courtesy of Majco Building Specialties, L.P. Reprinted by permission from *The Professional Practice of Architectural Working Drawings*, 2d Ed., © 1995 by John Wiley & Sons, Inc.)

Bends of 30° can be incorporated as the chimney goes through the space provided. This space, called the chimney chase, allows the chimney to pierce the ceiling or roof at a convenient point, so as not to interrupt the plane of the roof at an intersection (such as a valley) or bypass a beam or any other structural member. See Figure 16.56. Straps are then used to stabilize the chimney to the adjacent framing members. See Figure 16.57. Note the inclusion of a recommended 2″ clearance space.

A fire-stop spacer should be used on top of the ceiling joist if there is an attic, or on the underside of the roof joist when there is an attic space. See Figure 16.58.

The total area around the opening (chase) should be insulated even if the wall is an inside wall. If the fireplace is on a second floor or on a first floor constructed of wood, the space under the fireplace should also be insulated. In fact, it is always best to read the installation manual before detailing the framework around the structure. The detailer should not worry about how the smoke is drafted out of the fire chamber or the inner workings of the fireplace, because the fireplace engineering has already been done by the Majestic company designers.

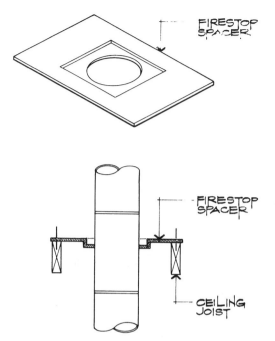

Figure 16.58 Chimney position. (Reprinted by permission from *The Professional Practice of Architectural Working Drawings*, 2d Ed., © 1995 by John Wiley & Sons, Inc.)

Framing. The walls around the prefabricated fireplace are framed in the same way as all other walls. Even the openings are framed in the same manner as other openings such as doors, skylights, windows, and so on. See Figure 16.59.

The framing on the Ryan Residence is rather unique because:

A. The fireplace is backed against a bearing wall.
B. The rafters of the main part of the roof will come down to the bearing wall.
C. The ceiling joists are running perpendicular to the main rafters.
D. The California framed roof also needs to be reframed with an opening.
E. The chimney will be contained inside a wood chase and capped with metal.

See Figure 16.60 for a model simulation of this area. Figure 16.61 for a sectional view of the fireplace, and Figure 16.62 for a good look at the total framing around the fireplace.

Putting the last two drawings together becomes the next task of the detailer. To see whether this approach works, a freehand sketch might be made, such as that in Figure 16.63.

Chimney Above Roof. In most cases, a chimney must rise two feet higher than the highest part of the roof within a ten-foot radius. See Figure 16.64.

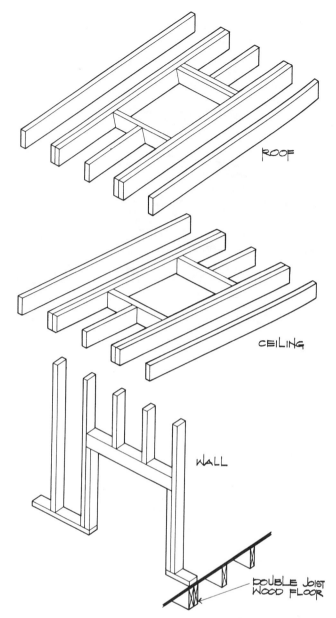

Figure 16.59 Framing an opening. (Reprinted by permission from *The Professional Practice of Architectural Working Drawings*, 2d Ed., © 1995 by John Wiley & Sons, Inc.)

Chimney Chase. There are a number of ways of terminating the chimney above the roof. A round top termination, as seen in Figure 16.65, can be used to "top it off," and the finish will be left in this state. A second possibility is to purchase a constructed metal chase to cover this metal termination. A third suggestion is to use a wood chase with a constructed or custom-made cap. As you will note, this is the method used for the Ryan's fireplace (wood chase), and a form trim will be used on the detail to show variation, as seen in Figure 16.66.

Figure 16.60 Model simulation of the framing through the roof. (Reprinted by permission from *The Professional Practice of Architectural Working Drawings*, 2d Ed., © 1995 by John Wiley & Sons, Inc.)

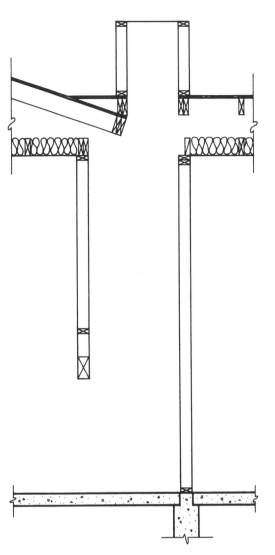

Figure 16.62 Surrounding framing. (Reprinted by permission from *The Professional Practice of Architectural Working Drawings*, 2d Ed., © 1995 by John Wiley & Sons, Inc.)

Figure 16.61 Outline of the fireplace. (Reprinted by permission from *The Professional Practice of Architectural Working Drawings*, 2d Ed., © 1995 by John Wiley & Sons, Inc.)

Development of the Ryan Residence Fireplace

A full section of the Ryan Residence fireplace is developed in four stages.

STAGE I (Figure 16.67). Fade-away pencil is used to detail the plate line, floor line, wall, and roof outline as this location is laid out. These lines establish the parameters within which the detailer can explore the framing members and place the prefabricated fireplace.

STAGE II (Figure 16.68). The ceiling joists and rafters are sized and positioned according to the framing plan. Because this is not a masonry fireplace, the drafter need not be concerned with a foundation. (For drafting full masonry fireplaces, read the chapter on fireplaces in the companion book, *The Professional Practice of Architectural Detailing*.)

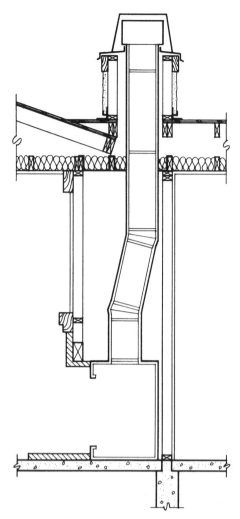

Figure 16.63 Full section of a fireplace. (Reprinted by permission from *The Professional Practice of Architectural Working Drawings*, 2d Ed., © 1995 by John Wiley & Sons, Inc.)

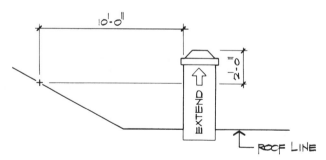

Figure 16.64 Chimney above roof. (Reprinted by permission from *The Professional Practice of Architectural Working Drawings*, 2d Ed., © 1995 by John Wiley & Sons, Inc.)

Next, the fireplace is positioned in this cavity, with the minimum clearances required by code. At this stage the drafter must be conversant with code restrictions as well as the method of installation. For exam-

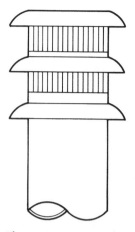

Figure 16.65 Round top termination. (Reprinted by permission from *The Professional Practice of Architectural Working Drawings*, 2d Ed., © 1995 by John Wiley & Sons, Inc.)

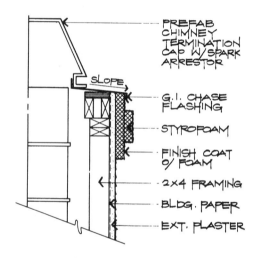

Figure 16.66 Half-section of chimney. (Reprinted by permission from *The Professional Practice of Architectural Working Drawings*, 2d Ed., © 1995 by John Wiley & Sons, Inc.)

ple, it is important to detail how the flue is stabilized within the cavity, what kinds of fire-stops are required, and where they are positioned. Manufacturers' literature includes installation instructions and standard manufactured pieces that are available to make such installation possible. The drafter should also check with the project book to verify finish materials for the face of the fireplace and the hearth.

STAGE III (Figure 16.69). Once the materials have been checked, material designation is included in the detail. Wood, insulation, concrete, and even the outside wall of the metal fireplace are shown. At this stage sheet

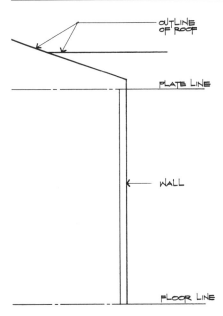

Figure 16.67 Establishing the parameters of the fireplace location—Stage I. (Reprinted by permission from *The Professional Practice of Architectural Working Drawings*, 2d Ed., © 1995 by John Wiley & Sons, Inc.)

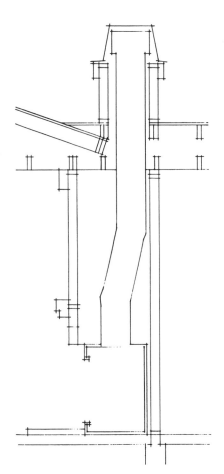

Figure 16.68 Ryan Residence fireplace—Stage II. (Reprinted by permission from *The Professional Practice of Architectural Working Drawings*, 2d Ed., © 1995 by John Wiley & Sons, Inc.)

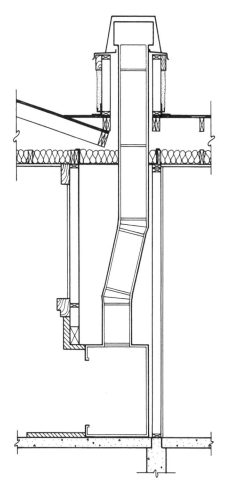

Figure 16.69 Ryan Residence fireplace—Stage III. (Reprinted by permission from *The Professional Practice of Architectural Working Drawings*, 2d Ed., © 1995 by John Wiley & Sons, Inc.)

metal, such as for the cap, is drafted with a single heavy line.

STAGE IV (Figure 16.70). There are a number of items of which the detailer must be aware on all details, as well as those that are unique to specific details, as is the case with a fireplace. Unlike the footing detail, which describes a structural part of a building, the fireplace detail is one for which there already exists a context. The second factor that the detailer must identify and describe accurately is the prefabricated unit itself. Thus, the final stage must be dealt with much in the same fashion as the detail was developed.

First, within the final sequence, is the identification of the context: the rafters, the ceiling joist, the floor, and the cell (surrounded with studs) within which the fireplace will be placed, including the housing for the chimney.

Next in this sequence is the identification of the fireplace and the flue, in such a way that the outline of

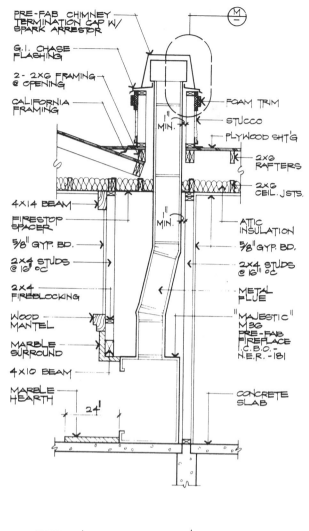

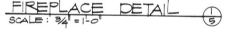

FIREPLACE DETAIL ①/⑤
SCALE: ¾" = 1'-0"

Figure 16.70 Half-section of fireplace-Stage IV. (Reprinted by permission from *The Professional Practice of Architectural Working Drawings*, 2d Ed., © 1995 by John Wiley & Sons, Inc.)

bles or notes should be included to direct the reader to these details. Although it may seem that this is referring a detail to a detail, it is really not. (See the chimney portion of Figure 16.67.) This drawing, as the title indicates, is a half-section—a hybrid between a building section and a full-blown detail.

Portfolio of Architectural Details for the Ryan Residence

A sampling of the architectural details that are used for the Ryan Residence are shown on Figures 16.71–16.88. They are shown at a larger scale than they would be if the details were incorporated into the working drawings in Chapter 16.

1.	Exterior bearing footing	Figure 16.71
2.	Interior bearing footing	Figure 16.72
3.	Porch connection	Figure 16.73
4.	Change of level	Figure 16.74
5.	Depressed slab	Figure 16.75
6.	Window	Figure 16.76
7.	Door	Figure 16.77
8.	Fireplace	Figure 16.78
9.	Wood column to beam	Figure 16.79
10.	Skylight	Figure 16.80
11.	Eave	Figure 16.81
12.	Trellis	Figure 16.82
13.	Upper cabinet	Figure 16.83
14.	Base cabinet	Figure 16.84
15.	Exterior bearing footing—garage	Figure 16.85
16.	Apron detail	Figure 16.86
17.	Eave at garage	Figure 16.87
18.	Half-section of chimney	Figure 16.88

the fireplace is clear in relationship to the surrounding structure.

The building code and the manufacturer's installation directions will reveal certain clearances that must be maintained and dimensioned, and attachments and fire-stop spacers which need to be identified. Positioning them is not alone sufficient.

Next, the decorative (noncombustible) portions that surround the opening, the chimney, the floor (hearth) and the wall plane of the fireplace, and the ceiling should be described and dimensioned.

Finally, if there are portions within this drawing that need to be enlarged and explored, reference bub-

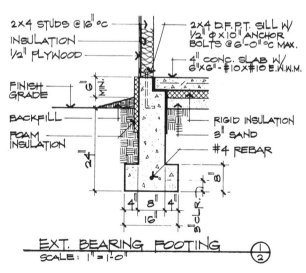

EXT. BEARING FOOTING ①/②
SCALE: 1" = 1'-0"

Figure 16.71 Exterior bearing footing. (Reprinted by permission from *The Professional Practice of Architectural Working Drawings*, 2d Ed., © 1995 by John Wiley & Sons, Inc.)

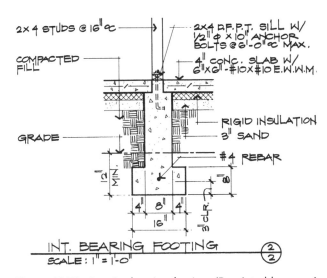

INT. BEARING FOOTING
SCALE : 1" = 1'-0"
②/2

2×4 STUDS @ 16" oc
COMPACTED FILL
GRADE
2×4 D.F.P.T. SILL W/ ½" ø ×10" ANCHOR BOLTS @ 6'-0" oc MAX.
4" CONC. SLAB W/ 6"×6"-#10×#10 E.W.W.M.
RIGID INSULATION
3" SAND
#4 REBAR

Figure 16.72 Interior bearing footing. (Reprinted by permission from *The Professional Practice of Architectural Working Drawings*, 2d Ed., © 1995 by John Wiley & Sons, Inc.)

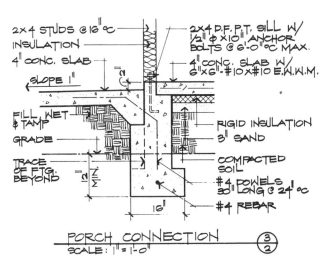

PORCH CONNECTION
SCALE : 1" = 1'-0"
③/2

2×4 STUDS @ 16" oc
INSULATION
4" CONC. SLAB
SLOPE 1"
FILL WET & TAMP
GRADE
TRACE OF FTG. BEYOND
2×4 D.F.P.T. SILL W/ ½" ø ×10" ANCHOR BOLTS @ 6'-0" oc MAX.
4" CONC. SLAB W/ 6"×6"-#10×#10 E.W.W.M.
RIGID INSULATION
3" SAND
COMPACTED SOIL
#4 DOWELS 30" LONG @ 24" oc
#4 REBAR

Figure 16.73 Porch connection. (Reprinted by permission from *The Professional Practice of Architectural Working Drawings*, 2d Ed., © 1995 by John Wiley & Sons, Inc.)

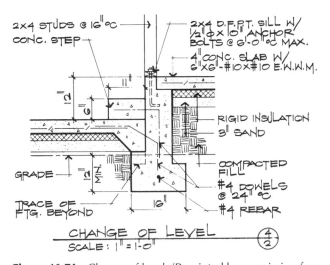

CHANGE OF LEVEL
SCALE : 1" = 1'-0"
④/2

2×4 STUDS @ 16" oc
CONC. STEP
GRADE
TRACE OF FTG. BEYOND
2×4 D.F.P.T. SILL W/ ½" ø ×10" ANCHOR BOLTS @ 6'-0" oc MAX.
4" CONC. SLAB W/ 6"×6"-#10×#10 E.W.W.M.
RIGID INSULATION
3" SAND
COMPACTED FILL
#4 DOWELS @ 24" oc
#4 REBAR

Figure 16.74 Change of level. (Reprinted by permission from *The Professional Practice of Architectural Working Drawings*, 2d Ed., © 1995 by John Wiley & Sons, Inc.)

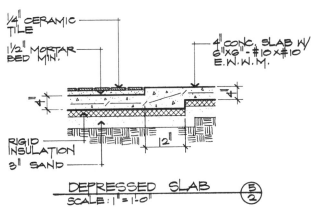

DEPRESSED SLAB
SCALE : 1" = 1'-0"
⑤/2

¼" CERAMIC TILE
½" MORTAR BED MIN.
RIGID INSULATION
3" SAND
4" CONC. SLAB W/ 6"×6"-#10×#10 E.W.W.M.

Figure 16.75 Depressed slab. (Reprinted by permission from *The Professional Practice of Architectural Working Drawings*, 2d Ed., © 1995 by John Wiley & Sons, Inc.)

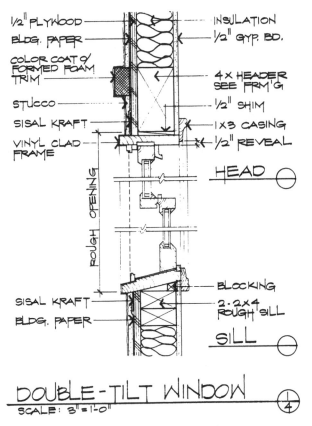

DOUBLE-TILT WINDOW
SCALE : 3" = 1'-0"
①/4

½" PLYWOOD
BLDG. PAPER
COLOR COAT OF FORMED FOAM TRIM
STUCCO
SISAL KRAFT
VINYL CLAD FRAME
ROUGH OPENING
SISAL KRAFT
BLDG. PAPER
INSULATION
½" GYP. BD.
4 × HEADER SEE FRM'G
½" SHIM
1×3 CASING
½" REVEAL
HEAD
BLOCKING
2-2×4 ROUGH SILL
SILL

Figure 16.76 Window. (Reprinted by permission from *The Professional Practice of Architectural Working Drawings*, 2d Ed., © 1995 by John Wiley & Sons, Inc.)

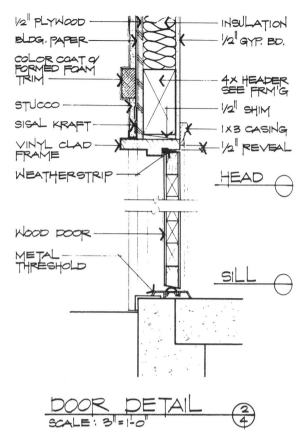

1/2" PLYWOOD
BLDG. PAPER
COLOR COAT O/ FORMED FOAM TRIM
STUCCO
SISAL KRAFT
VINYL CLAD FRAME
WEATHERSTRIP

INSULATION
1/2" GYP. BD.
4X HEADER SEE FRM'G
1/2" SHIM
1X3 CASING
1/2" REVEAL

HEAD

WOOD DOOR
METAL THRESHOLD

SILL

DOOR DETAIL
SCALE: 3" = 1'-0" 2/4

Figure 16.77 Door. (Reprinted by permission from *The Professional Practice of Architectural Working Drawings*, 2d Ed., © 1995 by John Wiley & Sons, Inc.)

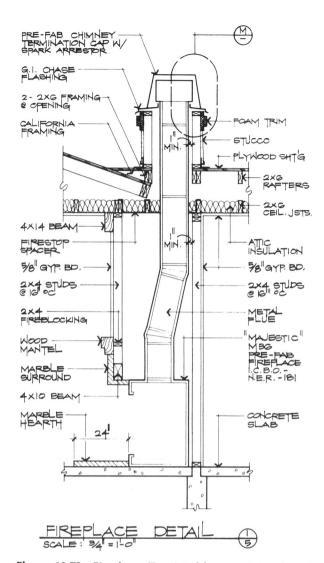

PRE-FAB CHIMNEY TERMINATION CAP W/ SPARK ARRESTOR
G.I. CHASE FLASHING
2- 2X6 FRAMING @ OPENING
CALIFORNIA FRAMING

FOAM TRIM
STUCCO
PLYWOOD SHT'G
2X6 RAFTERS
2X6 CEIL. JSTS.

1" MIN.
1" MIN.

4X14 BEAM
FIRESTOP SPACER
5/8" GYP. BD.
2X4 STUDS @ 16" OC
2X4 FIREBLOCKING
WOOD MANTEL
MARBLE SURROUND
4X10 BEAM
MARBLE HEARTH

ATTIC INSULATION
5/8" GYP. BD.
2X4 STUDS @ 16" OC
METAL FLUE
"MAJESTIC" M 36 PRE-FAB FIREPLACE I.C.B.O. - N.E.R. -181
CONCRETE SLAB

24"

FIREPLACE DETAIL
SCALE: 3/4" = 1'-0" 1/5

Figure 16.78 Fireplace. (Reprinted by permission from *The Professional Practice of Architectural Working Drawings*, 2d Ed., © 1995 by John Wiley & Sons, Inc.)

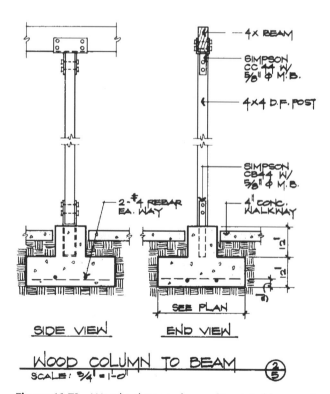

4X BEAM
SIMPSON CC 44 W/ 5/8" Ø M.B.
4X4 D.F. POST
SIMPSON CB44 W/ 5/8" Ø M.B.
4" CONC. WALKWAY
2 - #4 REBAR EA. WAY

SIDE VIEW   END VIEW
SEE PLAN

WOOD COLUMN TO BEAM
SCALE: 3/4" = 1'-0" 2/5

Figure 16.79 Wood column to beam. (Reprinted by permission from *The Professional Practice of Architectural Working Drawings*, 2d Ed., © 1995 by John Wiley & Sons, Inc.)

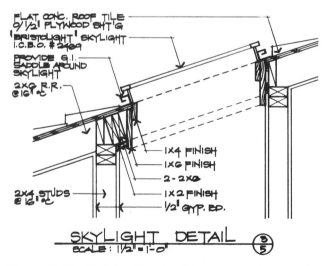

FLAT CONC. ROOF TILE O/1/2" PLYWOOD SHT'G
"BRISTOLIGHT" SKYLIGHT I.C.B.O. #2469
PROVIDE G.I. SADDLE AROUND SKYLIGHT
2X6 R.R. @ 16" OC
2X4 STUDS @ 16" OC

1X4 FINISH
1X6 FINISH
2 - 2X6
1X2 FINISH
1/2" GYP. BD.

SKYLIGHT DETAIL
SCALE: 1 1/2" = 1'-0" 3/5

Figure 16.80 Skylight. (Reprinted by permission from *The Professional Practice of Architectural Working Drawings*, 2d Ed., © 1995 by John Wiley & Sons, Inc.)

466

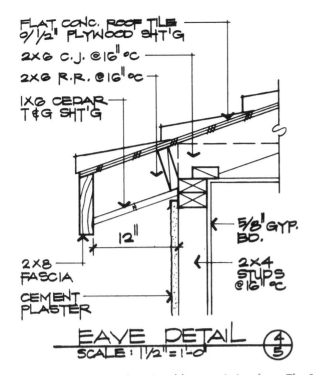

FLAT CONC. ROOF TILE
O/ 1/2" PLYWOOD SHT'G
2X6 C.J. @ 16" OC
2X6 R.R. @ 16" OC
1X6 CEDAR T&G SHT'G

12"

2X8 FASCIA

CEMENT PLASTER

5/8" GYP. BD.

2X4 STUDS @ 16" OC

EAVE DETAIL
SCALE: 1 1/2" = 1'-0"   (4/5)

Figure 16.81 Eave. (Reprinted by permission from *The Professional Practice of Architectural Working Drawings*, 2d Ed., © 1995 by John Wiley & Sons, Inc.)

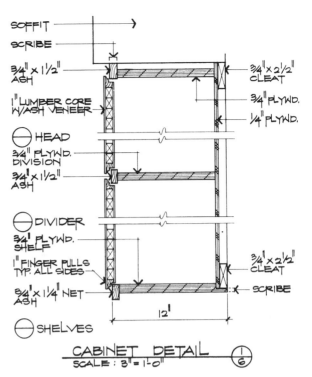

SOFFIT
SCRIBE
3/4" x 1 1/2" ASH
1" LUMBER CORE W/ASH VENEER
⊖ HEAD
3/4" PLYWD. DIVISION
3/4" x 1 1/2" ASH
⊖ DIVIDER
3/4" PLYWD. SHELF
1" FINGER PULLS TYP. ALL SIDES
3/4" x 1 1/4" NET ASH
⊖ SHELVES

3/4" x 2 1/2" CLEAT
3/4" PLYWD.
1/4" PLYWD.

3/4" x 2 1/2" CLEAT
SCRIBE

12"

CABINET DETAIL
SCALE: 3" = 1'-0"   (1/6)

Figure 16.83 Upper cabinet. (Reprinted by permission from *The Professional Practice of Architectural Working Drawings*, 2d Ed., © 1995 by John Wiley & Sons, Inc.)

2X8 FASCIA BD.
STEEL STRAP
3X6
2X6 C.J.
2X6 R.R.

4X BEAM
4X8 LEDGER

TRELLIS DETAIL
SCALE: 1" = 1'-0"   (5/5)

Figure 16.82 Trellis. (Reprinted by permission from *The Professional Practice of Architectural Working Drawings*, 2d Ed., © 1995 by John Wiley & Sons, Inc.)

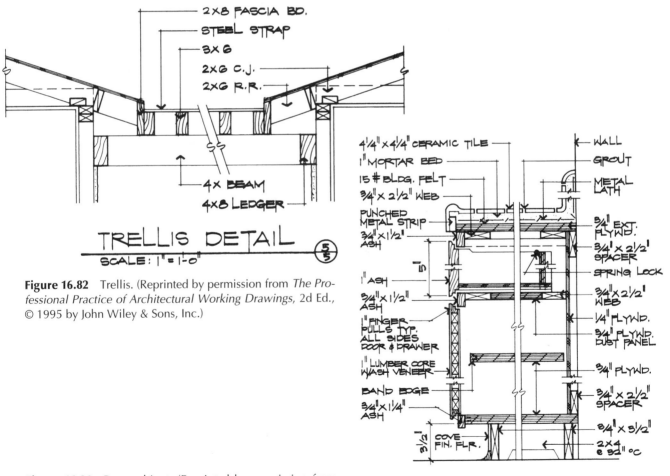

4 1/4" x 4 1/4" CERAMIC TILE
1" MORTAR BED
15 # BLDG. FELT
3/4" x 2 1/2" WEB
PUNCHED METAL STRIP
3/4" x 1 1/2" ASH
1" ASH
3/4" x 1 1/2" ASH
1" FINGER PULLS TYP. ALL SIDES DOOR & DRAWER
1" LUMBER CORE WASH VENEER
BAND EDGE
3/4" x 1 1/4" ASH
3 1/2"
COVE FIN. FLR.

5"

WALL
GROUT
METAL LATH
3/4" EXT. PLYWD.
3/4" x 2 1/2" SPACER
SPRING LOCK
3/4" x 2 1/2" WEB
1/4" PLYWD.
3/4" PLYWD. DUST PANEL
3/4" PLYWD.
3/4" x 2 1/2" SPACER
3/4" x 3 1/2"
2X4 @ 32" OC

BASE CABINET
SCALE: 3" = 1'-0"   (2/6)

Figure 16.84 Base cabinet. (Reprinted by permission from *The Professional Practice of Architectural Working Drawings*, 2d Ed., © 1995 by John Wiley & Sons, Inc.)

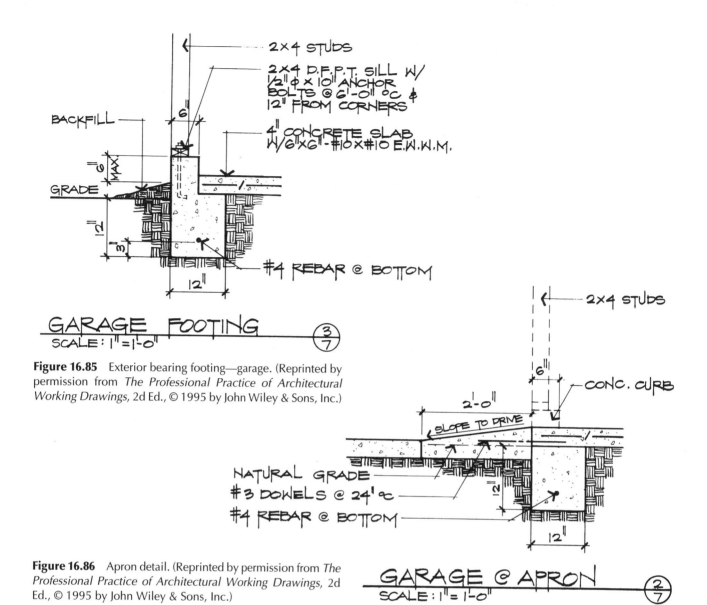

2×4 STUDS

2×4 D.F.P.T. SILL W/ 1/2"⌀ X 10" ANCHOR BOLTS @ 6'-0" OC & 12" FROM CORNERS

4" CONCRETE SLAB W/6"X6"-#10X#10 E.W.W.M.

BACKFILL

6"

6" MAX.

GRADE

12"

3'

12"

#4 REBAR @ BOTTOM

GARAGE FOOTING
SCALE : 1" = 1'-0"   ③/⑦

Figure 16.85 Exterior bearing footing—garage. (Reprinted by permission from *The Professional Practice of Architectural Working Drawings*, 2d Ed., © 1995 by John Wiley & Sons, Inc.)

2×4 STUDS

CONC. CURB

6"

2'-0"

SLOPE TO DRIVE

NATURAL GRADE
#3 DOWELS @ 24' oc
#4 REBAR @ BOTTOM

12"

12"

GARAGE @ APRON
SCALE : 1" = 1'-0"   ②/⑦

Figure 16.86 Apron detail. (Reprinted by permission from *The Professional Practice of Architectural Working Drawings*, 2d Ed., © 1995 by John Wiley & Sons, Inc.)

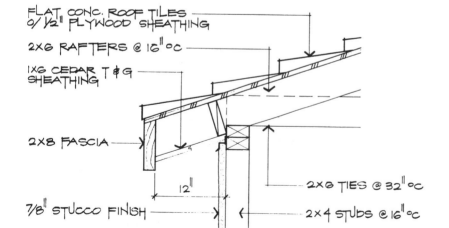

FLAT CONC. ROOF TILES O/ 1/2" PLYWOOD SHEATHING

2×6 RAFTERS @ 16" oc

1X6 CEDAR T & G SHEATHING

2×8 FASCIA

12"

2×6 TIES @ 32" oc

7/8" STUCCO FINISH

2×4 STUDS @ 16" oc

EAVE DETAIL
SCALE : 1 1/2" = 1'-0"   ①/⑦

Figure 16.87 Eave at garage.

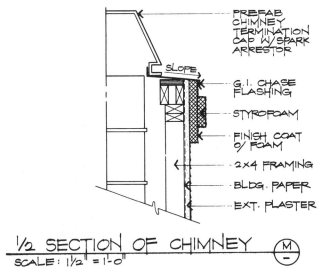

½ SECTION OF CHIMNEY (M)
SCALE: 1½" = 1'-0"

Figure 16.88 Half-section of chimney.

■ STAIR DESIGN AND VERTICAL LINKS

The stair design for any type of stairway will have to address the various physical and dimensional requirements while adhering to building code restrictions. The architect or designer will need to have some basic information prior to designing the stairs and the accompanying stair details. The first information required is the computed height between the floor levels. Second, the designer needs the dimensional requirements for the width of the stairs, and the length of the stair run to accommodate the number and width of the desired stair treads. After the floor-to-floor dimension is computed, this dimension will then become the basis for the number and height of the stair risers. An example of how this may be achieved is described mathematically as follows:

1. Floor to ceiling   = 8'-0"
2. Ceiling thickness   = 1"
3. Second floor wood joist   = 11 ½"
4. Second floor subfloor   = ¾"

Therefore, the floor-to-floor dimension is 9'-1 ¼" or 1091 ¼".

Desired riser height dimension = 6 ½" to 7"
Desired thread dimensions   = 10 ½" to 11 ½"

Riser Computation Example

Assume that there are 15 risers; therefore, 1091-¼" divided by 15 equals 7.26" risers or 7 ¼" risers. This does not meet current building code requirements. Try 16 risers. Thus, 1091-¼" divided by 16 equals 6.81" or 6 ¾" risers, which does meet building code requirements. Most building codes require that a rise in every step be not less than 4" nor greater than 7".

Tread Computation Example

Prior to computing the number and size of the treads for the preceding riser example, it is recommended that the governing building code requirements for the minimum width of the tread size be verified. Most codes require the tread size to be not less than 11" as measured horizontally between the vertical planes of the furthermost projection of the adjacent treads.

As determined by the foregoing riser computation, the stair calls for sixteen 6 ¾" risers. For most stairway designs the number of treads will be one less than the number of risers. Therefore, for the tread computation and code requirement, fifteen 11"-wide treads will be used in this example. To compute the dimensional length of the stairway run using fifteen 11"-wide treads, it would mathematically equate to 15 × 11" or 165". Therefore, the critical dimension to satisfy the number of treads in feet and inches would be 165" divided by 12, which converts into a minimum space requirement of 13'-10".

Stair Width. The desired or required stairway width will vary with the architect's design and the type of building that the stairway serves relative to the building code requirements. For most governing building codes, the required stairway width for commercial and public buildings must not be less than 44". In stairways serving residential structures or having an occupant load of less than 49, the stairway must not be less than 36" in width.

Handrails. Handrail designs and their projection into the required stairway width are governed by existing building code requirements. The allowed distance is 3 ½" from each side of a stairway. A three-dimensional drawing of an acceptable handrail design is shown in Figure 16.89. The height and tops of handrails and the handrail extensions must not be less than 34" nor more than 38" above the nosing of the treads and stairway landings.

Headroom. Another concern a stairway designer will need to consider is the minimum headroom clearance stipulated in most building codes. Generally, the headroom clearance must not be less than 6'-8". This clearance is to be measured vertically from a place that is parallel and tangent to the stairway tread nosings. Figure 16.90 graphically depicts a minimum headroom clearance requirement for a stairway.

The foregoing information and examples illustrate the basic concerns in designing stairways for a specific structure and the spaces required to meet these concerns. For further information on stairway designs and the various materials from which they may be constructed, refer to the third edition of *The Professional Practice of Architectural Detailing* (John Wiley & Sons Inc., Chapters 14, 15, and 16).

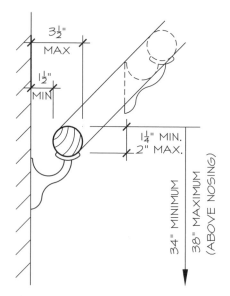

Figure 16.89 Handrail requirements.

Guardrails. Guardrails are safety devices found on stairway landings, balconies, and decks where their height is 30" or more above the adjacent grade or floor below. The structural design to stabilize the supporting vertical members is predicated on a horizontal force of 20 pounds per linear foot. Allowable openings in the guardrail assembly, as required by most building codes, depends on the occupancy classification and the use of the structure. For residential use the maximum clear openings must not exceed 4". For commercial and industrial structures the maximum

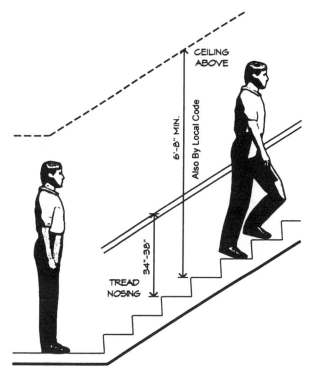

Figure 16.90 Headroom clearance.

clear openings must not exceed 8". In commercial and industrial-type structures that are not accessible for public use, the openings may be a maximum of 12". An example of a guardrail assembly is shown in a three-dimensional drawing in Figure 16.91.

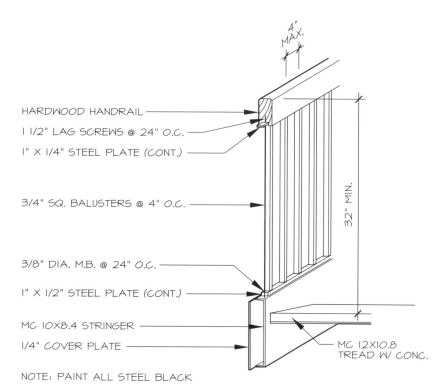

HARDWOOD HANDRAIL

1 1/2" LAG SCREWS @ 24" O.C.

1" X 1/4" STEEL PLATE (CONT.)

3/4" SQ. BALUSTERS @ 4" O.C.

3/8" DIA. M.B. @ 24" O.C.

1" X 1/2" STEEL PLATE (CONT.)

MC 10X8.4 STRINGER

1/4" COVER PLATE

MC 12X10.8 TREAD W/ CONC.

NOTE: PAINT ALL STEEL BLACK

Figure 16.91 Balustrade detail.

The construction materials used for stairways include wood, steel, poured-in-place concrete, precast concrete, or a combination of any of these materials. Figures 16.92, 16.93, and 16.94 illustrate a partial floor plan for a three-story residence incorporating a wood stairway construction at the different floor levels. The stairway designs will vary from a straight run and landings to a partial radial shape.

Starting at the basement level, as shown in Figure 16.92, and knowing the established basement floor-to-floor dimension of 10'-6", or 126", the designer can calculate the number and height of the stairway risers. Starting from the basement floor-to-floor, using 7" high risers, eighteen risers will be required. Therefore, when using 11"-wide treads, seventeen risers will be required. The length of the space required for seventeen 11"-treads

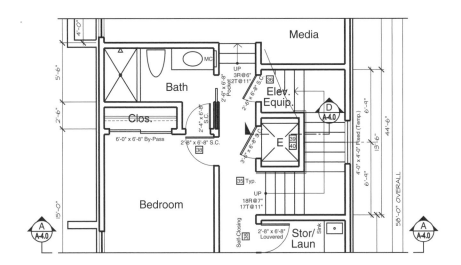

Partial Basement Floor Plan   SCALE: 1/4" = 1'-0"   N

0 1 2   4   8

Figure 16.92 Partial basement floor plan.

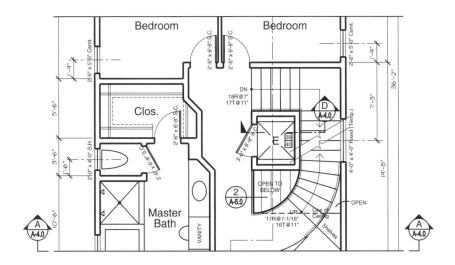

Partial 1st Floor Plan   SCALE: 1/4" = 1'-0"   N

0 1 2   4   8

Figure 16.93 Partial first floor plan.

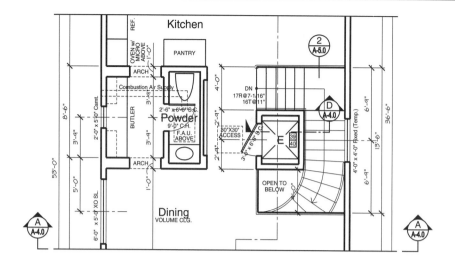

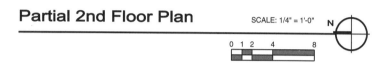

Partial 2nd Floor Plan

SCALE: 1/4" = 1'-0"

0 1 2   4   8

N

Figure 16.94 Partial second floor plan.

will be 15'-6" plus the width of the two stairway landings. The width of the landing is 42", as is the width of the stairway. The foregoing information is what was required to physically lay out this stairway design, which surrounds an elevator shaft enclosure.

The next step in this stairway design is to provide stair details as part of the project's working drawings. As shown in Figure 16.95, a section is cut at the bottom of the stairway, showing how the stringers are anchored at the basement concrete floor. Another detail will show

how the stringers occur at both landings. Figure 16.96 depicts this condition. The final detail, showing the method of attachment of the stringers to the floor joist, is illustrated in Figure 16.97.

As shown in Figure 16.93, the stairway access at the foyer has a partial radial curve in the design. An enlarged partial stair layout of this stairway segment is illustrated in Figure 16.98. This is done to show the inside and outer dimensions of a tread as a means for the construction of the stairway, while illustrating the building code re-

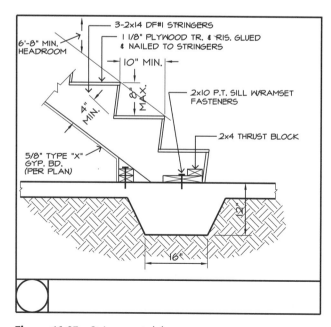

Figure 16.95 Stringers at slab.

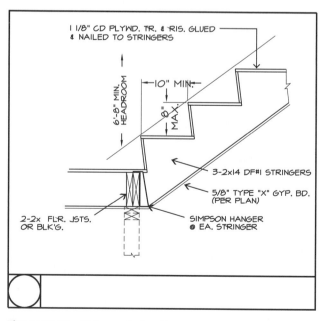

Figure 16.96 Stringers to landing.

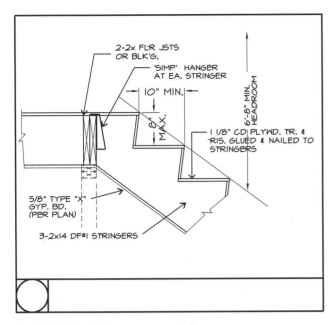

Figure 16.97 Stringers to second floor.

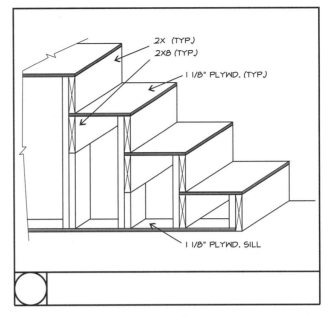

Figure 16.99 Circular stair detail.

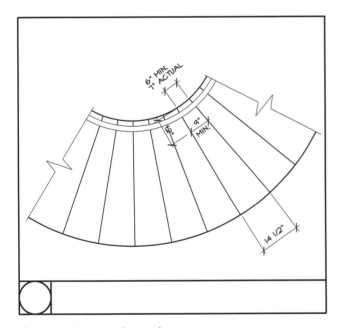

Figure 16.98 Partial stair plan.

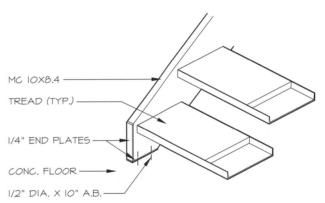

Figure 16.100 Stringer to concrete.

quirements for the tread design. A three-dimensional detail is added to the working drawings for the purpose of clarity for this circular portion of the stairway design. This drawing is depicted in Figure 16.99.

Steel Stairway Details

Details of the steel stairway assembly used in the Madison Building are found in Chapter 20 of this book. This all-structural-steel building utilizes an all-steel-and-concrete stairway assembly.

Beginning at the ground floor level, the steel stringers, fabricated from a standard steel channel, are attached to the concrete floor with $\frac{1}{4}$" steel plates and $\frac{1}{2}$'–0 × 10" anchor bolts. The typical tread design is a standard steel channel MC10x84 welded to the web of the channel stringer and filled with concrete. This detail assembly is illustrated in Figure 16.100.

The next connection detail is the stringer attachment at the intermediate landings and the support of the concrete at the landings, as shown in Figure 10.101. Note that the steel channel at the landing is used to support the steel stringers and the concrete at the landings. All connections are accomplished by assigned welds. The final detail for the steel stairway assembly is shown for the various floor levels. This detail illustrates a steel channel for the floor support and the support of the stringers. Steel angles are used for intermediate floor supports. These

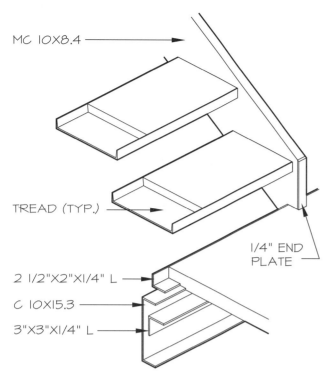

MC 10X8.4

TREAD (TYP.)

1/4" END PLATE

2 1/2"X2"X1/4" L

C 10X15.3

3"X3"X1/4" L

Figure 16.101 Stringer to landing.

quired steel reinforcing bars and then pouring the concrete in place. For many projects a precast concrete stairway is desirable, because there is no cost of forming and subsequently removing the forms. When using a poured-in-place concrete stair, it is necessary to provide details, with the required steel reinforcing as part of the working drawings. A three-dimensional detail for a poured-in-place concrete stairway is depicted in Figure 16.103.

Composite Stairway Assembly

Another type of stairway uses a manufactured precast concrete one-piece closed tread and riser assembly. These precast units can be assembled with wood or steel stringers. This composite stairway requires architectural detailing, because it is necessary to size wood stringers for their span and the weight of the precast treads and risers and to show how they are attached to the supporting beams. A three-dimensional detail illustrating a precast tread and riser unit attached to wood stringers is shown in Figure 16.104.

■ MECHANICAL VERTICAL LINKS

The drawings for elevators of all types and various lifting devices such as wheelchair lifts, chair lifts, and others must include the detailing necessary to satisfy the installation requirements. An example of a residential-type electric elevator is shown in Figure 16.92. The planned area for the wall framing and the openings that surround the electric elevator car must adhere to all the clearances required by the elevator manufacturer. The planning must also include the required space designated by the manufacturer for the machine room equipment. This room is located adjacent to and under the stairway run. A three-dimensional drawing of the framed opening is

members are illustrated in the detail shown in Figure 16.102.

Concrete Stairs

The construction of concrete stairways may be achieved in two ways. First, there are various precast concrete companies that manufacture different types of concrete stairs and will deliver and install them on the building site. Second, concrete stairways may be formed in the construction of the building by incorporating the re-

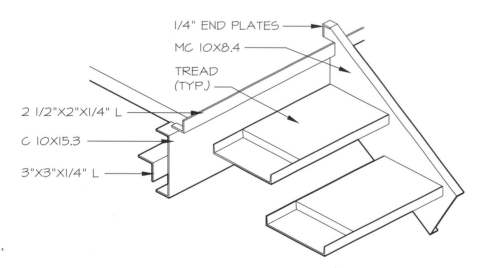

1/4" END PLATES

MC 10X8.4

TREAD (TYP.)

2 1/2"X2"X1/4" L

C 10X15.3

3"X3"X1/4" L

Figure 16.102 Stringer to floor.

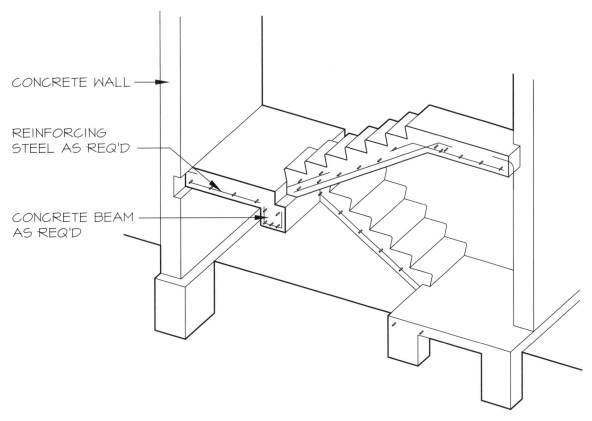

Figure 16.103 U-shaped concrete stairs.

shown in Figure 16.105. This particular elevator has a lift capacity of approximately 750 pounds.

A more detailed example of a manufacturer's requirements is shown in the plan view illustrated in Figure 16.106. This drawing, as furnished by a specific elevator manufacturer, shows the information an architect or de-

signer will need to integrate into the working drawings. Note that the shaft dimension requirements, the clearances for this specific elevator, and the electrical supply must be shown in the working drawings. A section through the elevator shaft and machine room is shown in Figure 16.107. This drawing depicts the length of the

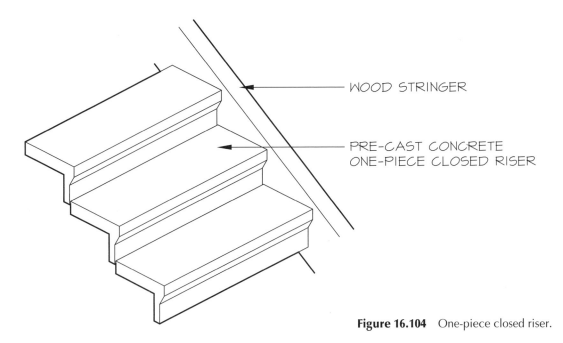

WOOD STRINGER

PRE-CAST CONCRETE
ONE-PIECE CLOSED RISER

Figure 16.104 One-piece closed riser.

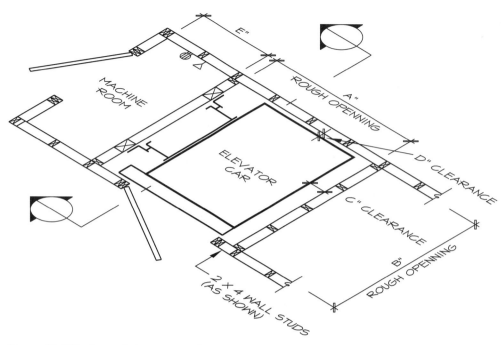

Figure 16.105 Framed elevator opening.

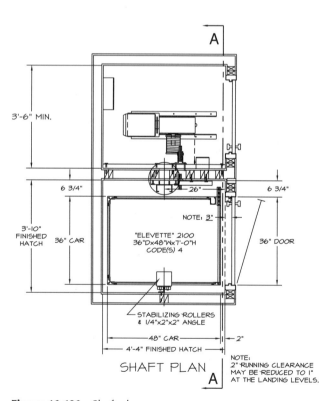

Figure 16.106 Shaft plan.

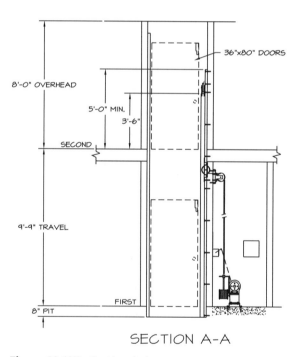

Figure 16.107 Section A-A.

vertical travel, the electrical supply location, and the required 8"-deep pit depression that is required for the cab clearance. The area and dimensions for the pit area must be shown accurately on the foundation plan of the working drawings.

For planning access to the electric elevator, there are various car configurations available from the manufacturer. Examples of car configurations are illustrated in Figure 16.108. A photograph of a finished electric elevator installation is shown in Figure 16.109.

Another manufactured device used in the development of a vertical link is a stair lift. This unit is ideal for persons with walking disabilities or other physical limitations. Figure 16.110 depicts a plan view of the stair lift

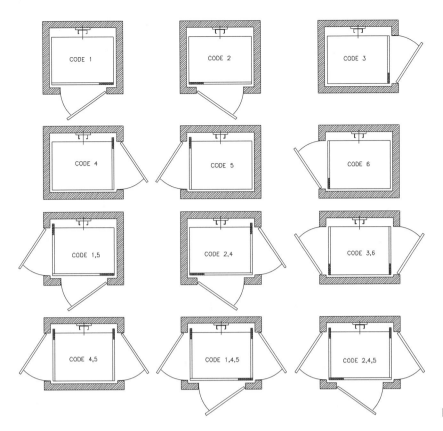

Figure 16.108 Car configurations.

Figure 16.109 Elevette. (Courtesy Inclinator Co. of America.)

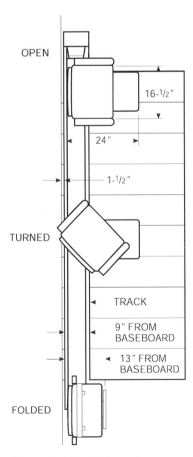

OPEN

16-1/2"

24"

1-1/2"

TURNED

TRACK

9" FROM BASEBOARD

13" FROM BASEBOARD

FOLDED

Figure 16.110 Stair lift diagram.

Figure 16.111 Stair lift. (Courtesy Inclinator Co. of America.)

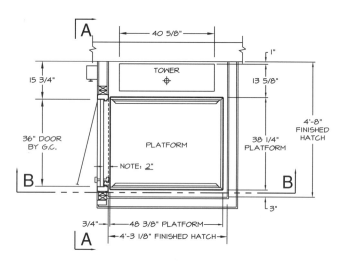

PLATFORM & TOWER

Figure 16.112 Vertical lift diagram.

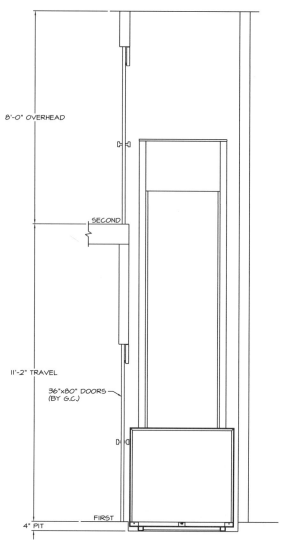

SECTION B-B

Figure 16.113 Section B-B.

positions and the dimensional aspects of the unit as it projects into the stairway run. A photograph of a stair lift installation is shown in Figure 16.111.

For persons who rely on the use of a wheelchair for vertical access, the use of a vertical lift is desirable. As in addressing the dimensional requirements of an elevator, the architect or designer will need to provide the dimensions, clearances, and electrical supply information as stipulated by the manufacturer's specifications. An example of a platform plan and its requirements for a vertical lift and the vertical travel dimensions are depicted in Figures 16.112 and 16.113. A photograph of a finished vertical lift installation is illustrated in Figure 16.114. This vertical lift unit is constructed of fiberglass that is rust-free and has a nonskid surface. Such units are available in various colors. Their maximum load capacity is 750 pounds.

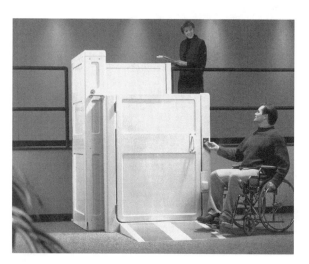

Figure 16.114 Spectralift. (Courtesy Inclinator Co. of America.)

A vertical linking unit that is convenient for lifting groceries and other heavy items from one level to another is a home waiter, frequently referred to as a dumbwaiter. These units vary in shaft size and maximum load capacity. The space planning and layout requirements for dimensions and clearances will be delineated in the working drawings, as shown for elevators and other lifting devices. A shaft plan illustrating dimensions and clearances for a two-landing home waiter installation is depicted in Figure 16.115. This particular unit is limited to a 75-pound lifting capacity. Figure 16.116 shows a section of this home waiter unit illustrating the vertical travel dimensions, clearances, machine equipment room location, and the desired counter height. The vertical link units described here are but a few examples of lifting units that are primarily found in residential projects.

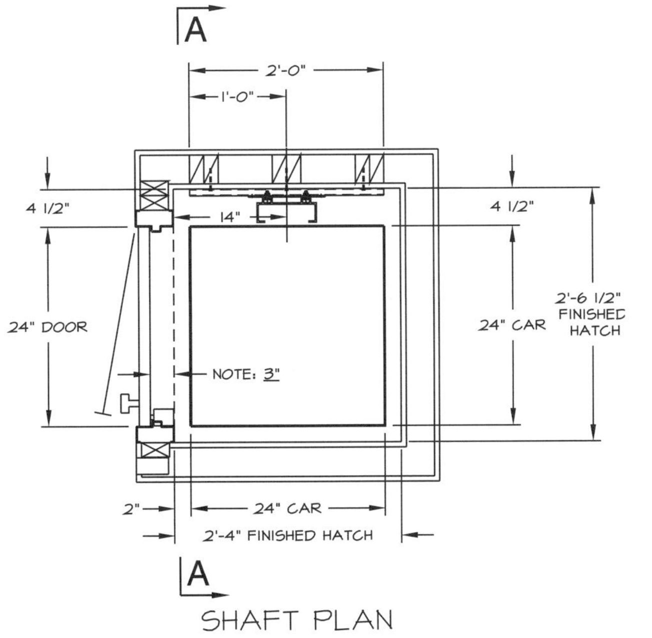

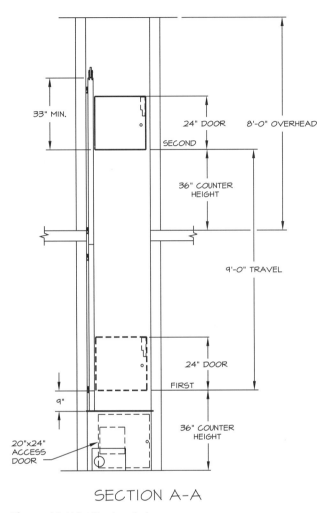

SECTION A-A

Figure 16.116 Section A-A.

SHAFT PLAN

Figure 16.115 Shaft plan.

PART

III

Case Studies

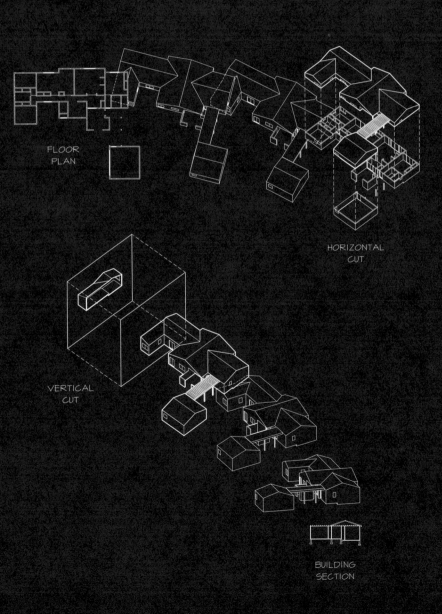

chapter

17

CONCEPTUAL DESIGN AND
CONSTRUCTION DOCUMENTS
FOR A CONVENTIONAL
WOOD RESIDENCE

FLOOR
PLAN

HORIZONTAL
CUT

VERTICAL
CUT

BUILDING
SECTION

■ CONCEPTUAL DESIGN

This chapter presents a hypothetical project, generated to provide a model for the student. The initial design and its subsequent changes are incorporated to illustrate the natural evolution of a design into a set of working drawings. Most of the changes are not based on design concepts or approaches, but rather create typical uncomplicated problems that might confront the beginning drafter. The rest of this book discusses a number of actually built projects.

Site Requirements

The design purpose is to create a three-bedroom, two-bath home that has room for growth. The site is a typical, yet irregular, city lot in Anytown, U.S.A. Because the zoning is R-1 (residential), the setbacks are the typical 20'-0" in the front, 5'-0" on the sides, and 15'-0" at the rear. Water flows to the rear in the direction of the lot's slope, which is greater beyond the rear property line. This slope created a city view to the rear of the lot.

With the neighbors' play area to the East, there is normal play-activity noise in the late afternoon and early evening. See Figure 17.1.

Client Requirements

Along with three bedrooms and two baths, the clients requested a family room, a kitchen, a living room oriented toward the view, and a formal dining room.

For security's sake, a security gate and entry were also requested. Most important, the structure had to be able

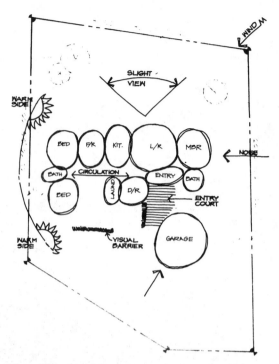

Figure 17.2 Bubble diagramming the Ryan Residence.

to expand by 100 to 150 square feet to accommodate a den, study, or guest room.

Initial Schematic Studies

Using what is commonly called bubble diagramming, room relationships were quickly established. Most of the rooms were oriented, as seen in Figure 17.2, to the rear of the lot to take advantage of the view and avoid the street noise. With the prevailing wind coming from the northeast, each of these rooms will be well ventilated, which is especially needed for the kitchen. The garage is positioned at an angle to produce an entry court. Circulation is through the center of the structure, which serves as a spline or connector to all rooms, and visual relief from the hall/tunnel effect is achieved with the space between the front bedroom and the laundry. This space is made private by incorporating a visual barrier (to be determined by client) of bushes or a sculptural wall. While the children are young, this space can be used as a play area, and, as they grow into their teens, a reading space or private patio. It is this space that can later house the final guest room, computer room, or den with minimal cost.

■ DESIGN AND SCHEMATIC DRAWINGS

The design sketches and schematic drawings represent the culmination of many hours of designer-client decisions. Some sets may even include the evolution of a design as a final presentation to the client, and the final changes incorporated by the client based on such things as financing

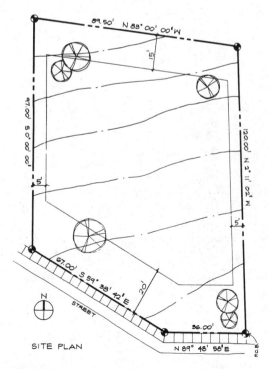

Figure 17.1 Ryan Residence site.

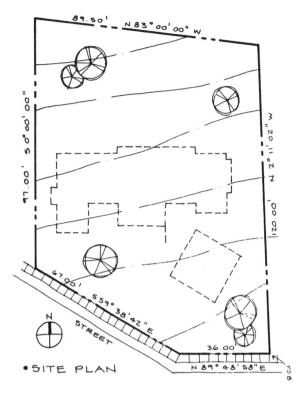

Figure 17.3 Preliminary site plan.

or the scaling-down of the structure because of the projected number of users. At some point a final decision is made, signed, and becomes the final design proposal used by the project manager to evolve as a set of drawings.

There are two kinds of design and schematic drawings to be considered. The first group is the first set of preliminary drawings developed by the designer in response to the client's needs. These provide the basis for the formulation and incorporation of changes and new ideas. Included are a site plan (Figure 17.3), floor plan (Figure 17.4), and a couple of elevations (Figure 17.5).

If this set of drawings is approved, additional preliminary structural drawings are conceived, which may include a foundation plan (Figure 17.6), a building section (Figure 17.7), and possibly a framing plan.

Client Changes

The preliminary floor plan plays a very important part in the development of a final configuration or shape of a structure. It gives the client time to look at and discuss some of the important family needs or to make major changes before the project progresses too far.

Figure 17.8 shows the changes generated by the client—the slight enlargement of all bedrooms and the

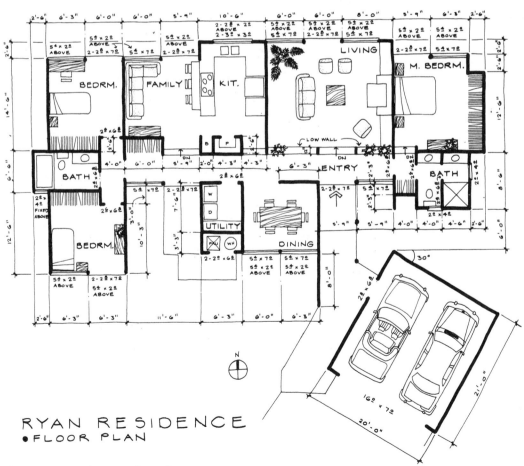

Figure 17.4 Preliminary floor plan.

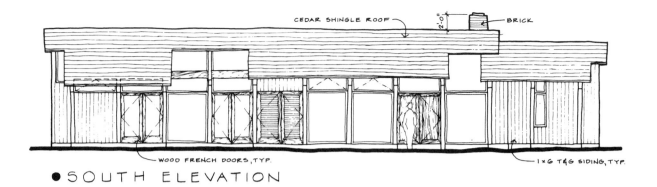

● SOUTH ELEVATION

CEDAR SHINGLE ROOF
2'-0"
BRICK
WOOD FRENCH DOORS, TYP.
1 x 6 T&G SIDING, TYP.

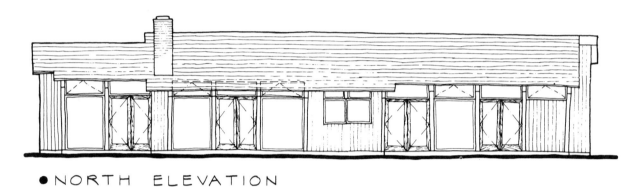

● NORTH ELEVATION

Figure 17.5 Preliminary elevations.

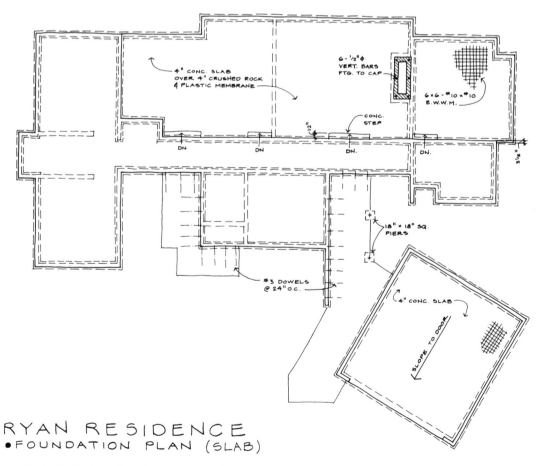

4" CONC. SLAB
OVER 4" CRUSHED ROCK
& PLASTIC MEMBRANE

6 - ½"Ø
VERT. BARS
FTG. TO CAP

6 x 6 - #10 x #10
E.W.W.M.

CONC.
STEP

12"

DN   DN   DN.   DN.

3½"

18" x 18" SQ.
PIERS

#3 DOWELS
@ 24" O.C.

4" CONC. SLAB

SLOPE TO DOOR

RYAN RESIDENCE
● FOUNDATION PLAN (SLAB)

Figure 17.6 Preliminary foundation plan—slab.

486

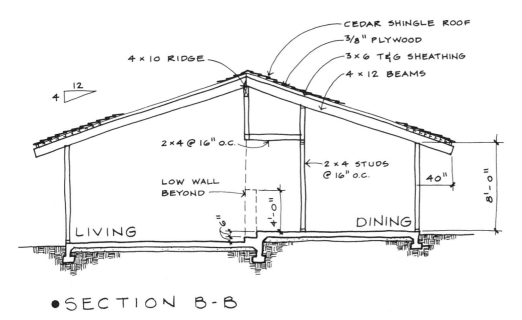

CEDAR SHINGLE ROOF
3/8" PLYWOOD
3×6 T&G SHEATHING
4×12 BEAMS

4×10 RIDGE

2×4 @ 16" O.C.

2×4 STUDS @ 16" O.C.

LOW WALL BEYOND

LIVING

DINING

•SECTION B-B

Figure 17.7 Preliminary building section.

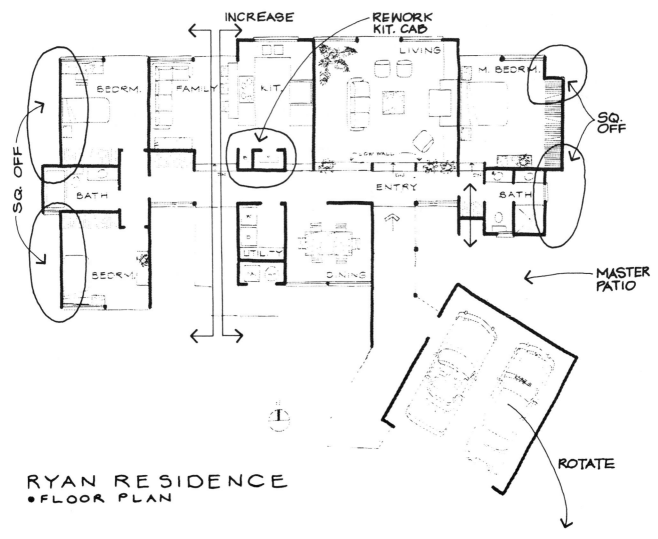

INCREASE

REWORK KIT. CAB

LIVING

M. BEDRM.

BEDRM.

FAMILY

KIT

SQ. OFF

SQ. OFF

LOW WALL

SQ. OFF

BATH

BATH

ENTRY

BEDRM.

W
D

UTILITY

DINING

MASTER PATIO

ROTATE

RYAN RESIDENCE
•FLOOR PLAN

Figure 17.8 Client changes—Ryan Residence.

master bath. This was an attempt to reduce the jogs in perimeter and to achieve cost reduction. The family room is to be expanded to about 15+ feet as the lot permits. The kitchen was redesigned so as to increase counter space, and the entry reworked to prevent the door from opening into the circulation pattern through the hall. Finally, and most significant, the possibility of the clients purchasing a boat or recreational vehicle mandated consideration of a storage and maintenance area. (The clients were leaning heavily toward the purchase of a boat.)

Adjusted Floor Plan

The adjusted floor plan is shown in Figure 17.9. Compare this with the original floor plan and note the changes. As indicated in Chapter 7, exterior and interior finishes are discussed with the client, along with the se-

lection of appliances, roofing materials, shapes of the roof, positioning of skylight, window quality and types, and other features.

Model

For the sake of visualization, a model was constructed over a copy of the preliminary floor plan. Because of the cost of model making, finished finite models are not always made, but simple massing models like those shown in Figure 17.10A and B can be. Figure 17.10A shows walls and door openings plus the change in level of one foot. The model was built of foam core board with black chart tape positioned to cover the top edge. Such a model allows the client to see the relationship of rooms three-dimensionally and the positioning of furniture in relation to the walls.

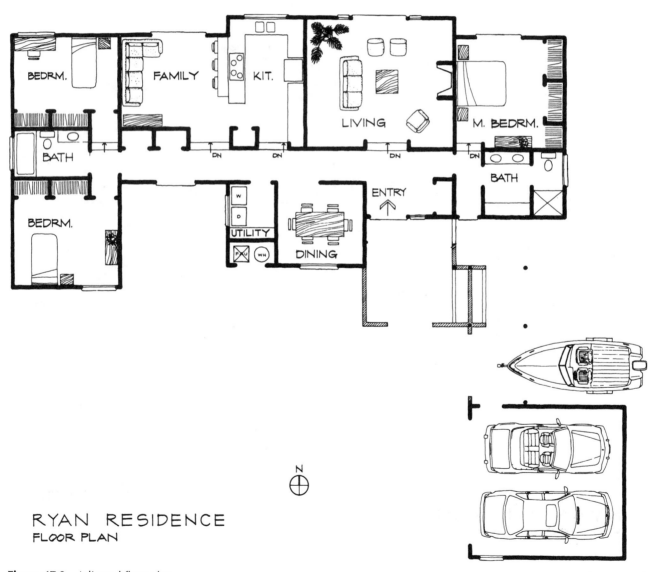

RYAN RESIDENCE
FLOOR PLAN

Figure 17.9 Adjusted floor plan.

A   B

Figure 17.10   Floor plan and massing model of Ryan Residence.

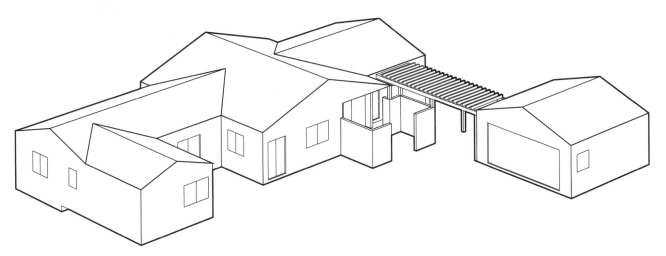

Figure 17.11   3-D model of Ryan Residence.

Figure 17.10B shows the roof and how it is structurally engineered. Additional information on this roof can be found at the end of Chapter 14.

Three-dimensional models can also be made on the computer. You will see an example of a 3-D model of the Ryan Residence in Figure 17.11. The model was initially drawn in 2-D, as shown in Figure 17.12A, and subsequently evolved as shown in Figures 17.12B through 17.12H. Figure 17.12H is the same model as that shown in Figure 17.11. Figures 17.12I and 17.12J show the Ryan Residence in other views as the object is rotated. These models of the Ryan Residence can be further rendered to show the suggested building materials, landscaped to scale, and then imported into a photograph of the vacant property to show the client an actual image.

Development of Elevations

The model helps the clients to visualize how the structure will look and to comprehend the preliminary exterior elevations, as seen in Figure 17.12.

■ EVOLUTION OF RYAN RESIDENCE WORKING DRAWINGS

In each of the subsequent chapters, the case studies will be evolved stage by stage within the confines of the specific topic. For example, for the beach house (Chapter 18), the site plan is evolved over a four-stage sequence with descriptive commentary at each stage as to what was done, in what order, and why. For the foundation, again four sages are encountered, with explanations given at each stage, and so on through the floor plan, exterior elevations, and so forth.

Preliminary design studies can also be scanned into the computer, sized, and positioned as shown in Figure 17.22 (Sheet A-1, Site Plan), Figure 17.23 (Sheet A-4, Elevations and Schedules) Figure 17.24 (Sheet A-5, Building Sections and Details), and a typical sheet layout for a garage, shown in Figure 17.25. This freehand cartoon can also be used in other projects. For example, if the roof configuration changes from a gable roof to a hip roof, the office manager only needs to scan the drawing,

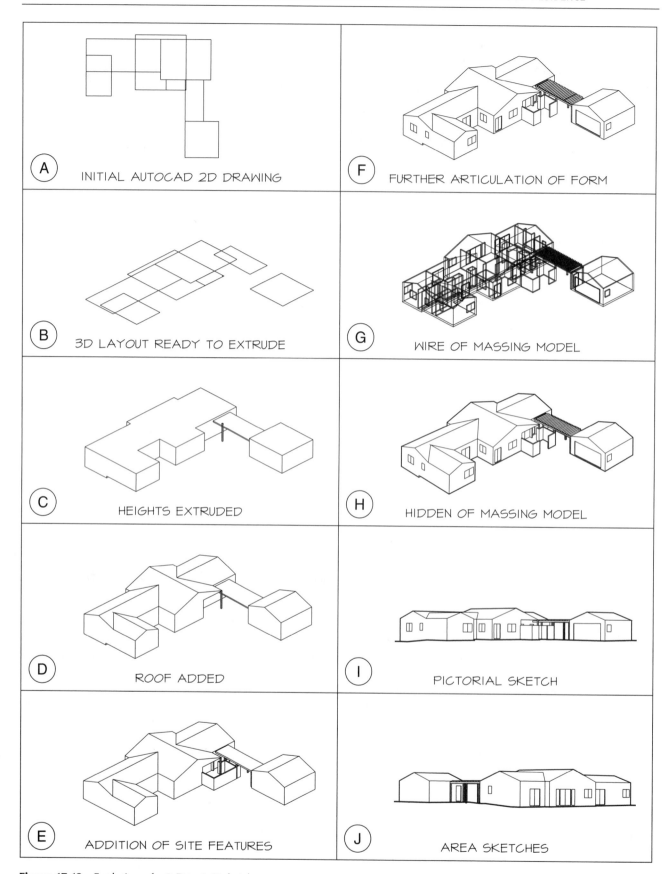

(A) INITIAL AUTOCAD 2D DRAWING

(B) 3D LAYOUT READY TO EXTRUDE

(C) HEIGHTS EXTRUDED

(D) ROOF ADDED

(E) ADDITION OF SITE FEATURES

(F) FURTHER ARTICULATION OF FORM

(G) WIRE OF MASSING MODEL

(H) HIDDEN OF MASSING MODEL

(I) PICTORIAL SKETCH

(J) AREA SKETCHES

Figure 17.12 Evolution of a 2-D to 3-D sketch.

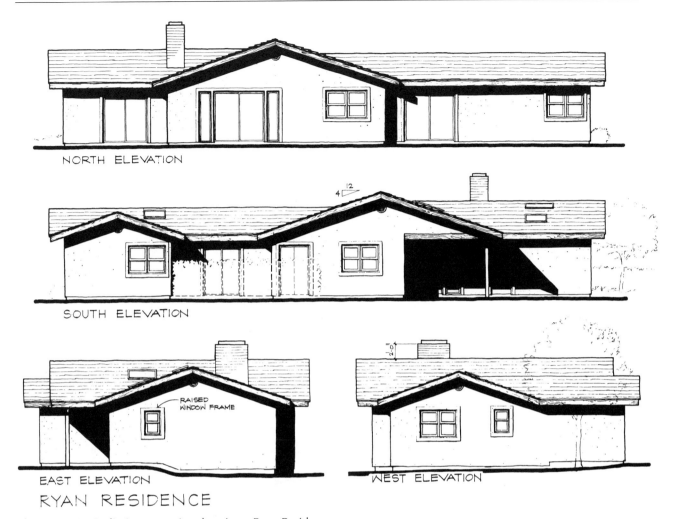

NORTH ELEVATION

SOUTH ELEVATION

RAISED
WINDOW FRAME

EAST ELEVATION

WEST ELEVATION

RYAN RESIDENCE

Figure 17.13 Preliminary exterior elevation—Ryan Residence.

make the necessary roof change, and give it to the drafter or red mark the change on a copy of the existing cartoon.

Other Preliminary Drawings

Other preliminary drawings may be evolved by the design and structural associates, making the task of the CAD drafter easier. This may take the form of a preliminary foundation plan, as shown in Figure 17.14, the revised preliminary building sections and roof plans shown in Figure 17.15, and the revised framing systems in Figure 17.16.

Cartoon of the Project

Cartoons can be created either manually or on the computer. Please review the section on cartoon development in Chapter 6.

A cartoon sheet format, or mock set as it is called in some regions, is a reduced replica of the distribution of

the drawings on each of the working drawing sheets drawn on an 8½″ × 11″ sheet of paper. These can be accomplished by substituting rectangles in place of the actual drawings, as shown in Figures 17.17 through 17.22 (Sheets A-1 through A-6), or the preliminary design studies can be reduced on a plain paper copier to the proper scale and pasted into place as shown in Figure 17.23. The second procedure is much faster, and the final image is a close replication of the final drawing.

Note the tick marks on the sheet around the borderline. If these are extended horizontally and vertically, they will form a matrix. The project manager will try to use this matrix to establish the drawing size limits and distribute the drawings in such a manner as to stay within these limits. In this way, general notes, details, schedules, and so forth can be drawn on separate sheets, reproduced onto sticky backs, and positioned onto the large sheets without encroaching onto other drawing on the sheet.

Throughout the development of the Ryan Residence, you will note the adherence to this matrix. There will be

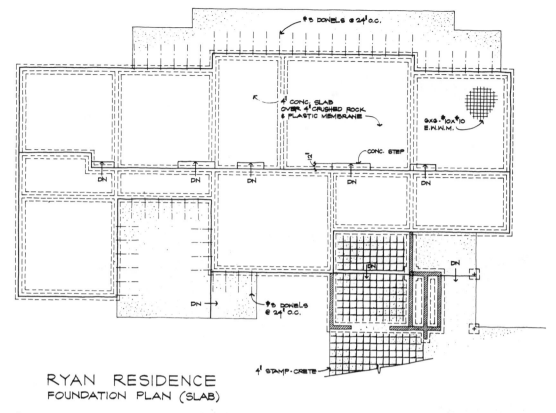

RYAN RESIDENCE
FOUNDATION PLAN (SLAB)

Figure 17.14 Revised preliminary foundation plan.

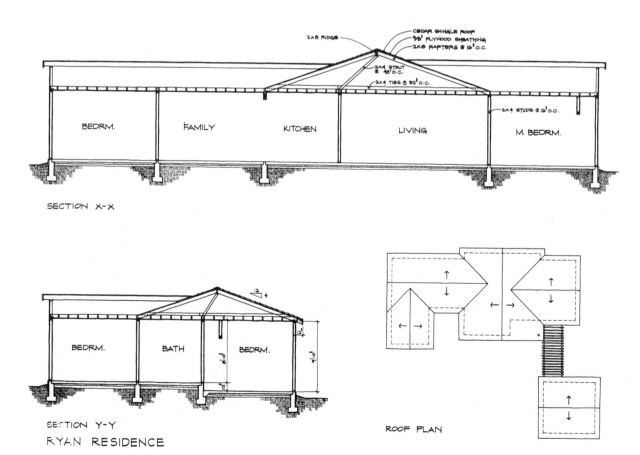

SECTION X-X

SECTION Y-Y
RYAN RESIDENCE

ROOF PLAN

Figure 17.15 Revised preliminary building sections and roof plan.

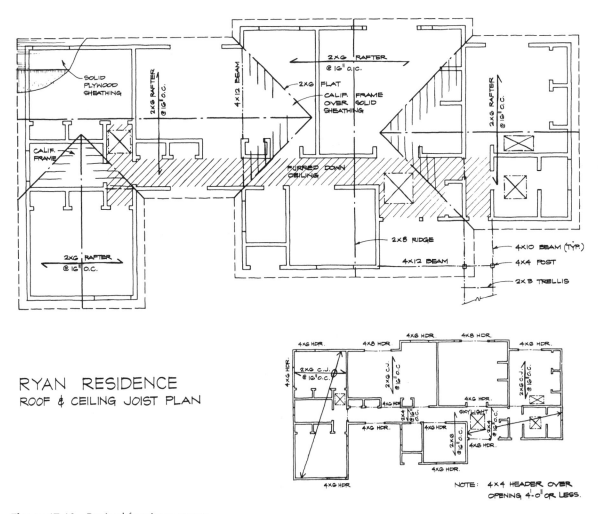

RYAN RESIDENCE
ROOF & CEILING JOIST PLAN

Figure 17.16 Revised framing systems.

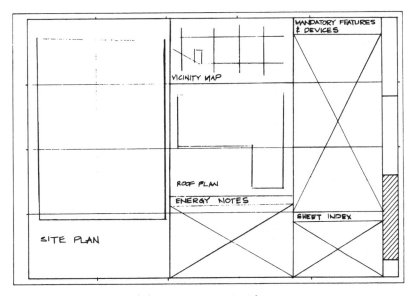

Figure 17.17 Cartoon of Sheet A-1—Ryan Residence.

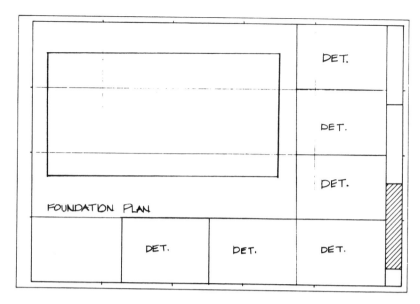

Figure 17.18 Cartoon of Sheet A-2—Ryan Residence.

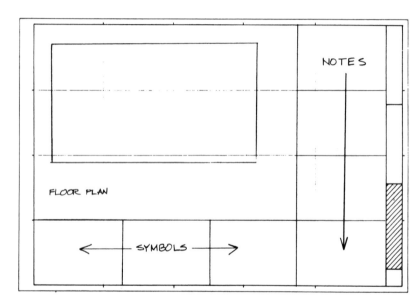

Figure 17.19 Cartoon of Sheet A-3—Ryan Residence.

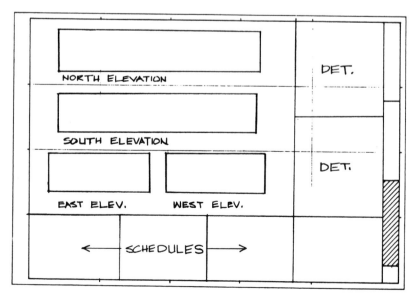

Figure 17.20 Cartoon of Sheet A-4—Ryan Residence.

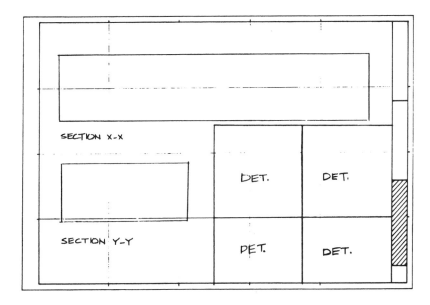

Figure 17.21 Cartoon of Sheet A-5—Ryan Residence.

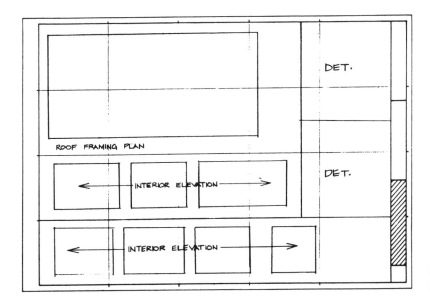

Figure 17.22 Cartoon of Sheet A-6—Ryan Residence.

Figure 17.23 Cartoon preparation.

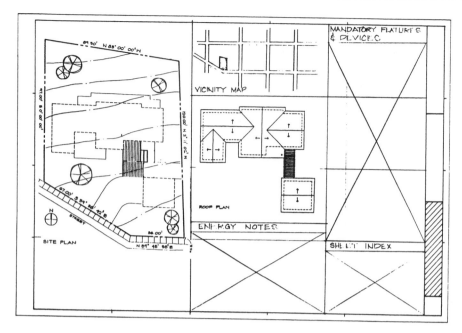

Figure 17.24 Cartoon of Ryan Residence site plan.

times that, owing to the scale or size of a detail, or the length of a note, we will not be able to adhere to this module. The fireplace detail is a good example of such nonadherence. The footing details adjacent to the foundation plan provide a good example of the use of the matrix.

For example, in dealing with the Ryan Residence, if you wish to find out how the roof is configured, read the section at the end of Chapter 14. Similarly, if you wish to understand the specific architectural features around the window or the type and shape of the fireplace, see the first half of Chapter 16.

The construction documents for the Ryan Residence are presented with two different approaches in this chapter. The evolution of the working drawings is shown first as a hand-drawn set, and is then presented as an entire set of working drawings drawn on the computer.

Single or Multiple Working Drawing Sheets Procedure

After looking at the cartoon of each sheet, the project architect must determine how these working drawing sheets will be evolved. Will a single drafter take on the

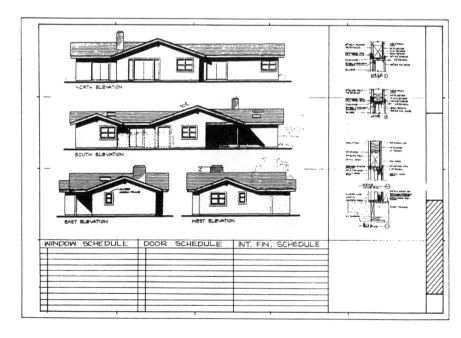

Figure 17.25 Cartoon of Ryan Residence exterior elevation.

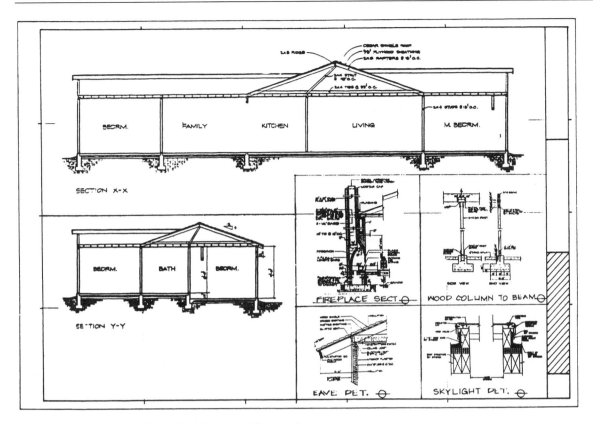

Figure 17.26 Cartoon of Ryan Residence building section.

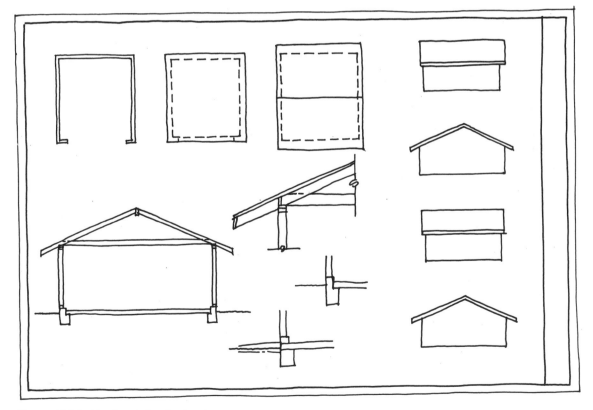

Figure 17.27 Freehand-sketched cartoon.

responsibility of a single sheet, or will there be a number of drafters working on it? Can parts of a single sheet be delegated to two or three individuals, drawn on separate sheets, and assembled photographically? Once this decision is made by the project architect, the drafters are selected and delegated the drawings for which they are responsible. The multiple-drafter, multiple-drawing approach is used throughout this chapter in dealing with the Ryan Residence, whereas subsequent chapters will have a single drafter responsible for each sheet in the set.

Evolving Construction Documents from a 3-D Model

The 3-D model is rotated into another position to obtain the roof plan and the corresponding elevations (See Figure 17.28). The 3-D model is sliced horizontally and vertically. The horizontal slice is used to produce the floor plan. If the roof half is rotated in the plan view, a reflected ceiling plan is produced. The vertical cut produces a view of the structure called a building section. For examples of the floor plan and building section, see Figure 17.29. A summary of the results of this exercise is shown in Figure 17.30.

The next step for the CAD drafter is to construct the structure as a 3-D model. See an example of such a section in Figure 17.31. Although this may seem like a lot of work at this stage, it is not when you consider that the floor plan will be used as the base (datum) for the fram-

ing plan, electrical plans, mechanical plans, and foundation plans, as seen in Figure 17.32. The sections can be enlarged to produce a base for partial sections and details, as shown in Figures 17.33 and 17.34, respectively. In this manner, the 3-D model becomes the datum and the glue that holds the entire set of drawings together.

■ SHEET A-1—SITE PLAN, VICINITY MAP, ROOF PLAN, NOTES

Check the cartoon of Sheet A-1 in Figure 17.7 for the basic layout, and you will be able to see the pieces come together.

As stated earlier, the drawings can be done by a single individual or by two drafters. If two drafters are used simultaneously, there must be a clear-cut delegation of responsibilities, a format that will allow such a procedure to work, and an understanding by the project manager as to skills of the drafters.

As can be seen in the cartoon, Sheet A-1 will include the following:

1. Site plan
2. Vicinity map
3. Roof plan
4. Energy notes
5. Mandatory features and devices
6. Sheet index

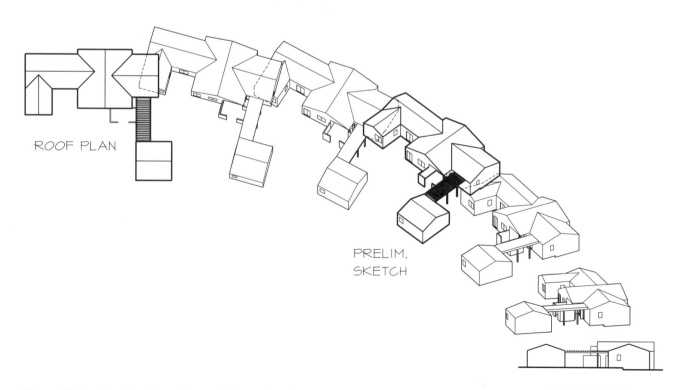

ROOF PLAN

PRELIM. SKETCH

ELEVATION

Figure 17.28   Rotation of massing model into ortho view.

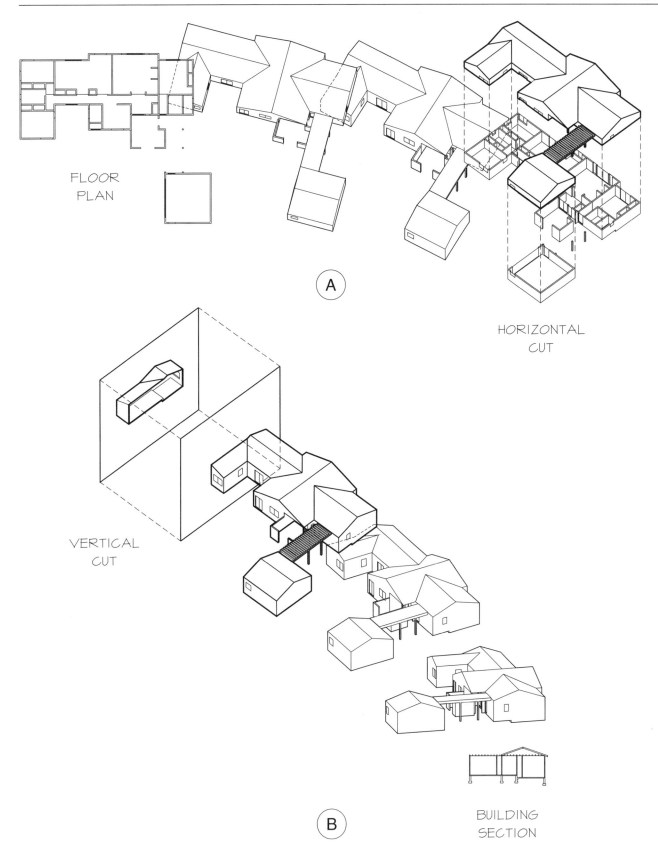

FLOOR
PLAN

A

HORIZONTAL
CUT

VERTICAL
CUT

B

BUILDING
SECTION

Figure 17.29 Horizontal and vertical sections through preliminary sketch.

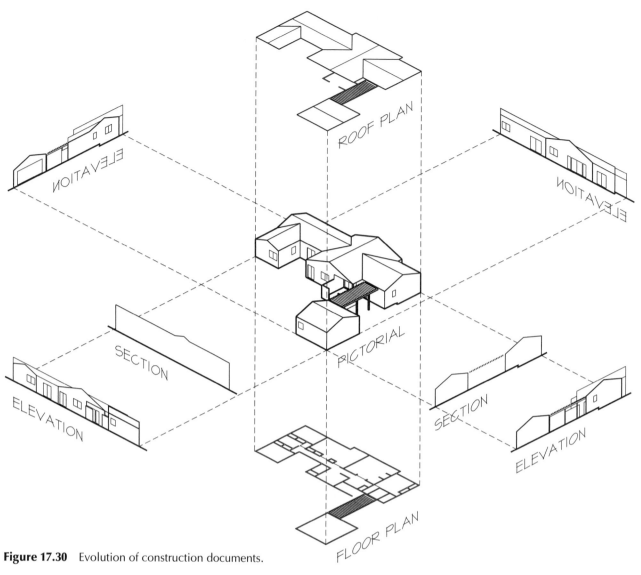

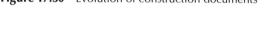

Figure 17.30 Evolution of construction documents.

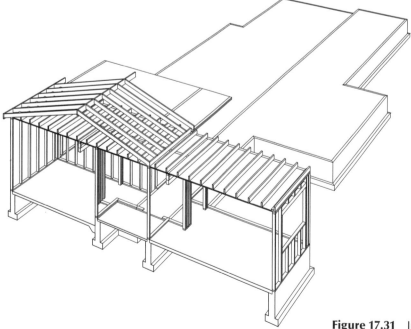

Figure 17.31 Incorporating the individual elements.

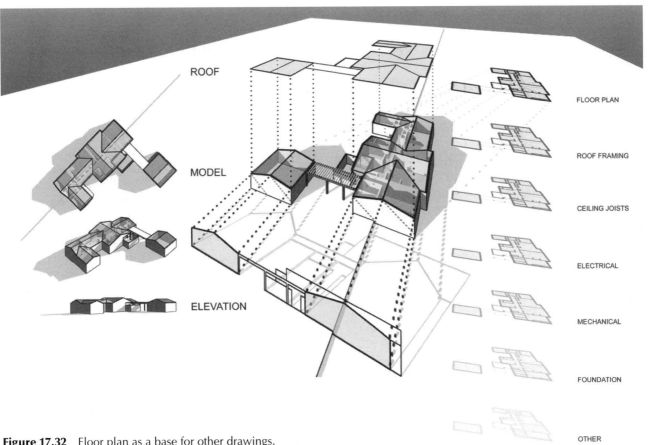

ROOF

MODEL

ELEVATION

FLOOR PLAN

ROOF FRAMING

CEILING JOISTS

ELECTRICAL

MECHANICAL

FOUNDATION

OTHER

Figure 17.32   Floor plan as a base for other drawings.

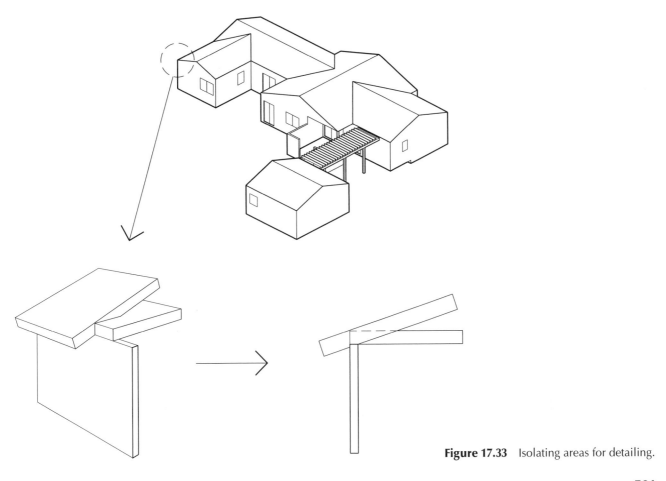

Figure 17.33   Isolating areas for detailing.

The first three components will be done by one drafter, and the remaining three by a second drafter. In fact, in some offices, an administrative assistant who is familiar with typing and word processing can receive additional training in scissor drafting and forward the notes to a CAD drafter, who can then insert the notes in the proper position.

If the office computers are networked and a third drafter is periodically available, this third drafter may be delegated the responsibility to draft only the vicinity map portion of the drawing. Thus, the entire site plan is done by multiple employees.

If the drawings are done by hand, each component part can be scissored and the parts assembled together to form the entire sheet, including the notes. Be sure to use repositionable glue. An engineering copier can then be used to make a single original on vellum.

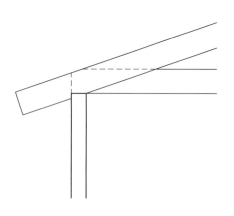

■ EVOLUTION OF RYAN ROOF PLAN

Ryan Residence Roof Plan

The roof plan is often superimposed on the site plan. In the evolution of the Ryan Residence these plans will be kept separate, which makes them easier to understand and is much better practice. When a roof plan is superimposed on a site plan, the building line and the roof outline are reversed, with the building line solid and the roof line dotted. On a true roof plan the outline of a roof is a solid line.

STAGE I   (Figure 17.33). The scale selected for the Ryan Residence roof plan is $1/8'' = 1'-0''$. The outline of the building can be drawn by taking the first stage of the floor plan and making a $1/2$ reduction and tracing. The garage plan is positioned adjacent to the main structure.

STAGE II   (Figure 17.34). The roof and building lines are darkened at this stage. Arrows are drawn to indicate the direction of the slope of the trellis that connects the residence to the garage via the master bedroom. The patio is drawn.

Next, an easing shield with a uniform series of circular openings is used in conjunction with an electric erase to produce near-perfect hidden lines, which represents the building line.

STAGE III   (Figure 17.35). Skylight and chimney locations are the first to be located at this stage. Some architectural offices show plumbing vents that come through the roof, as a confirmation of their positions. Detail and section reference bubbles are next and, finally, noting is completed.

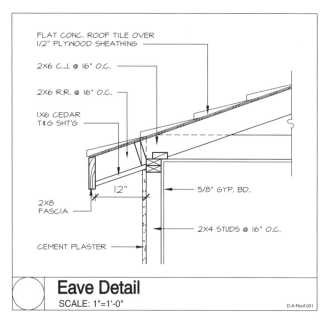

Figure 17.34   Isolating an area and detailing.

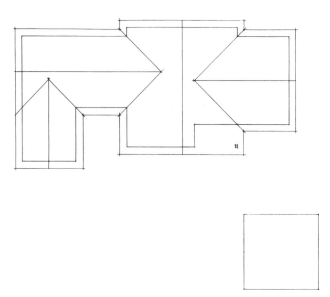

Figure 17.35   Roof plan—Stage I.

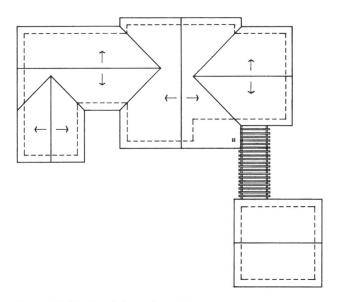

Figure 17.36 Roof plan—Stage II.

■ RYAN RESIDENCE SITE PLAN

As the site plan for the Ryan Residence was in its final phase, it became apparent that the trellis, which ties the house to the garage, could not be formatted the way originally proposed. A new study was executed, as shown in Figure 17.38. This drawing was sent to the client for approval and included in the project book for incorporation into the site plan, floor plan, and all other drawings it affected.

STAGE I (Figures 17.39). First, look at Figure 17.40, which is a set of notes that belong on Sheet A-1. Because there is a cartoon of this sheet (Figure 17.17), check the positioning of the notes, the vicinity map, the roof plan, the sheet index, and the site plan relative to each other. After positioning the outline of the site on the sheet, the setbacks should be drawn. In this instance they are 20'-0" in the front, 5'-0" on the side, and the rear has a minimum of 15'-0" but was not

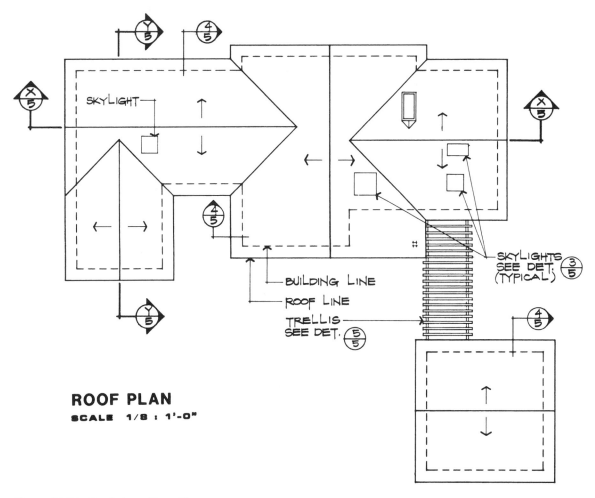

ROOF PLAN
SCALE 1/8 : 1'-0"

Figure 17.37 Roof plan—Stage III.

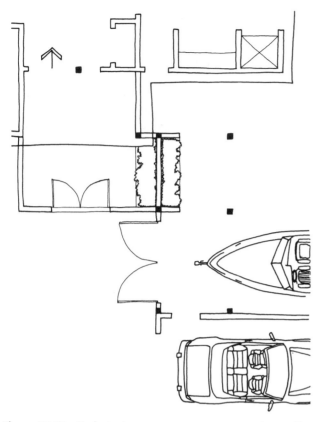

Figure 17.38   Redesigning entry court to accommodate trellis.

drawn in because the drafter knew in advance that this structure would not be very close to the rear property line. These setback lines should be drawn with non-printing lead. Such leads are usually blue or blue/purple. They are identified as nonphoto, nonprinting or fade-away lead. Although these setback lines appear black on this drawing, they do not appear in Stage II, as they have been drawn in face-away blue. These leads are also ideal for layout work and positioning drawings. Vellum can be purchased with fade-away lines already printed on it. These are helpful as guidelines for lettering, establishing the site and structure margins, or drawing anything of a tabular nature. This is drafted at an ⅛″ scale for the Ryan Residence.

Next, take this ⅛″ drawing of the floor plan and place it under the drawing for positioning. The garage was positioned as close as possible to the required setback on the bottom right corner, and the house as close as possible to the left limits. This positioning established the space between the two structures. The security and entry area was the next item to be drafted and positioned to align with the garage, leaving enough space for a gate to be added later for boat storage.

STAGE II   (Figure 17.41). The first step was to dimension the house and garage onto the site. Dimension lines were positioned to locate the structure from all sides of the property line. The sidewalk, parkway, and power pole were then drawn in, the driveway was positioned, and the textured concrete walk between the driveway

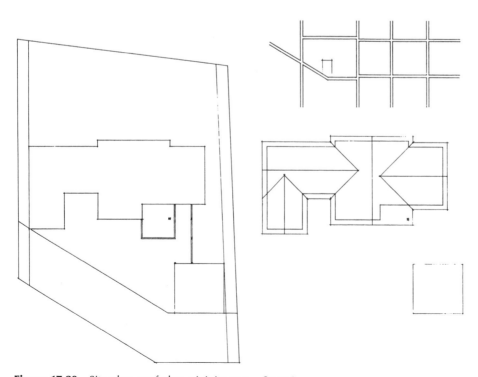

Figure 17.39   Site plan, roof plan, vicinity map—Stage I.

ENERGY NOTES

CERTIFICATE OF COMPLIANCE: Residential (Example)

Project Title --------------------
Project Address ------------

Documentation Author ------
Compliance Method ----------
Climate Zone -----------------

General Information
Conditioned Floor Area ------ 1500 S.F.
Building Type ----------------- Single Family
Number of Story -------------- One
Floor Construction Type ---- Raised Wood
Infiltration Control ----------- Standard

Building Shell Insulation

Component	Insulation	Location
Type	R-Value	Comments
Roof ---------------------	R-19	Vaulted Ceiling
Walls ---------------------	R-11	
Floor ---------------------	R-11	Floor over Crawl Space
Door ----------------------	R-0	

Glazing

Glazing Orientation	Area (S.F.)	Glass Type	Interior Shading	Exterior Shading	Roof Projection
Window 1 (SW)	24 S.F.	Double Pane	Shade	50% Screen	Yes
Window 2 (SW)	-	"	"	"	Yes
Window 3 (SW)	-	"	"	"	Yes
Window 4 (NW)	-	"	"	"	Yes
Door A (SE)	-	"	None	None	Yes
Door B (SE)	-	"	None	None	Yes

HVAC Systems

Heating			Cooling		
Make	Model	Capacity	Make	Model	Capacity
AJAX	C12345	65,800 B.T.u.	N/A	N/A	N/A

Heating Installed ------------------- 65,800 B.T.U.
Heating Allowed ------------------- 71,000 B.T.U.

Water Heating System

System Type	Tank Capacity	Make & Model	Energy Credit
Storage, Gas	40 Gal.	AJAX Rm 678	None

Special Features and Remarks
Compliance is based on performance method.

Compliance Statement
Provide performance specifications as is needed to comply with the governing State and/or Federal Regulatory Agency.

Designer	Owner
Name -------------	Name -------
Company --------	Company --
Address ----------	Address ----
Phone ----------	Phone -------
Signed ----------	Signed ------

Documentation Author	Enforcement agency
Name -------------	Name -------
Company --------	Company --
Address ----------	Address ----
Signed -----------	Signed ------

Figure 17.40   Notes for Sheet A-1.

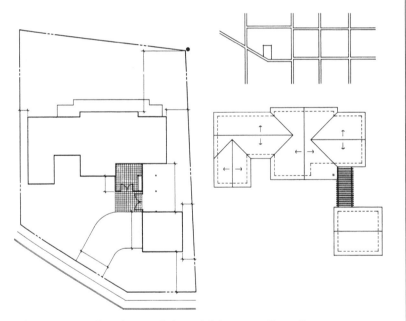

Figure 17.41   Site plan, roof plan, vicinity map—Stage II.

and house was completed. The walkway will be concrete, stamped with a pattern while still wet. This material is called stampcrete. Next in the sequence were gates to the entry and to the boat storage area, and these (drive, entry, and walk) were dimensioned. The living room, family room, and master bedroom are connected by a concrete walk as a final step. All lines were hard lined and the stampcrete texture was added, along with the posts that will hold up the trellis and a small planter positioned to the right of the entry court.

MANDATORY FEATURES & DEVICES

All openings marked * are security openings and the following notes shall apply:

A.   Wood flush-type doors shall be 1 3/8" thick minimum with solid core construction.

B.   Hollow core doors or doors less than 1 3/8" in thickness covered on the inside face with 16 gauge sheet metal attached with screws at 6" on centers around the perimeter or equivalent or

C.   Wood panel type doors with panels fabricated of lumber not less than 9/16 inch thickness, provided shaped portions of the panels are not less than 1/4 inch thick. Individual panels shall not exceed 300 sq. ft. in area. Stiles and rails shall be of solid lumber in thickness with overall dimensions of not less than 1 3/8 inches and 3 inches in width. Mullions shall be considered a part of adjacent panels unless sized as required herein for stiles and rails except mullions not over 18 inches long may have an overall width of not less than 2 inches. Carved areas shall have a thickness of not less than 3/8 inches.

D.   Glazed openings within 40 inches of the door lock when the door is in the closed position, shall be fully tempered glass or approved burglary resistant material, or shall be protected by metal bars, screens or grills having a maximum opening of 2 inches. The provisions of this section shall not apply to view ports or windows which do not exceed 2 inches in their greatest dimensions.

E.   Door stops of in-swinging doors shall be of one piece construction with the jamb or joined by rabbet to the jamb.

F.   All pin-type hinges which are accessible from outside the secured area when the door is closed shall have non-removable hinge pins. In addition, they shall have minimum 1/4 inch diameter steel jamb stud with 1/4 inch minimum protection unless the hinges are shaped to prevent removal of the door if the hinge pins are removed.

G.   The strike plate for latches and the holding device for projecting deadbolts in wood construction shall be secured to the jamb and the wall framing with screws not less than 2 1/2 inches in length.

H.   Specify deadbolts with hardened inserts; deadlocking latch key-operated locks on exterior; locks openable without key, special knowledge or special effort on interior; and type throw, and embedment of deadbolts for single swinging door, active leaf or pairs of doors.

I.   Straight deadbolts shall have a minimum throw of 1 inch and an embedment of not less than 5/8 inch.

J.   A hook-shaped or an expanding-lug deadbolt shall have a minimum throw of 3/4 inch.

K.   Cylinder guards shall be installed on all cylinder locks whenever the cylinder projects beyond the face of the door or is otherwise accessible to gripping tools.

L.   Sliding glass doors and sliding glass windows shall be capable of withstanding resistant tests and shall bear Force-Entry-Resistant labels.

M.   Door hinge pins accessible from the outside shall be non-removable.

A.   All equipment and materials to be certified by the manufacturer as complying with the governing Quality Standards established by the regulatory agency. Including HVAC equipment, water heaters, shower heads, faucets, thermostats and lamp ballasts.

B.   Ceiling insulation - The weighted average U-value shall not exceed that which would result from using R-19 batt insulation.

C.   Wall insulation - The weighted average U-value shall not exceed that which would result from using R-11 batt insulation.

D.   Slab edge insulation - Slab edge insulation shall have water absorbtion and water vapor-transmission rates of no greater than 0.3% and 2 perm/inch respectively.

E.   Masonry and factory built fireplaces shall be installed with tight fitting, closeable metal or glass doors, outside air intake with damper and flue damper. Continuous burning gas pilots are prohibited.

F.   Backdraft dampers for all exhaust and fan systems shall be provided.

G.   Heating system shall have an automatic thermostat with a clock mechanism which can program automatically to set back the thermostat set points for at least 2 periods within 24 hours.

H.   Storage type water heater and backup tanks for solar heating systems shall be externally wrapped with insulation having a thermal resistance of R-12 or greater.

I.   All return piping and recirculating hot water piping in unheated areas shall be insulated with a thermal resistance of R-3 or greater.

J.   Seal and caulk all plumbing, electrical and other openings that penetrate the building envelope.

K.   Ducts shall be constructed, installed and insulated as per Chapter 10 of the State Mechanical Code.

L.   Provide R-11 insulation in raised wood floor area.

M.   Post insulation compliance card in a conspicuous location in dwelling prior to final inspection.

SHEET INDEX

The planter area will be changed after the trellis is designed and aligned with the roof overhang.

STAGE III   (Figure 17.42). Prior to advancing to Stage III of the drawing sequence, the project manager will review the drawing and make some corrections and changes. This is done on a copy, which is often referred to as the "check print." In this case, three-dimensional errors were noted. These were the three-dimensional lines that locate the house and the garage on the right side of the site. The side yard dimension on the left side of the site is proper, because the property line and the building line are parallel to each other. The property line on the garage side is not parallel to the garage or the house. These will be the first to be corrected with extension lines.

Existing trees are positioned, and dimensioning continues with the location dimensions of the drive at the bend in the property line. Numerical values are now lettered. The positioning of the house and the garage onto the lot must be checked with the final overall dimensions of the Floor Plan. This is to ensure that the house *can* in fact fit onto the lot as shown. Remember, the house is dimensioned to the stud line outside of the house (the stucco). The overall dimension of the house (from the floor plan) must be added to side yard dimensions, *and* two inches must be added for the thickness of the stucco.

Public utility lines were next in the drawing order and included sizing and noting. Finally, the legal description and a description of the concrete block wall, curb break, and all other notes, including the North arrow, were given. The title and scale were produced by a lettering machine, a device that makes strips of letters on a sticky-back material. These strips are then placed on the drawing sheet. See Figure 17.43 for the entire assembly of Sheet A-1.

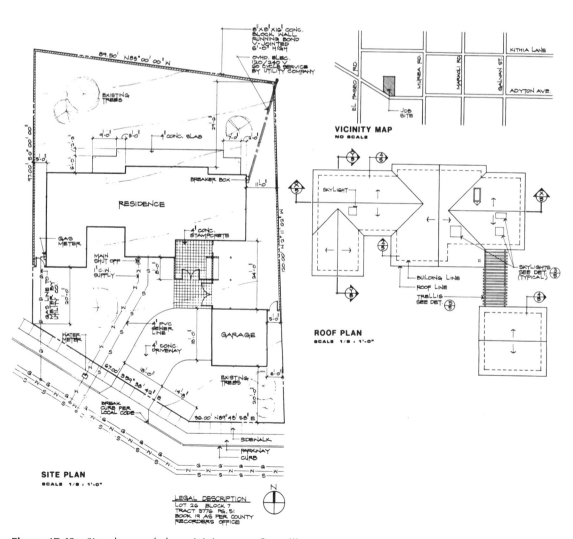

Figure 17.42   Site plan, roof plan, vicinity map—Stage III.

All openings marked * are security openings and the following notes shall apply:

A. Wood flush-type doors shall be 1 3/8" thick minimum with solid core construction.

B. Hollow core doors or doors less than 1 3/8" in thickness covered on the inside face with 16 gauge sheet metal attached with screws at 6" on centers around the perimeter or equivalent.

C. Wood panel type-doors with panels fabricated of lumber not less than 9/16 inch thickness, provided shaped portions of the panels are not less than 1/4 inch thick. Individual panels shall not exceed 300 sq. ft. in area. Stiles and rails shall be of solid lumber in thickness with overall dimensions of not less than 1 3/8 inches and 3 inches in width. Mullions shall be considered a part of adjacent panels unless sized as required herein for stiles and rails except mullions not over 18 inches long may have an overall width of not less than 2 inches. Carved areas shall have a thickness of not less than 3/8 inches.

D. Glazed openings within 40 inches of the door lock when the door is in the closed position, shall be fully tempered glass or approved burglary resistant material, or shall be protected by metal bars, screens or grills having a maximum opening of 2 inches. The provisions of this section shall not apply to view ports or windows which do not exceed 2 inches in their greatest dimensions.

E. Door stops of in-swinging doors shall be of one piece construction with the jamb or joined by rabbet to the jamb.

F. All pin-type hinges which are accessible from outside the secured area when the door is closed shall have non-removable hinge pins. In addition, they shall have minimum 1/4 inch diameter steel jamb stud with 1/4 inch minimum protection unless the hinges are shaped to prevent removal of the door or the hinge pins are removed.

G. The strike plate for latches and the holding device for projecting deadbolts in wood construction shall be secured to the jamb and the wall framing with screws not less than 2 1/2 inches in length.

H. Specify deadbolts with hardened inserts; deadlocking latch key-operated locks on interior, locks openable without key, special knowledge or special effort on interior and type throw, and embedment of deadbolts for single swinging door, active leaf or pairs of doors.

I. Straight deadbolts shall have a minimum throw of 1 inch and an embedment of not less than 5/8 inch.

J. A hook-shaped or an expanding-lug deadbolt shall have a minimum throw of 3/4 inch.

K. Cylinder guards shall be installed on all cylinder locks whenever the cylinder projects beyond the face of the door or is otherwise accessible to gripping tools.

L. Sliding glass doors and sliding glass windows shall be capable of withstanding resistant tests and shall bear Force-Entry-Resistant labels.

M. Door hinge pins accessible from the outside shall be non-removable.

A. All equipment and materials shall be certified by the manufacturer as complying with the governing Quality Standards established by the regulatory agency. Including HVAC equipment, water heaters, shower heads, faucets, thermostats and lamp ballasts.

B. Ceiling insulation - The weighted average U-value shall not exceed that which would result from using R-19 batt insulation.

C. Wall insulation - The weighted average U-value shall not exceed that which would result from using R-11 batt insulation.

D. Slab edge insulation - Slab edge insulation shall have water absorption and water vapor-transmission rates of no greater than 0.3% and 2 perm/inch respectively.

E. Masonry and factory built fireplaces shall be installed with tight fitting, closeable metal or glass doors, outside air intake with damper and flue damper. Continuous burning gas pilots are prohibited.

F. Backdraft dampers for all exhaust and fan systems shall be provided.

G. Heating system shall have a automatic thermostat with a clock mechanism which can program automatically to set back the thermostat set points for at least 2 periods within 24 hours.

H. Storage type water heater and backup tanks for solar heating systems shall be externally wrapped with insulation having a thermal resistance of R-12 or greater.

I. All return piping and recirculating hot water piping in unheated areas shall be insulated with a thermal resistance of R-3 or greater.

J. Seal and caulk all plumbing, electrical and other openings that penetrate the building envelope.

K. Ducts shall be constructed, installed and insulated as per Chapter 10 of the State Mechanical Code.

L. Provide R-11 insulation in raised wood floor area.

M. Post insulation compliance card in a conspicuous location in dwelling prior to final inspection.

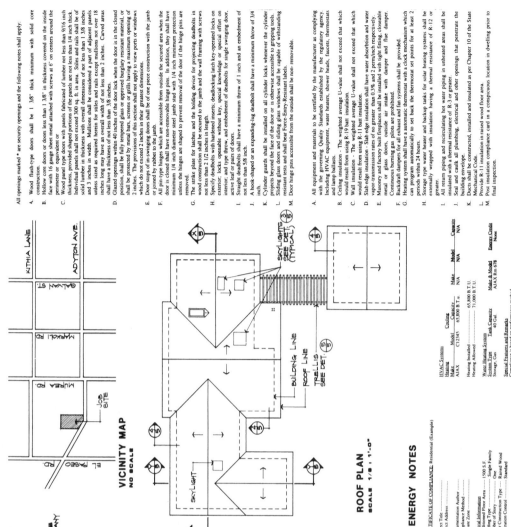

VICINITY MAP
NO SCALE

KITHIA LANE
ADYTON AVE.
GALWAY ST.
MARCELI RD.
MURELA RD.
EL PASEO RD.
JOB SITE

ROOF PLAN
SCALE 1/8 : 1'-0"

SKYLIGHTS SEE DET. (TYPICAL)
BUILDING LINE
ROOF LINE
TRELLIS SEE DET.
SKYLIGHT

ENERGY NOTES

CERTIFICATE OF COMPLIANCE: Residential (Example)

Project Title ....
Project Address ....

Documentation Author ....
Compliance Method ....
Climate Zone ....

General Information
Conditioned Floor Area .... 1500 S.F.
Building Type .... Single Family
Number of Story .... One
Floor Construction Type .... Raised Wood
Infiltration Control .... Standard

Building Shell Insulation
Component	Insulation Type	R-Value
Roof	R-19	
Walls	R-11	
Floor	R-19	
Door	R-0	

Glazing
	Area (S.F.)	Glass Type		
Glazing	24 S.F.	Double Pane		

Orientation		Interior Shade	Exterior Shading	Shading	
Window 2 (SW)				50% Screen	
Window 3 (SW)					
Window 4 (NW)					
Window 1 (SW)		None		None	
Door A (SE)		None		None	
Door B (SE)		None		None	

Location
Comments
Vaulted Ceiling
Floor over Crawl Space

Roof Projection
Yes
Yes
Yes
Yes
Yes

HVAC Systems
Heating
	Make	Model	Capacity
	AJAX	C12345	65,800 B.T.U.

Heating Installed .... 65,800 B.T.U.
Heating Allowed .... 71,000 B.T.U.

Cooling
Make	Model	Capacity
N/A	N/A	

Water Heating System
System Type	Tank Capacity	Make & Model	Energy Credit
Storage, Gas	40 Gal.	AJAX Rm 678	None

Special Features and Remarks

Compliance Statement
Provide performance specifications as as is needed to comply with the governing State and/or Federal Regulatory Agency.

Designer
Name ....
Company ....
Address ....
Phone ....
Signed ....

Documentation Author
Name ....
Company ....
Address ....
Signed ....

Owner
Name ....
Company ....
Address ....
Phone ....
Signed ....

Enforcement agency
Name ....
Company ....
Address ....
Signed ....

SITE PLAN
SCALE 1/8 : 1'-0"

8" x 6" x 16" CONC. BLOCK WALL RUNNING BOND V-JOINTED 6'-0" HIGH

COMB. ELEC. 120/240 V SERVICE BY UTILE SERVICE COMPANY

BREAKER BOX
4" CONC. SLAB
4" CONC. SLAB
RESIDENCE
GARAGE
4" CONC. STAMPCRETE
4" PVC SEWER LINE
4" CONC. DRIVEWAY
MAIN SHUT OFF IG'N SUPPLY
EXISTING TREES
GAS METER
WATER METER
SEWER TIE IN LINE
BREAK CURB PER LOCAL CODE
SIDEWALK
PARKWAY CURB
EXISTING TREES

LEGAL DESCRIPTION
LOT 26 BLOCK 7
TRACT 3776 PG. 51
BOOK 19 AS PER COUNTY
RECORDERS OFFICE

N

Figure 17.43 Two drawings merged to form Sheet A-1.

Because the required setback was drawn on a separate layer, or drawn manually with fade-away blue, the setbacks do not appear at this stage on the site plan.

RYAN RESIDENCE FOUNDATION PLAN

Having considered the ingredients of a foundation plan and the graphic (drafted) translation of these forms, we next sequentially draft a foundation plan for the Ryan Residence. It will be developed as a slab-on-the-ground system. Be sure to read Chapters 3, 5, and 6 to understand the structural system by which the building is assembled so that you can better appreciate the location and position of bearing and nonbearing footings, posts and their pads, and the need for and location of shear walls.

The process begins with the positioning of the foundation plan onto the vellum, as per the cartoon shown in Figure 17.18, and using the floor plan as an underlay. This is done to speed the drawing process, but more important, to ensure that the foundation does, in fact, sit under the floor plan and aligns with it.

If the foundation plan is drawn on a computer, the floor plan becomes the base or datum stage. The nonbearing walls are removed, and the dotted lines represent the width of the footing offset. The exterior walls that extend into the building and become the interior walls must be checked for plate alignment. Refer to Chapter 9 for an explanation of this problem and its resolution.

EVOLUTION OF THE RYAN RESIDENCE FOUNDATION PLAN

Because it was decided to have a separate (stock) garage sheet, the garage will appear in only three stages. The details for the entire residence, including the foundation

plan, are included in Chapter 16 on detailing and will not appear in drawing stages except for the last stage.

STAGE I   (Figure 17.44). After the wall line was traced in the correct position, a line was added on either side of these lines that represent the width of the footing. Next, the steps were positioned from the floor plan. An erasing shield with sequential holes was used in conjunction with an electric eraser to change these solid lines to dotted or hidden lines. In CAD, change the line type on the specific layer.

STAGE II   (Figure 17.45). Dimension lines were introduced at this stage. The project manager asked for a check print at the end of Stage II and noticed the absence of three interior bearing footings on the next stage. This process is called red marking in the industry. The red marking stage also incorporated the planter change at the entry. Note that two of the interior bearing footings are a result of the struts (see Chapter 14 on framing). A third is the result of the California frame in the front bedroom, also described in Chapter 14.

STAGE III   (Figure 17.44). A check print is used to perform Stage III of the foundation plan. The check print has blue or black lines, and the added information is usually of a different color (such as red) so that the information will stand out from the blue background and lines. As each task or series of tasks is performed, the drafter should cross out the information on the check print. A highlighter may be used; be sure that it is of a contrasting color. A highlighter is preferred because it does not cover the information and can again be checked if and when an error is made. Highlighting should always be done after the task has been done. All too often well-meaning drafters highlight information first, thinking they will get right to the original, only to be called away from the desk to work on some other task—and the job in question is filed away by another person, thinking it was completed.

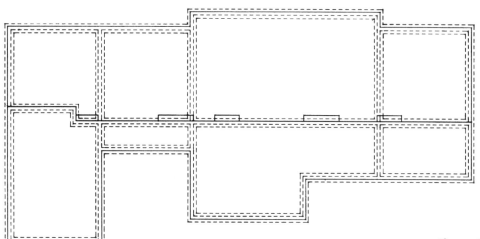

Figure 17.44 Foundation plan—Stage I.

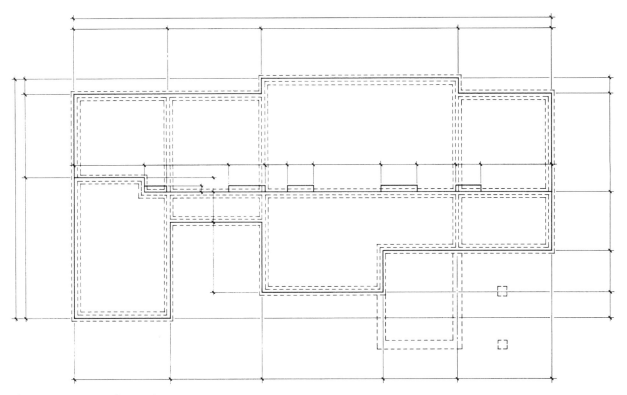

Figure 17.45 Foundation plan—Stage II.

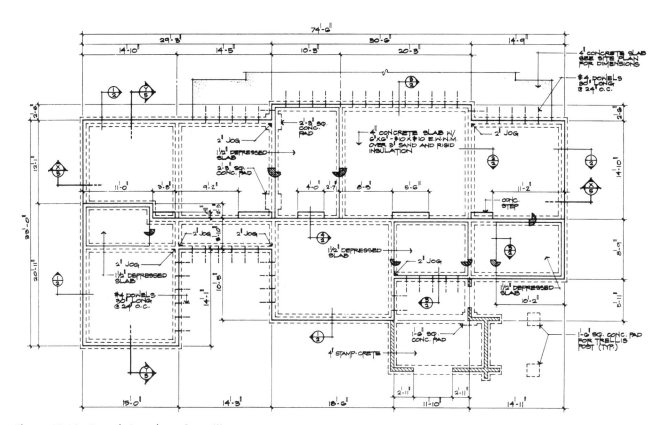

Figure 17.46 Foundation plan—Stage III.

Numerical values, noting, and referencing are done in that order. The small, pointed bubbles refer the viewer to the details that will be on this sheet but are drawn on a separate original and combined photographically. Each large bubble with a triangle drawn around half of it refers the viewer to the building section.

If there is only one area to be depressed, a simple notation, "1½ depressed slab," is sufficient. In this residence, we have four areas with depressed slabs and one major change of level. To ensure that the viewer reads the plans correctly, a half bubble with the horizontal portion showing the high and low sides, is employed. It is crosshatched so as to be noticeable.

In some offices all of the symbols—depressed slab, detail reference, North arrow, and so on—are predrawn and placed onto an adhesive back and scissored onto the drawing. On a computer, a library of symbols can be produced in the office, recalled, and positioned.

STAGE IV (Figure 17.47). A final check will be made of the set before it is considered finished. To avoid massive changes at the end, great care must be taken at each stage.

Finally, the titles and scale are positioned, thus concluding the foundation plan. Details are imported as per sheet format (cartoon).

■ RYAN RESIDENCE FLOOR PLAN

The Ryan Residence floor plan is evolved over several stages. The floor plan is by far the most important drawing in a set of working drawings, because it sets the stage for all dimensions in terms of width and length.

The Floor Plan (Sheet A-3)

Like Sheets A-1 and A-2, Sheet A-3 will be done by two individuals. While one evolves the floor plan, the other will position the construction notes, electrical and utility symbols, and abbreviations. Electrical and utility symbols and abbreviations, standard items in most offices, can be transferred to an adhesive sheet and then mounted directly on the floor plan sheet. With the computer, the task is much simpler. Just import the desired information, be it a set of construction notes, symbols, or the office standard that has been previously prepared.

The position of the floor plan, electrical and utility symbols, and the construction notes can be found in the cartoon of Sheet A-3.

To allow the drafter of the floor plan to work at his or her own speed without interruptions, two separate drawings will be made and merged photographically or electronically.

The positioning of the abbreviations, notes, and symbols can be done in one stage, as in Figure 17.48.

An intermediate stage is often reproduced several times using either a xerographic process onto vellum, a sepia using a diazo process, or an electronic file and given to associates to generate additional masters for framing plans, structural drawings, and/or separate electrical plans, to mention just a few.

It would be most convenient to have a ¼" scale drawing as well as a ⅛" drawing of the floor plan. An ⅛" drawing is easily obtained by reducing the ¼" drawing by mechanical means. Many copiers have enlarging and reducing capabilities. Thus, an ⅛" scale drawing can be produced in a matter of minutes. Many so-called blueprint shops can also provide you with enlargements or reductions, as well as erasable vellum "second originals." With CAD, you simply enter the scale factor (see Chapter 3), and the scale is changed immediately.

In addition to the normal information carried on the floor plan, as described in this chapter, we will superimpose an electrical plan and a ceiling framing plan onto this drawing. To understand the ceiling joist framing information, refer to the end of Chapter 14.

Notice that the garage floor plan is not included in this evolution because of the constraints and limits of the vellum. The garage plans, sections, elevations, and so on will be placed on a separate sheet.

STAGE I (Figure 17.49). The general shape of the structure is blocked out, possibly using fade-away (blue) pencil. The block-out is accomplished with a single line. The line that defines the perimeter is drawn with a solid line. This is the outside wall line, which allows the drafter to check outside overall dimensions to ensure proper positioning on the site. The interior walls are positioned with center lines. These will eventually become the extension lines during the dimensioning process. With CAD, this would establish the datum or base. In the case of a wood structure, grids are set at 1'-0" and snaps are set at 1" for stud line or face-of-stud dimensioning.

STAGE II (Figure 17.50). Into this single-lined floor plan, wall thickness is incorporated. Start with the outside perimeter. The only wall that does not use the single line as the outer surface is the wall opposite the family room and in between the utility room and the front bedroom. This wall starts at the left as an interior wall, becomes an exterior wall, and then becomes an interior wall again.

Next, a line is drawn on both sides of the center line defining the thickness of the interior walls. Openings in the wall (windows and doors) are located and positioned. As a drafter, be sure to verify the minimum openings for the door and be sure to comply with ADA and the sizes of the windows. Notice that jambs were left on both sides of the windows and doors to house

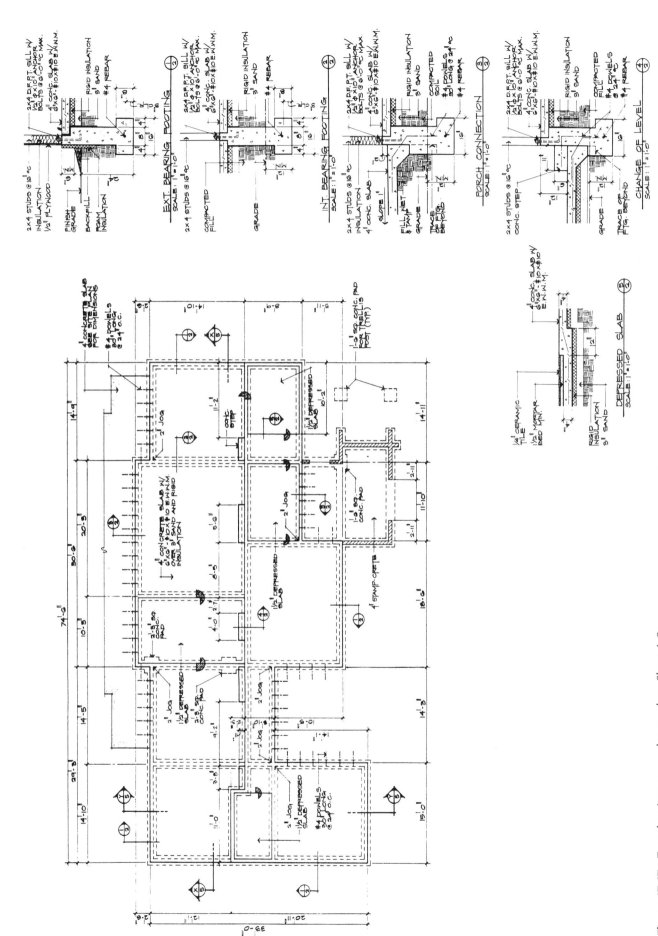

Figure 17.47 Two drawings merged to produce Sheet A-2.

CONSTRUCTION NOTES

1. The contractor and all sub-contractors shall verify all dimensions and conditions at the site, and shall notify the Engineer of any discrepancy. Cross-check details and dimensions shown on the structural drawings with related requirements on the architectural, mechanical, civil and electrical drawings.

2. Floor and wall openings, sleeves, variation in the structural slab elevations, depressed areas and all other architectural, mechanical, electrical and civil requirements must be coordinated before the contractor proceeds with construction.

3. In all cases where a conflict may occur such as between items covered by specifications and notes on the drawings, or between general notes and specific details, the Architect and/or the Engineer shall be notified and he will interpret the intent of the contract documents.

4. Details noted as typical shall apply in all cases unless specifically shown or noted otherwise.

5. Where no specific detail is shown, the framing or construction shall be identical or similar to that indicated for like cases of construction on this project.

6. Workmanship and materials shall conform to the requirements of the 1991 edition of the Uniform Building Code.

7. In no case shall working dimensions be scaled from plans, section or details on structural drawings.

8. The precise dimensions and locations of all doors and window openings shall be determined from architectural plans and details. Other wall and floor openings as required by mechanical, electrical or similar requirements shall be verified from shop drawings, equipment data, dimensions, etc., as required.

W O O D

1. Plywood roof sheathing shall be 1/2 inch thick, APA Rated Sheathing, Exposure 1. Plywood floor sheathing shall be 3/4" inch thick. APA Rated "STURD-I-FLOOR," Exposure 1, T & G. All plywood shall conform to U.S. Product Standard PS 1-83.

2. Plywood sheets shall be laid with the long dimension and face grain perpendicular to the rafters and the sheets shall be staggered as shown on the plans. Each sheet shall contain a minimum of 8 sq. ft. and shall extend to three bearing.

3. Plywood diaphragm shall be inspected and approved before the roofing is applied.

4. All horizontal framing members shall be Douglas Fir No. 2 grade or better for 2 x members and Douglas Fir No. 1 grade or better for 4 x members or larger (or as noted).

5. Minimum nailing shall be per Table 25-Q of the Uniform Building Code.

6. All bolt heads and nuts bearing on wood shall have washers.

7. Rafters, purlins or beams shall not be notched or dapped in any manner unless detailed.

8. All hangers and standard framing hardware unless otherwise noted shall be as manufactured by AJAX Company and are identified by numbers as shown in the latest catalog.

C O N C R E T E

1. All concrete shall be of 150 lb. per cu. ft. density and shall attain an ultimate compressive strength at 28 days of 2000 psi.

2. Cement shall be Type I or II Portland cement per ASTM C-150.

3. No pipes or ducts shall be placed in structural concrete unless specifically detailed.

4. Refer to architectural drawings for all molds, grooves, clips, ornaments, grounds, and other inserts to be cast in concrete.

5. All reinforcing, dowels, anchor bolts and other inserts shall be secured in proper position prior to placing concrete.

REINFORCING STEEL

1. All reinforcing bars shall be new billet steel conforming to ASTM A-615-81, Grade 60.

2. All bars shall be free from bends or kinks except as detailed and shall be free from any material which would tend to reduce the bond. Except for slabs on grade, concrete block shall not be used to support or space reinforcement.

3. Reinforcement marked "CONTINUOUS" spliced with a lap of 24 bar diameters (1'-3" minimum) in concrete (unless noted otherwise and 40 bar diameters (2'-0" minimum) in masonry. Stagger adjacent splices 10'-0" minimum.

4. All welding in conjunction with reinforcing steel shall be done with properly selected electrodes. Adequate preheat, interpass temperatures and controlled cooling shall be utilized to provide sound crack-free welds.

5. All reinforcing shall be supported in conformance with the latest edition of "Reinforcing Concrete -- A Manual of Standard Practice."

6. Reinforcing shall have the following minimum cover (or as noted on drawings):
   a. Formed surfaces in contact with earth — 2"
   b. Surfaces deposited against earth — 3"

7. Mesh reinforcement shall conform to ASTM A-185.

ABBREVIATIONS

A.B.	- anchor bolt	N.S.	- near side
M.B.	- machine bolt	F.S.	- far side
BLK	- block	I.S.F.	- inside face
BLKG	- blocking	O.S.F.	- outside face
BOT.	- bottom	OPG	- opening
C.M.U.	- concrete masonry unit	V.	- vertical
CL	- clear	H.	- horizontal
CLG	- ceiling	O.C.	- on center
CONC.	- concrete	NLR	- nailer
CONT.	- continuous	NLG	- nailing
E.S.	- each side	R.	- rafter
E.W.	- each way	STL	- steel
F.A.	- framing anchor	WL.	- wall
E.N.	- edge nail	TYP.	- typical
I.N	- intermediate nailing	MIN	- minimum
B.N.	- boundary nailing	EX.	- existing
T.N.	- toe nailing	E.G.	- exterior grade
P.T.	- pressure treated	F.G.	- finish grade

ELECTRICAL AND UTILITY SYMBOLS

1.	WALL SWITCH SINGLE POLE	13.	SINGLE FLOOR OUTLET W/ COVER PLATE
2.	WEATHERPROOF SWITCH SINGLE POLE	14.	WALL FIXTURE
3.	WALL SWITCH 3-WAY	15.	CEILING OUTLET DUPLEX
4.	CONVENIENCE OUTLET-DUPLEX	16.	CEILING FIXTURE
5.	WEATHERPROOF DUPLEX	17.	LIGHT & FAN/SEPARATE SWITCHING
6.	TRIPLEX	18.	HEAT, LIGHT, FAN/SEPARATE SWITCHING
7.	FOURPLEX	19.	EXHAUST FAN
8.	CONVENIENCE OUTLET 1/2 SWITCH	20.	PULL CHAIN
9.	CONVENIENCE OUTLET (WITH HEIGHT)	21.	RECESSED CEILING FIXTURE
10.	GROUND FAULT INTERRUPTER	22.	FLOOD LIGHT
11.	220V DUPLEX OUTLET	23.	FLUORESCENT LIGHT
12.	SPECIAL PURPOSE	24.	UNDERGROUND STUB-OUT W.P. BOX

25.	"J" BOX
26.	TELEVISION ANTENNA
27.	TELEPHONE JACK
28.	PUSH BUTTON
29.	DOOR BELL
30.	SMOKE DETECTOR
31.	POWER PANEL
32.	CIRCUIT BREAKER
33.	THERMOSTAT
34.	FUEL GAS
35.	KEY
36.	HOSE BIBB

Figure 17.48 Format of symbols, abbreviations, and notes.

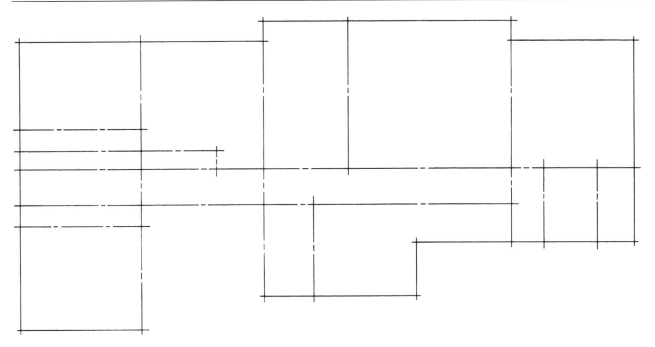

Figure 17.49 Floor plan—Stage I.

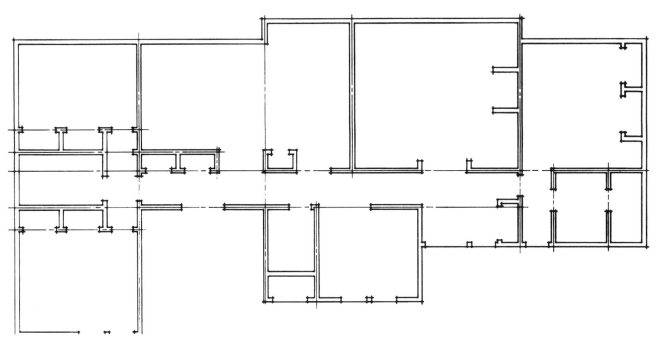

Figure 17.50 Floor plan—Stage II.

the support for the beam and/or headers that will eventually be used. The next step is to darken the complete floor plan. When printed, the center lines (drawn in fade-away lead) will disappear and look like the drawing in Figure 17.51.

STAGE III   (Figure 17.52). Before commencing Stage III, the draft should turn to the project book and glean all the specifics in reference to appliances, plumbing fixtures, and fireplaces. This information is then trans-

lated into drawings, as shown. Windows have also been incorporated into the drawing. Sizes are found in the preliminary schedule based on energy analysis.

STAGE IV   (Figure 17.52). This stage is the most critical, because all of the dimensions are established at this time. A check print was made of Stage III, and the dimensions and their numerical values established. This was all done rapidly in freehand, but with great accuracy.

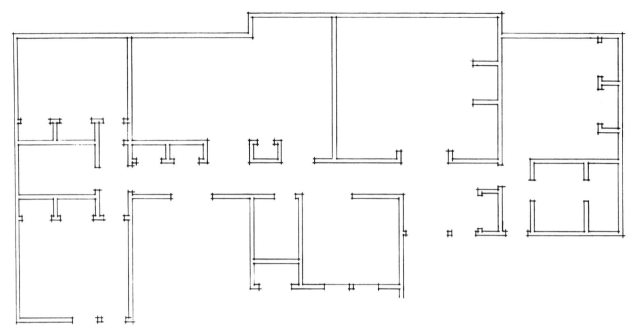

Figure 17.51   Floor plan as it will actually appear.

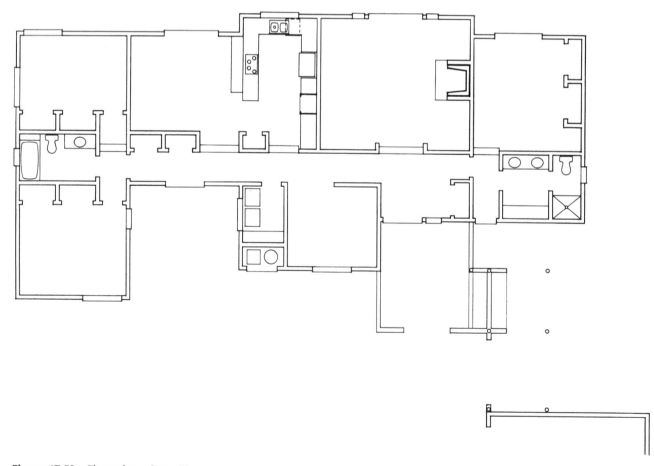

Figure 17.52   Floor plan—Stage III.

There are, in Figure 17.53, a number of exterior walls that become interior walls on this plan. For example, the wall that separates the family room from the bedroom is an interior wall but becomes an exterior wall on the opposite side. The total width is 15'-0" measured face-of-stud to face-of-stud. However, on the opposite side, this same wall becomes an interior wall, and the measurement reads 14'-0", measured face-of-stud to center-of-wall.

The 2 × 4 stud measures 3½", half of which is 1¾". This 1¾" measurement is rounded off to a 2-inch measurement, which accounts for the two-inch difference on either side. Notice how the drafter included what we call a 2" "look-out" dimension along the extension line. This is a drafter warning to the rough carpenter to watch out for the discrepancy.

This happens again at the wall between the living room and the master bedroom, and along the interior wall of the dining room and laundry room, which becomes an exterior wall for a short time, and then an interior wall again, as it separates the closet and the bathroom.

Notice the string of dimensions on the inside of the house, especially the one that goes through the kitchen.

If the wall is dimensioned on the face of the stud on the outside, then the interior dimensions should be dimensioned to this point; and if the wall had been dimensioned on the exterior dimension line to the center, then the interior dimension should use this position as a point of reference. The only exception might be that where 2" look-out dimensions exist, either position could be used—the center or face-of-stud.

Based on this positioning of extension and dimension lines, totals are carefully checked to ensure that the sum of the parts is equal to the totals.

The electrical plan is next superimposed onto the floor plan and the door and window conventions drafted, including the reference symbol adjacent to each door and window that connects the plan with schedules.

Cutting plane lines and their respective bubbles are drawn to refer the reader to the building section drawings.

A check print will be made at this stage, and dimensional corrections will be noted as well as any other change or correction to take place. The project manager may even overlay the original over the foundation plan to discover any other errors or omissions.

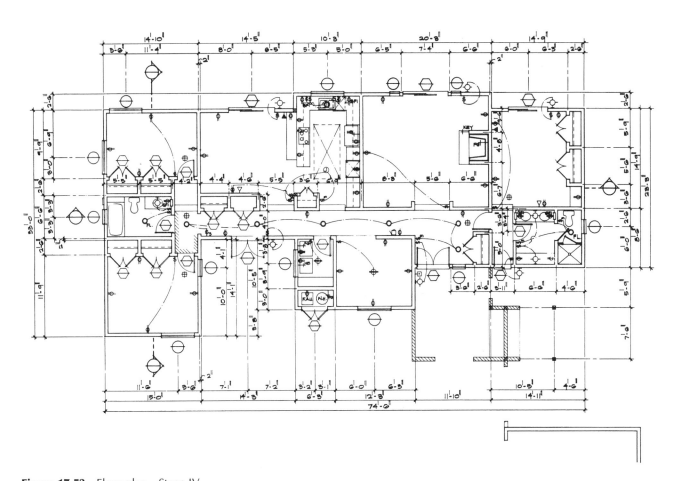

Figure 17.53 Floor plan—Stage IV.

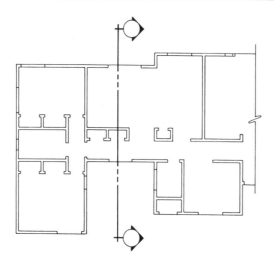

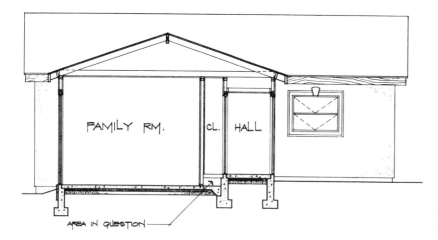

Figure 17.54 Section/elevation revealing unresolved space.

One such oversight is the floor of the pair of closets in the hall adjacent to the family room. If the change of level occurs at the face of the doors, the depth of these two closets will be at the same level as the family room, creating a 12-inch drop in the closet. A section/elevation shown in Figure 17.54 also reveals this problem. The solution was to build a wood floor even with the hall side and to use this space in one of five ways:

A. Leave the space under the wood floor as dead space.
B. Use this space, with a removable floor, to hide a floor safe.
C. Build low drawers openable to the family-room side. The top of the drawer space will be the floor of the closet.
D. Face the closet toward the family-room side and use it as a built-in entertainment center.
E. Move the interior bearing footing between the closet and the family room.

STAGE V (Figure 17.55). After receiving a check print from the project manager, a good procedure would be to follow up on this check print with a procedure sheet of your own. This could be done by using the floor plan checklist and adding to it with notation from the check print. Because this is a standard office form for all floor plans, not all items will apply. You can make this one a job-specific checklist by highlighting what you feel is critical information and/or have your immediate supervisor check the list for you. Armed with this new tool you can proceed, with confidence, to draft the final stage of this most critical sheet.

Most of the notes can be reduced to five categories:

A. Identification of the rooms, appliances, and equipment.
B. Identification of items that are in the contract and those that are to be provided by the owner. The wood planter shelves at the entry compound is a good example of such items.
C. Positioning and locating structural members (some of which are inside a wall). The posts for the trellis and the posts inside the wall between the family

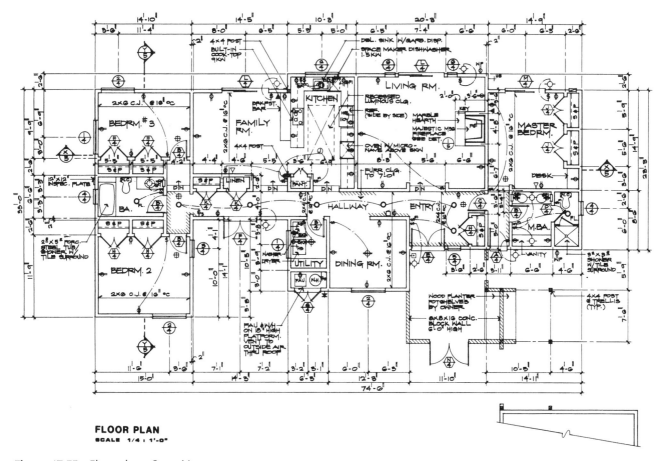

FLOOR PLAN
SCALE 1/4 : 1'-0"

Figure 17.55 Floor plan—Stage V.

room and kitchen are good examples of positioning and locating.

D. Special needs that may be established by codes, such as the inspection plates and notes dealing with the FAU (forced air unit) and W/H (water heater).

E. Finally, the superimposing of the ceiling joist plan over the floor plan. This can be identified by the directional line with half-arrowheads on each side, with a note about sizing and spacing the ceiling joists.

STAGE VI (Figure 17.55). This is the culminating stage for the floor plan, and as can be seen in Figure 17.56, "it all comes together" with the floor plan, construction notes, electrical symbols, abbreviations, and, of course, the border and title blocks (not shown).

■ EVOLUTION OF RYAN ELEVATIONS

The Ryan Residence exterior skin will be stucco. A three-coat system will be used, which includes an initial coat called "scratch," a second coat called "brown," and a thin final coat called a finished "color coat." If raised por-

tions made of wood are to be used, they will be installed prior to the three coats of exterior plaster (stucco). If Styrofoam is used to raise portions of the wall surface, two coats of plaster are placed first; then the foam and the final coat (color coat) is placed over the entire ensemble. See Chapter 16 for the method of installing these raised window and door frames in relation to the building paper and the placement of the stucco. The roof is gabled with vents in the gable end, which is called the rake.

■ SHEET A-4—EXTERIOR ELEVATIONS, SCHEDULES, AND WINDOW AND DOOR DETAILS

As can be seen in the computer-generated cartoon (Figure 17.25), there are three components to this sheet: the exterior elevation, the details, and the schedules. Three drafters will be used to bring this sheet to its conclusion—one for each of the components.

The exterior elevation will occupy 3 of the 4 vertical modules in the sheet, and 3³/₄ of the horizontal modules. This will leave a wider band at the right for the details

CONSTRUCTION NOTES

1. The contractor and all sub-contractors shall verify all dimensions and conditions at the site, and shall notify the Engineer of any discrepancy. Cross-check details and dimensions shown on the structural drawings with related requirements on the architectural, mechanical, civil and electrical drawings.

2. Floor and wall openings, sleeves, variation in the structural slab elevations, depressed areas and all other architectural, mechanical, electrical and civil requirements must be coordinated before the contractor proceeds with construction.

3. In all cases where a conflict may occur such as between items covered by specifications and notes on the drawings, or between general notes and specific details, the Architect and/or the Engineer shall be notified and he will interpret the intent of the contract documents.

4. Details noted as typical shall apply in all cases unless specifically shown or noted otherwise.

5. Where no specific detail is shown, the framing or construction shall be identical similar to that indicated for like cases of construction on this project.

6. Workmanship and materials shall conform to the requirements of the 1991 edition of the Uniform Building Code.

7. In no case shall working dimensions be scaled from plans, section or details on structural drawings.

8. The precise dimensions and locations of all doors and window openings shall be determined from architectural plans and details. Other wall and floor openings as required for mechanical, electrical or similar requirements shall be verified from shop drawings, equipment data, dimensions, etc., as required.

WOOD

1. Plywood roof sheathing shall be 1/2 inch thick, APA Rated Sheathing Exposure 1. Plywood floor sheathing shall be 3/4" inch thick, APA Rated "STURD-I-FLOOR" - Exposure 1, T & G. All plywood shall conform to U.S. Product Standard PS 1-83.

2. Plywood sheets shall be laid with the long dimension and face grain perpendicular to the rafters and the sheets shall be staggered as shown on the plans. Each sheet shall contain a minimum of 8 sq. ft. and shall extend to three members.

3. Plywood diaphragm shall be inspected and approved before the roofing is applied.

4. All horizontal framing members shall be Douglas Fir No 2. grade or better for 2 x members and Douglas Fir No. 1 grade or better for 4 x members or larger (or as noted).

5. Minimum nailing shall be per Table 25-Q of the Uniform Building Code.

6. All bolt heads and nuts bearing on wood shall have washers.

7. Rafters, purlins or beams shall not be notched or dapped in any manner unless detailed.

8. All hangers and standard framing hardware unless otherwise noted shall be as manufactured by AJAX Company and are identified by numbers as shown in the latest catalog.

CONCRETE

1. All concrete shall be of 150 lb. per cu. ft. density and shall attain an ultimate compressive strength at 28 days of 2000 psi.

2. Cement shall be Type 1 or II Portland cement per ASTM C-150.

3. No pipes or ducts shall be placed in structural concrete nless specifically detailed.

4. Refer to architectural drawings for all molds, grooves, ornaments, grounds, and other inserts to be cast in concrete.

5. All reinforcing, dowels, anchor bolts and other inserts shall be secured in proper position prior to placing concrete.

REINFORCING STEEL

1. All reinforcing bars shall be new billet steel conforming to ASTM A-615-81, Grade 60.

2. All bars shall be free from bends or kinks except as detailed and shall be free from any material which would tend to reduce the bond. Except for slabs on grade, concrete block shall not be used to support or space reinforcement.

3. Reinforcement marked "CONTINUOUS" spliced with a lap of 24 bar diameters (1'-3" minimum) in concrete (unless noted otherwise and 40 bar diameters (2'-0" minimum) in masonry. Stagger adjacent splices 10'-0" minimum.

4. All welding in conjunction with reinforcing steel shall be done with properly selected electrodes. Adequate preheat, interpass temperatures and controlled cooling shall be utilized to provide sound crack-free welds.

5. All reinforcing shall be supported in conformance with the latest edition of "Reinforcing Concrete -- A Manual of Standard Practice."

6. Reinforcing shall have the following minimum cover (or as noted on drawings):
   a. Formed surfaces in contact with earth .... 2"
   b. Surfaces deposited directed against earth .... 3"

7. Mesh reinforcement shall conform to ASTM A-185.

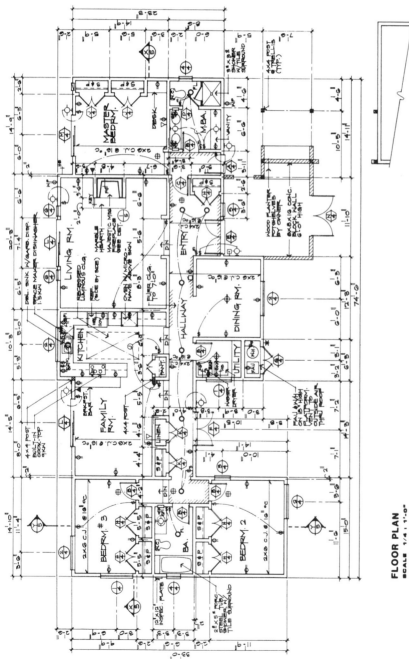

FLOOR PLAN
SCALE 1/4" = 1'-0"

ELECTRICAL AND UTILITY SYMBOLS

1.	WALL SWITCH SINGLE POLE	13.	SINGLE FLOOR OUTLET W/ COVER PLATE
2.	WEATHERPROOF SWITCH SINGLE POLE	14.	WALL FIXTURE
3.	WALL SWITCH 3-WAY	15.	CEILING OUTLET DUPLEX
4.	CONVENIENCE OUTLET-DUPLEX	16.	CEILING FIXTURE
5.	WEATHERPROOF DUPLEX	17.	LIGHT & FAN/SEPARATE SWITCHING
6.	TRIPLEX	18.	HEAT, LIGHT, FAN/SEPARATE SWITCHING
7.	FOURPLEX	19.	EXHAUST FAN
8.	CONVENIENCE OUTLET 1/2 SWITCH	20.	PULL CHAIN
9.	CONVENIENCE OUTLET (WITH HEIGHT)	21.	RECESSED CEILING FIXTURE
10.	GROUND FAULT INTERRUPTER	22.	FLOOD LIGHT
11.	220V OUTLET	23.	FLUORESCENT LIGHT
12.	SPECIAL PURPOSE	24.	UNDERGROUND STUB-OUT W.P. BOX

25.	"J" BOX
26.	TELEVISION ANTENNA
27.	TELEPHONE JACK
28.	PUSH BUTTON
29.	DOOR BELL
30.	SMOKE DETECTOR
31.	POWER PANEL
32.	CIRCUIT BREAKER
33.	THERMOSTAT
34.	FUEL GAS
35.	KEY
36.	HOSE BIBB

ABBREVIATIONS

A.B.	- anchor bolt	
M.B.	- machine bolt	
BLK	- block	
BLKG	- blocking	
BOT.	- bottom	
C.M.U.	- concrete masonry unit	
CL	- clear	
CLG	- ceiling	
CONC.	- concrete	
CONT.	- continuous	
E.S.	- each side	
E.W.	- each way	
F.A.	- framing anchor	
E.N.	- edge nail	
I.N.	- intermediate nailing	
B.N.	- boundary nailing	
T.N.	- toe nailing	
P.T.	- pressure treated	

N.S.	- near side	
F.S.	- far side	
I.S.F.	- inside face	
O.S.F.	- outside face	
OPG	- opening	
V.	- vertical	
H.	- horizontal	
O.C.	- on center	
NLR	- nailer	
NLG	- nailing	
R.	- rafter	
STL	- steel	
WL	- wall	
TYP.	- typical	
MIN.	- minimum	
EX.	- existing	
E.G.	- exterior grade	
F.G.	- finish grade	

Figure 17.56 Two drawings merged to form Sheet A-3.

and a full vertical module at the bottom for the schedules.

Descriptions of these stages are presented at the end of Chapter 13 and are repeated here.

The drafter selected to draft the exterior elevation should be the same person who drafted the building section, because both drawings reveal vertical dimensions and both use the same pitch development and ceiling heights.

STAGE I (Figure 17.57). This is the datum stage. The datum is based on the building section for vertical distances between the floor line and the plate line.

STAGE II (Figure 17.58). The basic shape is now drawn over the plate and floor line. The beginning and end points of the wall are constructed, and the pitch is measured from the intersection of these wall lines and the plate line. Once the pitch has been established, the drafter gives the roof thickness. The drafter obtains the

roof thickness via the rafter size and the outline of the roof's shape from the roof plan.

STAGE III (Figure 17.59). The drawing that was initially laid out lightly or drawn with a fade-away blue pencil is now hard-lined. It will go through one more stage of hard-lining during the profiling stage. Window and door locations are obtained from the floor plan, and the openings are defined.

Check Print—Figure 17.61

The check print reveals a couple of small omissions and a rather large error, which will be corrected in the final stage.

The small omissions are the skylights. Looking at the South elevation, you will notice that two of the skylights extend above the top of the ridge. Both of these skylights should be seen on the North elevation.

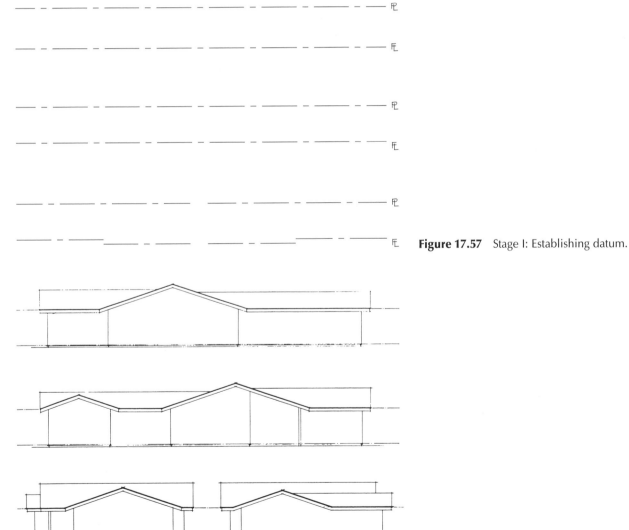

Figure 17.57 Stage I: Establishing datum.

Figure 17.58 Exterior elevations—Stage II.

Figure 17.59   Exterior elevations—Stage III.

Figure 17.60   Exterior elevations—Stage IV.

The large error is the overhang on the roof. It is drawn as a 2'-0" overhang, but it should be 12 inches. This makes a difference in the visual appearance of the elevations and in the height of the fascia. It will also place the trellis over the master bedroom door in a different location, but position the planter below it correctly.

Compare this check print with Figure 17.62, the final stage.

When done on a computer, the correction can be easily incorporated because you only need to locate the layer(s) on which the corrections are to be made, erase the area, and redraw. In years past a project manager would have suggested that a xerographic copy be made, the affected area cut out and printed onto an erasable vellum copy, and then repaired.

STAGE IV   (Figure 17.60). At this stage, many things have transpired. The material designation for the roof has been drawn. Notice how the drafter indicated the roof material on the outside edge of the roof. This serves two purposes: to save time and to profile the roof. Next, the outline of the chimney has been located, the chimney extending 2'-0" above the highest point within a 10'-0" radius, with the dotted lines representing flashing. Finally, the material designation for wood has been placed on the fascia and the beam that supports the roof at the entry.

The finished configuration for the windows and doors have also been drawn at the stage. This includes any changes requested by the client or the firm's design divi-

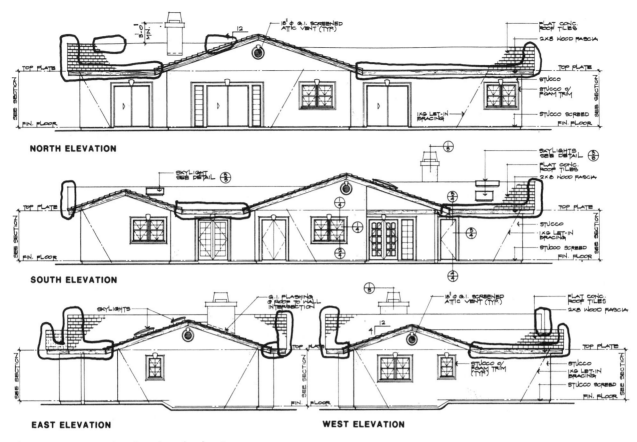

Figure 17.61 Exterior elevation check print.

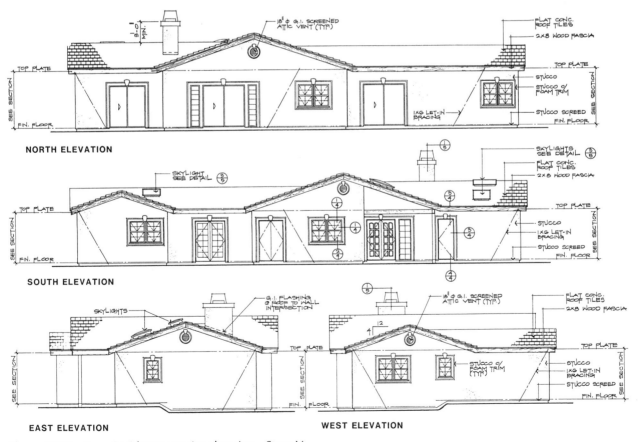

Figure 17.62 Ryan Residence exterior elevation—Stage V.

sion. In this case the raised wood frames around the windows and doors have been reduced in width, and a keystone form may be included on the vent, which will be dealt with at the next stage. A remark to this effect might be placed in the left margin of the drawing sheet as a reminder for the drafter to check on its inclusion.

If the project manager fails to inform the drafter about the final disposition of the vent keystone, the drafter can take the initiative and follow through. Through such action, a drafter can stay on top of the project and become a dependable and valuable asset to the firm.

In comparing this stage with the previous stage you will notice that additional hard-lining has taken place.

STAGE V   (Figure 17.61). This is the dimensioning, noting, and referencing stage. It is also the stage at which some items, required but held up for owner approval, were drawn. A keystone form for the vent is a carryover from the previous stage, as is the location and positioning of the skylights. These are now included. Notice the dimensioning procedure used on the exterior elevation. The floor-to-plate lines refer to the building section and roof pitch expressed as a ratio; the chimney as minimum clearances.

STAGE VI   (Figure 17.63). All parts of Sheet A-4—Exterior elevations are assembled. The elevations, the three schedules, and the window and door details are combined onto the sheet along with the title block and border, standard to the specific architectural office.

Referencing

Referencing is the process of referring a specific area to an enlarged detail. Thus, the top half of the reference bubble indicates the name of the detail, and the bottom number indicates the sheet on which the particular detail can be found. Had this been a complete set with details of all conditions, you would see detail reference bubbles around all windows, doors, beam connections, and so on.

Noting

Whenever possible, noting was done outside the elevation within the right margin. You cannot fit all of the notes in one place without having to use long leaders pointing to the subject. Therefore, certain notes were made inside the elevation to reduce the length of the leaders. A good rule of thumb in regard to leaders is not to allow them to cross more than one object line, never cross a dimension line, and keep the leader length to a minimum.

Keynoting is used by many offices. This is a procedure of numbering and placement of all of the notes on one side (usually the right). You then place a leader in the desired location and, rather than placing the note at the end of the leader, you use a reference bubble that refers to the correct note. A detail used to show the keynoting procedure can be seen in Chapter 16.

Keynoting can be done with either hand-drafted or CAD-drafted elevations. If computers are down, keynoting can still be done on the sheet with adhesives.

The advantage of keynoting is the standardization of the notes. Keynoting also allows the drafter to make direct references to the specification numbers right on the notes. Numbering systems recommended by the American Institute of Architects are similar to the numbering system used by our public libraries and can be incorporated here.

■ SHEET A-5—BUILDING SECTION AND DETAILS

Before a building section of any building is undertaken, it is essential to understand and comprehend the structural system at work and how the building will be assembled using this system. Be sure to read "Framing the Ryan Residence" in Chapter 14 before you proceed. The walls, bearing footings, their locations, and how the weight of the structure, starting at the roof, is distributed downward are explained in Chapter 14.

There are two major divisions to this sheet, the building section and the details. The two divisions can readily be seen in the cartoon in Figure 17.21 and will be delegated to two drafters. As in previous steps, the drawings will be merged in the final stage into one drawing.

The drafter who drafted the foundation plan and/or the roof framing plan is an ideal candidate to draft the building section because of his or her familiarity with the framing system involved.

Likewise, the drafter who developed the footing details and the window and door details is a logical choice to draft the detail portion of the sheet. Because of that person's familiarity with detail procedures as well as the finishes used in the décor of this house, he or she can ensure a degree of consistency and uniformity to the structure. Both building sections will remain in their original positions (as proposed by the cartoon), but the positions of the details will change. The change is caused by the increase of scale in the fireplace detail and the addition of the trellis detail.

The fireplace detail will occupy the position originally held by the wood column-to-beam and skylight detail.

The wood column-to-beam detail will now occupy the original position of the fireplace, and the skylight detail will move beneath the wood column-to-beam detail and replace the eave detail. The eave and newly added trellis detail will both occupy the space below building section Y-Y. The details and their final new positions on this sheet can be seen in the final stage.

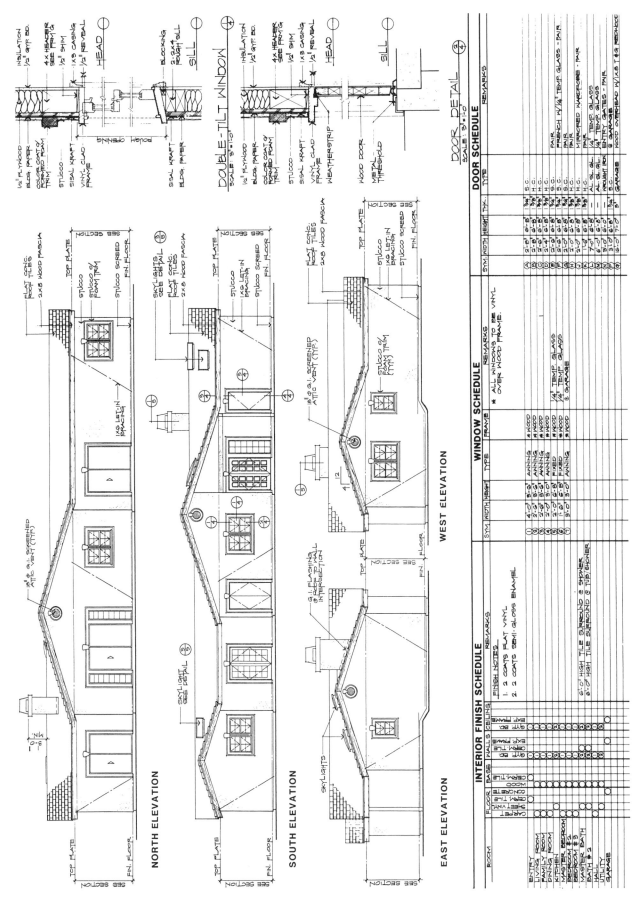

Figure 17.63 Merging of the three segments of Sheet A-4—Stage VI.

Each drawing will be reproduced many times during the course of the project. Many copies will go to contractors for estimates of cost, and the various municipalities will require sets of drawings. An art jury for a particular community might require as many as 15 sets for review. As a single contractor is selected, the subcontractors will also require sets (carpenters, plumbers, electricians, etc.). It is for this reason that formatting and a conservative use of space are essential; reformatting was done on this sheet.

STAGE I (Figure 17.64). This datum stage establishes heights. The floor line and plate line are the most critical from a building perspective. The Ryan Residence has two floor lines because of the change of level that occurs at the bearing wall located in the center of the structure. Dimensioning the top of the ridge is often required by many planning departments not to obstruct views for neighbors and is therefore often included in exterior elevations.

STAGE II (Figure 17.65). The outline of the roof and the positioning of the bearing walls are incorporated at this stage. Study the California frame in Chapter 14 to see how the loads are distributed onto the various interior walls. Templates can be used to construct the intersection of the walls and roof (see Figure 17.66).

STAGE III (Figure 17.67). As seen in the drawing, the building section is receiving detail at the various intersections. The top and bottom plates, as well as the seat in the stem wall for the slab, are drafted. Notice in particular the way the drawing illustrates the backfill at the end walls.

STAGE IV (Figure 17.68). This is a very critical stage, because it establishes all of the structural components, their position and direction, and even the direction in which the section was taken.

Note the inclusion of the material designation and the makeup of the foundation with its insulation and sand.

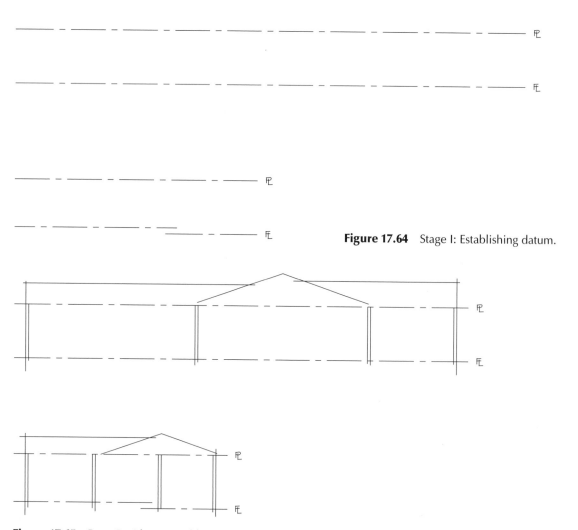

Figure 17.64 Stage I: Establishing datum.

Figure 17.65 Ryan Residence: Building section—Stage II.

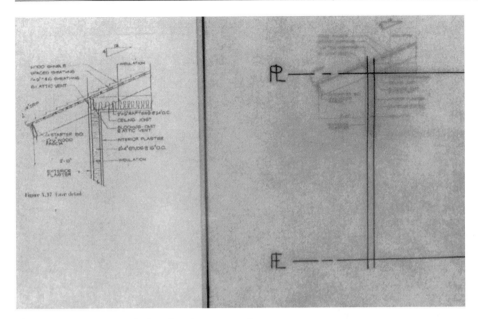

Figure 17.66   Using existing drawing as template.

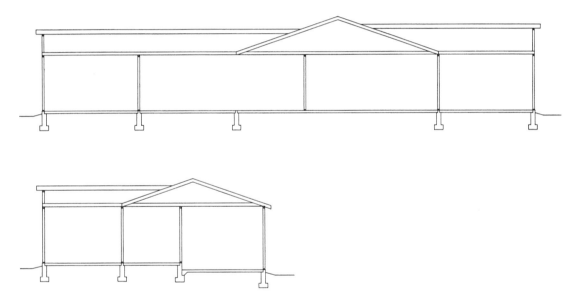

Figure 17.67   Ryan Residence: Building section—Stage III.

Walls show drywall, and the ceiling reveals the direction of the ceiling joist.

At this point a check print is made, and the project manager can freehand the errors, position dimensions, and notes for a beginning drafter right onto this check print.

Correction of Drawing Errors

As in all drawings, errors are made. It is no different with a building section. Some errors are simple to correct, whereas others are a bit more complex. Both types of er-

rors are addressed here, and possible solutions are suggested.

Because a building section is the result of the foundation plan, roof plan, and roof framing systems used, the framing is checked and corrections clearly noted on the check print. Compare the ceiling joist direction with Figure 17.85. It changes direction in the bedroom wing (left side), but this change of direction is not incorporated in either of the two building sections. This will most certainly be corrected in the final stage.

An even greater error is revealed if you compare this drawing with the various plans (floor plan, foundation

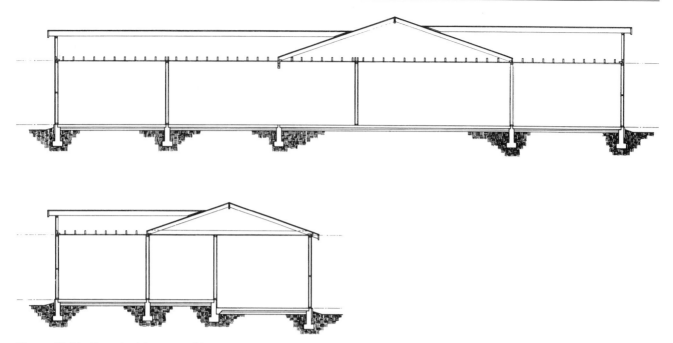

Figure 17.68   Ryan Residence: Building section—Stage IV.

plan, etc.) and the original cartoon. The building sections are drawn in the same way as the cartoon, yet the cut for the section is taken in the opposite direction that the arrows indicate in the various plans.

A quick fix of this problem would be to change the direction of the arrows on the cutting plane line, thus making the drawing technically correct. The arrows would be changed in the roof plan, foundation plan, floor plan, and roof framing plan.

Another and more complex approach would be to turn the bottom building section around to produce a mirror image. This would align the image with all of the cutting plane lines and produce a more comfortable look at the structure for the carpenters (framers) in the field. The mirror image would be a better look at the structure, because you are cutting away the smaller piece of the building and looking in the direction of the larger portion of the building.

If this drawing had been done on a computer, the solution would be simple. Most computers can isolate a drawing and produce a mirror image of it with a set of simple commands. However, if the drawing was hand drawn, the solution is a bit more complex.

Because an engineering or diazo copy will eventually be made of this drawing, a solution is feasible. Make the ceiling joist corrections, cut the lower building section out, scissor it back into the original vellum with the image on the back side (which will mirror-image the drawing) and continue to draft on the correct side of the vellum. In this way, the original is saved and the new information will be on the opposite side of the drawing. As

a copy is made, no one will ever know you have drawn on both sides of the vellum.

STAGE V   (Figure 17.69). Having made all the necessary corrections at the previous stage, this stage becomes very straightforward. Noting of the component parts and dimensioning become the utmost important tasks. All the parts should be identified as if you were labeling a drawing showing how to assemble a bicycle. Material designations for insulation, roof material, and concrete are done at this stage, as well as referencing to reveal footing details and eave details.

STAGE VI   (Figure 17.70). This is not really a stage in the evolution of the building sections, but more of an assembly stage for Sheet A-5. The final stages of the details and the building section are merged at this point and positioned onto the title block sheet in the final plotting. Note the use of almost every square inch of the sheet.

■ SHEET A-6—ROOF FRAMING PLAN, INTERIOR ELEVATIONS, AND CABINET DETAILS

As can be seen in the cartoon for Sheet A-6, Figure 17.22, there are three components to this sheet: the roof framing plan, the interior elevations, and the cabinet details. Again we will utilize the skills of three drafters. The cabinet details will be done in three stages and can be seen in Chapter 16. The interior elevation and the roof

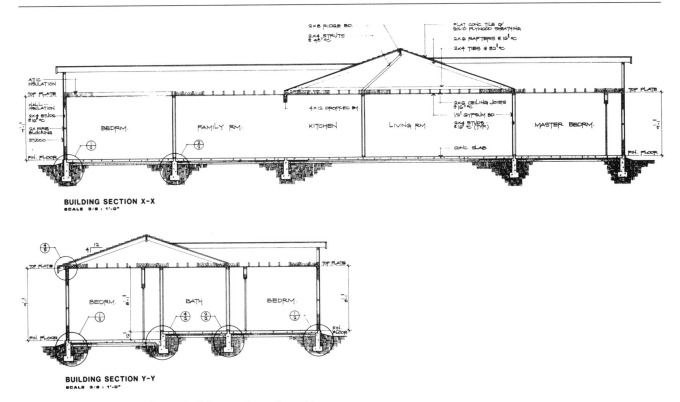

Figure 17.69   Ryan Residence: Building section—Stage V.

framing plan will be developed in this chapter and merged in the final stage of the roof framing plan.

RYAN RESIDENCE—INTERIOR ELEVATION

Seven examples of interior elevations are provided to show the basic progression of the drafter through various stages: three elevations for the kitchen, three for a bathroom, and one for a utility room.

STAGE I   (Figure 17.71). This is the block-out stage. Prior to this stage the drafter should consult the project book to become familiar with the shapes and sizes of the various kitchen appliances, plumbing fixtures, cabinets, and washer and dryer. The drafter starts by first laying out the ceiling line, the floor line, and the wall line. Next, changes are made in the ceiling level, owing to the presence of soffits or furred ceiling (lowered ceiling). With the use of a fade-away pencil, countertop levels and the underside of the upper cabinets are drafted.

STAGE II   (Figure 17.72). Once the basic outline of the room is established, the doors and drawers are lightly outlined. If preconstructed cabinets are to be used, the distributor can usually help you size the doors and drawers based on the available sizes. A catalog listing basic sizes may be available in the project book. Basic available sizes are usually displayed on the back of these catalogs. If the cabinets are to be custom-built, then the designer of the firm should be consulted for the basic distribution of sizes to be used. In *The Professional Practice of Architectural Detailing*, a companion book to this one, a complete chapter is devoted to cabinets.

With the use of a template, plumbing appliances and the surrounding area are drawn. If the ceramic tile extends on the wall surface for only a couple of rows, this area is called a "splash." If it extends the entire height of the wall or at least to the height of a person, it is called a wainscot.

After placing the kitchen appliances, windows, and plumbing appliances, clearances are checked to see that they meet code requirements. For example, the water closet in one of the bathrooms is located between the tub and the cabinets. A 30" minimum clearance is required by most municipalities. There are similar requirements for the space between the upper and base cabinets.

STAGE III   (Figure 17.73). All information about cabinet sizes and configuration, door swings, and shelves, as well as all necessary vertical dimensions, are included at this stage. Note the location of the General Electric Space-Saver Dishwater[1] as it is positioned in relation to the kitchen sink. Horizontal dimensions should not

---

[1]Courtesy of General Electric.

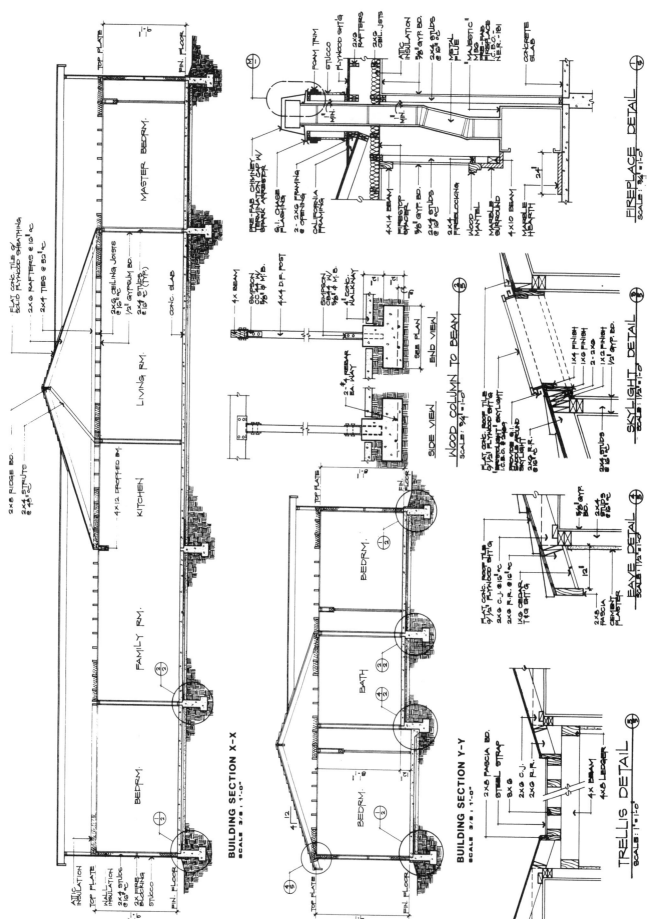

Figure 17.70 Sections and details merged to form Sheet A-5.

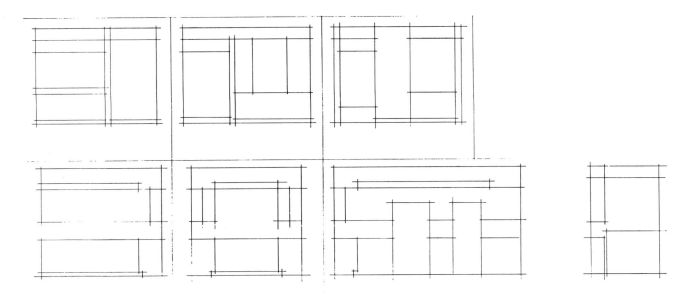

Figure 17.71   Ryan Residence: Interior elevations—Stage I.

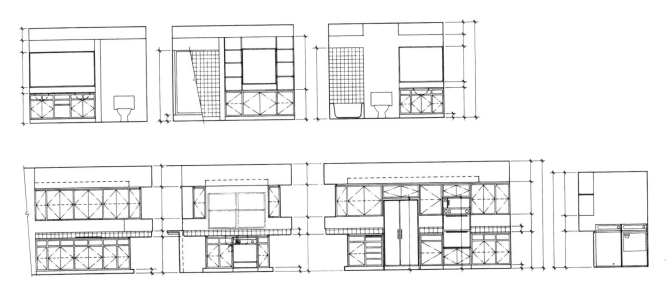

Figure 17.72   Ryan Residence: Interior elevations—Stage II.

Figure 17.73   Ryan Residence: Interior elevations—Stage III.

be included, as they are gotten from the floor plan. (An exception may be to size the width of a cabinet *not* bound on the ends with a wall and not dimensioned on the floor plan.)

STAGE IV (Figure 17.74). There are two ways to approach the final stage of a set of interior elevations. The first is to use a standardized office checklist. A second method is to develop one of your own, which should include the following:

A. Call-outs for all surface materials, other than those that exist on the finish schedule.

B. A description of all appliances, even those that are not on the surface facing the observer; for example, sinks, garbage disposals, recessed medicine cabinets.

C. A description of items that are not standard. The open shelves in the master bedroom is a classic example.

D. The use of standard conventions to denote shelves, cabinet door swings, drawers, and so forth.

E. Any clearances that need to be maintained. Refrigerator and oven/microwave are two good examples in this instance.

If a set of specifications are included in this set of drawings as a part of the construction documents, noting should be generic. For example, the note for tile should be stated simply as "ceramic tile"; the specific size, brand, color of grout, and so on would be covered in the specifications.

Profiling also plays an important part in the final stage. Notice how heavy the lines are around the perimeter so as to define the limits of the wall. Most other lines are drafted as a medium-dark line, except for objects that

can be seen on the exterior elevation as well. This is why the window above the sink is drawn as a medium-light line.

Also note the appearance of dark objects that have been sectioned. The bathtub in Bath 2 is a good representation of this procedure.

Put yourself in the position of a contractor who must build this interior and ask yourself, "What will prevent me from building this kitchen or bathroom? What description, dimension, or clearance is missing?" Then note or dimension any missing elements.

■ FRAMING A RESIDENCE

In considering the Ryan Residence, let's examine the specific detail as well as the overall look. A model of the Ryan Residence was constructed to illustrate the framing approach (see Figure 17.75A and B). This is not usually done in an office for such a simple structure.

As in all structural analysis, we first describe the overall structure, starting with the top of the building and working downward.

The roof, as you have seen, is a gable roof, built of rafter to form a triangle. The sides of the base of the triangle accept the weight of the roof (called the dead load) and the weight of movable objects (called the live load). Movable objects might be architectural décor, roofers walking about, and so on. Thus, in the photograph seen in Figure 17.75, notice how the main form of the roof places its weight on the wall between the master bedroom and the living room and necessitates a beam to bridge the opening between the kitchen and the family

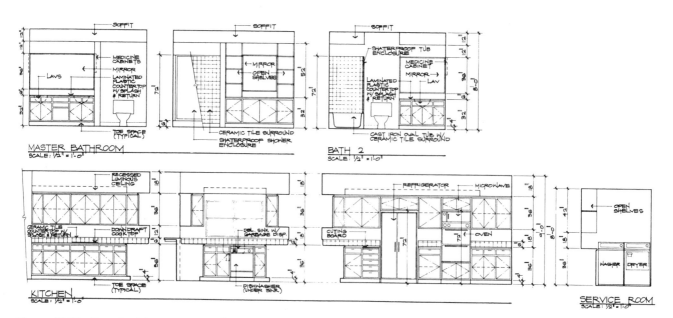

Figure 17.74 Ryan Residence: Interior elevations—Stage IV.

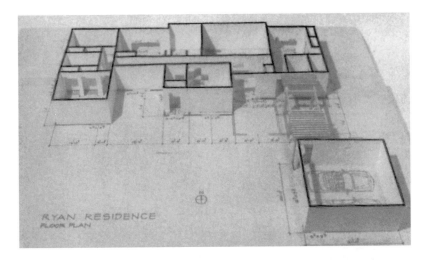

Figure 17.75 Floor plan model and roof system for the Ryan Residence.

room. This structural consideration is demonstrated in Figure 17.77. The walls in the two areas become load-bearing walls and must, in turn, have bearing footings beneath them.

The main roof is completely sheathed, and the two adjacent roofs are locked into the main roof by means of a framing system called a California frame. In this system, complete roofs are interlocked. See Figure 17.78. In reality, a 2x__member is laid flatwise onto the sheathed roof, as shown in Figure 17.78, the new ridge is attached, and the jack rafters (shaft rafters) and the common rafters (full-length rafters) are installed.

Now look at Figure 17.80. Because of the positioning of the new roof to the left of the main roof, there is a need for a new bearing wall between the bathroom and the front bedroom.

When the final segment of the roof is installed via a California frame, the total roof system is complete. See Figure 17.74B. In every instance, the previous roof is totally sheathed before the California frame roof is installed. The sheathing in turn acts as a diaphragm to resist

earthquakes, wind, or any other force acting upon this structure. In addition, the total wall surface will also be sheathed with plywood to resist any lateral forces acting upon the structure. This plywood wall membrane will also, along with other material, work to prevent heat loss on cold days and heat gain on hot days.

A second way of holding up the roof by changing the direction of the ceiling joist is to turn the ridge into a beam. This beam is subsequently supported by a post and by a concrete pad to distribute this concentrated load over the ground. Figure 17.81 shows a model illustrating this method, and Figure 17.82 shows a diagram for positioning the posts.

Next, consider the ceiling system. The ideal procedure is to install the ceiling joist in the same direction as the rafters, to complete the desired triangle. See Figure 17.83. The beginning, the end points, and the lap of other ceiling joists are well secured to form a solidly built triangle. In this system, the ceiling joist also rests on the wall between the kitchen and the living room, making this a bearing wall (structural wall) and requiring a bear-

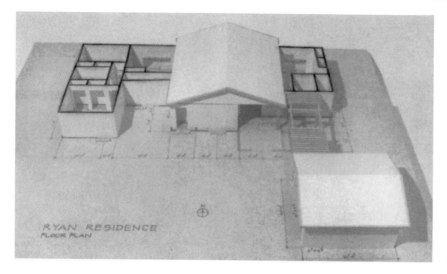

Figure 17.76 Main roof system.

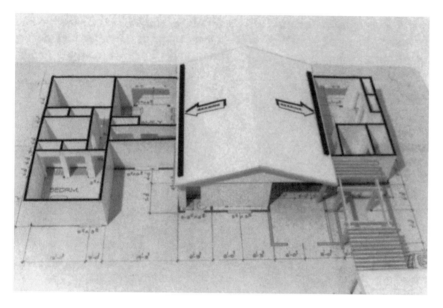

Figure 17.77 Distributing main roof load.

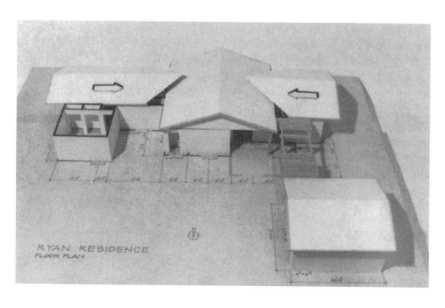

Figure 17.78 Interlocking roof system.

Figure 17.79 California frame method.

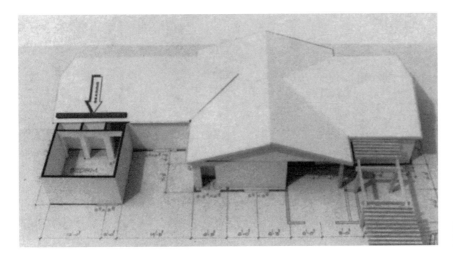

Figure 17.80 Additional bearing walls identified.

ing footing. Another solution is to use a wood truss system, as opposed to the conventional rafter/ceiling joist system.

In a wood truss, the rafter as seen in Figure 17.81 and ceiling joist are integrated as a total unit. Because of the way they are configured, the forces on trusses are distributed to the ends of the trusses and thus can span greater distances. They are prebuilt in the shop and delivered ready for erection. Light roof trusses (built of 2 × 4 and 2 × 6 members) are light enough that two framers can lift the units place. Spaced at 16 to 24 inches on center, these trusses can easily span between 20 and 30 feet, depending on exterior forces such as snow loads, wind, earthquake, and so forth. Heavy timber trusses can span upward of 100 feet. Look at Figure 17.84 and compare the appearance of the structure with the previous illustration. The metal plates used to connect the various components are toothed plates. (A piece of metal is

punched to form a nail like a tooth, which is pressed into position by the manufacturer of the truss.)

Perpendicular to the trusses and on the top side are members called purlins. Purlins keep the trusses from toppling over like dominos.

The negative aspect to the use of trusses, if you can call it a negative, is the reduction of attic space.

To show alternative solutions and their implications, we run the ceiling joist parallel to the ridge and perpendicular to the rafters. This shortens the span of the ceiling joist and runs them in the same direction as required by the two roofs adjacent to the main roof. However, this causes two additional problems. We have not created a triangle, and we must find a way to hold up the ridge.

We will hold up the ridge by the introduction of a member called a strut, placed at 4'-0" o.c. and resting on the kitchen/living room wall, as shown in Figure 17.85. We will produce the desired triangle by placing a series

Figure 17.81 Ridge beam and its support.

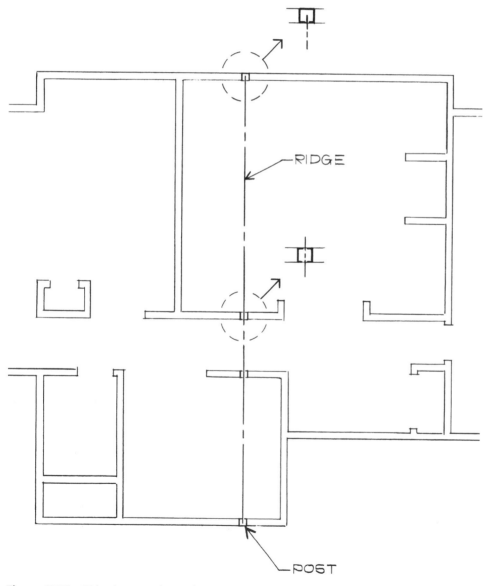

Figure 17.82 Ridge beam and post diagram.

Figure 17.83 Creating a structural triangle.

Figure 17.84 Truss system.

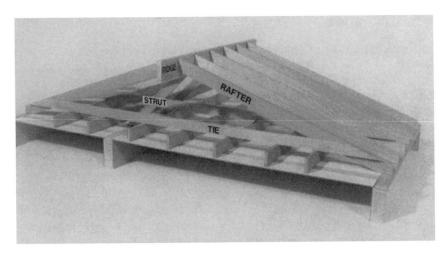

Figure 17.85 Configuration for ceiling joist perpendicular to rafters.

of members (32″ o.c.) parallel to the rafter. The members positioned above the ceiling joist are called ties. This is the way we will configure the ceiling joist during the evolution of the Ryan Residence.

The direction of the ceiling joist of the two-bedroom wing at the left will be changed, producing the necessity for still another bearing wall and, subsequently, a bearing footing. Figure 17.85 is a simple diagram for interior walls that become bearing walls for the ceiling joist. These bearing walls are added to those produced by the rafters and will determine the configuration for the foundation plan.

Within these bearing walls are openings. A header or lintel is used to distribute the weight of the ceiling and roof around the openings. These beams, headers, and lintels are marked on Figure 17.86.

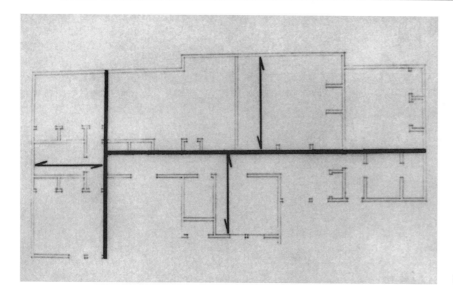

Figure 17.86 Bearing wall for ceiling joist.

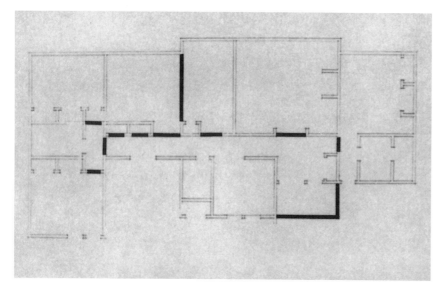

Figure 17.87 Required beams as result of roof and ceiling.

■ EVOLUTION OF RYAN ROOF FRAMING PLAN

Ryan Residence Roof Framing Plan

As described at the beginning of this chapter, there are two ways of developing framing plans; superimposition and separate development. For the Ryan Residence, the ceiling joist plan will be superimposed on the floor plan, making this plan a three-in-one plan; a floor plan, an electrical plan, and a ceiling framing plan.

For the roof framing plan, the initial procedure is as follows:

A xerographic copy of the floor plan, prior to the dimensioning stage, is printed onto vellum. If your office does not have a plain paper copier capable of producing the necessary reproduction size, local *blueprint shops often do and can make a copy for you, or a diazo process can be used. When a diazo copy is printed onto vellum, it is called a sepia copy. It is onto this copy that the roof framing plan is drawn.*

With CAD, you simply use an earlier layer of the floor plan without the notes and dimensions shown.

STAGE I (Figure 17.88). The outline of the floor plan is imported and becomes the datum sheet for this drawing. Be sure to pick a floor plan stage that shows only the openings for the windows and doors and does not have the doors and windows drawn in. This allows for the beams and headers to be easily shown. Lighten the lines to allow for easy reading of the framing members.

STAGE II (Figure 17.89). The roof plan is then drawn over the floor plan. If the roof plan is to be drawn over

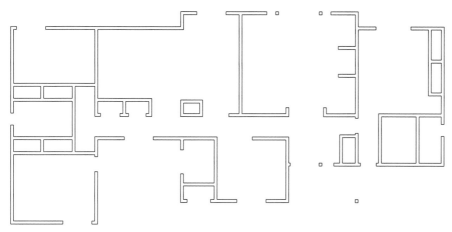

Figure 17.88 Roof plan datum.

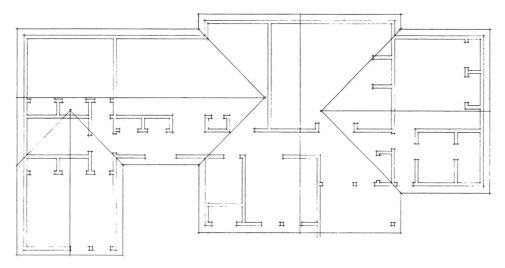

Figure 17.89 Ryan Residence: Roof framing plan—Stage II.

a printed copy of the floor plan, be sure to make a lighter copy so the lines of the roof and framing members stand out.

STAGE III (Figure 17.90). Skylights and beams over critical openings (in load-bearing walls) are placed. At this stage, two skylights and the fireplace opening are missing. This is an oversight on the part of the drafter. They are the skylight in the master bedroom and another at the end of the hall (near the rear bedroom). The second skylight conflicts with the beam placed to accept the weight of the struts, and should be discussed with the project manager and/or the structural engineer. The framing around the two existing skylights is indicated, which can be viewed from a different perspective as you look at the detail All of the rafters are positioned, except for the California framed areas.

STAGE IV (Figure 17.91). Bearing walls are identified by the pouché of the walls as in the California frame areas. The two missing skylights and the framing around the fireplace are incorporated at this stage.

STAGE V (Figure 17.92). The final stage of the roof framing plan is drawn in diagrammatic fashion and includes notations for the struts, California frame, ties, and so on.

All headers and beams are checked and labeled. To eliminate the redundant task of labeling every beam or header, a special note can be included to identify all 4 × 4 or less. A legend identifying bearing and nonbearing walls is also included.

Finally, locate a portion of the roof that is somewhat typical, that is, without beams or windows beneath it, and display the roof material plus the sheathing in this area.

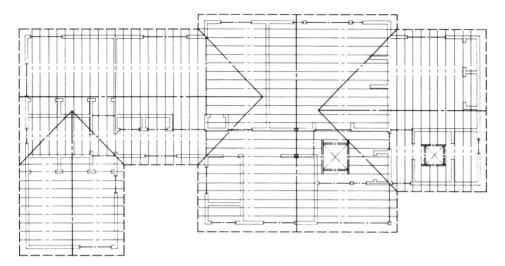

Figure 17.90 Ryan Residence: Roof framing plan—Stage III.

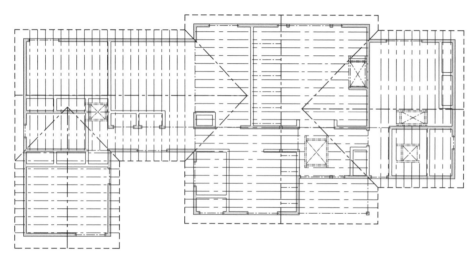

Figure 17.91 Stage IV: Roof plan.

STAGE VI (Figure 17.93). In the final stage of Sheet A-6, the three components that make up this set are merged: the roof framing plan, the interior elevations, and the cabinet details.

■ SHEET A-7—RYAN RESIDENCE GARAGE

The garage of the Ryan Residence was evolved entirely on a separate sheet. At a single glance, the reader can see the evolution of a complete set of drawings for the simplest of all structures, a garage.

Sheet A-7 contains the following:

A. Floor plan
B. Foundation plan
C. Roof framing plan
D. Building section

E. Exterior elevations
F. Three typical details

Compare the garage with the evolution of the Ryan Residence and you will find that the typical titles used in both sets will be alike.

In some offices that specialize in residential work, a sheet such as this might exist as a standard for a typical detached two-car garage. A xerographic master can be made of this master onto vellum and adjusted to meet the needs of each new project.

Let's say that the master was drafted as a hip roof for use with the Ryan Residence, but needed to be changed to a gable roof. The procedure is rather simple. The areas that have to be changed can be covered with white bond paper; for example, the entire roof framing plan, the tops of the exterior elevations, or any other areas.

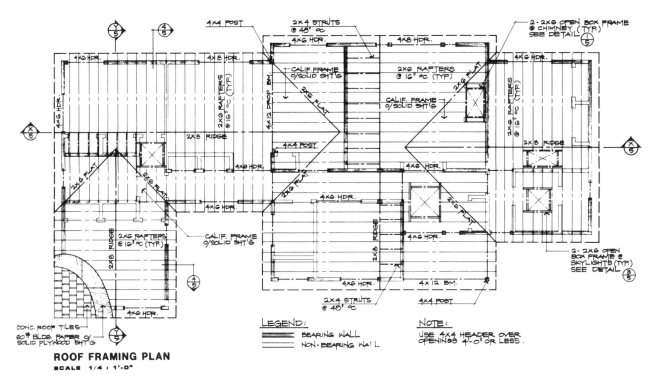

Figure 17.92 Ryan Residence: Roof framing plan—Stage V.

The drawing is then xerographically reproduced as a vellum original, and the new information hand drafted and incorporated into the system.

If the garage was developed by a computer and CAD drafted, it becomes a simple matter for the CAD drafter to recall the garage sheet, and delete, correct or change the drawing to suit the new requirements.

Sheet-size limits suggested that the garage be placed on a separate sheet for the Ryan Residence. Because we were using a rather small sheet to evolve this set of drawings (24 × 36), the format did not allow the floor plan of the garage to be included, for example, with the floor plan of the residence itself. The same was true of the roof framing plan, foundation plan, and so on.

The garage will be evolved in three stages. The cartoon of the garage can be found in the Student Manual, and the plan will be hand-drafted by one drafter.

STAGE I (Figure 17.93). Prior to starting sheet A-7, the plan of this garage was drafted onto an 8½ × 11 sheet of paper. This will be traced three times onto the original. Its position, based on the cartoon of the garage, can be drawn with a fade-away pencil. Slide the 8½ × 11 sheet under the vellum and trace the outline once for the floor plan; then slide the 8½ × 11 sheet to its new position and trace it again for the foundation plan. Finally, the 8½ × 11 drawing is moved again and traced as a basis for the roof framing plan.

Rather than measuring the width and depth on a scale (which might be faster) the 8½ × 11 can be positioned and used as a measuring device for the exterior elevations. It can also be used to measure the width of the building section when the required distance is measured off twice (you may find use of a divider to be much faster). What this does for the beginning drafter is to maintain accuracy of measurement throughout the complete sheet.

Details can be gotten from a standard file of details (which is often available in the office), traced, scissored, or reproduced onto an adhesive and mounted in the proper position, For this drawing, we will use details from the companion book *The Professional Practice of Architectural Detailing*.

STAGE II (Figure 17.95). The first thing the drafter did at this stage was to block out the details for the eave and the footing. These were then checked against the building section, the various plans, and the elevations.

Next, the floor plan and foundation plan were dimensioned. This included the diagonal dotted lines on the floor plan that represent the diaphragm bearing. These two 1 × 4 members stretch from one corner to the opposite corner. Because they are laid flatwise above the ties, they can be slightly bowed to miss each other as they cross. Much like reinforcing the open end of a cardboard box, the diaphragm bracing keeps the top end of the garage from becoming deformed.

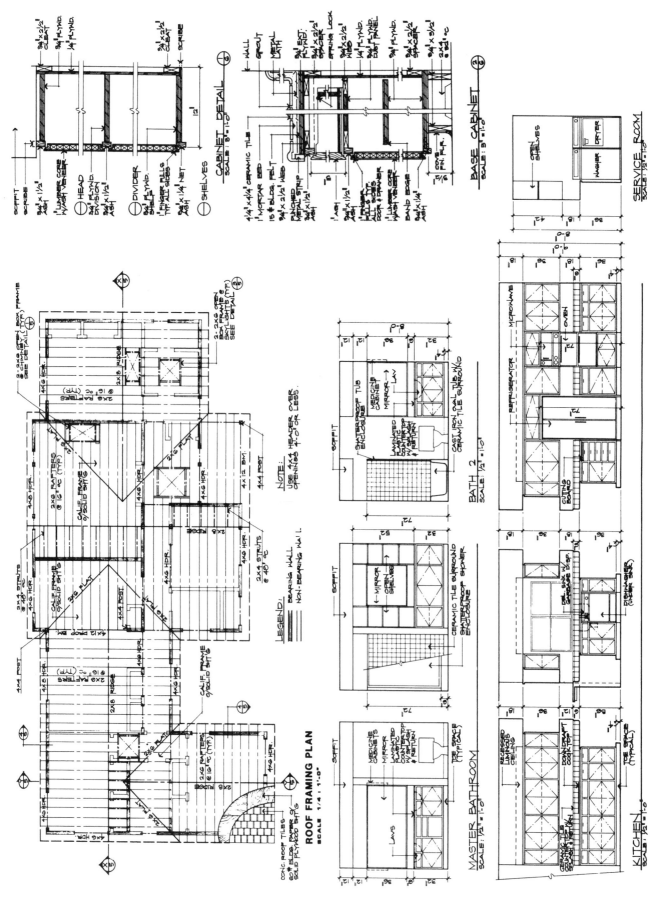

Figure 17.93 Three drawings merged to form Sheet A-6.

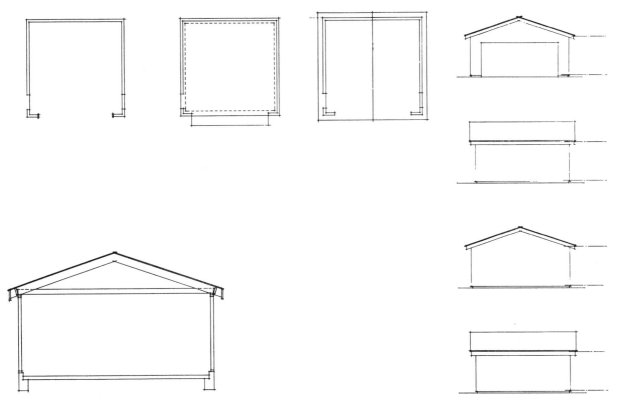

Figure 17.94 Ryan Residence: Garage—Stage I.

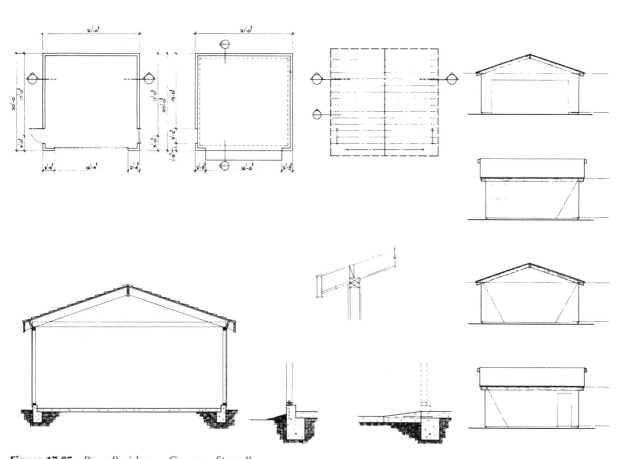

Figure 17.95 Ryan Residence: Garage—Stage II.

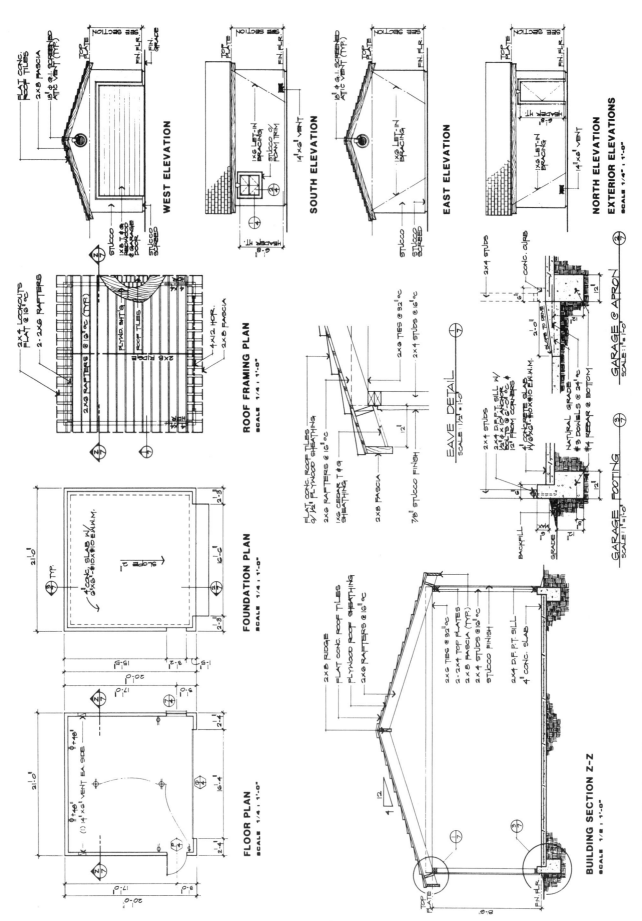

Figure 17.96 Ryan Residence: Garage—Stage III.

The rafters, the ridge, and the look-outs are next to be drawn on the roof framing plan. These members were drawn in their entirety. However, this is not the way an office would have you draft. Instead, the ridge and rafters would be drawn as center lines, or the roof would be drawn diagrammatically, as shown in Chapter 14.

The roof structure was drafted in this manner so that you can actually see, on a drawing, how it would appear.

Notice, next, how the material designations have been placed in the building section, details, and elevations.

Finally, the window and door are positioned and drawn onto the exterior elevations along with the let-in brace and the two required vents (one per car). These are placed between the studs and above the bottom plate. Look at the exterior bearing footing and note that the bottom plate is above the floor level. This factor should be taken into consideration when positioning the vents on the elevations.

STAGE III   (Figure 17.96). This is the noting and referencing stage and will be the final stage for this sheet. Because there is no checklist for the garage, the garage plan should be checked against the items listed in "Set Check," the following section of this chapter.

■ SET CHECK

In-House Plan Checker

Every office has a plan checker. It may be the architect, the project manager, or the job captain. Along with checking the plans for the same type of items that a Department of Building and Safety might check for, he or she will check to see that the sheets coordinate with each other and have correctly included all of the client's needs and changes.

Dimensions (Horizontal)

Even if the dimensions have been checked for errors in addition, the dimensions of one sheet are again checked against another. The floor plan measurements are checked with the dimensions posted on the foundation plan to validate, in fact, that this foundation will set properly under the walls shown and dimensioned on the floor plan.

The side yards on the site plan are added to the overall width of the building, as expressed on the foundation plan or floor plan; two inches are added for the thickness of the skin of the building (stucco, in the case of the Ryan Residence) and this total checked against the size of the lot as expressed around the perimeter of the site in the form of metes and bounds. This check validates

that, in fact, the structure will, with its measurements and setbacks, fit and situate itself correctly onto the property.

If the plan check was done properly at the various stages, this final check becomes nothing more than a pro forma check.

Remember, just because a dimension is given does not automatically mean that the component has been dimensioned properly. As expressed in Chapter 9, it is important to think in terms of size and location.

To merely size an object is of little value if the craftsperson does not know where to position it (location). The opposite is also true. A pier or a beam may be positioned (located), but if the craftsperson does not know its size, the information is of little use.

Dimensions (Vertical)

Because most of the main drawings included in this set are plans, it might appear that the horizontal distances are the main dimensions to check. Nothing could be further from the truth. Vertical dimensions should be checked throughout the set. With the floor plan as the main sheet for horizontal dimensions, the building section becomes the basis for most vertical dimensions. For example, anytime you extend a roof over an area, such as the entry, you should check the framing to see if there is enough space for a door and the header above the door. Head clearance above a stairwell should always be checked, as well as the space through which a beam might travel.

Anytime you pierce a horizontal plane or an angular plane—such as a roof, floor, or ceiling—with a skylight, stairwell, chimney, or some such object, a section should be drawn to check for clearances.

Cross-Referencing

A critical step is to check any cross-referencing. Especially if there is more than one drafter on a job, it is essential to see that all references to details actually refer to details that do in fact exist, and that the proper letter or number is included in each reference bubble. For example, the eave area of a building section may refer to an eave detail. The checker must be sure the name given to the detail, such as "D," is the same that exists in the detail. Remember, reference bubbles are divided in two. The upper half houses the name, and the lower half indicates the number of the sheet on which you can find this detail.

The most common error made by a beginning drafter is in the section lines and section references. The section line is most often drawn across plans. For example, when a section is taken through the center of a floor plan, there is a reference bubble on each end. Each bubble is split in two, with the top containing the letter name for the section and the bottom showing the page number of the building section.

Let us say the title to a particular section is X-X. Under the section, the title should read "Building Section X-X." On each of the bubbles on the floor plan there should be only one X. Therefore, the reader will look at one X and search for the other to complete the section (slice) through the building. Beginners often put an X-X in each of the reference bubbles, thinking that this is its name.

Plan Check and Correction

For the beginning drafter, it would be good practice to visit the local Department of Building and Safety to find out how it checks plans, or to obtain a set of simple plans that has gone through this process and study the list of corrections required by that particular municipality.

Over the years many offices have developed a check-list, often referred to as a punch list. Familiarity with these forms and lists cannot help but make you a more conscientious and effective drafter.

CONCEPTUAL DESIGN AND CONSTRUCTION DOCUMENTS FOR A WOOD BUILDING— BEACH HOUSE

■ CONCEPTUAL DESIGN

The site for this project was a small beach lot fronting the ocean in a southern California community. The site dimensions are 35 feet in width and 110 feet in depth, with the 35-foot dimension adjacent to a private road. The site ownership also included an additional 35 feet on the opposite side of the private road easement. Figure 18.1 graphically illustrates the site plan, showing its relationship to the ocean, access road, and compass direction.

Site Development Regulations

Site development regulations, enforced by the community's planning commission, covered building setback requirements, building height limit, parking requirements, and the allowable building coverage of the site. These are considered together with the site and floor plan development.

Other regulatory agencies included a design review board and a state coastal commission. The design review board primarily dealt with the architectural design of the building and the landscaping plan. The coastal commission is concerned with the protection of historical landmarks, access to the public beach, and energy conservation through, for example, the use of solar collectors to augment domestic water heating.

After researching all the site development regulations and gathering the design data for our clients' needs, we started the conceptual design process.

Clients' Requirements

The clients, a middle-aged husband and wife whose children no longer live at home, wanted to develop the site to its maximum potential. The site allowed a two-story residence with a maximum floor area of 2,900 square feet measured from the inside wall dimensions. Given these two factors, they wanted the following rooms: living room, dining room, kitchen, study or family room, guest bath, mud room and laundry, and three bedrooms with two full bathrooms. They also wanted a two-car garage and shop area. Because this was a beach site, they also wanted to have sun decks wherever possible, as well as a sheltered outdoor area for winter.

Initial Schematic Studies

Our initial schematic studies worked around relationships among the rooms as well as room orientation on the site. Room orientation required that we locate the major rooms, such as the living room, dining room, and master bedroom, so that they would face the ocean and capture a coastline view. The garage and entry court needed to be adjacent to the private road for accessibility.

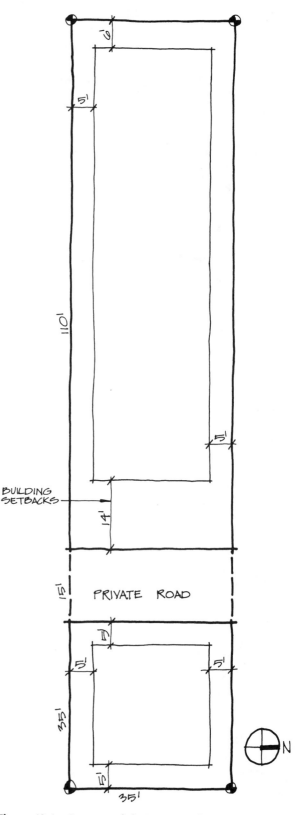

Figure 18.1 Conceptual design—site plan.

Because the site is small and because the setback regulations further reduced the buildable area, we obviously needed to design a two-story building to meet the clients' requested number of rooms.

First Floor. Figure 18.2 shows a schematic study of the first floor level. This figure also illustrates some early decisions we made: locating the entry court on the leeward side of the building; providing a view and access to the beach from the living, dining, and family rooms; locating the mud room and laundry in an area that would afford accessibility from the outside and to the beach; and providing a basement area for the mechanical system for space heating as well as a boiler for the solar collectors.

Second Floor. We developed a schematic study for the second floor level to show the desired location and relationships among the rooms as well as possible sun deck locations. We wanted all bedrooms to have direct access to a sun deck. See Figure 18.3.

Preliminary Floor Plans

Using the schematic studies as a basis for the various room locations, we developed scaled preliminary floor plan drawings.

First Floor. The first floor level, as Figure 18.4 shows, was planned to follow the site contour, which sloped to the beach. So we included floor transitions from the living room, dining room, and family room levels. Our choice of forty-five-degree angles on the exterior window wall areas was influenced by a coastline view in the Southwest direction. As you can see, these angles in turn influenced other areas of the floor plan. At this stage, the scaled plan adhered to all the setback requirements and was within the allowable floor area established by the design review board.

Second Floor. The second floor preliminary plan, as Figure 18.5 shows, was basically an extension of the first floor level. It provided a master bedroom with an ocean view and had sun decks adjacent to the bedroom areas. A portion of the hall, which provided the circulation to the various rooms, was opened to the entry below. This gave the entry a high ceiling and allowed both areas to have natural light from a skylight.

Roof and Exterior Elevation Studies

From these preliminary floor plans, we developed roof and exterior elevation studies to investigate any design problems that might require some minor floor plan adjustments. We made these adjustments as we drew the floor plans for the construction documents.

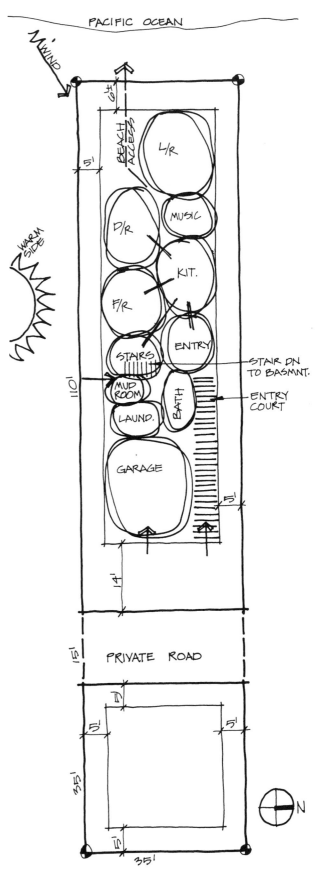

Figure 18.2 Schematic study—first floor.

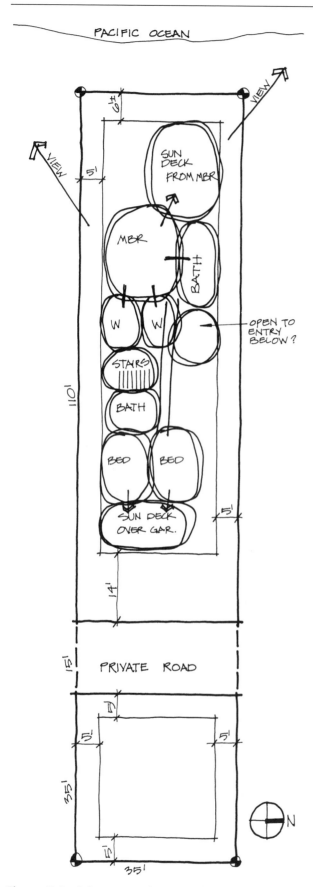

Figure 18.3   Schematic study—second floor.

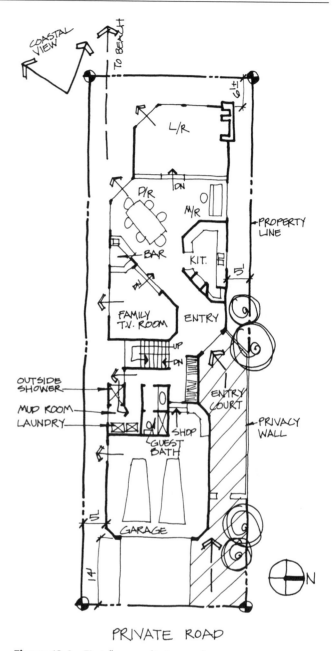

Figure 18.4   First floor preliminary plan.

Roof Design.   The development of the exterior elevations started with the roof design. We decided to use a roof pitch of 4½ in 12 to achieve an angle conducive to using solar collectors. We planned to locate these collectors on the recommended South side of the plane of the roof. This roof pitch provided the maximum height allowed by the design review board; it also determined the roof material. We selected shingle tile for the roof and cedar shingles for the exterior walls. Because salt air causes metal corrosion, we used wood windows and doors with a creosote stain finish. The glass was double

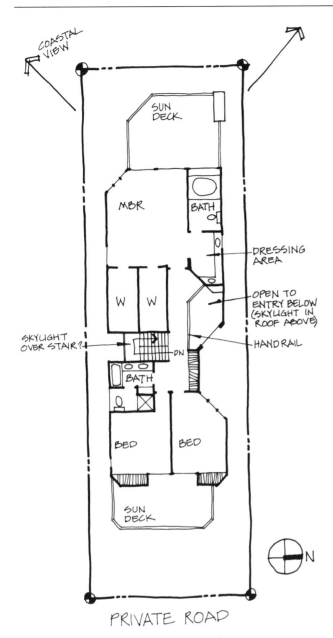

Figure 18.5 Second floor preliminary plan.

glazing throughout to provide greater insulation during both the winter and summer months.

Exterior Elevations. The window designs combined fixed glass and operable sections as well as separate operable sections. Using the previously mentioned design criteria, we developed sketches of the exterior elevations. Figure 18.6 shows the four sides of this residence using these exterior materials and window elements. Because the material on the exterior was wood, we also exposed the wood lintel over the windows and doors.

After we completed these studies, we submitted them to the clients and to the various regulatory agencies. We

incorporated their adjustments and refinements into the final drawing of the construction documents.

■ SITE PLAN

Stage I

If this set of drawing had been done on the computer, the civil engineer would have provided the office with a digital copy of the site plan, which would then have become Stage I and the datum sheet. The site, drawn full size in model space and positioned on the sheet (when plotting), will be done as per the cartoon for a hand-drawn site plan. The second stage, as described next, essentially becomes the first stage.

Stage II

The second stage of the site plan (see Figure 18.7) eventually results in a combination site plan and roof plan. After planning the sheet layout, we traced the site layout from the civil engineer's drawing. We established the perimeter of the structure from both the ground floor and upper floor plan. We also did a light layout of the vicinity map at this stage. The set of double lines at each end of the structure are second floor decks. Note the entry patio on one of the sides.

The roof is what is called a hip roof. The horizontal and perpendicular lines represent the top or peak of the roof (called the ridge), while the angular lines (always drawn at 45° to maintain a constant slope of the roof) represent what are called the hip and the valley. The hip and the valley mark the transition from one plane to another. See Figure 18.8.

Stage III

After confirming the correct setbacks and the size of the structure in relationship to the site, we began the line darkening process. See Figure 18.9. For the vicinity map, we cut the plastic lid from a coffee can as a template for darkening the outline of the beach at the left. This is good practice for irregular lines for a beginner. An experienced drafter performs this freehand.

All lines on the site plan were darkened. Notice the change in the roof outline at the rear of the structure. Figure 18.10 shows the geometry to perform this cutting of the roof.

The outline of the structure was changed to a hidden line. Had the roof plan been separate from the site plan, the building would have been solid and the roof outline would have been dotted. The lines representing the shape of the roof would also have been eliminated. Skylights were put in two locations, at the entry and on the opposite side of the roof.

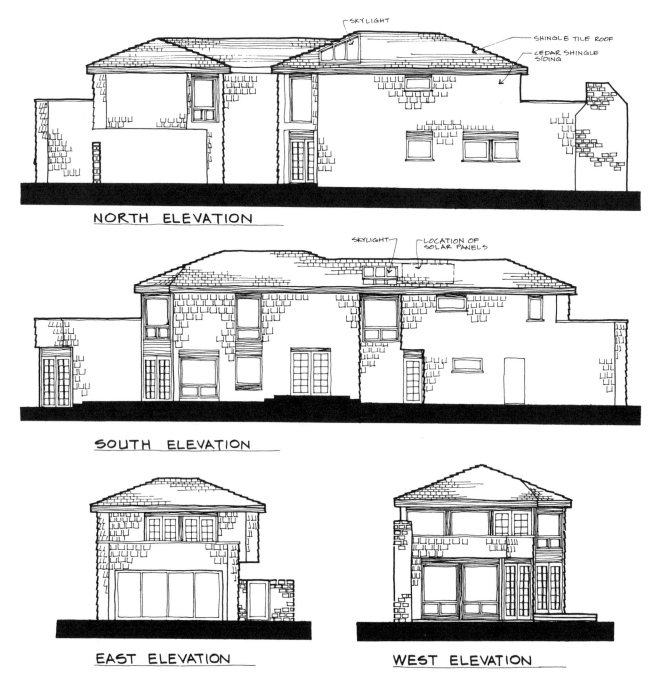

Figure 18.6 Conceptual design—exterior elevations.

The round shapes found around the perimeter are planters. We next included the material designation for brick pavers as well as the wood benches at the back of the lot. We also made a correction in the size of the fireplace at this stage.

The series of close parallel lines at the front and the rear of the building indicated the guardrail around the deck created by a smaller second floor. The very small rectangular pieces attached to these parallel guardrail lines represent scuppers. Scuppers are used for draining

water that accumulates on the deck and are usually made of sheet metal. In this case, they project through an opening in the guardrail and allow the water to drip to the ground. They protrude beyond the surface of the guardrail to stop water from flowing onto the surface of the guardrail.

There are various levels on the ground surface. A look at the final stage of the building section (Figure 18.34) shows the different heights. The area adjacent to the family room is the highest; the property slopes downward to

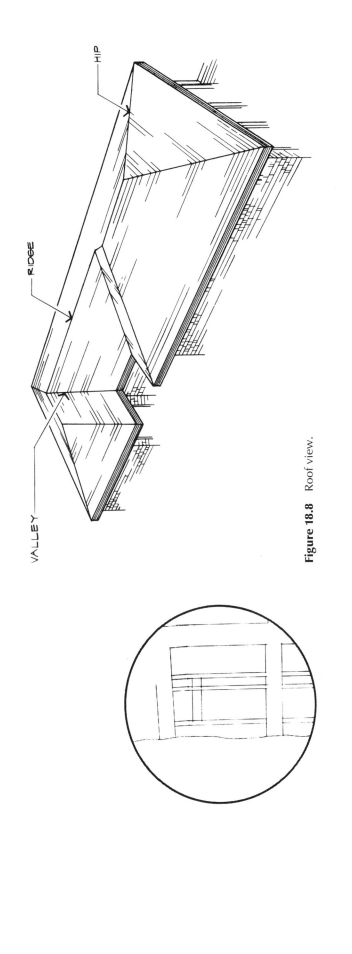

Figure 18.8 Roof view.

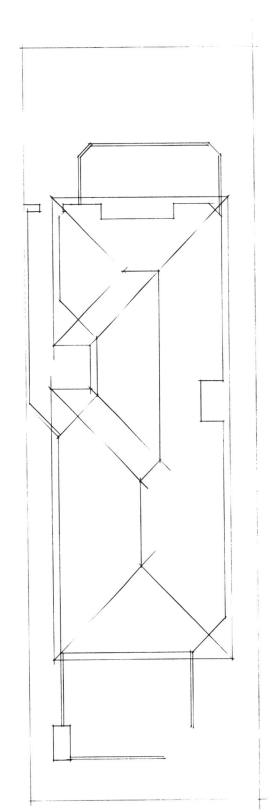

Figure 18.7 Site plan—Stage II.

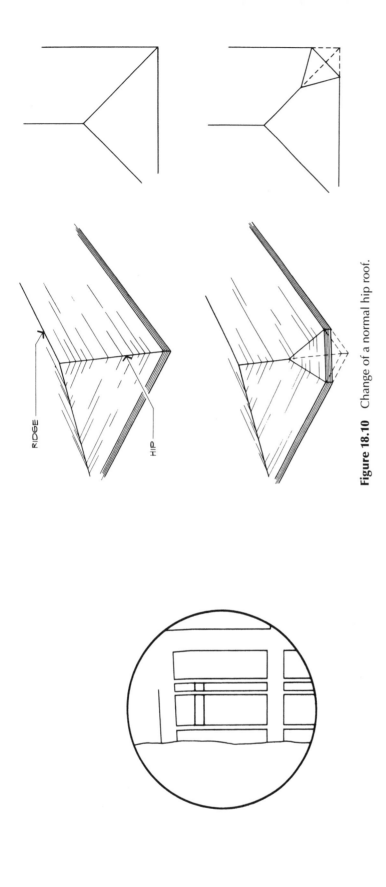

RIDGE

HIP

Figure 18.10 Change of a normal hip roof.

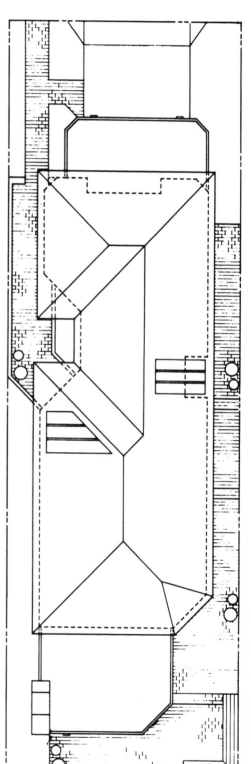

Figure 18.9 Site plan—Stage III.

the rear and to the front from here. The lot slopes up again on the other side of the private road.

Stage IV

Relocating the Vicinity Map. A check at this point showed that the vicinity map was in an inconvenient location. (See Figure 18.7). The general notes and sheet index still had to be located on this sheet. It was better to have the index on the right-hand side opposite the binding edge where it is more accesible. So the vicinity map was moved, but not redrawn. (See Figure 18.11). We did this as follows:

1. A new sheet of vellum was placed over the original sheet.
2. With the use of a mat knife and a straightedge, both sheets were cut in half lengthwise at the same time.
3. The upper half of the original sheet was replaced with the newly cut vellum and taped on the reverse side with transparent tape.
4. The original half sheet containing the vicinity map was placed over this newly assembled drawing in the now desired position.
5. Another cut around the vicinity map and through the two sheets of vellum was then made.
6. The cutout of the vicinity map was then taped in the new location with transparent tape on the reverse side.

The vicinity map was then finished by shading the subject property and identifying adjoining streets and the Pacific Ocean.

Setbacks, Improvements, and Notes. The setbacks— that is, the dimensions needed to locate the structure— were then added to the site plan. All improvements were dimensioned next. These improvements were located from the property line or the building itself. The direction of the slope of the roof, the decks, and even such areas as the driveway we indicated by arrows and/or notes.

Notes were next to be added, and we used broad general terms. Utility lines were shown. Notice the abbreviation "P.O.C." (point-of-connection) to the various utility lines. The sewer line is marked with an "S", the gas line with a "G", and the water main with a "W". We showed hose bibb locations (garden hose connections) as well as the various steps around the lot.

Reference bubbles for the skylight areas were drawn to refer to a specific detail. Finally, we added the legal description at the extreme right.

Stage V

The final stage for the site plan sheet is shown in Figure 18.12. In the previous stage we nearly finished the site

and roof plan. All that remained was to add roof texture, which we did to show a variety of techniques. Some architectural offices prefer not to invest a drafter's time in this type of activity and leave the roof as it was in the previous stage.

We made a correction to one of the skylights because we found that the exterior wall below forced a separation. Finally, we added the title, North arrow, construction notes, and sheet index. As you can see, the construction notes are not hand lettered, but they could have been. In this case, the notes were typed onto a piece of vellum cut from the larger sheet, then spliced back in when the typing was completed. Other methods already discussed in earlier chapters could have been used to apply the notes to the larger vellum.

■ FOUNDATION PLAN: SLAB

There are two foundation plans shown here, concrete slab and wood floor. These are shown to illustrate their differences and how they are drafted.

Stage I

The computer- and hand-drafted datum stage utilizes the floor plan, because it is usually laid out before the foundation plan. The materials used to build the structure are also studied so as to alert the drafter to the material datum to which the building subscribes. The datum for the building sections will be started after the foundation is evolved, so as to establish the floor and plate lines. If the sections include a cut through the stairs, this will also become a datum as it connects one floor with another.

Stage II

Figure 18.13 shows the layout stage for both the foundation plan and two building sections. The basement retaining wall footing size has been dictated by the fact that the top of the retaining wall is restrained by the concrete floor slab.

The dotted and solid lines of the foundation plan show the shape of the footing and foundation walls. The double solid line around the perimeter of the garage represents a 6" curb that extends above the grade far enough to keep the sill away from termites.

All walls are bearing walls except the two in the laundry room, represented by a pair of dotted lines. The rectangle between the family room and the dining room, drawn with a solid line, represents a step down.

The foundation plan and details are used to figure the shape of the building sections. The horizontal lines between floors in the sections represent the thickness of the slab floor. The three horizontal lines between the lower

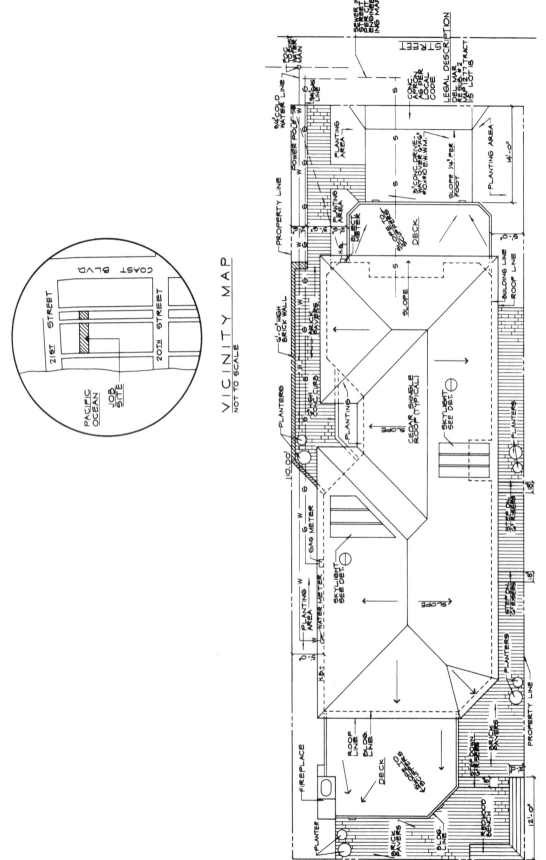

Figure 18.11 Site plan—Stage IV.

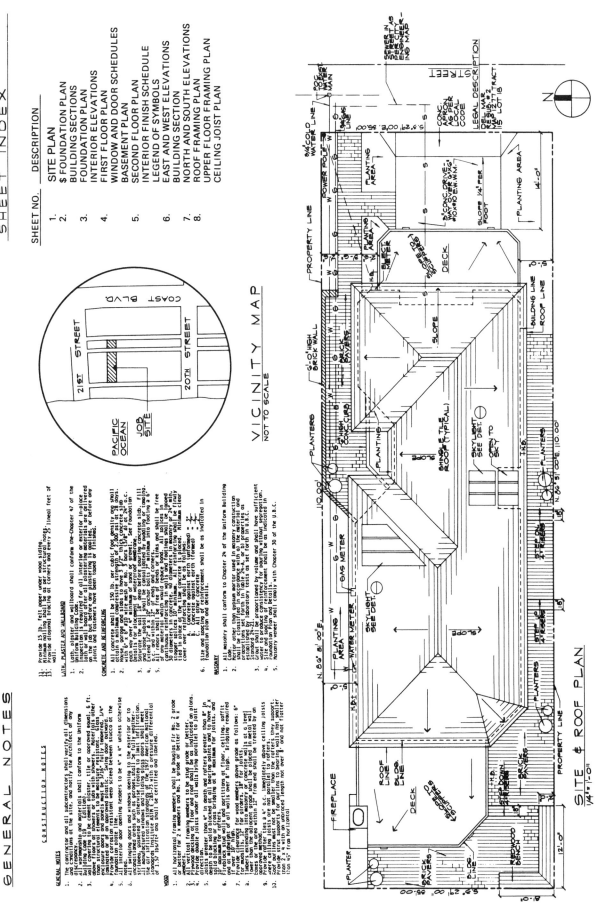

Figure 18.12 Site plan—Stage V.

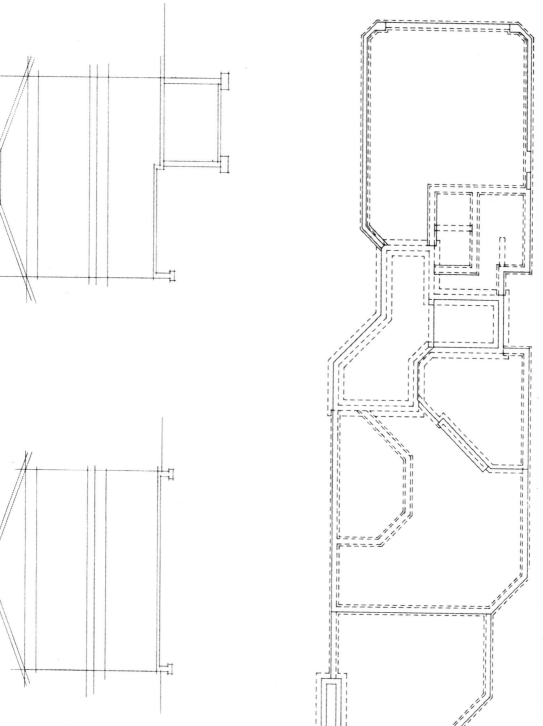

Figure 18.13 Foundation plan (slab)—Stage II, with building sections.

floor and the upper floor are the header (support beam at openings) line for windows and doors, the plate line, and the floor line.

The two lines between the upper floor and the roof are the header line and the plate line. The angular lines represent the rafters. The building section on the left was taken through the dining room and between the kitchen and living room. The other building section was taken through the family room and entry to show the basement and how the entry extends through both floors (this will become visible in the next stages of the drawing).

Stage III

Figure 18.14 shows the beginning of the dimensioning stage for the foundation and the refinement stage for the building sections. These cross-sections could appear on the same sheet as the longitudinal section in order to group similar drawings. However, for learning purposes, the building sections are shown here with the foundation plan.

The sizes for the various members in the building section were obtained from the structural engineer's framing plan. However, with this type of structure, this framing plan could have been done "in house."

Freehand sketches of details help greatly at this stage. See the illustrations in Chapter 16 for architectural details.

The dimensions at the corners of the structure for the angles are not really necessary but they are included to help the contractor. The rectangle at the left top corner is the foundation for the fireplace. Local codes should be checked for fireplace requirements. The dots represent the vertical steel included in earthquake areas. Check the sheets to make sure that every exterior and interior wall (and the foundation under them) can be located from either side. Check for size and location.

Stage IV

Building Sections. At this stage the building sections are being refined. See Figure 18.15. The quality of lines is improved, and the material designations for such items as concrete, masonry, and insulation is the delineation of the structural components such as joists, studs, beams, and rafters. Here we tried to show what the roof would look like based on the precise location of the cutting plane. Rather than seeing the ridge at the top of the building section, the cutting plane exposes this end view of the rafters. We could have taken, instead, an offset section by moving the cutting plane running through the building to expose the most comprehensible structure. If we had done this, we would have exposed the ridge at the top rather than the rafters.

Notice the location of the beam on the left building section and the furred (lowered) ceiling. On the right building section, notice too how the stud goes from almost the ground level to the roof, two stories tall. These are 2×6 studs rather than the normal 2×4 studs because of the increased vertical span. The eaves (intersection of the roof and wall) are closed off by a horizontal member.

Structurally, the building section shows the retaining wall in the basement. Because the slab is pinned (attached) to the outer walls, it stops the walls of the basement from caving inward.

Foundation Plan. This is the stage during which the numerical values are added. The dimensions must coincide with the floor plan. Both *must* be to the stud line. The edge of the concrete foundation wall is also the stud line. Detail reference bubbles are located and the material designation for the masonry in the fireplace is drafted. See Figure 18.15.

Stage V

This is the noting stage—the final stage for both the building sections and the foundation plan. See Figure 18.16.

Sections. We first established vertical distance, which were taken from floor line to plate line. Each room that the building sections cut through is labeled to make its cutting location clear. We next labeled parts of the building: floor, ceilings, and roof coverings, plus special beams, and so forth. Detail reference bubbles, scale, and titles completed this portion of the sheet.

Foundation Plan. After double-checking the dimensions, we put in the building section reference bubbles and their symbols. Notes were added next. These notes take the form of descriptions of the slab, sizes of spread footings, or notes describing the drafter lined, as in the case of the steps. Omission of the waterproof (W.P.) membrane in the garage area was also noted, as was the slope of the slab. The title, scale, and North arrow finished this sheet.

■ FOUNDATION PLAN: WOOD

Both a wood floor and a concrete slab floor system were developed for this beach house. Although preparing two foundation plans for a single project is not customary, it was done here for comparison so that the reader can see the difference in appearance between a wood and a concrete floor. The slab foundation will be used throughout the rest of this set of drawings.

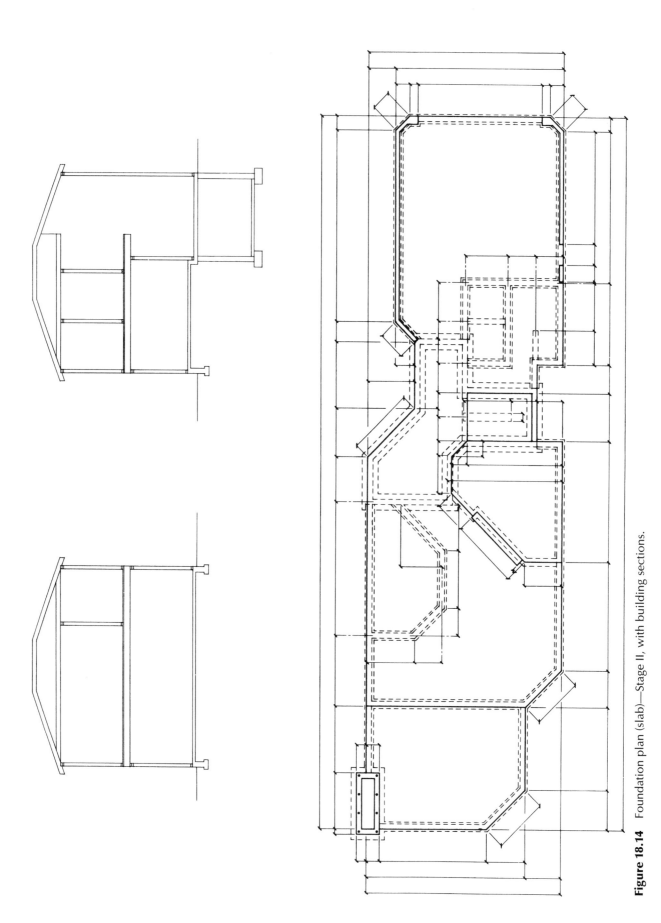

Figure 18.14 Foundation plan (slab)—Stage II, with building sections.

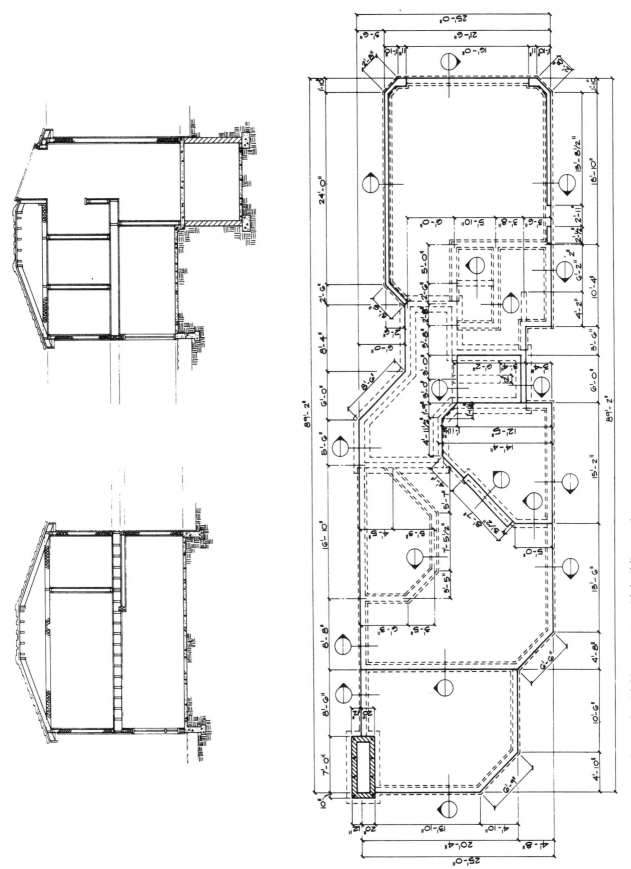

Figure 18.15 Foundation plan (slab)—Stage III, with building sections.

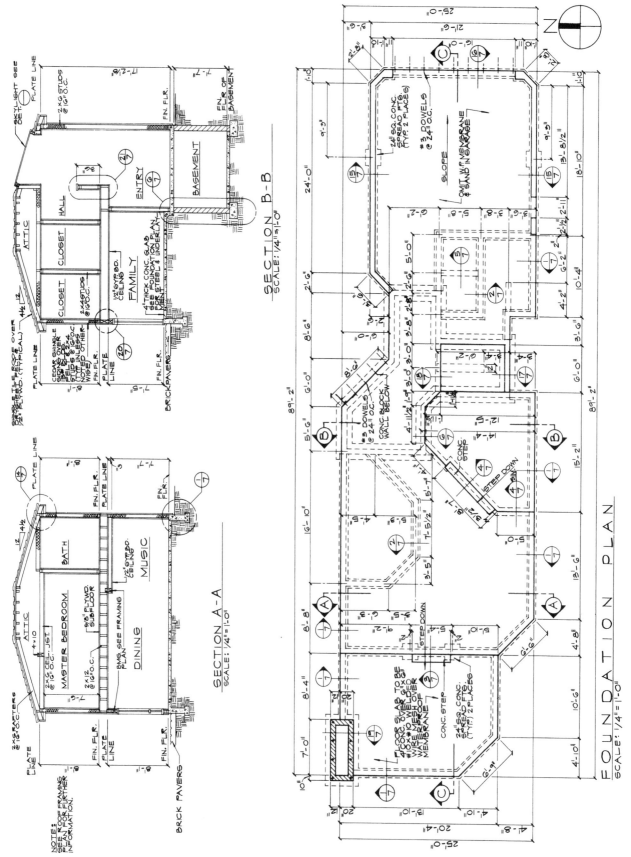

Figure 18.16 Foundation plan (slab)—Stage IV, with building sections.

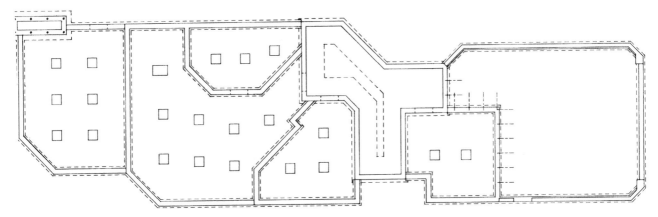

Figure 18.17 Foundation plan (wood)—Stage II.

Stage I

As in the case of the slab-on-ground drawing, the floor plan is the datum sheet and serves two additional purposes. One is for use in the floor plan, and the other is for identifying the load-bearing walls.

Stage II

The layout of the foundation plan (Figure 18.17) was done after the floor plan had been finalized to the point where all exterior and interior walls were established.

The structural considerations should always be analyzed so that the design of the foundation can take those considerations into account. Basically, there were three levels in this structure. On the first floor the rooms are on one level with the exception of the living room near the fireplace and the triangular family room. However, the foundation plan shows four levels: the three already mentioned plus the basement located directly below the entry.

The footing for the basement retaining wall is large because it is not restrained at the top and acts as a full cantilever. The dotted lines in the basement area represent footing shape. The dotted lines do not extend into the area below the hall between the garage and entry; because the leg of the footing is so large that the garage and entry overlap each other, they are treated as a solid mass. The garage is the only area that is a slab on the ground. The double lines around the edge represent the width of the 6″ wall. This extends above the ground to keep the wood sill away from the ground level, protecting it from termites.

The square forms represent the piers. One form, adjacent to the kitchen, is not square but rectangular. Because of the design of this structure, two girders were going to land on this pier, so the pier size was increased.

The rectangular shape at the corner of the living room represents the fireplace and the dots represent the reinforcing bars to be placed vertically. The series of center lines between the laundry room and the garage represents dowels that hold the slab of the garage to the foundation wall of the house.

Note the solid and dotted lines around the perimeter of the foundation walls. The solid line, like the one in the garage, represents a break in the portion that extends above the slab level and is for a door. The dotted lines represent an opening for access from one underfloor area to another. From the basement there is access to any of three underfloor areas. There is also access to the area below the kitchen from the area below the dining room. This access is located where there is no supporting wall or partition. There is also underfloor access near the fireplace.

The basement wall is concrete block and does not follow the block module. We decided to forgo the block module measurement because it was costly and unnecessary for a use this small.

Stage III

A check print was made, on which freehand dimension lines, actual dimensions, notes, and missing items like girders and so on were drawn. See Figure 18.18. This information was then transferred onto the final drawing. The following stages illustrate the placement of the information from the check print.

The space above the foundation plan on this sheet was allocated to the interior elevations. Stage III of the foundation plan also became Stage II of the interior elevations. Stage I is not shown with Stage II. The elevation on the top left is the downstairs bathroom; the one directly to the right is the bathroom on the upper floor; the last two on the right of the top row are the master bath. The three directly below are interior elevations of the kitchen.

The outline of the foundation plan was now confirmed and checked for size. Dimension lines were introduced. Because of the various angles throughout the structure, dimension lines were often crossed by extension lines

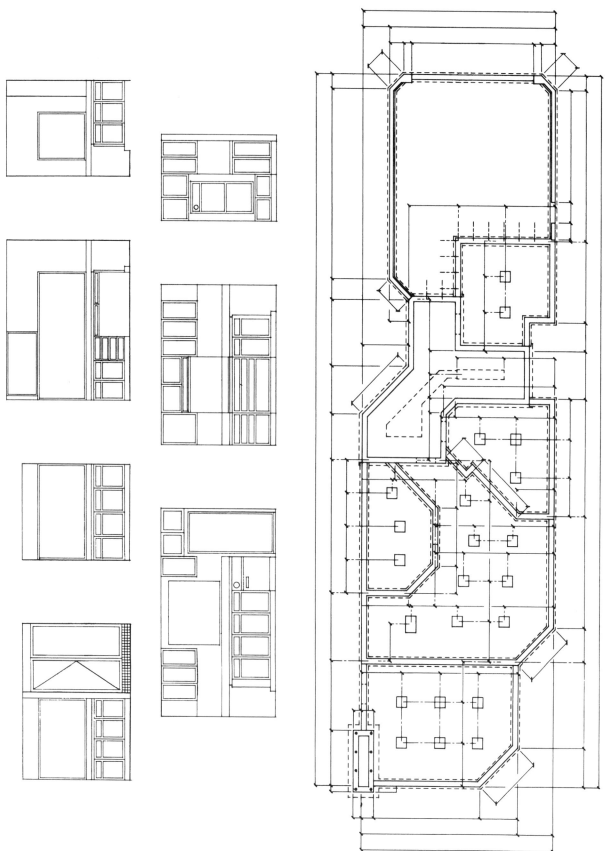

Figure 18.18 Foundation plan (wood)—Stage III, with interior elevations.

and other dimension lines. The extension lines on the bottom left corner were broken for the dimension lines. We did this because dimension lines take precedence over extension lines.

Girders were overlooked and were added at a later stage. For the drafting of piers and girders, see Chapter 9. A final correction that might be made later using this stage for comparison is a wall that separates the two sets of stairs. The dotted lines representing the end of the re-taining wall disappear, because the space between the dotted lines is filled with a footing for the new wall. A look at the building sections will explain this better.

Stage IV

Compare Stage III and IV drawings (Figures 18.18 and 18.19) at the stair, and notice the change in the pattern of the hidden lines. Because the walls of the basement and the fireplace were masonry units, the material des-ignation for masonry (diagonal lines) was drafted.

We next added the numbers for the dimensions. See Figure 18.19. These dimensions must always coincide with the floor plan's. We also included reference bubbles for details at this stage. We drew vertical dimension lines on the interior elevations, cleaned up all lines, and drafted additional details such as door swing designa-tions, shelves, and handles on doors and drawers.

Stage V

Interior Elevations.   Here we added material designa-tions such as ceramic tile on interior elevation #1 and kick space material. See Figure 18.20. We deleted the solid line for the refrigerator by using the erasing shield method. The numerical values for the vertical dimension lines were next to be included. We eliminated small cor-rections such as the lines above and below the oven. Fi-nally, we put the notes in. Remember that a set of written specifications is included as part of these construction documents. Our notes, therefore, were general in nature, and descriptive but not specific. Reference bubble num-bers and titles completed this step.

Foundation Plan.   The main difference between this stage and the previous stage was the inclusion of girders (floor beams to support floor joists). They are shown by a very dark center line. Joists are shown by a dark line and arrows (half arrowheads); these show the size, spac-ing, and direction of the floor joists. See Figure 18.20.

The floor joists were running parallel to the garage door in the area of the bathroom, stairs, and entry. The rest of the house—family room, dining room, kitchen, music room, and living room—had floor joists running perpendicular to the garage door.

A rectangle with a single diagonal line indicates the break in the foundation wall between one area and the next. On the computer, the use of hidden lines becomes

cumbersome, because the breaks in the dotted lines do not occur in the proper locations and may mislead the builders in the field. A note on the bottom left explains the drafting system being used. Additional notes about venting were added in the garage area. This would show up in drafted form on the exterior elevation if an exterior elevation of a wood floor system were drafted. Reference bubble num-bers, title, scale, and North arrow complete this drawing.

■ FIRST FLOOR PLAN

Stage I

Stage I uses face-of-stud and center-of-stud walls as a datum. Because the floor plan is the first construction document to be drawn, care must be taken to establish the correct datum for the materials being used.

Stage II

Although the lines in Figure 18.21 appear dark because of the photographic method used in textbook reproduc-tion, this is actually the light block-out stage. Measure-ments are carefully taken from the preliminary floor plan, verified, and checked against the site plan.

The door jambs of the garage and entry are enlarged to give the illusion of a thicker wall construction. The "U"-shaped area in the kitchen was designed to eventu-ally house a built-in oven. The area with the shower ad-jacent to the laundry room functions as the mud room. Here those coming in from the beach can wash off sand and change out of bathing suits before entering the main portion of the house.

Stage III

At this stage, all equipment was placed in the kitchen and the bathrooms. See Figure 18.22. Note the wet bar between the dining room and the family room. The stairs to the basement and to the upper level are shown. Most important are the level changes that are beginning to show between the living room and dining room and the dining room and family room, and the slight change be-tween the garage and the house. Windows and doors around the perimeter were also located. The wall lines were darkened. Sepia copies were made for the struc-tural, mechanical, and electrical consultants.

Stage IV

Figure 18.23 shows the preliminary layout stage for the window and door schedules. The format is normally es-tablished by office standards. This format follows the AIA standard with allowances for specific structures. This in-formation usually comes from the designer and/or architect.

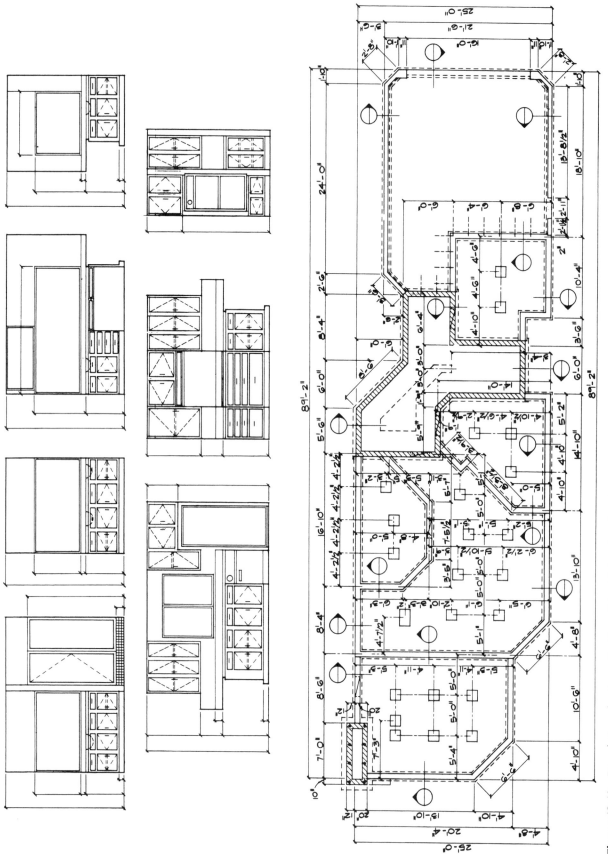

Figure 18.19 Foundation plan (wood)—Stage IV, with interior elevations.

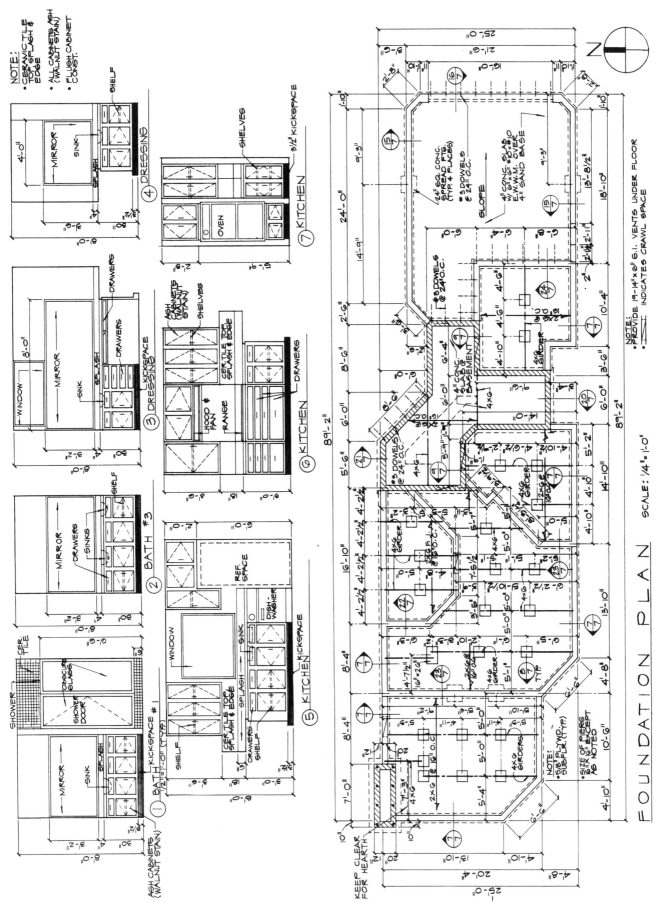

Figure 18.20 Foundation plan (wood)—Stage V, with interior elevations.

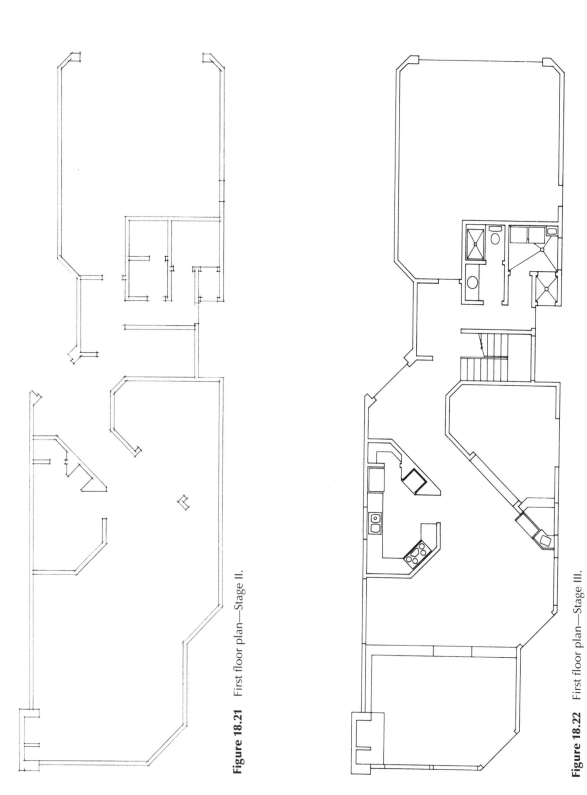

Figure 18.21 First floor plan—Stage II.

Figure 18.22 First floor plan—Stage III.

This is also the preliminary stage for the basement plan. The basement is made of concrete block but is so small it will not follow the block module. Had the area been larger, a standard block module would have been used. The basement area was designed to house the boiler for the solar collectors and the mechanical equipment for space heating.

This is a critical step in the plan because it is the dimension line stage. This step also includes variations of line quality because while the dimension lines must be precise, they must not take away from the main body of the drawing. Every wall and partition must be located and every door and window must be sized. See Chapter 10, on floor plans, for a method for wood structures.

The measurements on the angular walls were included to help the contractor check accuracy. These dimensions must not only be graphically correct but trigonometrically correct as well. Because of the many angles, many dimension lines may cross each other. This crossing should be kept to a minimum.

Electrical fixtures are also shown. This floor plan eventually incorporated a complete electrical plan. Larger buildings, however, often have a separate electrical plan.

At this stage, dimensioning could be established by indicating the dimensions directly on a check print of the floor plan. Door and window designations were also added at this stage.

Stage V

The window and door schedules were now due to be finished. See Figure 18.24. Remember that each door and window described is different. The schedules do not list every single door and window, just each different type of door or window. For example, the #2 window is used frequently in the plan, but is only listed once in the schedule.

Fixed windows are also listed here because they are manufactured and brought to the job. If fixed windows are built on the job site, the size is dimensioned on the exterior elevation and not listed on the schedule. The identification numbers for windows and doors found in the "SYM" (symbol) column of the schedule were put into reference bubbles on the plan. Because both the plan and the schedules were on the same sheet, the reference bubbles did not need to be divided into halves to show the sheet number.

Manufacturers' numbers and brand names are not on this sheet. These will be included on the specifications. However, switches to electrical outlet lines were included at this stage.

On the door schedule, the abbreviation "S.C." is for solid core, "H.C." for hollow core, and "P.P.T." for polished plate tempered. Some schedules also use numbers for doors and letters for windows.

Stage VI

Corrections were made on the schedules after checking with the senior drafter. Room titles were now included on the floor plan. See Figure 18.25. Various pieces of equipment such as the range, oven, and sink were described, as were other parts of the structure such as closets, garage doors, lift counter for the bar, and so on. The titles are general and do not include the construction method, finish, or function. Naturally, the dimensions were checked again and corrections made where necessary. Titles, scale, and North arrow completed this sheet.

■ SECOND FLOOR PLAN

Stage I

The first stage is, of course, that of establishing a datum. What makes structures with multiple floors unique is the multitude of datums. In the case of this two-story structure, we must consider a vertical datum as well as the normal horizontal ones. Along with wall alignment (load-carrying walls), we have stairs that link the two floors. As described in Chapter 16, the total rise and run of the stairway must be defined early in the development stage. The riser and tread design as described in the companion book, *The Professional Practice of Architectural Detailing* by the same authors and publisher, should be consulted for a better understanding of the proportion of treads to risers and how they are detailed for different building materials.

Stage II

The upper floor plan has many walls that align themselves with the walls below on the ground floor. Therefore, the light blockout of the upper floor plan (Figure 18.26) was done by first overlaying the vellum on top of the ground floor plan and using the information from the preliminary floor plan, or by using multiple layers.

The exterior walls, stairs, entry, and fireplace were good locations to register one drawing with another. Check the preliminary upper floor plan (Figure 18.5) for various room names. Note the deck areas, the upper entry area (the entry is two stories high), the cantilever (overhang without support) of one of the bedrooms near the entry, and the two walk-in wardrobe closets in the master bedroom.

Stage III

Figure 18.27 shows the stage at which bathroom equipment, closet poles, stairs, and several windows were located and the handrail around the opening at the upper

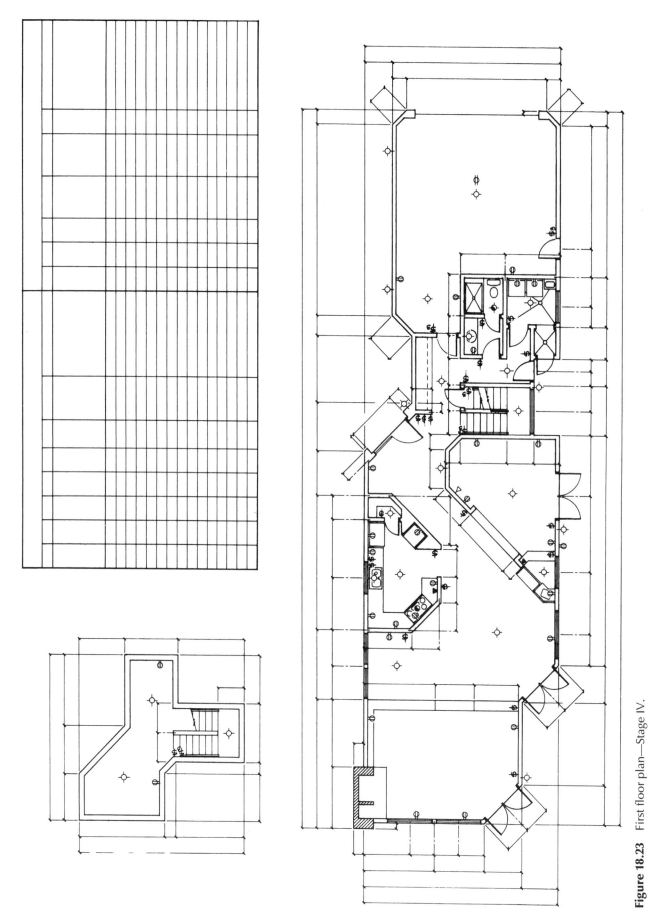

Figure 18.23 First floor plan—Stage IV.

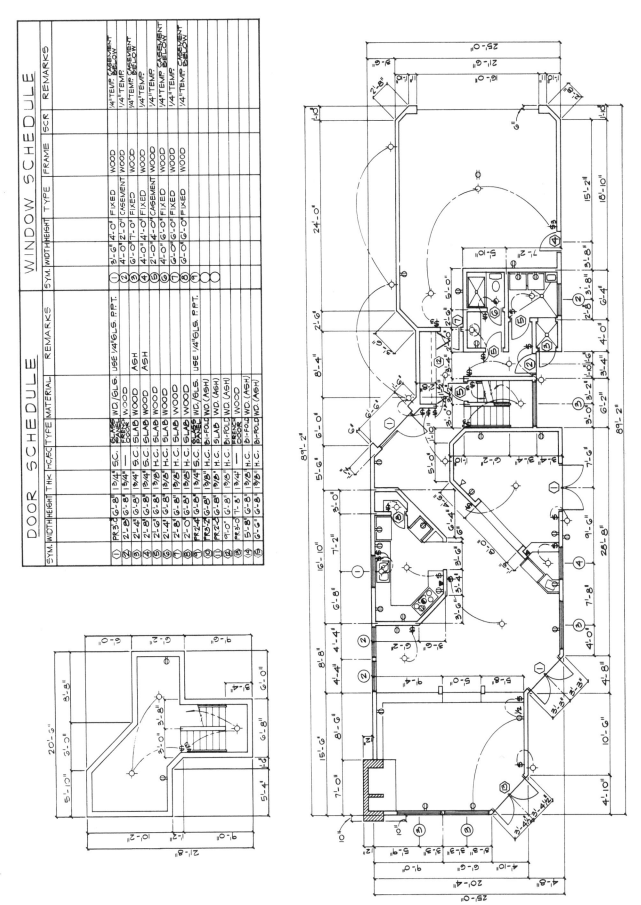

Figure 18.24 First floor plan—Stage V.

569

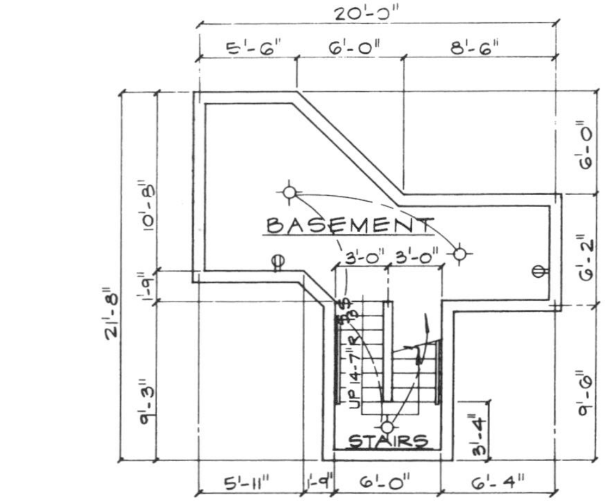

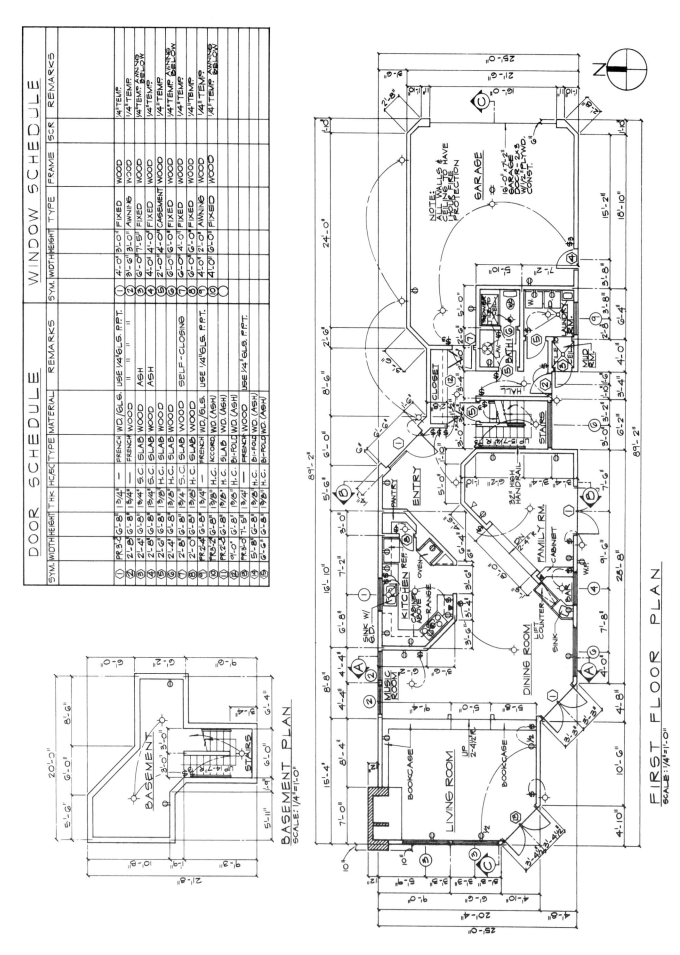

BASEMENT PLAN
SCALE: 1/4"=1'-0"

DOOR SCHEDULE								WINDOW SCHEDULE						
SYM.	WIDTH	HEIGHT	THK	HC/SC	TYPE	MATERIAL	REMARKS	SYM.	WIDTH	HEIGHT	TYPE	FRAME	SCR	REMARKS
1	PR.3'-0"	6'-8"	1 3/4"	—	FRENCH	WD./GLS.	USE 1/4" GLS. P.P.T.	1	4'-0"	3'-0"	FIXED	WOOD		1/4" TEMP.
2	2'-8"	6'-8"	1 3/4"	—	FRENCH	WOOD	" " " "	2	3'-6"	3'-0"	AWNING	WOOD		1/4" TEMP.
3	2'-4"	6'-8"	1 3/4"	S.C.	SLAB	WOOD	ASH	3	6'-0"	7'-5"	FIXED	WOOD		1/4" TEMP. AWNING BELOW
4	2'-8"	6'-8"	1 3/4"	S.C.	SLAB	WOOD	ASH	4	4'-0"	4'-0"	FIXED	WOOD		1/4" TEMP.
5	2'-6"	6'-8"	1 3/8"	H.C.	SLAB	WOOD		5	2'-0"	4'-0"	CASEMENT	WOOD		1/4" TEMP.
6	2'-4"	6'-8"	1 3/8"	H.C.	SLAB	WOOD		6	6'-0"	6'-0"	FIXED	WOOD		1/4" TEMP. AWNING BELOW
7	2'-8"	6'-8"	1 3/4"	S.C.	SLAB	WOOD	SELF-CLOSING	7	6'-0"	4'-0"	FIXED	WOOD		1/4" TEMP.
8	2'-0"	6'-8"	1 3/8"	H.C.	SLAB	WOOD		8	6'-0"	6'-0"	FIXED	WOOD		1/4" TEMP.
9	PR.2'-4"	6'-8"	1 3/4"	—	FRENCH	WD./GLS.	USE 1/4" GLS. P.P.T.	9	4'-0"	2'-0"	AWNING	WOOD		1/4" TEMP.
10	PR.3'-2"	6'-8"	1 3/8"	H.C.	ACCORD.	WD. (ASH)		10	4'-0"	6'-0"	FIXED	WOOD		1/4" TEMP. AWNING BELOW
11	PR.2'-0"	6'-8"	1 3/8"	H.C.	SLAB	WD. (ASH)								
12	9'-0"	6'-8"	1 3/8"	H.C.	BI-FOLD	WD. (ASH)								
13	PR.3'-0"	7'-5"	1 3/4"	—	FRENCH	WOOD	USE 1/4" GLS. P.P.T.							
14	5'-8"	6'-8"	1 3/8"	H.C.	BI-FOLD	WD. (ASH)								
15	6'-6"	6'-8"	1 3/8"	H.C.	BI-FOLD	WD. (ASH)								

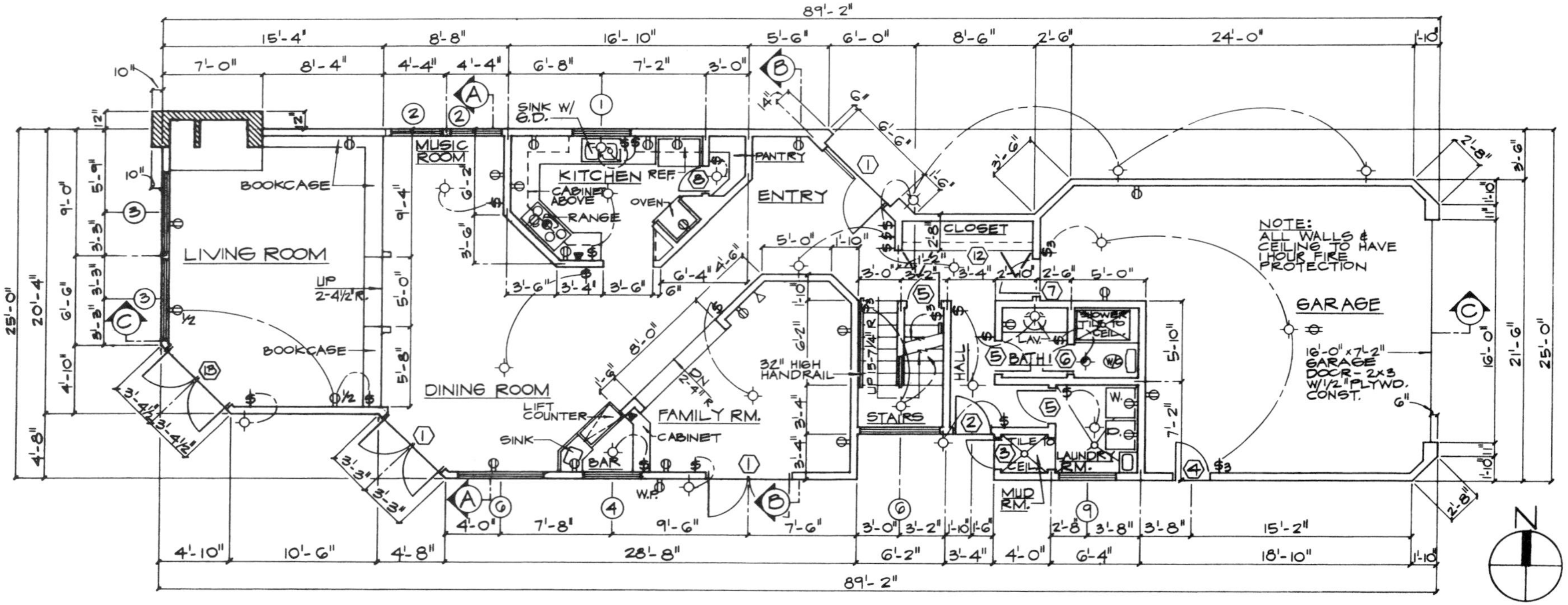

FIRST FLOOR PLAN
SCALE: 1/4"=1'-0"

Figure 18.25 First floor plan—Stage VI.

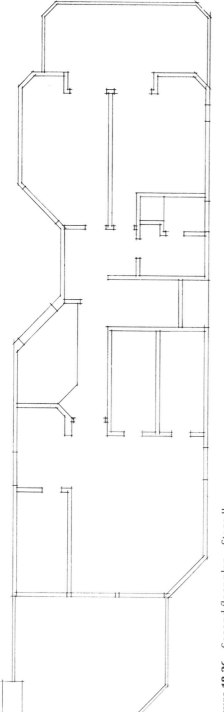

Figure 18.26 Second floor plan—Stage II.

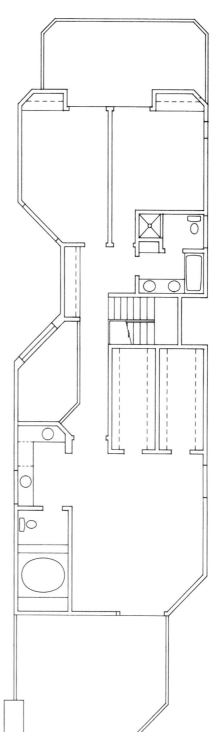

Figure 18.27 Second floor plan—Stage III.

entry was drawn. Hard lines were drawn for the walls and the intersecting corners were cleaned up with an eraser. The rectangle adjacent to the sunken tub is a planter. A planter over the entry would be added later.

Stage IV

A chart, called the finish schedule, for the description of the finish on the various wall and floor surfaces was begun in the top left corner. To the right of the finish schedule is the legend for the various symbols used, such as electrical outlets, switches, and telephone jacks. See Figure 18.28.

We added dimension lines to the floor plan. As with the foundation plan, the dimension lines were not done initially on this plan but rather were done freehand on a check print, checked for accuracy, and transferred to this sheet.

We decided to incorporate the electrical plan into the floor plan. So we included switches, outlets, duplex convenience outlets, and so on, here. Doors and windows were also completed. Compare this drawing with the final stage (Figure 18.30) and determine whether any dimensions were changed or corrected.

Stage V

The symbol legend, showing various symbols used on the floor plan, was now finished. See Figure 18.29. The interior finish schedule was partly finished. Window and door numbers were included on the floor plan. We also placed two smoke detectors in the hall.

After discussion with the clients, we decided to use bifold doors rather than sliding doors into the master bath. We changed the wall that separates the stairs. This change then affected the foundation plan. See Stage III of the foundation plan, Figure 18.14. The electrical switch to outlet lines were also included at this stage.

Finally, we added dimensions. These dimensions had to be checked against those on the lower floor plan. It is always important to check walls that line up under one another.

Stage VI

We then filled in the interior finish schedule on a check print, based on consultation with the clients. The information was then transferred to this sheet. See Figure 18.30.

We added notes at this stage, which included titles and necessary area descriptions. As with the ground floor plan, the notes are general in nature and do not describe construction methods, workmanship, or installation requirements that are described in the specifications. Addition of the main title completed this sheet.

■ BUILDING SECTION/ELEVATIONS

Because of the available space, the longitudinal section and two of the narrow elevations were combined. Many of the lines drawn on the first stages should be lightly identified in pencil and later erased, or done on a separate construction layer.

Stage I

This will be the datum setting stage for both the elevation and the building section. See Figure 18.31. The datum for the building section is threefold. It establishes measurements vertically from floor-to-floor and then to the plate line, as well as for the horizontal measurements from wall-to-wall. Because the positioning of the stairs is critical at this stage, we have isolated this area with a cloud (not actually drawn) to accent its importance. For the elevation, the building section datum becomes its datum.

Stage II

With the datum established in Stage I, both the building sections and the elevations are ready for outlining the roof shape, the precise location of the stairs and their handrails, and the footing shape. See Figure 18.32. The positioning of the walls and balconies can be done on the elevations. In fact, the building section of this drawing coordinates the first floor plan with the second floor plan, and the roof plan with the preliminary details or structural decisions that have already been made.

Stage III

Building Section. Compare the stair footing area in Figure 18.33 with the foundation plan (slab) in Figure 18.16. A basement wall between the stairs was now included. All interior and exterior walls were also outlined using Western frame construction, and the location of walls and guardrails was taken from the floor plan.

The upper floor level was definitely established as were the various horizontal members. Specific sizes of these members were obtained from the structural engineer, architect, or another supervisor. All of the lines were cleaned up and darkened.

Elevations. The previous stage had established all of the horizontal lines. This stage now produced all the vertical and angular roof lines. The vertical lines were obtained from the floor plans. The elevation on the left side now begins to show a cantilever. The elevation on the right begins to show the exterior form of the fireplace. Both elevations also begin to show the outline of the balcony and the roof forms.

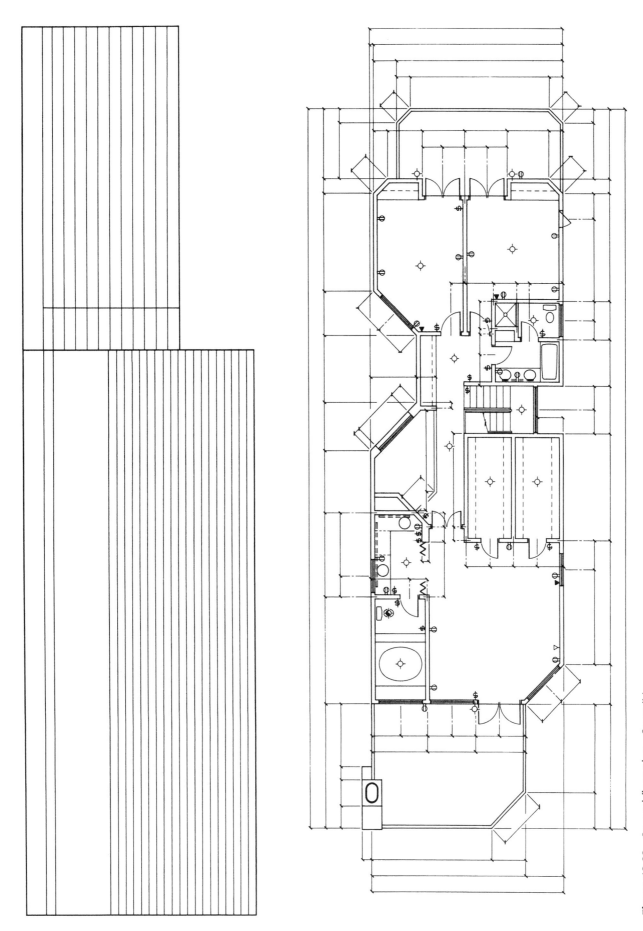

Figure 18.28 Second floor plan—Stage IV.

573

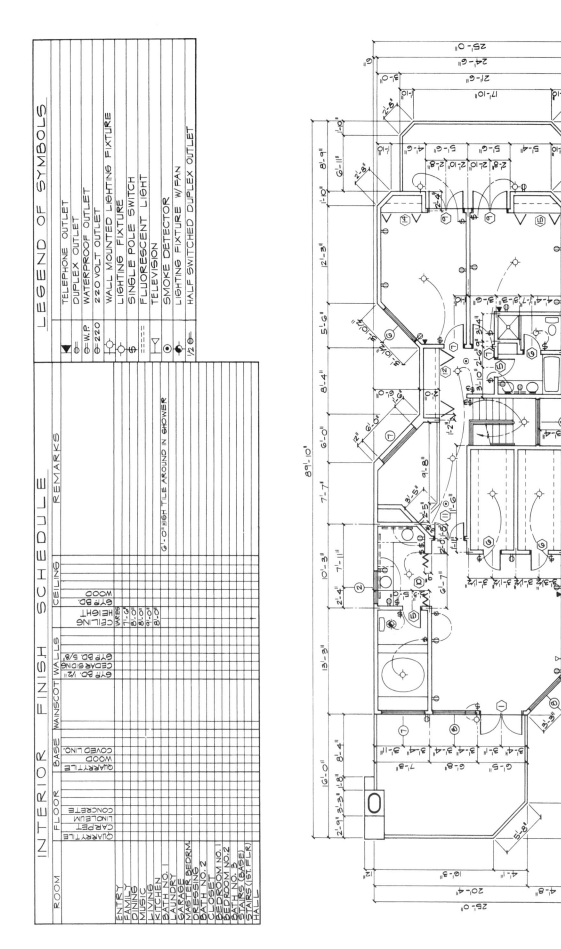

Figure 18.29 Second floor plan—Stage V.

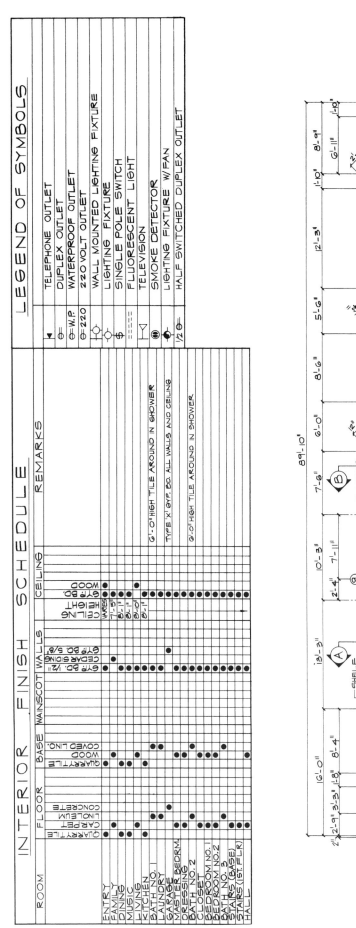

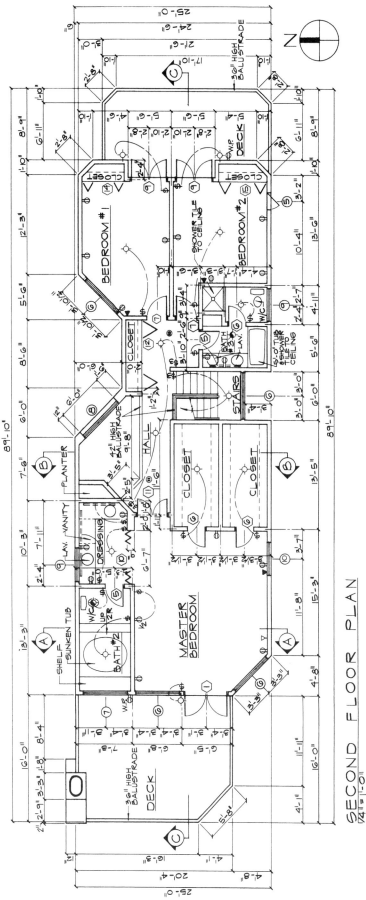

Figure 18.30 Second floor plan—Stage VI.

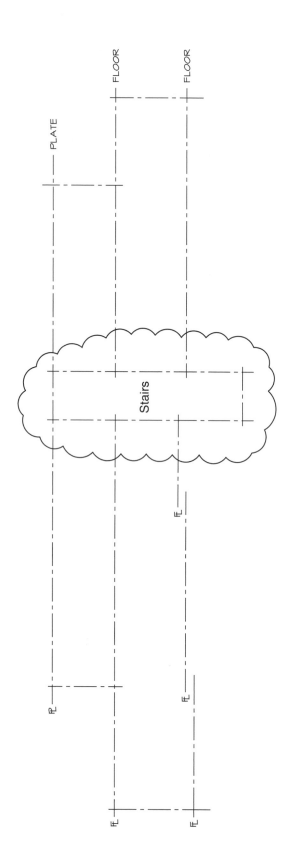

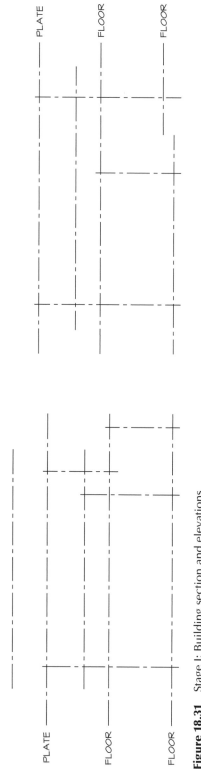

Figure 18.31 Stage I: Building section and elevations.

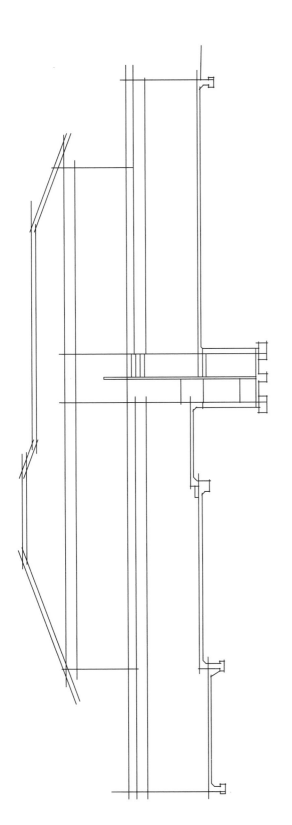

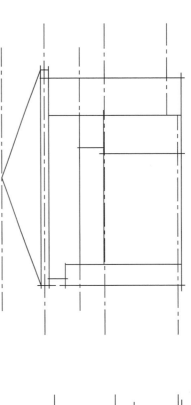

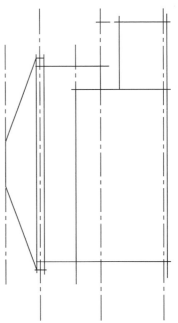

Figure 18.32 Stage II: Building section and elevations.

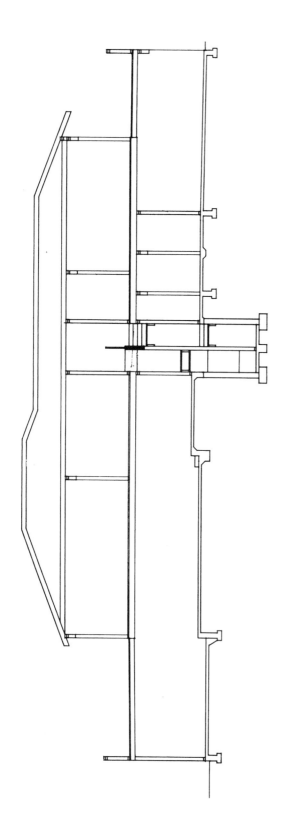

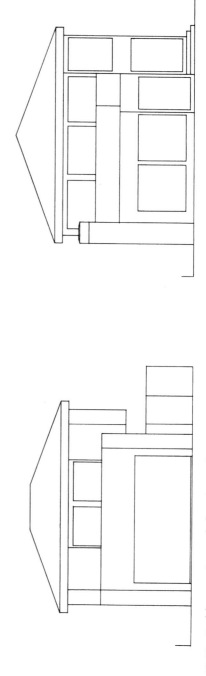

Figure 18.33 Building section and elevations—Stage III.

A drawing of a roof can be constructed from scratch, like a building section, or the shape can be obtained from the building section itself. Still another way is to orthographically project it from the roof plan, if such a drawing is available. Note that all of the horizontal lines that were drafted in the first stage do not appear here. They are there, but drafted so lightly that the reproduction process did not print them.

Stage IV

Building Section. All of the individual members were drafted in at this stage. Of particular interest is the top of the roof. See Figure 18.34. Examine the second floor plan (Figure 18.30) or the roof framing plan (Figure 18.41). These show where this actual section slice was taken.

The ridge, especially at the left, is missed by the slice and therefore shows the rafters coming forward. An offset section would pick up the ridge, but we decided to show a straight slice. Not shown is the ridge behind sloping up and receding away. You should refer to the details relevant to this structure that are found in Chapter 16. These details, such as footing details, guardrails, and eave details, help explain, in an enlarged form, some of the critical areas in the structure.

Material designations—earth, concrete block, concrete, and shingle tile—were added at this stage.

Elevations. Material designations for the roof, the surface of the wall, and the masonry units were drafted. The total surface material is *not* shown. There is, however, enough shown to identify the material and to help the profiling, which was also completed at this stage. Windows and door shapes were confirmed from the manufacturer's literature and drawn accurately.

Stages V and VI

The dimensioning and noting stages were combined, thus making this the final stage.

Exterior Elevations. Vertical dimensions were referred to the building section for the sake of clarity and to avoid duplication. See Figure 18.35. The hidden lines designating the swing of doors and windows were drafted, together with the divisions (called lights) in the french doors. Various notes were placed on the elevations to identify such items as the fascia, shingles, gate, and garage door.

Building Section. Vertical heights were established based on the type of framing chosen and the head clearance required by local code. We obtained basic framing member sizes and noted them from the structural engineering drawings. You should look at this drawing (Section C-C in Figure 18.35) together with the foundation plan and roof framing plan. Together, they answer many questions. Detail references, room titles, drawing title, and scale finished this drawing.

■ EXTERIOR ELEVATIONS

Stage I

Before starting the exterior elevations, you should always carefully study two drawings—the floor plans and building sections—and use the building section as a datum. The floor plans give the width and length of the structure. In this case, the upper floor is not the same size as the lower floor. The building section establishes all the heights.

In Figure 18.36, the heights were laid out lightly first and then identified lightly in pencil. The elevations to be drawn here were the North and South elevations. Looking at the upper (North) elevation, the first two lines at the bottom of the layout are floor lines. The next two lines above these are the header lines (tops of windows). And above these, two lines run the full width of the sheet. The lower is the plate line and the upper is the floor line for the second floor. The next short line is the top of the guardrail on the balcony.

The next two long lines above the guardrail line are the header line and plate line, respectively. Finally, the two top lines are the ridge of the roof. These should usually be lightly drawn in.

The lower (South) elevation resembles the upper, but the lines are reversed (left becomes right and right becomes left) because the elevation being drafted is a view in the opposite direction. Another difference is the variation in the floor lines and header lines for the first floor in the South elevation.

Stage II

Study Figure 18.37. This is the stage that gave the exterior elevation shape. The floor plan was used to locate exterior wall lines and windows, and the roof plan was used to help define the outline of the roof.

Stage III

At this stage, shown in Figure 18.38, lines were polished. Notice the extremely dark line at the bottom of the exterior elevations and the dark lines around the perimeter of the structure as well as those defining the changes of plane. Texture was added to the roof as well as to the walls. We did not waste time covering the entire surface of the wall or roof with the texture; we did only the perimeter to help the profile lines. The wall material

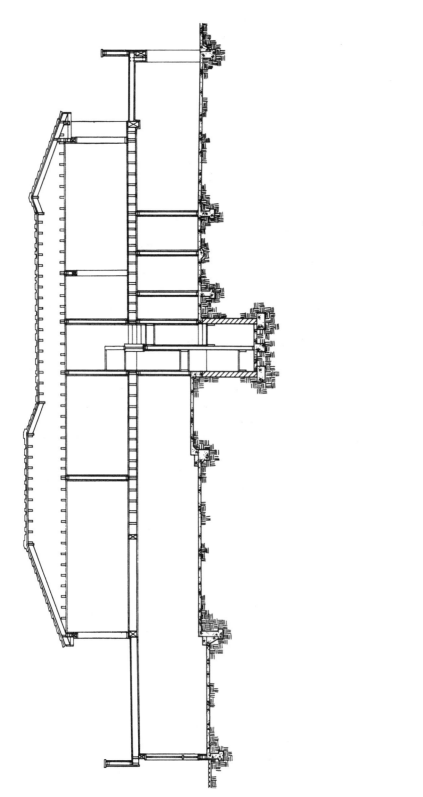

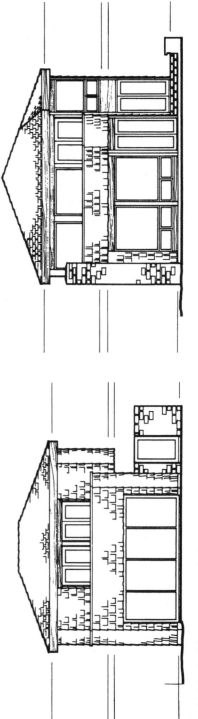

Figure 18.34 Building section and elevations—Stage IV.

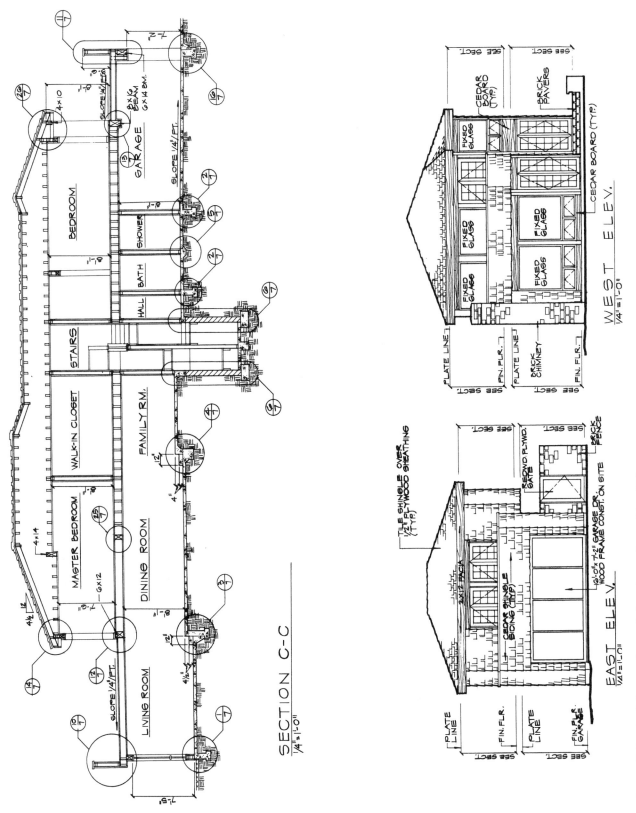

Figure 18.35 Building section and elevations—Stages V and VI.

Figure 18.36 Exterior elevations—Stage I.

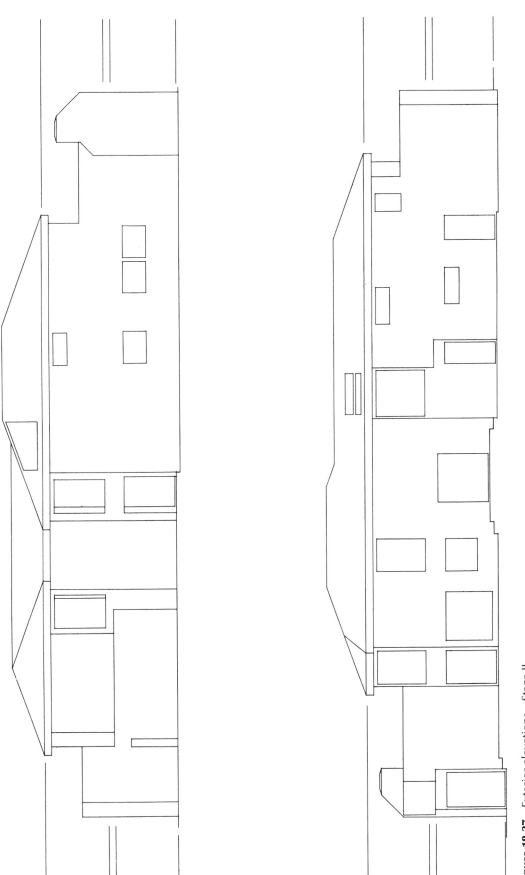

Figure 18.37 Exterior elevations—Stage II.

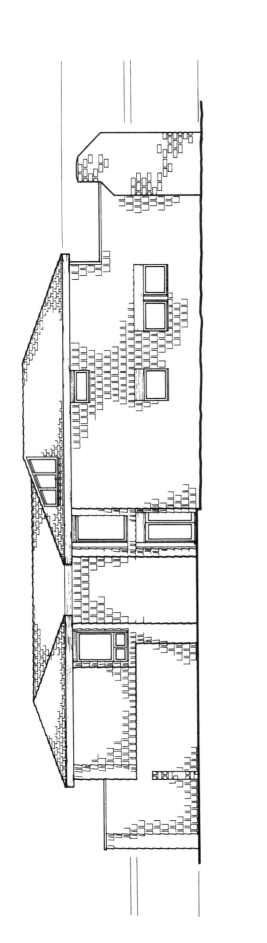

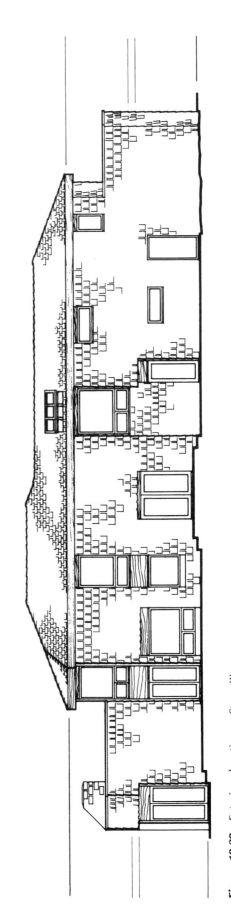

Figure 18.38 Exterior elevations—Stage III.

shown is cedar shingles and the roof material, tile shingles. Wood graining of the exposed lintel was used above the doors and windows.

Stage IV

Vertical dimensions in Figure 18.39 refer to the building sections. A special note is also included to direct the reader to the building sections for dimensions. All callouts are generic in nature and depend on the specifications for specific material, quality, size, and workmanship. Roof material and wall surface material are called out with such identifying notes as "chimney," "wall," and "fixed glass." Finally, the title and scale were drawn. Note location for future solar panels.

■ FRAMING PLAN

Stage I

Prior to drafting a framing plan we needed to make a number of decisions. These included approach, size, and method. First, we need to decide on our approach—that is, whether to use directional arrowheads or actually draft each framing member. Both approaches are shown in Figure 18.40. Scale (size) was the second major decision. Available sheet size and clarity were the deciding factors here. Third, we had to decide on method. We needed to draft a framing plan over a sepia copy of the specific plan involved.

First Floor and Second Floor Plans.   There are three plans here. The top left is the first floor plan showing the floor framing for the second floor. The drawing adjacent to it is a floor plan for the second floor which indicates the ceiling joists for the second floor. The largest of the three plans shows the second floor plan with the roof framing plan.

In our office, the two smaller plans could have been drafted from scratch or the specific floor plan involved could have been reduced photographically or by a plain paper copier onto vellum.

On the small framing plans, we decided to demonstrate the abbreviated method of showing the members, that is, drafting of all beams and headers but not all joists. The floor and ceiling joists are shown by a dimension-type line using a half arrowhead on each end. Beams are drafted showing the actual thickness of the members, and headers are shown over windows and doors as a center-line type line.

Second Floor with Roof Framing Plan.   On the roof framing plan, headers are shown as center lines, beams are drafted to actual size, and the ridge, hip rafters, and

valley members are drafted showing their full size. A hip rafter rests on the corner of the structure and is held in place by the forces from the rafters coming against it from either side. Rafters themselves are drafted with a center-line type line.

All exterior walls and interior bearing walls are drafted solid (i.e., using solid lines). All nonbearing walls are drafted using dotted lines.

Three things make this roof unique. First, the framing around the skylights. The skylight above the entry area (see the floor plan for roof description) is a single opening while the one over the stair area is two skylights. The framing around the skylights is not too unlike the opening for a roof access or an opening for an interior chimney.

Most corners of structures have 90° corners. One conventional framing for such a corner is to bisect the 90° corner with a hip rafter. A good example of such framing can be found at the corner where the master bathroom tub is found.

A variation can be found on the opposite corner where the wall angles at 45°. Here, we actually have two corners with a hip rafter near the ridge. This hip rafter joins other members, which in turn bisect the 45° corners. This creates a weak spot in the roof. To strengthen it, 4 × 4 posts are added to the wall and a beam is installed parallel to the 45° wall. Two additional 4 × 4 posts are placed on top of this beam to support the members that bisect the 45° bend in the wall.

If you look carefully, you can tell when a beam sits on a post or a post on a beam. If the beam sits on a post, you will see the two parallel lines that simulate the beam drafted over the post. If the post sits on top of the beam, the lines of the beam stop short of the post.

The use of a roof with a normal 90° angle over walls at 45° angles is also unique. This condition called for cantilevered beams that protrude from the wall parallel to the roof to form a 90° intersection which supports the roof. These beams enter deeply into the wall of the structure. This construction was used in a number of places, as you can see on the framing plan for the roof.

Stage II

To better understand the three drawings in Figure 18.41, look at the final stage of the building section and elevations shown in Figure 18.35. The top left drawing, the second floor framing plan, uses half-arrows to indicate the direction of the various members. A close look at this drawing shows many interesting features. The deck on the left side has 2 × 10 members while the area adjacent has 2 × 12 members. The two-inch difference allows for the difference between the floors of the deck and the inside of the house. The direction of the floor joists changes from one area to another and their spacing also changes.

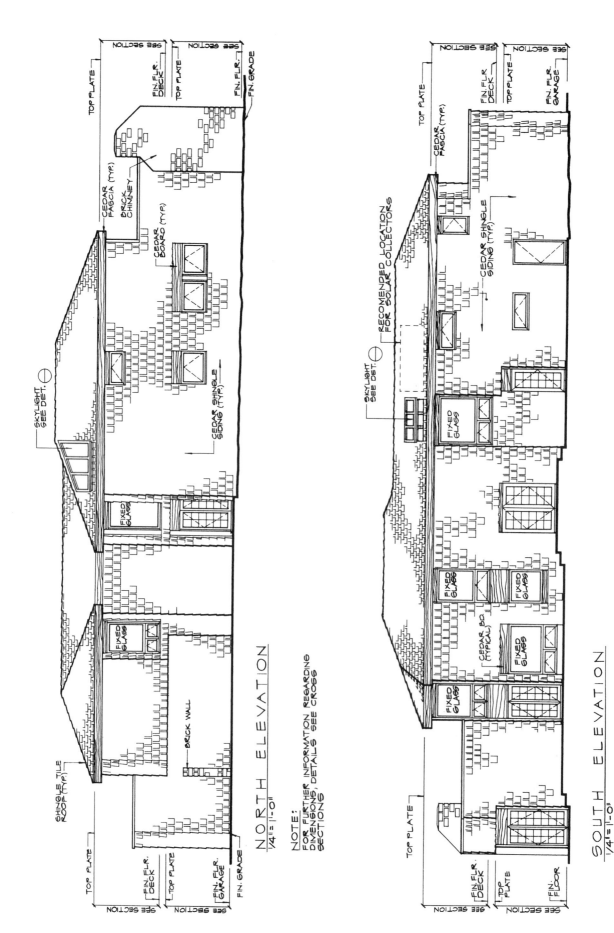

Figure 18.39 Exterior elevations—Stage IV.

NORTH ELEVATION
1/4" = 1'-0"

NOTE:
FOR FURTHER INFORMATION REGARDING DIMENSIONS, DETAILS SEE CROSS SECTIONS

SOUTH ELEVATION
1/4" = 1'-0"

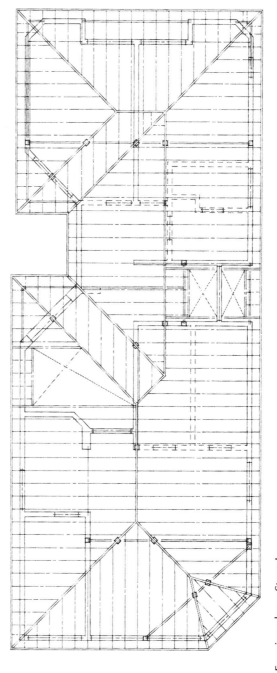

Figure 18.40 Framing plan—Stage I.

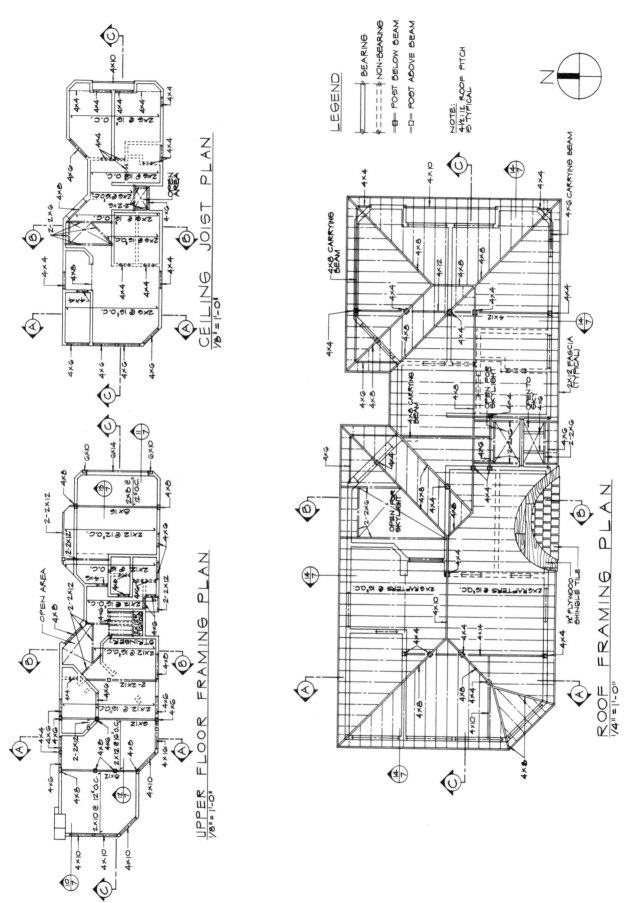

Figure 18.41 Framing plan—Stage II

Open areas are crossed out ("X") as in the entry area. Headers (beams over windows and doors) are also noted throughout the drawing as are certain beams to hold up posts which in turn will hold up the roof. Extremely large sizes were selected for the framing plan because the structure is in an earthquake area, and the roof material is heavy.

Above the garage, the members were again placed perpendicular to the floor joists under the floor of the house. Two things result from this change of direction. First, the floor of the deck can be sloped away from the house for water drainage. Second, the reduced size of the floor joists allows for a larger beam over the garage door without sacrificing head clearance.

The ceiling in the garage is therefore *not* flush as in the living room at the rear. The long building section (Figure 18.35) shows this clearly. The change of spacing of the floor joists above the garage was produced by the distance the joist had to travel: 2×12 at 12" o.c. (on centers) to start and eventually 16" o.c. A hidden line between these shows where the change of spacing took place.

The posts (square forms) drawn throughout must be looked for very carefully. Some are under the floor plan while others are above and often located inside walls of the second floor. Compare the floor plans here with the roof framing plan and you will find many post locations.

We also used the same method the structural engineer used in the roof framing plan to show the location of these posts. If the post is drawn solid with no lines interrupting the perimeter of the post, the post is above. If the lines of the joist or beam are drawn through it, the post is below. See the legend in Figure 18.41. All sizes and locations were obtained from the structural engineer.

The floor joists of the second floor become the ceiling joists of the lower floor. The ceiling joist plan of the upper floor is shown on the top right. We chose to show all of the headers for the second floor on this drawing rather than on the roof framing plan. Of special interest is the framing around openings like the skylights.

On the roof framing plan, the dotted walls are non-bearing and the solid wall lines are load bearing walls. An explanation is given on the legend on the far right.

The framing of the Northwest corner (top left corner of the roof framing plan) is the most typical framing for a hip roof with no special beams needed to carry the weight of the roof. However, such is not the case with the other corners. A careful look at the various corners reveals how the structural engineer designed the beams and posts to carry the weight of this unique roof.

The rafters are all 2×6 at 16" o.c. Title, scale, and North orientation completed this drawing.

CONCEPTUAL DESIGN AND CONSTRUCTION DOCUMENTS FOR A STEEL AND MASONRY BUILDING—THEATRE

■ CONCEPTUAL DESIGN

Site and Client Requirements

The client required a theatre building with six separate auditoriums of 200 seats each. The sloping site of approximately three acres also had stringent architectural restrictions.

The proposed structure, with six auditoriums, office, restrooms, storage and food areas, required approximately 26,000 square feet of area. The seating area dictated the required on-site parking of 400 automobiles.

To satisfy fire requirements, the primary building materials selected were structural steel and concrete block. The concrete block also would provide an excellent sound barrier between the auditorium and the lobby.

The initial concept provided for three auditoriums on each side of a central service core. This core would contain the lobby, toilet facilities, food bar, and storage areas. The core would provide controlled circulation and access to the auditoriums, facilities, and required fire exits. Efficient arrangements for the 200 seats and fire code requirements governed the auditorium dimensions. The wall dimensions also had to be compatible with the concrete block module. The upper floor level would contain the projection rooms, manager's office, employee toilet, and additional storage rooms. Stair location for this upper area was also governed by fire department and building code design criteria.

■ INITIAL SCHEMATIC STUDIES

After programming the basic physical requirements for this proposed project, we began schematic site development.

Stage I

The irregularly shaped site had a West-to-East cross fall averaging 22 feet from the lowest to the highest grade. See Figure 19.1. Complicating the site further was a 25-foot-wide utility easement located near the center of the site. We could not build any of the structure in this easement.

Stage II

In the initial schematic site study, shown in Figure 19.2, the structure is located north of the utility easement on the upper portion of the site. We thought this location would provide the most suitable parking layout for access to the theatre as well as a higher floor elevation for site drainage. The site entrance for automobiles is from the East property line only.

Stage III

After the schematic site development was completed, we designed the scaled preliminary first floor plan (Figure 19.3) and preliminary parking layouts. Client require-

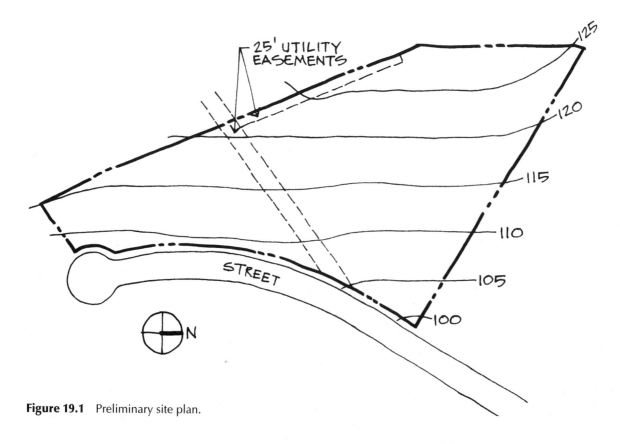

Figure 19.1 Preliminary site plan.

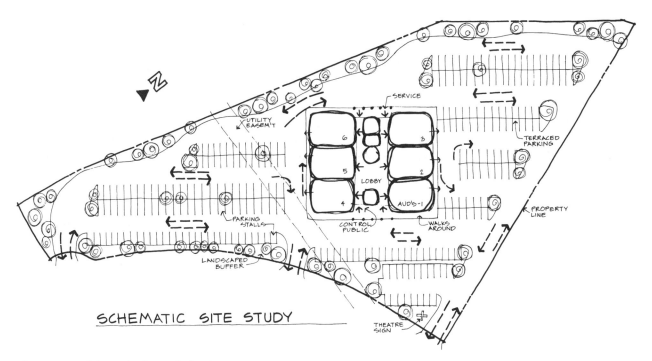

Figure 19.2 Schematic site study for theatre.

SCHEMATIC SITE STUDY

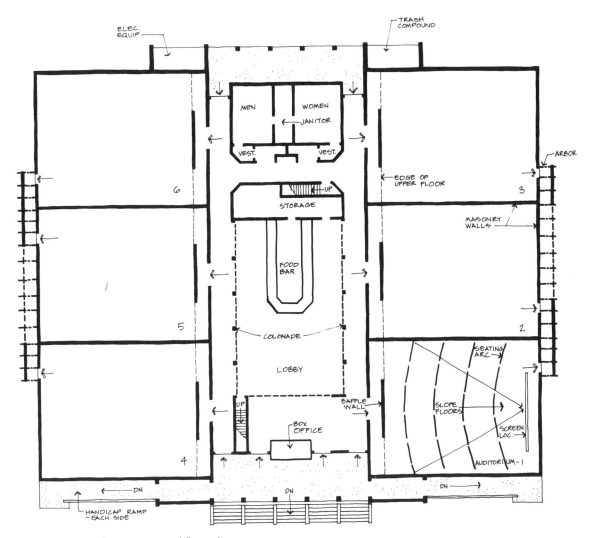

Figure 19.3 Preliminary ground floor plan.

ments determined the first level floor plan. Parking layouts and automobile circulation were designed to be compatible with the natural topography of the site; we paralleled the parking stalls and driveways with the existing grades. We also terraced the parking levels. This reduced the amount of rough and finish grading to be done. Stairs, as well as ramps for disabled persons, were provided at the front of the theatre.

Stage IV

From the scaled preliminary first floor plan, we made overlay studies of the second floor. Correct projector port locations for each auditorium, and required exit locations, determined the second floor design. Other spaces and their locations were more flexible. See Figure 19.4.

Stage V

Buildings in the area where this theatre is located are subject to the jurisdiction of an architectural review committee, with written criteria being given for exterior appearances and materials. One of these restrictions stated that the roof must be of mission tile with a minimum pitch of 4 in 12. Another requirement was that all roof-mounted mechanical equipment must be shielded from view. By providing the required sloping roof planes over the auditoriums and the rear and front lobby access, we created a well that would screen the roof-mounted heating and ventilating equipment.

For aesthetic reasons, we decided to soften the facade of the building by breaking up the long exterior blank walls at the rear of the auditoriums. We added a heavy timber arbor to provide shadows on the blank walls. See Figure 19.5A. The arbor stain and general design were chosen to be compatible with mission tile. To provide an acceptable finish, we covered the concrete block with a plaster finish. To enhance the exterior and further define the design elements, as well as to fulfill building department requirements, we added concrete columns in the colonnade. Instead of using three-dimensional drawings for presentation, a conceptual model was constructed defining the general massing of the building as well as major architectural features. This model is shown in Figure 19.5B.

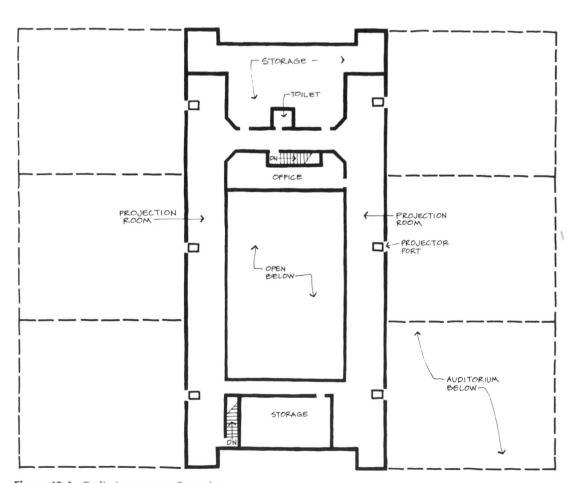

Figure 19.4 Preliminary upper floor plan.

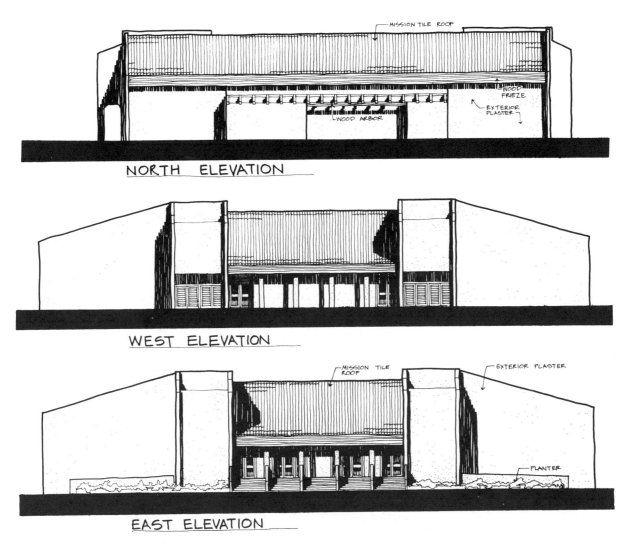

NORTH ELEVATION

WEST ELEVATION

EAST ELEVATION

Figure 19.5A Preliminary exterior elevations.

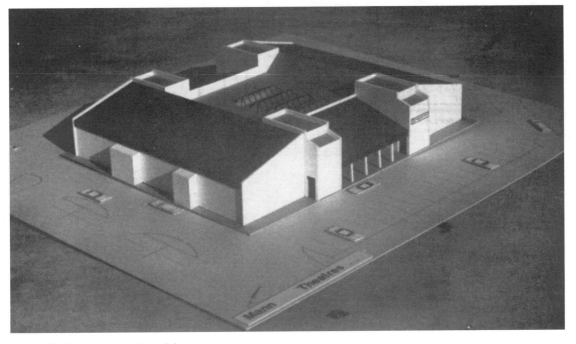

Figure 19.5B Conceptual model.

■ SITE PLAN

The primary purpose of the site plan was to locate the structure on the lot and indicate the proposed parking plan. Depending on its complexity, the site plan may or may not be combined with the grading plan. For this project, the grading plan, the site plan, and the paving plan were done separately. Figure 19.6 is an aerial photo of the completed project.

Stage I

Our first step was to describe with lines the perimeter of the lot. See Figure 19.7. A formal description of the site is obtained from the client or the civil engineer. The civil engineering survey shows and locates easements (right-of-access). In this case, the easement was a sewer easement, shown by dotted lines through the center and at the top of the lot.

The property contour is shown with a center-line type line to contrast it with the dotted lines of the easement. Property contours are shown with dotted lines or central-line type lines.

The center line of the road is shown here as a solid line, as are the road itself and the sidewalk. The circle at the left indicates a **cul-de-sac** (the end of the road with an area for turning around).

Stage II

Our main task at this stage was to locate the structure. See Figure 19.8. Location must always be done very carefully, using the preliminary site plan and the civil engineer's site plan. In this case, the easement through the center of the lot was a key factor in locating the structure.

The 400 parking stalls were next located. We needed to take into account such regulations as:

1. Turning radius of a standard car
2. Parking stall requirements
3. Permissible ratio of compact stalls to regular stalls
4. Aisles required between rows of parking
5. Dedicated green space requirement, if any
6. Ratio of parking spaces for persons with disabilities, their required distance to the point of entry, etc.

At this stage, also, the property line was darkened.

Figure 19.6 Aerial photo of finished site. (William Boggs Aerial Photography. Reprinted with permission.)

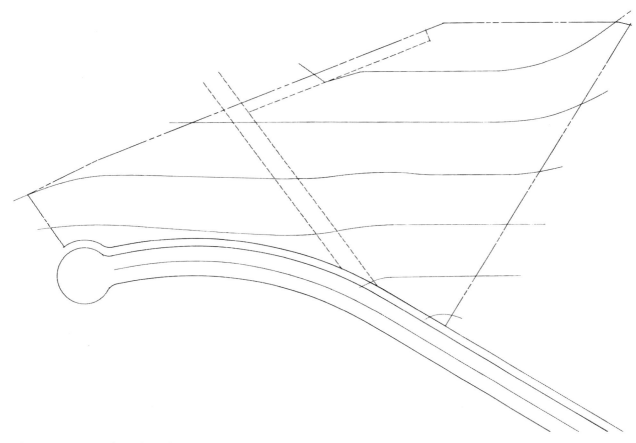

Figure 19.7 Site plan—Stage I.

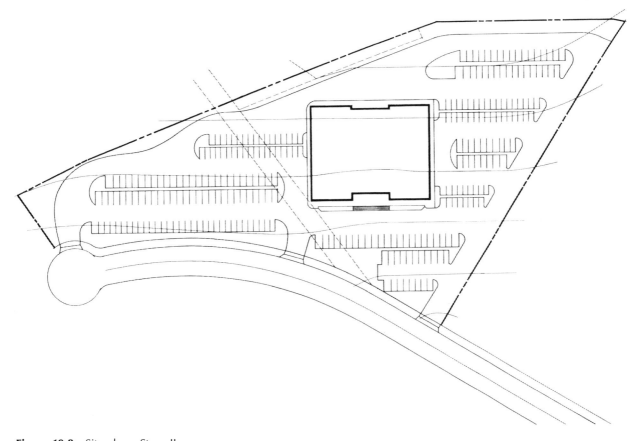

Figure 19.8 Site plan—Stage II.

Stage III

Look carefully around the perimeter of the structure in Figure 19.9 and notice the dimension lines locating the building from the property lines.

Stage IV

Here, we added the property lines with their North orientations and respective lengths. See Figure 19.10. The dimensions that located this structure were added next.

Parking stalls and islands were dimensioned and located next. Notice again that the parking layout follows the contour lines. Streets were labeled, and the drawing titled. The scale and North arrow were added.

The shape of the site was complicated and we had many parking stalls to show, so we drew a separate partial grading plan. Figure 19.11A shows the overall site with a shaded area that is enlarged in Figure 19.11B. The letters "T.C." means "top of curb." The number on the top indicates the elevation to the bottom of the curb. These numbers are expressed in decimals; a difference of 0.5 is equal to 6 inches. By following the numbers around the curb, the direction of water flow can be determined. A 1% and a 2% slope are also shown periodically.

◼ FOUNDATION PLAN

The floor plan is used as a base or datum when drawing the foundation plan (See Figure 19.26). Size and opening locations must conform to the block module. See Chapter 5 and the first stage of the floor plan.

Stage I

To better understand the evolution of this plan, see Figures 19.12 and 19.13. Both the aerial photograph and the ground level view show how the property is graded. Stakes were used to guide the large earth-moving equipment, as you can see in Figure 19.14. Figures 19.15 and 19.16 show the chalk lines indicating the position of the wall columns, and Figure 19.17 shows trenched footings. A **back hoe** (trenching machine) was then used to dig the required trenches.

Pilasters (periodic widenings of a wall) act as columns to support members above. On interior walls, pilasters are seen from either room, while exterior pilasters can be seen only from the inside, so that the face of the exterior wall can remain flat. Pilaster sizes are obtained from the structural drawing; a few typical sizes are used. If you start a foundation drawing before you have these re-

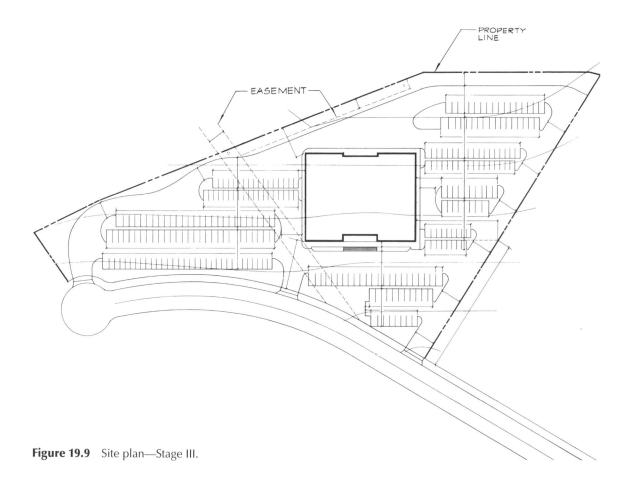

Figure 19.9 Site plan—Stage III.

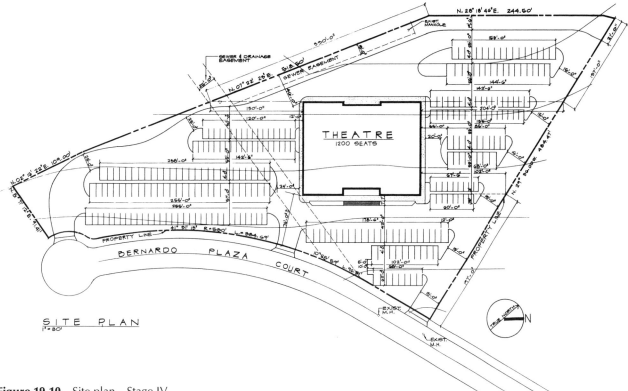

Figure 19.10 Site plan—Stage IV.

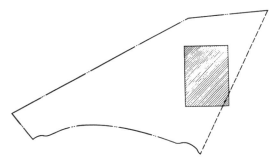

Figure 19.11A Portion of grading plan to be enlarged.

quired sizes, you can still trace the walls and indicate the tentative location of the columns and pilasters with light cross lines to show the center.

Figure 19.18 shows the first stage in the preparation of the foundation plan. In this drawing, lines are dotted lines, but often, at this initial stage, the outline is drawn with light solid lines.

Four lines are needed to represent the walls of concrete block and the footing below the grade. At some locations, where the footing is continuous but the wall is not, there are only two lines. The squares drawn with dotted lines represent concrete pads for steel pipe columns.

The exit doors at the rear of each auditorium are interesting features of this project. Each exit was designed to be sheltered by a wall with a trellis above.

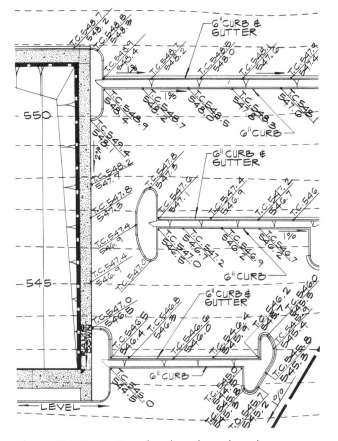

Figure 19.11B Portion of grading plan enlarged.

Figure 19.12 Graded site without structure. (William Boggs Aerial Photography. Reprinted with permission.)

Figure 19.13 Grading the property.

Figure 19.14 Stakes placed by surveyor.

Figure 19.15 Chalk lines for foundation.

Figure 19.16 Chalked lines ready for trenching. (William Boggs Aerial Photography. Reprinted with permission.)

Figure 19.17 Trenched footings.

The rectangular areas adjacent to the easterly side are ramps for handicapped persons. (Every feature of this theatre had to accommodate persons with disabilities. These features include restroom facilities, widths of openings and halls, and ramps for wheelchairs.)

The columns toward the center of the structure would hold up the upper floor. Figure 19.19 shows these columns and also the forms placed for the entry stairs adjacent to the ramps for disabled persons. The columns were carefully aligned with the upper floor walls and first floor walls.

Stage II

The inclusion of the stairs in Figure 19.20 clearly identifies the entry to the theatre. The two lines extending from each column with several perpendicular lines in them represent **brick pavers** (patterned brick on ground level).

The arc lines within one of the auditoriums represent the subtle changes of levels. This was done only once because the floors in all six auditoriums are the same.

All exterior and interior dimension lines were added next, taking care to ensure a proper block module.

The reference bubbles on the outside of the overall dimension lines are called, collectively, a matrix of the dimensional reference plane. This matrix is used to locate columns, walls, and structural members above (not seen in this drawing).

Stage III

Major section lines were added at this stage, as were detail reference bubbles. See Figure 19.21. Some of the section symbols break the overall dimension lines. This is not desirable, but we had to do it because of space limitations.

At the top right auditorium (looking at the building from the side where the entry is), notice two reference bubbles piggybacked. This indicates that two details of these columns are available elsewhere, one architectural and the other a structural detail. The section bubbles with a flag-like symbol on the opposite side indicate wall sections.

In the lobby, next to the columns, are hexagonal symbols. These are concrete pad symbols and will have numbers or letters in them corresponding with the chart introduced at the bottom right. Each concrete pad for the various columns varied enough to necessitate a chart rather than individual dimensions.

We finally added the material designation for the walls (the hatching lines within the wall lines).

Stage IV

Noting, referencing, and actual numerical values of dimensions were now added. See Figure 19.22. Noting included describing the floor material, such as the ceramic tile in the restrooms and brick pavers at the front of the theatre. We indicated slopes on the ramps for the disabled. We noted special widening instructions along the perimeter of the foundation wall as well as sizing of the pilasters. At the center of the structure around the concession stand, a note reads "3" × $^3/_{16}$" tube typ. unless noted otherwise." Many of the columns at the rear of the concession stand and around the restroom area have a diagonal line indicating a different size.

Numerical values were placed, each being checked to ensure that the overall dimension fell within the block module. Some of the values are missing near the schedule at the bottom. These dimensions are picked up later.

All of the detail and section reference bubbles were noted, and the axial reference planes (the numbers across the top and the letters along the right side) were finished.

Stage V

The dimensions overlooked in the previous stage were picked up here. See Figure 19.23. A set of dimensions describes the slope of the floor in the auditorium nearest the **column pad** schedule.

The hexagon-shaped symbols next to the column pads were now sized, using the column pad schedule. Size, depth, and reinforcing now are indicated. If this structure had had only a few pads, we would have dimensioned them at their location.

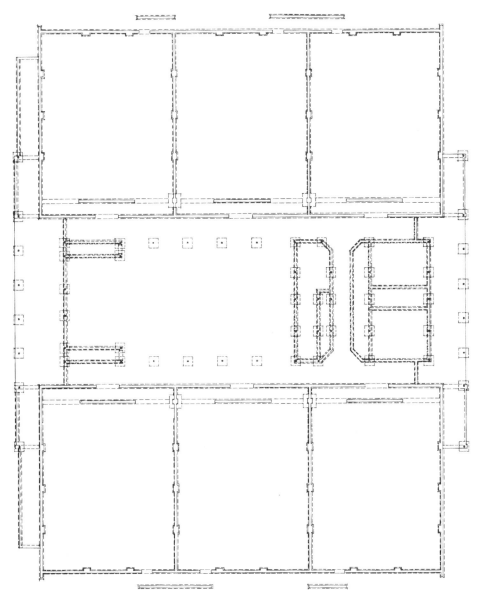

Figure 19.18 Foundation plan—Stage I.

Figure 19.19 Columns to support upper floor and forms for the stairs adjacent to the handicap ramps.

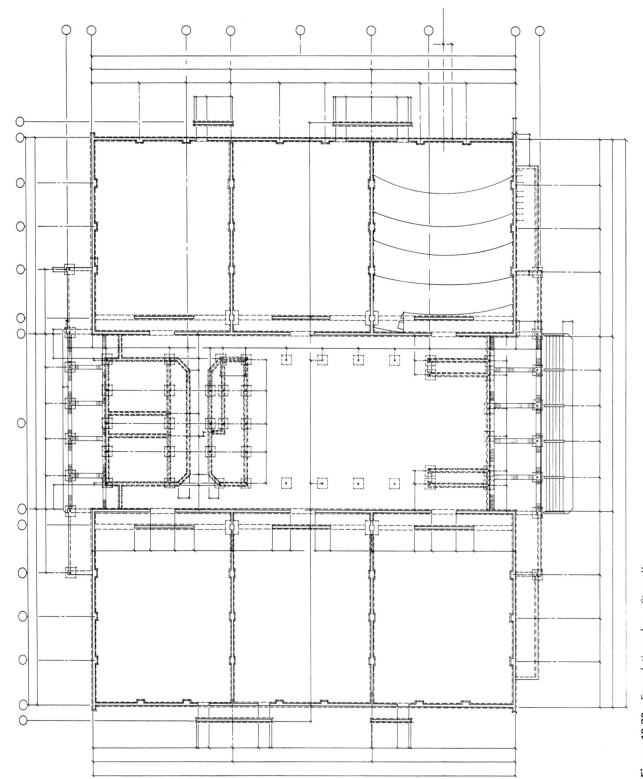

Figure 19.20 Foundation plan—Stage II.

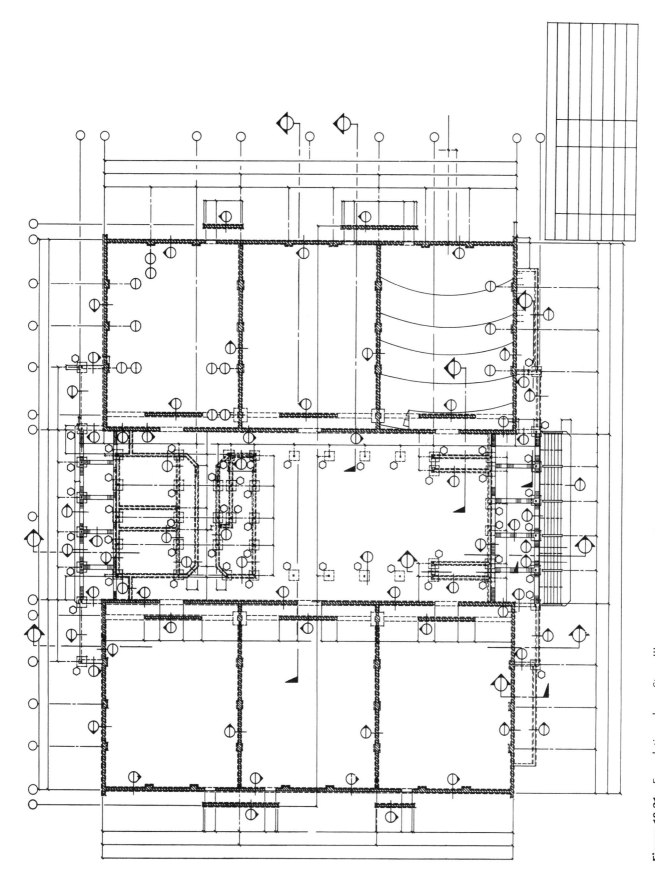

Figure 19.21 Foundation plan—Stage III.

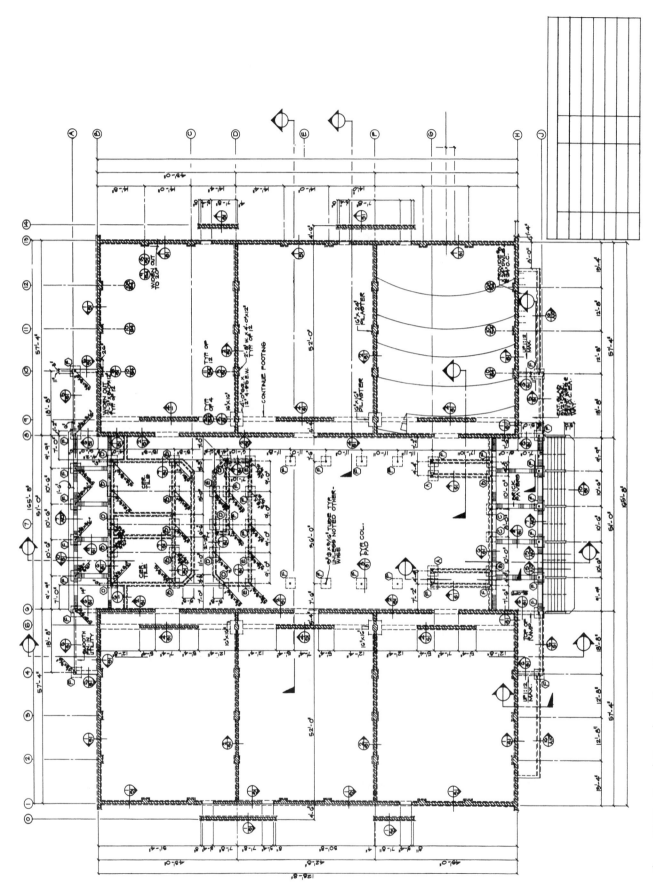

Figure 19.22 Foundation plan—Stage IV.

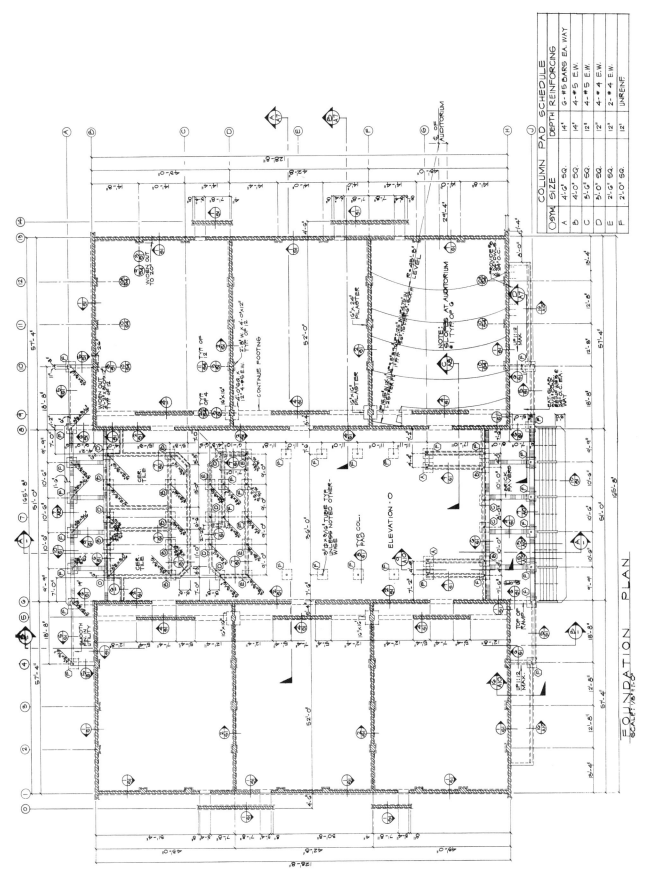

Figure 19.23 Foundation plan—Stage V.

607

The center of the arc that established the slope of the auditoriums was located on the outside of the building. Notice the broken 29'-4" dimension line on Figure 19.23. Because the arcs were symmetrical, we used a center-line type line to designate the middle of the auditorium. From this point we placed a series of numbers on a dimension line with arrowheads on it. Each arrowhead points to a specific arc and each arc was dimensioned with a note indicating two measurements. The first gives the distance traveled versus the change in the height; the second gives a ratio. For example, the first note closest to the center of the building reads, "up 16.15" in 12'-11" and 1.25" per ft," means the vertical distance traveled. In 12'-11" means the horizontal distance the 16.15" vertical distance is measured in. In other words, for every horizontal foot traveled, there is 1.25" vertical distance achieved. This ratio is based on the seating arrangement, viewing requirements, and the most comfortable walking slope for the audience.

Because all the auditoriums were to be the same, only one dimension was necessary, with a note to that effect placed in the center. Section references were labeled and the main sheet title and scale were added. This was the final stage.

■ GROUND FLOOR PLAN

Stage I

The floor plan is taken from the preliminary floor plan, because the floor plan is usually the first to be laid out. Thus, this stage must acknowledge the material that will be used to construct the building. In this instance 8" × 8" × 16" concrete blocks are used. When drawing the floor plan on the computer, a grid and snap must be built to the block module. See Figure 19.24 for an example of a block module chart. A chart similar to this one can be

BLOCK MODULE
(3/8" HORIZONTAL AND VERTICAL MORTAR JOINTS)

LENGTH	NO. 16" LONG BLOCKS	LENGTH	NO. 16" LONG BLOCKS	HEIGHT	NO. 4" HIGH BLOCKS	NO. 8" HIGH BLOCKS	HEIGHT	NO. 4" HIGH BLOCKS	NO. 8" HIGH BLOCKS
0'-8"	1/2	20'-8"	15 1/2	0'-4"	1		10'-4"	31	
1'-4"	1	21'-4"	16	0'-8"	2	1	10'-8"	32	16
2'-0"	1 1/2	22'-0"	16 1/2	1'-0"	3		11'-0"	33	
2'-8"	2	22'-8"	17	1'-4"	4	2	11'-4"	34	17
3'-4"	2 1/2	23'-4"	17 1/2	1'-8"	5		11'-8"	35	
4'-0"	3	24'-0"	18	2'-0"	6	3	12'-0"	36	18
4'-8"	3 1/2	24'-8"	18 1/2	2'-4"	7		12'-4"	37	
5'-4"	4	25'-4"	19	2'-8"	8	4	12'-8"	38	19
6'-0"	4 1/2	26'-0"	19 1/2	3'-0"	9		13'-0"	39	
6'-8"	5	26'-8"	20	3'-4"	10	5	13'-4"	40	20
7'-4"	5 1/2	27'-4"	20 1/2	3'-8"	11		13'-8"	41	
8'-0"	6	28'-0"	21	4'-0"	12	6	14'-0"	42	21
8'-8"	6 1/2	28'-8"	21 1/2	4'-4"	13		14'-4"	43	
9'-4"	7	29'-4"	22	4'-8"	14	7	14'-8"	44	22
10'-0"	7 1/2	30'-0"	22 1/2	5'-0"	15		15'-0"	45	
10'-8"	8	30'-8"	23	5'-4"	16	8	15'-4"	46	23
11'-4"	8 1/2	31'-4"	23 1/2	5'-8"	17		15'-8"	47	
12'-0"	9	32'-0"	24	6'-0"	18	9	16'-0"	48	24
12'-8"	9 1/2	32'-8"	24 1/2	6'-4"	19		16'-4"	49	
13'-4"	10	40'-0"	30	6'-8"	20	10	16'-8"	50	25
14'-0"	10 1/2	50'-0"	37 1/2	7'-0"	21		17'-0"	51	
14'-8"	11	60'-0"	45	7'-4"	22	11	17'-4"	52	26
15'-4"	11 1/2	70'-0"	52 1/2	7'-8"	23		17'-8"	53	
16'-0"	12	80'-0"	60	8'-0"	24	12	18'-0"	54	27
16'-8"	12 1/2	90'-0"	67 1/2	8'-4"	25		18'-4"	55	
17'-4"	13	100'-0"	75	8'-8"	26	13	18'-8"	56	28
18'-0"	13 1/2	200'-0"	150	9'-0"	27		19'-0"	57	
18'-8"	14	300'-0"	225	9'-4"	28	14	19'-4"	58	29
19'-4"	14 1/2	400'-0"	300	9'-8"	29		19'-8"	59	
20'-0"	15	500'-0"	375	10'-0"	30	15	20'-0"	60	30

Figure 19.24 Block module chart.

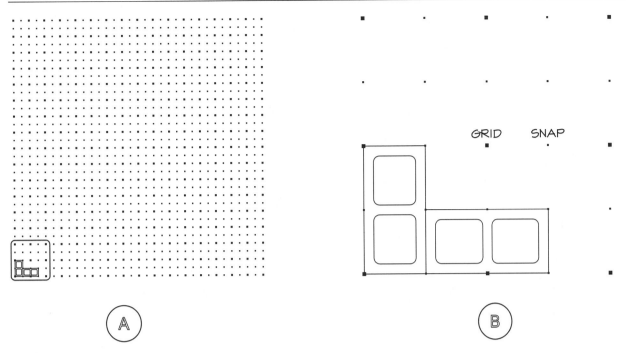

Figure 19.25 Grid and snap set to block module.

obtained from any of the manufacturers or associations that produce masonry units. A suggested layer might be set up with the grid set to 16″ increments and the snap set to 8″ (see Figure 19.25). The layout of Stage II will conform to this module.

Stage II

Clients may supply prototype plans based on their experience in a particular business. This particular client had determined that this would be a six-theatre structure with 200 seats in each theatre. Seating, the level for each row of seats, and fire restrictions were all design factors affecting the structure. We researched all of these factors prior to drawing the preliminary floor plan.

Compare the aerial photograph, Figure 19.26, with Figure 19.27 to see what was actually being constructed. Figures 19.26 and 19.27 show the construction sequence in relationship to the floor plan found in Figure 19.28.

In Figure 19.28, the columns toward the center of the theatre support the upper floor. (The upper floor accommodates the projectors and allows projectionists to move from one projector to another.) Near the rear of the building are the restrooms and snack bar storage. The two partial rectangles near the front of the theatre are stairwells.

Stage III

At the bottom of the left and right sides of the plan, we added a planter and a ramp for disabled people. See

Figure 19.29. Stairs were added throughout the plan, and we added a set of dotted lines in each auditorium to represent the motion picture screens. The size of the screen was determined by the seating capacity and client needs. Dividing walls were drawn within the stairs at the front. Notice at the front and rear of the building are brick pavers as described in the foundation plan. These pavers were drawn with textured concrete within them.

At the center of the structure is the concession stand. The textured area represents a tile floor and the blank space, the counter. We added toilet partitions and lavatories to the restrooms, leaving larger stalls for persons with disabilities. Toilets can be added here or later.

At the center of each restroom entry, the small area for telephones also accommodates disabled people. The small circles with a darkened cross indicate fire extinguishers. We added fire sprinkler symbols in the trash area in the rear of the building. Line quality becomes important here to differentiate between walls, floor patterns, and fixtures.

Stage IV

Interior and exterior dimension lines were now added. See Figure 19.30. These dimensions *must* always be double-checked with the foundation plan to insure proper alignment of the walls with the foundation. As the floor plan was dimensioned first, the concrete block module was followed.

Figure 19.26 Aerial view of completed wall. (William Boggs Aerial Photography. Reprinted with permission.)

Figure 19.27 View of entry, lobby, and back of theatres.

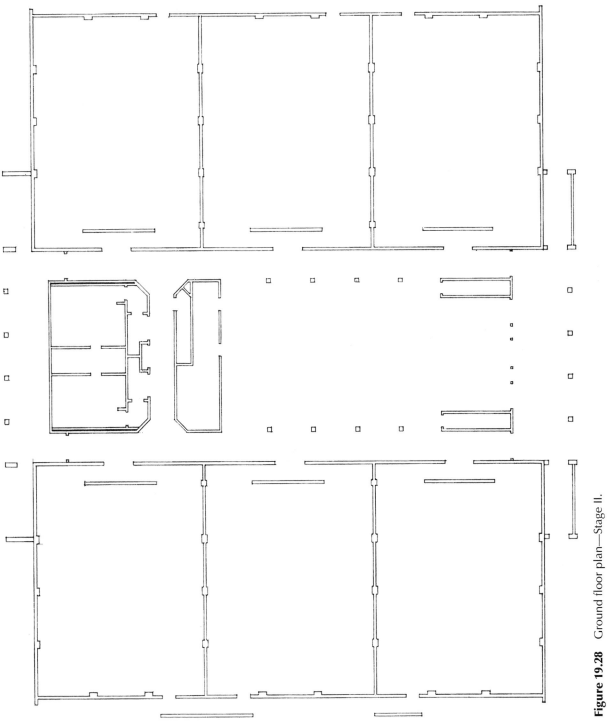

Figure 19.28 Ground floor plan—Stage II.

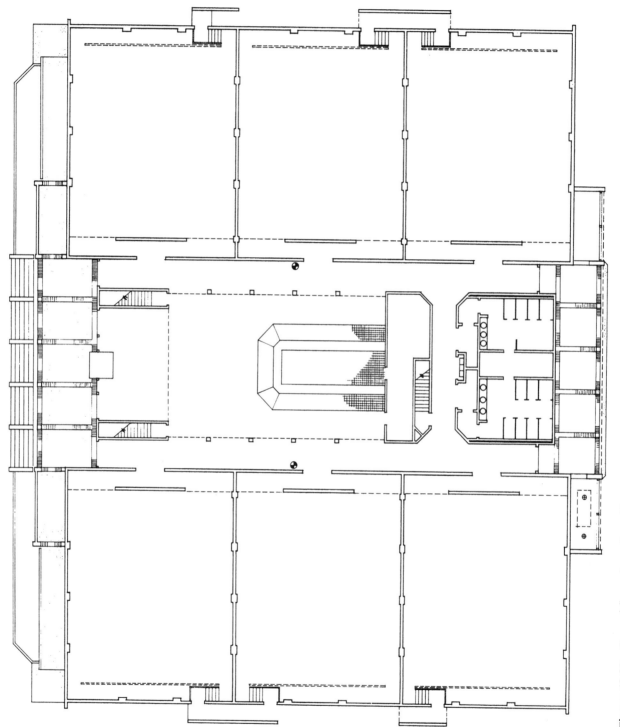

Figure 19.29 Ground floor plan—Stage III.

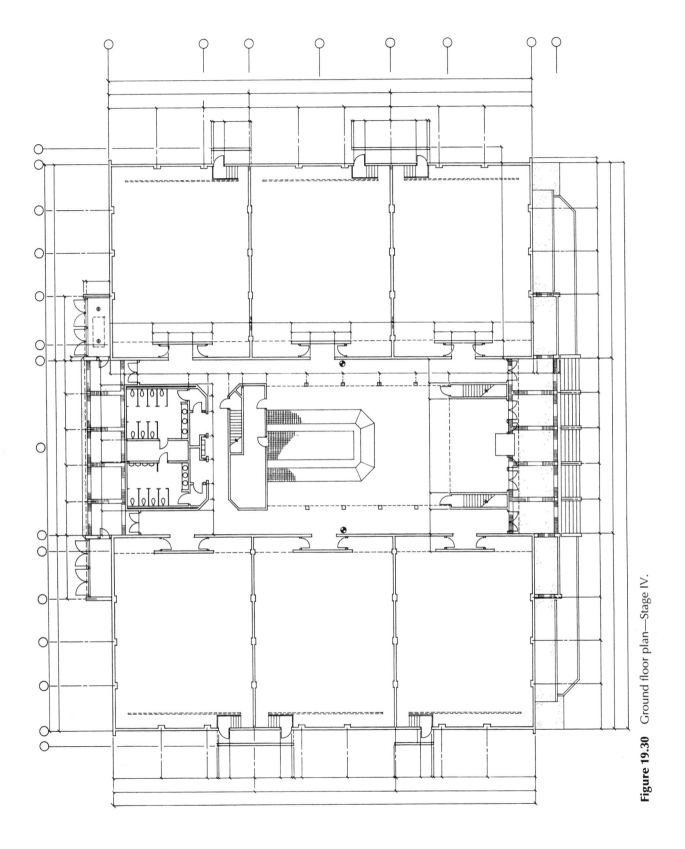

Figure 19.30 Ground floor plan—Stage IV.

The axial reference plane bubbles across the top and to the right correspond with walls, columns, and any structural members above, and form the reference plane matrix. We also indicated door swings.

Stage V

All of the reference bubbles were now located. See Figure 19.31. Full architectural section references, wall sections, door reference bubbles, and interior elevation reference symbols were included. Each room would later receive a number as well as a title, so we drew in underlines for the names and rectangular boxes for the numbers.

At the entry, we drew plants in the planters to clearly differentiate the planter areas from the ramps. The planters and plants were later included in the elevation (Figure 19.51) for clarity and consistency.

The material designation for the walls, indicated by hatching lines in the wall lines, was drafted next.

Stage VI

Numerical values for the dimension lines were now included. See Figure 19.32. Each dimension had to be checked with the foundation plan. Accuracy at this stage is critical. Compare the radial dimension line added in Auditorium #2 with Auditorium #1 on the foundation plan (Figure 19.25).

We noted typical items such as pilaster sizes and the location of the screens, and unique items such as the location of fire extinguishers. Area titles and room titles were the next items to be noted.

We labeled the reference plane bubbles next. The stair notations refer to the finish schedule in the same way that the door letters refer to the door schedule. Finally, the drawing title, scale, and North arrow were added.

■ UPPER FLOOR PLAN

Stage I

We included the six auditoriums in the upper floor plan (see Figure 19.33) because the upper portions of the auditoriums were adjacent to the upper floor. The center of the structure is the lobby, which extends to the roof.

We located the projection windows according to their required angle. Figure 19.34 shows the interior of the structure. Note the projection windows and the connectors below to attach the upper floor. We took care to align the walls of the upper floor with the walls below.

Another view of this relationship is seen in the structural sections (for instance, in Section B-B in Figure 19.55).

Stage II

This stage (Figure 19.35) shows the stairs, restroom facilities, two fire extinguishers (one circle on each side) and, most important, the projectors and the space they occupy. A rectangle with a line through it next to a circle was the symbol we selected to represent the projectors.

Stage III

The upper floor plan affects only the central part of the building, but the dimensions shown on it relate to the overall structure. So our first step was to add the necessary dimension line. See Figure 19.36.

The foundation plan and the first floor plan were consulted to maintain consistency in dimensioning. This correspondence would be checked again when numerical values were added to the drawing. Finally, we drafted the material designation for the concrete block and located the door symbols.

Stage IV

The main difference between this stage and the previous one is the addition of most of the dimension numbers. See Figure 19.37. The dimensions had to be checked against the floor plan of the floor below, and both had to be checked to ensure correct concrete block module dimensions.

Stage V

In this final stage, Figure 19.38, interior elevation reference bubbles were added, together with all necessary lettering. Some dimensions that were missing in Figure 19.37 now appear.

Doors and windows were checked with the schedule and filled in. Stair A and Stair B do not indicate the size or number of treads and risers. Details or sections provide their size, shape, and proportion. Look at the first floor plan (Figure 19.32) at the stair area and note the cutting plane line for a detail section.

The rooms in Figure 19.38 are numbered with three digits, beginning with a "2", for the floor reference. The auditoriums were previously numbered on the first floor plan; the upper floor plan shows the upper portion of the auditoriums (without room numbers).

The central portion of the plan is open to the area below as indicated. Using this scale, it was difficult to show the small toilet at the rear. Therefore, we made an enlarged floor plan and elevation of Room 208 on the partial floor plan and the interior elevation sheet.

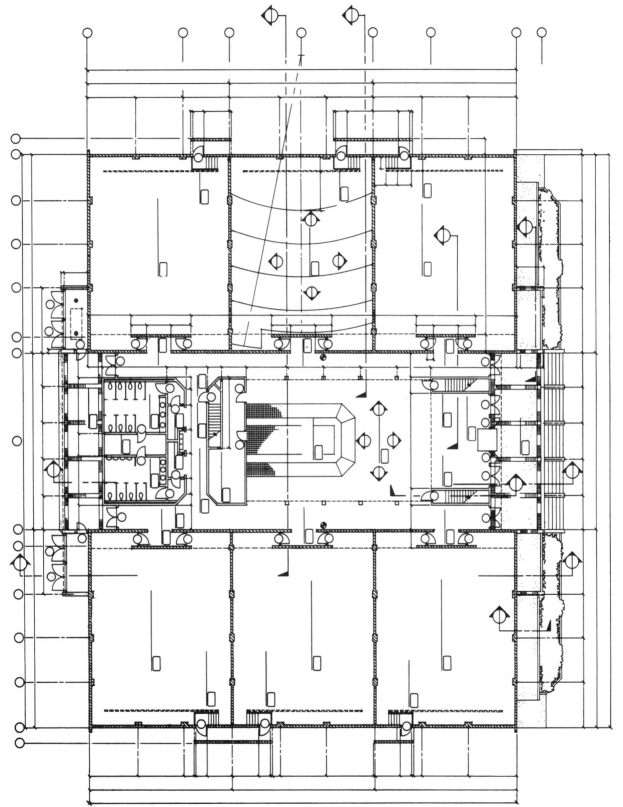

Figure 19.31 Ground floor plan—Stage V.

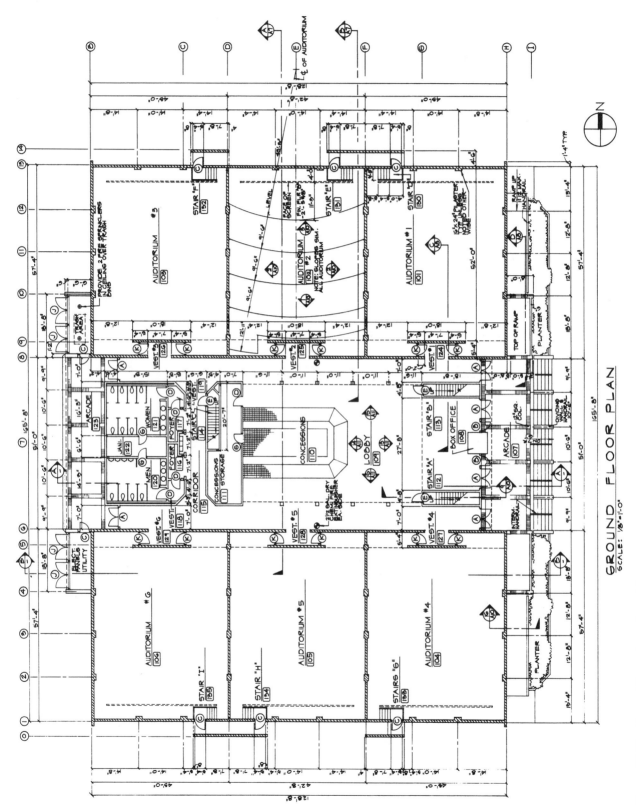

Figure 19.32 Ground floor plan—Stage VI.

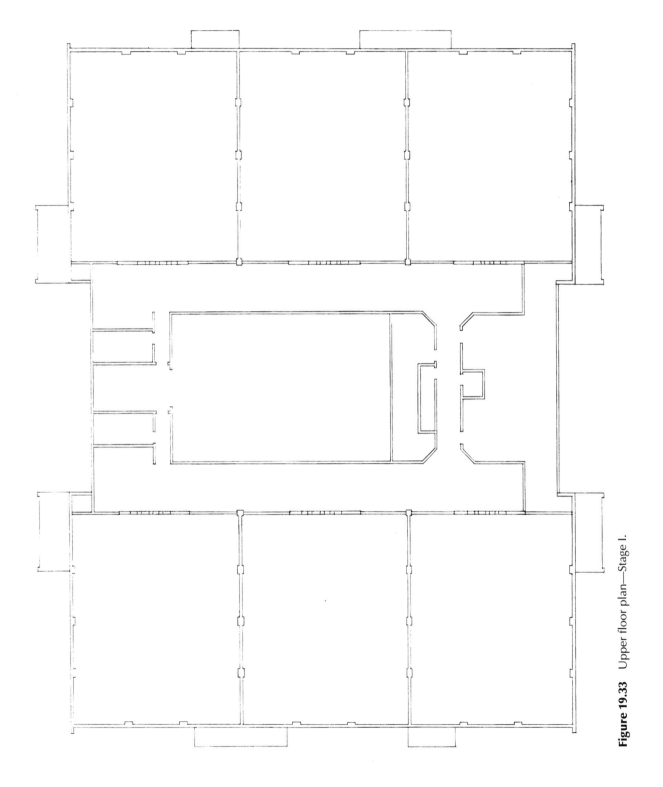

Figure 19.33 Upper floor plan—Stage I.

Figure 19.34 View looking toward lobby.

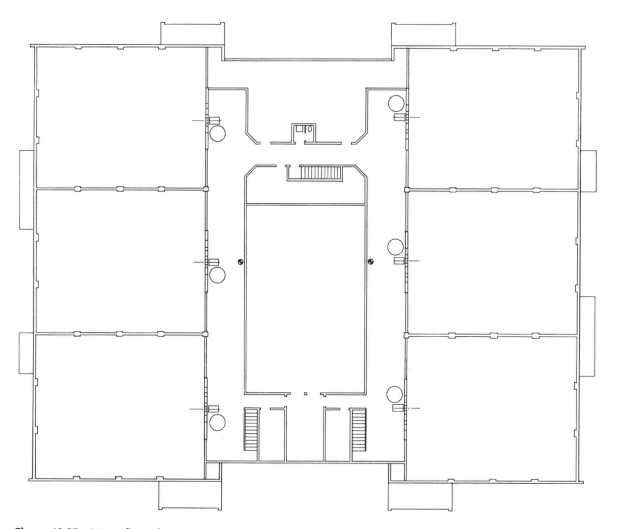

Figure 19.35 Upper floor plan—Stage II.

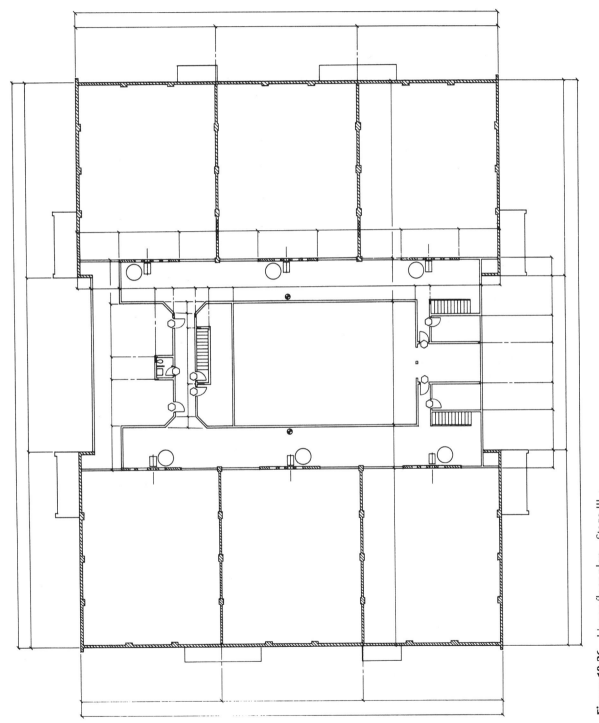

Figure 19.36 Upper floor plan—Stage III.

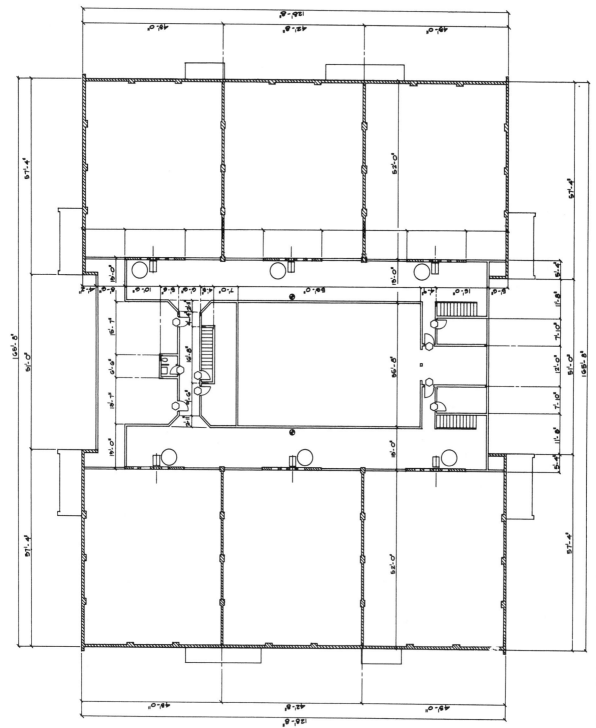

Figure 19.37 Upper floor plan—Stage IV.

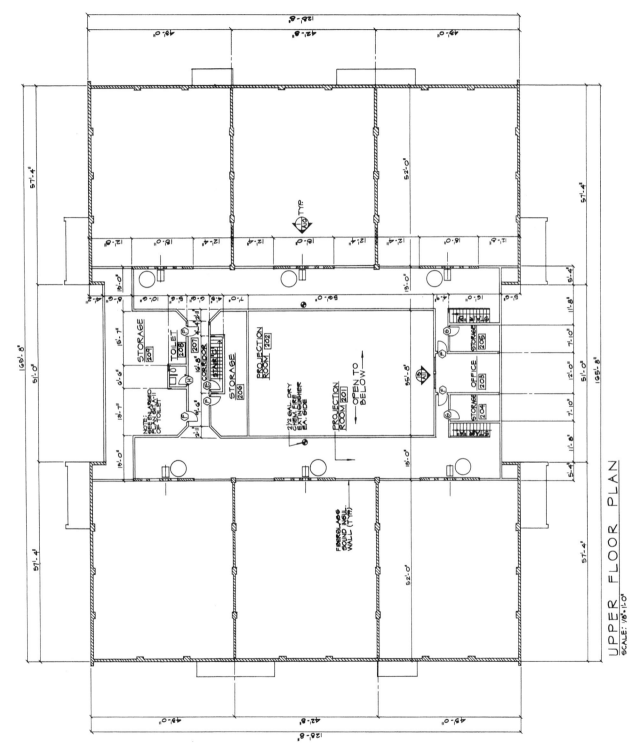

UPPER FLOOR PLAN
SCALE: 1/8" = 1'-0"

Figure 19.38 Upper floor plan—Stage V.

■ PARTIAL FLOOR PLAN AND INTERIOR ELEVATIONS

Stage I

The partial floor plan shown in Figure 19.39 was drawn at a larger scale than the other plans. It includes the concession areas and restrooms. Only a few interior elevations are drafted here.

Here, the partial floor plan is drawn twice the size of the first floor plan. We took the measurements from the first floor plan. At this scale, we could also show the double wall for the plumbing. (See the wall with toilets.)

The four rectangles at the bottom of the drawing represent columns. Two more columns appear to be located next to the walls but are actually inside the walls. They were included for visual continuity and have no structural implications.

The left half of the drawing was blocked out to receive the interior elevations, with one exception: the floor plan of the toilet on the upper floor level located slightly left of center on the drawing. The rectangle to the right of the upper floor toilet would become the interior elevation for that toilet, while the long rectangle at the bottom would become the interior elevation of the entry to the restrooms and telephone area.

Stage II

The partial floor plan now shows the plumbing fixtures and the floor material in the restrooms. See Figure 19.40. The rectangles at the center near the entry to the restrooms are drinking fountains. Across the hall are the stairs to the upper level.

The wall material was now added to the interior elevations. Various fixtures such as urinals, paper towel dispensers, grab bars for disabled persons, and drinking fountains were also added.

Stage III

All of the necessary dimension lines not included on the ground floor plan were located on this sheet (see Figure

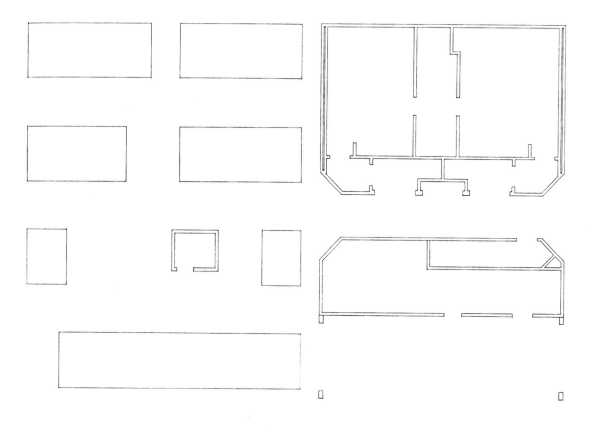

Figure 19.39 Partial floor plan and interior elevations—Stage I.

19.41), as well as some of the critical dimensions on the interior elevations. Door swings were shown by dotted lines. We added the designation of floor material in the concession area.

Stage IV

We established the numerical values for the dimensions shown in Figure 19.42 by checking the upper floor plan, foundation plan, and first floor plan. The dimension to the right side of the concession counter ends in a series of dots, indicating that the structure continues; break lines were not used.

The reference bubbles with arrows on them refer to the interior elevations. Only a few typical examples are shown here; in reality, there should be an interior elevation for every symbol shown.

Among the interior elevations, there is a plan and interior elevation for the upper floor toilet. This is unusual but the available paper space determined placement. Pay attention to the structural columns and the double stud wall behind the water closet designed for the plumbing.

Next, dimensions of the heights of the interior elevations were added. Various typical items such as mirrors were located and given sizes. Handicap requirements were again checked, and items such as grab bars were properly located.

Material indications for walls and floors were called out. This was done broadly (generically) because the written specifications would be used for a more defini-

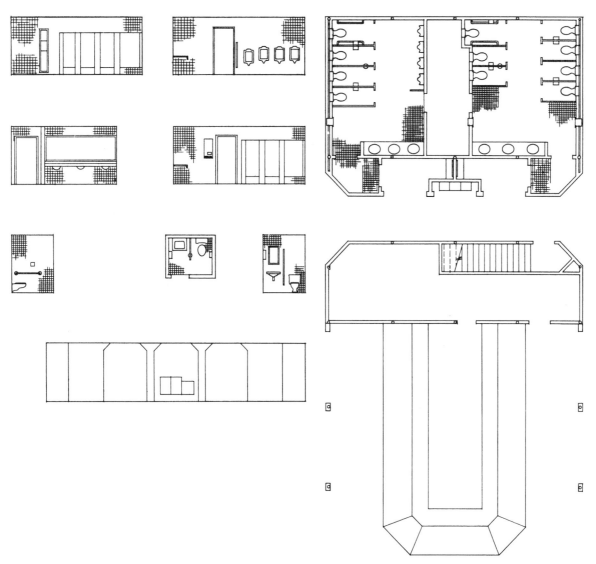

Figure 19.40 Partial floor plan and interior elevations—Stage II.

tive explanation. Last, additional notes, main titles, and scale were added.

EXTERIOR ELEVATIONS

Elevations are developed from scratch, and are not traced from any other drawings unless extremely accurate preliminary drawings have been prepared. In most sets of drawings, the elevations are among the last to be completed because they are dependent on the floor plan, sections, roof plan, and so on. To better see how exterior

elevations evolve, first read the chapter on building sections (Chapter 12). Figures 19.43 and 19.44 show how the exterior of the project actually appears as the construction proceeds, and Figures 19.45 and 19.46 show front and rear views of the construction when completed.

Stage I

We decided to draft only three exterior elevations rather than the normal four because the structure is symmetrical and the North and South elevations are similar. The horizontal lines in Figure 19.47 represent several items: the two floor levels, the top of the parapet, the tops of the

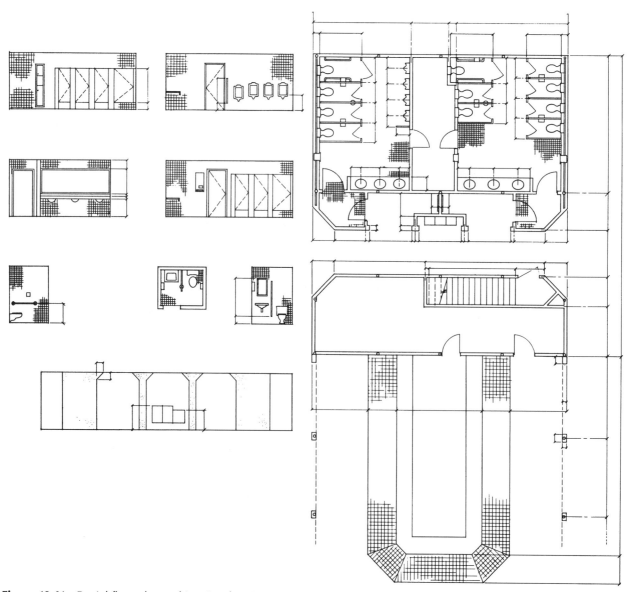

Figure 19.41 Partial floor plan and interior elevations—Stage III.

beams, and the tip of the beam at the canopy over the door. (The sloped, dotted line on the bottom elevation is the angle of the ramp for persons with disabilities.)

Stage II

The small, light vertical lines shown in Figure 19.48 locate the various beams and columns. These locations

were taken from the reference bubbles on the floor plan. The complete structure would later be referenced by the column locations.

Stage III

Where Stage II indicated the vertical heights, Stage III established the outline of the building itself. See Figure

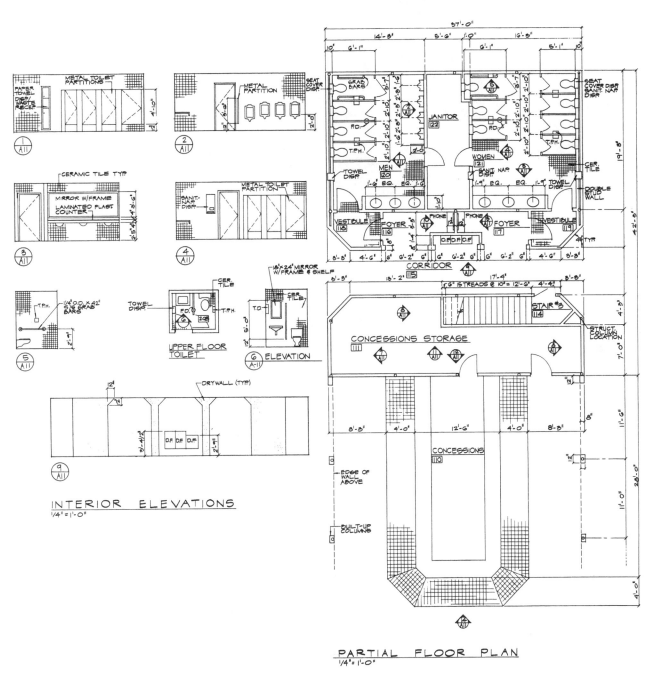

Figure 19.42 Partial floor plan and interior elevations—Stage IV.

Figure 19.43   Front of theatre. (William Boggs Aerial Photography. Reprinted with permission.)

Figure 19.44   Front of theatre showing ramp for disabled persons. (William Boggs Aerial Photography. Reprinted with permission.)

Figure 19.45 Front view of finished structure. (Photography: Kent Oppenheimer.)

Figure 19.46 Rear view of finished structure.

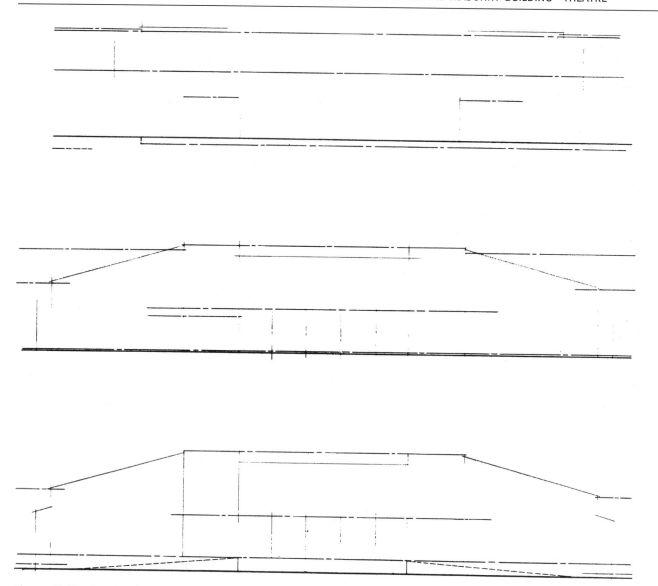

Figure 19.47 Exterior elevations—Stage I.

19.49. Column locations, wall thicknesses, independent walls at the exit were all established at this point. These measurements were obtained from the various plans, such as the floor plan, foundation plan, and the architectural sections. Each of these drawings used a dimensional system. This was helpful in the development of this structure because it gave specific points of reference. Heights, width, and depth of the structure were all referenced to this system.

For orientation purposes, the top elevation is the North elevation; the center is the West elevation; and the bottom is the East elevation and entry to the theatre. The two rectangular shapes toward the center of the North elevation represent the walls protecting the patrons at the exit.

The top center line on the West elevation is a point of reference. It is the top of the parapet wall extending

above the roof plan. The series of vertical lines toward the center represent columns, and the two horizontal lines above the columns represent the fascia.

The ramp on either side of the entry is indicated with dotted lines. See the East elevation, Figure 19.49. At the center are columns with handrails drawn in front of them. Stairs would be added later.

Stage IV

Now that we had a basic configuration, we could describe some of the smaller shapes. See Figure 19.50. We added the arbor, or shaded walk, to the North elevation. Refer back to Figure 19.46. The line above the wood arbor is the wood frieze (band of wood). The opening is located at the left.

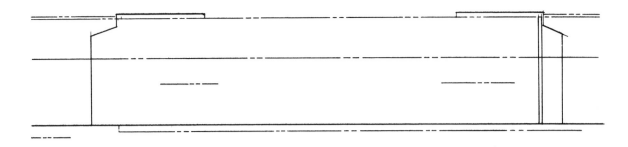

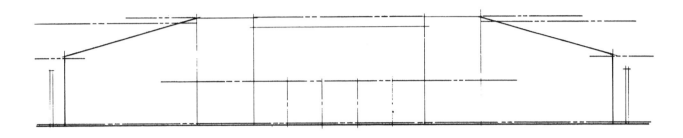

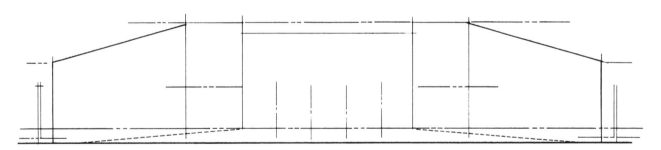

Figure 19.48 Exterior elevations—Stage II.

To the West elevation, we added rear doors, the doors for the storage area, and the arbor at each end. We positioned steps and doors on the East elevation.

Stage V

This was the final stage and included a multitude of items. See Figure 19.51.

Texture. Roof material was designated. We also stippled the cement plaster that was to cover the concrete masonry units. We added plants in the planter on the East elevation to be consistent with the plants we showed on the floor plan.

Dimensions. Dimensions of the two floor levels were added. Some dimensions were referenced to the building sections (Figure 19.55) for clarity.

Notes. The surface material was called out. We also added title and scale.

■ BUILDING SECTIONS

Stage I

The drawings developed in Figures 19.52 through 19.55 are architectural building sections, not structural sec-

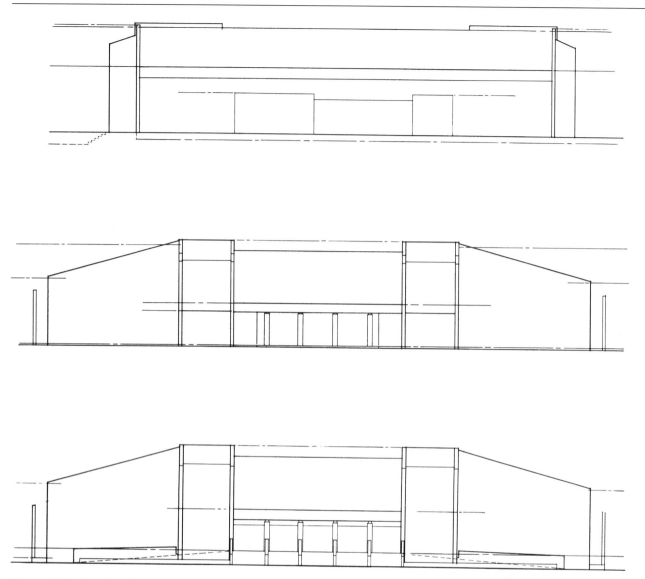

Figure 19.49 Exterior elevations—Stage III.

tions. This sheet is a classic example of how the available drawing area and number of sections to be drawn dictate the approach.

For example, the top section in Figure 19.52 has six break lines representing the removal of three areas. At this point, we could have changed scales or kept the same scale while eliminating the least important or the most redundant area. (We use the term *redundant* to mean an area that remains the same for long lengths.) We could either have two areas broken out and lose one major steel girder (see Figure 19.55) or have three areas broken out and save the girder. Because the location of the beams showed so much about heights and the structural assembly method, we decided to have three areas broken away and save the beam.

Another approach we could have taken would have been to use match lines and then slice the structure into two pieces, aligning one above the other. Because of the size of the structure, this would have left a lot of unused space on one side of the sheet and would have required our adding another sheet for the other section. This additional sheet would also have had extra space on it.

We approached the lower section by using a break line and eliminating a large portion of the theatre. The structure is symmetrical and the auditorium to the right would have been duplicated on the left. There would be no break in the center portion of the theatre (the lobby) or the auditorium on the right.

First, we located all of the steel beams as well as their corresponding foundation below. Using the framing and

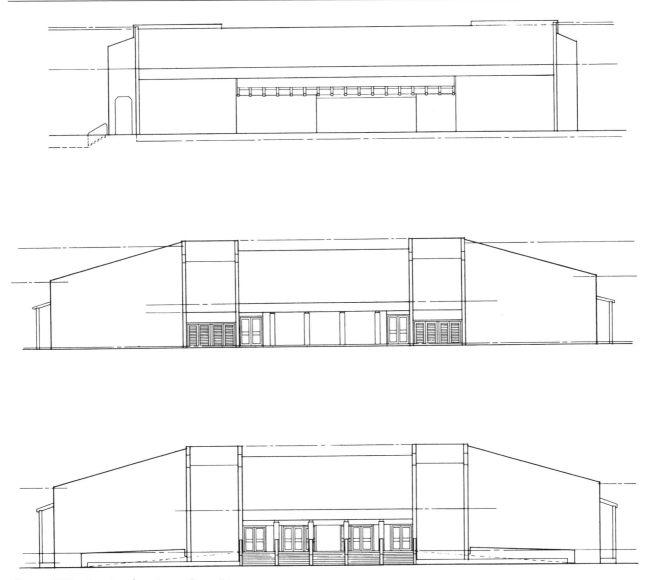

Figure 19.50 Exterior elevations—Stage IV.

foundation plans together with structural details helped greatly in developing this drawing.

Since the floor of the auditorium sloped, we used two floor levels to describe the structure: Level "A" and Level "B." Level "A" is the top of the auditorium slope and "B" the bottom.

The vertical lines above some of the beams in Figure 19.52 would have reference bubbles added to them in the next stage, so they could be keyed to other drawings.

Stage II

We added reference bubbles for the beams at this stage (Figure 19.53), but only above continuous beams, so some beams on the upper section and many on the lower sections have no reference bubbles.

We also studied available details at this time. When details are not available, freehand details should be sketched to solve many of the intersections of wall and floors or roofs. Based on this information, we drafted the interior walls and upper floor.

Stage III

As drawings become more complicated, the floor plan should always be reviewed to clarify the various parts of the section.

The sections now began to show the wall material designations, the soil under the foundation, the corrugated steel decking at the upper floor level, and the mission tile roof. See Figure 19.54. The steel decking under the mission tile is in side view in the lower section, so

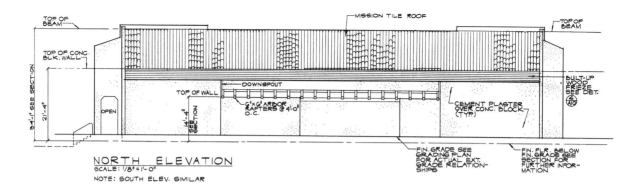

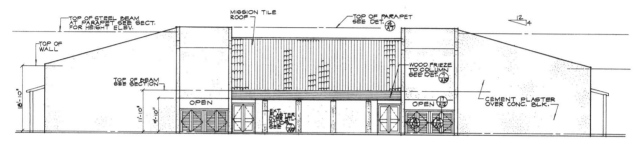

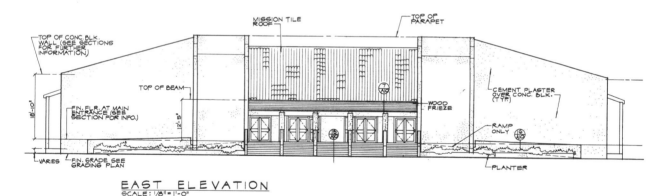

Figure 19.51 Exterior elevations—Stage V.

the corrugation does not show. The view of the floor decking in the upper section is an end view and shows the corrugation.

The suspended ceiling at various locations was now indicated. Because of the intended use of the structure and the materials chosen, we used many fireproofing techniques. For example, many of the steel beams have a freehand line drawn around them. These represent a sprayed-on fire protection material. A specific description of this spray material would be included later in the specifications.

Stage IV

At this stage, we completed the noting and dimensioning. See Figure 19.55.

Dimensioning. First we had to keep the dimensions consistent with the other drawings. Each letter of the matrix and each number had to align with the proper column, beam, or footing pad. After checking, they were vertically located. The term "T.B." means "top of beam." These beams were dimensioned by notation and were

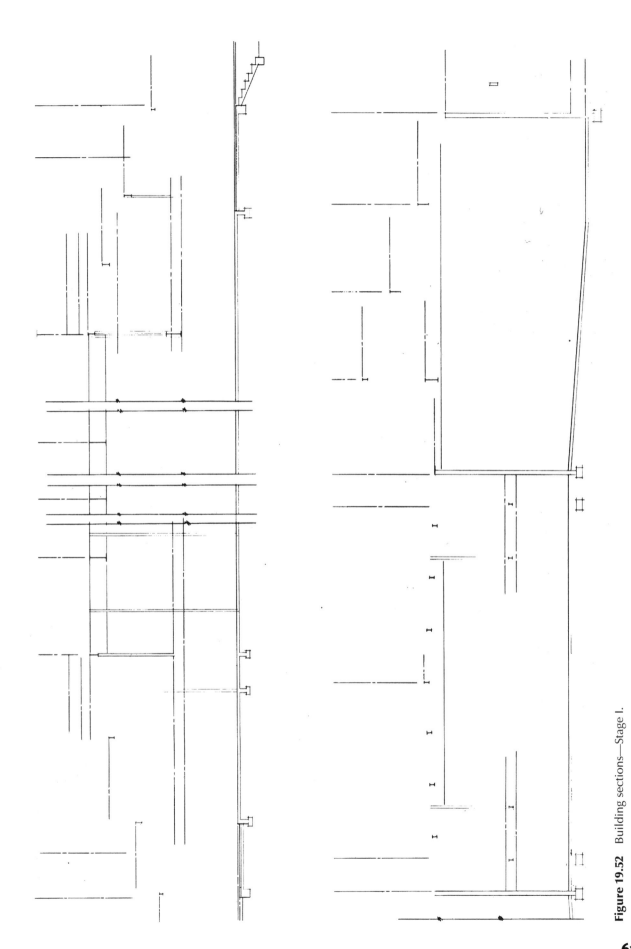

Figure 19.52 Building sections—Stage I.

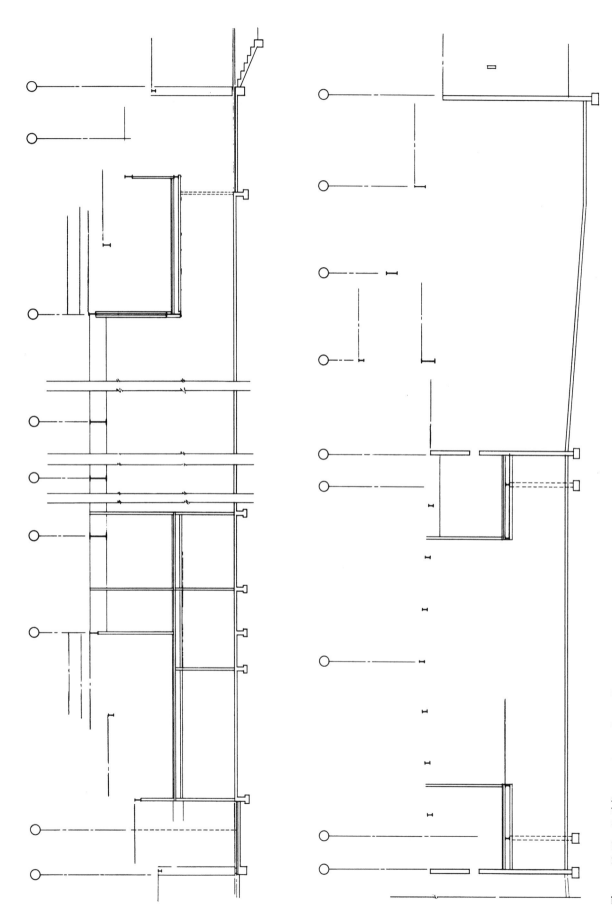

Figure 19.53 Building sections—Stage II.

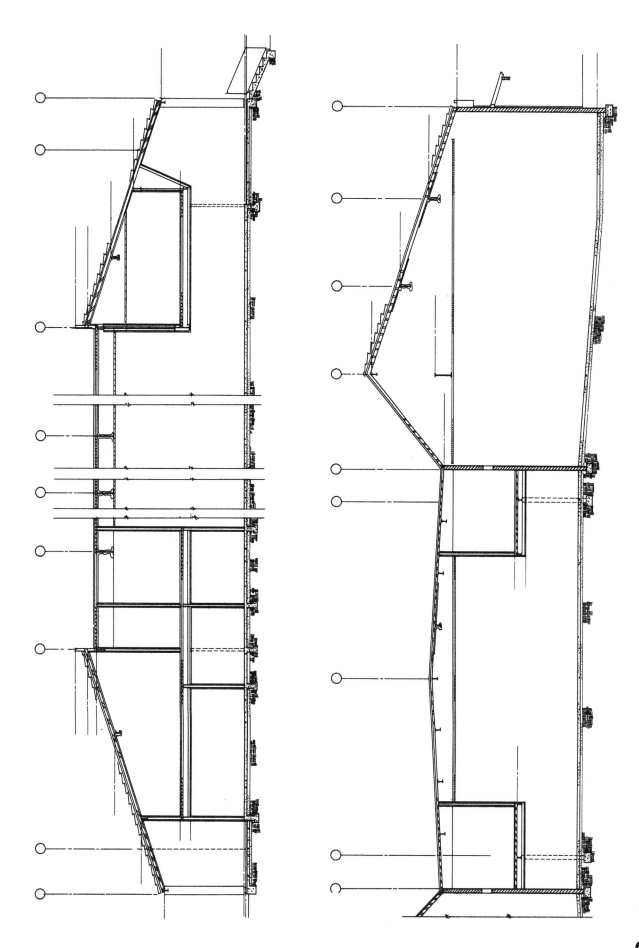

Figure 19.54 Building sections—Stage III.

635

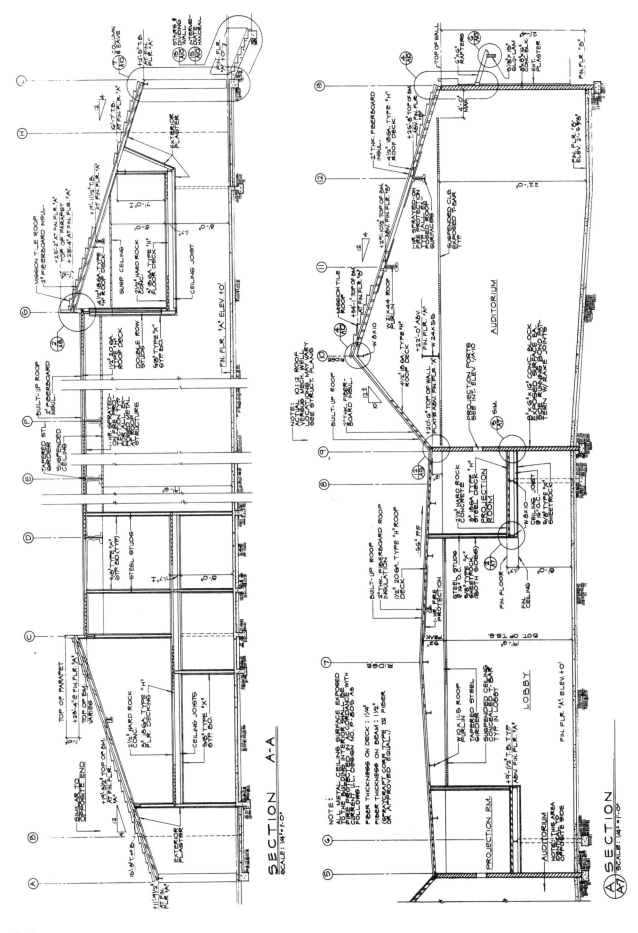

Figure 19.55 Building sections—Stage IV.

measured from one of the two floor levels. The abbreviation "T.S.G." means "tapered steel girder."

Dimension lines were now added to the floors and ceilings, and the top of walls. Because the space between the upper floor and the ceiling below it had been determined by details, it too was included.

Reference. We drew many reference bubbles showing locations of details or special wall sections. These were carefully selected.

Noting. Most of the noting explained a material or a method of erection or the dimensions themselves. The section titles, scales, and room names were added. There is also a special note about fire protection below the title "Section A-A."

■ ROOF PLAN

Review the first floor plan, the upper floor plan, the sections, and the preliminary elevations before starting to study this roof plan.

Stage I

First we traced the roof plan from the first floor plan. See Figure 19.56. The dotted lines located the major interior walls. Note that the design called for the exterior walls to extend above and beyond the tops of the roof.

The five major divisions of the roof are the top, bottom, left, right, and center. The top, bottom, left, and right portions all slope away from the structure. The center portion slopes in two directions with a ridge at the center.

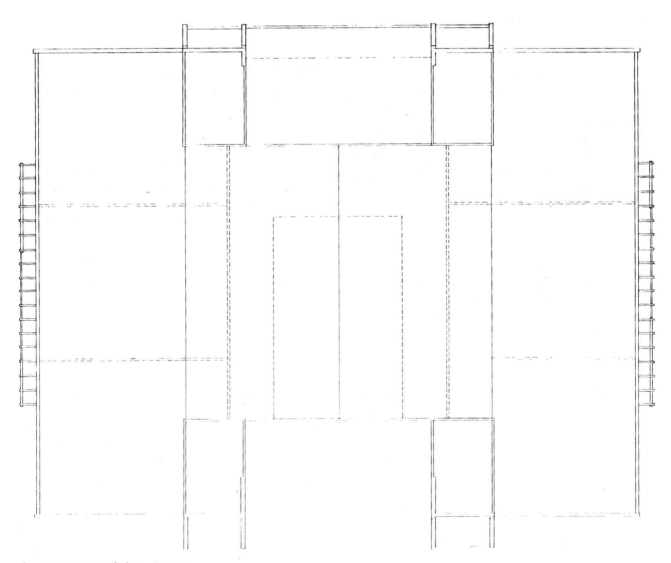

Figure 19.56 Roof plan—Stage I.

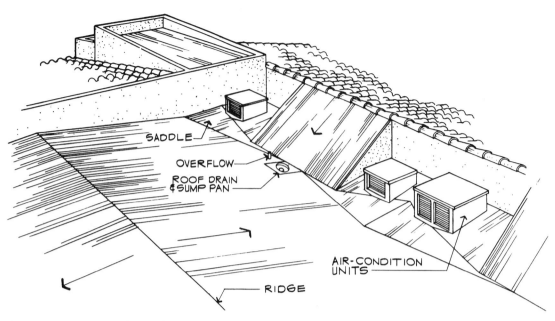

SADDLE

OVERFLOW

ROOF DRAIN
& SUMP PAN

AIR-CONDITION
UNITS

RIDGE

Figure 19.57 Corner of central portion of roof.

Because the four major portions around the center rose higher than the center, roof drains were required. See Figure 19.57. These drains and the surrounding areas will be mentioned later.

The exterior walls on Figure 19.56 were drawn slightly wider than the interior walls because they represented exterior plaster over concrete block. Note the configuration of the arbor over the exterior exits from each auditorium.

Stage II

To better understand this roof, as shown in Figure 19.58, look at the sketch of its central portion in Figure 19.57. The line at the very center is the ridge. This ridge produces a gable type roof at the central portions. The surrounding portions are higher and so the slope of this gable roof needs to be drained at its edges. Roof drains, commonly called scuppers, were added at strategic points.

As you can see by comparing the sketch with the plan, portions of the low point of the gable roof remained flat to accept air-conditioning equipment. Other portions sloped down from the vertical plane like a shed roof. Sheet metal saddles, called crickets, were positioned to control the flow of water on the roof and to direct it toward the roof drains. The small circles near the roof drains represent the overflow drains provided in case the regular scuppers clog.

On two sides of the structure, we added reference bubbles to correspond with those on the plans and sections.

Skylights (still visible in Figure 19.63) were not shown because they were deleted earlier at the request of the client.

Stage III

At this stage, the reference bubbles were numbered and lettered. See Figure 19.59. Numerical values for all the dimension lines were added next. The slope of the roofs were designated by arrows. Arrows at the edges of the roof show the slope of the gutters toward the downspout.

All dimensions were verified with the building section in this chapter, and the engineering drawings were checked for correct column and beam locations. Finally, detail reference bubbles were drawn. The details were selected at an earlier stage.

Stage IV

The final roof construction, described by the plan in Figure 19.60, actually differs from the drawing in Figure 19.59. This happens quite often as better solutions, the pressure of economic considerations, or construction restrictions change the final plans. Figure 19.61, the aerial photograph of the finished structure, shows how we departed from the original design.

All descriptive notes were included at this stage. In many of the notes, measurements, pitches, and ratios are indicated. Detail numbers, titles, and scale were the final items added. At each step, the water drainage system and the location of potential leakage areas were considered.

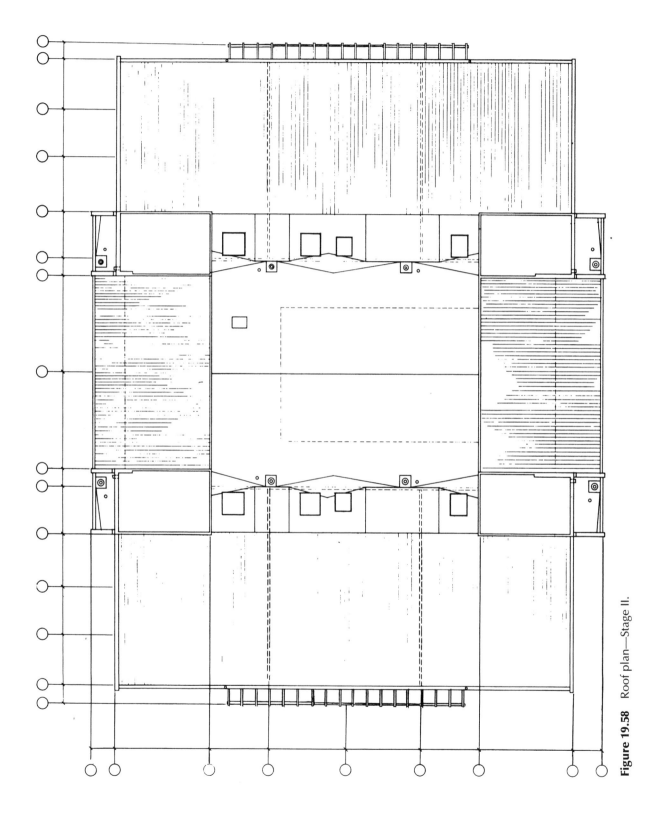

Figure 19.58 Roof plan—Stage II.

639

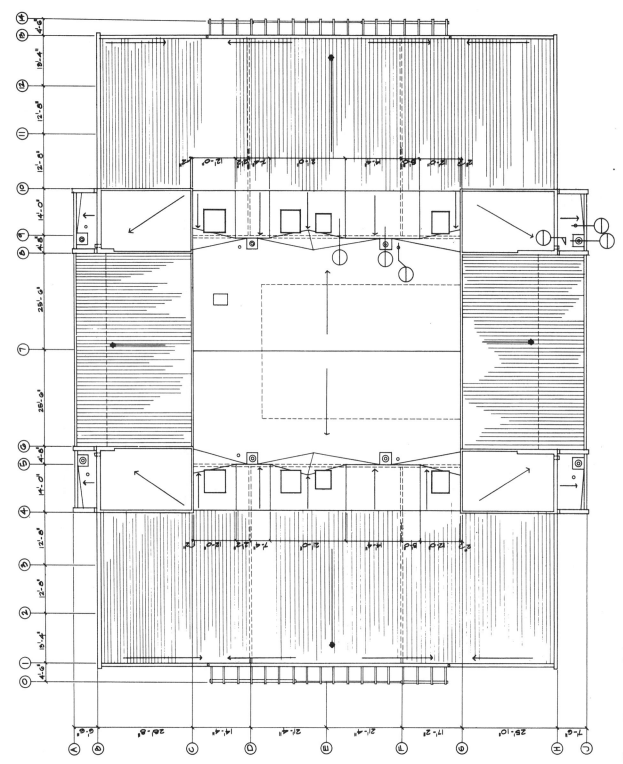

Figure 19.59 Roof plan—Stage III.

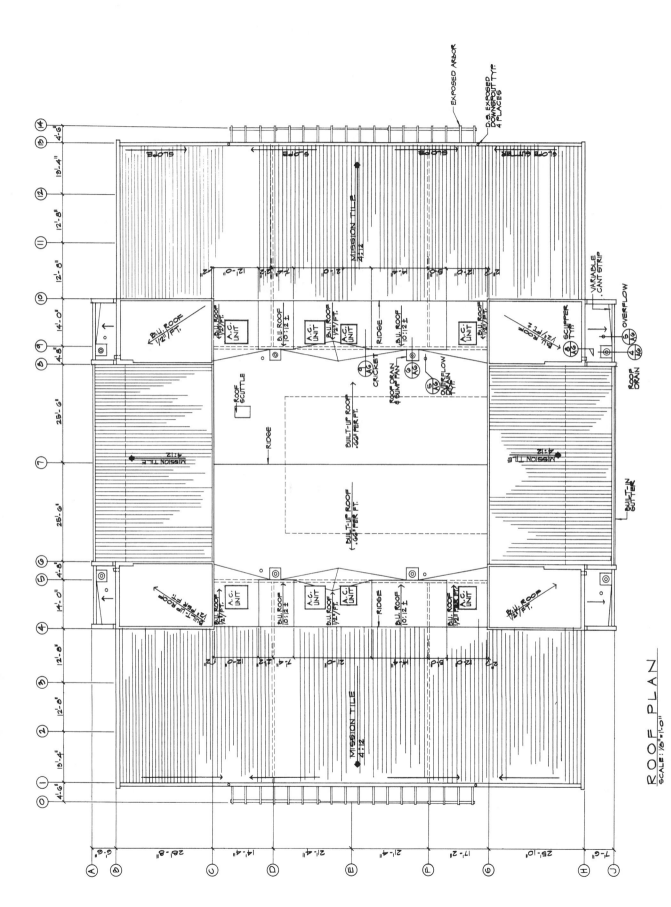

Figure 19.60 Roof plan—Stage IV.

641

Figure 19.61 Aerial photo of finished roof. (William Boggs Aerial Photography. Reprinted with permission.)

■ ROOF FRAMING PLAN

For a description of the parts of the roof framing plan, refer to the roof and ceiling framing chapter (Chapter 14). Here, we will describe the approach and method used to obtain the necessary information for this plan, and how the plan was drafted.

Stage I

First, a reproducible and a diazo print were made of the floor plan at an early stage without dimensions or notes.

See Figure 19.62. The diazo print was then sent to the structural engineer for structural information (column and beam locations, etc.).

Stage II

The engineer returned the diazo print with his sketches, and the refined sketches were then drafted onto the reproducible. See Figure 19.63. Notice the skylights and recall that they were deleted at a later stage, at the client's request.

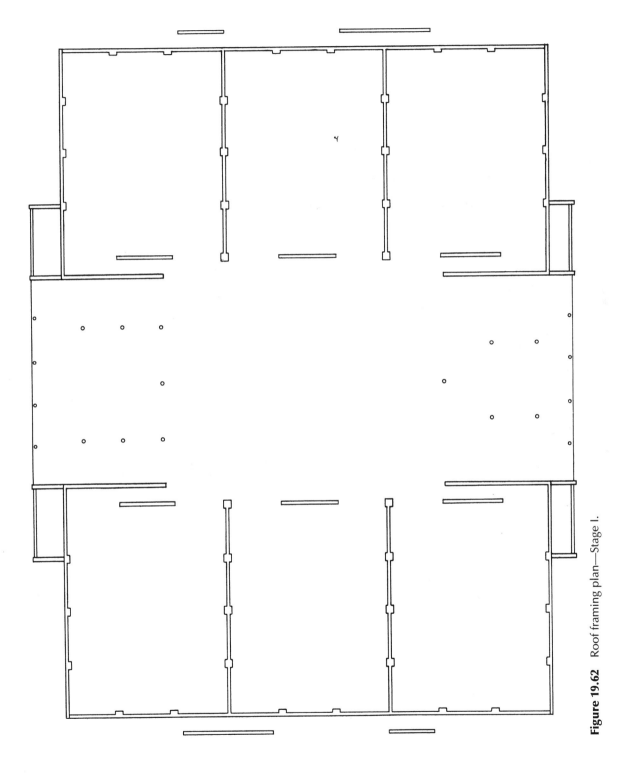

Figure 19.62 Roof framing plan—Stage I.

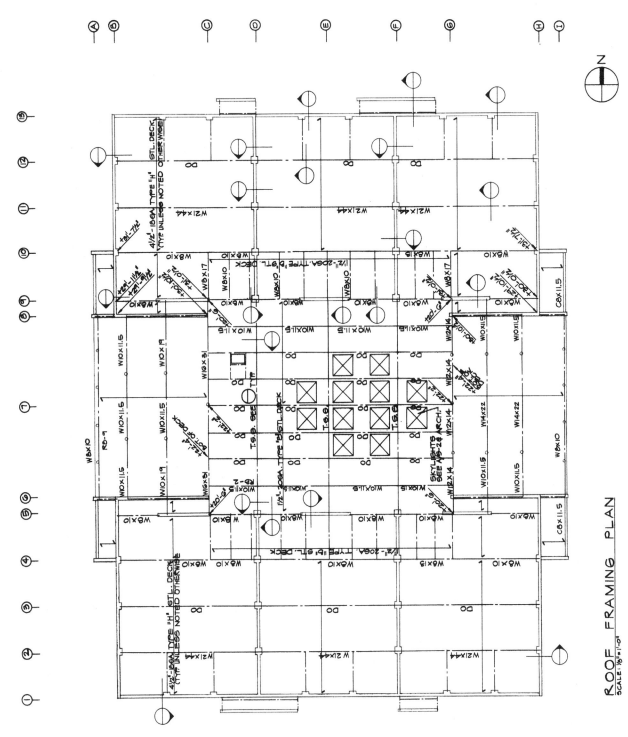

ROOF FRAMING PLAN
SCALE: 1/8" = 1'-0"

Figure 19.63 Roof framing plan—Stage II.

chapter

20

MADISON STEEL BUILDING

The client, an insurance company, requested an architectural firm to design an office building, titled the Madison Office Building, with a gross floor area of approximately 33,000 square feet and adequate ground level parking. The ground level parking requirement dictated that the office areas be located on the second and third floor levels. The remaining ground floor level would be used primarily for public access control and meeting existing building code requirements.

The long, rectangular shape of the property had one automotive access point on the West side. This dictated the parking design along with the locations of the supporting structural members including the steel columns and shear wall.

■ INITIAL SCHEMATIC STUDIES

Stage I

After members of our firm walked around the site and studied the adjacent commercial developments, the initial schematic studies were begun. As stated, the ingress and egress for automobile traffic was available only on the West end of the site. It was determined that parking

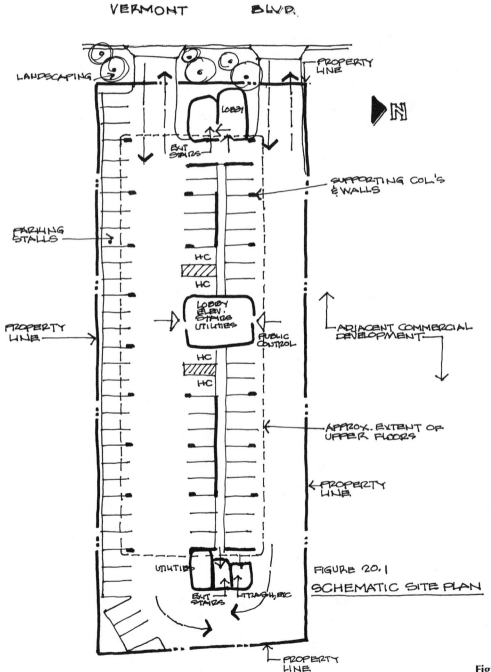

Figure 20.1 Schematic site plan.

stalls were best located adjacent to the South property line and with opposing parking stalls accessible from two traffic lanes. The use of 90° parking stalls provided the most efficient parking and satisfied the client's requirements. The schematic studies also included the desirable locations for lobbies, exit stairs, utilities, and a trash area. Figure 20.1 illustrates the initial schematic site plan design.

Stage II

After the initial schematic studies were completed, a scaled preliminary ground floor plan was developed.

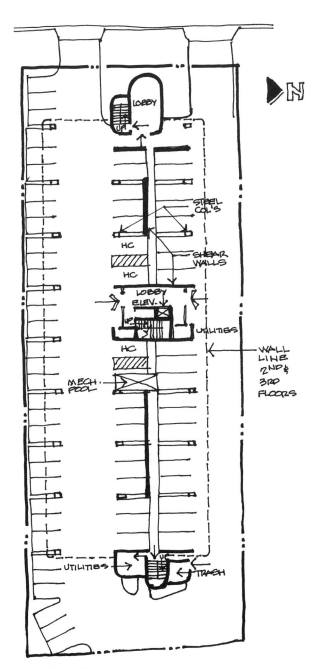

Figure 20.2 Preliminary ground floor plan.

This plan included the site plan, parking stall layout, lobbies, and exit stair locations. At this stage, a preliminary scaled drawing was used to establish the viability of the schematic approach. This initial scaled preliminary design established the locations of the supporting steel columns. The column locations were dictated by the parking stall design. Other important areas located on this drawing were the handicap parking stalls, lobbies, stairs, elevator, utility and machine rooms, potential shear wall locations, and a pool area that the mechanical engineer required for a possible ice bank cooling system. This scaled preliminary drawing also established the approximate locations of the second and third floor levels. The scaled preliminary ground floor plan is depicted in Figure 20.2.

Stage III

From the preliminary scaled ground floor plan, a study was made for an overlay for the second floor plan. This study established the steel column locations derived from the parking design. The exterior wall locations were established with reference to the steel column locations. The second floor preliminary floor plan also provided the locations for the required exit stairs, elevator, restrooms, and potential chase locations for the mechanical ducts. This plan also showed the floor square footage requested by the client for the second and third floors. Figure 20.3 illustrates the preliminary scaled second floor plan.

Stage IV

From the preliminary scaled second floor plan, overlay studies were created to establish the third floor plan. This preliminary third floor level incorporated the exact steel column locations that trace down through the second floor level and terminate at the ground floor level. A small mezzanine level and the stairway access was incorporated above the third floor level. Other space elements such as required exit stairs, elevators, and restrooms were provided. The scaled preliminary third floor plan is shown in Figure 20.4.

Stage V

The next stage in the preliminary studies for this steel structured office building was the design and development of the exterior elevations. Because the locations of the interior wall partitions had not been established for the interior space planning, a banding of windows was designed for all sides, using a window mullion module dimension that would conform to the varying dimensions for offices and other types of rooms. The exterior massing elements such as stairwells and lobbies were rounded and curved to develop a sculptural appearance. This approach was also applied to the corners of the building and the curved glazing at those locations. With

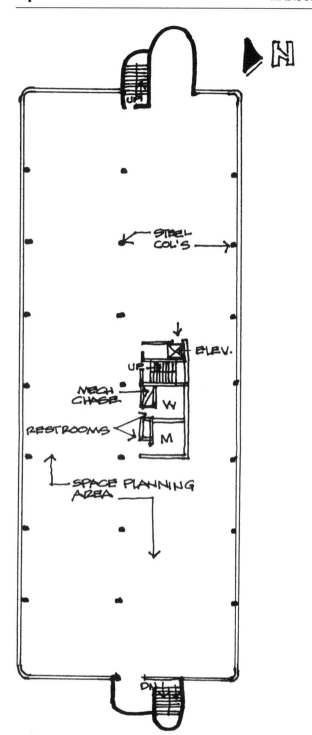

Figure 20.3   Preliminary second floor plan.

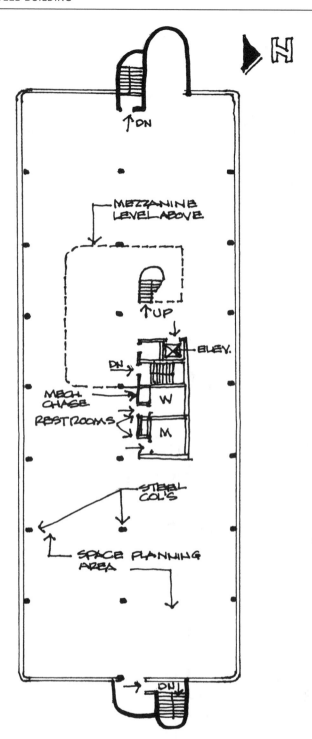

Figure 20.4   Preliminary third floor plan.

the approval of the consulting structural engineer, circular openings were designed in the shear walls to relieve the starkness of the solid walls and to continue the curved, sculptural appearance. After further study of the ground level steel columns, it was decided to increase the mass of the columns by forming a sculptured concrete element around the columns. These and other con-siderations were the initial design concepts for the exterior elevations. It should be noted that the architect and the design team envisioned an exterior wall finish material and substrate material that would be conducive to designing the round and curved shapes of the exterior building walls. Preliminary exterior elevation studies are depicted in Figure 20.5.

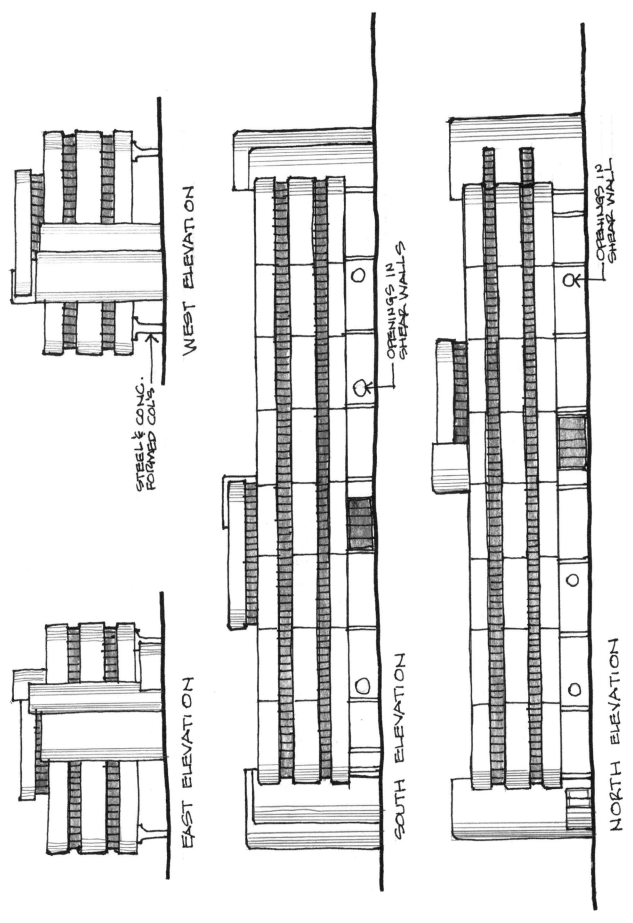

WEST ELEVATION

STEEL & CONC.
FORMED COL'S

EAST ELEVATION

OPENINGS IN
SHEAR WALLS

SOUTH ELEVATION

OPENINGS IN
SHEAR WALL

NORTH ELEVATION

Figure 20.5 Preliminary exterior elevations.

649

■ WORKING DRAWINGS

GROUND FLOOR PLAN

Stage I

The first step in the evolution of the working drawings was to precisely lay out the site plan, incorporating the parking stalls, traffic lanes, handicap parking stall, and spaces for public access locations. These accurately scaled areas were predicated on the schematic studies of the site plan and the ground floor plan.

Once the accurately scaled parking stalls were located, then the locations of the steel supporting columns could be established. From this drawing, a matrix identifying system designating the various column and wall locations was created. Refer to Chapters 2 and 3 for detailed information and explanations of the use of a matrix system. Figure 20.6 illustrates a site plan, parking layouts, and the initial structural matrix system with bubbles for the purpose of identifying the locations of the steel columns and wall. This drawing, which was prepared by the CAD operator for the project, was the first and the basis for the additional layering of succeeding drawings that were used in developing the various floor levels for the completion of the working drawings. In general, the layering process for drawings is the evolution of a series of drawings that have been formatted from initial drawings which become the basis for all succeeding drawings. For additional information relative to the layering process, refer to Chapter 3.

Stage II

From Stage I, a basic matrix system layout for all structural members was established in Stage II. This drawing became the primary structural template for all succeeding floors, incorporating the floor and roof framing plans, exterior elevations, and building sections. Note that on the West side matrix, there are symbols with a specific letter designation that may be followed by a number. This tells the viewer that there is an identifying wall located north of column "D". The basic matrix layout template is depicted in Figure 20.7.

Stage III

With the combination of layering from Stages I and II, a third stage for the ground floor plan was developed. This drawing illustrated the combination of the parking stalls, the matrix system, the supporting steel column locations, and the wall locations for public access and structural considerations. The drawing also defined the wall boundary location for the succeeding upper floor levels. As a result of the early schematic drawings, elliptical

wall shapes were incorporated into the stairwell walls and lobby locations at the West and East sides of the structure. In the main lobby area, which is located approximately in the center of the building, other spaces were established for facilities such as an elevator, stairwell, and machine and utility rooms. This drawing is shown in Figure 20.8.

Stage IV

The drawing for Stage IV incorporated the required number of risers and treads for the stairs while establishing the elevator size. The CAD operator designated the doors and the glass areas that are adjacent to the lobbies, along with the room numbers, for the various areas. These room numbers were eventually defined for their use on a room schedule.

As mentioned earlier in regard to the schematic studies, the architect and the mechanical engineer decided to incorporate an "off-peak cooling system," which can also be referred to as an "ice bank" system. This system requires a pool for the storage of the coolant. The pool is now shown at the matrix lines of D and E. The purpose for the off-peak cooling system is to save energy and costs by developing the coolant necessary for daily use. The system produces coolant in the late night or early morning hours when the demand for and cost of electricity is at a minimum. Finally, the title and the scale were established for this drawing. Figure 20.9 depicts the first floor plan for Stage IV.

Stage V

At Stage V, dimension lines and dimensions were established for the column and wall locations. These particular dimension lines related to the matrix system and provided a basis for the dimensioning of the various spaces. Parking stalls and automobile access areas were dimensioned, along with the handicap parking access areas. The dimensioning of the walkways, trash areas, and the off-peak cooling pool were shown at this stage. The drawing also defined the various curb radius dimensions within the parking and automobile access areas. This drawing stage is shown in Figure 20.10.

Stage VI

In Stage VI, the principal information added includes the various locations of the building structural sections. This is done at this time in order to allow the structural engineering firm to commence with the initial structural design and calculations. Note the bubble designations and the direction from which the building section will be viewed. This stage is illustrated in Figure 20.11.

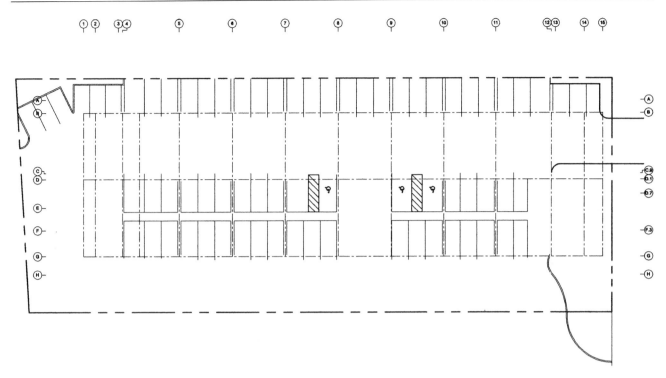

Figure 20.6 Matrix system.

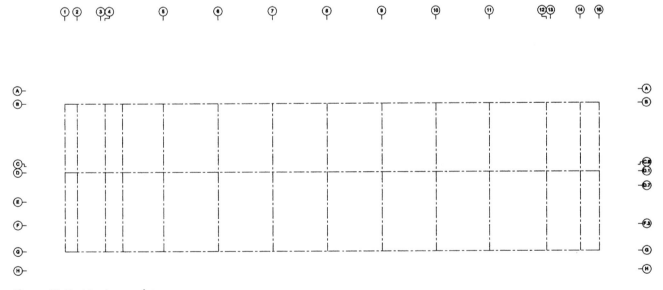

Figure 20.7 Matrix template.

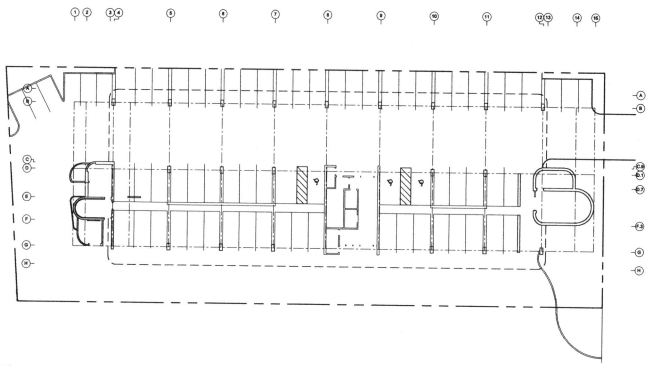

Figure 20.8   Ground floor development—Stage III.

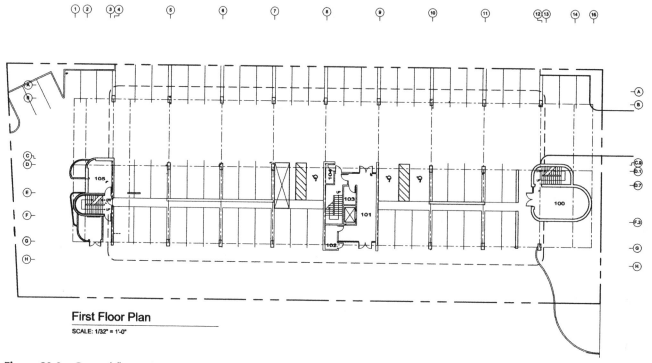

First Floor Plan

SCALE: 1/32" = 1'-0"

Figure 20.9   Ground floor—Stage IV.

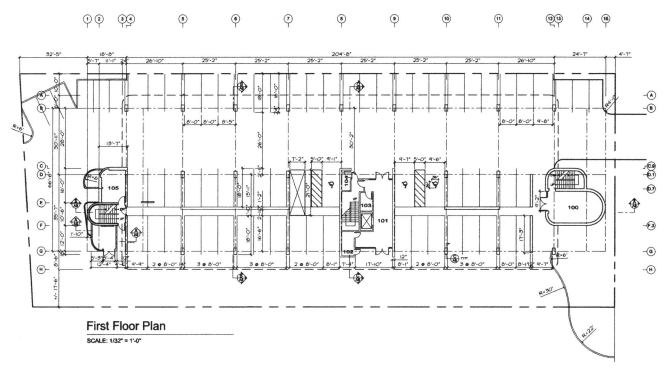

First Floor Plan
SCALE: 1/32" = 1'-0"

Figure 20.10 Ground floor—Stage V.

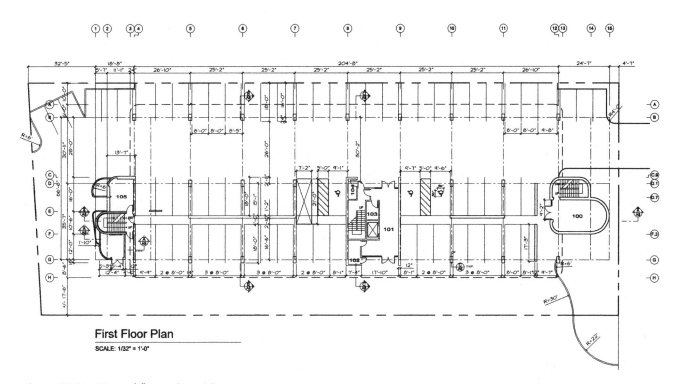

First Floor Plan
SCALE: 1/32" = 1'-0"

Figure 20.11 Ground floor—Stage VI.

Stage VII

The final stage for the first floor plan is to provide notes for items such as the building site lot bearings and dimensions, handicap designation requirements, steel and concrete column reference detail symbols, and the size and material for the automobile wheel stops. Also included are any notes in the trash area indicating the access gate size, and the steel arbor members for the open trellis above the trash compound.

The drawing depicts the extent of the floor pavers that are to be installed in the main lobby, or Room 101. Note that the columns and walls have been shaded to provide greater clarity in view of the fact that there are many other lines defining other spaces. A North arrow was located on this drawing to establish directional designations for reference on succeeding drawings. Figure 20.12 shows the final first floor plan at this stage. Door and window designation bubbles will be located on future enlarged drawings.

SECOND FLOOR PLAN

Stage I

The first task for Stage I of the second floor plan is to review and finalize the matrix symbolizing for all structural steel columns and exterior walls. This completed drawing is a culmination of a series of drawings evolving from the initial matrix that was shown in Figure 20.7. The finalized matrix drawing is depicted in Figure 20.13.

Stage II

With the use of the finalized matrix developed in Stage I as a basis for identifying the locations of steel columns and walls, a floor plan is developed that is primarily an overlay of the finalized first floor plan, as shown in Figure 20.12. This plan indicates the wall locations from the final first floor plan, including the walls for the elevator shaft and stairwells and the exterior wall extremities. This stage also shows the locations for all the vertical window mullions around the perimeter of the exterior walls. The drawing for Stage II is illustrated in Figure 20.14.

Stage III

The purpose of Stage III for the second floor plan is to delineate the risers and treads for all the stairwells, the elevator location, and the required vertical shafts for the housing of mechanical ducts. Restroom locations are also included in this stage. The room number designations are indicated, as well as door locations and the door swing directions. Finally, the second floor plan title

and drawing scale are shown graphically. This drawing is shown in Figure 20.15.

Stage IV

Stage IV of the second floor plan deals mainly with dimensioning and notes pertaining to the spacing of the vertical window mullions. The dimensioning values have been established primarily in the final stage of the first floor plan, with the main supporting columns aligning with the floors above. In addition, the referencing matrix symbols are identical to those of the first floor plan. This stage is depicted in Figure 20.16.

Stage V

The next step in completing the second floor plan is to designate the locations for the structural cross-sections and to provide a symbol for the referencing of these structural sections. These sections are taken in the North/South and East/West directions. Other details that are symbolized with a bubble and a detail reference are shown for a steel column and steel beam connection. These reference bubbles occur at the center supporting columns. Further detail symbols are indicated for the exterior window and wall assembly, while providing a reference detail symbol for the steel columns at the exterior walls. Notes for the exterior window mullion spaces are shown for the glazing areas found on the East/West walls and the North/South walls. The completion of Stage V is illustrated in Figure 20.17.

Stage VI

The intent of the overlay drawing in Stage VI, the final stage, of the second floor plan is to add additional notes for such items as a fire extinguisher cabinet, and areas that are to be drawn in a larger scale for clarity. Also noted are additional mechanical chase locations. A North arrow is added to the drawing, for the convenience of the viewer, to reference the building orientation while providing the directions for the exterior elevations. The foregoing information is shown in Figure 20.18.

THIRD FLOOR PLAN

Stage I

The first step in Stage I for the development of the third floor plan is to start and work from the governing matrix system as done for the second floor plan. The only difference between the matrix system for the second floor plan, as shown in Figure 20.13, and the matrix system for

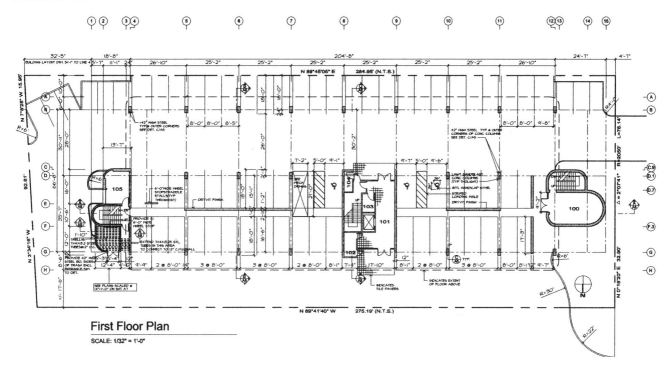

First Floor Plan

SCALE: 1/32" = 1'-0"

Figure 20.12 Ground floor—Stage VII.

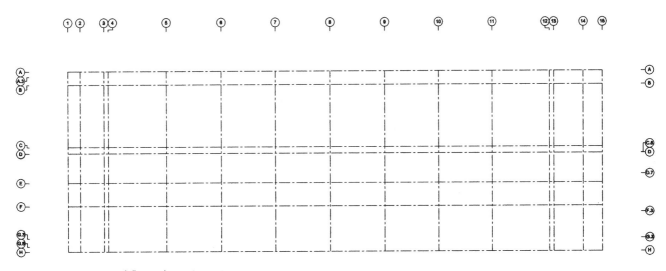

Figure 20.13 Second floor plan—Stage I.

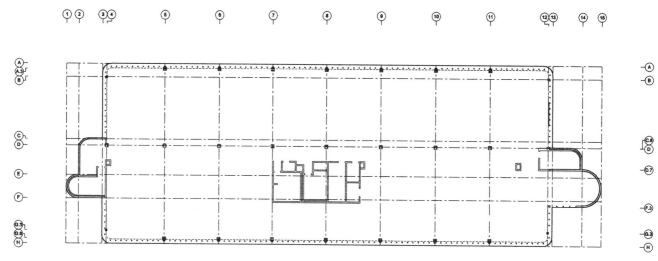

Figure 20.14 Second floor plan—Stage II.

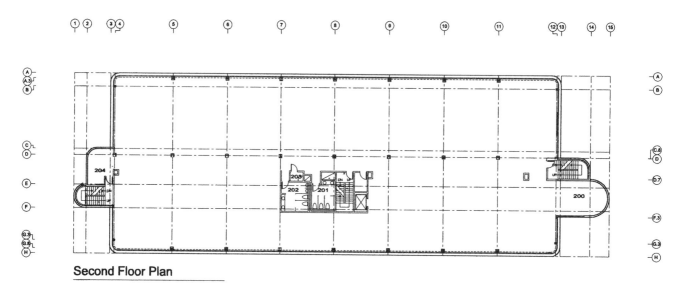

Second Floor Plan

Figure 20.15 Second floor plan—Stage III.

Second Floor Plan

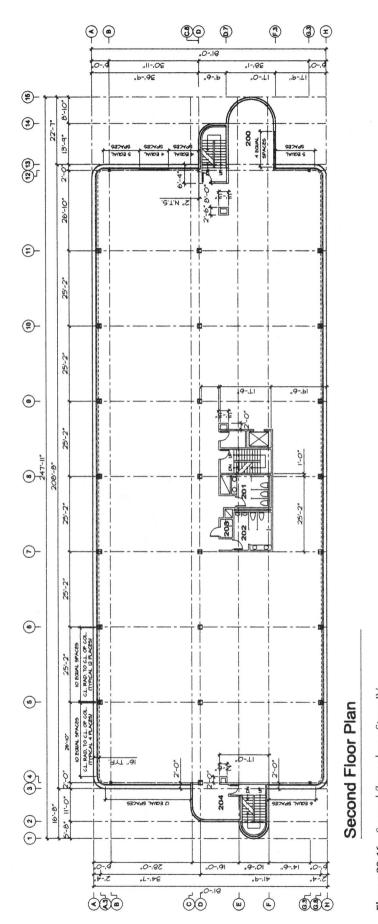

Figure 20.16 Second floor plan—Stage IV.

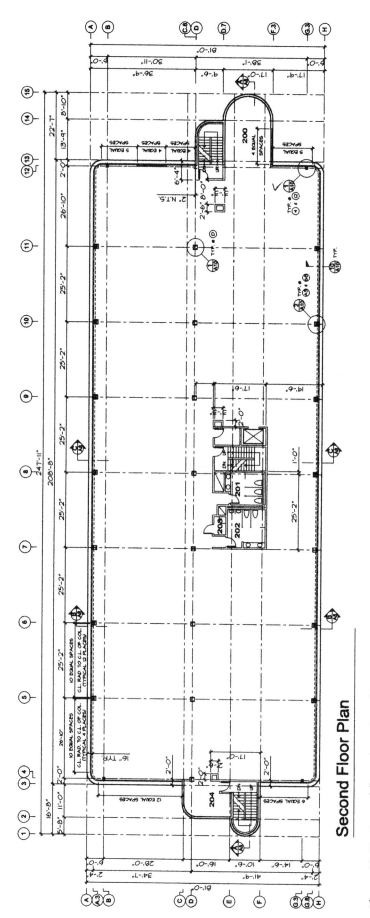

Second Floor Plan

Figure 20.17 Second floor plan—Stage V.

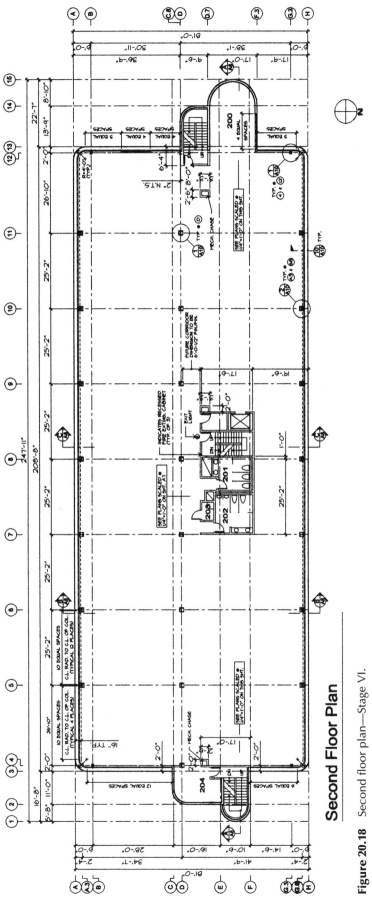

Second Floor Plan

Figure 20.18 Second floor plan—Stage VI.

the third floor plan is the addition of two matrix symbols identified as D/5 and F/1, which are located at two interior walls. Figure 20.19 illustrates the matrix system that is used for the third floor plan.

Stage II

Stage II for the third floor plan is a duplicate of the CAD drawing used in Stage II for the second floor plan, shown in Figure 20.14. The only variation from the second floor plan drawing is the addition of matrix symbols D/5 and F/1, as indicated in Figure 20.20. The locations of the vertical window mullions, corresponding to the second floor glazing, are also shown at this stage.

Stage III

Stage III shows the risers and treads for all the stairwells, which include an additional stair for access to a mezzanine level. The mezzanine level will be accessible only from the third floor. Broken lines are added to this drawing to depict the mezzanine floor area above. Also incorporated at this stage are the men's and women's restrooms, the elevator, the vertical mechanical shafts required for the air-conditioning ducts, and the room numbering for the various areas. The title identifying the third floor plan and the scale of the drawing are added at this stage as well. Figure 20.21 illustrates Stage III of the third floor plan.

Stage IV

The initial step for Stage IV is to lay out all the necessary dimension lines for all sides of the structure and the numerical values within the dimension lines. The numerical values are then checked to be sure that they relate to those values found in Figure 20.16 of the second floor plan. The drawing for Stage IV of the third floor plan is depicted in Figure 20.22.

Stage V

The main difference between Stage V and the previous stage is the addition of various detail reference symbols. These symbols illustrate where the building cross-sections are to be taken and the viewing direction. Detail bubbles indicating the detail number and sheet number are also shown. These particular bubbles are located at the steel column and steel beam connection in the center of the building and at the exterior walls. Figure 20.23 illustrates the drawing for Stage V.

Stage VI

The final stage for the third floor plan drawing is shown in Figure 20.24. This drawing provides additional notes describing the location of the recessed fire extinguisher cabinet and the exit light locations, and reference notes for reviewing of larger-scaled drawings located in the stairwell, the lobby areas, and the restrooms. These notes tell the viewer where to find the enlarged drawings. Finally, the directional North arrow symbol has been added to the drawing.

EXTERIOR ELEVATIONS

Stage I

The initial preparation for developing the exterior elevations begins with drawing in light broken lines, which will indicate the floor line level for the various floors. This is done for all four of the exterior elevations. In this stage, the ground level is represented with a solid line. The CAD operator uses this drawing for the layering or tracking of all future drawings of the exterior elevations. The initial drawing for Stage I of the exterior elevations is depicted in Figure 20.25.

Stage II

After determining the ground level and the other floor levels, we use a solid vertical line to identify the exterior wall extremities on the various sides of the exterior elevations. This drawing indicates the general massing of the building. Stage II is shown in Figure 20.26.

Stage III

In Stage II, the various exterior wall extremities for the building elements were established. Stage III is drawn to refine all the horizontal and vertical masses of the structure. This refined dimensional drawing illustrates the heights of the roof and floor masses while indicating the height of the continuous window band. Many design refinements are created at this stage. These refinements include avoiding square edges at the roof, floor, and wall masses. This was done to give the building a sculptured appearance. To provide compatibility with the sculpting of the building, it was decided to encase the exposed rectangular steel columns in concrete for two primary reasons. First, the fluid nature of concrete could be utilized in sculpting the columns. Secondly, the concrete could provide a larger proportional mass to the main supporting columns. Note the two vertical lines representing the main supporting columns. This particular column detail is illustrated later in the chapter.

The roof and window elements for the mezzanine level above the third floor are shown at this stage. Stage III of the exterior elevations is illustrated in Figure 20.27.

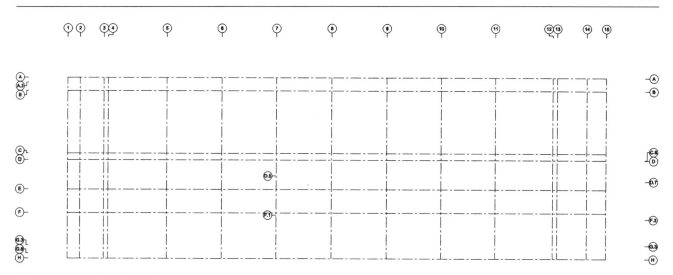

Figure 20.19 Third floor plan—Stage I.

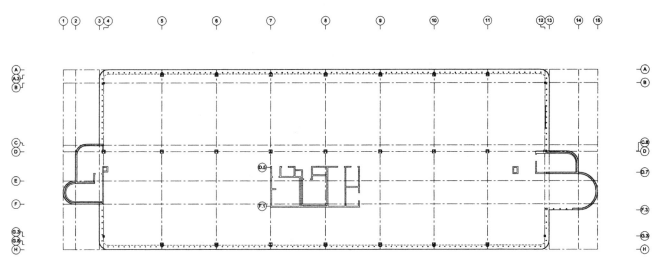

Figure 20.20 Third floor plan—Stage II.

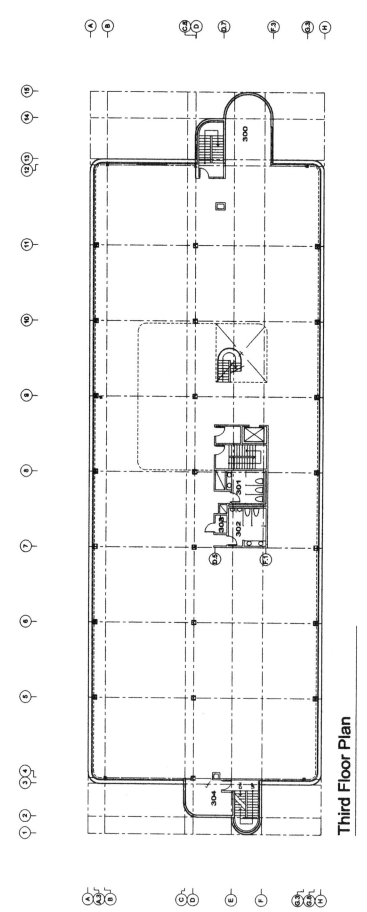

Third Floor Plan

Figure 20.21 Third floor plan—Stage III.

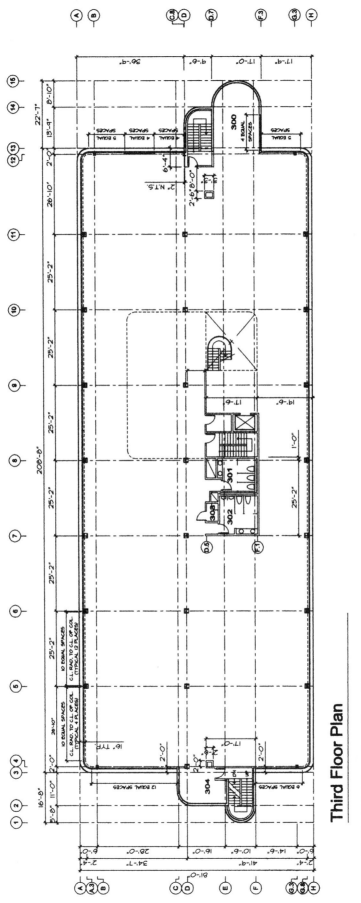

Third Floor Plan

Figure 20.22 Third floor plan—Stage IV.

Third Floor Plan

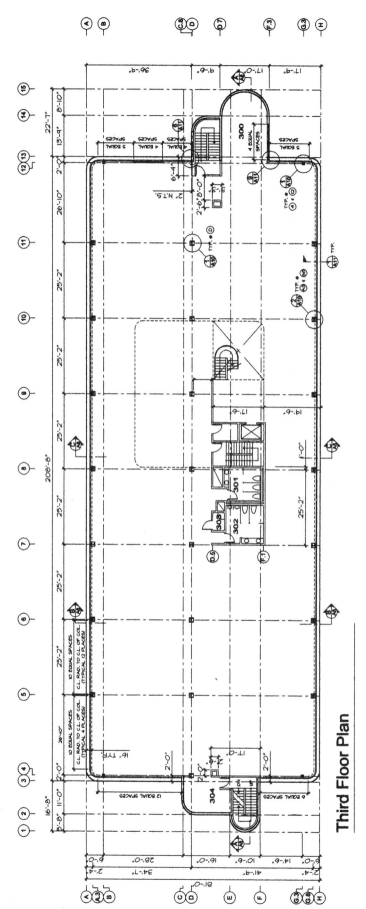

Figure 20.23 Third floor plan—Stage V.

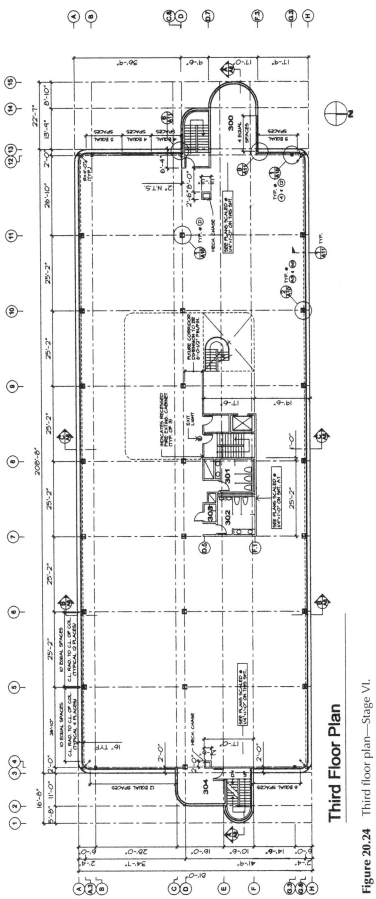

Third Floor Plan

Figure 20.24 Third floor plan—Stage VI.

Figure 20.25 Exterior elevations—Stage I.

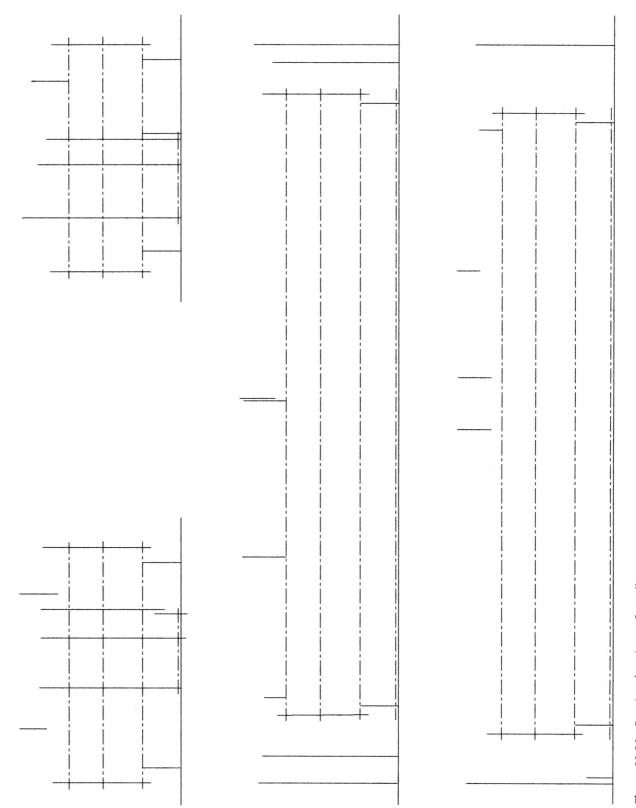

Figure 20.26 Exterior elevations—Stage II.

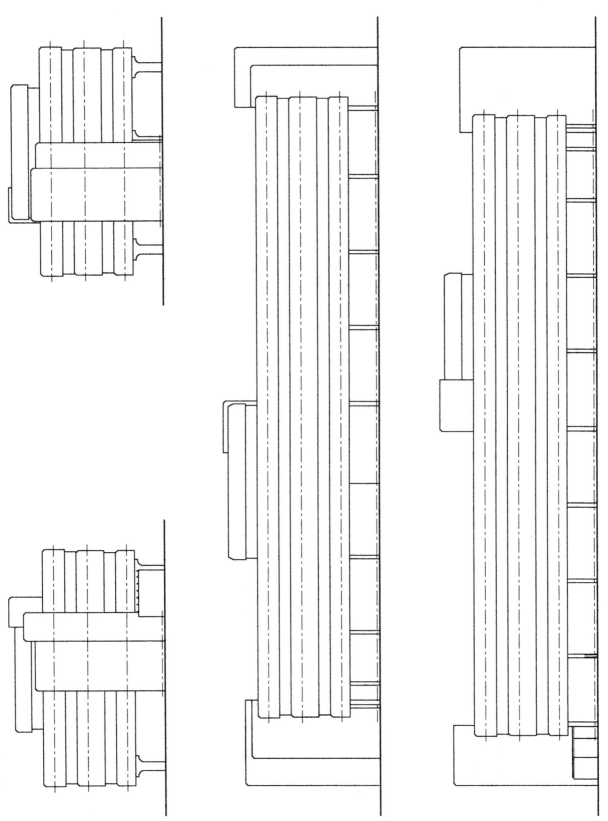

Figure 20.27 Exterior elevations—Stage III.

Stage IV

After establishing the basic elements for the four exterior elevations, refinements within those elements are added. These include the vertical window mullions, glass entry doors and the adjacent glazing in the lobby area, and the access gates at the trash area. It was decided to provide round sculptured openings in the masonry shear walls at this stage. This was done after consulting with the structural engineer. Figure 20.28 depicts Stage IV.

Stage V

The drawing of Stage V depicts the shading of all the glazing areas and the gradation of vertical lines that are simulating the curved wall edges, corners of the roof sections, and the floor masses. It was decided to shade the glazed areas for the purpose of providing greater clarity for the viewing of the exterior elevations. Note that the initial broken lines that were the basis for all the elevations are still indicated. This drawing is shown in Figure 20.29.

Stage VI

Stage VI is the final drawing for the exterior elevations. This drawing is a culmination of all the former stages with the following additions:

1. Lettering is included, indicating the direction of all four elevations (East, West, North, South).
2. The scale of the four drawings is shown.
3. Notes are added, indicating the sizes of the steel members for the open trellis work at the trash area.
4. Openings in the masonry shear walls are shown and noted with the size of the openings.
5. Detail bubbles are included, indicating the detail number and sheet number pertaining to the window sections.
6. Exterior wall and spandrel materials are designated.

Figure 20.30 illustrates the final stage for the exterior elevations.

THIRD FLOOR FRAMING PLAN

Stage I

The first step in developing the third floor framing plan is to recall the matrix layout that originally identified the locations of the columns and beams in the building. The matrix layout used for Stage I of the third floor framing plan is an amended portion of the matrix layout found in Figure 20.19. The initial matrix for the third floor framing plan deals with the matrix symbols 4 through 12 and

A/3 through G/8. Lettering identifying the third floor framing plan and the scale of the drawing are also shown at this time. This matrix drawing identifying the column and beam locations is depicted in Figure 20.31.

Stage II

Using the first stage drawing as the basis for the Stage II drawing, the perimeter exterior wall lines are drawn along with the exterior wall configurations of the stairwells and the lobbies. Also included in this drawing are the supporting column locations. These are shown at the perimeter walls and the main supporting center beam along the matrix line D. This drawing is illustrated in Figure 20.32.

Stage III

Prior to the completion of the drawing for Stage III, the drawings of Stage I and Stage II are sent to the consulting structural engineer for his or her use in developing the engineering calculations and the required intermediate beam locations. Required beams have also been shown in the stairwell and lobby areas. Framing members that provide the opening around the elevator are also shown. It should be noted at this stage that because this is an all-structural-steel building, the intermediate structural members spanning between the main North/South members have been spaced to receive a corrugated steel decking with a hard rock concrete topping. Figure 20.33 illustrates Stage III for the third floor framing plan.

Stage IV

On the Stage IV drawing, all the necessary dimension lines and the numerical values are shown. These numerical values have been carefully checked with the dimensional values found in Figure 20.22 of the third floor plan. Checking the dimensional values is critical to maintaining the structural simplicity of the steel frames. Notes referencing the architectural drawings and details in the elevator area are indicated. The fourth stage of this plan is shown in Figure 20.34.

Stage V

The main difference between the drawing in Stage IV and Stage V is the addition of the various structural detail bubbles and their symbols showing an enlarged drawing for a particular structural area. The numerous structural details that are designated by the detail bubbles are usually drawn and shown as part of the structural engineer's plans. The drawing for Stage V is depicted in Figure 20.35.

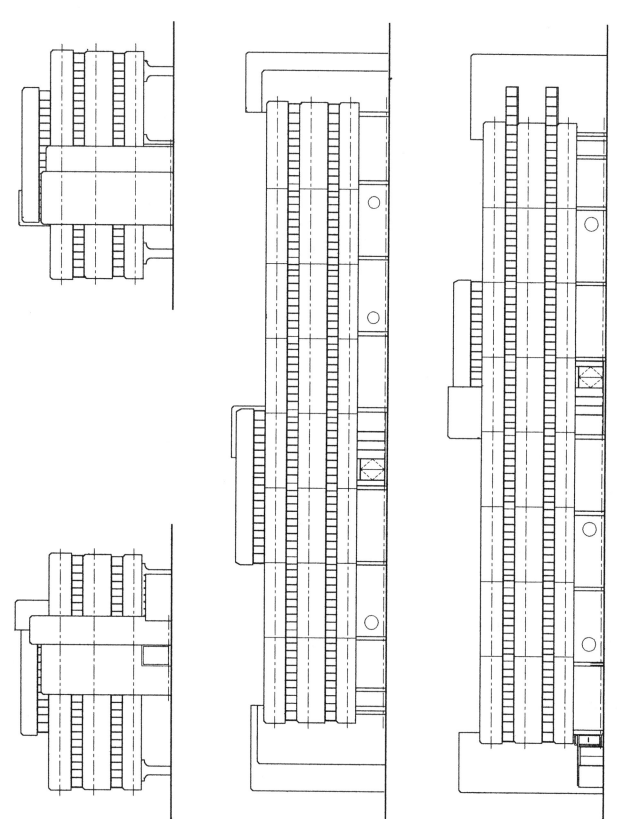

Figure 20.28 Exterior elevations—Stage IV.

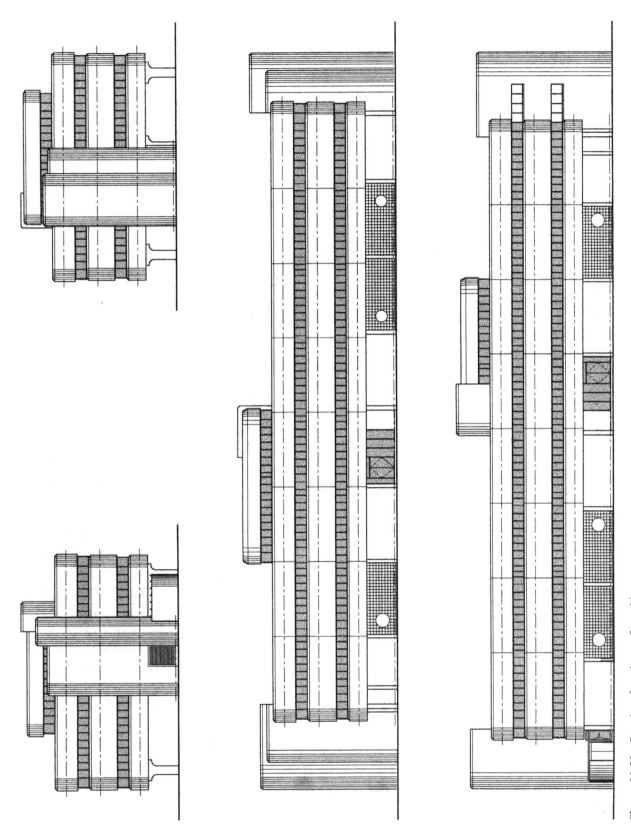

Figure 20.29 Exterior elevations—Stage V.

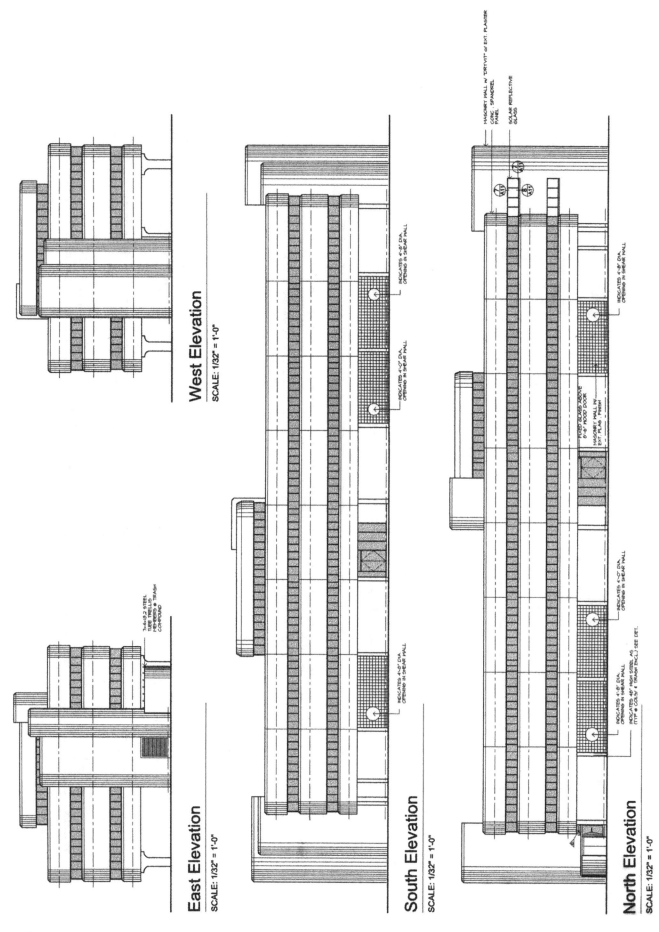

East Elevation

SCALE: 1/32" = 1'-0"

West Elevation

SCALE: 1/32" = 1'-0"

South Elevation

SCALE: 1/32" = 1'-0"

North Elevation

SCALE: 1/32" = 1'-0"

Figure 20.30 Exterior elevations—Stage VI.

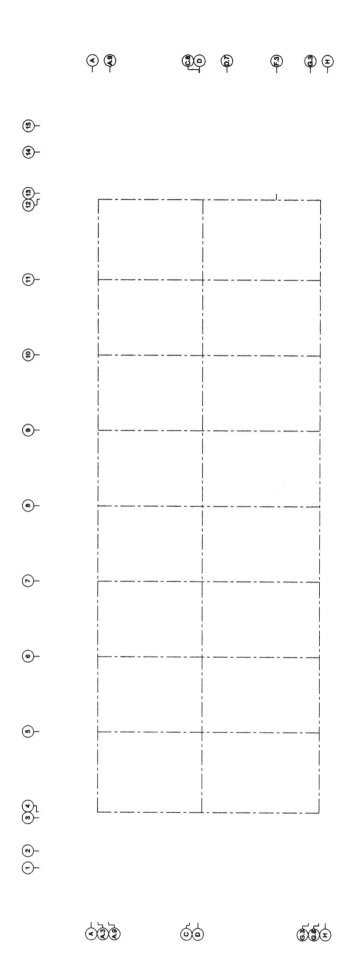

Third Floor Framing Plan

Figure 20.31 Third floor framing plan—Stage I.

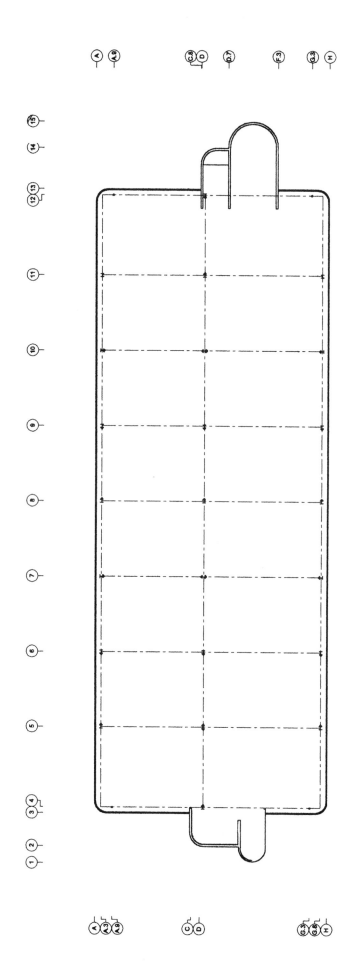

Third Floor Framing Plan

Figure 20.32 Third floor framing plan—Stage II.

Third Floor Framing Plan

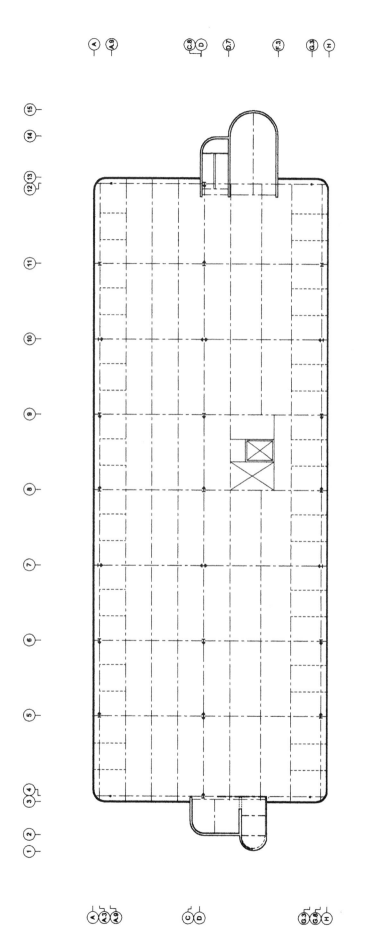

Figure 20.33 Third floor framing plan—Stage III.

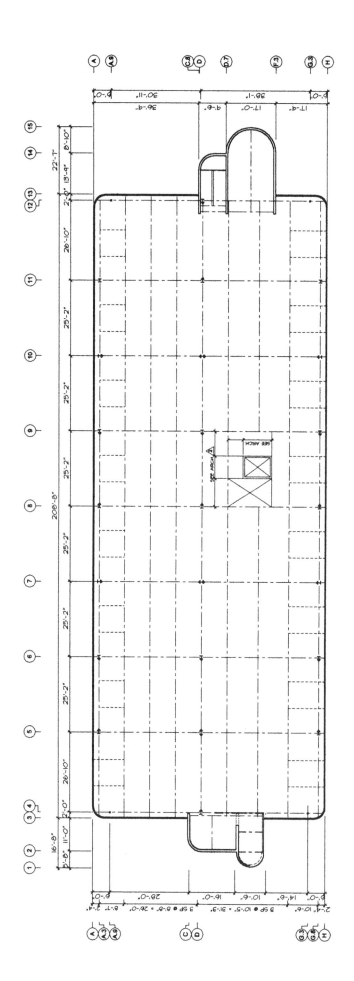

Third Floor Framing Plan

Figure 20.34 Third floor framing plan—Stage IV.

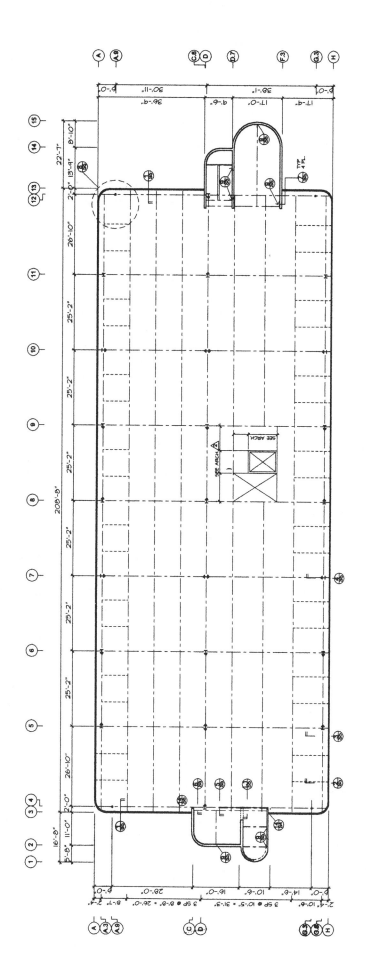

Third Floor Framing Plan

Figure 20.35 Third floor framing plan—Stage V.

Stage VI

Stage VI is the final drawing for the third floor framing plan. This drawing incorporates all the various steel beam sizes and steel column sizes. The structural engineer has opted to use the designation letters "DO" where a series of floor beams are identical in dimension and weight. This is indicated for many floor beams that span in an East/West direction. A general note defining the thickness of the concrete floor filling and the gauge of the corrugated steel decking substrate is included between matrix lines 6 and 7, as well as in the stairwell areas. A legend is provided directly above the third floor framing plan title. The legend shown in Figure 20.36 defines the abbreviations for the letters "TS," "BF," and "MF," which indicate that this structure is defined as a moment frame and braced frame building. In general, a moment frame is one in which all the lateral forces such as earthquakes or strong winds are resisted by the moment connections that are engineered and developed at the steel beam and column connections. For this building, those connections are done with welding techniques. The moment frame designation "MF" is shown in Figure 20.36 on the North and South walls. The braced frame designation "BF" is noted on matrix lines 4 and 12 in Figure 20.36. The braced frame concept depicted here uses horizontal steel beams for the bracing in those directions. The North directional arrow is shown to provide referencing orientation. Figure 20.36 illustrates the final drawing for the third floor framing plan. The stages and the drawings for the second floor framing plan and the roof framing plan are not shown; however, the procedures for their various stages and drawings are similar to those shown for the third floor framing plan.

BUILDING SECTION B-B

Stage I

The basic approach for implementing the initial drawing of a building section is to establish the correct direction of the given detail symbol and lay out the known floor elevation levels. It is also prudent at this stage to indicate the ceiling heights and to show the vertical lines that represent column and beam alignments. The location of these vertical lines is established from the matrix system shown on the floor plans. Broken lines are used for the horizontal floor and ceiling levels and for the column and beam locations. The basis for determining the various floor and ceiling levels is established from the drawing of Stage I, exterior elevations, found in Figure 20.25. It should be noted that the architect consulted with the structural engineer to determine the necessary heights and clearances that would be required to facilitate the

various steel structural members. The initial layout of the broken lines that have been discussed is depicted in Figure 20.37.

Stage II

The Stage II drawing is developed from a direct overlay of all the designated broken lines discussed in Stage I. Under the direction of the structural engineer, the required steel supporting members for the roof framing and the second and third floor framing members are now drawn in at the desired scale. Note that the finished floor level broken line is shown just above the steel floor members. This affords the required space for the installation of the steel decking and the concrete floor topping. Also shown at this stage are the main supporting steel columns at the ground floor level and the main exterior and interior supporting column locations at the second and third floor levels. In addition, this drawing depicts the initial shape of the concrete that will encase the steel columns in the parking area, along with the required spread footing for the support of the composite concrete and steel columns. A detail for the concrete-encased steel column is shown later in this chapter. The masonry shear wall and its required foundation footing are incorporated in this stage. Figure 20.38 illustrates Stage II for the drawing of the building section.

Stage III

The building section, which is taken on matrix line 6, is now profiled with darker lines in order to define the main supporting steel beams and the finished ceiling line at the first floor level. This drawing illustrates the exterior finish wall configuration and the extension of the exterior wall that establishes the parapet at the roof level. The window band around the perimeter of the building has been recessed for the purpose of defining the fenestration. An enlarged wall section taken at the window and wall area is shown later in this chapter. The drawing for Stage III is shown in Figure 20.39.

Stage IV

The main additions incorporated in the Stage IV drawing of building section B-B are the designations of the various matrix symbols and the vertical dimension lines with their numerical values between the floor levels. Note that "Varies" has been indicated on the dimension line that runs from the ground floor level to the second floor level. This is done because the parking level floor elevation varies owing to the necessary level changes to provide proper water drainage. Figure 20.40 depicts the Stage IV drawing.

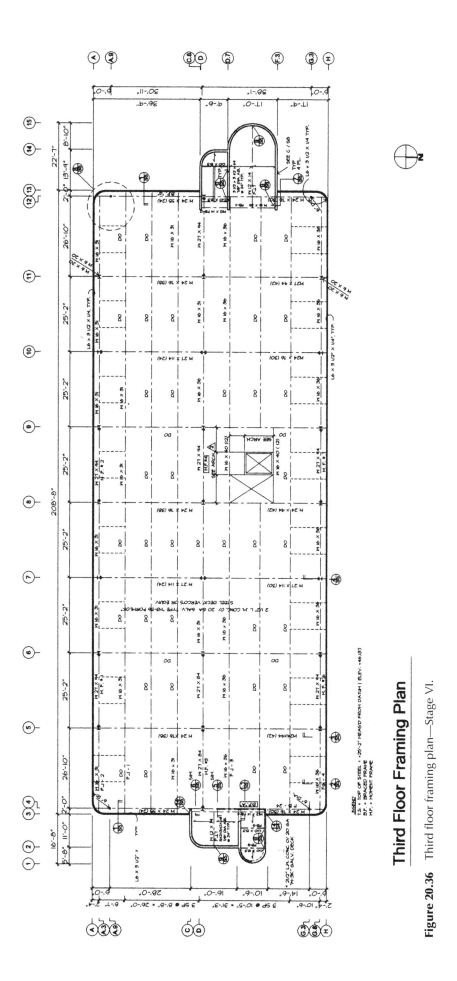

Third Floor Framing Plan

Figure 20.36 Third floor framing plan—Stage VI.

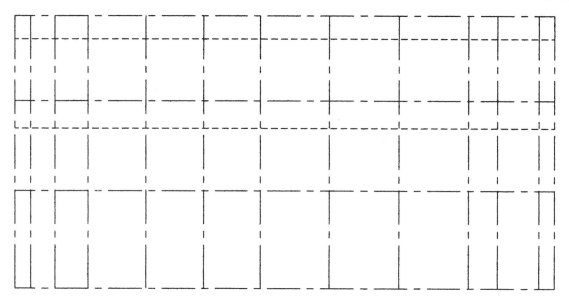

Figure 20.37 Building section B-B—Stage I.

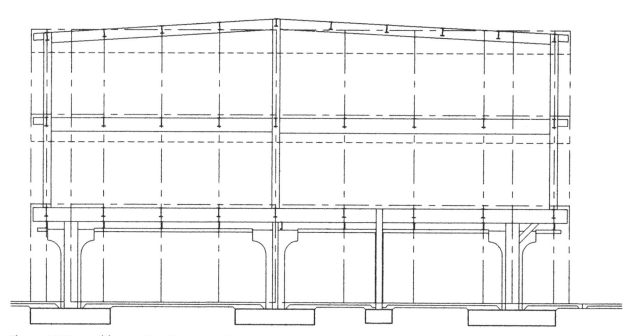

Figure 20.38 Building section B-B—Stage II.

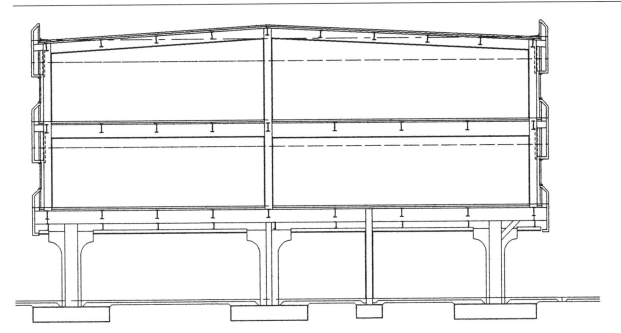

Figure 20.39 Building section B-B—Stage III.

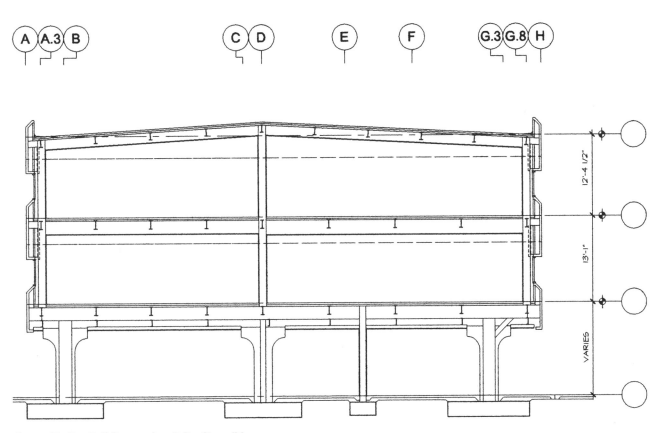

Figure 20.40 Building section B-B—Stage IV.

Stage V

The final stage for building section B-B is shown in Figure 20.41. Many items and notes have been added to complete this section:

1. The top of the concrete floor level elevation and the top of the roof insulation are located adjacent to the parapet wall.
2. Spaces have been designated for offices and garage use.
3. A broken line designates the extent of the suspended ceiling.
4. The steel roof and supporting floor beams are defined. The size and weight of these members will be designated on the framing plans.
5. The depth of the concrete floor topping and the gauge of the corrugated steel decking have been noted.
6. Detail references for items requiring a one-hour fire-rated assembly have been noted for the supporting columns and the ground floor ceiling.
7. The concrete block shear wall is crosshatched for definition, and the height of this wall is shown.
8. The types of roofing and insulation materials are indicated, and the steel decking and fire protection requirements are noted.
9. The size of the steel ceiling joists and their spacing are noted for the ground floor ceiling.
10. The thickness of the ground floor concrete and its substrate is noted.
11. The concrete shape encasing the steel columns at the ground floor level has been shaded for clarity.
12. The graphic designation for earth has been indicated for reasons of clarity.
13. Finally, the designation of the building section title has been lettered in, along with the scale of the drawing.

As you have seen, there are other building section designations that have been indicated. However, these will not be shown. Their method of development is similar to that discussed and shown for building section B-B.

Figure 20.42 illustrates a structural detail with a series of steel connections involving steel roof beams and steel floor beams and engineered assembly members for their

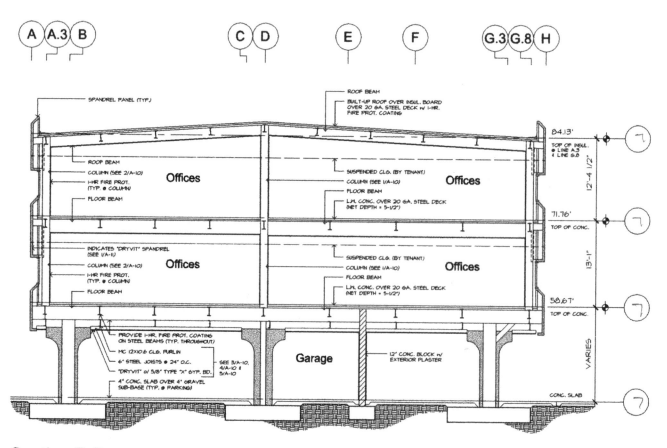

Section B-B

Figure 20.41 Building section B-B—Stage V.

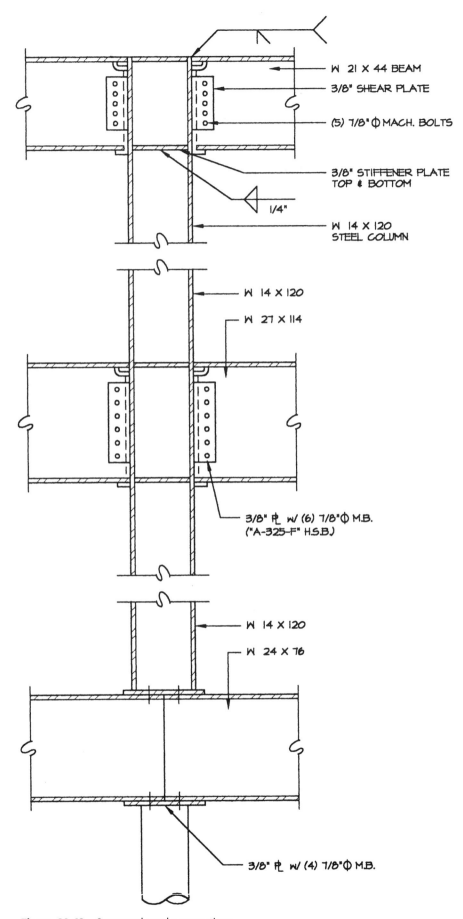

W 21 X 44 BEAM

3/8" SHEAR PLATE

(5) 7/8" Ø MACH. BOLTS

3/8" STIFFENER PLATE
TOP & BOTTOM

1/4"

W 14 X 120
STEEL COLUMN

W 14 X 120

W 27 X 114

3/8" PL w/ (6) 7/8" Ø M.B.
("A-325-F" H.S.B.)

W 14 X 120

W 24 X 76

3/8" PL w/ (4) 7/8" Ø M.B.

Figure 20.42 Structural steel connections.

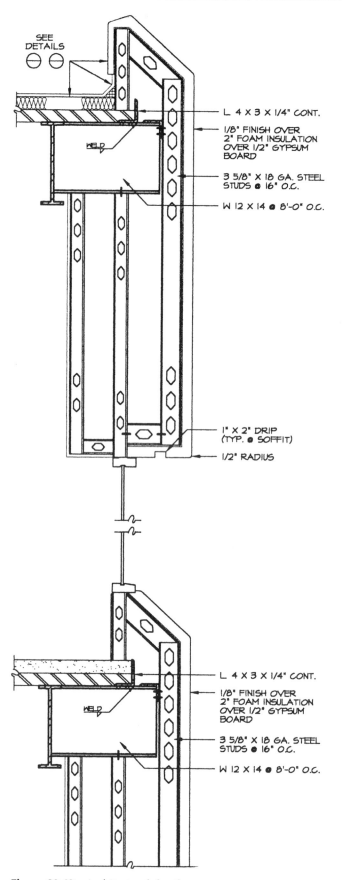

SEE DETAILS

L 4 X 3 X 1/4" CONT.

WELD

1/8" FINISH OVER 2" FOAM INSULATION OVER 1/2" GYPSUM BOARD

3 5/8" X 18 GA. STEEL STUDS @ 16" O.C.

W 12 X 14 @ 8'-0" O.C.

1" X 2" DRIP (TYP. @ SOFFIT)

1/2" RADIUS

L 4 X 3 X 1/4" CONT.

WELD

1/8" FINISH OVER 2" FOAM INSULATION OVER 1/2" GYPSUM BOARD

3 5/8" X 18 GA. STEEL STUDS @ 16" O.C.

W 12 X 14 @ 8'-0" O.C.

Figure 20.43 Architectural details.

connection to a steel column. This particular structural detail occurs on matrix lines D and 7. Note that a steel pipe column may be used as an alternative to a wide flange column for reasons of concealment at the first floor level. This detail is one of many to be found in the structural detail that is part of a set of working drawings.

Once the structural engineer and the architect have finalized the member sizes for the structural skeleton, the architectural detailing may commence. These details, and there will be many, will be predicated on the sizes and connections of the steel framing members. An example of an architectural detail that has been designed and detailed for the assembly of the exterior wall members and their attachment to the steel frame is shown in Figure 20.43. These members incorporate the use of light steel framing members, gypsum board, and 2" foam insulation board.

As previously mentioned, the steel columns at the ground floor level are to be encased in concrete and formed to give a desirable architectural appearance. The concrete encasement will also provide the necessary fire protection around the steel columns. This column detail is shown in Figure 20.44 and is applicable along matrix lines 4 through 12 and along lines B, D, and G. Note that the roof drainage pipe lines are concealed within the composite column, with their termination occurring 3" above the parking floor level. As mentioned earlier, the vertical dimension line titled "Varies" is so designated because of the change of floor levels in the parking floor for the purpose of providing proper water drainage.

Figure 20.45 is a pictorial view of the composite steel and concrete column found along the aforementioned intersecting matrix lines. Note that a portion of the spread concrete footing has been removed for the purpose of showing the concrete floor slab connection. Generally, the concrete spread footings are found to be symmetrical.

Figure 20.46 is a photograph showing the forming in preparation of pouring concrete for a spread footing, similar to that used in Figure 20.44.

The use of structural steel members and light steel framing members for the construction of various types of buildings is highly desirable and reduces the use of wood as a structural entity.

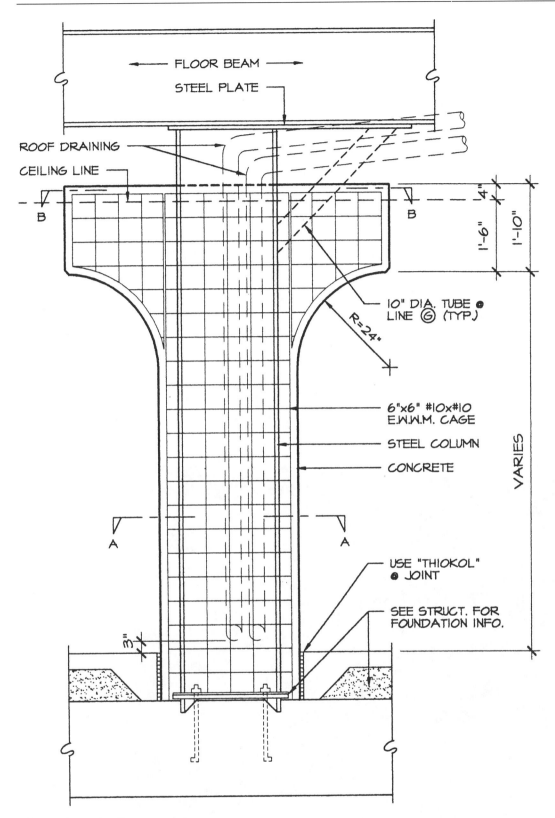

Figure 20.44 Steel/concrete column.

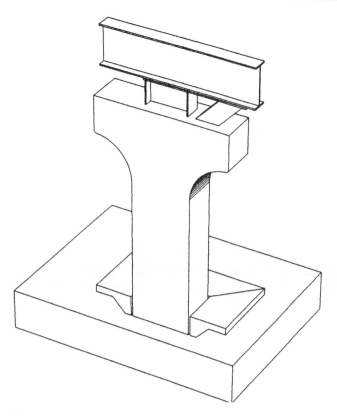

Figure 20.45 Pictorial view of composite steel and concrete column.

Figure 20.46 Formwork for concrete spread footing at steel columns.

chapter
21

TENANT IMPROVEMENTS

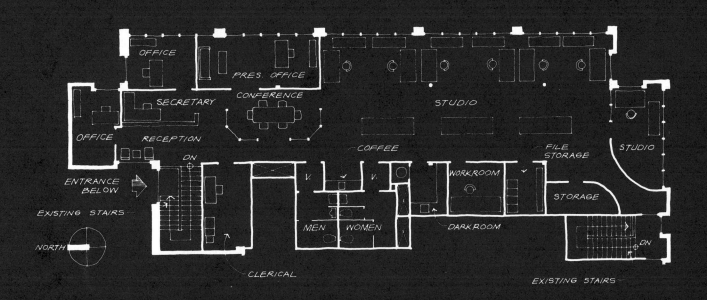

■ INTRODUCTION

The purpose of this chapter is to illustrate the procedures for the development of tenant improvements for specific spaces in two existing office buildings.

Building A, which has a large undeveloped open space with nonrequired travel and exit corridors yet to be constructed, will illustrate the necessary design procedures to satisfy corridor and exit travel to an existing lobby and two stairwells. Construction assemblies for exit corridor walls will be detailed to satisfy specific building code requirements.

Three tenant suite spaces will be illustrated as an example of the partial development for a large floor area. Exit requirements for these three spaces will be discussed, with an example of a tenant separation-wall assembly that will be constructed between the various suites. Building A and its illustrations provide an example of open space planning for tenant suites, required exiting, and wall construction requirements. Working drawings for the tenant suites are not illustrated.

Building B will demonstrate the entire procedure for developing an undeveloped floor area into a suite for a specific tenant. This procedure will include drawings for the assigned floor area reflecting the requirements of the tenant for the function of his or her business. At the end of this chapter, these drawings will be finalized into working drawings, with explanations of the various stages necessary to complete the drawings for construction and bidding purposes.

The term "tenant improvement," also referred to as "space planning, primarily deals with the internal planning of nonresidential buildings. Such buildings may be used for offices, industrial parks, medical facilities, manufacturing plants, and similar entities.

A "tenant" is defined as the user who will occupy a space, within one of the aforementioned types of buildings, for his or her type of business or professional use.

The "improvement" of a space, in most cases, is defined as the construction of the interior walls, doors, windows, ceilings, movable partitions, and specialty items that may be required for the function of the tenant's daily tasks. Improvements also include cabinetry, hardware, plumbing fixtures, finished floors, carpeting, and finished painting. Such improvement usually includes supplementary heating, ventilating, and air-conditioning systems, sized and installed for a designated space or area.

The internal planning deals with task areas enclosed within the walls with various construction assemblies. The tenant, that is, the user, will provide the necessary design criteria for the designer to plan the various task areas. Design criteria may include such information as room use, room sizes, and toilet facilities; electrical, telephone and equipment locations; special lighting requirements and desired floor, wall, and ceiling finishes.

In most cases, the designer or draftsperson will plan within a designated area of an existing structure or may plan an entire floor area. Generally, designated areas are found in multitenant buildings and vary in square footage. It should be noted that tenant improvement may also entail redeveloping an existing constructed space. This condition requires that the room dimensions, lighting fixtures, structural components, equipment locations, and existing electrical and mechanical locations are verified prior to the preliminary design process.

■ EXISTING FLOOR LEVEL—BUILDING A

With a given floor plan for an existing three-story undeveloped structure, we can explore potential floor areas for tenant use. Figure 21.1 illustrates the second floor level of this building. As illustrated, the existing stairwells, men's and women's toilet facilities, elevator shaft, telephone room, and janitor's room have been constructed according to building code requirements. The first prerequisite is to establish a corridor that satisfies all exit requirements of the governing building and fire codes.

Exit Corridors

Figure 21.2A shows a corridor that satisfies code requirements relative to width and location. A three-dimensional drawing illustrates the corridor in Figure 21.2B. The walls and ceiling construction of the corridor must meet the requirements for a one-hour fire-rated assembly. A detailed construction section of this assembly is depicted in Figure 21.3. Metal studs are illustrated; however, wood studs may be used if they meet the governing fire code requirements. It should be noted that most building codes require exit doors into the corridor to have a 20-minute fire-rated assembly, as designated in the corridor section in Figure 21.3.

Tenant Areas

After an exit corridor that will be used by various tenants on this floor is established, designated areas or floor areas required to satisfy the particular users' space requirements may now be formulated. In dealing with a tenant's area requirements, the designer must adhere to building code criteria relative to the number of exits required for a specific area.

An example of required exiting is depicted in Figure 21.4A showing that Suite A has a floor area of 3,200 square feet. Because of this suite's area and occupant load, the building code requires two exit doors to the corridor. According to the code, these two doors must be separated by a distance of one-half the length of the di-

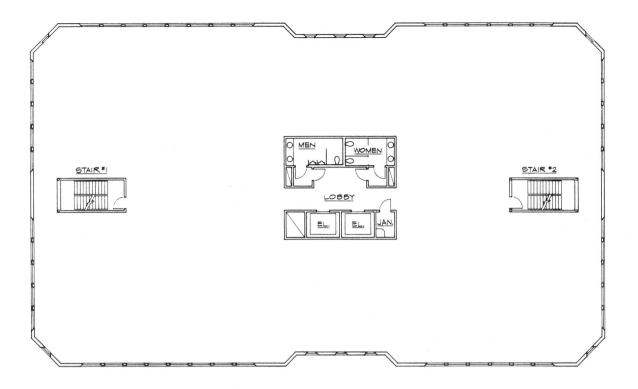

SECOND FLOOR PLAN
SCALE: 1/8" = 1'-0"

Figure 21.1 Existing undeveloped floor. (Reprinted by permission from *The Professional Practice of Architectural Working Drawings*, 2d Ed., © 1995 by John Wiley & Sons, Inc.)

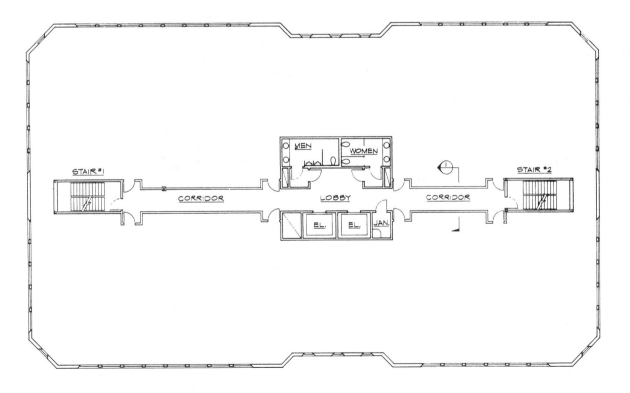

SECOND FLOOR PLAN
SCALE: 1/8" = 1'-0"

Figure 21.2A Exit corridor location. (Reprinted by permission from *The Professional Practice of Architectural Working Drawings*, 2d Ed., © 1995 by John Wiley & Sons, Inc.)

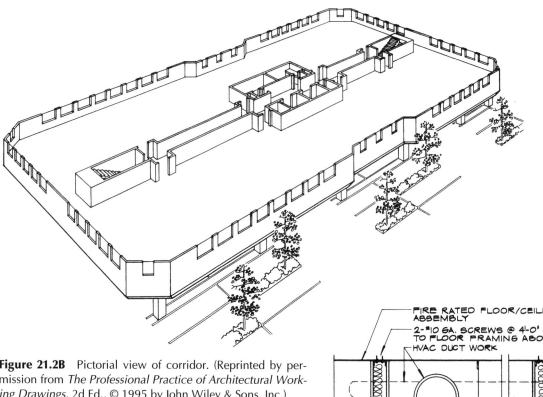

Figure 21.2B Pictorial view of corridor. (Reprinted by permission from *The Professional Practice of Architectural Working Drawings*, 2d Ed., © 1995 by John Wiley & Sons, Inc.)

agonal dimension of this area. See Figure 21.4A. Figure 21.4B illustrates this condition pictorially. This code requirement will be a primary factor in the internal planning of this suite. As shown in Figure 21.5A, the floor area of Suite C is less than 1,600 square feet; according to the building code this suite requires only one exit to the common corridor. It should be noted that additional toilet facilities may be required by the building code authorities, predicated on the number of employees occupying the particular suites. This would be a planning factor for the tenant improvement design. Figure 21.5B illustrates this suite pictorially.

Tenant Separation Wall

When there are numerous tenants on a given floor level, local building department authorities and building codes may require a one-hour fire-rated wall assembly between each tenant area and the next. Figure 21.6 illustrates a non-load-bearing, one-hour fire-rated wall assembly incorporating metal studs and gypsum board. A non-loading-bearing wall is one that does not support ceiling or floor weight from above or any other weight factors distributed to this wall. Wall insulation is shown as a means to decrease noise transmission between the various tenants.

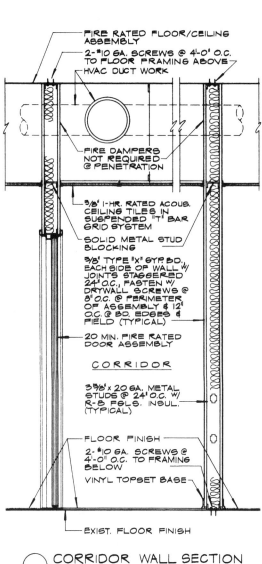

Figure 21.3 Fire-rated corridor construction.

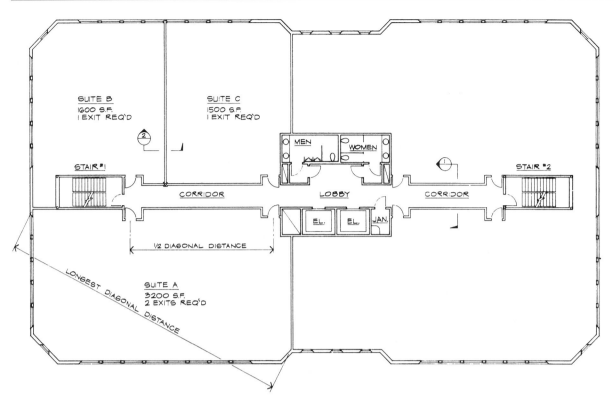

Figure 21.4A Suites A, B, and C. (Reprinted by permission from *The Professional Practice of Architectural Working Drawings*, 2d Ed., © 1995 by John Wiley & Sons, Inc.)

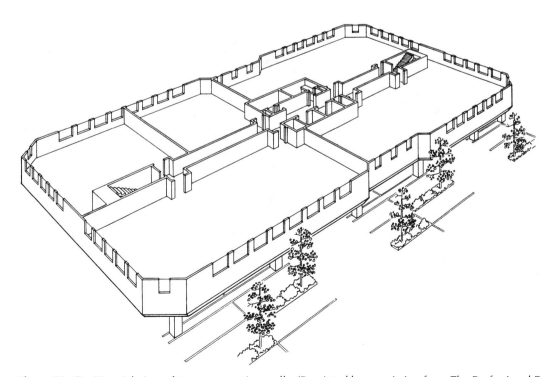

Figure 21.4B Pictorial view of tenant separation walls. (Reprinted by permission from *The Professional Practice of Architectural Working Drawings*, 2d Ed., © 1995 by John Wiley & Sons, Inc.)

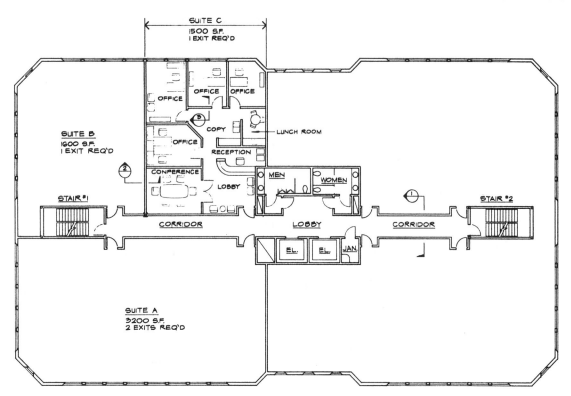

Figure 21.5A Floor plan—Suite C. (Reprinted by permission from *The Professional Practice of Architectural Working Drawings*, 2d Ed., © 1995 by John Wiley & Sons, Inc.)

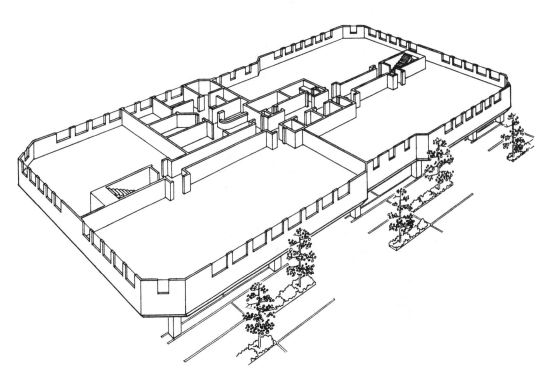

Figure 21.5B Pictorial view—Suite C. (Reprinted by permission from *The Professional Practice of Architectural Working Drawings*, 2d Ed., © 1995 by John Wiley & Sons, Inc.)

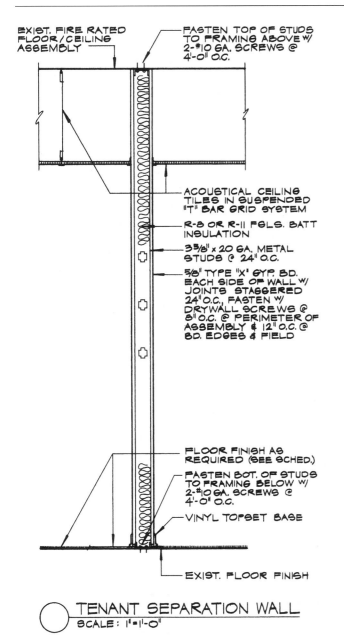

Figure 21.6 Tenant separation wall. (Reprinted by permission from *The Professional Practice of Architectural Working Drawings*, 2d Ed., © 1995 by John Wiley & Sons, Inc.)

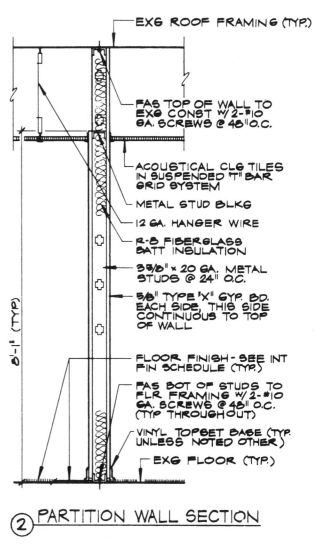

Figure 21.7 Partition wall section 3. (Reprinted by permission from *The Professional Practice of Architectural Working Drawings*, 2d Ed., © 1995 by John Wiley & Sons, Inc.)

The construction technique for a wall assembly used within a specific suite may vary. Figure 21.7 illustrates an example of a wall partition section used in offices for tenant improvements. Note that this wall partition extends to the roof framing in order to reduce the sound transmission between the various rooms and halls.

Building A has been used to illustrate the basic procedures and requirements for potential suite developments within a large, existing, undeveloped floor space. Building B, however, will illustrate the procedures imple-

mented in an architect's office for the tenant improvement design and the completion of working drawings.

■ DEVELOPMENT OF WORKING DRAWINGS—BUILDING B

As discussed earlier, internal suite planning is developed from the tenant's criteria that satisfy the needs for his or her business function.

In planning a given undeveloped space on the second floor of an existing office building, the designer will visit the space and verify the structural components such as columns and beam heights. The designer and staff will take measurements to verify existing inside area dimensions, column locations, window sizes, and the spacing of window mullions. In some cases, mechanical and/or plumbing components such as exhaust ducts, roof drainage pipes, and water lines for domestic and mechanical use may be located in this undeveloped space. If so, they should be plotted on the initial plan layout.

Figure 21.8A shows the undeveloped floor plan of an existing second floor level of a two-story office building. The working drawing process for the improvement of Suite 201, as shown in Figure 21.8B, will start with the tenant requirements and the verification of the existing space and conditions. Note in Figure 21.8B the existing steel columns, stairs, mechanical shafts, roof drain lines, windows, and window mullion locations.

Planning of Task Areas

The tenant for this designated space deals with graphic communications and has provided the designer with a list of the various rooms needed, their preferred sizes, their use, and their relationships to each other.

Schematic Study

The rooms specified by the tenant include a reception area, three offices, a conference room, a large studio accommodating numerous drawing boards, a small studio for airbrush media, a copy room, and a storage room. The tenant also desired a coffee area with cabinets and sink and a service area for cleanup of art implements. The location of walls and rough plumbing for the restrooms are existing; therefore, these rooms require only finishing.

Given the preceding information dealing with specific task areas, schematic studies can now begin in order to show tentative room locations and their relationship to one another. Figure 21.9 illustrates a conceptual floor plan in schematic form, which will be used in discussing the various areas and their locations with the tenant.

Following this procedure, a preliminary floor plan will be developed to scale, including suggested locations for the required furniture. This drawing may be done in freehand, as is shown in Figure 21.10.

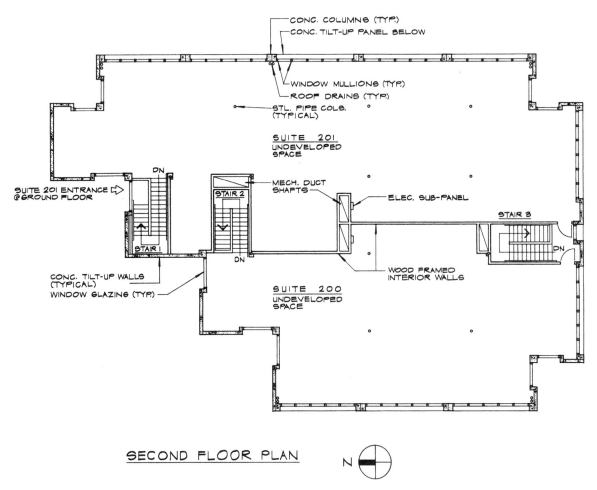

Figure 21.8A Undeveloped floor area plan—Building B. (Reprinted by permission from *The Professional Practice of Architectural Working Drawings*, 2d Ed., © 1995 by John Wiley & Sons, Inc.)

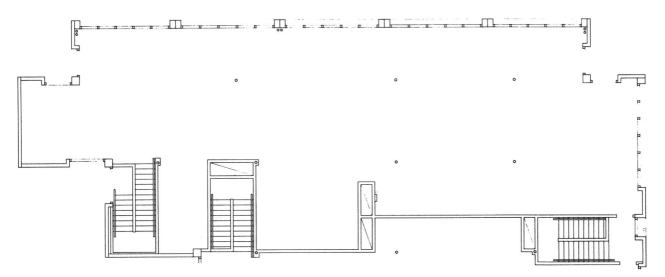

Figure 21.8B Existing undeveloped floor area—Suite 201. (Reprinted by permission from *The Professional Practice of Architectural Working Drawings*, 2d Ed., © 1995 by John Wiley & Sons, Inc.)

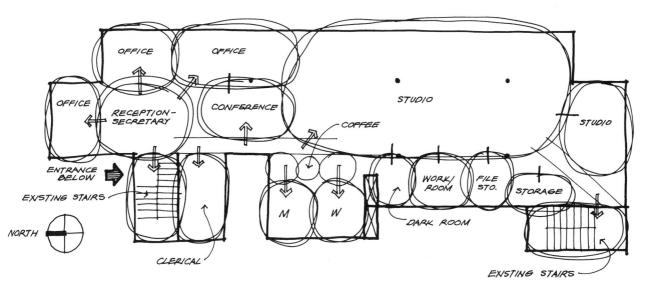

Figure 21.9 Schematic study. (Reprinted by permission from *The Professional Practice of Architectural Working Drawings*, 2d Ed., © 1995 by John Wiley & Sons, Inc.)

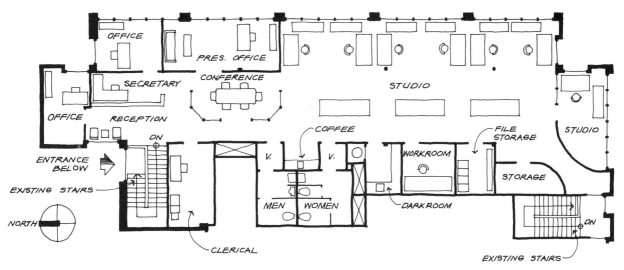

Figure 21.10 Preliminary floor plan. (Reprinted by permission from *The Professional Practice of Architectural Working Drawings*, 2d Ed., © 1995 by John Wiley & Sons, Inc.)

Upon the tenant's acceptance of the preliminary plan, Figure 21.11 now shows the required room locations and sizes. Note that the division walls between the offices, adjacent to the exterior wall with windows and mullions, are located to intersect at the window mullions and concrete column locations. This eliminates the problem of a division wall abutting into a glass area which obviously would be undesirable.

The location of existing structural columns presents planning obstacles as they relate to various spaces. It would be desirable to conceal a column within a division wall wherever possible. Note in Figure 21.11 that some of the existing steel pipe columns have been incorporated into various wall locations.

Interior Partition Wall Construction

Now that the locations of walls, doors, and windows have been established, details for the construction of these components will be designed as a part of the working drawings for this tenant improvement project.

For the sake of clarity, it is recommended that the existing walls and new walls be delineated differently. For example, the existing walls can be drawn with two separate lines, and new walls with two lines pouchéd or shaded in order to distinguish between them. Wall symbols can be used for reference. Note the wall shading and wall symbols in Figure 21.12. The main structural consideration in detailing nonbearing interior walls is to

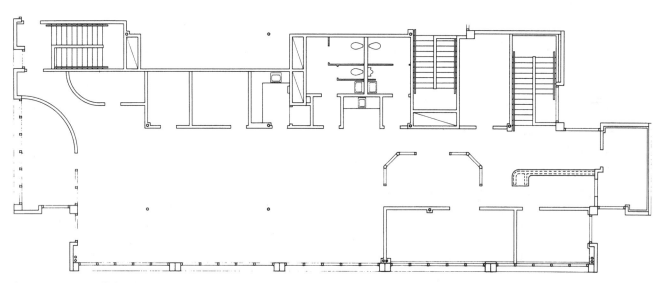

Figure 21.11   Wall development plan. (Reprinted by permission from *The Professional Practice of Architectural Working Drawings*, 2d Ed., © 1995 by John Wiley & Sons, Inc.)

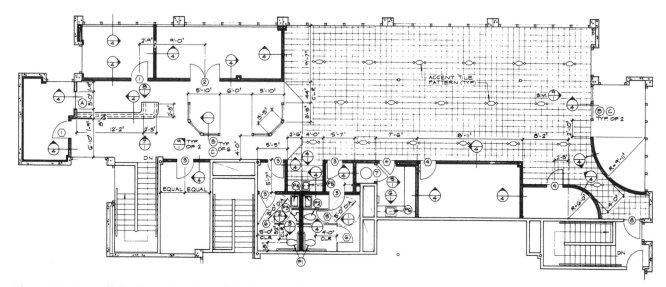

Figure 21.12   Wall shading and wall symbols. (Reprinted by permission from *The Professional Practice of Architectural Working Drawings*, 2d Ed., © 1995 by John Wiley & Sons, Inc.)

provide lateral stability. Figure 21.19 illustrates a partition wall section that is terminated a few inches above the ceiling finish material. For this assembly, the wall will be braced with metal struts in compression from the top of the wall to the existing structural members above, as shown in Figure 21.13. A photograph of a metal strut used for lateral wall support is illustrated in Figure 21.14. This wall assembly uses steel studs for the wall structure; however, wood studs are also used for partition wall assemblies. A photograph of steel stud framing members is shown in Figure 21.15. As shown in Figure 21.13, the finish ceiling members will terminate at each wall partition, because the use of this wall assembly will dictate that walls be constructed prior to the finished ceiling. This method provides more design flexibility for the ceil-

Figure 21.14 Stabilizing strut. (Reprinted by permission from *The Professional Practice of Architectural Working Drawings*, 2d Ed., © 1995 by John Wiley & Sons, Inc.)

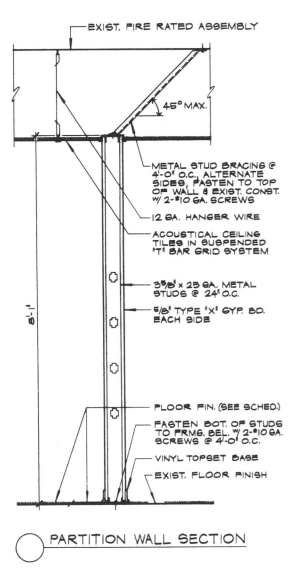

EXIST. FIRE RATED ASSEMBLY

45° MAX.

METAL STUD BRACING @ 4'-0" O.C., ALTERNATE SIDES, FASTEN TO TOP OF WALL & EXIST. CONST. W/ 2-#10 GA. SCREWS

12 GA. HANGER WIRE

ACOUSTICAL CEILING TILES IN SUSPENDED 'T' BAR GRID SYSTEM

3⅝" x 25 GA. METAL STUDS @ 24" O.C.

⅝" TYPE "X" GYP. BD. EACH SIDE

FLOOR FIN. (SEE SCHED.)

FASTEN BOT. OF STUDS TO FRMG. BEL. W/ 2-#10 GA. SCREWS @ 4'-0" O.C.

VINYL TOPSET BASE

EXIST. FLOOR FINISH

8'-1"

PARTITION WALL SECTION

Figure 21.13 Nonbearing partition wall. (Reprinted by permission from *The Professional Practice of Architectural Working Drawings*, 2d Ed., © 1995 by John Wiley & Sons, Inc.)

Figure 21.15 Wall framing—steel studs. (Reprinted by permission from *The Professional Practice of Architectural Working Drawings*, 2d Ed., © 1995 by John Wiley & Sons, Inc.)

ing and lighting layout, which is illustrated and discussed later in regard to the design and layout of the ceiling plan. Figure 21.13 illustrates a suspended ceiling, which is assembled with 12-gauge hangar wires and metal runners supporting the finish ceiling material. In regions of the country where there is earthquake activity, the suspended ceiling areas are braced to minimize lateral movement. One method is shown in Figure 21.13, where 12-gauge wire at a 45° angle is assembled in a grid pattern, providing lateral stability for the suspended ceiling.

In cases where the ceiling is installed prior to the construction of the wall partitions, a similar method for stabilizing the wall, as shown in Figure 21.16, will be

incorporated into the wall assembly. For the working drawings of this tenant improvement project, the wall section illustrated in Figure 21.13 will be used.

It often happens that in tenant improvements projects, the tenant or user will require additional soundproofing methods for the wall construction that separates specific areas. Figure 21.17 illustrates a separation wall terminating at the roof or floor system of an existing structure. This method helps to reduce the transmission of sound from one area to another through the ceiling and plenum areas. A plenum area, a space used primarily for the location of mechanical ducts and equipment, is usually located above the finished ceiling. Figure 21.18 is a

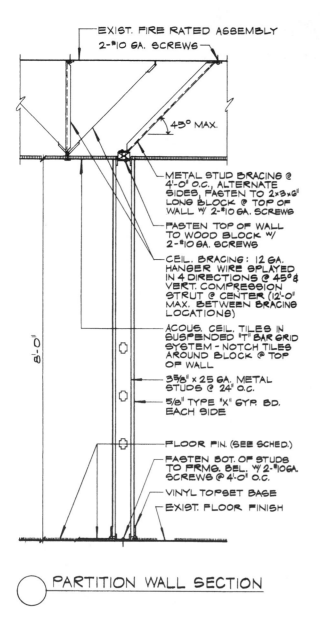

Figure 21.16   Nonbearing partition wall. (Reprinted by permission from *The Professional Practice of Architectural Working Drawings*, 2d Ed., © 1995 by John Wiley & Sons, Inc.)

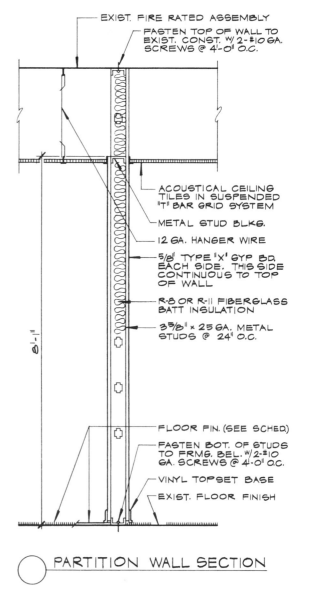

Figure 21.17   Sound deterrent partition wall. (Reprinted by permission from *The Professional Practice of Architectural Working Drawings*, 2d Ed., © 1995 by John Wiley & Sons, Inc.)

Figure 21.18 Mechanical unit. (Reprinted by permission from *The Professional Practice of Architectural Working Drawings*, 2d Ed., © 1995 by John Wiley & Sons, Inc.)

photograph of a small mechanical unit in the plenum area, which will distribute warm and cold air to the various tenant areas. It was decided that the studio would not have a finished ceiling so that the mechanical ducting for the heating, cooling, and ventilation could be exposed (shown later in the ceiling plan). In this case, the wall partitions will be detailed to extend to, and be secured at, the roof rafters (illustrated in Figure 21.19). Note that where the walls and rafters are not adjacent to each other, 2 × 4 blocking at 4'-0" o.c. is installed to stabilize the wall laterally.

Often, as in this project, a mechanical equipment room is required to enclose a mechanical unit that will provide cooling, heating, and ventilating for a particular suite only. However, because of the noise produced by certain mechanical units, it is good practice to detail the walls of the mechanical room in such a way that the noise of the motors is minimized. A detail of one of the walls is shown in Figure 21.20. Note that sound-absorbing board is installed on the inside of the mechanical room.

Existing Wall Furring

In projects where there are existing unfinished concrete or masonry walls, it will be desirable to furr out these walls in order to provide for electrical and telephone service and to develop a finished wall surface. Furring is adding a new inner wall to the main wall behind. Figure 21.21 illustrates a wall section where 1⅝ metal furring studs are attached to the existing unfinished concrete wall surface. In this detail, ⅝-inch thick gypsum wallboard has been selected for the interior wall finish.

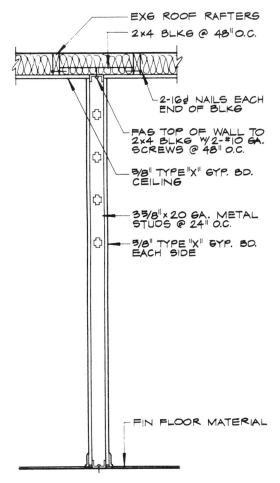

Figure 21.19 Wall section. (Reprinted by permission from *The Professional Practice of Architectural Working Drawings*, 2d Ed., © 1995 by John Wiley & Sons, Inc.)

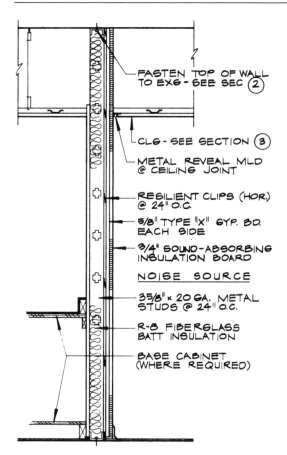

Figure 21.20 Sound wall section. (Reprinted by permission from *The Professional Practice of Architectural Working Drawings*, 2d Ed., © 1995 by John Wiley & Sons, Inc.)

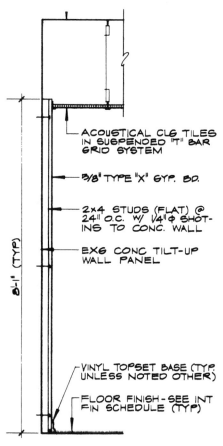

Figure 21.21 Existing wall furring. (Reprinted by permission from *The Professional Practice of Architectural Working Drawings*, 2d Ed., © 1995 by John Wiley & Sons, Inc.)

Interior Glass Wall Partition

The tenant requested the use of glass wall partitioning to partially enclose the conference room area. The use of glass and metal frames for wall partitions still requires horizontal stability, as is necessary for other types of wall partitions. A section through this glass wall partition is shown in Figure 21.22. Note that all glazing will be tempered glass, as required by building codes and for the safety of the user.

Low Wall Partition

A low wall and countertop are provided to separate the reception area from the secretarial area. This 42-inch high wall will be attached to the adjacent wall and anchored at the base, as indicated in Figure 21.23. The stability of a low wall is most critical at the base; therefore, the method of assembly will be determined by the structural components of the existing structure.

Interior Door and Window Assemblies

The door and window assemblies will be detailed to illustrate to the contractor the type of headers over the openings and the types of door and window frames that have been selected. The stabilization at the top of these assemblies will be identical or similar to the stabilization for the wall partitions. Figure 21.24 depicts the use of a metal header over the door opening, incorporating the use of a hollow metal door frame. The manufacturer and type of metal door frame will be called out on the door schedule.

Wall partitions that incorporate windows will be detailed to delineate the type of header, window frame material, and the construction of the wall portion in the assembly. The interior window located between office 3 and the secretarial area is detailed in a wall section illustrated in Figure 21.25.

The sizes, thickness, and types of doors and windows will be stipulated on the door and window schedules (il-

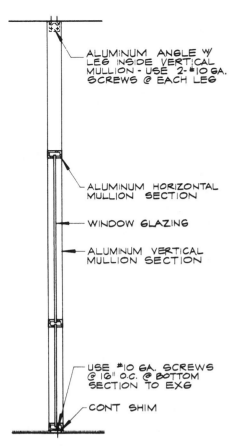

Figure 21.22 Glass wall partition. (Reprinted by permission from *The Professional Practice of Architectural Working Drawings*, 2d Ed., © 1995 by John Wiley & Sons, Inc.)

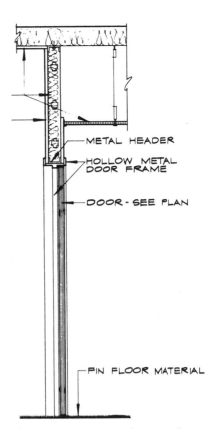

Figure 21.24 Interior door—wall section. (Reprinted by permission from *The Professional Practice of Architectural Working Drawings*, 2d Ed., © 1995 by John Wiley & Sons, Inc.)

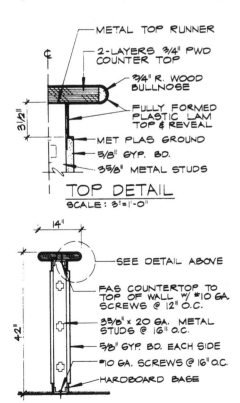

Figure 21.23 Low wall partition. (Reprinted by permission from *The Professional Practice of Architectural Working Drawings*, 2d Ed., © 1995 by John Wiley & Sons, Inc.)

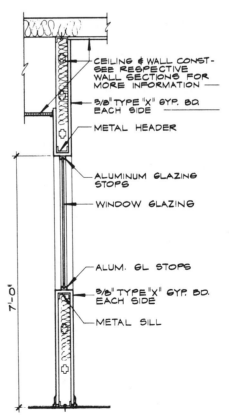

Figure 21.25 Interior window and wall section. (Reprinted by permission from *The Professional Practice of Architectural Working Drawings*, 2d Ed., © 1995 by John Wiley & Sons, Inc.)

lustrated later in this chapter). It should be noted that upon completion of the detailing for the various partition walls and door and window assemblies, these details will be referenced on the floor plan, using circles and numbers as a means of identification.

Electrical and Communication Plan

After the locations of partition walls, doors, windows, and furniture have been established, the architect or space planner, consulting with the tenant, may now proceed to develop an electrical and communication plan. The electrical portion of this plan will consist of the location of convenient electrical outlets installed approximately 12 inches above the floor, unless noted otherwise by a dimension at the outlet. The communication installation will comprise telephone jacks, a connection for the facsimile (fax) equipment, and a rough-in electrical service for the tenant's computer hardware. An electrical and communication plan prepared for this tenant of Building B is illustrated in Figure 21.26. It should be noted that on some projects the electrical and communication design may be so complex that separate plans must be provided and delineated for clarity.

Ceiling Plan

A ceiling plan will be drawn to delineate the following: location of ceiling lighting fixtures, symbolized for reference to the lighting fixture schedule; suspended ceiling design; the type of system to be specified; and other types of ceiling finishes. Switch locations for the various lighting fixtures will also be shown on this plan.

For this project, it was decided that a suspended ceiling system with recessed lighting fixtures would be specified for offices 1, 2, and 3. As mentioned earlier and detailed in Figure 21.13, the walls will be installed first, thus providing the designer with greater design flexibility for the layout of the suspended ceiling grid system and the location of lighting fixtures. To illustrate the design flexibility of this wall installation method, the ceiling plan shown in Figure 21.27 shows the suspended ceiling and lighting fixtures to be symmetrical within the offices, thereby creating a more pleasing ceiling design and lighting fixture location. Mechanical ducts for heating and cooling these offices will be installed and concealed above the suspended ceiling system. Note that the walls are drawn with two lines only, inasmuch as there are no wall openings at the ceiling level.

At the request of the tenant, the remaining rooms and task areas will not have a suspended ceiling system; rather, gypsum wallboard will be attached directly to the existing structural roof members, with the gypsum board being finished and painted. For wall reference, see Figure 21.19.

The selection of the ceiling finish and location was to allow the mechanical ducts to be exposed and painted. These round mechanical ducts, exposed and painted, will provide a decor compatible with the artwork and graphic design produced by this tenant. A photograph of the exposed mechanical ducts and lighting fixtures is shown in Figure 21.28. On the ceiling plan, as depicted in Figure 21.27, the designer has shown the desired location of the mechanical ducts and supply registers. The consulting mechanical engineer will specify the sizes of the ducts, type of supply registers, and type of equipment to be used, in the mechanical drawings.

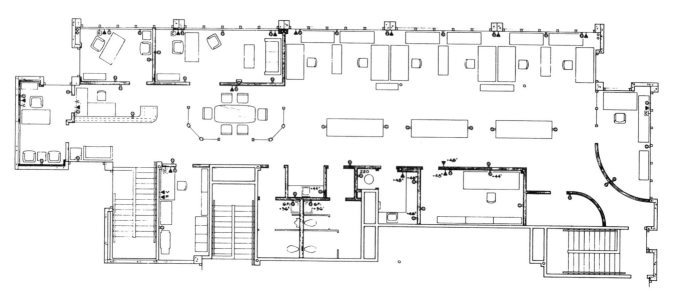

Figure 21.26   Electrical and communication plan. (Reprinted by permission from *The Professional Practice of Architectural Working Drawings*, 2d Ed., © 1995 by John Wiley & Sons, Inc.)

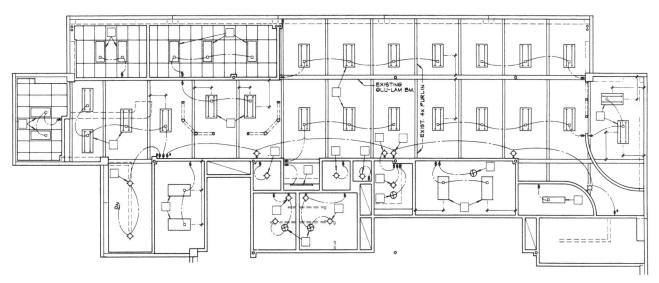

Figure 21.27 Ceiling plan. (Reprinted by permission from *The Professional Practice of Architectural Working Drawings*, 2d Ed., © 1995 by John Wiley & Sons, Inc.)

As previously mentioned, the lighting fixtures will be given a reference symbol that will also be on the electrical fixture schedule. The schedule will provide a description of the fixtures, including the manufacturer and model numbers. Designation of the finished ceiling material may be shown on the ceiling plan for convenience; in any case, these finishes will be designated on the interior finish schedule. Electrical and interior finish schedules, as well as other schedules, are discussed and illustrated later in the chapter.

Interior Elevations

Interior elevations will be provided to illustrate cabinets, counter heights, plumbing fixture locations, and location of hardware accessories. Restroom elevations will illustrate the clearances and hardware locations for

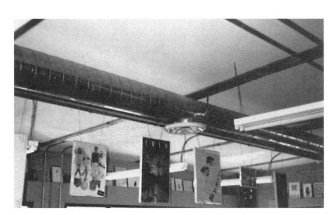

Figure 21.28 Exposed ducts and supply register. (Reprinted by permission from *The Professional Practice of Architectural Working Drawings*, 2d Ed., © 1995 by John Wiley & Sons, Inc.)

compliance with the American with Disabilities Act (ADA) requirements. There are only two restrooms, one for women and one for men, and each will be designed to satisfy the requirements set forth in the current ADA recommendations.

Figure 21.29 depicts one wall of a restroom, showing the required water closet seat heights, the length of grab bars, and their heights above the floor. In the final working drawings a reference symbol will be shown on the floor plan and included on the corresponding interior elevation. These corresponding symbols will provide clarity for those reviewing the working drawings. The cabinet dimensions and clearances delineated on the interior elevations are shown in Figure 21.30. In most cases, restroom walls will be delineated to show the location of toilet accessories and other types of hardware. Figure 21.31 is drawn to indicate the locations, as dimensioned, for the toilet paper and towel dispensers.

As requested by the tenant, cabinets have been provided in the coffee bar area for storage of dishes, utensils, coffee, and other necessities for the employees. See Figure 21.32. Low division walls will be drawn to illustrate the height, finish, and method of construction. Figure 21.33 depicts the low division wall between the reception and secretarial areas. Note that the wall construction method is referenced on the elevation. See Figure 21.23, which illustrates a section through the wall.

■ SCHEDULES

Schedules are incorporated into the working drawings for most tenant improvement projects. The schedules for this project include the door schedule, window sched-

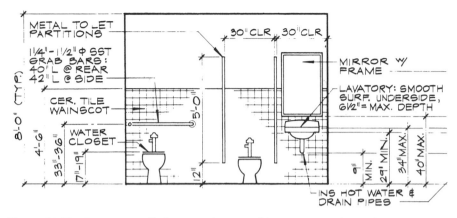

Figure 21.29 Restroom wall elevation. (Reprinted by permission from *The Professional Practice of Architectural Working Drawings*, 2d Ed., © 1995 by John Wiley & Sons, Inc.)

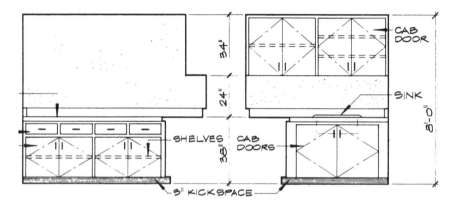

Figure 21.30 Cabinet elevations. (Reprinted by permission from *The Professional Practice of Architectural Working Drawings*, 2d Ed., © 1995 by John Wiley & Sons, Inc.)

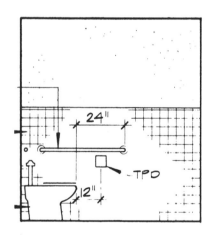

Figure 21.31 Hardware locations. (Reprinted by permission from *The Professional Practice of Architectural Working Drawings*, 2d Ed., © 1995 by John Wiley & Sons, Inc.)

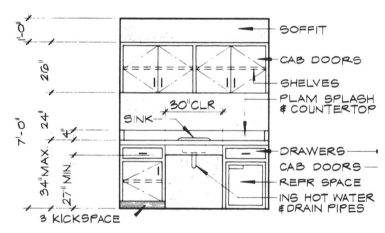

Figure 21.32 Coffee bar cabinets. (Reprinted by permission from *The Professional Practice of Architectural Working Drawings*, 2d Ed., © 1995 by John Wiley & Sons, Inc.)

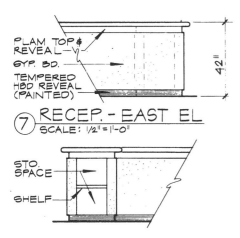

PLAM TOP & REVEAL—V

GYP. BD.

TEMPERED HDD REVEAL (PAINTED)

42"

⑦ RECEP. - EAST EL
SCALE: 1/2" = 1'-0"

STO. SPACE

SHELF

Figure 21.33 Low wall elevation. (Reprinted by permission from *The Professional Practice of Architectural Working Drawings*, 2d Ed., © 1995 by John Wiley & Sons, Inc.)

DOOR SCHEDULE

SYM	WIDTH	HEIGHT	THK	HC/SC	TYPE	MATERIAL	REMARKS
①	3'-0"	7'-0"	1 3/4"	SC	SLAB	WOOD	PLAM FIN (COFFEE)
②	PR 2'-8"	"	"	"	"	"	" " "
③	3'-0"	"	"	"	"	"	" " (BLACK)
④	2'-10"	"	"	"	"	"	" " "
⑤	2'-2"	5'-0"	1"	"	"	MET FACE	BLACK
⑥	2'-10"	"	"	"	"	"	"
⑦	"	"	1 3/8"	HC	"	PNT GD WD	WATER HEATER DR
⑧	3'-0"	7'-0"	1 3/4"	SC	"	WOOD	3/4 HR./SELF-CLSG.

Figure 21.34 Door schedule. (Reprinted by permission from *The Professional Practice of Architectural Working Drawings*, 2d Ed., © 1995 by John Wiley & Sons, Inc.)

WINDOW SCHEDULE

SYM	WIDTH	HEIGHT	GL THK	TYPE	FRAME MTL	REMARKS
Ⓐ	3'-0"	4'-0"	1/4"	FIXED	AL/DARK BRZ	CLEAR GL
Ⓑ	3'-2"	2'-6"	"	"	"	TINTED GL
Ⓒ	"	4'-2"	"	"	"	CLR GL, ABV Ⓑ

Figure 21.35 Window schedule. (Reprinted by permission from *The Professional Practice of Architectural Working Drawings*, 2d Ed., © 1995 by John Wiley & Sons, Inc.)

PLUMBING FIXTURE SCHEDULE

SYM	ITEM / MODEL NO.	MANUFACTURER	REMARKS
Ⓟ1	WC, ELONG. RIM, 18" RIM HT	FIXTURES INC.	WHITE
Ⓟ2	WATER CLOSET	"	"
Ⓟ3	WALL HUNG URINAL	"	"
Ⓟ4	" " LAV	"	"
Ⓟ5	BAR SINK	"	SST, 5" DEEP
Ⓟ6	SINK	"	" , 9" "

Figure 21.36 Plumbing fixture schedule. (Reprinted by permission from *The Professional Practice of Architectural Working Drawings*, 2d Ed., © 1995 by John Wiley & Sons, Inc.)

furniture sizes, manufacturers, and the desired finish materials. See Figure 21.39.

■ WORKING DRAWINGS

The following paragraphs describe the working drawings at various stages of the development for this tenant improvement project.

Floor Plan

STAGE I (Figure 21.40). At a larger scale, the draftsperson lightly blocked out all the existing exterior and interior walls for the area identified as Suite 201. This drawing included existing windows, structural columns, roof drain leaders, stairwells, and mechanical shafts. Also included in this first-stage drawing was the initial site plan layout.

STAGE II (Figure 21.41). After the required room locations and their sizes were determined from the schematic drawings in Figure 21.19, wall locations were established with their accompanying dimension lines only. All the existing and new walls were darkened for future clarity. Doors and their swing directions were now added, along with wheelchair clearances in the men's and women's restrooms. The various interior elevations were lightly blocked out,

ule, plumbing fixture schedule, interior finish schedule, electrical fixture schedule, and furnishing schedule. The door schedule, shown in Figure 21.34, provides the door symbol, door size and thickness, door material, frame material, and selected door finish. Even though few windows are incorporated, a window schedule is provided. See Figure 21.35.

Figure 21.36 depicts the plumbing fixture schedule, which lists the type of fixture, manufacturer, and model designation. Note on the floor plan the designated plumbing fixture symbols, which are referenced to the plumbing schedule shown in Figure 21.36. The interior finish schedule designates the various rooms and their respective floor, wall, and ceiling finishes. See Figure 21.37.

The electrical fixture schedule, shown in Figure 21.38, identifies the type of electrical fixture, the manufacturer, and the corresponding model number. Note that the electrical fixture symbols are designated only on the ceiling plan, shown in Figure 21.27. Other schedules are discussed and illustrated in Chapter 11.

Finally, to complete the necessary schedules, a furnishing schedule is provided. This schedule will depict

INTERIOR FINISH SCHEDULE

ROOM/AREA	Carpet & Pad	Vinyl Tile	Sheet Vinyl	Vinyl Topset	Coved Flr	"J" Molding	5/8" Type "X" G.B.			5/8"x2'x4' Sus Clg	5/8" Type "X" G.B.	Exp Framing	REMARKS
	FLOOR			*BASE*			*WALLS*			*CEILING*			
RECEPT./SEC.	●			●			●					●	
OFFICE - 1	●			●			●			●			
OFFICE - 2	●			●			●			●			
OFFICE - 3	●			●			●			●			
CONFERENCE	●			●								●	STOREFRONT GL WALLS (SEE EL)
CLERICAL WRKRM	●			●			●				●		
RESTROOMS			●		●		●				●		CT WSCT, ENAMEL PNT (SEE INT ELS)
VESTIBULES			●		●		●				●		
COFFEE BAR		●		●			●				●		
STUDIO - 1		●		●			●					●	SEE PLAN FOR FLR TILE PATTERN
DARKROOM		●		●			●				●		
PAINT/WORKROOM		●		●			●				●		
STORAGE		●				●	●				●		
STUDIO - 2	●			●			●					●	
STAIRS	●					●	●				●		
DNSTRS LOBBY	●			●			●				●		

Figure 21.37 Interior finish schedule. (Reprinted by permission from *The Professional Practice of Architectural Working Drawings*, 2d Ed., © 1995 by John Wiley & Sons, Inc.)

ELECTRICAL FIXTURE SCHEDULE

SYM	ITEM/MODEL NO.	MANUFACTURER	LAMP	
E1	2'x4' RECESSED w/ PRISMATIC LENS	LIGHTDESIGN INC.	4-40W	FLUR TUBES
E2	2'x4' SURF. MT w/ PRISMATIC LENS	"	"	"
E3	1'x4' DO	"	2-40W	"
E4	2'x4' OPEN TUBE INDUS. w/"ICE-TONG" HANGERS	"	4-40W	"
E5	4' STRIP/UNDER CAB	"	1-40W	"
E6	12"φ SURF. MT w/ OP ACRYLIC LENS	"	2-60W	A19 BULBS
E7	4"φ DO	"	1-75W	"
E8	SURF. MT/PORCELAIN	"PROPRIETARY"	1-60W	"

Figure 21.38 Electrical fixture schedule. (Reprinted by permission from *The Professional Practice of Architectural Working Drawings*, 2d Ed., © 1995 by John Wiley & Sons, Inc.)

and the site plan—illustrating the exact location of Suite 201 in this existing structure—was finalized.

STAGE III (Figure 21.42). At this stage of the floor plan, all the wall partitions were dimensioned, and the new walls darkened solid to distinguish them from the existing walls. Note that in the reference room, next to the darkroom, a wall was eliminated to provide more space for equipment. See Stage II. Door symbols and their numbers were now incorporated, along with plumbing fixture symbols and their accompanying designations. Also included are reference bubbles for the various wall sections with their designated numbers

and locations. Interior elevation reference symbols have been added and will later be located on their respective wall elevations. Symbols for glass sizes are shown at the various glass partition locations. At this stage of the floor plan, the specified tile floor and accent pattern locations are delineated in the studio area. The lines on the interior elevations are darkened and profiled for clarity with material designations, cabinet door swings, incorporating the various dimension lines.

STAGE IV (Figure 21.43). This is the final stage for the floor plan, interior elevations, and site plan. On the floor plan a wall legend is included, illustrating the various wall conditions. All final notes and room designations have been lettered, and the designated wall detail numbers placed in the various reference bubbles. Lettering and dimensioning on the interior elevations are now finalized, along with the titling and reference numbering for various wall elevations as they relate to the floor plan. Final notes are lettered on the site plan and titles provided for the site plan and floor plan. The scales used for various drawings are now lettered and located below the drawing titles.

Furnishing, Electrical, and Communication Plan

STAGE I (Figure 21.44). The initial step for this stage was to draft a floor plan incorporating the exterior walls, interior partitions, plumbing fixtures, and cabinet locations. Note that door swings and their directions are

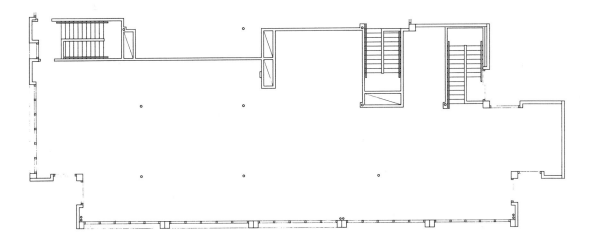

SYM.	WIDTH	DEPTH	HEIGHT	ITEM / MODEL NO.	MANUFACTURER	REMARKS
F1	60"	30"	29"	EXECUTIVE DESK	FURNITURE INC.	ROSEWOOD
F2	"	"	"	SECRETARIAL DESK	"	TEAK
F3	"	24"	26"	FREESTANDING TYPING TABLE	"	"
F4	90"	35"	28"	CONFERENCE TABLE	"	ROSEWOOD
F5	48"	24"	29"	WORKTABLE	"	BLACK PLAM TOP
F6	23"	26"	40"	HI-BACK DESK CHAIR	"	ROSEWOOD TRIM
F7	22"	24"	32"	ARMCHAIR	"	" "
F8	18"	20"	30"	SECRETARIAL CHAIR	"	BLACK
F9	22"	24"	31"	SIDECHAIR	"	ROSEWOOD
F10	80"	32"	26"	3-SEAT SOFA	"	COFFEE
F11	62"	"	"	2- "	"	"
F12	48"	21"	17"	COFFEE TABLE	"	ROSEWOOD
F13	18"	18"	19"	SQUARE TABLE	"	"
F14	24"	24"	"	" "	"	TEAK
F15	48"	13"	72"	BOOKCASE	"	ROSEWOOD
F16	36"	"	"	"	"	"
F17	72"	37½"	37"	DRAFTING/WORK TABLE	ARCHSTATION INC.	BLACK
F18	72"	24"	29"	FOLDING TABLE	FURNITURE INC.	BLACK PLAM TOP
F19	60"	21"	29"	3-DRAWER REF DESK	N/A	CUSTOM-SEE DRAWING
F20	96"	24"	29"	FOLDING TABLE	FURNITURE INC.	BLACK PLAM TOP
F21	72"	13"	60"	BOOKCASE	"	WHITE MELAMINE
F22	48"	"	"	"	"	"
F23	19"	21"	44½"	VARIABLE HT DRAFTING CHAIR	ARCHSTATION INC.	BLACK
F24	23"	26"	"	" " " ARMCHAIR	"	"

Figure 21.39 Furnishing schedule. (Reprinted by permission from *The Professional Practice of Architectural Working Drawings*, 2d Ed., © 1995 by John Wiley & Sons, Inc.)

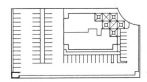

Figure 21.40 Floor plan—Stage I. (Reprinted by permission from *The Professional Practice of Architectural Working Drawings*, 2d Ed., © 1995 by John Wiley & Sons, Inc.)

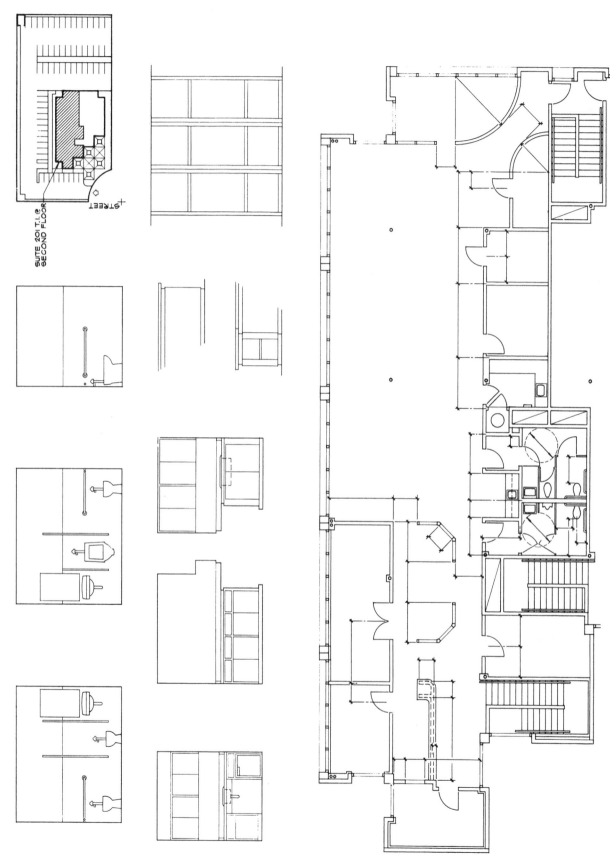

Figure 21.41 Floor plan—Stage II. (Reprinted by permission from *The Professional Practice of Architectural Working Drawings*, 2d Ed., © 1995 by John Wiley & Sons, Inc.)

SUITE 201 T.I. @
SECOND FLOOR

STREET

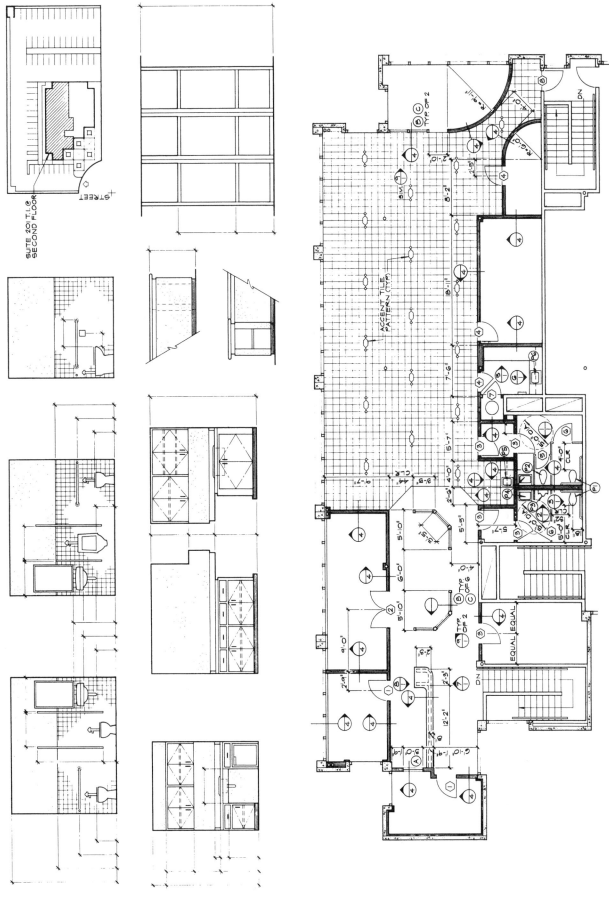

Figure 21.42 Floor plan—Stage III. (Reprinted by permission from *The Professional Practice of Architectural Working Drawings*, 2d Ed., © 1995 by John Wiley & Sons, Inc.)

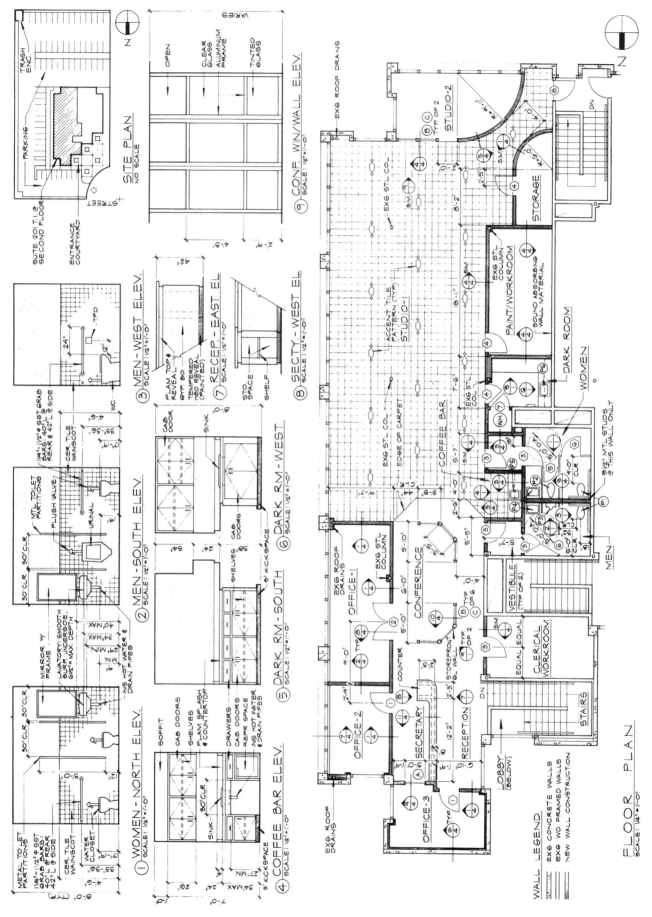

Figure 21.43 Floor plan—Stage IV. (Reprinted by permission from *The Professional Practice of Architectural Working Drawings*, 2d Ed., © 1995 by John Wiley & Sons, Inc.)

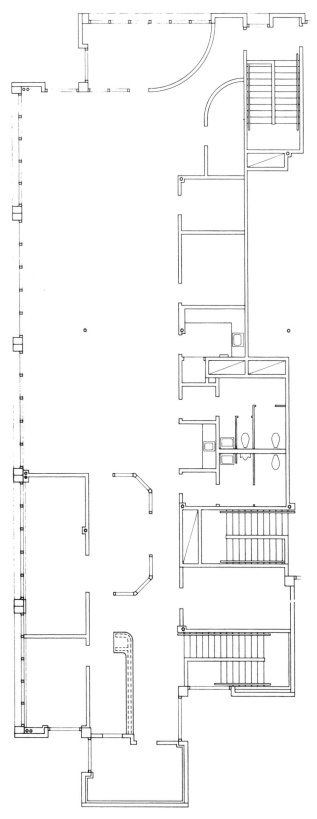

Figure 21.44 Electrical plan—furnishing layout—Stage I. (Reprinted by permission from *The Professional Practice of Architectural Working Drawings*, 2d Ed., © 1995 by John Wiley & Sons, Inc.)

not delineated. In many offices this stage may be a reproduction of an earlier floor plan stage.

STAGE II (Figure 21.45). The first concern at this stage was to lay out all the required furniture necessary for the function of the tenant's business. With the furniture location established, electrical, telephone, and facsimile outlets can now be located as required by the tenant. Also included at this stage is a furnishing schedule, which will be completed at a later stage.

STAGE III (Figure 21.46). For the completion of the electrical plan and furnishing layout, symbols for furniture identification are located accordingly and lettered for reference on the furnishing schedule. Final notes are provided for electrical outlet locations, as well as for the various furnishing items that will be supplied by the tenant. The furnishing schedule is now completed, providing symbol designation, sizes, and manufacturers' equipment designations. A legend is drawn and completed for the identification of electrical symbols, such as for the type of outlets and switched. General construction notes covering the various construction phases are now included with this drawing.

Ceiling Plan

STAGE I (Figure 21.47). At this stage the exterior and interior walls are lightly blocked out, illustrating the walls as they appear at the ceiling level.

STAGE II (Figure 21.48). The exterior and interior walls are darkened to provide greater clarity at this stage. The three office areas that will have a suspended ceiling system have been delineated to illustrate the grid pattern, lighting fixture location, and their symbols for identifications. Also shown are the light switched for the various lighting fixtures. All the surface-mounted lighting fixtures, exhaust fans, and accompanying switches for the various fixtures are completed in this stage. Fixture symbols are now located for the identification of the various electrical fixtures. The symbols will be completed at a later stage. Finally, schedules for the doors, electrical fixtures, plumbing fixtures, and room finishes are drawn in preparation for listing the various sizes, materials, and manufacturers' identification numbers.

STAGE III (Figure 21.49). The final stage of the ceiling plan is to letter all the lighting fixture symbols and locate the heating supply air ducts and diffusers. Dimensioning of some of the various lighting fixtures has now been completed, as have the final notes, the title of the drawing, and the scale designation.

The various schedules, which were blocked out in Stage II, are now completed, providing all necessary information and symbol identification.

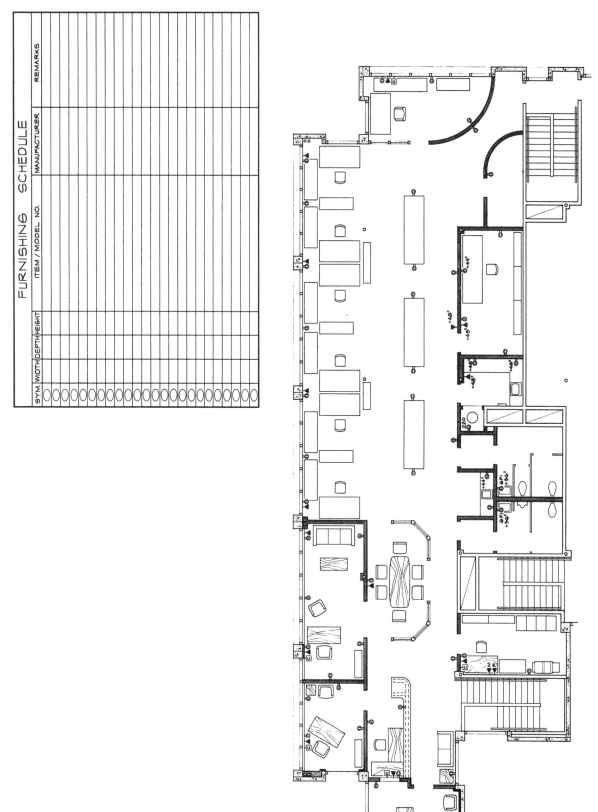

Figure 21.45 Electrical plan—furnishing layout—Stage II. (Reprinted by permission from *The Professional Practice of Architectural Working Drawings*, 2d Ed., © 1995 by John Wiley & Sons, Inc.)

FURNISHING SCHEDULE

SYM.	WIDTH	DEPTH	HEIGHT	ITEM / MODEL NO.	MANUFACTURER	REMARKS

FURNISHING SCHEDULE

SYM.	ITEM / MODEL NO.	WIDTH	DEPTH	HEIGHT	MANUFACTURER	REMARKS
F1	EXECUTIVE DESK	60"	30"	29"	FURNITURE INC.	ROSEWOOD
F2	SECRETARIAL DESK	"	"	"	"	TEAK
F3	FREESTANDING TYPING TABLE	"	24"	26"	"	"
F4	CONFERENCE TABLE	90"	35"	28"	"	ROSEWOOD
F5	WORKTABLE	48"	24"	29"	"	BLACK PLAM TOP
F6	HI-BACK DESK CHAIR	23"	26"	40"	"	ROSEWOOD TRIM
F7	ARMCHAIR	22"	24"	32"	"	"
F8	SECRETARIAL CHAIR	18"	20"	30"	"	BLACK
F9	3-SEAT SOFA	60"	24"	24"	"	ROSEWOOD
F10	SIDECHAIR	22"	24"	32"	"	COFFEE
F11	2- "	G2"	32"	2G"	"	"
F12	COFFEE TABLE	48"	18"	17"	"	ROSEWOOD
F13	SQUARE TABLE	24"	24"	19"	"	"
F14	"	24"	24"	"	"	TEAK
F15	BOOKCAGE	48"	13"	72"	"	ROSEWOOD
F16	"	3G"	"	"	"	"
F17	DRAFTING/WORK. TABLE	72"	37½"	37"	ARCHSTATION INC.	BLACK
F18	FOLDING TABLE	72"	24"	29"	FURNITURE INC.	BLACK PLAM TOP
F19	3-DRAWER REF DESK	60"	21"	29"	N/A	CUSTOM- SEE DRAWING
F20	FOLDING TABLE	90"	24"	29"	FURNITURE INC.	BLACK PLAM TOP
F21	BOOKCAGE	72"	13"	60"	"	WHITE MELAMINE
F22	VARIABLE HT DRAFTING CHAIR	48"	"	44½"	ARCHSTATION INC.	BLACK
F23	"	19"	2"	2"	"	"
F24	ARMCHAIR	23"	26"	26"	"	"

SYMBOL LEGEND

SYM.	DESCRIPTION
	TELEPHONE OUTLET, F=FAX M=MODEM
	COMPUTER NETWORK JUNCTION
	DUPLEX OUTLET
GFI	w/ GROUND FAULT INTERRUPTER
220	220 VOLT OUTLET
$	SINGLE POLE TOGGLE SWITCH
$3	3-WAY SWITCH
EXIT	EXIT SIGN (BATTERY)

GENERAL CONSTRUCTION NOTES

1. The contractor and all sub-contractors shall verify all dimensions and conditions at the site, and shall notify the Architect of any discrepancy.

2. All architectural, mechanical, plumbing and electrical requirements must be coordinated before the contractor proceeds with construction.

3. In all cases where a conflict may occur such as between items covered by specifications and notes on the drawings, or between general notes and specific details, the Architect shall be notified and he will interpret the intent of the contract documents.

4. Details noted as typical shall apply in all cases unless specifically shown or noted otherwise.

5. Where no specific detail is shown, the framing or construction shall be identical or similar to that indicated for like cases of construction on this project.

6. In no case shall working dimensions be scaled from plans, sections or details on the drawings.

7. Workmanship and materials shall conform to the requirements of the current edition of the Uniform Building Code.

8. All fire rated walls shall use fire rated gypsum board and be fire-taped.

9. All Plumbing, Electrical and Mechanical installations shall comply with their respective governing codes.

10. All legal exits shall be openable the from inside without the use of a key, special knowledge or effort.

11. Metal studs by "Metal Studs Inc." (or approved equivalent), ICBO #0000. See details and sections for more information.

12. Suspended Ceiling System by "Gypsum Ceilings Inc." (or approved equivalent), ICBO #0000. Installation shall be per Ch. 47 of the UBC & the following requirements:

A. Lateral support provided by 4- #12ga wires splayed in 4 directions at 90° apart. Connect wires to the main runner within 2" of the crossrunner & to the structure above at an angle not exceeding 45° from the plane of the ceiling. These lateral support points shall be at 12'-0" o.c. (max) in each direction, with the first point within 4' of the wall.

B. Provide vertical compression struts at the center of the lateral support points described above in item "A". Compression struts may be of metal stud material.

C. Discontinuous ends of main runners and crossrunners shall be vertically supported within 8" of the discontinuous end.

D. Lighting fixtures and air diffusers shall be supported directly by wires to the structure above.

ELECTRICAL PLAN / FURNISHING LAYOUT
SCALE: 1/4"=1'-0"

Figure 21.46 Electrical plan—furnishing layout—Stage III. (Reprinted by permission from *The Professional Practice of Architectural Working Drawings*, 2d Ed., © 1995 by John Wiley & Sons, Inc.)

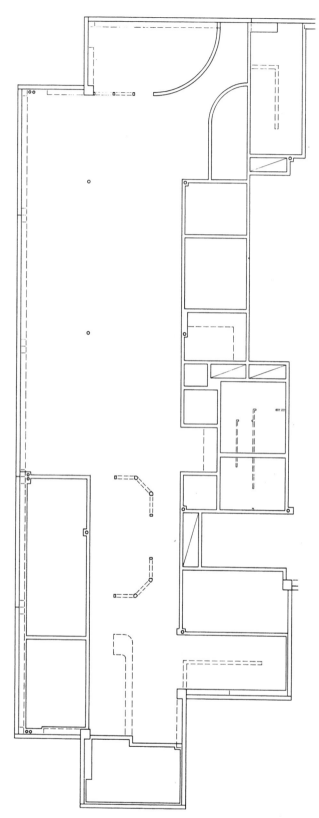

Figure 21.47 Ceiling plan—Stage I. (Reprinted by permission from *The Professional Practice of Architectural Working Drawings*, 2d Ed., © 1995 by John Wiley & Sons, Inc.)

Partition Walls and Sections

The final step in the development of the working drawings for this project is to provide sections for the various partition walls and other related wall assemblies. Initially, the drawing process for these partition walls is to lightly block out the partition wall section and progressively delineate the various members required for the completion of the detail. The completed detail is now profiled with line quality that will provide clarity to the drawing. Finally, lettering, leader lines, and arrows are incorporated in the detail. The progression of these partition wall sections is depicted in Figures 21.50 through 21.54.

Figures 21.55 and 21.56 illustrate additional partition wall sections as they progress toward completion of their respective details. Figure 21.57 depicts the completed drawings for all the partition wall sections.

The purpose and function of the various partition wall sections, as illustrated in Figure 21.57, are as follows: Partition wall section 1 illustrates the wall assembly between the studio and office 1, defining the size and gauge of the metal studs and their spacing. Wall insulation and the wall finish are defined, as well as the attachment to the floor and ceiling. Ceiling heights are also noted.

Partition wall section 2 indicates that the wall is to extend all the way to the roof framing in order to provide additional soundproofing between offices 1 and 2.

The assembly of partition wall section 3 illustrates the condition where the wall terminates just above the suspended ceiling members. To stabilize this wall for lateral support, metal wall braces are attached to the top of the wall and the roof framing. This partition wall assembly occurs in the coffee bar and restroom areas.

Partition wall section 4, which is to be erected between the darkroom and the paint/workroom, is detailed for the wall to continue up to the roof framing with sound-absorbing insulation board applied on the paint/workroom side. Note that resilient clips are called for to provide greater soundproofing capability.

The partition wall assembly that divides studios 1 and 2 is illustrated on partition wall section 5. This assembly provides for the partition wall to terminate at the roof framing, with no wall insulation. Note that there are no suspended ceilings in these areas, and that it will be necessary to provide 2 × 4 blocking between the existing roof rafters in order to attach the wall at that level when the roof rafters do not coincide with the wall locations.

Existing unfinished concrete walls, which are located in office 3, will be finished with the ⅝"-thick gypsum board. To attach the gypsum board and provide a space for electrical and telephone conduits, the wall will be furred out with 2 × 4 flat studs attached to the concrete wall. The detail is illustrated on furred wall section 6.

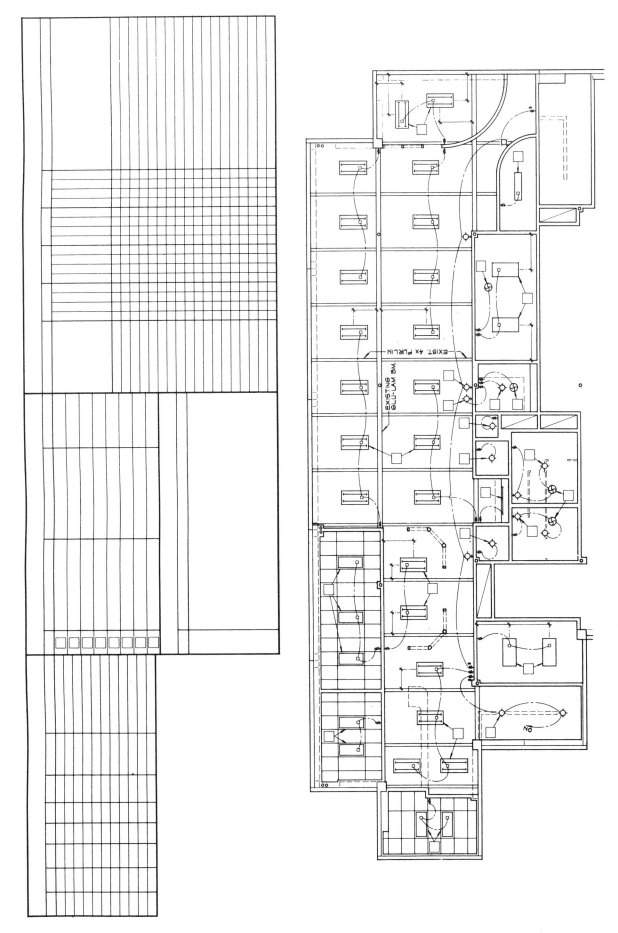

Figure 21.48 Ceiling plan—Stage II. (Reprinted by permission from *The Professional Practice of Architectural Working Drawings*, 2d Ed., © 1995 by John Wiley & Sons, Inc.)

EXIST. 4x PURLIN

EXISTING
GLU-LAM BM.

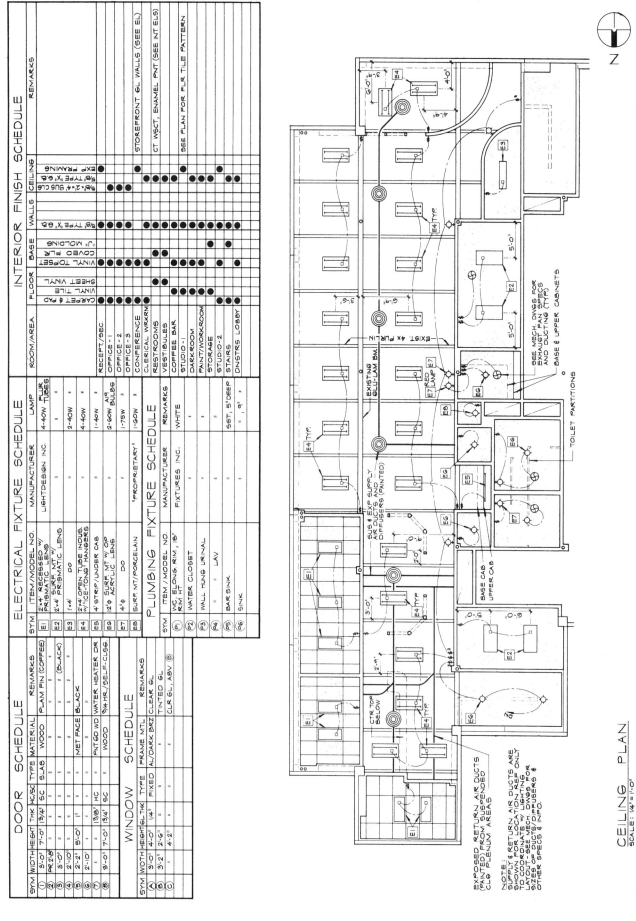

DOOR SCHEDULE

SYM	WIDTH	HEIGHT	THK	HC/SC	TYPE	MATERIAL	REMARKS
1	3'-0"	7'-0"	1¾"	SC	SLAB	WOOD	PLAM FIN (COFFEE)
2	PR 2-8	"	"	"	"	"	PLAM FIN (BLACK)
3	3'-0"	"	"	"	"	"	(BLACK)
4	2'-10"	"	"	"	"	DO	
5	2'-2"	5'-0"	"	"	"	MET FACE	BLACK
6	2'-10"	"	"	"	"	"	BLACK
7	"	7'-0"	1⅜"	HC	"	PNT GD WD	WATER HEATER DR
8	3'-0"	7'-0"	1¾"	SC	"	WOOD	¾ HR/SELF-CLSG

WINDOW SCHEDULE

SYM	WIDTH	HEIGHT	GL THK	TYPE	FRAME MTL	REMARKS
A	3'-0"	4'-0"	¼"	FIXED	AL/DARK BRZ	CLEAR GL
B	3'-2"	2'-6"	"	"	"	TINTED GL
C	"	4'-2"	"	"	"	CLR GL, ABV Ⓑ

ELECTRICAL FIXTURE SCHEDULE

SYM	ITEM/MODEL NO.	MANUFACTURER	LAMP	REMARKS
E1	2'x4' RECESSED w/ PRISMATIC LENS	LIGHTDESIGN INC.	4-40W FLUR TUBES	
E2	2'x4' SURF MT w/ PRISMATIC LENS	"	2-40W	
E3	1'x4'	"	"	
E4	2'x4' OPEN TUBE INDUS W/NICE-TONG HANGERS	"	4-40W	
E5	4' STRIP/UNDER CAB	"	1-40W	
E6	12"φ SURF MT W/ OP ACRYLIC LENS	"	2-60W AIR BULBS	
E7	4"φ DO	"	1-75W	
E8	SURF. MT/PORCELAIN	"PROPRIETARY"	1-60W	

PLUMBING FIXTURE SCHEDULE

SYM	ITEM/MODEL NO.	MANUFACTURER	REMARKS
P1	WC, ELONG RIM, 18" RIM HT	FIXTURES INC.	WHITE
P2	WATER CLOSET	"	"
P3	WALL HUNG URINAL	"	"
P4	LAV	"	"
P5	BAR SINK	"	SGT, 5" DEEP
P6	SINK	"	9", "

INTERIOR FINISH SCHEDULE

ROOM/AREA	CARPET & PAD	VINYL TILE	SHEET VINYL	VINYL TOPSET	COVED FLR	⅛"J⅛" MOLDING	⅝" TYPE "X" G.B.	STOREFRONT GL WALLS (SEE EL)	⅝" TYPE "X" G.B.	⅝" 2'x4' SUS CLG	EXP FRAMING	REMARKS
	FLOOR			BASE			WALLS		CEILING			
RECEPT/SEC.	●			●			●		●			
OFFICE-1	●			●			●		●			
OFFICE-2	●			●			●		●			
OFFICE-3	●			●			●	●		●		STOREFRONT GL WALLS (SEE EL)
CONFERENCE	●			●			●		●			
CLERICAL WRKRM			●	●			●		●			
RESTROOMS		●			●	●	●			●		CT WSCT, ENAMEL PNT (SEE INT ELS)
VESTIBULES		●				●	●			●		
COFFEE BAR				●		●	●			●		
STUDIO-1				●			●				●	SEE PLAN FOR FLR TILE PATTERN
DARKROOM				●			●				●	
PAINT/WORKROOM				●			●				●	
STORAGE							●				●	
STUDIO-2	●			●			●			●		
STAIRS	●										●	
DNGSTRS LOBBY	●			●			●			●		

CEILING PLAN
SCALE: ¼" = 1'-0"

EXPOSED RETURN AIR DUCTS
(PAINTED) FROM SUSPENDED
CLG PLENUM AREAS

NOTE:
SUPPLY & RETURN AIR DUCTS ARE
SHOWN FOR LOCATION REF ONLY
TO COORDINATE W/ LIGHTING
LAYOUT—SEE MECH DWGS FOR
SIZES OF DUCTS/DIFFUSERS &
OTHER SPECS & INFO.

Figure 21.49 Ceiling plan—Stage III. (Reprinted by permission from *The Professional Practice of Architectural Working Drawings*, 2d Ed., © 1995 by John Wiley & Sons, Inc.)

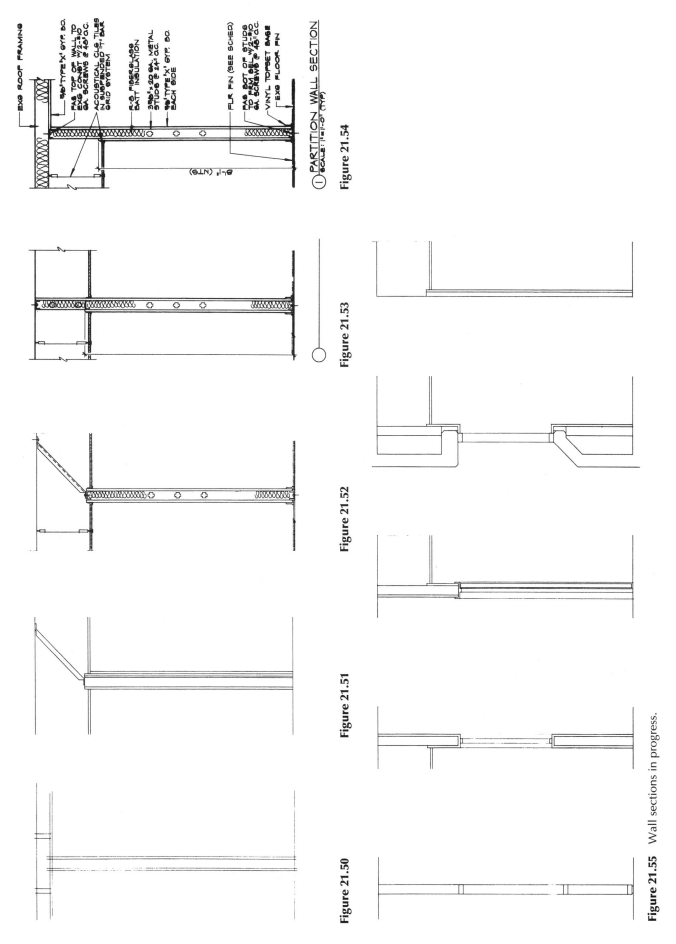

EXG ROOF FRAMING

5/8"TYPE'X' GYP. BD.

FAS TOP OF WALL TO EXG CONST W/2-#10 GA. SCREWS @ 48'O.C.

ACOUSTICAL CLG TILES IN SUSPENDED 1" BAR GRID SYSTEM

R-9 FIBERGLASS BATT INSULATION

3⅝"x 20 GA. METAL STUDS @ 24" O.C.

5/8" TYPE'X' GYP. BD. EACH SIDE

FLR FIN (SEE SCHED)

FAS BOT OF STUDS TO FLR BEL W/2-#10 GA. SCREWS @ 48"O.C.

VINYL TOPSET BASE

EXG FLOOR FIN

8'-1" (NTS)

1 PARTITION WALL SECTION
SCALE: 1"=1'-0" (TYP)

Figure 21.54

Figure 21.53

Figure 21.52

Figure 21.51

Figure 21.50

Figure 21.55   Wall sections in progress.

(Reprinted by permission from *The Professional Practice of Architectural Working Drawings*, 2d Ed., © 1995 by John Wiley & Sons, Inc.)

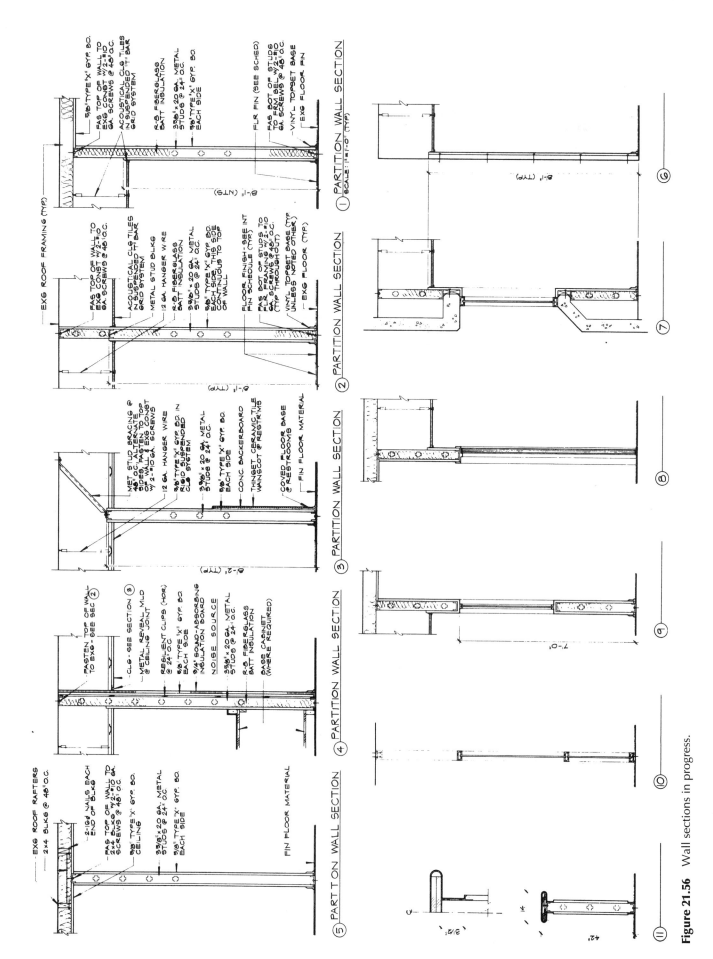

Figure 21.56 Wall sections in progress.

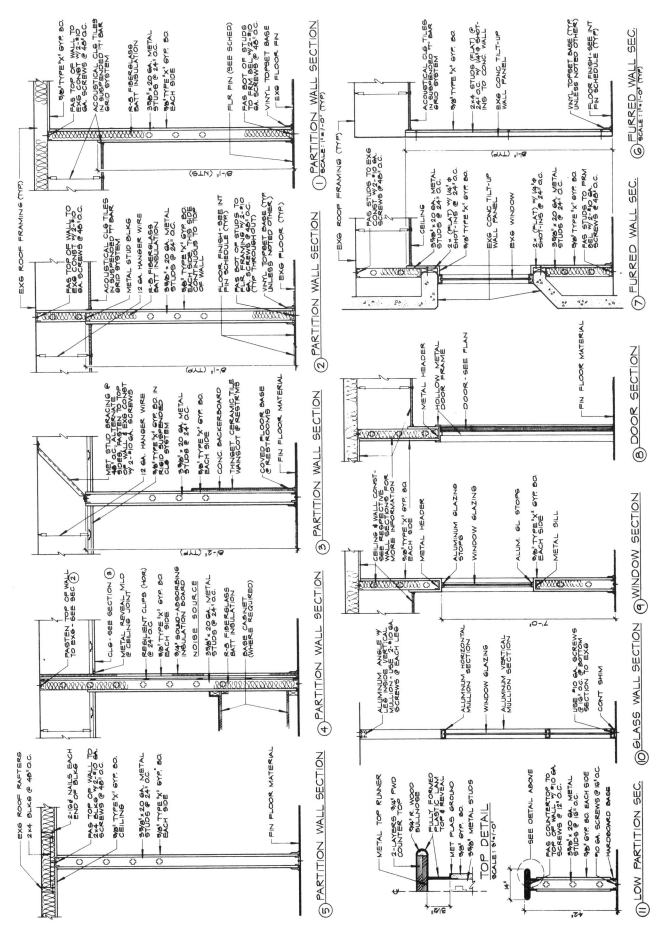

Figure 21.57 Completed partition wall sections.

Another furred wall condition that will be detailed occurs at the exterior walls that include unfinished concrete and window areas. Because of the wall configuration at the window locations, short sections of steel studs and gypsum board are detailed below and above the glass areas with various attachment methods. See furred wall section 7.

Interior passage door assemblies are detailed as shown on door section 8. This detail illustrates the type of door frame, door header, and wall construction and finish above the door.

As indicated on the floor plan, a window is located between office 3 and the secretarial area. This wall and window assembly will be detailed to illustrate the window height, type of glazing, glass stops, and wall construction and finishes above and below the window area. Note the change of ceiling heights and finishes between these areas. This detail is depicted on window section 9.

The conference area is to be partially screened with glass and aluminum wall partition. The design and location of the various aluminum members are illustrated on glass wall section 10. For lateral stabilization of this partition, the attachment of the vertical aluminum mullions at the floor and roof framing is most important.

The final partition section for this project is the low partition section 11. First, this detail illustrates the height and width of the low partition and the various members that are required for this assembly. Because the low partition acts as a space divider, it also serves as a countertop. A portion of this countertop is detailed at a larger

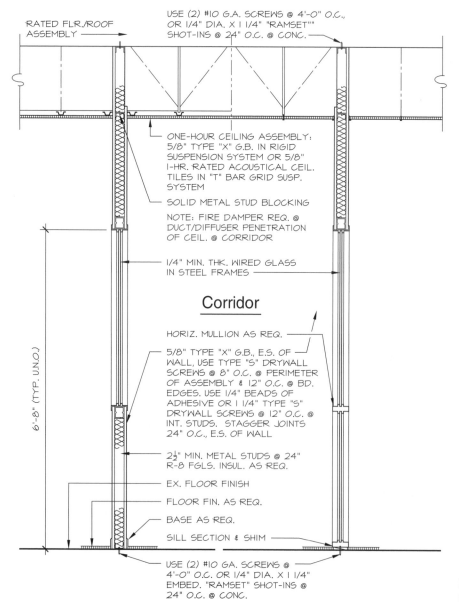

RATED FLR./ROOF ASSEMBLY

USE (2) #10 G.A. SCREWS @ 4'-0" O.C., OR 1/4" DIA. X 1 1/4" "RAMSET"" SHOT-INS @ 24" O.C. @ CONC.

ONE-HOUR CEILING ASSEMBLY: 5/8" TYPE "X" G.B. IN RIGID SUSPENSION SYSTEM OR 5/8" 1-HR. RATED ACOUSTICAL CEIL. TILES IN "T" BAR GRID SUSP. SYSTEM

SOLID METAL STUD BLOCKING

NOTE: FIRE DAMPER REQ. @ DUCT/DIFFUSER PENETRATION OF CEIL. @ CORRIDOR

1/4" MIN. THK. WIRED GLASS IN STEEL FRAMES

Corridor

HORIZ. MULLION AS REQ.

5/8" TYPE "X" G.B., E.S. OF WALL, USE TYPE "S" DRYWALL SCREWS @ 8" O.C. @ PERIMETER OF ASSEMBLY & 12" O.C. @ BD. EDGES. USE 1/4" BEADS OF ADHESIVE OR 1 1/4" TYPE "S" DRYWALL SCREWS @ 12" O.C. @ INT. STUDS. STAGGER JOINTS 24" O.C., E.S. OF WALL

2 1/2" MIN. METAL STUDS @ 24" R-8 FGLS. INSUL. AS REQ.

EX. FLOOR FINISH

FLOOR FIN. AS REQ.

BASE AS REQ.

SILL SECTION & SHIM

USE (2) #10 GA. SCREWS @ 4'-0" O.C. OR 1/4" DIA. X 1 1/4" EMBED. "RAMSET" SHOT-INS @ 24" O.C. @ CONC.

6'-8" (TYP. U.N.O.)

Figure 21.58 Glazed corridor wall (non-load-bearing).

scale, illustrating the countertop finish and shape, and showing the wall finishes directly below the countertop.

Miscellaneous Wall Sections

Depending on the governing building code requirements and the tenants' use of the operating space, there may be various wall construction requirements. In the case where a non-load-bearing, one-hour fire-rated corridor is designed to include some glazing on the corridor walls, it will be necessary to satisfy a building code requirement that calls for a ¼" (minimum)-thick wire glass secured in steel frames. A detail for this condition is illustrated in Figure 21.58.

The internal walls between the living spaces for tenants may require that the walls be constructed to solve two conditions. One is to satisfy a one-hour fire-separa-

tion requirement, and the other is to provide a means of reducing or eliminating sound transmission between the tenant spaces. Figure 21.59 depicts the recommended non-load-bearing wall construction between the living spaces to satisfy the fire and sound considerations.

Interior door designs will vary according to the desires of the tenant and the space plan designer. An example of an interior door design detail that includes a fixed matching panel above a door is shown in Figure 21.60. This detail is designed for a non-load-bearing wall and door condition.

When restrooms abut an office space or other area where people assemble, it is recommended that the dividing walls be constructed with sound insulation batts between the metal studs. Resilient clips are used to attach the gypsum board to the metal studs. This non-load-bearing wall section is illustrated in Figure 21.61.

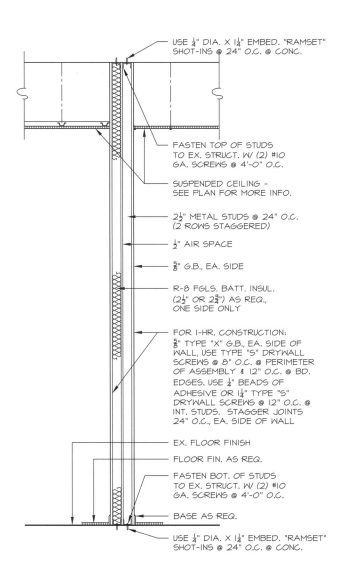

Figure 21.59 Fire and sound wall (non-load-bearing).

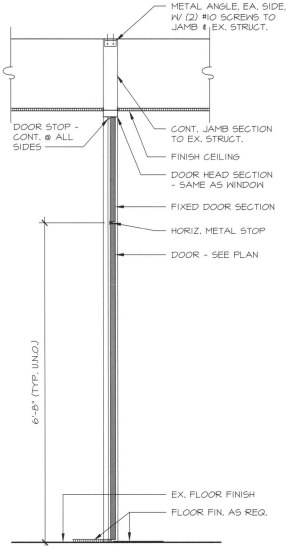

Figure 21.60 Interior door and fixed panel.

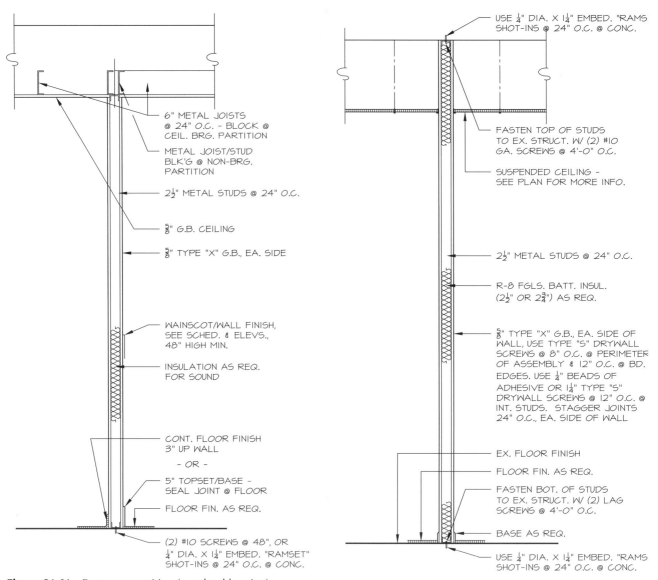

Figure 21.61   Restroom partition (non-load-bearing).

Figure 21.62   One-hour separation wall (non-load-bearing).

In cases where one-hour fire-rated division walls are required to meet a building code requirement, the walls will be constructed from the tenant floor to the floor system above. These wall sections, as viewed in Figure 21.62, illustrate the materials required to satisfy the construction of a one-hour non-load-bearing separation wall.

■ EXISTING BUILDINGS

It is imperative that the first step in drafting a set of construction documents for a tenant improvement project is to produce a drawing called **as built**. This drawing will feature the dimensions of the structure as it stands, hence the name "as built."

Often, the original set of construction documents is available to the tenant improvement drafter, but the parameters of the inside of the structure must be remeasured. The reason is that a structure is rarely built to the precise size shown on the original drawing.

The as-built drawing becomes the datum or base for the entire set of construction documents from this point on, whether drawn by hand or on the computer. If the original set of documents is available, the as-built drawing is derived by making the necessary corrections on the existing drawings: moving walls, column locations, and so forth.

INDEX